LIBRARY

OF

USEFUL KNOWLEDGE.

NATURAL PHILOSOPHY.

II.

POPULAR INTRODUCTIONS TO NATURAL PHILOSOPHY.	THERMOMETER AND PYROMETER.
NEWTON'S OPTICS.	ELECTRICITY.
	GALVANISM.
DESCRIPTION OF OPTICAL INSTRUMENTS.	MAGNETISM.
	ELECTRO-MAGNETISM.

WITH

AN EXPLANATION OF SCIENTIFIC TERMS,

AND

AN INDEX.

LONDON:
BALDWIN AND CRADOCK, PATERNOSTER-ROW.

MDCCCXXXII

CONTENTS.

		Page
I.	Popular Introductions to Natural Philosophy	1—6
II.	Sir Isaac Newton's Optics	1—64
III.	A Description of Optical Instruments	1—60
IV.	The Thermometer and Pyrometer	1—64
V.	Electricity	1—64
VI.	Galvanism	1—32
VII.	Magnetism	1—96
VIII.	Electro-Magnetism	1—196
IX.	Glossary	1—15
X.	Index	16—44

COMMITTEE.

Chairman—The Right Hon. the LORD CHANCELLOR.
Vice Chairman—The Rt. Hon. LORD JOHN RUSSELL, M.P., Paymaster General.
Treasurer—WILLIAM TOOKE, Esq., F.R.S.

W. Allen, Esq., F.R. & R.A.S.
Rt. Hon. Visc. Althorp, M.P. Chancellor of the Exchequer.
Rt. Hon. Visc. Ashley, M.P. F.R.A.S.
Rt. Hon. Lord Auckland, President of the Board of Trade.
W. B. Baring, Esq.
Capt. F. Beaufort, R.N., F.R. and R.A.S., Hydrographer to the Admiralty.
Sir C. Bell, F.R.S. L. and E.
The Rt. Rev. the Bishop of Chichester.
William Coulson, Esq.
Wm. Crawford, Esq.
J. Fred. Daniell, Esq., F.R.S.
Lt. Drummond, R.E., F.R.A.S.

Sir T. Denman, M.P., Attorney-General.
Viscount Ebrington, M.P.
Rt. Hon. Lord Dover.
T. F. Ellis, Esq., M.A.,F.R.A.S.
John Elliotson, M.D., F.R.S.
How. Elphinstone, Esq., M.A.
Thomas Falconer, Esq.
I. L. Goldsmid, Esq., F.R. and R.A.S.
B. Gompertz, Esq., F.R. and R.A.S.
G. B. Greenough, Esq., F.R. and L.S.
H. Hallam, Esq., F.R.S., M.A.
M. D. Hill, Esq.
Rowland Hill, Esq., F.R.A.S.
Edwin Hill, Esq.

Sir J. Cam Hobhouse, Bt., M.P.
David Jardine, Esq., A.M.
Henry B. Ker, Esq.
Th. Hewitt Key, Esq., A.M.
J. G. S. Lefevre, Esq., F.R.S.
Edward Lloyd, Esq., M.A.
James Loch, Esq., M.P.,F.G.S.
George Long, Esq., A.M.
J. W. Lubbock, Esq., F.R.,R.A. and L.S.S.
Dr. Lushington, D.C.L.
Zachary Macaulay, Esq.
B. H. Malkin, Esq., M.A.
A. T. Malkin, Esq., M.A.
James Manning, Esq.
F. O. Martin, Esq.
J. HermanMerivale,Esq.,F.A.S.
James Mill, Esq.
James Morrison, Esq., M.P.

W. H. Ord, Esq.
Rt. Hon. Sir H. Parnell, Bart., M.P., Secretary at War.
Professor Pattison.
Rt. Hon. T. S. Rice, M. P., F.A.S., Sec. to the Treasury.
Dr. Roget, Sec., R.S., F.R.A.S.
Sir M. A. Shee, P.R.A., F.R.S.
J. Smith, Esq., M.P.
Wm. Sturch, Esq.
Dr. A. T. Thomson, F.L.S.
N. A. Vigors, Esq., F.R.S.
H. Warburton, Esq.,M.P.,F.R.S.
John Ward, Esq.
H. Waymouth, Esq.
J. Whishaw, Esq., M.A., F.R.S.
Mr. Serjeant Wilde.
John Wrottesley, Esq., M.A., Sec., R.A.S.

Anglesea—Rev. E. Williams.
Rev. W. Johnson.
Mr. Miller.
Ashburton—J.F.Kingston, Esq.
Bilston—Rev. W. Leigh.
Birmingham Local Association.
Rev. John Corrie, F.R.S., *Chairman.*
Paul Moon James, Esq., *Treasurer.*
Jos. Parkes, Esq. } *Hon.*
W. Redfern, Esq. } *Secs.*
Bristol—J. N. Sanders, Esq., *Chairman.*
J. Reynolds, Esq., *Treas.*
J. B. Estlin, Esq., F.L.S., *Sec.*
Bury St. Edmunds—Bevan, Esq.
Cambridge—Rev. James Bowstead, M.A.
Rev. Prof. Henslow, M.A., F.L.S. & G.S.
Rev. Leonard Jenyns, M.A., F.L.S.
Rev. John Lodge, M.A.
Henry Malden, Esq., M.A.
Rev. Geo. Peacock, M.A., F.R.S. & G.S.
Rev. Prof. Sedgwick, M.A., F.R.S. & G.S.
Professor Smyth, M.A.
Rev. C. Thirlwall, M.A.
R. W. Rothman, Esq.
Canton—J. F. Davis, Esq., F.R.S.
Carnarvon—R. A. Poole, Esq.
William Roberts, Esq.
Chester—Hayes Lyon, Esq.
Rev. Mr. Aspland.

W. Cole, Jun., Esq.
Dr. Cumming.
— Granville, Esq.
Dr. Jones.
Henry Potts, Esq.
Mr. Swannick.
Dr. Thackery.
Rev. Mr. Thorp.
— Trubshaw, Esq.
— Wardell, Esq.
— Wedge, Esq.
Chichester—Dr. Forbes, F.R.S.
Dr. Sanden.
C. C. Dendy, Esq.
Corfu—Profess. Thistlethwaite.
Coventry—Arthur Gregory, Esq., *Stivichall*
Denbigh—Thos. Evans, Esq.
Derby—W. Strutt, Esq.
Devonport—Lt.-Col. J. Hamilton Smith, F.R. & L.S.
Dublin—Hon. Thos. Vesey.
Edinburgh—Right Hon. The Lord Chief Baron.
R. Greville, LL.D.
D. Ellis, Esq., F.R.S.
Rt. Hon. Fras. Jeffrey, M.P.
Prof. Napier, F.R.S.E.
W. Thomson, Esq.
Etruria—Jos. Wedgwood, Esq.
Exeter—Rev. P. Jones.
J. Tyrrell, Esq.
Glasgow—K. Finlay, Esq.
D. Bannatyne, Esq.
Rt. Grahame, Esq.
Professor Mylne.
Alexander McGrigor, Esq.
C. Macintosh, Esq., F.R.S.
Mr. T. Atkinson, *Honorary Secretary.*

Glamorganshire—
Dr. Malkin, Cowbridge.
Rev. B. R. Paul, Lantwit.
W. Williams, Esq., Aberpergwm.
Holywell—The Rev. J. Blackwall.
Hull—Dl. Sykes, Esq., M.P.
Keighley, Yorkshire—Rev. T. Dury, M.A.
Launceston—Rev. J. Barfitt.
Leamington Spa—Dr. Loudon, M.D.
Leeds—J. Marshall, Esq.
Benjamin Gott, Esq.
J. Marshall, Jun., Esq.
Lewes—J. W. Woollgar, Esq.
Liverpool Local Association—
Dr. Traill, *Chairman.*
J. Mulleneux, Esq., *Treas.*
Rev. W. Shepherd.
J. Ashton Yates, Esq.
Ludlow—T. A. Knight, Esq., P.H.S.
Maidenhead—R.Goolden, Esq., F.L.S.
Manchester Local Association—
G. W. Wood, Esq., *Chairman.*
Benj. Heywood, Esq., *Treas.*
T. W. Winstanley, Esq., *Hon. Sec.*
Sir G. Philips, Bart., M.P.
Monmouth—J. H. Moggridge, Esq.
Neath—John Rowland, Esq.
Newcastle—James Losh, Esq.
Rev. W. Turner.
Newport—Ab. Clarke, Esq.
T. Cooke, Jun., Esq.
R. G. Kirkpatrick, Esq.

Newport Pagnell—J. Millar, Esq.
Norwich—Rt.Hon. Ld. Suffield.
Rich. Bacon, Esq.
Plymouth—Geo. Harvey, Esq., F.R.S.
Portsmouth—E. Carter, Esq.
G. Grant, Esq.
D. Howard, Esq.
Rev. Dr. Inman, Nav. Col.
Rippon—Rev. H. P. Hamilton.
Ruthven—Rev. the Warden of.
Humphreys Jones, Esq.
Sheffield—J. H. Abraham, Esq.
Shrewsbury—R. A. Slaney, Esq., M.P.
South Petherton—John Nicholetts, Esq.
St. Asaph—Rev. Geo. Strong.
Tavistock—Rev. W. Evans.
John Rundle, Esq.
Truro—Wm. Peter, Esq.
Warwick—The Rev. William Field, (*Leam.*)
Dr. Conolly.
Waterford—Sir John Newport, Bart., M.P.
Wolverhampton—J. Pearson, Esq.
Worcester—Dr. Corbett, M.D.
Dr. Hastings, M.D.
C. H. Hebb, Esq.
Wrexham—J. E. Bowman, Esq.
Bartholomew Dillon, Esq.
Thomas Edgworth, Esq.
Yarmouth—C. E. Rumbold, Esq., M.P.
York—Rev. J. Kenrick, A.M.
John Wood, Esq., M.P.

THOMAS COATES, *Secretary*, 59, Lincoln's Inn Fields.

INTRODUCTION TO MECHANICS.

[The present Treatise is intended to furnish introductions to the study of different branches of Natural Philosophy, of the most elementary kind consistent with accuracy. Many readers have now, for a considerable time, found an excellent manual of this character in the well-known "Conversations on Natural Philosophy." The Author and Proprietors of that work have, with great liberality, authorized the Committee to use it freely for the purposes of the present Treatise, which accordingly is entirely founded upon it, with hardly any alterations except those which were necessary to adapt it to the form of the publications of the Society.]

SECTION I.—*On General Properties of Bodies.*

THIS Preface being intended as an elementary introduction to the Science of Mechanics, we shall consider our readers as entirely ignorant of natural philosophy, and endeavour to adapt our explanations to the comprehension of the most uninformed minds. No branch of Natural Philosophy can be understood without some previous knowledge of the general properties of bodies; we shall therefore begin by taking a survey of these properties.

There are certain properties which appear to be common to all bodies, and are hence called the *essential properties* of bodies: these are, *Impenetrability, Extension, Figure, Divisibility, Inertia,* and *Attraction.*

By *impenetrability* is meant the property which bodies have of occupying a certain space, so that, where one body is, another cannot be, without displacing the former; for two bodies cannot exist in the same place at the same time. A liquid may be more easily removed than a solid body; yet it is not the less substantial, since it is as impossible for a liquid and a solid to occupy the same space at the same time, as for two solid bodies to do so. For instance, if a spoon be put into a glass full of water, the water will flow over to make room for the spoon.

Air is a fluid differing in its nature from liquids, but no less impenetrable. If we endeavour to fill a phial by plunging it into a basin of water, the air will rush out of the phial in bubbles, in order to make way for the water; for they cannot both exist in the same space, any more than two hard bodies; and if we reverse a goblet, and plunge it perpendicularly into the water, so that the air will not be able to escape, the water will not fill the goblet; it rises, it is true, a considerable way into it, because the water compresses or squeezes the air into a small space in the upper part of the goblet; but, as long as the air remains there, no other body can occupy the same place.

If a nail be driven into a piece of wood, it will penetrate it, and both the wood and the nail will occupy the same space that the wood alone did before; but it must be observed, that the nail penetrates between the particles of the wood, by forcing them to make way for it; for not a single atom of wood remains in the space which the nail occupies; and if the wood is not increased in size by the addition of the nail, it is because wood is a porous substance, like sponge, the particles of which may be compressed or squeezed closer together; and it is thus that they make way for the nail.

We may now proceed to the next general property of bodies, *extension*. A body which occupies a certain space must necessarily have extension; that is to say, *length, breadth*, and *depth*: these are called the dimensions of extension, and they vary extremely in different bodies. The length, breadth, and depth of a box, or of a thimble, are very different from those of a walking-stick, or of a hair.

Height and depth are the same dimension, considered in different points of view; if you measure a body, or a space, from the top to the bottom, it is called depth; if from the bottom upwards, it is called height. Breadth and width are also the same dimension.

The limits of extension constitute *figure* or shape: a body cannot be without form, either symmetrical or irregular. Nature has assigned regular forms to her productions in general. The most perfect natural form of mineral substances is that of crystals, of which there is a great variety. Many of them are very beautiful, and no less remarkable by their transparency or colour, than by the perfect regularity of their forms, as may be seen in the various museums and collections of natural history. The vegetable and animal creations appear less symmetrical, and are still more diversified in figure than the mineral kingdom. Manufactured substances assume the various arbitrary forms which the art of man designs for them; and an infinite number of irregular forms are produced by fractures, such as broken china, or glass, or the fragments of mineral bodies, which are broken in being dug out of the earth, or decayed by the effect of torrents and other causes.

We may now proceed to *divisibility*; that is to say, a susceptibility of being divided into an indefinite number of parts. Take any small quantity of matter, a grain of sand, for instance, and cut it into two parts; these two parts might be again divided, had we instruments sufficiently fine for the purpose; and if, by means of pounding, grinding, and other similar methods, we carry this division to the greatest possible extent, and reduce the body to its finest imaginable particles, yet not one of the particles will be destroyed, and the body will continue to exist, though in this altered state. A single pound of wool may be spun so fine as to extend to nearly 100 miles in length.

The melting of a solid body in a liquid also affords a very striking example of the extreme divisibility of matter; when you sweeten a cup of tea, for instance, with what minuteness the sugar must be divided to be diffused throughout the whole of the liquid! And if a few drops of red wine be poured into a glass of water they will immediately tinge the liquid throughout. The odour of lavender-water, or any other perfume, will be almost as instantaneously diffused throughout the room if the bottle be opened. The odour or smell of a body is part of the body itself, and is produced by very minute particles or exhalations which escape from odoriferous bodies, and come in actual contact with the nose; and it would be just as impossible to smell a flower, the odoriferous particles of which did not touch the nose, as to taste a fruit, the flavoured particles of which did not come in contact with the tongue. If a bottle of lavender-water be left open a sufficient length of time, the whole of the liquid will evaporate and disappear. But though so minutely subdivided as to be imperceptible to any of our senses, each particle would continue to exist; for it is not within the power of man to destroy a single particle of matter; nor is there any reason to suppose, that in nature an atom is ever annihilated.

When a body is burnt to ashes, part of it, it is true, appears to be destroyed; the residue of ashes beneath the grate, for instance, is very small compared to the coals which have been consumed within it. In this case, that part of the coals, which one would suppose to be destroyed, evaporates in the form of smoke and vapour, whilst the remainder is reduced to ashes. A body in burning undergoes, no doubt, very remarkable changes; it is generally subdivided; its form and colour altered; its extension increased: but the various parts, into which it has been separated by combustion, continue in existence, and retain all the essential properties of bodies. Smoke, indeed, when diffused in the air, becomes invisible, but we must not imagine that what we no longer see no longer exists. Were every particle of matter that becomes invisible annihilated, the world itself would in the course of time be destroyed. The particles of smoke continue still to be particles of matter, as well as when more closely united in the form of coals: they are really as substantial in the one state as in the other, and equally so when, by being diffused in the air, they become invisible. No particle of matter is ever destroyed: this is a principle which must constantly be remembered. Every thing in nature decays and corrupts in the lapse of time. We die, and our bodies moulder to dust: but not a single atom of them is lost; they serve to nourish the earth, whence, while living, they drew their support.

It should be observed, that when a body is divided, its surface or exterior part is augmented. If an apple be cut in two, in addition to the round surface, there will be two flat surfaces; divide the halves of the apple into quarters, and two more surfaces will be produced.

Inertia, the next essential property of matter, expresses the resistance which inactive matter makes to a change of state. Bodies appear to be not only incapable of changing their actual state, whether it be of motion or of rest, but to be endowed with a *power of resisting* such a change. It requires force to put a body which is at rest in motion; an exertion of strength is also requisite to stop a body which is already in motion. The resistance of a body to a change of state is, in either case, called its inertia. In playing at cricket, for instance, considerable strength is required to give a rapid motion to the ball; and in catching it we feel the resistance it makes to being stopped. Inert matter is as incapable of stopping of itself, as it is of putting itself into motion. When the ball ceases to move, therefore, it must be stopped by some other cause or power, which we shall presently explain.

The last property which appears to be common to all bodies is *attraction*, under which general name we may include all the properties by which one atom of matter acts on another, so as to make the latter approach or continue near the former. Bodies consist of infinitely small particles of matter, each of which possesses the power of attracting or drawing towards it, and uniting with any other particle sufficiently near to be within the influence of its attraction. This power cannot be recognized in minute particles, except when they are in contact, or at least appear to be so: it then makes them stick or adhere together, and is hence called the *attraction of cohesion*. Without this power, solid bodies would fall in pieces, or rather crumble to atoms; although we are so much accustomed to see bodies firm and solid, that it seldom occurs to us that any power is requisite to unite the particles of which they are composed.

The attraction of cohesion exists also in liquids: it is this power which holds a drop of water suspended at the end of the finger, and keeps the minute watery particles of which it is composed united. But as this power is stronger in proportion as the particles of bodies are more closely united, the cohesive attraction of solid bodies is much greater than that of fluids.

The thinner and lighter a fluid is, the less is the cohesive attraction of its particles, because they are further apart; and in elastic fluids, such as air, there is no cohesive attraction whatever. Air, however, is of the same nature as other bodies in all its essential properties; nor is it probable that the particles of air are destitute of the power of attraction, but they are too far distant from each other to be influenced by it; and the utmost efforts of human art have proved hitherto ineffectual in the attempt to compress them, so as to bring them within the sphere of each other's attraction, and make them cohere.

It is owing to the different degrees of attraction of different substances, that they are hard or soft; and that liquids are thick or thin. This very frequently, especially in bodies of the same nature, corresponds with what we express by the term *density*, which denotes the degree of closeness and compactness of the particles of a body: in these cases, whether in solids or liquids, the stronger the cohesive attraction, the greater is the density of the body. In philosophical language, however, density is said to be that property of bodies by which they contain a certain quantity of matter, under a certain bulk or magnitude. *Rarity*, though opposed to density, as it denotes the thinness and subtlety of bodies, will admit of the same definition; for it implies merely a diminution of density: thus we should say that mercury or quicksilver was a very dense fluid; ether, a very rare one, &c.

We judge by the weight of the quantity of matter contained in a certain bulk, and bodies of the same bulk are said to be dense in proportion as they are heavy. Thus we say that metals are dense bodies, wood comparatively a rare one, &c. But it may be objected, that when the particles of a body are so near as to attract each other, the effect of this power must increase as they are brought by it closer together: so that one would suppose the body would gradually augment in density, till it was impossible for its particles to be more closely united. Now, we know that this is not the case; for soft bodies, such as cork, sponge, or butter, never become, in consequence of the increasing attraction of their particles, as hard as iron. The answer is, that in such bodies as cork and sponge, the particles which come in contact are so few as to produce but a slight degree of cohesion: they are porous bodies, which, owing to their peculiar arrangement, abound with interstices which separate the particles; and these vacancies are filled with air, the spring or elasticity of which prevents the closer union of the parts. But there is another fluid much more subtle than air, which pervades all bodies; this is *heat*. Heat insinuates itself more or less between the particles of bodies, and forces them asunder; it may therefore be considered as constantly acting in opposition to the attraction of cohesion, the one endeavouring to rend a body to pieces, the other to keep its parts firmly united.

The more a body is heated, then, the more its particles will be separated; consequently bodies generally swell or dilate by heat: this effect is very sensible in butter, for instance, which expands by the application of heat, till at length the attraction of cohesion is so far diminished that the particles separate, and the butter becomes liquid. A similar effect is produced by heat on metals, and all bodies susceptible of being melted. Liquids are made to boil by the application of heat; the attraction of cohesion, then, yields entirely to the expansive power; the particles are totally separated, and converted into steam or vapour. But the agency of heat is in no body more sensible than in air, which dilates and contracts by its increase or diminution in a very remarkable degree.

To return to its antagonist, the attraction of cohesion; it is this power which restores to vapour its liquid form, which unites it into drops when it falls to the earth in a shower of rain, and which gathers the dew into brilliant gems on the blades of grass: for rain does not descend from the clouds at first in the form of drops, but in that of mist or vapour, which is composed of very small watery particles; these, in their descent, mutually attract each other, and those that are sufficiently near in consequence unite and form a drop, and thus the mist is transformed into a shower. The dew also was originally in a state of vapour, but is, by the mutual attraction of the particles, formed into small globules on the blades of grass: in a similar manner the rain upon the leaf collects into large drops, which, when they become too heavy for the leaf to support, fall to the ground.

Among the wonderful phenomena of nature, we must not omit to point out a curious effect of the attraction of cohesion. It enables liquids to rise above their level in capillary tubes: these are tubes the bores of which are so extremely small that liquids ascend within them, from the cohesive attraction between the particles of the liquid and the interior surface of the tube. You may perceive the water rising in a small glass tube immersed in a goblet of water. It creeps up the tube to a certain height and there remains stationary, because the cohesive attraction between the water and the internal surface of the tube is balanced by the weight of the water within it. If the bore of the tube were narrower, the water would rise higher; and if you immerse several tubes of bores of different sizes, you will see it rise to different heights in each of them. In making this experiment, the water should be coloured with a little red wine, in order to render the effect more obvious.

All porous substances, such as sponge, bread, linen, &c., may be considered as collections of capillary tubes: if you dip one end of a lump of sugar into water, the water will rise in it, and wet it considerably above the surface of that into which you dip it.

We shall now explain the *attraction of gravitation*. It is unnecessary here to inquire whether it be only another modification of the same properties which produce the attraction of cohesion, which it certainly resembles in this, that it really results from the attractive force of the minute particles of matter of which bodies are composed. But, tracing it only in its effects, we now speak of it as a force acting, unlike that of cohesion, at considerable distances, and only perceptible in its effects when many particles of matter are combined together in one mass. It acts therefore on the largest bodies, and at immense distances as well as small ones. Let us take, for example, one of the largest bodies in nature, and observe whether it does not attract other bodies. What is it that occasions the fall of a book when it is no longer supported? You will say that all bodies have a natural tendency to fall. That is true; but that tendency is produced by the attraction of the earth. The earth, being much larger than any body on its surface, forces every other, which is not supported, to fall to it.

When you are accustomed to consider the fall of bodies as depending on this cause, it will appear to you as natural, and surely much more satisfactory, than if the cause of their tendency to fall were totally unknown. Thus all matter is attractive, from the smallest particle to the largest mass; and bodies attract each other with a force proportioned to the quantity of matter they contain.

When the attraction of cohesion and that of gravitation are opposed to each other, the former, within the limits at which it acts, is generally the stronger. Of this we have an instance in the attraction of capillary tubes, in which liquids ascend by the attraction of cohesion, in opposition to that of gravity. It is, however, necessary that the bore of the tube should be extremely small; for if the column of water within the tube is not very minute, the attraction would not be able either to raise or support its weight, in opposition to that of gravity. It may be observed, also, that all solid bodies are enabled, by the force of the cohesive attraction of their particles, to resist that of gravity, which would otherwise disunite them, and bring them to a level with the ground, as it does in the case of liquids, the cohesive attraction of which is not sufficient to enable them to resist the power of gravity. There is no attraction of cohesion between the separate parts of pulverized bodies; every grain of powder or sand is composed of a great number of more minute particles, firmly united by the attraction of cohesion; but amongst the grains themselves there is no sensible attraction, because they are not in sufficiently close contact.

The surface of bodies is so rough and uneven, that, when in actual contact, they touch each other only by a few points. Thus, if a book, the binding of which appears perfectly smooth, be laid on the table, so few of the particles of its under surface come in contact with the table, that no sensible degree of cohesive attraction takes place; it does not stick, or cohere to the table, and there is no difficulty in lifting it off. It is only when surfaces perfectly flat and well polished are placed in contact, that the particles approach in sufficient number, and closely enough to produce a sensible degree of cohesive attraction. Take two hemispheres of polished metal, press their flat surfaces together, having previously interposed a few drops of oil, to fill up every little porous vacancy. It now requires a weight of several pounds to separate them: but part of this effect is due, as will be explained hereafter, to a pressure of the air on their surface; the residue is the effect of cohesion. The same cause which occasions the fall of bodies produces also their weight; in other words it is the attraction of gravity which makes bodies heavy. The power which brings bodies that are unsupported to the ground causes those which are supported to press upon the objects which prevent their fall, with a weight equal to the force with which they gravitate towards the earth.

Attraction being mutual between two bodies, when a stone falls to the earth, the earth should rise part of the way to meet it. But when, on the other hand, you consider that attraction is proportioned to the mass of the attracting and attracted bodies, you will no longer expect to see the earth rising to meet the stone. You may possibly imagine that, according to this theory, the hills should attract the houses and churches towards them. The hills no doubt exert this influence, but they cannot move the buildings, because they can neither overcome the attraction of cohesion between the bricks and the mortar, nor that of gravity which fixes the wall to the ground. There are, however, some instances in which the attraction of a large body has sensibly counteracted that of the earth. If a man, standing on the declivity of an abrupt mountain, hold a plumb-line in his hand, the weight will not fall perpendicularly to the earth, but incline a little towards the mountain; and this is owing to the lateral or sideway attraction of the mountain interfering with the perpendicular attraction of the earth.

If no obstacle intervened to impede the fall of bodies, attraction would make them all descend with an equal velocity, or quickness; so that those which fall from the same height would reach the earth in the same space of time. It may be objected, that since attraction is proportioned to the quantity of matter which a body contains, the earth must necessarily attract a heavy body more strongly, and consequently bring it to the ground more rapidly than a light one. In answer to this, it must be observed that bodies have no natural tendency to fall any more than to rise, or to move laterally, and that they will not fall unless impelled by some force; and this force must be proportioned to the quantity of matter it has to move. A body consisting of 1000 particles of matter, for instance, requires ten times the force of attraction to bring it to the ground, in the same space of time, that a body consisting of only 100 particles does. If you draw towards you two bodies, the one of 100, the other of 1000lbs. weight, will you not be obliged to exert ten times as much strength to draw the heavier one to you in the same time that would be required for the lighter one? Therefore if the earth draw a body of 1000 lbs. weight to it in the same space of time that it draws a body of 100 lbs., it follows that it does actually, as we have stated it to do, attract the heavier body ten times more than the lighter one. So that the more matter there is in a body, the more forcibly it will gravitate; the more force there is, the more there is for the force to do. The consequence of this should be, that all bodies, whether light or heavy, being at an equal distance from the earth, should fall to it in the same time, or, in other words, that their velocities should be equal. But experience seems to contradict this, for we see bodies falling quickly or slowly in proportion as they are heavy or light. We must inquire, therefore, what is the cause which interferes with the regular action of gravity on bodies, and makes them fall with such various degrees of velocity. This cause is the resistance of the air through which bodies fall. They must force their way through this medium; and heavy bodies overcome this obstacle more easily than lighter ones, for the resistance which the air opposes to the fall of bodies is proportioned to their bulk, not to their weight; the air, being inert, cannot do more to support the weight of a cannon ball than that of a ball of leather of the same size; now as the cannon ball contains perhaps 100 times more matter than the leather ball, it would require 100 times more resistance to impede its fall equally. The larger the surface of a body the more air it covers and the greater is the resistance it meets with from it. A sheet of paper expanded descends gently to the ground. If rolled up in a ball it offers but a small surface to the air, encounters but little resistance, and falls with much greater velocity. The heaviest bodies may be made to float awhile in the air by extending their surface so as to counterbalance their weight; gold is one of the most dense bodies we know; but when beaten into a very thin leaf it offers so great an extent of surface in proportion to its weight that its fall is still more slow than that of a sheet of paper. When bodies have but little bulk in proportion to their weight, the resistance of the air has but a very trifling effect; and stones of different sizes let fall from the top of a house will reach the ground very nearly at the same time.

The air itself is also subjected to the law of gravity, the lower stratum is actually in contact with the earth, and the superior strata are supported by it, just as water at the bottom of a basin supports that which is at the surface. But the air is an elastic fluid, the peculiar property of which is, to resume, after compression, its original dimensions; and the air of the atmosphere must be considered as constantly in a state of compression, from the attraction of the earth; it has therefore a constant tendency to expand itself, and this is called the spring or elasticity of the air. This compression is increased in the lower strata of air by the weight of the upper strata, which rests upon them, and thus the air near the surface of the earth is more dense than in the superior regions. The pressure of the atmosphere has been compared to that of a pile of fleeces of wool, in which the lower fleeces are pressed together by the weight of those above; these lie light and loose in proportion as they approach the uppermost fleece, which receiving no external pressure is confined merely by the power of its own gravity.

There are some bodies which do not appear to gravitate: smoke and steam, for instance, rise instead of falling, but it is still gravity which produces their ascent. The air near the earth being heavier than smoke, steam, or other vapours, not only supports these light bodies, but, by its own tendency to sink below them, forces them to rise. The principle is just the same as that by which a cork, or a drop of oil, if forced to the bottom of a vessel of water, rises to the top as soon as it is set at liberty: the only difference being, that, in the case of the atmosphere, the weight or density continually diminishes; and the ascending body therefore does not rise through the whole extent of the atmosphere, but only till it reaches a stratum of which the weight is equal to its own; and there, if no other changes take place, it remains stationary. Smoke ascends but a very little way; it consists of minute particles of fuel carried up by a current of heated air from the fire below. Heat expands all bodies; it consequently rarefies air, and renders it lighter than the colder air of the atmosphere; the heated air from the fire carries up with it vapour and small particles of the combustible materials which are burning in the fire. When this current of hot air is cooled by mixing with that of the atmosphere, the minute particles of coal or other combustible fall, and it is this which produces the small black flakes which render the air and everything in contact with it, in London, so dirty.

Balloons ascend upon the same principle, the materials of which they are made are heavier than the air; but the air with which they are filled is an elastic fluid of a different nature from the atmospheric air, and considerably lighter; so that, on the whole, the balloon is lighter than the air which it displaces, and will consequently rise. Thus you see that it is the resistance of the air alone which prevents bodies of different weight from falling with equal velocities. Those which are lighter than the air are forced by it to ascend; those of an equal weight will remain stationary in it, and those that are heavier will descend through it, and their descent will be more or less retarded according to their weight. If you let fall a crown piece and a piece of writing paper of exactly the same dimensions, the crown piece will reach the ground much sooner than the paper, but if you place the paper upon it so closely that no air shall intervene, the paper will fall as rapidly as the crown piece. That bodies when not supported by the atmosphere fall with equal velocities may be proved by the air-pump, a machine by means of which the air may be expelled from any close vessel placed upon it. Glasses of various shapes, called receivers, are employed for this purpose, and bodies of whatever size or weight placed within them will fall from the top to the bottom in the same space of time. The experiment is usually made with a guinea and a feather: they are placed on a brass plate in the upper end of the glass, and as soon as the air is pumped out, by turning a screw the brass plate is inclined, and the two bodies fall at the same moment, and reach the ground at the same moment.

SECTION II.—*On the Laws of Motion, and the Centre of Gravity.*

THE science of mechanics is founded on the laws of motion; it will therefore be necessary to explain these laws before we examine the mechanical powers. Motion consists in a change of place. A body is in motion whenever it is changing its situation with regard to a fixed point. Now having observed that one of the general properties of bodies is inertia, that is, an entire passiveness either with regard to motion or rest, it follows that a body cannot move without being put into motion: the power which puts a body into motion is called *force;* thus the stroke of the hammer is the force which drives the nail; the pulling of the horse, that which draws the carriage. Gravitation is the force which occasions the fall of bodies, cohesion that which binds the particles of bodies together, and heat a force which drives them asunder. The motion of a body acted upon by a single force is always in a straight line, in the direction in which it received the impulse.

The rate at which a body moves, or the length of time which it takes to move from one place to another, is called its velocity; and it is one of the laws of motion that the velocity of the moving body is proportional to the force by which it is put in motion. The velocity of a body is called *absolute*, if we consider the motion of the body in space, without any reference to that of other bodies. When, for instance, a horse goes fifty miles in ten hours, his velocity is five miles an hour. It is termed *relative*, when compared with that of another body which is itself in motion. Thus a man sailing in a ship may remain at rest relatively to the vessel, though he partakes of its absolute motion; but if he walk the deck in the same direction as that in which the ship is sailing, his absolute motion will be increased by the rate at which he moves along it, and his relative motion will be the difference between his own absolute motion and that of the ship. So if two carriages go along the same road in the same direction, their relative velocity will be the difference of their absolute velocities; if in opposite directions, the same. If they start from the same point along two roads, making an angle with each other, their relative motion will be measured by their distance, in a straight line, from each other after a given time, and the direction of this relative motion will be the direction of that line. The absolute velocity of a body is measured by the space over which it moves, in some particular time, selected as the standard; the velocity *per hour*, for instance, would be shewn by dividing the number of miles travelled over by the number of hours occupied in the journey. Thus, if you travel one hundred miles in twenty hours, and wish to know what is your velocity, you divide 100 by 20, and the answer will be 5 miles an hour. We say, also, that space is equal to the velocity multiplied by the time; if your velocity be three miles an hour, and you travel six hours, you will have gone, in all, a space of eighteen miles.

Uniform motion is that of a body which passes over equal spaces in equal times. It is produced by a force having acted on a body once, and having ceased to act, such as the stroke of a bat on a cricket-ball. But it may be said, that the motion of a cricket-ball is not uniform, its velocity gradually diminishing till it falls to the ground. In answer to this objection, you must observe that the ball is inert, having no more power to stop than to put itself in motion; if it fall, therefore, it must be stopped by some force superior to that by which it was projected; and this force is gravity, which counteracts and finally overcomes that of projection. If neither gravity nor any other force (such as the resistance of the air or the friction of the ground) opposed its motion, the cricket-ball, or even a stone thrown by the hand, would proceed onwards in a right line, and with an uniform velocity for ever! Yet we have no example of perpetual motion on the surface of the earth; because the causes referred to ultimately destroy all motion, whether produced by natural or artificial means.

When we study the celestial bodies, we find that nature abounds with examples of perpetual motion, and that it conduces as much to the harmony of the system of the universe, as the prevalence of it would to the destruction of all stability on the surface of the globe. Providence has therefore ordained insurmountable obstacles to perpetual motion here below; and though these obstacles often compel us to contend with great difficulties, yet the general result is that order, regularity and repose, so essential to the preservation of the various beings of which this world is composed.

Retarded motion is produced by some force acting on a body in a direction opposed to that which first put it in motion, and thus gradually diminishing its velocity.

Accelerated motion is produced when the force which put a body in motion continues to act upon it during its motion, so that its velocity is continually increased. Let us suppose, that the instant after a stone is let fall from a high tower the force of gravity were annihilated: the stone would nevertheless descend, for a body, having once received an impulse, will not stop (unless some obstacle impede its course), but move on with a uniform velocity. If, then, the force of gravity be not destroyed after having given the first impulse to the stone, but continues to act on it during the whole of its descent, it is easy to understand that its motion will be thereby accelerated. Let us suppose that the impulse given by gravity to the stone during the first instant of its descent be equal to one; the next instant we shall find that an additional impulse gives the stone an additional velocity equal to one; so that the accumulated velocity is now equal to two; the following instant another impulse increases the velocity to three, and so on till the stone reaches the ground. The spaces described in a given time follow a law slightly different; for it has been ascertained, both by experiment and calculations, that heavy bodies descending from a height by the force of gravity, fall sixteen feet in the first second of time, three times that distance in the next, five times in the third second, seven times in the fourth, and so on, regularly increasing both their velocities and the spaces described according to the number of seconds during which the body has been falling. Thus the height of a building or the depth of a well may be measured by observing the length of time which a stone takes in falling from the top to the bottom.

If a stone be thrown perpendicularly upwards, it is the same length of time ascending that it is descending. In the first case the velocity is diminished by the force of gravity, in descending it is accelerated by it. The force of projection given to a body in throwing it upwards is equal to the force with which it strikes the ground when it descends again, and this latter force is the effect produced by gravity during the time of its fall. If a stone be thrown upwards gently it will not rise high, and gravity will soon make it descend; if thrown with violence, it will rise higher, and gravity will be longer in bringing it back to the ground. Suppose that it be thrown with a force which will make it rise only sixteen feet, in that case it will fall in one second of time. Now it is proved by experiment, that an impulse requisite to project a body sixteen feet upwards, will make it ascend that height in one second; here then the times of the ascent and descent are equal. But supposing it be required to throw a stone twice that height, the force must be greater. Thus the impulse of projection in throwing a body upwards, is equal to the accumulated effect produced by gravity during its descent; and it is the greater or less distance to which the body rises, that makes these balance each other, for it gives more time for the force of gravitation to act.

We must now explain to you what is meant by the *momentum* of bodies. It is the force, or power, with which a body in motion would strike against another body, so as to set the latter in motion. The momentum of a body is composed of its weight, multiplied by its velocity. The quicker a body moves, the greater will be the force with which it will strike against another body; so that a small light body may have a greater momentum than a large heavy one, provided its velocity be sufficiently great. For instance, the momentum of an arrow shot from a bow is greater than that of a stone thrown by the hand. We know also by experience, that the heavier a body is, the greater is its force, if it acts in other respects under the same circumstances, therefore the whole power or momentum of a body is composed of these two properties. But why should not these be added together, instead of being multiplied by one another? It is found by experiment, that if the weight of a body be represented by the number 3, and its velocity also by 3, its momentum will be as 9; not 6, as would be the case were these figures added, instead of being multiplied together. The same conclusion may very easily be deduced by reasoning. If two bodies, one of one pound weight, the other of two, have the same velocity, the moving force of the second, or its momentum, is double that of the first. If a third body, also of two pounds, move with three times the velocity of the second, its momentum, the weights being in this case equal, is three times that of the second. But the momentum of the second is twice that of the first; therefore the momentum of the third is three times this quantity, or six times that of the first. By thus dividing the process, and looking first to the effect of a change of the velocity, and afterwards to that of the change of the weight, it becomes evident that these effects are to be *multiplied* together.

The *re-action* of bodies is the next law of motion to be explained. When a body in motion strikes against another body it meets with resistance; the resistance of the body at rest will be equal to the blow struck by the body in motion; or, in philosophical language, action and re-action will be equal, and in opposite directions.

The most striking experiments on these subjects are made with elastic bodies. *Elasticity* is a property, by means of which bodies that are compressed return to their former state. If you bend a cane, as soon as it is at liberty it recovers its former position; if you press your finger upon your arm, as soon as you remove it, the flesh, by virtue of its elasticity, rises and destroys the impression. Of all bodies, those in the form of air or gas are the most eminent for this property. Hard bodies are in the next degree elastic: if two ivory or metallic balls be struck together, the parts at which they touch will be flattened, but no mark is perceptible, their elasticity instantly destroying all trace of it. If, however, a very small spot of ink be placed on one of the balls at the point of contact, it will be found after the contact to have spread, and will thus shew that there has been compression. Soft bodies, which easily retain impressions, such as clay, wax, tallow, butter, &c. have very little elasticity.

The cause of elasticity is not well ascertained. Elasticity implies susceptibility of compression, and the susceptibility of compression depends upon the porosity of bodies; for were there no pores or spaces between the particles of matter of which a body is composed, it could not be compressed. But you must not hence infer, that bodies whose particles are most distant from each other are most elastic. Elasticity implies not only susceptibility of compression, but the power of resuming its former state after compression. The pores of such bodies as ivory and metals are invisible to the naked eye; but it is well ascertained, that gold, one of the most dense of all bodies, is extremely porous, and that its pores are sufficiently large to admit water, under great pressure, to pass through them. In cork, sponge, and bread, the pores form considerable cavities; in wood and many kinds of stone, when not polished, they are perceptible to the naked eye; whilst in ivory, metals, and most varnished and polished bodies, they cannot be discerned. To give an idea of the extreme porosity of bodies, Sir Isaac Newton conjectured that if the earth were so compressed as to be absolutely without pores, its dimensions might possibly not be more than a cubic inch.

The elasticity of ivory is very perfect; that is to say, it restores itself, after compression, with a force very nearly equal to that exerted in compressing it. If two ivory balls of equal weight be suspended by threads (*fig.* 1), and one of them A be drawn a little on one side and then let go, it will strike against the other ball B, and drive it off to a distance equal to that through which the

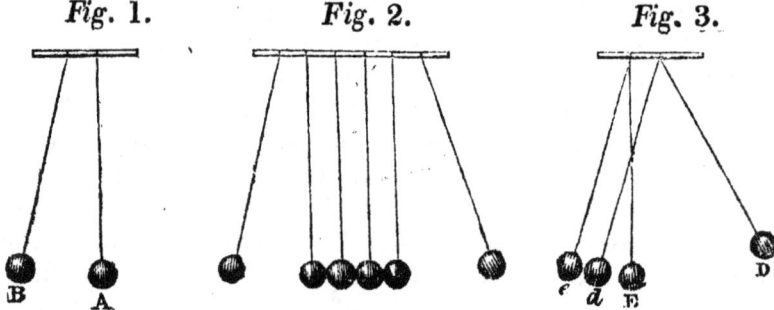

Fig. 1.   *Fig.* 2.   *Fig.* 3.

first ball fell; but the motion of A will be stopped, because, when it strikes B, it receives in return a blow equal to that it gave, and its motion is consequently destroyed. Therefore, when one body strikes against another, the quantity of motion communicated to the second body is lost by the first, but this loss proceeds—not from the blow given by the striking body,—but from the re-action of the body which it struck.

If six ivory balls of equal weight be hung in a row (*fig.* 2), and the first be drawn out of the perpendicular, and let fall against the second, none of the balls will appear to move except the last, which will fly off as far as the first ball fell. For when the first ball strikes the second, it receives a blow in return, which destroys its motion. The second ball, although it does not appear to move, strikes against the third; the re-action of which sets it at rest: the action of the third ball is destroyed by the re-action of the fourth, and so on, till motion is communicated to the last ball, which, not being re-acted upon, flies off. This effect takes place accurately only in the case of *perfectly* elastic bodies.

If two balls of clay (*fig.* 3), which are not elastic, be suspended, and one of them, D, be raised out of the perpendicular and let fall against the other E, only part of the motion of D, therefore, will be destroyed by it, and the two balls will move on together to *d* and *e*, which are less distant from the vertical line than the ball D was before it fell. Still, however, action and re-action are equal; for the action on E is only enough to make it move through a smaller space, but so much of D's motion is now also destroyed. If the elasticity of the balls be imperfect, the effect will be intermediate between the effects produced in the cases we have mentioned; that is to say, the ball struck will rise farther than in the case of non-elastic bodies, and less far than in that of perfectly elastic bodies; and the striking ball will be retarded more than in the former case, but not stopped completely, as in the latter. They will therefore move onwards both after the blow, but not together, or to the same distance; but in this, as in the preceding cases, the whole quantity of motion destroyed in the striking ball will be equal to that produced in the ball struck.

Birds, in flying, strike the air with their wings, and it is the re-action of the air which enables them to rise or advance forwards. The force with which their wings strike against the air must equal the weight of their bodies, in order that the re-action of the air may be able to support that weight; the bird will then remain stationary. If the stroke of the wings be greater than is required merely to support the bird, the re-action of the air will make it rise; if it be less, it will descend: the lark sometimes remains with its wings extended, but motionless; in this state it drops rapidly into its nest. A bird expands his wings when he gives the stroke, the re-action of which is to impel him onward, and contracts them when in the opposite direction. The swimming of fishes is on the same principle; their fins are expanded and contracted in a like manner; and a man in swimming strikes his hands out to produce the re-action which impels him forward, and turns them edgewise to lessen the effect of the contrary re-action. In rowing, the oars are lifted out of the water after every stroke, so as completely to prevent any re-action in a backward direction; and even in moving them through the air they are turned edgewise, or feathered, as it is called, from its resemblance to the action of the feathers of a bird in flying.

Let us now return to the subject of re-action, on which we have some further observations to make. It is re-action being contrary to action which produces *reflected motion*. If you throw a ball against a wall, it rebounds; this return of the ball is owing to the re-action of the wall against which it struck, and is called *reflected motion*. A ball filled with air rebounds better than one stuffed with bran or wool, for the elasticity of the air re-acts after compression. If the ball be thrown perpendicularly against a wall it returns straight towards the hand, though the action of gravity draws it downwards before reaching it; but if thrown obliquely upwards, it rebounds still higher. We use the term perpendicular in preference to the more familiar word straight, because straight is a general term for lines in all directions which are neither curved nor bent, and is, therefore, equally applicable to oblique or perpendicular lines. A perpendicular line has always a reference to something towards which it is perpendicular; that is to say, that it inclines neither to the one side nor the other, but makes an equal angle on either side.

Let the line A B (*fig.* 4) represent the floor of the room, and the line C D that in which you throw a ball against it: the line C D, you will observe, forms two angles with the line A B, and those two angles are equal. All circles are supposed to be divided into 360 equal parts, called degrees; the opening of an angle being, therefore, a portion of a circle, must contain a certain number of degrees; the larger the angle, the

INTRODUCTION TO MECHANICS.

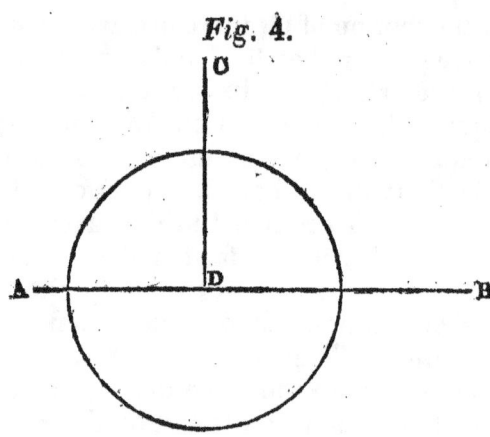

Fig. 4.

greater the number of degrees, and two angles are said to be equal when they contain an equal number of degrees: the two angles (A D C and C D B, *fig.* 4) are together just equal to half a circle; they contain, therefore, 90 degrees each: 90 being a quarter of 360. An angle of 90 degrees is called a right angle, and when one line is perpendicular to another, it forms a right angle on either side. Angles containing more than 90 degrees are called obtuse angles (*fig.* 5); and those containing less than 90 degrees are called acute angles (*fig.* 6). Thus the angles of a square

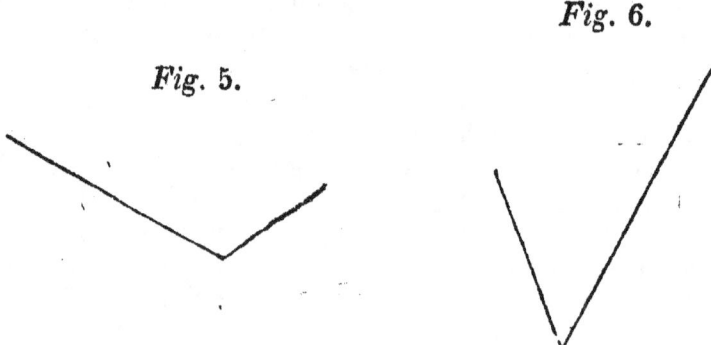

Fig. 5.   Fig. 6.

table are right-angles, those of an octagon table obtuse angles, and those of sharp pointed instruments, acute angles.

When a billiard player strikes the ball perpendicularly against the 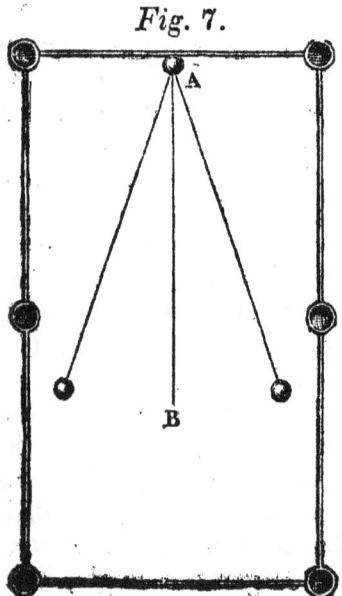cushion, it returns in the same direction; but when he sends it obliquely to the cushion it rebounds obliquely on the opposite side; the ball in this latter case describes an angle, the point of which is at the cushion. The more obliquely the ball be struck against the cushion, the more obliquely it will rebound on the opposite side, so that a billiard player can calculate with great accuracy in what direction it will return. *Fig.* 7 represents a billiard table: if a line A B be drawn perpendicular to the cushion from the point where the ball A strikes, it will divide the angle which the ball describes into two parts, or two angles; the one will show the obliquity of the direction of the ball in its passage towards the cushion, the other its obliquity in its passage back from the cushion. The first is called the

Fig. 7.

INTRODUCTION TO MECHANICS.

angle of incidence, the other *the angle of reflection*, and these angles are, if the bodies be perfectly elastic, equal.

We shall now explain the nature of compound motion. If a body be struck by two equal forces, in opposite directions, it will not move. But if the forces, instead of acting on the body in opposition, strike it in two directions inclined to each other, at an angle of 90 degrees, if the ball A (*fig.* 8) be struck by equal forces at X and at Y, the force X would send it towards B, and the force Y towards C; and since these forces are equal, the body cannot obey one impulse rather than the other. Yet as they are not in direct opposition, they cannot entirely destroy the effect of each other; the body will therefore move, but, following the direction of neither, it will move in a line between them, and reach D in the same space of time that the force X would have sent it to B, and the force Y would have sent it to C. Now, if two lines be drawn from D to join B and C, a square will be produced, and the oblique line which the body describes is called the diagonal of the square. Supposing the two forces to be unequal, that X, for instance, be twice as great as Y; then X will drive the ball twice as far as Y, consequently the line A B (*fig.* 9) will be

Fig. 8.   Fig. 9.   Fig. 10.

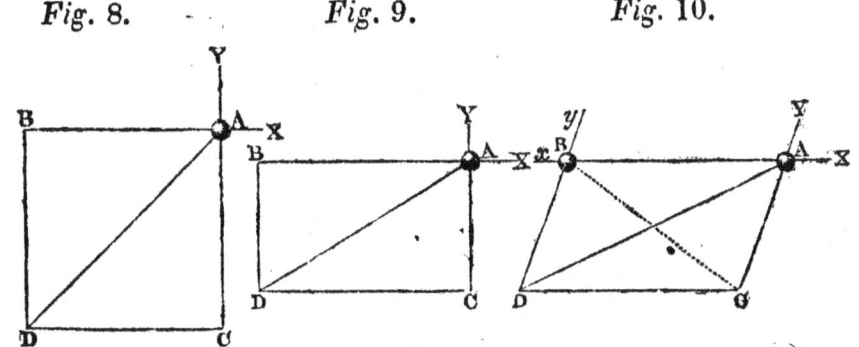

twice as long as the line A C; the body will in this case move to D; and if lines be drawn from that point to B and C, you will find that the ball will have moved in the diagonal of a rectangle. Let us now suppose the two forces to be unequal, and not to act on the ball in the direction of a right angle, but in that of an acute angle. The ball will move from A to D (*fig.* 10), in the diagonal of a parallelogram, A B D C. Forces acting in the direction of lines forming an obtuse angle will also produce motion in the diagonal of a parallelogram. For instance, if the body set out from B instead of A, and was impelled by the forces x and y, it would move in the dotted diagonal B C.

We shall now proceed to circular motion: this is the result of the action of two forces on a body, by one of which it is projected forward in a right line, whilst by the other it is continually directed towards a fixed point. For instance, if I whirl a ball fastened to my hand with a string, the ball will have a circular motion, because it is acted on by two forces, that I give it, which represents the force of projection, and that of the string, which confines it to my hand. If during its motion I were suddenly to cut the string, the ball would fly off in a straight line; being released from confinement to the fixed point, it would be acted on but by one force, and motion produced by one force is always in a right line. When a mop is trundled the threads fly from the centre; but being confined to it at one end, they cannot part from it; whilst the water they contain is thrown off in straight lines. In the same way, the flyers of a windmill, when put in motion by the wind, would be driven straight forward in a right line, were they not confined to a fixed point, round which they are compelled to move. The point to which the motion of a small body, such as the ball with the string, is confined, becomes the centre of its motion; for it may be considered as moving in the same plane or flat surface. But when a body is not of a size or shape to allow of our considering every part of it as moving in the same plane, it revolves round a line, which is called the *axis of motion*. In a top, for instance, when spinning on its point, the axis is the line which passes through the middle of it, perpendicularly to the floor. The axle of the flyers of the windmill is the axis of its motion. The centre of motion is not always in the middle of a body.

The middle point of a body is called its centre of magnitude, that is, the centre of its mass or bulk. Bodies have also another centre, called the centre of gravity, which shall be explained; but, at present, we must confine ourselves to the axis of motion. This line remains at rest, whilst all the other parts of the body move around it; when a top is spun, the axis is stationary, whilst every other part is in motion round it. A top, it is true, has also generally a motion forwards, besides its spinning motion; and then no point within it can be at rest. But what is said of the axis of motion relates only to circular motion; that is, to motion round a line, and not to that which a body may have at the same time in any other direction.

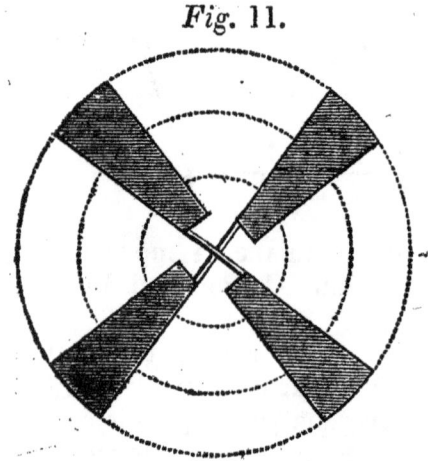

Fig. 11.

There is one circumstance in circular motion, which must be carefully attended to; it is, that the further any part of a body is from the axis of motion, the greater is its velocity: as you approach that line, the velocity of the parts gradually diminishes till you reach the axis of motion, which is perfectly at rest. The extremities of the vanes of a windmill move over a much greater space than the parts nearest the axis of motion (*fig.* 11). The three dotted circles describe the paths in which three different parts of the vanes move, and though the circles are of different dimensions, the vanes describe each of them in the same space of time.

The force which confines a body to a centre, round which it moves, is called the *centripetal* force; and the force which impels a body to fly from the centre, is called the *centrifugal* force: in circular motion, these two forces balance each other; otherwise the revolving body would either approach the centre or recede from it, according as the one or the other prevailed. And should any cause destroy the centripetal force, the centrifugal force would impel the body to fly off from the centre. It would not, however, fly off in a right line from the centre; but in a right line in the direction in which it was moving at the instant of its release: if a stone, whirled round in a sling, gets loose at the point A (*fig.* 12), it flies off in the direction A B: this line is called a *tangent*; it touches the circumference of the circle, and forms a right angle with a line drawn from that point of the

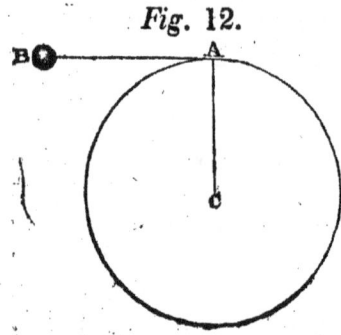

Fig. 12.

INTRODUCTION TO MECHANICS.

circumference to the centre of the circle C. This force would, therefore, with more propriety be called the tangential than the centrifugal force, or rather, the inertia of the body which inclines it to move in the direction of the tangent is the tangential force. But motion in the direction of the tangent would remove the body farther from the centre; a tendency, therefore, to such motion is a tendency to leave the centre, and that part of its force which tends to produce motion thus away from the centre is called the centrifugal force.

If a ball be thrown in an horizontal direction, it is acted upon by no less than three forces: the force of projection first given to it; the resistance of the air through which it passes; and the force of gravity, which finally brings it to the ground. Gravity and the resistance of the air act continually; and as the whole effect produced by them is always so great as to overpower any force of projection we can communicate to a body, the latter is gradually overcome, and the body brought to the ground; but the stronger the projectile force, the longer will these powers be in subduing it. A shot fired from a cannon, for instance, will go much further than a ball thrown by the hand. Bodies thus projected describe a curve line in their descent. If the forces of projection and of gravity both produced uniform motion, the ball would move in the diagonal of a parallelogram, but the motion produced by the force of projection alone is uniform, that produced by gravity is accelerated; and it is this acceleration which brings the ball sooner to the ground, and makes it fall in a curve instead of a straight line (see *fig.* 13). If a ball at A be projected, in a horizontal direction, with a force capable of carrying it to F (which we will suppose to be 100 feet) in a second, then, if it were not acted upon by gravity, it would proceed from F to G, another 100 feet, in the next second, and the same distance G H in a third, and H I in a fourth second. Now, if the ball, when at A, be allowed to fall, by the force of gravity alone, from A towards E, it will fall 16 feet to B during the first second*; then three times as much, or 48 feet the next second; and five times as much, or 80 feet, in the third second; and seven times as much, or 112 feet, in the fourth second. Then, in order to find the line in which the ball will move, by the united forces of projection and gravity, we must draw a line B K parallel to the horizontal line A F, and 16 feet below it; then another line C L, also parallel, at the distance of 48 feet more; then another line, D M, 80 feet further; then another, E N, 112 feet further. Then, at the end of the first second the ball will be at K, at the same distance from B as F is from A; at the end of the next second it will be at L, the same distance from C that G is from A; at the end of the third second it will be at M; and at the end of the fourth second at N; and thus you see the curve line A K L M N is described in its fall, instead of a straight line, which would be the case if A B, B C, C D, D E, were all equal.

Fig. 13.

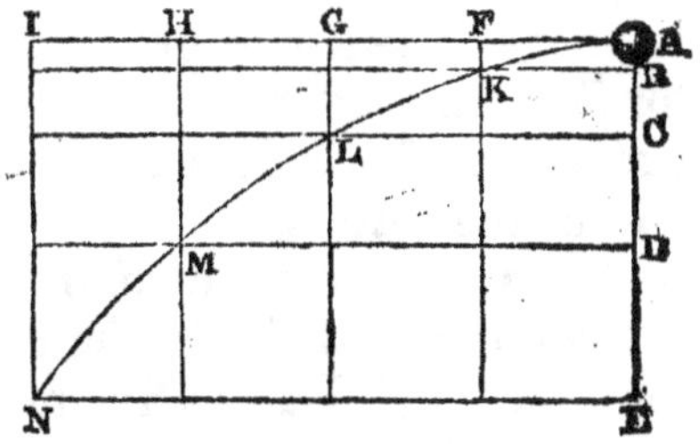

We have not taken notice of the resistance of the air, which much complicates these results in practice. The principles of its operation may easily be understood from the mode in which the other forces act; but the degree and manner in which it modifies their effects cannot be shown without much difficulty and intricacy of explanation. It is, how-

* See page x.

ever, sufficiently plain that this resistance increases with the velocity of the ball, for the particles of air re-act on the ball in proportion to the stroke they receive from it; so that if the force of projection be doubled, the resistance of the air is doubled also: nor is this all, for in doubling the velocity of the ball, it passes through twice the quantity of air in the same time, and receives twice the resistance from each particle; the whole of the resistance must, therefore, be four times as great as in the first instance. And if the velocity of the ball be tripled, it will pass through three times the quantity of air; will strike each particle with three times the force, and receive three times the re-action; which summed up will make nine times the resistance.

The shortest mode of calculating the resistance is to multiply the velocity by itself; thus, if the velocity be three, multiply it by three, and the product will be nine. The product of a number multiplied by itself is called its square.

The curve-line which a ball describes, if the resistance of the air be not taken into consideration, is called in geometry a *parabola*. But when the ball is thrown perpendicularly upwards, it will descend perpendicularly; because the force of projection, and that of gravity, are in the same line of direction.

We have noticed the centres of magnitude and of motion, but we have not yet explained what is meant by the centre of gravity. It is that point about which all the parts of a body exactly balance each other, in every position of the body; if, therefore, that point is supported, the body will not fall. Were any other point of the body alone supported, the surrounding parts no longer balancing each other, the body would fall on the side at which the parts are heaviest; therefore, whenever the centre of gravity is unsupported, the body must fall. This sometimes happens with an overloaded waggon winding up a steep hill, one side of the road being more elevated than the other: let us suppose it to slope as described in *fig.* 14. We will suppose that the centre of gravity of this loaded waggon is at the point A. Now the eye will tell you, that a waggon thus situated will overset; and the reason is, that the centre of gravity, A, is not supported; for if a perpendicular line be drawn from it to the ground at C, it does not fall under the waggon within the wheels, and is, therefore, not supported by them. A perpendicular line thus drawn from the centre of gravity to the earth, is called the line of direction. Let us in imagination take off the upper part of the load; the centre of gravity will then change its situation, and descend to B, as that will now be the point about which the parts of the less heavily laden waggon will balance each other; and the waggon will no longer upset, for a perpendicular line from that point will fall within the wheels at D, and be supported by them. You have heard that it is dangerous, when a boat is in any risk of being upset, for the passengers to rise suddenly; this is owing to their raising the centre of gravity, and thus increasing the chance of throwing it out of the line of direction. When a man stands upright, the centre of gravity of his body is supported by the feet. If he lean on one side, he will no longer stand firm. A rope-dancer performs all his feats of agility, by dexterously supporting his centre of gravity; whenever he finds himself in danger of losing his balance, he shifts the heavy pole, which he holds in his hands, in order to throw the weight

Fig. 14.

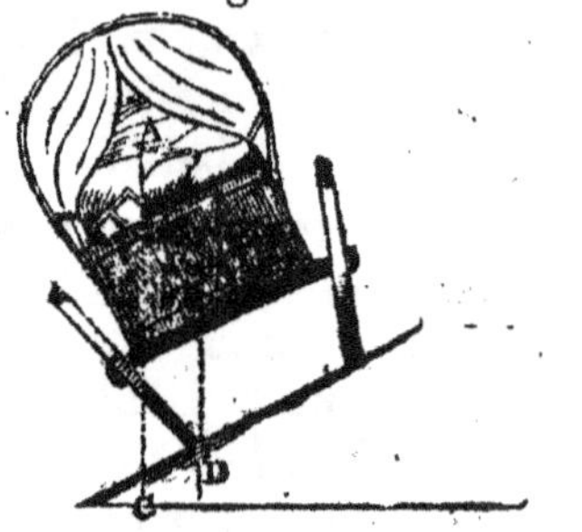

towards the side that is deficient; and thus by changing the situation of the centre of gravity, restores his equilibrium.

A stick is poised on the tip of the finger, by supporting its centre of gravity, and it is for want of this support that spherical bodies roll down a slope. A sphere being perfectly round, can touch the slope but by a single point, and that point is not perpendicularly under the centre of gravity, which therefore is not supported. The centre of gravity in this case coincides with the centre of magnitude, but when one part of the body is composed of heavier materials than another part, the centre of gravity, being the centre of the weight of the body, will generally no longer correspond with the centre of magnitude, though it may accidentally do so.

We defined the centre of gravity to be that point about which all the parts of a body balance each other: you must consider it as an abstract point, since there are cases in which it may be situated at some distance from the body. Such, for instance, is the centre of gravity of a ring, which is situated in the centre of the space which the ring encircles; and that point cannot be supported unless the ring be held so that the line of direction will fall within the base of the support, which will be the case, either if you poise the ring on the tip of your finger, or if you suspend it by a string, as in *fig.* 15.

Fig. 15.

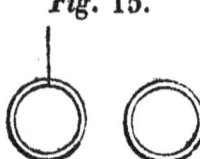

If a body be suspended by that point in which the centre of gravity is situated, it will remain at rest in any position indifferently; but if it be suspended by any other point, it can rest only in the two following positions:—Either when the centre of gravity is either exactly above or below the point of suspension, so that the point of suspension shall be in the line of direction.

Bodies having a narrow base are easily upset, for if they are the least inclined, their centre is no longer supported, as you may perceive in *fig.* 16.

Fig. 16.

A person carries a single pail of water with great difficulty, owing to the centre of gravity being thrown on one side, and the opposite arm is stretched out to endeavour to bring it back to its original situation. But two pails, one hanging on each arm, are carried with much greater facility, because they balance each other.

When two bodies are fastened together by a line, string, chain, or any power whatever, they are to be considered as forming but one body. If the two bodies be of equal weight, the centre of gravity will be in the middle of the line which unites them (*fig.* 17), but if one be heavier than the other, the centre of gravity will be proportionably nearer the heavy body than the light one (*fig.* 18). Were you to carry a rod or

Fig. 17.   *Fig.* 18.

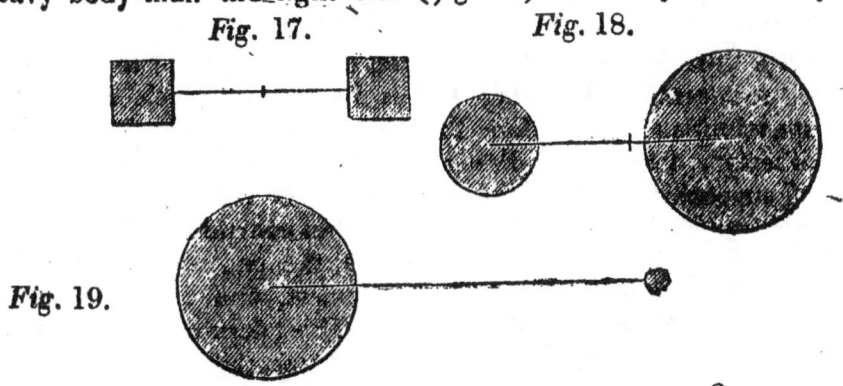

Fig. 19.

pole with an equal weight fastened at each end of it, you would hold it in the middle of the rod, in order that the weights should balance each other; whilst if it had unequal weights at each end, you would hold it nearest the greater weight, in order to make them balance each other; and if one were very considerably larger than the other, the centre of gravity would be thrown out of the rod into the heaviest weight (*fig.* 19).

Section III.—*On the Mechanical Powers.*

We will now proceed to examine the mechanical powers. They are six in number, one or more of which enters into the composition of every machine. The *lever*, the *pulley*, the *wheel* and *axle*, the *inclined plane*, the *wedge*, and the *screw*.

In order to understand the power of a machine, there are four things to be considered. 1st. The power that acts: this consists in the effort of men or horses, of weights, springs, steam, &c.

2dly. The resistance which is to be overcome by the power; this is generally a weight to be moved. The effect of the power, acting in the manner in which in each particular case it is applied, must always be superior to the resistance, otherwise the machine could not be put in motion. For instance, were the resistance of a carriage equal to the strength of the horses employed to draw it, they would not be able to make it move.

3dly. We are to consider the centre of motion, or, as it is termed in mechanics, the *fulcrum*, which means a prop; this is the point about which all the parts of the body move: and, lastly, the respective velocities of the power, and of the resistance.

We shall first examine the power of the lever. The lever is an inflexible rod or beam, that is to say, one which will not bend in any direction. For instance, the steel rod to which a pair of scales is suspended is a lever, and the point by which it is suspended, called the prop or fulcrum, is also the centre of motion. The two parts of a lever divided by the fulcrum are called its arms. Now, both scales being empty they are of the same weight, and consequently balance each other (*fig.* 20). We have stated that when two bodies of equal weight were fastened together the centre of gravity would be in the middle of the line that connected them; the centre of gravity of the scales must, therefore, be in the middle between them, as the fulcrum is, and, this being supported, the scales balance each other.

You recollect, that if a body be suspended by that point in which the centre of gravity is situated, it will remain at rest in any position indifferently; which is not the case with this pair of scales, for when we hold them inclined, they instantly regain their equilibrium; the reason of this is, that the centre of suspension, instead of exactly coinciding with that of gravity, is a little above it; if, therefore, the equilibrium of the scales be disturbed, the centre of gravity moves in a small circle round the point of suspension, and is therefore forced to rise, and the instant it is restored to liberty it descends and resumes its situation immediately below the point of suspension, when the equilibrium is restored. It is this property which renders the balance so accurate an instrument for weighing goods. If the scales contain different weights, the centre of gravity will be removed towards the scale which is heaviest, and being no longer supported the heaviest scale will descend. The fulcrum of the balance is moveable; the lever may be taken off the prop and fastened on in

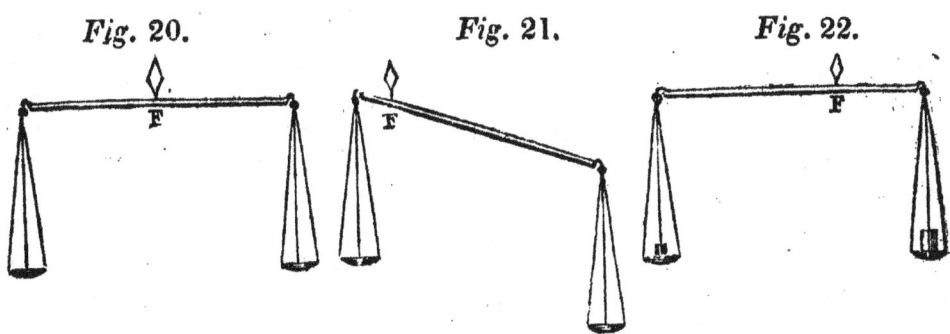

Fig. 20.   *Fig. 21.*   *Fig. 22.*

another point which then becomes the fulcrum. In this case the equilibrium is destroyed; the longest arm of the lever is heaviest and descends. The centre of gravity is not supported because it is no longer immediately below the point of suspension; but if we can bring the centre of gravity immediately below that point, as it is now situated, the scales will again balance each other. Now if a heavy weight be placed in the scale suspended to the shortest arm of the lever, and a lighter one into that suspended to the longest arm, the equilibrium will be restored. It is not, therefore, impracticable to make a heavy body balance a light one; and by this means an imposition in the weight of goods might be effected, as a weight of ten or twelve ounces might thus be made to balance a pound of goods. An ingenious balance called a steelyard has been invented on the principle that a weight increases in effect in proportion to its distance from the fulcrum. In this machine a single pound weight, for instance, answers the purpose of weighing any quantity of goods, simply by moving it along the lever; for, in proportion as it recedes from the fulcrum, it will balance five, ten, twenty, or perhaps even 100 lbs. weight. The hook by which the instrument is suspended, forms the fulcrum; it is, for instance, two inches distant from the basin which is to contain the articles to be weighed, while the opposite arm of the lever extends two feet; a small weight is suspended to it, and the graduations on the lever indicate the different powers of this weight according to the situation which it occupies on the long arm of the lever; when pushed to the extremity, a weight of 5 lbs. is equivalent to 60 lbs. placed in the basin. The same steelyard, when suspended by a second hook, which divides the lever with less inequality, and corresponds with another scale of graduation, is used for weighing smaller quantities of goods, and the same weight, when hung at the extremity, may be equal only to 20 lbs. placed in the basin.

Let us now return to the balance (*fig.* 22), and divesting it of the basins, consider the lever simply. In this state the fulcrum is no longer in the line of direction of the centre of gravity, but it is and must ever be the centre of motion, as it is the only point which remains at rest while the other parts move about it. When a lever is put in motion the longest arm, or acting part of the lever must move with greater velocity than the shortest arm, or resisting part of the lever, because it is furthest from the centre of motion. When two boys ride on a plank drawn over a log of wood, the plank becomes a lever, the log which supports it the fulcrum, and the two boys the power and the resistance at each end of the lever. When the boys are of equal weight the plank must be supported in the middle to make the two arms equal;—if they differ in weight, the plank must be drawn over the prop so as to make the arms unequal, and the lightest boy be placed at the extremity of the longest arm, in order that the greater velocity of his motion may compensate for the superior gravity of his companion, so as to render their momentums equal. But we know that the action of the power must be greater than the resistance in

xxii INTRODUCTION TO MECHANICS.

order to put a machine in motion. For this purpose each boy at his descent touches the ground with his feet, and the support he receives from it diminishes his weight and enables his companion to raise him; thus each boy alternately represents the power and the weight, and the two arms alternately perform the function of the acting and the resisting part of the lever.

A lever, in moving, describes the arc of a circle, for it can move only around the fulcrum or centre of motion. It would be impossible for one child to rise perpendicularly to the point A (*fig.* 23), or for the other to

Fig. 23.

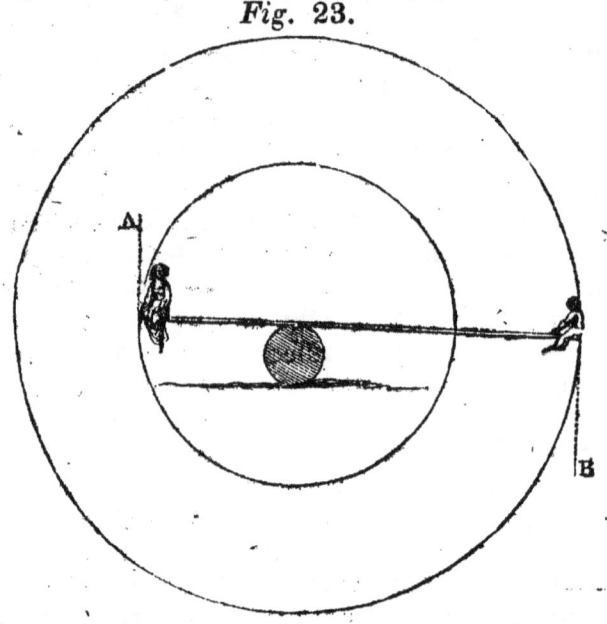

descend in a straight line to B, they each describe arcs of their respective circles; and you may judge from the different dimensions of the circle how much greater the velocity of the little child must be than that of the bigger one. Enormous weights may be raised by levers of this description, for the longer the acting part of the lever in comparison to the resisting part, the greater is the effect produced by it; because the greater is the velocity of the power compared to that of the weight. You have seen a heavy snow-ball rolled over (*fig.* 24) by thrusting the end of a strong stick beneath the ball, and resting it against a log of

Fig. 24.

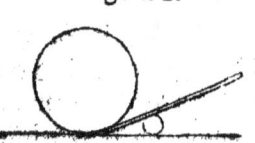

wood, or any object which can give it support, near the end in contact with the snow-ball? The stick, in this case, is a lever; the support, the prop or fulcrum; and the nearer the latter is to the resistance, the more easily will the power be able to move it.

There are three different kinds of levers; in the first, which comprehends the several levers we have described, the fulcrum is between the power and the weight. When the fulcrum is situated equally between the power and the weight, as in the balance, the power must be greater than the weight, in order to move it; for nothing can in this case be gained by velocity. The two arms of the lever being equal, the velocity of their extremities must be so likewise. The balance is therefore of no assistance as a mechanical power, but it is extremely useful to estimate the respective weights of bodies. But when the fulcrum F of a lever (*fig.* 25) is not equally distant from the power and the weight, and that in amount, though greater in effect, the power P acts at the extremity of the longest arm, it may be less than the weight W, its deficiency being com-

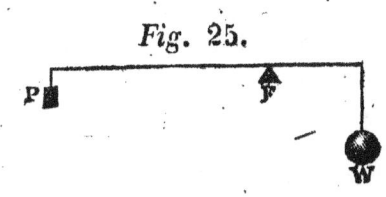

Fig. 25.

pensated by its superior velocity; as we observed in the *see-saw*. Therefore when a great weight is to be raised, it must be fastened to the shortest arm of a lever, and the power applied to the longest arm; but if the case will admit of putting the end of the lever under the weight, no fastening will be required, as you may perceive by stirring the fire. The poker is a lever of the first kind; the point where it rests against the bars of the grate, whilst stirring the fire, is the fulcrum; the short arm, or resisting part of the lever, is employed in lifting the weight, which is the coals, and the hand is the power applied to the longest arm, or acting part of the lever. A pair of scissars is an instrument composed of two levers, united in one common fulcrum; the point at which the two levers are screwed together is the fulcrum; the handles, to which the power of the fingers is applied, are the extremities of the acting part of the levers, and the cutting part of the scissars are the resisting parts of the levers; therefore the longer the handles, and the shorter the points of the scissars, the more easily will they cut. Thus when pasteboard, or any hard substance is to be cut, that part of the scissars nearest the screw or rivet, is used. Snuffers, and most kinds of pincers, are levers of a similar description, the great force of which consists in the resisting part of the lever being very short in comparison of the acting part.

In levers of the second kind, the weight, instead of being at one end, is situated between the power and the fulcrum (*fig.* 26). In moving it, the velocity of the power must necessarily be greater than that of the weight, as it is more distant than the centre of motion. You may, perhaps, have seen a snow-ball moved by means of a lever of the second order, as well as by one of the first. The end of the stick (*fig.* 27) that is thrust under the ball rests on the ground, which becomes the

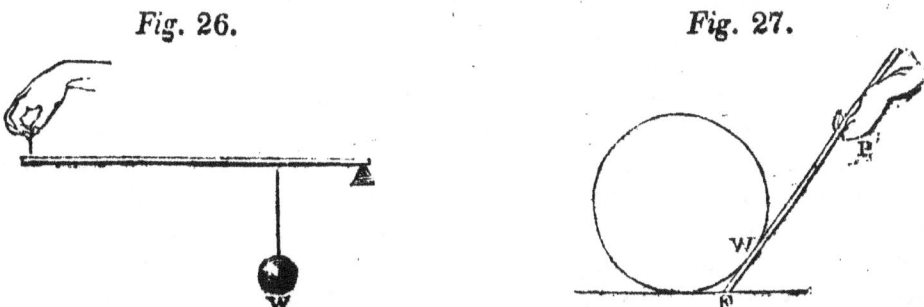

Fig. 26.   Fig. 27.

fulcrum; the ball is the weight to be moved, and the power the hands applied to the other end of the lever. In this instance there is an immense difference in the length of the arms of the lever, the weight being almost close to the fulcrum, and the advantage gained is proportional. Fishermen's boats are thus raised from the ground to be launched into the sea, by means of slippery pieces of board, which are thrust under the keel. The most common example that we have of levers of the second kind is in the doors of our apartments: in these the hinges represent the fulcrum, the hand, the power applied to the other end of the lever, and the door, or rather its inertia, is the weight which occupies the whole of the space between the power and the fulcrum. The whole weight and inertia of the door may be regarded as collected into its centre of gravity; that is to say, the resistance of the door is the same that would be offered by a force equal to the inertia of the door, and passing through its centre of gravity. Another very common instance is found in an oar: the blade is kept in the same place by the resistance of the water, and becomes the fulcrum; the resistance is applied where the oar passes over the side of the boat, and the hands at the handle are the power. Nut-crackers are double levers of this kind: the hinge is the fulcrum, the nut the resistance, and the hands the power.

In levers of the third kind (*fig.* 28), the fulcrum is also at one of the extremities, the weight or resistance at the other, and it is now the power which is applied between the fulcrum and the resistance. Thus the fulcrum, the weight, and the power, each in its turn, occupies some part of the middle of the lever between its extremities. But in this third kind of lever, the weight being further from the centre of motion than the power, the difficulty of raising it, instead of being diminished, is increased.

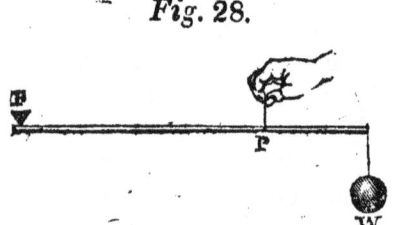

Fig. 28.

Levers of this description are used when the object is to produce great velocity. The aim of mechanics, in general, is to gain force by exchanging it for time; but it is sometimes desirable to produce great velocity by an expenditure of force. The treddle of a common turning lathe affords an example of a lever of the third kind employed in gaining time, or velocity, at the expense of force. A man, in raising a long ladder perpendicularly against a wall, cannot place his hands on the upper part of the ladder: the power, therefore, is necessarily placed nearer the fulcrum than the weight, for the hands are the power, the ground the fulcrum, and the ladder the weight, which, as in the case of the door, may be considered as collected in the centre of gravity of the ladder, about half way up it, and consequently beyond the point where the hands are applied. Nature employs this kind of lever in the structure of the human frame. In lifting a weight with the hand, the lower part of the arm becomes a lever of the third kind: the elbow is the fulcrum; the muscles which move the arm, the power; and as these are nearer to the elbow than the hand is, it is necessary that their power should exceed the weight to be raised.

You may perhaps wonder that nature should have furnished us with such levers, but the disadvantage is more than compensated by the convenience resulting from the structure of the arm. It is of more consequence that we should be able to move our limbs nimbly, than that we should be able to overcome great resistance; for it is comparatively seldom that we meet with great obstacles, and when we do, they can be overcome by art. Besides, the Creator has endowed the muscular fibres with prodigious strength, so that, upon the whole, this kind of lever is best adapted to enable the arm to perform its various functions.

The pulley, which is the second mechanical power we are to examine, is a circular flat piece of wood or metal, with a string running in a groove round it, by means of which a weight may be pulled up. Thus pulleys are used for drawing up curtains, the sails of a ship, &c. When, as in the examples alluded to, the pulley is fixed, it does not increase the power to raise the weight. If P represent the power, to raise the weight W (*fig.* 29), it is evident that the power must be greater than the weight, in order to move it. A fixed pulley is useful, therefore, only in altering the direction of the power, and its most frequent practical application is to make us to draw up a weight by drawing down the string con-

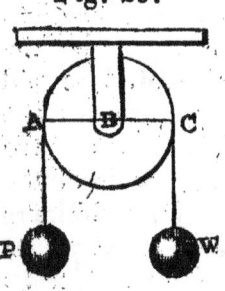

Fig. 29.

nected with the pulley. But a moveable pulley affords mechanical assistance (*fig.* 30). The hand which sustains the cask by means of the cord D E going over the moveable pulley, does it more easily than if it held the cask suspended to a cord without a pulley; for the fixed hook H, to which one end of the cord is fastened, bearing one half of the weight of the cask, the hand has only the other half to sustain. Now it is evident, that the hook affords the same assistance in raising as in sustaining the cask, so that the hand will have only one half of the weight to raise. But observe that the velocity of the hand must be double that of the cask; for in order to raise the latter one inch, the hand must draw the two strings (or rather the two parts D and E into which the string is divided by the pulley) one inch each; the whole string being shortened two inches, while the cask is raised only one. Thus the advantage of a moveable pulley consists in dividing the difficulty; twice the length of string it is true must be drawn, but only half the strength is required which would be necessary to raise the weight without such assistance; so that the difficulty is overcome in the same manner as it would be by dividing the weight into two equal parts, and raising them successively. The pulley, therefore, acts on the same principle as the lever, the deficiency of strength of the power being compensated by its superior velocity; and it is on this principle that all mechanical power is founded. In the fixed pulley (*fig.* 29) the line A C may be considered as a lever, and B the fulcrum; then the two arms A B and B C being equal, the lever will afford no aid as a mechanical power; since the power must be equal to the weight in order to balance it, and superior to the weight in order to raise it. In the moveable pulley (*fig.* 30) you must consider the point A as the fulcrum; A B or half the diameter of the pulley as the shortest arm; and A C or the whole diameter as the longest arm. It may, perhaps, be objected to pulleys that a longer time is required to raise a weight with their aid than without it: that is true, for it is a fundamental law in mechanics, that what is gained in power is lost in time: this applies not only to the pulley but to the lever and all the other mechanical powers. It would be wrong, however, to suppose that the loss was equivalent to the gain, and that we derived no advantage from the mechanical powers; for since we are incapable of augmenting our strength, that science is of wonderful utility which enables us to reduce the resistance or weight of any body to the level of our strength. This we accomplish, by dividing the resistance of a body into parts which we can successively overcome; and if it require a sacrifice of time to attain this end, you must be sensible how very advantageously it is exchanged for power. The greater the number of pulleys connected by a string, the more easily the weight is raised, as the difficulty is divided amongst the number of strings, or rather of parts into which the string is divided by the pulleys. Several pulleys thus connected form what is called a system, or tackle of pulleys (*fig.* 31). You may have seen them suspended from cranes to raise goods into warehouses, and in ships to draw up the sails. Here both the advantages of an increase of power and a change of direction are united;

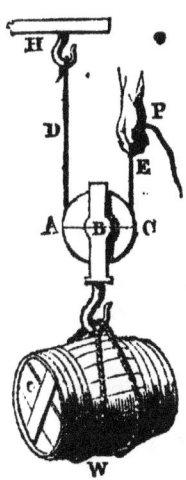

Fig. 30.

Fig. 31.

for the sails are raised up the masts by the sailors on deck from the change of direction which the pulley effects; and the labour is facilitated by the mechanical power of a combination of pulleys. Pullies are frequently connected, as described in *fig.* 32, both for nautical and a variety of other purposes; but in whatever manner pulleys are connected by a single string the mechanical power is the same in its principle.

The third mechanical power is the wheel and axle. Let us suppose (*fig.* 33) the weight W to be a bucket of water in a well, which is to be raised by winding the rope, to which it is attached, round the axle: if this

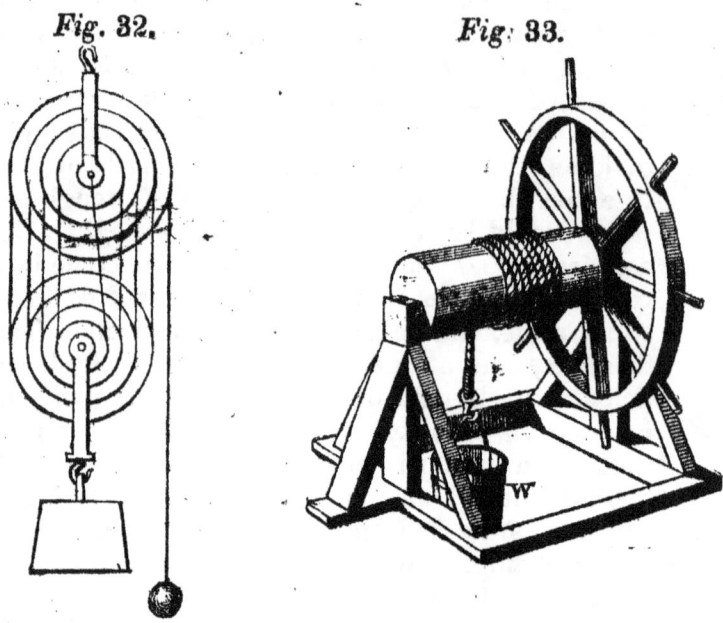

Fig. 32.   Fig. 33.

be done without a wheel to turn the axle, no mechanical assistance is received. The axle without a wheel is as impotent as a single fixed pulley, or a lever, whose fulcrum is in the centre; but add the wheel to the axle, and you will immediately find the bucket is raised with much less difficulty. The axle acts the part of the shorter arm of the lever, the wheel that of the longer arm. The velocity of the circumference of the wheel is as much greater than that of the axle, as it is further from the centre of motion; for the wheel describes a large circle in the same space

Fig. 34.

of time that the axle describes a small one, therefore the power is increased in the same proportion as the circumference of the wheel is greater than that of the axle. If the velocity of the wheel were twelve times greater than that of the axle, a power nearly twelve times less than the weight of the bucket would be able to raise it. Instead of a wheel there is commonly attached to the axle only a crooked handle, which answers the same purpose (*fig.* 34). For the branch of the handle A, which is united to the axle, represents the spoke of a wheel, and is as effectual as an entire wheel; the other branch, B, affords no mechanical aid, merely serving as a handle to turn the wheel. Wheels are a very essential part of most machines. They are employed in various ways; but, when fixed to the axle, their mechanical power is always the same; that is, as the circumference of the wheel exceeds that of the axle, so much will the energy of the power be increased. In mills and manufactures, you must have admired the immense wheel, the revolution of which puts the whole of the machinery into motion; and though so great an effect is produced by it, a horse or two has sufficient power to turn it; but a steam-engine is both the most powerful and the most convenient mode of turning the wheel. We have the advantage sometimes of a gratuitous force, such as the stream of water to turn a watermill; and the wind which turns the vanes of a windmill. One of the great benefits resulting from the use of machinery is, that it gives us a sort of empire over the powers of nature, and enables us to make them perform that labour which would otherwise fall to the lot of man. When a current of wind, a stream of water, or the expansive force of steam performs our task, we have only to superintend and regulate their operations.

The fourth mechanical power is the inclined plane. This is nothing more than a slope, or declivity, frequently used to facilitate the drawing up of weights. It is not difficult to understand, that a weight may with much greater ease be drawn up a slope than it can be raised the same height perpendicularly. But in this, as well as the other mechanical powers, the facility is purchased by a loss of time (*fig*. 35); for the weight, instead of moving directly from A to C, must move from B to C, and as the height of the plane is to its length, so much is the resistance of the weight diminished. Thus, if a pulley be fixed at F, so that the string from F to W may be parallel to B C, and a string fixed to the weight W were connected with another weight P; then if P bear the same proportion to W that the line A C does to the line B C, the two weights will balance each other, a considerable portion of the weight W being supported by the plane B C, and only the residue by the power P.

The wedge, which is the next mechanical power, is composed of two inclined planes (*fig*. 36): you may have seen woodcutters use it to

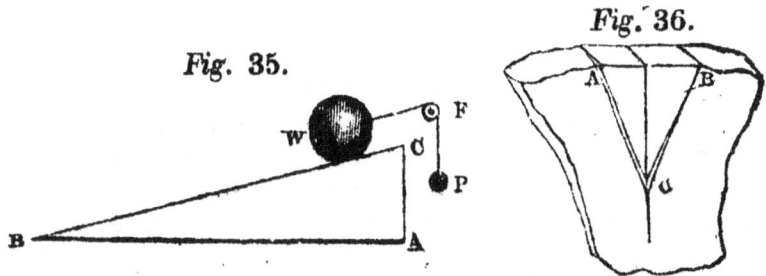

Fig. 35.　　Fig. 36.

cleave wood. The resistance consists in the cohesive attraction of the wood, or any other body which the wedge is employed to separate; and the advantage gained by this power is in the proportion of half its width to its length. The wedge, however, acts principally by being struck, and not by mere pressure: the proportion stated is that which expresses its power when acting by pressure only.

All cutting instruments are constructed upon the principle of the inclined plane, or the wedge. Those that have but one edge sloped, like the chisel, may be referred to the inclined plane; whilst the axe, the hatchet, and the knife (when used to chop or split asunder), act on the principle of the wedge. But a knife cuts best when drawn across the substance it is to divide, as it is used in cutting meat, for the edge of a knife is really a very fine saw, and therefore acts best when used like that instrument.

The screw, which is the last mechanical power, is more complicated than the others (*fig.* 37). It is composed of two parts, the screw and the nut. The screw S is a cylinder, with a spiral protuberance coiled round it, called the thread; the nut N is perforated to contain the screw; and the inside of the nut has a spiral groove, made to fit the spiral thread of the screw; just like the lid of a box which screws on. The handle which projects from the nut is a lever, without which the screw is never used as a mechanical power. The nut, with a lever L attached to it, is commonly called a winch. The power of the screw, complicated as it appears, is referable to one of the most simple of the mechanical powers, the inclined plane. If a slip of paper be cut in the form of an inclined plane, and wound round a pencil, which will represent the cylinder, it will describe a spiral line corresponding to the spiral protuberance of the screw (*fig.* 38). The nut then ascends an inclined plane, but ascends it in a spiral instead of a straight line. The closer the thread of the screw

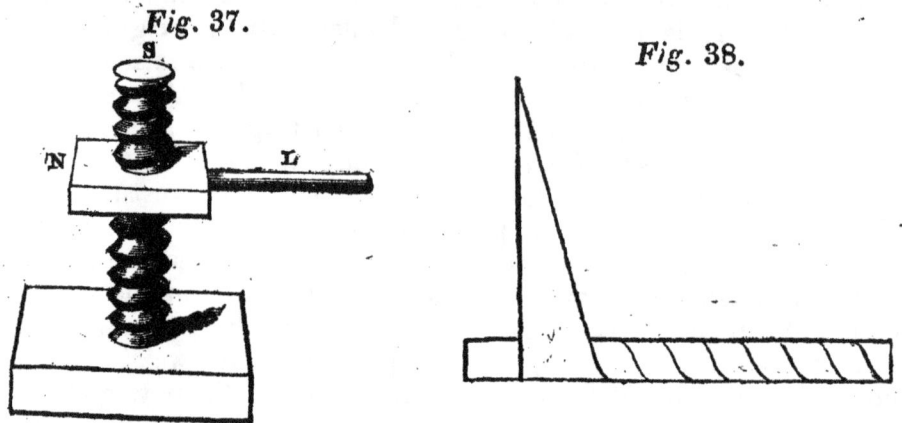

Fig. 37.   *Fig.* 38.

the more easy is the ascent, but the greater are the number of revolutions the winch must make; so that we return to the old principle,—what is saved in power, is lost in time. The power of the screw may be increased, also, by lengthening the lever attached to the nut; it is employed either for compression or to raise heavy weights. It is used in cider and wine presses, in coining, book-binding, and for a variety of other purposes.

All machines are composed of one or more of the six mechanical powers we have examined. One more remark must be made relative to them, which is, that friction in a considerable degree diminishes their force. Friction is the resistance which bodies meet with in rubbing against each other. There is no such thing as perfect smoothness or evenness in nature. Polished metals, though they wear that appearance, more than any other bodies, are far from really possessing it; and their inequalities may frequently be perceived through a good magnifying glass. When, therefore, the surfaces of the two bodies come into contact, the prominent parts of the one will often fall into the hollow parts of the other, and occasion more or less resistance to motion. In proportion as the surfaces of bodies are well polished, the friction is diminished; but it is always considerable, and it is usually computed to destroy one-third of the power of a machine. Oil or grease is used to lessen friction: it acts as a polish by filling up the cavities of the rubbing surfaces, and thus making them slide more easily over each other. It is for this reason that wheels are greased, and the locks and hinges of doors oiled. In these instances the contact of the rubbing surfaces is so close, and the rubbing so continual, that, notwithstanding their being polished and oiled, a considerable degree of friction is produced. It is a remarkable circumstance, that there is generally less friction between two bodies of different substances, than of the same. It is on this account that the holes in which the spindles of watches work, are frequently made of jewels; and that when two cog-wheels work in one another, the cogs of the one are generally made of wood, and of the other of metal.

There are two kinds of friction; the one occasioned by the sliding of the flat surface of a body, the other by the rolling of a circular body. The friction resulting from the first is much the most considerable; for great force is required to enable the sliding body to overcome the resistance which the asperities of the surfaces in contact oppose to its motion, and it must be either lifted over, or break through them; whilst, in the other kind, the friction is transferred to a smaller surface, and the rough parts roll over each other with comparative facility; hence it is, that wheels are often used for the sole purpose of diminishing the resistance of friction. When, in descending a steep hill, we fasten one of the wheels, we decrease the velocity of the carriage by increasing the friction, that is to say, by converting the rolling friction of one of the wheels into the dragging friction; and when casters are put to the legs of a table the dragging is converted into the rolling friction.

The great fly-wheel which is frequently attached to steam-engines and other large machines, acts in the first instance as a heavy weight to impede their free uncontrolled motion. However paradoxical this mode of improving machinery may appear, it is nevertheless of great advantage. The motion of a machine is always more or less variable, owing to the irregularity both of the power which works it, and of the resistance which it has to overcome. Whether the power consists in wind, water, steam, or the strength of animals, it cannot be made to act with perfect regularity, nor can the work which the machine has to perform be always uniform. Yet in manufactures, and most cases in which machinery is employed, uniformity of action is essentially requisite, both in order to prevent injury to the machine, and imperfection in the work performed. A fly-wheel, which is a large heavy wheel attached to the axis of one of the principal wheels of the machinery, answers this purpose, by regulating the action of the machine: by its weight it diminishes the effect of increased action, and by its *inertia* it carries on the machine with uniform velocity when the power transiently slackens; thus by either checking or impelling the action of the machine, it regulates its motion so as to render it tolerably uniform.

There is another circumstance which we have already noticed as diminishing the motion of bodies, and which greatly affects the power of machines: this is the resistance of the medium in which a machine is worked. All fluids, whether of the nature of air, or of water, are called mediums; and their resistance is generally proportioned to their density: for the more matter a body contains, the greater the resistance it will oppose to the motion of another body striking against it. It is therefore more difficult to work a machine under water than in the air. If a machine could be worked in *vacuo*, and without friction, it would be perfect; but this is unattainable. A considerable reduction of power must, therefore, be allowed for the resistance of the air.

INTRODUCTION TO ASTRONOMY.

Section I.—*The Earth's Annual Motion.*

In attempting to give some general notions on astronomy, we shall not begin by entering into an explanation of the system of the celestial bodies, but select that portion which is most interesting to us, the earth; and when you have formed a distinct idea of the part which it performs in the general system, lead you from thence to form some conception of the grandeur and immensity of the universe. Let us suppose the earth at its creation to have been projected forwards into universal space. We know that if no obstacle impeded its course it would proceed in the same direction, and with a uniform velocity for ever. In *fig.* 1, A represents the earth, and S the sun. We shall suppose the earth to be arrived at the point in which it is represented in the figure, having a velocity which would carry it on to B in the space of one month; whilst the sun's attraction would bring it to C in the same space of time.

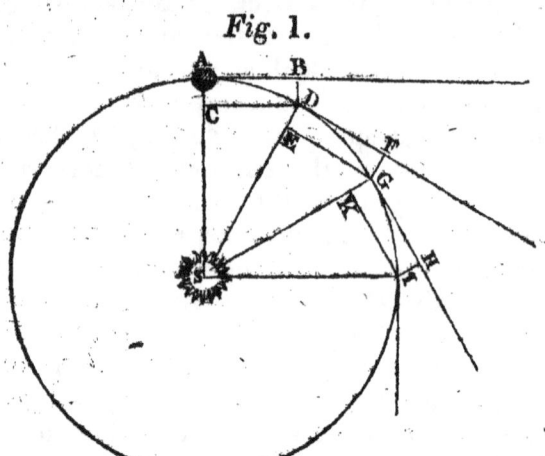

Fig. 1.

According to the laws of motion you would conclude that the earth would move in the diagonal A D of the parallelogram A B D C as a ball acted on by two forces will do. But it must be observed that the force of attraction is continually acting upon our terrestial ball, and producing an incessant deviation from its course in a right line, which converts it into that of a curve line; every point of which may be considered as constituting the diagonal of an infinitely small parallelogram.

Let us detain the earth a moment at the point D, and consider how it will be affected by the combined action of the two forces in its new situation. It still retains its tendency to fly off in a straight line; but a straight line would now carry it away to F, whilst the sun would attract it in the direction D S. In order to know exactly what course the earth will follow, another parallelogram must be drawn in the same manner as the first; the line D F describing the force of projection, and the line D S that of attraction; and you will find that the earth will proceed in the curve line D G drawn in the parallelogram D F G E: and if we go on throughout the whole of the circle drawing a line from the earth to the sun to represent the force of attraction, and another at a right angle to it, to describe that of projection, we shall find that the earth will proceed in a curve line passing through similar parallelograms till it has completed the whole of the circle. It will then recommence a course, which it has pursued ever since it first issued from the hand of its Creator, and which there is every reason to suppose it will continue to follow as long as it remains in existence. It affords an example, on a magnificent scale, of the circular motion which was taught in mechanics. The attraction of the sun is the centripetal force, which confines the earth to a centre; and the impulse of projection the force which impels the earth to quit the sun and fly off in a tangent, and which, therefore, by the inertia of the body, produces the centrifugal force.

A simple mode of illustrating the effect of these combined forces on the earth is to cut a slip of card in the form of a right angle (*fig.* 2), to describe a small circle at the angular point representing the earth, and to fasten the extremity of one of the legs of the angle to a fixed point, which we shall consider as the sun. Thus situated, the lines forming the angle will represent both the forces which act upon the earth; and if you draw it round the fixed point, you will see how the direction of the force which opposes the centripetal force varies, constantly forming a tangent to the circle in which the earth moves, as it is constantly at a right angle with the centripetal force.

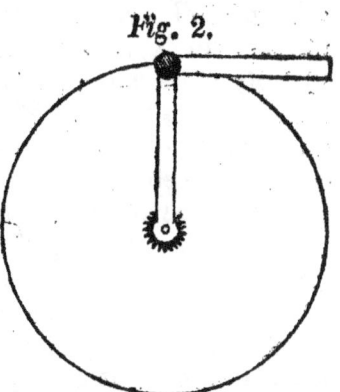
Fig. 2.

You will naturally conclude that if the two forces which produce this circular motion had not been so accurately adjusted, one would ultimately have prevailed over the other, and we should either have approached so near the sun as to have been burnt, or have receded so far from it as to have been frozen. But we have described the earth as moving in a circle, merely to render the explanation more simple, for in reality these two forces are not so proportioned as to produce circular motion; and the earth's orbit, or path which it describes round the sun, is not circular but elliptical or oval.

Let us suppose that when the earth is at A (*fig.* 3) its projectile force does not give it a velocity sufficient to counterbalance that of gravity, so as to enable these powers conjointly to carry it round the sun in a circle; the earth instead of describing the line A C, as in the former figure, will approach nearer the sun in the line A B. Under these circumstances, it will be asked what is to prevent our approaching nearer and nearer the sun till we fall into it; for its attraction increases as we advance towards it. There also seems to be another danger. As the earth approaches the sun, the direction of its motion is no longer perpendicular to that of attraction, but inclines more nearly to it.

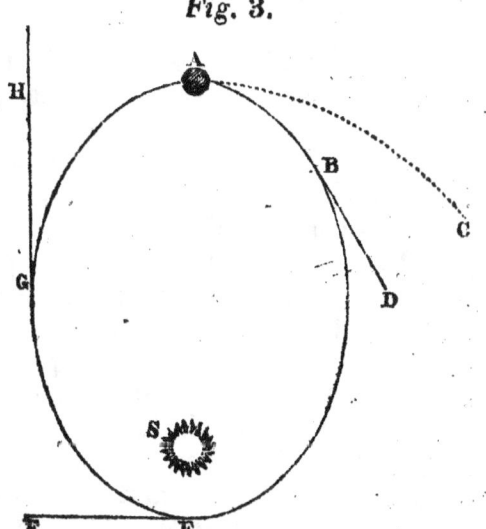
Fig. 3.

When the earth reaches that part of its orbit at B, the force of projection would carry it to D, which brings it nearer the sun instead of bearing it away from it; so that being driven by one power, and drawn by the other towards this centre of destruction, it would seem impossible for us to escape. But nature abounds in resources. The earth continues approaching the sun with an accelerated motion, till it reaches the point E: the projectile force now impels it in the direction E F. Here then the two forces act perpendicularly to each other, and the earth is situated as in the preceding figure, yet it will not revolve round the sun in a circle for the following reason. The centrifugal force increases with the velocity of the body, or in other words, the quicker it moves the stronger is its tendency to fly off in a right line. When the earth arrives at E, its accelerated motion will have so far increased its velocity and consequently its centrifugal force, that the latter will prevail over the force of attraction, and drag the earth away from the sun till it reaches G. It is thus that we escape from the dangerous vicinity of the sun; and as we recede from it, both the force of its attraction, and the velocity of the earth's motion diminish. From G the direction of projection is towards H, that of attraction towards S, and the earth proceeds between them with a retarded motion, till it has completed its revolution. Thus the earth travels round the sun, not in a circle, but an ellipsis, of which the sun occupies one of the *foci*; and in its course the earth alternately approaches and recedes from it, so that what at first appeared to be a dangerous irregularity, is the means by which the most perfect order and harmony are produced. The earth then travels on at a very unequal rate, its velocity being accelerated as it approaches the sun, and retarded as it recedes from it.

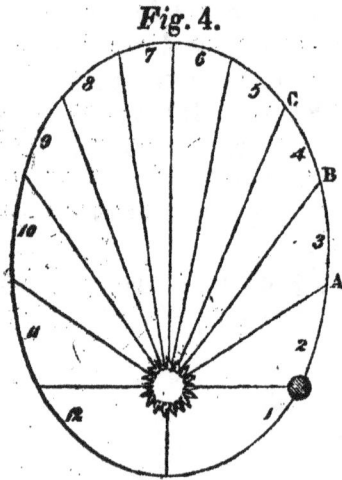

Fig. 4.

Now it is mathematically demonstrable, that when a body moves round a point towards which it is attracted, the areas included between the line it describes and the lines joining its place at different instants to the attracting point, are equal in equal times. The whole of the space contained within the earth's orbit is (*fig.* 4), divided into a number of areas, or spaces, 1, 2, 3, 4, &c., all of which are of equal dimensions, though of very different forms; some of them are long and narrow, others broad and short; but they each of them contain an equal quantity of space. An imaginary line drawn from the centre of the earth to that of the sun, and keeping pace with the earth in its revolution, passes over equal areas in equal times: that is to say, if it is a month going from A to B, it will be a month going from B to C, and another from C to E, and so on.

The inequality is not in fact so considerable as appears in figure 4; for the earth's orbit is not so eccentric as it is there described; and, in reality, differs but little from a circle. That part of the earth's orbit nearest the sun is called its *perihelion*, that part most distant from the sun its *aphelion*; and the earth is about three millions of miles nearer the sun at its perihelion than at its aphelion. You will learn with surprise that during the height of our summer, the earth is in that part of its orbit which is most distant from the sun, and it is during the severity of winter that it approaches nearest to it. The difference, however, of the earth's distance from the sun in summer and winter, when compared with its total distance from the sun, is but inconsiderable, for three millions of miles sinks into insignificance in comparison of 95 millions of miles, which is our mean distance from the sun. The change of temperature, arising from this difference, would in itself scarcely be sensible, and it is completely overpowered by other causes which produce the variations of the seasons; but the explanation of these must be deferred till we have made some further observations on the heavenly bodies. Since the earth moves with greatest velocity in that part of its orbit nearest the sun, it must complete its journey through one half of its orbit in a shorter time than through the other half; and in fact, it is about seven days longer performing our summer half of its orbit than the winter half. The planets are celestial bodies which revolve round the sun, on the same principle, and they are supposed to resemble the earth also in many other respects; and we are led by analogy to consider them as inhabited worlds.

Some of the planets are proved to be larger than the earth: it is only their immense distance from us which renders their apparent dimensions so small. Now, if we consider them as enormous globes, instead of small twinkling spots, we shall find it most consistent with our ideas of the Divine wisdom and beneficence, to suppose that these celestial bodies should be created for the habitation of beings, who are, like us, blessed by His providence. Hence, in a moral, as well as a physical point of view, it is most rational to consider the planets as worlds revolving round the sun; and the fixed stars as other suns, each of them probably attended by its system of planets, to which they respectively impart their influence. Our telescopes are brought to such a degree of perfection, that from the appearances which the moon exhibits when seen through them, we have probable reason to conclude that it is a habitable globe; its mountains and valleys are very perceptible, and some astronomers imagine that they have seen volcanoes in it.

The planets which are supposed to revolve round the fixed stars must of course be much smaller than the suns which give them light; and the distance which makes these suns appear to us like stars must render their planets quite invisible: besides the light of these planets would be much more feeble than that of the fixed stars; there would be exactly the same sort of difference as between the light of the sun and that of the moon, the first being a fixed star, the second a planet.

According to the laws of attraction, the planets belonging to our system all gravitate towards the sun; and this force, combined with that of projection, occasions their revolution round the sun, in orbits more or less elliptical, according to the proportion which these two forces bear to each other. But the planets have also another motion: they revolve upon their axis. The axis of a planet is an imaginary line which passes through its centre, and on which it turns; and it is this motion which produces day and night. With that side of the planet facing the sun, it is day; and with the opposite side, which remains in darkness, it is night. Our earth, which we consider as a planet, is 24 hours in performing one revolution on its axis; in that period of time, therefore, we have a day and a night. Hence this revolution is called the earth's diurnal or daily motion; and it is this revolution of the earth from west to east which produces an apparent motion of the sun, moon, and stars in the contrary direction.

Section II.—*On the Planets.*

The Planets are distinguished into primary and secondary. Those which revolve immediately about the sun are called primary. Many of these are attended in their course by smaller planets, which revolve round them: these are called secondary planets, satellites, or moons. Such is our moon, which accompanies the earth, and is carried with it round the sun. The sun is the general centre of attraction to our system of planets; but the satellites revolve round the primary planets, on account of their greater proximity. The force of attraction is not only proportional to the quantity of matter, but to the degree of proximity of the attracting body. This power being weakened by diffusion, diminishes as the squares of the distances increase. The square is the product of a number multiplied by itself; so that a planet situated at twice the distance at which we are from the sun would gravitate four times less than we do, the product of two multiplied by itself being four. The more distant planets, therefore, move slower in their orbits, for their projectile force must be proportioned to that of attraction. This diminution of attraction by the increase of distance also accounts for the motion of the secondary round the primary planets, in preference to the sun; for the vicinity of the primary planets renders their attraction stronger than that of the sun. But since the attraction between bodies is mutual, the primary planets are also attracted by their satellites. The moon attracts the earth, as well as the earth the moon; but as the latter is the smaller body, her attraction is proportionally less. The result is, that neither the earth revolves round the moon, nor the moon round the earth; but they both revolve round a point, which is their common centre of gravity, and which is as much nearer the earth than the moon, as the weight of the former exceeds that of the latter. It has been already stated (p. xix.) that if two bodies were fastened together by a wire or bar, their common centre of gravity would be in the middle of the bar, provided the bodies were of equal weight; and if they differed in weight, it would be nearer the larger body. Attraction is the tie which unites the earth and moon; and if these bodies had no projectile force which prevented their mutual attraction from bringing them together, they would meet at their common centre of gravity.

The earth then has three different motions: it revolves round the sun, upon its axis, and round the point towards which the moon attracts it; and this is the case with every planet which is attended by satellites. The complicated effect of this variety of motions produces certain irregularities, which, however, it is not necessary to notice at present. The planets act on the sun in the same manner as they are themselves acted on by their satellites; but the gravity of the planets (even when taken collectively) is so trifling compared with that of the sun, that they do not cause the latter to move so much as one-half of its diameter. The planets do not, therefore, revolve round the centre of the sun, but round a point at a small distance from its centre, about which the sun also revolves. The sun also revolves on his axis. This motion is ascertained by observing certain spots which disappear and re-appear regularly at stated times.

The great distance of the planets renders their motion apparently so slow, that the eye is not sensible of their progress in their orbit, unless we watch them for some considerable length of time: in different seasons they appear in different parts of the heavens: The most accurate idea which can be given of the situation and motion of the planets will be by the examination of the diagram (fig. 5), representing the solar system, in which the principal planets, with their orbits, are delineated. The sun is in the common centre of the whole, but, to avoid confusion in the figure, he is not represented.

The orbits of the planets are so nearly circular, and the common centre of gravity of the solar system so near the centre of the sun, that these deviations are not noticed in the diagram. The dimensions of the planets, in their true proportions, will be found delineated in fig. 6: the signs annexed to them are those used to represent the planets, which are also used in fig. 1.

INTRODUCTION TO ASTRONOMY.

xxxv

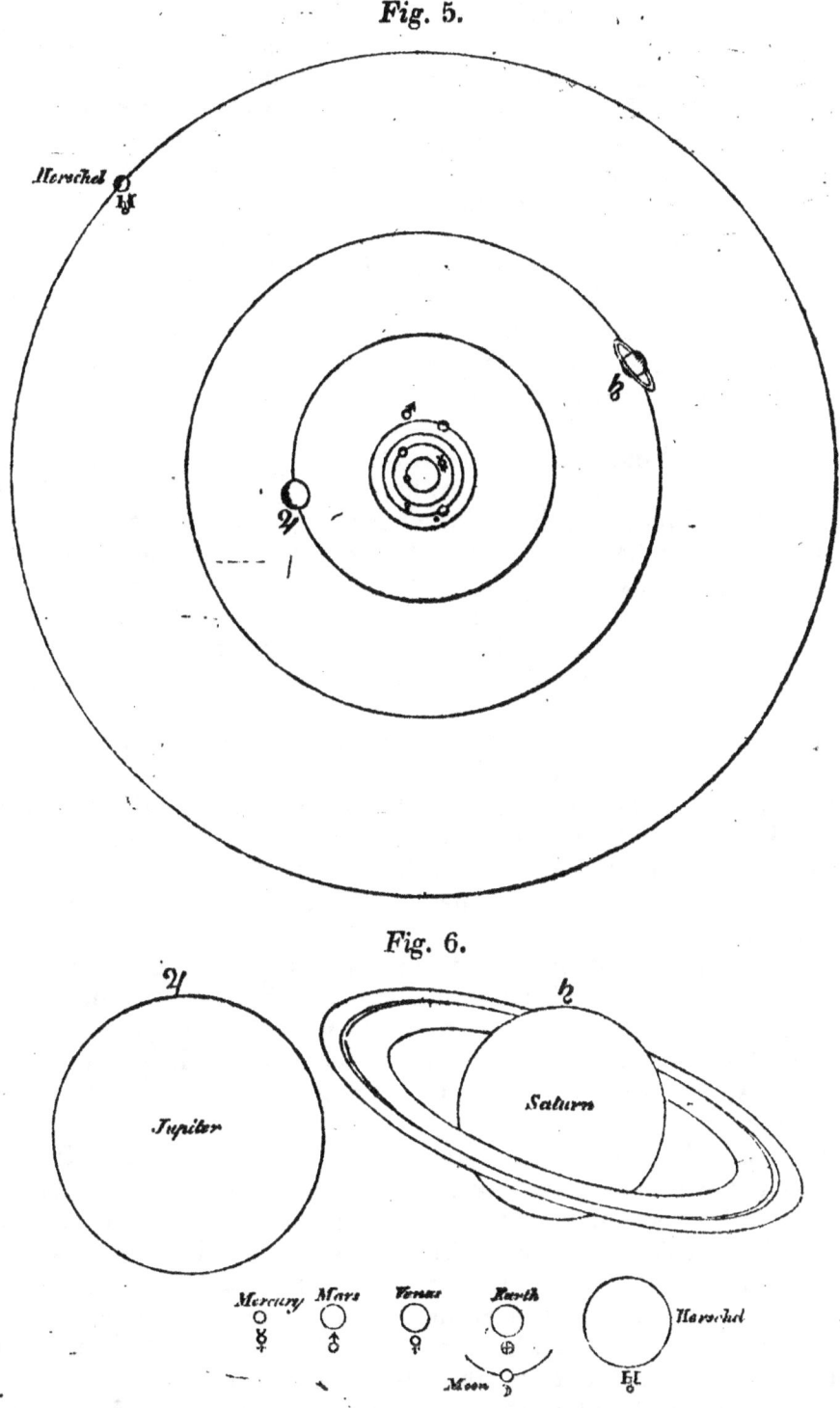

Fig. 5.

Fig. 6.

Mercury is the planet nearest the sun: his orbit is consequently contained within ours; but his vicinity to the sun occasions his being nearly lost in the brilliancy of his rays; and when we see this planet, the sun is so dazzling, that very accurate observations cannot be made upon him. He performs his revolution round the sun in about 87 days, which is consequently the length of his year; the time of his rotation on his axis is not accurately known; his distance from the sun is computed to be 37 millions of miles, and his diameter 3,224 miles. The heat of this planet is so great, that water cannot exist there but in a state of vapour, and metals would be liquefied.

Venus, the next in the order of planets, is 68 millions of miles from the sun; she revolves about her axis in 23 hours and 21 minutes, and goes round the sun in 224 days 17 hours. The diameter of Venus is 7,687 miles. The orbit of Venus is within ours; during nearly one-half of her course in it we see her before sunrise, and she is called the morning-star; in the corresponding part of her orbit, on the other side, she rises later than the sun. We then cannot see her rising, as she rises in the daytime; but she also sets later; so that we perceive her approaching the horizon after sunset: she is then called Hesperus, or the evening-star.

The planet next to Venus is the Earth, of which we shall soon speak at full length; at present we shall only observe, that we are 95 millions of miles distant from the sun—that we perform our annual revolution in 365 days, 5 hours, and 49 minutes—and are attended in our course by a single moon.

Then follows Mars. He can never come between us and the sun, like Mercury and Venus; his motion is, however, very perceptible, as he may be traced to different situations in the heavens; his distance from the sun is 144 millions of miles; he turns on his axis in 24 hours and 39 minutes; and he performs his annual revolution in about 687 of our days: his diameter is 4,189 miles. Then follow four very small planets—Juno, Ceres, Pallas, and Vesta, which have been recently discovered, but whose dimensions and distances from the sun have not been very accurately ascertained.

Jupiter is next in order. This is the largest of all the planets; he is about 490 millions of miles distant from the sun, and completes his annual period in nearly twelve of our years; he revolves on his axis in about ten hours; he is above 1,400 times as large as our earth, his diameter being 89,170 miles. The respective proportions of the planets cannot therefore, you see, be conveniently delineated in a diagram. He is attended by four moons.

The next planet is Saturn, whose distance from the sun is about 900 millions of miles. His diurnal rotation is performed in ten hours and a quarter; his annual revolution in nearly thirty of our years; his diameter is 79,000 miles. This planet is surrounded by a luminous ring, the nature of which astronomers are much at a loss to conjecture: he has seven moons.

Lastly, we observe the Georgium Sidus, discovered by Dr. Herschel, and which is attended by six moons. His numerous moons are, however, far from making so splendid an appearance as ours; for they can reflect only the light which they receive from the sun; and both light and heat decrease in the same ratio or proportion to the distances as gravity;—consequently Saturn, which is at nearly ten times the distance at which we are from the sun, has a hundred times less heat and light. To us such a climate would not be habitable; but this furnishes no argument against the supposition that these planets are worlds, peopled with beings whose bodies are adapted to the various temperatures and elements in which they are situated. Whether we judge from the analogy of our own earth, or from that of the great and universal beneficence of Providence, we may reasonably conjecture this to be the case: and an inhabitant of Mercury might with as much plausibility pity us for the intense coldness of our situation, or those of Jupiter and Saturn for our intolerable heat, as we can draw any inferences against their existence, from the circumstance that we, constituted as we are, could not live there.

Comets are supposed to be planets. The re-appearance of some of them at stated times proves that they revolve round the sun; but in orbits so extremely eccentric, and running to such a distance from the sun, that they disappear for a great number of years. If they are inhabited, it must be by a species of beings very different, not only from the inhabitants of this, but from those of any of the other planets, as they must experience the greatest vicissitudes of heat and cold: their heat in that part of their orbit nearest the sun is computed to be greater than that of red-hot iron. In this part of its orbit the comet emits a luminous vapour, called the tail, which it gradually loses as it recedes from the sun; and the comet itself totally disappears from our sight in the more distant parts of its orbit, which, in most cases, extends considerably beyond that of the furthest planet.

The number of comets belonging to our system cannot be ascertained, as some of them are several centuries before they make their re-appearance. The number that are known by their regular re-appearance is very small.

The ancients, in order to recognise the fixed stars, formed them into groups, to which they gave the names of the figures delineated on the celestial globe. In order to show their proper situations in the heavens, they should be painted on the internal surface of a hollow sphere, from the centre of which you should view them: you would then behold them as they appear to be situated in the heavens. The twelve constellations, called the Signs of the Zodiac, are those which are so situated, that the earth in its annual revolution passes directly between them and the sun. Their names are—Aries, the Ram; Taurus, the Bull; Gemini, the Twins; Cancer, the Crab; Leo, the Lion; Virgo, the Virgin; Libra, the Balance; Scorpio, the Scorpion; Sagittarius, the Archer; Capricornus, the Wild Goat; Aquarius, the Water-carrier; Pisces, the Fishes: the whole occupying a complete circle, or broad belt, in the heavens, called the Zodiac (*fig.* 7). Hence, a right line drawn from the earth, and passing through the sun, would reach one of these constellations, and the sun is said to be in that constellation at which the line terminates. Thus when the earth is at A, the sun would appear to be in the constellation or sign Aries; when the earth is at B, the sun would appear in Cancer; when the earth was at C, the sun would be in Libra; and when the earth was at D, the sun would be in Capricorn. This circle, in which the sun thus appears to move, and which passes through the middle of the Zodiac, is called the Ecliptic.

We have no means of ascertaining the distance of the fixed stars. When therefore they are said to be in the Zodiac, it is merely implied that they are situated in that direction, and that they shine upon us through that portion of the heavens which we call the Zodiac.

Whether the apparent difference of size and brilliancy of the stars proceed from their various degrees of remoteness, or of dimension, is a point which astronomers are not enabled to ascertain. Considering them as suns, we know no reason why they should not vary in size, as well as the planets belonging to them.

It may perhaps be objected to this system of the universe, that it is directly in opposition to the evidence of our senses, to which it is plain and obvious that the earth is motionless, and that the sun and stars revolve round it. But our senses, or at least the inferences we draw from them, too often mislead us, for us to place implicit reliance on them. When sailing on the water with a very steady breeze, the houses, trees, and every object appear to move, whilst we are insensible of the motion of the

INTRODUCTION TO ASTRONOMY.

Fig. 7.

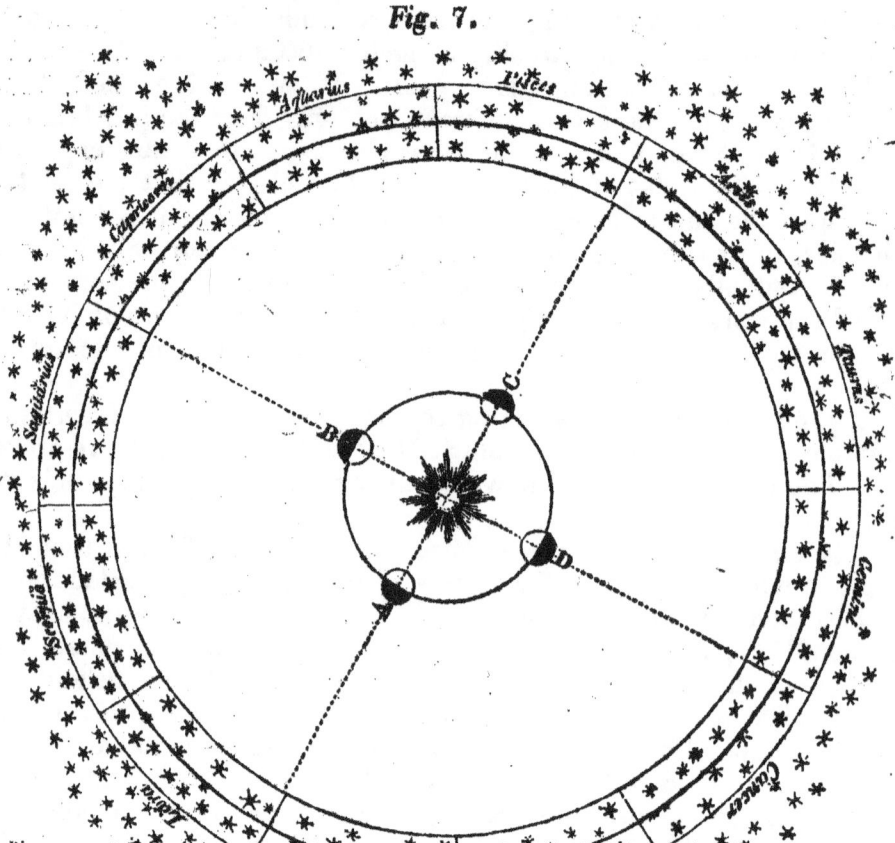

vessel in which we sail. It is only when some obstacle impedes our motion that we are conscious of moving; and were you to close your eyes while sailing on calm water, with a steady wind, you would not perceive that you moved, for you could not feel it, and you could see it only by observing the change of place of the objects on shore. So it is with the motion of the earth: every thing on its surface, and the air that surrounds it, accompanies it in its revolution—it meets with no resistance, therefore we are insensible of motion.

The apparent motion of the sun and stars affords us the same proof of the earth's motion that the crew of a vessel has of their motion from the apparent motion of the objects on shore. Imagine the earth to be sailing round its axis, and successively passing by every star, which, like the objects on land, we suppose to be moving, instead of ourselves. In balloons, the earth appears to sink beneath the balloon, instead of the balloon rising above the earth.

It is a law which we discover throughout Nature, and worthy of its great Author, that all its purposes are accomplished by the most simple means. We have no reason to suppose this law infringed, in order that our earth may remain at rest, while the sun and stars move round us: their regular motions, which are explained by the laws of attraction on the first supposition, would be unintelligible on the last, and the order and harmony of the universe be destroyed. What an immense circuit the sun and stars would make daily, were their apparent motions real! We know many of them to be bodies more considerable than our earth; for our eyes vainly endeavour to persuade us, that they are little brilliants sparkling in the heavens, while science teaches us that they are immense spheres, whose apparent dimensions are diminished by distance." If the heavenly bodies revolved round our earth in twenty-four hours, the centrifugal force implied in so rapid a motion would be quite destructive, and no power can be assigned which would be sufficient to balance it; grindstones driven by machinery in manufactories have been known to fly in pieces from their great velocity. Why then should these enormous globes traverse such an immensity of space, merely to prevent the necessity of our earth revolving on its axis? The motion produced by the revolution of the earth on its axis is about thirteen miles and a half a minute to an inhabitant of London. A person at the equator moves much quicker; and one situated near the poles much slower, since they each perform a revolution in twenty-four hours. But in performing its revolution round the sun, every part of the earth moves with an equal velocity, and this velocity is no less than a thousand miles a minute.

In ancient times, the earth was supposed to occupy the centre of the system; and the sun, moon, and stars to revolve round it. This was the system of Ptolemy; but so long ago as the beginning of the sixteenth century it was discarded, and the solar system, such as we have shown, was established by the celebrated astronomer Copernicus and his followers, and is hence called the Copernican system. But the theory of gravitation, the discovery of the source whence this beautiful and harmonious arrangement flows, we owe to the powerful genius of Sir Isaac Newton, who lived at a much later period.

It is far less difficult to trace by observation the motion of the planets, than to divine by what power they are impelled and guided. The idea of gravitation, it is said, was first suggested to Sir Isaac Newton by a circumstance from which one should little have expected so grand a theory to have arisen. During the prevalence of the plague in the year 1665, Newton retired into the country to avoid the contagion. When sitting one day in his orchard, he observed an apple fall from a tree, which led to a train of thought, whence his grand theory of universal gravitation was ultimately developed. His first reflection was, whether the apple would fall to the earth if removed to a great distance from it; then, how far it would be required to be removed from the earth, before it would cease to be attracted; would it retain its tendency to fall at the distance of a thousand miles, or ten thousand, or to the distance of the moon?—and here the idea occurred to him that it was not impossible that the moon herself might have a similar tendency, and gravitate to the earth in the same manner as the bodies on or near its surface, and that this gravity might possibly be the power which balanced the centrifugal force implied in her motion in her orbit. It was then natural to extend this idea to the other planets, and consider them as gravitating towards the sun, in the same manner as the moon gravitates towards the earth. He followed up this beautiful hypothesis by a series of calculations and demonstrations, unparalleled for their originality, and the industry and judgment with which they were conducted, until he established the stupendous doctrine of universal gravitation! Who would imagine that the simple circumstance of the fall of an apple would have led to such magnificent results? It is the mark of superior genius to find matter for observation and research in circumstances which, to the ordinary mind, appear trivial, because they are common, and with which they are satisfied because they are natural, without reflecting that Nature is our grand field of observation—that within it is contained our whole store of knowledge: in a word, that to study the works of Nature, is to learn to appreciate and admire the wisdom of God. Thus, it was the simple circumstance of the fall of an apple which led to the discovery of the laws upon which the Copernican system is founded; and whatever credit this system had obtained before, it now rests upon a basis from which it cannot be shaken.

Section III.—*On the Earth.*

As the Earth is the planet in which we are the most particularly interested, we shall explain the effects resulting from its annual and diurnal motions; but for this purpose it will be necessary to make you acquainted with the terrestrial globe. This globe, or sphere (*fig.* 8), represents the earth. The line which passes through its centre, and on which it turns,

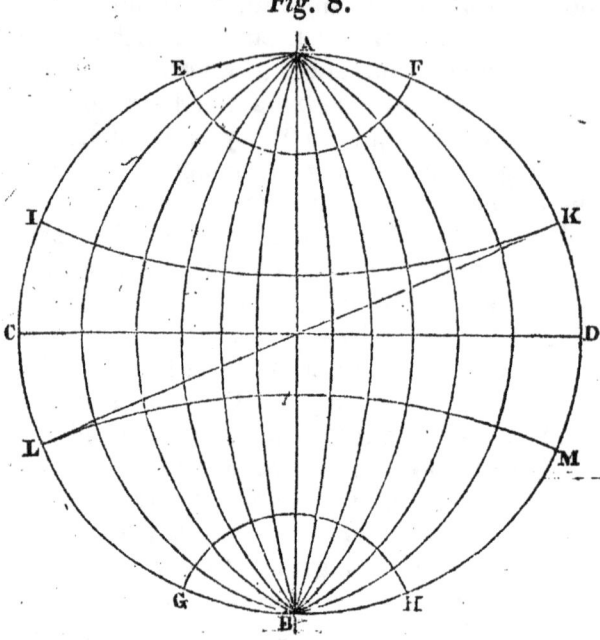

Fig. 8.

is called its axis; and the two extremities of the axis, A and B, are the poles distinguished by the names of the north and the south pole. The circle, C D, which divides the globe into two equal parts between the poles, is called the equator, or equinoctial line; that part of the globe to the north of the equator is the northern hemisphere; that part to the south of the equator, the southern hemisphere. The small circle, E F, which surrounds the north pole, is called the arctic circle; that, G H, surrounding the south pole, the antarctic circle. There are two intermediate circles between the polar circles and the equator,—that to the north, I K, called the tropic of Cancer; that to the south, L M, called the tropic of Capricorn. Lastly, this circle, L K, which divides the globe into two equal parts, crossing the equator, and extending northward as far as the tropic of Cancer, and southward as far as the tropic of Capricorn, is called the ecliptic. The delineation of the ecliptic on the terrestrial globe is not without danger of conveying false ideas; for the ecliptic (as has before been said) is an imaginary circle in the heavens, passing through the middle of the zodiac, and situated in the plane of the earth's orbit.

In order to understand the meaning of the plane of the earth's orbit, let us suppose a smooth, thin, solid plane cutting the sun through the centre, extending out as far as the fixed stars, and terminating in a circle, which passes through the middle of the zodiac. In this plane the earth moves in its revolution round the sun: it is therefore called the plane of the earth's orbit; and the circle in which this plane cuts the signs of the zodiac is the ecliptic. Let *fig.* 9 represent such a plane, S the sun, E the earth with its orbit, and A B C D the ecliptic passing through the

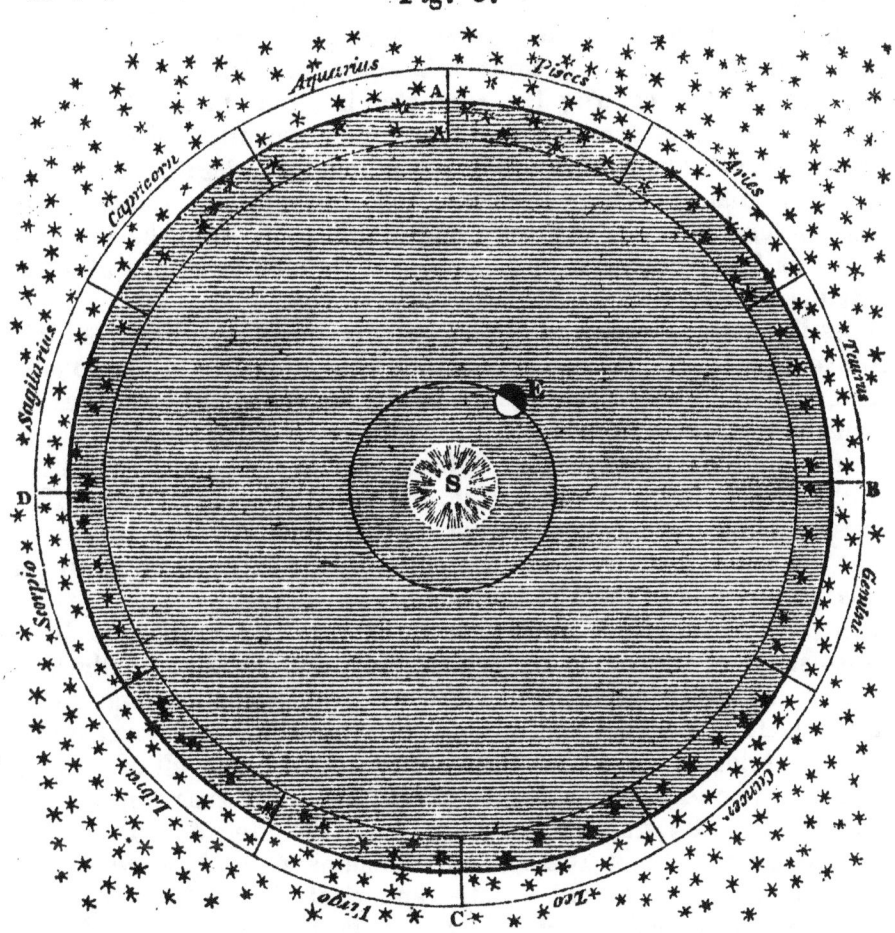

Fig. 9.

middle of the zodiac. Therefore the ecliptic relates only to the heavens; but it is described upon the terrestrial globe to facilitate the demonstration of a variety of problems in the use of the globes; and besides, the obliquity of this circle to the equator is rendered more conspicuous by its being described on the same globe; and the obliquity of the ecliptic shows the inclination of the earth's axis to the plane of its orbit. But to return to *fig.* 8.

The spaces between the several parallel circles on the terrestrial globe are called zones; that which is comprehended between the tropics is distinguished by the name of the torrid zone; the spaces which extend from the tropics to the polar circles, the north and south temperate zones; and the spaces contained within the polar circles, the frigid zones.

The several lines which, you observe, are drawn from one pole to the other, cutting the equator at right angles, are called meridians. When any one of these meridians is exactly opposite the sun, it is mid-day, or twelve o'clock in the day, with all the places situated on that meridian; and, with the places situated on the opposite meridian, it is consequently midnight. To places situated equally distant from these two meridians, it is six o'clock. If they are to the east of the sun's meridian, it is six o'clock in the afternoon, because the sun will have previously passed over them; if to the west, it is six o'clock in the morning, and the sun will be proceeding towards that meridian.

Those circles which divide the globe into two equal parts, such as the equator and the ecliptic, are called great circles—to distinguish them from those which divide it into two unequal parts, as the tropics and polar circles, which are called small circles. All circles are divided into 360 equal parts, called degrees; and these degrees into 60 equal parts, called minutes. The diameter of a circle is a right line drawn across it, and passing through the centre; the diameter is equal to a little less than one-third of the circumference, and consequently contains a length equal to nearly 120 degrees, or more accurately, about $114\frac{1}{2}$ degrees, of the circle itself. A meridian, reaching from one pole to the other, is half a circle, and therefore contains 180 degrees; and the distance from the equator to the pole is half of a meridian, or a quarter of the circumference of a circle, and contains 90 degrees.

Besides the usual division of circles into degrees, the ecliptic is divided into twelve equal parts, called signs, which bear the name of the constellations through which this circle passes in the heavens. The degrees measured on the meridians from north to south, or south to north, are called degrees of latitude; those measured from east to west on the equator, or any of the lesser circles parallel to it, are called degrees of longitude;—these lesser circles are called parallels of latitude, because being every where at the same distance from the equator, the latitude of every point contained in any one of them is the same.

The degrees of longitude must necessarily vary in length according to the dimensions of the circle on which they are reckoned: those, for instance, at the polar circles, will be considerably smaller than those at the equator. The degrees of latitude, on the contrary, never vary in length, the meridians on which they are reckoned being all of the same dimensions. The length of a degree of latitude is 60 geographical miles, which is equal to $69\frac{1}{2}$ English statute miles. The degrees of longitude at the equator would be of the same dimensions were the earth a perfect sphere; but its form is not exactly spherical, being somewhat protuberant about the equator, and flattened towards the poles. This form proceeds from the superior action of the centrifugal power at the equator. The revolution of the earth on its axis gives every particle a tendency to fly off from the centre. This tendency is stronger or weaker in proportion to the velocity with which the particle moves. Now a particle situated near one of the polar circles makes one rotation in the same space of time as a particle at the equator; the latter, therefore, having a much larger circle to describe, travels proportionally faster, consequently the centrifugal force is much stronger at the equator than at the polar circles: it gradually decreases as you leave the equator and approach the poles, where, as there is no rotatory motion, it entirely ceases. Supposing, therefore, the earth to have been originally in a fluid state, the particles in the torrid zone would recede much farther from the centre than those in the frigid zones: thus the polar regions would become flattened, and those about the equator elevated. According to the same rule, our heads move with greater velocity than our feet; and on the summit of a mountain, our velocity is greater than in a valley; for the head is more distant from the centre of motion than the feet—the mountain-top than the valley. Even at the equator, however, the force of gravity preponderates very considerably, being at the equator 288 times greater than the centrifugal force.

It would be natural to suppose that the prominence at the equator and depression at the poles would render the attraction of gravity stronger at the former, so that a body would weigh heavier at the equator than at the poles. This, however, is erroneous. The manner in which the force of gravity varies at different spots on the surface of the earth depends on considerations too complicated to be here explained; but the general result is that, although the difference in different situations is very small, the nearer any part of the surface is to the centre of attraction, the more strongly it is attracted. We refer, however, only to any situation on the surface of the earth. Were you to penetrate into the interior, the attraction of the parts above you would counteract that of the parts beneath you, and consequently diminish the power of gravity in proportion as you approached the centre; and if you reached that point, being equally attracted by the parts all around you, gravity would cease, and you would be without weight. Bodies therefore gravitate less, and consequently weigh less, at the equator than at the poles, while their centrifugal force is much greater; and as this force tends to drive bodies from the centre, it is necessarily opposed to, and must decrease the power of gravity. There are then two causes which render bodies lighter in weight at the equator than at the poles: the diminution of gravitation, and the increase of the centrifugal force. Men of science have travelled both to the equator and to Lapland, with a view of ascertaining this fact. The severity of the climate and the obstruction of ice has hitherto rendered every attempt to reach the pole abortive; but the difference of weight of a body at the equator and in Lapland is very considerable.

This difference cannot be discovered by simply weighing bodies; for if the body under trial at the equator decreased in weight, the weight which was opposed to it in the opposite scale must diminish in the same proportion. For instance, if a pound of sugar did not weigh so heavy at the equator as at the poles, the leaden pound which served to weigh it would not be so heavy either; therefore they would still balance each other. A pendulum is the instrument used for the purpose of discovering the variations of gravity in different situations on the surface of the earth. A pendulum consists of a line, or rod, to one end of which a weight is attached, and it is suspended by the other to a fixed point, about which it is made to vibrate. Without being put in motion, a pendulum, like a plumb-line, hangs perpendicular to the general surface of the earth, by which it is attracted; but if you raise a pendulum on one side, gravity will bring it back to its perpendicular position. It will, however, not remain stationary there, for the velocity it has received during its descent will impel it onwards, and it will rise on the opposite side to an equal height: from thence it is brought back by gravity, and again driven by the impulse of its velocity. Were the motion of a pendulum not opposed by the resistance of the air in which it vibrates, and by the friction of the part by which it is suspended, it would be perpetual; and were the force of gravity which produces these vibrations always the same, they would be perfectly regular, being of equal distances and performed in equal times. This is the natural result of the uniformity of the power which produces these vibrations: the force of gravity being always the same, the velocity of the pendulum must consequently be uniform. But if the force of gravity is less at the equator than at the poles, the vibrations of the pendulum will be slower.

It was thus that the difference of gravity was discovered, and the true figure of the earth ascertained; for after having made due allowance for the effect of the centrifugal force, gravity was still found to be greater in the polar than in the equatorial regions, owing to the spheroidal figure of the earth. If then a pendulum vibrates faster at the poles and slower at the equator, the inhabitants must regulate their clocks in a different manner from ours, in which the pendulum vibrates once in a second of time. The only alteration required is to lengthen the pendulum in one case, and to shorten it in the other; for the velocity of the vibrations of a pendulum depends on its length; and when it is said that a pendulum at the pole vibrates quicker than one at the equator, it is supposing them both to be of the same length. A pendulum which vibrates a second in this latitude is rather more than 39 inches in length. In order to vibrate at the equator in the same space of time, it must be shortened by a few lines; and at the poles, it must be proportionally lengthened.

We shall now explain the variation of the seasons, and the difference of the length of the days and nights in those seasons—both effects resulting from the same cause. In moving round the sun, the axis of the earth is not perpendicular to the plane of its orbit; in other words, its axis does not move round the sun in an upright position, but slanting or oblique. This you will understand more clearly if you carry a small globe round a lamp or candle, which is to represent the sun (*fig.* 10). You

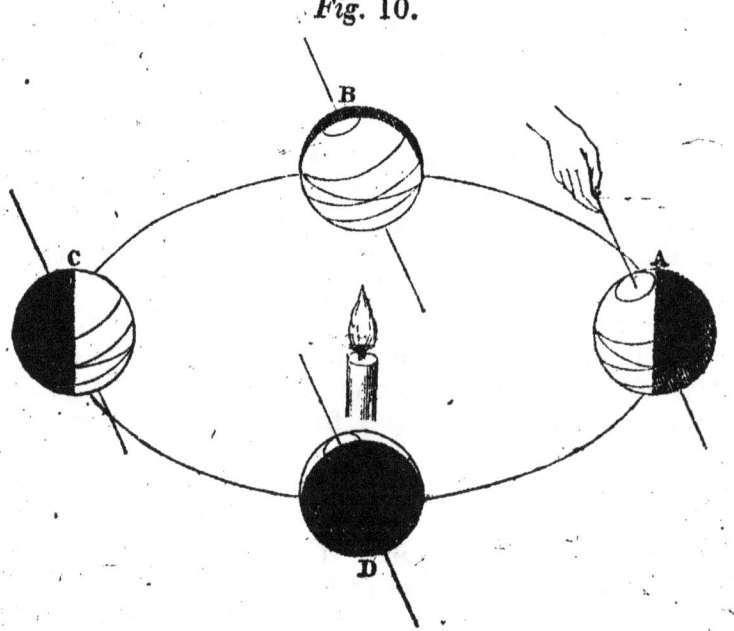

Fig. 10.

must consider the ecliptic drawn on the small globe as representing the plane of the earth's orbit; and the equator, which crosses the ecliptic in two places, shows the degree of obliquity of the axis of the earth in that orbit, which is exactly 23½ degrees. The points in which the ecliptic intersects the equator are called nodes. The globe at A is situated as it is in the midst of summer, or what is called the summer solstice, which is on the 21st of June. The north pole is then inclined towards the sun, and the northern hemisphere enjoys much more of his rays than the southern. The sun now shines over the whole of the north frigid zone; and notwithstanding the earth's diurnal revolution, which may be imitated by twirling the ball on the wire, it will continue to shine upon it as long as it remains in this situation, whilst the south frigid zone is at the same time completely in obscurity.

Let the earth now set off from its position in the summer solstice, and carry it round the sun: observe that the axis must be always inclined in the same direction, and the north pole point to the same spot in the heavens. There is a fixed star situated near that spot, which is hence called the North Polar Star. The earth at B has gone through one quarter of its orbit, and is arrived at that point at which the ecliptic cuts or crosses the equator, and which is called the autumnal equinox. The sun now shines from one pole to the other, as it would constantly do were the axis of the earth perpendicular to its orbit, the inclination of the axis being now neither towards the sun nor in the contrary direction. At this period of the year, the days and nights are equal in every part of the earth, excepting at the very poles; but the next step she takes in her orbit involves the north pole in darkness, whilst it illumines that of the south. This change was gradually preparing as the earth moved from summer to autumn; the arctic circle begins to have short nights, which increase as the earth approaches the autumnal equinox; and the instant it passes that point, the long night of the north pole commences, and the south pole begins to enjoy the light of the sun. As the earth proceeds in its orbit, the days shorten and the nights lengthen throughout the northern hemisphere, until it arrives at the winter solstice, on the 21st of December, when the north frigid zone is entirely in darkness, and the southern enjoys uninterrupted daylight. Exactly half of the equator, it will be observed, is enlightened in every position, and consequently the day is there always equal to the night.

Observe that the inhabitants of the torrid zone have much more heat than we have, as the sun's rays fall perpendicularly on them, while they shine obliquely on the temperate, and almost horizontally on the frigid zone; for during their long day, the sun moves round at no great elevation above their horizon without either rising or setting; the only observable difference is, that it is more elevated by a few degrees at mid-day than at midnight; but at the poles themselves, the sun travels round in the course of four-and-twenty hours nearly at the same elevation from the horizon, rising every day a very little higher from the vernal equinox till midsummer, and declining after that period till the autumnal equinox, when their long night begins.

To a person placed in the temperate zone, as we are in England, the sun's rays will shine neither so obliquely as at the poles, nor so vertically as at the equator; but will fall upon him more obliquely in autumn and winter than in summer. Therefore, the inhabitants of the earth between the polar circles and the equator will not have merely one day and one night in the year, as happens at the pole; nor will they have equal days and equal nights, as at the equator; but their days and nights will vary in length at different times of the year, according as their respective poles incline towards or from the sun, and the difference will be greater in proportion to their distance from the equator. During the other half of her orbit, the same effect takes place in the southern hemisphere as what we have just remarked in the northern. When the earth arrives at the vernal equinox, D, where the ecliptic again cuts the equator, on the 22nd of March, she is situated, with respect to the sun, exactly in the same position as in the autumnal equinox, excepting that it is now autumn in the southern hemisphere, whilst it is spring with us; for the half of the globe which is enlightened extends exactly from one pole to the other: the sun rises to the north pole, and sets to the south pole. On the two days of the equinox the sun is visible at both poles; but only half of it is seen from either, the other half being concealed by the horizon.

The sun is nearly three of our days in rising and setting at the poles. About thirty hours, or rather more, before he reaches the exact period of the autumnal equinox, the upper edge or limb of the sun begins to be visible at the south pole; and it is there seen constantly travelling round the horizon, and rising gradually higher and higher, till at the end of about sixty hours, after revolving nearly 2½ times round the horizon, the whole of its orb is visible.

At the same moment that the edge of the sun becomes visible at the south pole, the same edge which appears as the lower limb at the north pole begins to dip below the horizon; but the sun still continues visible, travelling round the horizon, more and more of it being hid, till, at the end of sixty hours, it totally disappears, just at the same moment when it is fully seen at the south pole. As the earth proceeds towards summer, the days lengthen in the northern hemisphere, and shorten in the southern, till the earth reaches our summer solstice, which brings it again to the spot whence we first accompanied her.

The mind can find no object of contemplation more sublime than the course of this magnificent globe, impelled by the combined powers of projection and attraction to roll in one invariable course around the source of light and heat; and what can be more delightful than the beneficent effects of this vivifying power on its attendant planet? It is at once the grand principle which animates and fecundates Nature.

The sun's rays afford less heat when in an oblique direction than when perpendicular, because fewer of them fall upon an equal portion of the earth. This will be understood better by referring to *fig.* 11, which represents two equal portions of the sun's rays, shining upon different parts of

Fig. 11.

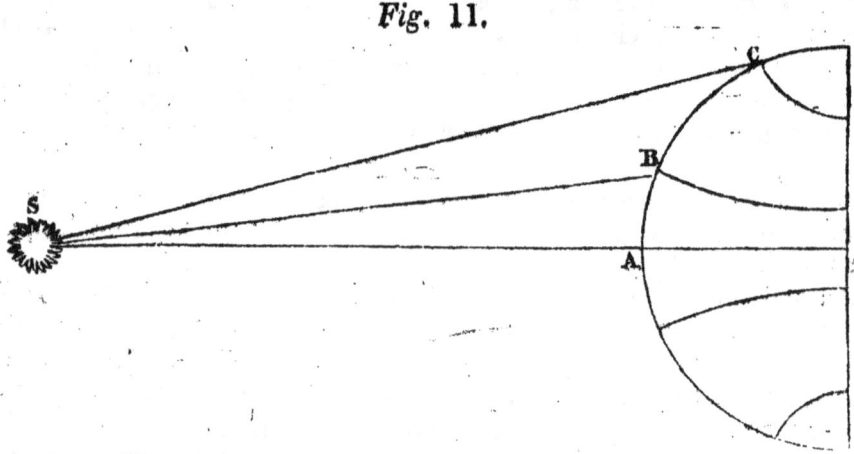

the earth. Here it is evident that the same number of rays fall on the space A B as fall on the space B C; and as A B is less than B C, the heat and light will be much stronger in the former than in the latter. A B, you see, represents the equatorial regions, where the sun shines perpendicularly; and B C the temperate and frozen climates, where his rays fall more obliquely. This accounts also for the greater heat of summer, as the sun shines less obliquely in summer than in winter.

In *fig.* 12, the earth is represented as it is situated on the 21st of June, when England receives less oblique, and consequently a greater number of rays than at any other season; and *fig.* 13 shows the situation of England on the 21st of December, when the rays of the sun fall most obliquely upon her. But there is also another reason why oblique rays give less heat than those which are perpendicular; the former have a greater portion of the atmosphere to traverse; and though it is true that the atmosphere is itself a transparent body, it does not admit the passage of the

INTRODUCTION TO ASTRONOMY.

Fig. 12.

Fig. 13.

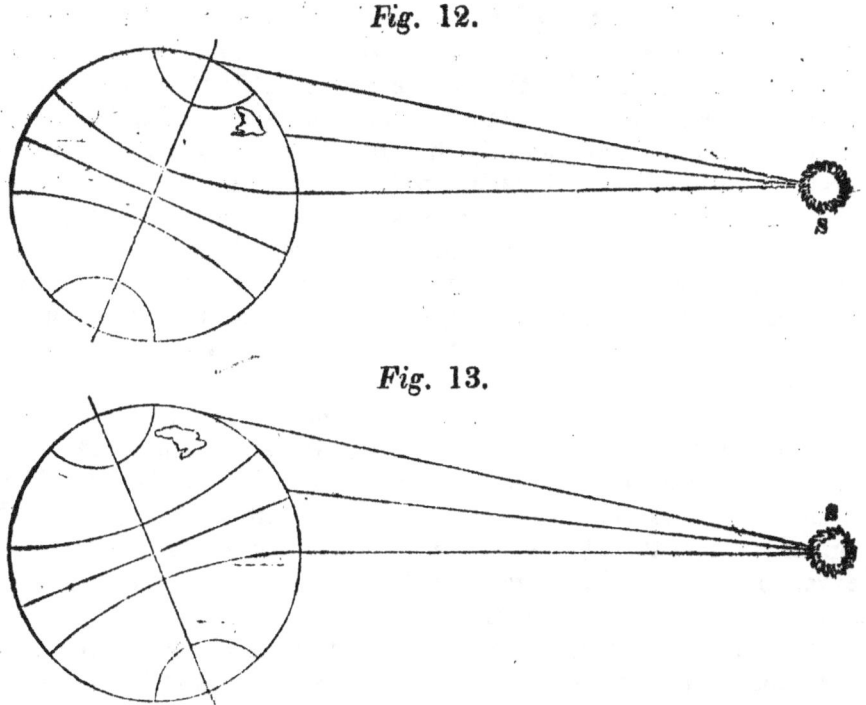

sun's rays quite freely; and besides, it is always loaded more or less with dense and foggy vapour, which the rays of the sun cannot easily penetrate; therefore the greater the quantity of atmosphere the sun's rays have to pass through in their way to the earth, the fewer of them will reach it. This will be better understood by referring to *fig*. 14. The dotted line round the earth describes the extent of the atmosphere, and the lines which proceed from the sun to the earth, the passage of two equal portions of the sun's rays to the equatorial and polar regions: the latter, from its greater obliquity, passes through a greater extent of atmosphere.

The diminution of heat, morning and evening, is also owing to the greater obliquity of the sun's rays; and, as such, they are affected by both the causes which have just been explained: the difficulty of passing through a foggy atmosphere is more particularly applicable to them, as mists and vapours are very prevalent about the time of sunrise and sunset. But the diminished obliquity of the sun's rays is not the sole cause of the heat of summer; the length of the days greatly conduces to it; for the longer the sun is above the horizon, the more heat he will communicate

Fig. 14.

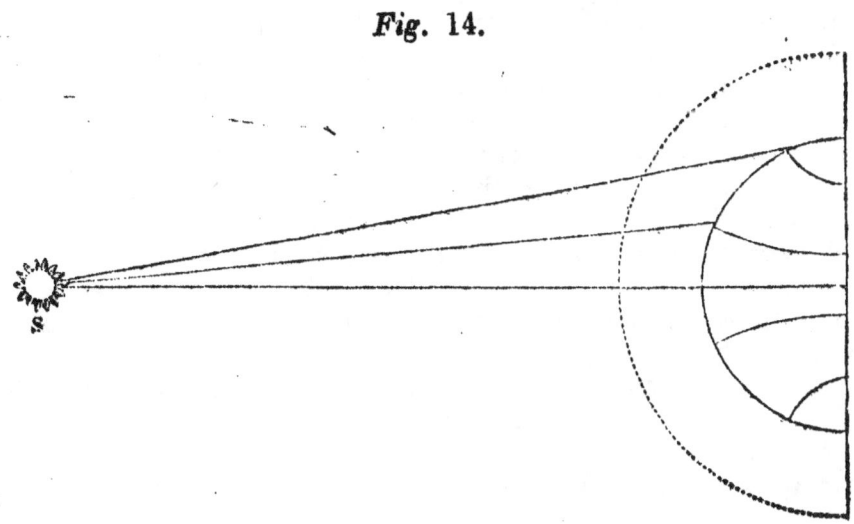

to the earth; and yet, though both the longest days and the most perpendicular rays are on the 21st of June, the greatest heat prevails in July and August. To account for this, you must reflect that those parts of the earth which are once heated retain the heat for a considerable length of time; and the additional quantity they receive occasions an elevation of temperature, although the days begin to shorten, and the sun's rays to fall more obliquely. For the same reason, we have generally more heat at three o'clock in the afternoon than at twelve, when the sun is on the meridian. As long as the sun continues to communicate more heat than the earth parts with in a given time, so long the heat of the earth will increase, even though the rate at which it receives new heat from the sun is diminished.

The vicissitudes of seasons of the other planets vary according as their axes deviate more or less from the perpendicular to the plane of their orbits. The axis of Jupiter is nearly perpendicular to the plane of his orbit; those of Mars and of Saturn are each inclined at angles of about 60 degrees; whilst the axis of Venus is believed to be elevated only 15 or 20 degrees above her orbit: the vicissitudes of her seasons must therefore be considerably greater than ours.

There is one more observation to make relative to the earth's motion, which is, that although we have but 365 days and nights in the year, she performs 366 complete revolutions on her axis during that time. This is owing to the progressive motion of the earth in its orbit whilst it revolves on its axis: as it advances almost a degree westward in its orbit, in the same time that it completes a revolution eastward on its axis, it must revolve nearly one degree more in order to bring the same meridian back to the sun. These small daily portions of rotation are each equal to the three hundred and sixty-fifth part of a circle, which at the end of the year amounts to one complete rotation. If the earth, then, had no other than its diurnal motion, we should have 366 days in the year; or rather, we should have 366 days in the same period of time that we now have 365; for if we did not revolve round the sun, we should have no natural means of computing years. If time be calculated by the stars instead of the sun, the irregularity which we have just noticed does not occur, and that one complete rotation of the earth on its axis brings the same meridian back to any fixed star; and yet the earth's advance in her orbit must change her position with regard to the fixed stars, as well as with regard to the sun! This difficulty is explained by the distance of the fixed stars, which is so immense, that our solar system is in comparison to it but a spot, and the whole extent of the earth's orbit but a point; therefore, whether the earth remained stationary, or whether it revolved in its orbit during its rotation on its axis, no sensible difference would be produced with regard to the fixed stars. One complete revolution brings the same meridian back to the same fixed star: hence the fixed stars appear to go round the earth in a shorter time than the sun by three minutes sixty-six seconds of time, the time which the earth takes to perform the additional three hundred and sixty-fifth part of the circle, in order to bring the same meridian back to the sun. Hence the stars gain every day three minutes fifty-six seconds on the sun, which makes them rise that portion of time earlier every day.

When time is calculated by the stars, it is called sidereal time; when by the sun, solar or apparent time; and a sidereal day is three minutes fifty-six seconds shorter than a solar day of twenty-four hours. The difference of the solar and the sidereal year must also be explained: the common year, called the solar or tropical year, containing 365 days, 5 hours, 48 minutes, and 52 seconds, is measured from the time the sun sets out from one of the equinoxes, or solstices, till it returns to the same again; but the year is completed before the earth has finished one entire revolution in its orbit. This is owing to the spheroidal figure of the earth, the elevation about the equator producing much the same effect as if a similar mass of matter, collected in the form of a moon, revolved round the equator. When this moon acted on the earth in conjunction with, or in opposition to, the sun, variations in the earth's motion would be occasioned, and these variations produce what is called the precession of the equinoxes. The equinoctial points are therefore not quite fixed, but have a retrograde motion: that is to say, instead of being every revolution in the same place, they move backwards. Thus, if the vernal equinox be at A (*fig.* 15, next page), the autumnal one will be at B, instead of C, and the following vernal equinox at D, instead of at A, as would be the case if the equinoxes were stationary at opposite points of the earth's orbit: so that though the earth takes half a year to move from one equinox to the other, it has not then travelled through half its orbit; and consequently, when it returns again to the first equinox, it has not completed the whole of its orbit. In order to ascertain when the earth has performed an entire revolution in its orbit, we must observe when the sun retires in conjunction with any fixed star; and this is called a sidereal year. Supposing a fixed star situated at E, the sun would not appear in conjunction with it till the earth had returned to A, when it would have completed its orbit. The sidereal is only about twenty minutes longer than the solar year, so that the variation of the equinoctial points is very inconsiderable.

In regard to time, we must further add, that the earth's diurnal motion, on an inclined axis, together with its annual revolution in an elliptic orbit, occasions so much complication in its motion as to produce many irregularities: therefore true equal time cannot be measured by the sun. A clock, which was always perfectly correct, would in some parts of the year be before the sun, and in other parts after it. There are but four periods in which the sun and a perfect clock would agree, which are—the 15th of April, the 16th of June, the 31st of August, and the 24th of December. The greatest difference between solar time and true time amounts to between fifteen and sixteen minutes. Tables of the equation of time are constructed for the purpose of pointing out and correcting these differences between solar time and equal or mean time, which is the denomination given by astronomers to true time.

Section IV.—*On the Moon.*

Let us now turn our attention to the Moon. This satellite revolves round the earth in the space of twenty-seven days eight hours, in an orbit nearly coinciding with the plane of the earth's orbit, and accompanies us in our revolution round the sun. Her motion, therefore, is of a complicated nature; for as the earth advances in her orbit whilst the moon goes round her, the moon proceeds in a sort of progressive circle. There are also other circumstances which interfere with the simplicity and regularity of the moon's motion, but which are too intricate for us to notice at present.

The moon always presents the same face to us, by which it is evident

INTRODUCTION TO ASTRONOMY,

that she turns but once upon her axis while she performs a revolution round the earth; so that the inhabitants of the moon have but one day and one night in the course of a lunar month. Since we always see the same hemisphere of the moon, the inhabitants of that hemisphere alone can perceive the earth. One half of the moon, therefore, enjoys our light every night, while the other half has constantly nights of darkness; and we appear to the inhabitants of the moon under all the changes or phases which the moon exhibits to us.

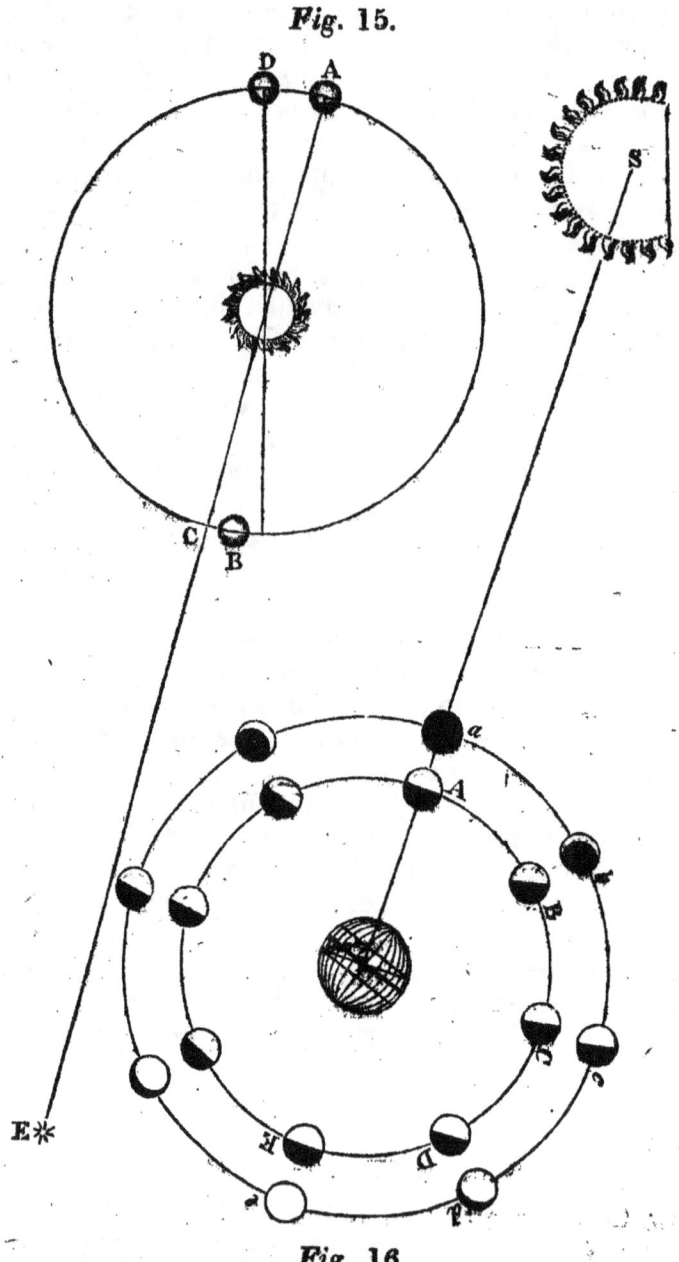

Fig. 15.

Fig. 16.

These phases require some explanation. In *fig.* 16, let us say that S represents the sun, E the earth, and ABCD, &c. the moon in different parts of her orbit. When the moon is at A, her dark side being turned towards the earth, we shall not see her; but her disappearance is of very short duration, and as she advances in her orbit we perceive her under the form of a new moon: when she has gone through one-sixth of her orbit at B, one quarter of her enlightened hemisphere will be turned towards the earth, and she will then appear horned, as in the figure *b*: when she has performed one quarter of her orbit, she shows us one half of her enlightened side, as at C, and appears as in the figure *c*; at D she is said to be gibbous, and at E the whole of the enlightened side appears to us, and the moon is at full. As she proceeds in her orbit she becomes again gibbous, and her enlightened hemisphere turns gradually away from us till she completes her orbit and disappears, and then again resumes her form of a new moon. The small exterior figures, *a, b, c, d*, &c., it will be seen, represent the phases corresponding to the situations A, B, C, D, &c.: the light part of the figures, *a, b, c, d*, &c., alone being supposed visible.

When the moon is at full, she is said to be in opposition; when a new moon, to be in conjunction with the sun. At each of these times, the sun, the moon, and the earth are in the same right line; but in the first case, the earth is between the sun and the moon; in the second, the moon is between the sun and the earth. An eclipse can take place only when the sun, moon, and earth are in a right line. When the moon passes between the sun and the earth, she intercepts his rays, or, in other words, casts a shadow on the earth: then the sun is eclipsed, and the daylight gives place to darkness, while the moon's shadow is passing over us. When, on the contrary, the earth is between the sun and the moon, it is we who intercept the sun's rays, and cast a shadow on the moon: she then disappears from our view, and is eclipsed.

Why then have we not a solar and a lunar eclipse every month?

The planes of the orbits of the earth and moon do not exactly coincide, but cross or intersect each other; and the moon generally passes either on one side or the other when she is in conjunction with, or in opposition to, the sun, and therefore does not intercept the sun's rays, or produce an eclipse; for this can take place only when the earth and moon are in conjunction near those parts of their orbits which cross each other (called the nodes of their orbits), because it is then only that they are both in the same plane, and in a right line with the sun. A partial eclipse takes place when the moon, in passing by the earth, does not entirely escape her shadow. When the eclipse happens precisely at the nodes, they are not only total, but last for some length of time.

When the sun is eclipsed, the total darkness is confined to one particular part of the earth. In *fig.* 17 a solar eclipse is exhibited: S is the sun, M the moon, and E the earth; and the moon's shadow is not large enough to cover the earth.

Fig. 17.

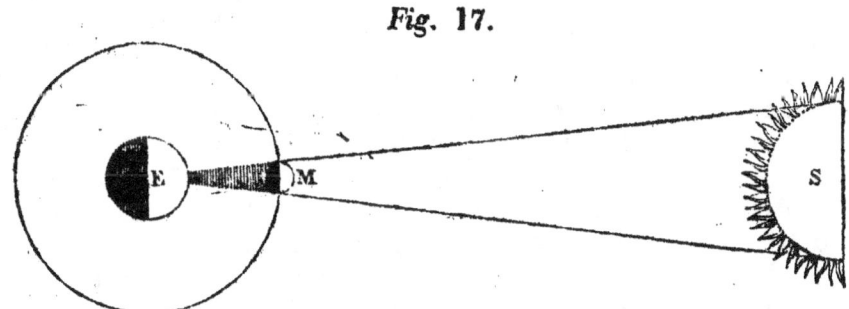

The lunar eclipses, on the contrary, are visible from every part of the earth, where the moon is above the horizon. In *fig.* 18, S represents the sun, which pours forth rays of light in straight lines in every direction; E is the earth, and M the moon. Now a ray of light coming from one extremity of the sun's disk in the direction AB will meet another coming

INTRODUCTION TO ASTRONOMY.

Fig. 18.

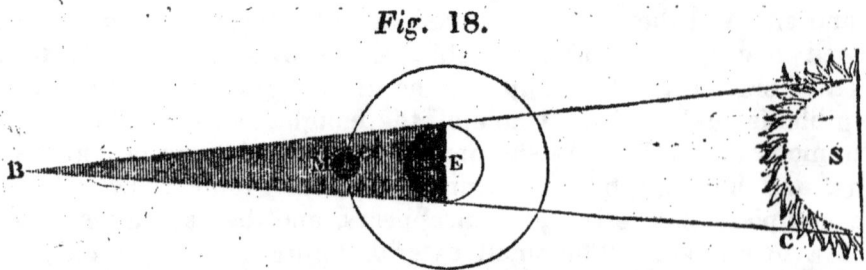

from the opposite extremity in the direction CB; the shadow of the earth cannot, therefore, extend beyond B. As the sun is larger than the earth, the shadow of the latter is conical: it gradually diminishes, and is much smaller than the earth where the moon passes through it, and yet we find the moon to be not only totally eclipsed, but some length of time in darkness. The moon, shining only by reflected light, disappears absolutely when the light of the sun is intercepted from her. She does not, therefore, become invisible, like the sun, only from particular spots on the earth's surface, but absolutely and universally, until the light of the sun begins to shine upon her again. The length of an eclipse depends on the respective distances and magnitudes of the sun, earth, and moon. The diameter of the moon is about $\frac{3}{11}$ of that of the earth, or the whole bulk of the earth about 49 times that of the moon.

When the moon eclipses the sun to us, the earth is eclipsed to the moon; for if the moon intercepts the sun's rays, and casts a shadow on us, we must necessarily disappear to the moon, but only partially—a black spot will appear to pass over the earth, as in figure 17.

In the distant planets, few days elapse without an eclipse taking place; for among the number of satellites, one or other of them is continually passing into the shadow of the planet, or between the planet and the sun. Astronomers are so well acquainted with the motion of the planets and their satellites, that they have calculated not only the eclipses of our moon, but those of Jupiter, with such perfect accuracy, that it has afforded a means of ascertaining the longitude. When, as on land, we know where we are situated, there is no difficulty in ascertaining the latitude or longitude of the place by referring to a map; but the question is to find out our situation when we do not know where we are: for instance, at sea, interrupted in our course by storms, a map would afford no assistance in discovering where we were. The latitude may be found by taking the altitude of the pole: that is to say, observing the number of degrees that it is elevated above the horizon, for the pole appears more elevated as we approach it, and less as we recede from it. It is true that the pole is not visible to us; but the north pole points constantly towards one particular part of the heavens, near which a star is situated, called the Polar Star. The altitude of the polar star is therefore nearly the same number of degrees as that of the pole; and, as this star is visible in clear nights from every part of the northern hemisphere, it furnishes an easy mode of ascertaining the latitude in all that half of the world. The latitude may be more accurately determined by other observations, which may be made on the sun or any of the fixed stars; the situation, therefore, of a vessel at sea, with regard to north and south, is easily ascertained. The difficulty is respecting east and west—that is to say, its longitude. As there are no eastern poles from which we can reckon our distance, some particular spot must be fixed upon for that purpose. The English reckon from the meridian of Greenwich, where the Royal Observatory is situated; in French maps the longitude is reckoned from Paris.

INTRODUCTION TO ASTRONOMY.

The rotation of the earth on its axis in twenty-four hours, from west to east, occasions, as we have already seen, an apparent motion of the sun and stars in the contrary direction, and the sun appears to go round the earth in the space of twenty-four hours, passing over fifteen degrees, or a twenty-fourth part of the earth's circumference every hour: therefore, when it is twelve o'clock in London, it is one o'clock in any place situated fifteen degrees to the east of London, as the sun must have passed the meridian of that place an hour before he reaches that of London. For the same reason it is eleven o'clock to any place situated fifteen degrees to the west of London, as the sun will not come to that meridian till an hour later. If, then, the captain of a vessel at sea could know precisely what was the hour at London, he could, by looking at his watch, and comparing it with the hour of the spot in which he was, ascertain the longitude. For this purpose he must be furnished with two watches—the one daily regulated by the sun, and the other unaltered. The former would indicate the hour of the place in which he was situated, and the latter the hour of London; and by comparing them together, he would be able to calculate his longitude: this mode of finding the longitude is universally adopted. Watches of a superior construction, called chronometers, or time-keepers, are used for this purpose; but the best watches are liable to imperfections, and should the time-keeper go too fast or too slow, there would be no means of ascertaining the error: implicit reliance cannot consequently be placed upon them.

Recourse is therefore had to the eclipses of Jupiter's satellites. A table is made of the precise time at which the several moons are eclipsed to a spectator at London. When they appear eclipsed to a spectator in any other spot, he may, by consulting the table, know what is the hour at London; for the eclipse is visible at the same moment from whatever place on the earth it is seen. He has then only to look at the watch which points out the hour of the place in which he is, and by observing the difference of time there, and at London, he may immediately determine his longitude.

Let us suppose that a certain moon of Jupiter is always eclipsed at six o'clock in the evening at London, and that a man at sea consults his watch, and finds that it is ten o'clock at night where he is situated, at the moment the eclipse takes place: he would be sixty degrees east of London; for the sun, which travels (apparently) fifteen degrees an hour, must have passed his meridian four hours before it reaches that of London; for this reason, the hour is always later than in London when the place is east longitude, and earlier when it is west longitude. Thus the longitude can be ascertained whenever the eclipses of Jupiter's moons are visible.

The latitude shows on what meridian you are situated, and the longitude on what part of that meridian; therefore, when you can ascertain both these, you discover the very spot in which you are situated. But it is not only the secondary planets which produce eclipses, for the primary planets near the sun eclipse him to those at a greater distance, when they come in conjunction in the nodes of their orbits; but as the primary planets are much longer in performing their course round the sun than the satellites in going round their primary planets, these eclipses very seldom occur.

Mercury and Venus have however passed in a right line between the earth and the sun, but being at so great a distance, their shadows did not extend so far as the earth. No darkness was therefore produced on any part of our globe; but the planet appeared like a small black spot, passing across the sun's disk: this is called a transit of the planet. It was by the last transit of Venus that astronomers were enabled to calculate with some degree of accuracy the distance of the earth from the sun, and the dimensions of the latter.

The tides are produced by the attraction of the moon. The cohesion of fluids being much less than that of solid bodies, they more easily yield to the power of gravity; in consequence of which the waters immediately below the moon are drawn up in a protuberance, producing a full tide, or what is commonly called high-water, at the spot where it happens. According to this theory, you would imagine that we should have full tide only once in twenty-four hours—that is, every time that we were below the moon—while we find that we have two tides in the course of twenty-four hours, and that it is high-water with us and with our antipodes at the same time.

This opposite tide is rather more difficult to explain than that which is drawn up beneath the moon. In order to render the question more simple, let us suppose the earth to be everywhere covered by the ocean, as in *fig.* 19. M is the moon, ABCD the earth. Now the waters on the surface of the earth about A, being more strongly attracted than in any

Fig. 19.

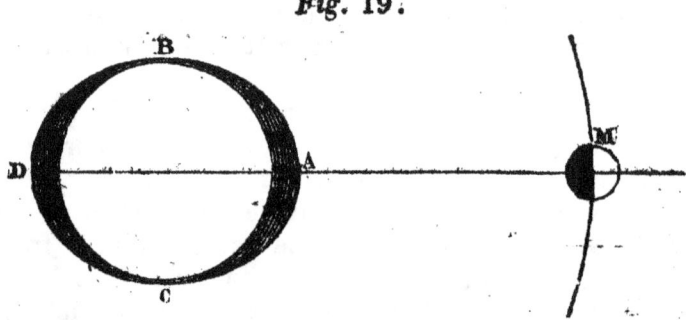

other part, will be elevated, the attraction of the moon at B and C being less; but still it will be greater there than at D, which is the part most distant from the moon. The body of the earth will therefore be drawn away from the waters at D, leaving a protuberance similar to that at A; so that the tide A is produced by the waters receding from the earth, and the tide D by the earth receding from the waters.

The influence of the sun on the tides is less than that of the moon; for observe, that the tides rise in consequence of the moon attracting one part of the waters more forcibly than another part: it is this inequality of attraction which produces full and ebb tides. Now the distance of the sun is so great, that the whole globe of the earth is comparatively but as a point, and the difference of its attraction for that part of the waters most under its influence, and that part least subject to it, is but trifling; no part of the waters will be much elevated above, or much depressed below their general surface by its action. The sun has, however, a considerable effect on the tides, and increases or diminishes them as it acts in conjunction with, or in opposition to, the moon.

The moon is a month in going round the earth; twice during that time, therefore, at full and at change, she is in the same direction as the sun. Both then act in conjunction on the earth, and produce very great tides, called spring-tides, as represented in *fig.* 20, at A and B; but when the moon is at the intermediate parts of her orbit, the sun, instead of affording assistance, weakens her power by acting in opposition to it, and smaller tides are produced, called neap-tides, as represented in *fig.* 21.

Fig. 20.

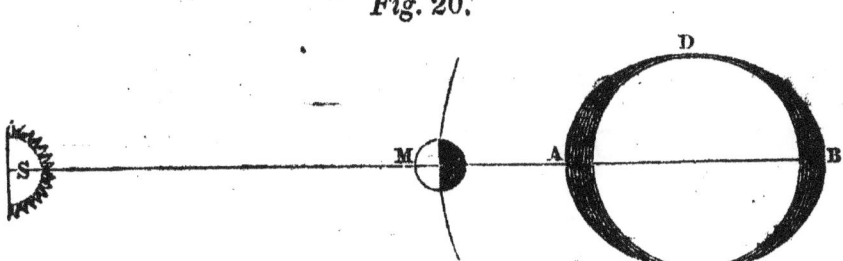

Fig. 21.

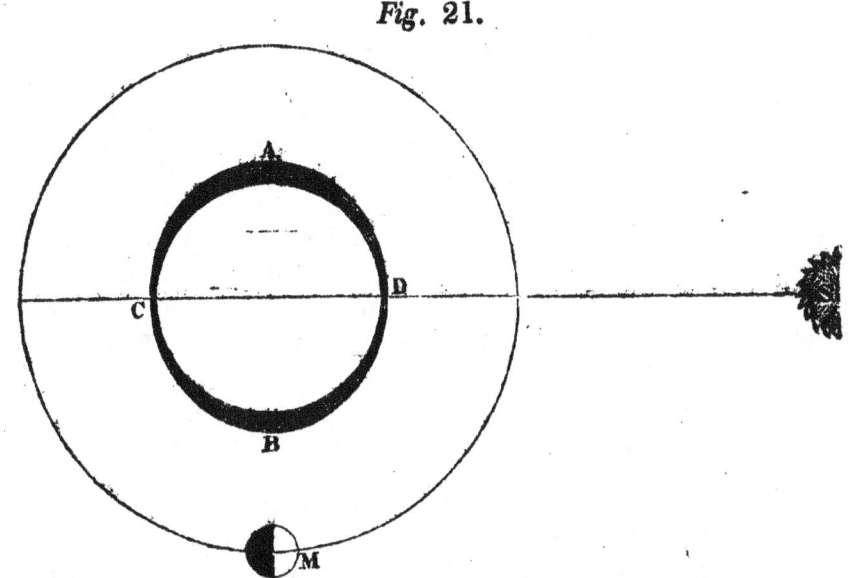

Since attraction is mutual between the moon and the earth, we produce tides in the moon; and these are more considerable, in proportion as our planet is larger. Neither the moon nor the earth in reality assume an oval form, for the land which intersects the water destroys the regularity of the effect. The orbit of the moon being nearly parallel to that of the earth, she is never vertical but to the inhabitants of the torrid zone: in that climate, therefore, the tides are greatest, and they diminish as you recede from it and approach the poles; but in no part of the globe is the moon immediately above the spot where it is high tide. All matter, by its inertia, offers some resistance to a change of state; the waters, therefore, do not readily yield to the attraction of the moon, and the effect of her influence is not complete until some time after she has passed the meridian.

The earth revolves on its axis in about twenty-four hours: if the moon were stationary, therefore, the same part of our globe would, every twenty-four hours, return beneath the moon; but as during our daily revolution the moon advances in her orbit, the earth must make more than a complete rotation in order to bring the same meridian opposite the moon: we are three-quarters of an hour in overtaking her. The tides, therefore, are retarded, for the same reason that the moon rises later, by three-quarters of an hour every day. This, however, is only the average amount of the retardation. The time of the highest tide is modified by the sun's attraction, and is between those of the tides which would be produced by the separate action of the two luminaries. The action of the sun, therefore, makes the interval different on different days, but leaves the average amount unaffected.

INTRODUCTION TO HYDROSTATICS.

SECTION I.—*On the Mechanical Properties of Fluids.*

THE science of the mechanical properties of fluids is called Hydrostatics. A fluid is a substance which yields to the slightest pressure. If you dip your hand into a basin of water, you are scarcely sensible of meeting with any resistance. Fluids, generally speaking, are bodies of less density than solids. From the slight cohesion of their particles, and the facility with which these slide over each other, it is conjectured, that they must be small, smooth, and globular; smooth, because there appears to be little or no friction among them; and globular, because touching each other but by a point would account for the slightness of their cohesion.

Fluids are divided into two classes, distinguished by the names of liquids and elastic fluids, or gases, which latter comprehends the air of the atmosphere, and all the various kinds of air with which chemistry makes us acquainted. We shall confine our attention at present to the mechanical properties of liquids or non-elastic fluids.

Water, and liquids in general, are little susceptible of being compressed, or squeezed into a smaller space than that which they naturally occupy. This is supposed to be owing to the extreme minuteness of their particles, which, rather than submit to compression, force their way through the pores of the substance which confines them, as was shown by a celebrated experiment, made at Florence many years ago. A hollow globe of gold was filled with water, and on its being submitted to great pressure, the water was seen to exude through the pores of the gold, which it covered with a fine dew. But more recent experiments, in which water has been confined in strong iron tubes, prove that it is susceptible of compression.

Liquids are porous, like solid bodies, but the pores are too minute to be discovered by the most powerful microscope. The existence of pores in liquids can be ascertained by dissolving solid bodies in them. If you melt some salt in a glass full of water, the water will not overflow, because the particles of salt will lodge themselves in the pores of the liquid, so that the salt and water together will not occupy more space than the water did alone. If you attempt to melt more salt than can find room within these pores, the remainder will subside at the bottom, and occupying a space which the water filled before, oblige the latter to overflow. Spirit of wine may also be poured into water without adding to the bulk, as the spirit will introduce itself into the pores of the water.

Fluids show the effects of gravitation in a more perfect manner than solid bodies; the strong cohesive attraction of the particles of the latter in some measure counteracting the effect of gravity. In a table, for instance, the strong cohesion of the particles of wood enables four slender legs to support a considerable weight. Were the cohesion so far destroyed as to convert the wood into a fluid, no support could be afforded by the legs; for the particles no longer cohering together, each would press separately and independently, and would be brought to a level with the surface of the earth.

INTRODUCTION TO HYDROSTATICS.

This deficiency of cohesion is the reason why fluids can never be formed into figures or maintained in heaps; for though it is true the wind raises water into waves, they are immediately afterwards destroyed by gravity. Thus liquids always find their level. The definition of the equilibrium of a fluid is, that every part of the surface is equally distant from the point to which gravity tends; that is to say, from the centre of the earth. Hence the surface of all fluids must partake of the spherical form of the globe and be bulging. This is evident in large bodies of water, such as the ocean; but the sphericity of small bodies of water is so trifling as to render their surfaces apparently flat.

The equilibrium of fluids is the natural result of their particles gravitating independently of each other; for when any particle of a fluid accidentally finds itself elevated above the rest, it is attracted down to the level of the surface of the fluid, and the readiness with which fluids yield to the slightest pressure, will enable the particle by its weight to penetrate the surface of the fluid and mix with it. But this is the case only with fluids of equal density, for a light fluid will float on the surface of a heavy one, as oil on water; and air will rise to the surface of any liquid whatever, being forced up by the superior gravity of the liquid. *Fig.* 1. represents an instrument called a water-level, which is constructed upon the principle of the equilibrium of fluids. It consists of a short tube, AB, closed at both ends, and containing water and a bubble of air; when the tube is not perfectly horizontal the water runs to the lower end, which makes the bubble of air rise to the upper end, and it remains in the centre only when the tube does not incline on either side. It is by this means that the level of any situation, to which we apply the instrument, is ascertained.

Solid bodies, therefore, gravitate in masses, the strong cohesion of their particles making them weigh altogether, while every particle of a fluid may be considered as a separate mass, gravitating independently. Hence the resistance of a fluid is considerably less than that of a solid body. The particles of fluids acting thus independently, press against each other in every direction, not only downwards but upwards, and laterally or sideways; and in consequence of this equality of pressure, every particle remains at rest in the fluid. If you agitate the fluid, you disturb this equality, and the fluid will not rest till its equilibrium be restored.

Were there no lateral pressure, water would not flow from an opening on the side of a vessel; sand will not run out of such an opening, because there is scarcely any lateral pressure among the particles. Were the particles of fluids arranged in regular columns, as in *fig.* 2, there would be no lateral pressure, for when one particle is perpendicularly above the other, it can only press it downwards; but as it must continually happen that a particle presses between two particles beneath (*fig.* 3), these last suffer a lateral pressure; just as a wedge driven into a piece of wood separates the parts laterally. The lateral pressure is the result therefore of the pressure downwards, or the weight of the liquid above; and consequently the lower the orifice is made in the vessel, the greater will be the velocity of the water rushing out of it. *Fig.* 4 represents the different degrees of velocity with which a liquid flows from a vessel furnished with three stop-cocks at different heights. Since the lateral pressure is entirely owing to the pressure downwards, it is not affected by the horizontal dimensions of the vessel, which contains the liquid, but merely by its depth; for as every particle acts independently of

INTRODUCTION TO HYDROSTATICS.

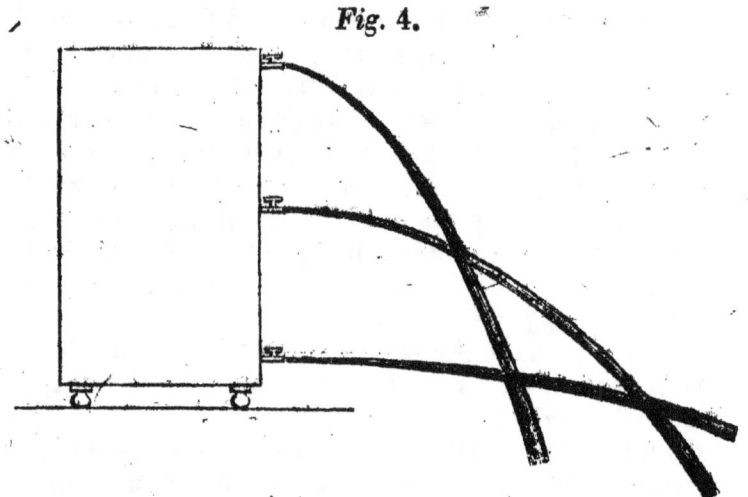

Fig. 4.

the rest, it is only the column of particles immediately above the orifice that can weigh upon and press out the liquid.

In a cubical vessel, the pressure downwards will be double the lateral pressure on one side, for every particle at the bottom of the vessel is pressed upon by a column of the whole depth of the fluid, whilst the lateral pressure diminishes equably from the bottom upwards to the surface, where the particles have no pressure.

The pressure of fluids upwards, though it seems in direct opposition to gravity, is also a consequence of their pressure downwards. When, for example, water is poured into a tea-pot, the water rises in the spout to a level with that in the pot. The particles of water at the bottom of the pot are pressed upon by the particles above them; to this pressure they will yield, if there is any mode of making way for the superior particles, and as they cannot descend, they will change their direction and rise in the spout.

Suppose the tea-pot to be filled with columns of particles of water similar to that described in *fig.* 5, the particle 1 at the bottom will be

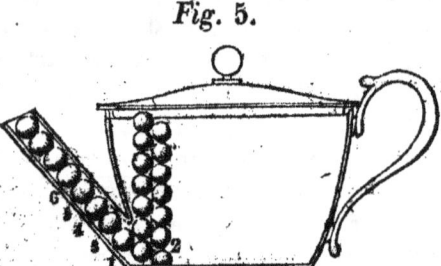

Fig. 5.

Fig. 6.

pressed laterally by the particle 2, and by this pressure be forced into the spout, where, meeting with the particle 3, it presses it upwards, and this pressure will be continued from 3 to 4, from 4 to 5, and so on, till the water in the spout has risen to a level with that in the pot.

You may also reverse the experiment by pouring water into the spout, and you will find that the water will rise in the pot to a level with that in the spout, for the pressure of the small quantity of water in the spout will force up and support the larger quantity in the pot. But this will be better exemplified by *fig.* 6, in which a goblet is filled by means of a narrow tube. In the pressure upwards, as well as that laterally, the force results entirely from the height, and is quite independent of the horizontal dimensions of the fluid. The tube, however, could never be filled by pouring water into the goblet, because the water in the goblet cannot force that in the tube above its own level, and as the end of the tube is considerably highest, if water be poured into the goblet after it is full, it will run over instead of rising in the tube above the level.

INTRODUCTION TO HYDROSTATICS.

The specific gravity of a body means simply its weight compared with that of another body of the same size. When we say that substances, such as lead and stones, are heavy, and that others, such as paper and feathers, are light, we speak comparatively: that is to say, that the first are heavy, and the latter light, in comparison with the generality of the substances in nature. Mahogany is a heavy body when compared to most other kinds of wood, but light when compared to stone. Chalk is a heavy body compared to coal, but light if compared to metal. You perceive therefore that our notions of light and heavy are vague and undefined, and that some standard of comparison is required, to which the weight of all other bodies may be referred. The body which has been adopted as a standard of reference is distilled water. It may perhaps appear surprising that a fluid should have been chosen for this purpose, as it must necessarily be contained in some vessel, and the weight of this vessel must be deducted. This is true, when the specific gravity of fluids is to be estimated; but with regard to solids, it is necessary simply to weigh the body under trial in water. If a piece of gold be weighed in a glass of water, the gold will displace just as much water as is equal to its own bulk: a cubic inch of water must make way for a cubic inch of gold. The bulk alone is to be considered, the weight has nothing to do with the quantity of water displaced; for a cubic inch of gold does not occupy more space, and therefore will not displace more water, than a cubic inch of ivory, or any other substance that will sink in water.

The gold will weigh less in water than it did out of it, on account of the upward pressure of the particles of water, which in some measure supports the gold, and by so doing, diminishes its weight. If the body under trial be of the same weight as the water in which it is immersed, it will be wholly supported by it, as was the water, the place of which it occupies; if it be heavier, the water will offer some resistance to its descent; and this resistance will in all cases be the same to bodies of equal bulk, whatever be their weight. All bodies of the same size, therefore, lose the same quantity of their weight when completely immersed in water. A body weighed in water loses as much of its weight as is equal to that of the water it displaces; so that were this water put into the scale to which the body is suspended, it would restore the balance.

These observations, however, require some modification when applied to the case of bodies lighter than an equal bulk of water, and which, therefore, do not sink entirely in water. The method of ascertaining their specific gravity will be presently pointed out. At present we may observe, that the rule given above has an application even to them, if forcibly immersed in water; but the resistance, or upper pressure of the water, being greater than the weight of the body, that weight is not merely diminished, but the body has a tendency *upwards* equal to the difference between the resistance and its weight.

When a body is weighed in water, in order to ascertain its specific gravity, it may either be suspended to a hook at the bottom of the basin of the balance, or, taking off the basin, suspended to the arm of the balance (*fig.* 7). Now, supposing that a cubic inch of gold weighed nineteen ounces out of water, and lost one ounce by being weighed in water, the cubic inch of water it displaces must weigh that one ounce: consequently gold would be nineteen times as heavy as water.

The specific gravity of a body lighter than water cannot be ascertained in the same manner. If a body were absolutely light, it would float on the surface without displacing a drop of water; but bodies have all some

INTRODUCTION TO HYDROSTATICS.

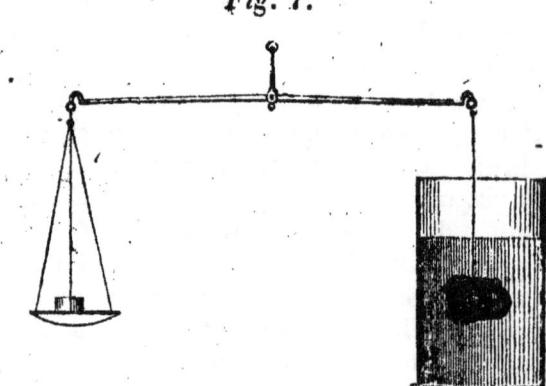

Fig. 7.

weight, and will, therefore, displace some quantity of water. A body lighter than water will not sink to a level with the surface of the water, and therefore will not displace so much water as is equal to its bulk, but a quantity equal to its weight. A ship sinks to some depth in water, and the heavier it is laden the deeper it sinks, the quantity of water it displaces being always equal to its weight. This quantity cannot, however, afford a convenient test of its specific gravity, from the difficulty of collecting the whole quantity of water displaced, and of measuring the exact bulk of the body immersed.

In order practically to obtain the specific gravity of a body which is lighter than water, a heavy one, whose specific gravity is known, must be attached to it, and they must be immersed together: the specific gravity of the lighter body may then be easily calculated.

Bodies which have exactly the same specific gravity as water, will remain at rest in whatever situation they are placed in water. If a piece of wood, by being impregnated with a little sand, be rendered precisely of the weight of an equal bulk of water, it will remain stationary in whatever part of a vessel of water it be placed. If a few drops of water be poured into the vessel (so gently as not to increase their momentum by giving them velocity), they would mix with the water at the surface, and not sink lower.

The specific gravity of fluids is found by means of an instrument called an hydrometer. It consists of a thin glass ball, A (*fig.* 8), with a graduated tube, B, and the specific gravity of the liquid is estimated by the depth to which the instrument sinks in it, for the less the specific gravity of the fluid, the further will the instrument sink in it. There is a smaller ball, C, attached to the instrument below, which contains a little mercury; but this is merely for the purpose of equipoising the instrument, that it may remain upright in the liquid under trial.

The weight of a substance, when not compared to that of any other, is perfectly arbitrary; and when water is adopted as a standard, we may denominate its weight by any number we please; but then the weight of all bodies tried by this standard must be signified by proportional numbers. If we call the weight of water, for example, 1, then that of gold would be 19; or, if we call the weight of water 1000, that of gold would be 19,000. In short, the specific gravity indicates how much more or less a body weighs than an equal bulk of water.

INTRODUCTION TO HYDROSTATICS.

Section II.—*On Springs, Fountains, &c.*

Let us now turn our attention to the various states in which the water belonging to our globe exists. It is the same water which successively forms seas, rivers, springs, clouds, rain, and sometimes hail, snow, and ice. We will follow it through these various changes, and consider how the clouds were originally formed. When the first rays of the sun warm the surface of the earth, the heat, by separating the particles of water, transforms them into vapour, which, being lighter than the air, ascends into the atmosphere. The atmosphere diminishing in density as it is more distant from the earth, the vapour which the sun causes to exhale, not only from seas, rivers, and lakes, but likewise from the moisture on the land, rises till it reaches a region of air of its own specific gravity, and there it remains stationary. By the frequent accession of fresh vapour it gradually accumulates, so as to form those large bodies of vapour which we call clouds; and these at length becoming too heavy for the air to support, fall to the earth in the form of rain. If the watery particles retained the state of vapour, they would descend only till they reached a stratum of air of their own specific gravity; but during their fall several of the watery particles come within the sphere of each other's attraction, and unite in the form of a drop of water. The vapour, thus transformed into a shower, is heavier than any part of the atmosphere, and consequently descends to the earth. Observe, that if the waters were never drawn out of the earth, vegetation would be destroyed by the excess of moisture; if, on the other hand, the plants were not nourished and refreshed by occasional showers, the drought would be equally fatal to them. Were the clouds constantly in a state of vapour, they could never fall to the ground; or were the power of attraction more than sufficient to convert the vapour into drops, it would transform the cloud into a mass of water, which, instead of nourishing, would destroy the produce of the earth. We cannot consider any part of Nature attentively without being struck with admiration at the wisdom it displays: we cannot contemplate these wonders without feeling our hearts glow with admiration and gratitude towards their bounteous Author.

Water, then, ascends in the form of vapour, and descends in that of rain, snow, or hail, all of which ultimately become water. Some of this falls into the various bodies of water on the surface of the globe, the remainder upon the land. Of the latter, part re-ascends in the form of vapour, part is absorbed by the roots of vegetables, and part descends into the bowels of the earth, where it forms springs. The only difference between rain and spring water consists in the foreign particles which the latter meets with and dissolves in its passage through the various soils it traverses. Spring water being more pleasant to the taste, and more transparent, is commonly supposed to be more pure than rain water. Excepting distilled water, however, rain water is really the most pure we can obtain: it is this which renders it insipid, whilst the various salts and different ingredients dissolved in spring water, give it a species of flavour, without in any degree affecting its transparency; and the filtration it undergoes through gravel and sand in the bowels of the earth cleanses it from all foreign matter which it has not the power of dissolving.

When rain falls on the surface of the earth, it continues making its way downwards through the pores and crevices in the ground. Several drops meet in their subterraneous passage, unite, and form a little rivulet: this, in its progress, meets with other rivulets of a similar description, and they pursue their course together in the interior of the earth, till they are stopped by some substance which they cannot penetrate; for though we have said that water under strong compression penetrates the pores of gold, when acted upon by no other force than gravity it cannot make its way even through a stratum of clay. This species of earth, though not remarkably dense, being of great tenacity, will not admit the passage of water. When, therefore, it encounters any substance of this nature, its progress is stopped, and the pressure of the accumulating waters forms a bed, or reservoir.

Fig. 9 represents a section of the interior of a hill or mountain. A is a body of water such as I have described, which, when filled up as high as B (by the continual accession of waters it receives from the ducts or

Fig 9.

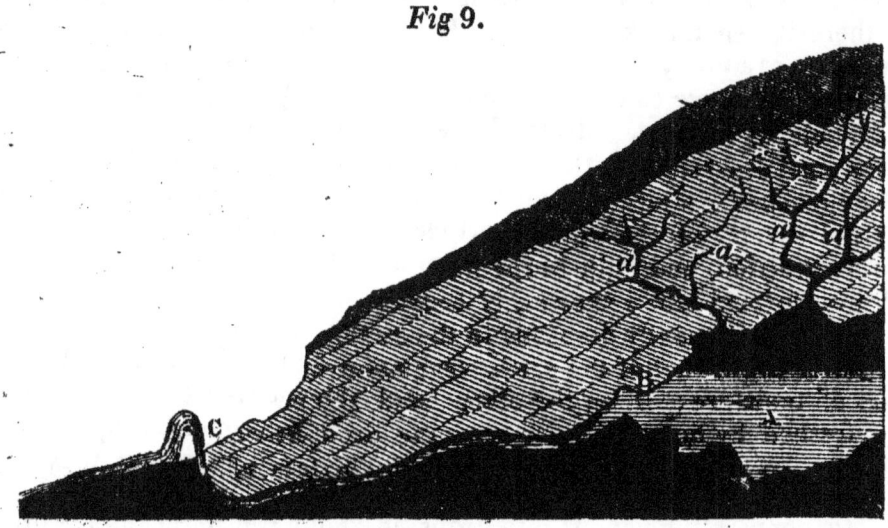

rivulets *a, a, a, a*), finds a passage out of the cavity; and, impelled by gravity, runs on, till it makes its way out of the ground at the side of the hill, and there forms a spring, C. The spring, during its passage from B to C, rises occasionally, upon the same principle that water rises in the spout of a tea-pot, but it cannot mount above the level of the reservoir, whence it issues; it must therefore find a passage to some part of the surface of the earth that is lower or nearer the centre than the reservoir. Water may thus be conveyed to every part of a town, and even to the upper stories of the houses, provided that it be originally brought from a height superior to any to which it is conveyed.

Reservoirs of water are seldom formed near the summit of a hill, for in such elevated situations there can scarcely be a sufficient number of rills to supply one; and without a reservoir there can be no spring. In such situations, therefore, it is necessary to dig deep wells, in order to meet with a spring; and then it can rise in the well only as high as the reservoir whence it flows.

When reservoirs of water are formed in very elevated situations, the springs which feed it descend from higher hills in the vicinity. There a lake on the very summit of Mount Cenis, which is supplied by the springs of the higher Alps surrounding it.

A syphon is an instrument commonly used to draw off liquids from large casks or other vessels which cannot be easily moved. It consists simply of a bended tube. If its two legs are of equal length, and filled with liquid, if held perfectly level, though turned downwards, the liquid will not flow out, but remain suspended in the tube (*fig.* 10); for there is no pressure of the atmosphere above the liquid, while there is a pressure from below upwards upon the open ends of the tube; and so long as this pressure is equal on both ends, the liquid cannot flow out; but if the smallest inclination be given to the syphon, so as to destroy the equilibrium of the water, it will immediately flow from the lowest leg. When syphons are used to draw off liquids, the legs are made of unequal lengths, in order to render the pressure of the liquid unequal; the shortest leg is immersed in the cask, and the liquor flows out through the longest. To accomplish this, it is however necessary to make the liquor rise in the shortest leg, and pass over the bended part of the tube, which is higher than the level of the liquor in the cask. There are two modes of doing this: one is, after immersing the shortest leg in the liquor to be drawn off, to suck out the air of the tube from the orifice of the longest leg; then the liquor in the cask, which is exposed to the pressure of the atmosphere, will be forced by it into the tube which is relieved from pressure. As long as the tube continues full, no air can gain admittance; the liquor will therefore flow on till the cask is emptied. The other mode is to fill the syphon with the liquor, then stopping the two ends with the fingers, immerse the shortest leg in the vessel, and the same effect will follow. In either case, the water in the highest part of the syphon must not be more than 32 feet above the reservoir; for the pressure of the atmosphere will not support a greater height of water.

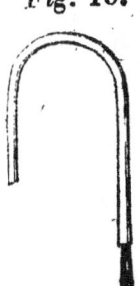

Fig. 10.

The phenomena of springs which flow occasionally, and occasionally cease, may often be explained by the principle of the syphon. The reservoir of water which supplies a spring may be considered as the vessel of liquor to be drawn off, and the duct the syphon, having its shortest leg opening in the reservoir, and its longest at the surface of the earth whence the spring flows; but as the water cannot be made to rise in the syphon by either of the artificial modes which we have mentioned, the spring will not begin to flow till the water in the reservoir has risen above the level of the highest part of the syphon: it will then commence flowing upon the principle of the equilibrium of fluids; but it will continue upon the principle of the syphon; for, instead of ceasing as soon as the equilibrium is restored, it will continue flowing as long as the opening of the duct is in contact with the water in the reservoir. Springs which do not constantly flow are called intermitting, and are occasioned by the reservoir being imperfectly supplied.

Reservoirs of water which are formed in the bosom of mountains generally find a vent either on their declivity, or in the valley beneath; while subterraneous reservoirs formed in a plain can seldom find a passage to the surface of the earth, but remain concealed, unless discovered by digging a well. When a spring once issues at the surface of the earth, it forms a rivulet, and continues its course externally, seeking always a lower ground, for it can no longer rise: if therefore it flows into a situation which is surrounded by a higher ground, its course is stopped, the water accumulates, and forms a pool, pond, or lake, according to the dimensions of the body of water. Thus the Lake of Geneva is filled by the Rhone, which passes through it. When the river enters the valley which forms the bed of the Lake, it finds itself surrounded by higher grounds: its waters, consequently, are pent up, and accumulate till they rise to a level with that part of the valley where the Rhone continues its course out of the Lake, and from whence it flows through valleys, occasionally forming other small lakes, till it reaches the sea.

A Fountain is a spring conducted perpendicularly upwards by a spout or adjutage, A (*fig.* 11). It would rise as high as the reservoir, B, were its motion not impeded by the resistance of the air and the friction against the sides of the spout whence it issues; besides, as all the particles of water spout from the tube with an equal velocity, and as the pressure of the air upon the exterior particles diminish their velocity, they will in some degree strike against the under parts, and force them sideways, spreading the column into a head, and rendering it both wider and shorter than it otherwise would be. Besides this, the resistance of the air prevents even the first particles projected from the tube from rising to the height of the water in the reservoir. Were there no such resistance, it would rise to that height, and no higher: of course, being resisted, the elevation to which it rises is diminished. On both accounts, therefore, the height of such a fountain falls very considerably short of the height of the water in the reservoir.

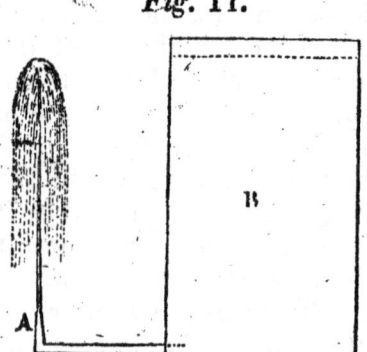

Fig. 11.

INTRODUCTION TO PNEUMATICS.

Section I.—*On the Mechanical Properties of Air.*

We shall now examine the second class of fluids, distinguished by the name of aëriform, or elastic fluids, the principal of which is the air we breathe, which surrounds the earth, and is called the atmosphere. There are a great variety of elastic fluids, but they differ only in their chemical, not in their mechanical properties; and it is the latter we are to examine. There is no attraction of cohesion between the particles of elastic fluids, so that the expansive power of heat has no adversary to contend with but gravity; any increase of temperature, therefore, expands elastic fluids prodigiously, and a diminution proportionally condenses them. The most essential point in which air differs from other fluids is by its spring or elasticity: that is to say, its power of increasing or diminishing in bulk, according as it is less or more compressed—a power of which liquids are almost wholly deprived.

The atmosphere is thought to extend to about the distance of 45 miles from the earth; and its gravity is such, that a man of middling stature is computed, when the air is heaviest, to sustain the weight of about 14 tons. Such a weight would crush him to atoms, were it not that air is also contained within our bodies, the spring or elasticity of which counterbalances the weight of the external air, and renders us insensible of its pressure. Besides this, the equality of pressure on every part of the body enables us more easily to support it: when thus diffused, we can bear even a much greater weight, without any considerable inconvenience. In bathing we support the weight and pressure of the water, in addition to that of the atmosphere; but this pressure being equally distributed over the body, we are scarcely sensible of it: whilst if the shoulders, the head, or any particular part of the frame were loaded with the additional weight of a hundred pounds, we should feel severe fatigue. On the other hand, if the air within a man met with no external pressure to restrain its elasticity, it would distend his body, and at length bursting the parts which confine it, put a period to his existence. The weight of the atmosphere, therefore, so far from being an evil, is essential to our existence. When a person is cupped, the swelling of the part under the cup is produced by taking away the pressure of the atmosphere; in consequence of which, the internal air distends the part. The air-pump affords us the means of making a great variety of interesting experiments on the weight and pressure of the air. We have already seen, that in a vacuum produced within the air-pump, substances of various weights fall to the bottom in the same time.

We shall now point out some experiments which illustrate both the weight and elasticity of air. If a piece of bladder be tied over a glass receiver, open both at the top and bottom, when the air is taken away from the under surface, so that there is no longer any re-action to counterbalance the pressure of the atmosphere, the bladder is pressed inwards in proportion as the receiver is exhausted; and before a complete vacuum or void is formed within the receiver, the bladder, unable to sustain the violence of the pressure, bursts with a loud report.

F

A shrivelled apple placed within a receiver becomes plump from the expansion of the air within it, as soon as the pressure of the external air is taken away, and shrinks to its former dimensions when the air is again let into the receiver. If two bodies be placed so close together that there is absolutely no air between them, to counterbalance by its elasticity the pressure of the air on their outer surfaces, that whole pressure resists their separation. It is thus that a stone may be raised by a string fixed to a piece of moistened leather pressed close upon it; and thus also that in the experiment detailed in page 6, the pressure of the atmosphere, as well as the cohesion of the metallic hemispheres, prevents their separation.

A column of air reaching to the top of the atmosphere, and whose base is a square inch, weighs 15 lbs. when the air is heaviest. The rule that fluids press equally in all directions applies to elastic fluids as well as to liquids: therefore every square inch of our bodies sustains a pressure of 15 lbs., and the weight of the whole atmosphere may be computed by calculating the number of the square inches on the surface of the earth, and multiplying them by 15.

The weight of a small quantity of air may be ascertained by exhausting the air from a bottle, and weighing the bottle thus emptied. Suppose that a bottle, six cubic inches in dimension, weighs two ounces; if the air be then introduced, and the bottle re-weighed, it will be found heavier by two grains, shewing that six cubic inches of air (at a moderate temperature) weighs about two grains. In estimating the weight of air, the temperature must always be considered, because heat, by rarefying air, renders it lighter. The same principle indeed applies, almost without exception, to all bodies. In order to ascertain the specific gravity of air, the same bottle may be filled with water, and the weight of six cubic inches of water will be 1515 grains: so that the weight of water to that of air is about 800 to 1.

A barometer is an instrument which indicates the state of the weather, by shewing the weight of the atmosphere. It is extremely simple in its construction, and consists of a glass tube, A B (*fig.* 1), about three feet in length, and open only at one end. This tube must first be filled with mercury, then stopping the open end with the finger, it is immersed in a cup, C, which contains a little mercury. Part of the mercury which was in the tube now falls down into the cup, leaving a vacant space in the upper part of the tube, to which the air cannot gain access. This space is therefore a perfect vacuum; and consequently the mercury in the tube is relieved from the pressure of the atmosphere, whilst that in the cup remains exposed to it: therefore the pressure of the air on the mercury in the cup supports that in the tube, and prevents it from falling: thus the equilibrium of the mercury is destroyed only to preserve the general equilibrium of fluids. This simple apparatus is all that is essential to a barometer. The tube and the cup or vase are fixed on a board, for the convenience of suspending it; the board is graduated for the purpose of ascertaining the height at which the mercury stands in the tube; and the small moveable metal plate serves to show that height with greater accuracy. The weight of the atmosphere sustains the mercury at the height of about

Fig. 1.

bodies send rays of light immediately to our eyes; but the rays which they send to other bodies are invisible to us, and are seen only when reflected or transmitted by those bodies to our eyes. Yet it may be observed that the ray of light on its passage from the sun to the mirror, and its reflection, have been spoken of as visible, though in neither case were those rays in a direction to enter our eyes. The fact is, that what is seen is the light reflected to the eye by small particles of dust floating in the air, and on which the ray shone in its passage to and from the mirror. So when, in common phrase, we speak of seeing the sun shining on an opposite house, it is impossible to see a single ray which passes from the sun to the house: no rays are visible but those which enter our eyes; therefore it is the rays which are reflected by the house, and not those which proceed from the sun to the house, that are seen. Why, then, does one side of the house appear to be in sunshine, and the other in the shade; for if we cannot see the sun shine upon it, the whole of the house should appear in the shade? That side of the house on which the sun shines reflects more vivid and luminous rays than the side which is in shadow, the latter being illumined only by rays reflected upon it by other objects: these rays are therefore twice reflected before they reach our sight; and as light is more or less absorbed by the bodies it strikes upon, every time a ray is reflected its intensity is diminished. Thus, on a large sheet of water the sun appears to shine on one part only, though the whole of it is equally exposed to its rays. This partial brilliancy of water is more remarkable by moonlight, on account of the deep obscurity of the surrounding parts. To account for this, it must be remembered that the direction of a reflected ray depends on that of the incident ray; the sun's rays, therefore, which fall with various degrees of obliquity upon the water, are reflected in directions equally various: some of these will meet the eye, and it will see them, but those which fall elsewhere are invisible to it*.

Let us now examine by what means the rays of light produce vision. They enter at the pupil of the eye, and proceeding to the retina or optic nerve, which is situated at the back of the eye-ball, there describe the figure, colour, and (with the exception of size) form a complete representation of the object from which they proceed. If the shutters be closed, and a ray of light admitted through the small aperture, a picture may be seen on the opposite wall similar to that which is delineated on the retina of the eye: it exhibits a picture in miniature of the garden, and the landscape would be perfect were it not reversed. This picture is produced by the rays of light reflected from the various objects in the garden, and which are admitted through the hole in the window-shutter. It is called a camera obscura (*dark chamber*), from the necessity of darkening the room in order to exhibit it.

The rays from the glittering weathercock at the top of the alcove, A (*fig.* 7), represent it at *a*; for the weathercock being much higher than the aperture in the shutter, only a few of the rays, which are reflected by it in an obliquely descending direction, can find entrance there. The rays of light moving always in straight lines, those which enter the room in a descending direction will continue their course in the same direction, and will, consequently, fall upon the lower part of the wall opposite the aperture, and represent the weathercock reversed in that spot, instead of erect in the uppermost part of the landscape; and the rays of light from the steps, B, of the alcove, in entering the aperture, ascend, and describe

* See Mechanics.

Fig. 7.

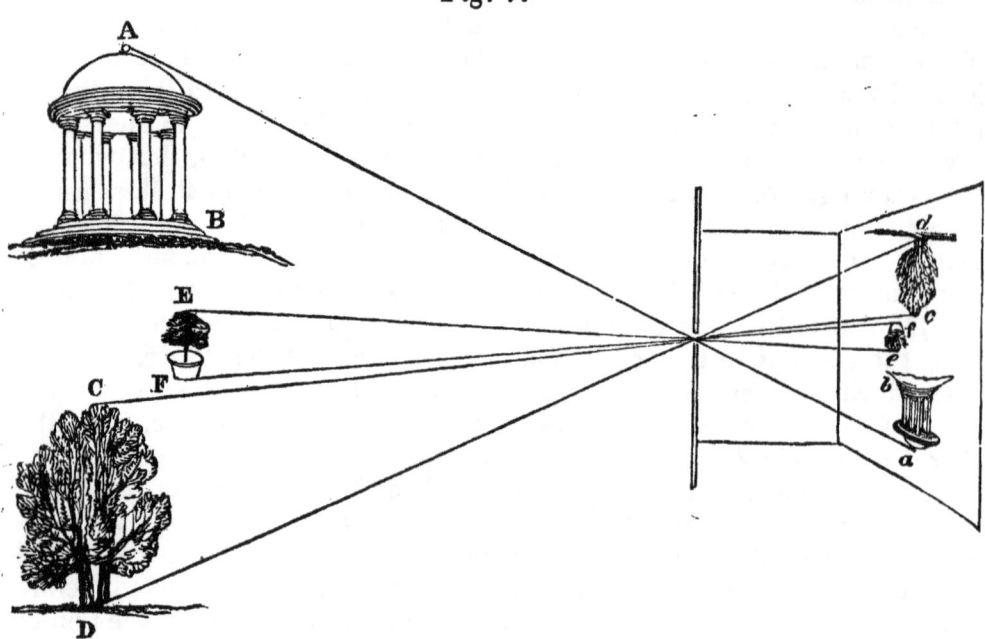

them in the highest instead of the lowest part of the landscape; whilst the rays proceeding from the alcove, which is to the left, describe it on the wall to the right. Those which are reflected by the walnut-tree, C D, to the right, delineate its figure in the picture to the left, *c d*. Thus the rays, coming in different directions, and proceeding always in straight lines, cross each other at their entrance through the apertures: those from above proceed below, those from the right go to the left, those from the left towards the right; thus every object is represented in the picture as occupying a situation the very reverse of that which it does in nature, excepting the flower-pot, E F, which, though its position is reversed, does not change its situation in the landscape; for being immediately in front of the aperture, its rays fall perpendicularly upon it, and consequently proceed perpendicularly to the wall, where they delineate the object. It is thus that the picture of objects is painted on the retina of the eye. The pupil of the eye, through which the rays of light enter, represents the aperture in the window-shutter; and the image delineated on the retina is exactly similar to the picture on the wall.

The retina of the eye exhibits a much more perfect image than any mirror: the extensive landscape beheld from the window is there represented with the greatest accuracy. Art would in vain attempt to paint so small and distinct a miniature; but Nature works with a surer hand and a more delicate pencil. That Power which forms the feathers of the butterfly and the flowerets of the daisy can alone pourtray so admirable and perfect a miniature. As the rays intersect each other on entering the pupil, in the same manner as they do on entering the camera obscura, the image is reversed. The scene, however, does not excite the idea of being inverted, because we always see an object in the direction of the rays which it sends to us. How it is that we do so is a point rather difficult to explain clearly. The following, however, seems to be the best explanation:—A ray which comes from the upper part of an object describes the image on the lower part of the retina; but experience having taught us that a ray which strikes the retina there comes from above, we consider that part of the object it represents as uppermost. The rays

piston formed the bottom. This common pump is, therefore, called the sucking and lifting pump, as it is constructed on both these principles.

The forcing pump consists of a forcing power added to the sucking part of the pump. This additional power is exactly on the principle of the syringe: by raising the piston, the water is drawn up into the pump; and by making it descend, it is forced out. The large pipe, A B (*fig. 3*), represents the sucking part of the pump, which differs from the lifting pump only in its piston, P, being unfurnished with a valve, in consequence of which the water cannot rise above it. When, therefore, the piston descends, it shuts the valve, *y*, and forces the water (which has no other vent) into the pipe, D: this is likewise furnished with a valve, V, which, opening outwards, admits the water, but prevents its return. The water is thus first raised in the pump, and then forced into the pipe, by the alternate ascending and descending motion of the piston, after a few strokes of the handle to fill the pipe, from whence the water issues at the spout.

Section II.—*On Wind and Sound.*

We are now to give some account of the nature of Wind and Sound. Wind is the motion of a stream or current of air, which may be produced by a variety of causes; but the most common one is a partial change of temperature in the atmosphere: for when any one part is more heated than the rest, that part is rarefied; and thus, becoming lighter than the air around, it rises, and the surrounding air presses in towards that part, in order to restore the equilibrum: this spot, therefore, receives wind from every quarter. Those who live to the north of it experience a north wind; those to the south, a south wind; and those who live on the spot where these winds meet and interfere have turbulent and boisterous weather—whirlwinds, hurricanes, rain, lightning, thunder, &c. This stormy weather occurs most frequently in the torrid zone, where the heat is greatest: the air being more rarefied there than in any other part of the globe, is lighter, and consequently ascends; whilst the air about the polar regions is continually flowing from the poles, to restore the equilibrium. This motion of the air, did no obstacles interfere, would produce a regular and constant north wind to the inhabitants of the northern hemisphere, and a south wind to those of the southern hemisphere; but these winds do not meet without previously changing their direction. The atmosphere accompanies the earth in its diurnal motion: it travels, therefore, with greater or less velocity as it is nearer the equator, or more distant from it. When therefore the air flows from the north or south to restore the atmospherical equilibrium at the equator, this air, not having acquired the velocity of the equatorial regions, cannot keep pace with the earth, which, travelling faster, passes through it; and as the earth moves from west to east, its motion through the air produces a regular east wind at the equator. The winds from the north and south combine with this easterly wind, and form what are called the tradewinds. The composition of the two winds north and east produces a constant north-east wind; and that of the two winds south and east produces a regular south-east wind. These winds extend to about thirty degrees on each side of the equator, the regions further distant from it experiencing only their respective north and south winds.

The light air about the equator, which expands and rises into the upper regions of the atmosphere, ultimately flows from thence back to the poles, to restore the equilibrium. If it were not for this resource, the polar atmospheric regions would soon be exhausted by the stream of air, which, in the lower strata of the atmosphere, they are constantly sending towards the equator. There is therefore a sort of circulation in the atmosphere: the air in the lower strata flowing from the poles towards the equator, and in the upper strata flowing back from the equator towards the poles. An example of this circulation on a small scale may be seen in the air of a room, which being more rarefied than the external air, a current is pouring in from the crevices of the windows and doors, to restore the equilibrium; but the light air with which the room is filled must find some vent, in order to make way for the heavy air which enters. If the door be set a-jar, and a candle held near the upper part of it, the flame will be blown outwards, showing that there is a current of air flowing out from the upper part of the room; and if the candle be placed on the floor close by the door, the flame will bend inwards, shewing that there is also a current of air setting into the lower part of the room. The upper current is the warm, light air, which is driven out to make way for the stream of cold, dense air which enters below.

There are also periodical trade-winds, commonly called monsoons, which change their course every half-year. This variation is produced by the earth's annual course round the sun, when the north pole is inclined towards that luminary one-half of the year, and the south pole the other half. During the summer of the northern hemisphere, the countries of Arabia, Persia, India, and China, are much heated, and reflect great quantities of the sun's rays into the atmosphere, by which it becomes extremely rarefied, and the equilibrium consequently destroyed. In order to restore it, the air from the equatorial southern regions, where it is colder (as well as from the colder northern parts) must necessarily have a motion towards those parts. The current of air from the equatorial regions produces the trade-winds for the first six months in all the seas between the heated continent of Asia and the equator. During the other six months, when it is summer in the southern hemisphere, the ocean and countries towards the southern tropic are most heated, and the air over those parts most rarefied; then the air about the equator alters its course, and flows in an opposite direction.

The breaking-up of the monsoons is the name given by sailors to the shifting of the periodical winds; they do not change their course suddenly, but by degrees, as the sun moves from one hemisphere to the other. This change is usually attended by storms and hurricanes, so that those seas are seldom navigated at the season of the equinox.

It is less easy to account for the great variety of winds which prevail in the temperate zones; but when we consider that so large a portion of the atmosphere is in continual agitation in the torrid zone, these agitations in an elastic fluid, which yields to the slightest impression, must extend every way to a great distance. The air in all climates will suffer more or less perturbation, according to the situation of the country, the position of mountains, valleys, and a variety of other causes: hence it is easy to conceive that almost every climate must be liable to variable winds. On the sea-shore a gentle sea-breeze generally sets in on the land in the afternoon, to restore the equilibrium which had been disturbed by reflections from the heated surface of the shore during the earlier part of the day; and about midnight, when the earth is cooled and the air condensed it flows back towards the sea.

The air, being a gravitating fluid, is affected by the attraction of the moon and the sun, in the same manner as the water, and must therefore have tides. These tides, however, are of no practical interest or importance.

We have considered the effects produced by the wide and extended agitation of the air; but there is another kind of agitation of which the air is susceptible—a sort of vibratory tremulous motion, which, striking on the drum of the ear, produces *Sound*. Sonorous bodies, such as bells, musical instruments, &c., are merely the agents by means of which that peculiar species of motion is communicated to the air. A bell rung in vacuo under the air-pump gives no sound.

Air, though by far the most common, is not the only vehicle of sound. Liquids are capable of conveying the vibratory motion of a sonorous body to the organ of hearing; for sound can be heard under water. Solid bodies also convey sound, as you may be convinced by a very simple experiment. If a string be fastened, round a poker, by the middle; the poker raised from the ground by the two ends of the string, and one end being held to each ear, if the poker be then struck with a key, the sound will be conveyed to the ear by means of the strings in a much more perfect manner than if it had no other vehicle than the air.

Bodies are called sonorous which produce clear, distinct, regular, and durable sounds—such as a bell, a drum, musical strings, wind instruments, &c. They owe this property to their elasticity; for an elastic body, after having been struck, not only returns to its former situation, but, having acquired momentum by its velocity, like the pendulum, it springs out on the opposite side. If the string A B (*fig.* 4), which is

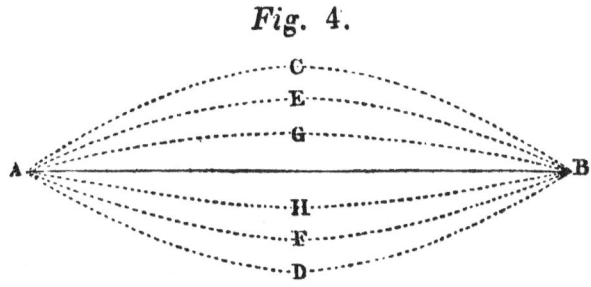

Fig. 4.

made fast at both ends, be drawn on one side to C, it will not only return to its original position, but proceed onwards to D. This is the first vibration; at its termination, the string, being stretched into the position A D B, will again tend to return to its natural state A B, and will, therefore, return to that line and pass on beyond it to E, and thence back again to F: then in the same manner to G and H; the resistance of the air continually destroying some of the motion, so that the extreme points, E F G H, are continually nearer to the line A B, until the whole motion is destroyed, and the string comes to rest in the position A B.

The tremulous motion given to the air by the vibration of a sonorous body is very similar to the motion communicated to smooth water when a stone is thrown into it. This first produces a small circular wave round the spot in which the stone falls: the wave spreads, and gradually communicates its motion to the adjacent waters, producing similar waves to a considerable extent. The same kind of waves are produced in the air by the motion of a sonorous body; but with this difference, that air, being an elastic fluid, the motion does not consist of regularly extending waves, but of vibrations composed of a motion forwards and backwards, similar to those of a sonorous body. The aërial undulations also take place in all directions, and are spherical. The first sphere of undulations which are produced immediately around the sonorous body, by pressing against the contiguous air, condenses it. The condensed air, though impelled forward by the pressure, re-acts on the first set of undulations, driving them back again. The second set of undulations which have been put in motion, in their turn communicate their motion, and are themselves driven back by re-action. Thus there is a succession of waves in the air. The air is immediately put in motion by the firing of a cannon; but it requires time for the vibrations to extend to any distant spot. The velocity of sound in air is computed to be at the rate of 1142 feet in a second.

The direction of the wind makes less difference in the velocity of sound than might be imagined. If the wind sets from us, it bears most of the aërial waves away, and renders the sound fainter; but it is not very considerably longer in reaching the ear than if the wind blew towards us. In fact, the wind cannot possibly retard the progress of the sound, by more than its own rate of motion: and as the velocity of sound is about 780 miles in an hour, the velocity of even a high wind bears too small a proportion to it to affect very materially the rate at which sound travels. The nearly uniform velocity of sound enables us to determine the distance of the object whence it proceeds: as that of a vessel at sea firing a cannon, or that of a thunder-cloud. If we do not hear the thunder till half a minute after we see the lightning, we conclude the cloud to be at the distance of six miles and a half.

An echo is produced when the aërial vibrations meet with an obstacle having a hard and regular surface, such as a wall, or rock: they may thus be reflected back to the ear, and produce the same sound a second time; but the sound will then appear to proceed from the object by which it is reflected. If the vibrations fall perpendicularly on the obstacle, they are reflected back in the same line; if obliquely, the sound returns obliquely on the other side of the perpendicular, the angle of reflection being equal to the angle of incidence.

Speaking-trumpets are constructed on the principle of the reflection of sound. The voice, instead of being diffused in the open air, is confined within the trumpet; and the vibrations which spread and fall against the sides of the instrument, are reflected according to the angle of incidence, and the form of the instrument is so regulated, that the whole of the vibrations are collected into a focus; and if the ear be situated in or near that spot, the sound is prodigiously increased. *Fig.* 5 represents the

Fig. 5.

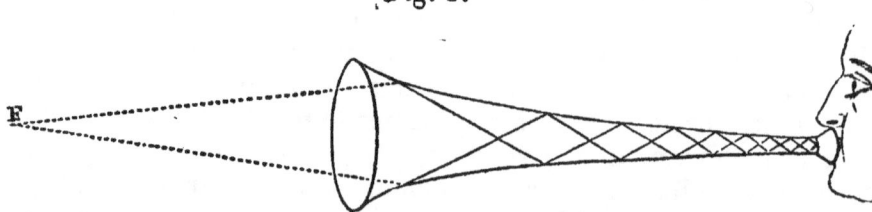

speaking-trumpet; the rays, as they issue from its mouth, are distinguished by being dotted; and they are brought to a focus at F. The

trumpet used by deaf persons acts on the same principle; the rays, in this case, being collected into a focus near the smaller end of the trumpet which is applied to the ear. The trumpets used as musical instruments are also constructed on this principle, so far as their form tends to increase the sound; but, as a musical instrument, the trumpet becomes itself the sonorous body, which is made to vibrate by blowing into it, and communicates its vibrations to the air.

If a sonorous body be struck in such a manner that its vibrations are all performed in equal times, the vibrations of the air will correspond with them, and be equal also; and thus, striking uniformly on the drum of the ear, they produce an uniform sensation on the auditory nerve, and excite the same uniform idea in the mind; or, in other words, we shall hear one musical tone. But if the vibrations of the sonorous body be irregular, there will necessarily follow a confusion of aërial vibrations; for a second vibration may commence before the first is finished, meet it half way on its return, and interrupt it in its course. The quicker a sonorous body vibrates, the more acute or sharp is the sound produced. The duration of the vibrations of strings or chords depends upon their length, the thickness or weight, and their degree of tension: thus the low, bass notes of a harp or piano are produced by long, thick, loose strings; and the high, treble notes, by those which are short, small, and tightly strung: so that the different length and size of the strings serves to vary the duration of the vibrations, and, consequently, the acuteness or gravity of the notes.

Among the variety of tones, there are some which, sounded together, please the ear, producing what we call harmony, or concord. This is thought to arise from the agreement of the vibrations of the two sonorous bodies; so that some of the vibrations of each strike upon the ear at the same time. Thus, if the vibrations of two strings are performed in equal times, the same tone is produced by both, and they are said to be in unison. If a violin is to be tuned in unison with another, the strings must be drawn tighter if too low, or loosened if at too high a pitch, in order to bring them to vibrate in equal times with the strings of the other instrument.

But concord is not confined to unison, for two different tones harmonize in a variety of cases. If one string (or any sonorous body whatever) vibrate in double the time of another, the second vibration of the latter will strike upon the ear at the same instant as the first vibration of the former; and this is the concord of an octave. If the vibrations of two strings are as two to three, the third vibration of the first corresponds with the fourth vibration of the latter, producing the harmony called a fifth: so that when the key-note is struck with its fifth, you hear every third vibration of one, and every fourth of the other at the same time. The key-note struck with the fourth is likewise a concord, and the vibrations are as three to four. The vibrations of a major third with the key-note are as four to five; and those of a minor third, as five to six.

There are other tones which, though they cannot be struck together without producing discord, if struck successively, give us the pleasure which is called melody.

INTRODUCTION TO OPTICS.

Section I.—*On Optics.*

Optics is one of the most interesting branches of Natural Philosophy: it is the science of vision, and teaches us how we see objects. In this science, bodies are divided into *luminous, opaque,* and *transparent.* A luminous body is one that shines by its own light—as the sun, the fire, a candle, &c. But all bodies that shine are not luminous: polished metal, for instance, when it shines with so much brilliancy, is not a luminous body, for it would be dark if it did not receive light from a luminous body: it belongs, therefore, to the class of opaque, or dark bodies, which comprehend all such as are neither luminous nor will admit the light to pass through them; and transparent bodies are those which admit the light to pass through them, such as glass and water. Transparent or pellucid bodies are frequently called mediums; and the rays of light which pass through them are said to be transmitted by them. Light, when emitted from the sun, or any other luminous body, is projected forwards in straight lines in every possible direction, or at least appears to move as it would on that supposition: so that the luminous body not only seems the general centre whence all the rays proceed, but every point of it may be considered as a centre which radiates light in every direction (*fig.* 1). A ray of light is a single line of light projected from a luminous body; and a pencil of rays is a collection of rays proceeding from any one point of a luminous body, as *fig.* 2.

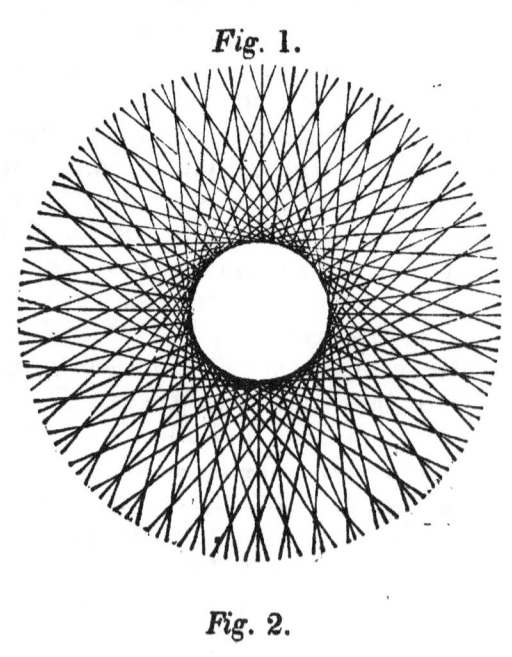

Fig. 1.

Fig. 2.

Philosophers are not agreed as to the nature of light. Some maintain the opinion that it is a body consisting of detached particles, which are emitted by luminous bodies, in which case the particles of light must be inconceivably minute, since, though they must cross each other in every direction, they are never known to interfere with each other; others suppose it to be produced like sound, by the undulations of a subtle fluid diffused throughout all known space. In some respects, light is obedient to the laws which govern bodies; in others, it appears to be independent of them. Thus, though its course corresponds with the laws of motion, it does not seem to be influenced by those of gravity; for it has never been discovered to have weight, though a variety of experiments have been made with a view of ascertaining that point. We are, however, so ignorant of the intimate nature of light, that an attempt to investigate it would lead us into a labyrinth of perplexity, if not of error. We shall therefore confine our attention to such of its properties as are well ascertained.

To return then to the examination of the effects of the radiation of light from a luminous body; since the rays are projected in straight lines, when they meet with an opaque body through which they are unable to pass, they are stopped short in their course, for they cannot move in a curve line round the body. The interruption of the rays of light by the opaque body produces therefore darkness on the opposite side of it; and if this darkness fall upon a wall, a sheet of paper, or any object whatever, it forms a shadow, for shadow is nothing more than darkness produced by the intervention of an opaque body, which prevents the rays of light from reaching an object behind it. You might suppose from this definition of a shadow, that it would be perfectly black; but it frequently happens that light from another body reaches the space where the shadow is formed, in which case the shadow is proportionally fainter. This happens if the opaque body be lighted by two candles: if you extinguish one of them, the shadow will be both deeper and more distinct. Yet it will not be perfectly dark, because it is still slightly illuminated by light reflected from the walls of the room, and other surrounding objects.

There are several things to be observed in regard to the form and extent of shadows. If the luminous body A (*fig.* 3) be larger than the opaque body, B, the shadow will gradually diminish in size till it terminate in a point; if smaller, the shadow will continually increase in size, as it is more distant from the object which projects it.

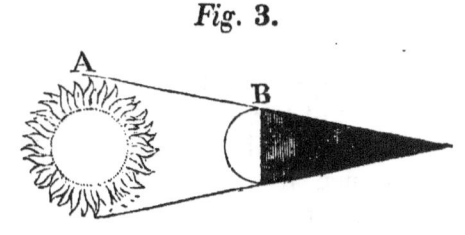

Fig. 3.

The shadow of a figure, A, (*fig.* 4) varies in size according to the distance of the several surfaces, B, C, D, E, on

Fig. 4.

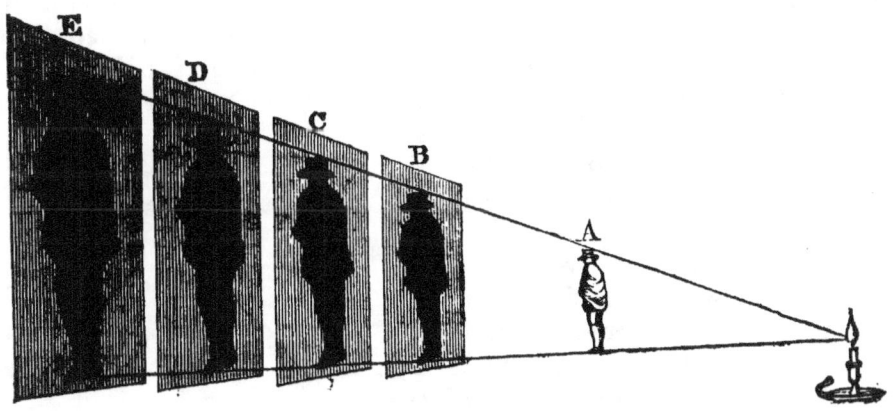

which it is described. Two lights produce two shadows from the same object. The number of lights (in different directions), while it decreases the intensity of the shadows, increases their number which always corresponds with that of the lights; for each light makes the opaque body cast a different shadow, as illustrated by *fig.* 5. It represents a ball, A, lighted by three candles, B C D: the light B produces the shadow *b*, the light C the shadow *c*, and the light D the shadow *d*. Now what becomes of the rays of light which opaque bodies arrest in their course, and the interruption of which is the occasion of shadows? This leads to a very important property of light, *Reflection*.

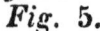

Fig. 5.

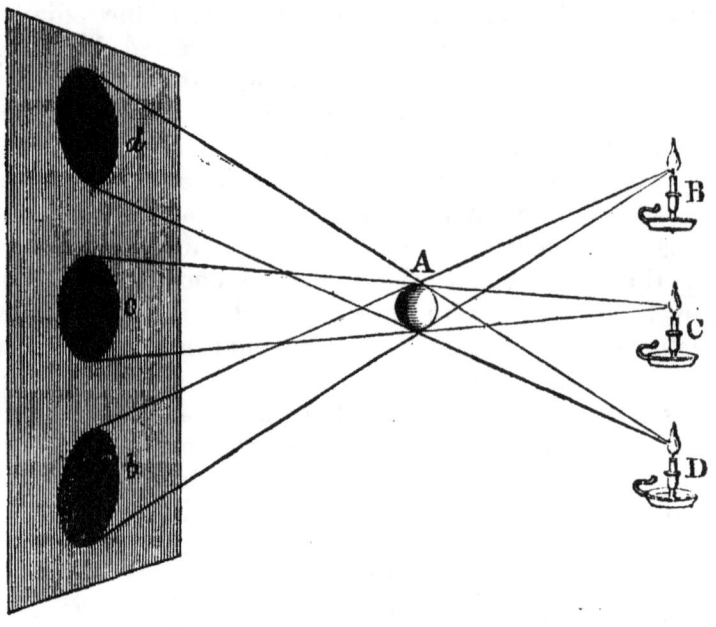

When rays of light encounter an opaque body, which they cannot traverse, part of them are absorbed by it, and part are reflected, and rebound as an elastic ball which is struck against a wall. Light in its reflection is governed by the same laws as solid perfectly elastic bodies. If a ray of light fall perpendicularly on an opaque body, it is reflected back in the same line towards the point whence it proceeded; if it fall obliquely, it is reflected obliquely, but in the opposite direction, the angle of incidence being equal to the angle of reflection.* If the shutters be closed, and a ray of the sun's light admitted through a very small aperture, and reflected by a mirror, on which the ray falls perpendicularly, but one ray is seen, for the ray of incidence and that of reflection are both in the same line, though in opposite directions, and thus are confounded together. The ray, therefore, which appears single, is in fact double, being composed of the incident ray proceeding to the mirror and the reflected ray returning from the mirror. These may be separated by holding the mirror, M (*fig.* 6), in such a manner that the incident ray, A B, shall fall obliquely upon it; then the reflected ray, B C, will go off in another direction. If a line be drawn from the point of incidence, B, perpendicularly to the mirror, it will divide the angle of incidence from the angle of reflection, and these angles will be equal.

Fig. 6.

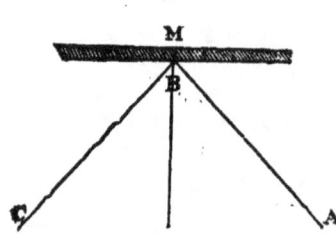

It is by reflected rays only that we see opaque objects. Luminous

* See Mechanics.

$29\frac{1}{2}$ inches; but the exact height depends upon the weight of the atmosphere, which varies much according to the state of the weather. The greater the pressure of the air on the mercury in the cup, the higher it will ascend in the tube. The air therefore generally is heaviest in dry weather, for then the mercury rises in the tube, and consequently that in the cup sustains the greatest pressure; and thus we estimate the dryness and fairness of the weather by the height of the mercury. We are apt to think the air feels heavy in bad weather, because it is less salubrious when impregnated with damp. The lungs, under these circumstances, do not play so freely, nor does the blood circulate so well: thus obstructions are frequently occasioned in the smaller vessels, from which arise colds, asthmas, agues, fevers, &c.

As the atmosphere diminishes in density in the upper regions, the air must be more rare upon a hill than in a plain; and this difference may be ascertained by the barometer. This instrument is so exact in its indications, that it is used for the purpose of measuring the height of mountains, and of estimating the elevation of balloons. Considerable inconvenience is often experienced from the thinness of the air in such elevated situations. It is sometimes oppressive, from being insufficient for respiration; and the expansion which takes place in the more dense air contained within the body is often painful: it occasions distension, and sometimes causes the bursting of the smaller blood-vessels in the nose and ears. Besides, in such situations, you are more exposed both to heat and cold; for though the atmosphere is itself transparent, its lower regions abound with vapours and exhalations from the earth, which float in it, and act in some degree as a covering, which preserves us equally from the intensity of the sun's rays, and from the severity of the cold.

Now since the weight of the atmosphere supports mercury in the tube of a barometer, it will support a column of any other fluid in the same manner; but as mercury is the heaviest of all fluids, it will support a higher column of any other fluid; for two fluids are in equilibrium, when their heights vary inversely as their densities: as, for instance, if a cubic foot of one fluid weighs twice as much as a cubic foot of the other, a column of the first ten feet in height will weigh as much as a column of the other twenty feet in height. Thus the pressure of the atmosphere, which will sustain a column of mercury of twenty-nine inches, is equal to sustaining a column of water of no less than thirty-four feet above its level. The weight of the atmosphere is therefore as great as that of a body of water surrounding the globe of the depth of thirty-four feet; for a column of air of the height of the atmosphere is equal to a column of water of thirty-four feet, or one of mercury of twenty-nine inches, each having the same base.

The common pump is constructed on this principle. By the act of pumping, the pressure of the atmosphere is taken off one part of the surface of the water: this part therefore rises, being forced up by the pressure communicated to it by that part of the water on the surface of which the weight of the atmosphere continues to act. The body of a pump consists of a large tube or pipe, whose lower end is immersed in the water which it is designed to raise. A kind of stopper, called a piston, is fitted to this tube, and is made to slide up and down it, by means of a metallic rod fastened to the centre of the piston.

The various parts of a pump are delineated in *fig.* 2 (next page). A B is the pipe or body of the pump; P the piston; V a valve, or little door in the piston, which, opening upwards, admits the water to rise through it, but prevents its returning; and *y* a similar valve in the body of the pump. When the pump is in a state of inaction, the two valves are closed by their own weight; but when, by drawing down the handle of the pump, the piston ascends, it raises a column of air which rested upon it, and produces a vacuum between the piston and the lower valve, Y: the air beneath this valve, which is immediately over the surface of the water, consequently expands, and forces its way through it; the water then, relieved from the pressure of the air, ascends into the pump. A few strokes of the handle totally exclude the air from the body of the pump, and fill it with water, which, having passed through both the valves, flows out at the spout. Thus the air and the water successively rise in the pump on the same principle that the mercury rises in the barometer. Water is said to be drawn up into a pump by suction; but the power of suction is no other than that of producing a vacuum over one part of the liquid, into which vacuum the liquid is forced by the pressure of the atmosphere on another part. The action of sucking through a straw consists in drawing in and confining the breath, so as to produce a vacuum, or at least to lessen materially the quantity of air, in the mouth: in consequence of which, the air within the straw rushes into the mouth, and is followed by the liquid, into which the lower end of the straw is immersed. The principle is the same; and the only difference consists in the mode of producing a vacuum. In suction, the muscular powers answer the pur-

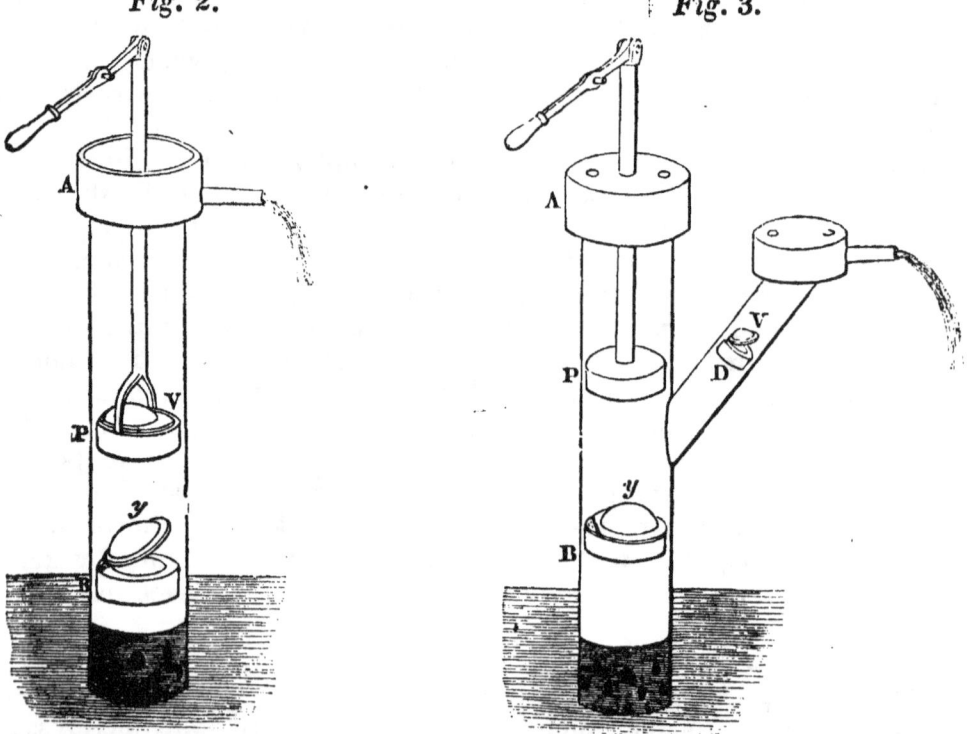

Fig. 2.   *Fig. 3.*

pose of the piston and valves. The distance from the level of the water in the well to the valve in the piston ought not to exceed thirty-two feet, otherwise the water would not be sure to rise through that valve, for the weight of the air is sometimes not sufficient to raise a column of mercury more than twenty-eight inches, or a column of water much more than thirty-two feet; but when once it has passed that opening, it is no longer the pressure of air on the reservoir which makes it ascend—it is raised by lifting it up, as you would raise it in a bucket, of which the

proceeding from the lower part of an object fall upon the upper part of the retina; but as we know their direction to be from below, we see that part of the object they describe as the lowest. When you wish to see an object above you, you look upwards; when an object below, you look downwards. You look up to see an elevated object, for it is only thus that the rays which proceed from it fall upon the retina of your eyes, and they must do so if you are to see the object; but the very circumstance of directing your eyes upwards convinces you that the object is elevated, and teaches you to consider as uppermost the image it forms on the retina, though it is in fact represented in the lowest part of it. When you look down upon an object, you draw your conclusion from a similar reasoning. It is thus that we see all objects in the direction of the rays which reach our eyes.

The different apparent dimensions of objects at different distances proceed from our seeing, not the objects themselves, but merely their image on the retina. *Fig.* 8 represents a row of trees, as viewed in the camera

Fig. 8.

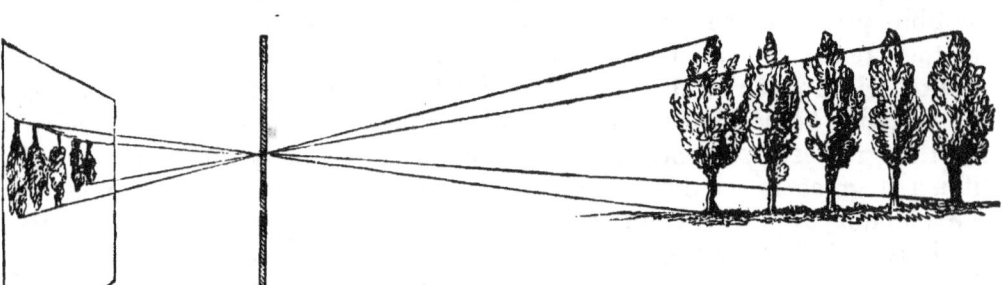

obscura; the direction of the rays from the objects to the image is expressed by lines. Observe that the ray which comes from the top of the nearest tree, and that which comes from the foot of the same tree, meet at the aperture, forming an angle of about twenty-five degrees: this is called the angle of vision, being that under which we see the tree. These rays cross each other at the aperture, and represent the tree inverted in the camera obscura. The dimensions of the image are considerably smaller than those of the object, but the proportions are perfectly preserved. The upper and lower ray, from the most distant tree, form an angle of not more than twelve or fifteen degrees, and an image of proportional dimensions. Thus two objects of the same size, as the two trees of the avenue, form figures of different sizes in the camera obscura, according to their distance, or, in other words, according to the angle of vision under which they are seen.

The experience we acquire by the sense of touch corrects the errors of our sight with regard to objects within our reach; we are so perfectly convinced of the real size of objects which we can handle, that we do not attend to their apparent difference. The opposite house does not appear to you much smaller than if you were close to it; and yet you see the whole of it through one of the windows of the room you sit in, and the image of the house on your retina must be very considerably smaller than that of the window through which you see it. Those accustomed to draw from nature are well aware of this difference. When we look up an avenue, the trees not only appear smaller as they are more distant, but **seem gradually to approach each other till they meet in a point, for the** road which separates the two rows forms a smaller visual angle, in proportion as it is more distant from us; therefore the width of the road seems gradually to diminish as well as the size of the trees, till at length the road apparently terminates in a point, at which the trees seem to meet.

In sculpture we copy Nature as she really exists; in painting we represent her as she appears to us—that is to say, we do not copy the objects, but the image they form on the retina of the eye.

If an object, with an ordinary degree of illumination, does not subtend an angle of more than half a minute of a degree, it is invisible. There are, consequently, two cases in which objects may be invisible, either if they are too small, or so distant as to form an angle less than one second of a degree. The fixed stars subtend much smaller angles, and yet are visible; but they are bodies luminous in themselves, and possess much more than an ordinary degree of illumination. In like manner, if the velocity of a body be so small that the arc which it describes in an hour does not subtend an angle of more than twenty degrees, its motion is imperceptible: consequently a very rapid motion may then be imperceptible, provided the distance of the moving body be sufficiently great; for the greater its distance, the smaller will be the angle under which its motion will appear to the eye. It is for this reason that the motion of the celestial bodies is invisible, notwithstanding their immense velocity; for the greatest *apparent* motion of any celestial body does not exceed fifteen degrees in an hour, being that seemingly produced in a body at the equator by the revolution of the earth. The greatest of the real motions is that of the moon, and even that does not exceed about thirteen degrees in a day. The real velocity depends altogether on the space comprehended in each degree; and this space depends on the distance of the object and the obliquity of its path. Now we cannot judge of the velocity of a body in motion unless we know its distance; for, supposing two men to set off at the same moment from A and B (*fig. 9*), to walk each to the end of their respective lines C and D, if they perform their

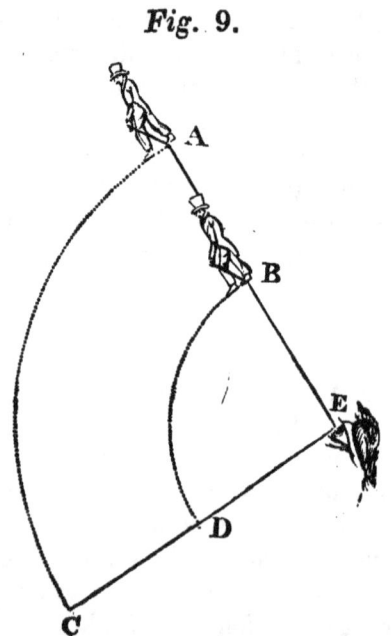

Fig. 9.

walk in the same space of time, they must have proceeded at a very different rate; and yet to an eye situated at E, they will appear to have moved with equal velocity, because they will both have gone through an equal number of degrees, though over a very unequal length of ground. Sight cannot be implicitly relied on: it deceives us, both in regard to the size and the distance of objects—indeed our senses would be very liable to lead us into error, if experience did not set us right. Nothing more convincingly shows how requisite experience is to correct the errors of sight, than the case of a young man who was blind from his infancy, and who recovered his sight at the age of fourteen, by the operation of couching. At first he had no idea either of the size or distance of objects, but imagined that every thing he saw touched his eyes; and it was

INTRODUCTION TO OPTICS.

not till after having repeatedly felt them, and walked from one object to another, that he acquired an idea of their respective dimensions, their relative situations, and their distances.

Since an image is formed on the retina of each of our eyes, it would seem that we ought to see objects double. In fact, however, we do not; and perhaps the best solution which has been offered of the difficulty is this, that the action of the rays on the optic nerve of each eye is so perfectly similar, that they produce but a single sensation: the mind, therefore, receives the same idea from the retina of both eyes, and conceives the object to be single. It is, however, safer to treat the fact as one established by experience, but not admitting of any satisfactory explanation; for the manner in which external objects act upon the mind admits of no direct observation, and all theories respecting it can therefore rest on no sound foundation. Persons afflicted with a disease in one eye, which prevents the rays of light from affecting it in the same manner as the other, frequently see double.

The image of an object in a looking-glass is not inverted, because the rays do not enter the mirror by a small aperture, and cross each other, as they do at the orifice of a camera obscura, or the pupil of the eye.

When a man views himself in a mirror, the rays from his eyes fall perpendicularly upon it, and are reflected in the same line; they proceed, therefore, as if they had come from a point behind the glass, and the same effect is produced, as if they proceeded from an image of the object described behind the glass, and situated there in the same manner as the object before it. This is not the case only with respect to rays falling perpendicularly on the glass, but with all others. Thus in *fig.* 10, a ray proceeding from the point C to D is reflected to A, and arrives there in the same manner as if it had proceeded from E, a point behind the glass, at the same distance from it as C is in front of it.

A man may see himself at full length in a mirror which is not more than half his height (*fig.* 10). The ray of light, A B, from his eye which falls perpendicularly on the mirror, B D, will be reflected back in the same line; but a ray, C D, from his feet, which falls obliquely on the mirror, will be reflected in the line D A; and since we view objects in the direction of the reflected rays, which reach the eye, and the image appears at the same distance behind the mirror as the object is before it, we must continue the line A D to E, and the line A B to F, at the termi-

Fig. 10.   Fig. 11.

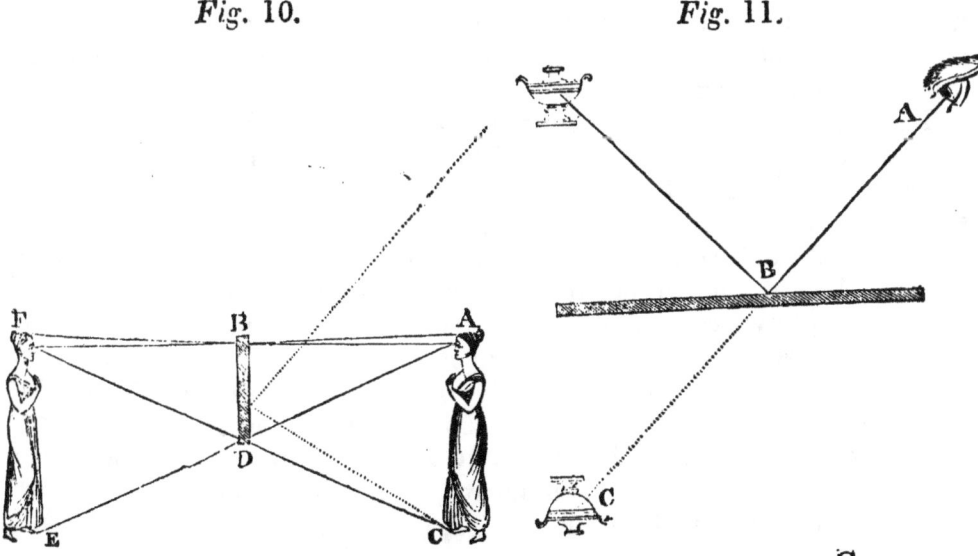

nation of which the image will be represented. The line D E is equal to D C, or to D A; and the line A B D therefore, which represents the necessary length of the mirror, is half the line E F, which represents the height of the person. The man could not see the whole of his person in a much smaller mirror; for a ray of light from his feet would fall so obliquely on it, that it would be reflected above his head, so that he could not see it. This is shown by the dotted line (*fig.* 10). A man cannot see himself in a mirror if he stand to the right or the left of it, because the incident rays falling obliquely on the mirror will be reflected obliquely in the opposite direction, the angles of incidence and of reflection being equal.

Fig. 11 represents an eye looking at the image of a vase, reflected by a mirror: it must see it in the direction of the ray A B, as that is the ray which brings the image to the eye; prolong the ray to C, and in that spot will the image appear. You must observe, that in a glass mirror it is not the glass that reflects the rays which form the image, but the mercury behind it. The glass acts chiefly as a transparent case, through which the rays find an easy passage. Could mirrors be made of mercury, they would reflect more perfectly; but mercury is a fluid. By amalgamating it with tin-foil, it becomes of the consistence of paste, attaches itself to the glass, and forms, in fact, a mercurial mirror, which would be much more perfect without its glass cover, for the purest glass is never completely transparent: some of the rays, therefore, are lost during their passage through it, by being either absorbed, or irregularly reflected. This imperfection of glass mirrors has introduced the use of metallic mirrors, for optical purposes. All opaque bodies would be mirrors, were their surfaces sufficiently smooth; but the surface of bodies in general is so rough and uneven, that their reflection is extremely irregular, which prevents the rays from forming an image on the retina. You may easily conceive the variety of directions in which rays would be reflected by a nutmeg-grater, on account of the inequality of its surface, and the number of holes with which it is pierced. Now all solid bodies resemble the nutmeg-grater in these respects, more or less; and it is only those which are susceptible of receiving a polish, that can be made to reflect the rays with regularity. As hard bodies are of the closest texture, the least porous, and capable of taking the highest polish, they make the best mirrors: none, therefore, are so well calculated for this purpose as metals.

There are three kinds of mirrors used in optics: the plane or flat, which are the common mirrors we have just mentioned, convex mirrors, and concave mirrors. The reflection of the two latter is very different from that of the former.

The plane mirror, we have seen, does not alter the direction of the reflected rays, and forms an image behind the glass exactly similar to the object before it: for it forms an image of each point of the object at the same distance behind the mirror, that the point is before it; and these images of the different points together make up one image of the whole object. A convex mirror has the peculiar property of making the reflected rays diverge, by which means it diminishes the image; and a concave mirror makes the rays converge, and, under certain circumstances, magnifies the image. Let us begin by examining the reflection of a convex mirror. This is formed of a portion of the exterior surface of a sphere. When several parallel rays fall upon it, that ray only which, if prolonged, would pass through the centre, or axis of the mirror, is perpendicular to it. In order to avoid confusion, we have, in *fig.* 12, drawn only three parallel lines,

AB, CD, EF, to represent rays falling on the convex mirror MN: the

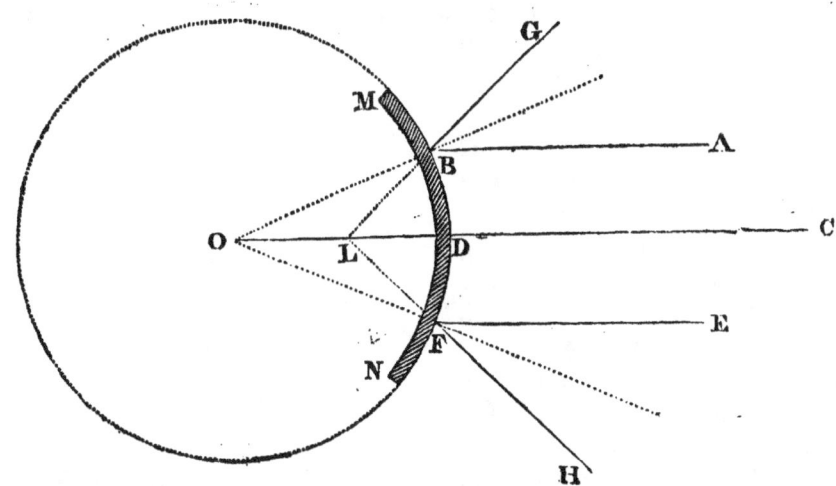

Fig. 12.

middle ray, you will observe, is perpendicular to the mirror, the others fall on it obliquely. The three rays being parallel would all be perpendicular to a flat mirror; but no ray can fall perpendicularly on a spherical mirror, which is not directed towards the centre of the sphere, just as a weight falls perpendicularly to the earth when gravity attracts it towards the centre. In order, therefore, that rays may fall perpendicularly to the mirror at B and F, the rays must be in the direction of the dotted lines, which meet at the centre, O, of the sphere, of which the mirror forms a portion.

Now let us observe in what direction the three rays AB, CD, EF, will be reflected. The middle ray falling perpendicularly on the mirror, will be reflected in the same line; the two others falling obliquely, will be reflected obliquely to G and H, for the dotted lines are perpendiculars, which divide their angles of incidence and reflection, or they will proceed as if they came from the point L; and since we see objects in the direction of the reflected ray, we shall see an image, answering to that which would be produced by a body placed at L, which is the point at which the reflected rays, if continued through the mirror, would unite and form an image. This point is equally distant from the surface and centre of the sphere, and is called the imaginary focus of the mirror. A focus is a point at which converging rays unite; in this case called an imaginary focus, because the rays only appear to unite there, or rather proceed after reflection in the same direction as if they came from behind the mirror, from that point: for they do not pass through the mirror, since they are reflected by it.

If the rays diverge before they fall on the mirror, they will diverge still more after reflection; but in this case also they will diverge as if they proceeded from a point within the mirror, which is the focus of those rays. The rays, therefore, which really proceed from a point in front of the mirror, will appear to proceed from a point within it, at which they would unite, and form an image. This point within the mirror, like the imaginary focus of parallel rays, is always a point in the line joining the centre of the sphere, with the point without the mirror, from which the rays really proceed.

If, instead of supposing a single luminous point, we imagine a body of some magnitude placed before the mirror, the rays of light which proceed from each point of it will be reflected exactly in the same manner as if that was a single luminous point; and an image of that point therefore will be formed as before, in the line joining that point to the centre of the sphere. An image being thus formed of each point in the object, there will be an image of the whole object, formed by the collection of these images of its different parts.

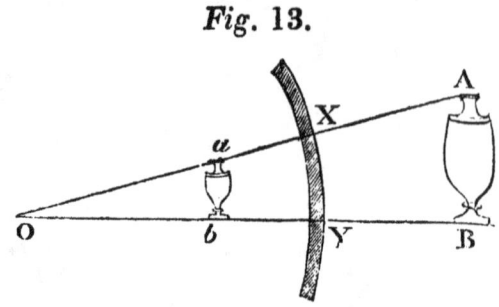

Fig. 13.

This image will necessarily be smaller than the object itself. If A B be an object placed before the convex mirror, X Y, and lines be drawn from its extreme points, A B to O, the centre of the sphere of which the mirror forms part, the image of the point A will be at *a*, a point in the line A O; that of B at *b*, a point in the line B O; and of course the image of every intermediate point somewhere between *a* and *b*. Or, in other words, the rays which really proceed from A are seen after reflection as if they proceeded from *a*; those from B as if they proceeded from *b*; and all others as if from some point between them. The lines A O, B O, converge to a point at O; and the points *a*, *b*, which are nearer to O than A, B are, are necessarily nearer together than A, B. The space, therefore, from which the rays after reflection appear to proceed is less than that occupied by the body itself, as the image is smaller than the object.

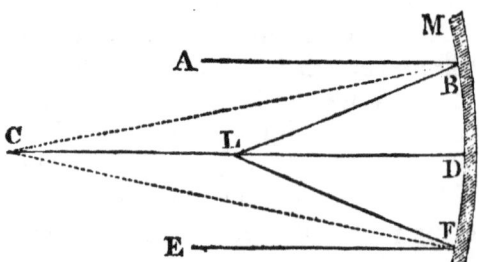

Fig. 14.

A concave mirror is formed of a portion of the internal surface of a hollow sphere, and its peculiar property is to make the rays of light converge. If three parallel rays, A B, C D, E F, fall on the concave mirror, M N (*fig.* 14), the middle ray will be reflected in the same line, being in the direction of the axis of the mirror, and the two others will be reflected obliquely, as they fall obliquely on the mirror. The two dotted perpendiculars divide their angles of incidence and reflection; and in order that these angles may be equal, the two oblique rays must be reflected to L, where they will unite with the middle ray. Thus, when any number of parallel rays fall on a concave mirror, they are all reflected to a focus: for in proportion as the rays are more distant from the axis of the mirror, they fall more obliquely upon it, and are more obliquely reflected: in consequence of which they come to a focus in the direction of the axis of the mirror; and this point is not an imaginary focus (as with the convex mirror), but the true focus at which the rays unite. If rays fall convergent on a concave mirror (*fig.* 15), they are sooner brought to a focus, L, than parallel rays: their focus is therefore nearer to the mirror MN. Divergent rays are brought to a more distant focus than parallel rays, as in *fig.* 16, where the focus is at L; but the true focus of mirrors, either convex or concave, is that formed by parallel rays, which is equally distant from the centre and the surface of the sphere, as in *fig.* 12 and *fig.* 14. If a metallic concave mirror of polished tin be exposed to the sun, the rays will be collected into a very brilliant focus; and a piece of paper held

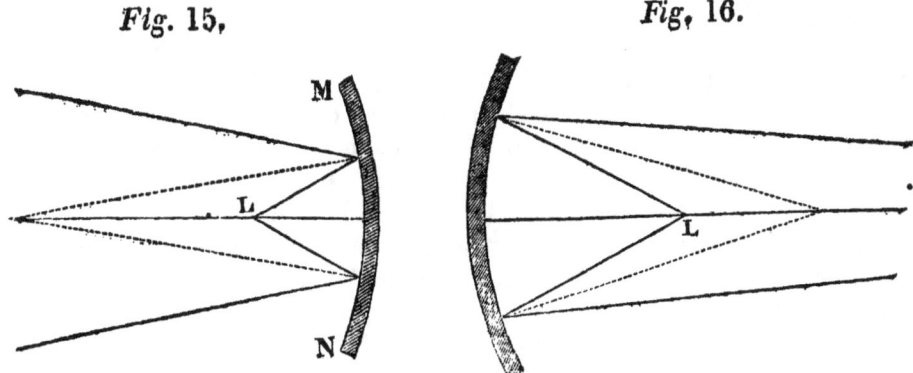

Fig. 15. Fig. 16.

in this focus will take fire; for rays of light cannot be concentrated without accumulating a proportional quantity of heat: hence concave mirrors have obtained the name of burning mirrors. If a burning taper be placed in the focus (*fig.* 17), the ray which falls in the direction of the axis of the mirror will be reflected back in the same line; but two other rays, drawn from the focus, and falling on the mirror at B and F, will be reflected to A and E. Therefore the rays which proceed from a light placed in the focus of a concave mirror fall divergent upon it, and are reflected parallel: it is

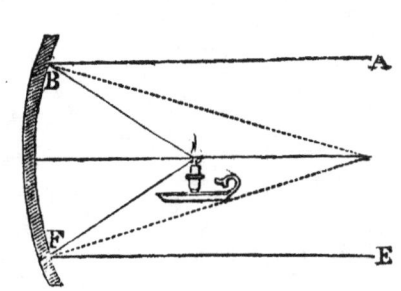

Fig. 17.

exactly the reverse of the former figure, in which the sun's rays fell parallel on the mirror, and were reflected to a focus. In other words, when the incident rays are parallel, the reflected rays converge to a focus; when the incident rays proceed from the focus, they are reflected parallel: this is a very important law of optics. We have said that the image was formed in the focus of a concave mirror, yet glass concave mirrors are often seen, where the object is represented within the mirror, in the same manner as in those which are convex. This is the case only when the object is placed between the mirror and its focus; the image then appears magnified behind, or within the mirror.

Section II.—*On Refraction and Colours.*

Refraction is the effect which transparent mediums produce on light in its passage through them. Opaque bodies reflect the rays, and transparent bodies transmit them; but it is found that if a ray, in passing from one medium into another of different density, fall obliquely, it is turned out of its course. The power which causes the deviation of the ray is not fully understood, nor completely ascertained; but the appearances are the same as if the ray (supposing it to be a succession of moving particles, which is for this purpose the most convenient way of considering it) were attracted by the denser medium more strongly than by the rarer. Let us suppose the two mediums to be air and water: when a ray of light passes from air into water, it appears to be more strongly attracted by the latter. If then a ray, A B (*fig.* 18), fall perpendicularly on water, the attraction of the water acts in the same direction as the course of the ray; it will not therefore cause a deviation, and the ray will proceed straight on to E; but if it fall obliquely, as the ray C B, the water will attract it out of its course. Let us suppose the ray to have reached the surface of a denser medium, and that it is there affected by its attraction. If not counteracted by some other power, this attraction would draw it perpendicularly to the water at B, towards E; but it is also impelled by its projectile force, which the attraction of the denser medium cannot overcome: the ray, therefore, acted on by both these powers, moves in a direction between them, and instead of pursuing its original course to D, or being implicitly guided by the water to E, proceeds towards F, so that the ray appears bent or broken. C B (*fig.* 19) represents a ray passing

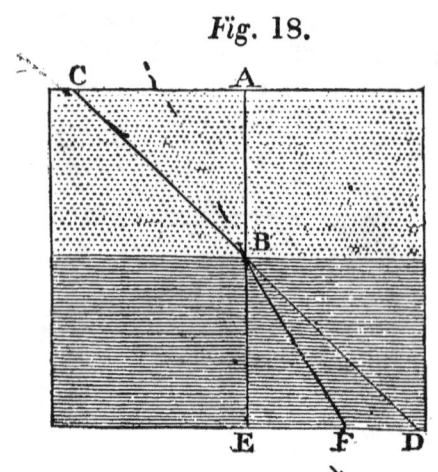
Fig. 18.

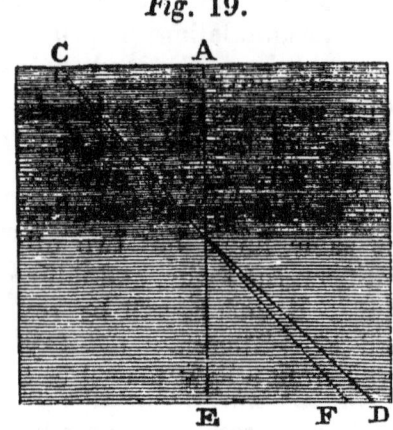
Fig. 19.

obliquely from glass into water; glass being the denser medium, the ray will be more strongly attracted by that which it leaves, than by that which it enters. The attraction of the glass would act in the direction A B, while the impulse of projection would carry the ray to F: it moves, therefore, between these directions towards D; so that when a ray passes from a dense into a rare medium, a refraction takes place in the opposite direction to that observed when the ray passes from a rare into a dense medium. The distance at which the denser medium produces its effect upon a ray is so small as to be insensible: the ray appears, therefore, to be refracted only at the point at which it passes from one medium to the other, and passes on in a straight course through each.

If a shilling (*fig.* 20) be placed at the bottom of an empty tea-cup, and the tea-cup at such a distance from the eye that the rim shall hide the shilling, it will become visible by filling the cup with water. In the first instance, the rays reflected by the shilling are directed higher than the eye, but when the cup is filled with water, they are refracted by its attraction, and bent downwards at quitting it, so as to enter the eye. When the shilling becomes visible

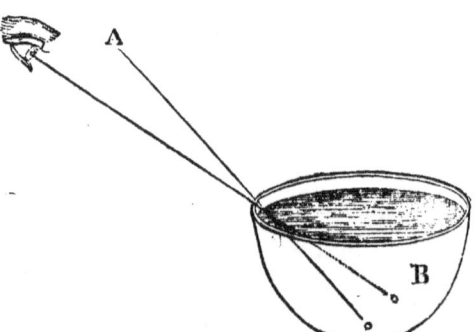
Fig. 20.

by the refraction of the ray, you do not see it in the situation which it really occupies, but an image of it higher in the cup; for as objects always appear to be situated in the direction of the rays which enter the eye, the shilling will be seen in the direction of the refracted ray at B.

The manner in which an oar appears bent in water is a similar effect of refraction. The line drawn from the point A to the shilling in the last figure may now be conceived to represent an oar plunged in water; the lowest point being represented in the figure by the little circle, will, as before, have an image of itself formed apparently above it, as at B. In like manner every point of the oar below the surface of the water will have an image of itself formed above it at some point in the dotted line in the figure, and the whole dotted line will represent the whole image of that part of the oar which is immersed. The part of the oar above the water, extending to A, is seen in its natural position; that below the water is seen as if reaching along the dotted line to B; the oar, therefore, appears bent or broken at the surface of the water. The fact of the formation of an image *above* the true place of the body does not depend on the situation of the eye. The representation of the eye in the figure therefore, which was introduced in the former paragraph, to explain the cause of a single ray, is not necessary or particularly applicable to the present subject.

When we see the bottom of a clear stream, the rays which it reflects, being refracted in their passage from the water into the air, will make the bottom appear more elevated than it really is, and the water will consequently appear more shallow. Accidents have frequently been occasioned by this circumstance; and boys who are in the habit of bathing should be cautioned not to trust to the apparent shallowness of water, as it will always prove deeper than it appears.

The refraction of light prevents our seeing the heavenly bodies in their real situation. The light they send to us being refracted in passing into the atmosphere, we see the sun and stars in the direction

Fig. 21.

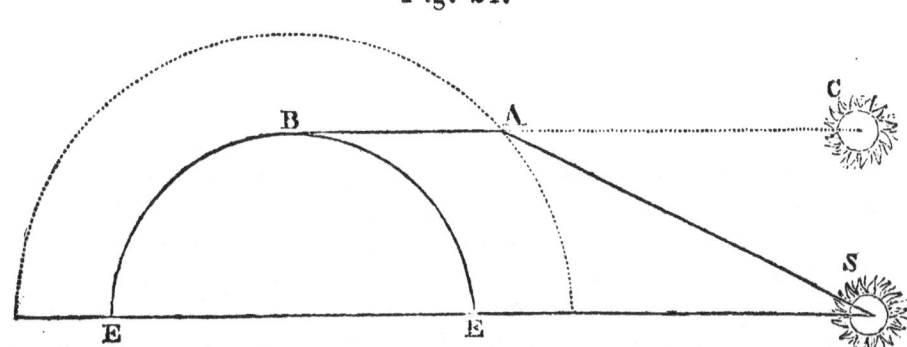

of the refracted ray, as described in *fig.* 21, where the dotted line represents the extent of the atmosphere, above a portion of the earth, E B E. A ray of light coming from the sun, S, falls obliquely on it at A, and is refracted to B; then, since we see the object in the direction of the refracted ray, a spectator at B will see an image of the sun at C, instead of the real object at S. If the sun were immediately over our heads, its rays falling perpendicularly on the atmosphere would not be refracted, and we should then see it in its true situation. To the inhabitants of the torrid zone, where the sun is sometimes vertical, its rays are then not refracted. There is, however, another obstacle to seeing the heavenly bodies in their true situation, which affects them in the torrid zone as well as elsewhere. Light is about eight minutes and a half in its passage from the sun to the earth; therefore, when the rays reach us, the sun has quitted the spot he occupied on their departure; yet we see him in the direction of those rays, and consequently in a situation which he had abandoned eight minutes and a half before. In speaking of the sun's motion, we mean his apparent motion, produced by the diurnal rotation of the earth, for the effect being the same whether it be our earth or the heavenly bodies which move, it is more easy to represent things as they appear to be, than as they really are. The refraction of the sun's rays by the atmosphere prolongs our days, as it occasions our seeing an image of the sun, both before he rises and after he sets; for below the horizon he still shines upon the atmosphere, and his rays are thence refracted to the earth. So likewise we see an image of the sun before he rises, the rays that previously fall upon the atmosphere being reflected to the earth.

In passing through a pane of glass the rays suffer two refractions, which being in contrary directions, produce nearly the same effect as if no refraction had taken place.

Fig. 22, A A represents a thick pane of glass seen edgeways. When the ray B approaches the glass at C, it is refracted by it; and, instead of continuing its course in the same direction, as the dotted line describes,

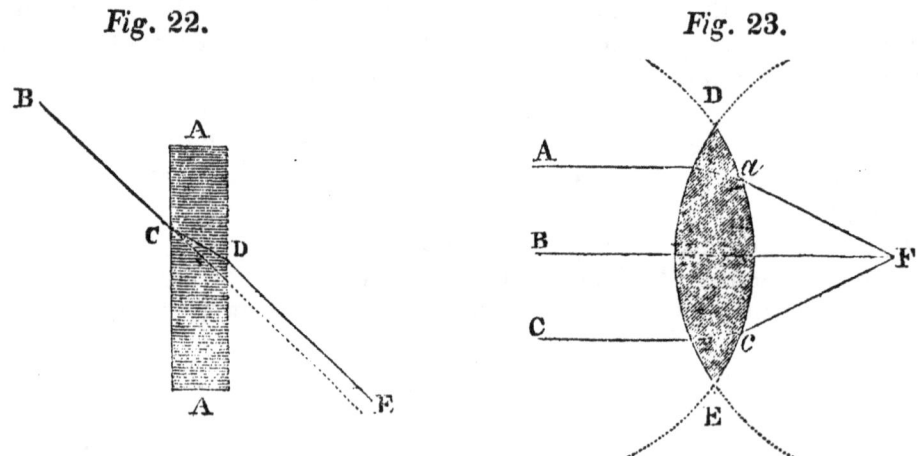

it passes through the pane to D; at that point returning into the air, it is again refracted by the glass, but in a contrary direction, and in consequence proceeds to E. Now the ray B C and the ray D E being parallel, the light does not appear to have suffered any refraction; for if a ray of light passes from one medium into another, and through that into the first again, the two refractions being equal and in opposite directions, no sensible effect is produced; for the direction is the same, and the little space by which the ray is thrown to one side, as represented in fig. 22, is necessarily less than the thickness of the medium, and the thickness of a pane of glass is too little to be worth considering. But this is the case only when the two surfaces of the refracting medium are parallel to each other; if they are not, the two refractions may be made in the same direction. Thus, when parallel rays (*fig.* 23) fall on a piece of glass having a double convex surface, which is called a lens, that only which falls in the direction of the axis of the lens is perpendicular to the surface; the other rays falling obliquely are refracted towards the axis, and will meet at a point beyond the lens, called its focus. Of the three rays A, B, C, which fall on the lens D E, the rays A and C are refracted in their passage through it, to *a* and *c*, and on quitting the lens they undergo a second refraction in the same direction, which unites them with the ray B, at the focus **F***. The focal distance, or distance of the focus from the surface of the lens, depends both upon the form of the lens and of the refractive power of the substance of which it is made; in a glass lens, both sides of which are equally convex, the focus is situated nearly at the centre of the sphere of which the surface of the lens forms a portion: it is at the distance, therefore, of the radius of the sphere.

There are lenses of various forms, which are represented in *fig.* 24. The property of those which have a convex surface is to collect the rays

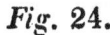

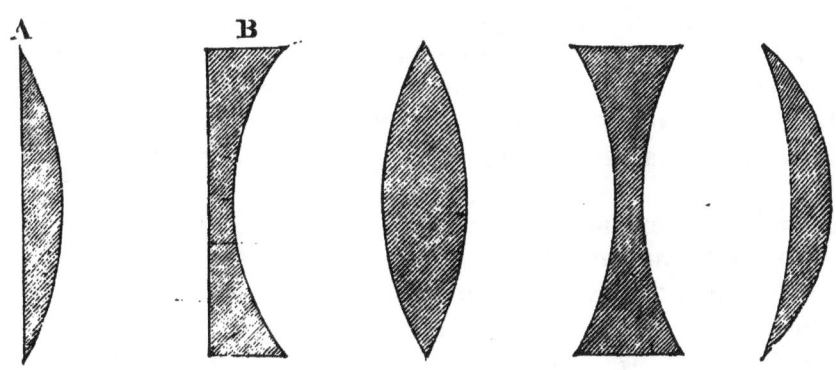

of light to a focus; and of those which have a concave surface, to disperse them: for the rays A, C, falling on the concave lens X Y (*fig.* 25), instead of converging towards the ray B, which falls on the axis of the lens, will each be attracted towards the lens, both on entering and quitting it, and will, therefore, by the first refraction, be made to diverge to *a, c*, and by the second to *d, e*. Lenses which have one side flat, and the other convex or concave, as A and B, *fig.* 24, are called plano-convex and plano-concave lenses. The focus of the former is at the distance of the

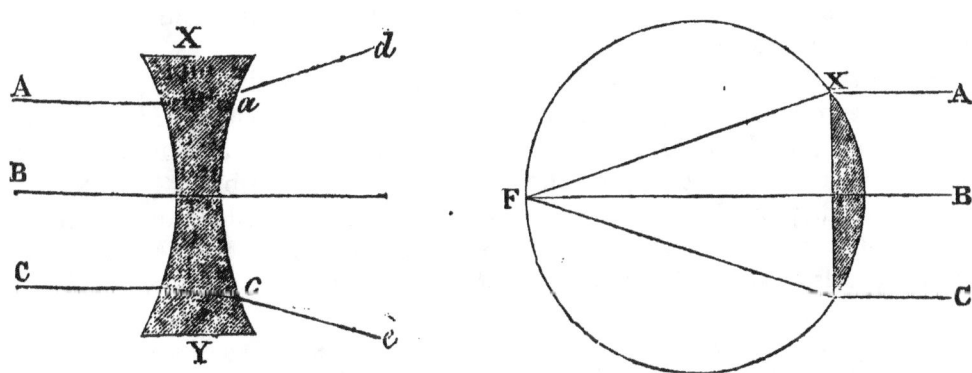

diameter of a sphere, of which the convex surface of the lens forms a portion, as represented in *fig.* 26. The three parallel rays, A, B, C, are brought to a focus by the plano-convex lens X Y at F.

Thus far we have only spoken of the refraction of *parallel* rays; if the

---

* The refractions will at once appear to be in the same direction if perpendiculars to the surface of the lens be drawn at the points where the ray enters and quits it: bearing in mind that the lens being denser than the air, the ray is drawn *towards* the perpendicular on entering, and *from* it on quitting the lens.

rays diverge originally, they will be less convergent or more divergent after refraction, but they would in general still finally meet at a point, or appear to diverge from one. Taking the case of a convex lens, the point at which they would meet would be farther from the lens than that in which parallel rays meet, and continually farther and farther, as the rays were more divergent, or as the body from which they proceeded was brought nearer to the lens. An image* would therefore be formed, but continually farther and farther from the lens, as the body approached it; and the image is smaller or larger than the body, as it is nearer to or farther from the lens than the body itself is. If the body is brought as near to the lens as the distance of the focus for parallel rays, no image would be formed, for the rays would be refracted parallel to each other; and if the body were brought still nearer, the rays would diverge after refraction. The case of a convex lens is one of the most simple and the most important; but the same principle may easily be extended to other cases.

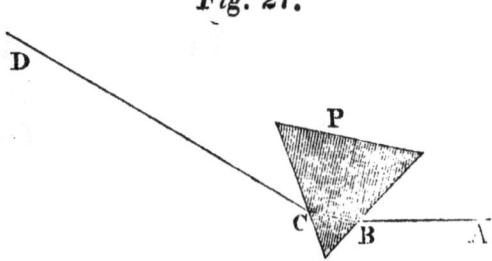

Fig. 27.

We shall next explain the refraction of a triangular piece of glass, called a prism (*fig.* 27). The sides are flat; it cannot therefore bring the rays to a focus, nor can its refraction be similar to that of a flat pane of glass, because it has not two sides parallel. The refractions of the light, on entering and on quitting the prism, are both in the same direction†. On entering the prism P, the ray is refracted from B to C, and on quitting it from C to D. If the window-shutters be closed, and a ray of light, admitted through a small aperture, fall upon a prism, it will be refracted, and a spectrum, A B (*fig.* 28), representing all the colours of the rainbow, will be formed on the opposite wall. It is difficult to conceive how a piece of white glass can produce such a variety of brilliant colours; but the fact is, that the colours are not formed by the prism, but existed in the ray previous to its refraction; for the white rays of the sun are composed of coloured rays, which, when blended together, appear colourless or white.

Sir Isaac Newton, to whom we are indebted for the most important discoveries respecting light and colours, was the first who divided a white ray of light, and found it to consist of an assemblage of coloured rays, which formed an image upon the wall, such as is exhibited (*fig.* 28), in which are displayed the following series of colours—red, orange, yellow, green, blue, indigo, and violet. Now a prism separates these coloured rays by refraction. It appears that the coloured rays have different

---

* We speak of the formation of an *image* at a point wherever the rays after reflection or refraction proceed, *as if they diverged from that point.* The object is then seen as an image of it placed there would be. This image, however, has not, under common circumstances, any real existence. The rays pass through the point in question; but as they are only seen by an eye in the direction of their motion, a spectator any where else will not see them at all, and the spectator who does see them will only know the direction in which they move. If, however, a screen be placed at the focus, so as to intercept and reflect the rays, the existence of the image will be proved by the actual formation of a distinct picture of the object upon the screen; if the screen be placed nearer or farther off, so that the rays have not yet accurately converged to, or have begun to diverge from, the focus, there will be a confused spot of light, but no distinct representation.

† This will at once appear, as in the case of the lens, by drawing perpendiculars to the surface of the prism where the ray enters and quits it.

Fig. 28.

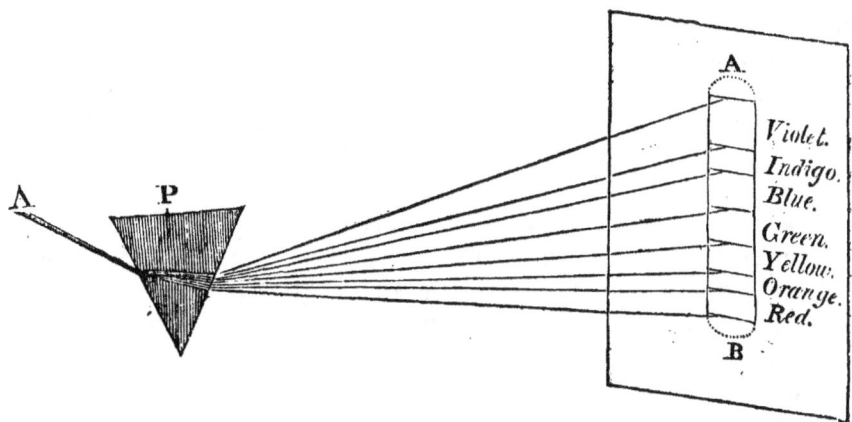

degrees of refrangibility; in passing through the prism, therefore, they take different directions, according to their susceptibility of refraction. The violet rays deviate most from their original course: they appear at one end of the spectrum A B. Contiguous to the violet are the indigo rays, being those which have somewhat less refrangibility: then follow, in succession, the blue, green, yellow, orange, and, lastly, the red, which are the least refrangible of the coloured rays. The union of these colours, in the proportions in which they appear in the spectrum, produces in us the idea of whiteness. If a card be painted in compartments with these seven colours, and whirled rapidly on a pin, it will appear white. But a more decisive proof of the composition of a white ray is afforded by re-uniting these coloured rays, and forming with them a ray of white light. This can be done by letting the coloured rays, which have been separated by a prism, fall upon a lens, which will make them converge to a focus; and when thus re-united, they will appear white as they did before refraction. The prism P (*fig.* 29) separates a ray of white light into seven coloured rays; and the lens L L brings them to a focus at F, where they again appear white: thus, by means of a prism and a lens, we can take a ray of white light to pieces, and put it together again.

Fig. 29.

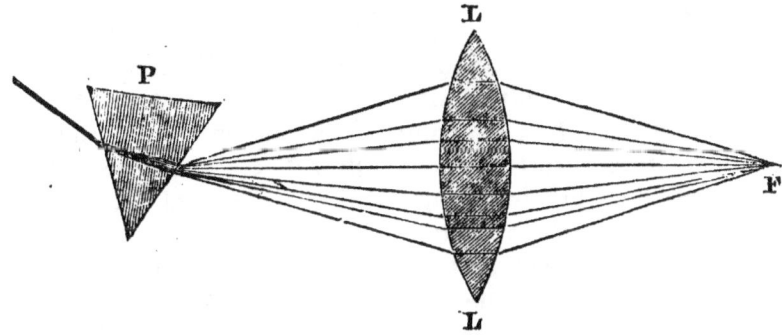

This division of a ray of white light into different colours, being caused by the unequal refrangibility of the different coloured rays, must take place, more or less, whenever the ray suffers refraction. Thus the rainbow, which exhibits a series of colours so analogous to those of the spectrum, is formed by the refraction of the sun's rays in their passage through a shower of rain, every drop of which acts as a prism, in separating the coloured rays as they pass through it.

The sun's rays may be collected to a focus by a lens in the same manner as they are by a concave mirror: in the first, the rays pass through the glass, and converge to a focus behind it; in the latter they are reflected from the mirror, and brought to a focus before it. A lens, when used for this purpose, is called a burning glass; and if, when the sun shines bright, a piece of paper be held in the focus of the rays, it will take fire. This experiment succeeds best with brown or any dark-coloured paper; for though it is true that the lens collects an equal number of rays to a focus, whether the paper held there be white or coloured, the white paper appears more luminous in the focus, because most of the rays, instead of entering into the paper, are reflected by it; and this is the reason that the paper is not burnt; whilst, on the contrary, the coloured paper, which absorbs more light than it reflects, soon becomes heated and takes fire.

It is supposed that the tendency to absorb or reflect rays depends on the arrangement of the minute particles of the body, and that the diversity of arrangement renders some bodies susceptible of reflecting one coloured ray, and absorbing the others; whilst other bodies have a tendency to reflect all the colours, and others again to absorb them all. A body appears to be of the colour which it reflects; as we see it only by reflected rays, it can appear but of the colour of those rays. Thus grass is green, because it absorbs all except the green rays: it is, therefore, these only which the grass and trees reflect to our eyes, and which make them appear green. The sky and flowers, in the same manner, reflect the various colours of which they appear to us: the rose, the red rays; the violet, the blue; the jonquil, the yellow, &c. If you imagine that these are the permanent colours of the grass and flowers, you are mistaken. Whenever you see those colours, the objects must be illuminated; and light, from whatever source it proceeds, is of the same nature, composed of the various coloured rays, which paint the grass, the flowers, and every coloured object in nature. Objects in the dark have no colour, or are black, which is the same thing. You can never see objects without light. Light is composed of colours, therefore there can be no light without colours; and though every object is black, or without colour in the dark, it becomes coloured as soon as it becomes visible.

An object placed in a coloured ray of light which has been refracted by a prism, will appear of the colour of the ray in which it is placed. A sheet of white paper will take all the colours indifferently, but a coloured body will appear most brilliant when placed in the ray which it naturally reflects. But though bodies, from the arrangement of their particles, have a tendency to absorb some rays and reflect others, yet they are not so perfectly uniform in their arrangement as to reflect only pure rays of one colour, and perfectly absorb the others. A body reflects, in great abundance, the rays which determine its colour, and the others in a greater or less degree, in proportion as they are nearer or farther from its own colour, in the order of refrangibility.

Bodies which reflect all the rays are white; those which absorb them all are black. Between these extremes they appear lighter or darker, in proportion to the quantity of rays they reflect or absorb. A rose is of a pale red: it approaches nearer to white than black, it therefore reflects rays more abundantly than it absorbs them. Pale-coloured bodies reflect all the coloured rays to a certain degree, which produces their paleness, approaching to whiteness; but one colour they reflect more than the rest: this predominates over the white, and determines the colour of the body. Since, then, bodies of a pale colour in some degree reflect all the rays of light, in passing through the various colours of the spectrum, they will reflect them all with tolerable brilliancy, but will appear most vivid in the ray of their natural colour. The green leaves, on the contrary, are of a dark colour, bearing a stronger resemblance to black than to white: they have, therefore, a greater tendency to absorb than to reflect rays. Blue often appears green by candle-light, because this light is less pure than that of the sun; and when refracted by a prism, the yellow rays predominate; and as the admixture of blue and yellow forms green, the superabundance of yellow gives to blue bodies a greenish hue.

The sun appears red through a fog, owing to the red rays having a greater momentum, which gives them power to traverse so dense an atmosphere. For the same reason the sun generally appears red at rising and setting: as the increased quantity of atmosphere which the oblique rays must traverse, loaded with the mists and vapours which are usually formed at those times, prevents a large proportion of the other rays from reaching us. The colour of the atmosphere, commonly called the sky, is blue;—now since all the rays traverse it in their passage to the earth, it would be natural to infer that it should be white; but we must not forget that we see none of the rays which pass from the sun to the earth, excepting those which meet our eyes; and this happens only if we look at the sun, and thus intercept the rays, in which case, you know, it appears white. The atmosphere is a transparent medium, through which the sun's rays pass freely to the earth; but when reflected back into the atmosphere, their momentum is considerably diminished, and they have not all of them power to traverse it a second time. The momentum of the blue rays is least; these, therefore, are the most impeded in their return, and are chiefly reflected by the atmosphere; or it may be that, without any question of momentum, the colour which the particles of air most readily reflect is blue—just as grass reflects the green, or a rose the red rays. This reflection is performed in every possible direction; so that wherever we look at the atmosphere, some of these rays fall upon our eyes: hence we see the air of a blue colour. If the atmosphere did not reflect any rays, though the objects on the surface of the earth would be illumined, the skies would appear perfectly black. This would not only be very melancholy, but it would be pernicious to the sight, to be constantly viewing bright objects against a black sky.

When bodies change their colour, as leaves which wither in autumn, or a spot of ink which produces an iron-mould on linen, it arises from some chemical change, which takes place in the internal arrangement of the parts, by which they lose their tendency to reflect certain colours, and acquire the power of reflecting others. A withered leaf thus no longer reflects the blue rays: it appears, therefore, yellow, or has a slight tendency to reflect several rays which produce a dingy brown colour. An ink-spot on linen at first absorbs all the rays; but, exposed to the air, it undergoes a chemical change, and the spot partially regains its tendency to reflect colours, but with a preference to reflect the yellow rays; and such is the colour of the iron-mould.

Section III.—*On the Structure of the Eye and Optical Instruments.*

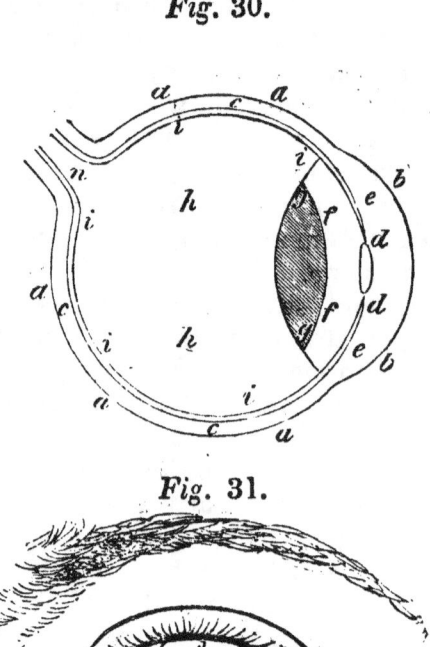

Fig. 30.

Fig. 31.

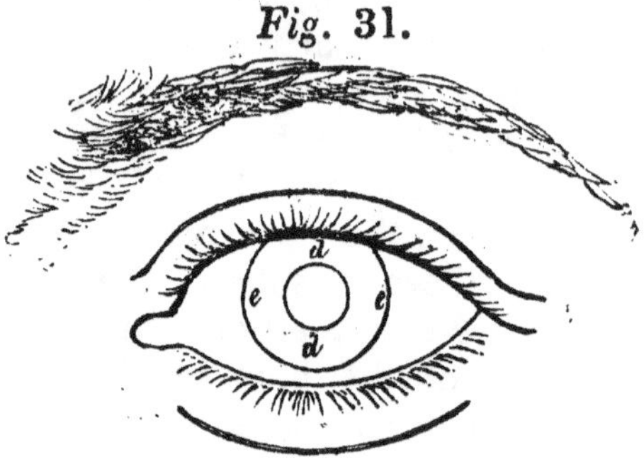

The body of the eye is of a spherical form (*fig.* 30). It has two membraneous coverings;—the external one, *a a a*, is called the sclerotica: this has a projection in that part of the eye which is exposed to view, *b b*, which is called the cornea, because, when dried, it has nearly the consistence of very fine horn, and is sufficiently transparent for the light to obtain free passage through it. The second membrane which lines the cornea, and envelopes the eye, is called the choroid, *c c c*: this has an opening in front just beneath the cornea, which forms the pupil, *d d*, through which the rays of light pass into the eye. The pupil is surrounded by a coloured border of fibres, called the iris, *e e*, which, by its motion, always preserves the pupil of a circular form, whether it be expanded in the dark or contracted by a strong light. (*Fig.* 31.)

The construction of the eye is so admirable, that it is capable of adapting itself, more or less, to the circumstances in which it is placed. In a faint light the pupil dilates so as to receive an additional quantity of rays; and in a strong light it contracts, in order to prevent the intensity of the light from injuring the optic nerve. The eyes suffer pain, when from darkness they suddenly come into a strong light; for the pupil being dilated, a quantity of rays rush in before it has time to contract; and when we go from a strong light into obscurity, we at first imagine ourselves in total darkness; for a sufficient number of rays cannot gain admittance into the contracted pupil to enable us to distinguish objects; but in a few minutes it dilates, and we clearly perceive what was before invisible. The choroid, *c c*, is imbued with a black liquor, which serves to absorb all the rays that are irregularly reflected, and to convert the body of the eye into a more perfect camera obscura. When the pupil is expanded to its utmost extent, it is capable of admitting ten times the quantity of light that it does when most contracted. In cats, and animals which are said to see in the dark, the power of dilatation and contraction of the pupil is still greater: it is computed that their pupils may receive one hundred times more light at one time than at another. Within these coverings of the eye-ball are contained three transparent substances, called humours. The first occupies the space immediately behind the cornea, and is called the aqueous humour, *f f*, from its liquidity and its resemblance to water. Beyond this is situated the crystalline humour, *g g*, which derives its name from its clearness and transparency: it has the form of a lens, and refracts the rays of light in a greater degree of perfection than any that have been constructed by art: it is attached by fibres, mm, to each side of the choroid. The back part of the eye, between the crystalline humour and the retina, is filled by the vitreous humour, $h\,h$, which derives its name from a resemblance it is supposed to bear to glass or vitrified substances. The membranous coverings of the eye are intended chiefly for the preservation of the retina, $i\,i$, which is by far the most important part of the eye, as it is that which receives the impression of the objects of sight. The retina consists of an expansion of the optic nerve, of perfect whiteness: it proceeds from the brain, enters the eye at n on the side next the nose, and is finely spread over the interior surface of the choroid. The rays of light which enter the eye by the pupil, are refracted by the several humours in their passage through them, and unite in a focus on the retina.

Rays proceed from bodies in all possible directions; we must, therefore, consider every part of an object which sends rays to our eyes as points from which the rays diverge, as from a centre. Divergent rays, on entering the pupil, do not cross each other; the pupil, however, is sufficiently large to admit a small pencil of them; and these, if not refracted to a focus by the humours, would continue diverging after they had passed the pupil, would fall dispersed upon the retina, and thus the image of a single point would be expanded over a large portion of the retina. The divergent rays from every other point of the object would be spread over a similar extent of space, and would interfere and be confounded with the first, so that no distinct image could be formed on the retina.

Fig. 32 represents two pencils of rays issuing from two points of the tree A, B, and entering the pupil, refracted by the crystalline humour D, and forming distinct images of the spot they proceed from on the retina, at a, b. *Fig.* 33 differs from the preceding, merely from not being supplied with a lens: in consequence of which the pencils of rays are not refracted to a focus, and no distinct image is formed on the retina. The rays issuing from two points of an object are alone delineated, and the two pencils in *fig.* 33 distinguished by describing one of them with dotted lines. The interference of these two pencils of rays will

Fig. 32.

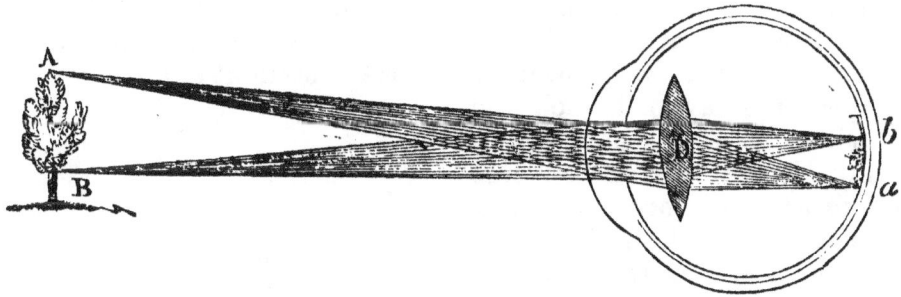

enable you to form an idea of the confusion which would arise from thousands and millions of points at the same instant pouring their divergent rays upon the retina. The refraction of the several humours unites the whole of a pencil of rays, proceeding from any one point of an object, in a corresponding point on the retina, and the image is thus ren-

Fig. 33.

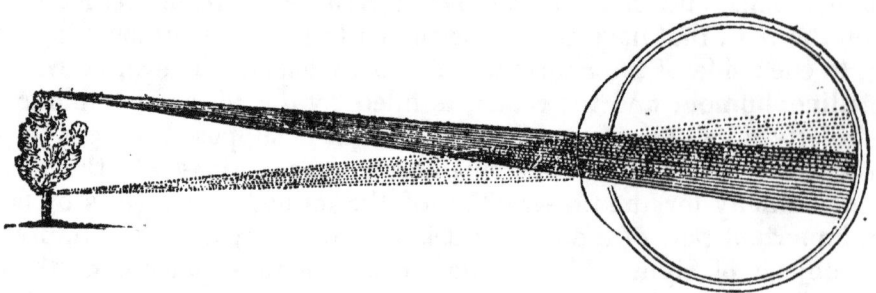

dered distinct and strong. If you conceive (in *fig.* 32) every point of the tree to send forth a pencil of rays similar to those, A, B, every part of the tree will be as accurately represented on the retina as the points *a, b*. You may perhaps inquire why, since the eye requires refracting humours in order to form a distinct representation on the retina, the same refractions are not necessary for the image formed in the camera obscura? It is because the aperture through which we receive the rays into the camera obscura is so extremely small, that but very few of the rays diverging from a point gain admittance; but if the aperture be enlarged, and furnished with a lens, the landscape will be more perfectly represented.

That imperfection of sight which arises from the eyes being too prominent, is owing to the crystalline humour, D (*fig.* 34) being too convex; in consequence of which it refracts the rays too much, and collects a pencil, proceeding from the object A B, into a focus, F, before they reach the retina. From this focus, the rays proceed diverging, and conse-

Fig. 34.

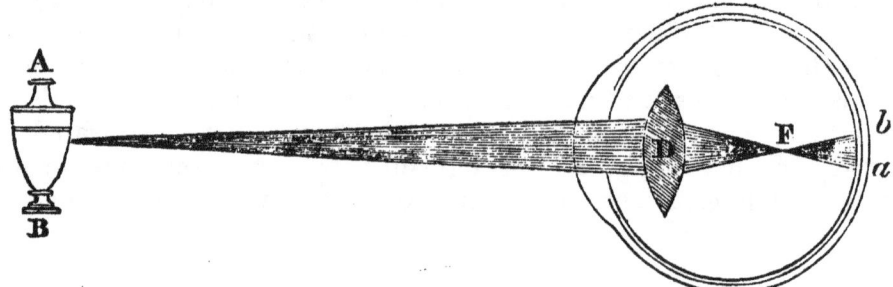

quently form a very confused image on the retina, at *a b*. This is the defect of short-sighted people; and it is remedied by bringing the object nearer to the eye; for the nearer an object is brought to the eye the more divergent the rays fall upon the crystalline humour, and consequently do not so soon converge to a focus: this focus, therefore, either falls upon the retina, or at least approaches nearer to it, and the object is proportionally distinct, as in *fig.* 35. The nearer, therefore, an object is brought to the crystalline or to a lens, the further the image recedes behind it.

Fig. 35.

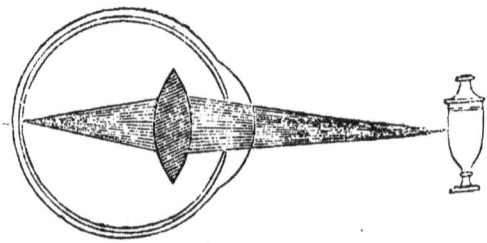

But short-sighted persons have another resource for objects which they cannot approach to their eyes: this is to place a concave lens, C D (*fig.* 36), before the eye, in order to

Fig. 41.

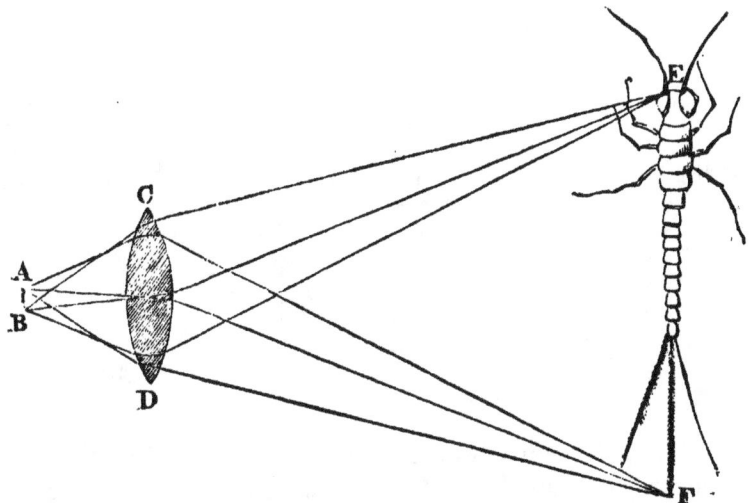

the lens itself being placed at such a distance from the opposite wall that an image may be accurately formed upon it; the image E F therefore will be represented on the opposite wall in the same manner as the landscape was in the camera obscura—with this difference, that it will be magnified, instead of being diminished, because it is farther from the lens than the object A B; while the representation of the landscape was diminished, because it was nearer the lens than the landscape was: a lens, therefore, answers the purpose equally well, either for magnifying or diminishing objects. In this state, the image produced by the solar microscope is faint and indistinct, a very small ray of light being diffused over a prodigiously magnified image; but if the aperture be enlarged, so as to admit a more considerable pencil of rays, and a lens X Y (*fig.* 42)

Fig. 42.

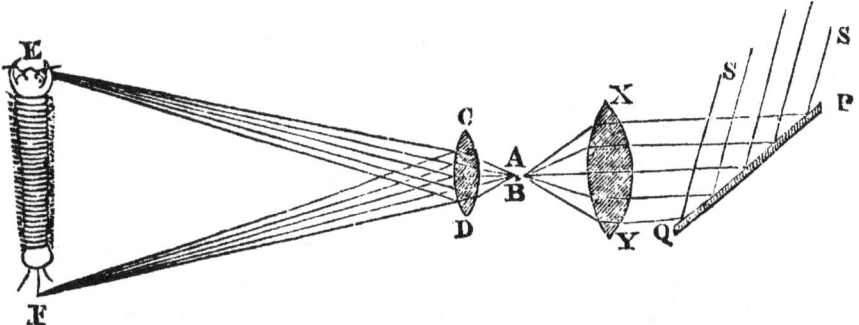

placed in it to bring it to a focus on the object A B, the image will be much more distinct. There is but one thing more required to complete the solar microscope, which is a small mirror, P Q (placed on the outside of the window-shutter), which receives the incident rays, S S, and reflects them on the lens X Y. This microscope can be used only when the sun shines, and is adapted to transparent objects. Very minute objects, such as are viewed in a microscope, are generally transparent; but when opaque bodies are to be exhibited, a second mirror M N (*fig.* 43) is used to reflect the light on the side of the object next the wall: the image is then formed by light reflected from the object, instead of being formed by rays transmitted by it. A magic lantern is constructed on the same principle—with this difference, that the light is supplied by a lamp instead

INTRODUCTION TO OPTICS.

Fig. 43.

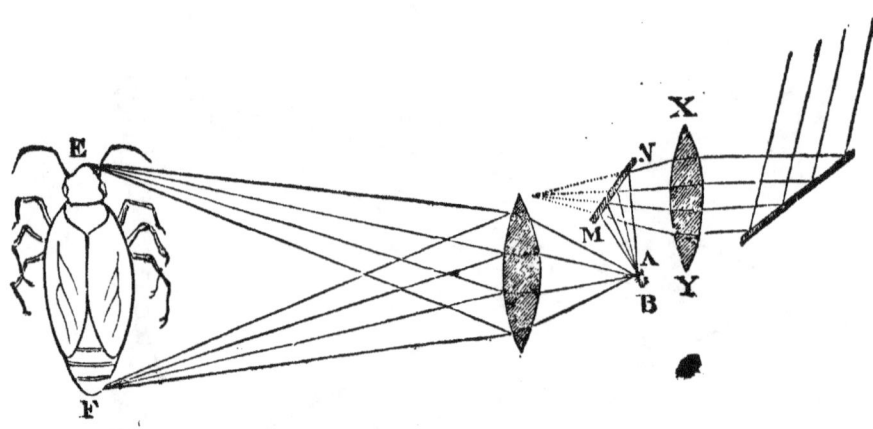

of the sun. The microscope thus enables us to see and distinguish objects which are too small to be visible to the naked eye. But there are objects which, though not really small, appear so to us, from their distance. To these we cannot apply the same remedy, for when a house is so far off as to be seen under the same angle as a mite which is close to us, the effect produced on the retina is the same: the angle it subtends is not large enough for it to form a distinct image on the retina. It is impossible in this case to bring the object to the eyes, but by means of a lens we may bring an image of it nearer to us; but then, the object being very distant from the focus of the lens, the image would be exceedingly smaller than the object itself, and in most cases it would even be so small as to be invisible to the naked eye. To obviate this difficulty, we must look at the image through another lens, which, acting as a microscope, enables us to bring the image close to the eye, and thus renders it visible. This instrument is a telescope. In *fig.* 44, the lens C D forms an image, E F,

Fig. 44.

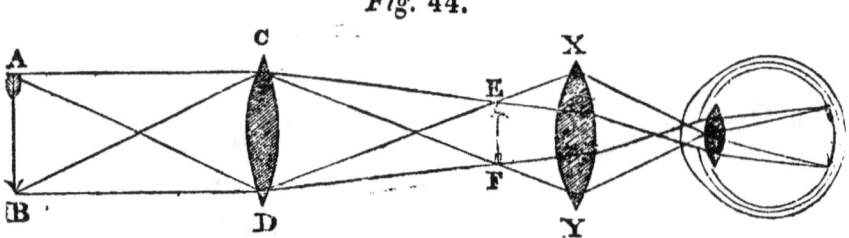

of the object A B; and the lens X Y serves the purpose of magnifying that image: and this is all that is required in a common refracting telescope. Observe that the image is not inverted on the retina, as it usually is: the object therefore appears to us inverted. When it is necessary to represent the image erect, two other lenses are required; by which means a second image is formed, the reverse of the first, and consequently upright. These additional glasses are used to view terrestrial objects, for no inconvenience arises from seeing the celestial bodies inverted.

When a very great magnifying power is required, telescopes are constructed with concave mirrors instead of lenses. Concave mirrors produce by reflection an effect similar to that of convex lenses by refraction. In reflecting telescopes, therefore, mirrors are used in order to bring the image nearer the eye; and a lens or eye-glass, as in the refracting telescope, to magnify the image. The advantage of the reflecting telescope is, that mirrors whose focus is six feet will magnify as much as lenses of a hundred feet.

Fig. 36.

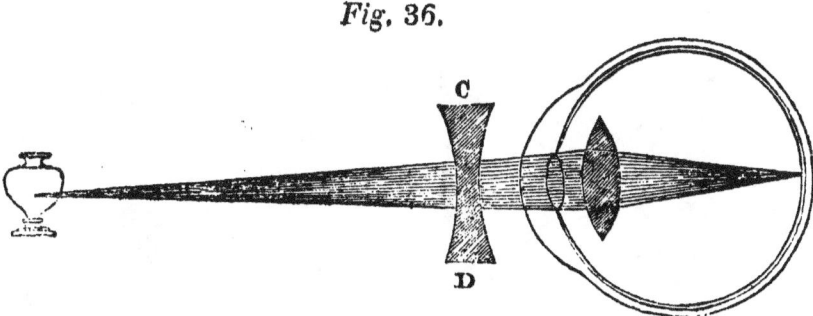

increase the divergence of the rays, the effect of a concave lens being exactly the reverse of a convex one. By the assistance of such glasses, therefore, the rays from a distant object fall on the pupil as divergent as those from a less distant object; and, with short-sighted people, they throw the image of a distant object back as far as the retina. Those who suffer from the crystalline humour being too flat, apply an opposite remedy: that is to say, a convex lens L M (*fig.* 37), to make up for the deficiency of convexity of the crystalline humour, O P. Thus elderly people, the humours of whose eyes are decayed by age, are under the

Fig. 37.

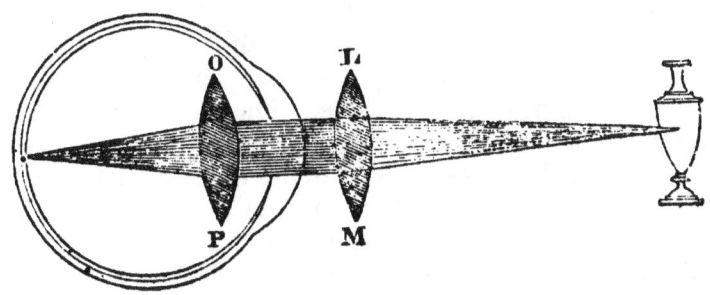

necessity of using convex spectacles; and when deprived of that resource, they hold the object at a distance from their eyes, for the more distant the object is from the crystalline, the nearer the image will be to it. These two opposite defects are easily comprehended; but it is difficult to conceive how any sight can be perfect, for if the crystalline humour be of a proper degree of convexity to bring the image of distant objects to a focus on the retina, it will not represent near objects distinctly; and if, on the contrary, it be adapted to give a clear image of near objects, it will produce a very imperfect one of distant objects. It is true, that every person would be subject to one of these two defects, were it not in our power to increase or diminish, in some degree, the convexity of the crystalline humour, and to project it towards, or draw it back from the object, as circumstances require. In a young, well-constructed eye, the fibres to which the crystalline humour is attached have so perfect a command over it, that the focus of the rays constantly falls on the retina, and an image is formed equally distinct both of distant objects and of those which are near. We cannot, however, see an object distinctly, if we bring it very near to the eye, because the rays fall on the crystalline humour too divergent to be refracted to a focus on the retina. The confusion, therefore, arising from viewing an object too near the eye, is similar to that which proceeds from a flattened crystalline humour; the rays reach the retina before they are collected to a focus (*fig.* 38). If it were not for this imperfection, we should be able to see and distinguish the parts of

Fig. 38.   Fig. 39.

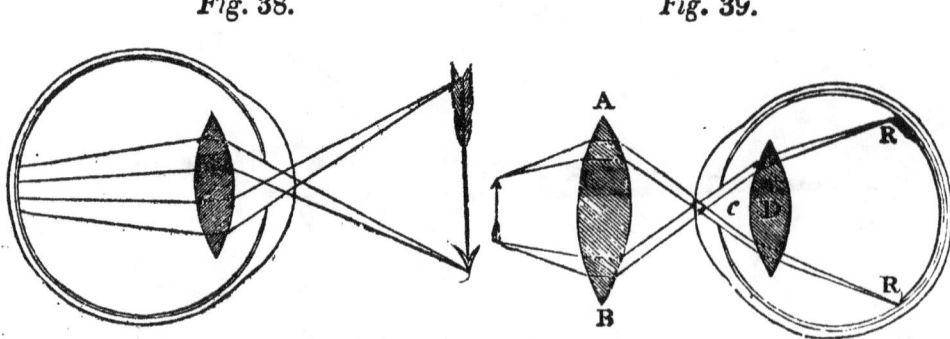

objects which are now invisible to us from their minuteness; for could we bring them close to the eye, their image on the retina would be so much magnified as to render them visible. The microscope is constructed on this principle. The single microscope (*fig.* 39) consists simply of a convex lens, in the focus of which the object is placed, and through which it is viewed. By this means, you are enabled to bring your eye very near the object, for the lens A B, by diminishing the divergency of the rays before they enter the pupil C, makes them fall parallel on the crystalline humour D, by which they are refracted to a focus on the retina, at R R. The lens magnifies the object merely by allowing us to bring it nearer to the eye; those lenses, therefore, which have the shortest focus will magnify the object most, because they enable us to bring the object nearest to the eye. On the other hand, a lens that has the shortest focus is most convex; and its protuberance will prevent the eye from approaching very near to the object. This inconvenience is remedied by making the lens extremely small: it may then be spherical without occupying much space, and thus unite the advantages of a short focus, and of allowing the eye to approach the object.

A double microscope is a more complicated instrument (*fig.* 40), in which you look not directly at the object A B, but at a magnified image of it, *a b*. In this microscope two lenses are employed: the one, L M, is placed so near the object, that the image which it forms is farther from the lens than the object itself is; the image therefore is larger than the object itself, and it is further magnified by being viewed through another lens,

Fig. 40.

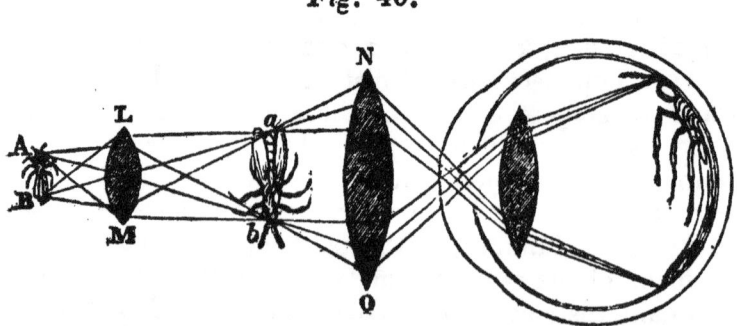

N O, which acts on the principle of the single microscope, and is called the eye-glass. The solar microscope is the most wonderful, from its great magnifying power: in this we also view an image formed by a lens, not the object itself. A ray of light is admitted into a darkened room through a small aperture in the window-shutter, and the object A B (*fig.* 41), which is a small insect, placed before the lens C D, and nearly at its focus:

A POPULAR ACCOUNT
OF
NEWTON'S OPTICS.

Chapter I.
Of the State of Optical Science before the time of Newton.

(1.) The splendid phenomena of optics must have been among the first natural appearances to attract the attention of mankind. Of all the objects in nature, light is perhaps the most pleasurable. Vision, at once the most perfect and useful of the senses, wholly depends on it. By its agency the sphere of our observation and experience is indefinitely enlarged. It brings us sure and immediate intelligence of existences and events, whose places are remote, and thus gives us a certain degree of omnipresence. Setting aside all the beautiful variety of form and figure, and the gorgeous phenomena of colours, which it is the means of disclosing, *light itself* is a delightful perception. Nature supplies it so continually and so abundantly, that we are apt to forget its value; but, in cases where habit has not blunted the sense of pleasure, it seems to produce singular enjoyment. The infant eagerly directs its gaze to the window or the lamp, and stretches forth its hand as if to grasp an object so agreeable. Persons blind from infancy, but whose organs are not absolutely opaque, derive exquisite pleasure from the perception of the cloudy light which the imperfectly transparent humors allow them.

The property of light soonest noticed was most probably its *rectilinear propagation*, by far the most important of its qualities, and one with which all the others are intimately connected. It was impossible to observe the effects of opaque bodies on light, the confines of their shadows and their effects on the sense of sight, without at once discovering this important law. An opaque body B (*fig.* 1.), placed in a right line A C joining another opaque body A and a luminous point C, deprived that other opaque body A of the light it received

Fig. 1.

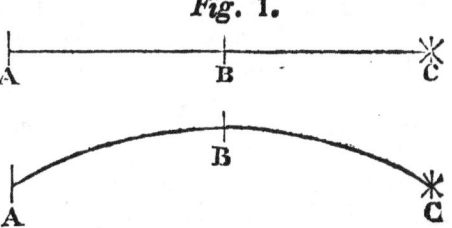

from the point C; but if the same opaque body B was placed in any curved or crooked line ABC, joining the luminous point C and illuminated body A, no such obscuration was produced. Again, if a straight line be drawn from the eye to a luminous point, and also any curved or crooked line drawn from the eye to the same point, an opaque body placed any where in the straight line will deprive the eye of the perception of light; but if the same opaque body be placed any where in the curved or crooked line, the perception of light continues. Facts like these must have occurred so constantly at all times, and in all places, the inference from them is so evident and immediate, that it is impossible to suppose that the rectilinear propagation of light was not known even in the most rude and savage state.

(2.) Some of the phenomena of *reflection* must also have attracted attention, and excited inquiry at a very early period. The inverted picture of a landscape in the placid water of the lake or river must have been viewed with astonishment. Polished surfaces, natural and artificial, presented themselves in sufficient abundance to furnish numerous experiments on reflection, and thus from the rectilinear propagation of light the step to the *law of reflection* was not very difficult. The equality of the angles of incidence and reflection was taught in the Platonic school, and probably was known considerably prior to that date.

Aristotle devoted considerable attention to the phenomena of rainbows, parhelia, halos, &c. He observed these with accuracy, and ascribed the rainbow to the imperfect reflection of the sun's rays by drops of rain. Some of the properties of concave and convex spherical mirrors appear to have been taught in the Alexandrine school, and are explained in a treatise on optics contained in the works of Euclid.

(3.) The phenomena of refraction not being of so striking a kind, or of such frequent occurrence as those of reflection, do not seem to have been noticed until a later period. The power of refractors to collect the sun's rays to a focus, so as to burn any substance exposed to their influence, was, however, long known. Burning refractors are very distinctly described in Aristophanes' comedy of *The Clouds*, and Aristotle observed the broken appearance of a stick held obliquely in water, and attempted to account for it. In the first century of the Christian era several optical phenomena were investigated by Seneca, and among others he observed that writing viewed through a glass bottle filled with water was magnified. This was, probably, the first discovery of the magnifying power of a refracting medium, bounded by convex surfaces. Seneca also noticed the colours produced by a prism or angular piece of glass, and observed that they were similar to those of the rainbow.

(4.) The most distinguished among the ancients for discovery in optical science was *Claudius Ptolemy*, the celebrated astronomer of Alexandria, who flourished in the second century of the Christian era. This philosopher was the first who observed, with any degree of scientific precision, the phenomena of refraction. He appears to have systematized, improved, and imparted a greater degree of accuracy to all that was previously known concerning the reflection of light at plane and curved surfaces, but he must justly be considered as the first and exclusive discoverer of the principal phenomena of refraction or dioptrics.

Ptolemy observed that if a visible object, a piece of money for example, be laid on the bottom of a vessel, and the eye so placed that the edge of the vessel just intercepts the view of the object, upon filling the vessel with water, the object will seem to be gradually raised, until at length it comes distinctly into view. This fact led him directly to the true nature of refraction, and shewed that the visual ray in passing out of the water at the surface, was bent towards the eye of the spectator, so as to make the object on the bottom of the vessel appear higher in the water than its real position. He invented an instrument to measure the deflection of the ray in passing from the water into air. This instrument consisted of a circle, carrying two *sights* on its graduated rim, and a third sight at the centre. The circle was immersed in the water, with its plane perpendicular to the surface, and so that the surface of the water coincided with one of its diameters, and that one of the sights on the rim was above and the other below the surface. The eye being placed at the sight above the surface, the sight below the surface was moved upon the rim, until the three sights appeared to lie in the same straight line. The distances of the sights on the rim, from the highest and lowest points of the circle, then shewed the angles of refraction and incidence.

With this instrument Ptolemy observed and calculated the refractions corresponding to every ten degrees of incidence in the quadrant, the refraction being made between air and water. He also measured and calculated the refractions between *air* and *glass* and *water* and *glass*, by cutting the glass into a semi-cylinder of the same diameter as the graduated circle, and applying the semicircle to the end of the semi-cylinder.

The results of these experiments showed that the deflection of the ray between glass and water was less than in either of the cases between water or glass and air. From this he was led to conclude that the difference of the densities of the media was the cause of refraction, since water and glass differed less in density than air and glass, or air and water. This fortunate observation suggested the probability that light from celestial objects, in passing into our atmosphere from the surrounding medium, whatever it be, might suffer a deflection, the consequence of which would be that our view of the whole face of the heavens must be distorted; objects appearing variously removed from their true places, according to their various positions with respect to the highest point or the *zenith*. The only point which would not be removed from its true place under such circumstances, ould be the zenith itself; for the ray passing from that point to the eye, must enter the atmosphere perpendicularly; and he observed that in his experiments, whenever the ray met the surface of the water or glass perpendicularly, there was no deflection.

Thus he perceived that the zenith was a fixed point, with reference to which he should be enabled to ascertain this interesting fact. The test to which he submitted this is a remarkable instance of philosophical acuteness. In his experiments he had observed that the more obliquely the ray met the refracting surface, the greater was the deflection of the refracted from the incident ray. Hence he supposed that those objects which were more remote from the zenith, and the light of which met the atmosphere more obliquely, were more removed from their proper places. In other words, that the distortion of the firmament by the refraction of the atmosphere was greater near the horizon than near the zenith. Accordingly, he observed the positions of the same star in different parts of its diurnal path in the heavens, and found that it appeared not to move in a *lesser circle* parallel to the celestial equator, but that it continually deviated in a slight degree from such a circle; that this deviation was greater, the more distant the star was from the zenith or highest point, and that the deviation always brought the star nearer to the zenith.

Such were the phenomena he observed, and they were precisely what his experiments suggested. The last mentioned circumstance, of the deviation being always towards the zenith, showed that the refracted ray was bent towards the perpendicular, which proved that the density of the atmosphere must be greater than that of the fluid, if such there be, which pervades the region beyond it.

(5.) A long interval elapsed after the age of Ptolemy, before the science of optics made any advance. About the beginning of the twelfth century, some steps were made towards improvement in the theory of vision. In the thirteenth century Roger Bacon devoted considerable attention to the study of optics; and although he cannot be said to have extended the bounds of the science by positive discoveries, yet he has so plainly described the effects on vision produced by lenses and their combinations, that we cannot, with any regard to justice, deny him a share in the honour of the invention of spectacles, telescopes, and microscopes. In describing the effects of convex lenses of glass, he states that " they are useful to old men, and to those that have weak eyes, for they may see the smallest letters sufficiently magnified." Respecting the effects of combinations of lenses, he says—" We shall see the object near at hand, or at a distance, and under any angle we please. And thus from an incredible distance we may read the smallest letters, and may number the smallest particles of dust and sand, by reason of the greatness of the angle under which we see them; and on the contrary, we may not be able to see the greatest bodies just by us, by reason of the smallness of the angles under which they appear; thus a boy may be as big as a giant, and a man as big as a mountain, forasmuch as we may see the man under as great an angle as the mountain, and as near as we please. Thus, also, the sun, moon, and stars, may be made to descend hither in appearance, and to appear over the heads of our enemies, and many things of a like sort, which would astonish unskilful persons."*

It will be perceived that Bacon not only describes the effects of telescopes, but also distinctly alludes to their causes. It is very difficult to conceive that he could have written thus, without having actually constructed the instruments, and witnessed the effects which he describes.

(6.) In the sixteenth century, Maurolycus explained, with great exactness, the structure and functions of the eye, more especially of the crystalline humor. He showed that those defects which are called long-sightedness, and short-sightedness, proceeded from too small or too great a refracting power in the eye, and showed how and why these defects were removed by the use of convex and concave lenses. Maurolycus failed to discover the formation of the picture on the retina, and the functions of that coat, from the difficulty of reconciling an inverted image with our perception of erect objects.

About this time Baptista Porta, a Neapolitan philosopher, invented the *camera obscura*. He observed that if a small hole be made in the window-shutter of a darkened chamber, the images of external objects will appear depicted in their proper colours on the opposite wall. He then tried the effect of a convex lens fixed in the aperture, and found that the

---

* See the Edinburgh Encyclopædia—OPTICS.

images became much more perfect and distinct. In this way the features of persons outside could be discerned, and known from the image. The pictures, however, thus produced, were inverted. To remedy this, he proposed that, instead of being projected on the wall, the rays from the lens should be received upon a convex mirror properly placed and adapted to the lens.

Observing that the images thus formed by the convex lens were magnified, and seen with more distinctness than with the naked eye, it occurred to him that if a convex lens were presented to an object so as to form an image at its focus, an eye placed a short distance behind that image would see the object magnified. Such an arrangement was, in fact, a telescope without an eye-glass.

(7.) The phenomenon of the rainbow could not have failed to attract attention at a very early period. A work has been brought to light by Venturi, written, in 1311, by Theodoric of Saxony, a Dominican friar, in which a rational explanation of the double bow is given. Extensive extracts from this work, with the figures of the single and double reflection within the drops, may be seen in the sixth volume of the *Annales de Physique et de Chimie*.

The art of printing not having been then invented, it is probable that the work of Theodoric did not gain publicity, and was not generally known. Accordingly, we find several eminent philosophers, at the end of the sixteenth and commencement of the seventeenth centuries, engaged in attempts to solve the problem of the rainbow. Some conceived the exterior bow to be a reflected image of the interior one, and thus accounted for the inversion of the colours. Fleschier, of Breslau, attributed the production of the colours of the rainbow to two refractions by the drop, but conceived that a reflection took place at another drop before the light reached the eye. It is curious to observe how slowly and gradually the laws of nature are discovered.

Soon after the year 1600, Antonio de Dominis, archbishop of Spalatro, reduced the phenomenon of the rainbow to actual experiment, and proved that one reflection only, with two refractions, is sufficient to produce the effect. He filled a hollow globe of glass with water, and having placed it in a proper position with respect to a beam of solar light, found that when viewed in the same direction, and under the same circumstances, as the drops of rain which form the bow, the same colours were produced, and were disposed in the same order. He conceived that a solar ray entering at the upper part of the drop, was refracted to the back of it, where it suffered a reflection by the inner surface; passing out again at the lower surface, that it reached the eye of a spectator properly placed, and produced a perception of the colours of the bow. He accounted for the colours in the following manner. The red rays issued from the nearest part of the inner surface of the drop, and having traversed a less quantity of water, preserved the greater degree of intensity; for the red colour was always considered to be produced by the most intense and active portion of the light. The green and blue rings, on the contrary, were those which were reflected from that part of the posterior surface of the drop which was most distant from the point of final emergence, and having, therefore, traversed a greater quantity of water, were more faint. The other colours of the bow were conceived to be formed by these three mixed in various proportions.

If a straight line be drawn from the sun to the centre of the drop, and continued through the centre, it will meet the posterior surface, at a certain point. De Dominis conceived that the rays which produced the same colour were similarly situate with respect to this point, and therefore that such rays ought to form with the line drawn from the sun to the eye of the spectator equal angles. Hence he inferred that each colour should appear in a circular band or in the surface of a cone of which the eye is the vertex, and the line from the eye to the sun the axis. Upon these principles he accounted for the shape of the bow and the order of the colours, and confirmed his theory by corresponding experiments with the glass globe.

It has been considered extraordinary that it should be reserved for De Dominis to make the first important step towards an explication of the most singular and beautiful phenomenon in nature. Montucla declares his work to be obscure and confused, and to betray an unusual ignorance even of so much of optical science as was generally known in that day. Some difference of opinion exists, however, as to the extent of his claims to a share in the merit of the explanation of this phenomenon. Montucla states, that he cannot concede to him greater merit than that of having had a glimmering of the true explanation of the interior bow. From the manner in which he explains the course of the rays, it seems doubtful whether he was even aware of the second refraction which the rays suffered on their emergence from the drop. Montucla, however, denies him any participation in the discovery of the cause of the exterior bow, and states that he had not the most remote idea of the double reflection which constitutes the character of this phenomenon. Dr. Brewster, on the other hand, an high authority on this subject, says, that although his attempt at explaining the interior bow is sufficiently absurd, yet that it is impossible for any philosopher, free from the influence of national partiality, to deny that the Italian prelate has given such an explanation of the general phenomena of the exterior bow, that any other philosopher of more optical knowledge, and of inferior acuteness, could not fail, without any stretch of intellect, to give precision and perfection to the explanation. Newton's own opinion appears to have been similar to that last quoted.

About the period at which De Dominis instituted his experiments, Kepler proposed an explanation of the rainbow, in a letter to Harriot. He conceives that the solar ray which touches a drop of rain is refracted, and penetrating the drop meets the posterior surface, from which it undergoes a partial reflection; that again penetrating the drop, it emerges, and at its emergence undergoes a second refraction, after which it reaches the eye of the spectator. Kepler here approximated very closely to the true solution of the problem. If, however, the ray which finally reached the eye were a tangent to the drop when incident on it, the bow would be much smaller than it is known to be. Harriot did not, on this occasion, give to the subject that attention to which its importance entitled it, but excused himself to Kepler by business and indisposition, promising that he would one day develop the mystery. It is evident that he agreed with Kepler in the necessity of a reflection intermediate between the two refractions, which, indeed, considering the relative positions of the sun, the drops, and the spectator, was sufficiently obvious. But he said nothing which can guide us to a knowledge of how far he was acquainted with the true theory of the phenomenon.

(8.) The accumulated facts and experiments furnished by various philosophers, and the numerous suggestions of optical writers, on the use and applications of lenses, and their combinations, among which those of Roger Bacon and Baptista Porta are more especially entitled to notice, had now prepared the way for the construction, we will not say invention, of telescopes and microscopes. The approach to the construction of the telescope, like the passage from darkness through twilight to broad day, is so gradual, that it is almost impossible, if we deny the invention to Bacon, to assign it to any other. Descartes assigns the discovery to James Metius, a Dutchman, and a citizen of Alkmaer. He commences his Dioptrics with this humiliating confession:—" To the shame of science, this admirable invention was the fortuitous result of experience. About thirty years ago, a person named James Metius, who had never studied, although his father and brother had devoted themselves to the profession of mathematics, but who took great pleasure in making mirrors and burning glasses, having occasion for glasses of different forms, happened to look through two of them, of which one was convex and the other concave. He applied them to the ends of a tube, and thus happily formed the first telescope."

Not satisfied with this origin of the telescope, some authors have sought for one still more humiliating to science, and to the pride of human intellect. It is said that the children of a spectacle-maker at Middleburg, happening to play in their father's shop, were amusing themselves with looking at a weathercock with two glasses, the one convex and the other concave; and happening to place them in a fit position, they beheld the object magnified, and brought close to them. They communicated their astonishment to their father, who, to make the experiment more convenient, fixed the glasses in a proper manner upon a board. Presently another person adjusted the lenses at the ends of a tube, so as to exclude the lateral light, which disturbed the vision, and thus made the objects appear more brilliant and distinct. The next improvement, which trod upon the heels of the last, was to use tubes which moved one within another, so as to admit of any adjustment of the lenses which might be found necessary.

Without insisting further on this account of the invention, which, besides being unsupported by evidence, is attended with circumstances which give it small probability, we shall notice the better substantiated claim of Zacharias Jansen, urged by Borelli, and attested by legal witnesses, who were regularly sworn by the consular magistrates of Middleburg in the year 1655. Zacharias Jansen appears to have been a spectacle-maker at Middleburg, and the witnesses were his children, a son and daughter. The son assigns the invention to the year 1590, and the daughter to the year 1610. Both, however, agree in the fact of the invention; and the difference in the dates assigned to it, instead of invalidating their testimony, ought to be considered favourable to its truth, since it shows that no conspiracy existed between them. Other witnesses give the honour of the invention to Jean Lapprey, a spectacle-maker in the same place.

All these circumstances, considered with reference to the general state of optical knowledge at the time, render it probable that telescopes were constructed by several persons nearly at the same period, each being ignorant of what had been done by the others. Effects so singular and so brilliant as those produced by the telescope could not be long confined to one country. It will easily be believed, that such an instrument could not continue a mere toy of amusement, or matter of curious observation to philosophers. Among those who applied it to the great ends of science, the name of Galileo stands foremost. If we could credit his own account, it would not be more than justice even to assign to this philosopher a share in the honour of the invention, although we cannot concede to him a priority. He states that he was at Venice when a report of the wonderful effects of this discovery was spread abroad. Doubtful at first to what degree of faith statements apparently so incredible were entitled, he awaited a confirmation of the intelligence, which he received in letters from Paris. Being credibly assured of the reality of the powers ascribed to the new instrument, but uninformed of the particulars of its construction, he applied himself to the investigation of those particulars, by the aid of the established theory of refraction, and completely succeeded in discovering them. He forthwith applied a convex object-glass, and concave eye-glass, to the extremities of a tube, and directing it to distant objects, found that it rendered them three times as large as they appeared to unassisted vision. The success of this first attempt stimulated him to further exertion, and he constructed a second telescope which magnified about eight times. Finally, sparing neither labour nor expense on a subject which seemed to promise results so important, he produced a telescope which magnified *thirty times*, and with this he discovered the satellites of Jupiter, the solar spots, and other phenomena.

This account of Galileo's proceedings is given upon his own authority. It does not seem, however, likely that Galileo could have remained in total ignorance of the means which produced the wonderful effects which had excited such general attention. Besides, he acknowledges that he did not trust to mere public report, but received a letter expressly on the subject from " the noble James Badovere at Paris." Of this letter, which was written to inform Galileo on the subject, he does not give the particulars. Is it likely that in such a communication, made to such a man, no allusion would be made to the means of producing the effects described, nor that lenses were not distinctly mentioned? Add to this, that the general problem of magnifying distant objects by the modification of the rays of light by refraction or reflection, or both, which we must suppose to be that which Galileo asserts that he solved, is very indeterminate, and such as would be extremely unlikely to be deduced from the general theory of optics as then known. Still less probable is it that of the infinite variety of solutions, which so indeterminate a problem admits, he would have chanced to be led to that particular one which had been practised in the north of Europe.

(9.) The honour of the invention of the astronomical telescope belongs indisputably and exclusively to Kepler. In his work on Dioptrics, he distinctly suggests the substitution of a convex eye-glass for the concave one previously used. He shows that in this case the image will necessarily be inverted; but the advantage of an enlarged field of view, in which this instrument excels the Galilean telescope, seems to have escaped his notice. To this we may, perhaps, impute the circumstance of Kepler's never having actually constructed telescopes upon the principle which he suggested, considering, probably, that as they presented inverted images, their use for terrestrial objects would be awkward and inconvenient, and that they possessed no advantage in astronomical observations over those used by Galileo and others. Kepler was, however, aware of the method of correcting the position of the image, by the use of additional eye-glasses; but probably considered that the complexity of the instrument, and the loss of light, would render it inferior to the Galilean telescope.

The optical discoveries of Kepler were not confined to the telescope. He made experiments on refraction by lenses, and succeeded in establishing some of the properties of their foci. He also explained the formation of the inverted image on the retina. He attributed erect vision from an inverted image to an operation of the mind, by which it refers the lower part of the image to the upper side of the eye, but considered it beyond our power to determine the manner in which the mind perceives the images of objects upon the retina. He investigated the power of the eye to accommodate itself to different distances, and attributed it to the contracting power of the ciliary processes.

(10.) At the period to which we now refer, the beginning of the seventeenth century, the most important discovery in the theory of refraction since the time of Ptolemy, was made by Willebrord Snellius, professor of mathematics at Leyden. This philosopher, by a careful comparison of numerous refractions at different incidences, found that if a sphere were described round the point of incidence, and a cylinder circumscribed this sphere, having its axis perpendicular to the refracting surface, the parts of the incident and refracted rays, between the centre of the sphere and the cylinder, were in a constant ratio, so long as the refracting medium remained the same.

To explain this important law more fully, let I, *fig.* 2, be the point of inci-

Fig. 2.

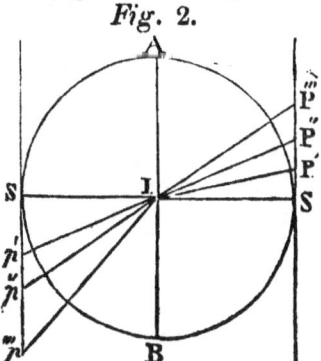

dence, and S I S the refracting surface, S B S being a vertical section of the refracting medium, or rather a section supposed to pass through the incident ray, and perpendicular to the surface. With I as centre, and any distance I S, describe a circle in the plane of the section, and draw tangents at S S, perpendicular to the refracting surface. Let the incident rays meet the upper tangent at P′, P″, P‴, &c.; and let the corresponding refracted ray meet the lower tangent at p', p'', p''', &c. It was found by Snellius, that the ratios $\frac{P'I}{p'I}, \frac{P''I}{p''I}, \frac{P'''I}{p'''I}$, &c. were equal so long as the media S A S and S B S remained the same. Taking the radius I A or I B as the unit, the lines P′I, P″I, P‴I, &c. are the cosecants of the angles of incidence; and the lines p'I, p''I, p'''I, &c. are the cosecants of the angles of refraction. These quantities are, therefore, in a fixed proportion. The cosecants of angles being the reciprocals of their sines, it follows that when the media on each side of the refracting surface are given, the sine of the angle of incidence bears to the sine of the angle of refraction an invariable ratio.

(11.) The discovery of the law of refraction has been sometimes erroneously ascribed to Descartes. With a degree of disingenuousness and want of candour, or rather of common justice, which not unfrequently characterised the conduct of that great philosopher, he has announced in his Dioptrics, published eleven years after the death of Snellius, the law of refraction as the result of his own inquiries, without taking the slightest notice of the previous discovery of Snellius, although there is no doubt that he was acquainted with it; and there is even strong reason to believe that Descartes had the manuscripts of Snellius in his hands, and availed himself of the full and unrestricted use of them.

About the time of the death of Snellius, which happened in 1626, at the early age of thirty, Descartes applied himself to optical investigations; and, in 1637, published his Treatise on Dioptrics. Guided by the law of refraction, with the recent discovery of which he was made acquainted, he made some important additions to, and improvements in, the science. The fact that spherical lenses were incapable of collecting rays of light into an exact focus, had been known by experience; and the cause of this spherical aberration, as well as its quantity and laws, were easily deduced from the Snellian law. To comprehend the nature of this defect of spherical lenses, let the light incident upon them be conceived to be divided into a number of concentrical rings; the exterior ring, or that which is most distant from the centre of the lens, will be collected by refraction into a focus, at a point on the axis of the lens at a certain distance from the surface. The next ring of light within the last will be also collected into a point, but at a greater distance from the surface; and so on, each ring of light is collected into a focus, the distance of which from the surface increases, as the distance of the ring from the centre of the lens diminishes. To illustrate this, let L L be a section of the lens at right angles to its axis; and suppose its surface divided into rings as represented in *fig.* 3, and let the order of the rings be reckoned from the edge of the lens towards the centre, calling the external ring *the first ring*, the next within that *the second ring*, and so on. Let L L, *fig.* 4, be a section of the lens by a plane through its axis;

Fig. 3.

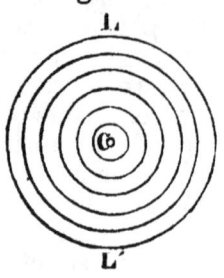

Fig. 4.

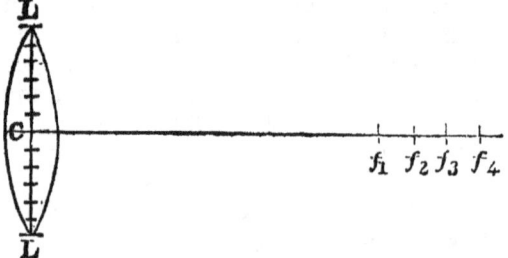

and suppose that the whole lens, except the first ring, be covered by an opaque circular cover, and light be incident on its surface, this light will be refracted to a certain point f_1 in the axis; and this point will, therefore, be the focus of the *first ring*. Again, removing the cover from the lens, let another be substituted, which will leave the second ring alone exposed to the light. The rays will now be collected in the point f_2. The same process being continued, and the third, fourth, and other rings being successively exposed to the light, their foci will be found at the points f_3, f_4, &c. the rings nearest to the centre of the lens having their foci most distant from its surface. It was easily deduced from the law of refraction, that the foci of the rings near the centre of the lens were much closer together than those near its surface.

Since the images of objects were known to be formed by collecting the rays emerging from them into the focus of the lens, it followed from these considerations that each of the rings, into which we have supposed the surface of the lens to be divided, must produce a separate image; and thus an indefinite number of images of the same object would be found at different distances from the lens, and arranged in regular succession along the axis. This effect, called *spherical aberration*, caused a confusion in the appearance of the image, which confusion was increased with the magnitude and curvature of the lens.

Seeing that this defect was essential to the very nature of spherical lenses, Descartes proposed to investigate the figure of a lens which should be free from this defect; and such that each ring, into which its surface would be divided, might collect the rays to a focus at the same distance from the lens. The high analytical acquirements of this mathematician, united with the knowledge of Snellius's law, rendered the solution of this problem a matter of no great difficulty. He accordingly found a class of curves, since called the *Cartesian ovals*, which possessed the required property. When the densities of the medium of incidence and the medium of refraction are given, the figure of the surface, which will collect into an exact focus rays emerging from any given point, will always be determined by one of these ovals. When the incident rays are parallel, the oval becomes a conic section *.

Ignorant of the cause of the principal defect of lenses, which was subsequently discovered by Newton, Descartes expected much greater results from this discovery than it was capable of producing. He invented machines, and engaged skilful artists to grind spheroidal lenses, according to the figures suggested by his theory. After the expenditure of much labour and ingenuity, no adequate advantage was obtained, and at this day, when practical science has attained such an extraordinary degree of perfection, the spherical lenses are still universally used.

(12.) In unfolding the theory of the rainbow Descartes has been singularly happy, and certainly has brought the explanation of this phenomenon as near to perfection as could be done by one who was ignorant of the different re-

---

* For an account of these curves, see Lardner's *Algebraic Geometry*, p. 452.

frangibility of light. Here, as in the case of the *law of refraction*, this geometer has fixed an indelible stain upon his fame, by a similar act of unprincipled selfishness and injustice towards Antonio de Dominis, to whom he never even alludes in his treatise. Descartes explained why the interior bow has a diameter of 42°; this was an easy inference from the theory of De Dominis and the law of Snellius. But the genius of Descartes was very conspicuous in his solution of the problem of the exterior bow. He shewed that the sun's rays entering the inferior part of the drop, emerged with a second refraction from the superior, after undergoing two reflections within. The double reflection accounted for the faintness of the exterior bow, and the inversion of its colours. Thus we see that ignorance of the different refrangibility of light alone prevented this philosopher from bringing the theory of the rainbow to absolute perfection.

(13.) In the middle of the seventeenth century a discovery was made by Erasmus Bartolinus, a Danish mathematician, which formed the first of the most brilliant train of experiments, and may be considered the basis of the most splendid speculations which ever adorned the annals of science; speculations which regard not merely the phenomena of light and vision, but which seem to furnish man with new sensibilities, which are to *touch* what the microscope is to *sight*, and disclose to his view wonders of nature which would refuse to unveil themselves to any other power. In this extensive field, more than in any other, has the philosophic genius of our own times shone forth.

Bartolinus received from some Danish merchants, who frequented Iceland, specimens of the crystal, of extraordinary transparency and dimensions, since known by the name of *Iceland spar*, which is *carbonate of lime*, in a crystallized form. While making optical experiments with pieces of this crystal, he discovered that it exhibited a double image of objects seen through it, and consequently inferred that each ray of light in passing through it was cloven into two rays, which were refracted at different angles, while the angle of incidence of the whole ray of which they were the component parts remained the same. Slight observation was sufficient to prove that both of these refracted rays did not obey the Snellian law, for if that were the case, both images of an object seen through the crystal would maintain the same position with respect to a perpendicular to the refracting surface, while the crystal was turned round that perpendicular as an axis. Such, however, he found not to be the fact. By the revolution of the crystal, one of the images only was observed to obey the above-mentioned law. Hence he inferred that one of the two refractions was performed according to the common law, but that the other obeyed an extraordinary law, not before noticed by opticians. The results of these experiments were published by Bartolinus, in a work, entitled *Experimenta crystalli Islandici dis-diaclastici quibus mira et insolita refractio detegitur*. Copenhagen, 1699.

The publication of this work soon drew the attention of the celebrated Huygens to the subject of double refraction. Previously to this he had published a theory of refraction and reflection, founded on the hypothesis, that light, like sound, was propagated by the undulations of a subtle and elastic medium, which he supposed to pervade all space permeable to light. Others held that light was corporeal, and composed of infinitely small and subtle corpuscles, which were emitted from every luminous body, and entering the eye impinged upon the retina, and produced sensation. This corpuscular theory, which is as old as Pythagoras, was adopted by Newton for the explication of the phenomena of optics; but it is proper to add, that he is careful not to intermingle with the reasoning from his experiments any assumptions from this theory, which could at all affect the validity of his results, all of which are entirely independent of any hypothesis, and such that any theory must account for before it can be admitted as a true one.

Huygens took up the subject of *double refraction*, in order to obviate any objections to his undulatory theory, which might arise from it. He accordingly explains distinctly the law which regulates the refraction of the extraordinary ray, and attempts to shew how the phenomenon may be accounted for by spheroidal undulations, while ordinary refraction is ascribed to spherical undulations. As, however, this part of the subject is not intimately connected with the discoveries of Newton, we shall not here enter into further detail upon it, but refer the reader to our history of optics, in which this and many other matters entirely omitted here will be treated at large.

While examining the two rays into which the incident ray is cleft by the Iceland spar, Huygens discovered one of the facts from which Newton subsequently deduced the polarisation of light. He found that if these two rays entered a second prism of the same crystal similarly placed with respect to the ray, each of the two rays were again refracted, according to the same law which regulated their refraction in the first crystal; but he found that if the second prism were placed at right angles to the first, the laws by which the rays were refracted were interchanged. In every intermediate position of the second crystal, each of the two rays from the first crystal were divided into two, so that the whole primitive ray was resolved into four. These complicated phenomena Huygens confessed himself unable to solve, and it remained for the genius of Newton to explain the curious and beautiful property of polarisation.

(14.) Newton was born in 1642, and in 1663 James Gregory published his invention of the reflecting telescope, consisting of two concave mirrors, the larger of which, receiving rays from the object, was perforated at its axis, and opposite to the perforation and facing the larger, the smaller was placed so as to receive the rays reflected from the larger, and reflecting them to bring them to a focus in a tube placed in the perforation. The image thus formed was viewed with an eye-glass as in the astronomical telescope.

Three years after this Newton invented his reflecting telescope, in which he dispensed with the perforation in the principal speculum, thereby preserving the central rays which were most essential to the formation of a perfect image. The rays reflected from the great speculum in Newton's telescope were again reflected to an aperture in the side of the tube by a plane reflector placed at an angle of 45° with the axis of the tube. At this aperture they were viewed in the usual way through an eyeglass.

(15.) In 1665 the work of Francis Maria Grimaldi, an Italian Jesuit, was published, containing his discovery of the *inflexion* or *diffraction* of light. He admitted a ray of light through a small hole into a darkened chamber, and observed that it was diffused into the form of a cone, and that the shadows of bodies placed in this light were larger than they would have been had the light passed without interruption or deflexion at their edges. Upon more minute and careful inspection, he observed that these shadows were skirted with three coloured fringes, which grew narrower as they receded from the body. He also observed, that when the light was strong there were similar streaks of colour within the shadow, which increased in number in the same shadow when it was received at a greater distance from the body. From these phenomena he concluded that light, in passing the boundaries of an opaque body, was turned from its rectilinear course, an effect which has been called *inflexion* or *diffraction*.

Another experiment instituted by this philosopher indicated a still more extraordinary property of light. Through two small apertures he admitted two cones of light into a darkened chamber, the apertures being so placed that the cones did not penetrate one another until they reached a considerable distance from them. Beyond this distance the light was received upon a screen, and it was observed that the part of the screen illuminated by both cones was the least bright, and that its degree of illumination was increased by depriving it of the light of one of the cones, by stopping one of the apertures. Thus it appeared that a body may actually become more obscure by increasing the quantity of light which shines upon it.

We have in this chapter attempted to give a short sketch of the principal discoveries in optics before the time of Newton. In doing this we shall perhaps be accused of having given an unequal or disproportionate attention to particular topics, and of having touched too slightly upon others. It must however be remembered that our design was not to write a history of optics, but to shew the reader how far the way had been paved for Newton, and what advances had been already made in some of those theories which he has the merit of completing; and on the other hand to shew that on other subjects, such as the unequal refrangibility of light, absolutely nothing was known, nor any advance made, even in the shape of conjecture.

We shall proceed in the next chapter

to give the reader, in a popular form, an account of Newton's Optics, a work which communicated to the world a series of discoveries of transcendent beauty, and which would themselves have been sufficient to have conferred immortality on the name of Newton, even had he never written his PRINCIPIA.

CHAPTER II.

The Compound Nature of Solar Light established by Experiments.

(16.) BEFORE he enters upon the interesting detail of the experiments which led to his great optical discoveries, Newton explains in eight axioms the leading principles and established results of the science before his time. We have, in the preceding chapter, enlarged more fully on the subject than he has done in the *axioms*, that the reader may be the better enabled to appreciate the discoveries we have to explain. The propositions respecting the properties of light which Newton gives under the title of *axioms*, are not to be understood as partaking of the nature of mathematical axioms. On the contrary, many of them are results, not only of careful experiment, but of very subtle and complex reasoning. "I have," says Newton, " now given, in axioms and their explications, the sum of what hath been hitherto treated of in optics. For what hath been generally agreed on, I content myself to assume, under the notion of principles, in order to what I have further to write. And this may suffice for an introduction to readers of quick wit and good understanding, not yet versed in optics; although those who are already acquainted with this science, and have handled glasses, will more readily apprehend what followeth."

The following are the propositions assumed by Newton as axioms:—

Axiom I.

The angles of reflection and refraction lie in one and the same plane with the angle of incidence.

Axiom II.

The angle of reflection is equal to the angle of incidence.

Axiom III.

If the refracted ray be turned directly back to the point of incidence, it shall be refracted into the line before described by the incident ray.

Axiom IV.

Refraction out of the rarer medium into the denser, is made towards the perpendicular; that is, so that the angle of refraction be less than the angle of incidence.

Axiom V.

The sine of incidence is either accurately or very nearly in a given ratio to the sine of refraction.

Axiom VI.

Homogeneal rays which flow from several points of any object, and fall perpendicularly, or almost perpendicularly, on any reflecting or refracting plane or spherical surface, shall afterwards diverge from so many other points, or be parallel to so many other lines, or converge to so many other points, either accurately or without any sensible error; and the same thing will happen, if the rays be reflected or refracted successively by two or three or more plane or spherical surfaces.

Axiom VII.

Wherever the rays, which come from all the points of any object, meet again in so many points, after they have been made to converge by reflection or refraction, there they will make a picture of the object upon any white body on which they fall.

Axiom VIII.

An object seen by reflection or refraction, appears in that place from whence the rays, after their last reflection or refraction, diverge in falling on the spectator's eye.

The work opens with the announcement of the discovery that LIGHTS WHICH DIFFER IN COLOUR, DIFFER ALSO IN REFRANGIBILITY.

For those readers who are not familiar with the science, we shall first explain the meaning of this property, and next describe the nature of the experiments by which Newton established it.

Let S S *s s*, *fig.* 5, be a section of any transparent medium, as water or glass. Let R be a ray of red light incident at I, and supposed to proceed from some red object in the direction I R, or to have been transmitted through red glass. In like manner, let B be a ray of blue light incident at I', in a direction B I', parallel to R I, and proceeding as before from a blue object in that direction or transmitted through blue glass. The angles of incidence formed by the rays R and B, with the perpendiculars P to the refracting surface will be equal, *Fig. 5.*

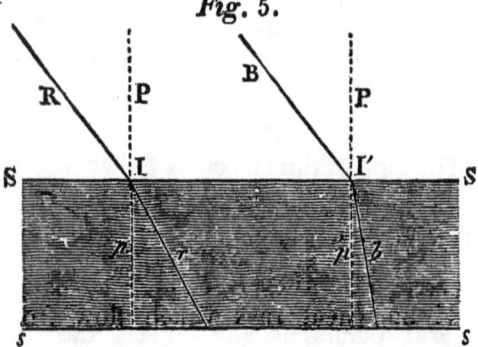

because the rays R and B are parallel. On entering the medium they will be both deflected by the law of refraction towards the perpendiculars *p*. Let *r* be the course after refraction of the red ray, and *b* the course after refraction of the blue one. If these rays were equally refrangible they would be equally deflected towards the perpendicular. Such, however, is not the case. The red ray *r* will be less deflected from its original direction than the blue ray *b*, and therefore the angle under the lines *r* and *p* will be greater than the angle under *b* and *p*. Hence, red light is said to be less refrangible than blue light.

We might expect that this effect would be easily reduced to experiment by colouring two sticks, one red, and the other blue, and placing them parallel to each other, obliquely in water. In this case, the broken appearance which the sticks should exhibit would be different, the angle formed by the parts in the water with those in the air being more obtuse in the red than in the blue stick. It happens, however, that the difference between their deflections is so small, that, in this way, it would be very difficult to render it perceptible.

To obviate this inconvenience, and render the difference of refractions so great as to be easily perceptible, Newton contrived that the different lights should each be twice refracted, so that being originally parallel, they should thus acquire the sum of the divergencies which such refraction alone would give them. This he accomplished by using a glass prism, in the manner which we shall now describe.*

---

* We advise every reader who has not seen the prismatic spectrum, before he proceeds further, to procure a prism, or a common angular piece of glass with plane sides, and to transmit through it a beam of the sun's light admitted through an aperture in the window-shutter of a dark room. The facility with which he will comprehend Newton's interesting experiments will thus be much increased.

(17.) Let A B C, *fig.* 6, represent a section of a triangular glass prism at right

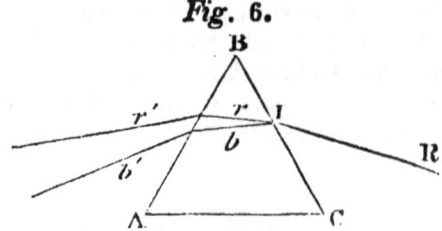

angles to its axis (an end view of it.) A ray of red light entering at I in the direction R I will, by the refraction of the glass, be deflected in the direction *r*, *towards* the perpendicular to the surface B C, on which it is incident. On meeting the second surface B A, it will emerge, suffering a second refraction on passing into the air. But here, as it passes from glass into air, it will be deflected *from* the perpendicular to the surface B A in the direction *r'*, which increases still more its deviation from its original course R. In like manner, a blue ray incident in the same direction at I will suffer two deflections at the surfaces of the prism; but in each case will be more deflected from its original direction R, than the red ray. The deviation of the blue from the red ray, on emerging from the surface B A, will evidently be found, by adding together the two deviations at the surfaces B C and B A. Thus, although either deviation alone might be too small to be perceptible, yet the sum of both will produce a sensible effect.

(18.) To reduce this to absolute experiment, Newton states that he took a black oblong stiff paper, terminated by parallel sides, with a line drawn from side to side, dividing it into two equal parts. One of these was coloured with an intense *red*, and the other with an intense *blue*. He then covered the wall and shutters, surrounding the window of the room with black cloth, to prevent the light reflected from them from interfering with his experiment. On a table before the window, also covered with black, he placed the coloured paper, the line dividing the colours being perpendicular to the plane of the window. Things being thus arranged, he held the prism, with its angle B, *fig.* 7, upwards, so that the light coming from the paper R B should be twice refracted before it reached the eye placed behind the prism, as represented in the cut. Upon viewing the appearance through the prism, he found that the blue half of the paper appeared a little more elevated than the red half, which plainly proved that the rays from the blue half were more deflected from their original direction than those of the red half. Had the rays been equally refrangible, the parts of the paper would have maintained the same relative position, although the place of the entire paper would appear to be elevated.

Fig. 7.

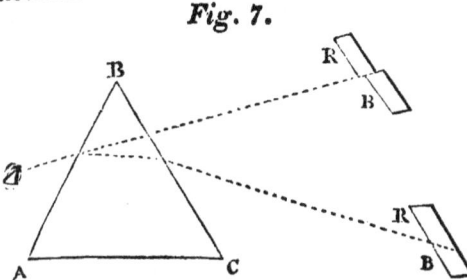

In order to confirm the conclusion deduced from this experiment, Newton viewed the same paper with the refracting angle B, *fig.* 8, of the prism presented downwards. He found, as he expected, that the blue half of the paper was lower than the red, being more depressed, owing to the greater refraction of the rays.

Fig. 8.

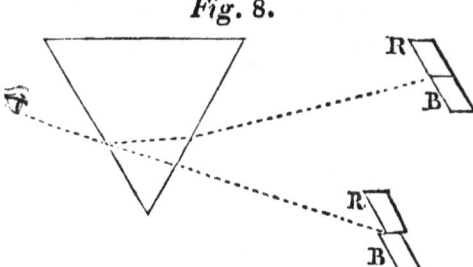

(19.) He now determined to submit the question to a different test. It was previously known that the position of the focus, in which rays from any luminous object are collected by a lens, depended on the refracting power of the glass upon the light. The greater that refracting power, other things being the same, the nearer to the lens will be the focus into which the rays are collected. It was also well known that the place of the focus might always be detected by the presence of an image of an object placed before the lens. We have already stated (p. 8), that a certain degree of indistinctness will attend this image, when the lens is spherical; but still a certain point of greatest distinctness will always be found, which may be regarded as the place of the focus, were all spherical aberration removed. Now, if it be true that light of different colours is differently refrangible, and that according to the result of the experiments already described, *red light* is less refrangible than *blue light*, it would follow that the images of red and blue objects, formed by the same lens, ought to be found at different distances from it.

To apply this test to the coloured paper already mentioned, Newton wrapped round it an extremely fine thread of black silk, so as to form fine black lines upon the red and blue ground, as represented in *fig.* 9; where, for distinction, the black lines are parallel on the red, and cross each other on the blue. He covered the wall of a dark chamber with black cloth, and attached to it the coloured paper, with the silk thread wound round it, as in the figure. Immediately under this he placed a light, so as to illuminate the paper thoroughly, the flame not rising above its lower termination; and, therefore, not intercepting any of the light reflected from it. He then placed a double convex lens M N,

Fig. 9.

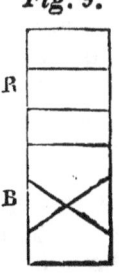

Fig. 10.

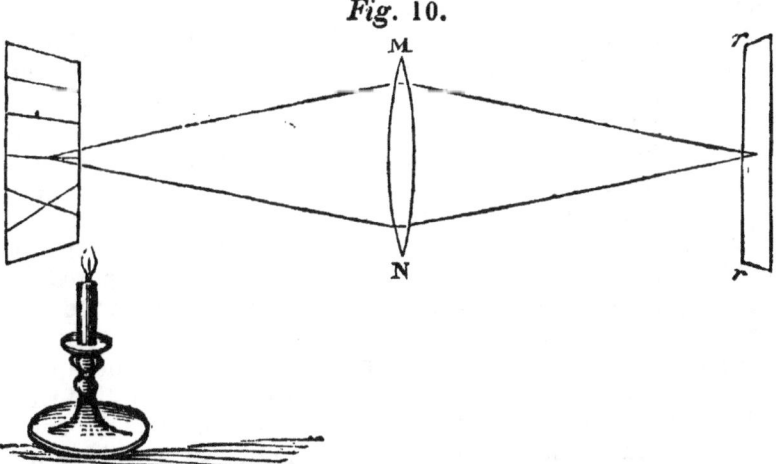

fig. 10, of about four inches and a quarter diameter, at about six feet two inches from the paper. The image of the paper was received upon a white screen, at the same distance behind the lens. This screen was slowly moved to and from the lens, until that position *rr* was obtained, in which the black lines upon red were seen with the greatest distinctness depicted in the image on the screen. This was evidently the focus of the red rays, because the black lines became distinctly visible only when the red boundary was precisely defined. In this position the black lines on the blue part of the image were faint, confused, and scarcely distinguishable. The screen was then moved slowly towards the lens. As it moved the lines on the red part became faint and confused, while those on the blue part became clear and distinct, being found to be as distinct when the screen was removed an inch and a half nearer to the lens, as the lines on the red had been in the first position; while, on the other hand, the lines upon the red part were scarcely observable. The conclusion was irresistible; the same lens placed at the same distance from red and blue surfaces illuminated by the same candle, brought the rays from the one surface to a focus nearer than those from the other; and, therefore, had a greater refracting power on the blue rays than on the red; which conclusion harmonized exactly with the results of the prismatic experiments previously instituted.

(20.) Notwithstanding the very conclusive nature of these experiments, Newton reasons from them with a degree of caution and circumspection truly philosophical. "From these experiments," he says, "it follows not that all the light of the blue is more refrangible than all the light of the red; for both lights are mixed with rays differently refrangible, so that in the red there are some rays not less refrangible than in the blue, and in the blue there are some rays not more refrangible than in the red; but these rays, in proportion to the whole light, are but few, and serve to diminish the event of the experiment, but are not able to destroy it: for if the red and the blue colours were more dilute and weak, the distance of the images would be less than an inch and an half; and if they were more intense and full, that image would be greater, as will appear hereafter."

These experiments were conclusive respecting light which proceeded from the colours of natural bodies. But it still remained to analyze the direct solar light, and to determine the nature of the beams of white light, which are the means of rendering all coloured objects visible, and of causing them to transmit the coloured light which emerges from them.

(21.) If a ray of light, direct from the sun, be admitted through a small aperture A, *fig.* 11, in the window-shutter of

Fig. 11.

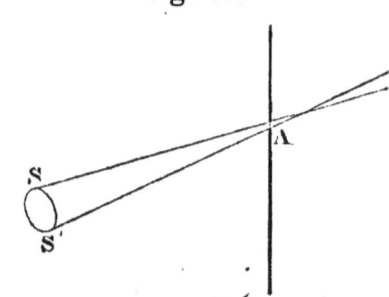

a dark chamber, a circular image of the sun will be formed by the rays admitted through the hole, and may be received upon a paper screen, as at S S'. We shall, for the present, suppose the hole to be so small, that its diameter may be neglected, and it may be regarded as a physical point. The rays which proceed from the several points of the sun's disc entering the aperture A, cross each other, and that from the highest point proceeds to S' the lowest point of the image, while that from the lowest proceeds to S the highest point of the image. In like manner the ray from the right-hand side of the sun proceeds to the left-hand side of the image, and that from the left-hand side to the right-hand side of the image. In the same way every point of the sun's disc is referred to that point of the image diametrically opposite in position. The image is therefore inverted in whatever way it be considered with reference to the sun.

The magnitude of the image, or illuminated spot, on the screen, evidently depends on the distance of the screen from the aperture A, increasing as that distance increases; and the diameter of this image subtends at the hole A the same angle as the sun subtends at it, or as the apparent diameter of the sun.

We have here supposed that the hole has no sensible magnitude, or is a physical point. If this be not the case, and, on the other hand, the aperture have a sensible diameter, all that we have above stated will be true of every separate point in it: so that there will be innumerable images of the sun; the centres of which will be diffused over a space upon the screen equal to the size and shape of the aperture. At present we will consider the aperture circular. To find, then, the magnitude of the illuminated spot upon the screen, first describe a circle A B, *fig.* 12, whose diameter is equal to that of the hole. Then, adding to the radius of this circle another line, A C, whose length is such as would subtend at the hole an angle equal to the sun's semidiameter, with the whole distance O C describe a circle. This circle will be the magnitude of the illuminated spot on the screen.

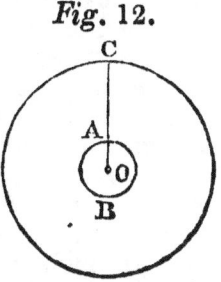

Fig. 12.

(22.) Instead of allowing the beam of light to pass directly from the aperture to the screen, let it be intercepted by a prism A B C near the hole, with its refracting angle B presented downwards. The refraction by the surfaces of this prism might be expected to deflect the beam from its original course, and raise it to an higher position, as represented in *fig.* 13. The part of the screen on

Fig. 13.

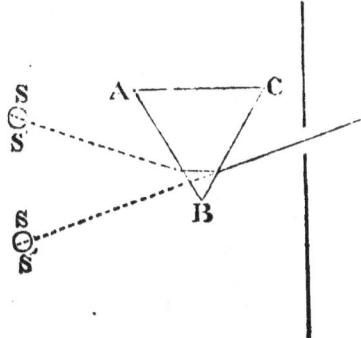

which the refracted ray falls, is, accordingly, elevated by the effect of the prism, but this is not the only effect produced. The breadth of this *spectrum*, as it is called, is exactly equal to the diameter of the illuminated spot which would be projected on the screen, if the prism were removed. But, instead of a circular image being projected on the screen, the illuminated part assumes an oblong form, such as R V, *fig.* 14. The sides are straight, and the ends semicircular—the length being perpendicular to the axis of the prism.

It appears, therefore, that of the rays which pass through the prism, some are refracted to a higher part of the screen than others, those toward the end V being more elevated by the refraction than those towards the end R. From this Newton inferred, that of the light which passed through the prism, some was more, and some less refracted, those rays which passed towards the highest points, V, being more refracted than those which passed towards the lowest points R.

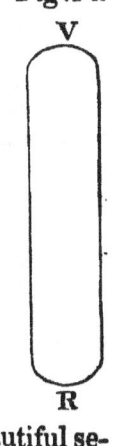

Fig. 14.

The oblong form given to the illuminated part of the screen, was not the most curious or surprising effect produced by the prism. This image or spectrum exhibited the most beautiful series of colours, each depicted on the screen with a degree of splendour and intensity far exceeding those of the colours of any natural object. Beside these the most brilliant colour which nature presents, or the most refined efforts of art could exhibit, would seem faded and dim. The lower extremity, R, exhibited the most dazzling *red*, and above this, in regular succession, were ranged the colours, *orange, yellow, green, blue,* and *indigo,* the upper termination, V, being *violet.* These colours were not separated by distinct limits, but the tints seem to melt imperceptibly one into another, it being impossible to determine exactly where any one ended and the next began. Thus the red was tinted off insensibly into the orange, the orange into the yellow, and so on.

From these observations, it is apparent that the red light, and all that portion of light which partook of this character, being deflected to the lower part of the spectrum, is less refracted than the blue light, and those colours of the same class which are refracted to the upper part. It would therefore seem to be an obvious inference, that the solar beam incident on the prism, was a mixture of different kinds of light; that the prism acting on the component parts refracted some of them in a greater, some in a less degree; those partaking of the blue character being more refracted than those of the red kind. This inference seems also to harmonize with the former experiments made upon coloured bodies (18, 19), whereby it was proved that red light is less refrangible than blue.

(23.) Newton repeated the preceding experiment in another way. The prism being placed as before, at the aperture in the window shutter, he placed his eye behind it, so as to receive the rays emerging after the second refraction from the prism. In this case the eye supplied the place of the screen in the former experiment, the rays which formed the spectrum entering the pupil as they emerged from the prism. He found the same effects to ensue. He beheld the oblong spectrum as before, the order of the colours being in all respects the same.

(24.) It appears by the experiment which we have described that the action of the prism was such as to dilate the ray in a direction at right angles to its length, and thereby to give the spectrum the oblong form. Now if this dilatation was the consequence of the action of the material of the prism, and not of the various refrangibility of the component parts of solar light, it must inevitably follow that a second prism placed with its length vertical, and consequently at right angles to the first, so as to refract the light sideways, would dilate the ray as much in the horizontal direction as the first did in the vertical. The inference from this would necessarily be, that the combined action of two prisms would be to give a square spectrum, as much length being obtained by the action of the one, as breadth by the action of the other.

Accordingly Newton tried this experiment. Let R V, *fig.* 15, be the spectrum produced by the first prism. He placed another prism with its length vertical, and consequently at right angles to the first, and when the rays were intercepted by it, the effect was, that instead of the spectrum, V R, being spread over a square surface, it retained its breadth, but was transferred to the position V'R'.

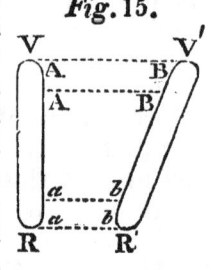

Fig. 15.

This result furnished a most convincing and beautiful confirmation of the theory of Newton. The rays at the upper end of the spectrum were deflected by the second prism, through the distances A B, from their former position, while the rays at the lower end were only deflected through the smaller spaces *a b*. The breadth of the spectrum remained unaltered, plainly shewing that the second prism had no power to dilate the rays which formed it. The rays which were most refracted by the first prism, were those of the blueish character, which occupied the upper part of the spectrum. These same rays were also most refracted by the second prism, being most removed from their first position (through the spaces A B). Also the rays which were least refracted by the first prism, were those of the reddish character which occupied the lower part of the spectrum; and these also are least refracted by the second prism, being those which are least removed from their places through the distances *a b*.

To put this question even more beyond dispute, Newton received the rays from the second prism on a third, placed with its length parallel to the length of the spectrum, and found the same effect repeated, the third position of the spectrum being inclined to the second in the same manner as the second was inclined to the first, but no dilatation taking place, and the breadth of the spectrum remaining the same. He states that he used a fourth prism with the same result.

It is important to remember that in all these experiments the light is all incident on each prism *at the same angle*. For if its parts fell upon the surface at different angles, different quantities of refraction would be the natural and necessary result.

(25.) Newton contrived a very elegant experiment to shew the regularity with which the prisms determined the magnitude, figure, and position of the spectrum. Before two small apertures F, *f*, *fig.* 16,

Fig. 16.

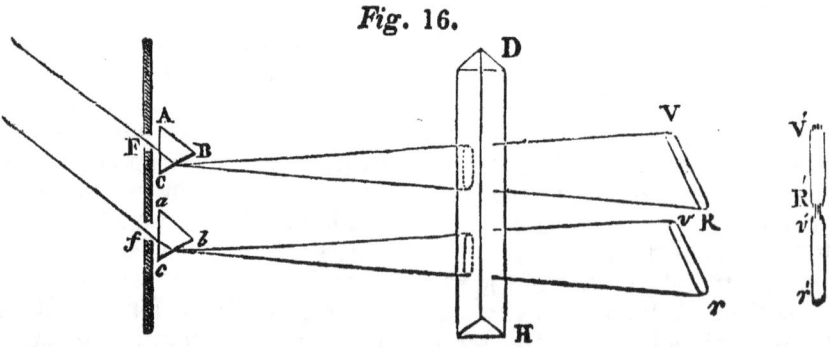

in the window shutter he placed two similar prisms A B C, *a b c*, the one immediately beneath the other, with their lengths parallel and horizontal. These cast two spectrums R′V′, r′v′, on the opposite wall so as to lie in the same right line, and having the lengths at right angles to the floor, the lowest point R′, or red end of one, being contiguous to the highest point v′, or violet end of the other. A third prism, DH, was now placed with its length vertical, and of course at right angles to the other two, and so as to receive the rays emerging from them. The two spectrums were immediately translated from their former positions to other positions RV, rv, no longer in the same line, but similarly inclined to the former, and therefore parallel to each other.

(26.) The next test to which Newton submitted the problem was even more conclusive and convincing than any of the preceding. Through an aperture, O, *fig.* 17, in the window-shutter he admitted a beam of the sun's light which he received upon a prism A B C, placed before

Fig. 17.

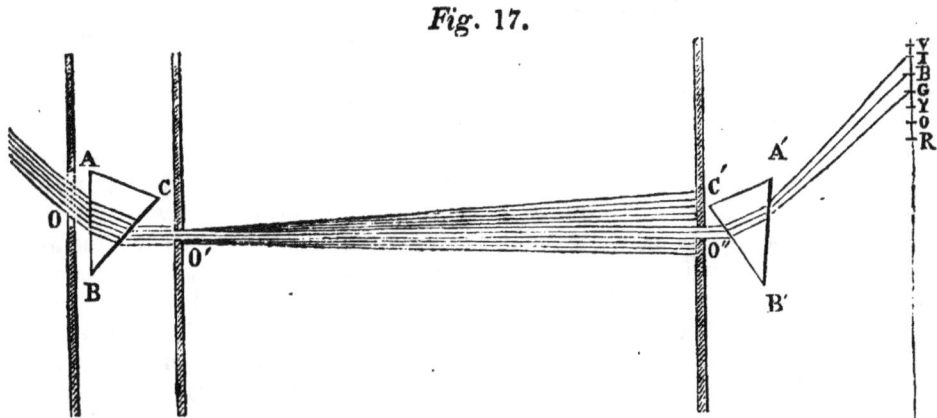

the aperture. The spectrum produced by the refraction of this prism was received upon a screen perforated by a small hole O′. The several coloured lights of the spectrum being diffused over a considerable space upon the screen, and the aperture O′ being small, the light of but one colour passed through it, while the prism A B C remained stationary; but when this prism was slowly turned round its axis, the spectrum moved upwards and downwards on the screen, so as to transmit in succession the lights of the several colours through the aperture O′. At a distance of about twelve feet from this screen another was placed, having, in like manner, a small aperture O″. The beam of coloured light transmitted through the aperture O′ was received upon the second screen, diffusing itself over a space of some magnitude. A small ray of this light passing through the aperture O″ was received upon a prism A′B′C′ placed immediately behind it, and by this prism was refracted to a certain point upon the opposite wall.

The prism A′B′C′ remaining fixed, the prism ABC was turned until the red end of the spectrum fell upon the hole O′. A ray of red light now passed from O′ to O″, and was refracted by the prism A′B′C′ to the point R on the wall. This point was marked. By a slight motion of the prism A B C, the *orange* light was next brought upon O′, and a ray of it passing in the direction O′ O″ fell upon the prism at the same angle as the red light had before been incident. This orange ray was refracted by the prism A′ B′ C′ to a point O on the wall a little above the point R to which the red had been brought. The *yellow, green, blue, indigo,* and *violet* rays were in succession transmitted in the same way to the prism A′ B′ C′, all being incident upon it at the same angle, and they were severally found to be refracted to the points Y, G, B, I, and V. Thus it appeared that the several coloured lights into which the sun-beam was resolved by the prism A B C were, under the same circumstances, differently refracted by the prism A′ B′ C′, each light being refracted the more, the nearer its situation to the violet end of the spectrum.

The conclusiveness of this result would have satisfied an ordinary inquirer, and it would have immediately been made the basis of a theory. The ardour of discovery was, however, in Newton tempered by philosophical circumspection, and in the unwearied patience of his research, he left untried nothing which could put his hypothesis to the proof, and overturn it if false. In the records of scientific discovery there is not a more splendid instance of an investigation in which theory and experiment mutually guide and support each other. In the first experiments, Newton found that the coloured lights

C

reflected from the surfaces of natural bodies were differently refrangible; and subsequently he shewed that the colours produced by the refraction of a sunbeam by a prism were also differently refrangible, and that the colours which, reflected from natural bodies, were most refrangible were also the colours most refrangible in the refracted solar light. But in order, as it were, to identify the two experiments on natural colours and coloured light, he instituted the following experiment.

(27.) By means of two prisms, as described in (25), he projected two spectrums on the wall, so as to be placed end to end in the same direction, and so that the violet end of the one joined the red end of the other. At some distance from the wall he placed a slender piece of white paper, with straight and parallel edges, and so arranged that the red light R, *fig*. 18, of the one spectrum

Fig. 18.

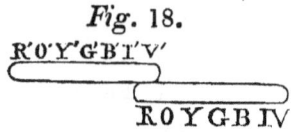

should illumine one half of the paper, while the violet light, V', of the other spectrum illuminated the other half. The paper thus appeared of two colours, red and violet, similar to the painted paper used in the experiment described in (18). The remaining lights of each spectrum passing beyond the paper fell upon the wall, which was hung with black, in order that light reflected from it might not disturb the experiment. It is evident that this arrangement was such as to place the coloured light produced by the refraction of the prism exactly under the same circumstances as the light reflected by the colours of natural bodies in the experiment already alluded to. Accordingly Newton viewed the illuminated paper through a prism held parallel to it, as in that experiment, and found exactly the same result, *viz.* that the violet half was separated from the red by a greater refraction, so that the parts of the paper, instead of forming one straight band, were now separated from one another, but placed in parallel directions. Instead of using a band of paper, he sometimes used a white thread, one half of which he placed in the violet, and the other in the red light, and observed the same effect, the thread appearing to be broken, and one half of it moved out of its place, but parallel to its former position.

In this experiment, by turning one of the prisms upon its axis, he was enabled to illuminate one half of the thread successively with the *violet, indigo, blue, green*, and the other prismatic colours, while the other prism, maintaining its position constantly illuminated the other half of the thread with *red light*. Upon viewing these phenomena successively with a third prism, he found that in each case the parts of the thread illuminated with lights of different colours were separated, but the separation was greatest between the red and violet, less between the red and indigo, still less between the red and blue, and so on, being very small between the red and orange. But when both parts of the thread were illuminated with the reds of the two spectra, the thread appeared no longer broken. It is scarcely necessary to observe, that all these phenomena were such as must have been easily foreseen from the supposed unequal refrangibility of differently coloured lights. Newton might have carried this experiment further, and probably he did so, although he has not particularly mentioned it. He might have thrown on the thread every possible distinct pair of the prismatic colours, by moving both prisms on their axis, and the result would be that the apparent separation of the parts of the thread, when viewed through the prism, would have been great in proportion to the distance between the two colours in the spectrum.

(28.) All those experiments instituted by Newton, in which the refracted light was received upon a screen, were repeated with the same success, the light being admitted immediately to the eye from the prism, without the use of the screen. Thus the experiment (25) in which the two spectra, lying in the same line, were refracted by the prisms to parallel lines, was repeated thus. The spectra were viewed through a prism without disturbing the screen, and their apparent position, as seen through the prism, was found to be the same as when refracted by the third prism, and received upon the screen.

Two prisms ABC, A'B'C', *fig*. 19, were also placed at apertures in the window-shutter, the refracting angle of one being directed upwards, and that of the other, downwards. The spectra produced by these prisms were both in an upright position; but had the colours arranged in an opposite order, the red end being the higher in the one, and the lower in the other. One of the prisms was slowly turned on its axis, until the spectrum produced by it was thrown upon the spectrum produced by the other. The two spectra thus appeared to form one, which, in its colours, differed from either

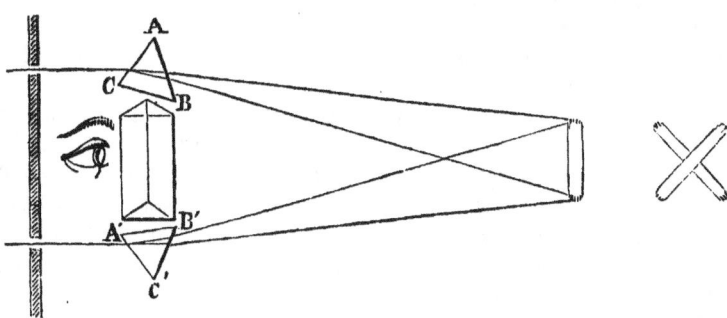

Fig. 19.

of them, the red of the one being mixed with the violet of the other, the orange with the indigo, and so on. This mixed spectrum was now viewed through a third prism, held as represented in the figure. The effect which ensued was, the separation of the spectra, which assumed the cross position shewn in the figure. This experiment is another variety of that which we last described; the inclined positions assumed by the spectra, with respect to their first position, was explained in (24) to arise from the different refrangibilities of the rays. In the present experiment, this inclined position is given at the same time to two spectra. The inclinations are in opposite directions with respect to the first position, because the lights which form the spectra are disposed in an opposite order.

(29.) The following experiment, mentioned by Newton, is another beautiful example of the analysis of mixed lights. A circular piece of white paper A, about one inch in diameter, was placed before a black wall, and using the two prisms mentioned in the last experiment, the paper A, *fig.* 20, was illuminated at the same time with the red light from the one, and a deep violet light from the other. By this mixture the paper assumed a rich purple colour. The circle A was then viewed through a prism at some distance, and the appearance exhibited was two circles, R and V, the circle R, nearer to the paper being *red*, and the more remote one, V, *violet*. The prism in this case refracted the red and violet light, mingled in the circle A, through different angles; the red being least refrangible was removed to R, and the more refrangible violet light carried so far as V.

Fig. 20.

To confirm this, the apertures before the prisms, which cast the red and violet lights on A, were in turns covered, so as alternately to deprive the circle A of these lights. It was accordingly found that the circles R and V alternately vanished, plainly proving that all the light of R came from the prism which cast the red light on A, and that all the light of V came from the prism which cast the violet light on A.

By turning one of the prisms at the window upon its axis, the circle A was successively illuminated with all the prismatic lights, while the other prism, being stationary, constantly projected on it an intense red light. The effect produced to an eye viewing these changes through the third prism was, that the circle V changed its colour according to the change in the light used with the red upon A. But the change of colour was not the only alteration observed in V. Its *position* was also changed. When the blue light was mixed with the red, it appeared nearer to R. Still nearer when green was mixed with red on A. In a word, the circles R and V always exhibited the colours mixed upon A, and their separation from A and from each other always corresponded to the separation of the prismatic spectrum from the direct course of the light, and to the separation of the two lights in the spectrum from each other.

From all these experiments no doubt could remain that lights which differed in colour differed also in refrangibility. One test more however remained, analogous to that which was applied to the colours of natural objects in (19). If the difference of refrangibility be admitted, it will necessarily follow that the same double convex lens will have different foci for differently coloured lights, the focus of the more refrangible light being nearer to the lens than that of the less refrangible. Thus if the lens be exposed to a beam of violet light proceeding from a given object, and collects that light to a focus at a certain point, it should collect red light to a focus at a more distant point, and the lights of intermediate colour to points between these extreme limits.

(30.) In order to reduce the doctrine to this test, Newton cast a strong red light, by means of a prism, upon the page of an open book in a dark room. At a certain distance from the book thus illuminated, he placed a double convex lens, so as to give an image of the book at its focus; this image was received upon a sheet of white paper properly placed behind the lens. The book and the lens being fixed in their respective positions, the paper was moved until that situation was found in which the image of the page and its letters were most distinctly depicted on the paper. This position was of course the focus to which the red light reflected from the book was collected by the lens. The prism in this experiment was so placed, that as the sun moved in the heavens, the several coloured lights of the spectrum were successively cast upon the book, without disturbing either its place or those of the prism or the lens. The position of the book was ascertained in which the letters appeared most distinct, and it was found that as the successive prismatic lights, in regular order from *red* to *violet*, passed over the book, the place of greatest distinctness gradually approached the lens, so that the full *violet* light required for distinctness that the book should be two inches and an half nearer to the lens than for the *red* light.

In this experiment it was necessary to render the chamber extremely dark, in order to prevent the pure prismatic light cast upon the book from being diluted by the white light which might be scattered about the room. In proportion as this adventitious light was admitted, it was found that the distance between the extreme foci became less. And this is plainly the reason why the distance between the extreme foci of prismatic light was found to be so much as two inches and an half, while the distance for light reflected from natural bodies was only one inch and an half (19). For the colours of natural bodies never have the extreme vividness, purity, and splendour which are obtained by the prism.

(31.) The doctrine of the different refrangibility of light led to an obvious consequence respecting its reflexibility, which Newton easily foresaw, and from which he derived another beautiful test to establish the truth of his theory. To render this intelligible to those who are not familiar with optical investigations, we must here be permitted a short digression.

It will be recollected that long before the time of Newton, it was known that the deflection of a ray of light, in passing from a denser into a rarer transparent medium, was *from* the perpendicular. Thus, let A, *fig.* 21, be air, and

Fig. 21.

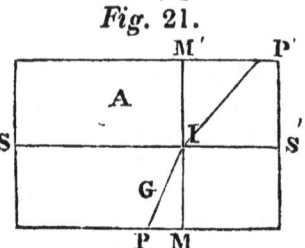

G glass, and let P I be a ray incident on the surface S S, which separates the air from the glass. Let M M′ be the perpendicular at the point of incidence I. Since air is less dense or heavy than glass, the ray P I, instead of persevering in the direction P I, will take a direction further from the perpendicular I M′, such as I P′. This fact was long known. The law of this deflection, as discovered by Snellius, has been already explained; but it may be explained under another point of view, as follows:—

Round the point of incidence I, *fig.* 22, describe a circle in a perpendicular

Fig. 22.

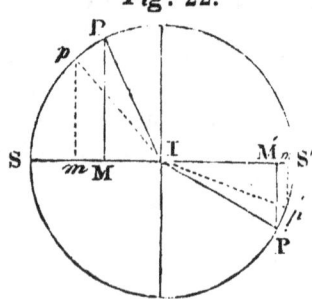

plane. Let P I be the incident ray in the denser medium, and P′ I the refracted ray in the rarer medium. Draw P M, P′ M′ perpendicular to the surface S S′. It was found, that at whatever angle P I might be incident, the proportion of M I to M′ I would be the same, so long as the media on each side of the surface remained unaltered. Thus, suppose M I were two-thirds of M′ I, *r* I being incident at I, its refraction may be thus found: take a distance I *m*′ from I, of which I *m* is two-thirds, or such that I *m*′ is equal to I *m* and the half of I m, and from m' draw m' p' perpendicular to I m'; the line I p' will be the direction which the ray p I will take in passing through the denser medium.

Now suppose that a ray P I, *fig.* 23,

Fig. 23.

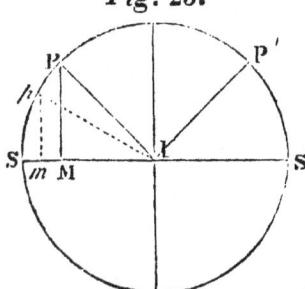

were to meet I in such a direction that M I is two-thirds of I S. If in this case, in conformity with the rule just explained, we take a length from I equal to I M, together with the half of I M, that length will be I S', and S' would be the point from which the perpendicular (m' p', see last *fig.*) should be drawn to meet the circumference. But this point S' being itself on the circumference, the perpendicular (m' p') altogether disappears, its length being reduced to absolutely nothing; and the point (p') of the circumference to which the ray is deflected, would be the point S' itself. Thus the Snellian law would shew that, in this case, the ray incident at I would not pass into the rarer medium. Experience, however, proved that, in this case, the ray P I was *reflected* according to the common law of reflection, in the direction I P', making the angle P' I S equal to I P S.

If the incident ray made any angle p I m less than P I M, the law of Snellius likewise became inapplicable. For, in this case, m I being more than two-thirds of I S, the distance from I taken upon I S would be beyond the point S, and therefore outside the circle, so that the perpendicular could never meet the circle; and accordingly the refracted ray could have no direction conformable to this law. In all such cases experiment shewed that the ray was reflected. In this illustration we have supposed the fixed proportion to be two-thirds, but the conclusion may be drawn if any other proportion be adopted.

It appears, therefore, that in passing from a denser medium into a rarer there is a certain degree of obliquity beyond which the ray cannot be refracted; and, on the contrary, will be reflected back into the denser medium, according to the common law of reflection. It further appears, by what has just been explained, that this degree of obliquity, which limits the possibility of refraction, depends on the degree of refraction which the ray suffers in passing from the one medium into the other, and that the limiting obliquity is greater where this refraction is greater.

Aware of this property of refracting media, Newton perceived, that if the doctrine of unequal refrangibility were granted, it would follow that the limiting obliquity, in passing from a denser medium to a rarer, would vary with the refrangibility of the light, being greater for the violet and more refrangible lights than for the red and less refrangible lights. Thus it would follow that those lights which had a greater aptitude for refraction, were also more susceptible of reflexion, and *vice versâ*. He accordingly submitted the doctrine to this test by the following ingenious experiment.

(32.) He took two prisms, B A C, *fig.* 24, and C D B, of the same quality of

Fig. 24.

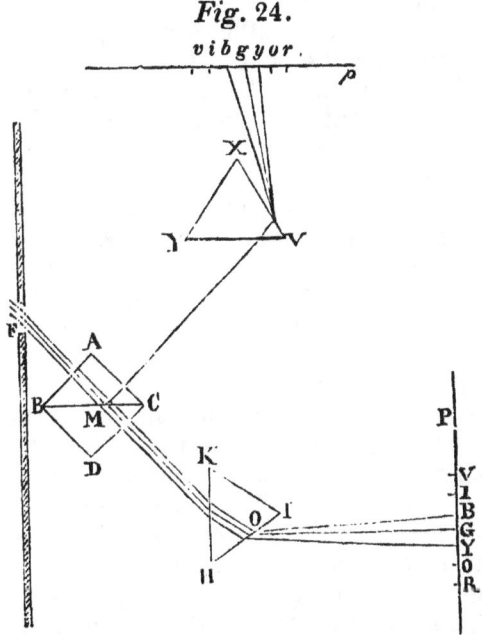

glass, having the angles A and D right, and the angles at B and C, in each 45°, and placing their broadest faces B C together, tied them in this position, so as to form a square prism. This compound prism was placed before an aperture F, which admitted a beam F M of the sun's light, so as to fall perpendicularly on the face A B of the prism. This ray was incident upon the thin plate of air B C between the prisms, which were not brought into absolute contact. Passing through this and the second prism, it emerged from the surface C D parallel to its incidence; for since the refracting angles of the two prisms, A C B and C B D, are turned in opposite directions, and are equal, they neutralise each other's effects, and the light emerges as it entered. The ray M O, emerging from the compound prism, was received upon another prism I H K, and was dilated in the same manner as if it had been received directly from the aperture F, and the spectrum was received in the usual way upon the screen at P.

Another prism X V Y was placed above the compound one, in such a position as to receive a ray reflected from the surface B C; and above it a paper screen, placed to receive the light refracted by it.

Let us suppose that in the position thus given to all the prisms, a vivid spectrum appears on P, and no appearance of light is exhibited on p. The compound prism is now slowly turned round its axis in the direction A C D B, so as gradually to increase the obliquity of the ray F M to the surface B C. At a certain position, a strong violet light will appear upon the screen p at v. Maintaining the prisms, for the present, in this position, let the circumstances of the experiment be examined. The violet part of the spectrum on P will be found to have disappeared. If a screen be interposed between the prism I H K, and the compound prism, it will be found that the light which falls upon it will be of a colour which would result from the mixture of all the colours of the spectrum, except the violet. If a screen be interposed between the prism X V Y and the compound prism, it will be found that the light which falls upon it is the violet. The inference is most obvious. The incident ray F M has obtained the limiting obliquity, corresponding to the most refrangible or violet light. This light is accordingly reflected by the surface B C, and is transmitted through the prism X V Y to the screen p, where it appears. The violet light not passing with the other parts of the sun-beam through the prism B C D, has disappeared from the spectrum on P, which, therefore, now terminates with the indigo light. The beam M O, before it is dilated by the prism I H K, is in fact the sun-beam F M deprived of the violet light, which has been reflected at M, and, therefore, it is composed of all the colours of the spectrum except violet, as appears by the spectrum, which is now exhibited on P. Thus it follows that violet light is totally reflexible at an obliquity, which is insufficient to prevent the refraction of lights of other colours.

The prism A C D B was now slowly turned round a little more in the same direction, and the effects observed. The screen p, in addition to the violet light v, was now illuminated by the indigo i, of which the spectrum on P was observed to be deprived. The place of the indigo light on p was also next to v, but so as to be less refracted. On interposing the screen between the prism I H K and the compound prism, it was found to be illuminated with a colour, which would result from the mixture of all the colours of the spectrum, except *violet* and *indigo;* and on the other hand, on interposing it between the prism X V Y and I H K, it was illuminated with a colour which would be produced by the mixture of violet and indigo.

The inference from these effects is consistent with the former one. The prism A C D B had now attained that position which gave the incident ray F M the limiting obliquity of the indigo light. It was accordingly reflected, together with the more reflexible violet light. The lights of other colours were transmitted, and produced the effects observed on P, and between I H K and A C D B.

This process was continued, the prism A C D B being slowly and gradually turned on its axis in the same direction. The lights, blue, green, yellow, orange, and red, successively disappeared from the spectrum on P, and at the same times appeared in succession in their proper places on p. In each case the colour of the light in the beam M O was such as would result from the mixture of the colours on P, and the colour of the light M N was such as would result from the mixture of the colours on p.

All these effects are obvious and beautiful consequences, and therefore confirmations of Newton's doctrine. As the obliquity of the incident ray F M to the surface B C is gradually increased, it becomes successively equal to the limiting obliquities of the several coloured lights, and in the same succession reflects them to the screen p; the other screen P being in the same order, and at the same instants of time, deprived of them. Thus it appears, not only that lights of different colours are differently refrangible, but also that they are differently reflexible; and that those which are more refrangible are also more reflexible, and *vice versâ*.

Chapter III.

Of the Methods of obtaining Homogeneous Light.

(33.) By the results of the experimental investigations described in the last chapter, Newton was convinced that solar light was not simple and homogeneous, but was a mixture or composition of many lights, differing from each other in certain respects, but more particularly in *refrangibility*. This quality he adopted as a test for pure unmixed or homogeneous light. A beam, every ray of which was equally refrangible, and which, therefore, did not admit of being dilated by a prism, he considered to be pure homogeneous light. Although the parts into which the solar beam was decomposed were shewn, by the experiment described in p. 17, to be incapable of further dilatation; yet this method did not give all the purity to the light which philosophical exactitude demanded, for the reasons which we shall now explain.

It will be recollected that the aperture in the window-shutter (p. 14) casts a circular illuminated spot on the opposite wall, the diameter of which is equal to the diameter of the hole, together with a line, which being drawn upon the wall would subtend at the hole an angle equal to the apparent diameter of the sun. But this circular spot is not uniformly bright. It is more faintly illuminated at its edges than at its centre, the cause of which will be easily understood. Let O O', *fig.* 25, be the hole in

Fig. 25.

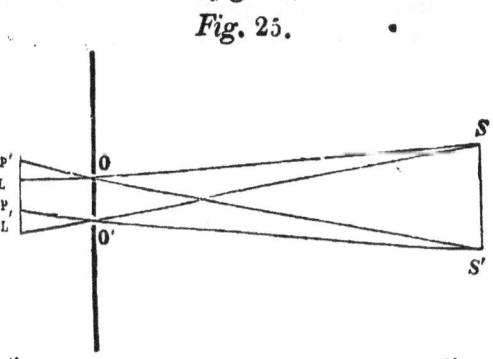

the window shutter; S S' the sun's diameter. A ray of light from S', passing the upper boundary O of the hole, falls upon a screen at P; and a ray from S, passing the lower edge O' of the hole, falls upon the screen at P'. Now, it is apparent that no part of the sun's disc, except the lowest point S', can shine upon P, the upper part of the window shutter intercepting the light from all the other points; and that no part of his disc, except the point S, can shine upon P', the lower part of the window shutter intercepting the light. Hence it appears that the points P P', and the entire of the edge of the illuminated circle on the screen, will be more faintly illuminated than any of the parts nearer to its centre.

The ray from S' passing above the lower edge of the hole at O' will illuminate L, and thus the point L will be exposed to light from the entire disc of the sun. The same may be said of L', and of all intermediate points. The several points from L to P' will be exposed to light from only a part of the sun's disc, that part being smaller the more distant the point is from L, so that the light becomes gradually more faint from L to P'. The same may be said of the light from L' to P. From this it appears that the circular illuminated spot on the screen is composed of a small circle whose diameter is L L', uniformly illuminated, surrounded to the distance L P' by a ring of light of gradually decreasing brightness, and fading away until it becomes insensible. This ring is called the *penumbra**.

Now since the effect of the prism, as has been already proved, is to stretch out this luminous circle into an oblong form, the breadth being the same, and the sides and ends being illuminated by the rays which form the penumbral ring surrounding the unrefracted circle, it follows that the sides and ends of the spectrum will be bounded by a penumbral skirt of the breadth of P L'; and such, in fact, was the result of the experiments.

In the experiments which Newton now desired to institute, it was necessary that the light should be obtained of as uniform an intensity as possible, and therefore it was necessary to remove or very much diminish the penumbral fringe which we have just described. But it was still more necessary that light should be obtained which was perfectly pure and homogeneous, and it so happened that the same cause which produced the fringe and varied the intensity of the light, also impaired its purity.

---

* The hole may be so small, that its apparent diameter at the screen will be less than that of the sun. In this case the part of the figure L L' will disappear, and the whole spot on the screen will have the character of penumbra, the centre being the most luminous point.

This will be understood by attending to the effects of the prism on the circular spot.

Let S, *fig.* 26, be the circular illuminated spot cast upon the screen by the light proceeding directly from the aperture without being intercepted by the prism. Let S A be the distance on the screen to which the least refrangible rays are deflected. These rays, which before fell upon the circle S, will now fall upon the circle A. Let S Z be the distance on the screen to which the most refrangible of the rays incident on S are deflected by the prism. These rays, which before fell upon the circle S, now fall upon the circle Z. The rays of all the intermediate degrees of refrangibility are deflected by the prism, so as to fall upon circles whose centres occupy the entire space from A to Z. From A take a distance A C, equal to twice the radius of the circle A, or, what is the same, to the breadth of the spectrum. A circle described round the centre C, with a diameter equal to A C, will evidently touch the circle A, but neither circle will be within or upon the other. It is evident, however, that every circle of the same diameter, whose centre lies between A and C, must lie partly upon the circle A, and partly upon the circle C. Hence it is evident, that the rays which, deflected from S, illuminate the circle A, and those which illuminate the circle C, are not intermixed. But between the points C and A is a considerable space, and between the degrees of refrangibility which would cause rays to be deflected to these points, are many intermediate degrees, in virtue of which rays would be deflected upon innumerable circles, whose centres lie between C and A. It follows, therefore, that all these lights of intermediate refrangibilities are intermixed with lights upon the circles A and C, neither of which, therefore, shine with pure homogeneous light. Since the lights of different refrangibilities which are thus intermingled are diffused over circles whose centres occupy the space A C, the number of such circles must be proportional to the space A C, or to the breadth of the illuminated circle S, increasing and diminishing as that breadth is increased or diminished. In this proportion, then, lights of different refrangibilities are mixed in the spectrum; and, therefore, every means which can diminish the breadth of the spectrum will proportionally increase the purity of the lights.

The first method which occurred to Newton to accomplish this, and, at the same time, to remove the penumbral fringe already mentioned, was to perforate the screen in the space L L' (*fig.* 25), and to receive the light transmitted through the perforation on a second screen behind the first. By this means the penumbral ring would be received upon the first screen at L' P, L P', and the uniform light of L L' would be admitted to the second screen through the perforation. In this case, the breadth of the illuminated circle on the second screen, and therefore that of the spectrum, would be nearly equal to that of the perforation. In proportion as the breadth of the spectrum would be thus reduced, the intermixture of heterogeneous lights would be diminished, and, as we have just explained, the penumbral light would be altogether intercepted.

He, however, accomplished what he aimed at more effectually by the following method. At a distance of ten or twelve feet from the hole O, *fig.* 27, he placed a lens L, which formed an image of the hole at O'. If the lens were so

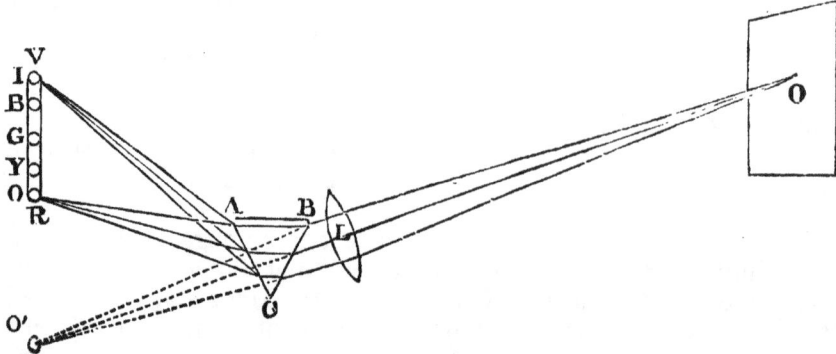

Fig. 27.

placed that O L and O' L should be equal, which was always possible, the magnitude of the image O' would be exactly equal to that of the hole. This image was therefore considerably less than the illuminated circle cast on the wall or screen without the interposition of the lens. A prism A B C, placed behind the lens, deflected the rays emerging from it, and formed the oblong spectrum R V, the breadth of which was equal to O', and which was free from any penumbra. The length of the spectrum in these experiments is never changed. In the present experiment he succeeded in reducing the breadth to about one-sixtieth of the length; and therefore diminished the mixture of heterogeneous lights in any part of it proportionally. Although it was impossible by this method, or perhaps by any other, to obtain a beam of absolutely homogeneous light, yet what was thus obtained was sufficiently simple and homogeneous for all the purposes of experiment.

Some other ingenious expedients were resorted to for the simplification of light. The diminished breadth of the spectrum, while it gave a purified homogeneous light, gave a very small quantity of it. To obtain it in greater abundance, it occurred to Newton to form a great number of small holes in the shutter, in the same horizontal row, so as to obtain several of these spectra placed parallel to each other, and thus form one broad one, in which the lights should be as homogeneous as in a single one of small breadth. Or what was equivalent, and still more effectual, instead of a row of holes, he formed one narrow slit in the shutter extending in an horizontal direction, so as to admit a thin sheet of light. By this means a spectrum of any required breadth may be formed, in which the light is as pure and homogeneous as in a spectrum formed by light admitted at a round hole, whose diameter is equal to the breadth of the slit.

Newton suggests another very ingenious means of obtaining a spectrum, in which lights would be supplied of different degrees of purity and intensity. Let a narrow triangular hole be cut in the shutter in an horizontal direction, as *fig.* 28, O o. The sunbeam admitted through this hole will have an edge like a knife. The broadest part O of the ray will form a spectrum R V, in which the intermixture will be in proportion to the base O of the triangle; but as the ray diminishes in breadth towards o, the corresponding parts of the spectrum, towards

Fig. 28.

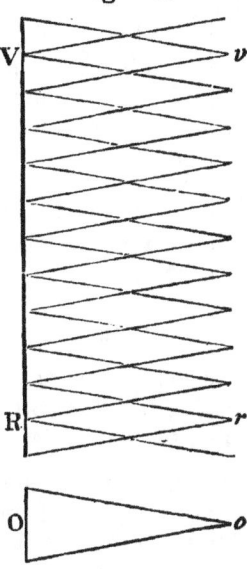

R V, are increased in the purity of the light, heterogeneous rays being less intermixed as the breadth of the triangle is diminished, as is evident from the figure. Having a spectrum of this kind, experiments may be tried either in its stronger, though less simple light, on the side R V, or in the weaker and more simple light on the side r v, as may seem more suitable to the objects of the investigation.

In all experiments on homogeneous light, Newton states that he found it necessary to use great precaution in order to be secure of success. The chamber should be carefully darkened to avoid the disturbance arising from rays of white light scattered casually about. The glass, both of the prisms and lens, should be free from veins, striæ, air bubbles, and other inequalities. He found it so difficult to procure good prisms, that he frequently used transparent liquids inclosed in hollow prisms, formed of pieces of plate glass fixed together at proper angles.

With light simplified by the methods we have now explained, he tried the experiment explained in (26), and found that a pure homogeneous ray admitted of no dilatation by the prism, and therefore concluded that the light of which it was composed was all equally refrangible. With a view of establishing the same principle, he took two small circular pieces of white paper, and illuminated one with light direct from the sun, and the other with homogeneous light obtained by one of the methods which we have just explained. Viewing these circles thus illuminated through a prism, he found that the white circle was dilated into an oblong spectrum; but that the other still appeared as perfectly circular as when viewed without the intervention of the prism. He now placed minute objects in the homogeneous light, and viewing them through the prism, found them distinct; but when the same objects in the sun's direct unrefracted beam were similarly viewed, they became confused and indistinct.

Chapter IV.

Law of refraction of homogeneous light—imperfection of refracting telescopes—Newton's reflecting telescope.

(34.) Newton having now succeeded in establishing the unequal refrangibility of the rays which compose solar light, his next step was to determine the law by which each species of light was refracted. It was about the year 1665, being then in his 25th year, that he appears to have commenced his investigations respecting the composition of light; and on the 8th of February, 1672, he communicated his discovery to the Royal Society, of which he had just been elected a Fellow. About fifty years prior to this period, Snellius discovered the *law of refraction*, which being afterwards adopted by Descartes, was well known, and generally received at the period to which we now allude. The philosophers who observed this law were not aware that all the rays of light were not equally refrangible; and Newton concluded that they adapted their measures to the mean rays, or those which lie in the middle of the spectrum, and which therefore have an intermediate refrangibility between those of the red and violet, the least and most refrangible rays. Hence he concludes from the experiments of his predecessors, that the green light of the prismatic spectrum is refracted according to the Snellian law.

Newton showed, by the experiment which we shall now describe, that when the sun's rays were all incident on the prism at the same angle, the sines of the refractions of the several component rays always have to each other the same proportion. It follows, therefore, that they must always have the same proportions to the sine of the angle of incidence, for since the green ray obeys this law, and they all have fixed proportions with respect to it, they must all obey a similar law. The experiment by which this was determined was as follows.

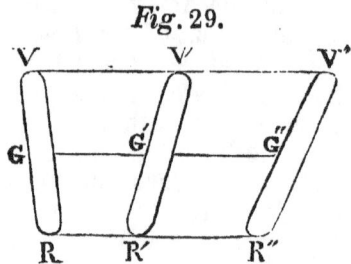

Fig. 29.

Let RV (*fig.* 29) be the spectrum produced by a prism in the usual way. Let another prism be placed at right angles to this, as described in (24), and let R'V' be the new position which the spectrum assumes. The distances RR', VV' measure upon the screen the deflections of the red and violet rays, and lines parallel to these, as GG', measure the deflection of the intermediate rays. From the proportion of these lines, that of the sines of the refractions of the several kinds of rays was determined by mathematical reasoning. The prism placed at right angles to the first was now removed, and another with a different refracting angle was substituted for it, which removed the spectrum to the position R"V". The proportion of the sines of the refractions was now deduced from measurement and computation as before, and was found to be unaltered. A third prism, with a different refracting angle, was used with the same result. Thus it appeared that the sine of refraction of each light bears a fixed proportion to that of the green light, while the sine of refraction of the green light bears a fixed proportion to the sine of incidence, by the law of Snellius; from whence it follows that in each kind of light the sine of the angle of refraction bears a fixed proportion to that of the angle of incidence, but that this proportion is different in light of different kinds.

Newton gives an investigation, by which he shows that this law of refraction may be deduced independently of experiment, by mathematical reasoning, from the supposition that bodies refract light by acting upon its rays in directions at right angles to their surfaces. We shall not give here the details of this investigation, which also furnishes an explanation of the fact we have already stated, namely, the total reflection of the light at the limiting obliquities. It is, however, in the Principia that this latter consequence is deduced from it.

(35.) Having determined the proportion of the sine of incidence and refraction for the red, green, and violet, supposed to pass from air into glass, to be as follows:—

Red Sin.inc. : Sin.ref. : : 77 : 50
Green Sin.inc. : Sin.ref. : : 77½ : 50
Violet Sin.inc. : Sin.ref. : : 78 : 50

he proceeded to investigate the effect which this difference in the proportion produces on the images of objects formed by the object-glasses of refracting telescopes. When the curvature of the object-glass is not great, compared with its diameter, the angles of incidence of rays proceeding from a point at any considerable distance are very small, the rays being evidently very nearly perpendicular to the surface of the glass. By a well known principle of mathematics, the sines of very small angles are in the same proportion as the angles themselves: and, therefore, in the case to which we now allude, the angles of incidence will be to those of refraction as the above numbers, and the deviations of the rays above mentioned will be as the differences of those numbers. That is to say, the deviations of the *red, green*, and *violet*, will be as 27, 27½, and 28.

Let L be a lens presented to a dis-

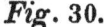
Fig. 30.

tant object from which the rays may be considered parallel. Let V be the focus to which the *violet*, or most refrangible rays are collected; and R the point to which the *red*, or least refrangible rays are collected; and let G be the focus of the medium or *green* rays. The places of the points, V, G, R, may be determined by geometrical reasoning, if the proportions of the sines of incidence and refraction as above given, and the curvature of the lens, be known. The result is, that if twice the distance, L G, be divided into 55 equal parts, the space V R is equal to one of these parts.

It may also be proved that if O be a lucid point, and V, G, R, the foci of the *violet, green* and *red* light from it, and as before twice the distance L G be divided into 55 equal parts, V R will have the same proportion to one of those parts as O G has to O L.

It will be observed that the violet rays diverging from V meet the red rays converging towards R at a certain point between V and R, and that at this distance all the rays which are refracted by the lens are collected into the smallest possible circle. The diameter of this circle being computed when the incident rays are parallel, was found to be about the 55th part of the diameter of the lens.

(36.) To verify these inferences, Newton repeated again the experiment described in (19), but adopted the method mentioned in p. 24, of rendering the prismatic light homogeneous. In the course of these experiments he encountered many practical difficulties arising from imperfections, such as veins, air bubbles, &c. in the glass of which his prisms were formed, of which, as well as of his efforts to avoid or remove them, he gives a very detailed and interesting account. He also found considerable difficulty in determining the exact foci of the lights of blueish character at the upper end of the spectrum, owing to their extreme faintness. On the whole, however, he succeeded in satisfying himself that the foci of the rays of different colours were at those points to which the computation made on their supposed unequal refrangibility assigned them. Thus it appeared that the object glass of a refracting telescope formed as many distinct images of an object placed before it, as there are lights of different degrees of refrangibility: that these images differed in colour, the blueish ones being nearest to the object glass, and the reddish most remote from it, and that between these were included images of a greenish and yellowish hue; that these images extended over a space along the axis of the telescope, equal to about 2-55ths of the focal length of that glass; and that the smallest space into which the innumerable images of the same point in the object can be collected on a plane at right angles to the axis of the telescope, is a circle, whose diameter amounts to about a 55th part of the diameter of the object glass. "So that it is a wonder," says Newton, "that telescopes represent objects so distinct as they do. But were all the rays of light equally refrangible, the error arising only from the sphericalness of the figures of glasses would be many hundred times less."

The effect called spherical aberration,

and its cause, have been already indicated in (11.) Let L L′, *fig*. 31, be the section of a plano-convex object-glass made by a plane passing through its axis, and let parallel rays of pure homogeneous light be supposed to fall on

Fig. 31.

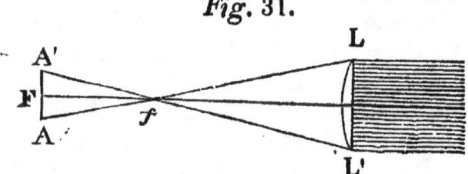

the plane side, perpendicular to the surface. If the surface of the lens be conceived to be divided into a number of concentrical rings, as described in (11), the foci of each ring will be more distant from the lens, the nearer the ring is to the edge of the lens. Let *f* be the focus of the marginal ring, and F that of the central rays. The foci of all the intermediate rings will lie between F and *f*. The rays diverging from all the foci between *f* and F are collected in a circle having the line A A′ for its diameter, and this is evidently the smallest space within which *all* these rays are collected. The diameter of this circle, therefore, measures the *lateral aberration* which parallel rays would sustain from the sphericity of the lens; and Newton calculated this, in order to compare the imperfection of telescopes, arising from this cause, with that imperfection which arises from the unequal refrangibility of light.

By geometrical reasoning, the details of which we cannot properly introduce here, it is proved that the square of the radius of the spherical surface of the lens, multiplied by the square of the sine of refraction, has to the square of half the breadth of the lens L L′ multiplied by the square of the sine of the angle of incidence the same proportion as half that breadth bears to the aberration A A′.

Newton then proceeds to show that if the object-glass were a plano-convex lens, having its plane side turned towards the object, having the radius of its convex surface 100 feet or 1200 inches, and the diameter of the lens four inches, the diameter of the smallest circle into which equally refrangible rays would be collected, would be about $\frac{1}{80000}$th of an inch. The calculation is as follows, the proportion of the sine of incidence to that of refraction being supposed to be 3 to 2.

Square of the radius of the spherical surface of the lens, (radius being 1200 inches) 1440000
Square of the sine (2) of refraction 4

Their product . . 5760000

Square of half the breadth of the lens, (the breadth being 4) . . 4
Square of the sine (3) of the angle of incidence 9

Their product 36

The proportion of these products is that of 160,000 to 1; and such is the proportion of half the breadth of the lens (*i. e.* two inches) to the aberration, which is, therefore, the 160,000th part of two inches, or the 80,000th part of an inch.

The diameter of the lateral aberration arising from unequal refrangibility of light, would, in the case of the lens just described, be the fifty-fifth part of four inches, or four fifty-fiths of an inch. The lateral aberration produced by the spherical form of the lens has, therefore, to that produced by the unequal refrangibility of light, so small a proportion as 1 to 5800.*

It follows, therefore, that the imperfection of telescopes, which arises from the spherical form of lenses, bears an exceedingly small proportion to that which is caused by the unequal refrangibility of light. But even the small error arising from the spherical form may be almost removed, as Newton suggests, by a compound object-glass, formed by two glass lenses with water between them. So that thus all the labours of Descartes, and others who devoted themselves to the formation of spheroidal lenses were fruitless, since even had they succeeded in producing lenses absolutely free from spherical aberration, the effect would not have been perceptible.

(37.) Reasoning thus, Newton did not hesitate to pronounce *the improvement of refracting telescopes desperate*, a conclusion which forms a striking exception to the almost superhuman sagacity which characterised all the philosophical researches of this extraordinary man. What renders this error the more wonderful, is that the property of light,

* This proportion is calculated with reference to the green or mean rays. If, however, it be taken with reference to those rays which produce the strongest effect in vision, it will only be as 1 to 1200.

on which the perfection of refracting telescopes has since been found to depend, seems to have pressed itself forward, and even to have courted his attention in the very experiments from which he deduced his erroneous conclusion. (*Fig.* 32.) Let A B C, A' B' C'

Fig. 32.

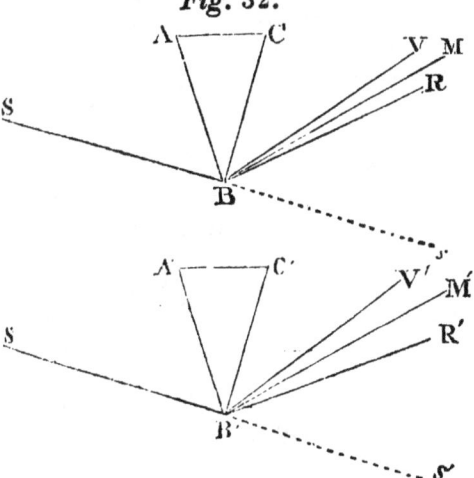

be two prisms, formed of different transparent substances. Let S B, S' B' be rays of the sun falling on them in parallel directions. Let B V, B' V be the most refracted or violet light in each, and B R, B' R' the least refracted or red light. The deviation of the rays from their original direction, produced by the refraction of the prisms, will be different for each component part of the incident light. Newton supposed that the deviations of the different coloured lights from the common direction when incident, have to each other a certain fixed proportion; so that with the same average refraction or deviation from their common original direction, they would be dilated or separated from each other in the same degree. This may perhaps be more easily comprehended if thus explained. Let A B C, A' B' C' be two prisms of different materials, receiving parallel rays S B, S' B', of solar light. Let the lines B M, B' M' divide the angles V B R, V' B' R', formed by the extreme red and violet rays into equal parts, or so that V B M shall be equal to R B M, and also V' B' M' to R' B' M'. Also, suppose the prisms to have such refracting angles, that the rays B M, B' M' shall be parallel. The deviations of these rays, *s* B M, *s'* B' M', from their original directions B *s*, B' *s'* must be equal. Under these circumstances Newton concluded that the angles V B R and V' B' R' would be equal, and that the deviation of every ray in the spectrum V R, from its original direction B *s*, would be equal to the deviation of the similar ray in the spectrum V' R' from its original direction B' *s'*. Such is not the fact, and it is almost inconceivable how Newton, who had avowedly examined the spectra produced, not only by prisms of different kinds of glass, but also by liquids contained in hollow glass prisms, could have escaped noticing a fact that would at once have led him to the discovery of achromatic telescopes.

In fact the prisms being circumstanced as we have just described, so as to produce equal deflections of the sunbeam from its original direction, the dilatation or *dispersion* of the rays from each other, and which may be measured by the divergence V B R, V' B' R' of the extreme rays, will be different according to the material of which the prism is composed. Newton, on the other hand, concluded that when the deflection of the sun's beam by different prisms was the same, the dispersion would also be the same. Had he thought of measuring the lengths of spectra produced by different prisms, equally deflecting the light, he could not have failed to have found them different, and would have naturally been led to the discovery of achromatic telescopes, as we shall now explain.

Since prisms of different materials, with an equal deflection of the beam, produce spectra of different lengths, and since also the length of a spectrum varies with the position of the prism, or, what is the same, with the deflection of the light, it follows that if two prisms of different materials be exposed to beams of the sun's light, one of them may be turned until such a position be given to it, that the length of the spectrum produced by it shall be equal to the length of the spectrum produced by the other prism.

In this case the deflection of the beam by the two prisms producing equal spectra must be different, for if not, as we have before stated, the spectra would have different lengths. If one of the prisms be inverted with respect to the other, all other things remaining the same, the spectra will still keep the same length, but the colours will be reversed. Now suppose that instead of transmitting different beams of light through the two prisms, the *same beam* be successively transmitted through them, the one being placed behind the other, but the former arrangement being in all other respects preserved, it is quite evident that the dispersion of the one prism will have a tendency to neutralise the dispersion of the other, and that in the beam emerging from the second prism, the prismatic lights will be so mingled as to render the emergent beam nearly colourless. This will appear from considering that the tendency of the one prism to disperse the rays in one way, bringing the violet ray highest and the red lowest, is exactly equal to the tendency of the other to disperse the light in the opposite way, bringing the violet lowest and the red highest. But this mutual compensation will not obtain in the deflection of the light, since the power of the second prism to deflect downwards is not, in its actual position, equal to the power of the first to deflect upwards; so that the prism which has the less deflecting power will destroy so much of the deflecting effect of the other as is equal to its own, but an effective deflection will remain, by which the beam will be turned from its original direction.

Thus we arrive at the important fact, that a beam of light may have its direction changed by refraction, so that the directions of all its component rays shall be equally changed, or nearly so, although they be differently refrangible. What may be done by prisms may also be effected by lenses; and therefore an object-glass of a telescope may be so constructed as to collect all the rays of different refrangibilities nearly to the same focus,* and thus an achromatic telescope may be formed. Such was the discovery that Newton left to adorn a future age, a discovery presented to him by his own experiments, a fact rendered not improbable by his own reasoning, consistent with his own theory, and soliciting investigation and inquiry at almost every step of his own researches, yet which investigation and inquiry he seems, by an unaccountable pertinacity, to have stepped out of his way to avoid.

Newton seems not to have maintained an uniform opinion at all times on this point. The first edition of his Optics was published in 1704, and the second in 1717. In both of these he pronounces the improvement of refracting telescopes to be *desperate*. And yet, in a letter to Mr. Oldenburg, dated July, 1672, three years before his " discourse about light was written at the desire of some gentlemen of the Royal Society," he vindicates himself from a charge of Dr. Hooke, " who reprehended him for laying aside the thoughts of improving optics by refractions," in the following words—" What I said was in respect of telescopes of the ordinary construction, signifying that their improvement is not to be expected from the well figuring of glasses, as opticians have imagined. But I despaired not of their improvement by other constructions, which made me cautious to insert nothing that might intimate the contrary. For although successive refractions which are made all in the same way do necessarily more and more augment the errors of the first refraction; *yet it seemed not impossible for contrary refractions so to correct each other's inequalities, as to make their difference regular, and if that could be conveniently effected, there would be no further difficulty.* Now to this end I examined what may be done not only by glasses alone, but by a complication of divers successive mediums; as by *two or more glasses or crystals, with water or some other fluid between them;* all which may together perform the office of one glass, especially of the object-glass, on whose construction the perfection of the instrument chiefly depends. But what the results in theory or by trials have been, I may possibly find a more proper occasion to declare."

In this passage he hints at the principle on which achromatic telescopes depend, and even the manner of applying that principle in their construction, and yet fifty years of his life after this employed in perfecting his theory, seem only to have confirmed his error.

(38.) Abandoning all further inquiry into the methods of improving refracting telescopes, Newton, at the part of his Optics to which we have now arrived, proceeds to explain his contrivances for the construction of a reflecting telescope. In the end of a tube he placed a concave spherical reflector, which he constructed of metal, and polished with his own hands. The image from this was deflected by another plane reflector placed in the axis of the tube, so as to be received by an eye-glass in the side of the tube at which it was viewed by the observer. He suggests the possibility of

---

* In strictness, two prisms or lenses will only bring two colours accurately together, the law of dispersion being different throughout the whole spectrum: the rest, however, will be very nearly coincident, and consequently colour very nearly got rid of. By the combination of three prisms or lenses, three colours may be accurately combined, and the rest still more nearly than before; and so in succession.

constructing a concave reflector of glass, as being in some respects preferable to metal, but does not seem to have carried this into effect. Newton was fully aware of the defects of reflecting telescopes compared with refractors, owing to the much greater loss of light in reflection, and the greater aberration proceeding from their spherical form. These, however, he thought inconsiderable when compared with those defects of the refracting telescope, which proceeded from the unequal refrangibility of light.

Chapter V.

The Theory of Colours.

(39.) The colours exhibited by refracted and reflected light were phenomena with which philosophers had been familiar before the time of Newton. These effects were generally ascribed to the action of the reflecting or refracting body, and to the edges of opaque bodies which marked the limits of shadow, in imparting to the light qualities which it did not possess before encountering these bodies. Thus it was thought, that in passing through glass or other transparent substances formed into a prism, the solar beam is endued with a virtue by the action of the medium upon it, by which it reddens, or otherwise colours any body which it afterwards illuminates. In like manner, it was supposed, that in passing the edge of an opaque body a similar effect might be produced.

Before he proceeds to explain and establish his theory of colours, Newton shows that this hypothesis of his predecessors is untenable and inconsistent with facts. The coloured spectrum being produced by the prism in the usual way, the lights of the several colours may be successively intercepted by the interposition of an opaque body, so that any one of the colours may bound its shadow. These colours will remain unaltered by thus passing the edge of the opaque obstacle; and therefore he concludes that the light in passing the body receives no modification which affects its colour.

He further shows, that the same light, refracted in the same manner, passing the same opaque edges, will throw upon the paper which it illuminates different colours, according to the direction in which the paper is placed with respect to the rays. He argues, that if the colorific property were a virtue imparted to the ray by the edges of the aperture through which the light is admitted, or by the refracting medium through which it has passed, this could not happen, inasmuch as the colouring quality would then be independent of the position of the paper.

But perhaps the most conclusive argument against this theory is derived from the experiment explained in (32). It appears in that experiment that the confines of shadow produce no effect whatever; for the colour of the whole of the light emerging from the compound prism is always the same, that in the middle of the beam being in nowise different from that at the borders. Neither can the colour proceed in this case merely from the action of the glass, because it changes from white to yellow, orange, red, &c., that action remaining the same. Besides this, the refractions being equal, and in contrary directions, would mutually destroy each other's effects. It may further be argued, that if the light owed its colour to the action of the glass, it would not have the colour before its passage through the prism K I H; yet it was found, in that experiment, that when all the colours in the spectrum P were made to vanish, except the red, the light producing that colour on the screen P was found to produce the same colour on a screen which received it between the compound prism and K I H, before it was refracted by the latter. Thus the light which reddens the screen P would also redden it if unrefracted by the prism K I H, and the same may be said of the lights of other colours.

From these and, indeed, all other experiments which have been described, it abundantly appears, that "all homogeneous light has its proper colour answering to its degree of refrangibility, and that this colour is unalterable, either by refraction or by reflection." When pure homogeneous light of any colour illuminates a body, whatever the natural colour of that body may be, it will appear, when so illuminated, to have the colour of that light only which shines upon it. The apparent colour of the body is that of the light which it reflects; and it can reflect no light but that which shines upon it. Thus if a body whose natural colour is blue be placed in a dark chamber, and illuminated by the red light of the prismatic spectrum, it will appear red; and, on the other hand, a body whose natural colour is red, illuminated in the same way with blue light, will appear blue.

(40.) In the theory derived by Newton from the experiments which have been explained, the white light of the sun is supposed to be compounded of several component lights which have qualities different each from the others. They are all refrangible according to the same law discovered by Snellius (10); but, as we have already shown, they possess this quality in different degrees. This property is accompanied by another intimately connected with it. Any two of the component parts of solar light which differ in refrangibility, differ also in *colour;* and therefore the light of the sun is composed of various species of light of different colours, the mixture of which produces whiteness.

Newton next proceeds to determine the degrees of refrangibility corresponding to the rays of different colours. To determine this by experiment, he delineated, on a paper, the outline of the spectrum, *fig.* 33, F A P G M T, and refracting the sun's light by a prism, as

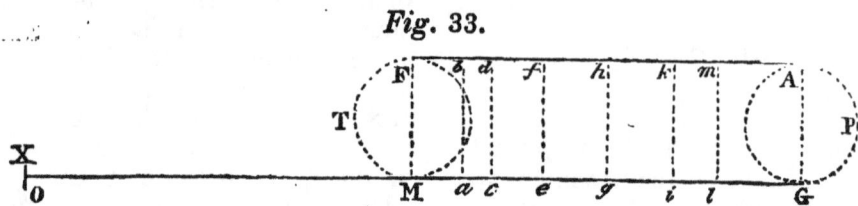

Fig. 33.

described in p. 15, he held the paper so that the spectrum might exactly fall upon the space marked out upon it. He employed an assistant, whose perception of colours he considered to be better than his own, who drew lines across the paper, marking the confines of the several colours. Thus *a b* divided the *red* from the *orange; c d*, the *orange* from the *yellow; e f*, the *yellow* from the *green; g h*, the *green* from the *blue; i k*, the *blue* from the *indigo; l m*, the *indigo* from the *violet*. This experiment was frequently repeated on the same, as well as on different papers, and the results were found to be generally accordant. Let G M be drawn to X, so that M X shall be equal to G M, the spaces measured from G to the several boundaries of the colours were found to have the following proportion:

X G, X *l*, X *i*, X *g*, X *e*, X *c*, X *a*, X M,

1, $\frac{8}{9}$, $\frac{5}{6}$, $\frac{3}{4}$, $\frac{2}{3}$, $\frac{3}{5}$, $\frac{9}{16}$, $\frac{1}{2}$.*

The spaces measured along the spectrum occupied by the lights of the several colours may be considered to measure the differences of the sines of refraction of those rays having one common sine of incidence. But the proportion of the sine of incidence to that of refraction from glass into air has been already ascertained to be 50 to 77 for the least, and 50 to 78 for the most refrangible rays; it follows, therefore, that if 50 be the common sine of incidence, the sines of refraction for the rays at the boundaries of the several colours, beginning from the *red*, will be $77\frac{1}{8}$, $77\frac{1}{5}$, $77\frac{1}{3}$, $77\frac{1}{2}$, $77\frac{2}{3}$, $77\frac{7}{9}$, 78, which may be familiarly explained thus. Let A B, *fig.* 34, be

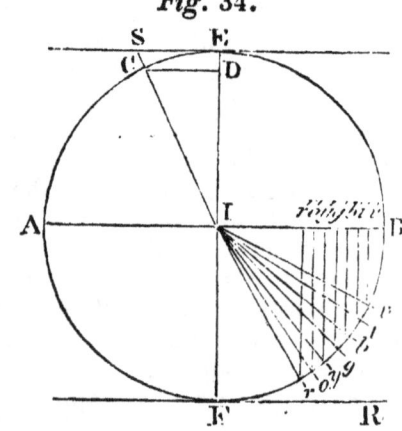

Fig. 34.

the surface of glass from which the ray S I passes at the point I into air. Let the ray S I be solar light. Round the point I as centre describe a circle, and through I draw a diameter E F perpendicular to the refracting surface A B. From the point C, where the ray meets this circle, draw C D: this is the sine of incidence. Let it be divided into 50 equal parts. Upon I B from I take a length I *r'* equal to 77 such parts, and draw *r'r* perpendicular to I B; again, take I *o'*, equal to $77\frac{1}{8}$ of those parts, and draw *o'o* perpendicular to I B. In the same manner, take I *y'*, I *g'*, I *b'*, I *i'*, I *v'*, equal to $77\frac{1}{5}$, $77\frac{1}{3}$, $77\frac{1}{2}$, $77\frac{2}{3}$, $77\frac{7}{9}$, 78 parts respectively, and draw, as before, *y'y*, *g'g*, *b'b*, *i'i*, *o'o*. From I draw I *r*, I *o*, I *y*, I *g*, I *b*, I *i*, I *v*. These lines will determine the directions of the *red*, *orange*, and the other rays corresponding

---

* The analogy observed by Newton between the proportion of these intervals and the musical intervals must be regarded as merely fanciful.

to the different degrees of refrangibility; the ray I B being after refraction resolved into I r, I o, &c.

If a ray of light be successively transmitted through several transparent media having different refracting powers, it may so happen that, on its emergence from the last of these media, it shall take a direction parallel to that which it had when incident upon the first of them. In this case the several refractions which the ray suffers in passing through the media, compensate and neutralise each other, so as to produce, on the whole, no deflection of the ray from its original course. Newton observed that, under these circumstances, whenever the incident ray was white, the refracted ray was also white. But he found, on the other hand, that if the refractive powers of the media were not thus related, and that a deflection of the incident ray from its original direction finally took place, a separation of the white ray into its component colours was produced. From these results he inferred that the same succession of media, which mutually neutralised the refractions of any one species of homogeneous light, also neutralised them on all the others, so that if one component part of the solar beam emerged parallel to its incident direction, all the others would emerge with it in the same directions, thus forming an emergent white beam. But, on the other hand, that if on the whole any deflection of the incident beam were finally produced, such deflection would be different for the different component lights; and, therefore, a decomposition or dispersion would ensue.

(41.) From these facts experimentally exhibited, Newton inferred, by mathematical reasoning, the following theorems:

I. The differences between the sines of incidence and refraction, when the ray passes from several different media into the same medium, are to one another in a given proportion.

II. The proportion of the sines of incidence and refraction for any one species of homogeneous light from one medium into another, is composed of the proportions of these sines from the first medium into any third medium, and from that third medium into the second medium.

By the first of these theorems, the refractions of all sorts of rays from any medium into air may be found, if the refraction of any one sort be known. By the latter, the refraction out of one medium into another may be found, if the refractions of both of them into a third medium be known.

"These theorems," says Newton, "being admitted into optics, there would be scope enough of handling that science voluminously after a new manner; not only by teaching those things which tend to the perfection of vision, but also by determining mathematically all kinds of phenomena of colours which could be produced by refractions. For to do this there is nothing else requisite than to find out the separations of heterogeneous rays, and their various mixtures and their proportions in every mixture. By this way of arguing, I invented almost all the phenomena described in these books, besides some others less necessary to the argument; and by the successes I met with in the trials, I dare promise, that to him who shall argue truly, and then try all things with good glasses and sufficient circumspection, the expected event will not be wanting."

(42.) Although colour is one of the qualities of homogeneous light, it is not, like the degree of refrangibility, a *test* of its purity or homogeneity. For compound lights may be produced, the tints of which will not be distinguishable from those of homogeneous light. If the red and yellow lights produced by a prism be projected on the same white paper, they will give it an orange tint, precisely the same as the pure homogeneous orange light, which lies between the red and yellow lights in the spectrum. If another white paper be illuminated by this pure orange light, it will have exactly the same appearance as to colour as the paper which receives the compound light. But if these two papers thus illuminated be viewed from a distance through a prism, it will be found that no change will take place in the appearance of the paper illuminated by the pure orange light, while that which receives the compound light will be divided into two images of its component colours, red and yellow. In the same manner any two alternate colours in the spectrum will, by their mixture, produce the intermediate tint. Thus blue and yellow will produce green, and so on.

(43.) "Whiteness, and all grey colours between white and black, are formed by mixtures of all the colours; and the whiteness of the sun's light is compounded of all the prismatic colours mixed in a due proportion." The experiments by which Newton verified and established this important proposition,

D

are characterised with such singular elegance and ingenuity, that we shall not apologise for giving the particulars of them at some length.

The prismatic spectrum being projected on a screen, a white paper was held before it, in such a manner as not to intercept the rays from the prism, and so that the paper should be as nearly as possible equally distant from all the colours. Under these circumstances, the paper appeared *white*. The colours which produced this white were evidently the several colours of the spectrum reflected from the screen upon the paper, and consequently reflected in the same proportions as they hold in the spectrum itself; from whence we may infer that the mixture of these colours produces white. If any of the colours of the spectrum be intercepted, the paper will appear to be illuminated with that colour which would be produced by the mixture of those which remain; a circumstance which further confirms the inference, that the white produced, when no light is intercepted, is the consequence of the mixture of all the colours.

Let the spectrum *fig.* 35, be projected upon a lens M N, which will

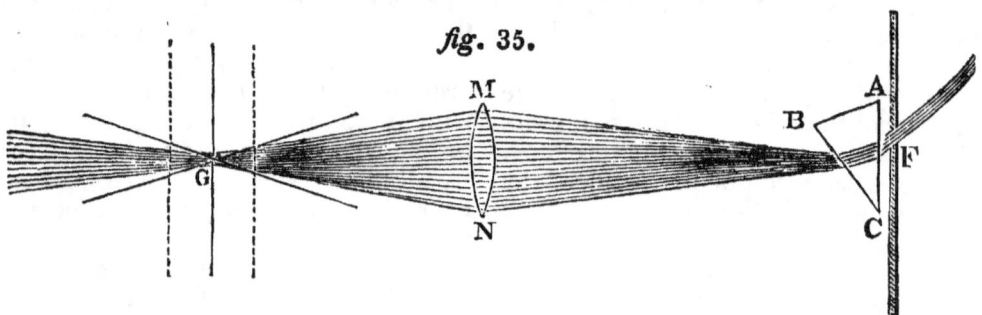

fig. 35.

cause the coloured light to converge to its focus G, and there to fall on white paper. If the paper thus illuminated be moved to and from the lens, it will be found that when near the lens the paper will be intensely coloured. As its distance from the lens is increased, the colours will seem to approach each other, and be collected into a smaller space, until at last, at the focus G, they will be collected and perfectly mixed together: here the illuminated spot on the paper will be white. By removing the paper to a greater distance from the lens, the rays which before converged, having crossed each other at the focus G, will now diverge. The colours also will be inverted, those rays which were above in the former case being now below, and *vice versâ*.

Let the paper be now placed at the focus, so as to be illuminated with white light free from colour. We are to prove that this whiteness arises from the admixture of all the coloured lights of the spectrum in their due proportions. Let all the colours except the *red* be intercepted by an opaque screen, placed between the prism and the lens. The spot on the paper will now appear *red*. By raising the screen let the orange be admitted with the red through the lens. The spot on the paper will now take a tint which would be produced by a mixture of red and orange. Again, let the yellow light be admitted, and a similar result will be obtained, the colour being one which would be produced by the mixture of red, orange, and yellow. In a word, let any number of the prismatic colours be intercepted between the lens and the prism, and the colour on the paper will be that due to the mixture of those colours which are not intercepted. From which we infer that if no colour be intercepted, the white light on the paper must arise from the mixture of all the colours.

Let X Y, *fig.* 36, be an instrument formed like a comb, with teeth about an inch and a half broad, at intervals of about two inches asunder. By interposing successively the teeth of this instrument between the prism and the lens, a part of the colours was intercepted, while the rest went through between the teeth. The teeth of this instrument being passed before the lens, all the colours are successively thrown upon the paper. Now, when this motion is rapid, so that the colours on the paper succeed each other in very quick succession, the eye loses all sense of colour, and the paper appears white. Yet it is certain that the paper is not at any instant white. In this case the perception of whiteness is produced by the continuance of the impression which each colour makes upon the sense of sight, until all the other colours have

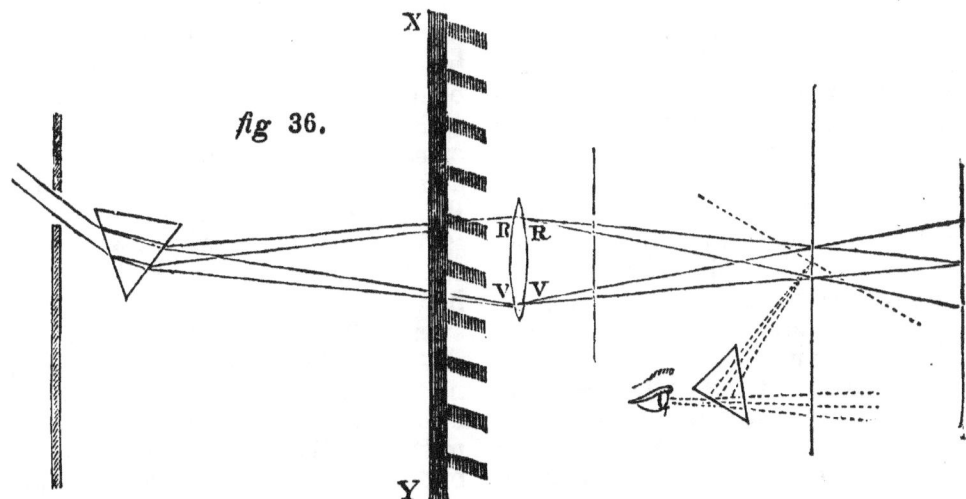

fig 36.

likewise affected the organ. The effect is thus compounded of the influences of the several colours upon the eye, as much as if they all affected it at the same moment.

(44.) In this explication of the phenomenon just described, we assume the fact, that when a visible object affects the eye, it continues to be perceived after it has ceased to be present. Thus, if a light be suddenly extinguished, the light itself and all the objects which it rendered visible continue to be seen for a certain short space of time after the extinction. This curious fact admits of very simple proof. If a burning coal or lighted stick be moved rapidly in a circle, it will be seen in every part of the circle at once, so as to have the appearance of a ring of fire; which proves that the impression which the light in one part of the circle makes upon the eye, continues until it returns again to the same part of the circle, to make another impression.

The colours of the spectrum may be recomposed, so as to form white light, by a second prism, instead of the lens mentioned in the last experiment. Let RV, *fig*. 37, be the spectrum formed by the prism A B C, and let this be viewed through another prism *a b c*, placed in such a manner that the rays which con-

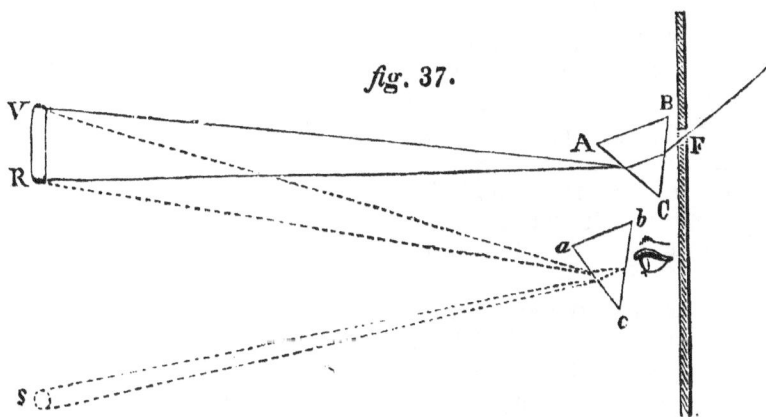

fig. 37.

verge from RV will be received as if they emerged from a circular image of the sun at *s*. In this case the rays enter the eye exactly as they would if it were placed before the aperture F, and presented towards it. The colours proceeding from RV are thus mixed on entering the eye, and appear white.

If any of the colours of the spectrum RV be removed by intercepting a part of the light between RV and the prism A B C, the colour which will be perceived through the prism *a b c*, will be that which would be formed by the mixture of the remaining colours. But if the comb mentioned in the last experiment be quickly moved between RV and A B C, so as to throw the several colours on the screen in rapid succession, the eye will again perceive white, for the reason already explained.

The same result was obtained by various other means, such as projecting several spectra produced by different prisms, on the same part of the same paper, by moving several spectra rapidly up and down, &c. &c. In all these cases the colours submitted to experiment were, however, *prismatic*. To establish his theory more completely, Newton now proceeds to inquire whether the colours of natural bodies were endued with qualities similar in all respects to those of prismatic light. To accomplish this, having procured powders of colours similar to those of the spectrum, he mixed them together as nearly as possible in the proportion which they were found to hold in the spectrum. He found that the mixture was not a pure white, such as that produced by the composition of the prismatic colours, but was a dim, greyish white; such, in fact, as would be produced by mixing a small quantity of black with a pure brilliant white.

(45.) It was not difficult to account for this circumstance, which Newton appears even to have foreseen. The colours of natural bodies arise from a quality, in virtue of which they reflect one component part of the solar beam more copiously than the others, and therefore affect the sense of sight with the colour so reflected. Thus a body which we call *red*, is one which reflects a very large portion of the red light of the solar beam, and absorbs nearly the whole of the other six colours. But it is found that no body reflects the light of its proper colour so copiously as a white body would reflect the same light. If a white and a red object be placed beside each other in a dark room, and both be illuminated with red homogeneous light, by means of a prism, the white object will be more intensely red than the red one.

(46.) Since then coloured bodies do not any of them reflect *all* the light of their proper colour, we are not to expect by their mixture to obtain a clear white, but rather such an obscure white as would result from imperfect illumination. That the colour produced by mixing powders in the manner already mentioned is exactly of this kind, Newton proved by the following ingenious experiment.

He placed the mixture of powders on the floor of the chamber, and beside it a piece of white paper. The room being darkened, a beam of light was admitted, so as to illuminate intensely the powder, the white paper remaining near it, but in the shade. Viewing them from a distance, he could perceive no difference, both appearing to have exactly the same whiteness. Another person happened to enter the room during the experiment, and Newton, without informing him of the previous arrangement, asked him, "Which of the two whites were the better, and in what they differed?" After he had deliberately viewed them, he answered, "That both were good whites, that he could not say which was better, nor wherein they differed." Thus it was evident that the colour produced by the mixture of the powders was a true white, but only deficient in the *degree* of whiteness; just as twilight is as true a light as broad sunshine, differing from it only in quantity.

(47.) Having established the important fact, that *white* must result from the mixture of all the colours of the spectrum in the proper proportions, Newton proceeds to the consideration of the more general question as to the colour which would result from the composition of any given colours in any assigned proportion. For this problem he gives the following very ingenious solution.

With the centre O, *fig.* 38, and a radius O D, describe a circle A D F, and let the circumference of this circle be divided into 447 equal parts. Take A B,

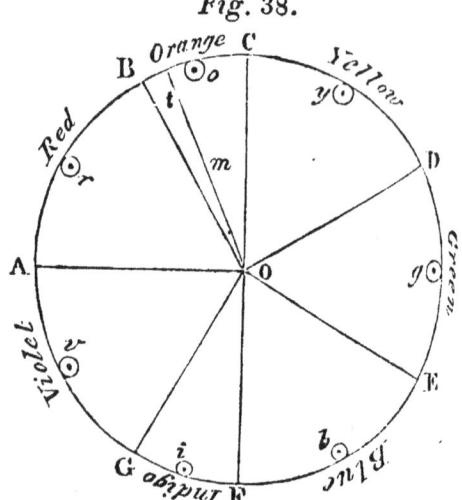

Fig. 38.

consisting of 80 parts, B C of 45, C D of 72, D E of 80, E F of 45, F G of 45, and the remaining part, G A, will consequently consist of 80 parts. Let the first part A B represent a *red* colour; the second B C an *orange*; the third C D a *yellow*, and so on in the order of the spectrum. Let it be conceived that these are all the colours of uncompounded light gradually passing one into another as they appear in the spectrum, so that, in effect, the circumference of the circle will exhibit, as it were, a *round prismatic spectrum*. By the principles of mechanics, let the centres of gravity of the arcs A B, B C, &c. be respectively found, and let these points be r, o, y, g, b, i, and v. Now, suppose that it be required to determine the tint which would result from the mixture of red, green, and blue, in certain given proportions. Let circles be described round the points r, g, and b, the magnitudes of which are to be made proportional to the quantities of the three colours in the proposed mixture. Let the common centre of gravity of these circles be found, and let it be m; and from the centre O through m draw Om, to meet the circle at t. The colour at the point t will be the tint sought, and the line Om will represent "its fullness, or intensity, that is, its distance from whiteness." Thus, if t should fall exactly in the middle of any of the arcs, A B, B C, &c. the tint will be the purest of the corresponding colour; but if it be distant from the middle point, it will partake of the colour which occupies the next arc, towards which it lies. Again, if m fall on the centre O, the colour will be, as it were, infinitely diluted, and will be a perfect white; but, on the other hand, the nearer m is to the circumference, the more intense and florid the tint will be.

Newton conceived this method to be sufficiently accurate for practice, although not mathematically true. This is a subject, however, in which much improvement has been introduced in later times. It would not be to our purpose here to enter upon it, our design being merely to present to the reader in a popular form a sketch of the labours of Newton in the *science of light*. Those who desire a short account of the modern discoveries, will find one in the admirable article on LIGHT, by Mr. Herschel, in the Encyclopædia Metropolitana.

In applying his theory of light to explain the phenomena of the colours of natural bodies, Newton assumes, "that every body reflects the rays of its own colour more copiously than the rest, and derives its colour from their excess, or predominance, in the reflected light." When a beam of solar light falls upon a violet, a decomposition immediately ensues. The red rays, and those of the less refrangible character, are either transmitted through the body, or absorbed and stifled; those of the bluish, or violet hue, and of the more refrangible species, are copiously reflected, and produce in the spectator the effect which in ordinary language is denominated the violet colour of the object.

Several ingenious experiments support this reasoning. A natural object, whatever be its colour, will, if placed in homogeneous light, take for the time the colour of that light, proving thereby its capability of reflecting, *in some degree*, lights of all colours. But when it is placed in homogeneous light of its own colour, it will appear much more resplendent than in light of any other colour. Hence we infer that it possesses a capability of reflecting light of its own colour more abundantly than light of any other colour. Thus cinnabar, a red substance, placed in homogeneous red light, exhibits a splendid red; let it, however, be illuminated with green or blue light, and it will assume these colours, but with great faintness.

The colours of transparent liquors vary with their thickness. If a red liquor be poured into a glass of conical or tapering shape, and held between the light and the eye, it will appear of a pale dilute yellow at the narrowest part of the glass; a little higher, where the glass is wider, it becomes orange; higher still it becomes red; and, finally, in the widest part, exhibits a deep dark red. We must, therefore, infer that a small quantity, or thickness of the liquor, intercepts a portion of the violet and indigo rays, so that the remaining rays which it transmits form a pale yellow. A greater quantity of the liquor, besides stopping the violet and indigo, also arrests the blue rays, and a part of the green, transmitting the other component parts of light, the mixture of which produces an orange. A still greater quantity of the fluid will intercept all the green, and a great part of the yellow, so that the transmitted light approaches to a red, becoming a deep dark red, when the quantity of the fluid is so great as to absorb the whole of the orange light.

We have in this description assumed several distinct effects, but the changes of colour are not sudden, but take place by an imperceptible gradation, an obvious consequence of the tapering form of the glass. If the glass were formed of a number of cylinders rising one above another, the diameter of each exceeding that below it by a certain magnitude, the changes of colour would be sudden and distinct; and the liquid in each cylinder would present, in the vertical direction, an uniform colour.

(48.) Connected with the power of transparent liquids to reflect and transmit the different component parts of solar light, Newton mentions two very remarkable facts noticed by Halley and Hooke, but which these eminent philosophers were unable to explain. Halley, having descended in a diving bell to the depth of several fathoms in the sea, observed, upon holding his hand in the sun's light, which penetrated the water, and shone into the bell through a small glass window in the top, that the light upon his hand was *red*. Whereupon he examined the lower part of his hand illuminated by light reflected from the water below, and found it *green*. This circumstance is thus accounted for by Newton. The sea-water reflects back the violet and blue rays most easily, and transmits most copiously the red. In the sun's light transmitted to considerable depths, the red rays therefore predominating, objects illuminated by them assume a red hue. At depths to which the violet rays cannot penetrate, the reflection of the blue, green, and yellow light separated from the red, which is transmitted, must compound a green.

Two liquids may be obtained, one of which transmits the rays of the red character, and the other those of the blue, the former intercepting the bluish light, and the latter the red. If both liquids be placed between a spectator and the light, they will be found perfectly opaque, although either alone is transparent. This is evident, since all the rays which can be transmitted by either are intercepted by the other. Hooke casually, and without anticipating or expecting the result, actually tried this experiment. He filled two hollow glass wedges, one with a red, and the other with a blue liquor. On placing the wedges together, and looking through them at the light, he found them absolutely opaque.

(49.) We have explained, according to the Newtonian theory, the most striking phenomena of coloured lights produced by prisms. The explication of others will be found in every elementary treatise on optics. One very singular prismatic phenomenon, however, still remains to be noticed, and is entitled to attention, as well for the strong confirmation of Newton's theory which it furnishes, as from the ingenious manner in which that theory is shown to account for it.

Let HKG, *fig.* 39, be a prism placed before an open window, with its base HEIG

Fig. 39.

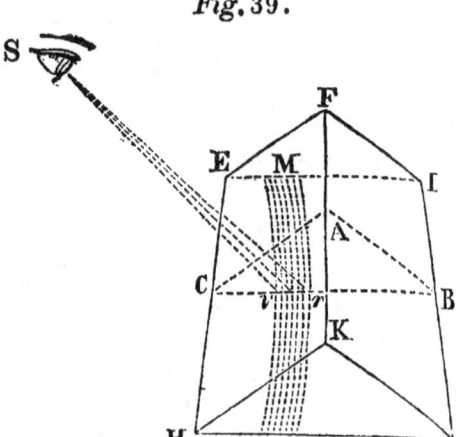

horizontal, the face F K G I presented to the light of the clouds, and let the base be viewed through the face F K H E by an eye at S. The base H E I G will now be observed to be separated into two parts by a beautiful iridescent arch, formed of colours of violet and bluish tints. This arch is concave towards the eye, and that part of the base which is towards the edge I G, or above the arch, exhibits a most vivid reflection of the firmament, not yielding in splendour to the direct view of the heavens. On the other hand, the lower division of the base next the edge E H, appears nearly dark, reflecting but a very small portion of the light incident upon it. The arch next this sombre space is fringed with a violet colour, which is gradually tinted off into a vivid blue towards the convex edge, which bounds the bright part of the base.

To account for this curious phenomenon, it must be remembered that the different parts of solar light are differently reflexible; also, that when rays of light are incident on the base of a prism, having previously passed through its side, there are certain angles of obliquity at which it will be impossible for the rays to pass through the base, and they will then be reflected. The limit of obliquity at which they will cease to penetrate the base, and will be reflected, depends on their degree of refrangibility. The most refrangible, and consequently the most reflexible rays, are the violet, next to these the indigo, then the blue, and so on through the other colours of the spectrum, the red being least reflexible. Let H E I G be the base of the prism. From the eye, let lines be supposed to be drawn to the base, inclined to it at that angle which limits the reflexion of the violet light. These lines being all equally inclined to the base, must meet it at points which lie in the arc of a circle. Let this arch be V V', fig. 40. Again, let lines be drawn at the

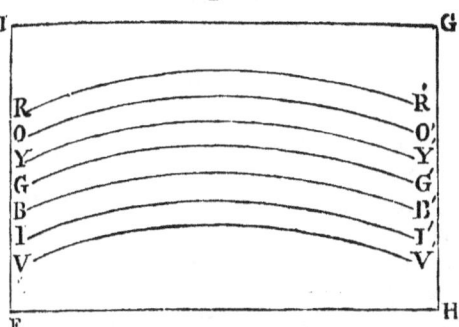

Fig. 40.

limiting angle of the indigo rays. This angle being less than that for the violet, the corresponding arc I I' will be beyond V V'. In the same manner the limiting arcs B B', G G', Y Y', O O', R R', corresponding to the other prismatic lights, *blue, green*, &c. may be drawn.

It follows then, that all the violet rays in the solar light will be reflected from the part of the base of the prism whose boundary is V V' G I; all the indigo from I I' G I; all the blue from B B' G I; all the green from G G' G I; all the yellow from Y Y' G I; all the orange from O O' G I, and all the red from R R' G I. Hence it appears that the space between the arcs, V V' and I I', is illuminated with a pure violet light only; that between I I' and B B' is illuminated by both violet and indigo mixed; between B B' and G G' there is a mixture of violet, indigo, and blue; between G G' and Y Y' is a mixture of the former colours, with the addition of green; from Y Y' to O O', yellow is added to the compound; the next arched band introduces orange, and the last the red. Now the last mixture constitutes a pure white. The former also a white, but one which, being deprived of the pure red rays, takes a faint tint approaching a bluish colour, but which is not distinguishable from a perfect white. In the next space the red and orange being removed, the mixture produces a greenish blue, which rapidly deepens, and becomes a strong blue, when the yellow rays are removed. The arc towards its inner termination is a pure violet.

Newton next applies his theory to explain the phenomena of rainbows. As this subject has been already fully discussed in our treatises on Optics according to the same principles, and in exactly the same manner as it is treated by Newton, it is not necessary to repeat it here.

CHAPTER VI.

On the phenomena exhibited by thin transparent plates—the theory of the fits of easy reflexion and transmission deduced from these phenomena.

(50.) THE first book of Newton's Optics contains the discussions which have been detailed in the last four chapters. In these investigations a ray of light upon its impact on the surface of any medium is considered to undergo one of two effects, viz. either to pass into the medium on which it impinges in a determinate direction, in which direction it is supposed to persevere through the entire medium; or to be reflected back from the surface into the medium from whence it came, following also and persevering in a rectilinear course. We are now about to accompany this great scrutineer of nature through a more subtle analysis of the process to which a beam of light is submitted when it encounters the surface which separates two media of different densities.

If it were possible to divide the medium which a ray of light penetrates into a series of plates, the thickness of which should be minute to an extreme degree, and to examine the state of the ray during its transmission through each of them, we should attain the end which we desire. Although it would perhaps be difficult to effect this very minute subdivision by direct mechanical means, yet numerous expedients present themselves, and those too of a character sufficiently familiar, by which the phenomena in question may be brought under examination. Indeed, these phenomena were long the subjects of daily observation, and may almost be said to have been the sport and toy of children; but, like many other natural effects, not less wonderful, which are continually passing under our eyes, they had failed to excite the attention or stimulate the curiosity of those who, by faculties and acquirements, were qualified to behold in them manifestations of the laws and principles on which the works of nature are constructed.

(51.) If a small quantity of soap be mixed with water, the latter acquires a tenacious or glutinous quality, in virtue of which it may be blown into bubbles, or it may be thrown into that state by mere agitation. Every one is familiar with the various colours which these bubbles reflect. Similar appearances are exhibited by glass when blown into bubbles of sufficient tenuity. Since these effects are not produced when the bounding surfaces of the medium are more distant from one another, we are compelled to suppose that when the light first enters the transparent medium, it is put into some state in which it does not continue during its entire course through the medium. This inference is as singular and important as it is inevitable. Suppose that the two surfaces of water impregnated with soap were at a distance of one inch asunder—a ray of light entering the first surface perpendicularly, would penetrate the water, and passing through the second surface, would issue from the water at the other side, preserving its original direction. Now, suppose that the second surface of the water, instead of intercepting the course of the ray at the distance of an inch from the first surface, meets it at a distance from that surface, equal to the thickness of a certain part of the soap-bubble, to which we have alluded—the ray will no longer be allowed to pass out in its original state at the second surface. On the contrary, if it be white solar light, that part of it which has a certain colour, say red, will be reflected back in the direction from which it came, while the remainder only of the ray which, combined with red, would produce white, will be transmitted. It therefore follows that, in this instance, after the ray has penetrated the water through a space equal to the supposed thickness of the bubble, that portion of it which is red is put into such a state, that were it to encounter the second surface, it could not penetrate it, and would be reflected. This state, however, does not continue; for when the white ray is allowed to proceed further into the water before it is intercepted by the second surface, it will be brought into a state in which it will penetrate that surface, and be transmitted into the ambient medium. Such is an example of the class of facts which form the basis of the experiments and investigations which we are now about to explain.

(52.) The property which we have instanced in water and glass is common to all transparent media. The evanescent and fluctuating nature of a water-bubble renders it an inconvenient object of experimental inquiry. Glass is better, but still is difficult to procure, and to retain in the highly attenuated state which is necessary to manifest the desired effects. By the following contrivance, Newton rendered *air*, though at the first view an unpromising agent, available for the purposes of deliberate and close experimental observation.

He procured a double convex lens, the object-glass of a fifty foot telescope, and consequently having a degree of convexity so small as to be scarcely perceptible. On this he placed the plane surface of another lens, so that the two surfaces were in absolute contact at the centre, the distance between them increasing with the increased distance from that centre. A lens of air was thus inclosed between two glass lenses. This air lens was plane on one side and concave on the other, losing all thickness at the centre at which may be conceived an infinitely small space, filled by the point of contact of the glass lenses. Taking this point of contact as a centre, let us suppose a number of concentric circles to be traced on the lenses as represented in *fig.* 41. Let the smallest circle be called 1, the next 2, the next 3, and so on. It is plain that the thickness of the air under the circle 1, is less than under the circle 2. In like manner the thickness under the circle 2 is less than under the circle 3, and so on. A section of the lenses exhibiting the thickness of the air between the lenses under the several circles 1, 2, 3, &c. is represented in *fig.* 42.

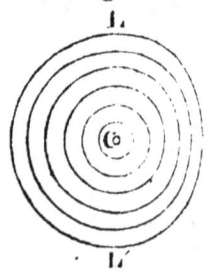

Fig. 41.

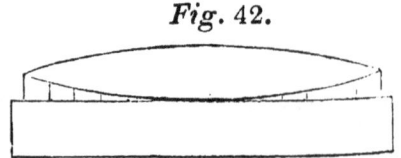

Fig. 42.

Upon exposing these lenses to a beam of light, a very minute black spot was observed at the centre. Immediately around this circular spot was a ring of blue colour, which gradually emerged from the black, so as to assume the perfect blue tint at some distance from the black spot. This blue ring was surrounded with a white one, into which it in like manner gradually melted, assuming tints more and more dilute, until it became absolutely white. This white ring was again bordered by a yellow one, which in its turn was tinted off in a red ring.

In this series of coloured circles the *blue* of the first circle was very faint; the *white* of the second was brilliant. The gradual tints assumed by the yellow of the third ring in passing into the red of the fourth, produced between them an *orange* ring.

A second series of rings succeeded, the first of which, surrounding the red ring of the last series, was *violet*, after which appeared in regular succession four other rings of *blue, green, yellow* and *red*. In this series the green was yellowish, the yellow brilliant, and the red partaking of a crimson hue.

After this came a third series. The first ring in this series surrounding the red of the last was purple, which was regularly succeeded by four rings of *blue, green, yellow* and *red*. Of these the green was brisk and copious, being a rich grass green, and the yellow was particularly splendid; but the red had a more faded appearance, and partook more of the pink and crimson, than the vermilion.

After these succeeded a fourth series, consisting of two colours, green and red. The green, in passing into the red, exhibited a yellowish *pink* hue. Then succeeded three other series, each consisting of two rings; the inner ones being various shades of green, and the outer ones various shades of red; each of the colours become more and more dilute, as the diameters of the rings increased.

(53.) Due consideration of these phenomena suggested some very important conclusions. Of the light which penetrated the glass within the central black circle none was reflected, for in that case the circle would take the colour of the reflected light. The incident light was, therefore, in this case, either stifled and absorbed by the glass, or was transmitted. To ascertain this, the eye was placed behind the lenses, so as to receive the transmitted light. The central spot now appeared white, proving that all the light incident on the glass was here transmitted. Again, of the light incident upon the first ring of the first series, the rays composing a bluish colour alone were reflected. The remaining rays were transmitted, as appeared by viewing the lenses on the other side; the colour of the first ring being that which was complemental to its reflected colour, or that which combined with the reflected colour would produce white. In the same way, each ring of each series was found to transmit the colour complemental to that which it reflected, which was proved by viewing the light through the lenses.

These phenomena were attended with many circumstances, which rendered it probable that some connexion subsisted between the colours of the reflected and transmitted light, and the thickness of the air-lens, at the place where these colours were produced. The same colour was observed to be arranged in a circle round the centre of the lens. It was evident, that in all parts of such a circle the thickness of the air-lens was the same. Again, in passing from one concentric circle to another, the tint was observed to undergo a change. In different concentric circles the thickness of the air-lens was different. Here, then, were two important steps towards the discovery of a connexion between the colour of the light, and the thickness of the air, which reflected or transmitted it.

By pressing the glass lenses together, so as to force them into closer contact, the diameter of each circle, at which the air-lens had a given thickness, would obviously be increased. If it were true, that the colour of the reflected light depended on the thickness of the air at the points of reflexion, it would follow, that upon pressing the glass lenses together, each coloured circle would be enlarged. It was accordingly found, that upon applying such *pressure*, the central spot was increased, and each coloured circle expanded its dimensions, and retreated from the centre. These indications were further confirmed, by pressing the lenses more closely at one side of the centre than at the other, the colours still retreating from the points of closest contact.

(54.) Aware of the heterogeneous nature of solar light by previous investigations, Newton considered it probable that these coloured rings were not the effects of one simple cause, or of a single action of the transparent medium on the solar ray, but conjectured that it might rather be the result of the combined actions on all or several of the component parts of light. To simplify the phenomena, and thereby facilitate the analysis, he determined to expose the lenses successively to the different species of homogeneous light, and to observe and carefully note the separate effects of each. He concluded, that these effects being severally known, there could be no difficulty in combining them, so as to account for the phenomena produced by compound solar light.

With this view, he decomposed a sunbeam, by means of a prism, and casting successively on the lenses the several coloured lights in the spectrum, he observed and carefully noted the phenomena. In each case the rings appeared, and even in greater numbers, than in the case of the compound solar light. They, however, no longer exhibited any variety of colour, the central spot being now surrounded by rings of the same colour as the light cast upon the lenses, separated by dark rings, in which, like the central spot, all light seemed to be transmitted, and none reflected. Upon looking through the lenses towards the light, the intermediate rings just mentioned, as well as the central spot, appeared of the colour of the prismatic light, to which the lenses were exposed; and, on the other hand, those rings which by reflected light appeared coloured, were now dark, no light being transmitted.

Let S S, *fig*. 43, be a section of the air-lens, and suppose a beam of homo-

Fig. 43.

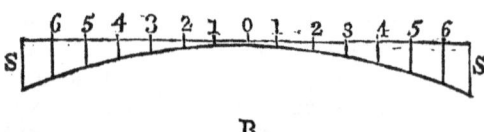

geneous red light projected on it from the direction A, and perpendicular to its surface. The centre of the lens being *o*, let 1 be the place of the first ring of red light, as viewed from A. At 2 will be a dark ring, at 3 a second ring of red light, at 4 a dark ring, and so on, the central spot *o* being dark. Now, let the lens be viewed from B, so as to receive the rays transmitted through it. The central spot *o* will appear red, the first ring 1, which before was red, will be dark, the ring 2 will be red, 3 dark, and so on; all the rings which were dark, when viewed from A, being red when viewed from B, and *vice versâ*.

Upon exposing the lenses to orange, yellow, and the other species of homogeneous light, similar effects were observable; the bright rings always taking the colour of the light incident on the lenses, and being separated by dark rings, which being viewed from B appeared bright,

the bright ones, as in the case of the red light, appearing dark. One difference, however, was remarkable, viz. that the rings formed by the less refrangible rays were larger than those formed by the more refrangible. Thus the first red ring was larger than the first orange one and this larger than the first yellow ring, and so on, the first violet ring being least.

(55.) The existence of a connexion between the colour of the reflected and transmitted light, and the thickness of the air-lens, being now manifest, Newton applied his attention to measure this thickness at the places of the several dark and bright rings. The extreme minuteness of the magnitude to be ascertained rendered the application of direct measures impracticable. The first principles of elementary geometry, however, furnished a method of effecting the measurement with the greatest accuracy.

* Let O T, *fig*. 44, be the plane side of

Fig. 44.

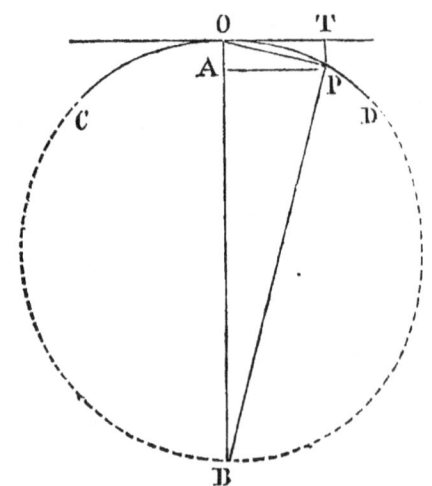

the air-lens, and C D the concave side, and let the circle, of which C D is an arc, be completed. Let O B be its diameter. By the principles of optics, the length of O B may be deduced, from observing the focus of the convex glass lens used in the experiments, provided the refracting power of the glass be known. Let it be required to ascertain the thickness T P of the air-lens at T. Draw the line P O, and from P draw P A parallel to T O. By actually measuring the diameter of the ring at the distance T, the line T O, or P A, will be determined; and from the extreme minuteness of T P, the line P A may be considered as practically equal to P O. The right angled triangles O P B, and O A P, are similar; and,

---

* This investigation may be omitted by those who are not familiar with the elements of geometry.

therefore, O P bears the same proportion to O B, as O A, or T P, bears to O P. Now, since the magnitudes of O P, and O B, are known, we know how many times O B is greater than O P. Then O P will be the same number of times greater than O A, or T P. Thus, if O B were 182 inches, and O P 8-79ths of an inch, the thickness T P is found by common arithmetic to be about $\frac{100}{1774784}$th part of an inch.

Calculating in this manner, Newton found a very singular analogy to subsist between the thicknesses at which the bright and dark rings of each colour were produced. Let the thickness at which the first bright ring of any homogeneous colour is produced, be called 1; the thickness at the next bright ring will be 3; the next 5; the next 7; and so on; the thicknesses of the successive bright rings being represented by the odd integers. Again, the thickness of the air at the dark ring, which immediately succeeded the first bright ring, was found to be twice its thickness at the first bright ring; and therefore the central spot being considered as the first dark ring, the second dark ring will be at the thickness 2. The third dark ring was found to be at the thickness 4; the fourth at 6, and so on: the thicknesses of the air at the several dark rings being represented by the even integers.

The proportion which we have now explained was found to prevail among the rings, whatever might be the colour of the light projected on the lens; but the absolute magnitudes of the rings was, as we have stated, different in each kind of light. This will, perhaps, be better understood by example. Suppose an inch divided into 180,000 equal parts, and let one of those parts be the thickness at which the first ring of a certain colour, say green, appears, homogeneous green light being projected on the lens. At a thickness equal to two of these parts will be a dark ring. At a thickness equal to three of these parts will appear the second bright green ring, and so on alternately.

The rings of the other colours will succeed each other in a similar manner, with this difference, that the thickness at which the first ring appears will be less for the more refrangible rays, i. e. those of a bluish tint, and greater for the less refrangible rays, which take the yellow or red hues, and that the intervals between the rings will also be less for the former rays than for the latter. Hence we may easily perceive how the succession of coloured rings is produced when compound solar light is projected on the lens. In this case each component part of the light forms its own set of rings, and the rings of one colour intermixing with those of another, form the several series of coloured rings already described.

(56.) All that has been observed respecting the rings produced by the light reflected from the lens will apply, with the requisite modifications, to the rings produced by the light transmitted through it. These latter, however, are much less vivid than the reflected rings.

Before we proceed further in our account of these phenomena, it may be useful, in impressing them on the memory of the reader, to give some account of the manner in which Newton explained them. He considers that every ray of light, in its passage through the surface which separates two media of different densities, is put into a certain transient constitution or state, which, in the progress of the ray, returns at equal intervals, and disposes the ray at every return to be easily transmitted through the next refracting surface, and between the returns, to be easily reflected by it. Let A B (*fig.* 45) be a ray of pure homogeneous light falling perpendicularly on a refracting surface, S S. Let us suppose that the medium through which

Fig. 45.

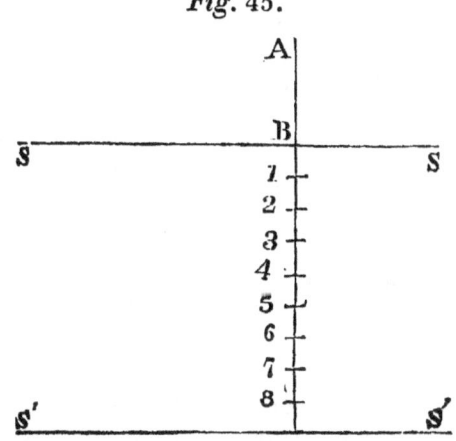

A B has passed is glass, and that the medium included between the surfaces S S and S' S' is air. Take B 1 in the direction of A B, and equal to the thickness of the air between the lenses at which the first ring of the homogeneous light, now supposed to fall on S S, appeared. From 1 take the intervals 2, 3, 4, &c. equal to B 1. The action of the surface, S S, upon the ray, is *supposed* to be such as to put it in a state in which it would be easily transmitted by another similar refracting surface, such as S′ S′, if that surface received the ray immediately after its passage through S S. But this state of easy transmission does not continue. When the light has arrived at 1 it is in a state of easy reflection, so that if it were intercepted at 1 by such a surface as S′ S′, it would be reflected back in the direction 1 B A. After passing the division 1, the state of the ray is again changed, and when it has arrived at the division 2, it is again in a state of easy transmission, as at B. If the surface, S′ S′, therefore, met the ray at 2, the ray would pass freely through it in the direction 3, 4, &c. In passing from 2 to 3 the ray again changes its state, and is found at 3 to be in the same disposition to be reflected as it was at 1; and such reflection would, in fact, take place if the surface, S′ S′, intercepted the ray at 3. In this manner the ray passes alternately into states of easy transmission and reflection, at the successive points, 4, 5, 6, &c.

(57.) These alternate states of the ray Newton calls *fits*, the light being in *fits of easy reflection* at the points 1, 3, 5, &c.; and in *fits of easy transmission* at the points 2, 4, 6, &c. The spaces B 2, 24, &c., or 13, 35, &c., he calls the *interval of the fits*. Although these phrases imply a theory or hypothesis, yet Newton intends them merely as names for *effects* which are known to exist, and distinctly disclaims the adoption of any hypothesis, endeavouring in every case to render his inferences independent of everything except the result of experiment or observation.

In describing the phenomena of physical science it is extremely difficult, if not impossible, to avoid expressions and terms which imply a theory or a supposed cause for effects. Every writer, but more especially he who promulgates new facts, should be cautious to remind the student that the *language of causation*, the use of which in physics is inevitable, is nothing more than a method of expressing the classification of effects; and that, when we are said to "discover the cause" of any appearance, nothing more is to be understood than that we have found a class of phenomena to which it belongs and must be referred. There is no philosopher who seems more conscious of the necessity of this than Newton; and, accordingly, in the introduction of the phraseology to which we have just alluded, he warns his reader that he does not pretend to affirm "what kind of action this (the fits) is; whether it consists in a circulating or a vibrating motion of the ray, or of the medium, or of something else. Those that are averse to assenting to any new discoveries but such as they can explain by an hypothesis, may for the present suppose that, as stones, by falling upon water, put the water into an undulating motion, and all bodies, by percussion, excite vibrations in the air; so the rays of light, by impinging on any refracting or reflecting surface, excite vibrations in the refracting or reflecting medium or substance, and by exciting them agitate the solid parts of the refracting or reflecting body, and by agitating them cause them to grow warm or hot; that the vibrations thus excited are propagated in the refracting or reflecting medium or substance, much after the manner that vibrations are propagated in the air for causing sound, and move faster than the rays, so as to overtake them; and that when any ray is in that part of the vibration which conspires with its motion, it easily breaks through a refracting surface; but when it is in the contrary part of the vibration, which impedes its motion, it is easily reflected; and by consequence, that every ray is successively disposed to be easily reflected or easily transmitted, by every vibration which overtakes it. *But, whether this hypothesis be true or false, I do not here consider.* I content myself with the bare discovery that rays of light *are*, by some cause or other, alternately disposed to be reflected or refracted for many vicissitudes."

(58.) By the observation of air between glass lenses, Newton ascertained the *fact* that, after passing through a certain thickness of air, a ray would be reflected or transmitted, according to the degree of thickness of the air and the species of the light. By actual admeasurement he ascertained the least thickness at which each species of homogeneous light would be reflected, a magnitude which will easily be perceived to be equal to half the *interval of the fits*. We have already observed that this interval is different in different kinds of light, being greater for the less refrangible rays than for the more refrangible. The following Table exhibits the interval for lights of the different degrees of refrangibility. If an inch be supposed to be divided into ten millions of equal parts, the number of these parts, in the interval for each ray, is expressed in the second column.

	Ten millionths of an inch.	Difference.
Extreme rays	133	0
Red rays	128	5
Intermediate	123	5
Orange rays	120	3
Intermediate	$117\frac{1}{2}$	$2\frac{1}{2}$
Yellow rays	$113\frac{1}{2}$	4
Intermediate	$109\frac{1}{2}$	4
Green rays	$105\frac{1}{2}$	4
Intermediate	$101\frac{1}{2}$	4
Blue rays	98	$3\frac{1}{2}$
Intermediate	$94\frac{1}{2}$	$3\frac{1}{2}$
Indigo rays	$92\frac{1}{2}$	2
Intermediate	$90\frac{1}{2}$	2
Violet	87	$3\frac{1}{2}$
Extreme rays	$83\frac{1}{2}$	$3\frac{1}{2}$

That the magnitudes, which appear in the third column of this Table, should be subjects of accurate computation, founded on measurements performed by the hand of man, must, we conceive, be matter of the greatest wonder and admiration. An inch being divided into five million of equal parts, a distance equal to one of these parts is ascertained by positive measurement, in the estimation of the intervals of the fits of indigo rays and those intermediate between them and the violet! Magnitudes of such minuteness far exceed even the powers of imagination. We have, perhaps, a distinct idea of the hundredth part of an inch, by imagining the tenth of an inch divided into ten equal parts. But when we are required to conceive one of these ten parts divided into fifty thousand equal parts, imagination altogether fails, and we cease to attach to the name of such a magnitude any positive conception. Nevertheless, this magnitude is, as we have seen, capable of measurement as accurately as any other, however gross and perceptible, so far does the power of reason exceed that of the imagination.

(59.) The principles which we have now explained will be found sufficient to account for all the phenomena of colours reflected, or transmitted by transparent media. Let us suppose that two glass surfaces are placed parallel at the distance of 120 ten-millionth parts of an inch, inclosing between them a plate of air. If pure orange light fall perpendicularly on the glass, it will pass through, being transmitted freely by the plate of air between the plates of glass. For on passing from the first glass plate into the air it is in a fit of easy transmission; and since the distance between the plates is equal to the interval between the fits (see Table), it will be again in a fit of easy transmission when it encounters the surface of the second plate and will consequently pass through. If, in this case, the eye be placed behind the second plate, the coloured light will be perceived to be transmitted.

Now suppose the two plates to be placed parallel as before, but only at half the former distance asunder. The orange light, on meeting the surface of the second plate, will be in a fit of easy reflection, and will consequently return through the plate of air in the direction from which it came. Having the same space to move through, it will be in a fit of easy transmission when it has again reached the surface of the first plate, and will consequently be transmitted. If the eye be placed before the first plate, it will be coloured over with the orange light.

Let us now suppose that the plates are placed at the distance of 240 ten-millionths of an inch asunder. This is equal to two intervals of the fits of orange light, and therefore that light being in a fit of easy transmission when it encounters it, will be transmitted at the surface of the second plate. An eye placed behind the second plate will receive the transmitted light, and the plate will take an orange hue.

In the middle of the interval between 120 and 240, that is, at the distance of 180 ten-millionths of an inch from the first plate, the ray will be in the middle of the second interval of its fits, and will therefore be in a fit of easy reflection. If it encounter the second surface at this distance, it will consequently be reflected. When it has returned to the distance 120, it will again be in a fit of easy transmission, which fit will return again after passing through the distance 120, at which point it will again meet the surface of the first plate, and will be transmitted through it. Thus an eye placed before the first plate will perceive the orange light reflected.

Thus the space followed by the ray in passing through the air being divided into parts equal to 60 ten-millionths of an inch, at each alternate point of division the orange ray will be in a fit of easy transmission, and at the intermediate points it will be in a fit of easy reflection. In the one case, the orange light transmitted will appear to an eye placed behind the second plate, while to an eye placed before the first no colour is apparent. In the other case the reverse will happen, the orange light being perceptible to an eye placed before the first plate, while no colour appears to an eye placed behind the second.

All that has been here observed of the orange light will be equally applicable to the red, yellow, and all the other colours, the interval of the fits only being different. It should, however, be observed, that the ray does not pass suddenly into its fits of reflection and transmission on arriving at the several points of division which we have mentioned, but passes gradually from its complete fit of easy reflection to its complete fit of easy transmission, and *vice versâ*, being, in the intermediate space, in a state to be partially reflected and transmitted.

(60.) When a beam of white solar light falls perpendicularly on the plates, each component part is put into fits separately, and in the same manner as would happen if that part alone had been incident on the plate. The thickness of the plate of air may be such, that several component rays may meet the second surface in fits of easy reflection, while the other parts meet it in fits of easy transmission. In this case, the tint exhibited to an eye placed before the first plate will be one which is compounded of the colours of those rays which meet the second plate, in fits of easy reflection, while the tint exhibited to an eye behind the second plate will be compounded of the colours of those rays which meet the second surface in fits of easy transmission. It will happen frequently that the second surface will encounter a ray in such a manner as to divide the interval of the fits unequally, so that the light will be partly reflected and partly transmitted. In this case, the tint seen on each side of the plates is determined as before, by the composition of the colours reflected and transmitted, due regard being had to their quantities.

(61.) Newton has given an ingenious scale for determining the colours reflected by the second surface, at any proposed distance from the first. We shall here, however, adopt another method of illustration, not differing in principle from that of Newton, but better adapted for popular illustration.

Draw two lines* A X (*fig.* 46) and A Y at right angles, and taking any

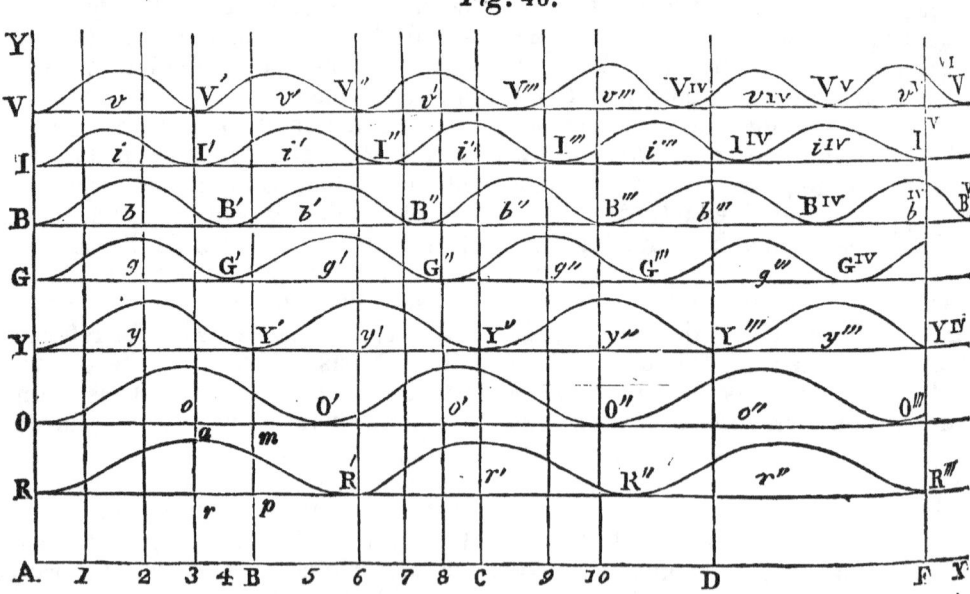

Fig. 46.

seven points R, O, Y, G, B, I, V on the line A Y, draw through them lines parallel to A X. Let R R' represent the interval of the fits of red light, and let this space be repeated, so that R' R'', R'' R''', &c. shall be equal to R R'. Draw a waving curve line touching the parallel through R in the points R, R', R'', &c., and let the points, at which the distance of the curve from the parallel is greatest, be situated exactly in the middle between every two successive points of contact, that is, perpendicularly above the points r, r', r'', &c. When the thickness of the air between the plates is equal to R R', or R R'', or R R''', &c. no red light is reflected, the ray being at those points in a fit of easy transmission. On the other hand, in the middle of each interval, or at the thick-

* This scale is used by Mr. Herschel in his able "Treatise on Light."

nesses Rr, Rr', Rr'', &c. the reflection of red light is most intense, the ray being at these points in a fit of easy reflection. From the first entrance of the red ray at the plate A Y until it reaches r, its disposition to be reflected is increasing, and consequently, the curve from R to r may be so shaped, that its increasing perpendicular distance from Rr may be proportionate to the quantity of red light reflected at each increasing thickness. If this be done, the perpendicular distance of the curve from r will represent the quantity of red light reflected when the ray attains its first fit of easy reflection. As the ray passes from r to R' it gradually changes its phase, and the reflected light constantly decreases like the distance of the curve from rR', until at length, like that distance, it dwindles into nothing at R', the entire light being here transmitted, the ray having attained its fit of easy transmission. The same process is repeated as the ray passes from R' to R'', from R'' to R''', and so on.

It thus appears, that the quantity of red light reflected by the plate of air intervening between the two plates of glass may be exhibited. Take R p equal to the distance between the plates, or the thickness of the plate of air. Draw pm perpendicular to Rp and meeting the curve at m. Then pm will bear the same proportion to ra as the quantity of red light reflected at the thickness Rp bears to the quantity reflected at the thickness Rr when the ray is in a fit of easy reflection. It is evident that the quantity of red light reflected at any other thickness may be similarly found.

Let O O' be taken to represent the interval of the fits of orange light, and let this interval be repeated O' O'', O'' O''', &c., as in the former case. Let a curve be drawn as before, touching the parallel at the points which mark the fits of easy transmission, and such that its distance from the parallel will always be proportionate to the quantity of orange light reflected at each thickness of the plate of air. The other curves are to be drawn in the same manner, the distances YY', GG', BB', II', VV' representing the intervals of the fits of the yellow, green, blue, indigo, and violet lights respectively. It is evident that, by this scale, the quantity of light of each colour which is reflected at any given thickness may always be exhibited, and the colours which compose the tint, perceived by reflection, may thus be determined, both in quantity and quality.

It will be observed, that the intervals R R', O O', Y Y', &c., continually diminish in passing from the red to the violet light. This is conformable to what has been explained; the interval of the fits being shorter for the more refrangible the lights. It is to this circumstance that the coloured rings between the lenses is owing; for if the fits of all the component parts of light were equal, the rings would be alternately white and black.

To explain more fully the manner of determining a tint corresponding to a given thickness, let the line A X be divided at 1, 2, 3, &c. Let A 1 be a thickness much less than R r, half the interval of the fits of red light. Through 1 draw a line parallel to A Y, and crossing all the curves. The parts of this line intercepted between each curve and the corresponding parallel to A X, express the quantities of the respective colours reflected by the air at this thickness. It thus appears, by inspection, that the quantities of red and orange are small; of yellow not much more, but that the proportion rapidly increases as we approach the blue and violet. The excess of light of a bluish tint, therefore, which enters the reflected light, will give that light a corresponding character. If the thickness of the plate of air be much less than A 1, the lines representing the reflected light will gradually disappear, and no light will be reflected. Accordingly, it was found in the experiment with the glass lenses described in (54), that at the centre, where the glasses were in contact, and for a small distance round it, a black spot was perceivable, arising from the absence of reflected light. In this case, the air immediately around the centre was too thin to reflect the light in any sensible quantity, as appears by the scale which we are now describing.

Let a parallel to A Y be drawn through 2. The lines which now represent the reflected lights are nearly equal. The red tints have not reached their maxima, and the blue tints have passed theirs. The intermixture of these produce a brilliant white.

Referring again to the experiments with the glass, we found that the blue ring which immediately succeeded the central black spot was followed by a ring of splendid white. Here, then, the thickness of the air between the lenses had so far increased as to be represented by A 2.

As the parallel to A Y is moved towards 3, the lines which are intercepted between the upper curves and their respective bases rapidly diminish and disappear, while those which correspond to the bases Y Y', and O O' attain their maxima. Hence it appears, that by this increase of thickness the reflection of the bluish lights is subdued, and the yellow and orange tints appear. When the parallel arrives at 3, the line ra representing the red light attains its maximum, the blues and violets altogether disappearing. Here the reflected tint will be red.

The first white ring which appeared between the lenses was succeeded by a yellow which passed through an orange into a red one. The increased thickness of the air between the lenses, in receding from the centre, accounts for this succession of colours as explained above.

As the parallel to A Y moves towards 4, 5, the lines representing the quantities of the red lights reflected gradually diminish and disappear, the indigo being on the increase, and the violet at its maximum. Hence the light reflected at this thickness will have a violet hue. Such is, in fact, the first ring of the second series between the lenses (54). As the parallel arrives at 5, the violet is on the decrease, the blue attains its maximum, and the reddish tints vanish. The colour reflected will, therefore, be blue, and corresponds to the blue ring in the second series between the lenses.

When the parallel to A Y arrives at 6, the lines representing the reds and violets disappear, the blue and green are only partially reflected, and the yellow is at its maximum. The partial reflexion of the blue and green mixed with the intense yellow, produces a yellowish green. This thickness of the air is that at which the green ring is reflected in the second series of rings between the lenses. After the parallel passes 6, the yellow predominates, the other lights being but faintly reflected, as appears by inspecting the curves. The yellowish green last mentioned, therefore, gradually changes into a bright yellow. This corresponds to the yellow ring of the second series.

As the parallel approaches 8, the red and orange increase; the greens, yellows, and blues nearly vanish; the violets are copiously reflected, but the stronger influence of the red and orange gives the reflected light a glowing crimson hue. This corresponds to the last ring of the second series between the lenses.

At C, the red and orange are copiously reflected; the yellow, green, and violet are not reflected in any perceptible quantity, but the indigo is abundant and the blue considerable. The result of the composition of these lights is a rich purple of a ruddy character, which corresponds to the first ring of the second series between the lenses. By following in this manner the parallel as it moves from A Y, we shall be able to trace distinctly the lights reflected by plates of air of every degree of thickness, and we shall perfectly account for the succession of coloured rings, as far as they are observable in the experiment with the lenses.

(62.) We have here constructed curves to represent the quantities of reflected light of seven distinct degrees of refrangibility. But it must be remembered that solar light consists of rays of every degree of refrangibility between certain extreme limits. To describe the phenomena perfectly, there should therefore be an infinite number of other curves between each pair of those already exhibited, and with bases of intermediate magnitude. Two such curves having bases nearly equal, correspond to lights which differ but little in refrangibility, and which have no perceptible difference in colour. When the thickness of the plate of air becomes considerable, the number of repetitions of the bases of two curves, whose bases have a very small difference, will be so great, that the points of contact will be separated by a considerable interval. Accordingly, it must at length happen, that when one ray is most copiously reflected, another of very nearly the same colour will not be reflected at all. As this is necessary to explain why a thick plate of air will only reflect white light, and that but faintly, we shall explain it more fully.

Let Y Y', instead of representing the interval of the fits of the yellow light, represent that of the fits of green light differing a little in refrangibility and not perceptibly in colour from the light whose fits are at the interval G G'. Suppose that the difference between Y Y' and G G' is the fortieth part of G G'; after passing through a thickness equal to twenty repetitions of G G', the highest point of the curve Y Y' will correspond to the lowest of G G', so that although no green light of the refrangibility of G be reflected, yet light of the same colour, but of the refrangibility of Y, will be reflected in abundance; so that at considerable thicknesses, green light, of some degrees of refrangibility, must always be reflected. Now, what we have to observe of green light is equally applicable to light of all other colours: so that it follows, that light of all colours will be both reflected and transmitted at considerable thicknesses.

(63.) Since a mixture of lights of all colours constitutes white light, it follows that the light reflected and transmitted by a thick plate of air will always be white; but since some is transmitted, and some reflected, neither the reflected nor transmitted light will be so intense as the lights which are reflected and transmitted by very thin plates.

The recurrence of the fits of lights of nearly equal refrangibility do not suddenly attain the state which we have described. They approach it gradually. Hence we may account for the dilute appearances of the colours reflected as the thickness of the air increases, as is perceived by observing the rings of colour at a considerable distance from the centre of the lenses. They become faint by degrees, and finally disappear.

(64.) Another circumstance attending the phenomena of the rings is accounted for on the grounds to which we have just adverted. When homogeneous light was projected on the lens, the rings appeared in much greater numbers, and more distinctly defined than when compound solar light was used. In fact, in this case their number seemed quite interminable. The colours were here not diluted and neutralized by the admixture of rays of all hues, as we have shown to be the case when white light was projected on the lenses.

(65.) Seeing that the interval of the fits changed with every change of refrangibility of the light, the problem to determine the relation between the interval of the fits and the degree of refrangibility obviously presented itself. This, however, Newton failed to solve. He fancied that the intervals of the fits of the seven coloured lights bore an analogy to the lengths of a string which sound the seven musical notes.

(66.) Hitherto we have conceived the light to fall perpendicularly on the plate of air, and therefore to be reflected perpendicularly by it. If the light enter the air obliquely to its surface, it will be reflected at the same obliquity. In this case the light is affected by the oblique incidence in a singular manner. The interval of its fits is lengthened, and bears a certain proportion to the length of the interval when perpendicular. Newton succeeded in detecting this proportion, and in showing how the length of the fit depended on the obliquity of the light.

Although the phraseology of mathematics may be considered in some degree necessary to express this curious relation, yet we hope to render it intelligible to the general reader, if a moderate portion of attention be given to the following explanation. Let the line P D (*fig.* 46.) represent the interval of the fits of any species of homogeneous light incident perpendicularly on a thin

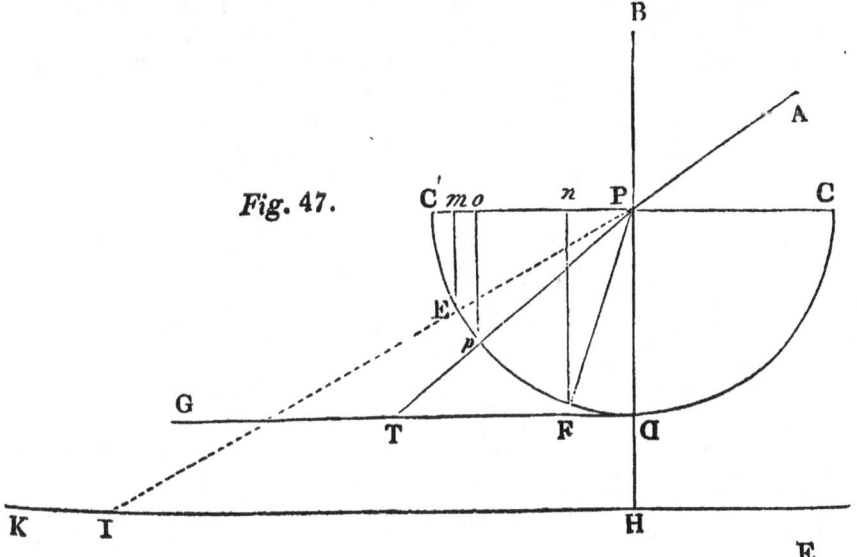

Fig. 47.

plate of air, having previously passed through a plate of glass. We are required to find the interval of the fits when the same ray enters the air obliquely to its surface, as in the direction A P.

With P as a centre, and P D as a radius, let a semicircle C D C′ be described, and let C C′ be considered as the surface of the plate of air. Let P F be the direction which the ray A P would take, if it were refracted by passing from air into glass. From F, draw Fn perpendicular to C P. Continue the line A P to the circle at E, and from E draw Em perpendicular to C P. Divide the interval mn into 107 equal parts, and let o be the point of division nearest to m. From o draw op perpendicular to C P, and meeting the circle in p. From D draw D G, touching the circle at D, and from P draw Pp, and continue it to meet D G at T. Continue P D below D, and take P H equal to P T. Through H draw H K perpendicular to H P, and continue P E until it meet it at I. Then P I will be the interval of the fits of the oblique ray, and P H will be the thickness of a plate of air through which the ray passes between two successive fits.

It appears from hence that the interval of the fits of an oblique ray depends on three things; first, the angle of obliquity; second, the refrangibility of the light; and third, on the refracting power of the media which bound the thin transparent plate through which the light passes. The relation by which the interval depends on these elements, appears complex in the preceding explanation. This complexity is, however, only apparent, and arises from the necessity of throwing our account of it into a popular form. Expressed in the language of Trigonometry and Algebra, it is sufficiently simple.*

(67.) The manner in which Newton deduced this relation from observation of the rings may easily be conceived, by recurring to the method by which he discovered the interval of the fits, when the incident light was perpendicular. In that case, the thickness of the plate of air, which reflected the colour in each ring, was found by measuring the diameter of the ring. When he viewed the rings obliquely, he found them enlarged, and, consequently, the thickness of the air at which the light was reflected was increased. Its increased thickness was computed in the same manner as before, by measuring the diameter of the ring. By a careful comparison of the thickness thus deduced with the thickness which reflected the same colour perpendicularly, he discovered the method already explained of finding the magnitude P H by knowing P D and the obliquity. The thickness at which a given tint will be reflected at a given obliquity being found, the interval of the fits was easily discovered. In the case where the ray penetrated the medium perpendicularly, twice the thickness of the air was equal to the length of the course of the ray in passing through it and returning, and this, therefore, was the interval of the fits. But when the ray, as in the present case, penetrates the air obliquely, the course of the ray in passing through it and returning is more than twice the thickness of the air. Let P H (*fig.* 48) be the

Fig. 48.

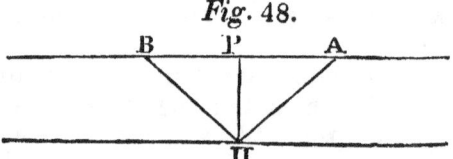

thickness of the air, and let A H be the ray entering, and H B emerging. The lines A H and H B taken together, form the course of the ray within the plate of air. These lines, therefore, taken together, or twice A H, is the interval of the fits.

In explaining the laws which govern these phenomena, we have referred constantly to a thin plate of air inclosed between two surfaces of glass. The presence of air, or any other material agent, is not necessary for the production of the effects. The lenses which we have described (54) would exhibit the same rings of colour if placed under an exhausted receiver. All that is necessary to produce the phenomena is, that two refracting surfaces should be placed close together, so as to include between a thin transparent space. In passing the first surface the rays will be

---

* It is very doubtful, as Newton does not give the details of his observations at great obliquities, and as the making the observations with accuracy at obliquities beyond 75° must be a matter of great difficulty, whether the construction is to be depended on; particularly as the observations, as far as from 0° to 75°, agree sensibly with the simple formula, secant < obliquity (or, if we use the figure in the text, P H, instead of being equal to P T, will be equal to the distance from P to the intersection of P E produced with D T). This formula is consistent with the theory of undulations. Biot does not say that he has repeated these observations at great obliquities, and found them to be correct. He is evidently at a loss to know how they were made.

put into fits of easy reflection and transmission, and those which meet the second surface in a fit of easy transmission will penetrate it, while those which meet it in a fit of easy reflection will be reflected from it.

(68.) The interval of the fits changes with the refracting power of the thin medium traversed by the light. The relation of this interval to the refracting power was detected by Newton, and may be exhibited as follows:

With a centre C (*fig.* 49) and a radius C A, describe a semicircle, and from any

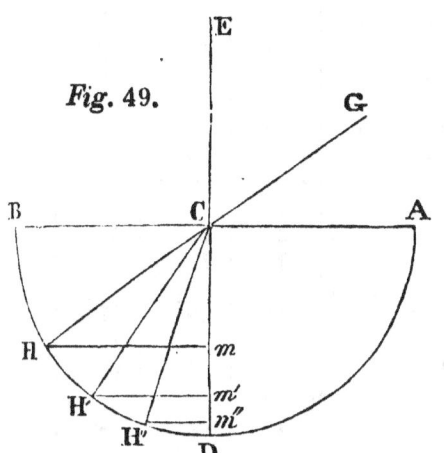

Fig. 49.

point G, through the centre C, draw the right line G C H. From H draw H *m* parallel to B A, and meeting at *m* a line E D drawn through the centre perpendicular to B A. Let H *m* represent the length of the interval of the fits when the ray traverses a vacuum. To find the length of a fit when the medium traversed by the ray is water, draw C H in that direction which a ray of light coming in the direction G C would take in passing from a vacuum, through the surface B A, into water. Let this direction be C H′, and from H′ draw H′ *m*′ parallel to B A. This line H′ *m*′ will be the interval of the fits when the ray passes through water. Again, if the medium be glass, draw C H″ in the direction which the ray G C would take in passing from a vacuum into glass, and H″ *m*″ is the interval of the fits.

Thus it appears that the greater the refracting power of the medium traversed by the light, the shorter will be the interval of its fits.

Newton discovered this law by introducing transparent liquids between the lenses, whose refracting powers were greater than that of air. "Upon wetting the object glasses at their edges the water crept in slowly between them, and the circles thereby became less and the colours more faint, insomuch that, as the water crept along, one-half of them, at which it first arrived, would appear broken off from the other half and contracted into a less room. By measuring them I found the proportion of their diameters to the diameters of the like circles made by the air, to be about seven to eight, and consequently, the intervals of the glasses at like circles, caused by the water and air, to be as three to four *. Perhaps it may be a general rule, that if any other medium more or less dense than water be compressed between the glasses, their intervals, at the rings caused thereby, will be to their intervals caused by interjacent air, as the sines are which measure the refraction out of that medium into air." These *sines* are the lines H *m*, H′ *m*′, H″ *m*″, &c. in our explanation.

(69.) It is remarkable, that whatever be the matter of which the then transparent medium traversed by the light is composed, the same colours will be reflected in the same order. This arises from the circumstance of the fits being regulated by the same law in all substances, one differing from another only in the length of the interval of the fits, and whenever the length of the fit for any one species of homogeneous light undergoes any change arising from a change in the refracting power of the medium, the intervals for all the other species of homogeneous light undergo a *proportional* change.

(70.) The scale for determining the tints corresponding to different thicknesses of the transparent medium would, accurately constructed, be a very exact method, not only of ascertaining those tints, but also the primary colours of which they are composed. Newton has given the following Table of the thickness of air, water, and glass, which reflect tints corresponding to the several series of rings described in (54). The numbers express millionths of an inch.

---

* The intervals of the glasses, being in the proportion of the squares of the diameters of the rings. are more accurately as 49 to 64; very nearly the same ratio.

THE THICKNESS OF COLOURED PLATES AND PARTICLES OF AIR, WATER, AND GLASS.

		Air.	Water.	Glass.
Their Colours of the first Order	Very Black	$\frac{1}{2}$	$\frac{3}{8}$	$\frac{10}{31}$
	Black	1	$\frac{3}{4}$	$\frac{20}{31}$
	Beginning of Black	2	$1\frac{1}{2}$	$1\frac{2}{7}$
	Blue	$2\frac{2}{5}$	$1\frac{4}{5}$	$1\frac{11}{20}$
	White	$5\frac{1}{4}$	$3\frac{7}{8}$	$3\frac{2}{5}$
	Yellow	$7\frac{1}{9}$	$5\frac{1}{3}$	$4\frac{3}{5}$
	Orange	8	6	$5\frac{1}{6}$
	Red	9	$6\frac{3}{4}$	$5\frac{4}{5}$
Of the second Order	Violet	$11\frac{1}{6}$	$8\frac{3}{8}$	$7\frac{1}{5}$
	Indigo	$12\frac{5}{8}$	$9\frac{5}{8}$	$8\frac{2}{11}$
	Blue	14	$10\frac{1}{2}$	9
	Green	$15\frac{1}{8}$	$11\frac{1}{3}$	$9\frac{5}{7}$
	Yellow	$16\frac{2}{7}$	$12\frac{1}{5}$	$10\frac{2}{5}$
	Orange	$17\frac{7}{9}$	13	$11\frac{1}{9}$
	Bright Red	$18\frac{1}{4}$	$13\frac{3}{4}$	$11\frac{5}{6}$
	Scarlet	$19\frac{2}{3}$	$14\frac{3}{4}$	$12\frac{2}{3}$
Of the third Order	Purple	21	$15\frac{3}{4}$	$13\frac{11}{20}$
	Indigo	$22\frac{1}{10}$	$16\frac{4}{7}$	$14\frac{1}{4}$
	Blue	$23\frac{2}{5}$	$17\frac{11}{20}$	$15\frac{1}{10}$
	Green	$25\frac{1}{5}$	$18\frac{9}{10}$	$16\frac{1}{4}$
	Yellow	$27\frac{1}{4}$	$20\frac{1}{3}$	$17\frac{1}{2}$
	Red	29	$21\frac{3}{4}$	$18\frac{5}{7}$
	Blueish red	32	24	$20\frac{2}{3}$
Of the fourth Order	Blueish Green	24	$25\frac{1}{2}$	22
	Green	$35\frac{3}{7}$	$26\frac{1}{6}$	$22\frac{3}{4}$
	Yellowish Green	36	27	$23\frac{2}{9}$
	Red	$40\frac{1}{3}$	$30\frac{1}{4}$	26
Of the fifth Order	Greenish Blue	46	$34\frac{1}{2}$	$29\frac{2}{3}$
	Red	$52\frac{1}{2}$	$39\frac{3}{8}$	34
Of the sixth Order	Greenish Blue	$58\frac{3}{4}$	44	38
	Red	65	$48\frac{3}{4}$	42
Of the seventh Order	Greenish Blue	71	$53\frac{1}{4}$	$45\frac{4}{5}$
	Ruddy White	77	$57\frac{3}{4}$	$49\frac{2}{3}$

A comparison of this Table with the scale in fig. 46 will give a tolerably accurate notion of the reflected tints and their composition. But it also answers the further purpose of measuring the thickness of a medium too minute to be estimated in any other way. Thus the size of the minute parts of natural bodies may be determined from their colours. "If two or more thin plates be laid upon one another, so as to form one plate equalling them all in thickness, the resulting colour may be determined. For instance: Hook observed that a faint yellow plate of Muscovy glass laid upon a blue one constituted a very deep purple. The yellow of the first order is a faint one, and the thickness of the plate exhibiting it is $4\frac{2}{3}$, to which add 9, the thickness exhibiting blue of the second order, and the sum will be $13\frac{3}{5}$, which is the thickness exhibiting the purple of the third order."

CHAPTER VII.

The Theory of Colours, continued.

(71.) In explaining the theory of colours, it was shown that the colours of natural bodies arose from an aptitude in them to reflect the rays of some colours rather than those of others. The experiments and investigations noticed in the preceding Chapter, now enabled Newton to advance a step further in the inquiry into the causes of the colours of natural bodies. He accordingly proceeds to discuss the principles to which bodies owe this *aptitude* to reflect some lights rather than others, and to trace this aptitude to the internal constitution and essential nature of the bodies.

A very close analogy may be observed between the phenomena of reflection and refraction. It has been proved that those species of light which were most refrangible were also most reflexible. But it further appears that those surfaces at which light is most powerfully refracted have a proportionately intense power of reflection.

A *surface* which separates glass from air has a considerable refractive power. That its reflective power is also great, will be seen by looking into the side of a prism at its base, the eye being placed so as to view the base obliquely and the side perpendicularly. The reflection of light from the base will be so intense, that every object seen in it has all the vivid splendour of reality.

The surface which separates glass from water has a much less refracting power, and, accordingly, we find the reflective power proportionately diminished. If the prism just mentioned be laid with its base upon water, the splendour of the reflection will be considerably impaired, and the images seen in the base will no longer have the intense brilliancy which was observable when the medium below the base was air. To this cause the diamond owes its lustre. Its refracting power is greater than that of most other substances. In conformity with the principle here laid down, its reflecting power is proportionately great, and we find the reflection of light from its inner surfaces of a corresponding intensity. On the other hand, if a surface separates two media of equal refracting powers, no refraction takes place in passing from the one medium to the other, and so neither do we find any reflection. Thus, at the point at which the lenses touched in the experiment described in (54), no light was reflected at whatever obliquity it was viewed.

(72.) Newton, therefore, concludes that the reason why uniform pellucid substances, such as water, glass, or crystal, reflect no light except from their surfaces, is, because every part within those surfaces has an uniform refracting power, or has in every place the same density. He infers that reflection of light may always be taken as an indication of a change of density in the medium at that point where the reflection is made, and that it is a test by which a change of density may be as certainly ascertained as by refraction.

A ray of light falling on the surface of a body in a fit of easy transmission, enters it. If, after penetrating to a small depth, it meet with a point at which there is a change of density, and be at the same time in a fit of easy reflection, it will retrace its course. According to this view, every body, how opaque so ever it be, is transparent to a certain depth within its surface. Experiments sufficiently evince the truth of this proposition. If a very thin lamina of the most opaque substance be suspended before a hole through which a beam of light is admitted into a dark room, it will be manifestly transparent, and light will be perceptible through it, provided it be sufficiently attenuated.

From all this it seems not impossible that the intimate particles or molecules of opaque or coloured bodies, are separated by minute pores or spaces, which are either entirely void or filled with some subtle material of a different density from the molecules of the body, in the same manner as a liquid pervades the particles of a solid substance which it holds in solution. If we admit that light penetrates the external surface of opaque bodies, a fact which experience proves, we must also admit the existence of spaces within that body, *filled by some medium* differing in density from the molecules of the body itself; for, without this difference of density, there could be no reflection, and, consequently, no opacity.

(73.) There are many experiments by which phenomena are elicited, which seem to support the hypothesis that the discontinuity of parts is the cause of opacity. If the pores of an opaque body be filled with any substance of nearly the same density or refracting power, it loses its opacity, and becomes diaphanous. Paper and oil have nearly equal refracting powers. Dry paper is opaque; but, when steeped in oil until its pores are in a great degree filled with that fluid, it acquires a proportionate degree of transparency. In the same manner, linen cloth, and many other substances of very imperfect transparency, will have that quality perceptibly increased by being steeped in liquids whose refracting power is nearly equal to their own.

On the other hand, the most translucent bodies may be rendered opaque by extricating from their pores the matter which pervades them, which may be done by separating their parts by mechanical division; or the subtle pervading agent may be banished by heat or chemical action. Thus, pulverised glass and the shavings of horn are no longer transparent. Wet paper becomes opaque upon evaporating the moisture by heat; and salts and other substances, held in solution, lose their transparency by precipitation.

On such grounds Newton assumes that the parts of opaque bodies are separated by interstices; but he even goes further. He affirms that these interstices must have certain determinate magnitudes, and there are limits within which they cannot come. In the experiment with the lenses (54), the black central spot, within which the transmission of the light was total, was much larger than the point of contact of the glass, and no light was reflected until the air attained a certain thickness. In like manner, if a soap-bubble be examined, it will be found that as the liquid which forms it subsides, the top becomes so thin as to reflect no light, and, consequently, appears black. In order, therefore, to reflect light, the distances between the particles of a body must be such as to allow the pervading medium, whatever it be, to exist in sufficiently thick parts; otherwise the distances between the particles would be less than half the interval of the fits, and the ray, throughout the whole thickness of the medium, would be in a fit of easy transmission.

This Newton considers to be the case with water, glass, translucid stones, and other transparent substances. That there are spaces between their particles is beyond doubt. But those spaces, relatively to the pervading medium, are circumstanced in the same way as the air immediately around the point of contact of the lenses; they are too small to reflect light, and the ray never has space enough in any of them to pass from a fit of easy transmission into one of easy reflection, and consequently it is wholly transmitted.

(74.) This theory derives some further support from the effects of the solution of solid substances in liquid. The particles, by a subdivision, inconceivably minute, are brought into closer contact; and, although the solid after solution, fills a greater space, and the *aggregate* of the interstices of its parts must therefore be increased, yet the subdivision is so minute that every *single interstitial space* is very much diminished. This diminution is carried so far, that it is less than the interval between a fit of easy transmission and one of easy reflection, and consequently the light is transmitted, and the solution is diaphanous.

(75.) There are many analogies which support the opinion, that the colours of natural bodies are produced upon the same principle, governed by the same laws, and attended with effects in all respects the same as those produced by their transparent plates, as explained in the last chapter. One of these thin transparent plates, provided it be of uniform thickness, will, in every part, reflect the same colour. Let it be slit into threads, or broken into fragments; every piece will separately reflect the same colour as the entire plate. A heap of these fragments will still appear of the same colour; and if a natural body be considered as a mass of such fragments, it must, on the same grounds, exhibit the same colours.

It will be recollected, that thin plates, viewed at different obliquities, shifted their tints, the length of the fits, and, therefore, the species of the light reflected, changing with every change in the obliquity of the light to the plate. In conformity with this, many natural bodies vary their hues with the point from which they are viewed. The plumage of birds, and more especially of the peacock, presents a splendid instance of this. Changeable silks, and almost all dyed clothes, are attended with a similar effect. A spider's web, when finely spun, exhibits colours. All these phenomena bear a close and obvious analogy to those which occupied our attention in the last chapter.

(76.) But, further, some substances reflect one colour and transmit another, like the air between the lenses in (54). Examples of this will be found in leaf gold, some species of stained glass, and the infusion of lignum nephriticum. The coloured powders used by painters change their tints by mere grinding. The parts being thus reduced in size, reflect various colours, in the same manner as a transparent plate would by reducing its thickness.

No example more strongly supports Newton's reasoning than those which are so common in chemical experiments, in which various changes of colour are produced by the admixture of different species of liquids. Two liquids, each of which is perfectly transparent, will frequently, when mixed, be strongly coloured. This may be conceived to arise from the mutual action of the corpuscles of the two liquids: they either create or destroy the connexion of particles, and cause the molecules to swell or shrink, whereby not only their bulk but their density may be changed.

This change of the magnitudes of the particles and their interstices is an adequate cause for the change of colour, according to Newton's theory.

It is observable in experiments such as those described in the last chapter, that when the thin transparent medium which reflects the colours is more dense than the surrounding medium, the colours are much more vivid and brisk, and less liable to shift their tints with a change in the direction in which they are viewed. This will be evident, by comparing the effect of thin films of glass or mica, the ambient medium being air, with that of a thin plate of air, inclosed between two pieces of plate glass. From this circumstance, Newton supposes that the parts of bodies on which their colours depend must be denser than those which fill the remaining spaces within the surface of the body. For the colour of a body being generally produced by light reflected at all angles, if the particles reflecting colour were rarer than the surrounding medium, all tints would be reflected at different obliquities, and so the body would appear white or grey. But if the parts reflecting colour be more dense than the others, the lights reflected nearly perpendicular will, by predominating over the oblique ones, give their own colour to the body.

(77.) All the preceding reasoning led Newton directly to the inference, that *the colour of a body furnishes a means of determining the magnitude of the ultimate transparent corpuscles of which it is composed*. Many circumstances render it probable, as Newton conceived, that the parts of bodies have, for the most part, the same refractive density as those of water or glass. This being assumed, it follows that the diameter of the corpuscle of a body, which has any proposed colour, is equal to the thickness of a plate of water or glass, which would reflect the same colour, and which may always be determined by the Table, p. 52, and by the Scale, fig. 46. Thus, if it be desired to know the diameter of a corpuscle, which, being of equal density with glass, will reflect green of the third order; $16\frac{1}{4}$ expresses the number of millionth parts of an inch in it.

(78.) The received opinion respecting the cause of reflection of light was, that its particles impinged upon the hard surface of the solid parts of the reflecting body, and were reflected by the reaction of that surface, in the same manner as an elastic sphere is reflected when it strikes a hard plane. This opinion seemed to be countenanced by the law of reflection of light, which is the same as that which regulates the reflection of all elastic spheres impinging upon hard surfaces. Newton, however, held that light does not impinge on the solid and impervious parts of bodies, but is reflected without having encountered these surfaces. He shows many difficulties which attend the hypothesis, that light impinges on the solid parts of bodies in reflection, among which the following may be noticed.

If light, after passing through glass, be reflected by the surface, the ambient medium being air, the reflection will be stronger than it would be if the light had passed through the air and been reflected by the surface of the glass, and much stronger than if the ambient medium had been water. This effect would lead to the conclusion, that the particles of air repelled the light with greater force than those of either water or glass. But it is still more unaccountable on this theory, that upon withdrawing the air from about the glass by an air-pump, the reflection of the light from the surface which separates the glass from the vacuum is still stronger than in either of the former cases.

If the light, after passing through the glass, be incident on the surface more obliquely than at an angle of 41°, it will be wholly reflected; but, at all obliquities less than this, it will be transmitted. Hence, if we admit that the impact on solid parts is the cause of reflection, and therefore the penetration of interstices the cause of transmission, we are compelled to suppose, that at obliquities greater than 41°, all the parts of the light encounter solid parts of air, but at less obliquities they all pass into pores or interstices; and, on the other hand, that in passing through air, and impinging upon glass, it never fails to meet pores enough to transmit nearly the whole of it, even at the most oblique incidences. Some may suppose that the light, after passing through the glass, is reflected—not by the parts of air contiguous to the glass, but by the last particles of the glass itself. This supposition, however, is scarcely intelligible, and, besides, is contradicted by wetting the surface of the glass, which immediately affects the reflection, which could not be the case, if the reflection were made by the parts of the glass.

It has been shown that two kinds of homogeneous light—say blue and red—might be incident at the base of a prism, with the same obliquity, and so that the red should be wholly transmitted, and the blue wholly reflected. In this case it seems inconceivable, that the red rays should everywhere fall on pores, and the blue rays on solid parts. A similar difficulty attends the explication of all the phenomena of thin plates explained in the last chapter, for we must there suppose, that the transmitted rays, being all of certain species, meet only with pores while the rays of the complemental colours encounter nothing but solid parts.

Still greater difficulties attend the explanation of the phenomena of reflection of light at polished surfaces, according to this theory. The substances used in polishing glass and other surfaces, only bring the roughness of the surface to a very fine grain, so that the inequalities become too small to be perceptible either to sight or touch. Hence, since innumerable inequalities exist, irregularly distributed over the most polished surface, it follows, that if the light were reflected by impinging on the surfaces of the solid parts, it would be as irregularly scattered about by such a surface as by the roughest.

(79.) Newton, therefore, considers that light is reflected—" not by a single point of the reflecting body, but by some power of the body which is evenly diffused over its surface, and by which it acts upon the ray without immediate contact."

By a comparison of the refracting powers of substances with their densities, Newton traced an evident connexion between them. In all bodies, whether solid, liquid, or aëriform, except such as be of an unctuous or sulphureous nature, the refracting powers are very nearly in the proportion of their densities. A body of an unctuous or sulphureous nature, compared with one which is not so, has a greater relative refracting power than the proportion of their densities indicates. But even in this case, bodies of this nature, when compared with one another, have refracting powers in a ratio not very remote from that of their densities.

The sulphureous principle, therefore, seems to increase the action of bodies on light; and Newton conjectures that this principle, existing more or less in all bodies, may be the cause of all the phenomena of reflection and refraction. " And as light congregated by a burning glass acts most upon sulphureous bodies to turn them into fire and flame, so, since all action is mutual, sulphurs ought to act most upon light. For that the action between light and bodies is mutual, may appear from this consideration; that the densest bodies which refract and reflect light most strongly, grow hottest in the summer sun, by the action of the refracted and reflected light."

This last observation of Newton has been since proved incorrect. The most dense bodies, if transparent and colourless, do not grow hot. However, the theory which has formed the subject of this chapter, and which has been given substantially as Newton himself has left it, must be received as matter of hypothesis. To discuss its merits, and compare it with subsequent experiments and theories, would greatly exceed the limits of the present treatise. Our object here is to give a succinct popular account of " Newton's Optics," and not to discuss the relative merits of the different theories which have been advanced to represent the phenomena.

Chapter VIII.
Thick transparent Plates.

(80.) The colours produced by the reflection and transmission of light by thin transparent plates are not peculiar to these, but may also be exhibited, under certain circumstances, by plates of considerable thickness. By a series of experiments with concave glass reflectors, silvered on the convex side, Newton made these phenomena manifest, and applied his hypothesis of the fits of easy reflection and transmission successfully, in accounting for them, and in reducing them to the laws which were explained in the sixth chapter.

Before we proceed to describe these experiments, it is necessary to remind the reader of the several effects which a beam of light undergoes when it encounters the surface of a transparent medium. A part is reflected, according to the regular law of reflection, and a part entering the medium is regularly refracted. But besides these, which may be considered as the principal parts, there is still another portion which is scattered about in all directions around each point of incidence, both within and without the refracting medium. It is this portion of the incident light which serves to render the surface visible to an eye placed in any situation with respect to it. For if no light proceeded in any other directions than those of the regularly reflected and refracted rays, the surface would be invisible to every eye, except to one placed in these directions. It is to the portion of light scattered thus irregularly that the phenomena, which we are now about to describe, are to be traced.

Newton procured a concave glass speculum or mirror, silvered on the convex side, and in every part exactly a quarter of an inch thick. This he placed in a darkened chamber opposite the window, through which a beam of light was admitted. The radius of the sphere on which the mirror was ground was about six feet, so that the centre of the mirror was at that distance from its surface. At the centre of the mirror he placed a white opaque paper screen, having a small hole in it, and so adjusted the mirror and the screen, that the beam of light, passing through the hole in the screen, should fall upon the mirror, and be reflected back from the mirror to the same hole.

Let A B (*fig.* 50) be the mirror, C D

Fig. 50.

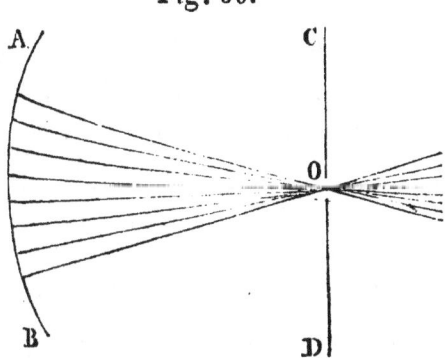

the screen placed before it, so that the hole O shall be at the centre of the mirror. The rays of light, passing from O to the mirror, will fall perpendicularly on it, and consequently all the regularly reflected rays will return to O; and as far as these rays are concerned, the side of the screen presented to A B will be as dark as if no light passed through O to the mirror. Nevertheless, upon observing the screen presented towards A B, Newton found this not to be the case. He observed upon the paper " four or five concentric irises or rings of colours like rainbows, encompassing the hole. These rings, as they grew larger, became fainter and diluter, so that the fifth was scarce visible. Yet, sometimes, when the sun shone very clear, there appeared to be faint lineaments of a sixth and a seventh."

There was a very obvious analogy between these rings, and those exhibited between the lenses in 54. The colours did not succeed each other in the order of the reflected rings, but in that of those which were in that case transmitted. In the centre, at and around O, was a white round spot. This was skirted or fringed with a dark grey, which insensibly brightened into a violet ring. This was followed by a circle of indigo, one of pale blue, a greenish yellow, a vivid pure yellow, and, finally, a red, which deepened into a purple on the outer edge. Such was the first iris which surrounded the white central spot.

This was encompassed by a second series of coloured rings, of which the first was a dark purple, the outer boundary of the red in the former series. This was followed in succession by circles of blue, green, yellow, and red.

The colours of the third and fourth series were green and red. Those of the fifth were so faint as to be scarcely distinguishable.

In order to trace their connexion with rings exhibited by air inclosed between the lenses, Newton now measured their diameters, and found exactly the same proportion subsist among them as prevailed among the rings seen by transmission in that case. In order to make the relation of these phenomena still more manifest, he now transmitted through the hole O, not a beam of compound solar light, but of pure homogeneous light, obtained in the usual way by a prism. Transmitting through O in succession each of the colours, he observed the effects on the screen. Rings now only appeared of that colour which fell upon the speculum. If the speculum were illuminated with red, the rings were totally red with dark intervals; if with blue, they were totally blue, and so of the other colours. With whatever colour they were illuminated, the same proportion subsisted among their diameters as was observed with the lenses.

But if the colour was varied, they varied their magnitude. In the red they were largest; in the indigo and violet least; and in the intermediate colours, yellow, green, and blue, they were of several intermediate sizes, answering to that colour.

Hence it was plain, as in the case of the lenses, that when the speculum was illuminated with white light, the several colours of the rings were produced by the superposition of the rings which were separately formed by projecting successively on the speculum the several component elements of white light. The several tints of the rings produced by the white light admitted, in this case, of being found by such a scale as was explained in 61.

The diameters of the corresponding rings of different colours varied with the refrangibility of the light, and varied exactly according to the same proportion, as in the case of the rings seen between the lenses.

In order to ascertain whether the colours seen upon the screen were the mere effects of light and shade, and not to be attributed to the lights proceeding from the mirror, Newton placed his eye where the rings appeared plainest, and directing his view towards the mirror, he beheld the speculum all tinged over with waves of colours, like those seen between the lenses; and, like these, the rings swelled and contracted as they were viewed more or less obliquely by moving the eye from or towards the centre of the speculum. A bystander, during this experiment, observed upon the eye of the observer the same coloured light as he perceived in the speculum.

On comparing the manner in which these rings were produced with that in which the like phenomena were caused, as described in Chapter VI., the only differences which are observable are the thickness of the glass, and the posterior surface of it being silvered. The thin transparent medium, forming a soap-bubble, has the same figure as the speculum used in the present case, with this difference, that the colours are seen on the convex side, whereas, in the present, they are seen in the concave side. This circumstance, however, so far from impairing the analogy, renders it more perfect when the order of colours is considered, for the rings are not those seen by reflexion in thin transparent mediums, but by transmission. Hence, if the soap-bubble were viewed upon the concave side by an eye placed within it, the colours would be identical with those exhibited by the concave speculum in the present case.

To ascertain whether the silvering upon the back of the speculum had any part in producing the phenomena of the rings, Newton tried the effect of a similar concave glass, without silvering. The result was the production of the same rings, but with more faint colours, owing to the reflecting power of the second surface being diminished by the want of silvering. It therefore appeared that the circumstance of the back of the speculum being silvered, had no other effect than that of increasing the intensity of the colours.

Notwithstanding the identity of the two phenomena, as well as the complete similitude which existed between the manner in which they were produced, Newton did not feel himself warranted in applying the theory of the fits of easy reflection and transmission in accounting for them, until he established the fact that the two surfaces of the glass were indispensable for their production. Were it possible for a single surface, *i.e.* the concave surface alone, to produce the phenomena, this theory would have been quite inapplicable, and altogether inadequate to explain them. To reduce this question to the test of experiment, Newton procured a concave speculum of polished metal, which reflected only from one surface. On presenting this to the light, in the same manner as the glass speculum, no rings were produced. This result was decisive of the point, and proved that the two surfaces were necessary to the production of the rings.

It was plain that the light, *regularly reflected* from the speculum, had no part in these phenomena; for, as all the incident light radiated from the centre of the sphere, it fell perpendicular on the speculum, and was therefore reflected back perpendicularly to the same centre. The rings, therefore, must owe their existence to the light irregularly scattered by the surfaces of the glass. By the experiment already mentioned to have been made with the metallic speculum, it appeared that they could not be produced by the light scattered by the irregular reflection of the first surface alone; for, if that were possible, the metallic speculum, by the surface of which the light was thus scattered, would have exhibited them. The cause of the phenomena was, therefore, to be looked for in the light irregularly refracted by the glass, and reflected by the posterior surface. The rays thus irregularly refracted by the first surface fell upon the second surface at various obliquities, and were reflected by it regularly and irregularly, so as to return through the first surface at various obliquities.

We must here call the recollection of the reader to a property of thin plates already mentioned. A plate of a certain thickness reflects or transmits a certain colour, the rays of light being perpendicular to it. The rays being still perpendicular, every change of thickness will produce a corresponding change of hue in the reflected and transmitted lights. The very same effects, the same shifting of tints, which is thus produced by a change of thickness, the rays remaining perpendicular, may also be produced by changing the direction of the rays, the thickness of the plate remaining unvaried. Thus a plate of a given thickness, at a certain obliquity, will transmit red light, at another yellow, at another green, and so on. Also, if a ray of a particular colour gradually increases its obliquity from the perpendicular direction, it will be alternately reflected and transmitted for many successions.

The glass mirror used in the experiment to which we now refer was, in every part, of exactly the same thickness; therefore the rings of colour could not, as in the case of the lenses, be ascribed to a regular variation of thickness. The light, however, reflected irregularly by the silvered surface of this speculum, encountered the first surface after reflection at various obliquities. Those rays which met the first surface at obliquities proper for transmission, were transmitted to the screen, where they depicted their proper colour, and those which fell upon it at other angles were intercepted. Thus, suppose a ray of homogeneous red light radiated from the centre to the speculum, all the regularly reflected rays returned to the centre. Those which being irregularly reflected by the second surface met the first surface at obliquities proper for transmission, were propagated in corresponding directions to the screen, and they produced a red tint. These rays being regularly disposed in circles round the axis of the speculum, depicted circles of red light on the screen, and the rays returning to the first surface at intermediate obliquities not being in fits of transmission, were intercepted, and thus caused the dark circles between the luminous red ones on the paper. What we have here said of red light may be equally applied to homogeneous lights of other colours; and, hence, will easily be collected the cause of the various coloured rings produced when the light which emanates from the centre of the speculum is compound solar light, this effect being nothing more than the result of the simultaneous exhibition of the rings of each colour.

(81.) Newton points out one difference between the effect of the speculum on the light and that of the thin plates, described in Chapter VII. In the latter case the colours are produced by alternate reflections and transmissions of the light at the second surface of the plate, after one passage through it; but here they pass from the first surface to the second, and then return from the second to the first, there being either transmitted to the screen or reflected to the silvered surface, according as they are in fits of easy transmission or reflection.

By measuring the diameters of the rings of the different lights, and comparing this with the distance of the screen from the speculum, Newton ascertained the obliquities at which the lights of different colours emerged from the speculum, and thence derived the angles at which they were incident on the first surface after reflection at the second. On comparing these with the obliquities corresponding to the lights of different colours deduced from the theory established in Chapter VII., he found a perfect accordance.

(82.) In order, however, to put the matter to a more decisive test, he calculated the effect which the thickness of the glass which formed the speculum would produce upon the diameters of the several rings, and found that, according to the theory of fits of easy reflection and transmission, the squares of the diameters of corresponding rings produced by different mirrors should be in the inverse proportion of the thickness of the mirrors. He, therefore, procured another speculum, ground on both sides, to the same sphere with the former. Its thickness was $\frac{5}{62}$ parts of an inch, and the diameters of the first three bright rings, measured between the brightest parts of their orbits, at the distance of six feet from the glass, were 3, $4\frac{1}{6}$, $5\frac{1}{8}$ inches. Now, the thickness of the other glass being $\frac{1}{4}$ of an inch, was to the thickness of this as $\frac{1}{4}$ to $\frac{5}{62}$, or as 62 to

20, or 31 to 10, or as 310,000,000, 100,000,000, which numbers are very nearly as the squares of 17,607 and 10,000, and in the proportion of the first of these to the second, are the diameters of the bright rings made by the thinner glass, 3, 4⅛, 5⅛, to the diameters of the corresponding rings made by the thicker glass, 1¼¼, 2⅜, 2¼½. This perfect accordance of the phenomena with the results of theory was considered by Newton to be conclusive as to the validity of his hypothesis.

CHAPTER IX.

Experiments on the Inflexion of Light.

(83.) In the account of the state of optical science before the time of Newton, which was given in the first chapter, the discovery of the diffraction or inflexion of light by Grimaldi was noticed. This phenomenon was too striking to escape the attention of Newton. He accordingly instituted some experiments with a view to the investigation of this property; but he seems not to have had leisure or inclination to pursue the subject to as great an extent, or to obtain results so satisfactory as those which have been discussed in the preceding chapters. In the commencement of his third book, however, he describes some experiments which he made, and hazards some conjectures on the probable cause of these phenomena, which, as well as some other matters connected with physical science in general, and with the phenomena of heat and light in particular, he proposes in the form of queries. He states that he was interrupted in his investigations; that he could not afterwards think of taking these things into further consideration; and as he had not finished his design, he leaves these queries, in order to a further search to be made by others.

The experiments which led Grimaldi to the discovery of inflexion were the following. Through a small aperture A B (*fig.* 51) he admitted a beam of

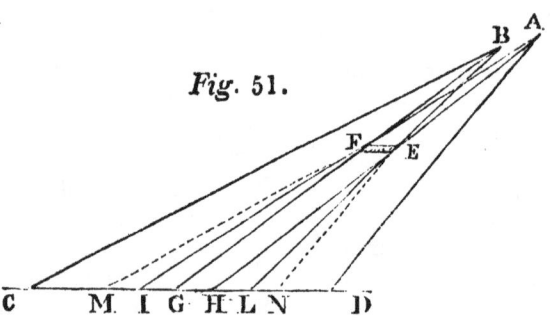

Fig. 51.

light into a dark room. He observed that the light thus admitted, spread itself in the form of a cone, and illuminated a large portion of a screen C D, held perpendicular to its direction, and at some distance from the hole, the illuminated part of this screen increasing with the increase of distance. When an opaque body E F was held in the light so as to cast a shadow on the screen C D, this shadow was found to be much larger than it would have been if the light had passed the edges of E F in right lines. From B draw the straight line B F G and from A the line A E H. Also from A draw the right line A F I, and from B the right line B E L. Now, if the light passes the edges of E F in right lines, it is plain that the space G H will be altogether deprived of light, and that from the limits G H to I and L respectively there will be a partial or penumbral illumination; but that beyond the limits I L, the illumination of the screen will be as complete as if the opaque object E F were not present. This was, however, found not to be the fact, for the shadow extended beyond I and L to wider limits, as M and N.

Beyond this shadow, and skirting it, Grimaldi observed three coloured fringes, the broadest and brightest of which was next the shadow. If X (*fig.* 52) represent the edge of the shadow, the space N N was *blue*, M was colourless, and O O red. In the second fringe, Q Q was faint blue, P colourless, and R R red. This fringe was narrower than the first and more faint. The third fringe T T, S and V V, was similar to the other two, but still narrower and fainter.

Fig. 52.

When the opaque body has a salient angle as D (*fig.* 53), the fringes were arched round it, and at a re-entrant angle they intersected each other as at C.

Newton repeated and varied these experiments of Grimaldi. He pierced a plate of lead with a pin, making a hole

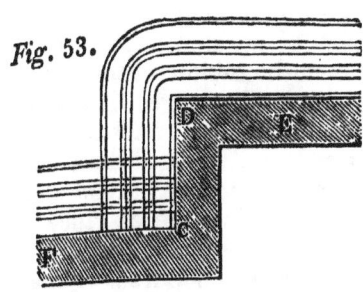

Fig. 53.

in it, the diameter of which was the 42nd part of an inch. Through this hole he admitted a beam of the sun's light, and found that the shadows of hairs, pins, straws, and such slender substances, appeared, when received upon a screen, to be much larger than they would be if the light passed their edges in unbroken straight lines. A human hair, the breadth of which was the 280th of an inch, held at 12 feet from the hole, cast a shadow upon a screen held at 4 inches from it, which was the 60th part of an inch broad, that is, above four times broader than the hair. Like effects were observable with other opaque bodies, and at all distances.

These effects were found to be entirely independent of the refractive power of the air, or of the nature of the body whose shadow was formed. When the hair was surrounded with moisture, or inclosed with a liquid between glass planes, the effect was the same. The scratches made on glass, and the veins in plates of that material, produced shadows of the same kind. Thus whatever was the origin of this effect, it was evident, that it did not proceed from the refractive powers of bodies, nor on any quality connected with the nature or properties of bodies of particular species.

The way in which Newton conceived the rays to be affected in passing the body may be thus explained. Let X (fig. 54) be a section of the hair at right

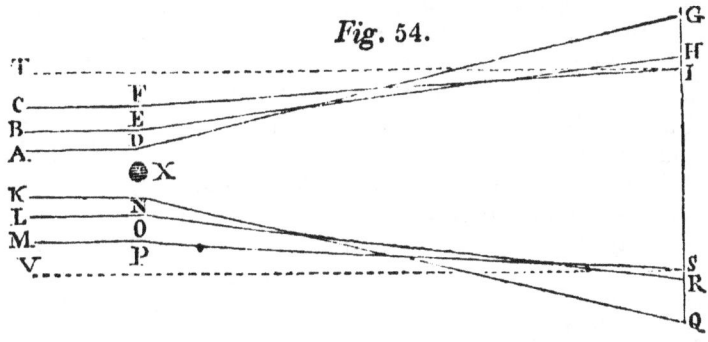

Fig. 54.

angles to its length. Let A D, B E, C F, K N, L O, M P, be rays of light approaching the hair in parallel directions. The ray A D is deflected at D in the direction D G, and falls upon the screen at G. In like manner the ray K N, at the same distance below the hair, is deflected in the direction N Q, meeting the screen at Q. Newton supposes that the force which deflects the light diminishes as the distance from the hair increases. Consequently, the rays B E and L O will be less deflected than A D and K N, and their deflected directions E H and O R will cross those of the nearer rays, if the screen be sufficiently distant from the hair.

In like manner, the more distant rays C F and M P will be still less deflected, and will also cross both the last rays. This continues until the distance of the ray from the hair becomes so great, that the deflecting power is lost, and the rays proceed in straight lines to the paper as T I and V S. These rays at I and S bound the shadow, and at the hair include within them the deflected rays, all of which they must cross between the hair and the screen.

The continued intersections of the deflected rays with each other between the hair and the screen form curves, which are concave towards the shadow, and the distance between which increases as the distance from the hair increases. It is evident also that the illuminated space on the screen, immediately beyond the boundaries L S of the shadow is exposed to the light of the deflected rays between T I or V S and the hair, as well as to the direct rays which proceed without T I and V S and parallel to them.

The shadows of bodies, such as metals, stones, glass, wood, horn, ice, &c., exposed to light in this way, were skirted with three coloured fringes. The colours observed by Newton in these fringes were as follows: the first or innermost fringe was violet, deep blue, light blue, green, yellow, and red. The second and third fringes which immediately succeeded this were blue, yellow, red; but their colours were faint.

Upon measuring the breadths of these fringes at their brightest parts, and also the breadths of their intervals, Newton found them nearly in the same proportion, and so that the fringes and intervals taken in regular succession were as the following quantities:

$$1, \frac{1}{\sqrt{2}}, \frac{1}{\sqrt{3}}, \frac{1}{\sqrt{4}}, \frac{1}{\sqrt{5}}$$

His next experiments were on the shadows produced by the edges of sharp knives placed across the aperture through which the light was transmitted. The light admitted between the edges being received upon a screen at some distance, the edges were moved towards one another, until their distance did not exceed the four hundredth part of an inch. The light upon the screen now parted in the middle, and formed two parallel lines. The intermediate shadow was so black and dark that all the light which passed between the knives seemed to be bent, and turned to the one side or the other. As the edges approached, the shadow grew broader, and the lines of light narrower, until at length, when the edges were in actual contact, the light wholly vanished. This experiment Newton considered conclusive of the greater deflection of the rays which were nearer the body.

From these experiments, he concluded that the light which formed the first fringe passed the edge of the knife at a distance not less than the eight hundredth part of an inch; that the light of the second fringe passed the edge of the knife at a greater distance than that of the first, and the light of the third fringe at a still greater distance.

From these and other circumstances, Newton concluded that the distances at which the light forming the fringes passed the knives are not altered by the approach of the knives, but that the angles at which the light is inflected are increased by their approach; the knife which is nearer each ray determining the direction in which it is bent, and the other knife increasing the deflection.

When the rays fell very obliquely on the ruler, at the distance of the third of an inch from the knives, the dark lines between the first and second fringes bounding each shadow, intersected each other at the distance of the fifth of an inch from the termination of the light. Hence Newton computed the distance between the edges, at the concourse of these lines, to be the hundred and sixtieth part of an inch. Since this concourse is in the middle of the light which passes between the edges, it follows that one-half of the light passes each edge at a distance not greater than the three hundred and twentieth part of an inch.

Upon increasing the distance of the ruler from the knives, he found that the distance of the concourse of the dark lines before mentioned, from the termination of the light, was more than the fifth part of an inch. Hence it appeared that the light, which in this case passed between the knives at the concourse of the dark lines, passed at a greater distance from the edges than the hundred and sixtieth part of an inch.

From these experiments Newton concluded that "the light which makes the fringes, is not the same light at all distances from the knives; but when the ruler is held near the knives, the fringes are made by light which passes the edges at a less distance, and is more bent than that which forms the same fringes at a greater distance." It will be perceived that this is consistent with the explanation of the phenomena of inflection already given.

When the shadows were received upon paper at a great distance from the knives, the fringes assumed the form of hyperbolic curves, being nearly straight where the distance between the edges was considerable, but bending into arches after intersecting. Let CA, CB, fig. 55, represent the projections of the edges of the knives upon the paper. The entire light would fall within the angle ACB, were there no inflection. Through C draw DE equally inclined to CA and CB. The curve eis represents the boundary of the shadow of the blade AC; fkt represents the dark line which separates the first and second fringe, and glo the dark line which separates the second and third fringe. The lines xip, ykg, zlr, are similarly related to the shadow of the other edge.

The two systems of curves, which are perfectly similar, intersect at the points i, k, l; so that the shadows of the edges are marked by the lines eis and xip, until the intersection of the fringes, and then each of those lines crosses the fringe corresponding to the *other* edge. Then those lines cross the fringes, distinguishing them from another light which begins to appear at i, and illuminates the triangular space $ipDEs$.

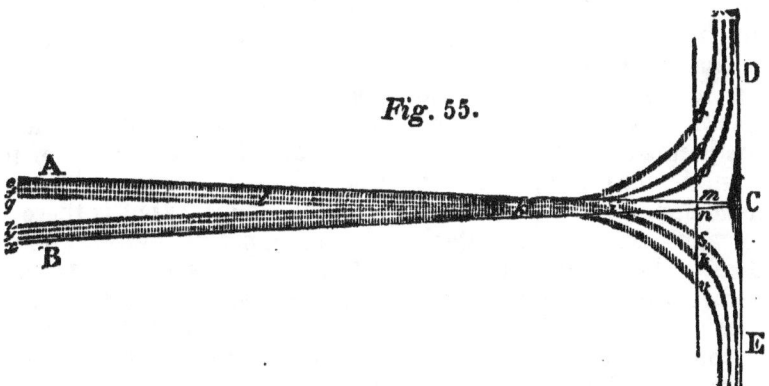

Fig. 55.

Newton now repeated the first experiment described in page 219; but, instead of using compound solar light, he used homogeneous light, obtained by a prism placed behind the hole through which the light was transmitted. He found the shadows of all bodies held in this light bordered with fringes, not as before of different colours, but of the colour of the transmitted light. Those made by the red light were largest, and those made by the violet, least; the intermediate colours having intermediate breadths.

From these experiments he inferred that the rays which formed the fringes in the red light passed by the body at a greater distance than those which formed the violet or any of the intermediate colours. So that the action of the body on the less refrangible rays at a given distance was equal to its action on the more refrangible rays at a less distance, and thus occasioned the tints of the fringes without changing the colour or properties of any component part of the solar light.

Such was the state to which Newton's experimental investigations had arrived, when they were unfortunately interrupted. In the queries, however, annexed to this book, and which have been already alluded to, he throws out some suggestions for the consideration of future inquirers. The following queries relate to the subject with which we have just been engaged.

1. Do not bodies act on light at a distance; and by their action bend its rays? and is not this action strongest at the least distance?

2. Do not the rays which differ in refrangibility differ also in flexibility? and are they not, by their different inflexions, separated from one another, so as, after separation, to make the colours in the three fringes above described? and after what manner are they inflected to make those fringes?

3. Are not the rays of light in passing by the edges and sides of bodies bent several times backwards and forwards with a motion like an eel? and do not the three fringes of coloured light above-mentioned arise from three such bendings?

4. Do not the rays of light which fall upon bodies, and are reflected or refracted, begin to bend before they arrive at the bodies; and are they not reflected, refracted, and inflected by one and the same principle, acting variously in various circumstances?

The theory hinted at in these queries is sufficient to represent the principal phenomena of inflexion; but it must be confessed that the undulatory theory affords rather a more satisfactory generalization of those complicated effects, and has been more generally adopted in the investigations of modern philosophers. Neither the material nor undulatory theory can be said to be satisfactorily established; but it would seem that every phenomenon which can be brought under the former, can also, with equal facility, be explained by the latter; while there are some known effects in strict accordance with the latter, which cannot, without great difficulty and the introduction of gratuitous hypothesis, be accounted for by the former. For the most part, however, the language of either may be translated into the other.

To discuss the question respecting the experiments which have been just described, and the inferences drawn from them, it would be necessary to refer to the original experiments and reasoning of Grimaldi, and the later investigations of Dr. Young and Fresnel. Such details are, however, foreign to the objects of the present treatise.

The remaining queries which terminate this book relate to the probable connexion and causes of heat and light, the sense of vision, the cause of gravitation, and other subjects in physics, which cannot properly find a place here. To this, however, we must make exception of that (the 26th) in which he points out the polarity of light, to the merit of having first suggested which he has an undoubted right. "If the planes of perpendicular refraction of one piece of Iceland spar be at right angles with those of another, the rays which are refracted after the usual manner by the first crystal will be all refracted after the unusual manner in passing through the second crystal; and the rays which are refracted after the unusual manner in passing through the first crystal will be all of them refracted after the usual manner in passing through the second." Hence Newton concluded, that the rays have *sides*, possessing different properties, in virtue of which they will be differently refracted, according to the direction in which the crystal is presented to them. If the ray be successively transmitted through two crystals, and is placed in the same manner with respect to the planes of both, it will be refracted in the same manner by both; but if that side of the ray which looks towards the coast of unusual refraction in the first crystal be at right angles with that side of the same ray which looks towards the coast of unusual refraction in the second crystal, the ray shall be refracted after several manners in several crystals. There is nothing more required to determine whether the rays of light, which fall upon the second crystal, shall be refracted after the usual or after the unusual manner, but to turn about this crystal, so that the coast of its unusual refraction may be on this or on that side of the ray. *And therefore every ray may be considered as having four sides or quarters, two of which opposite to one another incline the ray to be refracted after the unusual manner, as often as either of them are turned towards the coast of unusual refraction, and the other two, whenever either of them are turned towards the coast of unusual refraction, do not incline it to be otherwise refracted than after the usual manner. The first two may therefore be called the sides of unusual refraction.*

We cannot better conclude the rapid sketch which we have attempted to give of this extraordinary production of human genius, than by quoting some precepts which have been most admirably illustrated in the works of this illustrious philosopher. "The main business of natural philosophy is to argue from phenomena without feigning hypotheses, and to deduce causes from effects until we come to the very First Cause, which certainly is not mechanical; and not only to unfold the mechanism of the world, but chiefly to resolve these and such like questions: What is there in places almost empty of matter, and whence is it that the sun and planets gravitate towards one another without dense matter between them? Whence is it that nature doth nothing in vain? and whence arise all that order and beauty which we see in the world? To what end are comets, and whence is it that planets move all in one and the same way in orbits concentric, while comets move in all manner of ways, in orbits excentric; and what hinders the fixed stars from falling on one another? How came the bodies of animals to be contrived with so much art, and for what ends were their several parts? Was the eye contrived without skill in optics, and the ear without knowledge of sounds? How do the motions of the body follow from the will, and whence is the instinct of animals? Is not the sensory of animals that place to which the sensitive substance is present, and into which the sensitive species of things are carried through the nerves and the brain, that there they may be perceived by their immediate presence to that substance? And these things being rightly dispatched, does it not appear from phenomena, that there is a Being incorporeal, living, intelligent, omnipresent, who, in infinite space, as it were in his sensory, sees the things themselves, intimately and thoroughly perceives them, and comprehends them wholly by their immediate presence to himself; of which things the images only, carried through the organs of sense into our little sensoriums, are there seen and beheld by that which in us perceives and thinks. And though every step in this philosophy brings us not immediately to the knowledge of the First Cause, yet it brings us nearer to it, and on that account is highly to be valued. * * * And if natural philosophy in all its parts shall at length be perfected, the bounds of moral philosophy shall also be enlarged. For so far as we can know by natural philosophy what is the First Cause, what power he has over us and what benefits we receive from him, so far our duty towards him as well as that towards one another, will appear to us by the light of nature."

A

PRACTICAL TREATISE

ON

OPTICAL INSTRUMENTS.

AS PUBLISHED IN THE LIBRARY OF USEFUL KNOWLEDGE.

WITH AN APPENDIX,

GIVING

AN ACCOUNT OF NEW INSTRUMENTS AND IMPROVEMENTS
TO THE YEAR 1850.

ILLUSTRATED BY ONE HUNDRED ENGRAVINGS.

BY

ANDREW PRITCHARD, Esq., M.R.I.,

HON. MEM. SOC. ARTS, ED.; HON. MEM. MED. SOC., KING'S COLLEGE; AUTHOR OF A HISTORY OF
INFUSORIA, LIVING AND FOSSIL; MICROSCOPIC CABINET, ILLUSTRATIONS,
MICROGRAPHIA, ETC. ETC.

LONDON:—ROBERT BALDWIN,
47, PATERNOSTER ROW.

1850.

LONDON:
GEORGE WOODFALL AND SON,
ANGEL COURT, SKINNER STREET.

CONTENTS.

	Page
INTRODUCTION	1
CHAP. I. Mirrors.—Plane Looking glasses.—Concave Mirrors.—Burning Mirrors.—Convex Mirrors	2
II. Lenses.—Burning Lenses.—Polygonal Lenses	4
III. Spectacles.—Penscopic Spectacles	8
IV. Telescopes.—Common Astronomical Telescope.—Day Telescope.—Dynameters	9
V. Aberration of Reflectors and of Lenses.—Glass and Diamond Compared.—Huygens' Eye-Piece—Ramsden's Eye-Piece.—Newton's Parabolic Lenses.—Chromatic Dispersion	11
VI. Reflecting Telescopes.—The Newtonian.—The Gregorian.—The Cassegrainian.—Sir W. Herschel's.—Mr. Ramage's	15
VII. Theory of Achromatic Telescopes.—Double Object-Glass	19
VIII. Aplanatic Telescopes of Clairaut's Construction.—Mr. J. F. Herschel's Object-Glass.—Triple Object-Glasses.—Fraunhofer's and Tulley's Telescopes.—Galilean Telescope and Opera Glass.—Achromatic Opera Glass.—Dr. Brewster's Fluid Opera Glass	20
IX. Dr. Brewster's Telescope for measuring Distances.—Double Image Telescope.—Graphic Telescope.—Achromatic Eye-Pieces	25
X. Stands for Telescopes.—Method of Making, Grinding, and Polishing Specula and Lenses.—Method of Centering and Adjusting Lenses	29
XI. Microscopes.—History of.—Theory of Single Magnifying Powers of.—Illumination.—Forms of Lenses for Microscopes.—Globules.—Globule and Lens compared.—Mr. Pritchard's Diamond and Sapphire Microscopes.—Table of their Magnifying Powers	33
XII. Penscopic Microscopes.—Dr. Wollaston's.—Dr. Brewster's.—Mr. Herschel's for Mineralogy—Aplanatic	48
XIII. Fluid and Single Reflecting Telescopes	42

	Page
CHAP. XIV. Theory of Compound Microscopes.—Mechanical Arrangements of.—Eye-Pieces.—Magnifying Power of.—Object Glasses.—Dr. Goring's.—Mr. Tulley's.—M. Chevalier's.—S. Amicis.—Mr. Herschel's.—Dr. Brewster's.—The Amician Reflecting Microscope, with its Improvements	43
XV. Test Objects.—Opaque Microscope.—Solar Microscope, improved.—Lacernal Magic Lantern.—Phantasmagoria	49
XVI. Camera Obscura.—Portable Box.—Revolving Penscopic.—Camera Lucida.—Penscopic.—Amicis' improved.—Treinoscope.—Dr. Brewster's.—Amicis'.—Multiplying Glasses.—Kaleidoscope.—Telescopic	52
XVII. Micrometers	56

APPENDIX.

	Page
CHAP. XVIII. Improvements on Telescopes and their Stands.—Reflecting Telescopes of Lord Rosse	61
XIX. Microscopes:—On Stanhope and Coddington Lenses and Doublet Microscopes.—Achromatic Microscopes.—Microscopic Aphorisms.—Illumination.—Micrometers.—The Megaloscope.—Oxyhydrogen Microscopes	67
XX. The Chromatrope.—Physioscope.—Burning Mirrors	80
XXI. Opera Glasses.—Photographic Cameras.—Daguerreotype Mirrors	81

OPTICAL INSTRUMENTS.

INTRODUCTION.

THE construction of optical instruments has, in almost every instance, originated with eminent philosophers and mathematicians. Their gradual perfection has been a natural result of the difficulties which were presented to the progress of discovery, by the inefficient and inaccurate means which science possessed; and thus, the same great minds that have struck out and pursued vast and splendid ideas in their investigations of nature, have only been enabled to follow up their own conceptions by applying themselves to the practical improvement of the instruments with which they had commenced their discoveries. For instance, we are indebted to Newton for the construction of the first reflecting telescope that was ever made, although the idea had been previously suggested by Dr. Gregory. Leuwenhoek, one of the most assiduous naturalists of his day, carried on his curious researches in the animal and vegetable economy, with microscopes made by his own hands. The late Dr. Herschel, whose astronomical discoveries were the result of the profoundest mathematical knowledge, constructed the most powerful telescopes ever known, which, like the Gregorian, bear the name of their inventor. Indeed, the ordinary makers of optical instruments have been often men of considerable scientific attainments;—and it is from this union of a theoretic and practical knowledge, that these instruments, as is the case with almost every other important invention and improvement, have been conducted to their present very high state of perfection, in an almost unlimited adaptation to all the purposes of science, and all the wants and luxuries of common life.

In the limited extent of this treatise on Optical Instruments, the chief object will be to point out the principle of their construction, freed from *technical* mathematics, and to describe the improved state in which the more important are adapted to their several purposes. The various modes in which many instruments, not differing in their principle and end, are *mounted*, depend upon the varying taste of the artist, the caprice of fashion, or the demands of luxury. Any minute details of the *external* parts of the instruments would be therefore perfectly useless. Indeed, the external parts of the ordinary instruments can be much better understood by an inspection at the opticians' shops, than in volumes of description. So indifferent is the outward form of the common instruments, that makers living even in the same neighbourhood vary as much in their mountings as the artists of London or Paris. We shall, therefore, confine our observations to the *essential* parts in the construction of particular instruments, passing over their accidental varieties of mounting; — in the same way that the anatomist speaks of the various parts of the human body, without enquiring whether the *subject* upon which he has made his observations was dark or fair, tall or short.

The ancients seem to have been but little acquainted with dioptrical instruments, or those by which the light is refracted and transmitted; from their earliest history, however, they appear to have been conversant with the laws of the reflection of objects from the surface of water and polished metals, or that department of optical science called catoptrics. The first application of their knowledge of this branch of science, with which we are acquainted, is that of the burning mirrors employed by Archimedes, a philosopher of Syracuse, about 200 years before the Christian era, who, at the siege of that city, by Marcellus, the Roman Consul, employed them to destroy the besieging navy. The method by which this was probably accomplished is thus described by the historian Tzetzes:—"When the fleet of Marcellus was within bowshot, the old man Archimedes brought an hexagonal mirror, which he had previously prepared, at a proper distance from which he also placed other smaller mirrors of the same kind that moved in all directions on hinges, which when placed in the sun's rays directed them upon the Roman fleet, whereby it was reduced to ashes." We are also informed that Proclus in the same way destroyed the fleet of Vitalian at the siege of Byzantium.

CHAPTER I.—*Mirrors—Plane Looking-Glasses—Concave Mirrors—Burning Mirrors—Convex Mirrors.*

(1.) *Mirrors* are surfaces of polished metal, or glass silvered on its posterior side, capable of reflecting the rays of light from objects placed before them, and exhibiting to us their image. There are three classes of mirrors, distinguishable by the figure of their reflecting surface. These are *plane, concave,* and *convex.*— The reflection of light by either of these mirrors observes this constant *law*, that the angle which the incident ray makes with the reflecting surface, is equal to the angle of reflection. We may explain this law by a figure. Let *c d*, (*fig.* 1.) be a section of the reflecting surface:

Fig. 1.

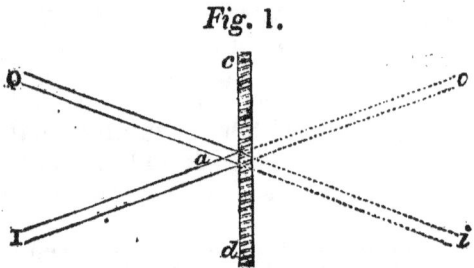

o an object before the mirror; and O *a* rays proceeding to the surface in the point *a*. The angle O *a c* which the rays make with the surface of the mirror is called the angle of *incidence;* and the direction in which an observer will see the object O in the mirror at *a*, must be I *a*, the angle of reflection I *a d* being equal to the angle of incidence O *a c*. If we suppose O I to be two persons viewing each other in a plane mirror or looking-glass *c d*, the direction in which each observeth the other at the point *a* is *a o* or *a i*, but the apparent place of their images will be behind the glass at the point *i* or *o*, the distance behind corresponding with that of their situation before the mirror. This deception proceeds from our common experience, which leads us to expect the object to be in the direction in which the rays come to our eyes, instead of in the real place of the object. The illusion is so complete, that domestic animals, when viewing themselves in a looking-glass for the first time, often have their passions strongly excited. When a person is viewing himself in a looking-glass, if he measure the size which he appears on the glass, the image will be one half his real magnitude, let his distance from the glass be in any manner varied. For, as it was stated above that the image appears behind the glass exactly at the same distance as the object is before it, it must be evident that as the mirror is half way between him and his apparent image, it will cut in half the cone of rays which proceed from his image to his eye. This is shown in *fig.* 2, where *c d* is a section

Fig. 2.

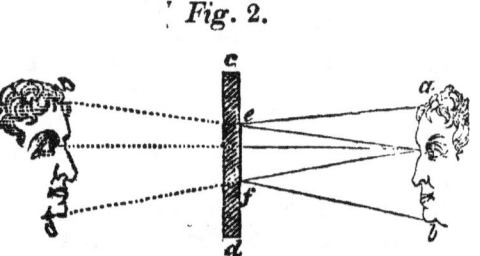

of a plane mirror or looking-glass, and *a b* the face of a person viewing himself in it; now rays from every part of his face fall upon the reflector, from which they are sent to the eye, forming a cone of rays whose apex enters the pupil; consequently, as this cone is cut by the glass half way between the apex and its base, which base is himself, the measure of the line *e f* will be half of *a b*.

(2.) *Concave Mirrors* are those whose polished surfaces are spherically hollow. The properties of these mirrors may be easily understood, when we consider

Fig. 3.

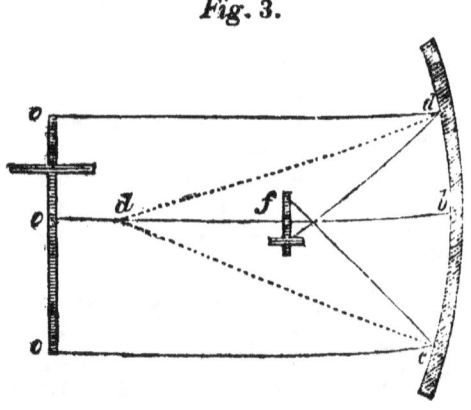

their surface as composed of an indefinite number of small planes all of which make a determinate angle with each other, so as to throw all the rays to a point. (See fig. 3.) Let *a b c* be a concave mirror, and let *d* be the centre of curvature, and *o o o* rays of light from a distant object (the cross in the wood-cut must be supposed at a considerable distance) falling on the mirror at *a b c*, making different angles with its surface; these rays when reflected at equal angles to their incidence, as may be seen by the dotted lines which are perpendicular, will meet in a point *f*, called the focus of the mirror, where an image of the object will be formed in an inverted position. The distance of this focal point from the surface of the mirror, when the curvature is moderate, will be equal to half its radius *d b*. The importance of concave mirrors in the construction of reflecting telescopes, in which construction they are commonly called specula, will be shown hereafter under that head.

The employment of concave mirrors in collecting the heat of the sun's rays from the whole of its surface to a single point, thus accumulating a very great degree of heat, for the combustion and fusion of various natural substances that are infusible in the greatest heat capable of being produced from ordinary fire, may be exemplified, amongst those of modern date, by the burning mirror of M. de Villette. The diameter of this metal speculum was 3 feet 11 inches, and its focal distance or point *f* from the surface was 3 feet 2 inches. The composition of this metal was of tin and copper, which reflects the light very powerfully, and is capable of a high degree of polish. When exposed to the rays of the sun, by Drs. Harris and Desaguliers, a silver sixpence was melted in $7\frac{1}{2}$ seconds when placed in its focus; a copper halfpenny melted in 16 seconds and liquefied in 34 seconds; tin was melted in 3 seconds; and a diamond, weighing 4 grains, lost $\frac{7}{8}$ths of its weight[*]. The intensity of heat, obtained by burning mirrors or lenses, will always be as the area of the reflecting surface exposed to the sun is to the area of the small circle of light collected in its focus; thus, the diameter of the spot of light at the focus of *Villette's* mirror was 0.358 of an inch, and the diameter of the mirror 47 inches; hence the area of these circles was as 0.358^2 to 47^2, that is, the intensity of the sun's rays was increased 17257 times at the focal point. The loss of light occasioned in passing through the medium of which the lens is composed, together with that lost by reflection from the surface of mirrors, must, however, be deducted from this theoretical calculation. See *Photometers*.

Concave mirrors afford many curious and pleasing illustrations of their peculiar properties. For example:—when a person stands in front of a concave mirror, a little further from its surface than its focus (or half the radius of its concavity), he will observe his own image pendant in the air before him, and in an inverted position: this image will advance and recede with him; and, if he stretch out his hand, the image will do the like. Exhibitions have been brought before the public in which a singular deception was obtained by a large concave mirror. A man being placed with his head downwards, in its focus an *erect* image of him was exhibited, while his real person was concealed, and the place of the mirror darkened; the spectators were then directed to take a plate of fruit from his hand, which in an instant was dexterously changed for a dagger, or some other dangerous weapon.

(3.) *Convex mirrors* are chiefly employed as ornaments in apartments. The objects viewed in these are diminished, but seen in an erect position; the images appear to emanate from a point behind the mirror; this point, which is its focus, will be half the radius of convexity behind their surface, and is called the negative, or imaginary focus, because the rays are not actually collected as by a concave mirror, whose focus is called real.[*]

---

[*] The burning mirror constructed by Count Buffon, was a polyhedron, 6 feet broad and as many high, consisting of 168 small mirrors, or flat pieces of looking-glass, each 6 inches square. By means of this instrument, with the faint rays of the sun in the month of March, he set on fire boards of beech wood at 150 feet distance. This machine had the convenience of burning downwards, or horizontally at pleasure, each speculum being moveable, so as, by the means of three screws, to be set to a proper inclination for directing the rays towards any given point. It thus turned either in its greater focus or in any nearer interval, possessing this great superiority over common burning glasses whose foci are fixed and determined. Buffon at another time burnt wood at the distance of more than 120 feet, and silver was fused at 50 feet. See the article Burning Apparatus, in the Edinburgh Enclyclopædia.

[*] The reflecting surfaces of cylinders have been occasionally used in optical amusements, for rendering *anamorphoses* (distorted or deformed pictures) of their proper shape when reflected from its surface.

CHAPTER II.—Lenses—Burning Lenses—Polyzonal Lenses.

Lenses.—(4.) A lens is any transparent substance, as glass, crystal, water, or diamond, having one or both of its surfaces curved to collect or disperse the light transmitted by it. The lenses in general use are made of glass, and are usually called magnifying glasses. Glass, however, does not possess a greater share of the magnifying property than other transparent substances. In *fig.* 4, there are six differently shaped lenses, shown in section. A is called a planoconvex, from having one side flat, and the other spherically rounded. B is a double convex, and has both sides spherically rounded. When these sides are unequally curved, as at C, it is termed a crossed lens. D is a plano-concave, having one side spherically hollow. E is a double concave with both sides hollow. F is a Meniscus (so called from its moon shape), and has one side convex and the other concave.

Fig. 4.

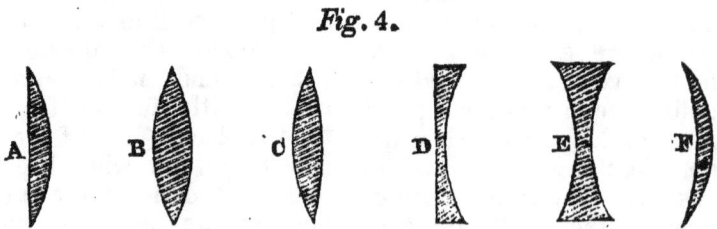

(5.) The passage of light, when transmitted by a plano-convex lens, is shown in *figs.* 5 and 6. Let A (*fig.* 5.) represent

Fig. 5.

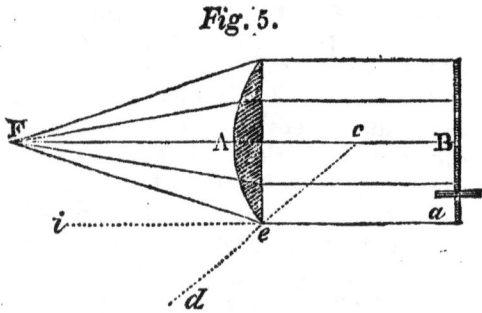

a section of the lens, and B an object at an infinite distance, as a star (in the figure a cross is placed to assist the conception). Now, the lines from B to A will represent the rays proceeding from every part of the object B, to every portion of the surface of the lens A, and from the distance of the object they will be parallel to each other. Only five rays are drawn in the figure, to prevent confusion; but it should be constantly remembered that the light strikes every part of the lens. The first surface of the lens next the object B is flat; and as all the rays fall perpendicularly on it, and the attraction on each side of the rays is equal, they will pass on in their right-lined direction, till they meet the curved surface of the lens, when all the rays will be bent or refracted, so as to meet in a point F, called the focus of the lens; but the central ray being perpendicular to the curved surface is not bent. This constant law of refraction, or bending, is always observed by rays of light in their passage from one medium to another of different density, whose surface is oblique to their direction; and the rays of light in passing from a dense medium, as glass, &c. into a less refractive medium, as air, will be bent so as to form a greater angle with a perpendiular to that surface, than it had at first. Let the dotted line *c d* be a perpendicular to the surface of the lens at the point *e*. Now, the angle *a e c*, called the angle of incidence, is less than the angle F *e d*, called the angle of refraction, as is shown by continuing the ray *a* to *i*.

(6.) But whenever light strikes an oblique surface in its passage from a rare medium, as air, to a denser, as glass, it will be refracted nearer the perpendicular, as shown by *fig.* 6, in which the lens is reversed. The ray of light *a e* is there bent nearer the perpendicular *c d*, as shown by the dotted line *e r*, and when this ray is transmitted by the plane side, it will be refracted to F,

Fig. 6.

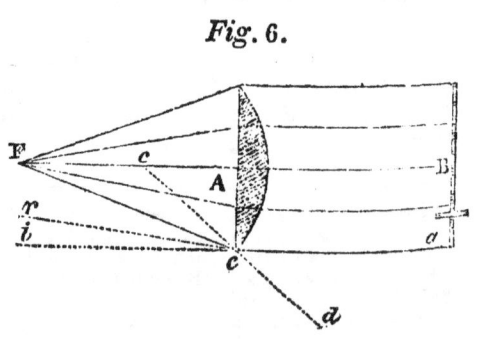

making a greater angle with the perpendicular to the flat side, as it now enters a rarer medium.

(7.) If, instead of supposing the object at an infinite distance, and consequently a point, we imagine it removed to some finite distance, a like action in a proportional degree will be observed, only the object will not be reduced to a point, but its image will be formed at F, whose size is equal to the angle under which the object would be seen without the lens. Let $a\,c$ (*fig.* 7.) be the object, and b the lens: now, this object will subtend the angle $a\,b\,c$ from every portion of the lens, and an inverted image $d\,e$ will be formed under the equal angle $d\,b\,e$; for whenever right lines intersect each other, the opposite angles are always equal. This experiment may be proved by a common convex glass lens. Suppose the distance of the focal point is six inches, and the lens two inches in diameter, the image of a distant object may be seen on a wall when the lens is held a little more than its focal length from it; then let the size of the image be measured: now remove the lens, and measure the apparent size of the object, while the eye of the observer is in its place, taking the distance of the focus of the lens for the point of measurement, and it will be found of the same size in both cases. If a wafer is made to adhere to the surface of the lens, so as to stop a portion of the light, the size is not altered, but the image will be formed less bright.

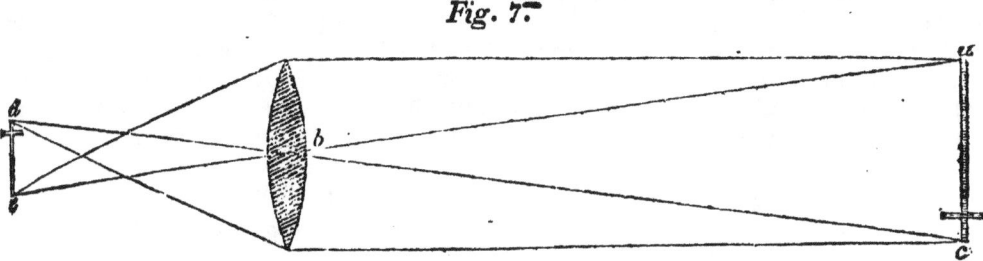

Fig. 7.

(8.) When an object is placed in the focus of a lens, the rays diverging from it will, by the action of the lens, be rendered parallel; this case, however, is only the reverse of the former, the place of the object and image being changed. But this astonishing circumstance will take place: when observed on the side for parallel rays, the objects will appear magnified or increased in size, should the distance of the object from the lens be less than the eye can see it without. Let $a\,b$ (*fig.* 8.) be the nearest distance at which an object can be seen distinctly without the assistance of a lens, and $b\,d$, the distance of the object when seen through the lens, equal to half the distance $a\,b$; now the angle $c\,b\,g$, which the object subtended without the lens, is only half the angle $e\,b\,f$; and, therefore, the object will be magnified twice, when seen by the lens; and if the distance had been only $\frac{1}{3}$, $\frac{1}{4}$, $\frac{1}{10}$, the object would have been magnified 3, 4, or 10 times in length and breadth, and, consequently, its surface increased 9, 16, or 100 times.

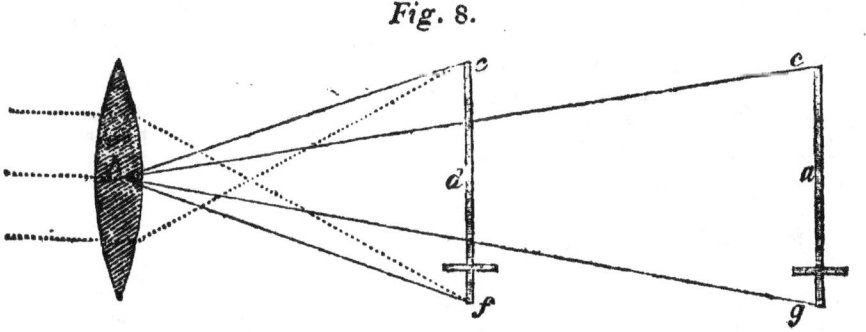

Fig. 8.

(9.) Concave lenses obey the same laws of refraction as convex, but as the curvature is reversed, the rays are bent outwards; hence a concave lens will render parallel rays diverging, as may be seen in *fig.* 9, where a is the object, $a\,b$ rays proceeding parallel to each other from the object. These rays, when transmitted by the concave lens, are made to diverge, as if they came from the point f, the imaginary focus of the lens; the perpendicular cd shews that the rays obey the same law of refraction as in a convex lens. It should be here observed, that when the lens is concave,

Fig. 9.

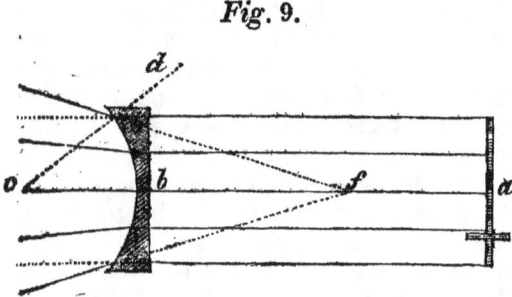

the focal point will be on the same side as the object, and it is termed negative, as objects are diminished by concave lenses.

When converging rays from a convex lens are transmitted by a concave, they are rendered parallel, as shewn in *fig.* 10, where the converging rays at c

Fig. 10.

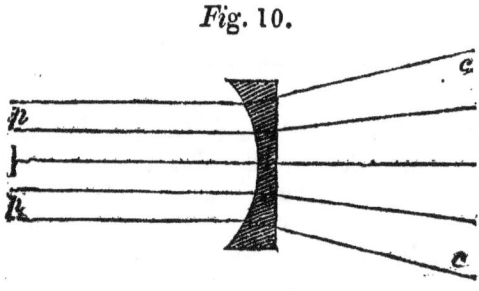

(from a convex lens) are brought parallel at p, after passing through the lens.

(10.) The manner in which the foci of lenses of different curves are calculated, and how the foci of combined lenses may be obtained, are as follows. When the lenses are made of plate glass, the focal distance is nearly the diameter of the sphere from which we may suppose a plano-convex lens to be cut, or it is equal to twice the radius of the circle that forms the convex surface of the lens. For example, if the globe of glass is one inch in diameter, and a portion is cut off to form a plano-convex lens, the focus will be one inch, or twice the radius of the circle. If the lens is double convex, the focus will be equal to the radius, or half the diameter. When the lens is crossed or unequally convex, the focal length will be twice the product of the two radii, divided by the sum of the radii. For example, let the radius on one side be 2 inches, and on the other side 6 inches; the focus of this will be $2 \times 2 \times 6 = 24$, divided by $2 + 6 = 8$ or 3 inches. The focus of the miniscus lens is found by dividing twice the product of the two radii by their difference. Example; let the radius on the convex side be 2 inches, and on the concave side 4, the focus is $2 \times 2 \times 4 = 16$ divided by $4 - 2 = 2$, or 8 inches, the focus of the lens*.

If two lenses are placed in contact, the compound focus, when each lens has the same power, will be half the focus of the single lens. When two convex lenses are in contact, having different focal lengths, then, as the sum of the two foci is to one of them, so is the other to the compound focus required. For example, let the foci of the lenses be 2 and 6; then, as $2 + 6 = 8 : 2 \therefore 6 : 1$, the compound focus. Lastly, if two lenses are not in contact, the compound focus is found by dividing the product of the two lenses by the sum lessened by their distance. Example: let the foci of the lenses be 2 and 4, their distance 2; then $2 \times 4 = 8$ divided by $(2 + 4) - 2 = 4$ gives 2 as the compound focus.

(11.) If lenses be made of different substances, although the curves may be the same, the focal lengths will vary; while, in like mediums, the action will always be equal. Let ab (*fig.* 11.) be a ray of light, and let it enter the medium cd at the point b; instead of continuing in a right line to e it will pass on in the direction bf, should the medium cd be denser than the first ab; now if on the point b a circle be drawn, and a line si, parallel to the surface of the medium, touching the incident ray ab be produced to e, this line will be the sine of incidence; and if another line pr be drawn in the same manner to the refracted ray, it will be the sine of refraction. Now if the angle abc be varied to any degree, the sine si will always be in the same proportion to the sine of refraction, pr. If the dense medium is water, the sine pr will be $\frac{3}{4}$ of si. When

---

* In many cases, it is found advisable to ascertain the radii of the two surfaces of a convex lens, as well as its focus, by a more accurate manner. This may be effected by forming a reflected image by the posterior surface, which distance will be half of the radius of curvature (or one quarter the focus of a plano-convex lens); then, by exposing the other side, we obtain the radii of the opposite surface. This method was adopted by Professor Robinson, to measure the different radii of double and triple achromatic object-glasses.

glass is used, the sines are as 2 to 3 nearly, and in diamond as 2 to 5.

Fig. 11.

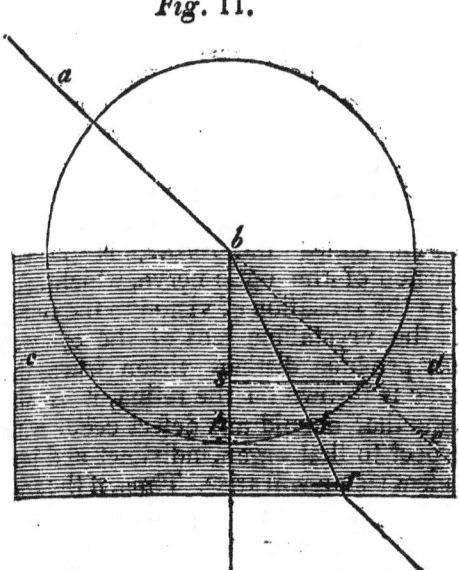

When a ray is passing out of a dense medium into a rarer, the direction will be changed, and the ray bf will now be bent further from the perpendicular, so as to make the sines the reverse of the former case. Out of water they will be as 4 to 3: from glass as 3 to 2, and from diamond as 5 to 2. The theorems just described for finding the foci of lenses are called geometrical, and will be nearly the same as the refracted, when the lens is made of plate glass. The refracted focus is only $\frac{1}{311}$st part less than the geometrical, when ascertained by accurate experiment. The refracted focus of lenses of other media may be obtained by dividing the geometrical focus by the quotient obtained when the sine of incidence (i), minus the sine of refraction (r), is divided by half the sine of refraction. $\left(\frac{i-r}{\frac{1}{2}r}\right)$

(12.) *Convex Lenses*, in their simple state, have been applied to collect the heat of the sun's rays for purposes similar to that of burning mirrors. One of the largest lenses that have been mounted for these purposes, was that made of flint glass by Mr. Parker. This lens was 3 feet in diameter, and when mounted, exposed a surface of 330 square inches to the sun's light; its focal distance was 3 feet 9 inches, and the diameter of the circular spot of light was one inch. But in order that the light might be condensed as much as possible, he employed another lens, 13 inches diameter, and of 29 inches focus, so as to decrease the diameter of the focal point to 3-8ths of an inch. The apparatus on which it was mounted is shown in *fig.* 12: a is the large convex lens mounted in a ring, and connected to the smaller lens b by wooden ribs cc; the lower rib has a piece e attached to it, capable of adjustment to or from the smaller lens: to this bar is fixed the holder d, having an universal joint. On this holder, the substance to be experimented on is placed. The following are some of its effects on bodies placed in its focus; 20 grains of pure gold was fused in 4 seconds; 10 grains of platina fused in 3 seconds, and a diamond, weighing 10 grains, exposed for 30 minutes, lost 4 grains. This lens, which is now in the posession of the Emperor of China, cost 700l.

Fig. 12.

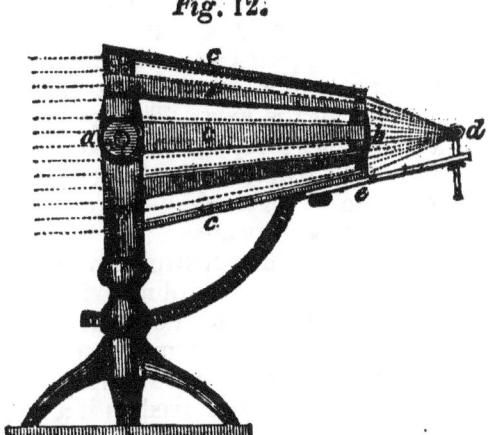

In large burning lenses the weight of the glass employed becomes of considerable importance; and to effect as great a saving as possible, Dr. Brewster has proposed to construct them of circular rings, as shown in *fig.* 13, where the lens

Fig. 13.

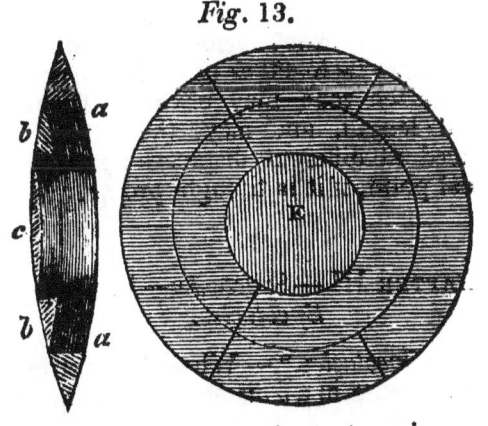

is composed of three pieces, two rings, a and b, and a lens c. When, however, the size is very great, the rings may be composed of several pieces, as shown by the front view E, where the lens is built of ten pieces. These instruments have been denominated by Dr. Brewster, *Polyzonal lenses*.

The following are the advantages of employing these lenses as laid down by Dr. Brewster.

1. The difficulty of procuring a mass of flint-glass proper for a solid lens of great dimensions, is in this construction completely removed.

2. If impurities exist in the glass of any of the spherical segments, or if an accident happen to any of them, it can be easily replaced at a very trifling expense. Hence, the spherical segments may be made of glass much more pure and free from flaws and veins than the corresponding portions of a solid lens.

3. From the spherical aberration of a convex lens, the focus of the outer portion is nearer the lens than the focus of the central parts, and, therefore, the solar light is not concentrated in the same point of the axis. This evil may, in a great measure, be removed in the present construction, by placing the different zones in such a manner that their foci may coincide.

4. A lens of this construction may be formed by degrees, according to the convenience and means of the artist. One zone, or even one segment may be added after another, and at every step the instrument may be used as if it were complete, without the rest of the zone to which it belongs; and it will contribute, in the proportion of its area, to increase the general effect.

5. If it should be thought advisable to grind the segments separately, or two by two, a much smaller tool will be necessary than if they formed one continuous lens. But, if it should be reckoned more accurate to grind each zone by itself, then the various segments may be easily held together by a firm cement.

6. Each zone may have a different focal length, and may, therefore, be placed at different distances from the focal point, if it is thought proper.

CHAPTER III.—*Spectacles—Periscopic Spectacles*.

(13.) *Spectacles*.*—When two lenses are mounted in a frame to fix before the eyes, they are denominated spectacles: the lenses are employed to render the objects before the wearer more distinct. The eye, which consists of a convex lens, called the *crystalline lens*, refracts the light proceeding from the object placed before it in the same manner as a convex glass: the image of the object is formed at the focus of the lens, where it is received on a screen at the back of the eye; this screen, called the *retina*, is an expansion of the optic nerve, which conveys the sensation of vision to the mind. As the crystalline lens of the eye will only produce distinct vision when the focus is thrown on the retina, it is obvious that should any defect occur with respect to that organ, indistinct and imperfect vision will arise. Thus, if the lens of the eye is not of a proper convexity to bring the image on the screen, an indistinctness must ensue. This is the case when the lens through age has become flattened; the image will then be thrown beyond the retina, and thus convey an imperfect representation of the object to the mind. To obviate this defect, we must make the rays pass through a glass of sufficient convexity to assist the eye, and enable it to form the image at the required place, which is in this instance done by shortening the focal distance of the crystalline lens of the eye. If, on the contrary, the eye should be too convex, or short-sighted, as is often the case with young persons, then the image will not be formed at a sufficient distance from the lens of the eye to reach the retina, and thus imperfect vision of distant objects is produced. To remedy this defect *concave lenses* must be resorted to, in order to diverge the rays before they enter the eye, and thus lengthen the focus of the crystalline lens to form an image on the retina. When the eyes are not directed near the centre of the spectacle-glasses, the obliquity of their surface to the rays will be increased, so as to occasion a confused appearance of the object. A great portion of this confusion is removed in the spectacles now usually made, when compared with those formerly employed, whose size, being very large, augmented the imperfection; for it may be observed that when objects are seen through spectacle-glasses, no more of the glass is employed at one view than a portion equal to the size of the pupil of the eye; this on an average may be reckoned at the *eighth of an*

---

* These instruments are said to have been invented about the year 1290.

inch in diameter. Thus, we see how small a portion is used for the purposes of vision; but as it would be tedious to require the eye always to look through a small aperture, the glasses are left of a sufficient size to admit of a moderate degree of motion; and, as we require a greater latitude horizontally than vertically, their figure is made of an oval form.

In the selection of spectacle-glasses great care should be used in examining them, and the first point of importance is the goodness of the material of which they are formed; this should be free from all veins or small bubbles, for if one of these occur in the portion through which we look, it will greatly impair the eyes. The next circumstance is the colour of the glasses; the best adapted for general purposes is a pale blue. The figure of their surfaces should be perfectly spherical, for if they are curved more in one direction than in another, they will injure the sight, unless they are cylindrically formed, as for some particular disease. The polish should be clean, and free from flare, which too often arises from the manner in which they are usually polished on heterogeneous surfaces, producing what is technically termed a *curdled glass*. See the method of grinding and polishing lenses, described in (48).

(14.) Dr. Wollaston, in order to allow the eyes a considerable latitude without fatigue, invented a peculiar form of glasses, called by him *periscopic*, from two Greek words signifying *seeing about;* their form is that of a meniscus with the concave side always turned towards the eye. When they are intended for *long-sighted persons*, or *old age*, the anterior surface, or that next the object, is formed spherically convex, with a curve deeper than the concave, so as both to gain the required power, and compensate for the divergency occasioned by the concave side; this form is shown at A, (*fig*. 14.). The *peri-scopic* form employed for correcting the defect of a short or near sight is shown in section at B, having its anterior surface convex, as in the former case; but here the concavity on its posterior side is increased to procure the required divergency, and compensate for the convex side.

CHAPTER IV. — *Telescopes — Common Astronomical Telescope — Day Telescope — Dynameters.*

(15.) *A Telescope* is an optical instrument employed for viewing distant objects, by increasing the apparent angle under which they are seen without its assistance; and hence the effect on the mind of an increase in size, or, as commonly termed, *magnified* representation. The construction of the Telescope is, perhaps, one of the most important acquisitions that the sciences ever attained, as it unfolds to our view the wonders of the heavens, and enables us to obtain *data* for astronomical and nautical purposes.

The invention of this instrument is somewhat uncertain, and is ascribed to different individuals, as John Baptista Porta, Jansen of Middleburg, and Galileo. The time of its first construction was about the year 1590.

The simplest construction of this instrument consists of two convex lenses, so combined as to increase the apparent angle under which distant objects are seen. If we take a convex lens, and place it in a similar position to the object, as that in *fig*. 7, and another of shorter focus in the position *fig*. 8, with a distance between them equal to the sum of their foci, a telescope will be formed, and the magnifying power will be in proportion to the focus of the two lenses. Let O (*fig*. 15) be the object lens, and suppose it 8 inches focus, and *e* the eye lens, of 2 inches focus, the distance between these two lenses must be ten inches, if the object be at an infinite distance, as a star; but when the object is terrestrial, the distance between the two lenses must be increased to adjust for distinct vision: on this account the eye lens is mounted in a tube, sliding within another tube in which the object-glass is fixed, and, therefore, can be drawn out for near objects. As the size of objects is dependent on the angle under which they are seen, the image F, formed by the object-glass, in the focus of the eye-glass *e*, will subtend

Fig. 14.

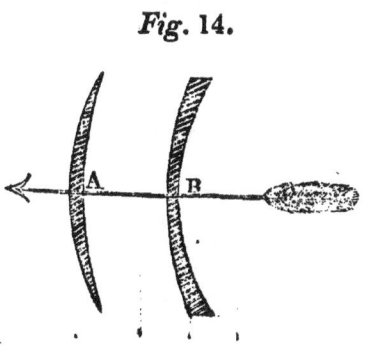

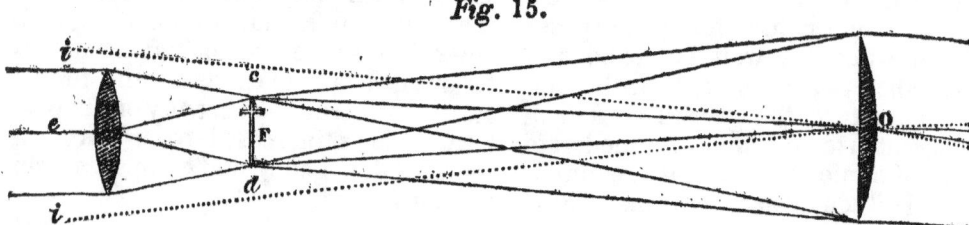

Fig. 15.

the angle $c\,e\,d$, which is four times the angle $c\,o\,d$ that the object subtends, for the distance Fo is four times Fe: hence the magnifying power may be found, by dividing the focal length of the object-glass by the focus of the eye-glass, when the quotient will be the power. Objects seen through this telescope are inverted, and on that account it is inapplicable to land observation; but at sea it is occasionally used at night, and in hazy weather when there is little light; it is hence called a night telescope.

(16.) The common *astronomical telescope* is of the same principle of construction as the preceding. The inversion of the object is immaterial in its application to celestial observations; but the disadvantage of this instrument is felt when very high powers are required, for then the objects are rendered dark and obscure, and if the aperture of the object-glass is increased to admit more light, the formation of the object is confused. M. Huygens, however, made a telescope of this construction, in which he was enabled to use an aperture of 6 inches, by making the focus of the object-glass 123 feet in length, and, by changing the eye-lenses, any required power was produced. From experiments on different combinations, he found that to obtain the greatest distinctness and light, the focus of the object-glass, its aperture, and the power of the instrument, should be according to the following table:

(17.) The common *day-telescope* is an instrument of this class, with the addition of two other lenses of the same power as the eye-lens e; these lenses will produce an erect image of the object when placed at a fixed distance from each other, equal to the sum of their two focal lengths. Let o (*fig.* 16.) be

Fig. 16.

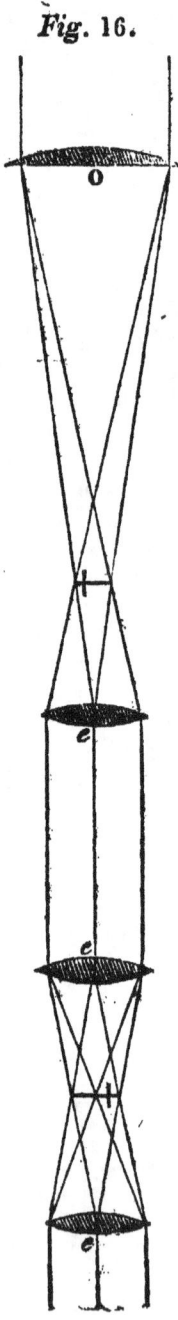

Focus of the Object Glass.	Aperture of the Object Glass.	Focus of the Eye Glass.	Magnifying Power.
Feet.	Inches.	Inches.	
1	0.545	0.605	20
2	0.76	0.84	27.6
3	0.94	1.04	33.5
4	1.08	1.18	39.5
5	1.21	1.33	44
10	1.71	1.88	62
20	2.43	2.68	88
30	3.00	3.28	108
40	3.43	3.76	125
50	3.84	4.20	140
100	5.40	5.95	197
120	5.9	6.56	216

the object-lens, which may be the same focus as that in *fig.* 16, *e e e* three lenses of equal power. Now, if the focus of each eye-lens *e* is two inches, as in the former case, then each eye-glass must be placed at a fixed distance of 4 inches from each other; and the distance between the object-lens *o*, and the nearest eye-lens, will be 10 inches, this distance increasing as the objects to be viewed approach the instrument. The power of day-telescopes may be calculated in the same manner as the astronomical; for the two additional lenses produce no effect in the amplification of the objects.

(18.) The magnifying power of telescopes may be ascertained without a knowledge of the foci of the glasses, by means of a *dynameter*; this apparatus simply consists of a strip of mother-of-pearl, marked with equal divisions, from the $\frac{1}{100}$ to $\frac{1}{1000}$ of an inch apart, according to the accuracy required; this measure is attached to a magnifying lens in its focus, in order to make the small divisions more apparent. When the power of a telescope is required, the person must measure the clear aperture of the object-glass; then holding the pearl *dynameter* next the eye-glass, let him observe how many divisions the small circle of light occupies when the instrument is directed to a bright object. Then by dividing the diameter of the object-glass by the diameter of this circle of light, the power will be obtained.

CHAPTER V.—*Aberration of Reflectors and of Lenses—Glass and Diamond compared—Huygens' Eye Piece—Ramsden's Eye Piece—Newton's Parabolic Lenses—Chromatic Dispersion.*

(19.) The field of vision, or number of objects seen by the telescopes, *figs.* 15 and 16, is very limited, the eye-lenses not being sufficiently large, as is shown by the dotted lines *i i* in *fig.* 15, which do not enter the eye lens *e*, and are not received by the eye. Now, if the diameters of these lenses were increased, the objects would be rendered indistinct, arising from the rays, spread over the surface of the lens from any point in the object, not being collected again in another point after refraction. This error is occasioned by the figure of the lens, and is called the spherical aberration by figure.

As a lens is formed with two surfaces, and, consequently, has two refractions, we shall first investigate the aberration of a spherical reflecting surface.

In (2) the focus of a concave spherical reflector was stated to be half the radius distant from its surface; this, however, is only the case with parallel rays near the centre. When we are desirous of employing specula for telescopes, they require to be made of the parabolic or hyperbolic form, to unite all the rays to one point: the rays that fall on the extreme parts of a spherical reflector, forming an image nearer the speculum than those that fall on its centre. In *fig.* 17, F is the focus of cen-

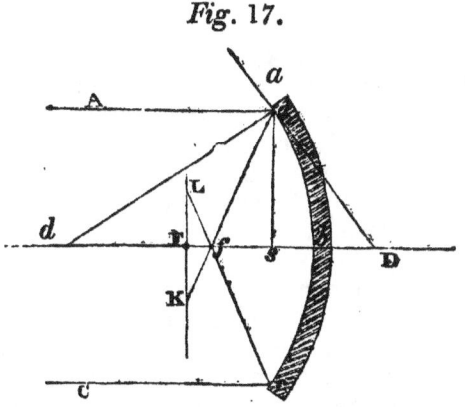

Fig. 17.

tral rays, and the point *f* the focus of the extreme rays A C, while, along the axis from *f* to F, images from the different parts of the reflector will be formed of the same object; these, not coinciding, will confuse one another. The quantity F*f* is called the longitudinal aberration, and will be equal to half the aperture of the speculum squared $(ab)^2$, divided by 4 times the radius of curvature (db), or $\frac{ab^2}{4bd}$ nearly, in specula whose surface is spherical.*

This spherical aberration produces an indistinctness of vision, by spreading out every mathematical point of the object into a small spot in its picture; which spots, by mixing with each other, confuse the whole. The diameter of this circle of confusion, at the focus of central rays F, over which every point is spread, will be L K (*fig.* 17.); and when the aperture of the reflector is moderate it equals the cube of the aperture, divided by the square of the radius

---

* The focus of rays reflected by any curve will be equal to half the distance of the tangent from the centre or half *d* D for A *a*.

$\left(\frac{a\ c_3}{b\ d_2}\right)$: this circle is called the aberration of latitude.

(20.) The aberration produced by a lens with a spherical surface is shown in *fig.* 18, where A B C is a section of a plano-convex lens. Let the plane side be exposed to parallel rays, and let a A be an extreme pencil of rays; D the centre of curvature; D f the axis of the

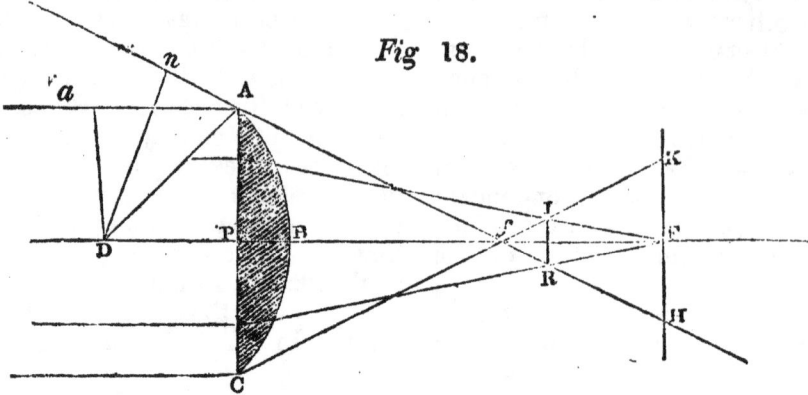

Fig. 18.

lens; and F the focus of a slender pencil of incident rays, at an infinitely smaller distance from the centre. Now, as the extreme ray a A is perpendicular to the plane surface, it will pass directly through to the convex side, where it will be refracted to f, crossing the axis in that point, for D A is perpendicular to the curve at A, and a D the sine of incidence, n D the sine of refraction; hence, an image of the object will be formed at F by the central rays, and another image of the same object will be formed at f by the extreme rays; while, from F to f, images of the same object will be formed by the intermediate portion of the lens. The longitudinal aberration F f bears a certain ratio to the thickness or versed sine B P; and when the lens is placed in the position shown in the figure, it is equal to $\frac{9}{2}$ or $4\frac{1}{2}$ times B P; this quantity will be decreased, when the curved surface of the lens is exposed to parallel rays, that is, when the refraction of the first surface is made nearer the perpendicular, or when the ray is bent in passing from a rare into a dense medium, and this difference out of air into glass, will be in the proportion of 27 to 7; so that when the convex side is placed next the radiant, the longitudinal aberration will be only $\frac{7}{6}$ of the thickness B P, or 1.166.

When a crossed convex lens is used, the proportions of the radii of whose surfaces are as 1 to 6, and the most convex side is exposed to the distant radiant, the longitudinal aberration will be the least possible quantity; viz. $1\frac{5}{14}$ or 1.0714 of the thickness of the lens. When the radii of a double-convex lens are equal, the aberration is $\frac{5}{3}$ of its thickness; therefore, this lens is not so good as a plano-convex of the same thickness, in its best position. *The longitudinal aberration F f increases as the square of the aperture, when the curvature of the lens is not altered; and is inversely as the focal distance, when the aperture is constant.*

The lateral aberration, which is the actual confusion of the image at the focus of central rays, is equal to the longitudinal aberration F f, multiplied by $\frac{A C}{B F}$, or the aperture of the lens divided by the focal distance, which is equal to K H. Now, if rays are drawn from the different parts of the lens, it will be found that they will be refracted through a small circular space I R, whose diameter will be $\frac{1}{4}$ of K H; hence, this point must be considered as the focus of the lens. *The lateral aberration of lenses increases as the cube of the aperture, if the radius remain the same, or inversely as the square of the radius when the apertures are the same.*

These laws may be considered as determining the relative aberration of all lenses; yet it is found that if we employ media of different refractive powers, and form each into lenses of like curvature, the separation or spreading out of the rays at their focal point will be different; that possessing the highest refractive power producing the least aberration, though its amplifying power will be greatest: thus, if three lenses were ground in the same tool, one of *plate glass*, and the others of *sapphire* and *diamond*, they would possess very different *magnifying powers, aberrations*, and *separation of colour*, or *chromatic dispersion*, (this latter error is explained in 23 :) their respective values are shown in the following Table:

Plano convex lenses with convex side exposed to parallel rays.	Magnifying powers.	Longitudinal aberration.	Chromatic dispersion.
Glass	150	1.167	48
Sapphire	250	1.005	26
Diamond	400	0.950	38*

But this difference in the longitudinal aberration would be much greater if the lenses were so formed as to give the same magnifying powers; for this error always decreases as the squares of their respective radii, while the lateral aberration or area of the circle of confusion will be as their *cubes*.

Hence, in *sapphire* and *diamond lenses* of high magnifying powers, the indistinctness arising from their figure would barely be discernible in practice, thus producing a kind of *natural aplanatic magnifier*.

The valuable properties possessed by these stones were known to Sir Isaac Newton, and Martin, and have been more particularly pointed out by Dr. Brewster, in his Treatise on *New Optical Instruments*. But their *hardness* and *crystalline form* probably occasioning difficulties in the formation of spherical polished surfaces almost insurmountable, has retarded their adoption as lenses: however, we have lately learned that *Mr. Pritchard* has succeeded in forming these substances into lenses, and their application to the microscope is so favourable, that, if any new discoveries are to be made in the *minutiæ of nature*, they seem most likely to develope them.

The process by which these lenses are worked, and their application to the microscope, are detailed in the Journal of Science of the Royal Institution, vol. ii. page 15 (New Series). This paper was communicated by Dr. Goring, who suggested to Mr. Pritchard the advantages which diamond lenses would most probably possess.

The adaptation of these lenses to telescopes in place of the ordinary eyeglasses would, in all probability, be attended with equal success, where every circumstance calculated to produce a perfect representation of the object is of the utmost importance.

* When it is considered, that the refraction of diamond is nearly three times that of glass, it follows, that in equal refractions its dispersion will be only one-third of the latter.—See Optics, p. 24.

21. The great advantage of duly considering the aberration of lenses will be evident, if we combine two lenses, of twice the focal distance, instead of one, to produce any given power, as the aberration will be decreased to one quarter of that of a single lens of equivalent power, and, therefore, the aperture of the compound lens may be increased, while the error will be less than in a single lens. In the common telescopes (*figs*. 15 and 16), if two lenses were used, instead of the single object and eye-glass, as there shown, the apertures of each might be increased, and, consequently, the instruments would be improved in light and field.

(22.) M. Huygens has demonstrated, that when the greatest possible distinctness is required for the eye-piece of a telescope, it may be obtained by two planoconvex lenses, placed as in *fig*. 19, with

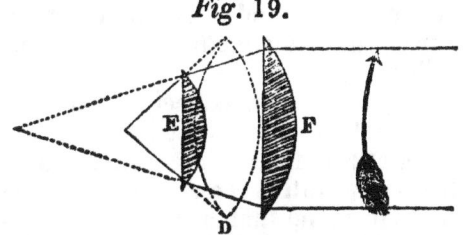

Fig. 19.

their plane sides outward, and the focus of the eye-lens E must be ⅔ of that of the field-lens F, with a distance between them equal to the difference of their focal lengths. This combination, from the purpose it has been adapted to, is called the astronomical positive eye-piece; and the telescope, by this addition, will have four times the distinctness of a single lens D, of equivalent power, while the distortion of the object will only be ¼ of that produced by a single lens; for the refraction of the object-lens brings the image of the marginal rays nearer to itself than the central, therefore the image will be formed convex next the lens F, as shown by the arrow; and as the radius of curvature of the lens F is twice that of the single lens D, the distortion will be decreased in the square of this ratio, or 4 times. On this account, a similar combination is used for the eye-pieces of telescopes for astronomical quadrants, and other graduated instruments, when the convex side of the field-lens is turned towards the eye-glass E, because equal divisions on a micrometer correspond with equal angles, subtended by objects measured by this instrument. This combination, which is called Ramsden's Micrometical Eyepiece, has one great disadvantage, viz. that it requires the eye to be placed exceedingly near to the eye-lens E.

(23.) Being now in possession of a combination that will diminish the aberration produced by the eye-piece of a telescope, our limit of magnifying power and light will arise from the errors occasioned by the object-glass; and this, we have seen, may be diminished by having the curves of the two surfaces as 1 to 6, with the most convex side outermost; for this lens has been shown to have less aberration than any other*. Secondly, by using two lenses of twice the focus in contact, to produce the required refraction, and thus diminish the error four times. But, although this error may, by the means here pointed out, be rendered very small and almost imperceptible, yet it is magnified in the same proportion as the objects; and when high powers are used, the indistinctness will become sensible.

Sir Isaac Newton conceived that the surfaces of the lens might be formed of some mathematical curve which would entirely obviate this error; and, by investigation he found that, if the surface were described by the revolution of a parabola, and the radiant or object be at an infinite distance, the rays would be collected to a point, and be free from all aberration. He afterwards formed tools to grind and polish lenses of this figure, but when made, although the error by figure was perfectly corrected, it was discovered that the white heterogeneous pencils of light (before that time considered as homogeneous) in their passage through the lens, were divided into their several constituents of red, orange, green, blue, and violet, in the same manner as by a prism, and hence lenses of this figure became useless.

---

* Dr. Brewster, in his Edition of Ferguson's Lectures (vol. ii. p. 299), states, that in order to render the common refracting telescope as perfect as possible without making it achromatic, the exterior surface of the object-glass should be ground to a radius equal to 5-9ths of its focal length; and the radius of the interior surface, or that next the eye, should be 5 times its focal length. In eye-glasses, the radius of the surface next the object should be 9 times its focal distance, and that of the surface next the eye 3-5ths of the same distance. By this means, the aberration arising from the spherical figure of the lenses will be nothing for objects placed in the direction of their axis, and the least possible for objects removed from the axis. According to Huygens, the spherical aberration was the least possible, when the radii of the surfaces are as 6 to 1. But though this be true for objects placed in the axes of the lenses, yet a considerable aberration remains when the objects are placed on one side of the axis.

(24.) To illustrate the chromatic dispersion produced by a lens, let a A, fig. 20, be a white compounded pencil of light proceeding from any luminous body, and falling on the lens B; parallel to its axis, at the point a, this pencil of light will not be refracted colourless, but the red rays will cross the axis at r, and

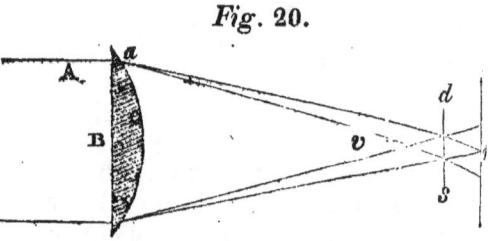

Fig. 20.

the violet, which will be attracted by the lens more than the other colour, crosses the axis at v; and along the intermediate space from r to v, will be formed a coloured spectrum of orange, yellow, green, and blue; the proportional quantity of these colours, and the total length, will vary according to the substance of which the lens is formed.* Sir Isaac Newton, by most accurate observations, found that in common glass, when the sine of the angle of the incident rays A a was 50°, the sines of refraction of the red and violet rays were 77° and 78°, the mean refraction of the pencil being $77\frac{1}{2}°$. Now, if we call the sine of incidence i, the sine of refraction for red rays r, and of the violet v, it is found that the diameter of the circle of dispersion $d\,s$, through which all the colours pass, will be as $(v-r)$ is to $(v+r-2i,)$ or as 1 to 55, so that the diameter is $\frac{1}{55}$th part of the aperture of the lens, which is equal to half the diameter of the circle of dispersion at the focus of central rays r. The circle of dispersion that will comprehend any particular colour, or set of colours, may be easily calculated. Thus, all the orange and yellow will pass through a circle, whose diameter is $\frac{1}{305}$th of the aperture of the lens. When it is considered that an object-glass $5\frac{1}{2}$ inches in diameter has a

---

* Sir Isaac Newton imagined, that the different colours divided the spectrum formed by all substances in the proportions of a musical canon. This is found to be a mistake; for when the spectrum is formed by a prism of crown glass, and another of precisely the same length is formed by the side of it with a prism of flint glass, the confines between the green and blue will be found precisely in the middle of the first spectrum; but in the second, it will be considerably nearer to the red extremity; indeed, there are hardly two substances that disperse the colours in the same proportions. Oil of cassia exerts the least action on green light, and sulphuric acid the strongest.

circle of dispersion $\frac{1}{70}$th of an inch in diameter, it may be surprising that any picture of an object can be distinguished; but the superior vivacity of the orange and yellow light in comparison with the rest, make the effect produced by the confusion of the colours much less sensible, and will allow this aperture to be used when the focal length of the lens is considerable.

(25.) We may now compare the diameters of the circles of the chromatic and spherical aberration together. If we take a standard telescope of approved goodness, it has not been found possible to give more than 4 inches aperture to an object-glass of 100 feet focal distance, so as to preserve sufficient distinctness; and if the diameter of the circle of spherical aberration is computed for this lens, it will not exceed $\frac{1}{120000}$th part of an inch, while the chromatic, if restricted to $\frac{1}{510}$th of the aperture, which is hardly a fifth of the whole dispersion, (or diameter of the circle of orange and yellow light,) is $\frac{1}{62\frac{1}{2}}$ of an inch, and is therefore about 1900 times greater than the other. But when the aperture of a lens is increased to 30°, the spherical aberration will be found equal to the chromatic in a glass lens; but this aperture can only be used for eye lenses or microscopes.

CHAPTER VI.—*Reflecting Telescopes— the Newtonian—the Gregorian—the Cassegrainian—Sir W. Herschell's— Mr. Ramage's.*

(26.) With these disadvantages to contend against in refracting substances, Sir Isaac Newton, in the year 1666, turned his attention to reflected light, in which the angle of all the coloured rays are equal. By pursuing this idea he entirely obviated the chromatic error. In the first telescope he made by reflection, the distinctness with which objects were seen through it was surprising, when compared with the refracting telescopes of those times; for though the focal distance of the metal was only $6\frac{1}{4}$ inches, it would carry a power of 38 with equal distinctness to a 4 feet refractor. The form of the metal was spherically concave; but by investigation he ascertained that if the form had been that of a parabola, there would not have been any spherical aberration produced; and if we examine the spherical aberration by figure of a spherically concave metal, and compare it with that of a plano-convex lens ground in the same tool, the former will be 4, while the latter is 9. But when it is considered that the focus of the glass lens is 4 times that of the metal, (for the focal distance of a plano-convex lens is twice the radius, and that of a concave reflector half the radius,) to make their foci equal, the curvature of the lens must be 4 times that of the speculum; and it has been shown that the error by figure increases inversely as the square of the radius: hence the aberration of the lens will be to that of the reflector as $4^2 \times 9$ to 4, or as 36 to 1, and the distinctness will be inversely as the areas of these circles, which are as the squares of their respective diameters; so that the distinctness of a reflector will be 1296 times greater than that of a lens of the same focus and aperture.

(27.) The Newtonian telescope *fig.* 21. consists of a concave parabolic metal A, fixed at the end of the tube $d\,d\,d$; the plane speculum c is fixed to

Fig. 21.

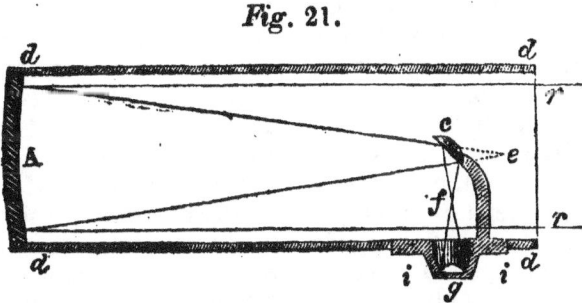

a wire, having its other end attached to a dove-tailed sliding-piece $i\,i$, and the face of the plane metal is inclined to the axis of the tube and the large speculum at an angle of 45°. In the sliding piece $i\,i$, opposite the small metal, is inserted a short tube to hold an eye-piece, which is a single lens with its flat side outermost, or the astronomical eye-piece (*fig.* 19.); but as the colour produced by these eye-lenses is not corrected, another combination, called the negative achromatic eye-piece, should be used, which will be described when treating on the chromatic correction of lenses. The adjustment of this instrument to distinct vision is made by a rack and pinion attached to the sliding piece and great tube of the telescope, by which the eye-piece and small speculum is brought nearer or farther from the large metal. Let $r\ r$ be the rays of light coming from a distant object, and falling on the large speculum A, these rays would be reflected to the focus e; but meeting with the oblique flat metal c, are reflected to f, where an image of the distant object will be formed, and is received by the eye-lens g, by which the rays are rendered parallel. The power of a Newtonian reflector is proportional to the relative focal distances of the concave metal and the eye-lens. For example, let the focal distance $A\ e$ be 40 inches, and the focus of the eye lens g, half an inch, the power will be 80. It should here be observed, that the same instrument which is free from aberration for astronomical observation will not be so for terrestrial uses; for the rays in the former case are parallel, while they are divergent in the other. The curve, therefore, of the large speculum when required for the latter purposes, should be elliptical, having the object in one focus, and the focus of the eye-lens in the other.

This telescope, which is more simple than other reflectors, may be greatly improved according to the method of Dr. Brewster, who has proposed, (for telescopes of moderate size, where a front view cannot be used,) to employ two glass prisms in place of the small plane. By the experiments of Major Kater, it appears that one-third of the rays of light is lost when reflected by a speculum at a vertical incidence, and probably not more than 68 out of 100 are reflected at an angle of 45°, as in the Newtonian small metal; in addition to this, the imperfection of surface and figure in metals, which makes the rays stray 5 or 6 times more than the same imperfection in a refracting surface,* as well as the difficulty of working metals as perfect as glass, induced him to suggest this improvement. Let $a\ b$, (fig. 22,) be the great speculum, and $r\ a$, $r\ b$ parallel rays from a distant object reflected to a focus at F; the cone of rays, however, is intercepted by the achromatic prism $c\ d$, and refracted to f, where a distinct image is formed in the anterior focus of the eye-glass e by which it is

Fig. 22.

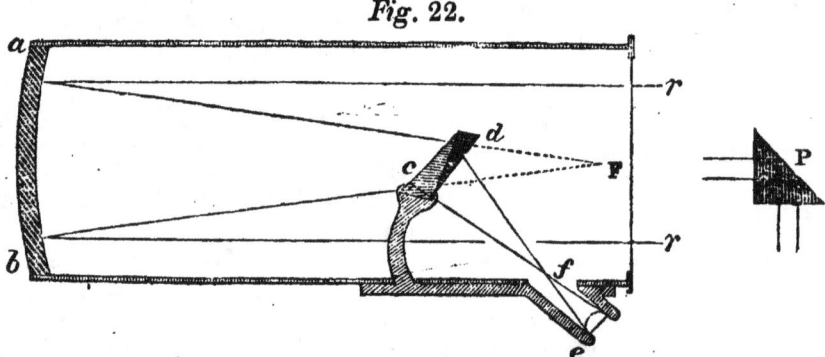

magnified. The double prism $c\ d$, being composed of a prism of crown glass c, and another of flint d, united by a cement of mean refractive power, the loss of light by transmission through the two prisms, says Dr. Brewster, will not exceed 600 rays out of 10,000, as the light transmitted through a lens of glass, according to Dr. W. Herschell, is 9,485 out of 10,000 incident rays. Hence, the light lost by the prism is only ¼ of that lost by reflection.

The Newtonian telescopes made by Hadley had, in place of a plane metal a right angular prism P substituted, having its sides perpendicular to the incident and emergent rays. In this, as is accomplished by the two prisms of Dr. Brewster, the image will be erect, and a less quantity of light lost than by a mirror of the common kind.

(28.) Another class of reflecting telescopes was invented by Dr. Gregory, in 1660, but they were not made till some years after the Newtonian, from the difficulty of forming the metals. The Gregorian reflector is, however, preferred to the Newtonian, and is most commonly used, because the observer is stationed in a line with the object, whereas, in the Newtonian he is at right angles to it. Fig. 23 is a section of the Gregorian reflector. B D is a concave metal, whose surface

---

* See Newton's Optics.

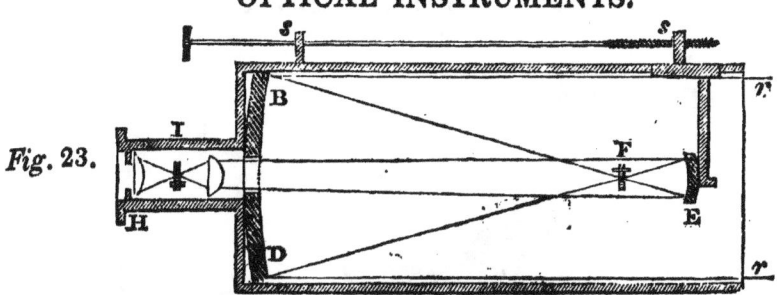

Fig. 23.

should be formed by the revolution of the hyperbolic curve: this speculum has a small hole in its centre. E is another concave elliptical small metal placed in the axis of the larger one, at a distance from it a little more than the sum of their focal distances. H are the eye-lenses sliding in a tube fixed behind the large speculum: the adjustment is made by the screw *s s*, which moves the small metal to or from the great speculum. Let *r* B and *r* D be two parallel rays from a distant object, these will be reflected to the focus F of the large metal, where an image will be formed, and the rays, crossing each other, fall upon the small speculum E; and if the focus of this metal had coincided with the focus F, the rays would have been reflected parallel, but now they form a direct image at I, and this image is viewed by the eye-piece or a single lens at H. The magnifying power of this instrument may be computed thus:—suppose the focus of the large speculum B F is 9 inches, and the focus of the small metal 1½ inch: then will the angle be increased six times; but this must be multiplied by the ratio of the distances I H, the focus of the lens, and the distance I F; and if these are as 1 to 8, the amplification of the object will be $6 \times 8 = 48$ times.

(29.) The Cassegrainian reflector is constructed in the same way as the Gregorian, with the exception of a small convex spherical speculum, instead of one a little concave; and as the focus of this metal is negative, it is placed at a distance from the larger metal, equal to the difference of their foci, and only one image is formed, viz. that in the focus of the eye-glass; on this account, the distinctness is considerably greater than in the Gregorian. Mr. Ramsden, in the 69th volume of the Philosophical Transactions, states, that this construction is preferable to either of the former reflectors, because the aberrations of the two metals have a tendency to correct each other: whereas in the Gregorian, both the metals being concave, any error in the specula will be doubled.

By assuming such proportions of the foci of the specula, as are generally employed in these instruments, which are about as 1 to 4, he asserts that the aberration or indistinctness occasioned by the figures of the reflectors (supposing each worked equally true) in the Cassegrainian construction, is to that in the Gregorian as 3 to 5.

(30.) In sidereal observations of nebulæ and small stars, abundance of light is necessarily required, and by whatever means a loss of light by reflection or refraction can be prevented, the adoption of such a construction would be advisable. Sir W. Herschel, from an investigation of the loss of light occasioned by the small speculum in reflectors, constructed an instrument which entirely obviated the use of the second metal, by what he called the *front view* telescope. The diameter of the polished surface of the speculum of his large instrument was 48 inches, and its focal distance 40 feet. This metal, which weighed when taken from the casting, 2118 lb., was placed at the end of an iron tube 4 feet 10 inches in diameter; the other end is elevated towards the object, and has attached to it a single eye-lens in the focus of the metal; the observer is mounted in a gallery moveable with the instrument, having his back to the object. The light obtained from so large a surface by this instrument was truly surprising, and enabled objects otherwise invisible to become extremely interesting. This telescope, erected at Slough, near Windsor, was completed on the 28th of August, 1789, and on the same day the sixth satellite of Saturn was discovered*. The frame of this instrument having greatly decayed, it has been taken down; and another, of 20 feet focus and 18 inches diameter, erected in its place, by his son Mr. J. Herschell, in 1822.

* A full description of this instrument will be found in the Transactions of the Royal Society for 1795, explained by means of 18 plates and 63 pages of letter-press; and an ample detail is given of every circumstance relating to the mechanical construction of this instrument.

Fig. 24.

MR. RAMAGE'S REFLECTING TELESCOPE, ERECTED AT THE ROYAL OBSERVATORY, GREENWICH, IN THE YEAR 1820.

(31.) The largest front view reflecting telescope at present in this country, is that erected at the Royal Observatory, at Greenwich, by Mr. Ramage, in 1820. The diameter of the concave reflector is 15 inches, and its focus 25 feet; the mechanical arrangement of the stand is greatly simplified. A perspective view of the whole instrument is shown at *fig.* 24. The tube is composed of a twelve-sided prism of deal ⅜ inch thick. At the mouth *c* is a double cylinder of different diameters on the same axis; around this a cord is wound by a winch, and passes up from the small cylinder over a pulley *a*, and down through the pulley *b*, on to the larger cylinder at *c*. Now, when the winch is turned to raise the telescope, the endless cord is unwound from the smaller cylinder, and wound on to the larger: the difference of the size of the two cylinders will be double the quantity raised, and a mechanical force to any extent may thus be obtained by duly proportioning the diameters of the two cylinders; by this contrivance the necessity for an assistant is superseded. The instrument, when not in use, is let down into the box *d d*, and covered with canvas, to prevent dust or moisture from tarnishing the speculum.

CHAPTER VII.—*Theory of Achromatic Telescopes—Double Object-Glass.*

(32.) Having noticed all the valuable modifications of the reflecting telescope, we must now return to the refracting one. The most obvious and important improvement in this instrument consists in the formation of object-glasses free from the errors of chromatic and spherical aberration, whence they were denominated achromatic telescopes. But as this word merely signifies freedom from colour, which in common telescopes is sometimes effected without a correction of the figure or spherical aberration, Sir W. Herschel has, therefore, very properly denominated a perfect telescope *aplanatic*, from two Greek words *a without*, πλάνος *error*, that is, *without errors*.

In (Note to 24) it was stated, that the length of the spectrum produced by lenses varied, when formed of different substances: thus, if two lenses are made of the same focal length, the one of flint glass and the other of crown, the the red and violet light, caused by the length or diameter of the coloured image in the flint will be to that produced by the crown lens as 3 to 2 nearly. Now, if we make the focal lengths of the lenses in this proportion, that is, as 3 to 2, the coloured spectrum produced by each will be equal; but if the flint lens be concave and the crown convex, when placed in contact they will mutually correct each other, and a pencil of white light refracted by the compound lens would remain colourless. Unfortunately in the formation of such a lens, the dispersion of the flint glass is so variable, that trials on each specimen require to be made, before the absolute proportional dispersion of the substances can be ascertained*. As the achromatic object-glass is the most delicate test of the dispersion of the medium, it is best found by forming a piece of the flint glass into a concave lens, and combining it with a convex of crown glass whose focal length is known, and varying the curvature of the flint till the dispersions are corrected, *i. e.* till the purple or lilac fringe surrounding a white object on a black ground is observed on one side of the focus, and a green on the other, when converted into the object-glass of a telescope and using a powerful eye-glass. Now, if the compound focus be accurately measured, and the focus of the convex lens known, the proportionate foci of each may be ascertained, and, consequently, the proportion of their dispersive powers is found. This correction of the spectrum will not correct the error of each colour, for the proportional lengths of the blue, green, or red light are variable in different substances*: thus flint glass is found to refract green light considerably less than crown glass, in the proportion of the whole refraction of the red and violet light: so that when the divergency of

---

* 1. It is ascertained that in all minerals in which a metal is the principal ingredient, [those] which have the greatest density have also the greatest faculty of producing colour, while in all the precious stones a high refractive power is attended with a low dispersive power.

2. The dispersive powers of *resins*, *gums*, *oils*, and *balsams* greatly exceed water, and correspond in some measure with their refraction.

3. The muriatic and nitric acids exceed water in dispersion, while the *phosphoric*, *citric*, *sulphuric*, and *tartaric* acids, surpassing them in refraction, possess very *low* dispersive powers. (See the Tables of Refractive and Dispersive Powers of different Substances in the Treatise on Optics.)

refraction of the two mediums, is equal, the divergency of the red and green light is always greater in the crown than in the flint, and the divergency of the violet is always less in the crown glass*. Hence it must be observed, that in order to have a complete correction of all the colours, more than two media must be used, and, therefore, the best telescopes have their object-lens composed of three kinds of glass. When the dispersive ratio is known, and the refractive focus of the compound lens is given, the refractive focus of each must be calculated, and to obtain the radius of the tools for working the lenses, their refractive foci must be converted into the geometrical shown as at (11), when the object-glass would be completed, and the task would not be difficult to perform; but the spherical aberration, although much less in quantity, is more troublesome to correct, and in making this correction, the proportion of the radii of the two surfaces of the convex lens must be assumed. When a suitable selection is made, the aperture of the lens being given, the spherical aberration must be calculated, when its thickness is ascertained†. And lastly, the curvatures and thickness of a concave flint glass must be found that will exactly balance the spherical aberrations produced by the convex glass; always keeping the foci of the two lenses in the *ratio of their dispersive powers.*

(33.) The radii of curvature of the different surfaces of the lenses necessary to form a double achromatic object-glass, when the sine of incidence is to the sine of refraction in the crown glass as 1.528 to 1, and in the flint as 1.5735 to 1, the ratio of their dispersive powers being as 1 to 1.524, and assuming the curvatures of the concave as 1 to 2, are shown in the following TABLE. The first column F is the compound focus of the object-glass in inches; r the radius of the anterior surface of the crown; R its posterior side; r' the radius of the anterior side of the concave lens of flint glass; and R' its posterior surface.

---

* Dr. Blair.
† The longitudinal aberration of a lens of glass may be found by the following general theorem, where r is the radius of the first surface, R the second surface, and T the thickness of the lens.

$$\left(\frac{27 r_2 + 6 r R + 7 R_2}{6 + (r \times R)_2} + T \right)$$

see Martin's new Optics, part vi, chapter 3; or Smith's Optics, book ii, chapter 18.

F	r	R	r'	R'
12	3.	4.652	4.171	8.342
24	6.	9.304	8.342	16.684
30	7.5	11.63	10.428	20.856
36	9.	13.956	12.552	25.027
48	12.	18.608	16.684	33.369
60	15.	23.260	20.856	41.712
120	30.	46.520	41.712	83.424

In these computations it may be remarked that the radius of the anterior surface of the concave being less than the posterior side of the convex, admits of its approach without touching in the centre, which should always be a necessary practical condition.

CHAPTER VIII.—*Aplanatic Telescopes of Clairault's Construction—Mr. J. F. Herschell's Object-Glass — Triple Object-Glasses —- Fraunhofer's and Tulley's Telescopes—Galilean Telescope and Opera Glass—Achromatic Opera-Glass — Dr. Brewster's Fluid Opera-Glass.*

(34.) The problem for the choice of the proportional curvature of the assumed convex lens is of the kind called *indeterminate*, or admitting of an infinite variety of solutions. In consequence of this, it allows an endless number of combinations of lenses, and each may be free from spherical aberration. It becomes therefore a matter of considerable delicacy to fix our choice among them, and numerous constructions have been calculated by different authors. Thus Clairault, a French mathematician, has given a construction in which the two internal surfaces are worked of equal radii, the one convex and the other concave, so as to admit of being cemented together, and thus avoiding the loss of light by reflections at the two surfaces. But having employed indices of dispersion in his computations, higher than what are usually met with in practice, and when those most likely to be obtained are used, the radii change so rapidly as to render this construction difficult to interpolate, where the artist is no algebraist; and hence it must lose much of its value to the practical optician.

(35.) Another construction has lately been proposed by Mr. J. F. Herschel, in which he states, that the destruction of the spherical aberration is ensured, not only for parallel rays from celestial objects, but also for those that diverge from objects situated at a moderate finite distance; and on these conditions he has rendered the problem determinate, while the radii resulting from the construction are such as will satisfy the following more important conditions:—1st. The curvatures assigned to each surface are more moderate than in any other theoretical combination. 2nd. The exterior surfaces of the compound lens vary within narrow limits by any variation in either the refractive or dispersive powers that generally occur in practice. 3rd. That the two interior surfaces approach in all cases so near to coincidence, that no sensible error can arise from neglecting their difference; finally, he states as a theorem, which will be found sufficiently exact in practice, that a double object-glass will be free from aberration, provided the radius of the exterior surface of the crown lens be 6.720, and of the flint 14.20, the focal length of the combination being 10.00, and the radii of the interior surfaces being computed from these data so as to make the focal lengths of the two glasses in the direct ratio of their dispersive powers. *Fig.* 25, is a section of this object-glass, the anterior glass A, or that which receives the incident ray, is an unequally convex

Fig. 25.

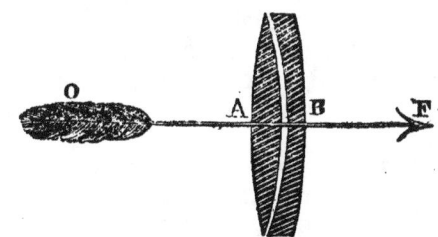

lens of crown glass, the flatter side being placed outermost; the posterior glass B is a meniscus of flint glass.

The rule here stated is given only as an approximation, and will no doubt be sufficiently exact for ordinary practical purposes; but when object-glasses of great aperture and value are to be constructed, their radii must be computed more strictly, and for this purpose we shall subjoin Mr. Herschell's TABLE, calculated upon the rigorous formulæ as given in the *Philosophical Transactions* for 1821:—

Dimensions of an Aplanatic Double Object-Glass.

Refractive index of the Crown Lens...... 1.524 } Compound Focal Length, 10,000.
Ditto ditto of the Flint Lens........ 1.585

Dispersive Ratio.	1st Surface Convex.			2d Surface Convex.	3d Surface Concave.	4th Surface Convex.			Focal Length of Crown Lens.	Focal Length of Flint Lens.
	Radius for the above Refractive Indices.	Variation of Radius for a change of +0.010 in Refractive Index of Crown Glass.	Variation of Radius for a change of +0.010 in Refractive Index of Flint Glass.	Radius.	Radius.	Radius for the above Refractive Indices.	Variation of Radius for a change of +0.010 in Refractive Index of Crown Glass.	Variation of Radius for a change of +1.010 in Refractive Index of Flint Glass.		
0.50	6.7485	+0.0500	−0.0036	4.2827	4.1575	14.3697	+0.9921	−0.3962	5.0	10.0000
0.55	6.7184	+0.0740	−0.0011	3.6332	3.6006	14.5353	+1.0080	−0.5033	4.5	8.1818
0.60	6.7069	+0.0676	+0.0037	3.0488	3.0640	14.2937	+1.1049	−0.5659	4.0	6.6667
0.65	6.7316	+0.0563	+0.0125	2.5208	2.5566	13.5709	+1.1614	−0.6323	3.5	5.3846
0.70	6.8279	+0.0335	+0.0312	2.0422	2.0831	12.3154	+1.1613	−0.7570	3.0	4.2858
0.75	7.0816	−0.0174	+0.0568	1.6073	1.6450	10.5186	+1.3847	−0.7207	2.5	3.3333

The dimensions in the table are computed on the supposition of the focal length of the object-glass being 10; and to adjust them to any other assigned focal length, all that is required is to increase or diminish the radii here set down on the proportion of the assigned focal length (in inches, feet, or parts of any given scale) to ten parts of the same scale.

When the refractive powers of the two media are exactly 1.524 and 1.585 (which are nearly their average values) respectively, and the dispersive ratio is any one of the numbers in the first column, this table gives at once the exact values of the radii required; but when this is not the case, we must proceed as follows:—Suppose (for example's sake) we would find the proper radii for the surface of an object-glass of 30 inches focal length: the refractive index of the crown lens being 1.519, and that of the flint 1.589, the dispersive power of the former being to that of the latter as 0.567.1 or 0.567 being the dispersive ratio.

The computation must first be made as for an object-glass of 10 inches focus, and first, we must determine the focal length of the separate lenses, to this end.

1. Subtract the decimal (0.567) representing the dispersive ratio from 1.000, and the remainder multiplied by 10, is the focal length of the crown lens (in this case 10 × 0.433, or 4.330.)

2. Divide unity by the decimal above mentioned (0.567,) subtract 1.000 from the quotient and multiply the remainder by 10, and we get the focal length of the flint lens. In this case before us $\frac{1}{0.567} = 1.7635$ and $0.7635 \times 10 = 7.635$ is the focal length required. We must next determine by the *tables* the radii of the 1st and 4th surfaces for the dispersive ratios their set down, (0.55 and 0.60), next *less* and next *greater* than the given one. For this purpose we have

$$\begin{array}{lrr}\text{Refractive powers given} & 1.519 & \text{and} \quad 1.589 \\ \text{Ditto ditto in the table} & \underline{1.524} & \text{and} \quad \underline{1.585} \\ \text{Differences} & -0.005 & \text{and} + 0.004\end{array}$$

The given refraction of the crown being less and the flint greater, than their average value on which the table is founded. Looking out now opposite to 0.55 in the first column for the variations in the two radii corresponding to a charge of + 0.010 in each of the two refractions, we find as follows:—

	1st surface	4th surface
For a charge = + 0.010 in crown	+ 0.0740	+ 1.0080
Ditto ditto = + 0.010 in flint	− 0.0011	− 0.5033

But the actual variation in the crown instead of + 0.010, being − 0.005, we must take the proportional parts of these, changing the sign in the case of the crown: Thus we find the variations of the first and last radii to be:—

	1st surface.	4th surface.
For − 0.005 variation in crown	− 0.0370	− 0.5040
For + 0.004 ditto in flint	− 0.0004	− 0.2010
Total variation from both causes	− 0.0374	and − 0.7053
But the radii given in the table are	+ 6.7184	and + 14.5353
Hence the radii interpolated are,	6.6810	and 13.8300

If we interpolate (by a process exactly similar) the same two radii for a dispersive ratio 0.60, we shall find respectively:—

	1st surface.	4th surface.
For − 0.005 variation in crown	− 0.0338	and − 0.5524
For + 0.004 ditto in flint	+ 0.0015	− 3.2264
Total variation	− 0.0323	and − 0.7788
Radii in the table	6.7069	14.2937
Interpolated radii	6.6746	and 13.5149

Having thus got the radii corresponding to the actual refractions, for the two dispersive ratios 0.55 and 0.60, it only remains to determine their values for the intermediate ratio 0.567 by proportional parts thus :—

		1st radius.	4th radius.
For	0.600	6.6746	13.5149
For	0.550	6.6810	13.8300
Diff. +	0.050	−0.0064	−0.3151

We then say as $0.050 : 0.567 - 0.550 = 0.017 :: -0.0064 : -0.0022$ and $.050 : .017 :: -0.3151 : -0.1071$, so that $6.6810 - 0.0022$ and $13.8300 - 0.1071$; or 6.6788 and 13.7229 are the true radii corresponding to the given data:

Thus we have in the crown lens :—

Focal length = 4.3300 }
Radius of first surface = 6.6788 }
Index of Refraction = 1.5190 }

From which data it is easy to compute, by rules familiar to every optician, the radius of the other surface, which will come out, 3.3868. Again in the flint lens we have for the

Focal length = 7.635 }
Radius of first surface = 13.7229 }
Index of refraction = 1.589 }

Whence we find 3.3871 for the radius of the other surface.

The four radii are thus obtained for a focal length of 10 inches; and to obtain them for 30 inches we have only to multiply them by 3, and we obtain finally. In the case proposed, the

Radius of 1st surface,	of 2nd,	3rd.	4th.
20.0364 inches,	10.1604 inches,	10.1613	and 41.1687.

So that here the radii of the two adjacent surfaces scarcely differ more than $\frac{1}{1000}$th of an inch, and may of course be cemented together, should it be thought desirable.

(36.) The triple object-glass is constructed in the same manner as the double, but as we have two convex lenses to produce the required refraction, the total spherical aberration will be less in a triple lens than in a double one, and, therefore, requires less correction by the flint; while the secondary spectrum may be greatly diminished by making one convex lens of crown, and the other of Bohemia, or Dutch plate glass. The theorems for finding the proportionate foci of the two lenses are indeterminate; for theoretically, it is immaterial whether their foci be equal, or in any other proportion, provided the compound lens be in the ratio of the dispersion of the flint. Again, the radii of the concave may be varied to any convenient curvature, as there are two convex lenses, and, therefore, the aberration cannot be greater than the convex lenses will correct*. When the radius of each surface is equal, and the ratio of dispersion and refraction is the same as in the double achromatic object-glass, and the compound focus of the lens is 30 inches, the radii of the first convex

will be $\begin{cases} r = 21.35. \\ R = 15.93. \end{cases}$

of the concave $\begin{cases} r' = 13.9. \\ R' = 13.9. \end{cases}$

second convex $\begin{cases} r'' = 21.35. \\ R'' = 15.93. \end{cases}$

(37.) The largest triple achromatic telescope ever constructed, has lately been erected in the observatory of the imperial university at Dorpat, on the 10th of November, 1824, and was made by Fraunhofer, the late director of the Optical Institute, at Benedictbauern, near Munich.

The concave is formed from a piece of dense flint glass made by Guinand, and has a greater dispersive power than any obtained before. It is perfectly free from veins; and the diameter of the object-glass exceeds that of any other telescope, having a clear aperture of $9\frac{6}{10}$ inches, and a focal distance of 25 feet. This instrument is mounted on a metal stand, and although of the immense weight of 5000 Russian pounds, is moveable in every direction with the slightest exertion, all the moveable parts being balanced by counter-weights. It has 4 eye-glasses, the lowest magnifying

---

* In a double achromatic object glass, the convex lens should be assumed first, as the flint might be formed with more aberration than the convex could correct.

175 times, and the highest 700 times: the cost of this instrument was 1300*l.* sterling. Another telescope has lately been made of similar materials in England by Mr. Tulley; the aperture of the object-glass is $6\frac{8}{10}$, and its focal length is 12 feet. This instrument is now in the possession of Dr. Pearson.*

(38.) The Galilean telescope was invented in 1590, by the illustrious person from whom it derived its name; but as it is susceptible of little improvement from the nature of its construction, it is seldom used except for opera glasses, in which the shortness of the construction renders it available. It consists of a single convex or achromatic object-glass, whose focal length is usually from 4 to 8 inches, which it rarely exceeds. The eye-glass is a double or plano-concave lens from $\frac{1}{2}$ an inch to 2 inches focus; the distance between the two glasses is equal to the difference of their focal lengths, and the power is in the ratio of their foci, as in the astronomical telescope. *Fig.* 26 is a section of the Galilean construction for an opera-glass. Let O be the object-glass of 6 inches focus, E the concave eye-glass 2 inches focus; the distance O E will be 4 inches, and the power will be expressed by 6 inches divided by 2 inches, equal to 3 times. The distinctness of the Galilean construction exceeds that of any other, and arises from the rays of light proceeding from the object directly through the lenses without crossing or intersecting each other; whereas, in the combination of convex glasses, they intersect one another to form an image in the focus of the object-glass; and this image is magnified by the eye-lens with its imperfections and distortions. With a power of 8 and a 12 or 16-inch object-glass, the satellites of Jupiter have been distinctly observed; while a common astronomical telescope of 4 or 5 feet focal length has scarcely rendered them visible. The area or field of view in this instrument is very limited, and, on that account, it cannot be used for high powers, as the objects seen at one

Fig. 26.

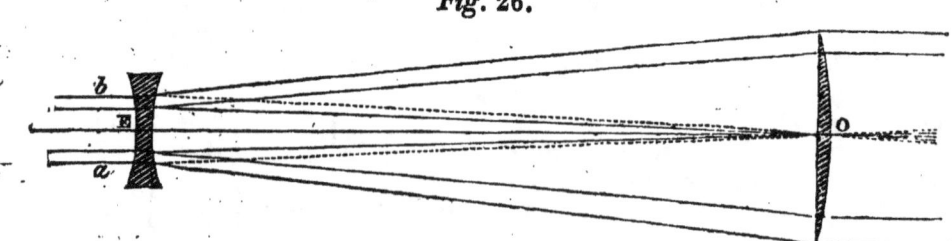

view are always as the area of the pupil of the eye, and not as the area of the eye-glass, as in convex lenses. Thus, if ab (*fig.* 20.) is larger than the pupil of the eye they will not be seen, although refracted by the lens E; but it should be remembered, that as the rays, when they have passed through the eye-glass, are not converged to a focus, the nearer the eye is placed to the lens E, the more numerous will be the objects seen at one view.

(39.) The construction of opera-glasses might be achromatic, when made with only two lenses, provided the focal length of the object and eye-lens are in the ratio of the dispersive and refractive powers of the media from which they are formed. Thus, if an object lens be made of rock-crystal, whose focal distance is 5, and the eye-lens be formed of oil of cassia, fixed between two parallel pieces of glass, or other convenient substance so curved as to give a focus of 1.02, the combination will be achromatic, with an amplyfying power of $4\frac{8}{10}$ times. If the concave lens had been formed of flint-glass, with the same object lens, a magnifying power of two might be obtained, and the combination would be free from all colour. If oil of aniseed were used for the concave, the power obtained to make the instrument achromatic would be 2.82 times*.

The following TABLE exhibits the refractive and dispersive powers of different substances capable of producing achromatic combinations; and it should be remarked, that the medium used for the eye-lens must have the greatest dispersive power:—

---

* See Astronomical Transactions, vol. ii.

* Dr. Brewster's treatise on new optical Instruments.

Substances to be employed for Eye-Lenses.	Refractive Power.	Dispersive Power.	Substances to be employed for Object-Lenses.	Refractive Power.	Dispersive Power.
1. Oil of Cassia	1.641	.139	Crown Glass	1.534	.036
2. ——— Aniseed	1.601	.077	Plate Glass	1.527	.032
3. ——— Cummin	1.508	.065	Water	1.336	.035
4. ——— Cloves	1.535	.062	Alcohol	1.374	.029
5. ——— Sassafras	1.532	.060	Sulphuric Acid	1.440	.031
6. ——— Sweet Fennel Seed	1.506	.055	Oil of Ambergris	1.368	.032
7. ——— Spearmint	1.481	.054	Rock Crystal	1.562	.026
8. ——— Pimento	1.507	.052 / .048	Topaz	1.638	.024
9. Flint Glass	1.616	.052 / .048	Diamond	2.470	.038

CHAPTER IX.—*Dr. Brewster's Telescope for measuring Distances — Double Image Telescope—Graphic Telescope—Achromatic Eye-Pieces.*

(40.) A telescope for measuring the distances of objects was invented by Dr. Brewster, for which he obtained a patent in 1810. When describing the telescope *figs.* 15 and 16, it was stated, that as the object approached the instrument, the eye-tube required to be drawn out to adjust the instrument for distinct vision: now the measure of the quantity required to be drawn out, if registered on the sliding tube by divisions, and by a corresponding mark on the outer tube, would determine the distances of the objects. The increase of the focal length of the object-glass may be found by dividing the square of the focal length of the object-glass by the distance of the object, minus the focus of the object-lens: thus, if the focus of the object-lens is 2 feet, and the distance of the object 50 feet, the tube must be drawn out $\frac{2^2}{50-2}$ or 1 inch from the solar focus, to adjust for distinct vision of the object; but the length of these divisions would be in a decreasing ratio, and the quantity is almost imperceptible for great distances: thus, if two objects be 100 feet apart, and the nearest 200 feet from the observer, the difference of adjustment for these two objects would be only $\frac{8}{100}$ of an inch. In the patent construction this quantity may be increased to almost any required length, by means of two object-glasses; the inner one is about ¼ of the focal length of the principal lens, and being fixed to the eye-tube slides along with the eye-piece. This instrument has been found useful at sea in determining the distance of head-lands, and in war, when an enemy's ship is gaining sail; this is determined by taking two observations, and noting the difference of the quantity required to be drawn out or pushed in to obtain a distinct vision; and when the time between each observation is known, the rate of the vessels sailing may be ascertained.

(41.) Another instrument, nearly for the same purpose as the one just described, but possessing more accuracy for measuring angles and distances, was constructed by the Abbé Rochon. This instrument is the ordinary telescope, with a double refracting prism of rock-crystal, placed before the eye-glass; this prism produces two images of an object. These images may be made to approach to or recede from one another by altering the distance of the prism from the eye-glass; but the object is better effected by a method proposed by Dr. Brewster, in which the first glass of the telescope, together with the prism, which may be cemented to it, is made to slide to or from the other glasses of the eye-piece, and the quantity moved is registered by divisions on the tube. This variable eye-piece, which changes the power of the telescope, is so adjusted, that the two images of the object shall be in accurate contact; when this is done, if an observation is made to find the angle, the index, by previous experiment, will give it; but when it is desired to know the rate of motion of the object, another observation must be made at a determinate interval, and the difference of adjustment required in the two observations to bring the images in contact will determine its distance, the scale being previously ascertained by experiment or calculation. The imperfect crystallization of quartz, and the difficulty of working it, led Dr. Brewster to adopt the *colourless topaz of New Holland* to form his double-refracting prisms, it being much freer from veins and imperfections, besides possessing the advantage of a lower dispersive power. In certain sections of the crystal, when we require only a very small separation of the images, we may preserve, on both sides, the natural surface of the cleavage. The other means of procuring a double image proposed by Dr. Brewster, we shall subjoin, as being well worthy consideration for micrometical purposes. 1. The double image may be produced by a small bisected plane speculum, placed between the eye-lens and the eye, and one of the halves may be made to move by a screw, not for the purpose of bringing the images in contact, but in order to vary the constant angle, according as it is wanted, for large or small discs. 2. The duplicature of the image may be effected by bisecting the eye-lens, or by placing a bisected lens between the eye-lens and the eye. 3. The two images may be formed by a slightly-inclined face, ground upon a highly-polished and parallel plate of fluor-spar, one image being seen by half of the pupil through the parallel plate, and the other through the inclined face. Fluor-spar is recommended because of its producing a less dispersion under a given angle than any other substance; and even this might be removed by the ordinary means.

(42.) The graphic telescope is employed for the delineation of objects situated at any distance from the instrument, which may be represented of any required size; and is used for drawing portraits, landscapes, and architectural subjects. It was invented in 1811, by Mr. C. Varley, who obtained a patent for it. This instrument consists of an astronomical telescope of low power, placed between two plane reflecting specula, with a particular construction of the eye-piece to correct the distortion of the image produced by the eye-glass. *Fig.* 27, is a section of the instrument.

Fig. 27.

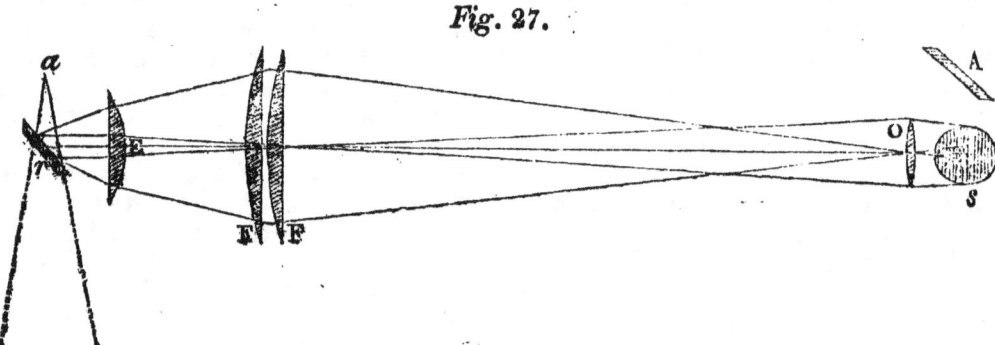

O is the object-glass, E the eye-glass, and F F two meniscus field-glasses, whose form and distance from the eye-glass are so adjusted as to produce a flat and enlarged field of view. The rays of light proceeding from an object enter the side of the tube, and impinge upon the flat speculum *s*, placed at an angle of 45° with the axis of the telescope, as is shown in section at A; the rays will be reflected by this speculum along the axis and through the object-glass O, and are converged to a focus near the field lens F, where an inverted image of the object will be formed and may be received by the eye-glass E; lastly, they will strike the other inclined flat reflector, and be reflected up to the eye placed above at *a*. When a piece of paper is placed below the speculum *r*, the observer being supposed to look down on the speculum, keeping both eyes open, he will be able to see an image of the object on the paper when the instrument is adjusted to its proper focus. This representation may be traced with one or both eyes, and the size of the image may be varied by altering the distance of the paper from the speculum, or by changing the magnifying power of the instrument. If the first speculum *s* be taken away, the sides of the objects are reversed (as on an engraved copper-plate,) the speculum *r* forms the image erect, which was inverted by the eye-glass E, and prevents the telescope from intercepting a view of the paper.*

---

* The inventor of this instrument has employed it very extensively in sketching from nature; and in the mountainous districts of Wales the views become of great value on account of their accuracy; he has also made with this instrument some very correct views of the seat of the late Lord Byron, at Newstead Abbey, Nottinghamshire. In drawing shipping and boats it is extremely valuable, as the numerous lines in the details of these objects are not of a geometrical figure. We have been informed that this instrument was the one employed in making the panoramic view of the metropolis from the top of St. Paul's, for the exhibition of which a building in the Regent's Park, called the Coliseum, has recently been erected.

(43.) The achromatic or negative eye-piece generally adapted to astronomical telescopes, is a combination of lenses intended to correct the dispersion produced by the eye-glass, independent of the object lens. Let O, *Fig.* 28, be the object-glass of a telescope free from chromatic dispersion, and E the eye-glass; let F be the focus of the object-glass O, where an inverted image is formed. Now the pencil of white light A a b, when transmitted by the lens E,

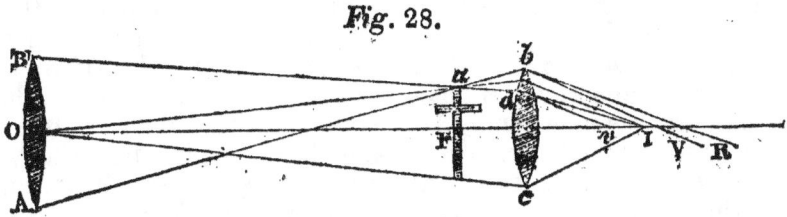

Fig. 28.

will be divided into its component colours, so that b R will be the direction of the red rays, and b V the path of the violet, and the angle V b R in crown-glass will be $\frac{1}{37}$ of $a\,b$ R. The rays B $a\,d$ passing through a part of the lens whose surfaces are less inclined to each other, will be less refracted and less dispersed in the same proportion nearly, and d I will be the path of the red rays, and $d\,v$ of the violet; therefore, the two violet rays will be very nearly parallel when the two red rays are rendered parallel. Hence it must happen, as coloured rays do not unite at the bottom of the eye, that the object will appear bordered with coloured fringes, and a black line seen near the margin on a white ground will have a ruddy and orange border on the outside, and a blue border within, and this confusion will increase nearly in the same proportion as the visual angle b I c.

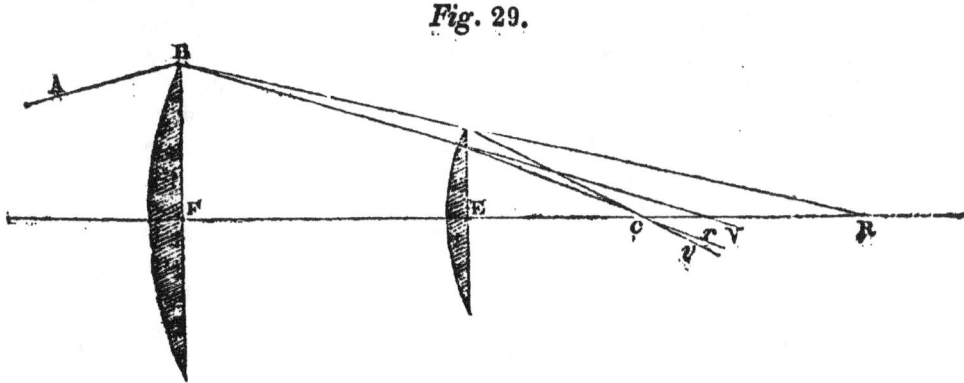

Fig. 29.

(44.) *Fig.* 29, is a section of the achromatic eye-piece. Let A B be a compounded pencil of white light proceeding from the object glass, B F a plano-convex field glass, with the plane side next the eye-glass E. Now the red rays of the pencil A B after refraction would cross the axis in R, and the violet rays in V, but meeting the eye-glass E, the red rays will be refracted to $c\,r$, and the violet to $c\,v$, when they will cross one another, in the axis at the point c and unite; for the violet ray being nearer the axis of the lens E, will suffer less refraction than the red, and when the eye is placed in the axis at c, the object will appear colourless. The distance of the two lenses F E, to produce this correction, when made of crown glass, whose dispersion is as 77 to 78, when the incidence is 50, must be equal to half the sum of their focal distances nearly; or, more exactly, the distance between the two lenses must be equal to half the sum of the focal distance of the eye-glass, and the distance at which the field-glass would form an image of the object-glass; for the point R is the focus to which a ray coming from the centre of the object-glass is refracted by the field-glass, consequently, this distance must be varied according to the distance of the objects, and also, as the length of the object-glass; for the same combination will not be correct for a long and a short object-glass, nor for celestial and terrestrial observations; for, when it is correct for one case, and the distance of the image or focal point is varied, the divergency of the rays will alter, and the dispersion will be either too much or too little corrected. The proportion of the foci of these two lenses should be as 2 to 3, to produce the largest field and the least distortion.

(45.) The eye-pieces employed to produce an erect image for terrestrial telescopes admit of numerous arrangements: the simplest was shown in *fig.* 16, composed of three similar lenses placed at equal distances; but as there is no field-lens in this construction, the view is limited, though the chromatic dispersion is in part corrected by the middle lens, and may be totally destroyed by using an eye-glass of shorter focal length than the other two, and at a less distance from the middle glass. Another combination may be produced by two glasses so placed that the lens which receives the inverted image formed by the object-glass shall form an image on the other side, inverted with respect to the first, but erect with the object, and this image may be viewed with an eye-glass. This construction is shown in *fig.* 30. Let *i* be the in-

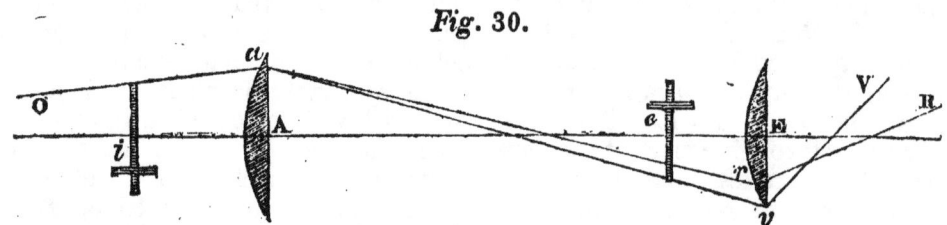

Fig. 30.

verted image formed by the object-glass, *o a* a pencil of light from the centre of the object-glass falling on the lens A; this pencil will be dispersed after refraction, and *a r* will be the path of the red rays, and *a v* of the violet; at the focal point *e* an erect image will be formed, and may be viewed by the lens E. Now the red rays at *r* falling on this lens will be less refracted than the violet at *v*, and will cross the axis in R, while the violet *v* crosses the axis at V; hence the dispersion will be greatly increased both by reason of the spherical aberration, and their greater refrangibility, so that objects seen through this eye-piece will be more fringed with colours than in any other construction.

(46.) The last construction might be improved by using two lenses disposed in a similar manner to the negative eye-piece (44,) instead of the lens E. These would enlarge the field and correct the dispersion; but as the spherical aberration is very great, two lenses should be used in place of the lens A, in order to make the combination complete; thus a four-glass eye-piece would be formed that is perfectly corrected, if duly proportioned distances and foci are used. This is accomplished in the following combination (*fig.* 31.) where the lenses are in the order of the

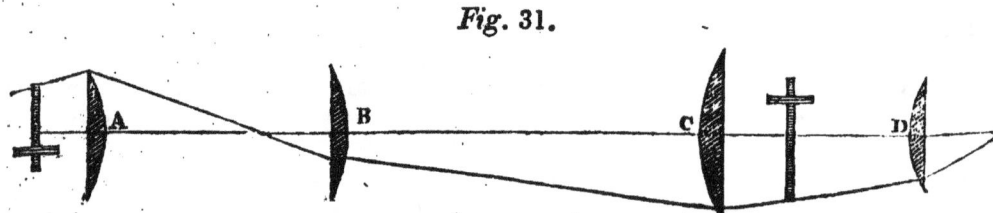

Fig. 31.

letters A B C D beginning with the lens next the object-glass, and the distances, &c. of each lens are as follows: focal length of A = $1\frac{1}{7}$ = B = $2\frac{1}{2}$, C = 2 and D = $1\frac{1}{2}$, and their distances A B = $2\frac{1}{4}$, B C = $3\frac{5}{8}$, C D = $2\frac{3}{8}$. This eye-piece will be nearly free from chromatic dispersion and aberration. In a very good eye-piece of Ramsden's, the focal lengths were found to be of A = .0775, B = 1.025, C = 1.01, D = .79; the distances A B = 1.18, B C = 1.83, C D = 1.105. Stops should be placed between the lenses A and B, and a larger one between C and D; these stops are to prevent any false light from passing through the lenses to the eye. The more black stops there are introduced into a telescope, provided they do not hinder the pencils of light proceeding from the object, the better will the instrument perform.

(47.) The brightness of any object seen through a telescope, in comparison with its brightness when seen by the naked eye, may, in all cases be easily found by the following formula. Let n represent the natural distance of a visible object at which it can be distinctly seen, and let d represent its distance from the object-glass of the instrument. Let m be the magnifying power of the instrument, that is, let the visual angle subtended at the eye by the object when at the distance n, and viewed without the instrument, be to the visual angle produced by the instrument, as 1 to m. Let a be the diameter of the object-glass, and p be that of the pupil. Let the instrument be so constructed that no parts of the pencils are intercepted for want of sufficient apertures of the intermediate glasses. Lastly, let the light lost in reflection or refraction be neglected.

The brightness of vision through the instrument will be expressed by the fraction $\left(\dfrac{a\,n}{m\,p\,d}\right)^2$ the brightness of natural vision being 1. But although this fraction may exceed unity, the vision through the instrument will not be brighter than natural vision. For when this is the case, the pupil does not receive all the light transmitted through the instrument.

In microscopes, n is the nearest limits of distinct vision nearly eight inches; but a difference in this circumstance, arising from a difference in the eye, makes no change in the formula, because m changes in the same proportion with n.

In telescopes n and d may be accounted equal, and the formula becomes $\dfrac{a^2}{m^2 p^2}$.*

CHAPTER X.—*Stands for Telescopes—Method of making Grinding and Polishing Specula and Lenses—Method of centering and adjusting Lenses.*

(48.) To describe the numerous varieties of stands or supports for telescopes would be both prolix and trifling, as different artists generally adopt such contrivances as they think most likely to please the fancy of the purchaser; but the chief consideration in a scientific point of view is, to obtain a steady and immoveable stand free from vibration. To effect this, the instrument should be supported at both ends, to give steadiness, and to prevent its being affected by the wind; for every vibration will be increased in the same ratio as the amplification of the instrument, and produce a tremulous or dancing motion in the objects. Thus a superior telescope badly supported may be rendered inferior to a common one fixed on an immoveable stand. The materials of which stands are composed should be capable of transmitting as little vibration as possible; thus, the vibration of a frame of cast iron in one piece, although perfectly steady, would be sufficient to destroy distinct vision. Wooden stands are preferable, provided firm diagonal braces are used, so as to form immoveable triangular frames. Where iron is required for durability, plates of lead should be screwed between each piece to stop the vibrations. In reflecting telescopes the difficulty of preventing vibrations greatly impairs their value; for the metals, particularly the small one, are easily set in vibration, and unless the arm of the small metal is damped, the vision is frequently indistinct. When a Gregorian telescope has been taken from its stand, and placed on a lump of soft clay, the distinctness has been such as to enable a person to read a bill placed at 900 feet; while on the stand it could be read only at the distance of 650 feet, although no apparent tremor could be discerned when on the stand.

(49.) *Specula.*—A good composition for the specula of reflectors is one of the most important desiderata in the making of telescopes. The qualities most in request are, a sound uniform metal, free from all microscopic pores; not liable to tarnish by absorption of moisture from the atmosphere; not so hard as to be incapable of taking a good figure and exquisite polish, or so soft as to be easily scratched; and possessing a high reflective power. The various compositions employed for specula differ more in the admixture of minor ingredients than in their essential materials. Copper and tin (bronze metal) are the metals mostly employed, with small quantities of arsenic, silver, and brass. The proportions generally employed are, copper 32 parts, grain tin 15, with the addition of two parts of arsenic to render it more white and compact. The Rev. Mr. Edwards, in a treatise annexed

* Barlowe.

to the Nautical Almanac for 1787*, says that if 1 of brass, and 1 of silver, be used with only one of arsenic, a most excellent metal will be obtained, which is whiter, harder, and more reflective than any other he ever met with. With respect to the practical value of this composition we cannot speak; but having made specula for reflecting instruments ourselves, we can vouch for the goodness of the following, both with respect to the exquisite figure and polish it is capable of assuming, and its freedom from pores. To make this composition, take two parts of copper, as pure as it is possible to be procured; (for the goodness of the speculum will depend on the purity of the materials employed) this must be melted in a crucible by itself; then put in another crucible, 1 part of pure grain tin†. When they are both melted, mix and stir them with a wooden spatula, keeping a good flux on the melted surface to prevent oxidation: this metal must be quickly poured into the moulds, which may be made of founders' loom; the intended face always being downwards. Where the speculum is required particularly good, the best mode of casting is to have an iron mould made with a vertical tube attached on one side, and the bottom of the tube to end in a bulb; the melted metal is then to be poured down the tube, and will fill the bulb and mould, leaving a sufficiency in the tube to give pressure. The bulb being lower than the mould will retain any dense impurities, and the tube the lighter ones; while the speculum will be uniform and dense.

Having thus procured the speculum, the next thing will be to grind it to the required figure; this is effected on a convex brass or hard metal circular tool, carefully turned to a gauge of the required curve. This tool is fixed on a post or upright, and the speculum is held in the hand by means of a convenient holder cemented on its back. The grinding is then commenced with coarse emery powder and water, when the roughness is taken off by moving the speculum across the tool in different directions walking round the post: finer emery is used in the same way, till the surface of the speculum has become uniform. The next step will be to smooth it by means of fine washed flour emery, gradually passing from one degree to the next finer, and washing the tool and speculum between each application of emery, to prevent any gritty particles from scratching the metal. When the speculum is completed, and of the required figure, it is next to be polished. This is done either by taking a convex tool similar to the grinder, or the grinder itself, and covering it with pure pitch evenly spread over its surface: while warm, a concave tool of the same figure as the speculum is then worked over its surface wet. When the proper figure is obtained, washed putty (*i. e.* combined oxide of tin and lead) is poured on the pitch, and the speculum polished thereon by moving it as before. During the process of grinding and polishing, the tools must be carefully examined by the *gauge*, and if they happen to get out of the true figure, the speculum must be worked more on the edge, or middle, as the case may require. Instead of the vertical *post* above mentioned, a *lap* is sometimes employed, which produces a much better figure and more expeditiously. A lap consists of a common lathe communicating a slow and regular motion to a vertical mandral, on which the grinding or polishing tool is fixed; in using the lap, the artist is enabled to stand in the same place, and has more command over the work.

Lenses are ground precisely in the same manner as specula, but the polishing is different. Here the concave or convex polishing tool is made of brass, and when turned of a proper curve, a smooth thick piece of felt (cloth) is stretched over the tool and cemented to it; the outer surface is then imbedded with washed putty powder. After this is done, the lens, or block of lenses, is worked on it with cross motions; if the powder be employed too wet the fibres of the cloth will rise up, and polish not only the surface, but also the small hollows left in the grinding. This effect, from the nature of the polishing surface being heterogeneous, generally takes place to a greater or less extent when viewed by a microscope; these cavities being polished admit the light and disperse it, instead of it being collected as with a uniform surface. When

---

* This treatise which is now very scarce, is republishing in the *Technological Repository*.

† It is most probable that the best proportions would be as their respective *atomic* weight, that is, thrice 32 of copper, and 58 of tin, as the metal would then be more intimately combined.

these faults are visible to the eye, the lens is called *curdled*. If we are desirous of procuring an uniform and perfect surface, the polishing tool must be homogeneous; and the best material for its formation is good clean *bees wax*, hardened by the addition of *red sulphate of iron*, dry and finely washed. This composition, when of the proper temper, is melted over the brass tool; and when cold can be turned to the required curve. The advantage of this improvement, besides its uniformity, is that should any hard scratching particles insinuate themselves between the tool and glasses, they sink and are imbedded in the wax, and thus their injurious effects are prevented. The polish of lenses made in this manner is clear and defined when examined by a microscope; when the shadow of a bar is brought across them. This method is now employed by one of the first opticians in the metropolis.*

Centering of Lenses.—The centering of lenses for accurate instruments is of great importance, more especially for the object-glasses of achromatic telescopes. Different opticians employ their own methods, but one of the best is done by reflection: let the lens to be centered be cemented on to a brass chuck, having the middle turned away so as not to touch the lens, but near the edge, which will be hid when mounted; this rim is very accurately turned flat where it is to touch the glass. When the chuck and cement is warm it is made to revolve rapidly: while in motion a lighted candle is brought before it and its reflected image attentively watched. If this image has any motion, the lens is not flat or central: a piece of soft wood must therefore be applied to it in the manner of a turning tool, till such time as the light becomes stationary. When the whole has cooled, the edges of the lens must be turned by a diamond, or ground with emery. This method of centering and adjusting object-glasses by their reflected images, was laid before the public by Dr. Wollaston, and has been used by our first opticians for a considerable time.

* The method of grinding and polishing lenses from diamonds for microscopes, by Mr. Pritchard, will be found in the Quarterly Journal of the Royal Institution, vol. ii, page 14, new series.

Concluding Remarks on Telescopes.

(48.) The applications of the telescope to the purposes of man are so numerous, that their details would far exceed the boundaries of our treatise. Amongst its principal uses, however, besides those accompanying the descriptions of the various modifications of that instrument, may be enumerated the following:—The accurate determination of the longitude of the various places on the earth's surface is ascertained by the telescope, by observing the immersions and emersions of the four satellites of the planet Jupiter; from thence, by the aid of a good chronometer, with the time of any known place, the situation of the unknown spot is determined. Before the invention of the telescope, navigators were compelled to keep within sight of the coast in sailing from one country to another, and thus were often endangered while passing an hostile or rocky shore : by the assistance of this instrument, the voyage is made direct to the intended place without fear or danger.

To the astronomer the telescope is his principal and most important guide. It enables him to determine, with precision, the transits of the planets and stars across the meridian. The computation of astronomical and nautical tables; to determine the revolution of the planets on their axes, and their relative polar, and equatorial diameters, is derived from observations by the telescope. We are by this instrument enabled to discover the analogy between the laws which govern the motions of the planets and those of our earth; their parallax, and from thence their distances. The aberration of light and the motions of the *siderial* systems in space, unfold wonders which must excite the imagination of the most profound philosophers in the highest possible degree. The harmony and simplicity displayed in such immense worlds prove the design and wisdom by which they were created; and the wonderful facts thus ascertained raise the most ordinary mind up to a sublime contemplation of the great Creator.

In surveying of land, the telescope is highly useful, and for this purpose is mounted on a stand, with an horizontal and vertical motion registering by divisions the degrees and minutes of inclination or position of the instrument. For the more accurate *reading off* these divisions, the two limbs are furnished with a *Vernier's scale*. Spirit levels and a magnetic needle are usually attached to the instrument; and from the purposes to which it is applied, a telescope with this mounting is called a *Theodolite*, derived from two Greek words θεαομαι *to see*, and οδος *the way or distance*,—that is, an instrument *for seeing or determining distances*. The method by which the distances and heights of remote objects are ascertained is by measuring the angles subtended by the object, and computing trigonometrically therefrom.

The continental writers have much exaggerated the powers and penetration of the telescope; indeed the time is not far distant, when it was gravely asserted, that works of art had been recognised in our satellite the moon. The fallacy of this circumstance may be easily shown to our readers by the following simple considerations.—Let a person direct the tubes of a telescope (without the glasses) to any celestial object, and there fix them; he will soon find that in a short space of time, the object will have removed from before the mouth of the tube. Now this motion of the celestial bodies, which is only *apparent*, arises from the revolution of our earth on her axis; and the quantity of this motion may be determined with facility, thus:—the earth is known to revolve once about her axis in 24 hours, and as every circle is supposed to be divided into 360 equal parts or degrees, the apparent time any celestial body takes to describe one degree, will be found by dividing the 24 hours by 360, which gives us 4 minutes as the time an object would pass the mouth of the tube if it only takes in one degree of the heavens.

Now, if we suppose the glasses to be placed in the tubes, the magnfying power of the instrument being 60, and we direct it (as before) to an object, as the moon, whose diameter is about half a degree, the time of her passing or transit will be one minute, if the field of view be, as in the ordinary telescopes, about 30', which the moon would exactly occupy. If the power of the telescope be increased 10 times, the eye-piece having the same angle of vision, only $\frac{1}{100}$ part of the moon would be seen at once, 100 being the square of 10, the increased power of the instrument; and the time in which this portion of the moon would pass the telescope is 6 seconds. Again, if we increase the power 10 times, so that its linear amplification of an object is 6000 times only a $\frac{1}{10000}$ part of the moon's surface could be seen in the field of view; or the planet Saturn, whose apparent diameter is 10 seconds, would just fill it, and the time of their passing the instrument would be only $\frac{1}{10}$ of a second.*

Having thus shown the amazing velocity with which a planet passes the mouth of a telescope with these high powers, we shall next proceed to point out the apertures and amplification necessary for observing some given measure on the surface of the moon. First, we must determine the angle every object must subtend to the eye, in order to render it visible: this is found on an average for different sights to be one minute, that is, when an object is removed from the eye about 3000 times its own diameter it will only be just distinguishable. From this we can now determine the extent of the smallest part of the moon's surface discoverable by the unassisted eye. Its real diameter being 2100 miles, which divided by the number of minutes which its apparent diameter subtends, (viz. 30,) gives us 70 miles as the measure of the least distinct spot seen by the naked eye; therefore, we know that, if a telescope magnifies 70 times, we can just discern a spot one mile in diameter on the moon's surface; and to recognise any object 10 feet in diameter, we shall find by this rule the magnifying power of the telescope must be 37100 times, and the diameter of an object-glass or metal for such an instrument may be found by the method described in (18); which if we suppose a pencil of rays $\frac{1}{10}$ of an inch in diameter will admit sufficient light to the eye, the diameter of the speculum must be 62 feet, and its focal distance 309 feet, when an eye-glass of $\frac{1}{10}$th of an inch is employed. These calculations must convince the reader of our inability to make such observations; for if the impossibility of procuring such enormous instruments were overcome, they would be so unwieldy as entirely to prevent our using them.

---

* It is necessary for us to state, that, for the observation of small stars and nebulæ with reflecting instruments this power is occasionally employed; as even under these circumstances they possess no sensible diameter, and a regular motion is communicated to the telescope in the plane of the equator by means of a clock or other mechanism.

CHAPTER XI.—*Microscopes.—History of.—Theory of Single.—Magnifying Powers of.—Illumination.—Forms of Lenses for Microscopes.—Globules.— Globule and Lens compared.—Mr. Pritchard's Diamond and Sapphire Microscopes.—Table of their Magnifying Powers.*

(49.) THE history of the microscope, like that of many other valuable inventions, has been veiled in considerable obscurity by the lapse of time: and the discovery, amongst the moderns, of so useful a class of optical instruments, has been claimed by several individuals. But it seems certain that the ancients were acquainted with the microscope, at least in one of its forms, as appears from the following passage in Seneca:— "Letters, though minute and obscure, appear larger and clearer through a glass bubble filled with water." Although we have no account that they understood the laws by which the magnifying power of the spherule was effected, yet their acquaintance with its application appears certain.

The invention of the microscope is attributed by the celebrated Dutch mathematician, Huygens, to a countryman of his, named *Drebell*, (for it must be observed that it was entirely lost in the middle ages.) He constructed them about the year 1621, or 31 years after the invention of the telescope. According to Borelli, the microscope was invented by Jansen, the reputed contriver of the telescope, who presented some instruments of his first construction to Prince Maurice, and Albert Archduke of Austria. These instruments were six feet in length, and consisted of a tube of gilt copper, one inch in diameter, supported by thin brass pillars in the shape of dolphins, on a base of ebony which was adapted to hold the objects to be examined. Of the internal construction of this microscope we have no precise account; though there is reason to think that it was nothing more than a telescope converted into a compound microscope.* Viviani, an Italian mathematician, also expressly informs us in his Life of Galileo, that this great man was led to the construction of the microscope from that of the telescope; and in the year 1612 he actually sent a microscope to Sigismund, King of Poland. The honour of making a microscope of two double convex lenses, like those at present in use (without their field-glass,) seems to belong to F. Fontana, a Neapolitan, who, in a work published in 1646, claims it as his own, and dates the invention from the year 1618.

The numerous forms of microscopes which have at different intervals been constructed, may be included in *three* distinct classes, however varying as to their external appearances;—these are, *Single*, *Compound Refracting*, and *Compound Reflecting* Microscopes.

(50.) *Theory of the single Microscope.*—It must have been observed by most persons, that when the distance of an object from a spectator is decreased, we are enabled to define its parts more readily, and that it appears larger; thus if we look at two men, the one 200 feet, and the other only 100 feet from us, the former will appear only half the height of the latter; or the angle which the latter subtends to the eye of an observer will be twice that of the former. Hence we must conclude, that the nearer we can bring an object to the eye the larger it will appear. Now, if we have to examine a very minute object, and in order to render its parts distinguishable if we bring it very near to the eye, (suppose one or two inches,) it will become very indistinct and confused. This effect is produced by the great divergency of the rays of light from the object, and the power of the crystalline lens of the eye not being sufficient to collect the rays, whereby an image of the object may be formed on the retina, at the proper distance on the back of the eye. Now if we employ a single microscope, which consists of a convex lens usually made of glass, (though it would have the power of magnifying or increasing the angle, if made of any other transparent substance, but in a different degree,) and mounted in a brass setting, and place it between the object and the eye, the former being in the focus of the glass, the diverging rays from the object will be refracted and rendered parallel by the lens: and thus we shall obtain a distinct and near view of the object.

To exemplify this fact more simply, let A (*fig.* 32) be a small object which we desire to examine. Now, bundles of rays will diverge from every part of this object in all directions, as shown by the lines A *r*, A *r*. And if there be placed before this object a convex lens B, whose focal distance is B A, those rays diverging from the object which fall on the

---

* See *Edinburgh Encyclopedia*, art. *Microscope*, for a more enlarged history of this instrument.

D

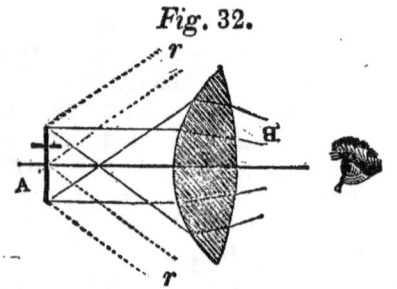

Fig. 32.

surface of the lens will be refracted at its two surfaces, and emerge from it nearly parallel to each other; consequently the object is capable of being received by the eye on the side B, under a greater angle than it could be seen without the lens.

(51.) Having shown that the magnitude is dependent on the distance of the object, we must now investigate the increase obtained by the employment of lenses; this we shall find to depend on the difference of the distance of the object from a lens, and the *distance* when seen without its assistance. This latter distance, however, (that is, the nearest distance at which we can distinctly discern a minute object,) is variable in different persons, and indeed in the same individual at different periods of life; therefore it becomes necessary to assume some measure as a standard, before we can express the amplifying power of a lens so as mutually to comprehend the same idea of the real magnitude of an object. In old optical works the distance at which the authors usually reckon the place of distinct vision is *eight* inches, but in latter works a shorter distance has sometimes been assumed. These distances are, however, variable, and are often determined by the writer to suit his own vision.

Dr. Brewster, in his optical works, has taken *five* inches as the distance for minute objects; "for," says he, "if we examine a small coin or insect, we naturally hold it nearer than an ordinary object, in order to inspect it more carefully." Again, we find that Professor Amici, of Modena, in determining the amplifying powers of his instruments, has adopted a standard of *ten* inches as the focus of the eye under ordinary circumstances. This latter number has also been employed by some authors, principally for the reason, that being a decimal number it offers greater facilities as a multiplier or divisor in optical investigations. We shall therefore assume this as our standard in subsequent calculations. Those who may think proper to adopt a shorter standard, as that of Dr. Brewster, will simply have to divide the magnifying powers hereafter given by *two*, which will give the required power according to that standard.

With this *decimal standard* we can now determine the magnifying power of lenses of any focal length, or formed of any substance (*media.*) Thus, if we are in possession of a lens which requires, for distinct vision, the object to be *one inch* from its centre (in a double convex,) we must divide the standard *ten* by *one*, which will give ten, therefore such a lens will increase the diameter of an object seen through it ten times: again, if we have another lens which requires the object to be the *twenty-fifth* of an inch distance from it, the power will be 250, which is found by simply adding a cipher (0) to the denominator of the fraction which expresses its distance (viz. $\frac{1}{25}$), and removing the numerator.

Now, in the first case, when we employed an inch lens, we called its magnifying power ten, from the number of diameters or increase of length and breadth of an object by the use of that lens. This, which is its usual denomination, is very defective; for we shall find, that if we draw the real object and its magnified view, the latter will occupy 100 times the surface of the former, so that the most proper expression of the magnifying power of this lens would be 100. This will be manifest from an inspection of *fig.* 33, where *a* is the real size

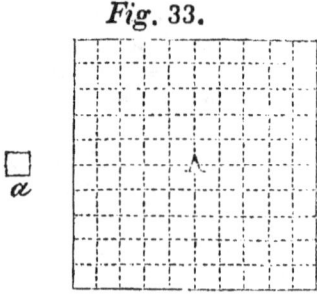

Fig. 33.

of a square object, and A its magnified view. Now, the dotted lines will show that it is ten times longer and broader than the object *a*, but it will be found to contain 100 such dotted squares all equal in size to the original square *a*: hence the proper magnifying power is 100, or the length squared.

The following table will exhibit the magnifying powers of lenses from two inches focus to the $\frac{1}{10}$th of an inch, according to the *decimal* standard; the column marked superficial is the true increase in size of an object by a lens of the focal length shown in the first column, formed from any transparent substance.

Focal lengths in inches.	Magnifying Powers.	
	Linear.	Superficial.
2	5	25
$1\frac{1}{2}$	6.6	43.5
1	10	100
$\frac{3}{4}$	13.3	176.8
$\frac{1}{2}$	20	400
$\frac{1}{4}$	40	1600
$\frac{1}{8}$	80	6400
$\frac{1}{10}$	100	10000

(52.) In a single microscope the circumstance requiring the greatest consideration, is the formation of the lens. The grinding of microscopic lenses is effected in a similar manner to that described in page 30, except that a quicker revolving motion of the grinding tool is necessary, and in the polishing great care is required to keep them of their proper figure (spherical.) When completed, they should be as thin as they can possibly be procured with a sufficient aperture, the reason for which will be hereafter explained. In the mounting or fitting up of the lenses, the intention of the instrument, whether it is to be used as *a hand, a pocket, or a table microscope*, must be considered. From the arrangement of the mountings to suit the nature of the objects to be examined, microscopes often derive their name, though the principle in all of them is similar, as *Botanical, Mineralogical, Anatomical, Natural History, Aquatic, Transparent,* or *Opaque Microscopes*, all of which are either *single* or *compound*. The focal distances of the lenses mounted in the single microscopes are usually $1\frac{1}{2}$ inch, 1 inch, $\frac{1}{2}$, $\frac{1}{4}$, $\frac{1}{10}$th, and $\frac{1}{20}$th of an inch, though the two last lenses seldom accompany the *pocket botanical*. One of these microscopes is shown in *fig.* 34, which is capable of having either lens adapted to it, and from its extreme simplicity is not liable to get deranged: *a* is the brass stem, having an internal screw cut in it to receive the cell *b* containing the lens *c*; at *d* there is attached an arm *e:* this arm being jointed at *d* is capable of lying flat when out of use, or can be altered to suit any other convenient position for holding the object, as shown by the dotted lines; on the round arm *e* is a sliding tube *f*, fixed to another sprung tube at right angles; this latter tube carries the forceps *h* moveable in every direction with respect to the lens *c*,

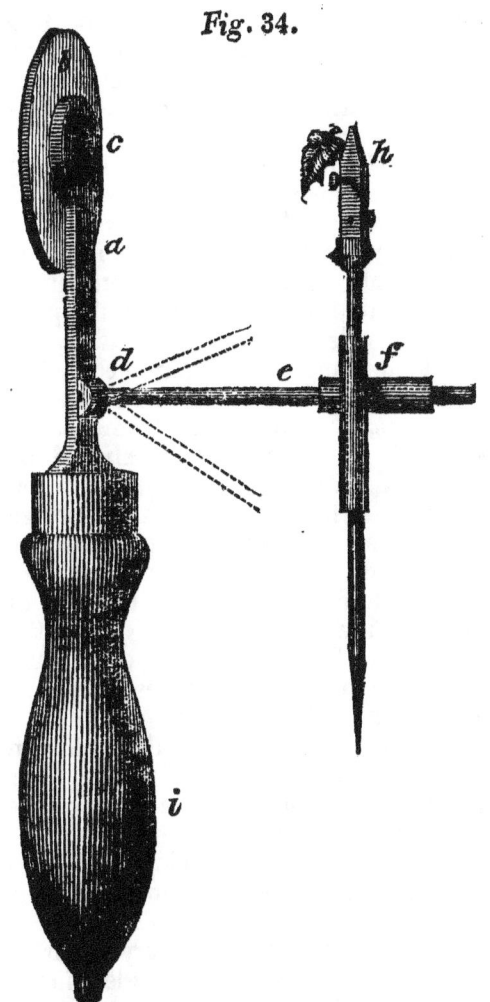

Fig. 34.

either as to distance or position; the handle *i* is screwed to the stem *a* when in use. If a lens of a different power is required to be employed, the cell *b* may be removed, and another with a deeper or shallower lens screwed into its place. If low power is wanted, as for the inspection of flowers, the cell with the lenses (shown in *fig.* 35) should be used,

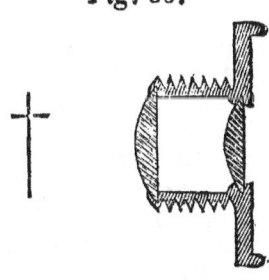

Fig. 35.

as that combination is superior to a single lens of equivalent power. This cell contains two plano-convex lenses, with their plane sides turned to the eye, the focus of the nearest being 2 and the other 3, with a distance between them equal to 1 of such parts; or their sidereal focal distances are usually about 1 inch and 1¼ inch. The advantage of this combination is, an increase of field (or number of objects seen at once,) and the diminution of aberration, as explained at page 13, (22.)

(53.) When microscopes are required for general purposes they are mounted on a stand, and usually called table microscopes. These, as we before remarked, are various, and accompanied with different implements for the purposes of dissecting and holding the various objects to be examined. The moveable parts of these, and of all microscopes, should be free from shake; while all their adjustments should be easy, and without *jolts* or *starts* when moving. The lenses should be so mounted as to be easily approached by the objects; and at the same time not too remote from the eye, as the field of view will always be increased with the nearness of the lens to the eye. Lastly, all shining or bright surfaces should be blackened on the anterior side of the lens, so that no glare or false light can be reflected towards the observer. For adjusting the object to the focus of the lens, a rack and pinion, or screw adjustment, is generally employed. These should be very fine, and sensible of the smallest motion.

(54.) With these preliminary remarks, we shall now describe a single microscope, suitable for the examination of any kind of object, in which the adjusting motions are of a novel and simple construction, as neither screw nor rackwork are employed. This instrument has recently been designed and executed by Mr. Holtzaffel, jun., on the basis of the microscope of Mr. Pritchard, who constructed the optical part. It consists of a circular brass stem a, (*fig.* 36,) capable of being fixed in every possible inclination, by the ball c attached to the clamp b, by which the whole may be firmly fixed to a table or board; the circular mirror d, working in the arm m, is attached to the tube x in the usual way. But it would be more convenient if applied in the manner shown below at *fig.* 37, where δ is the mirror, μ the arm, and ξ the tube: by this means the mirror is moveable in any position, to throw the reflected light on the slider or object e, (*fig.* 36,) by the screwheads fixed into the mirror case, which is loose in the arms. The whole slides upon the stem, that it may be placed nearer to, or farther from the object, according to the intensity of the light required for the

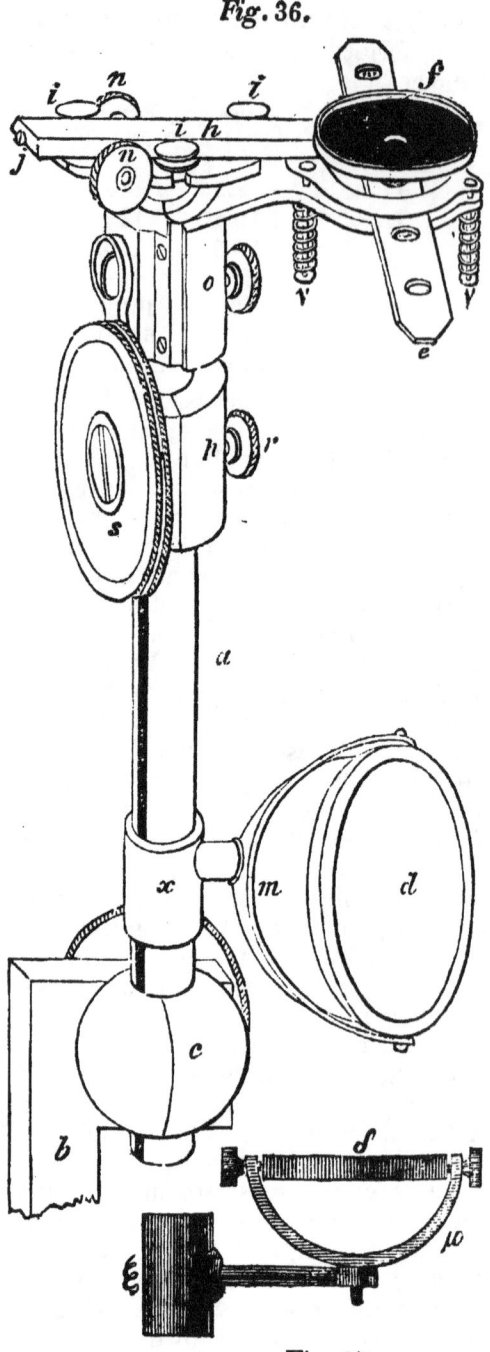

Fig. 36.

Fig. 37.

various subjects under examination. The back of this reflector is flat and polished, so that a monochromatic light reflected from the brass may be employed when necessary.

The lenses are mounted in cells as shown at f, and are screwed into the dovetail bar h, sliding between three stout pins i, i, i; the nearest one having a strong spring on the under side, which keeps the bar in close contact with the other two, without any shake. The bar is moved across the object by either of the milled nuts n, n, which, instead of having a pinion as usual, have a spring wound round their axis attached at each end to the bar *h*, with an adjusting screw to regulate the tension at the end *j*: the bar may also be turned round on the central pin, fitted in the top of the stem *a*, and thus a traversing motion in every direction may be given to the bar and lens, without disturbing the object, or altering in the least the distance between it and the lens.* The adjustment of the focus is first made by sliding the stage pieces *o*, *p* by the hand, until the object is seen nearly distinct; the thumb screw *r* being then turned, fixes the lower piece *p* to the stem *a*; then, by means of the large milled head *s*, the final adjustment is made by the intervention of a connecting bar *t*, attached to the stage piece; this bar works on an elastic eccentric movement under the milled head *s*, so that an adjustment of any small quantity can be obtained with extreme precision (similar in principle to the infinite lever.) The slider containing the object is kept close to the stage by two heliacal springs *v v*. A condensing lens and a pair of forceps are made to fit in the piece *o*, and can be employed either with or without the stage plate, which may be entirely removed by the thumb-screw in front, when necessary.

(55.) The quantity of light necessary to be employed in using a microscope, is dependent on the nature of the object under examination, and on the magnifying power of the lenses necessary for its developement.

The light, therefore, from the sun or a lamp may be condensed by a convex lens attached to the stage; or a condensing lens may be substituted in place of the reflector, and the light from the lamp allowed to fall on it direct. This light, in order that it may not produce the injurious prismatic colours, may be made of one uniform colour. In the monochromatic lamp introduced by Dr. Brewster, spirit of wine mixed with a little water is used. This produces a yellow flame, which he states is less injurious to the eye than that of the ordinary light. The glare of the common light may be removed by placing a plate of greyed glass under the object, by which means a cloudy light is obtained. This effect may likewise be produced by a circular disc of plaster of Paris used to reflect the light instead of the mirror; this contrivance, which was suggested by Dr. Goring, forms an excellent reflector for many interesting objects.

(56.) Having described the mechanical arrangements belonging to a microscope, it remains for us to treat of the magnifiers and the apertures necessary to be used. But before so doing, it may generally be remarked of all microscopes, that if the magnified representation of any object be not truly depicted on the retina of the eye, with its various parts and markings, of their true form and proportion, their outline distinctly defined, having a sufficient degree of brightness, and of their proper colour, the instrument cannot be depended upon to give a correct idea of the nature of the objects to be examined.

(57.) The common form of the magnifiers employed for microscopes are double-convex, and from what is stated in (20.) page 12, they should be made as thin as possible; for the *wandering* or *spreading out* of the rays proceeding from an object when refracted by a lens with spherical surfaces, whereby an indistinctness is produced in its image, will be decreased as the square of the thickness of the lens employed, while the loss of light in passing through the substance of the lens is increased in the same proportion as its thickness. But in page 12 the object was considered at an infinite distance, and the image was formed in its focus. Now in the microscope the *object* is placed in the focal point of the lens, and the rays are rendered parallel when refracted by it; hence, in order to diminish the aberrations* as much as possible when we employ lenses of unequal curvatures or plano-convex, the flattest side of the lens must be turned towards the *radiant* (object,) when the aberrations will be as there stated; or, according to the results of Mr. Herschel's recent investigation, they are as follows, calling the aberration of a lens of the best form and position, that is, with the convex side turned to parallel rays, and the radii of its surfaces as 1 to 6, *unity*.

Best form 1.000
Double convex or concave . 1.567

---

* The nuts *n n* might have a short ivory handle fixed to their axis, so that the same hand might turn it right and left, or backwards and forwards, at the same time.—See *Quarterly Journal*, vol. ii.

* The word *aberration* is derived from two Latin words, *ab*, *from*, and *erro*, to *stray* or *wander*; that is, the wandering or strayed rays of an object from the true image.

Plano-convex or concave, with the spherical surface exposed to parallel rays 1.081

Plano-convex or concave, the flat surface being exposed to parallel rays 4.2

In all these cases the lenses are supposed of equal thickness.

(58.) Now where the lens is of short focus, the proportional quantity of curvature required to be used with the necessary aperture will be greater than in lenses of long foci; besides which, as the quantity of light admitted by small lenses when thrown on the retina is attenuated in proportion to its magnifying power, it therefore becomes important to make it pass through glass of the smallest possible thickness, and of the utmost transparency. To show that this quantity is considerable, we shall give the thicknesses of two lenses of equal focus, each of which has an aperture sufficient for the vision of any class of objects.

Double Convex Lenses.	Thickness in hundredth of an inch.	Focus. Inch.
Ordinary manufacture	9	$\frac{1}{10}$
Executed in the best manner	4½	
Difference in thickness	4½	

From this statement it appears, that if we suppose the transparency of the glass in both lenses to be equal, the light lost in passing through the first will be double that of the last.*

(59.) When lenses of higher magnifying powers than those of the $\frac{1}{10}$th of an inch are required, small glass spherules are frequently mounted for microscopic purposes instead of them. These glass spherules or globules were first substituted for lenses, by Dr. Hooke, who describes the method of making them in his *Micrographia*, published in 1665.

(60.) The effects of employing globules practically, independent of the increase of aberration arising from their thickness, may now be considered. Let df be the focal distance of a double convex lens $c\,d\,e$ of crown glass, from its surface d to an object at f, (*fig.* 38,) which may be supposed equal 48,† or $\frac{1}{18}$th of an inch focus, and let its thickness be equal to the radius or 60. Now, when a globe of glass ‡ is

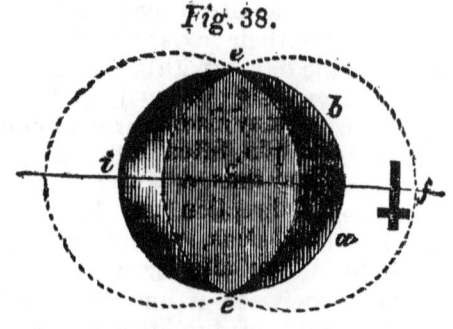

Fig. 38.

employed, the focal distance will be half the radius measured from the surface nearest the object, that is af, therefore, the radius of a globe of equal magnifying power to the lens must be $\frac{2}{3}$ of cf or
$$\frac{30 + 48 \times 2}{3} = 52.*$$
Hence the distance between the object and the surface of the globe i, c, b, a, e will be only 26 parts (or $\frac{1}{52}$th of an inch,) that is only half the distance a lens of equal power would be removed from the object nearly. Therefore, in adjusting the spherule to distinct vision, the liability of touching the object is doubled, and the danger of destroying it altogether by too near an approach is increased in the same proportion. While for viewing animalcula or moist objects, which require a thin plate of talc or glass over them to prevent the lens from being dewed by evaporation, and likewise to keep the surface flat, these disadvantages would in many cases render them useless. And the aberration is increased in the globule, both by its increase in thickness and the diminished radius of curvature, which also increases the distortion of its figure in the same proportion, (*viz.* inversely as the squares of their radii.)

(61.) The magnitude of the apertures used in small lenses is dependent on their aberration, and the nature of the object under examination; while the brightness of objects seen through a microscope (in regard to illumination) will be directly as the areas of their respective apertures. Hence, by whatever means the aperture can be increased without indistinctness, the instrument will always be improved.

For this purpose various contrivances have been suggested by many scientific individuals to improve the single microscope, by reducing the spherical and chromatic dispersions, and increasing the field of view. And here it may be

---

* The first lens here measured was taken from those made in the shops; the latter was executed expressly to examine the difference of the performance of lenses of different thicknesses, and experimentally proved the goodness of thin lenses,

† This number is here taken to avoid fractions.

‡ The focus of an hemisphere of plate glass with the convex side to parallel rays is $\frac{4}{3}$ of the radius.

* See *New Elements of Optics*, by B. Martin.—Theorems 429 and 552 for demonstrations.

remarked, that these improvements become of considerable importance in the investigation of minute natural objects, from the fact, that in the vision of objects through single microscopes we look at the *real* object; but in all compounds, however perfect their construction, we only see a magnified representation or *picture* of the object, which it is evident in point of accuracy cannot be relied upon with the same confidence as a magnified view of the object *itself*.

(62.) Dr. Brewster, in his *Treatise on New Philosophical Instruments*, speaking of single microscopes, says, "We cannot expect any essential improvement in that instrument, unless from the discovery of some transparent substance, which, like the *diamond*, combines a high refractive power with a low power of dispersion."* This substance has subsequently been formed into lenses by Mr. A. Pritchard, at the suggestion of Dr. Goring, who caused Mr. P. to commence the undertaking in July, 1824. The first diamond lens was completed at the end of that year. The difficulty of working this substance into a perfect figure was subsequently overcome. Mr. Pritchard finished the first diamond microscope in 1826; the focal distance of this magnifier, which is double convex, is about $\frac{1}{30}$th of an inch. Of the value and importance of the introduction of this brilliant substance for the formation of single microscopes, Dr. Goring states, "I conceive *diamond lenses* to constitute the ultimatum of perfection in the single microscope."†

The principal advantages of employing this brilliant substance in the formation of microscopes, arise from the naturally high refractive power it possesses, whereby we can obtain lenses of any degree of magnifying power, and that with comparatively shallow curves; the indistinctness occasioned by the figure of the lens is thus greatly diminished, and the dispersion of colour in the substance being as low as that of water, renders the lens nearly achromatic.

The curvatures of this substance and that of glass to produce the same amplification are shown in the following figures, where is also represented a lens of sapphire of the same power. This, next to the diamond, possesses all the qualities requisite for the formation of perfect magnifiers, and presents less difficulties in their construction; hence their expense is considerably lessened.* The lenses shown in the figure are plano-convex, having their flat sides exposed to the radiant (object,) which is the best position for divergent rays: their diameter is equal to their focal lengths, which is absolutely necessary for most transparent objects when the lens is less than $\frac{1}{20}$th of an inch focus. Fig. 39 is the diamond magnifier, which is the thinnest lens of the three; *fig.* 40, the sapphire; and *fig.* 41, the glass lens of the same power, but whose thickness being greater than the others has considerably more error by figure, (spherical aberration.)

Fig. 39.

Fig. 40.

Fig. 41.

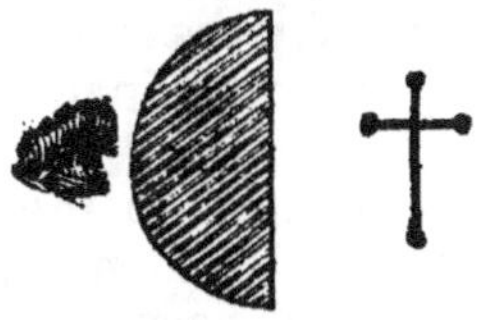

The aberration or indistinctness of lenses of the same aperture and substance are inversely as the squares of their radii. But when we compare a lens of diamond and glass of equal thickness their longitudinal aberrations are different.† And as the actual confusion is as the areas of the little circle into which every mathematical point on the surface of the object is spread over, it will be as their squares, or as .912 for the diamond, and 2.755 for the glass; and by multiplying these numbers by the squares of their radii inversely, it will be found that the indistinctness of a diamond lens of equivalent power is about *one twentieth* of that of a glass lens.

The magnifying powers of Mr. Pritchard's sapphire microscopes are shown in the following table, where their focal

---

* Page 402. 1813.
† *Quarterly Journal*, vol. xxii, p. 280.

* The same artist has also formed lenses of the other precious stones, but without any peculiar advantage, many of them producing two magnified images by double refraction, when their axis is not the axis of double refraction. The diamond has a very peculiar structure different from the other precious stones, some of which, when made into lenses, give a kind of treble image.
† See p. 18.

lengths, with their linear and superficial amplification, are given according to the decimal standard.

Table of Magnifying Powers of Sapphire Lenses.

Focal Lengths.		Magnifying Powers.	
Parts of an Inch.	Hundredths of an Inch.	Linear.	Superficial.
$\frac{1}{10}$	10	100	10000
$\frac{1}{15}$	..	150	22500
$\frac{1}{20}$	5	200	40000
$\frac{1}{25}$	4	250	62500
$\frac{1}{30}$	..	300	90000
$\frac{1}{40}$	2½	400	160000
$\frac{1}{50}$	2	500	250000
$\frac{1}{60}$	..	600	360000
$\frac{1}{70}$	..	700	490000
$\frac{1}{80}$	1¼	800	640000
$\frac{1}{100}$	1	1000	1000000

(63.) This table, which contains the foci of a complete set of sapphire microscopes, will also exhibit the amplification of a single microscope made of glass, or any other substance, by finding its focal length, and observing the number that stands against that measure. In glass, the curvatures being required so much greater than for the sapphire lenses, to produce the same magnifying power, very few have been made to exceed the $\frac{1}{60}$th of an inch focus when double convex, or the $\frac{1}{25}$th of an inch when plano-convex. In mounting the sapphire and diamond lenses, there are advantages which glass lenses do not possess. Their extreme hardness enables them to be burnished into brass settings, which is very difficult with those of glass. This facility of mounting renders them also more extensively useful in experimental research, from their capability of being applied in every possible way, with regard to the *object*, the *light*, or the *eye*.

CHAPTER XII.—*Periscopic Microscopes.*—*Dr. Wollaston's.*—*Dr. Brewster's.*—*Mr. Herschel's for Mineralogy.*—*Aplanatic.*

AMONGST the various contrivances that have been employed for the improvement of the single microscope, by diminishing its spherical aberration and increasing the field of vision, the following deserve particular attention:—

(64.) Dr. Wollaston, when treating of the single microscope, says, " The great desideratum in employing high magnifiers is a sufficiency of light, and it is accordingly expedient to make the aperture as large as is consistent with distinct vision. But if the object to be viewed is of such magnitude as to appear under an angle of several degrees on each side of the centre, the requisite distinctness cannot be given to the whole surface by a common lens (*of glass,*) in consequence of the confusion occasioned by the oblique incidence of the lateral rays, excepting by means of a very small aperture, and proportionable diminution of light."* To effect this purpose with glass lenses and render them *periscopic*, he unites two plano-convex lenses together by their plane surfaces, interposing a circular plate of brass between them, with a circular aperture in its centre, as shown in an enlarged section (*fig.* 42), where A and

Fig. 42.

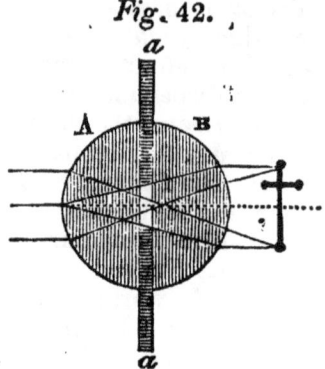

B are the two lenses fixed on each side of the perforated plate *a, a*. The diameter of the aperture in this plate which Dr. Wollaston found to answer best, was *one-fifth* of the focus of the combined lenses, and the visible field of view was about 20 degrees in diameter.

(65.) It has been remarked, that by doubling the number of surfaces in this combination a loss of light is occasioned. To remedy this inconvenience, and at the same time extend the limits of distinct vision, Dr. Brewster has ingeniously suggested the interposition between the lenses of a fluid of nearly the same refractive power as the glass. This fluid may either be oil of turpentine, castor oil, or Canada balsam; or the same effect might be produced more perfectly by grinding a groove in the circumference of a sphere or thick double convex lens, as shown in section *fig.* 43.

Fig. 43.

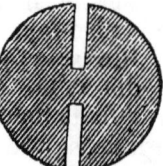

---

* *Philosophical Transactions*, 1812, vol. cii. p. 375.

(66.) Dr. Brewster has also suggested another improvement in this combination when we wish to diminish the aberration of colour; this is effected by means of two double convex lenses, having their internal surfaces of such radii as to form a concave lens in the aperture at the centre, which, when filled with a fluid of a different refractive and dispersive power from the glass, shall correct both kinds of aberrations. This combination is shown in *fig.* 44.

Fig. 44.

(67.) A plano-convex lens is well known to possess only one-fourth the superficial magnifying power of a double convex of like curvature. But Dr. Brewster has proposed a method of applying the former lens so as to produce the same magnifying power as the latter, by using it in the position shown in *fig.* 45, where A B C is a hemispheri-

Fig. 45.

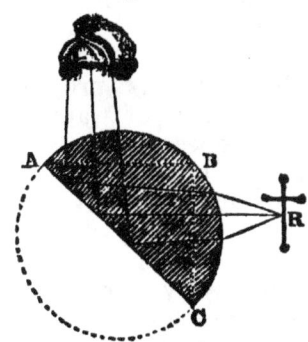

cal lens of half an inch radius, of which the inclination is as shown, with a microscopic object R before it, and the eye placed above. Now the rays issuing from the object R will, after refraction at the surface B C, fall upon the plane side A C, where they will be reflected up to the surface A B and suffer a second refraction. As the incidence of the rays upon A C is about 45° when the lens is hemispherical, and when the apertures are small, the rays will always be reflected at a greater angle than that at which total reflection takes place,* so that none of the rays will be lost by transmission

---

* The sine of the angle of total reflection being equal to $\dfrac{1}{\text{index of refraction}}$ it will be 41° in crown glass. *Edin. Phil. Jour.* vol. iii. p. 75.

at the surface A C. In this lens the source of error which arises from bad centering in a double convex lens is entirely obviated, as the surfaces through which the incident and emergent rays pass are ground simultaneously in one tool. To adapt the periscopic principle to this lens, we have only to remove the polish from an annular space of the plane side to exclude the lateral or obliquely incident rays.

(68.) The reflecting lens A B C Dr. Brewster also proposed to be employed as a *diagonal eye-piece;* for it may be considered as composed of a right-angled prism (shown by the dotted lines) A B and B C, and instead of an ordinary prism and two plano-convex lenses having five plane surfaces and two convex ones, the hemispherical lens has only one plane side and two convex, thus avoiding a great loss of light by reflection from such a number of surfaces.

(69.) Mr. Herschel's periscopic combination of lenses consists of a double convex lens of the best form (that is with the radii as 6 to 1,) but in its worst position. This lens is to be employed for that next the eye, as A, *fig.* 46, and a

Fig. 46.

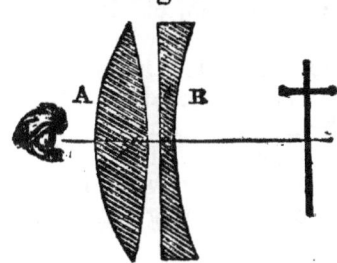

plano-concave lens B, with its concave side next the object; the proportion of the foci of the two lenses being as 5 to 13. By this construction a very extensive field of view is obtained with moderate distinctness. In *reading* glasses and magnifiers of low power, a distinct field of 40° on each side the centre may be obtained. In the investigations of *Entomology* and *Mineralogy,* or in the examinations of *Crystals,* this combination is of great value, from the extent of objects seen at one view; and although the spherical aberration is increased,* yet by the contrary prismatic refractions of the two glasses the edges are nearly freed from colour.

(70.) When the rigorous destruction of aberration for the central rays is re-

---

* 22,302 times greater than that of a single lens of equivalent power of the best form and position.—*Philosophical Transactions,* 1821, p. 248.

quired, Mr. Herschel has proposed the aplanatic combinations shown in *figs*. 47 and 48, where the aberration of rays

Figs. 47 *and* 48.

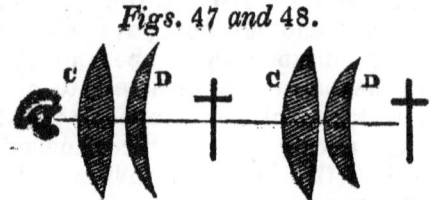

parallel to the axis is entirely destroyed. The lenses C in each of these cases are double convex, with the radii of their surfaces as 1 to 6, having the most convex side next the eye. The radii of the meniscus lenses D D are in the first case as 1 to 1.70, and in the other case as 1 to 3.957, with their concave sides exposed to the object; the focal lengths of the two lenses in *fig.* 47 are as 10 to 17.82, and in *fig.* 48, as 10 to 5.497. The compound focus of the lenses being 6.407, and in (*fig.* 48) 3.474.

(71.) The superior effect of these two latter combinations (which offer little impediment in their practical construction) has been sufficiently tried to warrant their application, where the rays are required to be as perfect as the case will admit. As object-glasses for compound microscopes when executed of short focus, they are, in many respects, equal to an achromatic; indeed quite so when the latter has only the same aperture as this combination. The details of their application will, however, be pointed out in treating on that instrument.

(72.) In the construction of burning glasses, this combination appears from an experiment made with one of 3-inch diameter, by Mr. Herschel, to be far superior to a single lens, as the temperature was raised much greater than by any, even of the best form, although it is certain some portion of heat must have been lost in passing through two lenses. Hence it is evident, that by far the greater portion of heat is lost by the aberration of the lens.

(73.) When we are desirous of decreasing the aberration in a lens, Mr. Herschel has shown that by employing two plano-convex lenses of equal focus with their convex sides in contact, the aberration will be only 0.603, while that of a lens of equivalent power is *unity*.

But in order to diminish the aberrations as much as possible, without employing a correcting lens, the foci of the two plano-convex lenses should be in the proportion of 1 to 2, 3, when the aberration will be 0.2481, or about one quarter of an equivalent lens of the best form. This combination, which is shown in *fig.* 49, has likewise the advantage of decreasing the distortion of the object, and diminishes the prismatic dispersion.

Fig. 49.

CHAPTER XIII.—*Fluid and single Reflecting Microscopes.*

(74.) FLUID microscopes have, in the absence of more permanent instruments, been resorted to with unexpected success. The first account of these microscopes is given in the *Philosophical Transactions*,* by Mr. Stephen Grey. They consist of a drop of water placed in a perforated plate of brass, the edges of the hole being made as thin as possible by forming a cavity on each side of the plate, so that the fluid forms a convex lens.

Dr. Brewster has proposed other fluids in the place of water, to render fluid microscopes more perfect. The disadvantages attendant on employing water is its low refractive power and speedy evaporation, by which their focal length, and, consequently, their power, are continually varying. In place, therefore, of this fluid he employs sulphuric acid† or castor oil, both of which possess a refractive power considerably greater than water. And as far as their optical properties are concerned, oil of ambergriese or alcohol might be used, but their volatility renders them less manageable.

(75.) Dr. Brewster describes the following as the best method of constructing fluid microscopes:— Take Canada balsam, balsam of capivi, or pure turpentine varnish, and drop either of them on a parallel piece of glass, when a plano-convex lens will be formed, (see *fig.* 50.) Their power may be varied by

---

* *Philosophical Transactions*, No. 221 and 223, or Dr. Smith's *Optics*, vol. ii. p. 394.

† It should be observed, that in using sulphuric acid great care must be had to prevent its contact with the eye, as it might destroy that organ.

the quantity of the fluid employed, or by allowing the plate of glass to be horizontal with the drop above or beneath it; thus if the plate be uppermost, the gravity of the fluid will make it more convex, as in *fig.* 51. If the drop be above the plate, the lens will be flattened, as in *fig.* 52.

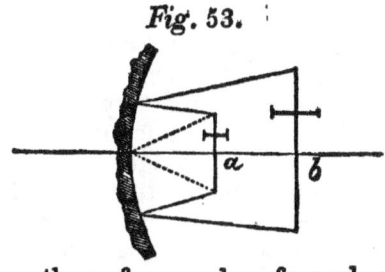

Fig. 53.

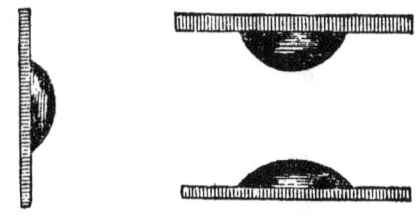

Fig. 50.   *Fig.* 51.

Fig. 52.

image thereof may be formed on a screen or wall, but the image will be inverted with respect to the object,* and when the object is not very luminous, the room should be darkened.

When the first of these substances is used it soon becomes indurated, and, if kept from dust, very durable. Dr. Brewster informs us, that he has made both object and eye-lenses of compound microscopes in this manner, which performed extremely well, and lasted a considerable time.

(76.) A single reflecting microscope may be formed by a concave speculum, having the object placed on its axis, and nearer to the surface of the reflector than the focus, as at *a*, *fig.* 53, when an enlarged view of the object will be formed in the same position as the object at *b*. This simple instrument is employed to enable a person to view his own eye, and show a magnified representation of the ramifications of the blood vessels, the pupil, and the iris.

When the object is placed between the focus and the centre, an enlarged

CHAPTER XIV.—*Theory of Compound Microscopes.— Mechanical arrangements of.—Eye-pieces.—Magnifying powers of.—Object-glasses.—Dr. Goring's.— Mr. Tulley's.— M. Chevalier's.—S. Amici's.—Mr. Herschel's. —Dr. Brewster's.—The Amician Reflecting Microscope, with its Improvements.*

(77.) A COMPOUND refracting microscope is an instrument consisting of two or more convex lenses, by one of which an enlarged image of the object is formed, and then, by means of the other employed as an eye-glass, a magnified representation of the enlarged image is obtained. The distance at which the two lenses of a compound microscope are placed from each other, must always exceed the sum of their focal lengths, in order that the image may be formed by the object-glass in the anterior focus of the eye-glass. *Fig.* 54 is a section of a compound instrument, *r* is the object intended to be magnified, which is placed in the focus

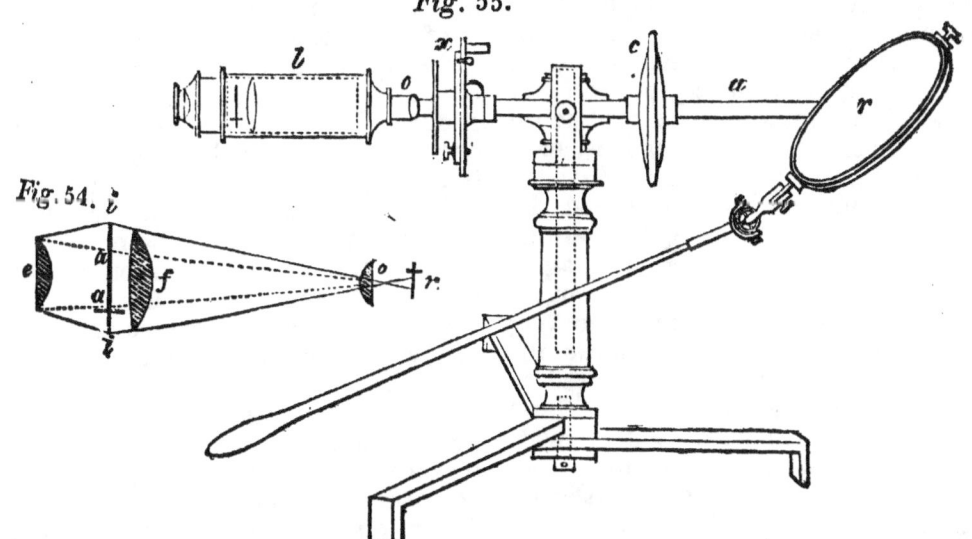

Fig. 55.

Fig. 54.

of the object-glass *o*; by this lens an enlarged and inverted image is formed at *a a*, in the focus of the eye-glass

---
* See p. 2.

e, by which the diverging rays from the image are rendered parallel, in the same manner as when a single lens was employed to magnify an object. Hence the great distinction, as before observed, between single and compound microscopes is, that in the latter we only view a magnified *image* of the object, while in the former we see the *object itself*. From this it must be evident, that unless the image formed by the object-glass is a perfect representation of the object in every particular, its imperfections, however small, will be increased by the eye-glass, in the same ratio as we magnify the image, or inversely as the focal length of the eye-glass.

With this disadvantage the compound instrument had been entirely laid aside, by the most distinguished naturalists and philosophers in their experimental researches, till very recently. For popular and general application it is preferred, on account of the extent of field obtained by it, which is far greater than that obtained by ordinary single glass lenses of equivalent power: and for these purposes there is usually introduced a field-glass *f*, by which the extent of the view is increased from *a a* to *i i*, by the rays being bent by this lens so that a greater portion may be refracted by the eye-glass *e*.

(78.) The compound microscope may be mounted nearly in the same manner as the single, or indeed the same stand may be employed for both. *Fig.* 55 is a compound microscope, having all its moveable parts sliding on a triangular bar *a*, which, from its mechanical properties, is better adapted for a microscope than any other form, provided the sliding pieces are sprung on one side only; *b* is the compound body, *o* the object end, *x* the slider attached to the stage, *c* the condensing lens, and *r* the reflector with a *hook's jointed* handle.

(79.) With the instrument just described, in order to bring the various parts of the object under the magnifier, the body of the instrument is moved by a rack and pinion working a triangular bar at right angles to the bar *a*, though it is often preferred to move the stage, as being of the least weight; for which purpose it is made to consist of *three* plates: the upper one carries the holder for the sliders, and is moved across the middle plate by means of a screw; while the middle plate is moved in a similar manner across the lower stage plate, but at right angles to the upper plate. In this way any position can be given to the object, by turning first the one and then the other screw. Different mechanical means have likewise been resorted to for effecting the same purpose. But when live objects, as *animalculæ*, are to be examined, it is preferable to make the stage a fixture, and to move the magnifier over the objects, as the most trifling motion will often disturb them for a considerable time.

(80.) Microscopic eye-pieces may be constructed in the same manner as those used for telescopes, (§ 22, 43—45) so as to correct the spherical and chromatic aberrations. But as the rays proceed from an object lens whose aperture is less than the field-glass, the distances of the two lenses will differ in a small degree from those employed for telescopes; this will also be the case if the distance between the object-glass and eye-piece of a microscope be varied.

(81.) If the field-glass *f* (*fig.* 54) were exactly in the focus of the eye-glass *e*, it would have no effect on the magnifying power of the microscope; in this case the amplification of an object might be determined, by dividing the distance from the object-glass at which the image is formed by the distance of the object from that glass, which gives the diameter of the image; by multiplying this number by the power of the eye-glass, we obtain the magnifying power of the instrument. Example: let the sidereal focus of the object-glass be one inch, and the distance *o i* be 6 inches; then $6 \div 1 = 6$, and 6×5 (the power of the eye-lens *e* of two inches focus) will give 30 times as the increase in the diameter of the object, or 900 its increase in surface. But here we have divided by one inch the sidereal focus of the object-lens; this, however, would not be its focus when it has to form an image at 6 inches distance on the other side, but to obtain distinct vision the object will require to be $1\frac{1}{5}$ from the lens, (see 40.) this would reduce the actual magnifying power to 25, or 625 in surface.

(82.) Having thus shown how the power of a compound microscope may be obtained with only *two* glasses, it is necessary to point out the means of determining the amplification when a *field* lens is introduced. If we proceed for this purpose by calculation, the process will be rather complex, and unless the *data* are very accurate the result will be incorrect; these data, which are the foci of the several lenses and their distances from each other, offer many practical difficulties. We shall therefore describe a practical and simple method by which it may be found with equal accuracy; either when the instrument is a compound *refractor*, or *reflector*, of any construction. This novel mode of Dr. Goring, for determining the amplification of a microscope, is as follows:*—*As the aperture of the object-glass or metal is to its acting focus, measured from the radiant point, (i.e.* distance of the object from the lens when seen distinctly,) *so is the size of its visual pencil (i. e.* the small circle of light described in § 18) *to the focus of a single lens equivalent in power to the compound instrument.*

By this method the sidereal focus is not required to be known for any of the lenses, however numerous; the acting focus of only one, *viz.* the object-glass or metal must be ascertained; and then by measuring its true acting diameter or aperture, together with the diameter of the small pencil of light seen through the eye-glass when the observer is at a little distance from it, the whole is accomplished.†

(83.) The eye-pieces of some compound microscopes consist of four or five glasses, the makers having considered the perfection of the instrument to consist in obtaining a *flat* and enlarged field of view with a high power and shallow object-glass; but the brilliancy and sharpness of the image is, however, destroyed by this arrangement, and the introduction of considerable fog and flare is occasioned by the reflection of so many surfaces: for it may be remarked, that each surface will produce a reflected image of the object in the axis of the instrument, and thus occasion a dark and undefined spot in the middle of the object, while the edges are bright and fringed with colour; from these defects the instrument is rendered unfit for the vision of all but the most common objects, and these cannot be seen of their natural figure. One of these eye-pieces is shown at *fig.* 56,

Fig. 56.

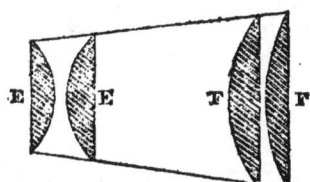

where E E are the eye and F F the field glasses.

(84.) The brightness and *penetration* of compound microscopes will be in proportion to their apertures under a given focus, from which circumstance the improvement of the instrument will always be as *the angle of aperture* of the object-glass free from aberration.

When a single plano-convex lens of about *half an inch* focus is used as an object-glass, the aperture must be about the 1/15th of an inch, with the flat side outermost; but if we employ *two* lenses to produce the required refraction, the aperture should be between them, which may be made larger than can be employed with a single lens of equivalent power. The most advantageous combination of convex lenses for low-powered object-glasses, is that contrived by Dr. Goring,* and shown in *fig.* 57. The outer lens

Fig. 57.

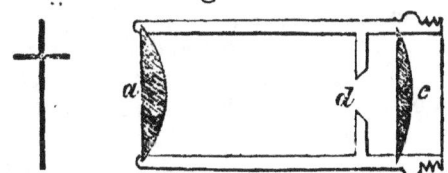

a is plano-convex, with its flat side next the radiant, whose focal distance is ½ or ⅔ of the crossed or plane lens *c*; the stop *d* is placed in the focus of the lens *a*; when the focus of the lens *a* is not less than ¼ an inch, the combination has been employed with considerable advantage both as regards distinctness and aperture.

(85.) The most improved object-glasses for compound microscopes are those

---

* *Quarterly Journal,* vol. xxi.
† To determine the magnifying power of a compound microscope by calculation, let D = distance of the radiant from the object-glass; d = distance of the image from the same; Δ = the distance of distinct vision; and f = the focal length of the eye-glass: then, if only two lenses are employed, the amplifying power $= A = \dfrac{d}{D} \times \dfrac{\Delta}{f}$. If a field-glass is introduced, as in most compounds, this formulæ must be multiplied by the fraction $\dfrac{L}{\varphi}$; φ being the focal length of the field lens, and $L = \dfrac{\delta^2}{\delta - \varphi} - \overline{d' - f}$; δ being equal the distance of the first and second glasses, and d' the distance of the first and third glasses. If the construction of the eye-piece is *negative*, the power is diminished by the introduction of the field-glass, but when positive (§ 22) the power is augmented.

* *Quarterly Journal,* vol. xvii. p. 202.

that are rendered achromatic, as a much larger angle of aperture can be obtained. These were first constructed at the suggestion and expense of Dr. Goring, by Mr. W. Tully, in the summer of 1824,* and more recently in France, by M. Chevalier.† The aplanatic of Mr. Tully consists of a concave of Guinard's flint glass placed between *two* convex lenses of *crown* and *Dutch* plate glass. The apertures obtained in these object-glasses are equal to half their focal distances, which are from 0.2 to 1.0 inch focus. By the increase of aperture which is here attainable, the penetrating power is augmented, so that the varied markings on objects are rendered visible with these large apertures, which with common object-glasses of the same power are wholly undiscernible. This property of the penetration of a microscope being always as the angle of aperture, was first pointed out by Dr. Goring, and is fully borne out by experiment. In the telescope the penetrating power necessary to observe *stars* and *nebula* is dependent on the area of the object-glass or metal, without relation to its focal distance; but in the microscope it is the result of *the aperture in proportion to their focal distance*. The difficulties that present themselves in correcting the aberrations of these object-glasses when of short focus is considerably increased, though their penetrating powers are always improved by a diminution of their focal length. The spherical aberration is greater and more difficult to correct than in telescopes, (the convex seldom having sufficient aberration to correct the concave,) and as the rays enter diverging from the object, the calculations of their radii are more abstruse than in a telescope for parallel rays. The curvatures and dimensions of one of Mr. Tully's object-glasses are as follows, and *fig.* 58 is a section twice its real size.

		Inch.
Sidereal focus of the object-glass		0.933
Total diameter of the lenses		0.55
Clear aperture		0.5

		Inch.	
Radius of 1st surface		0.825	convex.
Ditto	2nd	0.525	crown
Ditto	3rd	0.5	concave
Ditto	4th	0.5	flint
Ditto	5th	0.575	convex
Ditto	6th	0.575	Dutch plate

	Inch.
Specific gravity of crown	2.527
Thickness of ditto	0.15
Specific gravity of flint	3.627
Thickness of ditto	0.164
Specific gravity of Dutch	2.519
Thickness of ditto	0.175

(86.) The object-glasses of M. V. Chevalier are constructed on the principles laid down by Euler,* and consist of a double and equally convex lens of plate glass cemented to a plano-convex of Guinard's flint. The construction is remarkably simple, the radii of all their surfaces being alike. The measures of one of these achromatics obtained by Mr. Lister are as follows:—This object-glass is shown in section at *fig.* 59, of twice its real size.

Fig. 58.   *Fig.* 59.

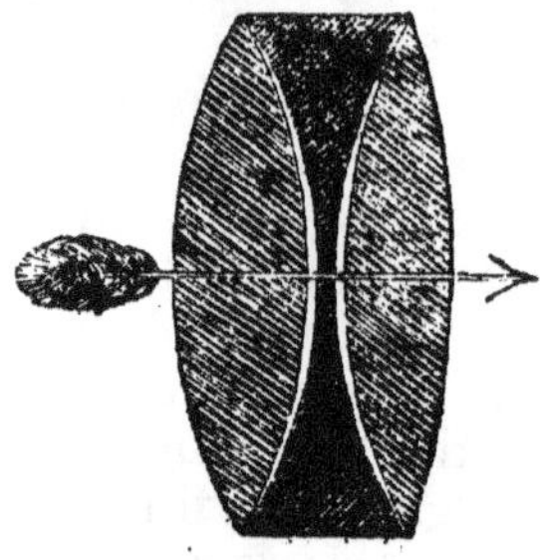

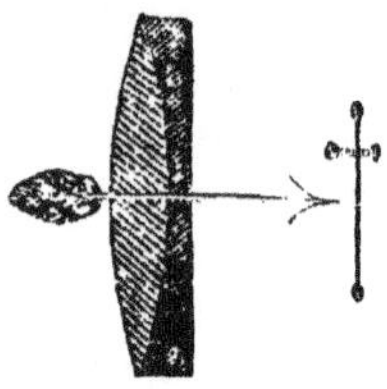

	Inch.
Radii of the isosceles convex	0.66
Radius of the plano-concave flint	0.66
Thickness of the concave at the edge	0.074
Thickness of the convex at the centre	0.072
Diameter of the lenses	0.36

When these object-glasses came first into this country, although achromatic, and two of them were combined, which is a considerable improvement on the single ones, they could not show the test objects, the aperture being cut off by a small stop; but on removing this stop Dr. Goring was enabled to make them *effective* on most of them.

(87.) The combination of three *sets* of achromatic lenses for an object-glass has recently been executed by Professor Amici, who, in order to have the body of the microscope horizontal and object-glasses vertical, introduces a right angular prism to change the direction of the rays, as at P, *fig.* 22. But the introduction of so many surfaces, *viz.* fifteen, has a tendency to weaken the outline of the objects. Mr. Dollond has, however, lately combined two triple object-glasses

---

* *Quarterly Journal*, vol. xxii. p. 265.
† Ibid. vol. ii. N. S.

* This theory was published at St. Petersburg, in 1774, and lately in the *Bulletin de la Société d'Encouragement de Paris*, No. ccliv. for August 1825.

of one inch focus, and about half an inch aperture, which perform extremely well: they can also be used separately. It is necessary for us to remark here, that as the ray after passing through the first aplanatic combination is in a different state to what it is on entering the second, due correction ought to be made when these glasses are intended to be used separately and combined; indeed, in those of short focus such correction is absolutely requisite, so that if they are perfect when combined, only one can be so if employed singly. When a triple one and a double one are combined the performance seems best of all.

(88.) If we are desirous of producing an aplanatic object-glass without using the achromatic combinations above described, that of Mr. Herschel, in *fig.* 48, will be found of great value, as it is free from all spherical aberration in the axis. One has been executed (which is in our possession) of only one-sixth of an inch focus, with an aperture of the $\frac{1}{18}$th of an inch, which brings out all the *test objects* and exhibits opaque ones with facility. This combination is made of crown glass. When it is not thought advisable to employ a correcting lens, (*i. e.* one with a concave surface,) it must be evident, from what has been stated respecting single microscopes, that the diamond or sapphire will be the most aplanatic as an object lens.

(89.) A compound microscope for viewing objects of natural history has been proposed by Dr. Brewster. In the ordinary instrument, from the objects being employed in a dry or shrivelled state, their " natural polish and brilliancy is impaired; the minute parts, such as the hairs and down, adhere to one another, and the general form, as well as the disposition of its individual parts, can no longer be distinctly seen." To remedy these defects, " several small glass vessels must be provided, having different depths from 1 to 3 inches, and having their bottoms composed of a piece of flat glass, for the purpose of admitting freely the reflected light which is intended to illuminate the object." The objects to be viewed must be preserved in a fluid which will cause them to retain their plumpness and impart that freshness of colour which they possessed when alive; these with the fluid are to be put into the vessel, " and being placed upon a glass stage, or, if necessary, fixed to it, the arm of the microscope and the lens is then brought into contact with the fluid in the vessel. The rays which diverge from the object emerge directly from the fluid into the object-glass, and therefore suffer a less refraction than if it had been made from air; but the focal length of the lens is very little increased;" as the radius of the immersed surface should be about 9 times its focal distance, and the side next the eye (or field lens) about three-fifths of the same distance.

(90.) This method of fitting up and using a compound microscope, says Dr. Brewster, enables us in a simple manner to render the object-glass achromatic, without the assistance of any additional lens. This may be effected by employing a fluid whose dispersive power exceeds that of the object-glass, and by accommodating the radius of the anterior surface of that lens to the difference of their dispersive powers, the image will then be formed free from any of the primary colours of the spectrum. The fluids most proper for this purpose are

Oil of cassia.
——— anise seeds.
——— cummin.
——— cloves.
——— sassafras.
——— sweet fennel seeds
——— spearmint.
——— pimento.

In order to render the object-glass achromatic, when it is made of crown glass, and the fluid in which the objects are immersed is oil of cassia, the radius of the surface next the object should be to that of the surface next the eye, as 2.5 to 1, or the radii may be made as 2.2 to 1, and the dispersion of the fluid let down (by any of the other oils which are here placed in the order of their dispersion) till the chromatic aberration is corrected.

(91.) Compound microscopes have been constructed of almost every possible dimensions, from a few inches in length to that of 20 feet; but from practical experience it appears evident, that when their magnitude is augmented beyond a certain point the performance of the instrument is deteriorated, though we suppose the amplifying power of both microscopes the same; indeed, those of the larger description, which have been made to examine objects of considerable dimensions, cannot be considered of any use except for amusement. The reason, however, why the smaller instrument produces a better representation of the object, has not been determined; for in both instruments (mathematically) the proportional errors are the same, but it may be that the errors in the smaller instrument, though existing, are not so divided as to be discoverable to the organ of vision. At present no certain proportion between the length of the body of the instrument and the focus of the object-glass has been determined, except that the body requires to be lengthened when the focal length of the object-glass is increased, to give its maximum effect. The average length of body for different object-glasses is from five to ten inches; for when the rays after once being acted upon are allowed to travel any considerable distance to form the image in the focus of the eye-piece, they will be so much separated and weakened that the eye-piece will not be able to collect them truly. And it may be further remarked, that the power should always be obtained by the object-glass in preference to the eye-piece; and although it is well known, that a flat and more extended field is obtained by the latter, yet when these are procured, no distinct idea of the structure of the object is discoverable, and thus the very intention of the microscope is destroyed, which ought to unfold to our perception the nature and functions of bodies too minute for ordinary inspection.

(92.) The Amician reflecting microscope was invented at Modena, by Professor Amici; it consists of a concave ellipsoidal reflector whose focal distance is $2\frac{6}{10}$ inches with an aperture of one inch. In the axis of this reflector, and at about half its focal distance, is placed a small flat reflector whose surface forms an angle of 45° with the axis of the instrument, (similar to the Newtonian telescope;) the object is placed opposite to the plane metal, and is adjusted to the focus of the concave reflector.* The rays, after reflection from the concave metal, form an image of the object in the other focus of the ellipse, which is viewed by an eye-piece attached to the tube at about 8 inches from the metal. The performance of this instrument was held in high estimation on the continent, being considered superior to any compound refracting microscopes then made; this induced the introduction of the Amician construction into England. But when carefully made of the proportion here stated it only equalled the compound refracting instruments, and like them it was unable to show the delicate markings on various test objects, particularly the lines on the dust from the wings of a certain class of moths and butterflies. This instrument, however, has since been improved in this country, so as to show in a distinct and satisfactory manner, free from chromatic and spherical aberration, almost every class of test objects. These improvements were made by Mr. Cuthbert, under the direction of Dr. Goring.* The most important improvement is the formation of the concave metal of very short focal distance, whereby less assistance is required from the eye-glass to obtain the required power, while its aperture is increased to more than half the focal distance; thus an increase of penetrating power is obtained. In the original Amician construction, the small flat metal occupied so large a portion of the central pencils of rays, as to produce a kind of nebulosity around the object, the image being formed on the retina of the eye by a narrow ring of reflected light, as represented at *fig.* 60. In Goring's improved construction the small metal is lessened, and, consequently, it does not occasion so much impediment to the central rays as shown at *fig.* 61.

Fig. 60.   *Fig.* 61.

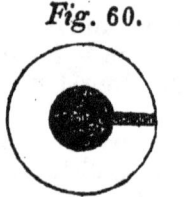 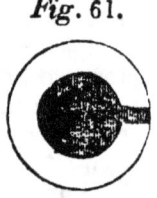

In the section of this *Engiscope*,† (*fig.* 62,) *a* is the object opposite the flat metal *c*, and in the focus of the concave ellipsoidal metal *d;* the image *i* is formed in the other focus of the ellipse between the lenses *e* and *f* of a negative Huygenian eye-piece; the adjustment of the object is effected by means of a rack and pinion *g*, attached to the tube at right angles to its axis. When the power is required to be changed, the metals are unscrewed from the body and others put on in their stead. Their usual apertures and foci are as follows:—

---

* The above measurements are those of the original instrument; the Professor having subsequently found, that, by shortening the focal length of the concave metal, the performance of the microscope is improved, less assistance being required from the eye-piece.

* See *Quarterly Journal*, vol. xxi. p. 34.
† This term has been applied by Dr. Goring to designate a microscope in its perfect form.

OPTICAL INSTRUMENTS.

Focus. Inch.	Apertures. Inch.
1.5	0.6
1.0	0.3
0.6	0.3
0.3	0.2

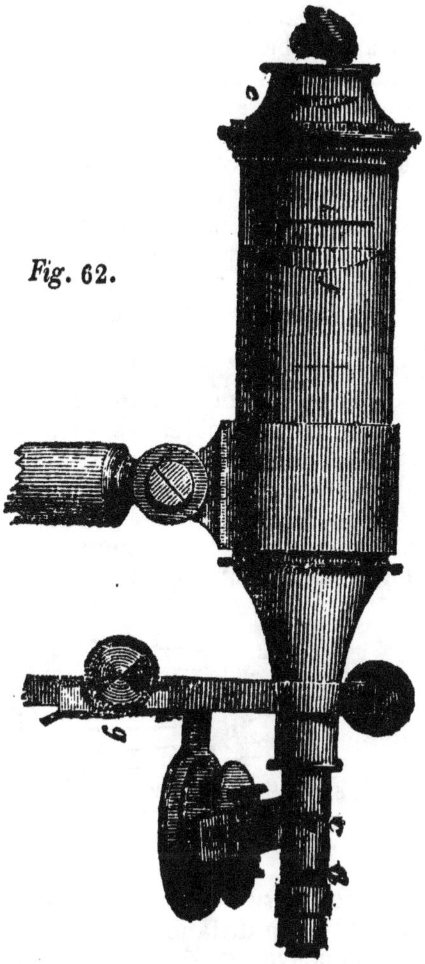

Fig. 62.

whether it will be efficient for the purposes intended. This can only be known by its capability of exhibiting those objects submitted to it: till very recently it was not ascertained that certain objects, in order to render their various markings or texture distinctly apparent, required the instrument to be of the best construction, whether single or compound, and possessing a considerable quantity of distinct light. These objects have therefore been denominated *tests*, by their discoverer, Dr. Goring. In order that our readers may be able justly to appreciate the efficiency of any microscope that may come within their observation, and determine its *penetrating* and *defining* powers, whether the instrument be single or compound, we shall describe the principal test objects necessary for that purpose. The objects best adapted to determine the penetrating power, are the dust or scales from the wings of certain classes of Papilio, (butterflies and moths.) Of these the *Menelaüs*, shown in *fig.* 63 and 64 (magnified) is a very useful object. The dust from the under side of the wing of the male papilio brassica (white cabbage butterfly,) shown in *fig.* 65, is a good proof-object, and a very peculiar one of the same kind is shown in *fig.* 66, (both magnified.) In viewing these objects a large angle of aperture is required (at least equal to half the focus,) in order that the lines and markings may be distinctly seen. There are, however, many of the scales from some kinds of papilio, on any of which the lines can be seen by an ordinary instrument. But the objects here selected, as well as the lines on the scales from the *small, brown, house moth*; the lines on the scales taken from the foreign curculio (diamond beetle) (*fig.* 67,) require a more perfect instrument to develope them. Lastly,

CHAPTER XV.—*Test Objects.*—*Opaque Microscope.* — *Solar Microscope.* — *Improved.*—*Lucernal.*—*Magic Lantern.*—*Phantasmagoria.*

(93.) *Test objects.*—It is perhaps one of the greatest requisites in the selection of a microscope, to be able to ascertain

Fig. 63. Fig. 65. Fig. 67. Fig. 66. Fig. 64.

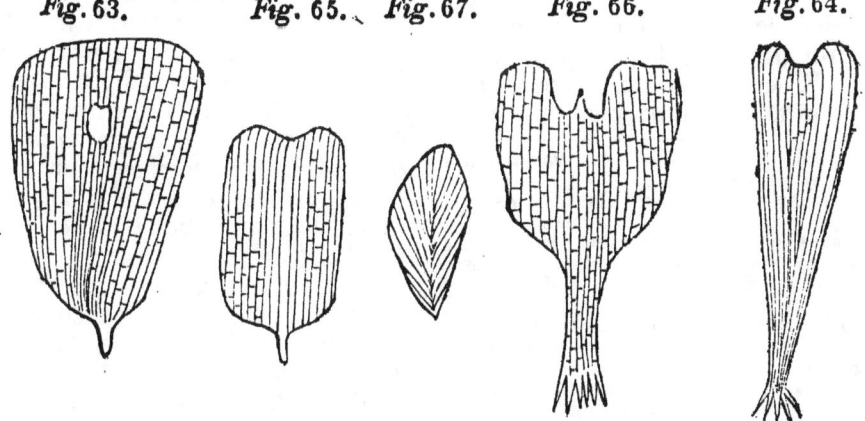

the most difficult of all the *test* objects are the lines on the scales from the *Podura springtail*, recently discovered by T. Carpenter, Esq., and on which the markings are only just discernible by the most perfect instruments. When the penetrating power is thus ascertained, its defining power may be determined by inspecting a leaf of the moss of a species of the genus *hypnum*,* which requires a considerable penetrating as well as *defining* power, fully to develope the lozenges which constitute its fabric, making out a luminous nucleus to each, which should be sharply defined and of the same shape with the outer lozenge.† As opaque test objects, the bat's hair shown in *fig.* 68 and 69, and the mouse hair (*fig.* 70 and 71,) may be considered excellent tests, when the outline and markings are well defined. These objects may be also examined with transmitted light with the same advantages.

Fig. 68. *Fig.* 69. *Fig.* 70. *Fig.* 71.

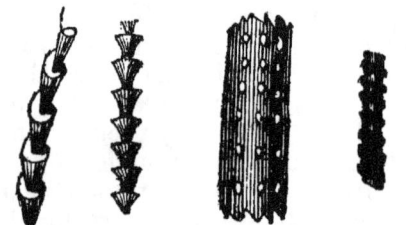

(94.) The white letters on a black ground seen on a piece of enamelled watch plate, is perhaps one of the best tests to determine the quantity of chromatic or spherical aberration in a lens: indeed to detect the latter error an artificial star ‡ may be used with advantage, which requires considerable *defining* power to show well.

(95.) In examining these test objects the direction and quantity of light must be carefully attended to, nor must it be injured or mutilated by the reflector, condensing lens, or other diaphanous body through which it may pass to the object. When an instrument can show these proof objects, it may with certainty be pronounced *effective*. It should be remarked, that when the objects are used as *opaque*, a smaller aperture will do best, *viz.* about ⅔ of its focus, (for any power less than 300 *decimal standard*,) but the magnifier requires to be more free from aberrations. For transparent objects a larger aperture is absolutely necessary; and for some *tests* it should be equal to its focal distance, to show the cross *striæ* between the lines on many of the scales, when the power of the instrument or lens is considerable. It is worthy of remark, that the same aperture that with advantage will develope one class of objects will not show another with the same success.

(96.) *Opaque Cups.*—When the focal distance of a magnifier, either employed singly or as the objective to a compound instrument, is too short to admit of an opaque object being illuminated by a light thrown between it and the lens, the magnifier is mounted in the manner shown in *fig.* 72, where the

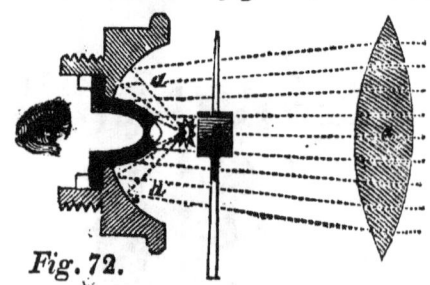

Fig. 72.

lens is set between two thin pieces of metal, at such a distance from the centre of the concave polished reflecting cup *a, a,* that the object *o* shall be in its focus and in the focus of the lens at the same time. When thus arranged the light is thrown on to the reflector (at the back of the object,) whence it is reflected to its focal point to illuminate the object placed therein. If the rays of light are not sufficiently condensed by this concave mirror, it may be assisted by a condensing lens *c,* by which the proper quantity of light required by the magnifier or object is obtained. When opaque objects are to be viewed in the Amician engiscope described in (92.) the silver reflector is made to be attached to the tube opposite the plane metal *c,* (*fig.* 62.)

(97.) *The solar microscope* consists of a common microscope connected to a reflector and condenser, the former being used to throw the sun's light on the latter, by which it is condensed to illuminate the object placed in

---

* The generic name of this moss was recently discovered by Mr. Carpenter.

† J. Pond, Esq., the Astronomer Royal, on recently examining this object with a deep sapphire-lens, discovered that they are not lozenges but hexagons, the two sides being very short in comparison to the others; he has also observed with a sapphire of the power of 250 all the lines on the *podura*.

‡ An *artificial star* may be made by taking a small globule of pure mercury kept in gum water, and securing it to a black ground, as burnt cork or black paper; or a globule of platina fused by electricity, and attached to a black ground may be employed.

OPTICAL INSTRUMENTS.

its focus; one of these instruments is shown in section *fig*. 73, with a double object-glass *e, c*. The rays from the sun *o, o, o* are received on

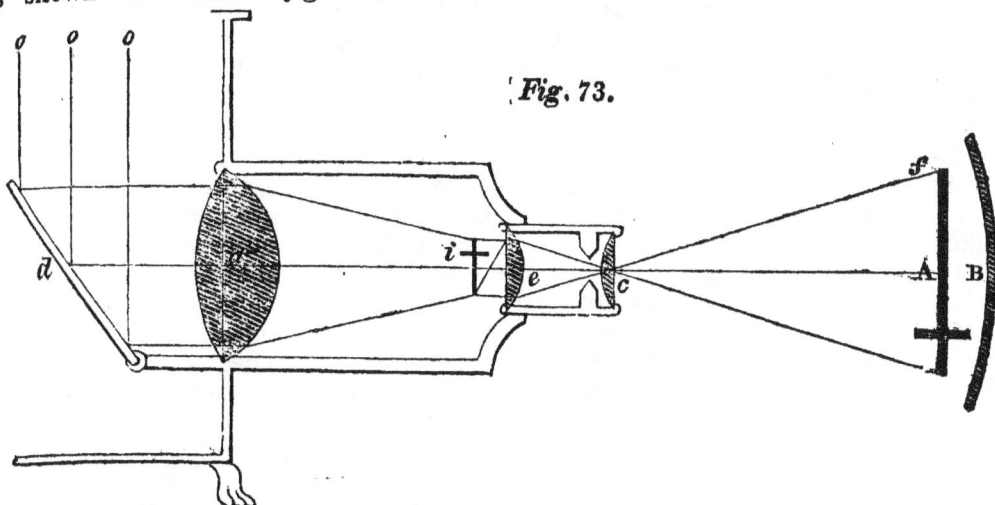

Fig. 73.

the looking-glass or reflector *d*, which is capable of being directed in any position, to throw the rays of the sun on the condensing-lens *a*; the object *i* is thus strongly illuminated by the condensed light of the sun. This object is placed in the focus of the microscopic lens *c*, which in the common instrument is the only one employed; but when the combination of two lenses is used the magnified image is improved; this representation, or picture of the object, is received on a wall or screen, and the magnifying power of the instrument will be always as the distances *i c* to *c* A; thus, if the acting focus of the lens *c* is 1 inch when it forms an image on the other side at 5 feet, the linear amplification will be 60 times, or the increase of surface 3600 times. When we decrease the distance of *c* A to about 10 inches, the *decimal* standard, although the magnitude of the image will not be so great yet its distinctness will be improved; and it will be likewise found, that when the image is thrown on a flat surface, the edges and middle are not distinct at the same time, for the rays *c f* are farther from the object-lens than *c* A: to remedy this, the white screen should be concave whose radius is C B, or distance of the lens from the screen; by this all the parts are made equally perfect.

(98.) An improved modification of this instrument is shown in *fig*. 74; *r* is the reflector, *c* the condenser, *o* the object, *b* the microscope, which is here the compound instrument with its eye-end fitting into the *darkened* box *d*, having a concave at the bottom to receive the representation of the object.

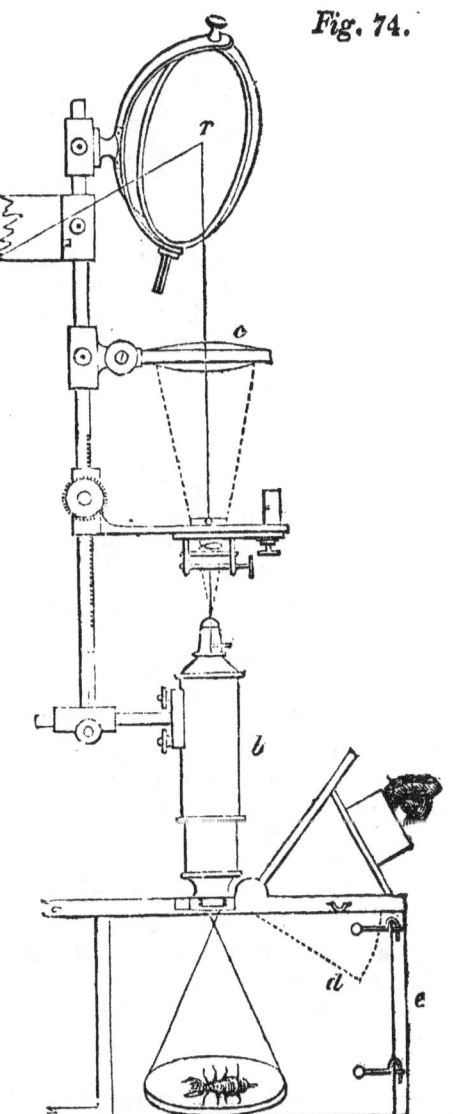

Fig. 74.

When it is to be used for drawing, the front *e* is let down to admit the hand; this modification of Dr. Goring's, having achromatic object-glasses adapted to it, renders the instrument *truly useful*, from the perfection of the magnified picture. These object-glasses may be used with or without the compound body, at option; but the most perfect object-glass for these purposes is formed by the continuation of a *triple* and *double* achromatic, by which a very large and distinct field is procured, free from colour and aberration.

(99.) The enclosing of objects in fluids, to exhibit them in a more natural form under the compound microscope (described in 89,) may be likewise applied with equal advantage to the solar instrument. This Dr. Brewster proposes to effect in the manner shown in *fig.* 75, where A B is the illuminating lens

Fig. 75.

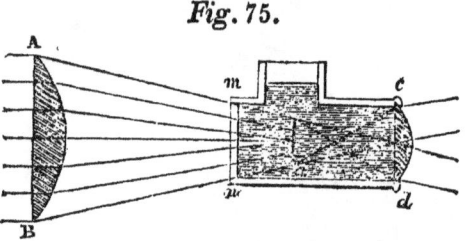

employed to throw the condensed light of the sun on the object *a*, enclosed in a tubular vessel of the fluid, having an opening in the upper side for the introduction of the object by a pair of forceps; *c d* is the object lens which forms one end of the tube, and *m n* a parallel plate of glass cemented to the other end. "The opacity which arises from a contraction of the parts is thus completely removed, and an additional transparency communicated to them from the fluid." This microscope may be rendered achromatic by using the same fluids and radii as proposed in § (90.)

(100.) *The lucernal microscope*, which was contrived by Mr. Adams, is constructed on the same principle as the solar instrument, having however a lamp to illuminate the objects instead of the sun; this lamp is enclosed in a lantern (*fig.* 76) to screen the light from the observers, in the same manner as in a magic lantern: the advantages of employing this instrument over the solar is, that we can command the light at any time, and in any situation, while in every other respect it is similar to that instrument.

(101.) *The magic lantern* is constructed similarly to the two former instruments, but having the object and field glasses of larger diameters and longer foci, to admit more extensive objects; these objects are usually painted representations of familiar or grotesque subjects on glass sliders, having the parts not occupied with the design blackened to obstruct the passage of light. These sliders are introduced by an opening cut in each side of the tube, in the same manner as in *fig.* 73; the diameter of the lenses *c* and *e* are nearly equal to that of the condenser or bull's eye *a*, and are made to slide within the outer tube to adjust the image on the wall at different distances. A part of the lantern is shown by the broken lines attached to the end of the tube at *a*. The reflector *d* is removed, and a lamp put in its stead to illuminate the lens *a*.

(102.) *Phantasmagoria.*—An exhibition some years ago was brought before the public under this appellation. It consists of a magic lantern constructed on a large scale, and having the object-sliders painted in the same manner; but instead of being exhibited on an opaque surface, the figures are thrown on a transparent substance. The manner in which this spectacle was exhibited at the Lyceum, has been described by Mr. Nicholson; but the kind of machinery then employed is not exactly known, though Dr. Young has given various ingenious methods of producing it.

CHAPTER XVI. — *Camera Obscura; Portable Box; Revolving; Periscopic.*— *Camera Lucida; Periscopic; Amici's improved.*— *Teinoscope; Dr. Brewster's; Amici's.*—*Multiplying Glass.*—*Kaleidoscope; Telescopic.*

(103.) *Camera Obscura,** or *darkened chamber*, is an optical apparatus for the representation of all surrounding objects under the same angle which they subtend to the unassisted eye, and which are exhibited in their proper colour and shape, so as to enable a person to delineate or trace both near and remote objects, without an acquaintance with the rules of perspective, when they are thrown on the paper.

In the construction of this instrument a convex lens and plane mirror are its principal parts; these are arranged differently, according as it is required to be *portable* or *stationary*. The first of these, called the *portable box camera obscura*, is shown in *fig.* 76, where the square box A has a

---

* Invented by Friar Bacon about the 13th century, but attributed by some to Baptista Porta, who published a work with an account of it, in 1560, at Antwerp.

OPTICAL INSTRUMENTS.

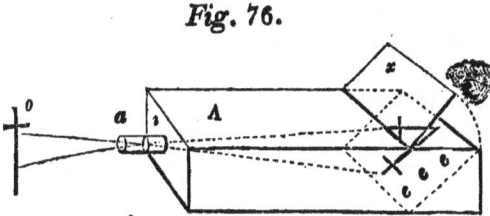

Fig. 76.

circular aperture in the front at *a*. Into this a short tube is inserted, having a convex lens at its outer end: this tube is made to slide out for adjustment; thus for near objects it requires to be drawn out more than for distant ones. Now the rays proceeding from the object *o* pass through the convex glass *a*, and form an inverted image *i* in the posterior focus of the lens; this image is received on a reflector or looking-glass *e, e, e*, inclined at an angle of 45°, by which it is reflected upwards on to a plate of ground glass at the top of the box; the lid *x* has two side wings to exclude the light when in use. The size of the image *i* to the object *o* will be as the distance *i a* to *o a*; and as the latter distance is usually the greatest, the image is less than the object.

(104.) *The revolving camera obscura* is shown at *fig.* 77, where *e* is the

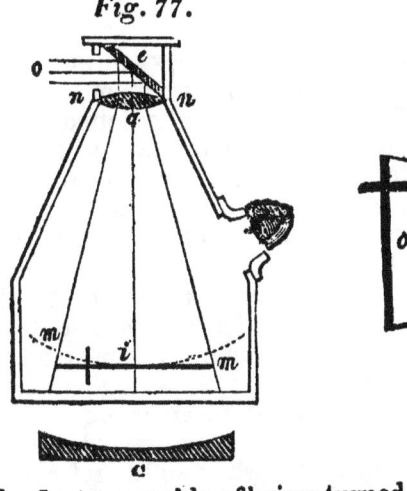

Fig. 77.

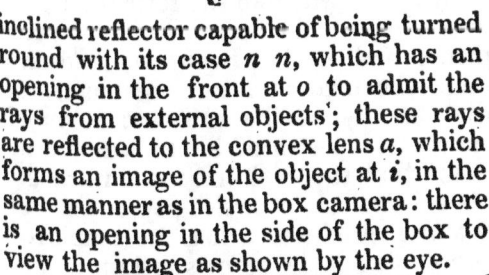

inclined reflector capable of being turned round with its case *n n*, which has an opening in the front at *o* to admit the rays from external objects; these rays are reflected to the convex lens *a*, which forms an image of the object at *i*, in the same manner as in the box camera: there is an opening in the side of the box to view the image as shown by the eye.

(105.) Although the modifications of this apparatus are numerous, they all depend on the same principle, which admits of the following improvement: the lens *a* being double convex converges the rays that pass through it to the same distance from every part of its surface, but as the image is received on a flat plane, the rays *a m* will have to diverge farther than those in the centre *a i*, which are nearer the lens; hence the image will be a distorted representation of the object: to remedy this, when not required for tracing, the image should be formed on a concave surface, like that shown in section at *c*. When, however, the instrument is wanted for the delineation of objects, Dr. Wollaston has proposed to make it *periscopic*, by having the lens *a* formed with such curves that the marginal rays *a m* are rendered longer than the central ones *a i*. The shape of the lens necessary to be employed for this purpose is meniscus, having the concave side next the object, and the radii of the two surfaces as 1 to 2, by which, he informs us, an aperture of 4 inches can be employed, with a lens of 22 inches focal distance; the light and brilliancy of the picture is thus greatly increased.*

(106.) The *camera lucida* was invented by Dr. Wollaston, in 1807, for the purpose of delineating distant objects, and for copying or reducing drawings. This instrument consists of a quadrangular glass prism, by which the rays from an object are twice reflected: its form is shown in *fig.* 78. The object *o* to be

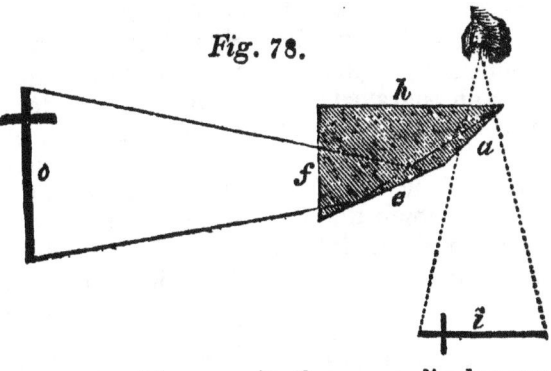

Fig. 78.

traced is opposite the perpendicular surface of the prism *f*, and the rays proceeding from *o* pass through this surface, and fall on the inclined plane *e*, making an angle with *f* of 67½°: from this they are reflected at an equal angle to the plane *a*, making an angle of 135° with *e*, and are again reflected to the eye above the horizontal plane, which makes an angle of 67½° with the last reflection. The rays of light from the objects proceeding upwards from *a* towards the eye of the observer, the observer will be led to imagine the image at *i*, and by placing the paper below in this place,

---

* *Phil. Trans.*

the image may be traced with a pencil. In order to increase or diminish the size of the picture, the prism is mounted in a brass frame supported by brass tubes, capable of being drawn out or shortened at pleasure. The picture always bears the same relation in size to the object as the distance from the eye to the image or paper is to the distance from the object to the eye; hence by lengthening the tubes the drawing is increased in size: it should be remarked, that by this prism no real image is formed, but it always appears as far below the prism as the object is before it. The brass frame of the prism has usually two lenses, one concave and the other convex, the former to be used in front at f for short-sighted persons, the latter above at h for long-sights. The periscopic principle of Dr. Wollaston has been applied to this instrument, by forming the upper surface at h slightly concave.

(107.) Various modifications and contrivances have been adopted to improve or construct different kinds of camera lucidas for tracing or delineating objects. A very simple one may be made with a plane reflector, either of speculum metal or plate glass, having its face inclined at an angle of 45°; but in this form, as there is only one reflection, the drawing or tracing will have those objects on the left side that in the original object are on the right side, in the same manner as an engraved plate for printing is the reverse of the impression taken from it.

(108.) The most ingenious camera lucida, in which the tracings are similar to the original, is shown in *fig.* 79, which consists of a parallel piece of

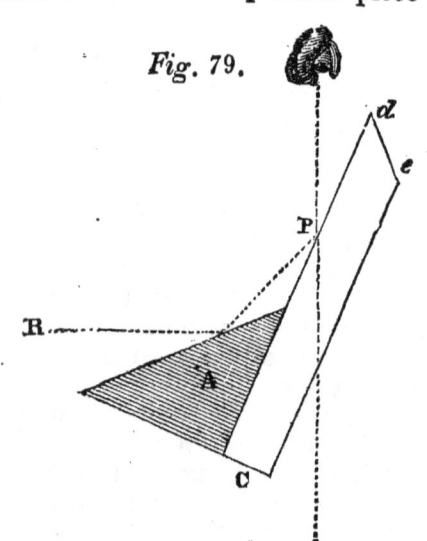

Fig. 79.

plate glass $d, e,$ C, connected to a reflecting speculum A. In this instrument, the invention of S. Amici, the rays from the object R are thrown on to the speculum A (inclined at an angle of 135°,) and reflected by it on to the plate glass at P, and from thence to the eye above. The instrument is mounted in brass, and has a rectangular opening at the top, whereby the eye is prevented from seeing a reverse image of the objects produced by the metallic mirror. Another construction, which Amici esteems the best, is shown in *fig.* 80, where the

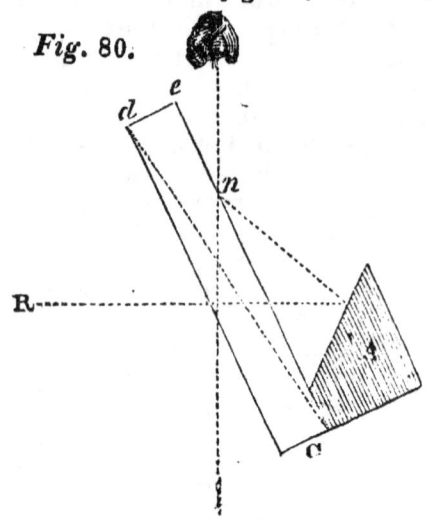

Fig. 80.

rays are made to pass through the plate glass before they impinge on the mirror A, (as shown by the dotted lines,) they are then reflected to n, and from thence to the eye, one half of the pupil being directed through the glass $d, e,$ C to the paper below, and the other half receiving the reflected rays.

(109.) *Teinoscope.*—We stated when treating of the achromatic telescope, that by combining a concave lens of a substance having a higher dispersive power than the convex object-glass, its colour might be corrected without destroying the whole of the refraction produced by it. From numerous experiments made by Dr. Brewster, to determine the irrationality or inequality of the lengths of the different coloured spaces in spectra of equal lengths, he found that the least and most refrangible colours might be destroyed, and *refraction* produced when he employed two prisms of the same substance, provided the prism with the least refracting angle was inclined so that the incident rays entered obliquely, by which means the dispersion is increased in a greater ratio than the refraction:—thus, if a flint-glass prism B (*fig.* 81,) with an

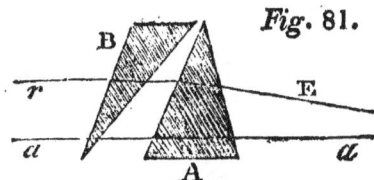

Fig. 81.

angle of 41° 11′, is corrected by another prism of flint-glass A having an angle of 60° 2′, the first being inclined to increase the dispersion; it will be found that the dispersion by this arrangement will be increased, so that the pencil r will be considerably refracted towards the axis $a\,a$ by the prism A, and yet emerge colourless at E. From this very curious circumstance of procuring refraction without colour by two prisms of the *same substance*, Dr. Brewster has proposed the construction of object-glasses on the same principle, by which he states that the spherical aberration of the two might more accurately be corrected by employing the form shown in section, *fig.* 82, where the lens A corresponds with the prism A in *fig.* 81, and the convex meniscus B with the prism B. The lens A is plano-convex, but probably the best form would be a convex meniscus, with the convex side turned towards the eye.*

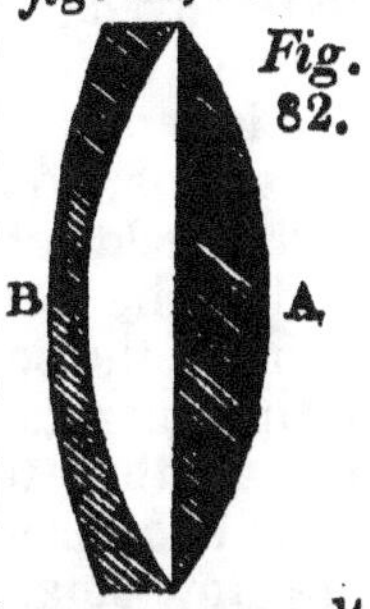

Fig. 82.

(110.) Signor Amici has very recenlty constructed a combination of prisms of the same glass on this principle, in which the chromatic aberration is corrected, and a power of about 3 times obtained. This plan is peculiarly well suited for *opera-glasses*, as the cluster of prisms requires no adjustment of focus for the different distance of the objects, a remote and near one being seen at the same time with equal distinctness; indeed, it does not possess a focus properly so called, a desideratum of great importance in this class of instruments; it is, therefore, superior to them in this respect.

Amici's teinoscope consists of four right angular prisms, having their refractive angles different and connected by pairs; the two pairs being similar, those next the eye or the first *pair* are vertical, and the second pair horizontal, so that equal refraction is produced in every direction. The distance between each pair is about an inch and a half.†

* See *Encyclopedia Edin.* art. OPTICS, p. 650.
† We have been informed that one of these instruments was made by Dr. Blair previous to that constructed by S. Amici, and that it is now in the possession of Dr. Brewster.

(111.) *The Kaleidoscope** is an instrument invented by Dr. Brewster while investigating the polarization of light by successive reflections between plates of glass, in the year 1814. The patent he obtained for it described it as a new optical instrument "for creating and exhibiting beautiful forms:" this is effected by two reflecting plates inclined to each other at any angle that is an aliquot part of a circle (or of 360°.) These plates are placed between the eye and certain objects to form the intended picture, as shown in *fig.* 83, where

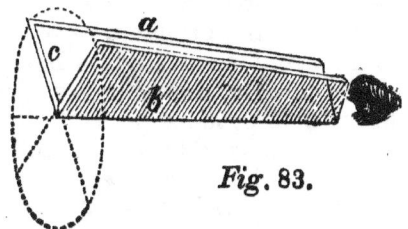

Fig. 83.

$a\,b$ are the two reflecting planes inclined at an angle of 60°, or the sixth of a circle; at the end c are placed the objects, and the eye is stationed at the other end: these two plates are usually enclosed in a tube, and the objects, consisting of pieces of coloured glass, beads, &c., are loosely confined between two circular pieces of common glass, the outer of which is usually *greyed*, to make the light uniform. In order to give the picture varied outlines, threads of coloured glass spun or twisted may be mixed with the pieces, being first formed into circles, ellipses, looped curves like the figure 8, curves like 3, or spirals like the letter S. On looking down the tube, through a small hole placed near the meeting of the plates, a beautiful circular figure will be seen having six angles, the plates being inclined the $\frac{1}{6}$th of a circle; if inclined the $\frac{1}{12}$, $\frac{1}{20}$, &c. twelve or twenty will be seen: these beautiful forms, by slightly turning the tube, will be changed, by which an almost infinite variety of patterns may be produced.†

(112.) In order to make this instrument capable of taking in distant objects, in the same manner as a telescope, a convex lens or object-glass fixed to a tube sliding for adjustment on the inner tube containing the reflectors should be annexed; by this means an inverted image of any distant object may be formed at the ends of the reflectors, as shown in *fig.* 84, where o

* This name is derived from three Greek words, καλος, *beautiful*, ιδος, *a form*, and σκοπεω, *to see*.
† For the theory of this instrument, see our *Treatise on Optics*, p. 19, fig. 28.

OPTICAL INSTRUMENTS.

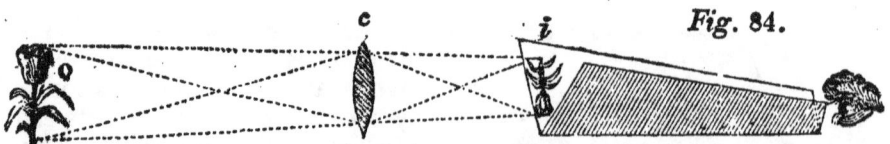

Fig. 84.

is the object, c the lens, and i the image formed with it. In this manner it has been employed for producing beautiful combinations of *flowers, trees, animals,* &c. When the lengths of the reflecting planes are less than the distance of distinct vision, a convex lens whose focus is the length of the plates should be attached to the eye-end of the tube. In this way polished speculums may be used, by which the brilliancy of the picture is increased, as less light will be lost by reflection. Dr. Brewster has found, that in order to produce perfectly beautiful and symmetrical forms, the following three conditions are necessary.

1. That the reflectors should be placed at an angle which is an *even* or an *odd* aliquot part of a circle, when the object was regular, and similarly situated with respect to both the mirrors, or an *even* aliquot part of a circle, when the object was irregular.

2. That out of an infinite number of positions for the object both within and without the reflectors, there was *only one* position where perfect symmetry could be obtained, namely, by placing the object in contact with the ends of the reflectors.

3. That out of an infinite number of positions for the situation of the eye there was *only one* where the symmetry was perfect; namely, as near as possible to the angular point, so that the whole of the circular field could be distinctly seen; and that this point was the *only one* out of an infinite number at which the *uniformity* of the reflected light was a maximum.

Chapter XVII.—*Micrometers.*

(113.) The micrometer is an instrument usually applied to telescopes and microscopes, for the purpose of measuring minute bodies or small angles subtended by bodies at a remote distance, by which their real magnitude is obtained. By the modern introduction of this instrument for the use of the astronomer, and the improvement of the telescope, may be attributed our accurate and extensive acquaintance with the universe of matter; while from the perfection to which the microscope has recently been brought, an equal acquaintance with the minute organization of bodies may be expected. By the application of the micrometer to this latter instrument the power of the naturalist is materially extended; while the micrometer is of the utmost value, for trigonometrical surveys, and in military or naval operations.

(114.) *The common wire micrometer,* usually attached to the eye-pieces of telescopes, is shown at *fig.* 85: it con-

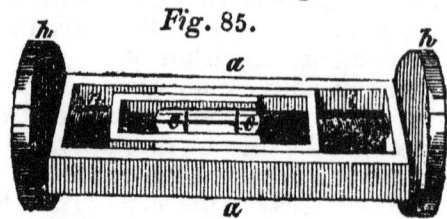

Fig. 85.

sists of a brass rectangular box $a\,a$, the upper and lower plate having an opening in the centre, (but in the figure both are removed;) this box is made to slide along an opening cut in the tube of the eye-piece of the telescope at right angles to its axis, so that the wires $c\,e$ may be in the field of view; these wires are fixed to the forks $i\,n$, moveable in each other by the screws i and n, connected to the micrometer heads $h\,h$: there is also another fixed wire at right angles to the two former from c to e. To measure any small angular distance with this instrument, as the diameter of a planet, the two parallel wires are made to approach or recede from each other by turning the screw-heads $h\,h$ till the body to be measured is exactly enclosed by them, while the longitudinal wire crosses the centre of the body. Having thus accurately measured the planet by the two cross wires, we must next ascertain their distance asunder, in the manner following: suppose there are 50 threads of the screw to an inch, and that the heads are divided each into 100 equal parts; now one of the screws is to be turned till one of the wires is brought into accurate contact with the other, when the number of turns and divisions requisite to effect this purpose will give the diameter of the planet, each division being equal to $\frac{1}{5000}$th of an inch. But if we are desirous of determining in seconds, or parts of a degree, it is found by previously measuring a known base, or by ascertaining the time an equatorial star takes in passing from one wire to the other, and from thence deducing the seconds or parts of a second agreeing with each revolution of the screw-head.

The essential requisite in this micrometer is, that the wires be perfectly parallel, and that there be no shake in the forks that carry them.

(115.) *The micrometrical telescope* of Dr. Brewster, (§ 40) for measuring distances, may be employed for determining the diameters of bodies by having two parallel wires fixed across the field of view in the focus of the eye-glass; these wires being immoveable will not be liable to any inaccuracies in the screws, or from the uncertainty of obtaining a correct zero. The manner of using it is thus: suppose the inner moveable object-glass to be in the focal point of the principal one, and that the wires, by experiment, exactly take in an object of known magnitude, this will be the *minimum* angle capable of being measured with it. But when we have a larger object than can be enclosed within the wires, the inner object-glass must be brought nearer the principal one, thus reducing the power of the telescope by shortening its focus, so that the angle between the wire will be increased to admit the object to be measured; and as by the laws of optics it is known that when the two object-glasses are in contact the focus is shortest, so the angle between the wires will then be a *maximum*. Hence, any angle between these two points ascertained by experiment, may be determined by divisions registered along the tube.

(116.) The preceding principle of a micrometer may be applied to the Gregorian or Cassagranian telescope, without any additional apparatus; for the magnifying powers of either of these instruments may be varied by altering the distance between the large metal and the eye-piece, and then adjusting for distinct vision by the little metal. In this way Dr. Brewster proposed to determine the angle subtended by any object, having experimentally formed the scale for adjustment.

(117.) *Fibres for micrometers.*—After the contact of brass plates, employed by Huygens, for micrometers was discontinued, *silver wire, hairs,* and *spiders' webs* were introduced; the former, however, till latterly, could not be produced finer than $\frac{1}{150}$th of an inch diameter in this country, which, consequently, led to the choice of the other fibres. But, by the ingenuity of Dr. Wollaston, wire can now be obtained of only the $\frac{1}{30000}$th of an inch in diameter: this he effects by having a fine platina wire thickly coated with silver, which is drawn out as fine as possible in the usual manner, through steel or jewelled holes, and then, by finally immersing this wire in an acid that will dissolve the silver and not the platina, he obtains a perfect wire of any fineness that may be required.

(118.) The spider's web was first successfully employed for micrometers by Mr. E. Troughton, who used the stretcher, or the long line which supports the web, for this purpose, the others being too weak. He found the thread to possess the valuable properties of fineness, opacity, and elasticity.* But the difficulty of procuring this particular thread has led to other contrivances in its stead.

(119.) The micrometer threads of Dr. Goring, which have been termed *artificial cobwebs*, were introduced by him to obviate the easy destruction of the natural ones when kept for any length of time, and from the difficulty of procuring those of the proper kind. These threads are formed from a thick solution of gum caoutchouc in oil of turpentine, and by not employing in their formation a heat greater than that of the human body: after the threads are drawn out, the essential oil evaporates, and leaves the *Indian rubber* in the same state as at first.† The cobwebs made in this manner are not liable to injury by keeping, like the ordinary ones, while they possess the essential properties of opacity, fineness, parallelism, and elasticity, and are far superior to them in strength.

(120.) *The divided object-glass micrometer* is composed of two semilenses $a, c,$ (fig. 86;) these act as two distinct

Fig. 86.

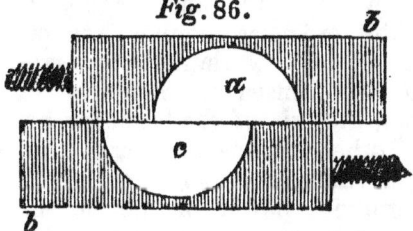

object-glasses, each producing an image of the same object, and in order that their foci shall be of the same length, they are made by dividing a circular

---

* This quality is lost by keeping.

† It should be observed, that the Indian rubber solution must not be kept in any vessel from which the air is entirely excluded, whereby the slow evaporation of the essential oil is prevented, as this consequence will decompose or change its nature, so that when drawn out into threads it remains in a clammy state and will not dry. This remark equally applies to all its solutions for making *water-proof* articles. The solution may be covered with a piece of wash leather.

lens across its centre. The centres of these semilenses are made to separate more or less, by means of a screw attached to the plates in which the lenses are mounted, as *b b*; and the distance of their centres is measured by a scale and vernier.

When it is required to measure the angle subtended by two objects, as O P, (*fig* 87,) the semilenses are separated till the images of both objects coincide at their foci F. This being accomplished, the angular distance of the two lenses, reckoning the vertex at E,

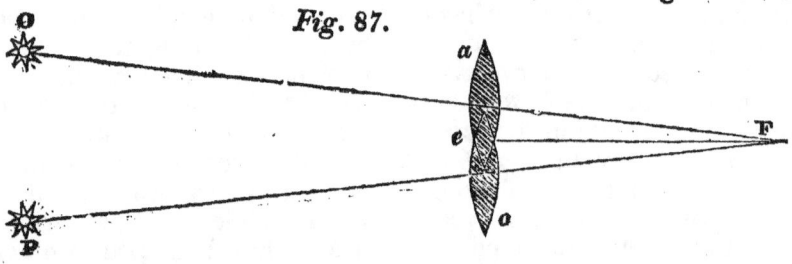

Fig. 87.

their focal distance will be equal to the real angle subtended by the two objects at F, or at the place of the object-glasses, (the real distance, of *a* F or *c* F being very small in comparison to the distance of the objects O P from the object-glasses:) to find, therefore, the angle of the semilenses, we have the sides *a c* (*i. e.* the distance of the two centres) and *e* F their focal distance, which are all the data necessary to determine it trigonometrically. But as the angle in practice is usually very small, it may with little error be considered simply as the subtense *a c*, having experimentally determined the distance of the semilenses corresponding to two objects making a known angle with each other, when by simple proportion the angle for any other distance may be found.

(121.) The improvements that have been made on this divided object-glass micrometer by Dr. Brewster, consist in having the centres of the two semilenses at a fixed distance from each other, and by employing another object-glass in the ordinary manner: to produce the requisite variation of angle, the fixed semilenses are made to traverse along the axis of the telescope between the other object-glass and the eye-piece, thus producing a change in the magnifying power of the instrument; and by means of a divided scale along the tube, showing the distance of the semilenses from the principal object-glass, the angle is ascertained.

(122.) The principle of the divided object-glass micrometer has been applied to the microscope, for the purpose of measuring the diameters of various fibres, and from thence determining the quality and value of the material for the manufacture of different articles; its principal application has been in the measurement of wool, from which it is called *an eriometer*. The instrument consists of a compound microscope, either refracting or reflecting, having two semi-concave lenses capable of adjustment by screws and a vernier's scale; this apparatus is fixed between the object and object-glass or metal, and the measurement of the fibre, by the contact of its two images, is effected in the same manner as in a telescope.

(123.) *The mother-of-pearl micrometer*, invented by Mr. T. Cavallo, and described by him in the *Phil. Trans.* for 1791, has, from its simplicity, been very extensively employed in practical astronomy, and is indeed admirably suited for measuring any small angle with expedition. The strip of pearl used for this purpose is minutely divided, and stretched across the diaphragm, or stop, usually placed in the anterior focus of the eye-glass, either of a telescope or compound microscope; so that the divisions may be distinctly seen by the eye at the same time as the object. When we are desirous to measure an object with the former instrument, any given number of equal divisions on the pearl corresponding to a known angle is first determined by experiment; then, on looking through the telescope at the object to be measured, and counting the number of divisions the diameter of the object occupies, the angle it subtends is determined from the proportion of that number to the number answering to the known angle. When this micrometer is applied to the compound microscope, in order to ascertain the magnitude of any minute object, the strip of pearl is stretched across the field-bar of the instrument; it is then brought in the direction of the length of the object to be measured, by turning the tube of the eye-piece till they coincide. Then, if we suppose the number of divisions on the pearl dynameter to be 100 in the space of an inch, and the part to be measured is found to occupy two of these divisions, to determine its real size we must ascertain how much the object has been amplified by the object and field glasses. But if no field lens is employed, the power will be as the distance of the object-glass from the image, divided by the distance of the object from that glass. As inaccuracies are however liable to occur in these measures, the best practical manner (which is equally simple, let the number of glasses be soever numerous) is to determine the increase in magnitude by using another scale of very fine divisions in place of an object; knowing how many there are in an inch, and ascertaining the number of divisions on the one employed as an object that are equal to any number of the equal divisions on the pearl dynameter across the field-bar, by dividing the one number by the other, the amplifying power will be obtained. Example. Suppose the divisions on the scale (used as an object) be 1000 in the space of an inch, and one of such divisions is magnified so as exactly to cover one of the divisions on the pearl, which are $\frac{1}{100}$th of an inch, it is evident the scale, or an object placed in its stead, is magnified 10 times. Hence we know that as the object we proposed to measure occupies *two* divisions, it is $\frac{2}{1000}$ths of an inch long; each division on the pearl being equal to the $\frac{1}{1000}$th of an inch on an object placed in the focus of the object-glass. In using the micrometer, the power of the eye-glass is not required to be known, as the divisions on the dynameter are magnified in the same ratio by it as the object.

(124.) *Circular micrometers.* The micrometer last described, as stretched across the field-bar for many astronomical purposes, is found objectionable from the three following circumstances. First, the central rays from the object are obstructed by the pearl, which likewise divides it into two portions. Secondly, the situation of the central portion of the pearl being nearer the eye-lens than the other parts, the various portions will be unequally magnified, although the pearl is really divided into equal parts; and therefore the measurements are inaccurate, unless taken from one particular part. Thirdly, the edge of the micrometer always requires to be in the direction of the parts to be measured: for this purpose, it is necessary always to turn the eye-piece to bring it in the proper direction; this, undoubtedly, is a loss of time, besides the liability of disarranging the instrument for distinct vision. Having thus stated the defects of that micrometer, it is only necessary to mention that the circular micrometer is entirely free from these evils; for the central space being clear, the rays are not obstructed, while the divisions are all equally magnified, and the object can be measured with equal facility and accuracy in any direction: indeed, the advantage of employing this instrument is so great, that we need only mention that the orbits of three out of the four new minor planets were determined by a circular micrometer alone.

(125.) *The circular pearl micrometer* was invented by Dr. Brewster, and consists of an annular portion of mother-of-pearl, *a, i, (fig.* 88,) fixed on its

Fig. 88.

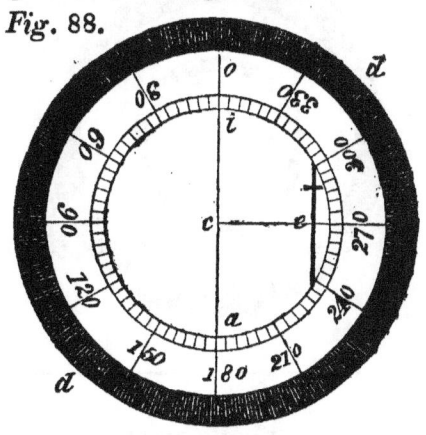

outer edge to the diaphragm *d, d,* at the end of a piece of brass tube, which is capable of being adjusted exactly to the anterior focus of the eye-glass of the telescope or microscope; the inner circumference of the pearl is divided into 360 equal parts or degrees; and when this micrometer is thus adjusted for use, the maximum angle must be determined experimentally: this angle will be subtended by the inner diameter of the pearl *a, c, i.* Now, if we suppose this angle, by observation, to be *two* degrees, we shall be able to find the value of the angle any other object subtends in any direction less than 2°; thus, let the object be represented by the line *e,* which, by inspection, is found to occupy sixty divisions; bisect the angle the object *e* subtends, and it will be equal to the sine of half the angle *a c i:* or the angle which this object subtends is equal to twice the sine of half the angle, *a c* being the radius; so that the object *e* subtends half the maximum angle, or *one degree.* In this manner, trigonometrically, might be found the angle answering to every division, which should be formed into a *table;* and thus it would be given by inspection.

(126.) *The circular suspended micrometer* is an instrument, simple in its construction, and admitting of extreme accuracy in its execution; it is less subject to injury, while it possesses many advantages over others in its application to astronomical observations. This micrometer was invented by the late M. Fraunhofer, and consists of a circular disc of parallel plate glass a, (*fig.* 89,) having in its centre a small circular hole of about *half an inch* diameter, and turned very true in a lathe; to the inner edge of this circle a narrow ring of steel c is securely fastened, when its inner edge is turned perfectly circular, and reduced very thin. The glass plate, with its steel ring, is then mounted in a brass tube or setting d, d, by means of which it can be adjusted to the focus of the eye-glass, (similar to the last micrometer.) This micrometer, when viewed in the telescope, appears like a narrow ring *suspended* in the heavens, from whence it derives its name. The chief advantage in this instrument is the accuracy by which the moment of *ingress* and *egress* of a planet or star is determined; for the body being seen in the field of view through the glass plate, before it comes to the inner edge of the steel ring, allows the precise moment of contact to be very readily observed. The angle subtended by the ring must be found in the same manner as with the other micrometers; or by noting the time an equatorial star passes when near the meridian, and deducing therefrom the angle which the inner edge of the ring subtends. The velocity of a planet may be determined in the same manner while near the meridian; or the difference of the time occupied by a star and the planet passing together, would determine the motion of the latter, making proper allowance when crossing above or below the centre.

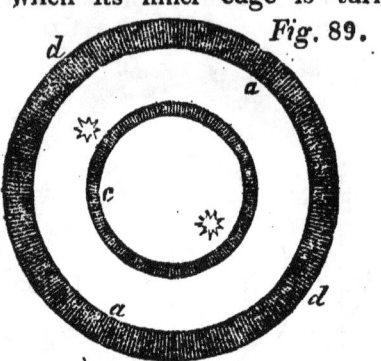

Fig. 89.

BOOKS UPON OPTICS AND OPTICAL INSTRUMENTS.

Optics in general. — Euclid's Optics, Paris, 1557. — Kepler's Dioptrics, Augsburg, 1611. — Descartes's Dioptrics, in his works, vol. ii.; published also in Baron Maseres's *Scriptores Optici*, London, 1823. — Huygens's Dioptrics, in his posthumous works. — James Gregory's Optica Promota, London, 1663; published also in Baron Maseres's Scriptores Optici. — David Gregory's Elements of Catoptrics and Dioptrics, Oxford, 1695. — Newton's Optics, London, 1701. — Newton's Lectiones Opticæ, 1728. — Smith's Optics, 2 vols. 4to., Cambridge, 1738. — Martin's New and Compendious System of Optics, London. — Le Caille's Lectiones Opticæ, Vienna, 1757. — Harris's Optics, 4to., London, 1775 — Priestley's History of Vision, Light, and Colour, 2 vols. 4to., London, 1772. — Emerson's Elements of Optics, London, 1768. — Euler's Dioptrics, 3 vols. 4to., Petersburg, 1769, 1770, 1771. — Hauy's Treatise on Natural Philosophy, translated by Dr. Olinthus Gregory, 2 vols., London, 1807. — Wood's Elements of Optics, Cambridge, 1811. — Biot's Traité de Physique, tom. iii. and iv. — Robison's Works, vol. iii., Edinburgh, 1823. The article Telescope in this volume is very excellent. — Euler's Letters to a German Princess, 2 vols., Edinburgh, 1823. Dr. Brewster's edition. This work contains a very full treatise on Optics, in which the various branches are illustrated in a most popular manner. — Ferguson's Lectures on Select Subjects in Mechanics, Optics, &c. 2 vols. 4to., Edinburgh, 1823. Dr. Brewster's edition. This work contains a very popular treatise on Optics. — Coddington's Elementary Treatise on Optics, Cambridge, 1823. — Optics, in Dr. Brewster's Encyclopædia, vol. xv. This article contains a very copious treatise on the various branches of Optics, historical, theoretical, physical, and practical, with minute references to all the works and memoirs. — Dr. Thomas Young's Elements of Natural Philosophy, 2 vols. 4to. This work is one of our most valuable books of reference.

Achromatic Telescope. — Boscovich's Opera Pertinentia ad Opticam et Achronomiam, 5 vols., Bassano, 1785. — Achromatic Telescope, in Dr. Brewster's Encyclopædia, vol. i. — Biot's Traité de Physique, vol. iii. — Dr. Blair, on the Inequal Refrangibility of Light, in the Edinburgh Transactions, vol. iii. p. 1. — Dr. Brewster's Treatise on New Philosophical Instruments, Edinburgh, 1813. — Clairaut, Mém. Acad. Par. 1756, 1757, and 1761. — D'Alembert, Opuscules Mathématiques, 3rd, 4th, 5th, 6th, and 7th vols., and Mém. Acad. Par. 1761. — Mr. J. F. W. Herschel, Phil. Trans., 1821. — Fraunhofer, in the Memoirs of the Bavarian Academy, 1814, 1815. — Professor Barlow, on his New Achromatic Telescope, in the Edinburgh Journal of Science, No. 15, 1828.

Physical Optics. — Grimaldi, Physico-Mathesis de Lumine, Bologna, 1665. — Dutour, Mém. Sav. Etrang. vols. iv., v., vi., and Rozier's Journal, vols. i., ii., v., vi., vii. — Comparetti, de Luce Inflexa, Padua, 1787. — Mr. Brougham, Phil. Trans. 1796, 1797. — Mr. Jordan's Observations on Light and Colours, London, 1797. — Dr. Thomas Young, Phil. Trans. 1800, 1303, 1808 and Sup. Encyclopædia Brit., Art. Chromatics. — Dr. Young, on Medical Literature, London, 1813. — MM. Biot and Pouillet in Biot's Traité de Physique, tom. iv. App. — M. Fraunhofer's Neue Modifikation des Lichtes. — M. Fresnel, Ann. de Chimie et de Physique.

Photometry. — Bouguer's Traité d'Optique. — Lambert's Photometria, Augsburg, 1760. — Prof. Leslie, on Heat, London, 1804. — Mr. W. Ritchie, Phil. Trans. 1825.

OPTICAL INSTRUMENTS.

APPENDIX.

More than twenty years have elapsed since the work for which this Appendix is now prepared was first presented to the public. It is, therefore, necessary to state that the principles therein described are still the same as those now employed in the construction of optical instruments. In this respect the science of Optics differs widely from that of chemistry and some others. Nevertheless the improvements which optical instruments have received since its publication renders it desirable to append a supplement. This, it is believed, contains the chief features of every improvement of practical value; and, although it was necessary to condense the matter into a limited space, it is hoped the information will be valuable to all who take an interest in these subjects. The author, who now cultivates this science as an amateur, regrets that he has not been allowed to extend the descriptions, but hopes an opportunity may occur at no distant time when he will be able to do so.

Canonbury Lane, Middlesex,
June, 1850.

CHAPTER XVIII.

IMPROVEMENTS ON TELESCOPES AND THEIR STANDS.

§ 127. The mounting of large telescopes has of late years been transferred from the workshop of the optician to the factory of the engineer. This change is a very beneficial one, and has led to many improvements. The massive supports necessary to carry instruments of such magnificent dimensions as the Reflector of Lord Rosse, or the Achromatic of Mr. Cooper, require the employment of gigantic machinery in their construction. We propose to give a brief description of these two instruments, which will serve to illustrate the scale on which such works of late years have been erected; premising that the reader should first make himself acquainted with the subjects described in Chapters IV. to X.

The largest achromatic telescope at present in this country is that belonging to Mr. Cooper of Markree Castle, in the county of Sligo. The object-glass, which is of foreign manufacture, is 13 inches in diameter[*] and 25 feet focal length. It is mounted on an equatorial stand, which enables an observer, with one motion only, to keep a celestial body constantly in the field of view of the telescope. This very desirable object may always be effected by inclining the vertical axis of a telescope stand so as to be parallel with the axis of the earth.

[*] The Munich Institute has just finished an object-glass 14·9 inches diameter for Russia.

OPTICAL INSTRUMENTS.

Fig. 90.

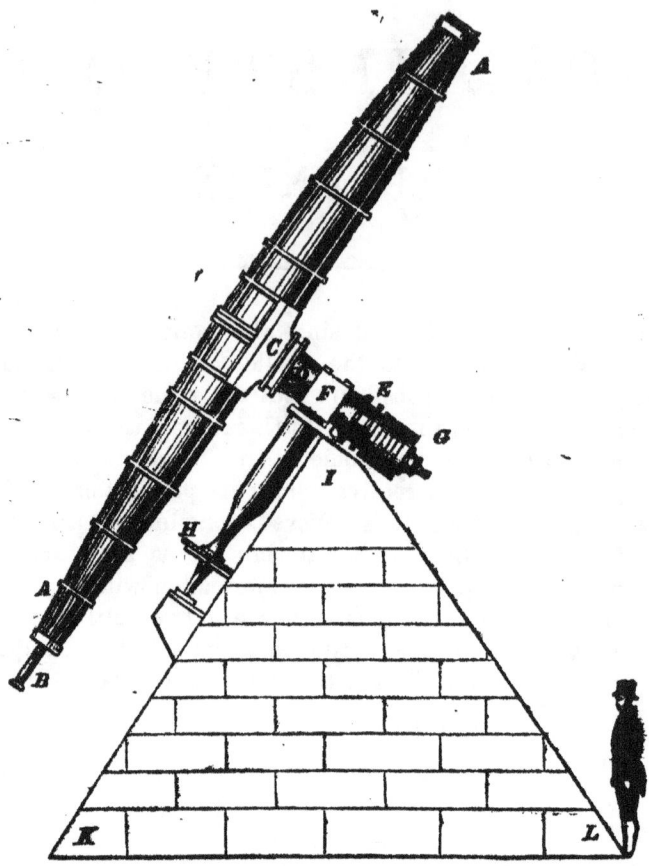

Figure 90 represents the achromatic telescope mounted on its stand. A A the tube of the telescope, which is made of sheet-iron, is strengthened with iron ribs and hoops forming pannels. This tube is further strengthened by being increased in size towards the center, where it is 24 inches in diameter; the ends being only 16 inches. It weighs 890 lbs. The tube is supported in the middle by the cast-iron cradle c, to which it is firmly attached by two jointed wrought-iron straps. Attached by four iron bolts to the cradle is the declination axis D E, which turns in the square top of the polar axis at F, which is furnished with friction-rollers. At E is the declination circle, which is divided and furnished with four microscopes to read off the divisions. G represents a series of circular rings of cast iron employed as weights to counterpoise the weight of the telescope. The interior of each ring has an annular cavity, divided by partitions into six parts, four of which are filled with lead; the others being left vacant afford a simple means of bringing the centre of gravity of the declination axis, &c., into its centre of revolution. The polar axis F H turns at its upper end between two large friction rollers attached to a cast-iron collar firmly fixed upon the top of the pier I K L. This pier is composed of large blocks of black marble well jointed and cramped together; it is 4 feet thick at the base, and the meridian face I K is sloped to the latitude of the observatory, which in this case is 54° 10′ north. The lower end of the polar axis has a hardened steel pivot, which works into a bell-metal bearing. This bearing has a lateral motion for adjusting the polar axis. At H is situated the hour circle carefully divided, and with it is a rachet wheel forming 720 teeth, which work into a pinion within the pier, a part being excavated to receive the clock. By this means, when the clock is wound up, and the pinion put into gear with the teeth of the wheel, the telescope moves around the polar axis, and thus when set to any given star, that star is always kept in the field of view.

So admirably has this telescope been mounted by Mr. Grubb, that a force of 3 lbs. applied to the eye-end B of the telescope is sufficient to move the instrument in any direction. The engraving is drawn to a scale of three quarters of an inch to ten feet. The weight of the iron work is as follows:—

	cwt.	qrs.	lbs.
Equatorial stand	25	3	21
Iron-tube, object-glass, eye-piece, &c.	9	0	14
Counterpoise G	12	1	19
	47	1	26

§ 128. *The reflecting Telescopes of Lord Rosse.*—These instruments, like the Refractor just described, are erected in Ireland; the natives of which have also the honour of constructing them. At a distant glance they resemble the chimneys of steam-boats. The smaller one has a tube 26 feet long, and 3 feet in diameter, which is capable of being directed to any part of the heavens. The large telescope, to which we propose to confine this description, with its tube and appendages, weighs 15 tons, and is placed between two high piers of masonry which limit the motion of the telescope in azimuth to about five degrees on each side of the meridian. Both telescopes are of the construction called *front view*, described in the treatise, § 30 and 31: though occasionally a small plane mirror is used, which is on the principle of the Newtonian. The two stone piers or walls which support the tube are erected parallel to each other, with a clear distance of 23 feet apart: they are 71 feet long, that is from north to south, and about 50 feet high.

The speculum is composed of 126 parts of copper, with $57\frac{1}{2}$ parts of tin, Earl Rosse having found, as suggested by us (see page 30), that when these metals are fused and mixed in the proportion of the atomic weights, they produce the best compound, both as regards the reflective power and the qualities for working. In casting large speculums of this brittle metal many difficulties arise from air bubbles, contraction in cooling, &c., that render ordinary sand or iron moulds valueless. The surmounting of these difficulties by his lordship is a triumph in science, and worthy of lasting renown. Lord Rosse forms the bottom of the mould, on which the face of the speculum is to be cast, of a close coil of iron hooping, the metal being poured upon the edges of the coil. By this contrivance the molten metal is prevented from escaping between the coils of hooping, while the interstices are sufficient to allow of the escape of air, steam, or gas. The diameter of this large speculum is 6 feet, which gives an area four times greater than that of any other telescope. It is $5\frac{1}{2}$ inches in thickness, and weighs $3\frac{3}{4}$ tons. The speculum is ground and polished under water by steam-power, and has a focal length of 54 feet. The tube is made of deal wood, $7\frac{1}{4}$ feet in diameter at the centre, and $6\frac{1}{2}$ at each end. The speculum is fitted into an 8-feet cubic box. A stout iron arc about 40 feet radius is firmly attached to the inner face of the eastern pier. This arc is provided with means for carefully adjusting it to the plane of the meridian—a matter of importance, seeing that by the contact with it of the telescope tube by rollers a few feet from the speculum end (the upper end being free), the position of the telescope in the meridian is secured, or any required deviation from it obtained, by altering this arc. The telescope rests on an universal joint, placed on masonry 6 feet below the ground, and is elevated by a chain and windlass. It is easily worked by two men, every part being counterpoised.

This telescope has commenced an important era in astronomical science, we purpose, therefore, to give a brief account of its performance, from the observations of Sir James South and of Dr. Robinson of Armagh.

Many nebulæ, says Sir James South, were observed by Lord Rosse, Dr. Robinson, and myself. Most of them were, for the first time since their creation, seen by us as groups or clusters of stars; whilst some, at least to my eyes, showed no such resolution. Never, however, in my life did I see such glorious sidereal pictures as this instrument afforded us. Most of the nebulæ we saw, I certainly have observed with my own large achromatic; but although that instrument, as far as relates to magnifying power, is probably inferior to no one in existence, yet, to compare these nebulæ, as seen with it and the 6-feet telescope, is like comparing, as seen with the naked eye, the dinginess of the planet Saturn to the brilliancy of Venus.

The most popularly-known nebulæ observed this night were the ring nebulæ in the Canes Venatici, or the 51st of Messieur's catalogue, which was resolved into stars with a magnifying power of 548; and the 94th of Messieur, which is in the same constellation, and which was resolved into a large globular cluster of stars, not much unlike the well-known cluster in Hercules, called also 13th Messieur. Although, however, the power of this telescope, in resolving nebulæ into stars hitherto considered irresolvable, was extremely gratifying, still it was in my mind little more than I had anticipated; for experience has long since told me that a telescope may show nebulæ, even those resolvable by it, very well; whilst, when directed to a bright star, with a very moderate magnifying power, its imperfections will be actually offensive. During Sir W. Herschel's lifetime, with the 20-feet reflector at Slough, I saw, amongst others, 3rd Messieur, 5th Messieur, 13th Messieur, 92nd Messieur, the annular nebulæ of Lyra, and the great nebulæ of Andromeda. No telescope of its size, probably, ever showed them better; yet, on the same night, the same instrument, when directed to Alpha Lyræ (a star of the first magnitude) broke under a power of about 300.

Perfection of figure, then, of a telescope must be tested, not by nebulæ, but by its performance on a star of the first magnitude. If it will, under high power, show the star round and free from optical appendages, we may safely enough take it for granted it will not only show nebulæ well, but any other celestial object as it ought. When about to buy my large object-glass at Paris, in 1829, I directed it to Alderbaran, viewed it in the telescope, certainly not one minute, and paid for it the next, without any one of the astronomers of Paris then present, and by my side, imagining I had even had the telescope on the star, much less that I had purchased it in consequence. Regulus on the 11th of this month (March) being near the meridian, I placed the 6-feet telescope on it, and, with the entire aperture and a magnifying power of 800, I saw, with inexpressible delight, the star free from wings, tails, or optical appendages; not, indeed, like a planetary disk as in my large achromatic, but as a round image resembling voltaic light between charcoal points; and so little aberrations had this brilliant image that I could have measured its distance from, and position with, any of the stars in the field with a spider's line micrometer, and a power of 1000, without the slightest difficulty; for not only was the large star round, but the telescope, although in the open air and the wind blowing rather fresh, was as steady as a rock.

On subsequent nights, observations of other nebulæ amounting to some thirty, or more, removed most of them from the list of nebulæ, where they had long figured, to that of clusters; whilst some of these latter, but more especially 5 Messieur, exhibited a sidereal picture in the telescope such as man before had never seen, and which for its magnificence baffles all description.

Several double stars were seen with various apertures of the telescope, and with powers between 360 and 800, and, as the Earl had told us before we should—before the speculum was inserted in the tube, in consequence of his having been obliged to quit the superintendence of the polishing at the most critical part of the process—we found that a ring of about 6 inches broad, reckoning from the circumference of the speculum, was not perfectly polished, and to *that* the little irradiation seen about Regulus was unquestionably referable.

The only double stars of the first class which the weather permitted us to examine with it were Xi Ursæ Majoris and Gamma Virginis: those I could have measured with the greatest confidence; whether, however, it would have separated some of the closest or of the most difficult double stars, I cannot say.

D'Arrest's comet we observed on the 12th of March, with a power of 400, but nothing worthy of notice was detected.

Of the moon a few words must suffice. Its appearance in my large achromatic of 12 inches aperture is known to hundreds of persons; let them then imagine that with it they look *at* the moon, whilst with Lord Rosse's 6-feet they look *into* it, and they will not form a very erroneous opinion of the performance of the Leviathan.

Dr. Robinson of Armagh, in his communication to the Royal Irish Academy, is reported to have said in reference to Earl Rosse's large telescope:—

"How far this instrument might have attained its limiting dimensions, how far it might have reached the bulk which could be used with effect under the circumstances of their atmosphere and the other physical influences which certainly war with astronomers, it was impossible to say; but the manner in which the experiments had already been made with it led him to hope that it might be possible to pass even these limits. The limits, they remembered, he had stated to be these:—A telescope had no advantage from its size, unless all the light which its mirror or object-glass collected was received into the eye. The dimensions of the pupil of the eye were limited; therefore, that telescope was uselessly large which magnified more than the diameter of the mirror or object-glass multiplied by 5; in the case of a 6-feet reflector it gave as the lowest a power of 360; upon the other hand, no advantage would be gained by employing a higher power than the lowest available power multiplied by 10, which would give a power of 3600. He had thought the nights were rare in which it would be possible to use a power of 360 with much advantage in this climate (Ireland); but to his surprise he found that he was deceived. He also thought that the difficulty would increase when the dimensions of the telescope were very great, but he found that it acted with double powers fully as well as the 3-feet reflector, therefore he would retract the observation which he had made, that he conceived it to be impossible that a still larger telescope could be used. How far it was practicable to construct a larger telescope he was unable to say, but it was impossible, when he saw the extraordinary amount of mechanical skill applied in the instance of the telescope in question, not to feel that the undertaking of a larger work would be exceedingly perilous and doubtful. There was another difficulty alluded to by the elder Herschel as giving a limit to the magnitude of the telescope—that was to say, the stars everywhere dotted over the sky, although faint when single, became very sensible in groups, amounting in instances to ten thousand times ten thousand; and on a starry night, when the field of the telescope was not full of light, it would obviously become necessary to secure artificial illumination. Long before the twilight he saw it approaching from the diminished brightness of the clusters of faint stars; and it was perfectly clear that during the whole of that portion of the summer, from the secondary twilight, or false dawn, as it was called, prevailing from the end of April to the end of August, it would be impossible to do anything with the telescope upon the faint clusters of stars. The light of the moon was so powerful during this period that it would most assuredly quench these faint objects, and present another limit to the magnitude of the instrument. Doubtless attempts would be made to extend this limit. They were aware of the proposal lately brought forward by their friend Arago, to construct at the expense of the French government an achromatic telescope of prodigious dimensions; he proposed to make it 30 inches in diameter. As to the inferiority of that telescope over the 6-feet reflector there could not be any doubt whatsoever; the optician who proposed to furnish the glass stated that the flint glass was to weigh about 400 lbs. Most of them knew that a piece of glass supported upon a ledge, and sustaining a pressure of 400 lbs., possessed the qualities of double refraction, which were of the most troublesome description possible; besides, an achromatic lens, by the excessive pressure of the brass of its mounting and its weight, interfered with the defining power of the instrument. But supposing the difficulty to be overcome, it was overlooked that light transmitted by an achromatic object-glass of large dimensions did not possess any remarkable supremacy over the brilliancy of service of a good-sized speculum. The only measurement made by Mr. Potter of the quantity of light transmitted by a 4-inch object-glass was, that it transmitted $\frac{2}{3}$ of a foot less light than that reflected by a good speculum which reflected $\frac{7}{10}$. It was said that, still further north, a speculum of 10 feet in diameter was about being contrived."

§ 129. Independently of these gigantic telescopes, several astronomers on both sides the Atlantic have lately constructed reflectors of great practical value. Of these we may mention the successful exertions of Mr. Lassell of Liverpool, whose speculums of the respective diameters of 9 inches and of 2 feet have achieved discoveries of no small amount, such as an eighth satellite of Saturn, satellites of Neptune, the sixth star in the trapezium of Orion, &c.

The casting and polishing of speculums of large diameters having attained a degree of perfection not known to the last generation, it is highly probable that telescopes of the reflecting construction will be much sought after. Such being our view of the matter, we strongly recommend to all those who may hereafter direct their attention to these productions, that the greatest improvement that can now be effected in their construction is the working of the speculums of *short* focal length in comparison with their diameter. To effect this very desirable end will require a large amount of skill and perseverance, but we do not foresee anything impracticable in the undertaking. We have now before us a very perfect reflector of $2\frac{1}{2}$ inches diameter and 5 inches focus (having two small metals), which give magnifying powers of 30, 44, 66, and 100 diameters. This *dumpy* exhibits the most delicate minutiæ in a distant landscape, or on the surface of the moon, with perfect sharpness. This telescope, with its brass tripod stand, is packed in a case 8 inches long by 5 inches wide and 3 inches deep. Now, when we compare the proportions of focal length and diameter of this speculum with those in Earl Rosse's, we find the first to be as 1 to 2 nearly, and the latter as 1 to 9. If we only consider the mechanical advantages and facilities of observation by a reduction of the focal length of large telescopes, the subject will be found of great importance. Consider the difference if the proportion were reduced to 1 to 4: then, in place of mounting a gallery 54 feet in the air, we should only have to ascend 24 feet. However, to enumerate all the advantages of rendering large reflectors dumpy would occupy far more space than is at our command; we must therefore leave the subject, seriously requesting all aspirants in this department of Optics not to let pass so important a hint.

CHAPTER XIX.

ON STANHOPE AND CODDINGTON LENSES AND DOUBLET MICROSCOPES.—ACHROMATIC MICROSCOPES.—THE MEGALOSCOPE.—OXYHYDROGEN MICROSCOPES.

§ 130. On referring to Chapters XI. and XII., various forms of magnifiers, and also combinations of lenses for microscopic purposes, are there figured and described. Of late years the grooved sphere (*fig.* 43) has been much used under the name of the Coddington lens, Mr. Coddington having in his admirable work on Reflection and Refraction demonstrated that the caustic, formed by the rays passing through it at a given distance from the axis, is flatter than that obtained by any other form. That gentleman also employed it as an object-glass of a compound microscope, and furnished the writer with a formula by which that instrument might be made achromatic when the eye-lens, field-lens, and grooved sphere were all of the same focus. The angular aperture of such a microscope is, however, necessarily very small, and hence, as shown by the authors of the *Microscopic Illustrations*, it is of little value for a compound microscope.

§ 131. The *Stanhope Lens* is made of a cylinder of glass, having both its ends ground and polished of a spherical shape, the convexity being such that an object placed on the one end shall be in focus when you look through the lens. These magnifiers are of little practical use for the investigation of minute bodies, and are mainly employed by the lovers of the marvellous. The late Earl Stanhope, who first employed a lens somewhat of this form, intended it as a field-glass of a telescope, which, when very thick, he found to exhibit bodies of their true shape; while an ordinary eye-piece magnifying the outer parts of an object more than the center distorts the form, thus giving to a square the figure of a pincushion.

§ 132. *Wollaston's Doublet Microscope* is by far the most perfect construction of microscope for high powers hitherto constructed, and only yields to the compound achromatic in not having so large a field of view; indeed it is one of those simple and elegant inventions for which the distinguished inventor was so renowned. This doublet consists of two plano-convex lenses whose foci are as 1 to 3, or thereabouts. The convex sides are placed next the eye, and the distance between them about half the sum of their focal lengths; the shallow lens being next the eye. *Fig.* 19, page 13, represents such a doublet greatly enlarged, the object being placed next the side E. These doublet microscopes are often made of very short focus: we have now before us a set whose foci varies from $\frac{1}{10}$ to the $\frac{1}{70}$ of an inch, that is to say, their magnifying powers are equal to single lenses of those foci.

Dr. Wollaston adapted to these microscopes an illumination equally simple and ingenious; it consists of a plano-convex lens of about $\frac{1}{4}$ of an inch focus fitted to one end of a tube of 3 inches in length, the other end having a stop or aperture of $\frac{2}{10}$ diameter. The light from the mirror being directed through this aperture, an image of it is formed by the lens, which image is carefully adjusted so as to be in the same plane as the object. To render this illumination perfect, an achromatic lens should be substituted for the plano-convex one mentioned above, and no light should be allowed to fall upon or pass through the object but that through the aperture and the lens.

Mr. Holland has, on the same principle as the Wollaston's Doublet formed a triplet, which, as its name implies, consists of three lenses. These magnifiers when carefully executed give exquisite definition, but, owing to the small space they allow in front of the lens, and the limited field of view, are not much in use.

§ 133. *Achromatic Microscopes.*—Referring the reader to Chapter XIV., we shall proceed to consider the improvements made since that was written. The great perfection to which this instrument has been brought of late years, both in this country and on the Continent, renders it desirable to trace the causes to which this is due; and, as it always happens that, where success ensues there are several claimants, we shall endeavour justly to record this matter. From the publication of this little treatise, until the appearance of the *Microscopic Cabinet* of Dr. Goring and Mr. Pritchard in 1832, little if any progress was made in this country. The practical principles on which object-glasses should be constructed and tested was therein fully detailed, and the attention of artists having been called to the subject by the previous writings of the same authors, and being now in full possession of the requirements, namely, *a large angle of aperture free from aberration*, the desired perfection was rapidly obtained, superior talents and great perseverance being employed on this subject. Messrs. Powell, Pritchard, Ross, and Smith greatly distinguished themselves in the production of achromatic object-glasses. Each, however, proceeded differently, but all availed themselves of the two essentials, first enunciated by those authors, namely, a large angle of aperture and the use of test objects. M. C. Che-

Fig. 91.

valier of Paris first employed a combination of three pairs of corrected lenses, whose foci was about 1, 2, 3, the shorter being in front, see *fig.* 91.

in which *o* is the object, *b*, *e*, *f*, the pairs of lenses; this form, or a modification thereof, is now usually adopted *.

The elegant investigations of Mr. Lister on the oblique pencils in double object-glasses is worthy of high commendation, though it has only been used by one or two artists, while the above essentials are aimed at by all opticians, English and Continental.

We have great pleasure in mentioning that Mr. Lister's method of measuring the angle of compound object-glasses is of great practical value, and should be generally resorted to by all makers and observers. The instrument for this purpose is figured in the *Microscopic Cabinet*.

§ 134. Many persons conceive that the chief value of a microscope is its magnifying power; but, so far from this being the fact, if two microscopes of unequal magnifying power be taken, but which exhibit the minutiæ of an object equally well, that which has the least magnifying power is the best. To explain this more fully, we shall extract a few sentences from Mr. Pritchard's *Microscopic Illustrations*:—

"Let me premise that, in order to render any object visible, it is necessary that rays of light should proceed from it, either by reflection from its surface, or by transmission through it, to the eye. Again, if the number of rays be insufficient, the object cannot be seen, notwithstanding we employ a microscope for the purpose. Bearing this in mind, I will endeavour to explain how an increase of angular aperture in an object-glass, independently of any increase of its magnifying power, will admit a greater quantity of light from any given point on the surface of an object to pass through the lens, so as to render the structure of the object visible.

"Let *figs*. 92 and 93 represent two objects in all respects alike, and let us employ two microscopes of equal magnifying power for the purpose of viewing them. Suppose that we are going to look at some spot on the surface of A or *a*, which we will imagine to be a delicate tissue. By a well-

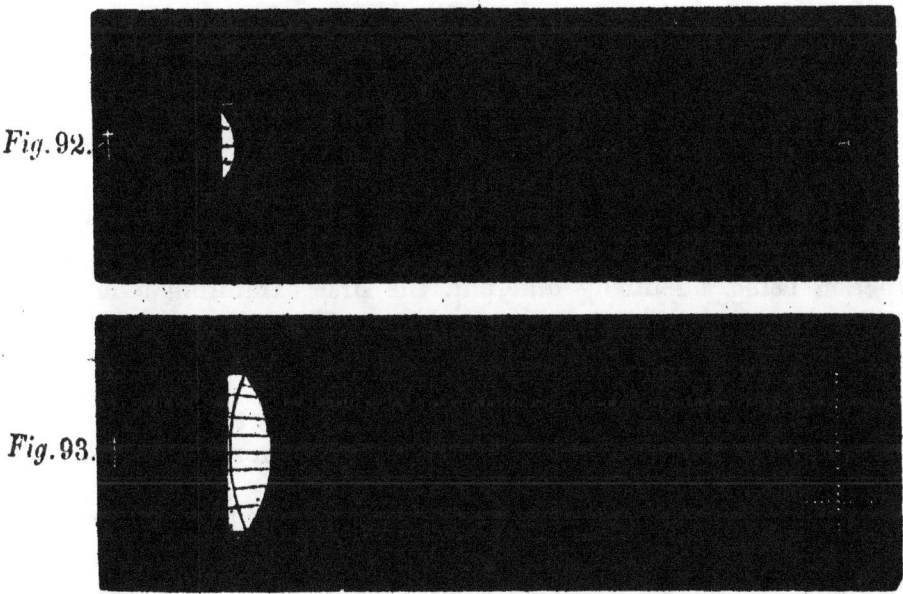

* On examining the surfaces of some fine achromatic object-glasses, eight or ten years old, we observed that the flint glass had undergone a change, the lead having revived. This, it is true, at present only occasions an absorption of light, but to what extent it will proceed it is impossible to conjecture. This change is serious, for when ten or twelve guineas are given for one object-glass, its durability is a consideration.

known law of light, the rays proceed in right lines in all directions from this spot, in the manner shown by the dotted lines in both figures. Suppose B B and *b b* to be two object-glasses of equal focal lengths; the former a single lens of the best construction, such as was used in the old compound microscope, and the latter a lens of the newest form, termed an achromatic. Now these object-glasses will form their respective images at I and *i*, and they will be of equal dimensions; but if the number of rays proceeding from A, and falling upon the single lens B B, is not enough when collected at I sufficiently to stimulate the eye, any minute pore, striæ, or other marking at A, will not be rendered visible, whilst, from the increase of aperture in the achromatic lens *b b*, allowing much more light from *a* to fall upon it and to be transmitted through it and collected at *i*, every marking, &c., at *a* will be clearly represented at *i*, and the eye, being powerfully acted upon by this increase of light, will become highly sensible of it.

"The angles B A B and *b a b* are the angles of aperture of the respective object-glasses, and the quantity of light collected and transmitted by each will be as the squares of B B and *b b*, the focal lengths being equal. Hence it is that the power of a microscope, or that faculty it possesses to render the structure of an object visible, depends upon the angle of aperture of its object-glass, and not upon its magnifying power alone."

Fig. 94.

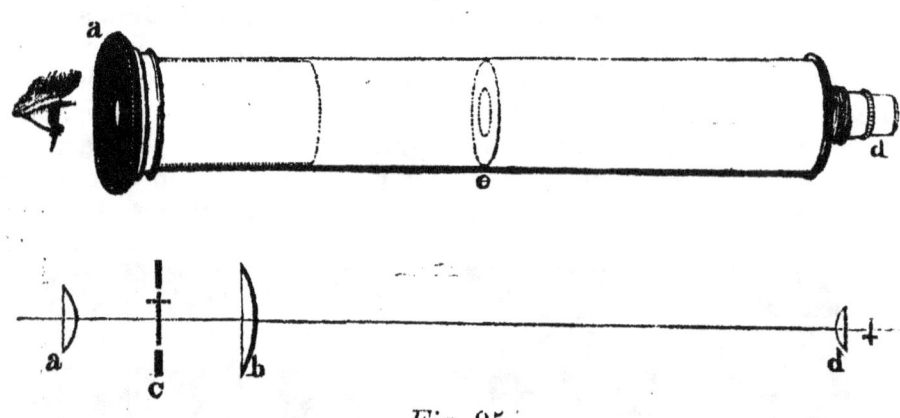

Fig. 95.

Figures 94 and 95 represent the body of a compound microscope, called by Dr. Goring an Engiscope, to distinguish it from compound magnifiers, their action being essentially different, the first exhibiting a magnified image, the latter, the object itself magnified. *a* is the eye-lens; *c* the diaphragm where the image is formed; *b* the field-lens; *e* a stop, and *d* the object-glass.

In concluding the account of the improvements on the optical part of microscopes, we select a few important aphorisms from the *Microscopic Illustrations*:—

"1. A *test* is an object which serves to render sensible both the perfection and imperfection of an instrument, as to defining and penetrating power.

"2. Proof objects may be ranged under three heads: first, those which render manifest chromatic and spherical aberration; secondly, those which give evidence of the presence of a large angle of aperture; and thirdly, those which shew the union of the above properties, and consequently the greater or less approximation of an instrument to its most perfect condition.

"3. Chromatic aberration is rendered sensible by almost any transparent object, *when the light falls upon it obliquely;* but more especially by such as are not transparent, but only illuminated by intercepted light, of which a very good example may be seen in a piece of fine wire gauze, treated like a diaphanous object, also in a thin plate of metal, perforated by very small holes. The various colours are seen according to the order of their refrangibility, by putting the object both without and within the focus, as well as by viewing it at the focal point; all brilliant opaque objects also exhibit chromatic aberration strongly, when managed in the same way.

"4. Spherical aberration is most sensibly felt in viewing opaque objects, especially if of the brilliant class; it shews itself in a variety of ways: first, as a diffused nebulosity over the whole field of view; secondly, as a confined nebulosity, extending only to a certain distance from the object; and thirdly, in a want of sharpness and decision in the outline caused by a penumbra or double image, which can never be made to lap perfectly over the stronger or true one. *Aplanatism,* or a destitution of the aberration of sphericity, is evinced by the absence of these appearances, and by the vanishing of the image immediately the object is put out of focus either way.

"5. A deficiency of angular aperture is shewn by a want of light, producing unsatisfactory vision, which is rather increased than ameliorated, by augmenting the intensity of the artificial illumination,—by an incapacity of shewing lined objects, except such as are of the lowest class, and by giving very large spurious discs, with artificial stars; also by shewing easy test objects, with the lines faint, while the spaces between them are darker and more opaque than they ought to be.

"6. When the spherical and chromatic aberration is small and faint, and the angle of aperture considerable, the lines on proof objects become fine, sharp, and dark, and the spaces between them clear and bright (provided the illumination is properly conducted): they moreover become visible in a very faint light; if the instrument is perfectly aplanatic, the outline and the lines are seen at once, and the spurious discs of all brilliant points are very sharp and small."

* * * * * * * * *

"16. The verification of the real nature, form, and construction of a vast variety of opaque objects, which elude the sense of touch by their extreme minuteness, can only be made out by an attentive study of their appearances under a variety of methods of illumination, conjointly with a consideration of the phenomena presented by bodies when seen in perspective, or, as painters term it, foreshortened. We are particularly perplexed in microscopic observations, by the circumstance that only a point of an object can be seen at a time, if the power used is considerable; we must, therefore, always begin to study them with *low powers* at first, and increase them gradually, so that we may always be able to recognise the particular part of the object we are looking at, otherwise all will be confusion. When we see an opaque object represented by a drawing, we see it as it never can be seen by a microscope, because, in the latter instrument, its various features can never be in focus at the same time, as before observed, and it would be impossible to represent it on paper exactly as seen at a variety of adjustments, without an infinite number of views of it.

"I particularly recommend observers, in examining and verifying opaque objects *too small to be dissected,* to use the simple light of a candle before the stage, as its divergent rays bring out more strongly their various component features, and render them more intelligible than can be done by any other method. The oblique light of the taper plays over their various prominences and depressions like that of the evening sun over common objects, giving broad lights and shadows; and, if the observer has any knowledge of the operation of light, and the manner in which it is broken and intercepted by ordinary bodies, he will hardly fail to arrive at a tolerably clear idea of the nature of the minutiæ he is contemplating. The light of the sun must never on any account be used, as it gives rise to an infinity of indescribable deceptions, both as to colour and form; it renders every opaque object a mass of confusion.

"17. There are a variety of optical deceptions produced by microscopes and engiscopes, against which observers cannot be too strongly guarded, as inadvertent persons have brought great disgrace on microscopic science by trusting too much to the testimony of their instruments. It requires long and repeated observation to enable us to be quite certain of the nature of what we see; for—1st, we are seldom or never in the habit of viewing common objects by *intercepted light;* vision by it is therefore altogether new to us, and the phenomena presented by bodies subjected to its influence are totally different to what they assume as opaque bodies, which is the usual way in which we see common objects;—2ndly, all microscopic vision may be considered as accomplished under very large angles, which is again a totally new way of seeing to the uninitiated. The object is in a manner placed in a most unnatural state of proximity to the eye, and consequently assumes a totally different character to that produced by objects at our common visual distance, which must inevitably perplex us till we become habituated to it. There is one general law to which all transparent objects are subjected; namely, that those parts which appear brightest and clearest in them are almost invariably the *thinnest;* a want of transparency nearly in every case argues thickness and substance. Much may be done towards their verification *by examining sections of them as opaque objects*, where this is practicable; and care should be taken *never to view them both as opaque and transparent bodies at the same time*, as this is sure to produce deception, and on this account they should be shaded from all incidental rays. Their true colours can never be seen properly by high powers: in order to ascertain them correctly, a low power should be employed, with the light of the sun reflected by a plaster of Paris disc.

"Observers should study the effect of intercepted light on ordinary transparent bodies, of the real nature of which there can be no doubt, in order to be able truly to appreciate microscopic phenomena. There are a number of glass toys made, which will make very good subjects of this description; and so do ordinary glass tubes, and solid rods of glass—the former being filled with other transparent objects, and afterwards with water. We frequently meet with bodies in transparent objects which operate like lenses on surrounding objects, of which they form miniature images, very remarkable to those who are not aware how the effect is produced.

"In short, we must consider, that in all bodies viewed by intercepted light, there is, properly speaking, neither light nor shade, in the ordinary acceptation of these terms; there are only dark and light parts, which again assume new aspects as the light is more or less direct or oblique. Thus depressions on transparent objects are almost sure, under the action of oblique light, to assume the effect of prominences; but prominences seldom or never the semblance of depression. As almost all diaphanous bodies can be examined as opaque objects, a scrutiny of them in this way will generally be found greatly to assist our judgment concerning their nature, whether they admit of being cut into sections or not. It would be easy to write a volume on this subject only, if we commenced an illustration of particulars which could not be rendered clear and satisfactory without a vast number of figures. Long practice must after all determine our opinions, and scepticism should ever form a leading feature in them; we should *suspect rather than believe.*

"18. Opaque objects are not upon the whole so liable to produce optical deceptions as transparent ones, because we are more in the habit of viewing ordinary bodies by reflected or radiated light. The most common illusion presented by them is that of shewing a *basso-relievo* as an *alto-relievo;* the reverse deception sometimes occur also, but more rarely. This effect occurs in ordinary objects viewed by the naked eyes, as well as in microscopes, especially if but one eye is employed. Thus, if we look intently for some time at a basso-relievo (a die of a coin, for example), *illuminated with very oblique light,* it at first appears in its true character; but, after a little while, some point on which we more particularly direct our gaze will begin to appear in *alt,* the whole rapidly follows; in a little time the effect wears off, and we again see it in bas-relief; then again in alt; and so on, by successive fits. This deception arises from the simple circumstance that *the lights and shades in bas-relief are very nearly like those of an alto-relievo of the same subject, illuminated from the opposite side;* our understanding in this case instantly corrects the false testimony of the eye, when we *consider from which side the light comes.* (If we observe with an engiscope, we must always remember that its image is inverted, and that in consequence the light must be considered as proceeding from the side of the field of view opposite to that where the source of illumination actually exists.) It will also be highly advisable, when we are in doubt as to the manner in which an instrument shews prominences and depressions, to verify its vision by observing some *known object* with it, of the real state of which, as to inequality of surface, we have been previously informed by the sense of touch, to which it has been well said there is no fellow *.

"19. Illumination, by cups or silver specula, does not produce these illusions, because they create no shade—the whole object is one mass of intense light; other false perceptions are, however, occasioned by them. Thus, all globular bodies, having polished surfaces, reflect an image of the cups, and the *pout,* if there is one, appears as a dark spot in the centre. The eyes of insects, illuminated in this way, shew the semblance of a pupil in the centre of each lens, which deception may be verified by examining small globules of mercury in the same manner. Spherical bodies, with bright surfaces, will even, on some occasions, reflect an image of the object-glass and its setting, on the same principle; so that we must perpetually consider the laws of the refraction and reflection of light, in all the conclusions we draw from the evidence even of the very best instruments, used with every possible precaution.

"20. Lastly, it must be observed, that in using engiscopes, we must

---

* We usually see objects illuminated from *above* with the *shadows below* the prominences; now, unless the light is below an opaque object, when we view it in an engiscope, we shall see the *shadows above,* giving the prominences the appearance of depressions, and producing a very unnatural effect.—A. P.

never attempt to verify an object concerning which we are uncertain, by increasing the depth of the eye-glass immoderately, so as in this way to obtain a very high power. A negative eye-glass, of about one-fourth of an inch focus, is the deepest which should ever be employed, even with a short body; for an engiscope only shews a *picture* of an object, and the more it is amplified the more its imperfections are developed. It is, on this account, much safer to trust to moderate powers in these instruments, in preference to high ones, *unless they are obtained through the medium of the depth and power of their objective part.* It is the nature of deep eye-pieces to cause all luminous points to swell out into discs, and to render the image soft, diluted, and nebulous; at length all certain vision fades away, and the imagination is left to its uncontrolled operation. Single and compound magnifiers, having to deal with the real object, may be made of any power which can be used; and if our eyes are strong, and habituated to their use, we may place great reliance on their testimony; but we must never allow them to persuade us to believe marvels which are manifestly impossible, or contrary to the known laws of nature and right reason."

§ 135. The mechanical construction of a microscope has of late years received great attention, and here again we must refer to the *Microscopic Illustrations* as containing the first set of rules laid down for its construction. As regards the stands of microscopes, the English artists have far outstripped those on the Continent, though in the optical part each country is equal; indeed some of the French object-glasses must be admitted to possess every quality that is desirable, though many inferior sets are sometimes sent to this country.

For descriptions of the continental stands we refer to C. Chevalier, *Des Microscopes et de leur usage,* and N. P. Lerabours' *Instructions des Microscopes.*

Stability in the stand of a microscope is of the utmost importance, any tremor being magnified in a direct ratio with the power of the instrument. This quality has been well secured by several of our opticians, indeed some have overstepped the mark and made their instruments heavy and cumbersome. In the later microscopes of Mr. Pritchard's construction he employs two bodies; a large one for low powers and a small one for the high ones. By this means a smaller and lighter stand is sufficient.

All the motions for adjustment of focus should be given to the optical part and triangular bars used for slides. The stage should be large and firmly supported. The axis of the instrument should be capable of being brought to any angle or direction, and the stand should be furnished with a motion to enable the stage *to turn* on one side.

As an example in which these principles are carried out, we insert a drawing of Mr. Pritchard's standard achromatic microscope (*fig.* 96), and refer to Mr. Queckett on Microscopes for other forms.

Description of the engraving:—*a* is the eye-piece; *b* the body; the arm into which the body screws. This arm and screw are sufficiently stout to carry the body without vibration, and therefore braces are unnecessary; *d* is the object-glass; *e* the triangular gun-metal bar, having a rack cut in its posterior truncated edge. This rack has a pinion working into it, the large triple milled head of which is represented at *f*. The stage *g* has four holes at the corners, either of which will receive forceps, condenser, or other apparatus. The center of the stage has an aperture one inch and a half in diameter, into which fits by a bayonet-joint the

Fig. 96.

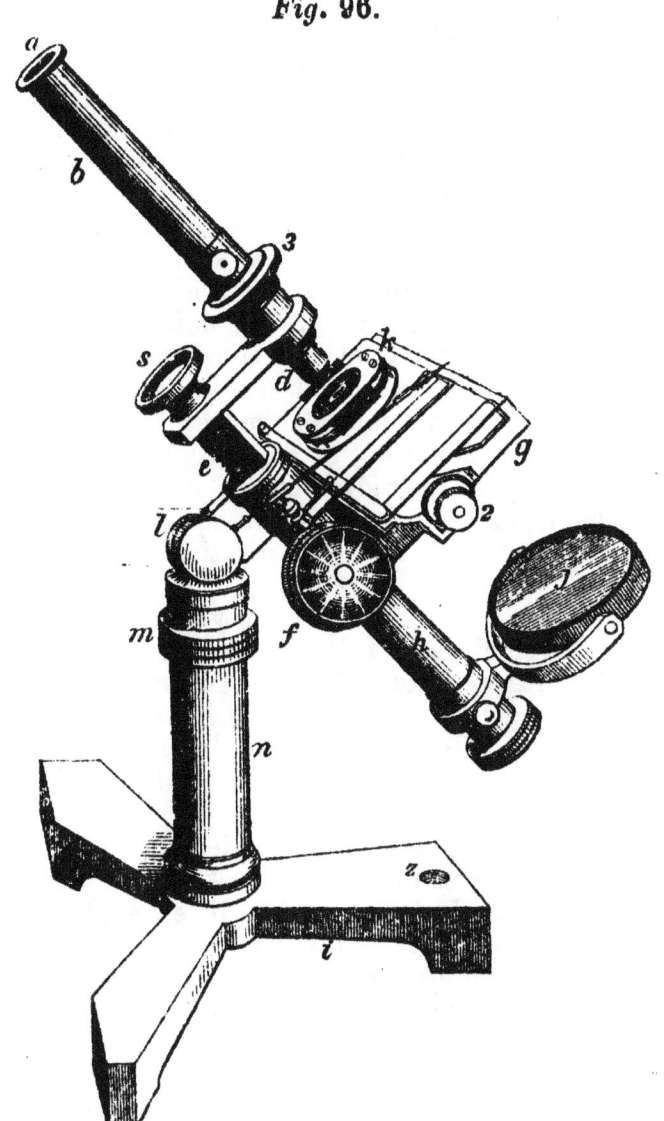

spring safety slider-holder k. This slider-holder has two moveable plates, so that in experiments with polarized light a plate of selenite inserted between them is not disturbed while the slider with its object, which rests upon the upper moveable plate, is moved about: h is the stem of the microscope, which can be brought into any position, either vertical, horizontal, or inclined at any angle. It will also *revolve* about its axis within the socket r. This latter motion is of great importance, and no microscope defective in this particular can do half the work it ought. j the mirror; n the pillar, which consists of two tubes, one sliding within the other, by means of which and the tightening ring m, the microscope can be raised or lowered at pleasure; i the solid tripod foot, which has its two posterior prongs squared so as to fit readily into a cabinet 9 inches wide by 7 inches deep. The anterior prong of the foot has a hole, z, to receive an arm for carrying a candle-holder, large condenser, and shade, when required. The traversing motions for moving an object under examination are effected by turning the heads 2. The fine adjustment of focus is obtained by the large milled head 3.

The application of a polarizing apparatus to a microscope, as originally described in Mr. Pritchard's list of 2000 objects published in 1835, has now become a necessary part of every first-rate microscope. We have not space to enter upon this subject in detail, but the only valuable improvement in this apparatus introduced since Mr. Pritchard's third edition of the *Microscopic Illustrations* is that proposed by M. C. Chevalier, namely, placing the analyzing prism close behind the object-glass.

Having in § 93 given an account of test objects, it remains to add that some others have since been added, as the shells of certain bacillarian infusoria, the striæ and sculpture on which are very delicate. To those who wish to understand the causes of the defects in microscopes, we recommend Dr. Goring's Memoir at p. 264 of the *Microscopic Illustrations*. With respect to microscopic objects in general, we refer to a volume under that title for full information; also Mr. Queckett's Essays on Microscopes. In the mounting of microscopic objects the most important modern discovery was that given by Mr. Pritchard, namely, immersing them in a fluid (gum-water) which subsequently indurated*. This idea has been further carried out by the substitution of varnishes and Canada balsam.

In mounting miscroscopic objects uniformity of size is of some importance, and the first proposal we find for effecting this purpose is contained in the List of 2000 Microscopic Objects published early in 1835. The lengths there given as convenient standards, being multiples of each other, are *three inches* and two inches. The former is now universally adopted, the width varying to suit the subject to be mounted, though it is generally *one inch*.

The best arrangement for microscopic objects is to lay them flat in drawers, and to cover each shallow drawer with a flat plate of glass. It will be well to adopt French measures for the sizes of the inside of the drawers, for reasons which will readily suggest themselves. A Cabinet now before us consists of 26 drawers, lettered. The inside dimensions are 16 inches by 12 inches, so that each drawer contains 64 of the 3-inch preparations, or 144 of the 2-inch objects.

Illumination.—The proper quantity, intensity, and direction of the light best adapted to bring out the various details of a microscopic object require considerable attention and care. The simple oblique rays of a candle, first employed to bring out the markings on test objects by Dr. Goring; the well-defined condensed spot of light used by Dr. Wollaston; the dark ground illumination by Mr. Reade; the achromatic illumination of Dujardin; and the well-defined, condensed, oblique light ingeniously contrived by Mr. Topping;—all have their uses. The first and last are in principle the same, but the elegant plan of Mr. Topping is greatly to be preferred. It consists of condensing the light by a small sphere of glass filled with water, the central rays being stopped out by a small disc of black paper stuck upon the sphere. We think it probable an achromatic illuminator with a similar disc might be more perfect.

Micrometers.—It would far exceed the limit of this work to describe in detail the various kinds of microscope micrometers. The simple plan of having finely-divided scales cut upon glass will always be of general use. Lines 10,000 in the space of an inch are now exquisitely cut by Mr. Jackson. The double-image micrometer of Dr. Leeson is described in the Trans-

---

* See Microscopic Cabinet, p. 230.

actions of the Chemical Society, and the different uses of micrometers by Mr. Bauer and Dr. Goring, are fully described in Pritchard's Micrographia.

As there are many French micrometers in this country, and some errors as to the value of their divisions have lately been published, it may be well to state they are usually divided into millimetres, or tenths or hundredths of that measure; and to convert measurements by them into English parts of an inch, it is necessary to know that a millimetre is equal to .03937, or rather less than the $\frac{1}{25}$ of an inch.

§ 136. *The Megaloscope.*—This instrument is in principle similar to the achromatic microscope, but constructed on a large scale, so as to show bodies of large dimensions moderately magnified. Dr. Goring, to whom we stand indebted for the megaloscope, gives the focus of the lenses and dimensions as follows:—length of body, $14\frac{1}{2}$ inches; diameter, $2\frac{1}{2}$ inches; focus of eye-lens, 2 inches; field-lens, 4 inches. Object-glasses (achromatic), three in number, are 1 inch aperture, and their foci $3\frac{1}{4}$, $4\frac{1}{4}$, and $4\frac{1}{2}$ inches, and are to be used separately or combined. For full particulars of the construction and use of this instrument we refer to the Doctor's Essay in the "Microscopic Objects," p. 187, from which the following is extracted:—

"When a megaloscope is properly constructed, and has all the optical excellencies it should have, its lowest power will be equal to that of its eye-glass: that is, the image formed by the shallowest objective will not be a magnified one, but of the same size as the object; consequently it will be capable of taking in an object not superior in size to the field-bar of the eye-piece, whatever it may be.

"Now as I do not think it is of much use to view objects with a magnifier of less focal distance than 2 inches, that power may be pitched upon for the lowest of the megaloscope; and the instrument I propose to describe has its proportions regulated accordingly.

"a, b, c, d, (*fig.* 97) is the optical part of the megaloscope $2\frac{1}{4}$ inches in diameter, and about $14\frac{1}{2}$ inches long, reckoning in the eye-hole, which screws on at a, and is represented at *fig.* 98; the object-glasses are three in number, and situated in the part c, d, and may be used together or separately. The object-glass at c is $3\frac{1}{4}$ inches focus; the other two are of the same focus, and are set in the same cell, giving a combined focus of about $2\frac{1}{4}$ inches. The glass at c is fixed in a separate tube, and made to slide within that which holds the others; thus it can be used either at a certain distance or in close contact with them; in the latter case the power of the combination is double what it is in the former. These three glasses are all achromatic, and should be so constructed that they will act either together or separately. A stop $\frac{3}{4}$ of an inch in diameter is made to slip into the exterior tube, and to be removed at pleasure. *This will in no degree diminish the size of the visual pencil or penetrating power of the glasses when they are all in combination*, though it greatly *reduces the quantity of light*, or what may be termed *the intrinsic brightness of the image*, while it *increases wonderfully* its distinctness; and for this purpose it may be advisable to use it occasionally, though the combination is *abundantly distinct* without it, *on any opaque objects not of extraordinary brilliancy*, such as globules of mercury, diamond beetles, and certain minerals. I need not observe, that *when the two glasses in front at d only are employed, the said stop reduces their aperture, and with it the size of the visual pencil and the penetrating power*. The focus of the body is adjusted by moving the milled head at e backwards and forwards; the entire body may also be moved in

G

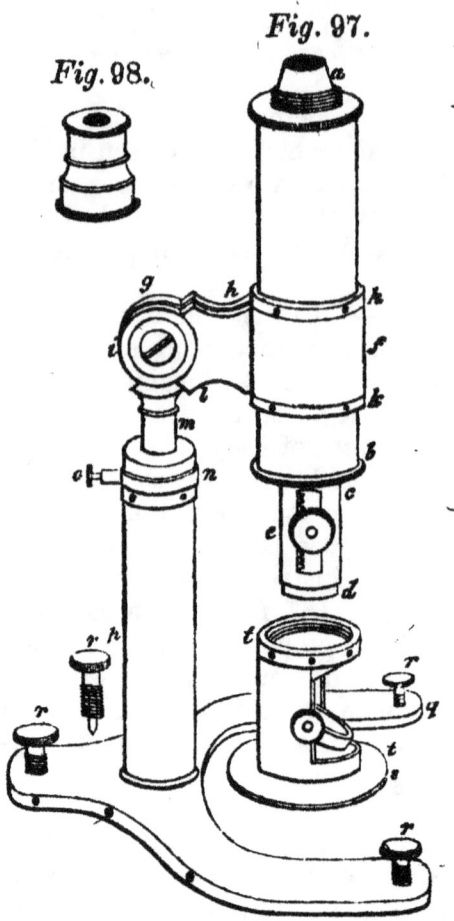

Goring's Megaloscope, one-sixth its real size.

its containing tube *f*, if micrometers are applied to the field-bar, whose value it is wished to disturb.

"As the instrument has a very shallow eye-piece, its visual pencil is of considerable length; thus camera lucidas, rectangular and other prisms, plane metals at different angles, may be applied *comfortably* to it *without preventing us from seeing the whole field of view*, as they are very apt to do in instruments having deeper eye-pieces. This will be found a great advantage in many cases, as the powers of a megaloscope are frequently those best adapted for drawings, giving general views of objects," &c.

§ 137. *Oxy-hydrogen Microscopes.*—At § 97 will be found a description of the solar microscope; since that article was penned, an instrument having the same object, namely, that of showing a magnified image upon a screen, has been invented, whereby we are not dependent upon the uncertainty of sunshine, an illumination being obtained by the light evolved by the ignited stream of hydrogen and oxygen gases upon lime. The perfecting of this invention is due to Messrs. Cary and Cooper; and the public were first made acquainted with the construction in Pritchard's Micrographia. This microscope mainly differs from the solar microscope in the condensing or illuminating part. In the solar, the illuminating rays being nearly parallel, a small refractive power only is necessary to bring them to a focus, while with artificial illumination the rays being strongly *divergent* require additional lenses to effect this purpose. Two or three condensers placed almost in contact are employed, and when the objects to be viewed are large butterflies or aquatic larvæ, to be magnified 20 or 30 feet in length, these lenses require a diameter of 7 to 10 inches. The optical part of these instruments is often constructed after the plan of Ramsden's eye-pieces, unless made achromatic, which Mr. Ross has done with success. In place of lenses a concave mirror is sometimes used to condense the light. We may also mention that achromatic magnifiers have been applied to solar microscopes. In all cases where the lime light is employed, minute and delicate objects have a milky appearance, and hence these microscopes are rarely employed as instruments of investigation; we suggest, therefore, the use of the electric light for this purpose, as likely to obviate this defect, and likewise as being perfectly safe, although at present not very manageable. Another kind of artificial illumination, namely, a small cylinder argand oil lamp, supplied with a central current of oxygen, has been found useful. For a full description of oxy-hydrogen microscopes, see Pritchard's Micrographia, Chapter VIII.

§ 138. The effects termed dissolving views are produced by employing two very large magic lanthorns, or gas microscopes, similar to those last described, but of such dimensions that an object 5 inches square can be introduced. For this purpose the condensing lenses require to have a diameter of 10 or 12 inches. The intrinsic magnifying power of the microscopes being small, the distance between them and the screen on which the images of the pictures are formed requires to be from 20 to 30 feet. The pictures are painted on glass similar to those used for the magic lanthorn; but the execution of the drawing and its finish more carefully attended to. They should be protected by cementing a plate of glass to the painted side. The effect of dissolving one picture into another is produced as follows:—being provided with two distinct, but similar microscopes, placed side by side, and as close together as convenient, the cone of rays from each is thrown upon the screen. This must be so adjusted that each microscope projects its light exactly on the same spot: when this coincidence is obtained, the microscopes should be firmly fixed. In front of the microscopes is an apparatus which slides up and down, and so constructed that whenever all the rays from one microscope fall upon the screen, the whole of the rays from the other are obstructed, or when half of one is open, half of the other is closed: the design being that under every condition the same quantity of light shall be thrown upon the screen; this quantity being equal to that emanating from one microscope only. This contrivance will be better understood by reference to *fig*. 99; where the circles A and B represent the front apertures of two microscopes; C and D are two blackened screens moveable upon the centers $a\ a$, and capable of sliding upon the upright rod E. This apparatus is fixed in front and close to the apertures of the microscopes. When the screens are in the position seen in the engraving, the rays from the microscope B are free to fall upon the screen, while those from A are wholly impeded. If the screens be gradually elevated, the screen D will cover a portion of the microscope B, while A will be gradually uncovered, and in every position there will be exactly the same quantity of light thrown upon the screen.

It may be remarked that other mechanical contrivances for effecting the same purpose have been adopted, such as a large circular plate, with apertures placed before the lanthorns, but, practically, the contrivance described is found to answer best.

The effects of lightning are produced by placing in the covered lanthorn

OPTICAL INSTRUMENTS.

Fig. 99.

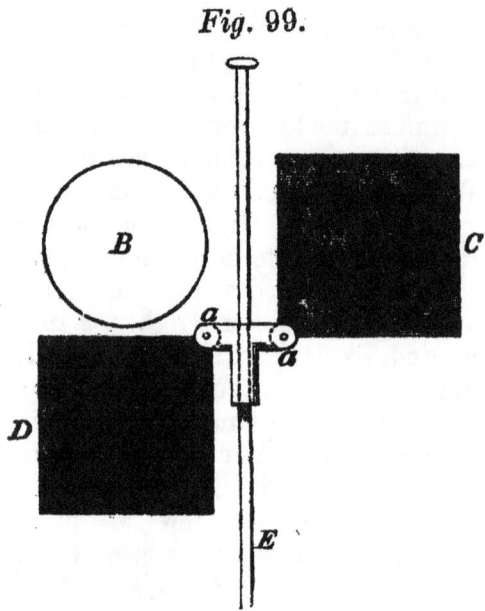

A a black opaque slider, with small portions to represent the forked light cut away, and when the effect is to be produced, turning down the shade c, which revolves about the centre *a*, and quickly replacing it. The Aurora Borealis rising with its arch of light is produced by the light from the covered microscope A, the light from which is thrown upon the view produced by the microscope B. The slide in A is moved by a rack-work, and the whole blackened, except the arch of light. Snow is very easily produced by having a long black slider, with numerous little holes or dots scraped out to allow the light to pass through and then in the lanthorn A (now uncovered), moving such slider *vertically upwards,* when the snow will appear to descend upon the picture produced by the lanthorn B.

The employment of two or more lanthorns at the same time allows the artist to exhibit the effects of nature in great variety and astonishing reality—motions of boats, ships, railway trains, a rainbow, fire, &c. &c. In the *Art Journal* for May, 1850, a description of a trioptric lanthorn invented by Mr. Beechey, is fully given. By this contrivance one light is made to produce the effects of two or three lanthorns as may be required, apertures at proper angles in the sides having microscopes inserted therein, and the rays reflected on to the screen by three-sided prisms. The illumination recommended is an oil lamp fed with oxygen, having a ball of lime suspended in the flame.

CHAPTER XX.

THE CHROMATROPE.—PHYSIOSCOPE.—BURNING MIRRORS.

§ 139. THE *Chromatrope* is an effect produced by the magic lanthorn, on a similar principle to that some years ago exhibited under the name of Chinese fireworks. The latter, however, was formed on a large scale, and consisted of several discs of mill-board, about 2 feet in diameter, mounted upon an axis, and so constructed that each disc may revolve with different velocities, and even in different directions when required. These opaque mill-board discs had radial curved and other apertures cut in them, over which Persian silk of different bright colours is glued. Strong lights are placed behind the circular discs, and when in motion a splendid effect is produced of different coloured rays flashing to and fro from the center, ever varying in form and position. The chromatrope slider is a contrivance employed in a magic lanthorn, and its effects when magnified are shown upon the screen and produced similar to the Chinese fireworks. The slide is furnished with two or three circular plates of glass, which are made to revolve about a common center, and before another fixed plate of glass. These discs are painted with curved radial and other lines in brilliant colours, and when put in motion produce " a mixed moving multitude of colours, vying in lustre with the precious stones, and producing numberless patterns which the eye attempts in vain to follow."

§ 140. The *Physioscope* is an optical contrivance for exhibiting upon a disc or screen magnified images of large bodies. Nearly a century ago these effects were produced by a single concave mirror of 2 or 3 feet diameter, in one of the foci of which an object is placed, and its image formed on the other, the mirror being slightly inclined and so placed in the dark that the spectators did not see it or the object. But as, in this arrangement, the bodies whose enlarged images it was desirable to view had to be inverted, the subjects were necessarily very limited. By the introduction of the strong light produced by the combustion of the oxy-hydrogen gases upon lime, lenses can be introduced to change the direction, and thus allow of more varied applications.

§ 141. *Burning Mirrors.*—A novel mode of producing a concave mirror for burning was exhibited at Birmingham, at a meeting of the British Association. The concavity was produced by atmospheric pressure. A circular disc of parallel plate glass, $\frac{3}{16}$ of an inch in thickness, and $3\frac{1}{2}$ feet in diameter, was fitted into a cast-iron box 1 inch deep, about half an inch of the margin of the glass resting upon the inner rim of the box. At the back of the iron box was attached an apparatus by which a vacuum could be produced; when this was effected, the pressure of the air on the outer surface of the disc of plate glass depressed the center and rendered the plate concave. By varying the rarefaction in the box the concavity, and consequently the focal length, of the mirror can be altered. The burning effects of this mirror were sufficient to ignite various articles, and to roast meat.

CHAPTER XXI.

OPERA-GLASSES.—PHOTOGRAPHIC CAMERAS.

§ 142. *Opera-Glasses.*—Great advance towards perfection in these instruments (the principles of whose construction are described in § 38) has been made of late years, especially by the labours of Herr Voigtlander of Vienna, who has not only constructed the object-glasses (see O, *fig.* 26) achromatic, of three lenses cemented together, but also constructs the eye-glass (E, *fig.* 26) of three lenses achromatized. By this arrangement the great defect of a small field of view, always observable in the Galilean telescope, is obviated. The luxuriant and perfect vision obtained by these instruments when binocular, with a magnifying power of four or five diameters, renders it desirable that they should be produced more readily and at a moderate cost.

This construction is well worthy the attention of opticians; there is little doubt short telescopes with a power of 10 or 12, and an object-glass of 2¼ to 3 inches diameter, would be invaluable to the tourist, and would show the moons of Jupiter, and many other celestial objects.

§ 143. *Solid Opera-Glasses.*—Some years ago these instruments were manufactured by Mr. Pritchard from a German model. They are made of single pieces of solid glass, in the form of truncated cones. One of these is shown of its real dimensions at *fig.* 100. The magnifying power of these

Fig. 100.

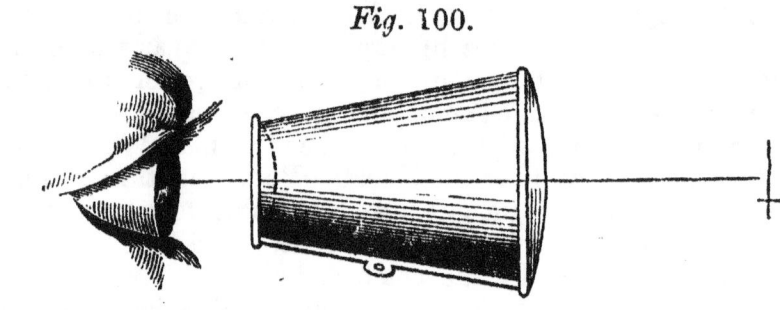

opera-glasses is about two diameters. They have no power of adjustment to suit the varied distances of objects to be viewed, and hence they are limited in their application, but they possess a large field of view compared with the other forms of Galilean construction, and even as an optical curiosity they are valuable.

§ 144. *Photographic Cameras.*—On referring to § 103 a general description of this instrument will be found. Since the invention of Daguerreotype great attention has been paid to these cameras, it being of the utmost importance to obtain a perfect image of an object on a plane surface. To effect this purpose they are usually made achromatic (see Chapters VII. and VIII.), and of such forms that the caustic shall be as flat as possible: were it not for want of achromatism, grooved spheres would effect the latter purpose, but for want of it they are inadmissible. These lenses are of various diameters and foci. For taking miniatures a diameter of 1⅜ is sufficient, the focus being from 4 to 7 inches. For taking distant views they are often composed of two distinct achromatic lenses, arranged at such a distance apart as shall give the flattest field to the image and have a diameter of 2 or 3 inches and a focus of about 12 inches. The best lenses we have seen for these cameras are those made at Vienna by Herr Voigtlander, and in Paris by C. Chevalier and M. Lerabours; the latter has been remarkably successful in constructing them of long focus for taking views. The investigation of the properties and peculiarities of different lenses for Daguerreotype processes has been made in this country by M. Claudet, whose discoveries therein are of the utmost value, not only in the art itself, but in the extension of our knowledge of the physical properties of light. Among other important facts, M. Claudet has found that the photogenic focus and the ordinary conjugate focus of a lens are not coincident, and further that this variation is not constant. We take this opportunity to refer the reader to an instrument of some importance to photographers, the invention of M. Claudet, whereby the ever-varying photogenic powers of the solar rays are accurately measured. This instrument, called a Photographometer, is described in the *Phil. Mag.* for November, 1849.

Daguerreotype Mirrors.—The early experimenters in Daguerreotype employed concave mirrors to form the image, instead of the camera obscura. By the adoption of mirrors the coloured dispersion of light was avoided. The mirrors used for taking miniatures were 7 inches in diameter and about the same focal length. When made of glass the two surfaces should be ground of different curves, so that the two images may be well separated. In some of the original sun-pictures made by M. Neipce, which we saw some years before Daguerre made the discovery public, the images were produced by a common lens not achromatized.

In taking portraits by a camera in the ordinary way the sides are changed; thus, a person having a blemish on the right cheek would be represented in the portrait as having one on the left cheek. To obviate this defect, which is sometimes a serious one, M. Claudet has invented an apparatus which, by passing the reflected image of the person through the camera, this error is rectified.

In taking panoramic views M. Lerabours has ingeniously constructed a camera, the lens of which revolves about a vertical axis; the plate is curved, and a screen is interposed, which revolves with the lens; this screen has a slit opposite the center of the lens, so that only a small part of the image impinges upon the plate at one time. By properly regulating the time and motion, to suit the varied brilliancy of the different parts of the landscape, and also by making the slit opposite the sky narrowest, a very perfect panoramic view is obtained.

THE END.

THE THERMOMETER AND PYROMETER.

The ancients were unacquainted with any more certain mode of marking the variations of temperature, than the indications of the senses, and the limited knowledge derived from observing the melting or combustion of different substances. In modern times, instruments have been invented for noting variable degrees of heat and cold, which, under the designation of *thermometers*, or *thermoscopes*, *pyrometers*, or *pyroscopes*, are now in general use in every part of the civilized world. Their names are derived from the Greek terms θεϱμος, πυϱ, signifying *heat*, *fire*, and μετϱον, σκοπος, a *measure*, an *investigator*.

The principle on which all such instruments are constructed, is *the change of bulk which every body undergoes by alteration of its temperature*.

All homogeneous bodies, except water, within a few degrees of its freezing point, expand by heat and contract by cold.* Their expansion, then, may afford a relative measure of the increase of temperature; and their contraction, of its diminution. This law holds good in gases, liquids, and solids; and, accordingly, matter in those three states of existence has been employed in the construction of instruments for measuring the intensity of heat and cold.

The changes of volume which gases or aeriform bodies undergo, were first employed for this purpose; liquids, such as spirit of wine, oils, or mercury were next used; and lastly, the changes in the bulk of solids were applied to measure the variations of higher temperatures, which would have too much expanded gaseous and liquid bodies.

The designation of *thermoscope* or *pyroscope* might be, with most propriety, applied to such instruments; but, in conformity to common usage, it is proposed in this treatise to apply the general term *thermometer* to the instruments depending on the expansions of aeriform and liquid bodies, and *pyrometer* to those in which the expansion of solids is the measure of the elevation of temperature; and the subject will be treated under the following heads.

I. Of the common Thermometer.
  1. Its history and construction.
  2. The precautions necessary in its construction and graduation.
II. Of the Pyrometer.
III. Of Register Thermometers.
IV. Of the Differential Thermometer, and its modifications.
V. Of some peculiar applications of the Thermometer.
VI. Of the imperfections common to all instruments for the indication of heat.

Chapter I.

Of the Common Thermometer.

§ 1. *History and Construction of the Thermometer.*

The invention of the thermometer, like almost every other discovery of great utility, has been claimed for different philosophers; and national vanity has occasionally been enlisted in support of the pretensions of rival claimants. There seem, however, but two whose titles are worthy of notice.

The Italian writers generally give the honour to their countryman *Santorio Santorio*, long a physician at Venice, and afterwards a professor at Padua, who flourished about the beginning of the seventeenth century; and who had obtained just celebrity by his discovery of the insensible perspiration of the animal frame: the Dutch philosophers as unhesitatingly ascribe it to *Cornelius Drebbel*, a physician of Alkmaar, who appears to have enjoyed a high reputation as a chemist, a mathematician, and an inventive mechanical genius,

---

* Clay, a seeming exception, is not a homogeneous substance, of which afterwards.

Santorio expressly claims the invention as his own,* and he is supported by Borelli † and Malpighi; ‡ the title of Drebbel is considered as undoubted by Boerhaave § and Musschenbroek.∥ It would now be difficult, perhaps, to decide the controversy; but it is worthy of remark, that Santorio, who was born in 1561, and died in 1636,¶ did not publish his claim to the invention till 1626;** and, although thermometers are alluded to by Robert Flud, within the first quarter of that century, yet as he travelled both in Germany and Italy for six years, we can draw no inference from that circumstance. Certain it is, that thermometers were constructed about the same time, both in Italy, and in Holland, on the same principle; and though the instruments of Drebbel were well known in Holland and England, before the fame of Santorio appears to have reached the North-West of Europe, the most recent writers have generally considered the latter as the real inventor of the thermometer. It is, however, by no means improbable that each may be justly entitled to the merit of a discoverer.

Be this as it may, the instrument was, from its imperfect construction, of little use in the hands of either, and required the successive labours of different philosophers to render it a tolerably accurate indicator of the variations of temperature.

The thermometer ascribed to Santorio and to Drebbel, is precisely the same in form and principle. It consists of a glass tube, with a ball blown on one of its extremities A, (*fig*. 1,) and having the other end open. A portion of the air in the ball is expelled by heat, and then the open end of the tube is immersed in any liquid contained in the cup *c*. As the ball cools, the included air diminishes in volume, and the liquid is forced into the stem, as at *b*, by the pressure of the atmosphere, until it replaces the volume of air which was expelled by the heat. When a heated body is applied to the ball A, the air will again be expanded, and depress the liquid in the stem; and, if this stem be a cylinder, a scale of equal parts applied to it will enable the observer to form some idea of the difference between the relative temperature of bodies applied to the ball. On the removal of the heated body, the volume of the included air again diminishes, and the liquid again rises in the stem by atmospheric pressure, until the elasticity of the air within the instrument is in *equilibrio* with that of the surrounding atmosphere. Instruments constructed on this principle are termed *air thermometers;* because their action depends on the elasticity of air; and from their having been originally employed to mark the changes of atmospheric temperature, they are described by the older writers under the name of *weather-glasses;* a denomination also given to barometers.

Drebbel appears to have devised a variety of the instrument more delicate in its indications. The globular form of the common bulb, and its small size, rendered it less susceptible of slight changes than a flattened bulb of larger diameter; and Boerhaave describes the bulb of Drebbel's thermometer, as composed of two shallow segments of large spheres, as in *fig*. 2. A, united at their edges, and in *fig*. 2. B, where it is seen in profile.

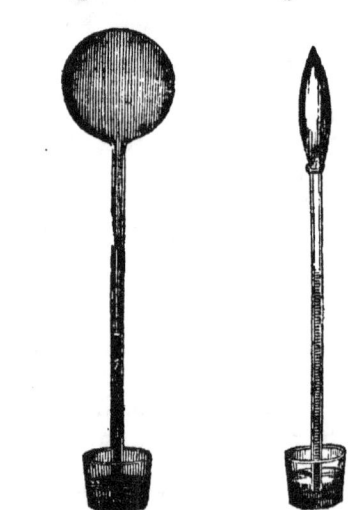

Fig. 2. A.   *Fig*. 2. B.

---

* Comment. in Galen. et in Avicen.
† De Motu Animalium. Prop. clxxv.
‡ Opuscula Posth. p. 30.
§ Elementa Chemiæ, tom. i. p. 152.
∥ Elem. Phil. Nat. § 780.—Tentam Exp. Acad. Cim.
¶ Tiraboschi Storia, tom. viii. P. 1, 323.
** Commentaria in Avicennam.

In the obscure, and often almost unintelligible, writings of our countryman, Dr. Robert Flud, published about the beginning of the seventeenth century, frequent mention is made of the thermometer, or, as he calls it, *speculum*

Calendarium; and the common air thermometer is repeatedly figured in his singular work, *De Philosophia Moysiaca,** with its stem equally divided into an ascending and descending series, each of 7 degrees, respectively appropriated to winter and to summer. It is obvious, that the size of an air thermometer, on such principles, is only limited by convenience, and the length of the column of liquid which the pressure of the atmosphere can sustain in the tube. As originally made, they were unwieldy, they could not be applied to high temperatures, and were, besides, liable to two very important objections, as indicators of the atmospheric changes of temperature,—they were liable to be affected not only by heat and cold, but by the varying pressure of the atmosphere; and the scales adapted to them were arbitrary, and without fixed points for the comparison of observations made with different instruments.

The first objection was foreseen and obviated by the scientific members of the Florentine academy *del Cimento,* assembled under the auspices and patronage of Fernando II., Grand Duke of Tuscany. In the first article in the published transactions of that learned body,† we find a full description and delineation of a thermometer from which the influence of atmospheric pressure is excluded. The expansion of spirit of wine is employed to ascertain the temperature, instead of the dilatation of air; and the instrument is sealed *hermetically,* as it is termed, or has its orifice closed by melting the glass, after the introduction of as much spirit as fills the bulb and a portion of the stem. The method employed by the Florentine academicians is nearly that still used by the makers of the instrument; namely, by heating the bulb in the flame of a lamp, to expel the air, and then immersing the open end of the tube in the liquid destined to fill the thermometer. As the ball cools, the atmospheric pressure forces the liquid into the stem and ball, to supply the *vacuum;* and the orifice is closed by melting with the blowpipe the end of the tube, from which any excess of the liquid may be previously expelled by again heating the ball. (*Fig.* 3.)

The Florentine academicians appear also to have been aware of the necessity of adapting some fixed scale to the tube; but their attempts were not very successful. They described the thermometer as consisting of a ball and tube of such relative size, " that on filling it to a certain mark of its neck with spirit, the cold of snow and ice will not cause it to fall below 20 degrees measured on the stem; nor, on the other hand, the greatest heat of summer expand it more than 80 degrees."* This method is undoubtedly erroneous, inasmuch as the last point could be of no determinate temperature; and their method of graduation is in itself rather rude. The tube is directed to be divided by compasses into ten equal parts, these divisions are to be marked " by a little button of *white* enamel; and these may be further subdivided by the eye, and the intermediate degrees marked by buttons of glass, or of *black* enamel."

Fig. 3.

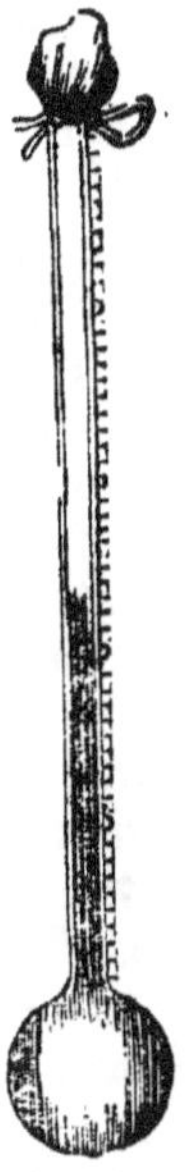

This instrument was variously modified by them to suit different purposes. The ball was occasionally enlarged, and the tube reduced in thickness to render the instrument more sensible; and in the work already quoted, we find a figure of a thermometer of this sort, with the stem spirally twisted to render it more portable, and less liable to accident.

Another invention of those philosophers to indicate changes of temperature may be here noticed. It consisted of hermetically sealed spherules of glass, of different specific gravities, introduced into a wide tube filled with pure spirit. The degree of the Florentine thermometer at which each sank was noted, and by hanging this instrument in an apartment, it somewhat slowly showed the variations of the temperature of the surrounding air.† Imperfect as these attempts were, they paved the way to very important improvements in thermometers.

The indefatigable Boyle appears early to have turned his attention to the improvement of the thermometer, and his first attempts were on the air thermometer, or the weather-glass, as it was then styled. He rendered the instru-

---

* Folio, Goydæ, 1638.
† Saggi di Naturali Esperienze.

* Saggi di Naturali Esperienze, p. 4.
† Saggi, p. 10.

ment more convenient, by making one reservoir for the liquid and for the air at the bottom of the tube; and thus the thermometer might be conveniently dipt in a fluid, or applied to any body for ascertaining its temperature. "The thermometer," he says, "being made by the insertion of a cylindrical pipe of glass (open at both ends) into a phial or bottle, and by exactly stopping with sealing wax, or very close cement, the mouth of the phial, that the included air may have no communication with the external, but by the newly mentioned pipe."* If a portion of any liquid sufficient to cover the lower extremity of the pipe, be contained in the bottle, it is obvious, that the expansion of the enclosed air will elevate the included liquid in the cylindrical pipe; and this liquid will again descend on the contraction of the enclosed air: *fig.* 4, 5. Mr.

Fig. 4.   *Fig.* 5.

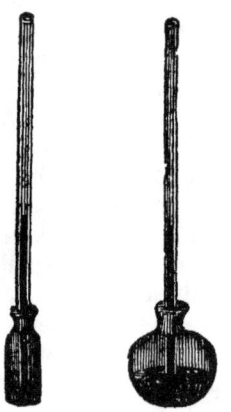

Boyle likewise showed that no dependence could be placed on the indications of *open* air thermometers, under different degrees of atmospheric pressure; and he states, that on plunging the bulbs of different thermometers in liquids of very different specific gravities, as mercury and water, the liquor in the stem stood at unequal heights, though both had been long exposed to the same temperature.

The Florentine thermometer was about that time introduced into England, and duly appreciated by both Boyle and Hooke. The specimen seen by these philosophers was filled with *colourless spirit*, but they made use of spirit of wine, tinged by cochineal, "of a lovely red;" and, says Boyle, "'tis pleasant to see how many inches a mild degree of heat will make the tincture ascend in the cylindrical stem of one of these useful instruments."* Boyle was fully aware of the imperfection of the scales hitherto applied to the thermometer, and sought to discover a remedy. He proposed to obtain a fixed point in the scale, by marking the height of the liquid in the stem of the instrument, when the ball was placed in thawing oil of aniseeds; a point which he preferred to that of thawing ice, because the former could be readily obtained at any time of the year. His method of making two or more comparable thermometers, however, would be found extremely difficult, if not impossible, in practice; it is best explained in his own words. "For if you put such rectified spirit of wine into a glass, the cavity of whose spherical, and that of its cylindrical part, are as near, as may be, equal to corresponding cavities in the former glass, you may by some heedful trials, made with thawed and recongealed oil of aniseeds, bring the second weather-glass to be somewhat like the first; and if you know the quantity of your spirit of wine, you may easily enough make an estimate, by the place it reaches to in the neck of the instrument, whose capacity you also know, whether it expands or contracts itself to the 40th, the 30th, or the 20th part, &c. of the bulk it was of, when the weather-glass was made."†

Boyle mentions that an "*ingenious man*"‡ had proposed the freezing of distilled water, as a fixed point in the scale of thermometers; but he himself evidently gives the preference to the congealing point of aniseed oil. Dr. Halley proposed to regulate the scale by the uniform temperature of such a cavern as that under the Observatory of Paris, or the point at which *spirit boils*; and he also suggests the fixing of the scale from the *boiling of water*. This point he considered as an invariably fixed one, not liable to alteration from external circumstances; and the same idea was entertained by Amontons. With a single point so fixed, the method attempted by Boyle, Halley, and Hooke was to calculate the proportion of the stem to the ball, and thus to determine the increase in bulk of the whole liquid, by a certain temperature. Dr. Hooke describes a method of obtaining this by comparing the expansions

---

* Works of Hon. Robert Boyle, folio, vol. ii. p. 247.

* Works, vol. ii. p. 249.
† Works, vol. ii. p. 247.
‡ He undoubtedly alluded to Hooke.

of the thermometer to be graduated, with those of the liquid in an accurately formed cylinder of metal, two inches in diameter and depth, and having cemented to its top a glass pipe, just $\frac{1}{10}$ of the diameter of the cylinder:* measure off two inches of the stem, above the cylinder of metal, and divide the space between them into 10 equal parts, so that each division of the stem will $= \frac{1}{1000}$ of the capacity of the cylinder. The thermometer to be graduated has the commencement of its scale, or 0°, fixed by marking the point at which the included liquid stands in the stem, when the bulb is plunged in distilled water just beginning to freeze; and the rest of the process he details in these words. " Fill this cylindrical vessel with the same liquid wherewith the thermometers are filled, then place both it and the thermometer you are to graduate in water that is ready to be frozen, and bring the surface of the liquor in the thermometer to the first mark, or 0°; then so proportion the liquor in the cylindrical vessel, that the surface of it may just be at the lower end of the small glass cylinder; then very gently and gradually warm the water, in which both the thermometer and the cylindrical vessel stand, and as you perceive the tinged liquor to rise in both stems, with the point of a diamond give several marks on the stem of the thermometer, at those places which, by comparing the expansion in both stems, are found to correspond to the divisions of the cylindrical vessel; and having by this means marked some few of the divisions on the stem, it will be very easy by these to mark all the rest of the stem, and accordingly to assign to every division a proper character."† This ingenious method is, however, more difficult in execution than any one, unacquainted with such operations, will readily suppose; and it presupposes, what is not easy to accomplish, a very perfect adjustment of the metallic cylinder and the glass stem in the standard instrument.

Dr. Hooke appears invariably to have used in his thermometers spirit of wine "highly tinged with the lovely colour of cochineal, which he deepened by pouring in it some drops of common spirit of urine."

The sagacity of our illustrious Newton saw the importance of improving thermometers. He appears to have been early aware of the inconvenience of spirit as a thermometric fluid, and employed linseed oil to fill his thermometer. It has the advantage of being able to endure a very considerable temperature, without endangering the bursting of the tube, and therefore can be applied to a higher range of temperature than a spirit thermometer. It has the disadvantage, however, to be more sluggish in its movements, and to adhere much to the inside of the tube, while it differs greatly in its fluidity at different temperatures. Newton perceived the convenience of having two fixed points in the construction of the scale; and he used the freezing and boiling points of water as the most suitable for this purpose.* His method of graduating his oil thermometer is given in the *Principia*. The oil, at the temperature of melting snow, was supposed to consist of 10,000 equal parts, which, when heated to the temperature of the human body, expanded to 10,256; at the temperature of water strongly boiling to 10,725; and at that of tin beginning to congeal, to 11,516 parts. In the first instance the ratio of expansion is as 40 to 39; in the second as 15 to 14; and in the third as 15 to 13 nearly. Hence, by taking the temperature of the oil in the ratio of the rarefaction and assuming 12 as the heat of the human body, the temperature of water briskly boiling will be 34 degrees, and of congealing tin 72 degrees.†

Newton continued his scale of temperature farther by observing the rate of cooling of heated bodies, until he could apply his thermometer to them, on the principle that equal decrements of temperature take place in equal times. It was thus he estimated the temperature of iron heated to the utmost intensity of a small kitchen fire equal to 194 degrees, and in a fire of wood about 200 or 210 degrees of the same scale.

It is perhaps unfortunate for the philosophy of heat that more sublime and dazzling objects drew Newton to other pursuits. Though he led the way to just views of the subject, neither he, nor any of his predecessors, appear to have been aware of the influence of the varying atmospheric pressure on the boiling points of liquids; nor do any of

---

* Micrographia.
† Micrographia, p. 39.

* Phil. Trans.
† " Ponendo caloris olei ipsius, rarefactione proportionalis, et pro calore corporis humani scribendo 12, prodest calor aquæ ubi vehementer ebullit partium 34, et calor stanni ubi liquescit prodest postea 72." Princip.

them seem to have considered that the varying expansions of the thermometric liquids at different temperatures, and the expansions of the glass of the instrument, must have materially affected every attempt to subdivide the stem of the thermometer into fractional parts of the whole bulk of the contained liquid.

One of these questions, however, seems to have about that time engaged the attention of philosophers, *viz.* whether equal increments of temperature caused equal expansions of the thermometric fluid. Dr. Brooke Taylor tried the experiment with an oil thermometer, by mixing definite portions of hot and cold water, and measuring the temperature of the mixture. His conclusion was in the affirmative, but the delicacy of his instruments was unequal to the solution of this nice problem, although he has the merit of pointing out how the problem is to be solved.

The construction and uses of thermometers early engaged the attention of the French *Académie des Sciences*; and several were constructed by Mr. Hubin for that learned body; but neither these, nor the thermometers placed in the observatory of Paris by De La Hire, appear to have been graduated on any fixed principle. The *Memoirs of the Academy* contain several descriptions of thermometers, and an account of many interesting observations, with these instruments; but the first alteration in their construction deserving of notice is the air thermometer of Geoffroy, which from the short description appears to be an improvement on that of Boyle, inasmuch as it is not affected by atmospheric pressure. He describes the tube as without any opening, except one, which descends almost to the bottom of the ball, and there dips into a small portion of coloured liquid.* There is no figure given in the original, and but a very rude one in our *Philosophical Transactions*,† seemingly from the description. It is not stated how the ball was joined to the tube, but it was most probably by cement, as represented in *fig.* 6.

M. Amontons clearly saw the importance of fixed points in the thermometric scale, and proposed to obtain them from the boiling point of water.* His thermometer consisted of a tube four feet in length, ending below in a ball bent upwards, as in *fig.* 7, and open at the other extremity. The measure of the temperature was the elasticity of a given portion of air included in the ball, and subjected to a pressure equal to *two atmospheres*, by adding to the usual atmospheric pressure that of a column of mercury of 28 French inches. Each half-inch of his tube is therefore equal to one inch under the usual pressure; and hence at a mean pressure of 28 French inches, the volume of the compressed air is really equal to 56 inches under the usual pressure.

In passing from the mean temperature of a Parisian spring to the heat of boiling water, Mr. Amontons found that these 56 inches were increased by one-third, or 18 inches 8 lines, and therefore he fixed the boiling point of his scale at $56 + 18,8 = 74$ inches 8 lines. To measure this on Amontons's principle a tube of 47 inches is quite sufficient; for 74 inches 8 lines minus 28 inches, the atmospheric pressure which need not be considered in the length of the tube, is equal to 46 inches 8 lines; and, indeed, as in Amontons's process, the compression at high temperatures is rather more than in the duplicate ratio of the air we breathe, the mercury in boiling water will not rise above 45 of his scale.† There is a slight discrepancy between the original account of Amontons's thermometer and that given by Martine, who states its boiling point at 73 inches, and its freezing point at $51\frac{1}{2}$ inches; but, according to the Academicians, the latter will be at 52 inches and about 8 lines. The ingenious contrivance of the double pressure enabled him to apply the instrument to measure the temperature of boiling water, by a tube less than four feet in length.‡

Although the idea of Amontons was a fine approximation to an universal standard for a thermometric scale, the instrument is liable to such objections

---

* Mém. Acad. tom. xiii. p. 120. It was read in May, 1709.
† Phil. Trans. vol. xxiii. p. 962.

* Mémoires de l'Acad. for 1702.
† Mémoires de l'Acad. des Sciences, tom. xv.
‡ Mém. Acad. des Sciences, tom. xv. for 1702

that its principle seems scarcely ever to have been put in practice, except by its inventor and the Marchese Poleni.* It is difficult to construct two instruments which shall correspond, from the varying expansibility of air according to its moisture or dryness; the indications are liable to be affected by the fluctuations of atmospheric pressure; it is liable to be deranged by the escape of a portion of the included air, when the instrument is moved about; it is, moreover, too unwieldy, and very liable to be broken.

Much about the period when those attempts to perfect the thermometer were made in France, important improvements on it were effected in the north of Germany and in Holland, by the introduction of quicksilver as the thermometric fluid.

The objections we have stated to the use of the spirit thermometers, and to the oil thermometer of Newton, led the way to the employment of quicksilver in the construction of the instrument. Dr. Halley alludes to several advantages of quicksilver as a thermometric fluid, but seems to have rejected it on the ground of its slight expansion by heat,† although this objection might have so easily been obviated by increasing the disproportion between the bulb and the diameter of the tube. On this account the claim set up for his title to priority of invention may justly be denied. It is most probable that science is indebted for this great improvement to Roëmer, the celebrated astronomer of Dantzic, to whom the invention is ascribed by Boerhaave, as well as the first idea of the scale now known as that of Fahrenheit. Boerhaave further adds, that as early as 1709, Roëmer observed with that instrument a natural cold so intense as to sink the mercury to the beginning of the scale.‡ Thermometers of this construction began to be made by Daniel Gabriel Fahrenheit, a native of Dantzic, who afterwards lived at Amsterdam, in so admirable a manner, that he has generally been considered the original inventor; they were speedily spread over the north of Europe under his name, and still maintain their ground in several countries, especially in Britain.

It has commonly been alleged, that at the time when Roëmer's or Fahrenheit's scale was proposed, its zero was derived from the artificial cold produced by a mixture of salt and snow, then supposed to be the lowest possible reduction of temperature. This, however, seems to be inaccurate: Boerhaave * gives a different account of the matter, which is repeated in the *Philosophical Transactions.* † The zero was fixed from " the lowest cold observed in *Ysland*," (Iceland); which was supposed to be as low a temperature as was likely to become the object of philosophic investigation: but when artificial methods of reducing the temperature of bodies much lower, and occasional natural colds brought the mercury below that point, a scale of equal parts was extended below the 0°; the ascending series of degrees being distinguished by sign + or *plus*, and the descending series by the sign — or *minus*.

The principle which dictated the *peculiar division* of the scale is as follows. When the instrument stood at the greatest cold of Iceland, or 0 degree, it was computed to contain 11,124 equal parts of quicksilver; which, when plunged in melting snow, expanded to 11,156 parts; hence the intermediate space was divided into 32 equal portions, and 32° was taken as the freezing point of water: when the thermometer was plunged in boiling water, the quicksilver was expanded to 11,336 parts; and therefore 212° was marked as the boiling point of that fluid.‡ *In practice*, Fahrenheit determined the divisions of his scale from two fixed points, the freezing and boiling of water: *the theory* of the division, if we may so speak, was derived from the lowest cold observed in Iceland, and the expansions of a given portion of mercury.

The mercurial thermometer was used by the Italian philosopher Renaldini before the end of the seventeenth century: and he proposed, in 1694, an ingenious method of graduating it between the freezing and boiling points of water, by successive mixtures of determinate weights of boiling and ice cold water.

The great advantages of Fahrenheit's thermometer over every other previous invention, consisted in its applicability to a greater range of tempera-

---

* Phil. Trans. No. 421.
† Phil. Trans. vol. xvii. p. 652.
‡ Boerhaavii Chemiæ, tom. i. p. 720.

* Chemiæ, tom. i. p. 720.
† Vol. xliv. p. 680.
‡ For 11156 — 11124 = 32, and 11336 — 1124 = 212.

ture, from the freezing to the boiling point of quicksilver, in its not soiling the containing tube, and in its receiving the impressions of heat and cold more readily, while its density rendered capillary tubes filled with it perfectly visible; and thus the instrument became more portable and delicate. We may also remark, that at the period of its invention, there was no other scale in use that could pretend to vie with it in accuracy; and it still possesses the peculiar advantages, that from the lowness of its 0°, the observer is seldom troubled with *negative* degrees, and from the number of its divisions has rarely, in ordinary operations, to use fractions of a degree.

We are indebted also to Fahrenheit for the knowledge of the fluctuation of the boiling point of water, according to the difference of atmospheric pressure.* Le Monnier, in 1739, confirmed this fact, by noting the temperature of boiling water on the top of Mount Canigou, one of the Pyrennees; and in 1744 it was fully established by Martin Folkes, who found that water boiled on the summit of Pic du Midi 15° of Fahrenheit's scale lower than at Bagneres; and at the latter place $3\frac{1}{2}$° lower than at Bordeaux; while he proved that elevation in the atmosphere had no sensible influence on the stability of the freezing point.† These facts led to an important correction in fixing the boiling point of water or other liquids.

It would now be a waste of time to describe minutely the various thermometers which were in use in France and England before the time of Fahrenheit. They were all without fixed points in the scale; and though they were vaunted as constructed after the models in the Royal Observatory at Paris, or in the apartments of the Royal Society of London, they gave most discordant results. An analysis of the most noted of them has been elaborately and ingeniously attempted by Dr. Martine in his valuable Essays, and the results presented in the very convenient form of a tabular view. We shall therefore pass at once to notice some of the other more accurate thermometers that have been employed in different parts of Europe, although the principle in them all is similar to what has been already described.

The thermometer with which the Dutch philosopher Cruquius made the observations published in the *Philosophical Transactions*, (vol. xxxiii. No. 381,) was an air thermometer, on which he states the freezing point of water to be indicated by 1070°, and boiling water by 1510°: the lowest known cold, which seems to have been the beginning of his scale, he gives = 1000°.

The objections to the thermometer of Amontons are clearly stated by Reaumur,* who proposed to adopt the freezing and boiling points of water as fixed points in the scale, but employed spirit as the thermometric fluid. He unquestionably fell into error when he stated that 1000 parts of strong spirit dilated to 1087.5 parts in passing from the freezing to the boiling point of water; for how could strong spirit sustain so high a temperature without being partially converted into vapour? His proposal was to use spirit of just such strength, that between these two temperatures it should expand from 1000 to 1080; and, commencing his scale or 0° at the freezing point of water, he made the boiling point 80°. The principle of this construction was good; but Dr. Martine has shown that from the large size of the bulbs of his thermometers, which were from 3 to 4 inches in diameter, and the short time they were immersed in the freezing mixture, they could not have acquired an uniform temperature; and accordingly Martine found their freezing point too high,† and the error in the boiling point from the cause already alluded to, must have been still greater.

These errors might have been obviated by the use of quicksilver instead of spirit. This was accordingly soon done; by whom first is uncertain, although there is strong reason to believe by De Luc; and the mercurial thermometer, with the 0° at the freezing point of water, and 80° as its boiling point, soon became general in France, and well known over Europe under the name of *Reaumur's Thermometer*. The only material objections to such a scale, when the instrument is accurately made, arise from the largeness of the divisions rendering fractional parts of a degree of frequent occurrence, and the elevation of 0° often introducing + and — degrees in a series of observations, even at common natural temperatures.

The mercurial thermometer of Mons.

---

* Phil. Trans. xxxiii. No. 381.
† Phil. Trans. vol. xliii. p. 32.

* Mémoires de l'Acad. des Sciences, for 1730
† Martine's Essays, Edin. 1792, p. 23.

J. De Lisle of St. Petersburg, differs little in principle from the instruments just mentioned; but its graduation is inverted. His 0° is at the boiling point of water, and he continues the graduation *downwards*: and conceiving the mercury, at that temperature, to be divided into 100,000 parts, he determined the degrees by the contractions of the whole mercury as it cooled, expressed in such parts.* The distance between the freezing and boiling points of water on this scale is 150°, as ascertained by Dr. Martine, who examined one of Dr. Lisle's original thermometers: but this thermometer seems to possess no advantage over those just described, and never came into general use except in Russia, where it is still employed.

Our countryman, Dr. Stephen Hales, employed another thermometer in his experiments on vegetable physiology. The 0° was at freezing water, and the highest point was ascertained by placing the instrument in hot water, on which wax was just beginning to congeal; the intervening space was divided into 100°.† This near approach to a true centesimal scale was defeated by the uncertainty of the upper point, arising from his using spirit instead of mercury in the tube, and the difficulty of ascertaining the exact moment of the congelation of the wax.

In the year 1742, the Swedish philosopher Celsius, professor at Upsal, divided *centesimally* the thermometer known in the north by his name, and which has, since its tacit adoption by the French chemists, obtained additional celebrity as the *Thermomètre Centigrade*. Celsius commences his scale at the freezing point of water, and divides the space between that point and the height of the mercurial column in boiling water into 100°. This appears a more natural and simple division than any that had been previously proposed, and it possesses several advantages; but it has two inconveniences of some importance in many practical operations. Thus, from the high position of the 0°, natural colds are frequently to be noted by a descending series of figures, and one column of observations may be hence embarrassed by + and − degrees; while from the large space intercepted between the degrees, the observer is frequently obliged to compute fractional parts of a degree.

M. de la Lande, in 1804, proposed a new thermometric scale, the 0° or mean point of which he would fix at the mean temperature of the earth; which he gives as = to 9°.5 of Reaumur's scale; and his degrees were to be the ten millionth part of the volume of the mercury in the instrument. Among the advantages of such a division, he considers the simplification of expression in meteorological observations—thus, 30° would express the heat of summer and cold of winter; 40° a hot summer and severe winter; while the smallness of the degrees would obviate the use of fractions of a degree. The boiling point of water would be at + 133, and the congelation of mercury at − 74°; ice would melt at − 18°, and the zero of Fahrenheit would be at − 44.*

This proposition has never been adopted; and its advantages seem overrated by the inventor. It only obviates one of the objections urged against the scale of Celsius, and is inferior in simplicity either to a millesimal division of the interval between the freezing and boiling point of water, or to the thermometric scale proposed by the late Dr. Murray of Edinburgh. That acute philosopher proposed to employ the freezing and boiling points of mercury itself as the extremes of his scale, and to divide the intervening space into 1000°. It is a more natural division than any hitherto proposed, inasmuch as it is taken from relations of the best thermometric fluid itself to heat: and if we suppose these two points to have been accurately fixed at − 40° and + 655° of Fahrenheit, the freezing point of water would be 99°, and its boiling point 347° on Murray's scale.

The advantages of this scale, are that it will very seldom, in natural temperatures, render the introduction of − degrees necessary, and the smallness of the divisions supersede the employment of fractional parts of a degree, in ordinary cases; two circumstances of considerable importance in a long series of thermometric observations.

Magellan informs us,† that M. Achard of Berlin invented a thermometer for ascertaining high temperature, which is a true *Pyrometer*, and might have been introduced in the next section. It consists of a ball and tube of semitranslucent porcelain, highly baked,

---

* Phil. Trans. vol. xxxix. p. 221, for 1736.
† Vegetable Statics, vol. i. p. 58.

* Journal de Physique, 1804. Nicholson's Journal, 8vo. vol. ii. p. 61.
† Sur la Théorie du Feu Elémentaire, 1780.

containing a fusible alloy of two parts of bismuth, one of lead, and one of tin. In the temperature of the air, it remains solid in the tube; it becomes fluid about the boiling point of water; then, as a fluid, expands by increase of temperature; and its expansion being seen through the semitranslucent tube, which is divided into equal parts or degrees, becomes an indication of the temperature applied to the ball.

This invention promises to be of considerable utility, and is capable of extension by the employment of less fusible metals. From the simplicity of its construction, it is rather surprising that it has not been more generally known, and employed in potteries, where the instrument could be easily made. An instrument on this construction would be a better method of uniting the scales of the common thermometer and pyrometer than any heretofore employed.

Of these various thermometric scales there are but three in very general use, *viz.* that of Fahrenheit, Celsius, and Reaumur. Fahrenheit's is chiefly used in Britain, North America, and Holland: the scale of Celsius was adopted by the French, and is now employed in most parts of the north and middle of Europe: Reaumur's was the only one used in France before the Revolution, and is still that best known in Spain and in some other continental states; but it is further important, as affording the terms in which numerous very valuable observations are recorded.

For these reasons it is useful to have formulæ for readily converting one scale into the equivalent degrees of the other two. The freezing point of *water* on Fahrenheit's scale is at 32°, and on those of Celsius and Reaumur at 0°, while it boils on each respectively at 180°, 100°, and 80°, above that point. Hence the degrees of Fahrenheit are to those of Celsius as $180:100 = 18:10 = 9:5$, and to those of Reaumur as $180:80 = 18:8 = 9:4$ —, or 9° of Fahrenheit are equal to 5° of Celsius and to 4° of Reaumur. Therefore, when we wish to convert the degrees of Celsius into those of Fahrenheit, we have to multiply the number of the former by 9, divide by 5, and add 32; to reduce the degrees of Fahrenheit into those of Celsius, the *converse* of the proposition will give the required result; that is, from the degree of Fahrenheit subtract 32, then multiply by 5, and divide by 9.

When we wish to convert the degrees of Reaumur into those of Fahrenheit, we have to multiply by 9, divide by 4, and add 32; and subtracting 32 from the given degree of Fahrenheit, multiplying the remainder by 4, and dividing by 9, will give the equivalent degree of Reaumur's scale.

The following short formulæ will apply to each case:

1. $F = \dfrac{9C}{5} + 32.$

2. $C = \dfrac{(F-32) \times 5}{9}.$

3. $F = \dfrac{9R}{4} + 32.$

4. $R = \dfrac{(F-32) \times 4}{9}.$

These formulæ apply to all degrees above the freezing point of water; but when negative degrees of Celsius are to be converted into the equivalents on Fahrenheit's scale, multiply the degree of Celsius by 9, divide by 5, and the difference between the quotient and 32 is the required degree of Fahrenheit: or when negative degrees of Fahrenheit are to be reduced to their equivalents on the scale of Celsius, add 32 to the given degree of Fahrenheit, then multiply by 5, and divide by 9. By substituting 4 for 5, the same formulæ will apply to Fahrenheit and Reaumur, all which may be thus expressed:

1. $-F = \dfrac{9C}{5} \backsim 32.$

2. $-C = \dfrac{(F+32) \times 5}{9}.$

3. $-F = \dfrac{9R}{4} \backsim 32.$

4. $-R = \dfrac{(F+32) \times 4}{9}.$

The formulæ are convenient for reducing a few examples from one scale to another; but when they perpetually occur in reading or writing it is very useful to have comparative tables, from which, by one glance, the desired information may be obtained.

§ 2. *Precautions necessary to be observed in constructing accurate Thermometers.*

A general idea has been already given of the mode of constructing a thermometer, but where much accuracy is required there are many niceties that demand attention.

1. The tube should be of equal diameter throughout the whole stem. As obtained from the glass-house, the tubes are in reality frusta of very elongated hollow cones, which, by extension, become more or less nearly cylindrical; and as the divisions of the scale are usually equal, it is very important that the tube should not perceptibly differ from a true cylinder.

For these purposes, after a tube has been chosen by the eye as equal in calibre as possible, the best makers blow a bulb on it, and introduce a short column of mercury into the stem, perhaps an inch in length, which is accurately measured on a fine scale of equal parts, in different portions of the tube, as the column is, by the heat of the hand, moved from the bulb to the open extremity of the tube. Should the mercurial column subtend the same number of divisions on the scale in every part of the tube, it may be considered as a perfect tube for a thermometer.

The late Mr. Wilson, of Glasgow, introduced thermometric tubes of an *elliptical* bore. The advantage of this form is, that a very small column of mercury is much more visible when it is expanded at right angles to the line of vision. If due precaution be taken to ensure the equality of the tube this form answers well, especially for ordinary purposes; but where great nicety is required, we would recommend the cylindrical tube.

2. The form and proportion of the bulb may vary according to the purpose for which the instrument is to be applied. The larger the bulb in proportion to the stem, so much more delicately susceptible of changes of temperature will be the thermometer. The spherical bulb is to be preferred, for this shape is least likely to be affected by the varying pressure of the air; but when the bulb is very large this form renders the thermometer less susceptible of minute changes of temperature, and pyriform or cylindrical bulbs are usually adopted. All large bulbs are more or less sensibly affected even by slight pressure. An examination of more than fifty common thermometers, with large spherical bulbs, in the work-shop of an excellent artist, afforded the writer of this article an opportunity of observing that by slightly compressing their bulbs between the finger and thumb, the mercury in the stem rose and fell alternately several degrees, as the pressure was increased or diminished. The bulb and stem are usually in the same straight line, but for various purposes the bulb is occasionally placed at various angles to the stem.

In forming the bulb the mouth must not be employed to blow it, otherwise moisture will condense in the tube, which is expelled with much difficulty, and if suffered to remain, will greatly impair the value of the thermometer. Good instrument-makers use a small bottle of caoutchouc, or elastic gum, fastened by a thread on one end of the tube, while the other extremity is softened by the flame of a tallow lamp, urged by a blowpipe. By compressing the bottle, after the orifice of the softened end of the tube is closed by the aid of another rod of glass, a bulb is formed of any required size; but a neat workman will rarely consider the first blown bulb sufficiently well formed for his purpose. It is generally dilated till it bursts; the glass, while still soft, is compressed into a rounded mass, and a fresh bulb formed of a regular shape, and size proportioned to the calibre of the tube. Should the artist not intend to fill the tube immediately, he usually hermetically seals the other end of the tube to prevent the entrance of damp air or dust.

3. The precautions necessary in filling thermometers with mercury are exceedingly well given in Nicholson's *Chemistry*.*

The mercury should be clean, dry, and recently boiled, to expel air as much as possible. Mercury is often cleaned by thermometer-makers by agitating it in a phial, for some time, with sand, and then straining it through leather; for nice instruments it should be distilled from iron filings, or reduced from its sulphurets, in clean iron vessels, at a moderate heat.

The bulb to be filled is heated in the flame of a lamp, and the open extremity of the tube is immersed in the mercury; as the bulb cools, the pressure of the atmosphere forces the fluid into the tube and ball. Mr. Nicholson recommends, that the bulb should be but moderately heated at first; so as, on cooling, to become only half filled. He advises the open end of the tube to be

---
* Edition 3rd, p. 24.

kept under the surface of the mercury, and the instrument to be retained as nearly in the horizontal position as possible, while the flame of a newly snuffed candle is applied to the bulb, so as to boil the included mercury. Thus the remaining air will be expelled; and on removing the candle, the mercury will suddenly fill the ball and part of the tube.

4. To ensure a delicate thermometer, the mercury is next to be boiled in the thermometer. For this purpose a slip of clean writing paper is to be rolled tightly around the upper part of the tube, so as to form, beyond the orifice, a cup or cylinder capable of containing as much mercury as the bulb: secure this round the tube with a thread, put a drop of mercury into the paper cavity, and again apply heat to the bulb, holding the tube by the part covered by the paper. The mercury will soon boil, and about one-half of the contents of the ball will rush up into the paper cup. On removing the bulb from the candle, the mercury will suddenly return. Repeat this operation again and again, until the speedy boiling of the mercury, and the diminished noise and agitation, show that the whole has been well heated, and air and moisture expelled from it.

Should there be the least moisture in the tube before this part of the operation, it is very likely to burst the bulb; and the same accident is likely to happen, if the mercury be too strongly boiled the first or second time.

An experienced eye will readily judge what range of scale the thermometer will have; but this point can easily be ascertained, before the tube is closed, by heating the bulb in the mouth, and then immersing it in cold water or melting ice. When the latter is used, the operator can at pleasure fix how far from the bulb he will have the freezing point; for, by keeping the tube more or less filled, he can adjust that point to any desired height.

5. The tube is now to be *hermetically sealed*, that is, closed by the fusion of the glass at the upper extremity, which for this purpose is previously drawn to a capillary orifice. When it is intended to free the tube entirely from air, which is the best method with mercurial thermometers, heat is again to be gently applied to the bulb, which at the same moment is to be softened by another flame, and closed in the usual way, as soon as the mercury reaches the extremity of the tube. When the ball has cooled a little the sealing is rendered more secure by fusing the glass more fully around the top, so as completely to obliterate the orifice. If the vacuum be perfect, the mercury will fall to the extremity of the tube on inverting the thermometer, unless the calibre be absolutely capillary; in which case capillary attraction will overcome the force of gravity, and the mercury will retain its position in the tube, in every situation of the instrument.

Where there is a complete vacuum in the tube, the mercury must be well boiled before the sealing, as above directed; and when we choose a thermometer, the ready falling of the mercury, on inversion of the tube, is the best test we can have that the mercury has been well freed from air and moisture. This vacuum is not, however, so essential to the true action of the thermometer as was once supposed. A thermometer with a small dilatation of the tube when sealed, containing some common air, has lately been recommended as preferable to the instrument with a vacuum on the surface of the mercury.

M. Flaugergues[*] first called attention to the fact, that when old thermometers are placed in melting ice, they seldom fall quite so low as the mark of freezing on their stems, especially when the whole air has been expelled from them. This difference he found to amount sometimes to 0.9 of a degree. The same fact has been confirmed by MM. De la Rive and F. Marcet,[†] and also by Bellani[‡] and Arago.[§] The writer of this article possesses three thermometers; one very delicate, made by Ramsden, and two well made instruments by Lovi of Edinburgh, all which have been in his possession upwards of a quarter of a century. On lately placing them in a vessel filled with pounded ice, in a warm apartment, they all showed a slight elevation of the freezing point. That made by Ramsden has a capillary tube and small spherical ball; the other two have small pyriform bulbs, and the mercury readily falls to the extremity of the tube on inverting them: yet Ramsden's stood about 0.6 of a degree above the freezing point, and the other were just perceptibly above it.

---
[*] Bibliothèque Universelle, tom. xx. 1823.
[†] Ib. tom. xxii.
[‡] Giornale di Fisica, tom. v.
[§] Annales de Chimie, tom. xxxii.

M. Flaugergues attributes this change to the effect of long continued atmospheric pressure on the bulbs of thermometers, in which there is no air to counteract it. De la Rive and Marcet give the same explanation, and remark how this circumstance must affect the result of all experiments on the cold produced in vacuo.

Arago is not inclined to attribute this elevation of the zero to atmospheric pressure on the bulb; since he found it equally affecting thermometers with very thick and very thin bulbs. He inclines to ascribe it to the disengagement of air, which either adhered to the glass or the mercury, and its accumulation in the upper part of the bulb, so as to affect the column in the stem.

The most complete observations on this point are those of Bellani,* who acknowledges two sources of variation in the zero of thermometers. That elevation of the zero, first noticed by Flaugergues, according to him, goes on gradually increasing for a limited period, but ceases after a year or two. He ascribes it to the extreme slowness with which glass once softened has the equilibrium among its particles restored. He found, that some months after graduation, a thermometer did not sink quite to the freezing point when immersed in melting ice; if laid by for some months, and again tried, its zero will be still higher; but after some time this irregularity ceases. He found that this effect was not diminished by leaving the thermometer open at the top, and it was sensible even in spirit thermometers.

The other irregularity noticed by Bellani is detected in the following manner.—Let a thermometer, having such a range that $\frac{1}{10}$ of a degree is appreciable, after lying by for some months, be plunged into melting ice, and its height accurately noted, then into boiling water, and again into ice, it will now stand *lower* by about $\frac{1}{10}$ of a degree than at its first immersion in the liquefying ice. This effect he ascribes to the extreme slowness with which the expanded glass can regain its former state of contraction, compared to the mercury.

These deductions appear to be perfectly just; and we are further indebted to Bellani for an ingenious method of showing that the air, if not wholly, is chiefly retained in thermometers and barometers by the glass, not by the mercury. He introduced a portion of unboiled mercury into a bulb, containing mercury which had ceased to give out any air, and found that this introduction did not renew the agitations which the first application of heat to the bulb had occasioned.

The difficulty of freeing thermometers from air is admitted by Arago, while he recommends boiling the mercury in the bulb as the best method of effecting the expulsion of the air; and he quotes some unpublished experiments of Dulong, to show the tedious manipulations which are necessary for this purpose.

We would recommend the boiling to be performed in the manner stated, until the agitation of the fluid caused by the air ceases; and after the tube is closed, the observations of Bellani would incline us to recommend, for delicate instruments, that the attempt to fix the freezing point should be deferred, until the glass might be supposed to have contracted to its state of equilibrium; after which, there would probably be little change in the dimensions of the bulb.

6. We come now to the last and most delicate step of the process, the adaptation of the scale to the instrument.

In the *manufacture* of thermometers this is conveniently done by plunging the new instrument, along with a standard thermometer, into two liquids at different temperatures: but the graduation of *this standard instrument* is a work of such nicety and importance, that a committee of seven members of the Royal Society was formed to investigate the subject, and their elaborate report is given in vol. lxvii. part ii., where all the requisite circumstances are distinctly noticed, and the best manipulations minutely described.

Two fixed points are sought; and the freezing and boiling points of water are most convenient for that purpose. To find the first, nothing more is necessary than to place the thermometer to be graduated, after it is filled, in melting snow or ice, in such quantity around the ball and tube, as to bring it to the desired temperature. When the mercury has become stationary in the tube, a mark is to be made on the tube with a file, just opposite to the top of the mercurial column; and that mark fixes the freezing point of the scale of the instrument. The determination of the boiling point

---

* Bellani, Giornale di Fisica, tom. v.

is much more difficult, because it is affected by atmospherical pressure, and even by the form of the vessel in which the water is heated.

The Committee of the Royal Society* recommend that the boiling point ought to be fixed under a barometrical pressure of 29.80 inches. For the graduation of the thermometer they recommend that the bulb should not be immersed in the water; because they found, that according to the depth of this immersion the mercury rose to a greater height in the tube. They recommend a vessel of tin plate, provided with a cover which fits easily on, and rendered steam-tight by a ring of woollen cloth between it and the vessel. This cover has two apertures—a chimney, with an area not less than half a square inch, and two or three inches high, to carry off the steam of the boiling water; and a hole for a cork, through which the thermometer tube is inserted in such a manner, that the ball does not touch the surface of the water, but may be surrounded with an atmosphere of steam; while no more of the tube should be above the cork than is sufficient to show the height to which the mercury rises when the water is briskly boiling. When all things are thus adjusted, a thin plate of metal is to be laid over the chimney, to prevent the escape of the steam as it is formed; heat is to be applied to the bottom of the vessel; and when the mercury has remained a few minutes stationary in the atmosphere of steam, its height is carefully to be marked with a file on the tube.

The water may be distilled, or any soft water, such as clear rain water, be used; for, if there be much saline ingredient in the water, this will affect the boiling point, and may lead to error.

Various mechanical contrivances have been proposed for more conveniently fixing the tube in the cover, but they are of little comparative importance. Some prefer plunging the ball into the water to the depth of two or three inches: in this case there is no necessity for a plate of metal on the chimney, nor for the tightness of the cover; but the adjustment of the boiling point is to be made for the barometer at 29.50 inches. To those unprovided with such a vessel the following method is recommended. Wrap several folds of linen, or flannel, round the tube, nearly as high as the supposed boiling point, which may be guessed at by previous immersion of the bulb in boiling water: hold the thermometer in an ascending current of boiling rain water about two or three inches below the surface; pour boiling water three or four times on the covering of the tube, at intervals of some seconds; and waiting a few seconds, after the last affusion, to allow the water to be in brisk ebullition, mark the height of the mercury in the tube, which will be the boiling point of the instrument.

Having thus obtained two fixed points, the freezing and boiling points of water, it is easy to mark off corresponding divisions on the scale which is to be graduated. If the tube be truly cylindrical, nothing more is necessary than to divide the intervening space into as many equal parts as it is intended to have degrees between those points. Should the tube not be of uniform bore, the size of the divisions ought to be accommodated to the inequalities of the tube. This may be done by taking intermediate points in mixtures of water at different temperatures; and after marking them on the tube, proportioning the size of the degrees, at short intervals, to the varying diameter of the tube. This method of graduating from intermediate points ought, in nice instruments, to be adopted, however true the tube may appear; but a tube with sensible inequalities is in general to be avoided.

Although it would be advisable to fix the boiling point when the barometer is at the height above recommended, this may be attended with serious inconvenience to artists; and philosophers have therefore investigated the correction to be made for every ordinary variation of atmospheric pressure.

The first considerable series of experiments on this subject are those of De Luc, in 1762, published in his interesting *Recherches sur les Modifications de l'Atmosphere*,* which were extended and verified by Sir George Shuckburg† in 1775 and 1778. Employing Reaumur's scale, De Luc ascertained, that if y represent the height of the barometer, T the height of the thermometer above the freezing point, expressed in hundredths of a degree of this scale, when immersed in boiling water; and a the constant number

---

* Phil. Trans. vol. lxvii. part ii.

Vol. i. 382; vol. ii. 333.
† Phil. Trans. vol. lxix. part ii.

10387, the following formula will express the height of such thermometer when plunged in boiling water under every variation of barometric pressure.

$$\frac{99}{200000} \log y - a = T;$$

or, as expressed in the more usual way of considering all the figures after the index as decimals, De Luc's formula would stand thus:

$$\frac{99 \times 100}{2} \log y - a = T.$$

De Luc's researches and his formula are reduced to English measures, and adapted to Fahrenheit's thermometer by Horsley, in a valuable paper in the *Philosophical Transactions*;* where a table is computed for the direction of artists in adjusting the boiling point. It is unnecessary to give his equation of the boiling point, because the later experiments of Shuckburg, and of the Committee of the Royal Society, enable us to present a more complete table for the direction of British artists in correcting the height of the boiling point in every ordinary fluctuation of the barometer.

Barometer when the boiling point is found by immersion in		Correction in 1000ths of the interval between freezing and boiling of water.
Steam.	Water.	
	30·60	10
	·50	9
30·71	·41	8
·50	·29	7
·48	·18	6 Lower.
·37	·07	5
·25	·95	4
·14	·84	3
·03	·73	2
29·91	·61	1
·80	·50	0
·69	29·39	1
·58	·28	2
·47	·17	3
·36	·06	4
·25	28·95	5 Higher.
·14	·84	6
·03	·73	7
28·92	·62	8
·81	·51	9
·70		10
·59		

The use of this table requires no further explanation: but it is necessary to remark, that it presupposes the thermometric tube to be cylindrical, or of equal

---

* Vol. lxiv. part i.

dimensions throughout, before the indications of the table can be received as *quite* correct; yet, unless the irregularity of the tube be considerable, a *small* correction will scarcely produce any sensible error in the instrument.

In proportioning the bulb to the tube, the eye and experience of the artist are usually judged sufficient for the purpose; or they are copied as nearly as possible from standard instruments. M. Durand has, however, thought it necessary to propose an algebraic formula for determining the proportions they ought to bear to each other; but there are practical difficulties in the way of its application, which render his formula an exercise rather of his own ingenuity than of utility to the artist.

During the various improvements of the common thermometer, the air thermometer was almost wholly neglected until of late years; but the attention of philosophers was directed to the changes of bulk which *solids* undergo by alterations of temperature, as a measure of the relative degrees of heat.

Chapter II.

History and Construction of Pyrometers.

1. The impracticability of applying the known modifications of the thermometer to bodies much heated, induced the celebrated Musschenbroek, before the middle of the last century, to employ the expansions of solid rods of metal to indicate the temperature of such bodies; and he gave the name of *pyrometer* to his invention.

As the expansions of solids are extremely minute, it was necessary to devise some method of rendering them perceptible; and the mechanism represented in *fig.* 8 was the Dutch philosopher's arrangement for this purpose. *a* is a metallic prism 5.8 inches in length and 0.3 in thickness, resting in a notch in the upright *i*, where it is secured by a screw, and heated by the lamp *b* with five wicks. The prism is pinned to the end of a bar *c*, which has twenty-five teeth in one inch of its length, and forms a rack sliding smoothly on the table of the instrument through the two holdfasts seen in the figure, and playing in the six-leaved pinion *d* on the same axis as the wheel *f*, which is furnished with sixty teeth. This wheel plays in another pinion *e*, of six leaves also, which is on the axis carrying the index *g*, which

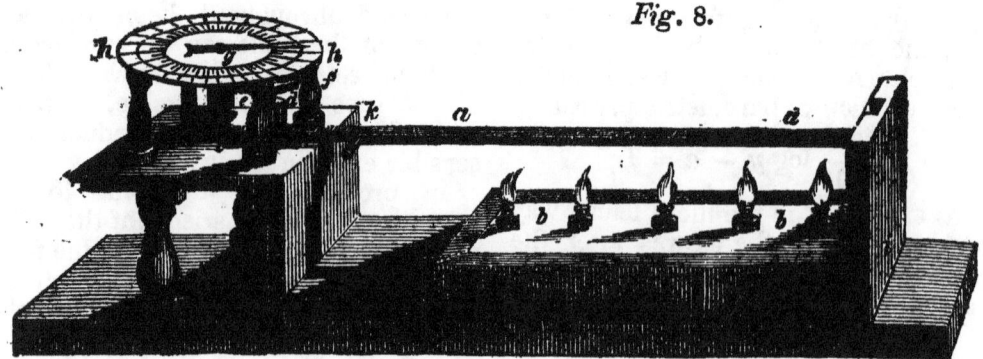

Fig. 8.

moves round the circle *h*, divided into 300°. The consequence of this arrangement is, that if the expansion of the metal were to push the rack *e* one inch forward, it would turn the pinion *d* $4\frac{1}{6}$ times round; and the wheel *f*, moving at the same rate, will carry the pinion *e*, and consequently the index $(10 \times 4\frac{1}{6})$ = $41\frac{2}{3}$ round. Hence the index would have moved over $(41\frac{2}{3} \times 300)$, or 12,500 divisions of the scale; or each degree of the instrument is equivalent to $\frac{1}{12500}$ of an inch of the expansion of the prism *a*. Similar prisms of different metals applied in like manner to the instrument, enabled Musschenbroek to measure the different expansibility of steel, iron, copper, brass, and lead, with considerable accuracy:[*] but there is always some uncertainty in the movements of so many loosely connected teeth and pinions; and this pyrometer was improved by

2. Desaguliers,[†] who instead of prisms substituted cylinders, as wires are more easily procured than prisms of equal dimensions. For the first pinion he employed steel slightly roughened by the file in the same direction as the teeth. Thus a more equable motion was given to the instrument. The toothed wheel and second pinion were supplied by a wheel and roller, having grooves in their circumference for receiving a watch-chain, by which motion was communicated to the index. The dial plate was square and movable, in order to stretch the watch-chain as there might be occasion. A thin plate of rough steel $\frac{1.5}{100}$ inch wide, slightly convex towards the first roller, was substituted for the rack; and this last, which in Musschenbroek's pyrometer was made to travel lightly over a small bit of fine watch-spring, moved in Desaguliers over a well constructed friction wheel, or roller.

These changes improved the delicacy of the instrument very considerably; but it soon underwent other modifications.

3. The pyrometer of Mr. John Ellicot,

Fig. 9.

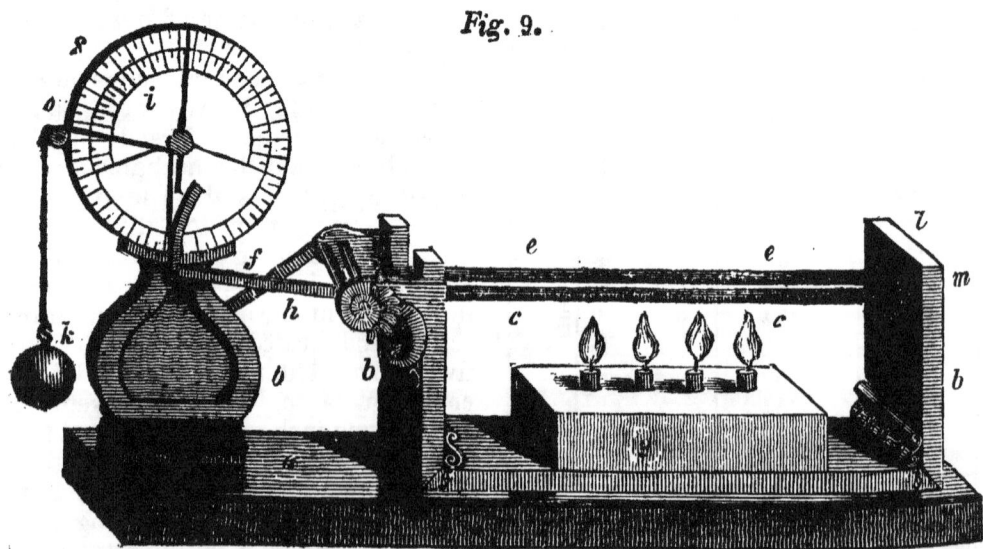

of London, is seen in *fig.* 9, *a a* is a flat plate of brass screwed to a thick mahogany sole, to which the three brass uprights *b b b* are firmly attached.

The pyrometric pieces consist of two metallic bars: the flat one *c c* is of

---

[*] Tentam Acad. del Cimento.
[†] Desagulier's Experimental Philosophy, i. 421.

steel, and is that by which the expansions of all the other metals are to be compared together. Its extremity to the right passes through a hole in the upright, and is fixed to a spring which may be tightened by the screw *m*. Its other extremity is free, and presses against a *snail* on the axis of the lever *f*. The other bar *e e* is a prism of any metal, the right end of which rests on the end of the screw *l*, while its other bears on a snail on the axis of the lever *h*. When the bars are expanded by the heat of the spirit lamp *g*, they move the levers, to each of which is attached a slender watch-chain: the chain from the lever *f* passes round a pulley $\frac{1}{4}$ inch in diameter, fixed on the axis round which the inner graduated circle *i* of the dial moves; the chain from the lever *h* passes round a similar pulley on the axis of the index, as seen in the figure; and the expansions of this bar are marked by the index on the fixed outer circle. Both pulleys have a thread wrapped round them in a contrary direction on each, and then passing over the pulleys at *o* to the weight *k*, which acts as a counterbalance to bring back the index and movable circle as the bars cool. The index and circle are both adjusted to the beginning of their scales by means of the screws *l, m*, at the commencement of each experiment; and when the temperature applied expands the standard bar to a given degree, as indicated on the inner circle, the index will show on the outer circle the relative expansibility of whatever metal is applied to the instrument at *e e*.*

This instrument was chiefly intended by its ingenious inventor, a chronometer-maker by profession, for ascertaining the relative expansion of the metals usually employed in the construction of pendulums; an important object, for which many of the best pyrometers have been devised.

In this instrument the dial is about three inches in diameter; the levers two inches and a half in length, and the proportions of the several parts such that the expansion of $\frac{1}{20}$ inch in the bar will move the index wholly round the circle; or each degree will mark the $\frac{1}{7200}$ of an inch in the lengthening of the bar. From the mean of numerous experiments, Ellicot ascertained the following to be the relative expansions of seven metals:—

Steel.	Iron.	Gold.	Copper.	Brass.	Silver.	Lead.
56	60	73	89	95	103	149,*

which is more nearly in the ratio of the *conducting power* of the different metals, than of any other of their physical properties.

4. In the 44th volume of the *Philosophical Transactions* is a description of another pyrometer by Dr. Cromwell Mortimer, which, though less accurate and convenient than Ellicot's, is worthy of notice, especially as it may be employed to show the alterations of atmospheric temperature.

a, b, fig. 10, is a round rod of brass

Fig. 10. A.

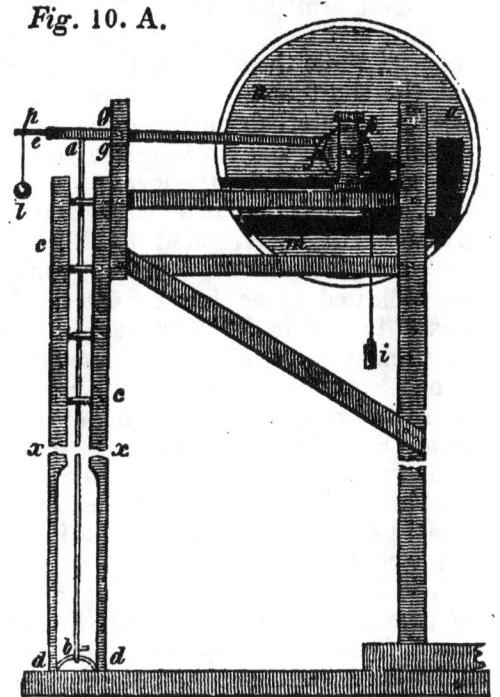

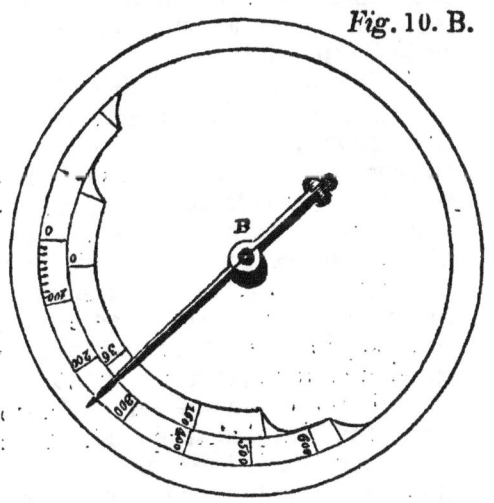

Fig. 10. B.

or steel, $\frac{1}{4}$ inch in diameter and three

---

* This description is taken from an original instrument now before the author.

* Phil. Trans. vol. xxxix. p. 297.

feet long, its upper extremity terminating in a hardened steel point one inch more in length, and entering a hole in a steel plate on the under side of the lever *e*, while its lower end rests on a point attached to the metallic plate at *d*. *c, d* are plates of iron joined at *d*, and at different other points, as in the figure: at *x, x* they are turned half round, to allow the application of heated bodies, as sand or water, to the bar, which is immersed in the heated bodies to a certain mark as at *b*. In the original instrument this mark was at 1½ inch from the bottom: *e, f* is a lever moving round an axis in *g*. A string from the end of its longest arm passes twice round the pulley *h*, and is kept tight by a weight *i* of ¼ lb., while there is another weight *l*, at the short arm of the lever, sufficient to counterbalance the weight of the longer arm, and to keep the point *a* in close contact with the lever. *m, n, o*, a dial, of which the face is seen at B, graduated to correspond to Fahrenheit's and Reaumur's degrees, which are indicated by an index fixed on the axis of the pulley *h*. The frame of the instrument is of oak. The lever from *p* to *a* = 4 inches; from *a* to *g* = 1.5 inch; from *g* to *f* = 12 inches; the pulley = 0.5 inch; the dial = 11 inches in diameter. In the original the melting point of different substances is indicated by their chemical signs in the outer circle of the dial.

This instrument appears to have been of considerable delicacy, and to have marked minute changes of atmospheric temperature very readily: but the size is inconvenient; and it must now be regarded rather as an instrument of curiosity than utility.

5. The pyrometer, figured 11, the invention of Mr. Froteringham, a Lincoln grazier, combines simplicity with considerable delicacy. It was also intended to indicate the changes of atmospheric temperature. *a, a* is a bar of iron four feet long and 1¼ inch wide, having a polished brass surface screwed to it with steel screws, which are fitted to short slips in the brass that allow the expansion of the iron bar, without that of the brass ornamental surface, to affect the hardened steel apex *b*. This apex moves the lever *c*, which raises the lever *d*; both turning on well made central disks. A chain from the extremity of the lever *d* is lapped twice round the pulley *f* on the axis of the

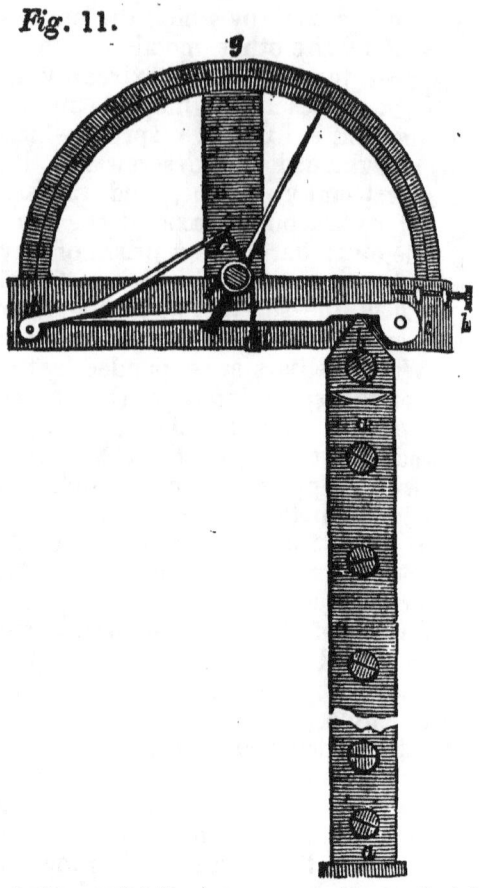

Fig. 11.

index, which moves round a graduated circle *g*. The counterpoise *i* brings back the index as the levers fall. The screw *h* is for adjusting the index to the beginning of the scale. It is very obvious that such an instrument would be capable of showing the expansions of the bar in proportion to the difference between the arms of the levers; and, it is said, that the original instrument, in the library of a philosophical society at Spalding, indicated the changes of the heat of the weather with great precision.*

6. All these instruments, however, yield in accuracy to the invention of the celebrated Smeaton, which is described in the *Philosophical Transactions*.†

In this instrument the expansions of the metallic bars, heated by water, are measured by means of a micrometer screw; a principle which had been before employed by the great chronometer-maker Graham, for the adjustment of the rods of a pendulum.

From the principle of its construction, this instrument is called the Micrometer-Pyrometer, *fig.* 12.

The basis of this instrument *a, b, c, d* is of solid brass, which was chosen as

---

* Phil. Trans. vol. xlv. p. 125.
† Phil. Trans. vol. xlviii. p. 487.

Fig. 12.

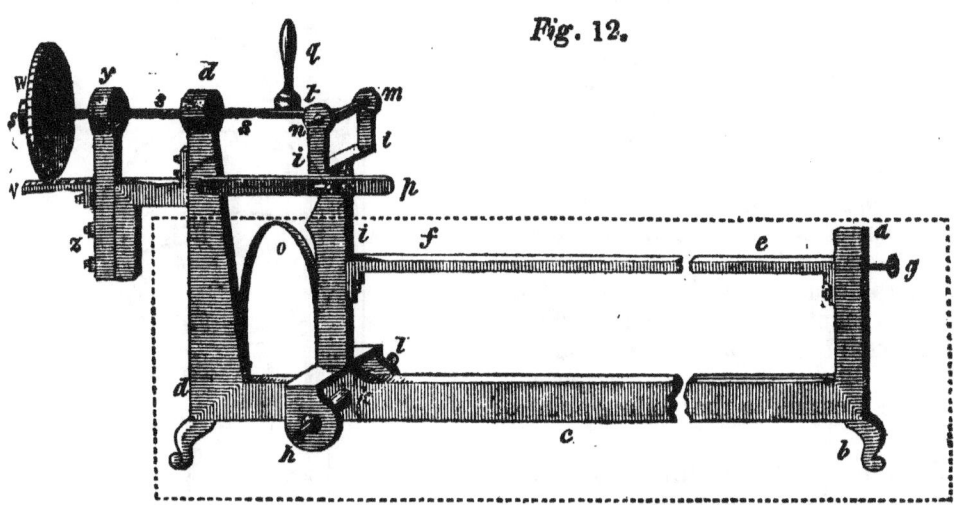

of a mean expansibility among the metals. ef is the bar to be measured, resting on two notches, one attached to the fixed upright $a\,b$, and the other to the principal lever $h\,i$. k is a strong arbor fixed to the basis, and intended to receive the ends of two screws h, l, upon which the principal lever h, i turns; o is a slender steel spring intended to press the lever against the extremity of the bar; and p is a checkrod to support the lever, when the bar is removed. t is called the *feeler*; it is in the form of the letter T, and is suspended freely, but without shake, between the points of the screws m, n. q is the handle of the feeler, which is movable on a loose joint, so that the feeler may be moved by the handle without being irregularly affected by the pressure of the hand. The principal part of the instrument is s, the micrometer screw, and w the graduated circle or index-plate fixed on the screw, which indicates the revolutions of the screw on the index v. The micrometer screw passes through two solid heads perforated by a corresponding screw; the piece $y\,z$ is made somewhat springy, and tends to draw the micrometer screw backward from d; by which its threads press uniformly against the corresponding threads in the holes, and keep the motion equable and easy.

When the instrument is used, its basis and the bar are immersed in a tin vessel containing water, as marked by the dotted line, which is heated by seven lamps applied below. The vessel is provided with a cover; and a delicate mercurial thermometer is suspended in the water, for regulating and ascertaining the temperature employed, which is not intended to exceed that of boiling water.

The expansion of the bar presses the lever and feeler towards the end of the micrometer screw, which, as well as the extremity of the feeler, is tipt with hardened steel. The handle q is laid hold of, and by it the feeler is moved up and down, while the screw is turned, until its steel point comes in contact with the end of the screw. Mr. Smeaton found that he could judge of that contact more accurately by the *ear*, than by the *eye* or the *touch*.

The turns of the index-plate counted by its edge and the divisions of the index, show the expansion of the bar; and its length when cool may be found in the same manner, either before or after the experiment above described. In this instrument the bar acts against the centre of a lever of the *second order*, the fulcrum of which is in the basis; and when both are expanded, the free extremity of the lever moves through a space double of the difference between the expansion of the bar and of the basis: hence, when we know the length of the lever from its axis to the point of suspension of the feeler, the distance from that axis to the point of contact of the bar, the number of threads of the micrometer screw in an inch, and the number of degrees on the circumference of the index-plate, we can compute the value of these degrees in fractions of an inch. In the original pyrometer the following were the proportions:

	Inches.
From axis of lever to point of suspension	5.875
—— fulcrum to point of contact	2.895
Length of 70 threads of the screw	2.455
Division of index-plate	100°.

Hence the value of each division of the index-plate will $= \frac{10}{57888}$ds of an inch; and as, when the instrument was well adjusted, the difference of contact was very perceptible when the screw was moved through $\frac{1}{4}$ of a division, the $\frac{1}{23133}$th of an inch of expansion was determinable by this pyrometer, with which Mr. Smeaton ascertained the expansibility of many solids.

The following table is the result of his experiments, showing in 10,000dths of an inch the expansion of rods of different kinds of matter, in passing from the freezing to the boiling point of water.

White glass barometer tube	100
Martial regulus of antimony	130
Bistered steel	138
Hard steel	147
Iron	151
Bismuth	167
Copper hammered	204
Alloy, 8 copper, and 1 tin	218
Cast brass	225
Alloy, brass 16, tin 1	229
Brass wire	232
Telescope speculum metal	232
Alloy, 2 brass, 1 zinc	247
Fine pewter	274
Grain tin	298
Soft solder, 2 lead, 1 tin	301
Alloy, 8 zinc, 1 tin, slightly hammered	323
Lead	344
Zinc	353
Zinc hammered out 1 inch per foot	373

These experiments correspond as nearly with the results obtained by Ellicot, as the difference of the instruments admit. They introduced a precision hitherto unknown in the law of expansion of solid bodies; and are still quoted with approbation in those nice disquisitions which have paved the way to the perfection of *horology*, and the modern refinements in *geodesical* operations, while they have extended our knowledge of the effects of heat.

7. The *metalline thermometer* of Mr. Keane Fitzgerald comes next in order of time; but it is chiefly applicable to mark the alterations of atmospheric temperature. Its general construction will be readily learnt from *fig.* 13.*

The basis of the instrument is a piece of well seasoned deal, on which a system of levers is fixed; $a\,a$ is the pyrometric bar, 2 feet long, the upper extremity of

---

* Phil. Trans. vol. li. p. 523.

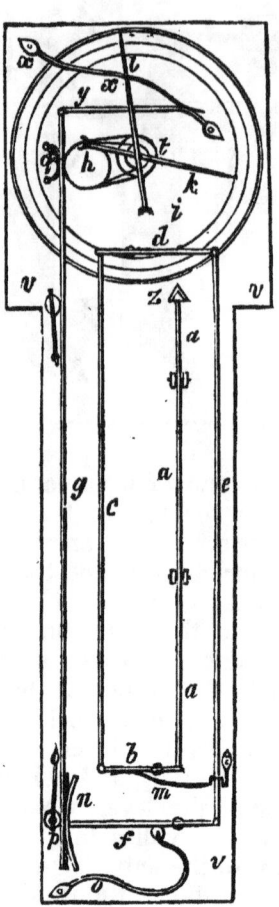

Fig. 13.

which bears against the fulcrum z, while its other end rests on a small hemisphere of metal on the short arm of the lever b. The long arm of this lever is $2\frac{1}{2}$ times as long as the other; b is joined by a pivot to the rod c, 2 feet 2 inches in length, which bears against the short arm of d, and the long arm of d is $2\frac{3}{4}$ times as long as the former. The rod e is 2 feet 4 inches long, and is jointed to f, as in the figure. The long arm of f is 4 times the length of its short arm, and terminates in a slender arch-head, which is attached to the lower end of the rod g by a watch-chain, as in the figure. This last rod is 3 feet long, and is kept perpendicular by sliding between two friction rollers p, v, its connection with the arch-head, its suspension from the lever y, and its friction on the pulley h. The weight of the levers, &c. is counterbalanced by the springs m and o, and the spring of y is nearly neutralized by the pressure of x. The pulley h is fixed at 2 feet 6 inches from the lower end of g, and is 3 inches in diameter. Two cords fixed to the spring q, pass twice round

THERMOMETER AND PYROMETER.

the pulley h in different ways, and thence go over the pullies at t, respectively, 1 inch and $\frac{1}{4}$ inch in diameter. These last are put on the common axes of the indices k, l, in the same manner as the hands of a clock. The face of the dial is 12 inches in diameter, and from the construction, the index l ranges 48 times, and the index k 12 times as much as the bar g. The dial has on it three circular scales; the inner is divided into 240°, corresponding to those of Fahrenheit's thermometer; the middle is divided into 360°; and the outer into 1080 parts, marking 18 for each degree of the thermometer, and 12 for each degree of the circle.

This instrument may be used as a pyrometer in low temperatures; for the bar a is removable; and from the construction, each division of the outer circle is equivalent to an expansion of $\frac{1}{73870}$th of the bar.

Used in this way, Mr. Fitzgerald informs us that the dilatations of metallic bars 2 feet long, at the same temperature, were as follows:

	Divisions.
Spelter or zinc	= 1570
Zinc 18, copper 2 parts	= 1550
Brass	= 1120
Iron	= 785
Steel	= 695

which agrees pretty well with the experiments of Smeaton and Ellicot.

When used as a thermometer the index k marks 74 divisions in passing from the usual extremes of temperature in our climate, and 212 divisions from freezing to boiling water.

Mr. Fitzgerald experienced some difficulty in proportioning the strength of the springs to the weight sustained by the levers, and he improved the instrument by the adoption of pulleys and counterpoise weights, as in *fig.* 14, which he ingeniously converted into a register thermometer, by adapting two light index hands a, a, fixed to two brass circles moving between friction wheels, attached to a fixed circle d. They were so nicely fitted as to move readily by a weight of 8 grains hung on them. These hands are moved in opposite directions, by a small stud in the under surface of the index f, which receives its motion from a cord passing from the pulley h round a small wheel on its axis.

This alteration of the instrument was intended only to note the changes of the atmosphere, which it seems to have done with much delicacy; for it had a range

Fig. 14.

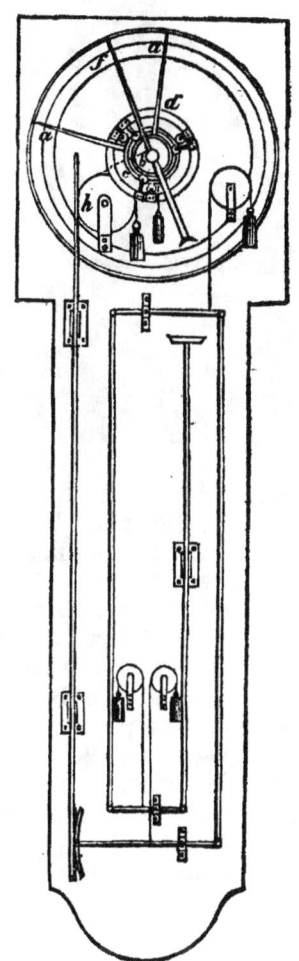

of 72 inches from the common changes of the heat of the weather in London; and it would show an alteration amounting to 50 or 60 degrees of its scale, when the pyrometric bar of the instrument was five or six times breathed upon.*

8. In Ferguson's *Lectures* two pyrometers, the invention of that great self-taught mechanician, are described.

Fig. 15 was merely intended to exhibit to his audience the expansions of bodies by heat, yet is worthy of notice.

$a\,a$, a mahogany board, on which are fixed four brass studs; of these b supports a screw for adjusting the pyrometric bar f, which rests in notches in the studs $c\,d$. The extremity of the bar presses against the crooked lever g, which acts on the index $i\,i$; the stud e holds the spring h, which brings back the index when the bar cools. The lever g (of the second order) has the portion between the point of contact of the

---

* Phil. Trans. vol. lii. p. 146.

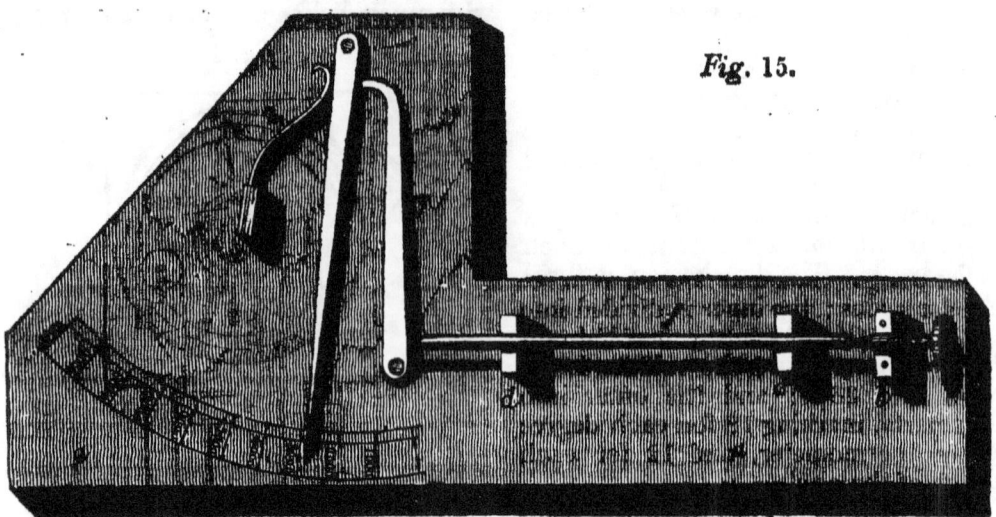

Fig. 15.

bar, and where it touches the index 20 times as long as the space between the point of the bar and its fulcrum; and the space between the end of the lever and the free end of the index is just 20 times the length of that between the point of the lever and the axis of the index; hence, when the bar expands $\frac{1}{100}$th of an inch, the point of the index will have moved over $(20 \times 20) = 400$ times as much space, or one inch; or if the bar expand $\frac{1}{1000}$th of an inch, the index will move $\frac{1}{10}$th.

The scale is divided into inches and tenths; and the mere friction of the bar f, which is removable at pleasure, with a piece of flannel till it becomes sensibly warm, will be sufficient to show variations of the index. Ferguson states that it gave the following results:— with bars of iron and steel, 3; copper, $4\frac{1}{2}$; brass, 5; tin, 6; lead, 7.

9. In the supplement to his lectures there is however a much more delicate pyrometer described, (*fig.* 16,) which will show the expansion of a bar of metal to the $\frac{1}{7500}$th of an inch, or even to the 90,000th.

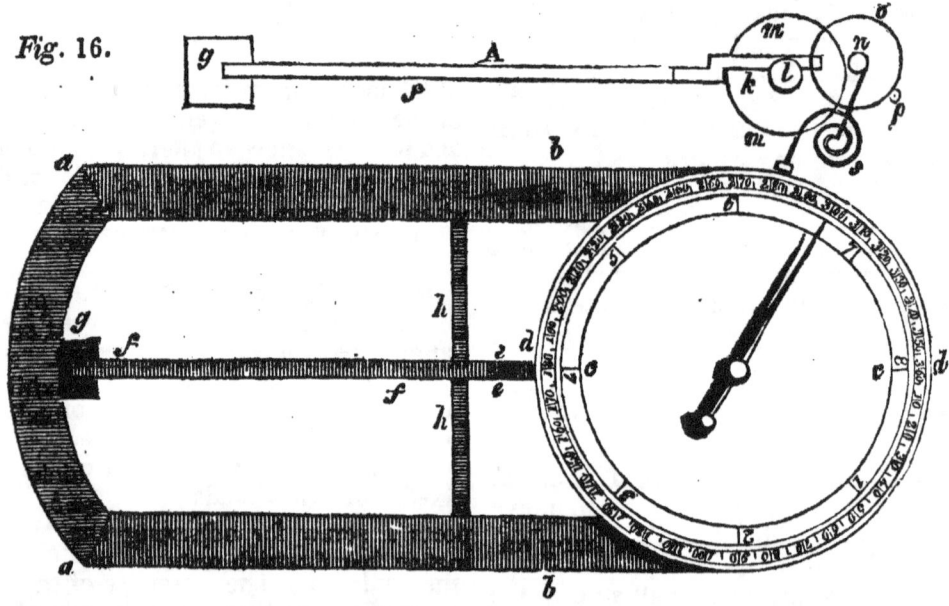

Fig. 16.

The frame $a\,b$ is of mahogany, supported on short pillars, so as to admit a lamp under it for heating the bar f; one end of which lies in a cavity in the piece of metal g, and the other, after passing on a friction wheel over the cross-bar $h\,h$, presses against the short lever $e\,e$. The manner in which this short lever acts on the index is seen in the adjoining diagram A, where k is the short lever that moves under the dial d between friction wheels. On the side of k are 15 teeth in the space of one inch, which play in the twelve leaves of the pinion

l on the axis of the wheel $m\,m$. This wheel has round its circumference 100 teeth, which work in the ten leaves of the pinion n, on the axis of the wheel o of 100 teeth, that gives motion to the pinion p of ten leaves, on the axis of which the index is fixed.

As the wheels m and n have each 100 teeth, and the pinions n and p ten leaves, it is obvious that when the wheel m has made one revolution the pinion p, and of course the index, will have made 100 revolutions; as the pinion l has twelve leaves, and the bar $i\,k$ has fifteen teeth to one inch (equivalent to $12\frac{1}{2}$) it is obvious that while $i\,k$ moves one inch the pinion p will have moved $100 + \frac{1}{4}$ or 125 times round, and the index would at the same time be carried 125 times round the circle $d\,d$. This circle is graduated into 360 degrees, and being eleven inches in diameter, it is subdivided into half degrees. Hence each degree of that circle will be equivalent to an expansion of $125 \times 360 = \frac{1}{45000}$th of an inch of expansion in the bar f; and as the half degrees can readily be distinguished on the dial, the instrument will show expansions only amounting to $\frac{1}{90000}$th part of an inch. A silk thread is several times wound round the axis of n and passes to the slender spring s, which keeps the teeth of the pinions and wheels in close contact, and pulls back the train of wheels when the cooling of the bar f allows the short bar $i\,k$ to recede.

The inner circle of the dial is divided into eight parts, corresponding to so many thousandths of an inch in the expansion of the bar f, or $\frac{1}{1000}$th of an inch for each degree of the outer circle over which the index has moved. Bars of different metals laid in g for a given time, and exposed to the same lamp, afford an indication of their relative expansibility; and to ensure equality in the bars it is recommended to have them *wire drawn* through the same hole. There is, however, in this instrument no accurate measure of the temperature applied to each bar; and, notwithstanding the delicacy of the movement, it seems inferior to Ellicot's pyrometer, as it wants a constant and uniform standard by which to compare the expansions in each separate experiment.

10. A new method of ascertaining the expansibility of different substances was suggested by the late Mr. Jesse Ramsden, and on his hint it was attempted by the ingenious and indefatigable De Luc, whose researches on the barometer gave this subject an increased interest to his mind. The object in view was to determine the relative expansion of solids by observation with a microscope furnished with a micrometer. The *microscopic pyrometer* of De Luc is seen in *fig.* 17, where $a\,b$ represents a

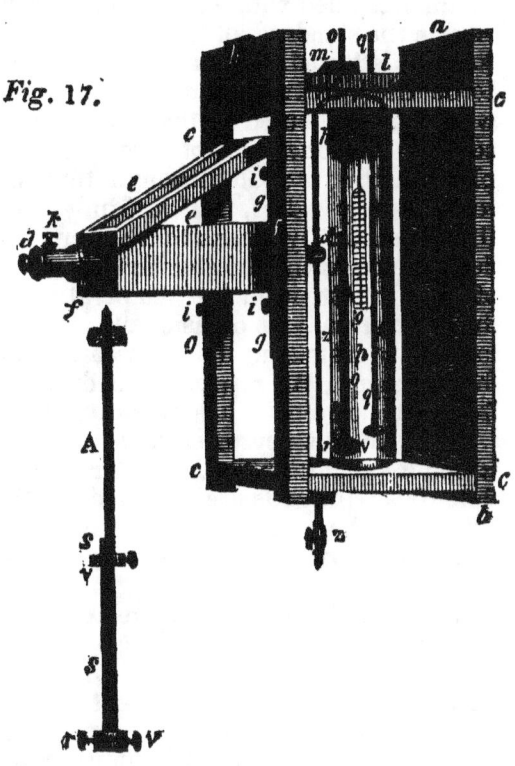

Fig. 17.

strong board of even-grained deal; to which the frame $c\,c\,c\,c$ is firmly joined, that when $a\,b$ is suspended vertically from a strong post, the front of the instrument bearing the microscope $d\,d$ is towards the operator.

The microscope is securely united to the frame by the braces $e\,e$ and the cross-bar f; and the whole of this part of the apparatus can be moved up or down by the slides $g\,g$, which fit so tightly on their centres as to require slight blows with a hammer on the frame to cause them to move down, and may be further tightened by the screws $i\,i\,i$. The microscope is kept horizontal by the cross-pieces, and by an inner sliding frame not seen in the figure. The microscope is so adjusted that an object is distinctly seen when a full inch from its lens; and it is furnished with a micrometer, movable by k, for ascertaining the expansions of the rods subjected to experiment. A piece of thick deal l is seen at the top of the frame lying horizontally from a groove cut in the board *a b* to the front of the frame; this is movable by means of the screw *h*, and is perforated by a piece of cork *m* firmly driven into it until level with its lower surface. The cork is then pierced vertically to receive the glass rod *o o o*, which is thus suspended in a thin cylindrical glass jar *p*, 21 inches high, and 4 inches in diameter, filled with water. The glass rod is the standard of comparison, and to it is attached a rod *s s*, of the metal to be tried, by two connected rings *r r*, which are tightened on the rods by two screws. Another set of rings *v* is applied higher up; but through this the rod *s s* freely slides, while it firmly clips the glass rod by means of a screw. A delicate thermometer hangs in the centre of the jar *p* to note the temperature of the water, which is occasionally agitated to secure uniformity of temperature by the rod *q q*. A syphon *z* to draw off the water completes the apparatus.*

In using this pyrometer, warm water is poured into the jar, in order to heat the rods; the rods are adjusted to the focus of the microscope by the screw *n*; the thermometer gives the degree of heat employed; and, by means of marks on the bars, their relative expansion is given in divisions of the micrometer, the value of which is known by previous experiments. The connection of the rods is more distinctly seen at A; but it is unnecessary to give a more minute description of an instrument which has been superseded by the more accurate and more elegant contrivance of Ramsden, so elaborately detailed by General Roy, to which we shall presently advert.

11. From experiments with this instrument, De Luc ingeniously applied a correction to the scale of barometers for temperature, by what, in the same paper, he calls "*metallic thermometers*." The scale of the barometer was fixed on a bar of metal of known expansibility, so as to raise the scale in exact proportion to the expansion of the mercury; and thus the mere inspection of the barometric scale will give the true height, without the trouble of applying the equation or formula of correction for temperature, as in ordinary observations.

12. We come now to certainly the most complex, but the most perfect of all contrivances for determining the relative expansions of solids, the *microscopic pyrometer of Ramsden*, contrived by that eminent artist, for determining with the utmost possible precision, the expansibility of the rods employed by General Roy, in the geodesical operations that are the foundation of the great trigonometrical survey of Britain. Fig. 18 contains plans and sections of this beautiful contrivance, and although we do not propose to enter into a minute detail of the different parts of the instrument, a general description will show, to those who have not considered such subjects, the nice precautions which are necessary to accuracy in like operations, while it explains its construction. Ramsden's pyrometer is attached to a strong and well joined deal table, or frame 5 feet long, 28 inches broad, and 42 inches high; of which an end elevation is seen *fig.* 18, B; the plan of its top will be best understood from an inspection of A. *a b* and *c d* are troughs of deal, (firmly screwed to the table) 3 inches in diameter, and a little longer than the frame; *a b* projects a little over the table, but *c d* is in a line with the frame, as may be seen at B. Each trough contains a cast iron prism, $1\frac{1}{4}$ inch on each side, firmly fixed in the troughs, at the ends *a* and *c*, by means of brass collars embracing the prisms, and tightened by screws as at G, while the ends *b* and *d* pass freely through loose collars, without any shake, when their dimensions are altered by temperature. The prism *a b* is called the *eye prism*; because it carries at each end the eye-pieces of the microscopes *l m n*, and *o p r*; which are figured on a larger scale at F and E. The other prism *c d* is called the *mark prism*; because it carries at one end the mark I, and at the other cross wires H; *e f* is a copper boiler $2\frac{3}{4}$ inches wide, and $3\frac{1}{2}$ deep, rather shorter than the wooden troughs. The centre of the boiler, or rather of the object lens standing perpendicular to it, is 5.81 inches from the cross wires of the mark in *c d*, and 20.33 inches from the wire of the micrometer attached to the corresponding eye-piece. The boiler rests on five small rollers, seen in the enlarged section D. The boiler, like the troughs, has a cock to the right hand; and in the plan A, it is represented with a bar in it, to show the position of the rods to be tried. The water in the boiler is heated by the 12 spirit lamps *g g g g*, standing on four

---

* Phil. Trans. vol. lxviii. part i. p. 437.

THERMOMETER AND PYROMETER. 25

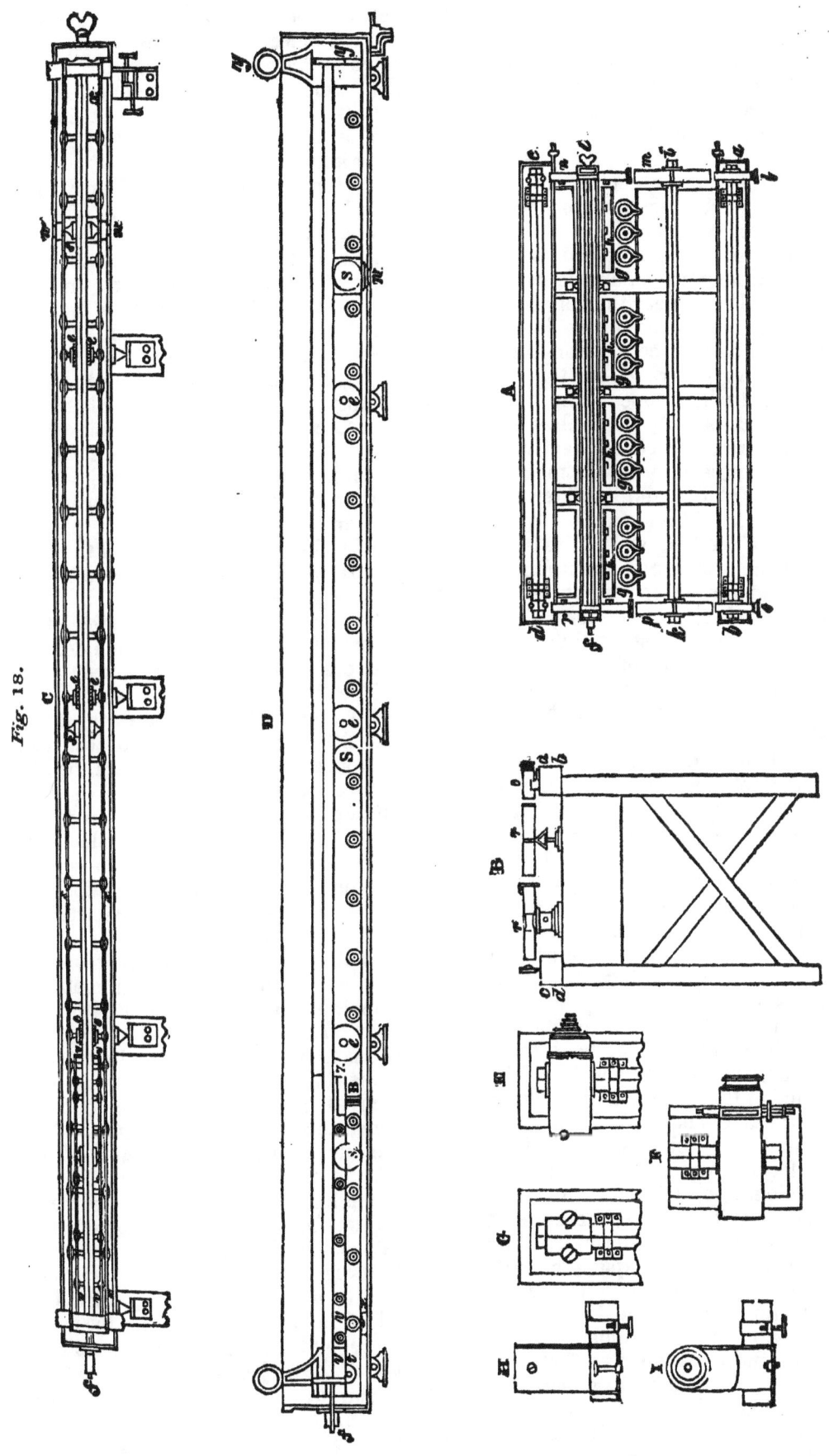

Fig. 18.

movable shelves, and showing only their handles *h h h h*, when under the boiler.

The boiler contains another essential part of the apparatus, *viz.* two brass slides, composed of two cheeks, kept at equal distances by cross bars as in C, where a prism or bar is represented as resting in the centre of the slides. The long slide reaches from microscope to microscope, and has its cheeks $1\frac{3}{4}$ inch deep. It is attached to the boiler only at the point *w*, and it rolls on the small roller *x*, near the left hand of D. The right hand end of the long slide is shut up by a piece of strong brass *y, y*, supporting two rings, for the part *n* of the fixed microscope. The short slide *v, v, v, v,* is only $14\frac{1}{2}$ inches long; its cheeks are $1\frac{1}{4}$ inch deep, kept parallel by braces, as seen in D. It moves within the long slide; and its outer end rests on the cylindrical surface of the last brace of the long slide, fitted to receive it, while a narrow longitudinal bar *z* moves freely in the notch of a bridge B, framed for it in the long slide. The outer end of the short slide is shut up by a similar piece of brass to that closing the opposite extremity of the long one. The bar or rod to be examined abuts against the piece of brass *y*, it rests on the three rollers *s s s*, 1 inch in diameter, and is kept in the centre of the slides by three milled nuts *e e e*, that screw up so as not to press too much on the sides of the bar. At *f* is a tube and wire moving through a collar of oiled leather, that by means of a helical spring presses a flat piece of metal attached to the wire, against the shut end of the short slide and rod to be measured, so as to keep the other extremity of the rod in contact with *y*. On the application of heat, the rod expands, and overcoming the slight resistance of the spring, carries before it the short slide, and with it the tube containing the object lens of the micrometer microscope *o, p, r*, a space proportional to the temperature applied; and it is this space, measured by the micrometer, that determines the numerical value of the expansion of the rod.

The microscope tubes are divided into three pieces, for the convenience of applying the instrument to measure rods shorter than five feet. For this purpose the central screening tube of the fixed microscope, supported on the mahogany prism *i k* by a collar, may be moved and *clamped* at any part of that prism; the eye-piece, in like manner, may be moved along the eye prism; but the object lens tube was left in the rings of the slide, and another lens of the same focus was clamped to the cheeks of the slide at suitable distances.

The standard prisms, during each experiment, were kept at the freezing temperature, by being surrounded with pounded ice. The microscopes were then accurately adjusted to the marks, by bringing the cross wires to bisect them, and until this was accomplished, the rod to be measured was also surrounded with ice. The lamps were then applied to the boiler, and the elongation of the rod, at the boiling heat, was ascertained by the micrometer attached to the microscope *o, p, r*. In these delicate investigations there were two observers, who simultaneously used both microscopes, lest any alteration had taken place in the fixed end of the rod; and to ensure accuracy, the experiments were twice at least repeated.

The value of the indications of the micrometer, on which so much depends, was previously thus ascertained:

The head of the micrometer screw = 0.9 inch in diameter, and was divided into fifty equal parts, each of which was reckoned two; and they were therefore numbered to 100. Fifty-five revolutions of the head were found equal to 0.77175 of an inch; it follows that there are 71.27 threads of the screw in one inch; and seven revolutions and *nearly* $\frac{13}{100}$ths move the micrometer wire $\frac{1}{10}$th of an inch; consequently $\frac{1}{100}$th of part of a revolution, or half a division of the head, will answer to a motion of something more than 0.00014th of an inch. Having found 7.13 revolutions equal to 0.1 inch at the wires, it is obvious that the number answering to 0.1 inch at the *mark* being also found and added to the former, their sum will give the measure of 0.1 inch at the object lens of the microscope *o, p, r*, or the space through which the free end of the rod has moved by the change of temperature. This last point was ascertained by experiment to be = 24.93 revolutions of the micrometer head; which being added to 7.13 = 32.06, " for the number of revolutions measuring a motion of 0.1 at the object lens, or an expansion of $\frac{1}{10}$th of an inch," or half a division of the micrometer head is equivalent to an expansion of the rod under examination of $\frac{1}{32000}$ of an inch; and $\frac{1}{4}$ of a division, which may readily be seen by the eye, $= \frac{1}{14000}$.

Such is the *microscopic pyrometer* of Ramsden; an instrument not indeed suitable for ordinary purposes, but admirably adapted for obtaining an accurate estimate of the comparative expansibility of different solids; an object of the highest importance, not only in bringing to perfection the delicate instruments required by the refinements of modern philosophical investigations, but essential to the perfection of different kinds of machinery in daily use, and even to a successful investigation of the laws and nature of heat itself. With this instrument Roy determined the expansion of the seven solids in the annexed table.

Expansion of

	By 180°. Revolutions.	Parts.	By 1°. Parts.	Inch. on 5 feet.	Inch. on 1 foot.
Dutch brass	35.69	=	$19 \frac{83}{000}$	= 0.111323	= 0.0222646
English plate brass, a rod	36.41	=	$20 \frac{23}{100}$	= 0.113568	= 0.0227136
Ditto, in the form of a trough	36.45	=	$20 \frac{25}{100}$	= 0.113693	= 0.0227386
Steel rod	22.02	=	$12 \frac{23}{100}$	= 0.068684	= 0.0137368
Cast iron prism	21.34	=	$11 \frac{86}{100}$	= 0.066563	= 0.0133126
Glass rod	15.54	=	$8 \frac{63}{100}$	= 0.048472	= 0.0096944
Ditto tube	14.93	=	$8 \frac{29}{100}$	= 0.046569	= 0.0046569

13. The instruments hitherto noticed are inapplicable to very high temperatures, or to ascertain the heat of closed fire-places; an object, in many processes in the arts, of the utmost importance. To supply this deficiency, our celebrated Wedgwood took advantage of the property which clay has of *contracting by heat*, and remaining afterwards in that state of contraction. This property is not, strictly speaking, an exception to the general law of expansion by increase of temperature: clay is not a homogeneous body, but a mechanical mixture of argil and silex, which by the influence of heat are brought into more intimate union, and therefore diminish in bulk; until a temperature sufficiently high to melt them, that is, to convert them into a homogeneous mass, is applied: after which the product obeys the general law of expansion by heat. Availing himself of this property, Mr. Wedgwood employed as *pyrometric pieces* cylinders of fine porcelain clay, slightly flattened on one side, as seen in A B, *fig.* 19,*

Fig. 19.

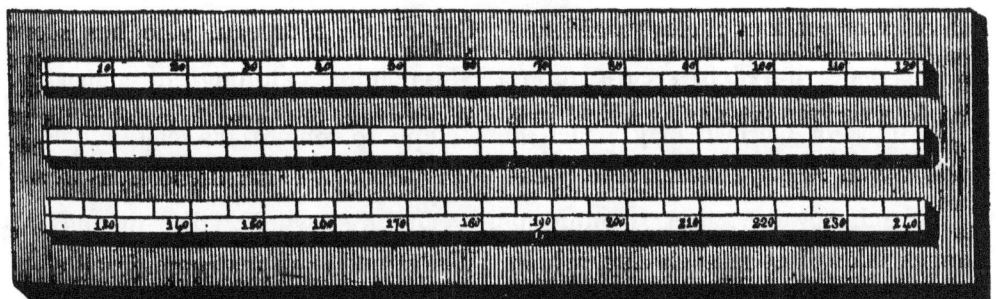

formed by pressing the clay into an iron tube, and baked in a potter's furnace. It was found, after repeated trials, that the pieces of clay contracted more and more in an uniform ratio to the degree of heat communicated to them, and permanently retained this contraction; so that by applying them when cold to a scale, an indication of the degree of heat was obtained.

The scale employed by Wedgwood consisted of two brass rods ¼ inch square, and two feet in length, fixed on a brass plate *convergingly*, so that they were distant at one end just 0.5, and at the other 0.3 inch. For convenience the rods are usually divided and fixed as in the figure on the plate, forming two nearly parallel grooves.† With the above-stated convergence the whole

---

* Phil. Trans. vol. lxxii. lxxiv. lxxvi.
† The degree of convergence being only one-tenth of an inch in a foot, is not perceptible in the figure.

groove is divided into inches and tenths, making 240 degrees in the whole scale; and the higher the temperature to which the pyrometric piece has been exposed, the further will it slide up the scale.

In order to compare his scale with Fahrenheit's mercurial thermometer, which cannot measure a temperature much beyond 600°, Mr. Wedgwood was compelled to make use of the *expansions* of a pyrometric piece of fine silver, applied to a gage on the same principle as that above described. By this, the expansions of the silver for 50° and 212° Fahrenheit were first noted; and then the silver and clay pyrometric pieces were compared at the same temperature. By such means Wedgwood estimated the value of each degree of his scale at 130° of Fahrenheit; and he reckoned that the 0° of his scale corresponded with the 1077°.5 of the common scale. On this principle comparative tables of the two thermometers have been constructed; but their accuracy depends on two circumstances which have not been determined to the satisfaction of the philosophic world. Clay being a heterogeneous mixture, it by no means follows that its contractions are equable at different temperatures; and even were this ascertained, there is great doubt how far the means employed by Wedgwood did accurately estimate the degree of Fahrenheit at which his scale commences.

There is still another serious objection to the general use of such an instrument. It occurred to the ingenious inventor, that different portions of clay would possess different degrees of contractibility; and he endeavoured to secure uniformity, to a certain extent, by laying in a large stock of Cornish clay, which he hoped would supply innumerable pyrometric pieces of the same quality. It was found, however, that spontaneous changes take place in such clay, which render its indications liable to variation at distant intervals; or pieces, now formed of the same clay, will not give the same indication with pieces baked several years ago. Attempts were made to remedy this inconvenience by forming a clay of uniform quality of fixed proportions of silex and alumine. Fine Cornish clay yielded, on analysis, two parts of silex and three of alumine; and such a mixture made into a paste with $\frac{2}{3}$ths their weight of water, has been recommended for the fabrication of pyrometric pieces. The method detailed by Wedgwood should then be followed in moulding them. The paste is first to be rammed into a metallic mould 0.6 inch wide, 0.4 deep, and 1 inch long: they should be dried in the air, and when quite desiccated, Wedgwood gaged them in another mould exactly 0.5 of an inch wide, and of the form given in the figure. Before they are baked they will, of course, just enter the widest end of the scale, resting at 0°. When contracted by baking to $\frac{1}{2}$th of their bulk, they will pass to the 120°; and when reduced to $\frac{2}{3}$ths, they would pass to the 240°, or the extremity of the scale; but Mr. Wedgwood never did obtain a higher temperature than 160°. From these proportions each degree of Wedgwood's scale is equivalent to a contraction of $\frac{1}{800}$th part of the pyrometric piece.

The difficulty of obtaining clay of an uniform quality, and not liable to spontaneous change, has lately given rise to a suggestion of employing pyrometric pieces formed of Chinese agalmatolite; a suggestion of Mr. Sivright of Meggetland, well worthy of attention.*

A more formidable objection was started by some foreign chemists to Wedgwood's scale; one, indeed, that would have overturned the theory of the instrument. It was alleged, that the effect of a long continued, or often repeated, exposure to even *inferior degrees of heat*, would cause contraction of the clay, after it had undergone the action of a higher temperature. This point has been examined with much care by Guyton de Morveau, who has shown, in his valuable essay,† the inaccuracy of this opinion; although he contends that Wedgwood has greatly erred in the attempts to convert his scale into degrees of Fahrenheit's thermometer, as we shall immediately notice.

On the whole, the pyrometer of Wedgwood is an instrument well adapted to the purposes of the potter, or to convey some idea of the relative heat of furnaces; but we cannot regard the determination of the celebrated inventor as giving even a tolerable approximation to relative degrees of high temperatures by other scales. As, however, Mr. Wedgwood's tables of temperature are often quoted, we shall here subjoin them, with the corresponding degrees of Fahrenheit, according to his calculation.

---

* Edinb. Phil. Journal, vol. vi. p. 179.
† Annales de Chimie, vol. lxxiv. lxxviii. xc.

	W.		F.
Red heat in full day-light	0°	=	1077°
Enamel heat	6	=	1857
Brass melts	21	=	3807
Swedish copper melts	27	=	4587
Fine silver melts	28	=	4717
Settling heat of flint glass	29	=	4847
Fine gold melts	32	=	5237
Delft ware baked	41	=	6407
Working heat of plate glass	57	=	8487
Flint glass furnace, low heat	70	=	10,177
Cream coloured ware baked	86	=	12,257
Welding heat of iron, least	90	=	12,777
Ditto ditto greatest	95	=	13,427
Stone ware, baked	102	=	14,337
Derby China vitrefies	112	=	15,637
Flint glass furnace, high heat	114	=	15,897
Inferior Chinese porcelain softened	120	=	16,677
Bow porcelain vitrified	121	=	16,807
Plate glass furnace, greatest heat	124	=	17,197
Smith's forge, greatest heat	125	=	17,327
Cast iron begins to melt	130	=	17,977
Bristol porcelain vitrifies	135	=	18,627
Hessian crucible melted	150	=	20,577
Cast iron thoroughly melted	150	=	20,577
Chinese porcelain, best sort softened	156	=	21,557
Greatest heat of an air furnace eight inches in diameter; deduct soften Nankeen porcelain at all	160	=	21,877
Extremity of Wedgwood's scale	240	=	32,277

These results are rendered doubtful by the causes already noticed; and the experiments of Morveau and Daniell with pyrometers of platina lead to very different results.

14. The metallic thermometer of Regnier is described in a report of the French Institute for 1798.* The inventor had remarked, that when a thin metallic rule, resting on a table, is raised by the middle, it forms a segmental arc of which the *versed sine*, that is a line perpendicular to the chord, drawn to the centre of the arc, is twelve times longer than the space through which the extremity of the bar has moved; and, on this principle, he proposed to construct an instrument for noting variations of atmospheric temperature. The small models which he exhibited answered perfectly; but his intention was, to apply his invention to instruments on a larger scale for public use.

The instrument consists of two plates of yellow copper, two mètres long, fixed in an iron frame, in a bent position, with their concave surfaces toward each other, as in the sketch, *fig.* 20. On one is fixed a pinion of eight leaves, on an axis, the end of which supports an index to mark the temperature. To the centre of the other plate is attached a toothed rack, in the position of the versed sine of the curve, playing in the leaves of the pinion. When the plates are cooled they approach each other, when heated their centres recede; and the only circumstances of consequence in the position of the bars or plates are,

* Mémoires de l'Institut. Nationale, tom. ii. an. 7.

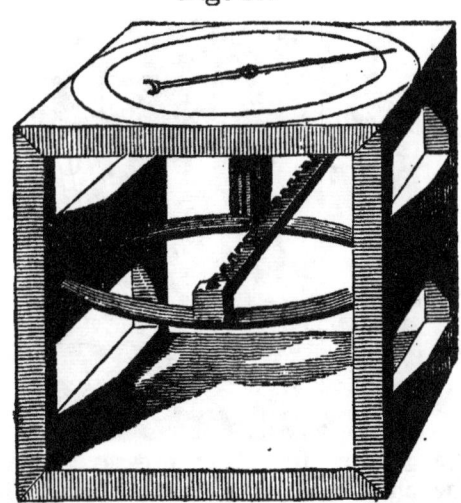

Fig. 20.

that they should be at some little distance from each other, and so bent that they cannot become parallel by any reduction of temperature to which they may be exposed. Regnier found, that two such bars, of two mètres in length, by a change of temperature equal to 60 centesimal degrees, changed the relative position of their centres, or *had a play* equal to 65 millimètres; but the correction for the expansion of the iron frame reduces this by $\frac{2}{3}$; so that there remains about 26 millimètres for the real play of the centres of the bars; and if the frames, in public instruments of this sort, are made of stone, that change, by diminishing the expansibility of the frame, will increase that of the bars. Regnier gave a radius of 659 millimètres to his index; so that it will traverse over a circle of 1.299 mètres in diameter. The pinion has 8 leaves in a diameter of 27 millimètres; and these proportions are such, that a temperature of 60 degrees centesimal will nearly cause a whole revolution of the index round a dial 4.085 mètres in circumference. Hence each degree would be about 68 millimètres in size, or rather more than $2\frac{1}{2}$ inches; and consequently might be distinctly seen at some distance.

15. The platina pyrometer of Guyton de Morveau, *fig.* 21, was laid before the French Institute in 1804, and was designed to measure the heat of open fireplaces and of furnaces.

Its basis is a small, yet solid plate *a, b* of highly baked porcelain, in which is a grove capable of containing a flat bar of platina *c*, 1.75 inch in length, 0.2 of an inch broad, and about 0.1 of an inch in thickness. One end of this bar rests or abuts against the bottom of

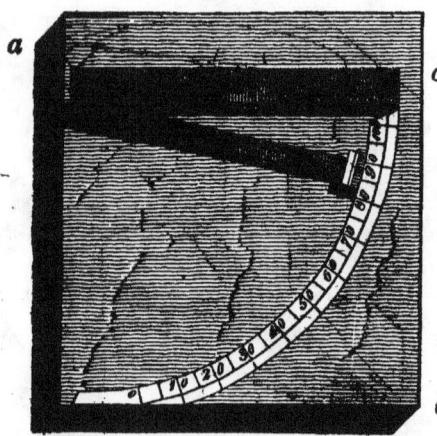

Fig. 21.

the groove; the other presses against the short arm of a bended lever, the long arm of which, moving on a pivot, becomes the index of the instrument. The short arm of this lever is just one twentieth of the length of the long arm, which in the original instrument was equal to 1.8 inch; consequently the space moved over by the long arm will be twenty times as great as the motion caused in the short arm by the expansion of the bar.

A finely graduated arc of a circle, of which the index is a radius, is fixed on the porcelain; and each degree of this arc is subdivided into ten parts by a vernier on the extremity of the index itself, and thus the instrument is capable of indicating an expansion of $\frac{1}{3730}$th part of the radius. All these parts are of platina.

With this instrument Guyton made many experiments, the general result of which proves, that Wedgwood has greatly erred in assigning too high a temperature for the degrees of his scale, a result confirmed by the later experiments of Daniell. Guyton ascribes Wedgwood's error to his estimating the fusing point of *silver* much too high. It was by means of a pyrometric piece of fine silver that Wedgwood connected his scale with that of Fahrenheit; and an error with respect to that metal must viciate all the results. According to Morveau, the fusing point of silver ought to have been at 22° W. instead of 28°: and each degree, instead of being equivalent to 130° of F., ought to have been no more than 62°.5; while the commencement of his scale should have been at 517° F., instead of at 1077°.5.

There is some reason, however, to believe, that Morveau has stated a red heat in day rather too low; for thermometers of mercury and of oil can sustain a temperature of 517° F. without any luminousness even in the dark.

Morveau appears to have taken great pains to connect the scale of his pyrometer with the common thermometer; and he is probably nearer the truth than Wedgwood.*

His corrected table of Wedgwood's temperatures is as follows :—

	Wedg.		Fah.
Mercury boils	2°	=	642.75
Zinc melts	3	=	705.26
Antimony melts	7	=	955.23
Silver melts	22	=	1822.67
Copper melts	27	=	2205.19
Gold melts	32	=	2517.63
Iron welds	95	=	6508.83
Cast iron melts	130	=	8696.24
Porcelain melts	155	=	9633.68
Manganese melts	160	=	10517.12
Malleable iron melts	175	=	11454.56
Nickel melts	175	=	11454.56
Platina melts	175	=	11454.56

16. In 1803, Mr. James Crighton, of Glasgow, published a new "metallic thermometer," in which the unequal expansion of zinc and iron is the moving power. A bar is formed by uniting a plate of zinc, *fig.* 22, *c, d*, 8 inches long, 1

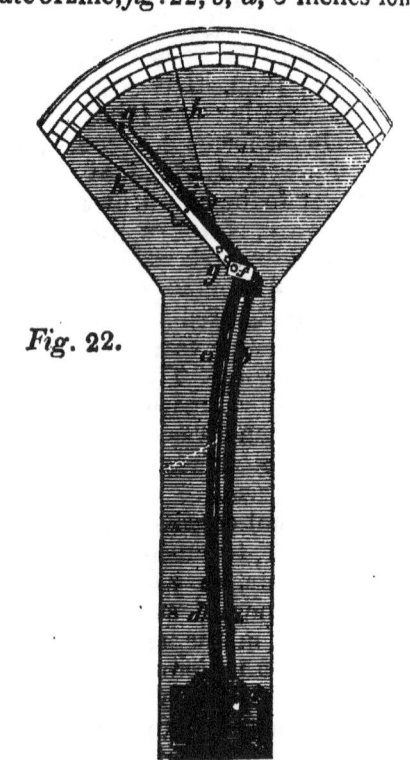

Fig. 22.

inch broad, and ¼ inch thick, to a plate of iron *a, b* of the same length. The lower extremity of the compound bar is firmly attached to a mahogany board at *e, e*; a pin *f* fixed to its upper end plays in the forked opening in the short arm of the index *g, g*. When the temperature is raised, the superior expan-

---

* Annales de Chimie, tom. lxxiv. lxxviii. xc.

sion of the zinc *c d* will bend the whole bar, as in the figure; and the index *g* will move along the graduated arc, from right to left, in proportion to the temperature. In order to convert it into a *register thermometer*, Crighton applied two slender hands *h, h* on the axis of the index: these lie below the index, and are pushed in opposite directions by the stud *i*, a contrivance seemingly borrowed from the instrument of Fitzgerald.

On the whole, the principle of this pyrometer is just; but it does not seem to possess any considerable advantages over several of those already noticed.

17. We have some doubts of the propriety of noticing a sort of *air pyrometer, fig.* 23, proposed by M. Schmidt

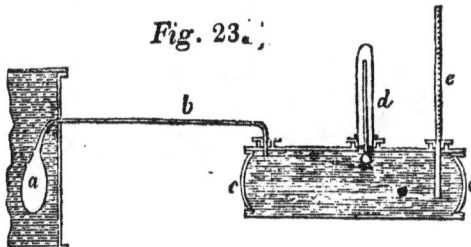

Fig. 23.

of Jasy in Moldavia.* It is so evidently a mere theoretic proposal, and is, besides, an expensive, clumsy, and probably not very accurate mode of ascertaining high temperatures. It consists of a bottle *a*, and narrow tube *b* of platina, the former to receive the impression of the heat, and the latter to convey the expanded air into *c c*, an air-tight cistern partially filled with water. The cover of the cistern is perforated by three holes; in one of which the end of the platina tube is cemented; in the second is fixed a glass tube *d*, containing a common thermometer; and in the third, a slender graduated tube *e*, which dips into the water in the cistern. The thermometer is for ascertaining the temperature of the included air of the cistern before the experiment; the graduated tube for ascertaining the temperature communicated to the platina bottle by the ascent of this water raised by the pressure of the expanded air on the surface of the fluid in the cistern. Any further description would be superfluous.

The pyrometer of Mr. Daniell (*fig.* 24) was first described in Brande's *Quarterly Journal.** The moving power is a rod or wire of platina 10.2 inches in length, and 0.14 inch in diameter, fixed in a tube of blacklead ware *a, b, c*, by a flanch within and a nut and screw without the tube at *a*. This tube has a shoulder moulded on it at *b*, for the convenience of always inserting it into the furnace, or muffle, to the same depth. From the extremity of the pla-

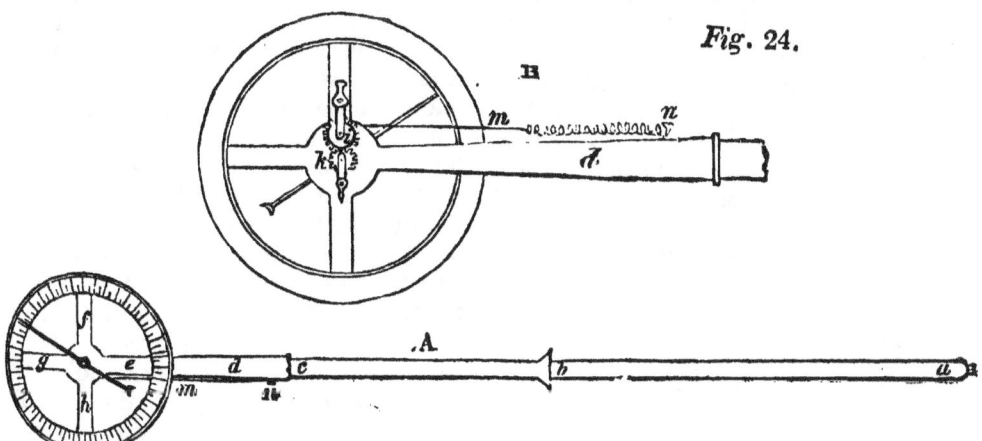

Fig. 24.

tina rod at *b* proceeds a fine wire of the same metal, $\frac{1}{100}$ inch in diameter, which comes out of a brass ferrule *d*, and passes two or three times round the axis of the wheel *i*, B, *fig.* 24. It then bends back, and is attached to a slender spring *m n*, which is fixed by one end to the pin at *n*, on the outside of the ferrule.

The substitution of a silk string for that part of the platina wire lapped round the wheel, and connecting it with the spring, has rendered the motions of the index more sensible. The axis of *i* is = 0.062 inch, and the diameter of the wheel one inch: its teeth play in the teeth of another wheel just one-third of its diameter, by which the wheel *k* has three times the movement of *i*; and the index on the axis of *k*

---

* Nicholson's Journal, 8vo, series, vol. ii. 141.   * Vol. xi. p. 309.

moves therefore three times round for every revolution of i. The action of the spiral spring m draws round the wheel i and the index, when the expansion of the platina rod permits it to act. The dial is divided into 360 degrees. By experiment, Daniell ascertained that each degree of his scale = 7 degrees of Fahrenheit's: and he has published an account of some well conducted experiments on the fusing points of some of the metals with this instrument, which very widely differ from the results obtained by Wedgwood, but nearly agree with those of Morveau. Mr. Daniell found, that after being exposed to high temperatures, the pyrometer did not fall to the point from which it set out; a circumstance which he attributes, with justice, to changes in the form of the tube induced by a high temperature. This is certainly an imperfection in the principle of the instrument; but if the degrees of heat be marked by the ascending series, its indications seem tolerably correct, and, although perhaps little to be depended on in nice investigations, it may become an useful instrument to manufacturers who make use of high temperatures. The tube should not be exposed to a naked fire, except it be of wood charcoal; because the foreign ingredients of fossil coal will adhere or incorporate with the blacklead ware of the tube. On these grounds we should feel more inclined to recommend the pyrometer of Morveau, which, besides, is extremely portable; and, being wholly exposed to the heat, is less liable to be affected by extrinsic circumstances in its indications.

The following table exhibits some of Daniell's comparative results.

50° Fahrenheit = 7°.2′ Daniell.
100 = 14 0
150 = 22.5
200 = 30.5
250 = 38.5
300 = 45.4
350 = 51.5
400 = 58.5
450 = 66.9
500 = 73 5
550 = 77 0
580 = 84 0

600° by calculation he estimates at 86°.4.

	D.	F.
Melting point of tin	63	441
——— bismuth	66	462
——— lead	87	609
Boiling point of mercury	92	644
Melting point of zinc	94	658
Red heat in full daylight	140	980
Heat of a parlour fire	163	1141
Melting point of brass	267	1869
——— silver	319	2233
——— copper	364	2548
——— gold	370	2590
——— cast iron	497	3479

18. Messrs. Breguet, the celebrated chronometer-makers, have lately constructed a most elegant and delicate pyrometer, or metalline thermometer, of which we give a figure. (See *fig.* 25.)

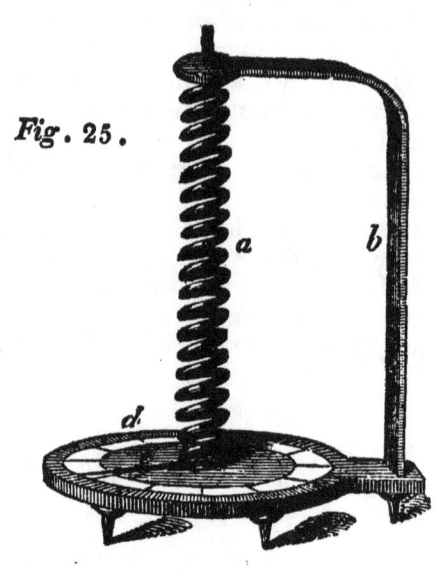

Fig. 25.

It consists of a helix formed of three metals of unequal expansibility. The exterior plate of this delicate helix is of silver, the interior of platina, and between them is one of gold. Two only are necessary to the perfect action of the instrument; but from the difference of expansibility between silver and platina, they would be liable to separate by sudden changes of temperature; and a thin plate of gold, which is of intermediate expansibility, is interposed. The whole form a single flat plate or wire about $\frac{1}{100}$th of an inch in thickness. The upper extremity of the helix is fixed to the brass support b, which by its form insulates the helix, and permits its coiling and uncoiling freely. To its lower extremity is attached a gold needle e, kept horizontal by a small counterpoise. This needle moves round a graduated circle representing degrees of the centigrade scale. When the ambient air is heated, the expansion of the metals carries round the needle in the direction of the coils of the helix, and a diminution of temperature moves it in the opposite direction by relaxing the coils. Experiment has proved that equal increments of temperature move the needle over equal spaces of the scale, so that it is comparable with other thermometers.

THERMOMETER AND PYROMETER.

The sensibility of the instrument is represented as very great, when compared to a mercurial thermometer; and it is applicable to such purposes as ascertaining the temperature of a *vacuum*, which the mercurial thermometer is able to do less accurately, because of the dilatability of its bulb by the removal of pressure.

The height of the instrument, from which this description is drawn, is 3 inches, including the feet, which are half an inch; the diameter of the helix is rather less than $\frac{3}{10}$; and its length is $1\frac{1}{2}$; the diameter of the graduated circle is 2 inches inside, and its breadth $\frac{1}{4}$.

19. The instrument delineated in *fig.* 26, from one now before us, is a

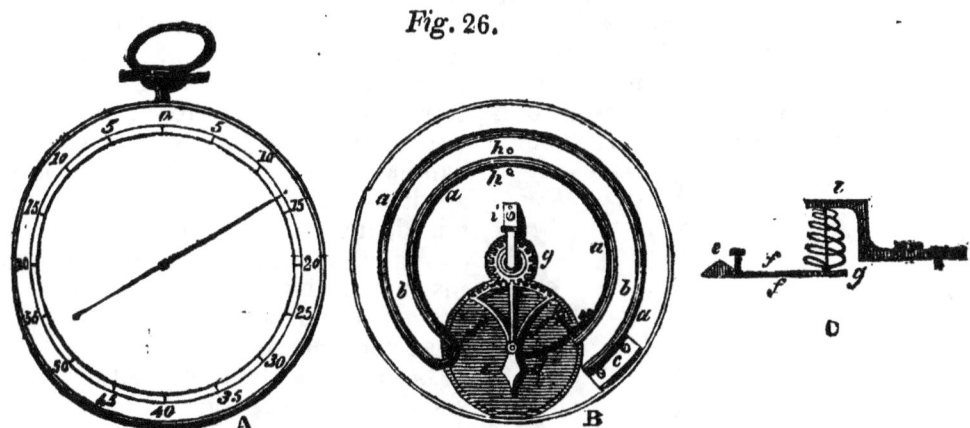

Fig. 26.

beautiful instrument of the same kind, the work of the Parisian artist, Frederick Houriet, which appears to be little known in this country. It is of the size of a thin ordinary watch, with a dial A divided according to the centigrade scale. The mechanism is covered by a thin plate of metal, which opens like a hunting watch; and the instrument is so delicate as to move, in less than a minute, after it is laid on the hand, at an ordinary temperature of 60° F.

The pyrometric piece is the bent compound bar a, b, a, b, composed of a plate of steel on the side a, and of another of brass on the side b, united together into one bar. The steel plate is $\frac{1}{10}$ inch in thickness, and the brass twice as much, forming a bar 9.5 inches in length, and about $\frac{1}{4}$ inch in depth. One extremity is firmly secured to the frame at c: the rest of it is free, bent up for the convenience of size, and secured against any accidental injury from rude handling by passing between two steel studs h, h. Its free extremity is terminated by a plate of steel d screwed to it, and projecting 0.3 inch beyond it, to press against the short arm e of the lever ff. The long arm of the lever ends in an arch-head with thirty teeth, that play in the teeth of a small wheel g with twenty-two teeth, which is fixed on the axis of the slender hand. The lengthening of the bar pushes the short arm of the lever, and the arch-head moves over a space proportional to the difference in length of the arms of the lever. How this motion is communicated in an increased ratio to the index is obvious from the construction. Under the cock i, which supports the common axis of the index, and g, is a spiral spring of flattened gold wire, intended to bring back the index when the contraction of the bar allows it, and to retain the piece d in contact with the short arm of the lever e. The instrument is adjusted by means of a steel screw k working in a small tube, which perforates the end piece d.

The whole instrument is most delicately made, and it accords in its indications with a mercurial centigrade thermometer, with which it has been carefully compared; forming one of the most elegant metalline thermometers hitherto described.

CHAPTER III.

History and Construction of Register Thermometers.

THE original suggestion of a thermometer which could register its own indications in the absence of the observer, is due to the celebrated John Bernoulli, who describes such an instrument in a letter to Leibnitz;[*] and an instrument

---

[*] Leibnitzii et Bernoulli Commercium Philosoph. et Mathemat.

on nearly the same principle was constructed by Kraft:* but their contrivances are inferior to several others of a later period, and do not require a detailed notice. We shall therefore proceed to describe the most approved register thermometers.

1. Lord Charles Cavendish communicated to the Royal Society different forms of thermometers, intended to register the *maximum* and *minimum* temperature in the absence of the observer.† His lordship's thermometer for showing the maximum is represented in fig. 27. It consists of a cylindrical bulb,

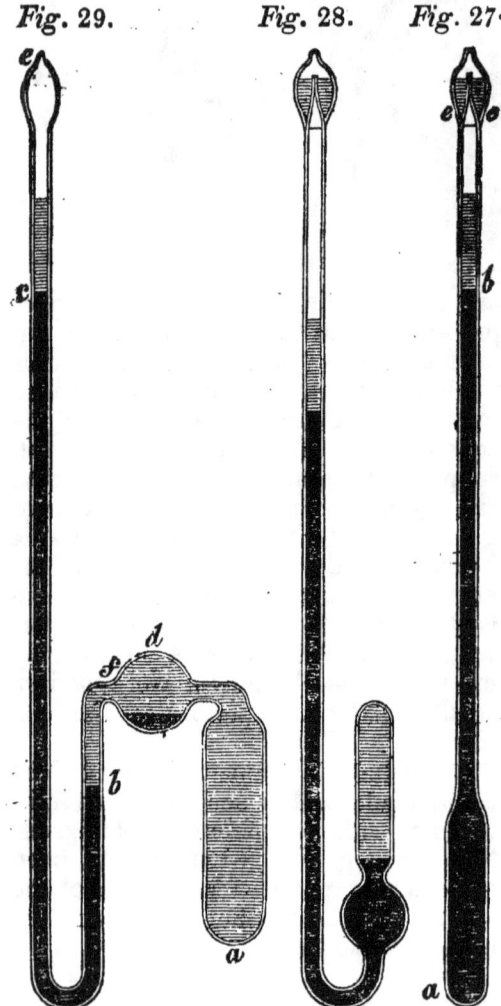

Fig. 29.   Fig. 28.   Fig. 27.

and a stem terminating in an open capillary orifice, covered by a glass cap or ball e completely closing the thermometer. The bulb and part of the stem are filled with mercury, the rise and fall of which indicate the temperature in the usual way; above the mercury a portion of alcohol is introduced, sufficient to fill the rest of the tube and a small part of the cap. When the mercury rises it drives the spirit before it into the cap e, from which it cannot return while the instrument remains erect; and the deficiency of spirit in the tube, on the subsiding of the mercury, measured by a proper scale, will show how much the maximum rise of the thermometer exceeded its height at the time of the observation.

To prepare it for a fresh observation, the thermometer is to be heated by the hand until the spirit fills the whole tube, which is then to be inclined so that the spirit in the cap may cover the capillary orifice: as the ball cools, the spirit will drain into the tube thus inclined, and fill it as completely as before.

Fig. 28 is a construction of the same instrument, intended to obviate the inconvenience of so weighty a bulb as that filled with mercury must be.

Lord C. adds a correction which should be made on account of the difference of expansion of mercury and spirit, in computing the deficiency, if this be measured by the same scale as the ascent of the mercury: the degrees computed by the column of spirit will exceed those of the mercurial column by $\frac{1}{8}$ of a degree for every $10°$ of Fahrenheit of difference between them.

Fig. 29 is his lordship's minimum thermometer. Its bulb, $\frac{3}{4}$ of the ball d, and part of the leg b, are to be filled with spirit of wine; from b to c is occupied by a column of mercury, and about $\frac{1}{4}$ of d contains a portion of this fluid; a little alcohol is likewise introduced above the mercury before the orifice of the tube at e is closed in the usual manner. The mercury at c will, when furnished with a proper scale, indicate the present temperature in the ordinary way; but, when the spirit in the bulb contracts by cold, the mercury will rise in the short leg of the siphon from b into the ball d, from which it cannot get back into the tube b. This will therefore occasion a deficiency of mercury in that leg, which, measured by a proper scale attached to the short leg of the siphon, and subtracted from the present height of the mercury in the long leg, will show the lowest point to which the thermometer had fallen during the absence of the observer. To prevent the mercury falling in too large drops into the ball d, by which the delicacy of the instrument would be impaired, a solid but fine thread of glass passes through the short leg to the

---
* Van Swinden, Comparaison des Thermomètres.
† Phil. Trans. vol. l. for 1757.

narrow neck f of the ball d, by which the passage is still further contracted, so that the mercury trickles through in most minute division. The instrument is prepared for a new observation by being inclined so as to bring the mercury in d to cover the orifice at f; the bulb is then heated, and the mercury is expelled from the ball into the short leg of the siphon, until it be filled with that fluid.

Fig. 30 is another form of the last

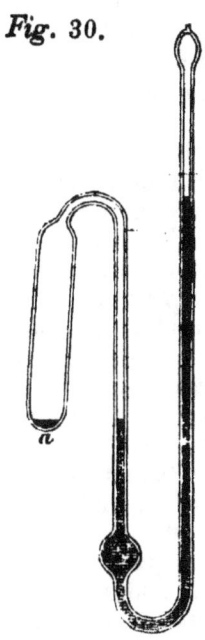

Fig. 30.

instrument, which has the advantage of being more easily adjusted, and is less liable, from slight motion, to have the mercury which has passed into a brought back into the tube.

These instruments are extremely ingenious contrivances; but there are some practical difficulties in their construction; and the minimum thermometer is rather liable to be broken from the size of the bulb, and the several bendings of the tube. Hence Lord C. Cavendish's thermometers never appear to have come into general use, although very well adapted for certain purposes, as for ascertaining the temperature of the ocean at great depths. It is therefore unnecessary here to notice the corrections pointed out by Mr. Cavendish in its applications to various purposes.

2. Next in point of time is the contrivance of Fitzgerald; which has been already noticed, as well as that of Crighton; for rendering their metallic thermometers indicators of the maxima and minima of temperature during the absence of the observer.

3. The Register Thermometer invented by Mr. James Six, of Colchester, was first described in the *Philosophical Transactions*,* and is represented in fig. 31. It is, in fact, a spirit of wine

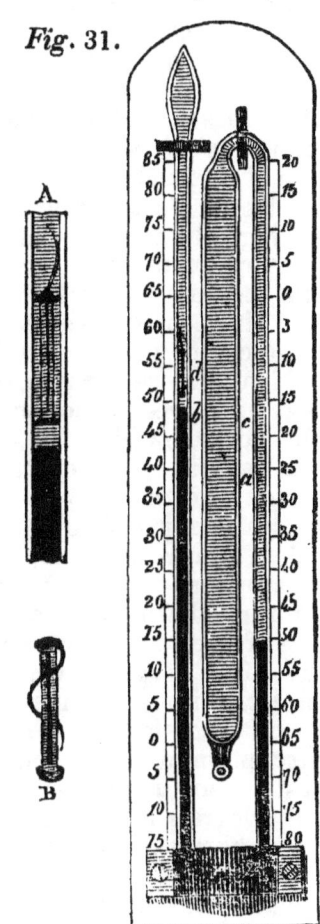

Fig. 31.

thermometer, with a long cylindrical bulb, and a tube bent in the form of a siphon with parallel legs, and terminating in a small cavity. A portion of the two legs of the siphon from a to b is filled with mercury; the bulb, and the remainder of both legs of the siphon, as well as a small portion of the cavity, are filled with highly rectified alcohol. The double column of mercury is intended to give motion to the two indices c, d; the form of which is better seen at A. Each index consists of a bit of iron wire inclosed in a glass tube, which is capped at each extremity by a button of enamel. Their dimensions are such, that they would move freely in the tube, were it not for a thread of glass drawn from the upper cap of each, and inclined so as to press against one side of the tube, forming a delicate spring of sufficient power to

---

* Vol. lxxii.

retain the attached index at any part of the tube, to which it is raised by the column of mercury. The action of the instrument will now be readily understood. When an increase of temperature expands the spirit in the bulb, it depresses the mercury in the limb a, and proportionally raises it in the limb b of the siphon: the mercurial column in the latter raises the index d before it; and when the mercury sinks in that leg, the bottom of the index d, retained at that height by the glass spring, will indicate how high the mercury had risen. When the spirit in the bulb contracts by cold, the mercury in the limb b descends, and the consequence is a proportional ascent of the column in the side a; which likewise carrying the index c before it, leaves its lower extremity at the point to which the column of that side had risen. In this manner the *maximum* and *minimum* temperatures are seen at any desired interval of time; and all that is necessary to prepare the instrument for a fresh observation is to bring down both indices to the surface of their respective columns by means of a magnet, which will act on the bit of iron wire included in the body of each index. From the above description, it is obvious, that there must be an *ascending* scale to measure the degrees of expansion in b, and a *descending* scale applied to a to mark the contraction of the spirit. Mr. Six graduated his thermometers by placing them in water at different temperatures, and marking on his scales the heights corresponding to every 5° of a standard mercurial thermometer immersed in the same liquid. This elegant invention has become a common instrument; and on account of the ease with which the glass spring of the index may be broken off, many instrument makers substitute a slender bristle, tied to the upper part of the index, and lapped round its body, as at B. This renders the spring less easily spoiled by the careless shifting of the index; but the hair, by being long steeped in spirit, is liable to have its elasticity destroyed; and a slender silver or platina wire would be preferable. The usual dimensions of the instrument are, a bulb from 6 to 16 inches in length, and from 0.2 to 0.3 inch in internal diameter; the siphon from the $\frac{1}{48}$ to the $\frac{1}{20}$ of an inch in width, and of a length proportioned to the size of the bulb; the indices about 1 inch long; the terminal expansion of the tube is, in most of the instruments now made, rather too small; in Six's original instrument, this part was a cylinder of 2 inches in length, by half an inch in diameter, to a bulb of 16 inches in length, and $\frac{1}{10}$ inch in internal diameter.

The chief defect of Six's thermometer arises, as in most other contrivances of this sort, from the unequal expansion of the spirit, and the introduction of two liquids of very different expansibility in the instrument; while, from the construction, it would be difficult to apply any general correction to its indications. It does not indicate the expansion of the spirit only, but also that of the mercurial column; which, where nice observation is required, would be of some moment; and the necessary friction of the indices will also tend to diminish the effect of expansion. Yet this instrument is a valuable addition to meteorology; and is probably the most convenient for ascertaining the temperature of the ocean, at great depths, of any hitherto given to the public.

4. The day and night thermometers of Dr. John Rutherford, from the simplicity of their construction, and low price, have in some measure superseded the register thermometer of Six. This ingenious and elegant device was first published in the Transactions of the Royal Society of Edinburgh,[*] and is represented in *fig.* 32; where A represents a spirit, and B a mercurial thermometer, each provided with its own scale, placed horizontally on the same piece of box wood or ivory. B contains, as an index, a bit of steel wire, which is pushed before the mercury, and is left in that situation to mark how high the temperature had been. A contains a glass index half an inch long, with a small knob at each end; it lies in the spirit, which can freely pass beyond it when expanded by heat; when contracted by cold, from the attraction between spirit and glass, the last film of the column of spirit is enabled to overcome the slight friction of the index on the inside of the tube, and to carry it back towards the bulb. This attraction is so considerable, that although the index will move freely up and down in the spirit, on inclining the instrument, it will rest on the last film, and require several smart concussions given to the thermometer, to make it

---

[*] Edin. Phil. Trans. vol. iii.

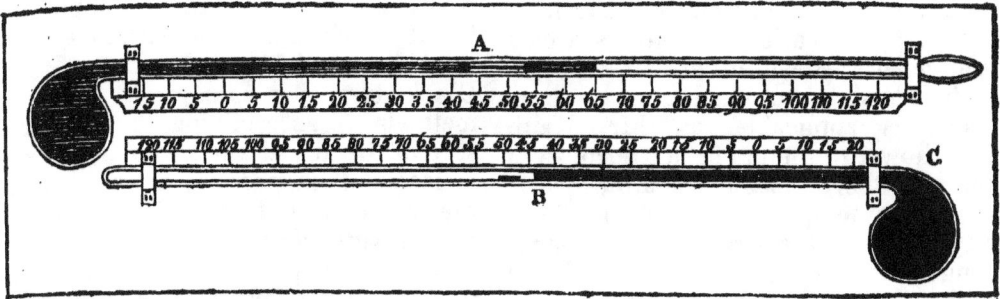

Fig. 32.

escape into the empty part of the tube. From the position of both thermometers it is obvious, that to bring both indices to the surface of the respective fluids, it is only necessary to incline the instrument toward C; and it is thus prepared for a fresh observation.

The accuracy of Rutherford's thermometers depends on the ease with which they are constructed, and the application of a due correction for the inequalities of expansion between them; this can be more readily accomplished than with Six's thermometer; because the indications of each fluid are independent of each other. The discrepancies between both thermometers have been carefully examined by De Luc,[*] and more lately by De Wildt, of Hanover;[†] the results will be given in the sixth chapter, from which the correction can be applied. Such a correction will render them applicable to the nicest meteorological observations of maxima and minima. For more ordinary purposes they are very convenient, as not being easily deranged, and being adjusted, for each observation, with the utmost facility.

5. In the *Transactions* of the same society,[‡] we find another register thermometer, by Mr. Alexander Keith, a gentleman of great mechanical invention, and long an active member of that society. It is represented in our *fig.* 33; where $a\,b$ is a glass tube, 14 inches long, and ¾ inch in calibre, sealed at the top, and below communicating with a bent tube b, d, 7 inches long, and 0.4 inches in diameter, open at the top, where it is cemented to a metallic plate e, which supports the ivory scale e, e, 6½ inches long. From a to b, the tube is filled with highly rectified alcohol, and from b to c with mercury. At c is a conical float of ivory or glass, resting on the surface of the quicksilver, and

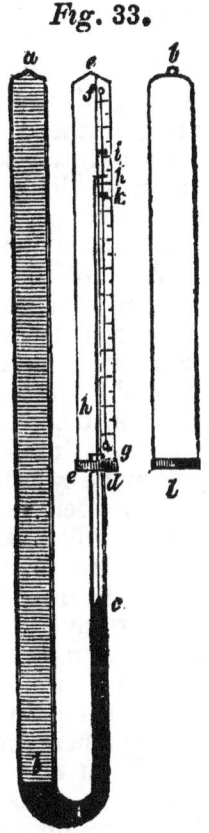

Fig. 33.

supporting a kneed wire h, intended for moving two indices of black silk i, k, that slide along the fine gold wire g, f, as will be readily seen from the figure.

To prepare the instrument for observation, the indices are drawn, by means of a crooked wire prepared for the purpose, till they touch each side of the knee of the *float wire*. It is obvious that, as the heat alters the dimensions of the column of spirit in a, b, the mercury will rise or fall in the small tube, and the float swimming on the surface of the mercury will raise or depress the knee h, which will move the indices accordingly on the wire g, f. The instrument is defended from wind or rain by the glass case l, l, which, by means of its metal collar, fits tight on e, and is only removed to adjust the indices.

This instrument, it is true, is influ-

---

[*] Recherches sur les Mod. de l'Atmosphère.
[†] Jameson's Edin. Phil. Journal for October, 1826.
[‡] Edin. Phil. Trans. vol. iv.

enced by atmospheric pressure, when its cover is removed; but the effects of barometrical variations are scarcely appreciable except in an air thermometer; and when made on a large scale, is applicable, as Mr. Keith has shown, to the important purpose of marking the *periods* of the atmospheric changes of temperature. This he effected by making the large tube 40 inches long, but retaining the original width; while the small tube is increased in diameter, but not in length. The float c is enlarged, and the float wire carries, instead of the knee, a soft pencil, which is made to press lightly against a hollow vertical cylinder, 7 inches long and 5 in diameter, moved by clock-work, once round in 31 days. This cylinder is covered with smooth paper, ruled longitudinally into 31 columns, to correspond to the days of the month; and every column is subdivided into 6 equal parts, each corresponding to 4 hours. The cylinder is ruled across into 100 divisions, intended to correspond to the 100° of Fahrenheit marked on the ordinary scale of the instrument, which is unnecessary when the cylinder is applied. Thus, as the cylinder revolves, the point of the pencil will trace a line on the paper more or less deviating from a horizontal line, as the mercury rises and falls; and thus the paper will present a *chart* of the variations of the thermometer for a whole month, the value of which, in degrees of Fahrenheit, will be indicated by the numbers on the margin of the paper. Keith recommends the observer to have a copper plate for giving ruled impressions on smooth paper, to be applied monthly to the cylinder; and these, bound up together, will present tabular views of the fluctuations of the thermometer for every month. It is hardly necessary to state that a similar contrivance is applicable to the indications of the barometer.

6. We are indebted to Mr. Henry Home Blackadder, for some very ingenious methods of ascertaining the temperature of the air, at any given hour, by a subsequent inspection of a thermometer. His first invention resembles one of Rutherford's thermometers, suspended on a pivot. If a spirit thermometer be preferred, it is to be hung vertically and inverted, so that the index may rest on the last film of the liquid. Suppose that we desire to know the temperature at 5 o'clock, A. M., a lever connected with a clock is applied, so as to bring the thermometer to a horizontal position at that hour; and, at the same time, the motion causes the bulb of the thermometer to approach some source of heat a little higher than that of the air; as, for instance, a small lamp, by which the spirit would rise beyond the now horizontal index, leaving it at the point to which the spirit had contracted before the reclination of the instrument. When a mercurial thermometer is employed, the instrument is also hung vertically, but with its bulb lowermost; and the index, therefore, resting on the mercury. It is brought to a horizontal position by the same means as the other thermometer; and then its bulb, coming into contact with a camel-hair pencil, kept continually moist with water, is cooled so as to cause the mercury to shrink, and leave the index at the height of the column while the instrument was in the upright position.

By a subsequent improvement he has contrived to dispense with the index altogether. This modification is seen in *fig.* 34, where two thermometers are placed parallel on the same piece of box

Fig. 34.

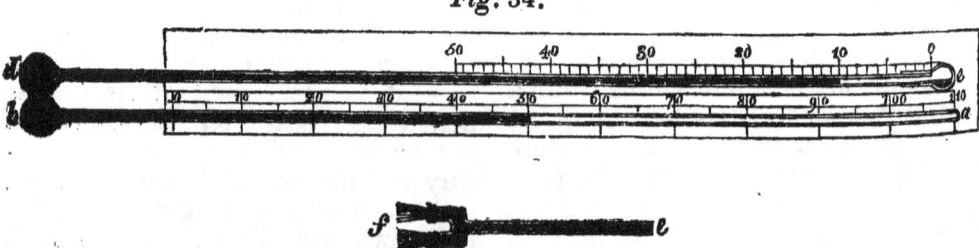

wood or ivory: $a\,b$ is a common mercurial thermometer; $c\,d$ is of the same size, but is not hermetically sealed. The end of its stem is ground flat, and is introduced into the neck of a small ball at e; which, as well as the stem, contains some mercury. The stem is pushed up until it just reaches the ball, to which it is cemented by colourless varnish.

When these thermometers are in the upright position, the globule of mercury in e covers the orifice of the tube; and on applying the heat of the hand to *d*, the mercury in the stem joins that in the ball; and the stem will remain filled with the mercury while the instrument is vertical: but when it is brought into a horizontal position by the machinery above mentioned, and the bulbs approximated to the pencils *e f*, suspended over them for that purpose, and supplied with liquid through the channels in them, the mercury in the ball will leave the orifice of the stem, and that in the latter will descend, as represented in the figure; and its subsequent contraction is marked by an inverted scale; which, with the indications of the other thermometer, will enable us to ascertain the temperature at the moment of the reclination of the instrument. Thus, as both instruments are equal, if the same diminution of temperature has sunk *a b* to 50°, and has produced a contraction of 10° in *e d*; it is evident the sum of both numbers will show the degree at which the common thermometer stood at the moment of the change of position; which in this case has been 60°.

This idea is most ingenious, and is said in practice to work exceedingly well. It promises to be useful in meteorological investigations, although not so complete as the register thermometer of Keith, which continues to note its own indications for a whole month; while that requires to be readjusted for each observation.

7. We shall conclude this chapter by a notice of another register thermometer invented by Dr. Traill, and seen in *fig.* 35. It is a single spirit thermometer,

Fig. 35.

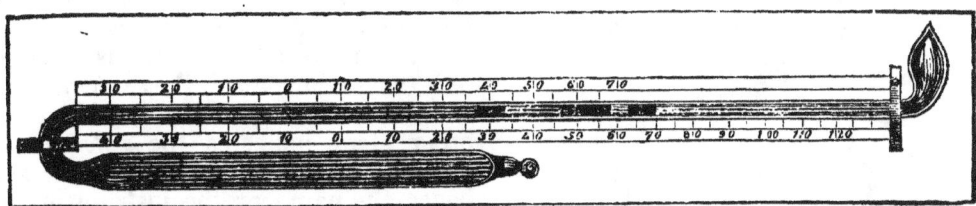

in which a column of mercury ⅓ of an inch in length is introduced: at each end of this column lies an index of fine steel wire, gilded by means of a galvanic circuit, to prevent oxidation in the spirit. An inspection of the figure will show how the variations of bulk of the spirit in the bulb will move the column of mercury; and by this the indices are pushed in opposite directions, but will remain at the lowest and highest points to which they are driven by the mercury. The difference between the two scales will be the length of the mercurial column. The indices are brought in contact with the mercury by a magnet.

This thermometer has the advantage of giving the *maxima* and *minima* by the changes in volume of a single fluid; for the expansion of so short a column of mercury is quite inappreciable. The defect of this construction is the liability of the mercury to separate by sudden motions of the instrument. This is least likely to happen when the mercurial column is short and the calibre of the tube is minute; and it is to admit of a fine tube that gilded steel wire is preferred to an index coated with glass.

Chapter IV.

Differential Thermometers, and their Modifications.

Thermometers of this kind are not affected by general changes of temperature in the surrounding medium; but are delicate indicators of partial changes affecting one of their balls. Some of the forms of the air thermometer described by Van Helmont, bear a general resemblance to the instrument known by the name of *differential thermometer*: but they were rudely constructed, without a fixed scale, and unsusceptible of accuracy, or of application to the delicate investigations required by modern experimental philosophy. We are indebted to the ingenuity of Professor Leslie of Edinburgh for a perfect differential thermometer, and its application to some very important purposes.

In January 1800, he published a description of a new *hygrometer* and *photometer*,[*] of which the principle depends on the difference in the volume of air contained in two equal balls of glass, connected by a tube bent in the

---

[*] Nicholson's Journal, 4to, vol. iii. p. 461.

form of a letter U, when the balls are unequally heated. This difference is measured by the motion of a coloured liquid contained in the bent tube. "In ordinary cases," says Leslie, "the intermediate liquor would continue stationary; for the air in both balls having the same temperature, and, consequently, the same elasticity, the opposite pressures would exactly counteract each other;" but if one ball becomes colder than the other, "it is manifest that the liquor would be pushed towards it by the superior elasticity of the air included in the other." This is the principle which suggested to him the

1. *Differential Thermometer*, used with so much skill and ingenuity in those delicate investigations *on heat*, with which he was occupied from the above period, until the publication of his work early in 1804. The differential thermometer in its most usual form is represented in (*fig.* 36,) where *a, b*, are two

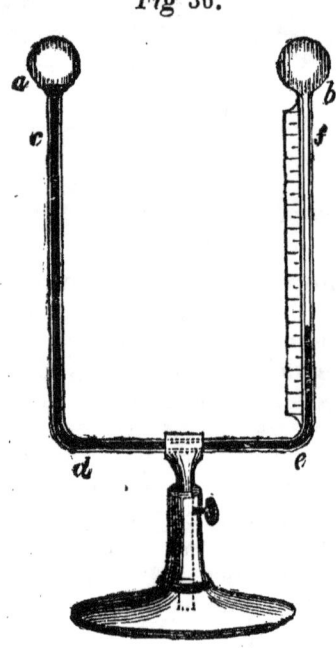

Fig 36.

equal glass spherules, connected by the tube *c, d, e, f*, slightly dilated just below the ball *a*, and at *e*, and partially filled with a coloured liquid, as represented in the figure. The dilatation below *a*, is intended as a reservoir of liquid; and that at *e*, for the more easy adjustment of the liquor to the commencement of the scale, by passing bubbles of air from one ball to the other. The liquid recommended by Leslie,* after many trials, is strong sulphuric acid, tinged by carmine. The scale he adopts, is *millesimal*, from the freezing to the boiling point of water; or 10 degrees of it are equal to one of the scale of Celsius. The instrument is cemented to a wooden foot, either immediately, or is furnished with a sliding stem to adapt it to different heights. Each leg of the instrument is usually from 3 to 6 inches in length, and the balls are from 2 to 4 inches apart. The calibre of the stem *e, f*, is from the 1-50th to 1-60th of an inch; that of the rest of the syphon a little larger.

When exposed in a room, or in the open air, the differential thermometer remains stationary at 0°, whatever may be the temperature of the ambient air; but if one of its balls be more heated than the other, the unequal expansion of the included air puts the coloured fluid in motion. In employing this instrument in experiments on the radiation of caloric, its principal use, the ball *a* is that to which the heat is applied; or is, as Leslie calls it, the *sentient* ball; and the mounting of the liquid in the other stem indicates the *difference* of elasticity of the air in both balls, and hence the name of the instrument. It owes to its insensibility to general changes of temperature, its peculiar fitness for measuring the influence of radiation.

The theory of the instrument supposes that *gases expand uniformly with equal increments of temperature*: this is, perhaps, not strictly true; yet, as Leslie remarks, it is so nearly correct, that, in the limited range of the instrument, the irregularity from that cause is quite inappreciable.

It is worthy of remark, that, a few weeks after the publication of Mr. Leslie's "Inquiry," a part of the "Philosophical Transactions" of London appeared, which contained a set of experiments almost similar to many of his, and a description of an instrument, in principle precisely similar to his differential thermometer. This was

2. *Rumford's Thermoscope*.

It consisted also of two horizontal balls, united by a syphon; and the only difference from Leslie's thermometer is, that the scale is attached to the horizontal part of the tube (which is the longest portion); and the coloured liquid is a bubble moving to and fro, when the balls are unequally heated, in the horizontal part of the tube. Rumford pro-

---

* Experimental Inquiry, p. 417, 1804.

fesses to have borrowed the idea of the thermoscope from Leslie's hygrometer; but the latter has roundly charged him with a more direct plagiarism from the *differential thermometer;* to which accusation we do not recollect that any satisfactory answer has been published.

The differential thermometer has undergone several alterations of form to adapt it to particular purposes as an air thermometer. One of the most common is seen at *fig.* 37, where the ball *b* is cemented to the tube, after the introduction of the liquid, as in the old air thermometer, but this form has been rendered more elegant and convenient by the modification of *Dr. De Butts of Baltimore,* (See *fig.* 38,) in which no cement is necessary; for the stem and both balls are united by the blow-pipe. These instruments are to be either fixed perpendicularly on a stand, or suspended. The liquid is contained in the lower ball, and the heat is applied to the upper one; so that the stem is provided with a *descending scale.*

3. *Leslie's, or the Thermometric Hygrometer.*

When the ball of the differential thermometer containing the supply of coloured liquid is coated with several folds of tissue paper, and kept moist with distilled water, the instrument becomes an *Hygrometer:* for the descent of the coloured liquid in the other stem will mark the diminution of temperature caused by the evaporation of the water from the humid surface; and as this effect is proportional to the relative dryness of the ambient air, it will give an indication of the comparative quantity of water suspended in the atmosphere, at the different times of observation. In most cases, two minutes are sufficient to produce the full effect on the instrument; and the included liquid then becomes stationary, until the whole moisture is exhaled from the ball. The drier the ambient air is, the more rapidly will the evaporation go on; and the cold produced will be greater. When the air is nearly saturated with moisture, the evaporation goes on slowly; the cold produced is moderate, because the ball regains a large portion of its lost heat from surrounding bodies; and the degree of refrigeration of the ball is an index of the dryness of the air. Could we ascertain with precision the capacity of air for moisture, at different temperatures, this hygrometer would likewise afford a measure of the absolute quantity of water suspended in the air. The most approved form of the instrument, according to Leslie, is seen in *fig.* 39. The balls are parallel, and bent from each other; *a* is covered smoothly with several folds of tissue paper, which is to be kept continually moistened with pure water, drawn from the vase *d,* by the capillary attraction of a few fibres of silk. In order to obviate any inequality from the disturbing effect of light, the ball *b* is formed of pale blue glass; and the *papered* ball is covered with thin Persian silk of the same hue.

Should the water become frozen on the ball, this hygrometer will still act; for evaporation goes on from the sur-

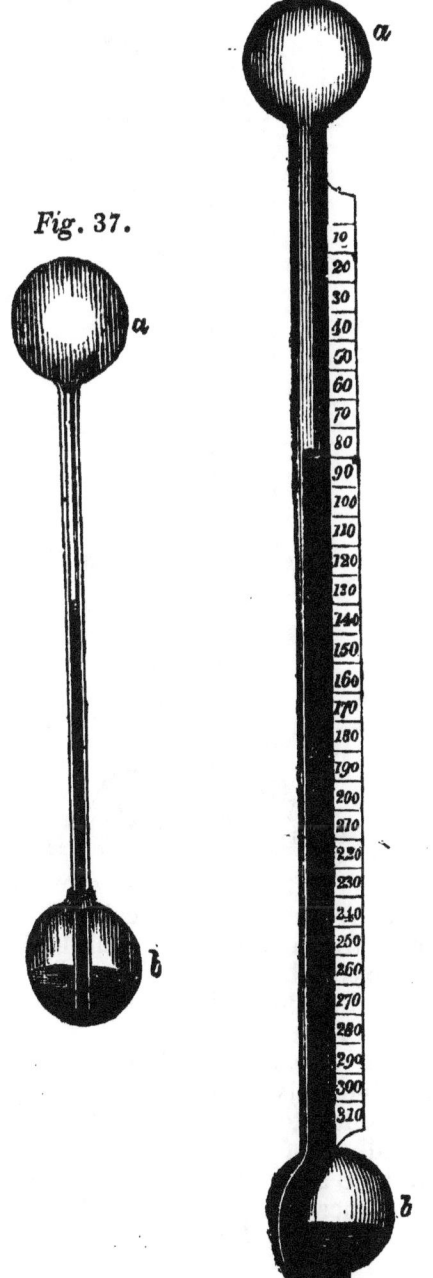
Fig. 37.
Fig. 38.

THERMOMETER AND PYROMETER.

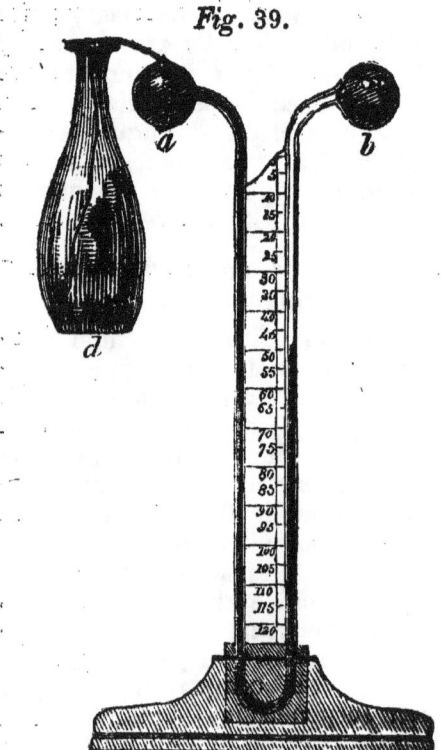

Fig. 39.

The thermometric hygrometer is of two forms; the *stationary*, (*fig.* 39,) and the *portable*, which resembles the instrument delineated in (*fig.* 41), without its glass shade. This last form is defended by a wooden case which screws over it, to fit it for the pocket.

4. *Leslie's Photometer.*

This elegant instrument is the differential thermometer, covered by a case of transparent glass, and having one of its balls either painted black, or, what is better, formed of black glass enamel.

The *Stationary* Photometer (*fig.* 40)

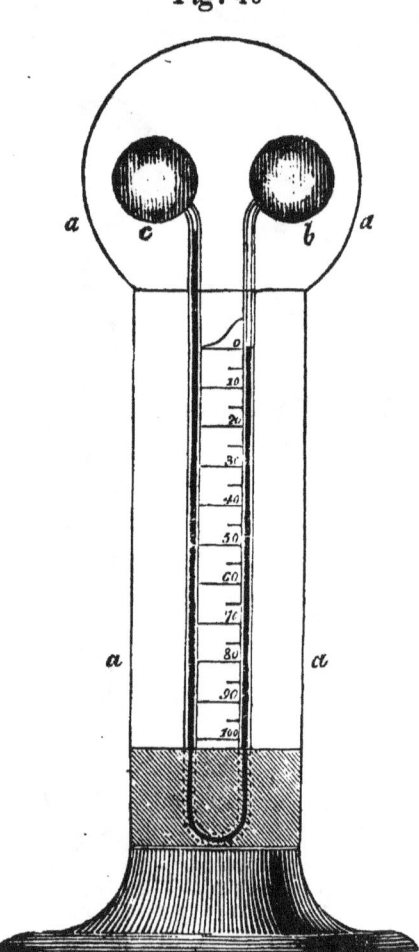

Fig. 40

face of ice, in proportion to the dryness of the air. Mr. Leslie estimates, that when the ball is moist, air, at the temperature of the ball, will take up moisture equal to the sixteen thousandth part of its weight, for each degree of his hygrometer; and as ice in melting, requires 1-7th of the caloric consumed, in converting water into vapour, when the papered ball is frozen, the hygrometer will sink more than when wet by 1° in 7°; and hence in the frozen state, we must increase the value of the degrees 1-7th: so that each of them will correspond to an absorption of moisture, equal to one-fourteen thousandth part of the weight of the air.

When this hygrometer stands at 15°, the air feels damp; from 30° to 40°, we reckon it dry; from 50° to 60°, very dry; and from 70° upwards, we should call it intensely dry. A room will feel uncomfortable, and would probably be unwholesome, if the instrument in it did not reach 30°.* In thick fogs it keeps almost at the beginning of the scale. In winter, in our climate, it ranges from 5° to 15°; in summer often from 15° to 55°; and sometimes attains to 80° or 90°. The greatest degree of dryness ever noticed by Leslie, was at Paris in the month of September, when the hygrometer indicated 120°.

has both its balls at the same height, and covered by a spherical shell of the most transparent glass; which, with the annexed glass tube, defend the balls from the disturbing influence of currents of air.

The *Portable* Photometer (*fig.* 41) has the balls in the same vertical line, in order to admit a turned tube of wood A, of the same form as its cover *a, a,* to screw on the brass collar *d,* as a defence to the instrument when in the pocket; and for further convenience

---

* Leslie "On the Relations of Air, Heat, and Moisture," p. 70.

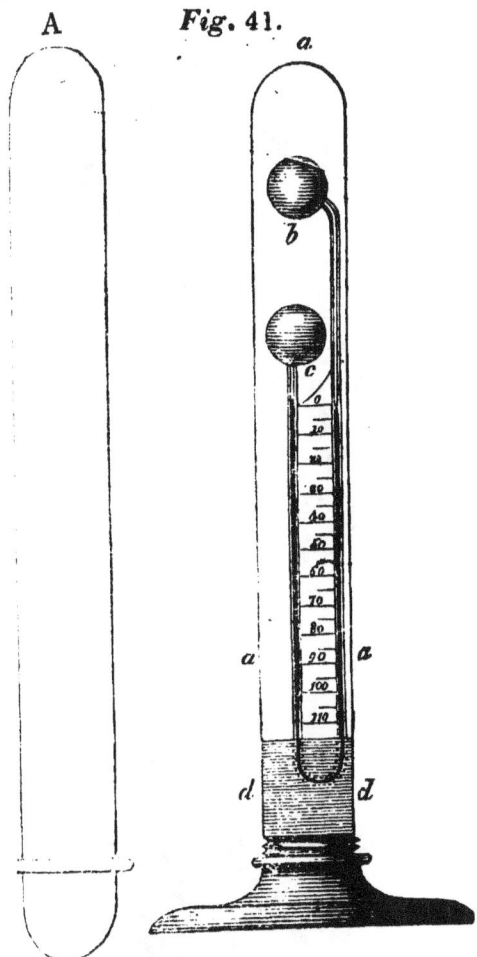

Fig. 41.

the socket is made to unscrew from the sole of the instrument. The ball, b, is of black, or deep reddish-brown enamel, while c is as diaphanous as possible. The graduation, and other parts of the photometer, are on the same scale and construction as in the differential thermometer.

Dr. Franklin, and others, had remarked the superior power which dark colours possessed of absorbing the calorific influence of the sun's rays; and Dr. Watson, afterwards Bishop of Llandaff, had, in 1773, observed, that when a thermometer, having its ball blackened, was exposed to the sun's light, it rose 10° higher than it had previously done in a similar situation. The researches of Mr. Leslie put this fact in a more striking point of view, and led to the invention of this instrument.

The theory of the photometer hangs on the supposition, that the intensity of light emitted from any body, is always proportional to the temperature excited by its incidence on the blackened ball. This is probably true with regard to the undecomposed rays of the sun, in which the caloric and the light, if different kinds of matter, are intimately blended; but there is strong reason to suspect, that light emitted by terrestrial bodies is not always proportional to the concomitant temperature. Thus the intense splendour of phosphorus burning in oxygen gas, gives out far less heat than the comparatively dull combustion of hydrogen in the same gas; and we have found this photometer often more affected by the emanations from a fire so dull, that not a single letter could be discerned in a well-printed page, than by the degree of daylight, by which we could read the same print with pleasure and facility. It is differently affected too by light of different colours, where their illuminating property appears the same; and the experiments of Herschel, Englefield, and others, show that the maximum of heat in the solar beam, decomposed by the prism, by no means corresponds with the illumination, but is even altogether beyond the margin of the spectrum.*

As a measure, however, of the intensity of undecomposed solar light, it appears to support the character it receives from the inventor.—" The photometer," says he, " exhibits distinctly the progress of illumination from the morning's dawn to the full vigour of noon, and thence its gradual decline till evening spreads her sober mantle. It marks the growth of light from the winter solstice to the height of summer, and its subsequent decay through the dusky shades of autumn; and also enables us to compare, with numerical accuracy, the brightness of different countries—the brilliant sky of Italy, for instance, with the murky air of Holland."

The direct impression of the sun's rays at noon, about the summer solstice, in this country, equals from 90° to 100° of this instrument; and at midwinter, the force of the solar beams is from 25° to 28°. The indirect light, from a summer's sky, at noon, is from 30° to 40°; in winter, it is from 10° to 15°. In the most gloomy weather, in summer, the photometer rarely indicates less than 10° at noon; but in winter it sometimes barely exceeds a single degree.

The observations on the light of day with this instrument should always be made in the open air; and the direct

---

* Herschel, Phil. Trans. 1800; Englefield, Journ. Roy. Institution, vol. i.

effect of the sun's rays noticed, as well as the indirect reflection from the sky.

5. *Pyroscope.*

When one ball of the differential thermometer is smoothly covered with thick silver leaf, or inclosed in a polished sphere of silver, and the other ball is naked, it forms the *pyroscope;* an instrument intended by its inventor, Mr. Leslie, to measure the intensity of heat radiating from a fire into a room, or the frigorific influence from a cold body. A figure is unnecessary, as the instrument is usually made either like the differential thermometer, like that represented in (*fig.* 37,) or the hygrometer, (*fig.* 39.) The theory of its construction and application is, that all the rays incident on the metallic surface, are returned from it; while those that reach the transparent ball expand the air within it, and depress the coloured liquid in the stem. In this way the comparative radiation from various bodies may be ascertained; and it is so delicate an instrument, that in a warm room it will be visibly affected by a pitcher of cold water, at the distance of a few inches.

6. The *Æthrioscope of Leslie* is another modification of the differential thermometer which we shall here notice. One of its most usual forms is given in *fig.* 42; and is what the inventor calls the *Pendant Æthrioscope.* The ball *a* of the thermometer is inclosed within a brass sphere, *d, d,* without touching it; and for the convenience of adjustment, this sphere may be unscrewed in the middle. The other ball, *b,* which is about one half the diameter of the first, is in the centre of an oblong spheroidal cup, *c, c,* which may be covered by a top that fits on at *f, f.* The coloured liquid in the stem is supported by capillary attraction in the dilated extremity of the tube, where it joins the ball *a.* The brass work is highly polished, and the inside of the spheroidal cup is well gilt.*

This very elegant instrument is intended, in the language of Mr. Leslie, " to indicate the *cold pulses* emanating from the sky;" or, in other words, to give a comparative idea of the radiation proceeding from the surface of the earth toward the region of perpetual congelation in the atmosphere. The brass coverings defend both balls from the influence of the sun's rays, or

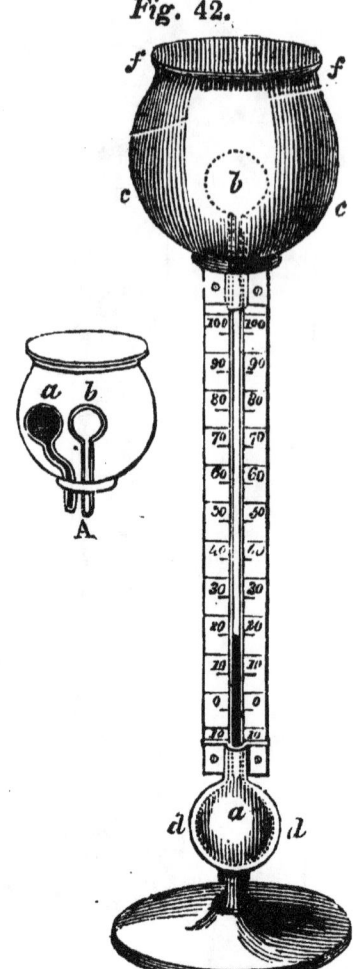

Fig. 42.

other adventitious sources of heat; and when the ball *b* is cooled by radiation toward the heavens, the air within it contracts, and the elasticity of that within *a,* forces up the liquid in the stem, the height of which marks the intensity of the radiation.

When the cover is on, the liquid remains at 0°; but when it is removed, and the instrument presented to a clear sky, either by night or by day, it instantly begins to rise, and continues to mount until the ball *b* has sustained the greatest diminution of temperature, which radiation at that time can produce.†

The circumstances which favour radiation from the surface of the earth toward the sky, namely, a clear and calm atmosphere, are admirably pointed out by Dr. Wells, in his excellent Essay on *Dew:* and this instrument becomes a

---

* Edin. Phil. Trans., vol. viii.

† Leslie appears to have been led to this invention by some of his own experiments on radiant caloric; but it is proper to state, that Dr. Wollaston had shown, that when a delicate thermometer, in the focus of a concave metallic mirror, is presented to the sky, cold is indicated.

valuable indicator of the state of the air favourable to the deposition of that interesting meteor. Such is its extreme delicacy, that, when rising, its progress is checked by the smallest cloud sailing over it; and it may be kept in a state of oscillation, by being alternately stretched beyond the edge of a parasol, and drawn within its shade, when the sky is clear and serene.

Besides the forms given above, Leslie describes two others, the *Standard* and the *Sectorial*. The first has the stem bent up as in the hygrometer, and one of the balls covered with silver leaf or gilt, near the side of the cup *c, c*, with the naked ball in the centre, as the balls *a, b*, in **A**. The second has the cup, *c, c*, formed with a notch in its bottom, for admitting a partial vertical motion round the ball *b*. The motion is given by means of a toothed sector and pinion; from which the name is derived. This form is applicable to ascertain the radiation from the earth, when we ascend a mountain, or rise in a balloon.

7. The differential hygrometer and photometer would have come into more general use had they indicated the maximum and minimum between any two times of observation. In their present construction they only show the state of the atmosphere at the moment of observation, and, therefore, require an attention which few have leisure or inclination to bestow on meteorological observations. To render them more extensively useful the following alteration is suggested, by which they are brought nearly to the thermoscope of Rumford in form. The tubes connecting the balls have the upright part of their stems shortened, and the horizontal part extended: instead of a coloured fluid filling the stems, there is a short column of mercury introduced into the horizontal part of the stem; the motion of which, towards either ball, carries before it a piece of steel wire, which constitutes the index of maximum and of minimum change during the absence of the observer. This construction will be readily understood from the figure 43, which represents the register hygrometer. A double scale lies along the horizontal part of the instrument. When the indices are adjusted for a fresh observation, they are brought by a magnet to each extremity of the little column of mercury.*

CHAPTER V.

Of some peculiar Applications of the Thermometer.

THERE are a few applications of the thermometer to certain useful purposes, which ought to find a place in the history of the instrument; I allude particularly to the Statical Thermometer of Dr. Cumming, the Balance Thermometer of Mr. Kewley, the Hygrometrical Instrument of Mr. Daniell, and the Barometrical Thermometer of Mr. Wollaston.

1. The *Statical Thermometer* of Dr. Cumming, now of Chester, was contrived by that gentleman, in 1808, and intended by him as a mode of opening and closing windows and ventilators in apartments, by the variations in temperature of the included air. This ingenious application of statical principles was shown to numerous friends at different times, in his residence at Denbigh, and was afterwards, for a considerable time, exhibited in the Denbigh Dispensary. The general form of the instrument is represented in *fig.* 44, where *a b* is a glass matrass, or a ball and tube of iron; the globular termination of which is capable of containing four or five pints of air, and the tube is about twenty-five inches in length, and from one to two inches in diameter. A portion of the tube is filled with mercury; and in this state it is inverted, and its extremity plunged in a cylindrical jar for containing the same fluid. The ball is covered by a net of strong cord, or of wire, which forms a ring at the top, for the suspension of the ball and tube. From this ring passes a cord over the pulley, *d;* and it may either pass upward under the pulley, *e*, to be attached to the frame of a swing window, as shown at *g;* or downwards over the pulley *f*, to be fixed to the ventilator *h*. When the heat of the apartment expands the air in the ball, it depresses the mercurial column in the tube, *b;* by which the whole instrument

Fig. 43.

* This instrument acts rather slowly, and the motion of the indices is not quite smooth; but it appears capable of supplying a desideratum in meteorological observations—a register hygrometer.

becomes as much lighter as the weight of the mercury expelled from the tube,

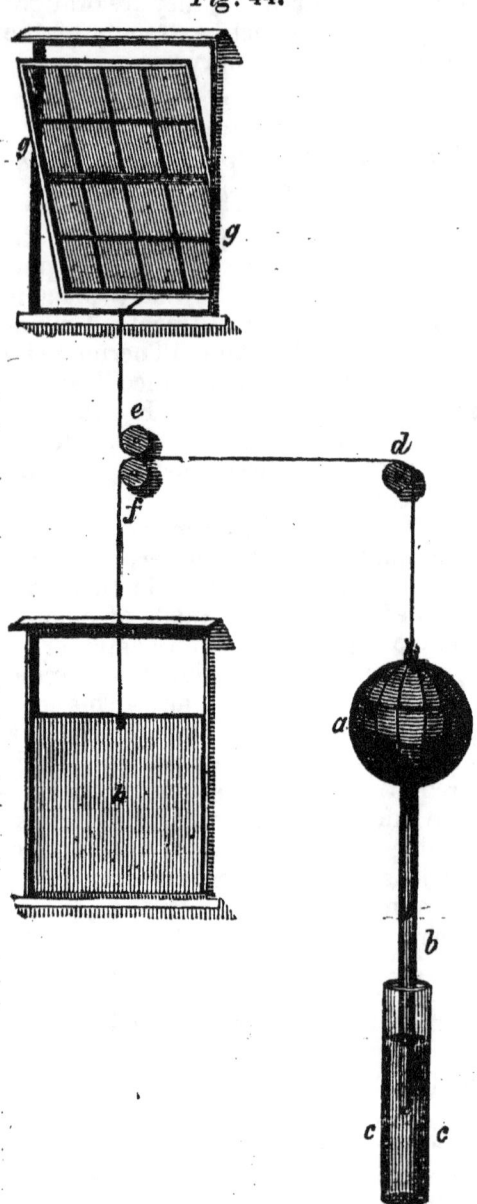

Fig. 44.

and the weight at the top of the window, or of the ventilator, opens these apertures which were kept shut by the weight of the statical tube and ball. On the other hand, when the cooling of the air in the chamber causes the contraction of the air included in the ball, the pressure of the atmosphere forces the mercury into the tube, which thus becomes so much heavier; and as it descends, it drags with it the window frame, or ventilator, attached to it.

This simple and very ingenious contrivance is applicable to hot-houses, rooms, and apartments of every description, that are liable to considerable changes of temperature; and it possesses considerable powers: for in a tube two inches in diameter, every inch in the rise or fall of the mercury is equivalent to a moving power of about one pound. It is liable to be slightly altered also by changes in atmospheric pressure.

Dr. Cummings's attention was drawn to the importance of regulated temperature in the treatment of disease, whether in public institutions or in private practice, and the contrivance above noticed was the method by which he endeavoured to obtain this important object: but he soon perceived that the principle was applicable to various meteorological purposes; and the instrument has, in his hands, undergone successive modifications and improvements, until it has become the basis of a thermometer, hygrometer, and photometer, capable of registering their own indications, by the aid of clock-work, at any given time. Details of these different contrivances would lead us into too

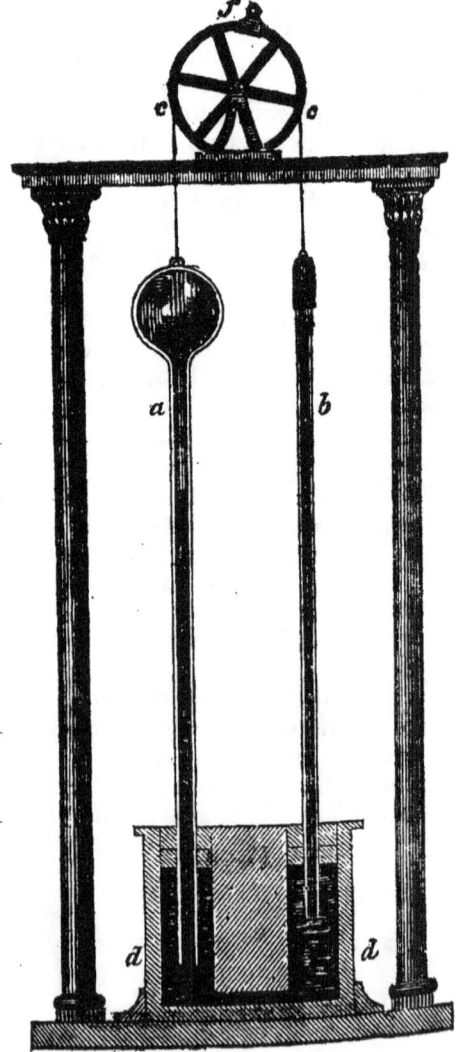

Fig. 45.

wide a field; but it may be proper to state, that finished drawings of them all have been in the possession of a distinguished member of the Meteorological Society of London for upwards of four years. The principle of them will be readily understood from the preceding figure, (*fig*. 45,) in which *a* represents an air thermometer; *b* a barometer, suspended from the opposite side of the wheel *c c*, to compensate the influence of variations in atmospheric pressure on the instrument; *d d* is a siphon-cistern, in both sides of which the mercury will always remain on the same level; *f* is an index, to which a pencil may be fixed, for tracing the variations of the instrument on a plate revolving by means of clock-work.

The portions of the tubes which dip into the mercury should be of equal substance; and the tube of the air-thermometer should be a cylinder capable of containing twice as much mercury as the corresponding portion of the barometer which counterpoises it. A small correction may be required for the varying immersion of the tubes, produced by the oscillations of the instrument. This must be determined by experiment, and allowed for in the graduation of the scale.

2. The *Balance Thermometer* of Mr. Kewley is a contrivance for a similar purpose, and is represented in *fig*. 46, A.

This instrument is the subject of a patent, the date of which is 1816. It

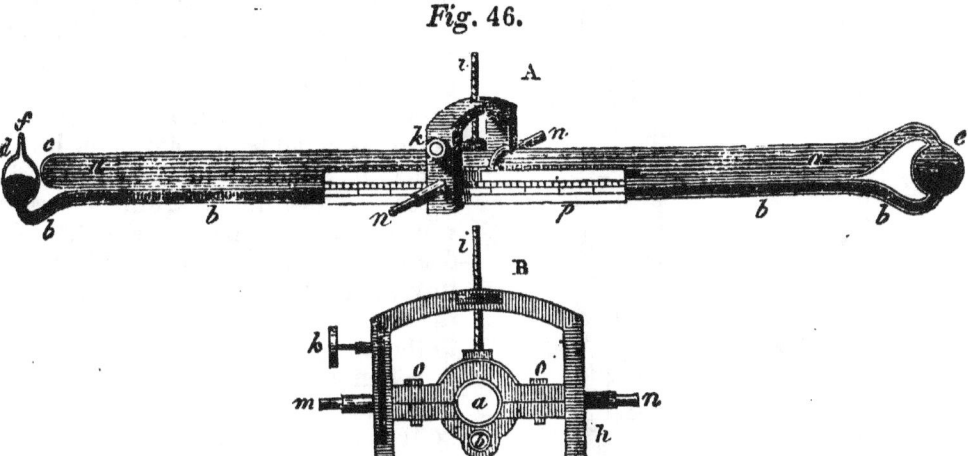

Fig. 46.

consists of a tube of glass, *a, a*, closed at *c*, and terminating at *e* in a ball, which communicates with another tube of smaller diameter, which also terminates in a ball at *d*, having a communication with the external air at *f*. The tube *a, a*, and one half of the ball, *e*, are filled with spirit, or any light easily expansible fluid. The other tube, from *e* to *d*, is filled with mercury. The whole is suspended in the iron frame, *h, i, k, m*, B, by means of two clamping pieces, which are adjusted to the tubes by the screws, *o, o*. The centre of gravity is suitably adjusted by means of the milled nut, sunk in the transverse part of the frame, and receiving the screw, *i*; in order that the whole may librate on the knife edges, *m, n*, destined to rest on surfaces resembling the suspension frame of a common balance. A brass scale, *p*, is moved by the nut, *k*, on the arbor of which is a pinion playing in the *teeth* of the plate, *p*.

It is obvious, that by adjusting the mercury in each arm of this balance, it will be in *æquilibrio*; but when the spirit in *a* is expanded by heat, it will force some more of the mercury into the ball, *d*, and that arm of the instrument will preponderate; when it again contracts, the atmospheric pressure will cause the mercury to resume its original situation.

The instrument may be used as a thermometer, by ascertaining at what temperature it is in equilibrio, and when either end preponderates, finding how much is necessary to restore the balance by the motion of the brass plate, *p*; but its chief value arises from its applicability to shut and open doors or windows, according to the temperature of the apartment; in which case, a lever, or tooth-wheel, is fixed on one of its centres of oscillation. It is almost needless to remark, that the whole may be constructed of iron, and of any convenient size. In point of simplicity and cheapness, however, it is inferior to that proposed by Dr. Cumming, which preceded it in date; although until now no detailed account of that invention has been published.

3. The *Barometrical Thermometer* of the Rev. F. Wollaston is seen in *fig.* 47, A. It is a thermometer with a

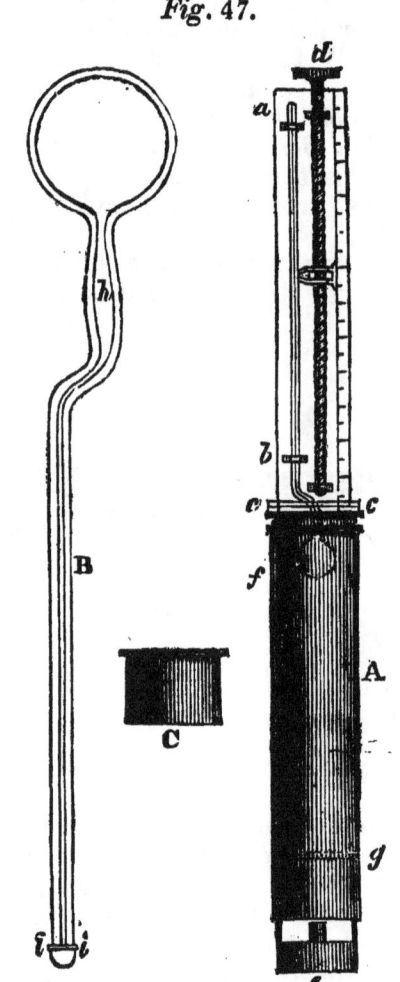

Fig. 47.

large bulb, devised for the measurement of altitudes, by observing the temperature at which liquids boil on different elevations;* on the principle first pointed out by Fahrenheit,† that the boiling of a fluid varies with the pressure of the atmosphere. Cavallo first applied this principle to the measurement of heights,‡ and the instrument proposed by Mr. Wollaston is intended to facilitate this method.

The bulb of the mercurial thermometer he proposed to use, is one inch in diameter, with a dilatation *h*, as seen in B, and ending in a capillary tube, five inches long, which is not closed in the usual manner, but, after being broken off smoothly, is sealed by a little cap of glass, as at *i, i*. The scale is 4.15 inches long, divided into 100 parts, and may be subdivided by a vernier into 1000 parts; giving 241 parts to each inch of the scale; and to facilitate observation, these are read off by a small lens jointed to the index, but not represented in our figure. The index is moved by a micrometer screw, *d*. The thermometer is supported by means of stuffing between two circular plates of metal, *c, c*, through which it passes, and which are tightened by screwing them together. They form a metallic collar, that may be screwed by either end into the top of the copper boiler, *f, g*, which becomes the case of the thermometer on inverting it; and then the bulb is protected by a copper cap C, which also serves as a measure of the due quantity of water to be used in the experiment. The portion of the copper tube below the bottom, *g*, of the boiler, is capable of holding the lamp, *e*, which is attached to it by two sliding wires. Thus the instrument becomes very portable. The boiler is 5.5 inches deep and 1.2 in diameter, with an aperture at the top to permit the escape of the steam, by which the heat is applied to the bulb.

When we have to determine an altitude, the boiling point is noted at the bottom of the eminence, and again when we have ascended; and the value of the difference between those points on the scale having been ascertained by experiment, we can estimate the height ascended, provided no change has, in the mean time, taken place in the barometrical pressure; or these points may be simultaneously found by two observers. The only correction required is, for the specific gravity of air at different temperatures, which may be found by General Roy's tables. The use of the dilatation, *h*, is to receive the expanded mercury, before it arrives at the boiling point: and the small cap, *i, i*, is intended to receive a globule of mercury, to be detached occasionally from the column in the stem, when it is wished to alter the range of the scale to suit various altitudes. The method of separating this globule is, to elevate the mercury, by heating the bulb until the thread of metal may be shaken over the flat end of the capillary tube; and when we wish to join the globule again to the thread, the two portions of mercury are brought into contact by heat, and then as the in-

---

* Phil. Trans. for 1817.
† Phil. Trans. vol. xxxii.
‡ Phil. Trans. vol. lxvi.

strument, held in the vertical position, cools, the globule will follow the thread into the stem.

This instrument is of great delicacy; being capable of showing a difference of altitude of not more than three feet; but, unfortunately, although not very bulky, it is not very portable, from the liability of the stem to be broken by the weight of the bulb, even from the usual jolting of a carriage; an accident which happened thrice to the writer of this, within one month. From this circumstance, and its price, it is not likely to supersede the barometer in geological surveys.

4. M. Le Roi was the first who suggested the temperature at which dew begins to be deposited as a method of ascertaining the moisture of the air. De Luc has the merit of having proved that the quantity and force of vapour in a vacuum of any given dimensions, are equal to its force and quantity, in an equal volume of air, at the same temperature; or that the force and quantity of vapour in the air are dependant on its temperature.* This was confirmed by Mr. J. Dalton,† who investigated the force of vapour, at every temperature, from 0° to above 212° Fahrenheit, and expressed this force by the height of the mercurial column, which it could support in a Torricellian tube. These results are given in a tabular form, and are thus easily applied to hygrometric purposes. Dalton finds the *dew point*, like Le Roi, by pouring *cold* water into a glass, and marking the temperature at which it just ceases to cause the deposition of dew on the sides of the glass, in the open air. This is the point at which, in an air of that temperature, dew would just begin to be formed. From this fact he is able to infer, not only the force exerted by the vapour, but its quantity in a perpendicular column of the whole atmosphere, and the force of evaporation at the time of observation.

Thus, if the *dew point* be 45°, the force of vapour in Dalton's table = 0.316 of an inch of the mercurial column, or the one-ninety fifth of the whole atmospheric pressure; or, if the specific gravity of steam be 0.70, the weight of the steam or vapour in a given volume of air will be the one hundred and thirty-sixth part of the whole. Now, as the force of a *whole atmosphere of steam*, at the surface of the earth, would be the weight of a perpendicular column of it, and as in a mixed atmosphere of steam and air, the force exerted by each is as their relative weights, it follows, that when the dew point is 45°, the whole superincumbent column of vapour in the atmosphere, being equal to the one-ninety-fifth of the whole atmospheric pressure, will be equivalent to a pressure of 4.30 inches of water; or the vapour, if condensed, would afford that depth of water. From these data, Dalton has shown how we can find the force of evaporation at a given time: for the quantity of water evaporated from a given surface is proportional to the maximum force of vapour at the temperature of that surface; it being understood that the vapour is still in contact with a surface of water. Hence, if we have the dew point 45°, while the temperature of the air is 50°, by subtracting the force of vapour at 45° from that of 50°, we shall obtain the force of the evaporation at that time—thus, .375—.316=.059, the force of evaporation.

5. It is on this principle that *Daniell's Hygrometer* is constructed; the invention of a gentleman distinguished for his meritorious labours in meteorology. It was published in 1820, along with a meteorological table, and seems to have been suggested by the cryophorus of Wollaston.‡ The form of the instrument is seen, as last improved by Mr. Daniell, in (*fig.* 48.) The ball *a* is of

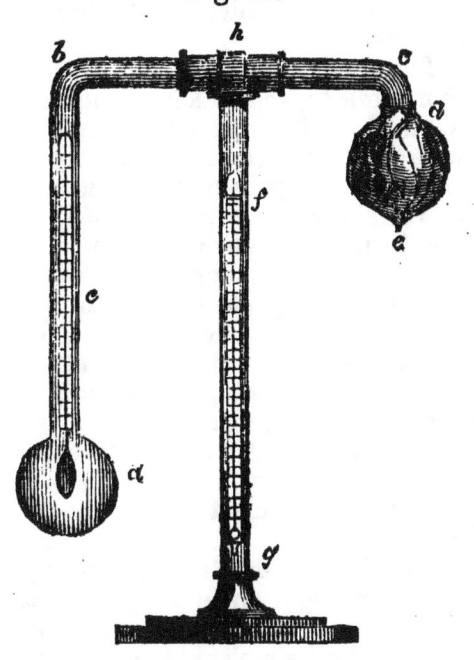

Fig. 48.

* Recherches sur les Modifications de l'Atmosphère.
† Manchester Memoirs, vol. v. 535.—vol. i. new series, p. 252.

‡ Quarterly Journal of Science, vol. viii. 299—see also vol. ix. &c.

black glass, about one and a quarter inch in diameter, and is connected with a ball *d* of the same size, by a bent tube one-eighth of an inch in diameter. A portion of sulphuric æther, sufficient to fill three-fourths of the ball *a*, is introduced; a small mercurial thermometer, with a pyriform bulb, is fixed in the limb *a b*, the atmospheric air is expelled as completely as possible; and the whole is sealed at *e*. The ball *d* is covered with muslin; the whole is supported on a brass stand *f, g*, on which is another delicate mercurial thermometer. The tube can be removed from the spring tube *h*; and the whole, together with a phial of æther, packed neatly in a box, that goes easily into the pocket. The method in which the dew point is indicated by this instrument, is as follows:—The æther is all brought into the ball *a*, by inclining the tube; the balls are placed perpendicularly; the temperature of the ambient air is now noted; æther is poured from a dropping tube that fits the mouth of the small phial, on the muslin cover of *d*; and, the cold produced by its evaporation, causing a condensation of the elastic æthereal vapour within the ball, produces a rapid evaporation from *a*, by which the temperature of the thermometer in it sinks; and when the black ball is thus cooled to the dew point, a film of condensed vapour, like a ring, surrounds the ball. If the thermometer be at that instant noticed, we obtain the true dew point of air at the temperature indicated by the other thermometer.

The observation is made in a very short period; and much of the labour required in the method of Le Roi is saved. There seems but one objection to this very ingenious instrument, and it is one, which, even with much practice, is not easily obviated. The surface on which the dew condenses, is small, and requires a peculiar light to be well seen; while the attention of the observer, distracted between the close inspection of the surface of the black ball, and the included thermometer, is not always able to fix with absolute precision the dew point.

6. This instrument has been modified in

Mr. Thos. Jones's Hygrometer; an instrument on exactly the same principle as the original invention of Daniell, but simpler in construction, more compact, and less expensive. It is seen in *fig.* 49, consisting of a deli-

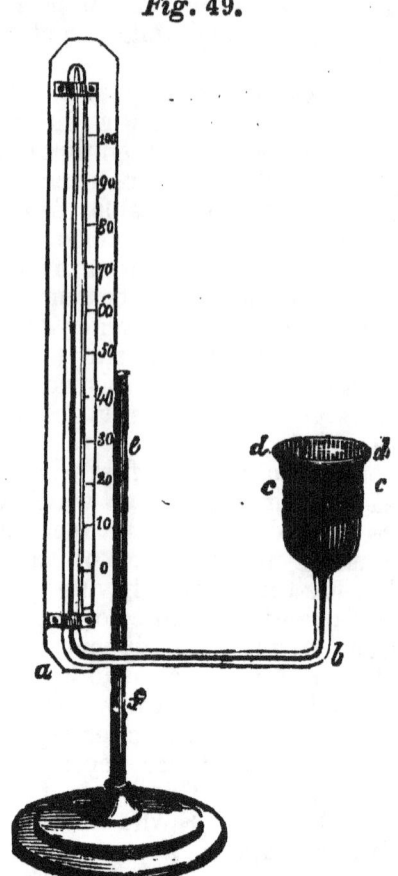

Fig. 49.

cate mercurial thermometer, with its tube at *a, b*, bent so as to bring its cylindrical ball *c*, parallel with, and at a little distance from, its stem. The bulb is one inch long, and is terminated by a flattened surface *d*, of black glass, which projects a little beyond the sides of the bulb. The bulb below the flattened surface is covered with black silk. The instrument is supported on the wire *e f*, which is attached to the scale by a pivot, that allows the black surface to be inclined to the light, and the whole, with a phial of æther, are contained in a small case. *

When used, the temperature of the air is first noted; then æther is poured on the silk cover of the bulb; and the condensation of the dew is seen on the black extremity of the bulb.

The difficulty of marking the incipient condensation on these instruments is the same; and it has produced various modifications of the instrument.

7. Dr. Cumming, of Chester, finds that the dew point is most conspicuously shown, by inclosing the bulb of a delicate thermometer, covered by a sponge, in a tube of planished tinned iron, silver, or platina. When the sponge is moist-

---

* Phil. Trans. for 1826, part ii. p. 23.

ened with any very evaporable fluid, such as æther or alcohol, and a stream of air blown through the tube, a more rapid and more conspicuous deposition of dew takes place on the surface of the metallic tube, than we ever recollect to have observed in similar experiments.

Fig. 50 is Dr. Cumming's hygrometer fitted to a portable air-syringe, by which a current of air is produced through the tube B B. The bulb of the delicate thermometer within it is surrounded with fine sponge, to retain the evaporable fluid; the tube B B is of highly polished metal, with an aperture in its upper part covered with a glass tube, for the inspection of the thermometer, as represented in the figure.

Fig. 50.

Chapter VI.

On the Imperfections common to all Instruments for the Indication of Heat.

1. The terms *thermometer* and *pyrometer* might lead to the supposition, that the instruments so designated were actual indicators of the quantity of caloric contained in those bodies to which they are applied; but a single experiment is sufficient to show that this view is erroneous. If we place equal quantities of water and of snow, both at temperature 32°, in a room at 60°, the temperature of the water will, as indicated by the thermometer, after some time, rise considerably; but the effect of the heat on the ice will only be to melt it partially, while its temperature remains steadily at 32°. Here we have *caloric* received by the ice which does not affect the thermometer.

The principle upon which the thermometer and the pyrometer act is, the tendency which heat or *caloric* has to diffuse itself among contiguous bodies. When applied to a hot body, they acquire a portion of the heat from that body; and when applied to a cold one, they communicate to that body a portion of their own caloric. These changes in the quantity of its own caloric are indicated by changes in the bulk of the thermometric fluid, or pyrometric piece; and such instruments, therefore, do no more than show a certain excess of heat given out by the hottest to the coldest body. On this ground the names of *thermoscope* and *pyroscope* are more suitable for such instruments than their more common designations.

That different bodies, in equal quantities, whether measured by weight or volume, contain unequal quantities of caloric, has been established by the investigations of Boerhaave, Black, Wilcke, Irvine, Crawford, Lavoisier, &c. It does not belong to this place to enter into this subject, but it is sufficient to mention the grounds for this important conclusion.

If we mix one pound of water at 212°, and as much water at 32°, when due precautions are employed to mix them without loss of heat or the addition of extraneous temperature, the thermometer plunged in the mixture will indicate very nearly 122°, or the arithmetical mean between the extremes; which proves that equal quantities of the *same body* contain quantities of caloric proportional to their temperature. If, however, we mix a pound of mercury with a pound of water, at different temperatures, when the mercury is the hottest, the temperature of the mixture will be greatly *below* the mean; and when the water is the hottest body, the mixture will be greatly *above* the mean temperature. A series of such experiments have shown that the same quantity of caloric which can raise the temperature of water only 4°, will raise that of mercury 112°. If this be the case at every temperature, which is most probable, the *quantity of caloric* in water is to that in an equal weight of mercury, at the same temperature, as $112 : 4 = 28 : 1$.

Besides this method of finding out the comparative quantity of caloric in bodies, there is another founded on the fact, that ice in melting absorbs an uniform quantity of caloric. Professor Wilcke, of Copenhagen, first conceived the idea of employing the melting of ice or snow, for the purpose of ascertaining the comparative quantity of caloric in different bodies; and this method was improved in the hands of Lavoisier and Laplace, by the invention of the *Calorimeter*.

It consists of two vessels of tinned iron, and a wire cage, which are fitted so that one may be inserted within the other, leaving a cavity between the sides of each. (See *fig.* 51.) The wire-cage,

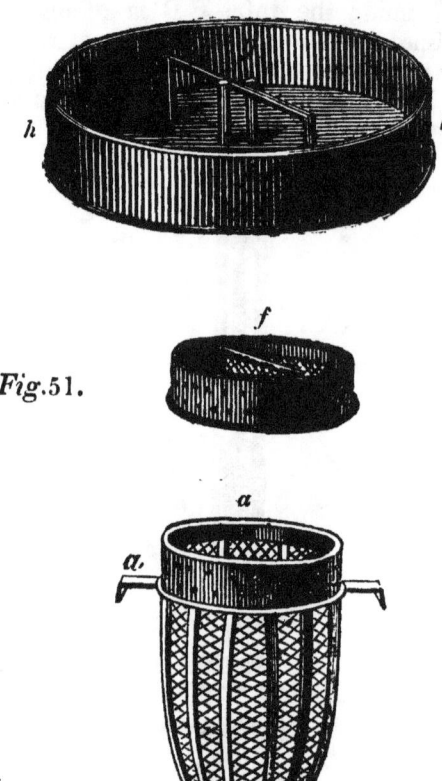

Fig. 51.

a, is the innermost; and is destined to receive the heated body, the subject of experiment. The space between it and the second vessel, *b*, is to be filled with pounded ice, or snow, as well as the perforated cover, *f*, of the cage *a*. It is the melting of this snow which affords the indication of the comparative quantity of caloric in the bodies submitted to experiment; it rests on a wire sieve, at the bottom of the cylinder *b*, and is received at the orifice of the pipe *d*. To guard against the effects of external temperature, the cavity between the vessel *b*, and the exterior one, is filled also with pounded ice or snow; the general lid *h*, of the whole being also covered with snow, and its edges resting in a groove *e*, lined with the same material, the interior of the instrument is defended from all direct access of external temperature. The two tubes, *g*, in the lid, are for the introduction of thermometers; but during experiments those tubes are shut up, to prevent the access of currents of air through the calorimeter. The water collected between the outer and second vessel may be drawn off by the pipe *i*. Experiments of this kind should be made in a room at a temperature of 32°. Before commencing the experiment, the snow is saturated with moisture by its melting, to obviate as much as possible the error from not collecting the whole of the water.

The indications of this instrument,

from the cause just alluded to, and the impossibility of altogether obviating the effects of currents of air through it, during experiments, are not susceptible of such accuracy as the more simple method of mixture; although this also is liable to lead to erroneous conclusions, from the difficulty of obtaining the true result of the effect of the different mixtures.

2. There is an obvious source of error in the indications of all instruments employed to measure temperature, in as much as the apparent changes in the volume of the thermometric substance are not the real augmentation or diminution of bulk it undergoes. The glass of the thermometer, and the frame of the pyrometer, are also expanded and contracted by changes of temperature; so that our instruments only show the *excess of the expansions* of the thermometric fluid, or pyrometric bar over those of the glass and frame; by which the true indications are diminished.

From the extreme nicety of some of the investigations in which the mercurial thermometer is employed, a comparative ratio of the expansions of mercury and glass has been most diligently sought after by De Luc, Ramsden, Roy, and others. From their investigations it has been ascertained that all solids and liquids vary in their rate of expansion; but that the expansibility of glass depends so much on the manufacture of that article, and varies so much in the different kinds, that no general equation as a correction for this source of error can be of practical utility. Even the form of the glass rod is material. Roy gives the expansion of a glass tube = 0.0046569th; of a solid glass rod = 0.0096944th, in passing from the freezing to the boiling point of water.[*]

An important series of experiments by Lavoisier and Laplace have been published by Biot,[†] from which it appears that of twenty-three solids tried, glass was the least expansible of them all.

The length of different glass rods, which at $32°$ Fahrenheit $= 1.00000000$, at $212°$ Fahrenheit is augmented as follows:

Glass of St. Gobain ......$1.00089089 = \frac{1}{1122}$
Glass tube, without lead $1.00087572 = \frac{1}{1142}$
Ditto ....$1.00089760 = \frac{1}{1114}$
Ditto ....$1.00091751 = \frac{1}{1090}$
French glass, with lead ...$1.00087199 = \frac{1}{1147}$
English flint glass ....$1.00081166 = \frac{1}{1248}$

This will show the impossibility of any general correction being applied; and the adoption of any formulæ for this purpose would be an affectation of accuracy, of which, unfortunately, the subject is incapable. If, however, such formula is considered desirable, it may easily be constructed from the experiments of De Luc on glass tubes [‡] at different temperatures, which, reduced to the scale of Fahrenheit, are,

Temp.	Bulk.	Temp.	Bulk.
32°	100000	150°	100044
50	100006	167	100056
70	100014	190	100069
100	100023	212	100083
120	100032		

3. Another error of some magnitude is produced by the inequalities of the expansions of the same substances by equal increments of temperature.

If we could consider expansion simply as the effect of the application of heat, equal increments of temperature should produce equal rates of increase of volume; but the expansion is the *resultant*, in solids and in liquids, of two opposite forces—of the repulsive energy of caloric opposed by the cohesion of the particles of matter; and, accordingly, it not only differs in the different kinds of solid and liquid matter, but in the same body at different temperatures. As might be expected from this view, it must be in an increasing ratio with the temperature; because the force of cohesion must diminish with the distance of the particles of matter.

In aëriform bodies, the force of cohesion does not exist; and we might infer that equal increments of heat would produce equal expansions, in all gases, at all temperatures. In gases, the ratio might even be expected to decrease, in a minute but inappreciable degree, with the temperature; because the increased distance of the particles will tend to diminish the repulsive energy.

Experiment in these particulars accords with theory. The ratio of expansion in solids and liquids is found to be an *increasing* one, as the temperature is augmented, and is very different in each substance; while in the gases, it is not only equable in the same gas, but equal in all.

The manner in which an increasing

---

[*] Phil. Trans., vol. lxxv.
[†] Traité de Physique, t. ii. 153.
[‡] Recherches, t. i.

ratio of expansion must affect thermometers and pyrometers, graduated on the principle of equal degrees between two fixed points, is obvious; and it early became an object of solicitude. Drs. Halley and Brooke Taylor devised the method of investigation—namely, by mixing together equal weights of water at different ascertained temperatures, and finding how much the thermometer, plunged in that mixture, differed from the mean temperature. From not sufficiently attending to the various requisites to obviate error, they did not arrive at the true conclusion. We owe to De Luc the more successful investigation of this problem; by a train of nice experiments, in which he endeavoured to guard against the sources of error arising from the cooling effect of the vessel containing the mixture, and of the escape of vapour, he proved that the different thermometric fluids do not expand in a uniform ratio to the quantities of caloric applied; but follow an increasing rate as their temperature is raised. Mercury he found to be the most regular in its expansions; yet it also showed very sensible deviations. When equal weights of water at 32° and 212° were mixed, the mercurial thermometer did not indicate the mean temperature 122°, but only 119°; an oil thermometer, in the same experiment, stood no higher than 117°, and one of spirit of wine at 108°; while, with a thermometer filled with water, the temperature of the mixture appeared only to be 75°. His experiments showed the great superiority of the mercurial over the alcoholic thermometer; but this superiority, it probably owes, as Mr. John Dalton has remarked, in a great measure to the distance of the ordinary range of temperature, from the freezing and boiling point of mercury; for the experiments of De Luc show that the irregularities of all fluids are much augmented about the points of their consolidation and passing into vapour.

From the usual method of graduating the mercurial thermometer from two fixed points only, the error from inequality of expansion will be greatest at the mean between the two points; when, according to De Luc, it amounts to about 3° Fahrenheit below the real temperature. In the following table are given the result of De Luc's researches, on the two fluids chiefly used for thermometers—mercury and alcohol. In the first column are the indications of the mercurial thermometer, according to De Luc's or Reaumur's scale; in the second, the indications of the alcoholic thermometer at the corresponding temperatures; and in the third, are, what ought to be, the real temperatures as discovered by experiment.

Mercurial Ther.	Alcohol Ther.	Real Tem.
80	80.0	80.0
75	73.8	75.28
70	67.8	70.56
65	61.9	65.77
60	56.2	60.96
55	50.7	56.15
50	47.3	51.26
45	40.2	46.37
40	35.1	41.40
35	30.3	36.40
30	25.6	31.32
25	21.0	26.22
20	16.5	21.12
15	12.2	15.94
10	7.9	10.74
5	3.9	5.43
0	0.0	0.0

There is reason to believe, however, that De Luc states the irregularity of the mercurial thermometer too high. Dr. Crawford investigated this point with great care, and concluded, that when the difference of temperature of the two portions of fluid did not exceed 100° F., the average deviations of the mercurial thermometer were not above 0.25 of a degree. De Luc himself allows, that the result of the mixtures must be inaccurate, if the *capacity* of the water operated on is changed during the experiment. In mixing together hot and cold water, the probability is, that the diminished volume of the mixture causes a diminution of capacity; and, consequently, an *increase* of temperature, beyond what is due to the heat of the two portions mixed together. By exposing a mercurial thermometer in a vessel, in which the included air was exposed to the frigorific influence of melting snow, and the heat of watery vapour at 212°, he found that it indicated 121°, or only a single degree less than the arithmetical mean.* From comparison with air thermometers, Gay Lussac inferred that the mercurial thermometer was equable in its expansions,

---

* Experiments on Animal Heat.

between the freezing and the boiling point of water.* Petit and Dulong have investigated the subject, by a comparison with the air thermometer, and with the expansions of a pyrometer of very infusible metals (platina and copper) which appear, by the experiments of Lavoisier and Laplace, to be very equable in their expansions, below the boiling point of water. They found that the irregularity in mercury increases with the temperature; and would even appear to be greater than the rise of the mercurial thermometer indicates, were not the increasing expansion of the mercury diminished by the increasing ratio of the dilatation of the glass itself.† Hence the source of error in thermometers arising from the expansion of the glass, is rather advantageous than detrimental to their accuracy.

The difference between the indications of the alcoholic and mercurial thermometers, as lately ascertained by Dr. De Wildt, do not materially differ from the determinations of De Luc; and having been obtained for every 5° of Reaumur's scale, apparently with much care, we give the result as a table of correction for Rutherford's thermometers; for which purpose they were intended by the author.

Mercury.	Spirit.	Mercury.	Spirit.
−45° =	−28°.50	+20°...	+16°.48
40	25 .92	25	20 .97
35	23 .19	30	25 .60
30	20 .32	35	30 .38
25	17 .30	40	35 .31
20	14 .13	45	40 .38
15	10 .82	50	45 .60
10	7 .36	55	50 .97
5	3 .75	60	56 .48
0	0 .00	65	62 .14
+5	+ 3 .90	70	67 .95
10	7 .95	75	73 .90
15	12 .14	80	80‡.00

The indications of air thermometers were at one time supposed liable to uncertainty, from the inequalities of their expansion. Guyton and Prieur imagined that they progressively expanded in a greater ratio than the temperature,§ but this has been proved to be erroneous; and the mistake probably arose from their neglecting the effect of hygrometric water in the gases. General Roy* found that their expansion followed a ratio, *decreasing* with the elevation of temperature; and the same result was obtained by Mr. Dalton,† Dr. Murray,‡ Gay Lussac,§ and Petit and Dulong;|| but there is reason to conclude that this apparently decreasing ratio in the expansion of gases is owing to the error caused by the unequable expansions of the mercury in the thermometer, and the dilatation of the bulb of that instrument; and philosophers now agree to consider the expansions of gases equable and equal, as before stated; especially as the decreasing ratio disappears, if we apply De Luc's correction of the real mean between 32° and 212°.

From the foregoing observations, we may conclude, that the air thermometer requires no correction of its indications; that the accuracy of the mercurial thermometer is not materially affected by the inequalities of the expansions of the mercury, in ordinary ranges of temperature; that the expansion of alcohol is pretty uniform, until about 30° R. or 100° F.: above that point its expansions become more irregular; but it has the advantage over every other liquid, of marking the lowest degrees of natural or artificial cold hitherto observed.

The irregularities affecting pyrometers, except from alteration in the size of the substances supporting the bars, are extremely minute. The experiments of De Luc and Roy would lead to the conclusion, that the expansibility of solids is not quite equable. Roy thinks that this slight irregularity may be apparent rather than real; but Lavoisier and Laplace state, that the expansions of solids keep pace with those of the mercurial thermometer, from the freezing to the boiling point of water; and Petit and Dulong assert, that the expansion of metals is progressive above 212° F.

These irregularities, if they exist, are so minute, as not, in any ordinary practical purpose, to affect the indications of pyrometers; and at high temperatures extreme accuracy is seldom of much consequence.

The differences arising from two pyrometers of different materials may be corrected by Table IV. in the appendix

---

* Annales de Chimie, t. xliii.
† Annales de Chimie et Physique, t. ii. p. 240.
‡ Jameson's Edin. Phil. Journal, Oct. 1826, and Kastner Archiv fur die Gesammte Natural, Decem. 1825.
§ Journal de l'Ecole Polytechnique.

* Phil. Trans. vol. lxvii.
† Manchester Memoirs, vol. v. p. 599.
‡ Edin. Phil. Trans. § Ann. de Chim. t. xliii.
|| Annales de Chim. et Phys. t. ii.

of the results obtained in 1782, by Lavoisier and Laplace, lately recovered by Biot. Each substance at 32° F.= 1.00000000.

There is one precaution in graduating thermometers, which will render any irregularities of little consequence; that is, in forming the scale, not to rest satisfied with only two fixed points, and *equally dividing* the intervening space; but to obtain intermediate points by means of mixtures, or by comparison with a standard instrument so formed; and by the shortness of the intervals adapting the scale to inequalities in the bore of the tube, or to the less important irregularities just now considered.

APPENDIX.

No. I.—TABLES OF CORRESPONDENCE OF THE DIFFERENT THERMOMETRICAL SCALES.

(From Dr. Murray's *System of Chemistry*).

TABLE FOR THE CENTIGRADE THERMOMETER.

Centigrade.	Reaumur's.	Fahrenheit's.	Centigrade.	Reaumur's.	Fahrenheit's.	Centigrade.	Reaumur's.	Fahrenheit's.
100	80.	212.	53	42.4	127.4	6	4.8	42.8
99	79.2	210.2	52	41.6	125.6	5	4.	41.
98	78.4	208.4	51	40.8	123.8	4	3.2	39.2
97	77.6	206.6	50	40.	122.	3	2.4	37.4
96	76.8	204.8	49	39.2	120.2	2	1.6	35.6
95	76.	203.	48	38.4	118.4	1	0.8	33.8
94	75.2	201.2	47	37.6	116.6	0	0.	32.
93	74.4	199.4	46	36.8	114.8	−1	−0.8	30.2
92	73.6	197.6	45	36.	113.	−2	−1.6	28.4
91	72.8	195.8	44	35.2	111.2	−3	−2.4	26.6
90	72.	194.	43	34.4	109.4	−4	−3.2	24.8
89	71.2	192.2	42	33.6	107.6	−5	−4.	23.
88	70.4	190.4	41	32.8	105.8	−6	−4.8	21.2
87	69.6	188.6	40	32.	104.	−7	−5.6	19.4
86	68.8	186.8	39	31.2	102.2	−8	−6.4	17.6
85	68.	185.	38	30.4	100.4	−9	−7.2	15.8
84	67.2	183.2	37	29.6	98.6	−10	−8.	14.
83	66.4	181.4	36	28.8	96.8	−11	−8.8	12.2
82	65.6	179.6	35	28.	95.	−12	9.6	10.4
81	64.8	177.8	34	27.2	93.2	−13	−10.4	8.6
80	64.	176.	33	26.4	91.4	−14	−11.2	6.8
79	63.2	174.2	32	25.6	89.6	−15	−12.	5.
78	62.4	172.4	31	24.8	87.8	−16	−12.8	3.2
77	61.6	170.6	30	24.	86.	−17	−13.6	1.4
76	60.8	168.8	29	23.2	84.2	−18	−14.4	−0.4
75	60.	167.	28	22.4	82.4	−19	−15.2	−2.2
74	59.2	165.2	27	21.6	80.6	−20	−16.	−4.
73	58.4	163.4	26	20.8	78.8	−21	−16.8	−5.8
72	57.6	161.6	25	20.	77.	−22	−17.6	−7.6
71	56.8	159.8	24	19.2	75.2	−23	−18.4	−9.4
70	56.	158.	23	18.4	73.4	−24	−19.2	−11.2
69	55.2	156.2	22	17.6	71.6	−25	−20.	−13.
68	54.4	154.4	21	16.8	69.8	−26	−20.8	−14.8
67	53.6	152.6	20	16.	68.	−27	−21.6	−16.6
66	52.8	150.8	19	15.2	66.2	−28	−22.4	−18.4
65	52.	149.	18	14.4	64.4	−29	−23.2	−20.2
64	51.2	147.2	17	13.6	62.6	−30	−24.	−22.
63	50.4	145.4	16	12.8	60.8	−31	−24.8	−23.8
62	49.6	143.6	15	12.	59.	−32	−25.6	−25.6
61	48.8	141.8	14	11.2	57.2	−33	−26.4	−27.4
60	48.	140.	13	10.4	55.4	−34	−27.2	−29.2
59	47.2	138.2	12	9.6	53.6	−35	−28.	−31.
58	46.4	136.4	11	8.8	51.8	−36	−28.8	−32.8
57	45.6	134.6	10	8.	50.	−37	−29.6	−34.6
56	44.8	132.8	9	7.2	48.2	−38	−30.4	−36.4
55	44.	131.	8	6.4	46.4	−39	−31.2	−38.2
54	43.2	129.2	7	5.6	44.6	−40	−32.	−40.

TABLE FOR REAUMUR'S THERMOMETER.

Reaumur's	Centigrade.	Fahrenheit's.	Reaumur's	Centigrade.	Fahrenheit's.	Reaumur's.	Centigrade.	Fahrenheit's.
80	100.	212.	42	52.5	126.5	4	5.	41.
79	98.75	209.75	41	51.25	124.25	3	3.75	38.75
78	97.5	207.5	40	50.	122.	2	2.5	36.5
77	96.25	205.25	39	48.75	119.75	1	1.25	34.25
76	95.	203.	38	47.5	117.5	–0	0	32.
75	93.75	200.75	37	46.25	115.25	–1	–1.25	29.75
74	92.5	198.5	36	45.	113.	–2	–2.5	27.5
73	91.25	196.25	35	43.75	110.75	–3	–3.75	25.25
72	90.	194.	34	42.5	108.5	–4	–5.	23.
71	88.75	191.75	33	41.25	106.25	–5	–6.25	20.75
70	87.5	189.5	32	40.	104.	–6	–7.5	18.5
69	86.25	187.25	31	38.75	101.75	–7	–8.75	16.25
68	85.	185.	30	37.5	99.5	–8	–10.	14.
67	83.75	182.75	29	36.25	97.25	–9	–11.25	11.75
66	82.5	180.5	28	35.	95.	–10	–12.5	9.5
65	81.25	178.25	27	33.75	92.75	–11	–13.75	7.25
64	80.	176.	26	32.5	90.5	–12	–15.	5.
63	78.75	173.75	25	31.25	88.25	–13	–16.25	2.75
62	77.5	171.5	24	30.	86.	–14	–17.5	0.5
61	76.25	169.25	23	28.75	83.75	–15	–18.75	–1.75
60	75.	167.	22	27.5	81.5	–16	–20.	–4.
59	73.75	164.75	21	26.25	79.25	–17	–21.25	–6.25
58	72.5	162.5	20	25.	77.	–18	–22.5	–8.5
57	71.25	160.25	19	23.75	74.75	–19	–23.75	–10.75
56	70.	158.	18	22.5	72.5	–20	–25.	–13.
55	68.75	155.75	17	21.25	70.25	–21	–26.25	–15.25
54	67.5	153.5	16	20.	68.	–22	–27.5	–17.5
53	66.25	151.25	15	18.75	65.75	–23	–28.75	–19.75
52	65.	149.	14	17.5	63.5	–24	–30.	–22.
51	63.75	146.75	13	16.25	61.25	–25	–31.25	–24.25
50	62.5	144.5	12	15.	59.	–26	–32.5	–26.5
49	61.25	142.25	11	13.75	56.75	–27	–33.75	–28.75
48	60.	140.	10	12.5	54.5	–28	–35.	–31.
47	58.75	137.75	9	11.25	52.25	–29	–36.25	–33.25
46	57.5	135.5	8	10.	50.	–30	–37.5	–35.5
45	56.25	133.25	7	8.75	47.75	–31	–38.75	–37.75
44	55.	131.	6	7.5	45.5	–32	–40.	–40.
43	53.75	128.75	5	6.25	43.25	–33	–41.25	–42.25

TABLE FOR FAHRENHEIT'S THERMOMETER.*

Fahrenheit's.	Reaumur's.	Centigrade.	Fahrenheit's.	Reaumur's.	Centigrade.	Fahrenheit's.	Reaumur's.	Centigrade.
212	80.00	100.00	170	61.33	76.66	128	42.66	53.33
211	79.55	99.44	169	60.88	76.11	127	42.22	52.77
210	79.11	98.88	168	60.44	75.55	126	41.77	52.22
209	78.66	98.33	167	60.00	75.00	125	41.33	51.66
208	78.22	97.77	166	59.55	74.44	124	40.88	51.11
207	77.77	97.22	165	59.11	73.88	123	40.44	50.55
206	77.33	96.66	164	58.66	73.33	122	40.00	50.00
205	76.88	96.11	163	58.22	72.22	121	39.55	49.44
204	76.44	95.55	162	57.77	72.77	120	39.11	48.88
203	76.00	95.00	161	57.33	71.66	119	38.66	48.33
202	75.55	94.44	160	56.88	71.11	118	38.22	47.77
201	75.11	93.88	159	56.44	70.55	117	37.77	47.22
200	74.66	93.33	158	56.00	70.00	116	37.33	46.66
199	74.22	92.77	157	55.55	69.44	115	36.88	46.11
198	73.77	92.22	156	55.11	68.88	114	36.44	45.55
197	73.33	91.66	155	54.66	68.33	113	36.00	45.00
196	72.88	91.11	154	54.22	67.77	112	35.55	44.44
195	72.44	90.55	153	53.77	67.22	111	35.11	43.88
194	72.00	90.00	152	53.33	66.66	110	34.66	43.33
193	71.55	89.44	151	52.88	66.11	109	34.22	42.77
192	71.11	88.88	150	52.44	65.55	108	33.77	42.22
191	70.66	88.33	149	52.00	65.00	107	33.33	41.66
190	70.22	87.77	148	51.55	64.44	106	32.88	41.11
189	69.77	87.22	147	51.11	63.88	105	32.44	40.55
188	69.33	86.66	146	50.66	63.33	104	32.00	40.00
187	68.88	86.11	145	50.22	62.77	103	31.55	39.44
186	68.44	85.55	144	49.77	62.22	102	31.11	38.88
185	68.00	85.00	143	49.33	61.66	101	30.66	38.33
184	67.55	84.44	142	48.88	61.11	100	30.22	37.77
183	67.11	83.88	141	48.44	60.55	99	29.77	37.22
182	66.66	83.33	140	48.00	60.00	98	29.33	36.66
181	66.22	82.77	139	47.55	59.44	97	28.88	36.11
180	65.77	82.22	138	47.11	58.88	96	28.44	35.55
179	65.33	81.66	137	46.66	58.33	95	28.00	35.00
178	64.88	81.11	136	46.22	57.77	94	27.55	34.44
177	64.44	80.55	135	45.77	57.22	93	27.11	33.88
176	64.00	80.00	134	45.33	56.66	92	26.66	33.33
175	63.55	79.44	133	44.44	56.11	91	26.22	32.77
174	62.11	78.88	132	44.55	55.55	90	25.77	32.22
173	62.66	78.33	131	44.00	55.00	89	25.33	31.66
172	62.22	77.77	130	43.55	54.44	88	24.88	31.11
171	61.77	77.22	129	43.11	53.88	87	24.44	30.55

* All the decimals in this Table are circulating decimals.

TABLE FOR FAHRENHEIT'S THERMOMETER CONTINUED.

Fahrenheit's.	Reaumur's.	Centigrade.	Fahrenheit's.	Reaumur's.	Centigrade.	Fahrenheit's.	Reaumur's.	Centigrade.
86	24.00	30.00	43	4.88	6.11	0	−14.22	−17.77
85	23.55	29.44	42	4.44	5.55	−1	−14.66	−18.33
84	23.11	28.88	41	4.00	5.00	−2	−15.11	−18.88
83	22.66	28.33	40	3.55	4.44	−3	−15.55	−19.44
82	22.22	27.77	39	3.11	3.88	−4	−16.00	−20.00
81	21.77	27.22	38	2.66	3.33	−5	−16.44	−20.55
80	21.33	26.66	37	2.22	2.77	−6	−16.88	−21.11
79	20.88	26.11	36	1.77	2.22	−7	−17.33	−21.66
78	20.44	25.55	35	1.33	1.66	−8	−17.77	−22.22
77	20.00	25.00	34	0.88	1.11	−9	−18.22	−22.77
76	19.55	24.44	33	0.44	0.55	−10	−18.66	−23.33
75	19.11	23.88	32	0.	0.	−11	−19.11	−23.88
74	18.66	23.33	31	−0.44	−0.55	−12	−19.55	−24.44
73	18.22	22.77	30	−0.88	−1.11	−13	−20.00	−25.00
72	17.77	22.22	29	−1.33	−1.66	−14	−20.44	−25.55
71	17.33	21.66	28	−1.77	−2.22	−15	−20.88	−26.11
70	16.88	21.11	27	−2.22	−2.77	−16	−21.33	−26.66
69	16.44	20.55	26	−2.66	−3.33	−17	−21.77	−27.22
68	16.00	20.00	25	−3.11	−3.88	−18	−22.22	−27.77
67	15.55	19.44	24	−3.55	−4.44	−19	−22.66	−28.33
66	15.11	18.88	23	−4.00	−5.00	−20	−23.11	−28.88
65	14.66	18.33	22	−4.44	−5.55	−21	−23.55	−29.44
64	14.22	17.77	21	−4.88	−6.11	−22	−24.00	−30.00
63	13.77	17.22	20	−5.33	−6.66	−23	−24.44	30.55
62	13.33	16.66	19	−5.77	−7.22	−24	−24.88	−31.11
61	12.88	16.11	18	−6.22	−7.77	−25	−25.33	−31.66
60	12.44	15.55	17	−6.66	−8.33	−26	−25.77	−32.22
59	12.00	15.00	16	−7.11	−8.88	−27	−26.22	32.77
58	11.55	14.44	15	−7.55	−9.44	−28	−26.66	33.33
57	11.11	13.88	14	−8.00	−10.00	−29	−27.11	−33.88
56	10.66	13.33	13	−8.44	−10.55	−30	−27.55	−34.44
55	10.22	12.77	12	−8.88	−11.11	−31	−28.00	−35.00
54	9.77	12.22	11	−9.33	−11.66	−32	−28.44	−35.55
53	9.33	11.66	10	−9.77	−12.22	−33	−28.88	−36.11
52	8.88	11.11	9	−10.22	−12.77	−34	−29.33	−36.66
51	8.44	10.55	8	−10.66	−13.33	−35	−29.77	−37.22
50	8.00	10.00	7	−11.11	−13.88	−36	−30.22	−37.77
49	7.55	9.44	6	−11.55	−14.44	−37	−30.66	−38.33
48	7.11	8.88	5	−12.00	−15.00	−38	−31.11	−38.88
47	6.66	8.33	4	−12.44	−15.55	−39	−31.55	39.44
46	6.22	7.77	3	−12.88	−16.11	−40	−32.00	−40.00
45	5.77	7.22	2	−13.33	−16.66			
44	5.33	6.66	1	−13.77	−17.22			

No. II.—TABLES OF EXPANSIONS OF BODIES BY HEAT.

I. TABLE OF EXPANSIONS ACCORDING TO SMEATON.

SUBSTANCES.	DILATION FOR A LENGTH EQUAL TO UNITY.	
	In decimal fractions.	In vulgar fractions.
Blistered steel	0.00115000	$\frac{1}{870}$
Tempered steel	0.00122500	$\frac{1}{816}$
Bismuth	0.00139167	$\frac{1}{719}$
Copper hammered	0.00170000	$\frac{1}{588}$
Copper 8 parts with 1 of tin	0.00181667	$\frac{1}{550}$
Cast brass	0.00187500	$\frac{1}{533}$
Brass, 16 parts with 1 of tin	0.00190833	$\frac{1}{524}$
Fine pewter	0.00228333	$\frac{1}{438}$
Grain tin	0.00248333	$\frac{1}{403}$
Iron	0.00125833	$\frac{1}{795}$
Brass wire	0.00193333	$\frac{1}{517}$
Speculum metal	0.00193333	$\frac{1}{517}$
Lead	0.00286667	$\frac{1}{349}$
Antimony	0.00108333	$\frac{1}{923}$
Lead 2 parts with 1 of tin	0.00250533	$\frac{1}{390}$
Copper 2 parts with 1 of zinc	0.00205833	$\frac{1}{486}$
White glass (barometer tube,)	0.00083333	$\frac{1}{1175}$
Zinc	0.00294167	$\frac{1}{340}$
Zinc hammered	0.00310833	$\frac{1}{322}$
Zinc 8 parts with 1 of tin	0.00269167	$\frac{1}{372}$

II. TABLE OF EXPANSIONS ACCORDING TO ROY.

SUBSTANCES.	FOR A LENGTH EQUAL TO UNITY.	
	In decimal fractions.	In vulgar fractions.
Steel rod	0.00114450	$\frac{1}{874}$
Brass scale, Hamburgh	0.00185550	$\frac{1}{589}$
Brass plate rod, English	0.00189296	$\frac{1}{528}$
Brass plate trough, English	0.00189450	$\frac{1}{528}$
Cast Iron prism	0.00111000	$\frac{1}{901}$
Glass tube	0.00077550	$\frac{1}{1289}$
Glass rod	0.00080833	$\frac{1}{1237}$

III. TABLE OF EXPANSIONS ACCORDING TO TROUGHTON.

SUBSTANCES.	LINEAR DILATATIONS FROM THE TEMPERATURE OF FREEZING TO BOILING WATER.	
	In decimal fractions.	In vulgar fractions.
Steel	0.0011899	$\frac{1}{848}$
Silver	0.0020826	$\frac{1}{480}$
Copper	0.0019188	$\frac{1}{521}$
Iron Wire	0.0014401	$\frac{1}{694}$
Platina	0.00099218	$\frac{1}{1008}$
Palladium (according to Wollaston)	0.0010000	$\frac{1}{1000}$

IV. TABLE OF THE LINEAR DILATATION OF DIFFERENT SUBSTANCES FROM THE TEMPERATURE OF FREEZING TO THAT OF BOILING WATER, ACCORDING TO THE EXPERIMENTS OF LAVOISIER AND LAPLACE.

SUBSTANCES	DILATATION FOR A LENGTH EQUAL TO UNITY.	
	In decimal fractions. At 212°	In vulgar fractions.
Glass of St. Gobain	0.00089089	$\frac{1}{1123}$
Glass tube without lead	0.00087572	$\frac{1}{1142}$
Ditto	0.00089760	$\frac{1}{1114}$
Ditto	0.00091751	$\frac{1}{1090}$
English Flint Glass	0.00081166	$\frac{1}{1248}$
French glass with lead	0.00087199	$\frac{1}{1147}$
Copper	0.00172244	$\frac{1}{581}$
Ditto	0.00171222	$\frac{1}{584}$
Brass	0.00186671	$\frac{1}{535}$
Ditto	0.00188971	$\frac{1}{529}$
Hammered Iron	0.00122045	$\frac{1}{819}$
Iron Wire	0.00123504	$\frac{1}{812}$
Hard Steel	0.00107875	$\frac{1}{927}$
Soft Steel	0.00107956	$\frac{1}{926}$
Tempered Steel	0.00123956	$\frac{1}{807}$
Lead	0.00284836	$\frac{1}{351}$
Malacca Tin	0.00193765	$\frac{1}{516}$
Cornish Tin	0.00217298	$\frac{1}{462}$
Cupelled Silver	0.00192974	$\frac{1}{518}$
Parisian Standard Silver	0.00190868	$\frac{1}{524}$
Pure Gold	0.00146606	$\frac{1}{682}$
Parisian Standard Ditto not softened	0.00155155	$\frac{1}{645}$
Ditto, softened	0.00151361	$\frac{1}{661}$

V. TABLE OF THE EXPANSIONS OF LIQUIDS.

The expansions in this table were determined by Mr. Dalton. They are equal to what would be produced by an elevation of temperature from the freezing to the boiling point of water; the volume at the former being 1.

Mercury	.0200	= $\frac{1}{50}$
Water	.0466	= $\frac{1}{21.5}$
Water saturated with salt	.0500	= $\frac{1}{20}$
Sulphuric acid	.0600	= $\frac{1}{17}$
Muriatic acid	.0600	= $\frac{1}{17}$
Oil of turpentine	.0700	= $\frac{1}{14}$
Æther	.0700	= $\frac{1}{14}$
Fixed oils	.0800	= $\frac{1}{12.5}$
Alcohol	.0110	= $\frac{1}{9}$
Nitric acid	.0110	= $\frac{1}{9}$

No. III.
TABLE OF REMARKABLE TEMPERATURES ACCORDING TO FAHRENHEIT'S SCALE.

	°
Iron red hot in the twilight	884
Heat of a common fire (Irvine)	790
Iron bright red in the dark	752
Zinc melts	700
Quicksilver boils (Irvine)	672
——————— (Dalton)	660
——————— (Crichton)	655
Linseed oil boils	600
Lead melts (Guyton, Irvine)	594
Sulphuric Acid boils (Dalton)	590
The surface of polished Steel acquires a deep blue colour	580
Oil of Turpentine boils	560
Phosphorus boils	554
Bismuth melts (Irvine)	476
The surface of polished steel acquires a pale straw colour	460
Tin melts (Crichton, Irvine)	442
A Compound of equal parts of Tin and Bismuth melts	283
Nitric Acid boils	242
Sulphur melts	226
A saturated Solution of Salt boils	218
Water boils, (the barometer being at 30 inches); also a Compound of 5 of Bismuth, 3 of Tin, and 2 of Lead, melts	212
A Compound of 3 of Tin, 5 of Lead, and 8 of Bismuth, melts	210
Alcohol boils	174
Bees' Wax melts	142
Spermaceti melts	133
Phosphorus melts	100
Æther boils	98
Medium Temperature of the Globe	50
Ice melts	32
Milk freezes	30
Vinegar freezes at about	28
Strong Wine freezes at about	20
A Mixture of 1 part of Alcohol, and 3 parts of Water, freezes	7
A Mixture of Alcohol and Water in equal parts, freezes	7
A Mixture of 2 parts of Alcohol and 1 of Water, freezes	11
Melting point of Quicksilver (Cavendish)	39
Liquid Ammonia crystallizes (Vauquelin)	42
Nitric Acid, spec. gr. about 1.42, freezes (Cavendish)	45
Sulphuric Æther congeals (Vauquelin)	47
Natural Temperature observed at Hudson's Bay	50
Ammoniacal Gas condenses into a liquid (Guyton)	54
Nitrous Acid freezes (Vauquelin)	56
Cold produced from diluted Sulphuric Acid and Snow, the materials being at the temperature of 57	78½
Greatest Artificial Cold yet measured (Walker)	91

ADDENDA ET CORRIGENDA.

Page 6. The description of the *fig.* 7, in the text, is taken from the Memoirs of the Academy of Sciences. It is probable that in the construction of the instrument, Amontons employed a tube of narrow calibre, to enable the included air to support the mercurial column. The proportion between the tube and ball may be inferred from what is stated of the expansion of the whole, by the heat of boiling water.

P. 10. In the beginning of the paragraph, just after the first set of formulæ, there is an error which requires correction. Instead of *these formulæ applying to all degrees above the freezing point*, read, "these formulæ apply to all degrees above the zero of each scale;"

P. 14. The notation employed by De Luc requires some explanation. y denotes the height of the barometer *in sixteenths of a Parisian line;* T the height of a thermometer, plunged in boiling water, above the melting point of ice, in hundredths of a degree of De Luc's scale; and a the constant quantity 10387, which Horsley thinks, from some of De Luc's experiments, should have been 10369; but in his investigations he retains the first number, as probably adopted on good grounds.

The logarithms used by De Luc are the tables of Briggs, in which the seven figures of the tables, as well as the indices, are reckoned integers; or he considers the *eighth* figure in the place of units: but it is most convenient to reckon all the figures after the index as decimals, and the formulæ will be $\frac{99 \times 100}{2}$ Log. $y - a = T$; or $\frac{}{99 \times 50}$ Log. $y - a = T$.

P. 15. In the second column of the table, 29 should be opposite to .95, *instead of* .39.

The terms *lower* and *higher*, in the third column of the same table, are so in the original paper; but the directions will be more plain, if the reader will recollect, that where *lower* is indicated, the correction is "to be subtracted;" and when *higher* is used, the correction is "to be added."

P. 23, *Col.* 1. The action of the pinions in Ferguson's Pyrometer is ill expressed in the text; and the reader is requested to substitute for the member of the sentence commencing with "*and the bar, &c.*" in the 14th line, the following—"and as the bar k has fifteen teeth to one inch, it is obvious that when k moves one inch, the pinion l will have made one revolution and a quarter, and the pinion p will have moved $100 \times 1\frac{1}{4}$, or 125 times round."

P. 29. In Wedgwood's table, *Col.* 1, line 27, for *deduct*, read, "did not."

In the same page, *Col.* 2, the radius of Regnier's instrument should have been 649 millimètres, its diameter 1.298 mètres, and its circumference 4.079 mètres.

ELECTRICITY.

CHAPTER I.

General Facts and Principles.

(1.) THE science of ELECTRICITY, which now ranks as one of the most important branches of Natural Philosophy, and which embraces so many subjects of inquiry, exceedingly curious in themselves, and highly interesting from their relations with every department of nature, is wholly of modern creation. The ancients were, indeed, acquainted with a few detached facts, depending on the agency of electricity; such as the attractive power which amber acquires by being rubbed, the benumbing shocks which are experienced on touching the *torpedo* (or electrical eel), and the appearance of those sparks or streams of light which, on some occasions, are seen to issue from the human body. But no suspicion was entertained that these phenomena had any connexion with one another; and far less was it imagined that they were the effects of a power pervading all material bodies, and extensively concerned in all the operations of nature.

(2.) It was only by slow degrees that this knowledge was acquired. The first step towards a generalization of the phenomena was made by Dr. Gilbert, an English physician, who, in the year 1600, published a very original and valuable treatise on the magnet. He remarked that several other bodies besides amber can, by friction, be made to attract light bodies; and he was thus led to the discovery of a property common to all of them. The Greek name for amber being ηλικτρον (*Electron*), the bodies possessed of this property were denominated *Electrics*; and the power they manifested was termed ELECTRICITY. The observations of Boyle, Otto Guericke, Newton, and a few other philosophers of the same period, contributed somewhat to the extension of our knowledge on this curious subject; but even the information collected during the whole of that century amounted to nothing that could be entitled to the name of science. The real science of Electricity can, properly speaking, be considered as taking its rise only in a later age; and it was the first fruit of that active spirit of investigation, which at the commencement of the eighteenth century was rapidly diffusing itself over Europe. The establishment of the Royal Society of London appears to have had considerable influence in promoting the cultivation of electricity: for we find that almost every discovery of importance in this science was made by the members, and is recorded in the Transactions of that Society. But it was not until the present century that the extensive relations which connect electricity with so many other branches of physical science, were discovered, and their importance appreciated. Already have we seen, in this short era, the rise of a new science, founded on that peculiar modification of Electricity, which is known by the name of GALVANISM. Hence, have we derived new instruments of analysis, new paths of research, and new powers of extending the dominions of science; hence, have we been able to trace alliances between several of the great agents concerned in the phenomena of the material universe. ELECTRO-CHEMISTRY has thus arisen as one of the connecting branches between remote divisions of the Philosophy of Nature. Still more recently there has been opened to us, in the subject of ELECTRO-MAGNETISM, another new province of science, which establishes a natural connexion between two powers hitherto regarded as distinct.

So rapid has been the march of scientific improvement, that it is difficult for those whose attention has not been steadily and exclusively devoted to these particular objects, to keep pace with the progress of discovery. The materials collected by the numerous labourers in these wide fields of inquiry have poured in upon us so fast, that there has scarcely yet been time for marshalling them in their proper places, and for disposing them in the order best fitted for instruction. It is to be lamented that there exists as yet no general and comprehensive treatise embracing the whole of these extensive and complicated subjects of modern research; and that the student has still to gather the information he seeks from a multitude of journals and other miscellaneous sources, where they lie irregularly scattered, and are not to be arranged, or even found, without a great expenditure of time and labour. It is the aim of these treatises to supply, in some degree, this deficiency, in as far, at least, as relates to the instruction of those who have no previous acquaintance with the subject, and are desirous of being initiated in the principles of the science.

(3.) In order to convey the clearest and most philosophical views of the subject we are about to treat, we shall begin by stating, independently of all theory, the most general facts relating to Electricity; presenting them at first in their simplest form. We shall, in the second place, review the theories which have been framed for the purpose of connecting these facts in the mind. We shall thus be enabled, lastly, to study their combinations, to unravel their complicated results, and to follow them in their practical applications.

(4.) The general facts relating to Electricity may be reduced to the six following heads:—
1. EXCITATION.
2. ATTRACTION.
3. REPULSION.
4. DISTRIBUTION.
5. INDUCTION.
6. TRANSFERENCE.

§ 1. *Of Excitation, Attraction, and Repulsion:*

(5.) If a piece of amber, or sealing-wax, or a smooth surface of glass, perfectly clean and dry, be briskly rubbed with a dry woollen cloth, and immediately afterwards held over small and light bodies, such as pieces of paper, thread, cork, straw, feathers, or fragments of gold leaf, strewed upon a table, these bodies will be seen to fly towards the surface that has been rubbed, and adhere to it for a certain time. The surfaces which have acquired by friction this attractive power are said to be *excited;* and the substances thus susceptible of excitation are termed *electrics,* in contradistinction to such as are not excitable by a similar process and which are, therefore, termed *non-electrics.*

(6.) The principal electric substances in nature are the following: viz. amber, gum-lac, resin, sulphur, glass, talc, the precious stones, silk, the fur of most quadrupeds, and almost all vegetable substances (excepting charcoal), which have been thoroughly deprived of moisture, as, for example, baked wood, and very dry paper.

(7.) After the bodies which had been attracted by the excited electric have remained in contact with it a certain time, the force which held them together ceases to operate: the bodies then recede from the electric, and if the latter be again presented to them, they will, provided they have touched no other body, be repelled, or driven off, instead of attracted. This change from attraction to repulsion takes place more slowly with some substances than with others: some bodies will adhere to the electric a considerable time before they recede; while others, and especially metallic bodies, are repelled the instant after contact:—the reason of this will afterwards be seen.

(8.) It is also to be noticed that two bodies which have both of them been in contact with the same electric, mutually repel each other.

(9.) The phenomena of electrical attraction and repulsion are best observed when electrics of considerable size are employed. For the experiments we are about to describe, it is convenient to have them of a cylindrical shape, which admits of their being more easily carried in the hand, and more readily transferred to wherever we may wish to place them. We may employ as our electric a thick cylinder of sealing wax, or one of sulphur. If glass be chosen, it should be in the form of a tube of considerable diameter, and should, previously to the experiment, be gently warmed before the fire, in order to expel all moisture from its surface. As a rubber we may use a silk handkerchief, a piece of clean flannel, or the fur of a quadruped; but the material which produces the greatest effect when rubbed with glass is an amalgam (or mixture) of mercury with tin or zinc. Whatever be the substance employed, it should be perfectly dry; to ensure which condition it should, previously to being used, be held for some time before the fire.

(10.) When, by attending to these precautions, a sufficiently powerful excitement of the cylinder has been obtained, we may observe several other remarkable phenomena, besides those of attraction. If the experiment be performed in a dark room, flashes of light, of a bluish colour, will be perceived during the friction, extending over every part of the surface rubbed; and sparks, attended with a sharp snapping sound, will be seen to dart around it in various directions. If a round body, as a metallic ball, be presented to it, and moved from one end to the other, a succession of sparks will be obtained as the ball passes along the surface; and if the knuckle be presented instead of the metallic ball, each spark will be accompanied by a pricking sensation. When the excited cylinder is brought near to the face, an unpleasant sensation of tickling is felt in the skin, as if it had been covered with a cobweb.

(11.) If a globe of metal be suspended in the air by silk threads, and if, while in this situation, it be rubbed by an electric, such as silk, fur, or the outside of the skin of a cat, it will also become electrical, and exhibit the same properties of attraction and of repulsion as if it had been itself an electric. The circumstance of its being thus insulated or cut off from the contact of any substance, except the air and the electric which sustains it, is essential to the success of this experiment.

(12.) Various modes have been devised for exhibiting distinctly the attractive and repulsive agencies of electricity; and for obtaining indications of its presence, when it exists only in a feeble degree. Instruments for this purpose are termed *Electroscopes*. One of the simplest of these is the Electroscope of Haüy, which is very similar to that formerly proposed by Dr. Gilbert. It consists of a light metallic needle, terminated at each end by a light pith ball, which is covered with gold leaf,

Fig. 1.

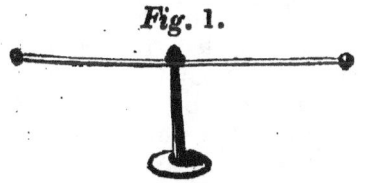

and supported horizontally by a cap at its centre, on a fine point. The attractive or repulsive power of any electrified body presented to one of the balls, will be indicated by the movements of the needle.

(13.) In some cases it is more convenient to employ a pair of similar balls, suspended from a brass ball fixed to the end of a glass handle, by very fine silver wires, or by hempen threads, previously steeped in a solution of salt, and afterwards dried. See *fig.* 2.

Fig 2.

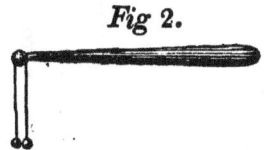

(14.) Cavallo has contrived an electroscope of the same kind, which has the advantage of being more portable than that of Haüy, while it is, perhaps, equally sensible. It is formed by two fine silver wires, each carrying at one of their ends a little ball made of cork, or of the pith of the elder tree; the other ends of the wires being suspended from a cork, which is rather long, and tapering at both ends, so as to fit either way into the mouth of a varnished glass tube, serving both as a handle to the instrument when in use, and as a case for it when carried in the pocket. When it is to be employed as an electroscope, the wires with pith balls are placed so as to hang out from the end of the tube, and will indicate by their divergence any electricity which may be communicated to them. (*Fig.* 4.) When

Fig. 3.   *Fig.* 4.

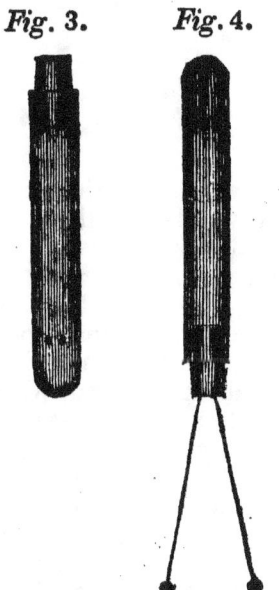

the instrument is not in use, the wires are put into the tube, by inverting it, and closing it with the other end of the cork. (*Fig.* 3.)

(15.) For studying the circumstances

attending electrical attraction, we should be provided with stands, from the ends of which are suspended by their respective threads one or two pith balls, about the size of a small pea, as shown in *fig.* 5.

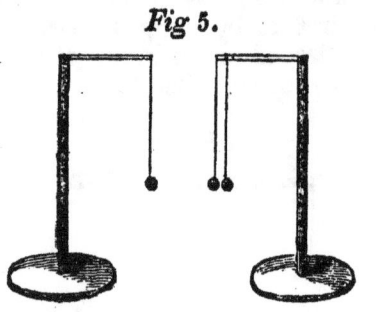

Fig 5.

§ 2. *Distribution and Transference.*

(16.) If an excited electric be brought near a pith ball suspended by silk, the ball will, in the first place, approach the electric (*fig.* 6.), indicating an attraction towards it, and if the position of the electric will allow, the ball will come into contact with it and adhere to it for a short time; but it will presently afterwards recede from the electric, showing that it is now repelled. (*fig.* 7.) If we

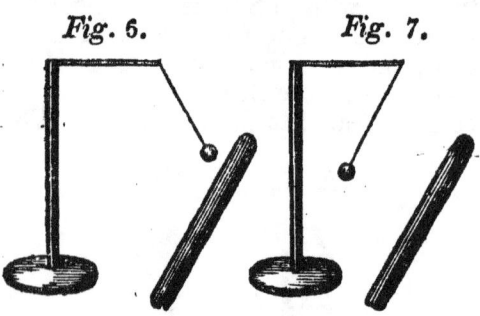

Fig. 6.   Fig. 7.

now remove the electric, and present to the ball which has thus touched it, a second ball which has had no previous communication with any electric, we find that these two balls attract one another, and come into contact. The same actions are repeated between this second ball and a third, which may be presented to it; and so on in succession, but with a continued diminution of intensity. This diminution plainly indicates a diminished power, in consequence, as it would seem, of its being distributed among a number of bodies.

(17.) In the prosecution of these experiments, therefore, the effects will be more distinct, if, instead of small pith balls, we employ a globe of metal of larger size, which will allow of the reception of a considerable quantity of this electric influence by contact with the excited electric. A globe, suspended by silk threads, as the pith balls are, and which has extensively touched the electric, will act upon these balls precisely in the same way as the original electric would have acted upon them, and may accordingly be substituted for it in all these experiments. It is, indeed, exactly in the same condition as the globe rubbed by an electric, already mentioned. (§ 11.)

(18.) From the whole of these facts we necessarily infer that the electric has imparted to the ball or globe which came in contact with it, properties exactly similar to those which had been excited in itself by friction. By repeated contact with a number of bodies, an excited electric is found to lose its electrical powers in the same degree as these powers have been acquired by the bodies themselves; and fresh excitation alone can renew them. It is evident, then, that the unknown agent, which we have termed *Electricity*, is capable of transference, in the same sense in which we speak of heat being communicated or transferred from one body to another, and that, like heat, it is weakened by diffusion among a number of bodies.

(19.) If the electrified ball be touched with the finger, it will be deprived of the whole of its electricity, which will pass into the body of the person who touches it. It is now reduced to its original or natural state, and is again susceptible of being attracted, either by an excited electric, or by another body to which electricity has previously been communicated.

If the electrified body, instead of being touched with the finger, had been touched by a rod of metal held in the hand, the effect would have been the same in both cases: hence we may infer that the metallic rod is capable of conveying away from the body the whole of its electricity. But if a glass rod be substituted, the result is very different; the body touched is found to retain the whole of its electricity, notwithstanding the contact of the glass rod. We are thus led to the conclusion that some substances, such as glass, are incapable of conducting electricity; while others, such as the metals and the human body, readily convey that influence.

(20.) It is invariably found that all *electrics* are, at the same time, *non-con-*

ductors. Conductors, on the other hand, are *non-electrics*. The two qualities of a capability of excitation, and a power of conducting electricity, appear to be incompatible with each other—for the one is always found to diminish in proportion as the other increases. The permanence of electricity in metallic bodies, which are suspended in the air by silk threads, shows that the air as well as the silk is a non-conductor. Bodies which are in this way surrounded on all sides by non-conductors are said to be *insulated*. When this condition is not observed, that is, when the body is in contact with conducting bodies which communicate with the earth, its electricity will escape by the channel which is thus opened for it, and will be lost by diffusion in the mass of the earth, which is formed of conducting materials, and which may be regarded as the great reservoir both for the absorption and supply of electricity. Hence we see why it is not possible to accumulate electricity in a conducting body while it is held in the hand, and why electrics alone are capable of permanent excitation.

(21.) The insulating power of atmospheric air depends principally upon two circumstances, its density and its dryness. Air with the density which it has under the ordinary pressure of the atmosphere, if perfectly dry, is a remarkably good insulator, even although it be rapidly renewed on the surface of the electrified body. This is shown by an experiment of Franklin's, in which he whirled an electrified ball round his head, by means of a silk line, with great rapidity, so as to make it perform many hundred revolutions, without being able to perceive that it had thereby lost any sensible portion of its electricity. Neither an increase, nor a diminution of temperature, appears to lessen its insulating power. But in proportion as the air is rarefied by the removal of the superincumbent pressure, its power of confining electricity diminishes, till, at last, when the rarefaction is very great, it opposes scarcely any resistance to the passage even of very feeble electricity; and it may be then classed among conductors. This is the case with the imperfect vacuum produced by the air-pump, from which it is almost impossible to exclude minute quantities of air. Even in the space left in the upper part of the tube of a barometer by the descent of the mercury, or the Torricellian vacuum, as it is called, there is in general present a minute portion of air, as well as of mercurial vapour, which are sufficient to conduct electricity. Small globules of air usually adhere to the mercury, and to the sides of the tube; and these, upon the removal of pressure, expand into an atmosphere. It has been asserted by Mr. Morgan that if great care be taken to remove every source of error, by the employment of very pure mercury, and by boiling it for a long time in the tube, a perfect vacuum may be obtained, which does not conduct electricity. His experiment, however, was made long ago, and requires careful repetition, before the result can be confided in.

(22.) The circumstance which chiefly determines the conducting power of common air is that of its containing a greater or less quantity of moisture. Water is a very good conductor of electricity; and that portion which is suspended in the air tends powerfully to carry off electricity from the bodies which are charged with it, and which are surrounded by air. Moisture also easily attaches itself to glass and other electrics, and deprives them of the power of insulation. Hence, the same experiments which succeed in a clear dry day, will often fail when tried in damp weather: and hence we see the utility of previously drying every part of the apparatus, in order to exclude as much as possible the interference of moisture.

(23.) The conducting powers of most bodies are influenced by changes of temperature, and also of form. Thus, although water in its liquid state is a good conductor, yet, when congealed, in the form of ice, its conducting powers are much impaired; and at a very low temperature, namely, at $-13°$ of Fahrenheit's scale, ceases altogether. Mr. Achard, who observed this fact, formed ice of this temperature into a spheroid, and mounting it upon an axis, was able to excite it by friction as any other electric. On the other hand, by raising the temperature of water, its conducting powers are increased. Charcoal is also found to transmit electricity with more facility when hot, than when cold. Glass, which is a non-conductor when cold, becomes a tolerably good conductor when heated to redness; and a similar change takes place in sulphur and in resinous bodies when melted; and also in baked wood when heated. Reducing substances to powder has often an effect upon their powers of conducting electricity. Snow conducts less readily than ice of the same temperature. The same is the case with powdered charcoal, when compared with the same substance in its entire state. But glass, on the contrary, acquires some conducting power by being pulverized, as was ascertained by Van Swinden, who extended the same observation to sulphur.

Many bodies, which, in their usual state, are good conductors of electricity, lose this power when they are made very dry. This is the case with recent vegetable and animal substances, their conducting power appearing to be derived solely from the fluids they contain.

(24.) Strictly speaking, there is no substance hitherto known that is perfectly impervious to electricity; for the intensity of that agent may be so increased as to force it, for a certain small distance, through all bodies: neither is there any body in which the conducting power is infinitely great; that is, which opposes no resistance to the transmission of electricity. If the degree of conducting power which bodies possess could be ascertained with sufficient precision, they might be arranged in progressive order; but the present state of our knowledge affords only an approximation to such a series. As a table of this kind, however, with all its imperfections, may be of great use, we subjoin the following, in which the different bodies are arranged in one series, beginning with those which have the greatest conducting power, and terminating with those that have the least. The order in which they possess the power of insulating is, of course, the reverse of this.

Catalogue of Bodies in the Order of their conducting Power.

The perfect, or least oxidable metals.
The more oxidable metals.
Charcoal prepared from the harder woods, and well burned.
Plumbago.
The concentrated mineral acids.
Powdered charcoal.
Dilute acids.
Solutions of metallic and neutral salts.
Metallic ores.
Animal fluids.
Pure water.
Snow.
Living vegetables.
Living animals.
Flame.
Smoke.
Steam.
Metallic salts.
Salts with alkaline or earthy bases.
Rarefied air.
Vapour of alcohol.
Vapour of ether.
Earths and stones in their ordinary state.
Pulverized glass.
Flowers of sulphur.

Dry metallic oxides.
Oils.
Vegetable ashes.
Animal ashes.
Dry transparent crystals.
Ice below —13° Fahrenheit.
Phosphorus.
Lime.
Dry chalk.
Native carbonate of barytes.
Lycopodium.
Caoutchouc, or Indian rubber.
Camphor.
Siliceous and argillaceous stones in proportion to their hardness.
Dry marble.
Porcelain.
Baked wood.
Dry atmospheric air, and other gases.
White sugar, and sugar crystallized.
Leather.
Dry parchment.
Dry paper.
Cotton.
Feathers.
Hair, especially that of a living cat.
Wool.
Dyed silk.
Bleached silk.
Raw silk.
Transparent gems.
Diamond.
Talc.
Metallic vitrifications.
Glass, and other vitrifications.
Fat.
Wax.
Sulphur.
Resins, and bituminous substances.
Amber.
Gum-lac.

Although the precise point in the scale which forms the separation between conducting and insulating bodies must, of course, be somewhat indefinite, we have endeavoured to mark it by the division in the above table.

(25.) It appears, from the experiments

of Mr. Coulomb, that a thread of gum-lac is the most perfect of all insulators, and is ten times more effectual than a silk thread as dry as it can be made; for the former, when only one inch and a half in length, insulated as well as a fine silk thread of fifteen inches. When the thread of silk was dipped in fine sealing-wax, it was equal in power to a thread of pure lac of four times its length. Professor Robison found that the conducting power of silk thread depends greatly on its colour; or, in other words, on the nature of the drug with which it is dyed. When of a brilliant white, or a black, its conducting power is the greatest; and a high golden yellow, or a nut brown, renders it the best insulator. Glass, even in its dryest state, and in situations where it was impossible that moisture could have access to it, is stated by the same author to insulate considerably better than silk; and when drawn into a slender thread, and coated with gum-lac, it acted as well as a thread of lac of one-third of the length. It was found, however, at the same time, that extreme fineness was requisite; for it dissipated in proportion to the square of its diameter. The insulating power of glass is remarkably injured by having a bore, however fine, unless that bore admits of being also coated with lac. Human hair, when completely freed from every thing that water could wash out of it, and then dried by lime, and coated with lac, was equal to silk. Fir, cedar, larch, and the rose-tree, when split into filaments, and first dried by lime, and afterwards baked in an oven, which just made paper become faintly brown, seemed scarcely inferior to gum-lac. The white woods, as they are called, and mahogany, were much inferior. Fir, baked and coated with melted lac, seems, therefore, the best support when strength is required. The lac may be rendered less brittle by a minute portion of pure turpentine, which has been cleared of water by a little boiling, without sensibly increasing its conducting power. Lac, or sealing-wax, dissolved in spirits, is far inferior, for these purposes, to what it is when melted by heat.

(26.) The laws which regulate the gradual dissipation of electricity from bodies in a state of imperfect insulation have been investigated with great ability by Coulomb. Three causes chiefly operate in depriving a body under these circumstances of its electricity:—First, the imperfection of the insulating property in the solids by which it is supported. Secondly, the contact of successive portions of air, every particle of which carries off a certain quantity of electricity. Thirdly, the deposition of moisture upon the surface of the insulating body, which establishes communications with its remote ends, and may be considered as virtually increasing its conducting power.

(27.) With regard to the first cause, Mr. Coulomb has completely ascertained that for all fine cylindrical fibres, such as hair, silk, filaments of gum-lac, &c. if the nature of the substance, the diameter of the fibre, and the dispersive state of the air are supposed constant, the length of the fibre requisite for the complete insulation of a given intensity of electricity, varies as the square of that intensity. Theory, therefore, leads to the conclusion that, however great may be the intensity, there is always a certain length beyond which a filament of any of these bodies becomes a perfect insulator; and we find, in practice, that by diminishing the intensity of the electricity, or increasing the length of the substance it has to traverse, a sufficiently accurate degree of insulation may be obtained. With respect to the second source of dissipation, it was found that in a given state of the atmosphere, as far as it could be determined by the indications of the barometer, thermometer, and hygrometer, the dissipation at each instant of time, varied directly as the intensity of the electricity.

(28.) There is one very material circumstance relating to the dissipation of electricity that should here be mentioned, although its explanation must be deferred till the principles on which it depends have been developed; and it is, that the power of retaining electricity in any body is much influenced by its shape. The form most favourable to its retention is that of a sphere; next to which is a spheroid, and a cylinder terminated at both ends by a hemisphere. On the other hand, electricity escapes most readily from bodies of a pointed figure, especially if the point projects to a distance from the surface. In such bodies it is scarcely possible, indeed, to accumulate any sensible degree of electricity, on account of its rapid dissipation from the point. In like manner pointed bodies receive electricity more readily than those of any other form.

§ 3. *Of the two species of Electricity.*

(29.) We have hitherto viewed electrical phenomena as arising from the operation of a single agent, which could be called into action, and transferred from one body to another. We have seen that bodies, which have received their electricity from excited glass, repel one another, and are likewise repelled by the excited glass. The same thing happens with respect to those bodies which have received their electricity from excited sealing-wax. But upon examining the action of any of the bodies belonging to the one set, upon any of those belonging to the other, we find, that instead of repelling, they attract each other. Thus, the ball which has received its electricity from the glass, attracts that which has been electrified by the sealing-wax, and is attracted by it; but, what is still more remarkable, the moment these balls have come into contact, provided they have both been electrified in the same degree, they cease at once to exhibit any signs of electricity, as if the electricities of both were suddenly annihilated by their mutual communication. Thus there appears to be two different, and, in some respects, opposite kinds of electricities; the one obtained from glass, the other from sealing-wax. Du Fay, by whom this distinction was first noticed, denominated the former the *vitreous*, and the latter the *resinous* electricity.

(30.) The mode of action which these two electricities exert on matter, may be expressed by the following law: namely, that *bodies charged with either species of electricity, repel bodies charged with the same species, but attract bodies charged with the other species; and that, at equal distances, the attractive power in the one case is exactly equal to the repulsive power in the other.*

Accordingly, if we wish to ascertain what is the species of electricity with which a given body is charged, we have only to approach it to a small insulated pith ball, which has previously been touched either with excited glass or with excited sealing-wax. If the body in question repel it in the former case, or attract it in the latter, its electricity is vitreous; if the contrary happens, it is resinous.

(31.) Although each of these two electricities, when taken separately, acts in a manner precisely similar to the other, they nevertheless exhibit in all their relations to each other a marked contrariety of nature. Hence they are naturally viewed as agents having opposite qualities, which completely neutralize one another by combination.

(32.) Another remarkable circumstance which characterizes these agents, is, that the excitation of one species of electricity is always accompanied by the excitation of the other; and both are produced in equal degrees. Thus, when glass is rubbed by silk, or flannel, just as much resinous electricity is produced in the silk, or flannel, as there is vitreous electricity produced in the glass; and whatever electrified bodies are repelled by the one are attracted in the same degree by the other. If one of the substances happen to be a conductor, and be held in the hand, the whole of the electricity which the friction excites in it will disappear as soon as it is produced, from its escaping through the body of the person holding it, and being lost in the earth. But if the precaution be taken of insulating the rubber, its electricity will become manifest, and is always found to be of the opposite species to that which is excited in the body which is rubbed.

(33.) Since the two surfaces rubbed acquire opposite electricities, it follows as a consequence of the law above stated, that they must attract one another; and this is found invariably to be the case. If a white and a black ribbon of two or three feet long, and perfectly dry, be applied to each other by their flat surfaces, and are then drawn repeatedly between the finger and thumb, so as to rub against each other, they will be found to adhere together, and if pulled asunder at one end, will rush together with great quickness. While united they exhibit no sign of electricity, because the operation of the one is just the reverse of that of the other, and their power is neutralized and inoperative. If completely separated, however, each will manifest a strong electrical power, the one attracting those bodies which the other repels.

(34.) The very act of separation is accompanied by appearances which indicate that considerable portions of the electricities excited on each of the surfaces fly back to the opposite surface, and by their union become as it were extinguished or inoperative; and it is only the remaining quantities which have adhered more tenaciously to the surfaces, that retain their activity. When the experiment is made in the dark, flashes of light attend these sudden exchanges of electricity, passing between the two surfaces, and accompanied with a rustling noise.

(35.) Numberless experiments have been made with a view of ascertaining the conditions that determine the species of electricity excited in the respective bodies of which the surfaces are made to rub against each other, but they have led to no satisfactory conclusion. The mechanical configuration of the surface appears to have a greater influence in the result than the peculiar nature of the substance itself. If a plate of glass with a polished surface be rubbed against one which is roughened, the former always acquires the vitreous, and the latter the resinous electricity. No approach to an explanation of this peculiarity has ever been made. Smooth glass acquires vitreous electricity by friction with almost every substance, except the back of a cat, which gives it the resinous electricity; but roughened glass, if rubbed with the same substances, becomes charged with resinous electricity, while the rubbing bodies acquire the vitreous. Sealing-wax, rubbed with an iron chain, acquires, if polished, the resinous electricity; but if its surface is previously rough with scratches, the vitreous. Silk, rubbed by resin, takes the vitreous, but with polished glass, the resinous electricity. The following is a list of several substances which acquire vitreous electricity when rubbed with any of those which follow it in the order in which they are set down; and resinous electricity if rubbed with any of those which precede:—

> The back of a cat.
> Polished glass.
> Woollen cloth.
> Feathers.
> Wood.
> Paper.
> Silk.
> Gum-lac.
> Roughened glass.

In the experiment just mentioned, in which a black and a white ribbon are rubbed together, the former is found to be resinously and the latter vitreously electrified. But if two pieces of the same ribbon of the same length be rubbed, the one being drawn lengthwise and at right angles over a part of the other, the one which has suffered friction in its whole length acquires vitreous, and the other resinous electricity. In like manner, when the whole length of the bow of a violin is drawn over a limited part of the string, the hairs of the bow exhibit a vitreous, and the string a resinous electricity, the body whose excited portion is of the least extent being generally found to be resinously electrified. But in truth, the slightest difference in the conditions of these and similar experiments on the species of electricity arising from friction, will be often sufficient to produce opposite results.

(36.) Electrical excitation may also be produced by the friction of liquids or of gases against solid bodies. This is the case when mercury is made to fall, in a fine shower, under the exhausted receiver of an air-pump, against the glass. If a current of atmospheric air be directed against a pane of glass, by means of a pair of bellows, the glass becomes vitreously electrified.

§ 4. *Induction.*

(37.) Another class of electrical phenomena must here be noticed. Whenever a body is charged with electricity, although it be perfectly insulated, and of course all escape of that electricity prevented, it tends to produce an electrical state of the opposite kind in all the bodies in its vicinity. Thus the vitreous electricity tends to induce the resinous electricity in a body that is situated near it; and this with greater energy, as the distance is smaller. This effect is termed the *induction* of electricity, and may be ranked among the general facts, or laws of the science. The further development of the consequences it leads to, must, for the present, be postponed, as we shall hereafter be better prepared to understand them. But there is one of its results which we shall now point out, as it refers immediately to the phenomena that have already occupied our attention.

(38.) If an electrified body, charged with either species of electricity, be presented to an unelectrified or neutral body, its tendency, in consequence of the law of induction, is to disturb the electrical condition of the different parts of the neutral body. The electrified body induces a state of electricity contrary to its own in that part of the neutral body which is nearest to it; and consequently a state of electricity similar to its own in the remote part. Hence the neutrality of the second body is destroyed by the action of the first; and the adjacent parts of the two bodies, having now opposite electricities, will attract each other. It thus appears, that the attraction which is observed to take place between electrified bodies and those that are unelectrified, is merely a consequence of the altered state of those bodies, resulting directly from the law of induction; and that it is by no means itself an original law, or primary fact in the science.

(39.) The effects of induction will be in proportion to the facility with which changes in the distribution of electricity among the different parts of a body can be effected, a facility which corresponds with the conducting power of the body. Hence the attraction exerted by an electrified body upon another body previously neutral, will be much more energetic if the latter be a conductor, than if it be an electric, in which these changes can take place only to a very small extent. This is confirmed by the following experiment: suspend by fine silk threads of equal length, two small balls of equal dimensions, both made of gum-lac, but one having its surface covered with gold leaf. Place these two pendulums, as they may be called, at a little distance from one another, so as to admit of a comparison of their motions; and then present to them an excited electric, which may be either a tube of glass, or a cylinder of sealing-wax. It will at once be seen that the ball, with a metallic covering, which readily admits of the transfer of electricity from one side to the other, will be much more readily and powerfully attracted, than the other ball which allows of no motion in its electricity. The latter ball will, by slow degrees, however, assume electrical states of the same kind as the gilt ball, and will be feebly attracted. As this change is very slowly effected, so it is more permanent when once produced; and the plain ball adheres for a considerable time to the electric which has attracted it. The gilt ball, on the contrary, is sooner repelled, by its readily receiving the charge of electricity imparted to it by the electric. A degree of permanent electricity, however, is also induced on this ball, in consequence of its gradual penetration into the substance of the gum-lac.

Chapter II.

Theories of Electricity.

(40.) It is impossible to arrive at the full comprehension of the multifarious facts relating to any of the physical sciences without the aid of some leading principles, or modes of viewing them, by which their connexions can be represented to the mind, so as to combine them into an intelligible system. We begin by classing the different agents in nature, designating them by specific names; we next endeavour to conceive these agents as possessed of certain powers or qualities adapted to the production of the observed effects. In the case of light, for example, we may conceive the phenomena to result from the action of material particles, emanating in all directions from the luminous body, and obeying certain laws in their course; or we may adopt another hypothesis, namely, that they proceed from the undulations of an elastic medium pervading space. By employing either the one or the other of these hypotheses, we acquire great facility in tracing the connexions of the phenomena of optics, and retaining them in our minds. This advantage is not immediately dependent on the truth of the particular hypothesis we employ for that purpose: for, in the example before us, it is evident they cannot both be true, and yet they both answer this end. But, of course, the utility of an hypothesis will be proportionate to the degree of exactness with which it accords with the phenomena. No inconvenience can arise from its adoption, as long as we bear in mind that our reasonings are founded on a mere hypothesis, and as long as we hold ourselves in readiness to abandon it, the moment we meet with facts with which it is decidedly inconsistent.

(41.) The hypothesis which naturally suggests itself for the explanation of electrical phenomena is that of a very subtile and highly elastic fluid, pervading the earth and all other material bodies, but itself devoid of any sensible gravity. We must suppose this fluid to be capable of moving, with various degrees of facility, through the pores or actual substance of different kinds of matter. In some, as in those we call *conductors*, or *non-electrics*, such as the metals, it moves without any perceivable obstruction: but, in glass, resin, and, in general, in all bodies called *electrics*, or *non-conductors*, it moves with great difficulty. Moreover, as the phenomena appear to point out the existence of two distinct kinds of agencies, we may further assume that there are two distinct species of electric fluid, which we shall, for the present, name the *vitreous* and the *resinous electricities*. They must each have, when separate, the same general properties as have already been enumerated; but, in relation to each other, there must be a complete contrariety in their natures, so that when combined together, their actions on the bodies in their vicinity, or on the particles of electric fluid contained in those bodies, are exactly balanced; and all visible action ceases. It is in this state of union, in which they perfectly neutralize one another, that they exist in bodies which may be said to be in their *natural state* with regard to electricity.

(42). Thus, then, may the problem be solved, in which it is required to conceive an agent, analogous, in many respects, to other known agents, and to assign to it such properties as will, in their results, correspond to all the observed phenomena. In order to apply to it this latter test, we must trace all the consequences which flow from the suppositions we have made, and strictly compare them with the facts both as presented to us by nature, and as resulting from experiment. These facts, it will be recollected, are reducible to those of excitation, attraction, and repulsion, distribution, induction, and transference.

(43.) *Excitation*. From various causes, of which the friction of surfaces is one, the state of union in which the two electricities naturally exist in bodies, is disturbed; their latent powers are called forth by their separation; the vitreous electricity is impelled in one direction, while the resinous is transferred to the opposite side; and each can now manifest its peculiar energies. When accumulated in any body, or part of a body, each fluid acts in proportion to its relative quantity, that is, to the quantity which is in excess above that which is still retained in a state of inactivity by its union with electricity of the opposite kind. Thus when glass is rubbed with a metallic amalgam, a portion only of the electricities at the two surfaces is decomposed; the vitreous electricity resulting from this decomposition attaches itself to the glass; the resinous, to the amalgam. What remains in each surface undecomposed continues to be quite inert, and has no other influence on the phenomena, than being ready, on the continuance of the decomposing action, to furnish a fresh supply of both fluids to the bodies in the vicinity.

(44.) *Distribution*. Each of these fluids, being highly elastic, their particles repel one another with a force which increases in proportion as their distance is less: and this force acts at all distances, and is not impeded by the interposition of bodies of any kind, provided they are not themselves in an active electrical state. From the most careful analysis of the phenomena, it has been deduced that the exact law of this force is the same as that of gravitation, namely, that its intensity is inversely as the square of the distance.

The mode in which the electricity imparted to a conducting body, or to a system of conductors, is distributed among its different parts, is in exact conformity to the results of this law, as deduced by mathematical investigation. But we reserve the examination of this subject for a future chapter.

While the particles of each fluid repel those of the same kind, they exert an equally strong attraction for the particles of the other species of electric fluid. This attraction, in like manner, increases with a diminution of distance, and follows the same law as to its intensity, namely, that of the inverse ratio of the square of the distance. This force, also, is not affected by the presence of any intervening body.

(45.) *Transference*. Since the two electricities have this powerful attraction for each other, they would always flow towards each other and coalesce, were it not for the obstacles that are opposed to their motion by the non-conducting properties of electrics. When these obstacles are overcome, and a free channel is open for the passage of the electricities, they rush into union with great force and velocity, producing, in their transit and confluence, several remarkable effects. After their coalescence, their power seems to be at once annihilated, or, more properly speaking, it remains dormant, until called into play by the renewed separation of the fluids.

(46.) *Attraction and Repulsion*. The repulsion which is observed to take place between bodies that are insulated and charged with any one species of electricity, for other bodies similarly charged, is derived from the repulsive power which the particles of this fluid exert towards those of their own species. Let us suppose a body charged with electricity to be suspended in the air, or otherwise surrounded by a non-conducting medium, which allows it to move freely. As long as this body remains alone, the outward pressure which the electric fluid exerts against the insulating medium that confines it, will, by the laws of hydrostatics, be equal on all sides; and the body, thus balanced by equal and opposite pressures, will have no tendency to move. But if another body, similarly circumstanced, be brought near it, the repulsive action between the similar electricities contained in these bodies, will diminish the outward pressures of each fluid against the sides of the bodies, (*b, c, fig.* 8.) which are adjacent to each

Fig. 8.

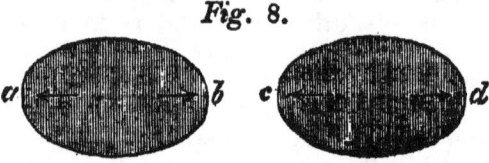

other; and it will, at the same time, increase the outward pressure on the opposite or remoter sides (*a, d*.) Both these causes conspire to destroy the equilibrium; each body is impelled in the direction of the preponderating force, that is, in a direction from the other body; and an effect, which may be called repulsion, takes place. The very same explanation, it is evident, applies to both kinds of electricity, their properties being in this respect exactly alike.

If, on the other hand, a body charged with vitreous electricity be presented to one that is charged with resinous electricity, the attraction of these two fluids will diminish the outward pressure on the remote sides of the bodies, and increase it on the adjacent sides; hence, the bodies will be urged towards each other, and motions indicative of attraction will result. Thus, in all cases, do the movements of the bodies represent the forces themselves which actuate the particles of the developed electricities they contain.

(47.) *Induction.* The law of induction is a direct consequence of the hypothesis we are considering. Wherever one of the electricities exists in an active state, it must repel the particles of the same electricity in all surrounding bodies, and attract those of the opposite species: or, in other words, it tends to decompose their united electricities, accumulating the electricity of the opposite species towards the nearest side, and impelling that of the same species towards the remote side. The body thus acted upon is no longer neutral, although it contains, on the whole, its natural quantities of both electricities; but, in consequence of their partial distribution, electrical appearances will be exhibited in its different parts. The further prosecution of this branch of the subject must also be postponed to a subsequent chapter, our present object being merely to point out, in a general way, the coincidence of the fundamental facts with the proposed theory.

(48.) Thus far we have proceeded upon the hypothesis of there being two distinct electric fluids, having certain properties in common, but each being characterized by a certain modification of these properties. It is, however, equally possible to account for all the phenomena with the same exactness, on the supposition of their resulting from the agency of a single electric fluid. This simplification of the theory may be considered as the discovery of the immortal Franklin, although it had occurred at the same period to Dr. Watson; for it was Franklin who first pointed out the mode in which it might be successfully applied to explain some of the most remarkable phenomena of the science. Several particular points in his theory, as he originally proposed it, were defective, and were found on strict examination to be at variance with ascertained facts. It is to Æpinus and to Cavendish that we owe the rectification of these errors: and the theory of Franklin, as thus amended, whatever alterations the future progress of discovery may oblige us to make in it, will ever remain one of the most beautiful specimens of this kind of reasoning which philosophy has produced. Of this hypothesis we shall now present a brief outline; and point out the mode in which it explains the phenomena.

(49.) We set out, then, with supposing that there exists in all bodies a subtile fluid, which we shall call the *electric fluid*;—that its particles repel one another with a force varying inversely as the square of the distance;— that they attract the particles of all other matter, or some specific ingredient in that matter, with a force following the same law of the inverse square of the distance;—that this fluid is dispersed through the pores of bodies, and from some unknown peculiarity, can move through them with various degrees of facility, according as they are conductors or non-conductors. Bodies are said to be in their natural state with regard to electricity, when the repulsion of the fluid they contain for a particle of fluid at a distance is exactly balanced by the attraction of the matter in the body for the same particle. In this state they may be considered as *saturated* with the electric fluid. Whenever they contain a quantity of fluid greater than this, they are said to be *positively electrified*, or to have *positive electricity*. When, on the other hand, there is a quantity less than that required for saturation, the body is said to be *negatively electrified*, or to have *negative electricity*. In the former case, it is the fluid that is redundant, or in excess; in the latter, it is the matter which is left unsaturated that should be considered as the redundant principle. The state of positive electricity, then, consists in a redundance of fluid, or in matter that is *over-saturated*, as it has been termed; that of negative electricity, in a deficiency of fluid, or in matter *under-saturated*, or, what is an equivalent expression, in *redundant matter*. In mathematical language, the former condition may be expressed by the sign *plus;* the latter by that of *minus*. In considering the mutual electrical actions of bodies, the portions in which the matter and the fluid mutually saturate each other, need not be taken into account, since their actions, as we have seen, are perfectly neutralized: and we need only attend to those of the redundant fluid and the redundant matter.

(50.) When a body contains more than its natural proportion of electric fluid, the surplus will, by the repulsive tendency of its particles, overflow and escape, if such escape be allowed, until the body is reduced to its neutral state. When under-saturated, the redundant matter will attract fluid from all quarters from which it can receive it, until it is again brought to its neutral state. This efflux, or influx, is prevented either when the body is surrounded on all sides by substances, through the pores of which the fluid cannot pass, or when the body itself is of that nature.

(51.) The mutual recession of two positively electrified bodies is a direct consequence of the repulsion of the redundant fluids contained in each, which, being attached to the matter by their attraction for it, impel it in the direction of their own repulsion. In the same way the mutual approximation of two bodies in opposite electrical states is the immediate effect of the attraction of the redundant fluid in the one, for the redundant matter in the other; and *vice versâ*, for this attraction is mutual.

(52.) A difficulty does, indeed, occur when we attempt to apply the theory to the case of two bodies which are both in a state of negative electricity, that is, in which there exists in both certain quantities of matter unsaturated with electric fluid. What action does the theory, as hitherto stated, point out as the result in this particular case? Plainly none. All those portions of the matter of each body which are still saturated, together with the fluid which saturates them, can have, as we have already seen, no effect either of attraction or repulsion. The only active element is the unsaturated matter; but the hypothesis does not assign any action of this matter upon other matter at a distance. Yet we learn from experience that the bodies, under these circumstances, actually repel one another. In order, therefore, to render the hypothesis conformable to fact, we are obliged to annex to it another condition; namely, that the particles of simple matter, that is, of matter uncombined with the electric fluid, exert a repulsive action on one another. It is singular that so acute a mind as that of Franklin should not have discerned this defect in his own theory, or perceived that this further condition was absolutely requisite for the explanation of the phenomena. Without it, indeed, we should be unable to explain the want of action between two neutral bodies; for the repulsion of the fluids in both bodies being balanced by the attraction of the fluid in the one for the matter in the other, the remaining attraction of the fluid in the second body for the matter in the first would be uncompensated by any repulsion, and the forces would not be held in equilibrium, as we find they really are.

(53.) The law of electrical induction is an immediate consequence of the Franklinian theory. When a body charged with electricity is presented to a neutral body, the redundant fluid of the former exerts a repulsive action on the fluid in the latter body; and if this happens to be a conductor, it impels a certain portion of that fluid to the remote end of this body, which becomes at that part positively electrified; while its nearer end, which the same fluid has quitted, is consequently in the state of negative electricity. If the first body had been negatively electrified, its unsaturated matter would have exerted an attractive force on the fluid in the second body, and would have drawn it nearer to itself, producing an accumulation or redundance of fluid at the adjacent end, and a corresponding deficiency at the remote end: that is, the former would have been rendered positive, and the latter negative. All this is exactly conformable to observation.

(54.) The phenomena of transference are easily explicable on this hypothesis; and they arise from the destruction of the equilibrium of forces, which confined the fluid to a particular situation or mode of distribution.

(55.) There is, indeed, no fact explicable by the hypothesis of a double fluid, which is not explained with equal facility by that of a single fluid, with the condition already stated. The explanation by the first is easily converted into an explanation by the second, by substituting the expressions of *positive* and *negative* for those of *vitreous* and *resinous electricities*; and considering the action of the latter as arising from the influence of redundant or unsaturated matter, to which is ascribed in the Franklinian hypothesis a similar operation to that of the resinous electricity in the hypothesis of Du Fay. The hypothesis of a single fluid has, it must be allowed, the advantage of greater simplicity: but, on the other hand, it lies open to the objection of its involving a condition which appears, at first view, to be at variance with our preconceived notions of the primary laws of matter, and more especially with that of gravitation; namely, that which implies the mutual repulsion of its particles when void of electricity.

When viewed as a mere hypothesis calculated to facilitate our comprehension of the phenomena and of their connexions, it is a matter of indifference which we employ, for they will either of them answer the purpose. In our future explanations we shall, in general, adhere to the language of the Franklinian theory, as being the simplest, and generally the most convenient; and because a conversion of terms the reverse of that just now pointed out will in all cases enable us to supply the explanation of the same phenomenon according to the theory of Du Fay. As to the question which of these two hypotheses approaches the nearest to the real state of things, we are not yet prepared to discuss the arguments that could enable us to decide it; and we must, therefore, wait till we can resume the subject in the sequel.

The further development of these theories, and of the law of induction, in particular, must, for the present, be postponed, since they require us to be acquainted with many practical details relating to the accumulation of electricity, and its management when applied to various objects of experimental research.

Chapter III.

Electrical Machines.

(56.) The essential parts of an instrument for procuring large supplies of electricity for the purposes of experiment, or an *electrical machine*, as it is called, are the electric, the rubber, the prime conductor, the insulator, and the machinery for setting the electric in motion.

(57.) The electric, by the excitation of which the electricity is to be developed, may be made of various materials. Globes of sulphur were employed by the earlier electricians for that purpose; but polished glass is found, on the whole, to be the most convenient substance. The original form given to it by Hauksbee, who was the inventor of the electrical machine, was that of a globe, which he caused to revolve upon a vertical axis. The most convenient forms, however, are those of a hollow cylinder, or of a flat circular plate, revolving upon a horizontal axis. When used in the form of a globe or cylinder, it has sometimes been found advantageous to line the inside of it with a thin layer of a resinous composition, consisting of four parts of Venice turpentine, one of resin, and one of bees' wax. This must be introduced in sufficient quantity into the inside of the globe or cylinder, and, when the glass is brought gradually to an equal degree of heat throughout the melted substances, is allowed to spread itself over the interior surface, by turning the globe or cylinder about its axis. The principal use of such a coating is to improve bad machines, for it is not required in good ones.

The earlier electricians contented themselves with using the hand as a rubber, till a cushion was introduced for that purpose by Professor Winkler, of Leipsic. The cushion is usually made of soft leather, generally basil skin, stuffed with hair or wool, so as to be as hard as the bottom of a chair, but yet sufficiently yielding to accommodate itself, without much pressure, to the surface of the glass to which it is applied.

(58.) Of cylindric machines, the simplest and most perfect construction is that invented by Nairne, and which is represented in *fig.* 9. The glass cylinder C is from 8 to 16 inches in diameter, and

Fig. 9.

from one to two feet long, supported, for the purpose of insulation, on two upright pillars of glass, which are fixed to a firm wooden stand. Two hollow metallic conductors P, N, equal in length to the cylinders, are placed parallel to it, one on each side, upon two insulating pillars of glass, which are cemented into two separate pieces of wood that slide across the base so as to allow of their being brought within different distances from the cylinder. To one of these conductors N, the cushion is attached, being fastened to it by the intervention of a bent spring, the purpose of which is to keep it equally pressed against the cylinder in every part of its revolution. The pressure of the cushion is also further regulated by an adjusting screw adapted to the wooden base, on which the glass pillar that supports the conductor is fixed. From the upper edge of the cushion there proceeds a flap F of thin oiled silk, which is sewed on the face of the cushion about a quarter of an inch from its upper edge. It extends over the upper surface of the glass cylinder to within an inch of a row of metallic points, proceeding like the teeth of a rake from a horizontal rod, which is fixed to the adjacent side of the opposite conductor P. The motion of the cylinder must always be given in the direction of the silk flap; and it may be communicated either by a single handle, or by a multiplying wheel W, as in the figure: the latter produces more electricity in the same time, but the labour of turning is increased nearly in the same proportion. On some accounts it is more convenient to place the conductor to which the rubber is not attached, at right angles to the cylinder; and this is the plan adopted in the common electrical machines.

(59.) The conductor P, to which the rubber is not attached, is generally called the *prime conductor*, or the *positive conductor*, as the electricity with which it becomes charged is positive. It is a cylindrical tube, each end terminating in a hemisphere. There is no advantage in its being made of solid materials, for the electricity is contained only at the surfaces. It may be made of thin sheet brass, or copper, or tin, or of pasteboard, covered with gold leaf or tin foil. Care must be taken that its surface be free from all points and asperities; and the perforations which are made in it, and which should be about the size of a quill, for the purpose of attaching wires, and other kinds of apparatus, should have their edges well rounded and smoothed off. For the more perfect insulation of the conductor, it is advisable to apply upon the glass pillar which supports it, a varnish of gum-lac, or of sealing wax.

(60.) The degree of excitation produced in the glass depends much upon the substance employed as a rubber. Mr. Singer observes that dry silk is very efficacious, but that the most powerful effects are obtained by the use of an amalgam of tin, zinc, and mercury, applied by means of hog's lard, to the surface of leather or oiled silk. That part of the cushion which comes in contact with the glass cylinder, should be coated with an amalgam of this kind, spread evenly over its surface, until level with the line formed by the seam which joins the silk flap to the face of the cushion. No amalgam should be placed over this seam, nor on the silk flap; which last should be wiped clean whenever the continued motion of the machine shall have soiled it, by depositing dust or amalgam on its surface. The same attention is requisite to the surface of the glass, which often becomes covered with black spots and lines, more particularly when the amalgam has been recently applied. It is essential to remove these as often as they are formed in any quantity, since they tend to lessen the power of the machine. The surface of the amalgamated cushion is also soon soiled; for the excited glass constantly attracts dust from surrounding bodies, and this dust is collected by the rubber as the glass passes it. If the dust is removed after every course of experiments, by separating the cushion from the negative conductor, and gently rubbing its surface, and the surface of the silk flap, with a dry linen cloth, the machine may be kept in good order without a frequent renewal of the amalgam; such renewal being only necessary when that which has been applied becomes irregularly distributed over the cushion, or impregnated with dust.

(61.) The amalgam recommended by Mr. Singer, is made by melting together one ounce of tin and two ounces of zinc, which are to be mixed, while fluid, with six ounces of mercury, and agitated in an iron, or thick wooden box, till cold. It is then to be reduced to very fine powder in a mortar, and mixed with a sufficient quantity of hog's lard to form it into a paste. When amalgams have a large proportion of mercury, their action is variable and transient. The best cement for attaching the cylinder to its pivots, is made by mixing five pounds of resin, one pound of bees' wax, one pound of red ochre, and two table-spoonfuls of plaster of Paris. The ochre and plaster of Paris should be well dried, and then added to, and alternately mixed with the other ingredients, when they are in a state of fusion.

The plate machine, *fig.* 10, was originally proposed by Dr. Ingenhouz, and has been since much improved by Cuthbertson. This machine, in its most per-

Fig. 10.

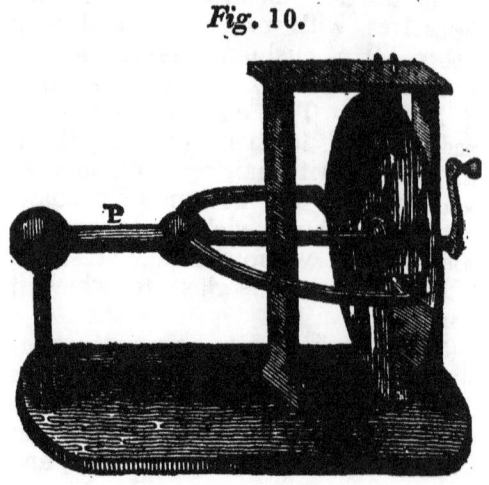

fect form, consists of a circular plate of glass, turning on an axis that passes at right angles through its centre: it is rubbed by two pair of cushions, fixed at opposite parts of the circumference by elastic frames of thin mahogany, which are constructed so as to press the glass plate between them with the requisite force, by means of regulating screws. A brass conductor P, supported by glass, is fixed to the frame of the machine, with its branched extremities opposite to each other, and near the extreme diameter of the plate, in a direction at right angles to the vertical line of the opposite cushions. The branched extremities of the conductor are furnished with pointed wires, that serve to collect the electricity from the surface of the excited plate.

(62.) It is not quite determined which of these two arrangements affords the greatest quantity of electricity from the same surface; but the cylinder is less expensive, and less liable to accidents than the plate, and it appears to possess nearly equal power.

(63.) From what has already been explained of the general laws of electricity, the mode in which these machines act will readily be understood. The friction of the cushion against the glass cylinder produces a transfer of electric fluid from the former to the latter; that is, the cushion becomes negatively, and the glass positively, electrified. The fluid which thus adheres to the glass, is carried round by the revolution of the cylinder; and its escape is at first prevented by the silk flap which covers the cylinder, until it comes to the immediate vicinity of the metallic points, which being placed at a small distance from the cylinder, absorb nearly the whole of the electricity as it passes near them, and transfer it to the prime conductor. Positive electricity is thus accumulated in the prime conductor, while the conductor connected with the cushion, being deprived of this electricity, is negatively electrified.

But if both these conductors are insulated, this action will soon have reached its limit: for when the cushion and its conductor have been exhausted of their fluid to a certain degree, they cannot by the same force of excitation supply any further quantity to the glass. In order to enable it to do so, we must replenish it, as it were, that is, restore to it a quantity equal to what it has lost. This purpose will be answered by placing it in communication with a conducting body of large dimensions; or, what is still more effectual, by making it communicate with the earth, which is an inexhaustible source of electric fluid. In order, therefore, to supply the prime conductor with a constant stream of electricity, we must destroy the insulation of the cushion, by placing on the conductor to which it is fixed, a metallic chain, or wire, extending to the ground. If, on the other hand, we wish to obtain negative electricity, by means of the same machine, we must keep the negative conductor insulated, and connect the prime conductor with the ground, in order to allow the fluid to escape from it as soon as it is collected from the cylinder. The fluid will thus continue to be drawn without interruption from the negative conductor, as it now meets with no impediment to its discharge on the opposite side of the machine.

That the quantity of positive electricity produced in one conductor is exactly equal to that of the negative electricity in the other, is proved by the fact that, if the two conductors are connected by a wire, no signs of electricity are obtained in any of the conductors on turning the machine: but if the wire be not continuous, but interrupted by short intervals, a succession of sparks appear at each interval, indicating the passage of a stream of fluid from the one side to the other of the apparatus.

(64.) A person standing on a stool with glass legs is thereby insulated; and if, in this situation, he touch the prime conductor, either with his hand, or through the intermedium of a metallic rod, or chain, he may be considered as forming part of the same system of conductors. When the machine is worked, therefore, he will partake with the conductor of its charge of electricity, and sparks may be drawn from any part of his body by the knuckle of any other person who is in communication with the ground.

Chapter IV.

Effects of Electrical Attraction and Repulsion.

(65.) Having obtained, by the electrical machine, the means of accumulating considerable quantities of electricity, we are enabled to multiply and extend our observations of the phenomena, and to examine with more precision their correspondence with the results of theory. The effects of electrical attractions and repulsions may be exhibited much more distinctly, and on a larger scale than with the simpler instruments we had previously employed. The experiments formerly mentioned on the alternate approach and recession of light bodies, may be repeated with either conductor of the machine, when charged with electricity, and we may note with more accuracy the differences which occur in the rapidity with which the changes from one electrical state to another take place according as the bodies are more or less good conductors of electricity. A pith ball, or a fragment of gold leaf, is very strongly and immediately attracted by the electrified conductor, and the instant after it has come into contact with it, is repelled; but it is now attracted by the other bodies in its neighbourhood, to which it communicates its own electricity, and then is again in a state to be influenced by the conductor, and to be again attracted: and this alternation of effects will continue as long as the conductor remains charged.

(66.) These alternate and rapid movements are best seen by placing these small bodies between two metallic plates, placed as in fig. 11, the one over the other, at a certain distance; the upper one communicating with the prime conductor, the lower one with the ground. If figures of men and women are cut out of paper and placed between the two plates, they will exhibit a rapid dance, while they fetch and carry the electricity from the upper to the lower plate; or contrariwise, if the conductor be in the negative state.

Fig. 11.

(67.) This alternation of attractions and repulsions accompanying the transferring electricity by moveable conductors, is also illustrated by the motions of a ball (*fig.* 12.), suspended by a silk

Fig. 12.

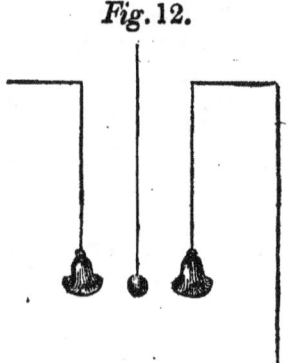

thread, and placed between two bells, of which the one is electrified, and the other communicates with the ground. The alternate motion of the ball between the two bells will produce a continued ringing. As thus described, it is a mere toy, but the same arrangement has been applied to the philosophical purpose of giving notice of changes taking place in the electrical state of the atmosphere.

(68.) The mutual repulsion of bodies that are similarly electrified gives rise to many amusing appearances. The filaments of a feather will separate from each other and diverge, when electrified, presenting a singular and unnatural appearance. A small figure in the shape of a human head, covered with hair, when placed upon the conductor and electrified, will exhibit the appearance of terror from the general bristling up and divergence of the hair. A lock of wool highly charged with electricity will, in like manner, swell out to a large size, in consequence of the mutual repulsion of the filaments which compose it. On approaching a needle to it, held in the hand, whereby its electricity is quickly drawn off, the cotton will suddenly shrink into its original dimensions.

(69.) We have already adverted to the effects of fusion in rendering some bodies conductors, which in their solid state had the contrary property. This is the case with sealing-wax; and accordingly, if melted sealing-wax be electrified, its particles will tend to separate by their mutual repulsion, and to draw out into filaments. Let a piece of sealing-wax be fixed on the end of a wire, and be set fire to, but the flame immediately afterwards blown out. While the surface of the wax is still melted, present it, at the distance of some inches, to the electrified conductor, a number of extremely fine filaments will immediately dart out from the sealing-wax to the conductor, on which they will be condensed into a kind of net-work resembling wool. If the wire with the sealing-wax be stuck into one of the holes of the conductor, and a piece of paper be presented at a moderate distance to the wax, just after it has been ignited, on setting the machine in motion, a net-work of wax will be formed on the paper. The same effect, but in a slighter degree, will be produced, if the paper be briskly rubbed with a piece of Indian rubber, and the melting sealing-wax be held pretty near the paper immediately after it has been rubbed. If the paper, thus covered with filaments of sealing-wax, be gently warmed before the fire, the wax will adhere to it, and exhibit permanently the result of the experiment. Still more beautiful are the appearances produced by camphor subjected to a similar process. For the purpose of obtaining them, a spoon, holding a piece of lighted camphor, must be kept electrified by working the machine, while it communicates with the conductor; the camphor will then throw out curious ramifications, which appear to shoot like those of a vegetable.

(70.) It is on the same principle that

the escape of a conducting fluid, such as water, through a narrow aperture, is promoted by electrifying it. If a small metallic vessel filled with water be suspended from the prime conductor, and there be placed in the water one end of a glass syphon, with a capillary bore of such a diameter as that the water will scarcely drop from it; upon turning the cylinder of the machine so as to convey electricity to the vessel and its contents, the water immediately flows in a stream, and, if the electrical charge be very powerful, the descending current will be seen to separate into several branches.

(71.) If a sponge, saturated with water, be suspended from the prime conductor, the water will at first only drop gradually from the sponge; but when the conductor has become strongly electrified, the drops will fall plentifully, and, in the dark, will produce the appearance of a luminous shower of rain.

(72.) Advantage is taken of the repulsive property of electrified bodies for the construction of an *Electrometer*, or instrument adapted to measure the intensity of the electricity they may contain. Henley's electrometer (*fig.* 13.)

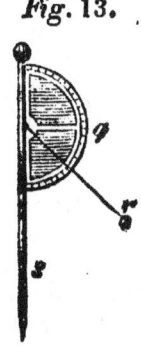

Fig. 13.

consists of a slender rod of very light wood, r, serving as an index, terminated by a small pith ball, and suspended from the upper part of a stem of wood, s, which is fitted to a hole in the upper surface of the conductor. An ivory semicircle, or quadrant, q, is affixed to the stem, having its centre coinciding with the axis of motion of the rod, for the purpose of measuring the angle of deviation from the perpendicular, which the repulsion of the ball from the stem produces in the moveable rod. The number of degrees which is described by the index, affords some evidence of the quantity of electricity with which the apparatus is charged; though the instrument has obviously no pretensions to being an exact measure of its intensity.

(73.) One of the most delicate instruments for detecting the presence of electricity is that which was invented by Mr. Bennet, and is usually called the *gold-leaf electrometer*; although it is, properly speaking, only an electroscope. It consists (*fig.* 14.) of two

Fig. 14.

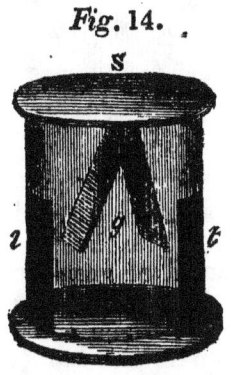

narrow slips of gold leaf, g, suspended parallel to each other, in a glass cylinder, which secures it from disturbance by accidental currents of air, and attached to the end of a small metallic tube, which terminates above either in a flat surface, S, of metal, or in a metallic ball. Two slips of tin-foil t t, are pasted to the inside of the cylinder, on opposite sides, in a vertical position, and so placed as that the gold leaves may come in contact with them, when their mutual repulsion is sufficiently powerful to make them diverge to that extent. These slips of tin-foil terminate in the foot of the instrument, and thus are in communication with the earth. A very minute charge of electricity communicated to the upper end of the tube, is immediately transmitted to the gold leaves, which are thus made to repel each other; but if the repulsion is such as to make them strike against the tin-foil, their insulation ceases, and their electricity is carried off; and being now rendered neutral, they cease to repel one another, and, collapsing, resume their original position.

(74.) The most perfect electrometer for measuring very small quantities of electricity, is the apparatus contrived by Coulomb, and to which he has given the name of the *torsion balance*. It is represented in its simplest form in *fig.* 15, and consists of a cylindrical glass jar, covered at the top by a circular glass plate, with a hole in its centre. Through this hole a single fibre of the web of the silk-worm descends nearly to the bottom of the jar, and

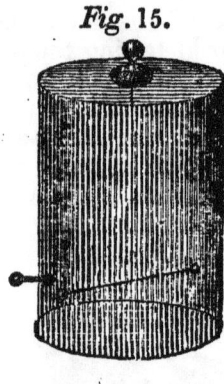

Fig. 15.

carries at its lower extremity a transverse needle. This needle consists of either a filament of gum-lac, or a silk thread or piece of straw coated with sealing-wax. At one end it is terminated by a small pith-ball, and at the other by a disc of varnished paper, acting merely as a counterpoise to the ball. The upper end of the silk fibre is affixed to a kind of button having a small index, and capable of being turned round upon a circular plate divided into degrees. One side of the jar is perforated to allow of the insertion of a short horizontal bar, having a small metallic sphere at each of its ends, the one being in the inside and the other on the outside of the jar; and the former being so situated as just to allow the ball of the suspended needle to come in contact with it in the course of its revolution. By turning the button, or the index, the needle may be brought into this, or any other required position with regard to the ball. It is found by experiment that the angle of torsion of the silk fibre is, within a certain range of distance, very nearly in the direct ratio of the force which acts in producing the torsion; and therefore, if the two balls be placed in contact by turning the button, and then similarly electrified, the distance to which they are repelled by the angular motion of the suspended ball, affords a measure of the repulsive force exerted. In like manner, the distance which the suspended ball is made to move when it is attracted by the fixed ball, when the two have opposite electricities, gives accurate measures of the attractive forces. It was by the employment of this apparatus, in a very elaborate series of experiments, that Coulomb was enabled to establish very satisfactorily the exact law of variation, both of the attractive and repulsive forces, arising from electricity, with relation to the distance, which we have already stated.

Chapter V.

Distribution of Electricity.

(75.) It had long been observed, that the quantity of electricity which bodies are capable of receiving, does not follow the proportion of their bulk, but depends principally upon the extent of their surface. It was found, for instance, that a metallic conductor in the form of a globe, or cylinder, contains just as much electricity when hollow, as it does when solid. Hence it was evident that the electricity resides altogether at the surface, or at least does not extend equally throughout the whole mass of the body. But it was only by applying to the theory all the refinements of mathematical investigation, that precise notions could be formed of the exact distribution of the electric fluid in bodies of different shapes. The labours of Cavendish, Coulomb, Poisson, and Ivory, have furnished the means of determining this problem in every case, however complicated; and whenever a comparison has been instituted between the results of experiment and of theory, the most perfect agreement has been found between them. Thus all the phenomena of electricity are found to be in exact conformity with the mechanical consequences of the theory: they can be anticipated with rigorous precision, and can even be reduced to numerical calculation in their minutest details, as well as in their most intricate combinations.

(76.) For the purpose of measuring the proportional quantities of electricity with which different parts of the same, or of different bodies are charged, no instrument is so well fitted as the balance of Coulomb, of which an account has just been given. What peculiarly adapts it for these experiments, is its extreme sensibility, by which the slightest variation in the intensity of the attractive or repulsive force produces a very considerable effect in the movement of the horizontal needle. In some of the experiments related by Coulomb, a force only equal to the 279th of a grain was sufficient to make the needle perform an entire revolution round the circle: the 360th part of this force, therefore, or less than the 100,000th of a grain, might be estimated by each degree of its angular motion.

In order to apply to the instrument only such forces as it is capable of measuring, and of collecting at the same time from the different parts of bodies such minute quantities of electricity as are exactly proportional to those with which they are themselves charged, Coulomb employed what he calls a *proof plane*, which is simply a small circular disc of gilt paper, *d*, (*fig.* 15,) fixed to the extremity of a very slender cylinder of gum-lac, and thus completely insulated. If we wish, then, to ascertain the proportions in which electricity is distributed on the surfaces or interior of any particular body, we first insulate that body as completely as possible, and impart to it a small quantity of electricity by a spark from the prime conductor. We next touch any of the points on its surface, the electricity of which we may wish to measure, with the little gilt disc, holding it by the other end of its insulating handle; then carrying the plane to the torsion balance, of which the moveable ball has been previously charged with an electricity of the same kind, we bring it for an instant in contact with the fixed ball. We then withdraw it, and the fixed ball being now electrified in the same manner as the moveable one, repels the latter with a force measured by the angle of torsion, at which the moveable ball stops. While the little plane and the balls of the balance remain the same, the division of the electricity between the little plane and the moveable ball preserves the same uniform proportion; and thus the repulsive force which results, and which drives off the moveable ball, is proportional to the quantity of electricity with which the little plane is charged. It has been proved, by a series of well-contrived experiments, that this quantity is exactly proportional to the quantity of electricity which really exists at the point of the body with which it has been placed in contact. By applying the same test and method of admeasurement to various other points of the body we are studying, we may determine the manner in which the electricity is distributed in all its parts; for the method is applicable even to the interior of the body, if we pierce it with a small hole terminating at the part whose electricity we wish to examine, and pass the proof plane into it till it is applied to the bottom of the aperture. Care must be taken, however, in conducting these last experiments, that the proof plane be not suffered to touch any other part of the body except that of which the electricity is to be determined, and not even the sides of the aperture through which it is introduced, as such contact would entirely falsify the result.

The following are among the principal results of these investigations:—

(77.) In a solid body having the form of a perfect sphere, and charged with positive electricity, the whole of the fluid is, in consequence of the repulsion of its own particles, which is everywhere directed from the centre outwards, accumulated in a thin stratum at the very surface of the sphere. If the body be charged with negative electricity, the deficiency of fluid will take place only in the superficial stratum of matter.

(78.) If, instead of being spherical, the body have any other form, the electricity will still be chiefly confined to the surface; and if it have an elongated form, there will be a greater charge in the remoter parts than in those nearer to the middle.

(79.) This result of theory, respecting the limitation of electricity to the mere surface, is confirmed in the most decisive manner by the experiments of Coulomb. A conducting body of the form represented by the section, *fig*. 16,

Fig. 16.

had small pits made in various parts of its surface. They were half an inch in diameter, and some of the most shallow were not depressed more than one-tenth of an inch below the surface. When the body was electrified, and the small proof plane applied in accurate contact to the bottom of these pits and depressions, care being taken that it should not touch their margin, and then applied to the electrometer, no indication of its having received any electricity could be perceived; whereas the contact of the same proof plane with any part of the even surface showed the latter to be strongly electrified.

(80.) The following experiment of Biot's contains also a striking practical illustration of the same truth. Let *a* (*fig.* 17.) represent a section of any spheroid of conducting matter, suspended by a thread which perfectly insulates it. Let *c c* be two caps formed of gilt-

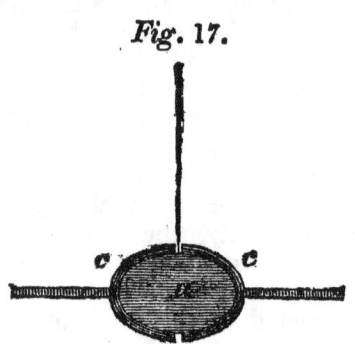

Fig. 17.

paper, tin-foil, or any conductor, and such that, when united, they accurately fit the surface of the spheroid; and let them be also furnished with insulating handles of gum-lac. Let there be communicated to the ball, *a*, any degree of electricity; and then let the two caps, held by their insulating handles, be carefully applied to its surface. Upon the removal of these caps, it will be found that the whole of the electricity has been abstracted from the spheroid, so that it will no longer affect the most delicate electrometer; whilst the two caps will be found, upon accurate trial, to have acquired precisely the same quantity of electricity which had at first resided in the body *a*.

We may conclude, both from theory and experiment, therefore, that although, strictly speaking, the electricity must reside within the substance of conducting bodies, it extends, in fact, to a depth so small as to be inappreciable by any known methods of observation.

(81.) The effect of an expansion of surface in lessening the intensity of electricity, while its absolute quantity remains the same, is well illustrated by the following experiment mentioned by Biot. *Fig.* 18 represents an insulated cylinder, *a b*, moveable round a horizontal axis, and capable of being turned by an insulating handle *h*. Around the cylinder is coiled a thin lamina of any metal, *c*, the end of which is semicircular, and has attached to it a silk thread *f*. The whole apparatus communicates with an electroscope *e*, formed of two linen threads, each terminating in a pith ball. On communicating a charge of electricity to the cylinder, the threads and balls of the electroscope diverge. Upon taking hold of the silk

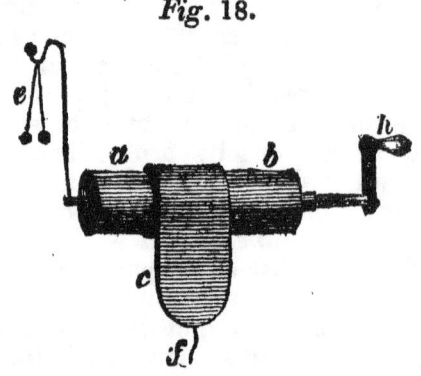

Fig. 18.

thread, and unrolling the metallic lamina from the cylinder, the balls gradually collapse; thus indicating a diminution in the intensity of electrical repulsion. If the lamina be sufficiently long, the electrical charge may be spread over so great an extent of surface, as to allow the balls to hang perpendicularly and come in contact. But on winding up the lamina, the intensity of the electricity is restored, and the balls diverge to the same extent as before, allowance being made for the small dissipation of electricity which may have occurred from the contact of the air during the experiment.

(82.) In the case of a long and slender lamina of conducting matter, charged with electricity, Coulomb found that its intensity continued nearly uniform from the middle of the lamina to within a short distance from the ends; at that part it rapidly increased; and at the very extremity it became twice as much as at the middle part. In a circular plate, the electricity is accumulated in much greater quantities at the circumference than about the centre; the intensities being in the proportion of 2.9 to 1: that is, the intensity at the centre is nearly one-third of that at the circumference.

(83.) If the body be an oblong spheroid, arising from the revolution of an ellipse on its greater axis, the thickness of the strata of electricity, or, in other words, its intensity, at the extremities of the two axes, is exactly in the proportion of the respective axes themselves. It thus appears, that if the ellipsoid be much elongated, the intensity must be very feeble at the equator, but very great at the poles. A still more rapid augmentation of the relative intensity at the extremities takes place in bodies of a cylindric or prismatic form; and the more so as their length bears a greater proportion to their breadth. Coulomb found by experiment that, in a cylinder thirty inches long and two inches in diameter, the intensity of the electricity at the ends was to its intensity at the middle, or at any part more than two inches from the extremity, as 2.3 to 1. Pursuing this train of reasoning, it will lead us to a conclusion of some importance, namely, that if the conducting substance be drawn out into a point, the intensity of the electricity at that point will be exceedingly great; and that the point will accordingly absorb and draw into itself nearly the whole of the electricity that is contained in the body. This vast concentration of electricity is found actually to take place in all points that project beyond the general surface.

Chapter VI.

Transference of Electricity.

(84.) We are next to consider the condition of bodies during the prevalence of those forces which tend to overset the electric equilibrium, over those which tend to preserve it. The pressure exerted by the electric fluid against the non-conducting medium, such as the air, which opposes an obstacle to its escape, is in a ratio compounded of the repulsive force of its own particles at the surface of the stratum of fluid, and of the thickness of that stratum; but as one of these elements is always proportional to the other, the total pressure must, in every point, be proportional to the square of the thickness. If this pressure be less than the resistance, or coercive force, as it has been called, of the air, the electricity is retained; but the moment it exceeds that force, in any one point, the electricity suddenly escapes, just as a fluid confined in a vessel would rush out if it were to burst open a hole in the side of the vessel.

(85.) It is only a certain proportion of the whole quantity of electricity in the conducting body that thus suddenly escapes; but the irruption of it is marked by many very striking phenomena, all indicative of the abruptness and violence with which the change is effected. A sharp snap is heard, accompanied by a vivid spark, and there are evidences of an intense heat being evolved in the line which the electricity takes.

(86.) The passage of the electric fluid through a perfect conductor is unattended with light. Light appears only where there are obstacles in its path by the interposition of imperfect conductors; and such is the velocity with which it is transmitted, that the sparks appear to take place at the very same instant along the whole line of its course. Thus, if a row of small fragments of tin-foil be pasted on a piece of glass, *fig.* 19, and electricity be sent through

Fig. 19.

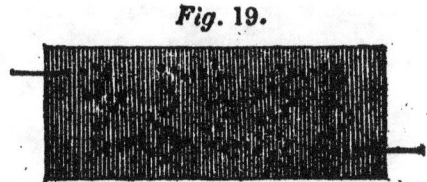

them by connecting one of its ends with the conductor of an electrical machine, while the other end communicates with the ground, it will not be possible to detect any difference of time in the occurrence of the light in the different parts, so that the whole series of luminous points, if sufficiently near, appear, in the dark, like a vivid and continuous line of light. By varying the arrangement of the tin-foil, we may distribute the light in any manner we please, so as to exhibit a brilliant delineation of the figure they represent. Even when conducting bodies appear to be in contact, if the experiment be made in the dark, a spark is generally seen to pass between them, unless the bodies be pressed together with considerable force. Hence, a chain appears luminous at each link, while conveying a charge of electricity.

(87.) The longest and most vivid sparks are obtained between two conductors having a rounded form, and the more so in proportion as they are both portions of spheres of large diameter. This may be exemplified in a common electrical machine, by presenting a metallic ball of large size to that side of the prime conductor which is furthest from the cylinder of the machine. In such cases, however, the electricity being of weaker intensity, the distance between the conducting bodies requisite for the transfer of electricity through the air, or what is termed *the striking distance*, is necessarily small. If the ball is of smaller diameter, or the conductor of a more elongated shape, the electricity at its surface is of higher intensity, and will therefore pass through a greater extent of air; the spark is in this case of considerable length, appearing as a long streak of fire extending from the conductor to the ball, and instead of being directed towards one point, being distributed to various points throughout a certain extent of the surface of the ball.

Often, when very long, the spark is seen to have an angular or zig-zag course, (see *fig.* 20.) exactly like that of a flash of lightning.—This irregularity

Fig. 20.

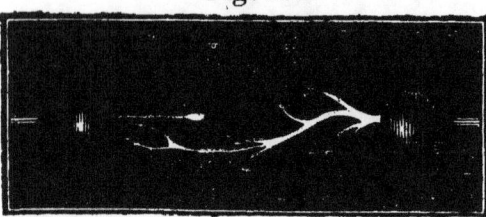

is probably occasioned by the fluid darting obliquely in its course to minute conducting particles that are floating in the air, a little removed from the direct line of passage. Even particles of moisture suspended in the air would be sufficient to occasion these deviations. The presence of such particles will account also for the appearance of lateral scintillations, which frequently seem to diverge from the principal stream of electricity. The greater the number of such intermediate conductors, or stepping-stones, as it were, for the electricity, the more readily will the balance between the forces be overset, and the irruption of electric fluid determined.

When the air is either sufficiently moistened, or sufficiently rarefied, the electric fluid passes through it with comparative facility, and its track is indicated by streams of light, probably occasioned by many parallel series of minute sparks passing from particle to particle.

(88.) Electrical light differs in no respect from the light obtained from other sources. Dr. Wollaston found that, when observed through a prism, the ordinary colours arising from the decomposition of light are obtained; but the prevailing tint of colour will vary according to the different substances through which the sparks pass, or to the nature of the surface from which they emanate, or by which they are received. Dr. Brewster found that it is capable of undergoing polarization, either by transmission through a doubly refracting crystal, by reflection at the proper polarizing angle from a polished plane surface, or by oblique refraction through a series of glass plates.

(89.) The brilliancy of the electrical spark is proportional to the conducting power of the bodies between which it passes. When an imperfect conductor, such as wood, is employed, the electric light appears in the form of faint red streams; but metals afford them of great brilliancy. Its colour is subject to variation, from a great number of different circumstances. Sparks passing through balls of wood or ivory, are of a crimson colour; but this depends also upon their position with regard to the surface. If two pointed wires be inserted obliquely and in opposite directions into a piece of soft deal, having their points an inch and a half distant, but penetrating to different depths below the surface, and so that the line joining them is in the direction of the fibres, the sparks passing from the one to the other, will exhibit different colours at different depths; and if one of the points be inserted deeper than the other, all these colours will appear at once, according as the electric light is transmitted at various depths. Electric sparks passing from one polished metallic surface to another are white; but if the finger be presented to an electrified conductor, the sparks obtained are violet. They are green when taken from the surface of silvered leather; yellow when taken from finely powdered charcoal; and of a purple colour when taken from the greater number of imperfect conductors. If one of the bodies between which the spark takes place is a green plant, the light is red; and the same is the case with water or ice. In the vapour of ether green sparks are seen when the eye is placed close to the tube: but they appear reddish when viewed at a considerable distance. Even between the same two metallic conductors the colour may vary from the most brilliant white to the most delicate violet, according to the distance through which the electricity is transmitted, and according to the resistance of the medium which it is compelled to traverse. In exceedingly rarefied air, the colour of the spark is green; in denser air, it acquires a blue tint, and passes to a violet and purple, in proportion as the condensation of the air is increased. Transmitted through other gases, the colour varies according to their density.

In carbonic acid gas, the spark is white and vivid; in hydrogen gas, it is faint and red.

(90.) It should be recollected, in making these experiments, that in proportion as the medium is more rare, its conducting power increases, and a smaller intensity of electricity is required for the production of light. In the ordinary vacuum produced by the air-pump, the passage of electricity is rendered sensible by streams or columns of diffused light occasionally varying in their breadth and intensity, and exhibiting movements which give them a marked resemblance to the coruscations of the Aurora Borealis. After rarefying the air contained in a glass jar, about one foot long and eight inches in diameter, to the 500th part, Mr. Smeaton placed the jar upon a lathe, and caused it to revolve rapidly, whilst at the same time he rubbed it with his hand. A considerable quantity of lambent flame appeared under his hand, variegated with all the colours of the rainbow. The light was steady; but every part of it was constantly changing colours. When a very perfect vacuum is made in a glass cylinder covered with a brass plate, the electric stream will pass between it and the plate of the receiver of the air-pump, in a continued stream of the same size throughout its whole length. If a Torricellian vacuum be formed in the upper portion of a long bent glass tube filled with mercury, and inverted, by placing the legs of the bent tube in separate basins of mercury, when electricity is transmitted through the tube, light is seen to pervade the vacuum in a continued arch of lambent flame, without the least divergency.

(91.) It was natural to suppose, before sufficient consideration had been bestowed upon the subject, that the light which appears during the passage of electricity, was actually the electric fluid itself, which, at some certain degree of accumulation, was in itself luminous; and such was the notion entertained by the early electricians. But since we know that common atmospheric air becomes luminous by violent compression, and we must also presume that electricity exerts a very sudden and powerful pressure upon the air by its passage through that resisting medium, we are certainly justified in drawing the inference that the same phenomena proceed in both cases from the same cause. Biot has adopted this opinion, which appears to be more consonant with philosophical views of the subject than any other: for it is certain that the whole of the electrical light that appears is not more than what may proceed from the mechanical compression of the air, the vapours, and other constituents of the medium through which the passage of the electricity is effected.

(92.) The sound which accompanies these various modes of transference is subject to corresponding modifications, dependent likewise, no doubt, upon the degree and the suddenness of the impulses given to the air. The full, short, and undivided spark is attended with a loud explosion; the more lengthened spark, with a sharper snap, which becomes more broken and rattling in proportion to the distance it has to traverse. The luminous streams produced by a succession of minute sparks are scarcely productive of noise, but are accompanied only by a faint rustling sound, like that of a stream of wind through a narrow chink.

(93.) A peculiar odour has sometimes been perceived in the neighbourhood of an electrical machine which has been briskly worked, so as to emit for some time a great number of sparks; and it has been thought to resemble that of phosphorus. This is also probably owing to some unknown chemical decomposition effected by the electricity during its passage through the air.

(94.) We have already had occasion to remark the great increase of intensity which the electric fluid acquires at the extremity of all elongated parts of conducting bodies; and the indefinite augmentation of this intensity which takes place at the apex of all projecting points. This high intensity will necessarily be accompanied with a powerful tendency in the fluid to escape; a circumstance which furnishes a natural and exact explanation of the rapid dissipation of electricity which takes place from all bodies of a slender and pointed form.

The following experiments illustrate these positions. Let the insulated conductor of a machine be furnished with a pair of pith-balls, suspended by a fine wire, and charged with either species of electricity; the divergence of the balls will indicate the presence and degree of this electricity. If a metallic rod with a ball at one end be held in the hand,

and the ball presented to the conductor, taking care not to bring it sufficiently near to draw a spark, the balls will be but little affected, and their divergence will continue for a considerable time. But if the rod terminate in a sharp point, instead of a ball, and the point be presented to the conductor at the same distance as the ball was in the former case, the electroscope will immediately collapse, showing that the electrical charge has entirely disappeared: it has, in fact, been rapidly drawn off by the pointed rod. It is quite immaterial to the success of the experiment whether we affix a point to the conductor itself, or whether we present to it a point held in the hand; the escape and dispersion of the electricity being equally promoted by the presence of a point, whether the fluid be given out or absorbed; for it is scarcely necessary to remark that the very same kind of reasoning applies equally to both the positive and negative conditions of electricity.

(95.) Currents of air always accompany the discharge of electricity, whether positive or negative, from pointed bodies; for each particle of air, as soon as it has received its electricity from the point, is immediately repelled by the body. These currents tend powerfully to increase the dissipation of the electricity, by bringing in contact with the point a continued succession of particles of air, that are not yet electrified, and are, therefore, ready to receive a charge. Many amusing experiments are founded on this principle. Let two cross wires, (fig. 21.) the ends of which terminate in

Fig. 21.

points, bent in a similar direction with respect to the axis, be supported by means of a cap upon a fine point, and electrified by being placed upon the prime conductor of a machine. Each of the points will give off a stream of electricity: this will remove a part of the pressure which the fluid would have exerted on that side if no efflux had taken place; but as the pressure of the fluid on the opposite side of the wire, in the opposite direction, still operates in full force, the wire will be impelled in the direction of that force, that is, in a direction opposite to that of the stream; and this taking place at all the four points, the whole system will revolve backwards with considerable rapidity.

The following is another form in which this experiment may be made. Two wires, (fig. 22.) are stretched in

Fig. 22.

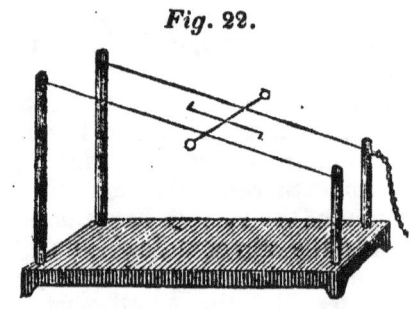

the direction of a plane, slightly inclined to the horizon, between four insulating pillars. Across these wires, another wire is made to rest, terminating by small balls at each end, and having a cross wire fixed to it at right angles, with two bent points, as in the former experiment. When this system is electrified, the dispersion of the electricity from the points produces a revolution of the bars, which makes the transverse bar roll up the inclined plane.

An apparatus consisting of wires terminating in points, and having balls annexed to them to represent the planets, may be constructed so as to revolve when electrified; and thus to imitate the planetary motions. Such an apparatus has been called an electrical orrery.

(96.) It should be observed, however, that a point loses its power of concentrating and dispersing electricity when it is surrounded by other parts of the conducting body which are equally prominent; as when it is placed between two balls, or inclosed in a tube, or when it does not rise above the general surface of the body. The effect of one point is much diminished even by the vicinity of another point; so that if several points placed near each other be presented to the conductor, the electricity is drawn off much less rapidly, and will be transferred by sparks instead of forming a continued stream.

(97.) When the transfer of electricity takes place between smooth surfaces of a certain extent, no difference can be perceived in the nature and appearance of the spark, whichever be the position of the negative surface. But in the passage of electricity through points, the effect is considerably modified by the species of electricity with which the bodies are charged; or, in other words, by the direction in which the fluid moves. When the electric fluid is escaping out of a pointed conductor, the luminous appearance is that of diverging streams, as represented in *fig*. 23; forming what is termed a *pencil of light*, and

Fig. 23.

resembling the filaments of a brush. When, on the contrary, the electric fluid is entering into the pointed body, the light is much more concentrated at the point itself, having a resemblance to a *star*, in which, if any streams appear, they are disposed like radii, and equally so in all directions. An approach to these different modifications may be remarked when sparks pass between balls of small diameter, especially if the charge is high. Thus the direction of the lateral ramifications sent out from the principal line, in the branched spark, *fig*. 20, is from the positive to the negative surface.

(98.) In describing the above appearances, we have, as usual, referred to the hypothesis of Franklin: but if we adopt that of the two electricities, we have only to consider the appearance of the pencil of light as arising from the double current of the vitreous electricity issuing from the point, and of the resinous electricity passing into it: while the star will be the effect of the irruption of the resinous, and the absorption of the vitreous electricities. But this remarkable difference in the phenomena produced, according to the particular species of electricity with which the point is charged, has always been urged as a convincing argument in favour of the Franklinian theory. They appear very strongly to indicate the emanation of some material fluid from the positive, and its reception by the negative point. The diverging lines on the one side, and their inflections on the other, represent exactly the paths of particles flowing out as from a pipe, and urged forwards by a force which gives them such a projectile velocity as to prevent their spreading out beyond a certain distance from the direct line of projection. But this very velocity will carry the particles that happen to have deviated most, somewhat beyond the point to which they are attracted: while the attraction to this latter point will tend to deflect them from the line of their path, and gradually turn them back, so that they will arrive at the point of attraction by very different paths, and some even by a retrograde motion. Hence, while in the first case they form a diverging cone of rays, in the latter they must be distributed on all sides of the point like the rays of a star. The annexed diagram, *fig*. 24, will sufficiently illustrate this explanation by

Fig. 24.

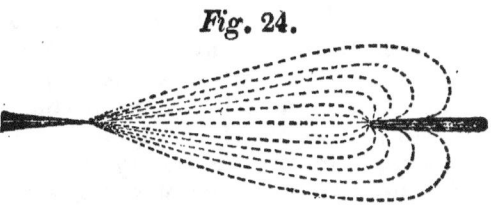

representing the supposed course of the particles of electric fluid, passing through the air from the positive to the negative point. What weight the argument derived from this phenomenon may be allowed in deciding the question, will be discussed in the sequel.

(99.) The difference which we have now described in these two appearances, may be employed, on many occasions, as a useful criterion of the species of electricity, at least, which is passing from one conductor to another, if not of the absolute direction of its motion. For, if a needle be presented to an electrified body, the appearance of a star on the needle will show that the electricity of that body is positive; while, on the contrary, a luminous brush on the needle will indicate that the body is negative.

(100.) The influence of a point projecting a short distance from the surface of a body, is greater when that body is negative than when it is positive. Hence, a spark is more readily obtained in the latter case than in the former.

On this principle an instrument has been invented by Mr. Nicholson for distinguishing the negative from the positive electricity. It consists simply of two metallic balls fixed at the ends of two curved rods of glass, and moveable like branches on a joint, so as to admit of the balls being placed at different distances from each other, when held by a handle proceeding from the joint. A short point projects from one of the balls on the side adjacent to the other ball; and this point affords a spark at a shorter distance when positively, than when negatively electrified.

Chapter VII.

Development of the Law of Induction.

(101.) We have next to trace the consequences of that important law of electricity which has been called the Law of Induction.

Active electricity existing in any substance tends always to induce the opposite electrical state in the bodies that are near it. Now it is impossible, as we have already seen, to induce one electrical state in any body without at the same time producing the opposite state in the same body, or in the one which is immediately contiguous. According to the simpler theory, the accumulation of electricity in any one part can be effected in no other way than by withdrawing it from another part, nor can it be abstracted from the one without being received by another; so that there is always an equal degree of negative as of positive electricity, and *vice versâ*, in every case. According to the more complex theory, if we decompose the natural electricities residing in any body, we must at the same moment obtain equal quantities of both the vitreous and resinous electricities. It follows, therefore, that if the bodies subjected to the inductive influence are non-conductors, although the tendency to produce the opposite electricity still exists, yet in consequence of the immobility of the fluid, it can produce no visible change. In proportion as the body opposes less resistance to the passage of electricity, the operation of the disturbing force becomes sensible; and in order to fix our ideas, let us first take the case of a positively charged electric, acting by induction on an insulated conducting body. The redundant fluid in the former will tend to repel all the fluid contained in the latter: a portion of this fluid will, therefore, be driven from the side adjacent to the first body, towards the remoter side. The adjacent side will thus be rendered negative; the remote side, positive. But this will take place to a certain extent only: for there is a limit at which the repulsion of the fluid accumulated at the remote end, will just balance the repulsion of the fluid in the electric, added to the attraction of the under-saturated matter, in the near end; and when this limit has been attained, the flow of electric fluid from the near to the remote end of the body will cease, and an equilibrium will be established.

(102.) Experiment shows the perfect coincidence of theory with the actual fact. Let a cylinder of metal, NP, (see *fig.* 25,) of some length, with rounded ends, and furnished in different parts

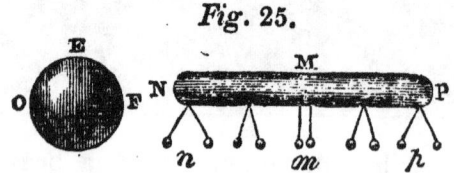

Fig. 25.

with pairs of suspended pith-balls, to serve as electroscopes, being previously insulated, be placed in the vicinity of an electrified globe of glass, E, taking care that it be not sufficiently near to receive any quantity of electricity by transference.

We shall find that every pair of balls, except those situated in a particular plane M*m*, about the middle of the cylinder, will immediately diverge, indicating the electrical states of the parts from which they are suspended. Those at either extremity of the body, *n, p,* diverge the most; and the divergence diminishes as we approach the middle plane before mentioned, at which the body is in the natural or neutral state. The position of this plane of neutrality, M*m*, varies according to the distance of the electric, and the relation which that distance bears to the length of the body itself. If we further examine the species of electricity residing in the different parts, we shall find it to be negative in all the parts nearer to the electric than the neutral plane, and positive in all those more remote. We may ascertain with much greater accuracy these electrical states by the employment of the proof plane and electrometer of Coulomb, than by the pith-balls; and the results are then found to correspond, with the most rigorous precision, with the deductions from the theory of electrical action.

(103.) These effects, it should be remarked, are simply the result of the action of electricity at a distance; for they depend upon no other circumstance.

They take place in an equal degree whatever substance be interposed between the bodies which are exerting this action on one another, provided the interposed substance undergoes no change in its own electrical state; a condition which is fulfilled in electrics only. Thus, induction will take place just as effectually through a plate of glass, as if no such substance had intervened.

(104.) Let us now suppose that the acting body, E, is, instead of an electric, a conducting body, a globe of metal, for example, charged with positive electricity. The primary effects of this globe on the cylinder will be the same as in the former case; but the electrical state which the globe has induced on the cylinder will re-act upon its own electricity. The negative electricity, that is, the under-saturated matter at the nearer end of the cylinder N, exerts a tendency to induce positive electricity in the globe, and more especially upon the adjacent side, F: that is, it will tend, by its attraction for the fluid, to draw it to that side, and thus render it still more highly positive than it was before. This can only be done at the expense of the other side, O, from which the fluid must be taken, and which is, therefore, rendered less charged with fluid, that is, less positive than before. But this new distribution of the electric fluid in the globe, by increasing the positive state of the side, F, next to the cylinder, tends to augment its inductive influence on the fluid in the cylinder; that is, to drive an additional quantity of fluid from the negative to the positive end. This is followed, in its turn, by a corresponding reaction on the globe, and so on, constituting a series of smaller adjustments, until a perfect equilibrium is established in every part. When this has been attained, the electrical states will, it is evident, be of the same kind as those consequent upon the immediate actions, though somewhat increased in intensity by the series of reactions.

The following experiment is a practical illustration of the preceding reasoning. Furnish the metallic globe with electroscopes on its opposite surfaces; when the globe is insulated and alone, any electricity communicated to it will diffuse itself equally over the surface, and both the electroscopes will diverge equally. But no sooner do we bring near to it a conducting body, than the balls of the electroscope at the side most distant from that body begin to collapse, while those at the nearer side diverge to a greater degree than before; thus showing the nature of the reflex operation of the induced electricity of the conductor upon the body from which the induction originated.

(105.) It should be recollected that in all the changes we have thus traced as the effects of induction, there has been no transfer of electricity from either of the bodies to the other; as was sufficiently proved, indeed, by their taking place equally if a plate of glass be interposed. Another proof is afforded by the circumstance that the mere removal of the bodies to a distance from one another, is sufficient to restore each of them to their original state. The globe remains as positively electrified as before; the cylinder returns to its condition of perfect neutrality; nothing has been lost, and nothing gained on either side. The experiment may be repeated as often as we please, without any variation in the phenomena. But this would not be the case if the cylinder were divided in the middle, and one or both of the parts were removed separately, while they still remained under the influence of the globe. The return of the electric fluid from the positive to the negative end being thus prevented, each part will retain, after its separation, the electricity which had been induced upon it. The nearer portion will remain negative; the remoter portion, positive. If the division had been in three parts, the middle part only would have been neutral. The experiment may be made by joining two or more conductors endwise, as shown in *fig.* 26, so that they

Fig. 26.

may act as a single conductor when placed near to the electrified globe, and after induction has thus been produced, removing them separately, and examining their electrical states. If E be positive, N will be found negative, P positive, and M neutral.

(106.) Another modification of effect will take place when an insulated conductor, rendered electrical at both ends by induction, is made to communicate with another conductor. Let us first suppose that a long metallic conductor is brought into contact with the remote end of the first cylinder P, (*fig.* 25), which has been rendered positive by induction. The fluid accumulated at this end will now pass into the conductor, and will remove to the most distant part of the conductor. The transit will now take place before actual contact, and will be manifested by the appearance of a spark when the bodies are brought within the striking distance. The removal of this fluid to a greater distance will occasion a disturbance in the equilibrium that had before been established. The repulsion which that fluid had excited, and which had contributed to prevent any more fluid from being propelled from the negative end N, is now considerably weakened by the greater distance at which it acts; and more fluid will leave the negative end, which end will consequently become more highly negative. This change of distribution will again occasion a further effect, by its reaction on the fluid in the globe whence the action originally proceeded; and another series of changes and adjustments will follow, until a new condition of equilibrium takes place, and then the fluid will be at rest.

(107.) Thus we learn that the effects of induction on a conductor are augmented by increasing its length; they would, therefore, be greatest of all, if we could give it infinite length: but the same condition is attainable by placing the conductor in communication with the earth, which will accordingly carry off all the fluid which the electrified body is capable of expelling from the nearest end. Accordingly, if we touch with the finger, or with a metallic rod held in the hand, the remote end of an insulated conductor under the influence of induction, we obtain a spark, more or less vivid according to the intensity of the electricity so induced; and the conductor so touched has now only one kind of electricity, namely, the one opposite to that of the electrified body which is acting upon it. The part touched is brought into a state, in which it appears to be neutral as long as it remains in the vicinity of the electrified body; because the actions of the redundant fluid, and unsaturated matter in the two bodies, exactly balance one another. But it all the while really contains less fluid than its natural share, in consequence of the repulsive tendency of the fluid in the body which produces the induction; and this negative state will readily become active, if the conductor that has been touched be again insulated, and then removed from the influence of the former. This peculiar condition of a body, in which its parts are really undercharged or overcharged with fluid, although, from the action of electrical forces derived from bodies in its vicinity, a state of equilibrium is established, and no visible effect results, has been denominated by Biot, *disguised electricity*.

(108.) It is also worthy of remark, that if the communication between the insulated conductor and another longer conductor, or the earth itself, be made at either end of the former, the same effect will result, and the electric fluid accumulated at its remote end will be carried off by the longer conductor, although, it will have, in one case, to pass round through the end nearest to the body which repels it. The operation which here takes place may be illustrated by the motion of a fluid in a syphon. A repulsive force is acting upon the fluid, both in the shorter and the longer column; but with regard to the motion of the fluid in the bent channel, the one force is in opposition to the other, and the tendency of the fluid in the longer column prevailing over that in the shorter, will draw off the latter, round the bend of the supposed syphon. Thus in the bent conductor A N P (*fig.* 27,), the repulsion exerted by the fluid in E for that in the longer column N P,

Fig. 27.

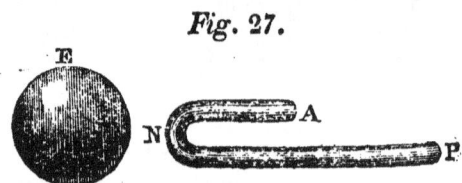

being greater than its repulsion for that in the shorter column N A, the fluid in A will be carried over the bend N, notwithstanding its tendency to move from N towards A.

(109.) We have hitherto supposed the acting body to be positively electrified; but precisely the same effects would happen with regard to degree, although opposite as to the species of electricity, if it had been negatively electrified: and the same explanations will in every respect apply, with the requisite substitution of the terms negative for positive, and of attraction for repulsion, and *vice versâ*. A little reflection will also easily show the application of the theory of the double electricities to explain the same phenomena.

(110.) Another consequence of the induction of electricity must not be overlooked, namely, that the bodies between which it takes place, necessarily attract one another: for the action of the adjacent sides F and N (*fig*, 25), which are brought into opposite electrical states, is greater than the action of those sides which are in the same electrical states, F and P, and which are more distant: hence the attractive force always exceeds the repulsive. We have already seen that this circumstance sufficiently explains the fact that conducting bodies, previously neutral, are attracted by electrified bodies. Another fact, which appears more singular, and which cannot be accounted for on any other principle, is also a direct consequence of the law of induction. If a small body weakly electrified, be placed at a distance from another and a larger body, more highly charged with the same species of electricity, it will, as usual, be repelled; but there is a certain distance within which if it be brought, attraction will take place, instead of repulsion. This happens in consequence of the inductive influence producing so great a change in the distribution of electricity, as to give a preponderance to the attractive forces of the adjacent parts of the two bodies, over the repulsive forces that take place in the other parts, and which would have alone acted if the fluid had been immoveable.

(111.) From the principles now laid down, it will be easy to understand how induction may operate through a succession of conductors, which are all of them insulated, except the last; and which are separated from each other by distances greater than that at which a transfer of electricity would take place. If, under such circumstances, the first be electrified, alternate states of opposite electricities will be produced in the two ends of each conductor in succession. In all the ends nearest to the first body, the electricity will be of the opposite kind to that with which the first has been charged; in the other ends it will be of the same kind as that of the first body. The vicinity of these opposite electricities will tend powerfully to retain them in that condition, and will diminish their electric action on surrounding bodies. A large portion of the electricities so arranged and retained, is, therefore, in the condition designated by the term *disguised electricity*.

(112.) In proportion as the interruptions to the continuity of the line of conductors are more numerous, the more nearly will such a system approach to the condition of an imperfectly conducting body. The same principle admits of being extended, with some modifications indeed, to the constitution of electrics themselves, as we shall have occasion to notice in the sequel.

Chapter VIII.

Accumulation of Electricity by Induction.

(113.) The most important application of the principle of induction is that by which a vast accumulation of electricity is obtained in a small space, while its intensity, or tendency to escape, is at the same time rendered exceedingly small. This condition exactly corresponds to that which has been termed *disguised electricity*.

(114.) Let two circular metallic plates P and N (*fig.* 28), be placed the one immediately over the other, but separated by a non-conducting medium, such as the air, or, what is still better, a plate of glass. Let the upper one P, commu-

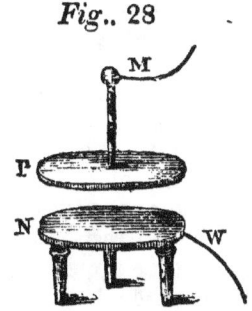

Fig.. 28

nicate, by a wire M, with the prime conductor of the electrical machine; and let the lower one N, be insulated by resting upon three glass supporters. Let P be charged with a certain quantity of electric fluid. The fluid naturally contained in N, will be repelled by the fluid in P, and will quit the upper surface of N in order to occupy its lower surface. When this change has taken place, let N be touched by a wire W, establishing a communication between it and the ground. All the fluid which was accumulated in the lower surface of N, will be carried off by the wire, and the whole plate will thus be negative, or undercharged with fluid. The redundant matter in N will, by its attraction for the fluid, draw more of it into the upper plate, which will be supplied from the conductor of the machine through the wire M; and such an additional quantity will be accumulated in P, as will balance the increased attraction of the matter in N, and maintain it at the same intensity as the fluid in the prime conductor. That this is what really happens will be rendered evident by placing an electroscope upon the prime conductor; for the moment the plate N communicates with the ground, the balls of the electroscope collapse, showing that the intensity of the fluid in the prime conductor is suddenly reduced by the great quantity that has been absorbed by the plate P. The machine must now again be set in motion, in order to supply the electricity which has been thus abstracted from the conductor. The operation of each plate on the other may be considered as that of increasing its electrical capacity, or of rendering a large proportion of its electricity latent or disguised.

(115.) It is evident that the quantity of electric fluid driven out of the lower plate by the action of the fluid in the upper one, can never be quite equal to that of the fluid with which the upper one is itself charged, and the difference will be greater in proportion to the distance of the plates. When they are very close to each other, these two quantities approach very near to an equality; and this circumstance it was that misled Franklin into the belief that they were actually equal.

(116.) The capacity for accumulating electricity corresponding to a given intensity in the upper plate depends upon the distance between the plates, provided always that the intervening electric opposes a sufficient obstacle to the direct transfer of the electricity from the one to the other; and is in some inverse ratio to that distance. The lower plate, N, which communicates with the ground by the wire W, although strongly negative, is rendered, by the vicinity of the fluid in the upper plate P, neutral with respect to fluid in the wire W: that is, the attraction of its unsaturated matter, although nearer, is exactly balanced by the repulsion of the redundant fluid in the upper plate, which, although really stronger, is, from the greater distance at which it acts, only equal to the former. With reference to fluid in the wire M, however, the action of the redundant fluid in P, is not balanced by that of the unsaturated matter in N, which latter is both weaker in itself and more distant. Thus, while N is neutral with respect to the conductors which touch it, P is in a slight degree active, in consequence of this small preponderance of force, and a portion of its fluid tends to escape. Hence, if N be again insulated, by removing the wire W, and the wire M be now made to communicate with the ground, this portion of the fluid in P will pass off by it; but not any larger quantity, for the remaining portion is retained by the attraction of the unsaturated matter in N. P is, by this loss, rendered neutral, as N had before been, and it now no longer acts on the fluid beyond it in M. The influence of P on that fluid is greater than that of N in respect to its greater vicinity, but less in as far as regards the intensity of action, and the compensation is exact. But under these circumstances, N, which was before neutral, becomes in its turn active, and now that the repulsion of the fluid in P is diminished, will absorb a certain quantity of the fluid as soon as it is touched by W, after P has been again insulated. By this contact, N is again restored to the neutral state, a fresh portion of fluid in P is released from the attraction of N, and P is again active. By repeating these alternate contacts a sufficient number of times, we gradually deprive the plates of their whole charge of electricity; alternately imparting small portions to the negative plate, and taking away the like portions from the positive one, until they are both brought to their natural unelectrified state. The quantities of fluid which are thus successively added and abstracted were found, by the calculations of Laplace, to be in geometrical progression.

(117.) The most convenient mode of obtaining the accumulated electricity arising from induction is by the employment of *coated glass*, that is, of a plate of glass, on each side of which is pasted a sheet or coating of tin-foil. Care must be taken to leave a sufficient margin of glass uncovered by the metal, for preventing the transfer of electricity from the one coating to the other round the edge of the glass; and all sharp angles, or ragged edges in the coatings, should be avoided, as they have a great tendency to dissipate the charge.

(118.) The following experiment of Professor Richman, (the philosopher who fell a sacrifice to his zeal for electrical science by a stroke of lightning from his apparatus,) is very instructive. Let a pane of glass placed vertically, and seen edgewise in *fig.* 29, be coated on both sides, and furnished with two

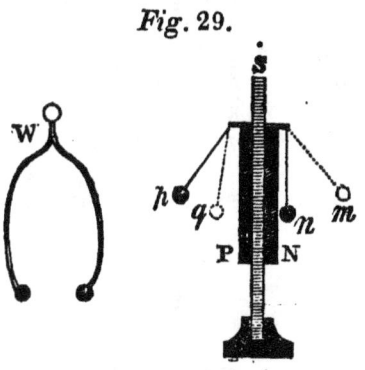

Fig. 29.

small electroscopes, *p, n*, consisting of two pith-balls, one attached to each of the coatings. Let the coating P be charged positively, while the coating N is made to communicate with the ground. The electroscope *p* will stand out from the plate, and *n* will hang down close to its coating, as long as N communicates with the ground. But in proportion as P loses electricity by gradual dissipation in the air, the ball *p* will gradually, but very slowly descend. If we now insulate N, *p* will fall down at first very speedily, and then more slowly, till it reaches *q*, about half its first elevation. The ball *n* will at the same time rise to nearly the same height; the angle between the two electroscopes continuing nearly the same as at first. When *n* has ceased to rise, both balls will very slowly descend, till the charge is lost by dissipation. If we touch N during this descent, *n* will immediately fall down, and *p* will as suddenly rise nearly as much; the angle between the electroscopes continuing nearly the same. Remove the finger from N, and *p* will fall, and *n* rise, to nearly their former places; and the slow descent of both will again recommence. The same thing will happen if we touch P, *p* will fall down close to the plate, and *n* will rise to *m*, and so on; and this alternate touching of the coatings may be repeated some hundreds of times before the plate is entirely discharged. If we suspend a crooked wire, bent, as shewn at W, (*fig.* 29,) having two pith-balls, from an insulated point, *s*, above the plates, it will vibrate with great rapidity, the balls striking the coatings alternately, and thus restoring the equilibrium by steps; each contact being attended by a spark.

(119.) If, instead of this gradual discharge, a direct communication is made between the two coatings by a metallic wire extending from the one to the other, the whole of the electric fluid which was accumulated in the positive coating rushes with a sudden and violent impetus along the conductor, and passes into the negative coating, thus at once restoring an almost complete equilibrium, and rendering every part very nearly, though not absolutely, neutral; for as there must always be some slight difference in the quantity of electrical charge in the two coatings, where one of them is in communication with the ground, there must always be a certain excess, however minute, of electricity, after the balance has been struck.

(120.) This sudden transfer of a large quantity of accumulated electricity is a real explosion; it gives rise to a vivid flash of light, corresponding in intensity to the magnitude of the charge. The effect of its transmission is much greater than that of the simple charge of the prime conductor of the machine; for while the latter gives a spark only, the former imparts what is called *an electric shock*, and the sensation it produces when passing through any part of the body is of a peculiar kind. We shall describe their effects in a future chapter; at present we must confine our attention to the purely electrical conditions of the phenomenon.

(121.) The presence of the coating is not absolutely essential to the charge and discharge for the two surfaces of the glass plate; for if the glass be furnished with moveable coatings, and charged in the usual manner, upon removing the coatings (taking care that they be touched only by electrics,) the greater part of the electricity will be found to have attached itself to the surfaces of the glass plate, where they are retained by their mutual inductive influence. In this state the charged plate of glass may be gradually discharged by making a communication between its several parts in succession. It cannot be discharged at once, for want of a common intermedium for the simultaneous transference of the electricity of the different parts of the surface. But if this be supplied by replacing the former coatings, or adding new ones,

D

the complete discharge may be effected as before.

(122.) By peculiar management a charge may be given to a plate of glass independently of any coating whatever. For this purpose, it must be held by one corner, and passed before a ball, connected with the prime conductor of a machine, so that it may successively come in contact with every part of the middle of the plate of glass, while the finger, or any conducting body communicating with the ground, is held opposite to it on the other side. Thus the glass will be charged, and will be in the same state as the glass from which the coatings had been removed.

(123.) We often find, a short time after the discharge of coated glass, that t has acquired spontaneously a small charge, producing a faint spark when a second communication is made between the coatings by the discharging wire. This, which is called the *residual* charge, arises from two causes: first, a portion of the electricity adheres to the uncoated surface of the glass: and secondly, another part has penetrated from the coating for some little depth below its surface. Both these portions slowly return to the coatings after they have been deprived of their original charge, and give it a fresh charge. When a very large extent of coated glass is employed, this residual charge may even amount to a considerable quantity, and the experimenter should be cautious not to expose himself to the shock which he might thus receive, if he inadvertently touched the apparatus before he had properly discharged it. That charges are capable of penetrating even through the entire thickness of the glass is proved by the curious fact, that a coated, cylindrical jar may be discharged merely by keeping up for a sufficient time a continuance of the minute vibrations excited by rubbing it with the finger, or by making it ring. A discharge may also be effected by heating the glass, which renders it a conductor of electricity.

(124.) The most convenient form for coated glass for experimental purposes, is that of a cylinder or jar. In the earlier periods of electrical research, jars were filled with water, mercury, or iron filings, which furnished the interior coating, while the exterior coating was supplied either by water, in which the jar was immersed, or by the hand of the operator, who for that purpose grasped the outside of the jar: a rod of metal was employed to communicate the charge from the prime conductor of the machine to the inner coating. On making a communication between the exterior and interior coatings, by means of a circuit of conducting substances, the discharge took place, and the shock made to pass through the circuit thus formed. This instrument having been made known principally through the experiments of Kleist, Cuneus, and Muschenbroeck, at Leyden, the name of the *Leyden phial*, or *jar*, was generally applied to it. It is at present constructed as shewn in *fig.* 30, by apply-

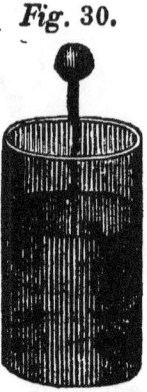

Fig. 30.

ing coatings of tin-foil on both sides of the jar or bottle, leaving a sufficient space uncovered at its upper part to secure it from the risk of a spontaneous discharge, which might take place if the coatings were not separated by a sufficient interval. A metallic rod, rising two or three inches above the jar, and terminating at the top in a brass ball, which is often called the *knob* of the jar, is made to descend through the cover, till it touches the interior coating. It is through this rod that the charge of electricity is conveyed to the inner coating, while the outer coating is made to communicate with the ground. We have already seen, that if this last condition be not observed, the inner coating can receive no charge, and only a feeble spark will pass from the conductor to the knob.

(125.) The outer coating may be made to communicate with the ground by holding it in the hand; and on presenting the knob of the jar to the prime conductor when the machine is in motion, a succession of sparks will pass between them, while at the same time nearly an equal quantity of electricity will be passing out from the exterior coating, through the body of the person who holds it, to the ground. If, instead of this, the jar be placed on an insulating stand, and a ball of metal, or the knuckle of the finger, be held near the outside of the jar, we have evidence of the escape of the electricity from the latter by a succession of sparks simultaneous with those that occur between the prime conductor and the knob of the jar.

(126.) If, instead of touching the outer coating of a jar supported on an insulating stand, we bring into contact with it the knob of a second jar, of which the outer coating communicates with the ground, as shewn in *fig.* 31,

Fig. 31.

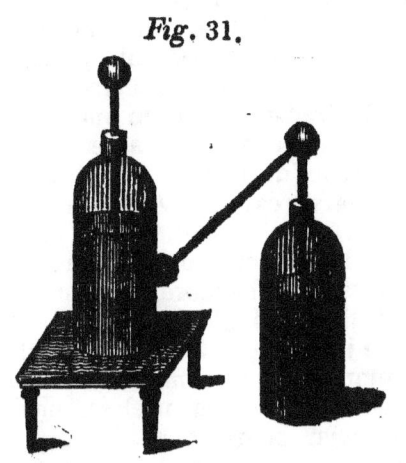

the electricity which is expelled from the outer coating of the first jar passes into the inner coating of the second jar, and thus both jars are charged. Thus may charges be given to a succession of jars, so placed as that the inner coating of each shall communicate with the outer coating of the one that precedes it in the series; taking care that the outer coating of the last jar communicates with the ground. All the jars will be found to be charged in a similar manner. It is evident, however, that the charge must diminish in intensity as it is conveyed from each jar to the next, because the quantity of electricity which is expelled from the exterior is never quite equal to that which passes into the interior.

(127.) For the sake of greater distinctness we have all along supposed the interior of the jar to be charged with positive electricity, but the very same effect would take place if the knob of the jar were charged negatively by communication with the negative conductor. A similar change in the electrical state of the coatings would result from placing the jar on an insulating stand, and then forming a communication between the outer coating and the prime conductor, while the knob is made to communicate with the ground. The only difference is, that the outer coating would then be active and the inner one neutral; but these conditions would again be reversed as soon as the knob was disconnected with the ground, and the outer coating touched with the hand.

(128.) If two jars, the one charged positively, the other negatively, be placed on two separate insulating stands, and their knobs then connected by a conductor, which is itself insulated, no explosion will take place, although the two coatings, which are thus brought into communication, are in opposite electrical states. But if the two outer coatings be at the same time connected, an explosion will take place, and both jars will be discharged.

(129.) Since the susceptibility of receiving a charge depends upon the proximity of the metallic surfaces, while the passage of the electricity from the one to the other is interrupted by the interposition of a non-conducting substance, it is evident that, in the construction of the Leyden jar, the thickness of the glass is an important consideration. The thinner the glass, the greater will be the power of taking a charge; but the power of retaining the charge will be less, on account of the diminished resistance which the glass will afford to the passage of the electricity through it. If the charge be higher than what the jar will bear, the glass will be broken by the violence with which the electricity forces a passage through its substance. Muscovy talc, even in very thin laminæ, resists much better than glass, and is, therefore, capable of receiving and of retaining a much higher charge. Another limit to the charge which a jar is capable of retaining, arises from the liability of the electricity to pass from one coating to the other, round the edges of the glass.

(130.) These spontaneous discharges, as they are called, are facilitated by the deposition of moisture on the glass, forming a chain of conducting particles in the very line which the electricity has a strong tendency to take. Hence, it is a requisite precaution to keep the apparatus in as dry a state as possible; and the deposition of moisture may be guarded against most effectually by covering the uncoated part of the glass with a layer of sealing-wax, or other resinous varnish. The liquid should be applied with a flat, camel-hair pencil, the glass being previously warmed.

On the other hand, it is a curious circumstance, that there is a degree of humidity in the inside of the jar, not only compatible with a high charge, but which even contributes to retain it. This effect was accidentally observed by Mr. Brooke, and afterwards by Mr. Cuthbertson, who states that a jar will take a much greater charge, namely, one-third more, if its inside be considerably damped by blowing into it with the mouth through a tube reaching to the bottom. The explanation of this remarkable fact has been given by Professor Robison on the principles formerly explained, namely, that there is no electric intensity so great, but that it may be insulated by the least imperfect conductor, provided the latter be long enough, and so constituted as that the intensity of the electricity it contains shall diminish by sufficiently gentle gradations. An uniform dampness, indeed, will not do this; but it will diminish the abruptness of the variations of intensity, and thus give security against a spontaneous discharge. A similar protection against the breaking of the glass is afforded by placing a layer of paper between the glass and the tin-foil, and making it extend also an inch beyond the coating.

(131.) Glass balloons of a spherical shape, being of more uniform thickness than jars, would be much preferable for the construction of an apparatus of this kind, were it possible to apply an uniform coating to the inside. Professor Robison recommends the following construction for a portable jar, which he found to answer exceedingly well. A long-necked phial was made of sheet tin, and then coated entirely on the outside with fine sealing-wax, one thirtieth of an inch thick. The sealing-wax was then coated with tin-foil, all but the neck. It is evident, that the wax here acts the part of the glass in the common jar, the tin plate corresponding to the inner coating and wire, and the tin-foil to the outer coating. The dissipation is almost nothing if the neck be very small; and it only requires a little caution to avoid bursting by too high a charge. Even this may be prevented by coating the sealing-wax so near to the end of the neck, that a spontaneous discharge must happen before the accumulation is too great. Alternate layers of tin-foil and hard varnish form also a very compendious battery. It admits of a surprising accumulation, without shewing any vivid electricity; but it must be used with more caution, lest it should be spoiled by a spontaneous discharge, in which case we cannot discover where the flaw has happened, and the whole is rendered useless.

(132.) By combining together a sufficient number of jars we are able to accumulate an enormous quantity of electricity: for this purpose all the interior coatings of the jars must be made to communicate by metallic rods, and a similar union must be established among the exterior coatings. When thus arranged, the whole series may be charged, as if they formed but one jar; and the whole of the accumulated electricity may be transferred from one system of coatings to the other, by a general and simultaneous discharge. Such a combination of jars is called an *Electrical Battery*.

(133.) It is evident, that an apparatus of this kind, consisting of a great number of parts, must be more liable to derangement than a single jar: for if any one of the jars should happen to break by a spontaneous explosion, the whole battery would be rendered useless, until the broken jar be removed. It is prudent, therefore, to secure the adjacent jars from actual contact, by fixing them in a box having thin partitions; the coated bottoms of the jars resting on a trellis of wire, or on a sheet of tin-foil, which may establish a general communication between them; while the rods from the interior coatings are connected above by cross wires, having balls at their extremities in order to obviate the dissipation of the electricity. On the other hand, by limiting the communications to a certain number of jars, we have it in our power to charge only a part of the battery, without employing the whole.

Chapter IX.

Management of Electrical Jars and Batteries.

(134.) For the purpose of making the direct communication between the inner and outer coating of a jar or battery, by which a discharge is effected, the instrument shown in *fig*. 32, and which is

Fig. 32.

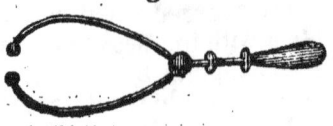

called the *Discharging Rod* or *Jointed Discharger*, may be conveniently employed. It consists of two bent metallic rods, terminated at one end by brass balls, and connected at the other by a joint, which is fixed to the end of a glass handle, and which, acting like a pair of compasses, allows of the balls being separated at different distances. When opened to the proper degree, one of the balls is made to touch the exterior coating, and the other ball is then quickly brought into contact with the knob of the jar, as represented in *fig.* 33, or with

Fig. 33.

any part of the system of the interior coatings, and thus a discharge is effected; while the glass handle secures the person holding it from the effects of the shock.

(135.) If we wish to send the whole charge of electricity through any particular substance which may be the subject of experiment, we must so arrange the connecting conductors, as that the substance shall form a necessary part of the *circuit of the electricity*, as it is termed. With this view, we must place it between two good conductors, one of which is in communication with the outer coating; and the circuit may then be completed by connecting the other conductor with the inner coating by means of a discharging rod, to one branch of which, if necessary, a flexible chain may be added.

(136.) In order to direct the charge with more certainty and precision, an apparatus, called the *Universal Discharger*, was contrived by Mr. Henley, and is represented in *fig.* 34. It con-

Fig. 34.

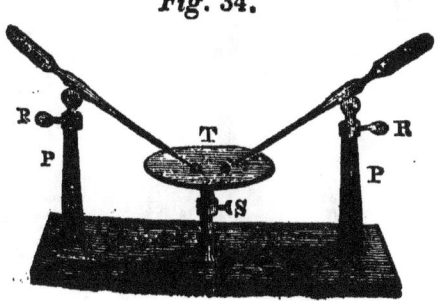

sists of a wooden stand with a socket fixed in its centre, to which may be occasionally adapted a small table T, having a piece of ivory (which is a nonconductor) inlaid on its surface. This table may be raised and kept at the proper height by means of a screw S. Two glass pillars P, P are cemented into the wooden stand. On the top of each of these pillars is fitted a brass cap, having a ring R attached to it, and containing a joint, moving both vertically and horizontally, and carrying on its upper part a spring tube, admitting a brass rod to slide through it. Each of these rods is terminated, at one end, either by a ball, a point, or a pair of forceps, and is furnished at the other extremity with a handle of solid glass. The body through which the charge is intended to be sent, is placed on the table, and the sliding rods, which are moveable in every direction, are then, by means of their insulating handles, brought in contact with the opposite sides, and one of the brass caps being first connected with the outside of the jar or battery, the other may be brought in communication with the inner coatings, by means of the discharging rod above described. For some experiments it is more convenient to fix the substance, on which the experiment is to be made, in a mahogany frame, consisting of two boards, which can be pressed together by screws, and which may then be substituted for the table T. In either of these ways the charge can be directed through any part of the substance with the greatest accuracy.

(137.) The quantities of electricity which can be accumulated in any given extent of coated glass, are in the inverse proportion to the thickness of the glass. Different jars or batteries, therefore, will, according to the thinness of their sides, and the quantity of coated surface they contain, have different capacities of holding charges of electricity. But in any given instrument of this kind, the quantity of the charge communicated to it by a machine may be measured by the intensity of the electricity in the prime conductor, which communicates with the interior coating. Some estimate of the intensity may be obtained by the employment of Henley's quadrant electrometer already described, (§ 72,) the index of which rises very slowly while the battery is charging, till it reaches a certain elevation, corresponding to the capacity of the battery. If the electricity be accumulated beyond this limit, a spontaneous discharge takes place, and the process must then be renewed in order to obtain a full charge. It is more prudent, however, to stop before this degree of accumulation is attained: and one great advantage of Henley's electrometer is, that it shows us the progress of the charge, and how far we may proceed with safety.

(138.) But the most effectual security against fracture from a spontaneous discharge, is to form an interrupted circuit, of which the parts, where the interruption occurs, terminate by metallic balls, placed at a certain distance from each other. By varying the interval between them, we may regulate the quantity of electricity which we shall allow to accumulate in the battery; for the moment it exceeds the quantity of which that interval is the *striking distance* (§ 87,) an explosion happens, by the electricity forcing its way through the air from one ball to the other. If the balls be brought very near each other, a discharge will take place with a comparatively small accumulation: when farther separated, a greater charge will be retained, because a higher intensity of electricity is required in order to pass through the larger intervening space. It is on this principle that the instrument, called *Lane's Discharging Electrometer*, is constructed. It consists of a brass ball, B, *fig*. 35, placed at the end

Fig. 35.

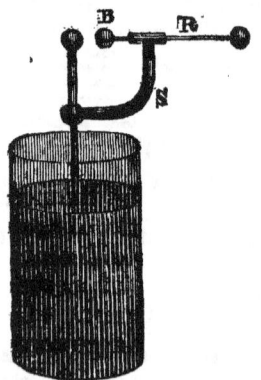

of a short metallic rod R, which moves through a tubular piece, supported by a bent glass stand S. This stand is made so as to be capable of being fixed, by its other extremity, to the rod passing up from the interior coating, and adjusted so that the ball B is immediately opposite to the knob of the jar, and may be brought to the exact *striking distance* from it which may be required: the other end of the moveable rod must be connected, by means of a chain or wire, with the outer coating.

The chief use of this instrument is to allow a jar to discharge itself spontaneously through any previously arranged circuit, without employing a discharging rod, or moving any part of the apparatus; and also to produce successive explosions nearly of the same strength. The magnitude of the charge is measured by the distance at which the balls are placed; and the power of the machine may be estimated by the number of explosions, which, at any given distance, take place in equal times. In Mr. Lane's experiment the shocks were twice as frequent when the interval between the balls was 1-24th of an inch, as when twice as much: hence he concluded that the quantity of electricity required for a discharge is in exact proportion to the distance between the surfaces of the balls. But the indications of this instrument are in reality subject to great fallacy, on account of the variable state of the atmosphere, which affects its conducting power; the quantity of dust which, even during the course of an experiment, is liable to be attracted, and to collect upon the balls; and also from the roughening and tarnishing of the metallic surfaces produced by frequent electric explosions. This last imperfection is one to which brass balls are particularly exposed; and might, if it were worth while, be remedied by having the balls made of fine silver.

(139.) Another contrivance for regulating the amount of the charge which we may wish to send through any substance, is that invented by Cuthbertson, and termed the *Balance Electrometer*. It consists of a metallic rod, R, *fig*. 36, terminated by two equal balls A, B, and balanced, like a scale-

Fig. 36.

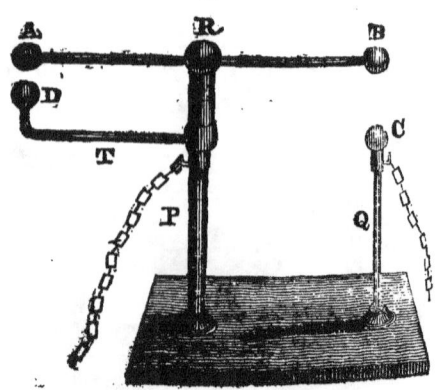

beam, upon knife-edged centres. One of the arms of this beam is graduated, and carries a slider, which, when set at different distances from the centre of motion, acts on the lever with a proportionate weight from one grain to sixty. The ball A, at the extremity of this loaded arm, rests on a similar ball D, below it, which is supported by a bent metallic tube T, proceeding from the same stand as that which supports the rods; the whole being insulated by a glass pillar P. At a little distance below the ball B, at the other extremity of the beam, another ball C, insulated by the glass pillar Q, is placed; this last ball is to be connected by a chain with the outer coatings of the battery, while the metallic support of the balance is connected with the inner coatings. When a charge is communicated to the battery, the two balls A and D, which are in contact, become repulsive of each other; and when the force of this repulsion is sufficient to raise the weight on the loaded arm of the beam, the other arm will be forced down, and the ball B coming in contact with the ball C, the circuit will be completed and a discharge take place. As the force of the repulsion depends upon the intensity of the charge, the weight it has to overcome affords a measure of this intensity, and enables us to regulate its amount.

The practical application of accumulated electricity to various purposes of experiment, involves considerations which relate to the laws observed by electricity in its movements, and which more properly belong to the subject of the ensuing chapter.

Chapter X.

Of the Motion of accumulated Electricity.

(140.) In forming arrangements for directing the passage of accumulated electricity, it should be borne in mind that the electric fluid will, on these occasions, always pass through the best conductors, although they may be more circuitous, in preference to those which are more direct, but have inferior conducting power: and it must also be recollected, that when different paths are open for its passage, along conductors of equal power, the electricity will always take that which is the shortest. Thus if a person, holding a wire between his hands, discharges a jar by means of it, the whole of the fluid will pass though the wire, without affecting him: but if a piece of dry wood be substituted for the wire, he will feel a shock; for the wood, being a worse conductor than his own body, the charge will pass through the latter, as being the easiest, although the longest circuit. During its transit through the human body, in like manner, the shock is felt only in the parts situated in the direct line of communication; and if the charge be made to pass through a number of persons who take one another by the hand, and form part of the circuit between the inner and outer coatings of the jar, each will feel the electric shock in the same manner and at the same instant; the sensation reaching from hand to hand, directly across the breast. By varying the points of contact, however, the shock may be made to pass in other directions, and may either be confined to a small part of a limb, or be made to traverse the whole length of the body from head to foot.

(141.) By accurate experiments it appears that the force of the electric shock is weakened, that is, its effects are diminished, by employing a conductor of great length for making the discharge. But it is difficult to assign a limit to the number of persons through which even a small charge of electricity may be sent, so that all shall experience the shock; or to the distance along which it may be conveyed by good conductors. At an early period of electrical inquiries, much interest was attached to the determination of these points. The Abbé Nollet passed an electrical shock from a small phial through a hundred and eighty of the French guards in the presence of the king; and at the Carthusian convent in Paris, the monks were formed into a line of above a mile in length, by means of iron wires held between them: on the discharge of the phial, the sensation was felt at the same moment by all the persons composing this extensive circuit. Many experiments were made both by the English and French electricians with a view to ascertain the space which a discharge can be made to traverse, and the velocity with which it is transmitted. Of these the most ingenious and satisfactory were the experiments planned and executed by Dr. Watson, with the assistance of the leading members of the Royal Society. A circuit was formed by a wire which extended the whole length of Westminster bridge, at a considerable height above the river: one end of this wire communicated with the outer coating of a charged phial, the other being held by a person on the opposite side of the river, who formed a communication with the water by dipping into it an iron rod held by the other hand. The circuit was completed by another person, who stood near the phial, and who likewise dipped an iron rod into the river with one hand, and was enabled, by means of a wire held in the other, to effect a contact with the knob of the phial. Whenever the discharges took place, the shocks were felt by both persons: thus proving that the electric fluid must have been in motion along the whole line of the circuit, including both the wire above and the river below.

In another experiment, made on Shooters'-hill, at a time when the ground was remarkably dry, the electricity was made to perform a circuit of four miles; being conducted for two miles along wires supported upon baked sticks, and for the remaining distance, also of two miles, through the dry ground. As far as could be ascertained, by the most careful observation, the time in which the discharge was transmitted along that immense circuit was perfectly instantaneous: nor has any other trial that has yet been made afforded the least approach to a measurement of the velocity with which electricity moves.

(142.) On this subject, however, an important distinction should be made between the actual movement of each individual particle of electric fluid, and the transmission of an impulse along a series of such particles, for the one may bear hardly any proportion to the other: just as we find that sound proceeds with a velocity incomparably greater than that of the particles of air which are concerned in its propagation. In like manner the portion of blood, which raises the artery at the wrist, where the pulse is felt, is not the identical portion of blood which is thrown out from the heart by the contraction of that organ producing that pulsation: the impulse, in all these cases, being propagated like a wave, from one particle to another. There is, therefore, no reason to suppose that the same particles of electric fluid, which enter at one part, have traversed from one end to the other the whole line of conducting substances which form the circuit.

(143.) If we conceive the conducting bodies which compose the circuit to be divided into an indefinite number of filaments, every one of which is capable, in an equal degree, of conveying the electric fluid, it is evident that the united power of these filaments, or what is the same thing, the capability of the body itself to convey a charge of electricity, is in proportion to the number of these elementary filaments which it contains, that is, to the magnitude of its transverse section, without any relation to its form. Thus, the same metallic rod will conduct a charge equally well, whether it be flattened, or divided into several smaller wires, or whether it consist of a single cylinder of the same area.

(144.) If the size of the conductor be sufficiently great, the whole charge may be conveyed without any sensible obstruction or retardation, and therefore without any tendency to deviate from the direct line of its course. But it is otherwise when the conductor is too slender to afford a ready passage to the fluid which is pressing onwards: and it is important to inquire into the consequences to which these obstructions may give rise.

(145.) The first effect of an impediment to the free passage of accumulated electricity must be a retardation of its motion. It is reasonable, therefore, to expect that with a circuit composed either of bad conductors, or of conductors of inadequate size, although good, the discharge will not be effected so instantaneously, nor so completely; and that the shock which accompanies it will be diminished in its violence. This principle may find its application on occasions where it is desirable to soften the intensity of the shock, as in the medical employment of electricity, where imperfect conductors are on this account sometimes preferable, both for taking sparks and shocks.

(146.) A second effect resulting from an obstruction to the flow of electricity, is a tendency in the fluid to diverge from the direct line of its course, and to fly off to different objects in the vicinity. This is frequently exemplified in the case of lightning, which, on striking a building, is apt to take a very irregular and seemingly capricious route, darting towards conducting bodies which may happen to attract it, although at some distance from the immediate direction it was pursuing. The position of such conducting bodies would appear to have a material influence in determining the striking distance. It was remarked by Dr. Priestley, that the explosion from a large battery extends to a greater distance over the surface of water than in air alone.

(147.) An effect which seems to depend upon this tendency in the fluid to divergence in consequence of obstruction, although it has by some been referred to a different principle, is that which has been termed *the lateral explosion*. When a large jar or battery is discharged by a metallic wire which is held in the hand without the protection of any glass or other insulating handle, it often happens that a slight shock is felt in the hand that grasps the wire, especially if the charge of electricity be very considerable. This apparent divergence or overflow of electric fluid, when rushing in large quantities through a narrow space barely sufficient to contain it, may also be rendered visible in other ways. If one end of a chain be connected with the outer coating of a charged jar, while the remainder of the chain is lying loosely upon a table, on discharging the jar in a darkened room, by a discharging rod, in the usual way, it will be found that the chain, although it makes no part of the circuit, is rendered luminous by the passage of sparks from one link to another. The following experiment, made by Dr. Priestley, may also be regarded as a case of lateral explosion. Let a thick metallic rod R, *fig*. 37, be sup-

Fig. 37.

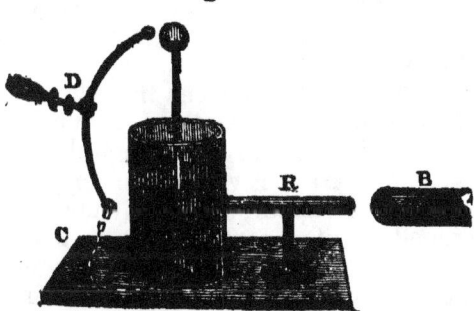

ported on an insulating stand, and placed with one of its ends in contact with the outer coating of a Leyden jar; and at a distance of half an inch from its other extremity place a long conducting body B, of at least six or seven feet in length, and only a few inches in breadth. Let a chain C, be now placed upon the table, so that one of its ends may be about an inch and a half dis-

tant from the outer coating of the jar, and apply one end of the discharging rod D, to the other extremity of the chain. As soon as the other ball of the discharging rod is made to touch the knob of the jar, so as to effect a discharge, a brilliant spark is seen to extend between the insulated rod R, and the adjacent conductor B. This lateral spark has the same length and brilliancy whether it be received on flat or smooth surfaces, or on sharp points.

It is stated by Dr. Priestley, that the effect we have been describing takes place without any apparent change in the electrical state of the conductor B; and hence Cavallo conceived that the lateral spark was sent out from the jar, and returned to it almost at the same instant, allowing of no perceptible time for an electrometer to be affected. Dr. Robison, however, always observed, on repeating the experiment, that a very delicate electrometer was affected under these circumstances: and the same observation is confirmed by Biot.

The phenomena of the lateral explosion have been attempted to be explained by the electricity exerting, during its passage, an inductive influence, of which the effects may be expected to cease the moment the cause is removed. But this explanation appears to be less satisfactory than the one which attributes the phenomena to an expansive propulsion, followed by an immediate recession of electric fluid, produced by obstructions to its free passage in the circuit of conductors.

Chapter XI.

Effects of Electricity upon Bodies.

(148.) Having considered the circumstances attending the motion of electricity with reference chiefly to the fluid itself, we next proceed to give an account of the effects which it produces upon bodies by its passage through them.

(149.) Independently of electrical attraction and repulsion, it does not appear that the simple accumulation of electricity in any quantity in bodies, as long as it remains quiescent, produces the least sensible change in their properties. A person standing upon an insulating stool may be charged with any quantity of electricity from a machine, without being perceptibly affected, until the equilibrium of the fluid is disturbed, by drawing sparks from his body, or from the prime conductor with which he may be in communication.

We have already seen, indeed, (§ 78, 79, 80,) that it is only a very small part of an electrified body, namely, the mere surface, that is in an active state, either of positive or negative electricity, and that the rest of the substance of the body is in a state of perfect neutrality.

(150.) It also appears that the uninterrupted passage of any quantity of electricity through a perfect conductor, such as a rod of metal which is of sufficient thickness to convey it, occasions no perceptible alteration in the mechanical properties of the conducting body.

(151.) On the contrary, very considerable effects are produced when a powerful charge is sent through a wire, which from the smallness of its size will not admit of the whole quantity to pass with perfect freedom; or through a substance which, although large, is deficient in conducting power; or, in other words, which opposes a degree of resistance to the passage of electricity. Thus, an iron conductor will carry off the whole electricity of a thunder-cloud in safety and in silence, while a beam of wood, or a tree, struck by lightning, is shivered into a thousand fragments.

(152.) When electricity thus changes the physical properties of bodies, its operation may, in general, be referred to that of separating their particles in the line of its course. This separation is effected with more or less violence, according to the intensity and quantity of the charge, and is frequently attended by the evolution of heat and light. The mechanical effects of electricity resemble those which would be produced by a material agent driven with great velocity and force through the substance of the body. Some of these effects, on the other hand, seem to be the consequences of the expansion produced by heat; but many of the changes induced by electricity are of a chemical nature, and such as mechanical agencies alone are insufficient to explain. We proceed to describe these several effects more particularly.

§ 1. *Mechanical Effects of Electricity.*

(153.) The cohesion of the particles of solid bodies may be conceived to oppose some resistance to the tendency of electricity to separate these particles from one another; for we find that fluids are more violently acted upon than solids, by the passage of the electric discharge. If the stem of a capillary tube, such as is employed for making thermometers, be filled with mercury, and placed so that the filament of this metal forms part of the circuit; on the discharge being made, the glass tube will be burst, and its fragments, together with the mercury, will be completely dispersed. If a fluid of inferior conducting power, such as water, be contained in a tube of larger diameter than in the preceding experiment, the passage, even of a moderate charge, will be sufficient to break the tube, and scatter its contents. Oil, alcohol, and ether, oppose still greater resistance than water to the passage of electricity, and they are expanded and scattered with still greater violence by a discharge being made to pass through them.

(154.) Beccaria introduced two wires through holes in the opposite sides of a perforated ball of solid glass of two inches diameter, the ends of the wires being separated by a drop of water, which occupied the centre of the perforation. On passing a shock through the wires and intervening drop, the ball was shattered with great violence. By a similar arrangement, Mr. Morgan succeeded in breaking green glass bottles filled with water, when the distance of the wires between which the explosion passed exceeded two inches. In this way, also, glass tubes, half an inch thick, with a bore of the same diameter, were burst with a very moderate charge, in Mr. Singer's experiments. If a cup-like cavity be turned in a piece of ivory, capable of receiving the half of a light wooden ball, with a small conical cell at the bottom of the cavity, and two wires be inserted into it through the sides of the ivory; on putting a drop of water, alcohol, or ether between the wires, and placing the ball over them in its cavity, and sending a charge through the drop of fluid, part of it will be suddenly converted into vapour, and the ball will be propelled with great violence. Even a common drinking glass, filled with water, may be broken by the explosive force with which vapour is formed at the point where the electricity passes. Beccaria constructed a small mortar with a ball, behind which a drop of water was placed, so as to be between the two wires that passed through the sides of the mortar. The charge being sent through the two wires, the drop of water was expanded with such force, as to drive out the ball with great velocity. Mr. Lullin, of Geneva, found that, by using oil instead of water in this experiment, the ball was projected with still greater force.

(155.) If two wires be introduced into a soft piece of tobacco-pipe clay, so that their ends be near each other, and a shock passed through them, the clay will be curiously expanded in the interval between the wires. The experiment will not succeed if the clay be either too dry or too moist. If the clay be too dry, or the shock too powerful, the mass will be shivered into innumerable fragments. If the clay be placed in the tube of a tobacco-pipe, or in a glass tube, the expansion of the clay will be so considerable as to shatter the tube which contains it.

(156.) The expansion of air by the passage of the electrical fluid, either in the form of sparks or shocks, is shown in the following experiment of Kinnersley, the apparatus for which has been called the *Electrical Air Thermometer*. It consists of a glass tube closed at both ends by air-tight brass caps, through which two wires slide in the direction of the axis of the tube. These wires are terminated by brass balls, which are made to approach within the striking distance. To an aperture in the bottom of the lower cap is fitted a bent tube of glass which turns upwards, and is open at both ends; the bent part is filled with mercury, or with a coloured fluid, which may indicate by its rising or falling in the tube any dilatation or contraction that may take place in the air within the vessel. It is found that every time a spark passes between the brass balls, the fluid suddenly rises, but descends again to its former level immediately after each explosion; thus showing that the dilatation of the air, produced by the abrupt passage of electricity, is but of momentary duration.

(157.) When a strong electrical charge is sent through a very confined portion of air, the explosive effects produced by it are as considerable as those we have seen exhibited by denser fluids. Thus if a piece of plate glass of the size of a square inch, and half an inch in thickness, be laid flat upon the small table of Henley's universal discharger, (§ 136,) and pressed down by a weight, and the points of the sliding wires be set opposite to each other and against the under edge of the glass, so that the electricity may pass beneath it, the charge of a large jar transmitted in this way will break the glass into innumerable fragments, and even reduce a portion into an impalpable powder. If the mouth of a small mortar made of ivory, with a cavity of half an inch diameter and an inch deep, be stopped by a cork, fitted so as to close the aperture accurately, yet without much friction, and if two wires be inserted through the sides of the mortar so that their points within the cavity be separated by an interval of about a quarter of an inch, a strong charge being sent through the wires will expand the air within the cavity so suddenly as to project the cork to some distance.

(158.) Solid bodies of a porous texture, such as wood, are easily torn asunder by an electric charge. If two holes be drilled in the opposite ends of a piece of wood, about half an inch long, and a quarter of an inch thick, and the ends of two wires inserted in the holes, so that their points may be at the distance of a quarter of an inch; on passing a strong charge through them, the wood will be split in pieces. Stones, loaf-sugar, and other brittle and imperfectly conducting substances, may be broken in a similar way.

Place a piece of dry writing paper upon the table of the universal discharger, and having removed the balls from the ends of the sliding wires, press the points of the wires against the paper at the distance of two inches from each other; if a powerful shock be now sent through the wires, the paper will be torn in pieces. If a number of wafers be placed on the table, instead of paper, they will be dispersed in a curious manner, and many of them broken into small fragments.

(159.) A singular result is obtained by the following variation in the circumstances of the last experiment, which was made by Mr. Lullin. Suspend a varnished card by silk threads, (see *fig.* 38,) in such a manner that two blunt

Fig. 38.

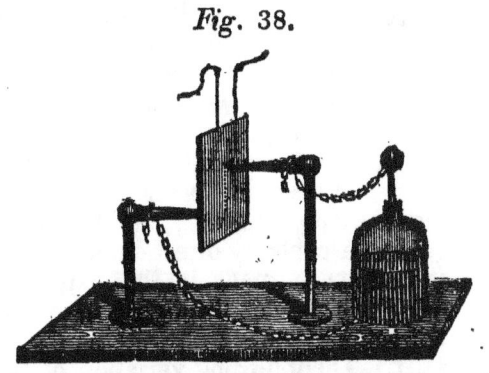

wires proceeding from the two sides of a jar or battery, may be in contact with the opposite sides of the card, but at the same time half an inch distant from each other; when the discharge is made between the wires, and along the surface of the card, the latter is found to be perforated, but always at the point where the wire communicating with the negative side of the battery had touched it. The same perforation takes place at this point, even when a hole has been previously made at the point, where it is touched by the positive wire.

The course of the electric fluid may be traced with more precision, by having both sides of the card coloured, previously to the experiment, with vermilion, for it will then leave on the card a well defined black line extending from the point of the positive wire to the perforation; and a diffused black mark on the opposite side of the card, around the perforation, and next to the negative wire.

(160.) When the electrical discharge is made to pass in a perpendicular direction through the thickness of a card, which may be effected by placing it against the outer coating of a Leyden jar, and setting the lower ball of the discharging rod against the other side of the card, so that its thickness may be interposed between it and the tin-foil, and making the explosion in the usual way, as represented in *fig*. 33, (§ 134,) the card will be perforated. At the edge of the perforation, on each side of the card, there will be a small bur or protrusion, which is always larger on the side next to the jar, than on that next to the discharging rod; the former being the negative, and the latter the positive side. By passing the shock through a quire of paper, instead of a single card, the progress of this effect at different depths from the surface may be accurately analysed. Mr. Symmer, who devised this experiment, observed that the ragged edges were for the most part directed outwards from the body of the quire. Upon examining the leaves separately, however, he found that the edges of the holes were bent regularly two different ways, and more remarkably so about the middle of the quire; one edge of each hole being throughout its course forced one way, and the other edge in the contrary direction, as if the hole had been made in the paper by drawing two threads through it in opposite directions.

(161.) The following variation of the experiment illustrates the nature of the mechanical impressions made by electricity. Let a sheet of tin-foil be placed in the middle of a quire of paper; on making the discharge through it, the tin-foil is found to have received two indentations in opposite directions, and the leaves of paper are rent in such a manner, that on both sides of the tin-foil the burs point towards the outsides of the quire; but the indentations upon the tin-foil, and the burs on the paper, are in opposite directions. If another quire of paper be taken, and two sheets of tin-foil be placed within it, so that they are separated by the two middle leaves of the quire, the result will be that all the leaves will be perforated, excepting the two within the tin-foil, and in these two leaves there will be two impressions or indentations in opposite directions.

(162.) The mechanical effects we have just described have been often adduced, not only as proofs of the materiality of the electric fluid, but also as positive indications of the direction of its motions, according as either the one or the other of the two theories of electricity is adopted. But this is a subject which we reserve for future discussion.

(163.) The fracture of glass by the electrical explosion has already been adverted to, (§ 129;) but there are still a few circumstances attending it which deserve to be noticed. The edges of the fractured portion appear well defined on the positive side; while on the negative side they are splintered, as might be expected from the passage of a material agent from the former to the latter. It is remarkable also, that a perforation may be made in glass by a very moderate discharge, when the glass is in contact with oil or sealing-wax. Thus if a small phial, or glass tube, closed at one end, be filled with olive oil, and a pointed wire, bent at right angles, and passing through a cork fitted to the mouth of the phial or tube, be introduced into it, so that the point may touch any part of its inside beneath the surface of the oil; on suspending the vessel by its wire to the prime conductor of an electrical machine, and applying to the outside, either the knuckle, or a brass ball, exactly opposite to the point of the wire within, so that a spark may pass between them, it will be found to have made a small perforation through the glass; by bringing the wire in contact with different parts of the glass, a great number of holes may thus be made in it. The effect of the oil appears to be that of controlling the tendency of the electric fluid to diverge, and of concentrating the whole power of the charge into a single point.

(164.) This repulsive tendency is also well illustrated by the following experiments made by Dr. Priestley. If a clean brass chain, previously dipped in melted resin, be laid upon paper, and the charge of a battery of at least 32 square feet be sent through it, the resinous coating will be thrown off from every part of the chain, which will be left perfectly clean, and free from resin. If a brass chain be laid upon a piece of glass, and a similar charge passed through it, the glass will be marked in a beautiful manner on every part of its surface, where it had been touched with the chain, every spot having the width and colour of the link. The metal may be scraped off the glass at the outside of the marks, but in the middle part it is forced within the pores of the glass. Dr. Priestley communicated a similar tinge to glass, by means of a silver chain, and small pieces of other metals; but he could not succeed with large pieces.

(165.) The effects of accumulated electricity upon metallic bodies, are referable, for the most part, to the agency of the heat produced by its passage through them; yet the phenomena, in many cases, indicate also the operation of other forces. By the transmission, through a piece of metal, of repeated shocks, which are not powerful enough to effect its fusion, or even ignition, a permanent alteration may be produced in its form, such as would not have resulted from heat alone. Dr. Priestley and Mr. Nairne found by experiment, that a chain through which an electrical charge had passed, undergoes a diminution in its length. A piece of hard drawn iron wire, ten inches long and one hundredth of an inch in diameter, was found, after fifteen discharges, to have lost one inch and one tenth of its length; and the increase of thickness seemed to be in proportion to this longitudinal contraction, for the wire had not perceptibly lost any of its weight during the experiment. A copper wire plated with silver, of the same dimensions as the former, underwent, by the same treatment, a diminution of length two thirds as great as that of the iron wire.

On the other hand, if the shocks be transmitted through a wire which has a weight suspended by it, so as to give it considerable tension, the length of the wire becomes increased instead of diminished, as in the above experiment. This is evidently owing to the influence of the heat which accompanies the passage of the electricity, and which diminishes the cohesion of the particles of the metal, and disposes them to yield to the extending force which the weight supplies.

§ 2. *Evolution of Heat by Electricity.*

(166.) The ignition and fusion of metals by the electric discharge, are phenomena which have been long observed. Thus by passing a strong charge through slender iron wires, they are ignited, and partly melted into globules. It was formerly believed that very large batteries were necessary for obtaining this effect; but if the wire be sufficiently fine, the electricity accumulated in a single jar of moderate size will suffice for its production. The best material for exhibiting this effect, is the finest flatted steel sold at the watchmakers' tool shops, under the name of watch pendulum wire. Van Marum has given a statement of the lengths of wires of different diameters, and of different metals, which his powerful machine enabled him to melt; when they were drawn to the thirty-second part of an inch in diameter, he found that he could fuse 120 inches of lead wire, and the same quantity of tin wire; five inches of iron wire; three inches and a half of gold wire; and only one quarter of an inch of wires of silver, copper, or brass.

(167.) From the experiments of Brooke and of Cuthbertson, it has been inferred that the length of wire which is thus melted by the electric discharge, varies as the square of the quantity of accumulated electricity which is sent through it; thus a combination of two jars, charged to an equal degree, will melt four times the length of wire which one jar will melt.

(168.) While the electric battery thus effects the fusion, and even in some cases the volatilization of metals, the phenomena appear also to indicate the action of propelling or dispersive forces, as if the agent concerned in their production was endowed with great mechanical momentum. Thus the densest metals are rent and dispersed with violence by the passage of accumulated electricity If a slip of gold or silver leaf be placed on white paper, and a strong shock passed through it, the metal will disappear with a bright flash, and the impulse with which its particles are driven against the paper will produce a permanent stain of a purple or grey colour. Franklin found that if the metallic leaf be placed between two panes of glass firmly tied together, the explosion, provided the glass withstands the concussion, will leave on each of its surfaces an indelible stain, in consequence of some of the metallic particles being actually forced into the substance of the glass, and being then inaccessible to the action of chemical solvents applied to the surface of the glass. Sometimes it is found that these metallic stains extend to a greater distance than the breadth of the piece of metal. It often happens, however, that the pieces of glass themselves are shattered to pieces by the discharge.

(169.) The colours produced by the electric explosion of metals have been applied to impress letters or ornamental devices on silk and on paper. For this purpose Mr. Singer directs that the outline of the required figure should be first traced on thick drawing paper, and afterwards cut out in the manner of stencil plates. The drawing paper is then placed on the silk or paper intended to be marked; a leaf of gold is laid upon it, and a card over that; the whole is then placed in a press or under a weight, and a charge from a battery sent through the gold leaf. The stain is confined by the interposition of the drawing paper to the limit of the design, and in this way a profile, a flower, or any other outline figure may be very neatly impressed.

(170.) The heat evolved by electricity, like most other of its effects, is in proportion to the resistances opposed to its passage. The less the conducting power of a metal, the greater is the portion of it which the same shock can ignite or destroy. A rod of wood of considerable thickness being made part of the circuit, has its temperature sensibly raised by a very few discharges. Most combustible bodies are capable of being inflamed by electricity, but more especially if it be made to strike against them in the form of a spark or shock obtained by an interrupted circuit, as by the interposition of a stratum of air. In this way may alcohol, ether, camphor, powdered resin, phosphorus, or gunpowder be set fire to. The inflammation of oil of turpentine will be promoted by strewing upon it fine particles of brass filings. If the spirit of wine be not highly rectified, it will generally be necessary previously to warm it, and the same precaution must be taken with other fluids, as oil and pitch; but it is not required with ether, which usually inflames very readily. But, on the other hand, it is to be remarked that the temperature of the body which communicates the spark appears to have no sensible influence on the heat produced by it. Thus the sparks taken from a piece of ice are as capable of inflaming bodies as those from a piece of red-hot iron. Nor is the heating power of electricity in the smallest degree diminished by its being conducted through any number of freezing mixtures which are rapidly absorbing heat from surrounding bodies.

(171.) Light, as well as heat, is emitted during the electric discharge at every point where the circuit is either interrupted, or is occupied by bodies of inferior conducting powers. A moderate charge will produce a bright spark when made to pass through water, and the spark is still more luminous in oil, alcohol, or ether, which are worse conductors than water: on the contrary, in fluids of greater conducting power there is greater difficulty of eliciting electric light. Thus a much higher charge is required to produce a spark in hot water than in cold; a still higher in saline solutions; and in concentrated acids, light can be obtained only when their volume is very small; so that it is necessary for that purpose, to draw a line of the acid upon a plate of glass with a camel's hair pencil. This is illustrated by the following experiment mentioned by Singer. Draw a line with a pen dipped in water on the surface of a slip of glass; place one extremity of the line in contact with the coating of a Leyden jar, and at six inches distance upon the line place one knob of the discharging rod; when the jar is fully charged, bring the other ball of the discharger to the knob of the jar, and the discharge will take place luminously over the six inches of water. Next, trace a line with a pen dipped in sulphuric acid on a slip of glass, as in the former experiment, and place one extremity of it in contact with the outside of the jar; the ball of the discharger may then be placed on the glass at twelve inches distance, and the electric fluid will pass as brilliantly over that interval as over the six inches of water. In either of these experiments, if the line of fluid be wider in any particular part, the light of the discharge will appear less brilliant in passing that portion; this must arise from the greater division of the fluid when passing over an extended conductor than over one that is narrow.

§ 3. *Chemical Effects of Electricity.*

(172.) Electricity exerts a most extensive and important influence in effecting changes in the chemical composition of bodies; but as this influence is most conspicuously exerted in that particular mode of agency, which is known by the name of *Galvanism*, this subject will more properly be considered in the treatise on that branch of electrical science. For the present, we must content ourselves with adducing a few instances, illustrative of the chemical effects of electricity in the forms under which it has now been presented to our notice.

(173.) Some of the chemical changes consequent on powerful electrical explosions, appear to be merely the effects of the heat which is evolved in that process. The surfaces of metallic bodies through which accumulated electricity is made to pass are frequently oxidated; this is seen more especially in the case of wires that have been fused or volatilized by the electric discharge. It is known that metals intensely heated are disposed to combine with the oxygen of the atmosphere, and, consequently, to assume the state of oxides; it is simpler, therefore, to ascribe this effect in the present case to a cause which is known to be in operation at the same moment, than to any peculiar or determining agency of electricity. A multitude of experiments are on record in which the partial oxidation of metals has been effected by electric explosions. This subject was prosecuted with minute and laborious attention by Van Marum, by Cuthbertson, and more lately by Singer. It is remarked by this last experimentalist, that the oxides of metals produced in this way appear to consist of several distinct portions of different degrees of fineness; when a wire is exploded in a receiver, part of the oxide immediately falls to the bottom, but another portion remains suspended in the air for a considerable time, and is at length gradually deposited. It is probable that this circumstance may in part account for the different colours of oxides produced in close receivers and in the open air, for in the latter case a portion of the oxide is always lost.

(174.) Under other circumstances, electricity is found to exert a power the reverse of the former; for it decomposes metallic oxides, extricating their oxygen, and restoring them to the metallic state. This deoxidating power was known to several of the earlier electricians. Beccaria reduced the oxides of tin and of mercury to their metallic state by electricity. In order to effect this change, a quantity of the oxide may be introduced into a glass tube, and pointed conducting wires inserted through corks at the opposite ends of the tube, so that a portion of the oxide may lie between them. This apparatus is then to be placed on the table of the universal discharger, (§ 136,) and repeated shocks are to be sent through the oxide until its partial or total reduction is accomplished. Vermilion, which consists of sulphur and mercury, is very easily decomposed by this process, and by a very moderate charge.

(175.) When a succession of electric discharges from a powerful electric machine are sent through water, a decomposition of that fluid takes place, and it is resolved into its two elements of oxygen and hydrogen, which immediately assume the gaseous form. This fact was discovered in 1789, by Messrs. Dieman, Paetz, and Van Troostwyck, who had formed themselves into a society for experimental research in Holland; and it completed the chain of evidence by which the great discovery of the composition of water, made five years before by Cavendish, is established. The abovementioned Dutch chemists being occupied, in conjunction with Mr. Cuthbertson, in investigating the effects of electricity when passed through different bodies, were desirous of ascertaining its effect on pure water. They employed for this purpose an apparatus consisting of a glass tube, twelve inches long and one-eighth of an inch in diameter, through one end of which a gold wire was inserted, projecting about an inch and a half within the tube; that end was then hermetically sealed. Another wire was introduced at the other end of the tube, which was left open, and passed upwards, so that its extremity came to a distance of five-eighths of an inch from the end of the first wire. The tube was then filled with distilled water, which had been freed from air by an excellent air-pump, and inverted in a vessel containing mercury. A little common air was let into the top of the tube, in order to prevent its being broken by the discharge. Electrical shocks were then passed between the two ends of the wires through the water in the tube by means of a Leyden jar, which had a square foot of coated surface. This jar was charged by a very powerful double plate machine, which caused it to discharge twenty-five times in fifteen revolutions. At each explosion bubbles of air were formed, and rose to the top of the tube. As soon as a sufficient quantity had collected to leave the upper end of the wire uncovered by the water, so that the shock had now to pass through a portion of the mixed gases, they were instantly kindled; a reunion of the elements took place; water was again formed, and the space they had occupied was immediately filled with fluid from below, so as to restore every thing precisely as at the outset of the experiment. It was ascertained by the most decisive chemical tests, that the gases thus obtained consisted of a mixture of oxygen and hydrogen gases.

(176.) It may appear somewhat paradoxical that the same agent should, in the course of the same experiment, produce at one time decomposition, and at another combination of the same elements. The simplest way of reconciling this apparent discordance, is to suppose that the combination of the gases is the effect of the heat evolved during its forcible transit through an aëriform fluid that opposes considerable resistance to its passage; while the decomposition of the liquid is the direct consequence of the agency of electricity when not interfered with by heat.

(177.) Until lately, it was thought necessary to employ powerful machines and large jars in order to effect the decomposition of water by electricity, and that mere sparks from a common machine were inadequate to accomplish this purpose. That there is in this respect, however, no essential distinction in the operation of these two forms of electricity has been satisfactorily shown by Dr. Wollaston. This distinguished philosopher, perceiving, with his accustomed sagacity and penetration, that the decomposition would depend on duly proportioning the strength of the charge to the quantity of water, and that the quantity exposed to its action at the surface of communication depends on the extent of that surface, inferred that by reducing the surface of communication the decomposition of water might be effected by smaller machines, and with less powerful excitation than had hitherto been applied to this object. Having procured a small wire of fine gold, and given to it as fine a point as possible, he inserted it into a capillary glass tube; and after heating the tube, so as to make it adhere to the point, and cover it in every part, he gradually ground it down, till, with a pocket lens, he could discern that the point of the gold was exposed. When sparks from a prime conductor of an electrical machine were made to pass through water by means of a point so guarded, a spark, extending to the distance of one-eighth of an inch, would decompose water when the point exposed did not exceed one 700th of an inch in diameter. With another point, estimated at one 1500th, a succession of sparks one-twentieth of an inch in length afforded a current of small bubbles of air. With a still finer filament of gold, the mere current of electricity, without any perceptible sparks, evolved gas from water.

(178.) When a solution of sulphate of copper was subjected to the action of electricity by means of these slender conducting wires, the metal was revived around the negative wire; but upon reversing the direction of the current of electricity, so that the same wire now became positively electrified, the copper which had collected around it was redissolved, and a similar precipitate was deposited on the opposite wire, which was now the negative one. Similar experiments made with other metallic solutions were attended with analogous results; the negative wire always separating oxygen from its combinations, the positive wire always attracting it, and effecting its union with the bases presented to it. With solutions of neutral salts, the alkaline or earthy bases were attracted by the negative, while the acids were attracted by the positive wire. The experiments of Sir Humphry Davy have confirmed these results as far as concerns the chemical action of common electricity; but as this is a subject which bears more immediate relation to chemistry and to galvanism, it would not be right to enlarge upon it in the present treatise.

(179.) The magnetic effects of electricity will likewise form the subject of a distinct treatise, as they now constitute a new branch of science, under the title of ELECTRO-MAGNETISM.

§ 4. *Effects of Electricity upon Animals.*

(180.) Having seen that the effects of electricity on inanimate matter are of various kinds, we should be led to expect that its operation on living bodies would be still more complicated; for in addition to its mechanical and chemical agencies, it can hardly fail of exerting considerable influence on the living powers, and more especially on the functions of the nervous system. It is unnecessary to describe the sensations excited in the body by receiving electric sparks or shocks, since most persons in the present day are familiar with them. It is curious, however, to take a retrospective view of the mode in which the effects of the Leyden phial were announced to the world, on their first discovery. The philosophers who first experienced, in their own person, the shock attendant on the transmission of an electric discharge, were so impressed with wonder and with terror by this novel sensation, that they wrote the most ridiculous and exaggerated account of their feelings on the occasion. Muschenbroek states, that he received so dreadful a concussion in his arms, shoulder, and heart, that he lost his breath, and that it was two days before he could recover from its effects; he declared also, that he should not be induced to take another shock for the whole kingdom of France. Mr. Allemand reports, that the shock deprived him of breath for some minutes, and afterwards produced so acute a pain along his right arm, that he was apprehensive it might be attended with serious consequences. Mr. Winkler informs us, that it threw his whole body into convulsions, and excited such a ferment in his blood, as would have thrown him into a fever, but for the timely employment of febrifuge remedies. He states, that at another time it produced copious bleeding at the nose; the same effect was produced also upon his lady, who was almost rendered incapable of walking. These strange accounts naturally excited the attention and wonder of all classes of people; the learned and the vulgar were equally desirous of experiencing so singular a sensation, and great numbers of half-taught electricians wandered through every part of Europe to gratify this universal curiosity.

(181.) As it is probable that the electric fluid meets with greater impediment in passing from the surface of one bone to another, at the parts where the continuity of substance is interrupted by the joints, this circumstance explains why the shock is often more especially felt at the joints than in any other part of a limb. But if the shock be directed more particularly through muscles, its effects are chiefly shown by exciting a convulsive and involuntary action of those muscles. This is often observed to take place in a paralysed limb, when electric shocks are sent through it, although the nerves of the limb are at the time incapable of conveying the impressions which produce sensation. Mr. Morgan states, that if the diaphragm be included in the circuit of a coated surface of two feet in extent, fully charged, the sudden contraction of the muscles of respiration will act so violently upon the air in the lungs, as to occasion a loud and involuntary shout; but if the charge be small, a fit of convulsive laughter is induced, presenting a most ludicrous exhibition to the by-standers.

(182.) It is on the nervous system, however, that the most considerable action of electricity is exerted. A strong charge passed through the head, gave to Mr. Singer th sensation of a violent but universal blow, and was followed by a transient loss of memory and indistinctness of vision. If a charge be sent through the head of a bird, its optic nerve is usually injured or destroyed, and permanent blindness induced: and a similar shock given to larger animals, produces a tremulous state of the muscles, with general prostration of strength. If a person who is standing receive a charge through the spine, he loses his power over the muscles to such a degree, that he either drops on his knees, or falls prostrate on the ground; if the charge be sufficiently powerful, it will produce immediate death, in consequence, probably, of the sudden exhaustion of the whole energy of the nervous system. Small animals, such as mice and sparrows, are instantly killed by a shock from thirty square inches of glass. Van Marum found that eels are irrecoverably deprived of life when a shock is sent through their whole body; but when only a part of the body is included in the circuit, the destruction of irritability is confined to that individual part, while the rest retains the power of motion. Different persons are affected in very different degrees by electricity, according to their peculiar constitutional susceptibility. Dr. Young remarks, that a very minute tremor, communicated to the most elastic parts of the body, in particular to the chest, produces an agitation of the nerves, which is not wholly unlike the effect of a weak electricity.

(183.) The bodies of animals killed by electricity, rapidly undergo putrefaction, and the action of electricity upon the flesh of animals is also found to accelerate this process in a remarkable degree. The same effect has been observed in the bodies of persons destroyed by lightning. It is also a well-established fact, that the blood does not coagulate after death from this cause.

(184.) It has not been determined with any degree of certainty, whether electricity, in its ordinary mode of application, exerts any sensible influence on the functions of the animal system. The Abbé Nollet persuaded himself, from the experiments he made on man and animals, that the perspiration was increased during the time they were electrified; and De Bozes had noticed that the pulse was quickened under the same circumstance. But Van Marum, on repeating these experiments in a variety of ways, met with such variable and contradictory results, that he could deduce from them no satisfactory conclusion respecting the real operation of electricity; and, indeed, if we take into account the powerful influence which the imagination exerts on most persons who are the subjects of such experiments, as well as on those who witness them, there appears but little chance, amidst such multiplied sources of fallacy, of arriving at the truth. The only general fact, perhaps, which appears to be established, is that electricity acts as a stimulant both to the muscular and the nervous systems.

(185.) When the energetic effects of the shock from the Leyden phial were first made known, the most sanguine expectations were immediately raised, that electricity would prove an agent of considerable power in the cure of diseases. It was supposed that as a stimulant, it would have many advantages over other remedies; for it can be administered in various degrees of intensity, which may be regulated with great exactness; and its application can be directed especially to the organ we wish to affect, and can be limited to that organ, so as not to interfere with the functions of the general system. Accordingly we find, that at one period electricity was in great repute as an efficacious remedy in a number of diseases; but at present it is seldom employed except in a very few. It is not unfrequently had recourse to in palsy, contractions of the limbs, rheumatism, St. Vitus's dance, and some kinds of deafness, and impaired vision; it has also been applied to discuss tumours, to remove obstructions, and to relieve pain.

(186.) Electricity may be administered medicinally in four different ways. The first and most gentle is under the form of a continued stream, or *aura* as it is termed, derived from a wire or pointed piece of wood connected with the prime conductor of the machine, held by an insulated handle, at the distance of one or two inches from that part to which it is to be directed; an impression is felt similar to a current of air; and in this way it may be borne by parts of great sensibility, such as the eye. The second mode is by directing sparks of various sizes to the affected part, by means of a metallic ball at the extremity of a brass rod, which is within a moderate distance from the part; or else by placing the patient on an insulating stool, and while he is in communication with the prime conductor of the machine, taking sparks from him by another person with a metallic ball at the end of a rod which he holds in his hand. The size and intensity of the spark will, of course, be regulated by the distance at which the ball is placed from the body, provided the machine be steadily worked. The third mode is that by shocks from the discharge of a Leyden phial, which is, of course, the most severe and painful method of applying electricity. Great caution is required against the indiscriminate application of this last method, which is not wholly free from danger. The fourth mode is by Galvanism, hereafter to be noticed.

§ 5. *Effects of Electricity upon Vegetables.*

(187.) It has also been imagined that electricity acts as a stimulus to vegetable life: and many fanciful projects of improvements in horticulture by the aid of artificial electricity have been entertained. It is needless, however, to enlarge upon these visionary speculations, the fallacy of which has been sufficiently shown by the late Dr. Ingenhouz, who, upon the most accurate inquiry, found that the vegetation of plants was in no sensible degree either promoted or retarded by common electricity. The experiments of Van Marum, however, in which be found that electricity increased the evaporation of plants, appear to be entitled to some confidence; but still the effect observed, may, as he himself remarks, have been occasioned by the increased current of air from the parts of the electrified leaves. His observations on the influence of electricity on the sensitive plant, (*Mimosa pudica*,) deserve also to be noticed. The mere approach of an electrified conductor, whether charged with positive or negative electricity, produced no effect upon the plant; but when sparks were taken from it, the leaves collapsed, just as they would have done by concussions of a mechanical nature, and in other respects the plant underwent no change. In the *Hedysarum gyrans*, a plant remarkable for the continual rotatory motions of its leaves, electricity appeared to have no sensible influence either in accelerating or retarding these movements.

(188.) The passage of shocks through living plants immediately destroys the vitality in the parts through which the shock has been sent. It is, indeed, very easy to kill plants by means of electricity. A very small shock, according to Cavallo, sent through the stem of a balsam, is sufficient to destroy it. A few minutes after the passage of the shock, the plant droops, the leaves and branches become flaccid, and its life ceases. A small Leyden phial, containing six or eight square inches of coated surface, is generally sufficient for this purpose, which may even be effected by means of strong sparks from the prime conductor of a large electrical machine. The charge by which these destructive effects are produced, is probably too inconsiderable to burst the vessels of the plant, or to occasion any material derangement of its organization; and, accordingly, it is not found, on minute examination of a plant thus killed by electricity, that either the internal vessels or any other parts have sustained perceptible injury.

(189.) It appears from the experiments of Mr. Achard, that the fermentation of vegetable matter is accelerated by electricity.

(190.) The general conclusion deducible from these inquiries is, that feeble electricity exerts no perceptible influence on either animal or vegetable life: but when transmitted in powerful shocks, its destructive effects are similar to those which are produced by lightning.

Chapter XII.
Instruments adapted to collect weak Electricity.

(191.) Before we proceed to consider the developement of electricity under various circumstances, it will be proper to give a description of several instruments which have been contrived for the purpose of collecting and exhibiting weak degrees of electricity, that would otherwise escape detection. All these instruments derive their efficacy from the principle of electric induction; and their mode of operation will be best understood by previously directing our attention to the electrophorus.

(192.) The instrument termed the *Electrophorus* was invented about the year 1774 by Professor Volta, a name which is associated with many important discoveries in the science of electricity. It consists of three parts: the essential part, which supplies the electricity, being a cake of some electric substance, (E, *fig*. 39,) such as sulphur,

Fig. 39.

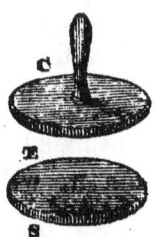

gum lac, sealing-wax, pitch, or other resinous composition; this is melted on a conducting plate S, called *the sole*, which is formed with a rim to contain it, and the fluid then allowed to congeal. The third part of the apparatus consists of a circular metallic plate C, provided with an insulating handle fixed upon its upper surface. This is called *the cover;* and is sometimes made of wood, covered on all sides with tin-foil well rounded at the edges to prevent the dispersion of electricity. In order to bring the apparatus into a state of activity, the surface of the cake is excited by friction with fur or flannel, and is thus rendered negatively electrical. The cover, held by its insulating handle, must now be placed on the cake: in this situation it does not come sufficiently in contact with the cake to receive its electricity; but acquires by induction an opposite state at its lower surface, and a similar state at its upper; that is, the cake being negative, the under side of the cover will be positive, and the upper side negative. If, while in this state, the upper negative surface be touched with the finger, or with any other conductor communicating with the earth, a spark will pass from the latter to the cover, so as to restore the electric equilibrium; the quantity of electricity thus superadded being retained in the cover by the inductive influence of the cake. But when the plate is raised, provided it be held by its insulating handle, the action of the cake being withdrawn, the cover is found to be charged with positive electricity, which may be imparted to an insulated conductor, or to a Leyden jar. This operation may be repeated an indefinite number of times, since the electricity of the cake continues unimpaired during the process, and thus may a charge be communicated to the jar of an intensity equal to that of the cover of the electrophorus when raised. The instrument has been known, indeed, to retain its power undiminished for months, and may therefore be regarded as a sort of magazine of electricity. It is obvious, that if the cover were simply placed on the cake, and again raised without previously touching it, it would then exhibit no sign of electricity. If the sole of the electrophorus be insulated, a spark may be obtained from it, when the cake has been excited; and if while placed on the cake the cover be touched with the finger, and at the same time the sole be touched with the thumb, a sensible shock will be felt in that part of the hand.

(193.) Volta is also the inventor of an instrument acting on the same principle as the electrophorus, and which he termed *the condenser*, of which the purpose is to collect a weak electricity, spread over a large surface, into a body of small dimensions, in which its intensity will be proportionably increased, and therefore become capable of being examined. A small metallic plate, connected with the substance of which the electricity is to be determined, is brought within a very small distance of another plate communicating with the earth. The small portion of electricity received from the substance to be tried by the first plate, acts by induction on the second plate, and occasions it to acquire the opposite electrical state: this latter state reacts upon the first plate, increasing its capacity for the electricity which it had first received, and tends to accumulate a larger quantity in it, which quantity it must derive from the substance with which it communicates. This mutual action and reaction continues till an equilibrium is attained. If the communication between the substance tried and the first plate be broken off, and the plate thus insulated be removed from the contiguity of the second plate, the accumulated electricity with which it is charged will become evident upon its application to an ordinary electroscope, such as those described in § 13 and 14.

(194.) Various have been the forms given to the condenser, according to the fancy of electricians, without any change in the principle on which it acts. In general, the two plates are merely separated by a thin stratum of air. Sometimes their surfaces are covered with a non-conducting varnish, which prevents any communication of electricity from the one plate to the other, while it allows of a very near approach of the plates to each other; but this method is liable to objection, from the permanent electricity which the varnish sometimes contracts by friction, and which may interfere with the regular operation of the instrument. One of the most convenient forms is that of the condensing electrometer, (*fig.* 40,)

Fig. 40.

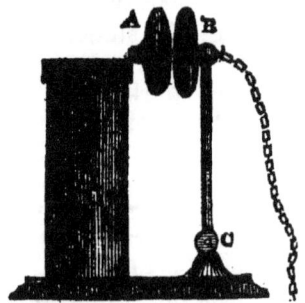

in which the first plate of the condenser A, is fixed to the cap of the gold-leaf electroscope; the second plate B, which communicates by a chain with the ground, being moveable round a joint C, and thus capable of being turned back and removed from the first plate, so as to allow its electricity to be manifested by the divergence of the gold leaves.

(195.) The instruments called *Doublers* are so contrived, that by executing certain movements, very small quantities of electricity communicated to a part of the apparatus may be continually doubled, until it becomes perceptible by an electroscope. The first invention of this kind was that of Mr. Bennet, which consists of three brass plates, which we shall call A, B, and C. The plate A has an insulating handle fixed in its centre, while the plate B has a similar handle fixed in its circumference. The under side of A, and both sides of B are covered with varnish. The third plate C is also of brass, and is only varnished on its upper side, the lower side communicating with the gold-leaf electroscope. The body whose electricity is to be tried, is made to communicate with the under side of the plate C, which touches the electroscope, while B is placed upon C, and then touched with the finger: the communication with the electrified body is then removed, and B is lifted up by its insulating handle. A is then placed, by means of its handle, upon B thus elevated. A is then touched, and, after withdrawing the finger, is separated from B. In this process B acquires an electricity contrary to that of C; and A an electricity contrary to that of B, that is, the same as that of C. If the plate A, thus electrified, be next applied to the under surface of C, and B be again applied over C, and touched with the finger as before, it will be acted upon by the electricities contained both in C and A, and thus acquire, by induction, nearly double the quantity which it had done in the first operation. The consequence of this will be that nearly all the free electricities of A and C will be concentrated in C. A may now be removed, and after withdrawing the finger from B, B may also be removed, and C will be left with double the quantity of electricity which it had received from the body with which it was originally made to communicate.

If after this duplication the electricity of the plate C be still too feeble to be indicated by the electroscope, the same series of operations must be repeated ten or even twenty times; when by doubling it every time, the smallest conceivable quantity of electricity must at last be rendered sensible; since, at the end of the twentieth operation, it will be augmented more than 500,000 times. Although the frequent repetition of the operations may appear tedious, yet, by a little practice, the art is readily acquired, and the whole process need not occupy a minute. Great care must be taken in conducting these experiments, not to excite any electricity by the friction of the finger, or by any other means, in the varnished sides of the plates. In order to obviate this source of error, Cavallo contrived a form of the instrument, that enabled the plates to be brought within a very small distance of one another, yet without actual contact, so as to enable him to dispense altogether with the employment of varnish. But notwithstanding every precaution of this kind, it is always found that the instrument exhibits electricity of itself, although none has been previously communicated to it: so that its indications cannot be at all depended upon for the detection of very minute quantities of electricity. It is unnecessary, therefore, to describe the particular mechanisms invented by Dr. Darwin, and improved by Nicholson, for bringing the plates into the requisite positions, and effecting in succession the necessary contacts, by the simple rotation of a winch, aided by wheelwork: instruments which have gone by the names of the *moveable*, or *revolving doubler*, and the *multiplier of electricity*, and which are now superseded in practice by instruments more sensible and certain in their operation.

Chapter XIII.
Developement of Electricity by Changes of Temperature and of Form.

(196.) There are certain mineral bodies, which, from being in a neutral state at ordinary temperatures, acquire electricity simply by being heated or cooled. This property is possessed only by regularly crystallized minerals; and of these the most remarkable is the tourmalin, which is a stone of considerable hardness, found in many parts of the world, and particularly in the island of Ceylon. The Dutch, who first became acquainted with it in that island, gave it the appellation of *Aschentrikker*, from its property of attracting ashes when it is thrown into the fire. It appears from the researches of Dr. Watson, that its attractive properties were known to Theophrastus, who describes it under the name of *Lyncurium*. Linnæus has termed it the *Lapis Electricus*, (Electric stone.) The form of its crystals is generally that of a nine-sided prism, terminated by a three-sided pyramid at one end, and by a six-sided pyramid at the other. Lemery noticed its electric properties in the year 1717; but the first scientific examination of them was made by Æpinus in 1756, and published in the Memoirs of the Berlin Academy. He found that when a crystal of tourmalin has its temperature raised to between 100° and 212° of Fahrenheit, one extremity, which is that terminated by the six-sided pyramid, becomes charged with positive electricity, while the other extremity is negative; so as to be capable of affecting a delicate electroscope. When the stone is of considerable size, flashes of light may be seen along its surface. Mr. Wilson, who made many experiments on this subject, observed that a flat tourmalin retained its electricity without diminution, after exposure to intense heat for half an hour; but Canton, upon repeating these experiments, did not obtain the same result. Hauy states, that very high degrees of heat destroy the electricity of the tourmalin. After this has been effected, it recovers its electricity as it gradually cools: but in that case the electric states are generally reversed; that extremity, or *pole*, as it has been called, which was before positive, is now negative, and *vice versâ*. It is only at the summits of the pyramids, by which the crystal is terminated, that the electricity is manifested; the intermediate portions exhibiting no sign of electrical excitation, unless the stone be broken in pieces; and then each fragment is found to possess a positive and a negative pole, like the entire crystal. This fact bears a striking analogy to a corresponding property in magnets. At the ordinary temperature of the atmosphere, the tourmalin may be rendered electrical by friction.

(197.) There are several other gems and crystallized minerals which possess the same property as the tourmalin. The luminous appearance of some diamonds, when heated, is ascribed by Sir Humphry Davy to their electrical excitation. The substance called the *Boracite*, composed of borate of magnesia, which crystallizes in cubes, having its edges and angles defective, becomes electrical by heat, and in one variety presents no less than eight sides, alternately in different states; that is, four positive and four negative; the opposite poles being in the direction of the axes of the crystal. In those varieties in which only four of the angles of the crystal are truncated, that is, cut off by planes, while the rest are either entire, or are replaced by more than one plane, it is always the former of these angles that become positive, and the latter negative.

(198.) Similar properties are possessed by the Topaz, which consists of siliceous fluate of alumina; its electric poles are situated upon the two opposite summits of the secondary crystal. In some varieties, Hauy found a series of consecutive poles alternately positive and negative. Axinite, Mesotype, and Prehnite, become electrical by the application of heat: as also the two following metallic oxides, namely Calamine, which is an oxide of zinc, and Sphene, or calcareo-siliceous oxide of titanium. Mr. Dessaignes has lately shown that all metallic bodies are capable of a feeble electric excitation by changes of temperature. It results from the researches of Hauy, that this electrical property in mineral bodies is intimately related to the laws of their crystallization, and also to the direction in which the light is most readily transmitted through them.

(199.) There are a great many substances which become electrified on passing from the liquid to the solid form. This happens to sulphur, gum lac, bee's wax, and in general all resinous bodies. Unless proper precautions be taken, however, we frequently obtain no indications of this electricity, because it is usually *disguised*, that is, rendered inactive by the opposite electricity of the contiguous substances. Thus, if sulphur be melted over the fire in an iron ladle, and then set by to cool and harden, it exhibits no sign of electricity; because the negative electricity of the sulphur is exactly counterbalanced by the positive electricity accumulated in the iron vessel which contains it. But if the sulphur be removed from the vessel, which may be done by again heating it for a short time, so as just to melt the surface in contact with the iron, and allow of its being detached when the ladle is inverted, on suffering the sulphur to cool in this situation, its electricity becomes very apparent. If sulphur be melted in a wine glass, the conical shape of which admits of its being taken out when cold, the opposite electricities of the two surfaces will then manifest themselves, that of the sulphur being negative, and that of the glass positive; but when the sulphur is replaced in the glass, all indications of electricity disappear. The electricity developed by the process of cooling was called by Wilke, who first observed it, *spontaneous electricity*, in contradistinction to that which, originating from friction, he called *excited electricity*. Van Marum, however, attributes the electricity developed by the separation of the two substances, to a species of friction; for he remarks, that the electricity does not manifest itself till the sulphur begins to contract in the act of congelation, and that it attains its maximum at the point of the greatest contraction.

(200.) It is reasonable to suppose that whatever change was produced in the electrical state by congelation, the reverse would be produced by liquefaction. We are not aware of any experiments which bear directly upon this question.

(201.) The conversion of bodies into the state of vapour, as well as the condensation of vapour, is generally attended by some alteration of their electrical condition; and the bodies in contact with the vapour are thereby rendered electrical. Thus, if a plate of metal strongly heated be placed upon a gold-leaf electroscope, and water be dropped upon the plate, at the moment the vapour rises the leaves of the electroscope diverge with negative electricity. The general fact was noticed by Laplace, Lavoisier, and Volta, in the year 1781; and was found to extend both to solids and to liquids passing into a gaseous form. De Saussure made an extensive series of experiments on the ebullition of water and other fluids, with a view to ascertain the degree and kind of electricity developed during this process. But investigations of this kind are attended with great difficulty, from the multitude of minute circumstances which are liable to affect the results; and we accordingly find, that different experiments of the same kind often afford the most opposite conclusions.

(202.) In general it is found, that the vaporization of water by simple ebullition produces negative electricity in the remaining fluid, or vessel which contains it: the vapour itself being positive. On the contrary, when aqueous vapour is condensed into water, it becomes negative, leaving the bodies with which it was last in contact in a state of positive electricity. Yet in some of De Saussure's experiments, when the heat was communicated to a quantity of water contained in an insulated metallic vessel, by throwing into it a mass of red-hot iron, the electricity was very strongly positive. This difference in the result was probably owing to the chemical decomposition of the water in the latter experiment, a circumstance which, as we shall presently see, is itself a source of electricity. It is principally on account of the interference of chemical actions with the regular operations of temperature, and of the complications introduced by electric induction, that experiments on this subject have hitherto presented such anomalous, and, apparently, discordant results.

Chapter XIV.

Developement of Electricity by Contact, Compression, and other mechanical Changes in Bodies, and also by their Chemical Action.

(203.) It had long been suspected, rather than proved, that a feeble degree of electricity is evolved by the contact or collision of different metals: but this important fact was established in the clearest manner by Volta, about the year 1801. The apparatus he employed in his investigations on this subject consisted of two discs, the one of zinc, the other of copper, (*fig.* 41,) rather more

Fig. 41.

than two inches in diameter, ground perfectly plane, and having in their centres insulating handles perpendicular to their surfaces, by means of which the plates could be brought into contact, without being actually touched with the hand. With this precaution the discs were made to approach till they touched one another; they were then separated, by keeping them parallel as they were drawn back. The electricity they possessed after this separation was then examined by means of the condenser; and, that the effects might be rendered more distinct, the electricity produced by a number of successive contacts, (taking care to restore the discs to the neutral state after each contact,) was accumulated in the same condenser. It was constantly found that the copper disc charged the condenser with negative, and the zinc disc with positive electricity. Thus it was established as a general fact, that these two metals, insulated, and in their natural state, are brought, by mutual contact, into opposite electrical states; the zinc acquiring positive electricity, and the copper becoming, in an equal degree, negative.

(204.) No explanation has yet been given of this curious fact, which seems to be at variance with all the previously ascertained laws of electric equilibrium. The transfer of electricity from one metal to the other during their contact, implies the operation of some new force which no theory has yet embraced. While the contact is preserved, neither of the metals gives any indication of its electrical state, the electricity being *disguised*; as would be the case of that of the coatings of a Leyden jar, if we could suppose them both in actual contact, but yet incapable of allowing any transfer of the electricity from the one to the other, so as to restore both to the state of neutrality.

We shall have occasion to resume the consideration of this curious subject in the treatise on Galvanism, with the theory of which it appears to have an intimate relation.

(205.) There are some bodies which are rendered electrical by pressure. This property is possessed in the most remarkable degree by that transparent variety of carbonate of lime which is known by the name of *Iceland spar*. According to Hauy, if a crystal of this spar, which has the form of a rhomboid, be held in one hand by two of its opposite edges, and if at the same time two of its parallel planes be lightly touched by two fingers of the other hand, and then brought near to the small needle of the electroscope, (§ 12) a decided attraction will be perceptible. By applying a more powerful pressure, the electrical effects will be still more considerable; the electricity being in all cases positive. Hauy observes that this property resides principally in those crystalline minerals that are capable of being reduced by mechanical division to plane and smooth laminæ: such as the Topaz, especially the colourless variety; Euclase, Arragonite, Fluate of lime, and Carbonate of lead. Among those substances in which friction excites negative electricity, there are some which require only to be pressed, for the production of the same effect. An instance occurs in elastic bitumen, when it has been cut into a proper shape for the experiment. Mr. Becquerel has lately discovered that many other substances, such as cork, bark, hairs, paper, and wood, possess the property of producing electricity by compression.

(206.) Many substances, when reduced to powder, exhibit electricity, if they are made to fall upon an insulated metallic plate. This fact was first noticed by Mr. Bennet, after he had invented his gold-leaf electroscope. He found that powdered chalk, put into a pair of bellows, and blown upon the cap of the electroscope, communicates to the instrument positive electricity, when the pipe of the bellows is about six inches from the cap; but the same stream of powdered chalk electrifies it negatively at the distance of three feet. On being blown in a more copious stream from a pair of bellows without the pipe, the electricity is always negative; and the same effect takes place when the powder is let fall from another plate upon the cap of the instrument. This subject was pursued by Cavallo; but the most complete set of experiments relating to it is that of Singer, who employed in his researches the two following methods: first, that of sifting the powders on the cap of a delicate electrometer through a fine sieve, which was thoroughly cleaned after each operation; and secondly, that of bringing an insulated copper plate repeatedly in contact with extensive surfaces of the powders spread on a dry sheet of paper; the copper plate being brought in contact with the condenser after every repetition of the contact, until a sufficient charge was communicated.

(207.) The following substances, according to Singer, produce negative electricity when sifted on the cap of the electrometer: *viz.* copper, iron, zinc, tin, bismuth, antimony, nickel, black lead, lime, magnesia, barytes, strontites, alumine, silex, brown oxide of copper, white oxide of arsenic, red oxide of lead, litharge, white lead, red oxide of iron, acetate of copper, sulphate of copper, sulphate of soda, phosphate of soda, carbonate of soda, carbonate of ammonia, carbonate of potash, carbonate of lime, muriate of ammonia, common pearl-ashes, boracic acid, tartaric acid, cream of tartar, oxymuriate of potash, pure potash, pure soda, resin sulphur, sulphuret of lime, starch, orpiment.

(208.) The following substances produce positive electricity under the same circumstance: *viz.* wheat flour, oatmeal, lycopodium, quassia, powdered cardamom, charcoal, sulphate of potash, nitrate of potash, acetate of lead, oxide of tin.

(209.) The following catalogue exhibits the results of the experiments of contact with a copper plate; the different substances being arranged under the head of the electricity they really acquire, which is contrary to that of the copper plate. *Positive:* lime, barytes, strontites, magnesia, pure soda, pure potash, common pearl-ashes, carbonate of potash, carbonate of soda, tartaric acid. *Negative:* benzoic acid, boracic acid, oxalic acid, citric acid, silex, alumina, carbonate of ammonia, sulphur, resin. These experiments were several times repeated with uniform results.

(210.) The above mode of electrical excitation is probably merely a species of friction, differing only from the more ordinary instances by the mode of its application. But in other cases the electrical effects of contact are more distinctly exhibited, as when zinc filings are poured through holes in a plate of copper, upon the cap of an electrometer.

(211.) The following experiment, founded on one devised by Professor Lichtenberg of Gottingen, is an elegant illustration of the opposite electrical states of different powders. With the knob of a charged jar, trace on the surface of a smooth plate of glass, or of any resinous substance, various lines at pleasure; and then repeat the same operation in other parts with the knob of a jar charged with the opposite electricity. Let the surface thus prepared be gently dusted, by means of a powder-puff, with a mixture of powdered sulphur and red lead, previously triturated together in a mortar. By the contact and friction thus produced, the sulphur has been rendered negative, and the red lead positive; and each of the powders, when projected on the plate, will attach itself to the oppositely electrified lines, forming a series of red and yellow outlines. It is also observable, that the configurations assumed by these and other powders differ according to the species of electricity impressed upon the plate; positive electricity producing an appearance resembling feathers, and negative electricity an arrangement more like stars.

(212.) The most important circumstance in this inquiry, is the connection between electricity and the chemical properties of matter. It is observed by Sir H. Davy, that most of the substances that act distinctly upon each other electrically, are likewise such as act chemically, when their particles have freedom of motion: this is the case with the different metals, with sulphur and the metals, with acid and alkaline substances. Of two metals in contact, the one which has the greatest chemical attraction for oxygen acquires positive electricity, and the other the negative: so that if arranged in the order of their oxidability, as follows, zinc, iron, tin, lead, copper, silver, gold, platina, each will become positive when brought into contact with any that follow it in the series, and negative with any of those which precede it. In contacts of acids with bases, as of crystals of oxalic acid with dry quicklime, the former is negative, the latter positive. All acid crystals when touched by a plate of metal render it positive, the crystals themselves becoming negative.

(213.) Bodies that exhibit electrical effects by mutual contact, previous to their chemical action on each other, lose this power during combination. Thus if a polished plate of zinc be made to touch a surface of dry mercury, and quickly separated, it is found positively electrical, and the effect is increased by heat; but if it be so heated as to amalgamate, that is, unite chemically with the mercury, it no longer exhibits any signs of electricity. The case is analogous with copper and sulphur; and iron, when applied to mercury, produces more electricity than zinc, apparently from its being incapable, under ordinary circumstances, of forming a chemical combination with mercury.

(214.) On the other hand, there can be no question that electricity is occasionally, if not universally, elicited during chemical action. We have just seen that a dry acid becomes negative by contact with a metal, which is consequently thereby rendered positive. In this case no chemical combination had taken place. But Becquerel has shown that if the acid, instead of being in a dry crystalline form, be in a liquid state, and capable of acting chemically on the metal, the acid will become positive and the metal negative. The same conclusion may also be deduced from the experiments of Lavoisier and Laplace, on the action of dilute sulphuric acid on iron filings. That the oxidation of metals gives rise to electricity has been also shown by the experiments of Dr. Wollaston, from which it would appear that the electricity obtained in the common electrical machine is derived principally from this source. When he employed as the rubbing substance an amalgam of silver or of platina, which are metals very little subject to oxidation, he could obtain no electricity. An amalgam of tin, on the other hand, supplied a large quantity of electricity. Zinc acts still better than tin; but the best amalgam for this purpose is made with both tin and zinc, a mixture which oxidates more readily than either metal separately. As a further trial whether oxidation assists in the production of electricity, a small cylinder with its cushion and conductor was arranged in a vessel so contrived that the contained air could be changed at pleasure. After ascertaining the degree of excitement produced in atmospheric air, carbonic acid was substituted, but the excitement could not be renewed; while it was immediately reproduced on the readmission of common air. It must be acknowledged, however, that Sir H. Davy, in repeating these experiments, arrived at opposite results; for he states, that the machine acted equally well in hydrogen gas as in atmospheric air, and was even more active in carbonic acid gas, a circumstance which he attributes to the greater density of this gas.

(215.) Electricity is often developed by processes quite independent of chemical changes. This is evident from its production by the friction of two bodies of the same kind upon one another, as has been already noticed, (§ 35;) and also by the strong electricity which is manifested on the separation of the parts of the same body. Thus, if a piece of dry and warm wood be suddenly rent asunder, the two surfaces which have separated are found to be electrified, the one positively, the other negatively; and a flash of light is perceived if the experiment be made in the dark. The same phenomenon is observed when the plates of mica (Muscovy glass) are suddenly torn asunder; and even when a stick of sealing-wax is broken across; the two surfaces of fracture being in each case positive and negative respectively. Dr. Brewster discovered that the fracture of the unannealed glass tears, called *Prince Rupert's drops*, was attended with the evolution of electrical light, which pervaded the whole drop, so that its form was distinctly visible in the dark. The light appears even when the experiment is made under water.

(216.) There is every reason to presume that electricity is essentially concerned in the processes that are carried on in the living system both of animals and vegetables. In the animal economy more particularly, the operation of this agent is indicated in the processes of secretion, in the actions of the muscles and nerves, and probably, indeed, in all the vital functions. There are several kinds of fish, which are endowed with the power of accumulating large quantities of electricity, which they can discharge at pleasure through conducting bodies that come in contact with them, and thus communicate powerful shocks. This power is possessed in an eminent degree by the torpedo, which is a species of ray; but it is also met with in the Gymnotus electricus, the Silurus electricus, the Trichiurus indicus, and the Tetraodon electricus. But as this, as well as other subjects relating to animal electricity, involve considerations which properly belong to Galvanism, we must defer treating of them until this branch of electrical science is before us.

Chapter XV.

Electricity of the Atmosphere.

(217.) As the subject of atmospheric electricity is more especially a branch of the science of Meteorology, we shall content ourselves, in this place, with a very brief outline of the principal facts relating to it.

(218.) The atmosphere is very generally in an electrical state. This may be ascertained by employing a metallic rod elevated to some height above the ground, and communicating at its lower end, which should be insulated, with an electroscope. In order to collect the electricity of the higher regions of the air, a kite may be raised, in the string of which a slender metallic wire should be interwoven, so as to conduct the electricity. If the electroscope be sufficiently sensible it will usually indicate the prevalence of positive electricity in the atmosphere, the intensity of which increases according as the stratum examined is more elevated. In the ordinary state of the atmosphere its electricity is invariably found to be positive: and is stronger in winter than in summer; and during the day than the night. From the time of sunrise it increases for two or three hours, and then decreases towards the middle of the day, being generally weakest between noon and four o'clock. As the sun declines its intensity is again augmented, till about the time of sunset, after which it diminishes, and continues feeble during the night. In cloudy weather the electrical state is much more uncertain; and when there are several strata of clouds, moving in different directions, it is subject to great and rapid variations, changing sometimes from positive to negative, and back again, in the course of a few minutes. On the first appearance of fog, rain, snow, hail, or sleet, the electricity of the air is generally negative, and often highly so; but it afterwards undergoes frequent transitions to opposite states. On the approach of a thunder-storm these alternations of the electric condition of the air succeed one another with remarkable rapidity. Strong sparks are sent out, in great abundance, from the conductor; and it becomes dangerous to prosecute experiments with it in its insulated state.

(219.) The analogy between the electric spark, and more especially of the explosive discharge of the Leyden jar, with atmospheric lightning and thunder, is too obvious to have escaped notice, even in the early periods of electrical research. It had been observed by Dr. Wall and by Gray, and still more pointedly remarked by the Abbé Nollet. Dr. Franklin was so impressed with the many points of resemblance between lightning and electricity, that he was convinced of their identity, and determined to ascertain by direct experiment the truth of his bold conjecture. A spire which was erecting at Philadelphia he conceived might assist him in this inquiry; but, while waiting for its completion, the sight of a boy's kite, which had been raised for amusement, immediately suggested to him a more ready method of attaining his object. Having constructed a kite by stretching a large silk handkerchief over two sticks in the form of a cross, on the first appearance of an approaching storm, in June 1752, he went out into a field, accompanied by his son, to whom alone he had imparted his design. Having raised his kite, and attached a key to the lower end of the hempen string, he insulated it by fastening it to a post, by means of silk, and waited with intense anxiety for the result. A considerable time elapsed without the apparatus giving any sign of electricity, even although a dense cloud, apparently charged with lightning, had passed over the spot on which they stood. Franklin was just beginning to despair of success, when his attention was caught by the bristling up of some loose fibres on the hempen cord; he immediately presented his knuckle to the key, and received an electric spark. Overcome with the emotion inspired by this decisive evidence of the great discovery he had achieved, he heaved a deep sigh, and conscious of an immortal name, felt that he could have been content if that moment had been his last. The rain now fell in torrents, and wetting the string, rendered it conducting in its whole length; so that electric sparks were now collected from it in great abundance.

It should be noticed, however, that about a month before Franklin had made these successful trials, some philosophers, in particular Dalibard and De Lors, had obtained similar results in France, by following the plan recommended by Franklin. But the glory of the discovery is universally given to Franklin, as it was from his suggestions that the methods of attaining it were originally derived.

(220.) This important discovery was prosecuted with great ardour by philosophers in every part of Europe. The first experimenters incurred considerable risk in their attempts to draw down electricity from the clouds, as was soon proved by the fatal catastrophe, which, on the 6th of August, 1753, befel Professor Richman, of Petersburg, whose name has already been before us, (§ 123.) He had constructed an apparatus for observations on atmospherical electricity, and was attending a meeting of the Academy of Sciences, when the sound of distant thunder caught his ear. He immediately hastened home, taking with him his engraver, Sokolow, in order that he might delineate the appearances that should present themselves. While intent upon examining the electrometer, a large globe of fire flashed from the conducting rod, which was insulated, to the head of Richman, and passing through his body, instantly deprived him of life. A red spot was found on his forehead, where the electricity had entered, his shoe was burst open, and part of his clothes singed. His companion was struck down, and remained senseless for some time; the door-case of the room was split, and the door itself torn off its hinges.

(221.) The protection of buildings from the effects of lightning, is the most important practical application of the theory of electricity. We have only room for a few observations on the principles on which conductors for this purpose should be constructed. They should be formed of metallic rods, pointed at the upper extremity, and placed so as to project a few feet above the highest part of the building they are intended to secure; they should be continued without interruption till they descend into the ground, below the foundation of the house. Copper is preferable to iron as the material for their construction, being less liable to destruction by rust, or by fusion, and possessing also a greater conducting power. The size of the rods should be from half an inch to an inch in diameter, and the point should be gilt, or made of platina, that it may be more effectually preserved from corrosion. An important condition in the protecting conductor is, that no interruption should exist in its continuity from top to bottom: and advantage will result from connecting together by strips of metal all the leaden water pipes, or other considerable masses of metal in or about the building, so as to form one continuous system of conductors, for carrying the electricity by different channels to the ground. The lower end of the conductors should be carried down into the earth till it reaches either water, or at least a moist stratum.

For the protection of ships, chains made of a series of iron rods linked together, are, by their flexibility, most conveniently adapted. They should extend from the highest point of the mast some way into the sea, and the lower part should be removed to some distance from the side of the ship, by a wooden spar or outrigger.

The air of close rooms, vitiated by respiration, is found to be negatively electrified.

Chapter XVI.
Theoretical Views of the Nature of Electricity.

(222.) The preceding history of the phenomena relating to electricity, may prepare us for the discussion of some interesting inquiries concerning the real nature of this powerful and mysterious agent, and the theory of its operation.

The first question that presents itself is with respect to its materiality. Besides the well-known mechanical forces which belong to ordinary ponderable matter, the phenomena of nature exhibit to our view another class of powers, the presence of which, although sufficiently characterised by certain effects, is not attended with any appreciable change in the weight of the bodies with which they are connected. To this class belong heat, light, electricity, and magnetism: each of which, respectively, produces certain changes on material bodies, either of a mechanical or chemical nature, which it is natural to regard as the effects of motion communicated by the impulse of material agents, of so subtile and attenuated a kind, as to elude all detection when we apply to them the tests of gravity or inertia. If we admit heat and light to be material, analogy will lead us to ascribe the same character to electricity and to magnetism, notwithstanding their being imponderable.

(223.) But the materiality of electricity has also been maintained on other grounds. The pungent sensation of the electric spark, the smart blow which accompanies the shock, the vivid line of light which marks its course, the varied sounds which attend its passage through the air, and the irresistible fury with which it bursts asunder the densest textures, all seem to denote the mechanical effects of sudden and powerful impulse; all seem to imply the rushing of a stream of fluid possessed of momentum adequate to produce these energetic motions. Can we refuse to ascribe the character of materiality to that which we not only see and hear, but feel also?

(224.) This argument has been endeavoured to be strengthened by a variety of experiments, from which the communication of impulse in a particular direction with respect to the species of electricity has been inferred. The stream of air, which proceeds from a pointed conductor when electricity is issuing from it, appears as if the air were carried forward along with the electric fluid. The direction of its motion is still more decidedly indicated by the different luminous appearances which accompany the escape of the fluid from, or its reception by, a pointed conductor. (See fig. 23.) We have already had occasion to notice the manner in which this curious fact appears to support the hypothesis of Franklin, implying the singleness of the electric fluid, (§ 98.)

(225.) The following experiment has also been adduced by Cavallo and by Singer, in support of the same opinion. Place on the table of the universal discharger a card bent lengthwise over a round ruler, so as to form a hollow cylindrical groove; or, what is still better, two straight sticks of sealing-wax, laid parallel to each other, so that the junction of their rounded edges may form a groove. In this groove place a pith-ball of about half an inch in diameter, and arrange the wires of the discharger with their points in the direction of the groove, and at four inches from each other, the ball being equally distant from each. On passing a small charge from one wire to the other, the ball will be driven from the positive to the negative wire, and this effect will be constant if the wires terminate in points; but if they are knobbed, the ball frequently vibrates between them, because the influence of the attracting surfaces upon the ball interferes with the regularity of the effect, and often renders the result equivocal.

(226.) The nature and place of the perforation effected in a card by the passage of an electric charge, of which we have already given an account (§ 159), appear to favour the same view of the subject. The following experiment, also, shews that the impulse is communicated most forcibly in the direction from the positive towards the negative conductor. A light float-wheel, the vanes of which are made of card paper, inserted in the circumference of a cork turning freely on a pin passed through its centre as an axle, will be put in motion by presenting to it an electrified point, apparently in consequence of the impulse of the stream of air which issues from the point. Whether the point be positively or negatively electrified, the direction of the motion, as well as of the stream of air, is always the same. But if the wheel be placed on an insulating stem, as in *fig.* 42, and introduced between the pointed

Fig. 42.

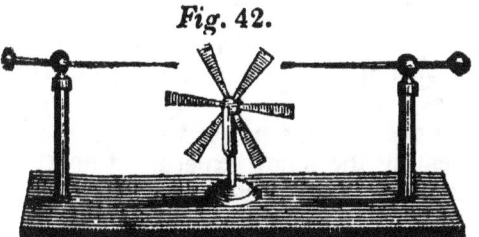

wires of the universal discharger, which are to be placed as accurately as possible opposite to each other, and at the distance of an inch or more from the upper vanes; on connecting one of the wires with the positive, and the other with the negative conductor of an electrical machine, and exciting it, the wheel will move as if impelled by a stream from the positive to the negative wire. On reversing the connections, so that the electricity of each wire is changed, the motion of the wheel will likewise be reversed.

(227.) If a card be placed vertically, by inserting it in a small piece of cork that may form a base of about a quarter of an inch wide for it to stand upon, but so that it may be overthrown by the smallest impulse; and the pointed wires of the universal discharger be brought opposite to each other, and about a quarter of an inch below the upper edge of the card, which stands at an equal distance between them; on connecting the wires with a machine, or with an insulated jar, so as to effect an electric discharge between them, the card will be thrown down, and will constantly fall from the positive, and towards the negative wire.

(228.) The determination of a stream of electrified air in this direction is also rendered very sensible by the motions of smoke or vapour placed in the circuit of the electricity. Thus the flame of a taper placed between two oppositely electrified balls will constantly be blown from the positive to the negative side. *Fig.* 43 represents two hollow metallic

Fig. 43.

balls, about three quarters of an inch in diameter, insulated on separate glass pillars, by which they are supported at a distance of two inches from each other: the upper part of each ball is hollowed into a cup, into which a small piece of phosphorus is to be put. A small candle has its flame situated mid-way between the balls, one of which is connected with the positive, and the other with the negative conductor of the machine. When the balls are electrified, the flame is agitated, and inclining towards the one which is negative, soon heats it sufficiently to set fire to the phosphorus it contains, whilst the positive ball remains perfectly cold, and its phosphorus unmelted. On reversing the connections of the balls with the machine, the phosphorus in the other ball will now be heated and will inflame.

(229.) However plausibly it may have been inferred, from a superficial view of these facts and experiments, that the electric fluid actually possesses momentum, and that it moves in a particular direction, a more rigid analysis of the phenomena will show that they in no degree warrant such an inference. All the mechanical effects that attend the transfer of electricity are ultimately resolvable into the sudden action of a repulsive power exerted among the particles of matter which are situated in the line of its course. They are only particular instances of the fundamental law of electric action, that bodies charged with the same kind of electricity repel one another. Thus the particles of air electrified by a pointed conductor are repelled by that conductor, and repel it also; and, moreover, repel one another: and the same effect takes place whether their electric state be of the positive or negative kind. Hence the stream of air which proceeds from any electrified point is very naturally accounted for. If the quantity of electricity which is transferred is considerable, it excites a more violent commotion among the particles which it influences in its passage. The intense energy of its repulsive action produces the most sudden and forcible expansion of that portion of the air which occupies this line; this air thus expanding must be impelled laterally against the surrounding particles, and must occasion their sudden compression. The evolution of heat and light is the necessary consequence of this violent compression; and the vibratory impulse being propagated in all directions is the source of the sound which attends the electric explosion. The sensation to which the passage of the electric shock through our bodies gives rise, is also, evidently, referable to an impression made on the nerves by the same repulsive action. In all this we can discern no positive proof of the operation of a material agent extraneous to the body itself and acting by mechanical impulse. The materiality of electricity, therefore, must still rest upon a similar foundation with that of heat, or of light.

(230.) If the electric power, or fluid, if we choose to consider it as such, does not act by its mechanical momentum, the arguments in favour of the motion of a single fluid from the positive to the negative body, derived from the appearances of the streams of electric light, (§ 97, 98,) the impulsion of a pith-ball, (§ 225,) the perforation of a card, (§ 159,) the rotation of a windmill, (§ 226,) and the determination of the flame of a taper (§ 228) in one constant direction, must fall to the ground, and can evidently be of no avail in deciding the great question, whether there be two electric fluids or only one. But, still, it is incumbent upon us to inquire upon what principle these remarkable differences in the phenomena of positive and of negative electricity can be accounted for, consistently with either hypothesis.

(231.) On an attentive examination of the phenomena they appear to be explicable on the supposition that the air, or medium through which the electricity passes, is, in the language of one theory, more disposed to admit of the passage of the vitreous than of the resinous electricity; or, to speak consistently with the Franklinean theory, that it is more disposed to receive the electric fluid from a conductor which is charged with it, than to part with it to an undercharged conductor which absorbs it. The consequences of this hypothesis are, that the vitreous electricity meets with less resistance in passing out from a body into the air, and is therefore carried forward more readily and more directly than the resinous electricity. The latter, in consequence of meeting with greater resistance to its exit, is more diffused in the surrounding space.

On the Franklinean theory the same effects will follow with reference to the propulsion of the electric fluid from the positive, and its absorption by the negative body.

(232.) That the peculiarity of the mechanical effects of the different species of electricity depends upon the properties of the air, which is the vehicle of its agency, and not upon any specific power in the agent itself, is shown by a modification of the experiment described in § 159, in which a varnished card, suspended between two conductors, was perforated at the point where it was touched by the negative wire. On repeating the same experiment under the receiver of an air-pump, Mr. Tremery found, that in proportion as the air is exhausted, the place where the card is perforated by the electric shock approaches nearer to the positive wire. When the pressure of the air is reduced to one-half, the hole is at the middle point between the two wires. At every discharge, a flash is seen to pass from each conductor to the place of perforation. The curious appearances presented by the edges of the perforations made in the leaves of a quire of paper, already detailed (§ 160, 161,) are not reconcileable with the supposition of a mechanical impulse acting only in one direction, but indicate the equal repulsive action of both kinds of electricity, when the disturbing influence of the air is withdrawn. It is a confirmation of this hypothesis, respecting the peculiar kind of obstruction which air opposes to the passage of electricity, that other substances have been discovered in which a similar property exists. Mr. Ermann, of Berlin, has found that the flame of alcohol is possessed of a greater conducting power with regard to positive, than to negative electricity. Alkaline soap, on the contrary, conducts negative electricity better than positive; and will, therefore, serve to insulate a feeble degree of the latter, at the same time that it permits the passage of the former.

(233.) It has always been urged as a strong objection to the theory of a single electric fluid, that it necessarily involves the condition of a mutual repulsion among the particles of ordinary matter. See § 52. Before attempting to combat this objection, it will be proper to enter into a somewhat fuller illustration of the position than we have already done; and for this purpose we shall avail ourselves of the assistance of a few diagrams, calculated to aid our conceptions of the forces concerned in the mutual actions of electrified or neutral bodies. For the sake of greater distinctness, we shall suppose the whole of the matter in the body, of which we are studying the actions, to be concentrated in a small space, and we shall represent this matter by a black square. In like manner, we shall suppose that the whole of the electric fluid contained in the same body is condensed into a small space, denoted by a white circle. The mutual actions of the matter or electric fluid in two adjacent bodies, are expressed by lines passing from the one to the other respectively; the attractions being distinguished by unbroken lines, and the repulsions by dotted lines.

(234.) *Fig.* 44 represents a body B in

Fig. 44.

a neutral state of electricity, by which is to be understood, that the quantity of fluid it contains exists in a proportion so exactly adjusted to the quantity of matter, as that its repulsion for a particle F of electricity at any distance, precisely balances the attraction of the matter, for that same particle. While this equilibrium is preserved among the forces which would impel any electric fluid external to the body both from it and towards it, it is evident that the body will neither acquire nor lose electricity, but remain quiescent, whether it be insulated or not.

(235.) The state of the forces operating between two similar neutral bodies is shown in *fig.* 45. Here it

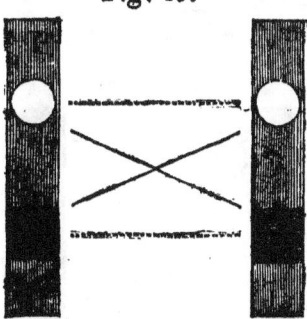

Fig. 45.

follows *from the condition of neutrality, as above defined*, that the two attractive forces, denoted by the two whole lines, are *each of them* equal to the repulsive force between the two fluids, denoted by the upper dotted line. Actuated by these forces only, therefore, the two bodies would attract each other. The addition of a second repulsive force between the two portions of matter, as represented by the lower dotted line, is therefore necessary to account for the state of equilibrium which we find, under these circumstances, really obtains. Some persons have conceived, that by assuming the repulsive force of the electric particles to be double the attractive forces of the same particles for matter, the equilibrium might be explained without having recourse to the mutual repulsion of the particles of matter: forgetting, that such an assumption is incompatible with that of the neutral state of the bodies, which is the condition under which we are now examining them.

(236.) The repulsion of two bodies, each containing twice the quantity of electric fluid requisite for the saturation of their respective matter, is illustrated by *fig.* 46. All the forces represented

Fig. 46.

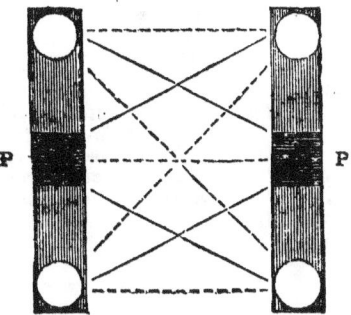

by the lines must, from the hypothesis, be regarded as equal in point of intensity: but the number of repulsive forces is as five, while that of the attractive forces is only as four: the former therefore will prevail.

(237.) Precisely the same result will obtain in the case of two negatively electrified bodies, in which, as represented in *fig.* 47, the quantity of matter

Fig. 47.

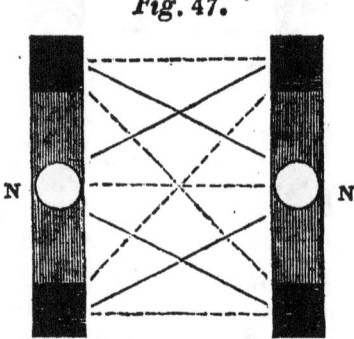

is twice as much as the fluid can saturate. In the former case it was the repulsion between the two portions of fluid which were in excess that destroyed the equilibrium; while in this case the same effect is produced by the mutual repulsion of the unsaturated portions of matter.

(238.) Lastly, we may collect from an examination of *fig.* 48, where a body

Fig. 48.

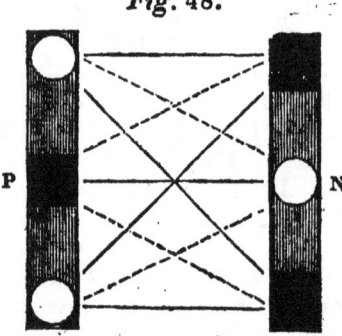

positively electrified is supposed to be placed near one that is negatively electrified, that the ultimate effect will be determined by the attraction between the fluid in excess in the former, and the unsaturated matter in the latter; all the other attractions and repulsions exactly compensating each other.

(239.) It is a great, though a common error to imagine, that the condition assumed by Æpinus, namely, that the particles of matter, when devoid of electricity, repel one another, is in opposition to the law of universal gravitation established by the researches of Newton; for this law applies, in every instance to which inquiry has extended, to matter in its ordinary state, that is, combined with a certain proportion of electric fluid. By supposing, indeed, that the mutual repulsive action between the particles of matter is, by a very small quantity, less than that between the particles of the electric fluid, a small balance would be left in favour of the attraction of neutral bodies for one another, which might constitute the very force which operates under the name of gravitation: and thus both classes of phenomena may be included in the same law.

(240.) An objection has been urged by Biot against the hypothesis of a single fluid, on the ground that it implies an equal degree of attraction between the fluid and every species of matter, whereas in the case of other agents, such as heat and magnetism, the degree of their attraction is very different towards different kinds of matter. This objection does not apply to the hypothesis of the two fluids, for they are assumed as acting independently of any specific attractions for the bodies which contain them: hence their distribution in those bodies follows the same law, whatever be the specific nature of the materials of which the latter are composed.

(241.) We arrive, then, at the conclusion that there is no fact in electricity which cannot be explained on either of the two hypotheses: but to which side the balance of probabilities may incline, when the respective merits and demerits of each are taken into account, remains, perhaps, to be decided more by the taste than the judgment of the inquirer.

ERRATA IN PART I.

Page.	Col.	Line.	
6,	1,	3, *from bottom, omit the line*—"Ice above—13° Fahrenheit."
7,	1,	10, *omit*—"of six inches, that is."
9,	1,	36, *for* "resinous," *read* "vitreous."
ib.	1,	37, *for* "vitreous," *read* "resinous."
20,	1,	1, *for* "silken," *read* "silk."
22,	1,	10, *for* "spheroids," *read* "spheroid."
ib.	2,	10, *from bottom, for* "smaller," *read* "greater."

GALVANISM.

Chapter I.

Origin of Galvanism.

(1.) The term GALVANISM is employed to designate a peculiar form of electric agency, elicited under particular circumstances, and capable of producing certain effects on bodies, not usually resulting from the ordinary modes of excitation. The first notice that we find of any phenomenon referable to this branch of electricity, occurs in a metaphysical work, published in 1767, and entitled, *The General Theory of Pleasures*, by a German writer of the name of Sulzer, who observed, that by applying two metals, one above, and the other below the tongue, and then bringing them into contact, a peculiar taste was perceived. He ascribed this sensation to some vibratory motion, excited by the contact of the metals, and communicated to the nerves of the tongue. Content with this loose and fanciful explanation, Sulzer appears to have pursued the inquiry no farther; and the curious fact he had announced remained for many years unnoticed, until the attention of the philosophic world was drawn to the subject, by the discovery of Galvani. Important discoveries in science seem often to arise from accident; but, on closer examination, it is found that they always imply the exercise of profound thought. As the fertility of the soil is essential to the germination and growth of the seed which the wind may have scattered on its surface, so it is principally from the qualities of mind in the observer that an observation derives its value, and may be made eventually to expand into an important branch of science. This has been remarkably exemplified in the origin of galvanism. Its founder, Galvani, was professor of anatomy at Bologna, and had early distinguished himself by his attainments and his zeal in his profession, and especially by the ardour with which he cultivated comparative anatomy. It happened, in the year 1790, that his wife, being consumptive, was advised to take, as a nutritive article of diet, some soup made of the flesh of frogs. Several of these animals, recently skinned for that purpose, were lying on a table in the laboratory, close to an electrical machine, with which a pupil of the professor was amusing himself in trying experiments. While the machine was in action, he chanced to touch the bare nerve of the leg of one of the frogs with the blade of the knife that he held in his hand; when suddenly the whole limb was thrown into violent convulsions. Galvani was not present when this occurred, but received the account from his lady, who had witnessed, and had been struck with the singularity of the appearance. He lost no time in repeating the experiment, in examining minutely all the circumstances connected with it, and in determining those on which its success depended. He ascertained that the convulsions took place only at the moment when a spark was drawn from the prime conductor, and the knife was at the same time in contact with the nerve of the frog. He next found that other metallic bodies might be substituted for the knife; and very justly inferred that they owed this property of exciting muscular contractions to their being good conductors of electricity.

(2.) Far from being satisfied with having arrived at this conclusion, it only served to stimulate him to the further investigation of this curious subject; and his perseverance was at length rewarded by the discovery, that similar convulsions might be produced in a frog, independently of the electrical machine, by forming a chain of conducting substances between the outside of the muscles of the leg, and the crural nerve. Galvani had previously entertained the idea that the contractions of the muscles of animals were in some way dependent on electricity; and as these new experiments appeared strongly to favour this hypothesis, he with great ingenuity applied it to explain them. He compared the muscle of a living animal to a Leyden phial, charged by the accumulation of electricity on its surface; while he conceived that the nerve belonging to it performed the function of the wire communicating with the interior of the phial, which would, of course, be charged negatively. In this state, whenever a communication was made, by means of a substance of high conducting power, between the surface of the muscle and the nerve, the equilibrium would be instantly restored, and a sudden contraction of the fibres would be the consequence.

(3.) The discoveries of Galvani were no sooner made known to the scientific world, than they excited very general interest; and philosophers in every country in Europe vied with each other in repeating his experiments, in varying them in all possible ways, and in inventing all kinds of hypotheses to account for the phenomena. Some regarded them as the effects of a new and unknown agent, differing altogether from electricity; while others, adopting the views of Galvani, recognised them to be electrical, but attributed them to a peculiar modification of that power, residing in the animal system only, and which they accordingly distinguished by the name of *Animal Electricity*. But the discovery of new facts contributed more and more to multiply and strengthen the analogies between galvanism and electricity: till at length all doubt of the identity of the agent concerned in all these phenomena was removed by the discovery of the *Galvanic*, or *Voltaic Pile*. Whatever share accident may have had in the original discovery of Galvani, it is certain that the invention of the pile, an instrument which has most materially contributed to the extension of our knowledge in this branch of physical science, was purely the result of reasoning. Professor Volta, of Pavia, a name already familiar to electricians,* was led to the discovery of its properties by deep meditation on the developement of electricity at the surface of contact of different metals.† We may justly regard this discovery as forming an important epoch in the history of galvanism: and indeed, since that period, the terms, *Voltaism*, or *Voltaic Electricity*, have often, in honour of this illustrious philosopher, been used to designate that particular form of electrical agency, which is the subject of the present treatise.

Previously to our entering into a detailed exposition of the facts relating to this science, and of the theories which have been proposed for their explanation, it will be necessary to direct our attention to the nature of those arrangements of bodies, which are the sources of galvanic power.

CHAPTER II.

Simple Galvanic Circles.

(4.) THE process usually adopted for obtaining galvanic electricity is to interpose between two plates of different kinds of metal a fluid capable of exerting some chemical action on one of the plates, while it has no action, or at least a different one, on the other plate: and then to establish a communication between the plates at some other part, either by their direct contact with one another, or by the intervention of conducting substances. Let us take, for example, a plate of zinc, Z, and another of copper, C, (*fig.* 1.) and immerse

Fig. 1.

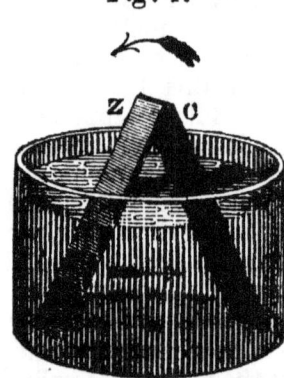

them, to a certain depth only, in diluted sulphuric acid, A, contained in a glass vessel, keeping their lower edges at a little distance from one another: then, inclining them towards each other, let us bring their upper edges, which are out of the fluid, into contact, as represented in the figure. The arrangement we have thus formed constitutes what is called a *galvanic circle*, in its simplest form, of which the three parts, or elements, are zinc, acid, and copper; each of these bodies being in contact with the two others. Under these circumstances it is found that a quantity of electricity is set in motion; a continued current of electric fluid passing from the zinc to the

---

* See *Treatise on Electricity*, § 192, 193.
† Ibid. § 203.

acid—from the acid to the copper—from the copper back again to the zinc—and so on, in a perpetual circuit. Such at least must be the explanation of the phenomena on the hypothesis of Franklin, implying the singleness of the electric fluid. But if the theory of Du Fay, which recognises two different fluids, be adopted, what has just been stated must be understood to refer exclusively to the current of vitreous electricity. Now, according to that theory, every such transfer of electricity consists of an interchange of the two fluids: the current of vitreous electricity just mentioned, must, therefore, necessarily be accompanied by an opposite current of resinous electricity; that is, of one flowing from the zinc to the copper; from the copper to the acid; and from the acid to the zinc. Hence in our future explanations of the phenomena of galvanism, it will be sufficient to express the former of these currents only; provided we bear in mind that the transfer of any quantity of vitreous electricity in a given direction, implies the transfer of an equal quantity of resinous electricity in the opposite direction.

(5.) The same effects will take place, if, instead of allowing the metallic plates to come in direct contact, the communication between them be effected by wires, (as shewn in *fig.* 2.) extending from the

Fig 2.

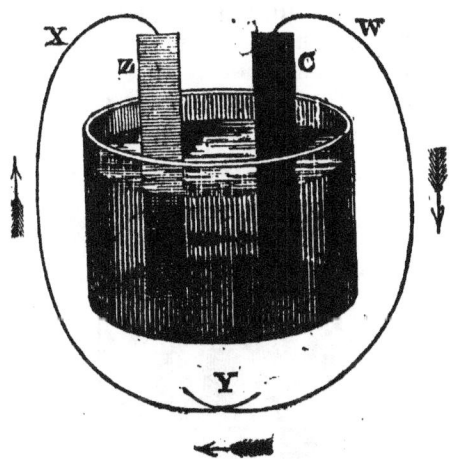

one to the other. The circuit of electricity will thus be lengthened, but the currents will move in the same direction as before; that of the positive electricity being denoted in the figure by the position of the arrows; namely, in the fluid, from the zinc towards the copper; and along the wires, from the copper to the zinc. The completion of the circuit by means of wires, enables us to direct the electric current through such bodies as we may wish to subject to its operation, and at the same time gives us the power of interrupting or renewing at pleasure the communication between the two metallic plates, by merely separating or joining together their remote extremities at Y. When united, the wire W, which proceeds from the copper-plate C, is imparting electricity to the wire X, which touches the zinc plate Z; hence, the former is considered as being in a positive, and the latter in a negative state.

(6.) The electrical effects of the simple apparatus just described are, in general, too feeble to be perceived, unless by very delicate tests. The fact mentioned by Sulzer, and the experiments of Galvani on the muscles of frogs, in their original form, afford, however, examples of the operation of simple galvanic circles. When the tongue is interposed between zinc and copper, the saliva in contact with the metals performs the part of the acid in the experiment above mentioned, and the stream of electricity in its passage from the zinc to the copper, through the substance of the tongue, affects the nerves of that organ, so as to give rise to sensations of taste. In Galvani's experiment, muscular contractions were produced by forming a connection between two different metals, one of which was applied to the nerve, and the other to the muscles of a frog's leg. It is evident that such an arrangement composes a galvanic circle, deriving its activity from the chemical properties of the fluids in those parts of the frog that are in contact with the metals. Although the quantity of electricity set in motion by this slight action, must be supposed to be exceedingly minute, it is yet sufficient, when passing over the exquisitely sensible nerves of the tongue, or through the highly irritable fibres of a frog, to produce a very considerable impression.

(7.) It has even been found possible, by means of a very small galvanic circle of the same simple kind as that which we have described, to produce some of the more energetic effects of galvanism, such as raising the temperature of the wire which conducts it to a red heat. We are indebted to the ingenuity of Dr. Wollaston for the contrivance of an apparatus, which he calls an *elementary galvanic battery*, capable of exhibiting this effect.* He found that a single plate of zinc, of the size of a square inch, when properly mounted, and suspended in dilute sulphuric acid, between two copper plates of similar dimensions, was more than sufficient to ignite a wire of platina, one three-thousandth of an inch in diameter, which formed part of the connection between the two metals.

(8.) It will readily be conceived, that by enlarging the size of the plates, their power will be proportionally increased. The first battery of this kind, on a very large scale, was that constructed by Dr. Hare, professor of chemistry in the university of Philadelphia, and called by him a *Calorimotor*, from its remarkable power of producing heat.† It consisted of sheets of zinc, and of copper, formed into coils, so as to encircle each other, separated only by interstices of a quarter of an inch in width. This construction is shown in *fig.* 3, which exhibits a hori-

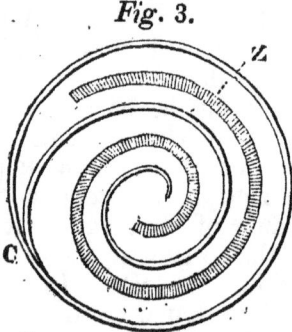

Fig. 3.

zontal section of the plates as they are coiled together: the thick line Z, representing the zinc, and the thinner line C, the copper plate. The zinc sheets were nine inches by six; the copper fourteen by six; more of the latter metal being required; as in every coil it was made to commence within the zinc, and completely to surround it on the outside. Each coil was about two inches and a half in diameter; their number amounted to 80; and by means of a lever they could all be let down at the same moment into as many glass jars, two inches and three quarters diameter inside, and eight inches high, placed so as to receive them, and containing the acid liquor intended to act upon the zinc.

(9.) To the class of simple galvanic circles must also be referred the magnificent battery belonging to the London Institution, and which was constructed under the direction of Mr. Pepys.* It consists of two plates only, the one of zinc, and the other of copper, coiled round a cylinder of wood, and prevented from coming into contact by ropes of horse hair, which is a non-conducting substance, interposed in various places between them. The length of each plate is 60 feet, and its breadth two feet; the total surface being 400 square feet. In order to charge this battery, the whole coil is immersed in a tub containing acid of the proper strength.

CHAPTER III.

Compound Galvanic Circles.

(10.) MANY of the effects of galvanism require for their production the combined influence of a number of plates, arranged so as to form what is termed *a compound galvanic circle*. To this class belongs the galvanic pile, discovered by Volta, and announced by him in a paper which he transmitted, in the year 1800, to the Royal Society. He had been led by theory to conceive that the effect of a single pair of metallic plates might be increased indefinitely by multiplying their number, and disposing them in pairs, with a less perfect conducting substance interposed between each pair. For this purpose he provided an equal number of silver coins, and of pieces of zinc, of the same form and dimensions; and also circular discs of card, soaked in salt water, and of somewhat less diameter than the metallic plates. Of these he formed a pile or column, as shown in *fig.* 4: in which the three sub-

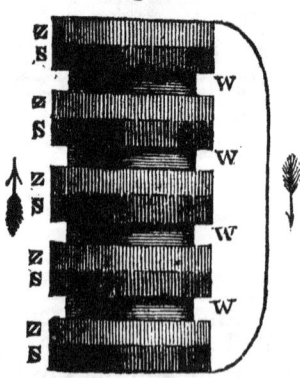

Fig. 4.

stances, silver,† zinc, and wet card, denoted by the letters S, Z, and W, were

---

* See Thomson's *Annals of Philosophy*, vol. vi. p. 209. While these pages were in the press we have sustained an irreparable loss in the death of Dr. Wollaston, a philosopher whose unrivalled acuteness of observation, soundness of judgment, and integrity of mind, directed to the highest objects of science, place his name among the most eminent of its benefactors.

† Silliman's *Journal*, iii. 105, and *Annals of Philosophy*, New Series, i. 330.

* *Philosophical Transactions* for 1823, p. 187.
† Copper might have been used instead of silver, as in the single galvanic circle already described, (§ 4, 5.) with the same effect.

made to succeed one another in the same regular order throughout the series. The efficacy of this combination realized the most sanguine anticipations of the discoverer: it far exceeded in power the single circle already described. If the uppermost disc of metal in the column be touched with the finger of one hand, previously wetted, while a finger of the other hand is applied to the lowermost disc, a distinct shock is felt in the arms, similar to that from a Leyden phial, or still more nearly resembling that from an electrical battery weakly charged. A repetition of shocks is obtained for an indefinite period, whenever the circuit is completed by touching the two ends of the pile with the moistened fingers. The strength of the shock is, as might be expected, greater in proportion to the number of plates of which the pile is composed.

If the pile were raised to any considerable height, it would obviously be in danger of oversetting: this may be prevented by placing the discs between three vertical glass rods, properly varnished, and cemented into two thick pieces of wood, one of which serves as a base, and the other as a cover to the pile. See *fig*. 5.

(11.) Any number of these piles may be combined so as to form a battery, by making a metallic communication between the last plate of the one and the first of the next, and so on; taking care that the order of succession of the plates in the circuit be preserved inviolate, as is shown in *fig*. 6, where the dark

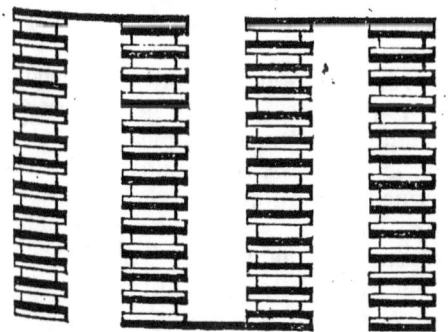

Fig. 6.

lines represent the copper, and the light lines the zinc plates.

(12.) The component parts of the pile may be arranged in a form somewhat different from the preceding, and corresponding more nearly to the elementary galvanic circle in its simplest state already described (§ 4, 5). In this new arrangement the metallic plates, instead of being piled one above the other, are placed side by side in a vertical position, and combined together in pairs, consisting each of one zinc and one copper (or silver) plate, connected at their upper edges by slips of metal, passing from the one to the other. A sufficient number of glasses being provided, and filled with water, or some acid or saline solution, they are to be placed side by side, so as to form a circle. The two plates belonging to each pair are then to be immersed in the fluids contained in two different, but adjoining, glasses; the zinc plate, for instance, in the first glass, and the copper in the second. The plates of the second pair must be immersed, in a similar way, in the second and third glasses; and so on successively throughout the series, taking care to preserve the same order of alternation in the metals. It is evident that by this arrangement, (of which an horizontal section is shown in *fig*. 7, where the dark

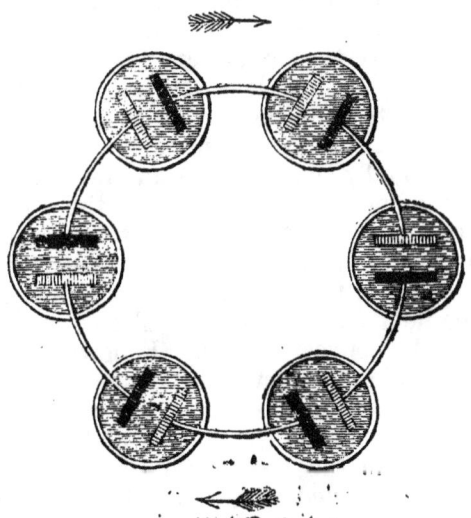

Fig. 7.

lines indicate the copper, and the lighter lines the zinc plates in each pair,) each vessel will contain one plate of zinc and one of copper, which, as they belong to different pairs, are not connected together, except through the medium of the intervening fluid in that particular vessel.

(13.) The first apparatus of this kind was constructed by Volta, who employed for that purpose a circular series of cups, and hence gave it the name of

Couronne de tasses. If the circuit be interrupted at any one point, by removing one or more of the vessels, the instrument is rendered similar in its operation to the pile, and the metallic plates at each end of the series which are not immersed in fluid, may be connected together by means of wires in order to complete the circuit: Such an arrangement is shown in *fig.* 8, where the zinc

Fig. 8.

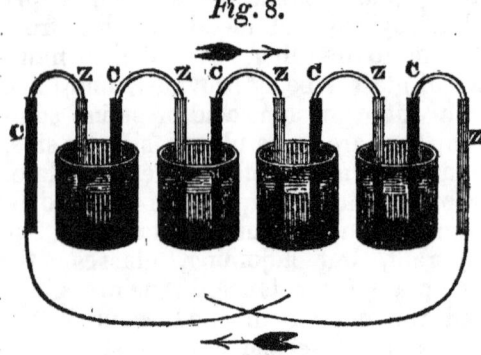

and copper plates are marked respectively with the letters Z and C: and the course of the electric fluid denoted by the arrows.

(14.) It is also to be observed, that in every compound galvanic circle, such as is exemplified in this apparatus, the direction of the electric current is precisely the same as in a simple galvanic circle composed of the same elements. In the present case, where zinc and copper are the metals employed, and the fluid acts upon the former so as to oxidate it, a stream of positive electricity is continually circulating from the zinc to the copper plate contained in the same vessel, through the oxidating fluid which separates them; and is transferred from the copper to the zinc plate contained in the next vessel, along the slip of metal which connects them. Following its course in this manner to the end of the series, we find the electric current passing on from the last copper plate, contained in the last vessel, to the zinc plate connected with it, and thence conveyed along the wires of communication, round to the copper plate at the other end of the series. The direction of this current is shown in the figure by the arrows above and below. It is evident, therefore, that that end of the battery which is terminated by a zinc plate is that from which electricity is given out to the wire, and is, consequently, the **positive end**, or *pole,* as it is called, of the battery. For the same reason, the **opposite end**, or that terminated by the **copper plate**, and which receives the electricity from the wire, is the **negative pole.** The same observations apply to the galvanic pile; the zinc end being the positive, and the copper (or silver) end the negative pole.

(15.) It will be perceived that the denominations of the zinc and copper ends of the pile or compound battery, as being positive and negative, are exactly the reverse of what obtains in the single galvanic circle, where, as we have seen, it is the copper plate which is positive, and the zinc negative, with relation to the communicating wires. But as the direction of the electrical currents is the same in the compound as in the simple circle, this contrariety in the qualities of the poles appears, at first sight, paradoxical. But the difficulty vanishes when we advert to the circumstance, that in the simple galvanic circle the conducting wire communicates directly with that plate which is in contact with the fluid part of the apparatus; while in the compound circle it proceeds, not from the plate immersed in the fluid, but from that which is associated with it, and, therefore, of a different kind. The compound circle reduced to its condition of greatest simplicity would be represented by the following series, consisting of five parts, namely,

copper—zinc—fluid—copper—zinc.

In this arrangement the copper end is negative, and the zinc end positive. By merely removing the two terminal plates,* which, in fact, are no ways concerned in the effect, we bring it to the state of the single circle, consisting simply of

zinc—fluid—copper:

here we find the zinc end negative, and the copper end positive. It is highly necessary to possess clear ideas of this difference, since much ambiguity has arisen from inattention to it in describing experiments, and reasoning upon their results, more especially in the study of electro-magnetism, hereafter to be considered.

(16.) A much more compendious form may be given to a battery constructed on the principle of the *Couronne de tasses,* by employing a trough divided into numerous compartments by partitions, the whole being made of non-conducting materials. This will admit of the plates being brought nearer to each other, and of a much greater number

---

* Volta, in conformity with the theory he had adopted, considered these terminal plates as adding to the galvanic power. But we shall afterwards point out the incorrectness of that theory.

being contained in a given space. The zinc and copper plates are united in pairs, as before, by a slip of metal passing from the one and soldered to the other: each pair being placed so as to enclose a partition between them, and each cell containing a plate of zinc connected with the copper plate of the succeeding cell, and a copper plate joined with the zinc plate in the preceding cell. Such an apparatus is called a *trough battery*, and is represented in *fig.* 9.

Fig. 9.

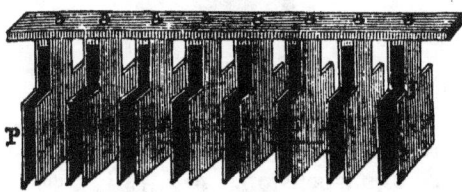
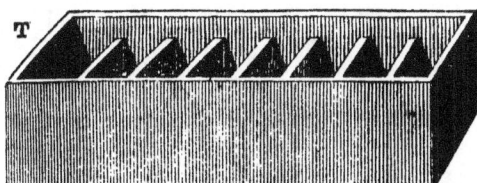

The trough, T, may be made of baked mahogany, with partitions of glass: but it is found more convenient to construct the whole of one material, and Wedgwood ware answers best for this purpose. Each trough is usually fitted up with ten or twelve cells. The plates, P, adapted to them, are connected together by a slip of baked wood, so as to allow of their being let down into the cells, or lifted out, together. A further advantage arises from this construction, that the plates and the fluid being independent of each other, the former may be readily cleaned or replaced, when worn or injured, without disturbing the fluid: and the latter may, in like manner, be removed and changed with the utmost facility. A number of these troughs may be combined with great ease, by connecting together the terminal plates of the adjoining troughs, by slips of copper; taking care, as in the case of the pile, (§ 11.) to preserve throughout the whole series the same order of alternation in the plates, by connecting the zinc end of one battery with the copper end of the next.

The voltaic battery belonging to the Royal Institution, which is of immense power, is constructed on the plan above described, and consists of 200 separate parts, each part composed of ten double plates, and each plate containing thirty-two square inches. The whole number of double plates is 2000, and the whole surface 128,000 square inches.

(17.) A trough battery on another construction was invented by Mr. Cruickshanks, and is represented in *fig.* 10. Plates of zinc and of copper,

Fig. 10.

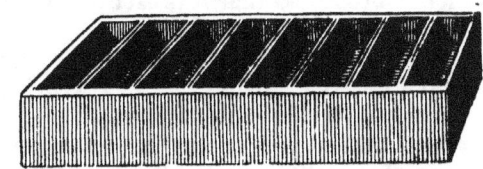

united by their flat surfaces by soldering, are employed to form the partitions themselves, and are fixed into grooves in the sides of a trough of baked wood, which is a bad conductor of electricity, so as to leave sufficient intervals to hold small quantities of fluid. They must, of course, be arranged so that all the zinc surfaces shall be on one side, and all the copper surfaces on the other. The battery is charged by filling the cells with a saline solution, or with dilute acid, and the galvanic circuit completed by bringing the two wires proceeding from the ends of the battery in contact with one another. The section, *fig.* 11,

Fig. 11.

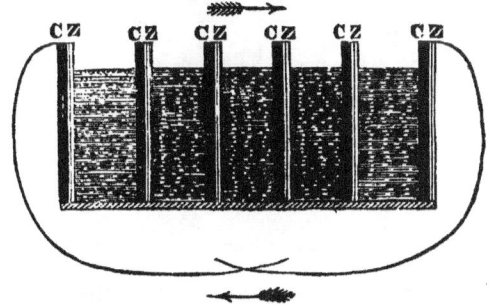

will tend to elucidate the principles of its action. Troughs of this construction, however, are exceedingly liable to get out of order, from the action of the liquid on the wood, which it tends to warp. The plates require to be fixed into the grooves by cement, in order to render them water tight; but this cement is apt to crack from the warping of the wood, and other causes, and the liquid insinuating itself into the fissures, impairs the power of the instrument by destroying the insulation of the cells.

(18.) The power of a battery is considerably increased when both surfaces of each plate of zinc, in contact with the oxidating fluid, are opposed to a surface of copper. In order to accomplish this, it will be necessary to add a second copper plate to each pair, so that every cell may contain one zinc and two copper plates, the former being placed between the latter. This plan, which was suggested by Dr. Wollaston, was adopted by Mr. Children in the construction of a very large battery, in which each plate was six feet long, by two feet eight inches broad, so that it presented thirty-two square feet of surface.*

(19.) An ingenious application of this principle was made by Mr. Hart of Glasgow, in the construction of a galvanic battery, requiring no other material for confining the fluid, than the metals themselves which form the circles. This he accomplished by converting the double copper plates into cells, by adding sides and bottoms, so as to enable them to hold the acidulous fluid into which the zinc plates are immersed. The cells are formed by cutting a sheet of copper into the form shown in *fig.* 12.† They are then folded

Fig 12.

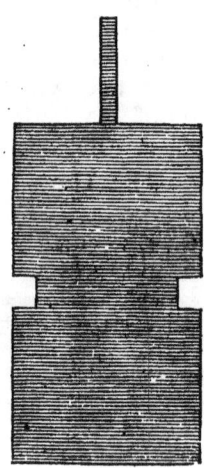

up as seen in *fig.* 13, and the seams

Fig. 13.

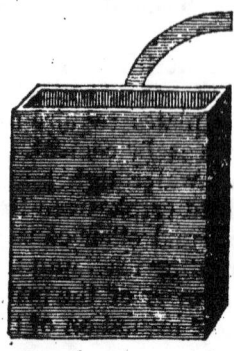

grooved. A drop of tin is run into each lower corner to render the cells perfectly tight. *Fig.* 14 represents the zinc

Fig. 14.

plate, having a piece of screwed brass-wire cast into the top of it for the purpose of suspension. *Fig.* 15 is a section

Fig. 15.

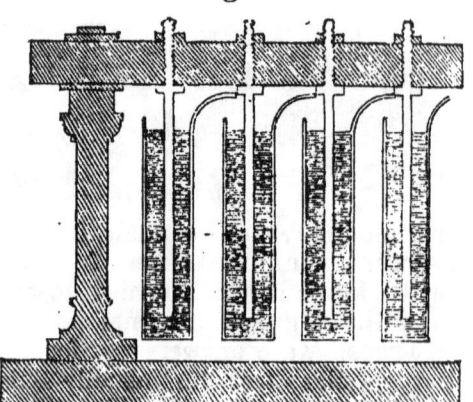

of the battery, showing how the copper tail of the first cell is connected with the zinc plate of the second, and so on. The connexion is rendered perfect by joining them with a drop of solder. Each zinc plate is kept firmly in its place by three small pieces of wood. The whole series is then fixed, by means of screw-nuts fitted on to the brass wires, to a bar of baked wood, previously well varnished. When the battery is to be used, it must be lifted off the frame, and dipped into a wooden trough, lined with lead, containing the acid. It is then placed on the frame and is ready for action. Such a battery, with an equal number of zinc plates, is found to possess considerably greater power than the best batteries of the ordinary construction.*

(20.) Various contrivances have been employed for converting a compound voltaic battery, consisting of a certain number of alternations of plates, into a

---

* *Philosophical Transactions* for 1815, p. 363.
† The engraving fig. 12, is here reduced in its dimensions from the original drawing. It should have been of the size required to form, when folded, the cell represented in fig. 13.

* *Edinburgh Journal of Science*, iv. 19.

battery having a smaller number, or even into one corresponding in principle to the simple battery with a single pair of plates, such as the calorimotor. These changes may be effected by altering the connexions of the plates, and uniting several plates of the same metal together, so that they may act as only one plate; or if the effect of a calorimotor be desired, connecting all the zinc plates together, and also all the copper plates, so that the whole may act only as a single pair.

CHAPTER IV.

Effects of Galvanism.

(21.) THERE are three principal circumstances in which the electricity produced by the voltaic battery differs from that obtained from the ordinary electrical machine; first, the very low degree of intensity in which it exists in the former, when compared with the latter; secondly, the very large quantity of electricity which is set in motion by the voltaic battery; and thirdly, the continuity of the current of voltaic electricity, and its perpetual reproduction, even while this current is tending to restore the equilibrium. The effects of the voltaic pile have been compared by the inventor of that instrument to those of an electric battery of large dimensions, but charged only to a low degree; in which case, as appears from what has already been said on this subject in the Treatise on Electricity, a large quantity of electricity may be contained, with a very small tendency to escape, or, in other words, with a very feeble intensity. The comparison is, in many respects, just; but it fails in regard to the third property we have noticed as belonging to the voltaic apparatus; namely, the continuity of the current arising from its perpetual reproduction and circulation.

However considerable may be the power collected in a highly charged electric battery, the whole of that power is at once expended as soon as the circuit is completed. Its action may, while it lasts, be sufficiently energetic; but it is exerted only for an instant; and, like the destructive operation of lightning, can effect, during its momentary passage, only sudden and violent changes, which it is beyond the power of the experimentalist to regulate or control. On the contrary, the voltaic battery continues, for an indefinite time, to develop and supply vast quantities of electricity, which, far from being lost by returning to their source, circulate in a perpetual stream, and with undimished force. The effects of this continued current on the bodies subjected to its action, will, therefore, be more definite, and will be constantly accumulating; and their amount will, in process of time, be incomparably greater than even those of the ordinary electrical explosion. We shall accordingly find that changes in the composition of bodies are effected by galvanism which can be accomplished by no other means. Hence may be conceived the advantages which have accrued to science from the acquisition of an instrument of such vast power, and admitting of such extensive application in the wide field of chemical research.

It will be convenient to study the effects of galvanism in their relation to the three circumstances which have been noticed as characterizing its operation when contrasted with those of ordinary electricity.

§ 1. *Ordinary Electrical effects resulting from Galvanism.*

(22.) The degree of intensity in which the electricity developed by a single galvanic circle exists, is so extremely low, that its action produces none of the usual phenomena exhibited by the common electrical machine. Even from the largest calorimotor that has yet been constructed, it is not possible to obtain indications of electrical attraction and repulsion, such as are given by the feeblest degree of excitation to a piece of sealing-wax. With a few alternations of plates and interposed fluid, as in the pile or trough battery, electrical indications may be obtained, by means of an ordinary condenser. It is necessary in these experiments to advert to the distinction already pointed out (§ 15.) between single and compound circles as to the denomination of the extremities or poles of the battery. In the compound circles the zinc side is found to be positive and the copper negative. When fifty pairs of plates are employed, a delicate gold-leaf electrometer will be affected, without the aid of the condenser, and with a series of one thousand groups, even pith balls are made to diverge. In order to exhibit these effects, the wire proceeding from one extremity of the battery should be connected with the foot of the electrometer; while the wire proceeding from the opposite extremity is made to touch the cap. It was by means of the revolving doubler (see Electricity, § 195.) that the electrical states of the two ends of the voltaic pile were first ascertained by Messrs. Nicholson and Carlisle.*

(23.) Since the ends of the two wires, which proceed from the two poles of the voltaic battery, are in opposite states of electricity, we might naturally expect that they would attract one another. Such an attraction actually does take place, as Biot found by experiment;† but it does not become sensible, unless a battery composed of a great number of plates is employed.

(24.) The general conclusion deducible from the facts that have now been stated, is that the intensity of the electricity developed by galvanic combinations is increased, according as the number of alternations in the elements which compose them is greater, and that it bears no proportion to the magnitude of their surfaces.

(25.) If the voltaic battery be of sufficient size, its electricity may be transferred to a common electrical battery, which will then become charged to the same degree of intensity. Nothing more is necessary for this purpose than to connect the outer and inner coatings of the electrical battery, respectively, with the two poles of the voltaic battery; when the charge will be instantly communicated to the former. If on removing it from the voltaic battery this electricity be discharged, and the same communications be renewed, a similar charge will again be received; and the same process may be repeated an indefinite number of times. If, instead of removing the electrical battery, we allow it to remain connected with the voltaic battery, a rapid succession of sparks may be obtained from it by connecting a wire with the outer coating, and repeatedly striking the knob of the phial with the other end of the wire. If the series of plates in the voltaic battery consist of three or four hundred alternations, these rapid explosions are so powerful as to ignite the end of the wire, if it be of iron, and to cause it to throw off an abundance of sparks, consisting of small particles of iron in a state of intense combustion. With a series of one thousand, each discharge is attended with a sharp sound, and will burn thin metallic leaves. This is the more remarkable as the same voltaic battery may not have sufficient power to produce these effects by itself, or unconnected with an electrical battery. The shortest possible contact with the voltaic battery is sufficient for giving the whole of the charge which it is capable of communicating. This was apparent in some experiments made by Van Marum and Pfaff with a battery having 137½ square feet of coated surface, and which was charged to the same degree of intensity as the pile with which it was made to communicate, by a contact which did not last for the twentieth part of a second.*

§ 2. *Luminous effects of Galvanism.*

(26.) It is only when the electricity of a voltaic battery possesses a sufficient intensity, that it becomes capable of passing through air. With the calorimotor the intensity is too feeble to enable it to traverse the smallest perceptible interval between metallic conductors, so that they must be brought into actual, or at least apparent, contact, before any sensible effect is produced. In a pile or trough battery, on the other hand, composed of a considerable number of alternations of plates, on bringing together the wires from the opposite poles, the transfer of electricity begins while they are yet at a sensible distance from one another: and as in the case of ordinary electricity, this transit through the air is accompanied by vivid light. The sparks occur every time the contact between the wires is broken, as well as when it is renewed. This phenomenon, which does not take place with the electricity furnished by the ordinary means, is characteristic of voltaic electricity, and is a consequence of its continuous supply. The stream continues to flow, notwithstanding the interruption to the line of circuit, and as long as the conductors remain within the striking distance; and although this happens only for an instant, there is still sufficient time for the appearance of a spark.

(27.) The most splendid exhibition of electric light is that obtained by placing pieces of charcoal, shaped like a pencil,

---

* *Nicholson's Journal*, 4to, iv. 174.
† Biot, *Traité de Physique*, ii. 511.

* *Annales de Chimie*, xl. 289.

at the ends of the two wires in the interrupted circuit, and bringing their points into contact. When the experiment was tried with the powerful battery of the Royal Institution, already noticed (§ 16.), a bright spark passed between the two points of charcoal, when they came within the distance of the thirtieth or fortieth of an inch; and immediately afterwards more than half of each pencil of charcoal, the length of which was one inch, and the diameter one-sixth of an inch, became ignited to whiteness. By withdrawing the points from each other, a constant discharge took place through the heated air, in a space at least equal to four inches, forming an arch of light in the form of a double cone, of considerable breadth, and of the most dazzling brilliancy. This phenomenon is represented in *fig.* 16; in

Fig. 16.

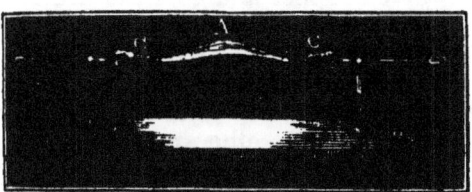

which W, X, are the conducting wires communicating with the ends of the battery; C, C, the pieces of charcoal, and A the luminous arch of electrical light, making the passage of electricity through the air. When any substance was introduced into this arch, it instantly became ignited: platina melted in it, as wax in the flame of a candle: some of the more refractory substances, as quartz, the sapphire, magnesia, and lime, all entered into fusion: fragments of diamond, and points of charcoal and of plumbago quickly disappeared, and seemed converted into vapour, even when the connection was made in highly rarefied air, and apparently without having undergone previous fusion. When the pieces of charcoal were placed in the receiver of an air-pump, in proportion as the air was abstracted, the distance at which the discharge took place increased: and when the height of the mercury in the barometrical gage was only one quarter of an inch, the sparks were nearly half an inch in length; and by then withdrawing the points from each other, the discharge passed through a space of six or seven inches, producing a most brilliant coruscation of purple light. The whole of the charcoal became intensely ignited, and some platina wire attached to it melted with bright scintillations, and fell down in large globules.* A battery of a hundred pair of plates of six inches square will suffice to exhibit these phenomena on a smaller scale. Charcoal, carefully prepared from some of the harder woods, such as beech, lignum vitæ, or box wood, answers best for these experiments. The arched form of the stream of light passing between the two charcoal points is perceptible even when the points are within half an inch of each other.

The light obtained by voltaic electricity in the manner now described exceeds in intensity any other that art can produce. It often exhibits in succession a variety of the prismatic colours; and supplies some of the rays which are deficient in the solar beams. It is so dazzling as to fatigue the eye even by a momentary impression; and it effaces, by its superior lustre, the light of lamps in an apartment otherwise brilliantly illuminated, and which, on the sudden cessation of the galvanic light, appears for a short time as if left in darkness. It is a light which so nearly emulates the brightness of the sun's rays, as to be applicable for the purpose of illuminating objects in a solar microscope; and even with the magic lantern it has been found capable of exhibiting on a large scale, as was done by Mr. W. Allen in his lectures, all the pleasing and endless variations of the kaleidoscope.

(28.) The employment of charcoal in these experiments might lead to a suspicion that the light might, in part at least, arise from combustion; but many circumstances concur to prove that it is quite independent of this cause. During the continuance of the light, although the charcoal be in a state of ignition, yet it suffers but little loss of weight. The light is evolved with equal splendour when the experiment is made in gases that contain no oxygen, such as azote or chlorine, and in which therefore combustion could not be maintained: and it is moreover found that during the ignition, neither the gas nor the charcoal has undergone any chemical change.† Light from voltaic electricity may also be obtained, though with diminished in-

* Davy's *Elements of Chemical Philosophy*, p. 152.
† Children, *Philosophical Transactions* for 1815, p. 369.

tensity, under water, alcohol, ether, oils, and other fluids of inferior conducting power.

§ 3. *Evolution of Heat by Galvanism.*

(29.) The evolution of heat is one of the effects which accompany the action of the voltaic, as well as of the electric battery; but there is a remarkable difference in the circumstances which favour its production in the two cases. In the common electrical apparatus, heat is not sensibly evolved where the electricity moves with perfect freedom, but only when some resistance is opposed to its passage, and when there is a sudden restoration of its equilibrium, accompanied with light and sound. But in the voltaic battery, an elevation of temperature is observed to take place when the circuit remains complete, when no light is evolved, and when the stream of electricity is conducted in the most silent manner. That the mere passage of voltaic electricity through bodies raises their temperature, is proved by making a wire, forming part of the circuit, pass through a known quantity of water, contained in a vessel, with a thermometer immersed in the fluid. The heat acquired by the water soon becomes sensible by the rise in the thermometer, which even attains the boiling point; and the water continues in ebullition as long as the experiment is continued.

(30.) The circulation of voltaic electricity produces an elevation of temperature, not only in that part of the circuit which connects together the poles of the battery, but also in the battery itself, every part of which, both the plates of metal and the fluid in the cells, become heated when the apparatus is in an active state. But the elevation of temperature is found not to be equal throughout the series; and the difference is dependant on causes which have not yet been accurately determined. Mr. John Murray found a gradual increase of temperature in the successive cells from the negative to the positive pole; and when a number of different troughs were joined together, the cells at the extremities of each were less heated than those towards the middle; the maximum of heat was at a part situated nearer to the positive pole; and the temperature gradually diminished in the direction of the negative pole.*

(31.) Ignition, in various degrees, is produced by the passage of voltaic electricity through metallic wires, when their size and length are properly proportioned to the kind of apparatus, and to the quantity of electric fluid they have to convey. Iron wire is in general easy to ignite, and is often fused into globules; and steel wire is made to burn with a rapid and brilliant combustion. A wire of platina, a metal not susceptible of being acted on by the air, may be kept at a red, or even white heat, for an indefinite length of time, by voltaic electricity. As long, indeed, as the battery retains its power, there appears to be no limit to the continual evolution of heat.

(32.) The order in which the different metals are raised to a red heat by the action of galvanism, was ascertained by Mr. Children, with the aid of a very powerful apparatus of his own construction, to be as follows, namely, platina, iron, copper, gold, zinc, silver. Between copper and gold the difference is inconsiderable; and with regard to platina and iron, their relative places in the scale seem to depend upon the temperature acquired. The relations of tin and lead to the other metals could not be ascertained in these experiments, on account of their melting before they could be raised to a red heat. A beautiful illustration of the difference existing in metals as to their capacity of ignition, is obtained by placing in the circuit a wire or chain composed of alternate portions, or links of platina and silver soldered together; it will then be found that the silver links are not sensibly heated, while all those of platina become equally and intensely ignited.

(33.) It would appear that the heat produced by the voltaic battery is more intense than can be excited by any other process. In the experiments detailed by Mr. Children,* the action of his powerful apparatus raised to a red heat, visible in full daylight, the whole of a wire of platina, one tenth of an inch in diameter, and five feet and a half in length. It also effected the fusion of a variety of substances on which the heat of the best wind-furnaces makes no impression.

(34.) When very thin metallic leaves are placed in the electric current of a powerful voltaic battery they take fire, and by continuing the action, may be made to burn with great brilliancy. In

---

* *Edinburgh Philosophical Journal*, xiv. 57.

* In the *Philosophical Transactions* for 1815, p. 368—370.

order to exhibit these effects, the metallic leaves should be suspended to a bent wire proceeding from one extremity of the battery, and then a broad metal plate connected with the opposite extremity should be gradually brought near to them till contact is produced. The brilliancy of the effect is heightened by covering the plate with gilt foil. Gold leaf, thus treated, burns with a vivid white light tinged with blue, and produces a dark purple or brown oxide. Silver leaf gives out a brilliant emerald green light, and leaves an oxide of a dark grey colour. Copper produces a bluish white light, accompanied with red sparks; its oxide is dark brown. Tin exhibits nearly the same phenomena, excepting that its oxide is of a lighter hue. Lead burns with a beautiful purple light; and zinc with a vivid white light, inclining to blue, and fringed with red. For the distinct appearance of these colours, it is necessary that the contacts should be made with a metal, and not with charcoal; for the intense white light emitted by the latter, would overpower the peculiar colours arising from the combustion of the metal.*

(35.) A beautiful effect, noticed by Van Marum, is produced by connecting a slender iron wire with one of the poles of a powerful voltaic battery, and bringing its end in contact with the surface of some mercury connected with the other pole. Vivid combustion takes place both in the mercury and in the wire; giving rise to an abundant emission of sparks, and appearing like a star or sun dispersing thousands of rays on every side. This splendid spectacle may be prolonged at pleasure, by taking care to continue the depression of the iron wire, in proportion as the metallic particles are dispersed by the combustion.

(36.) Inflammable bodies, such as oils, alcohol, ether, and naphtha, are easily inflamed by means of galvanism, when charcoal points in the circuit of the battery are brought near each other on the surface of these fluids; and gunpowder may readily be made to explode under the same circumstances.

(37.) The difference in the operation of voltaic and ordinary electricity is very manifest in their mechanical effects. The forcible separation of the particles of bodies, and destruction of their cohesion, characterize more especially the electrical explosion, in which the fluid appears to force for itself a passage through every obstacle; while the heat which occasionally manifests itself during this sudden effect, seems as if it were merely the effect of the compression and collision of the particles which are thus forcibly impelled. But the elevation of temperature which accompanies the passage of voltaic electricity, on the contrary, appears to be its immediate and direct effect; for the mechanical texture of the substance which conveys the electricity remains unaltered. If electricity in its common form possess any power of igniting bodies, its operation is too transient and momentary to produce any extensive effect; and its tendency is rather to separate and disperse the body into minute fragments, than to unite the particles into globules by fusion. We have seen that charcoal is very readily ignited by galvanism, but it will sustain a strong discharge from an electric battery without any perceptible rise in its temperature; nor is it possible to ignite it by this means. Whether reduced to fine powder, or cut into thin plates, or made to taper to a point, it resists all attempts to raise it to a red heat, or even to impart to it any sensible warmth, though subjected to the action of the most powerful battery that has yet been tried. Even when an apparently continuous stream of electricity, obtained from a large electrical machine, was made to pass through pointed wires coated with spermaceti, no part of the spermaceti was melted.

§ 4. *Electro-Magnetic Effects of Galvanism.*

(38.) We must rank among the more remarkable of the physical effects produced by the transit of voltaic electricity through conducting bodies, the induction of magnetism in iron, and the influence exerted on bodies which possess magnetic properties. But as the study of the connections which subsist between these phenomena implies a previous knowledge of magnetism, and constitutes, indeed, a distinct branch of science, it will be proper to reserve their consideration for a future treatise. It may be as well, however, to remark in this place, that the discovery of the electro-magnetic effects of galvanism have furnished us with the most delicate tests for detecting very minute portions of voltaic electricity, so that many of the results of simple galvanic arrangements,

---

* Singer's *Elements of Electricity*, p. 408.

to be hereafter mentioned, have been obtained by magnetic galvanometers.

§ 5. *Chemical changes effected by Galvanism.*

(39.) In the Treatise on Electricity, some of the chemical changes which result from the operation of this agent in its ordinary form were noticed; and experiments were described in which water, and a few saline bodies were decomposed by a succession of electric discharges from a powerful machine. But the power of galvanism to effect changes in the composition of bodies subjected to its action is incomparably greater; and its application has led to a series of discoveries which constitute a new era in chemistry, and rank among the most brilliant in the annals of physical science.

(40.) The chemical agency of galvanism, unlike its power of eliciting heat, is manifested, not while it is traversing substances of great conducting powers, but, on the contrary, when it meets with impediments to its passage; and it is exerted chiefly on substances, generally fluids, which convey electricity only partially and imperfectly. That we may acquire clear ideas of the connection of the chemical phenomena relating to galvanism, it will be necessary to trace them from their origin, and attend to what takes place in the simplest galvanic circle composed of two dissimilar metals and an interposed fluid.

(41.) If a plate of zinc, and another of copper, be immersed in very dilute sulphuric acid, without touching or communicating with each other, the zinc will be acted upon by the acid; part of the water will be decomposed, its oxygen combining with the zinc and forming oxide of zinc; and its hydrogen will be disengaged in the form of gas from the surface of the zinc plate. The oxide of zinc, in proportion as it is produced, will be dissolved by the acid, thereby forming sulphate of zinc. The plate of copper, which has been immersed in the same fluid, will, during all this time, have undergone no change; the acid, in its diluted state, being incapable of acting upon it. But if, while the above process is going on, the metals be brought into contact, either directly, or by the intervention of some metallic intermedium, the following changes will ensue. In the first place, the oxidation and solution of the zinc will proceed with much greater rapidity and energy than it did before; and in the second place, it will not be accompanied by the evolution of the same quantity of hydrogen gas from the oxidating surface. There will, indeed, be a disengagement of hydrogen from the whole fluid, in quantity exactly corresponding to that of the oxygen derived from the water; but the greater part of this hydrogen will now make its appearance on the surface of the copper plate, whence it will arise in a copious stream of bubbles. But still the copper will itself remain apparently unaffected by this change in the circumstances of the experiment. In process of time, indeed, when a considerable proportion of sulphate of zinc has been dissolved in the fluid, the quantity of disengaged hydrogen is found gradually to diminish, and a thin film, composed partly of metallic zinc and partly of filaments of oxide of zinc, is deposited on the surface of the copper; as soon as this happens the galvanic action ceases.

(42.) If an acid, such as the nitric acid, capable of acting upon the copper, as well as upon the zinc, be employed instead of the sulphuric acid, similar phenomena will take place, with this additional circumstance, that the action of the acid upon the copper will cease the instant the galvanic circuit is completed; and instead of nitrous gas being formed on the surface of the copper, which happens before the circuit is formed, only bubbles of pure hydrogen will make their appearance; and the copper is protected from all further action, the zinc being, as in the former case, oxidated and dissolved with additional energy. It is on this principle that Sir H. Davy has effected the protection of the copper sheeting of ships from the corrosion of sea water, by placing in contact with it pieces of zinc or iron, on which sea water exerts a greater chemical action than on copper. See Phil. Trans. for 1824, p. 151, and 242; and for 1825, p. 328.

(43.) In compound voltaic batteries, the same chemical changes which have been just described as occurring in the simple galvanic circle, take place in each of the portions of fluid intervening in the compartments between the plates.

(44.) The chemical agency of galvanism is exerted in a no less remarkable manner on fluid conductors placed in the circuit between the poles of the battery. Among the simplest of its effects is the resolution of water into its two gaseous elements, oxygen and hydrogen. The discovery of this fact is due to the united researches of the late Mr. Nicholson and of Mr. (now Sir Anthony) Carlisle, and was one of the immediate consequences of the invention of the pile by Volta.

(45.) The most convenient mode of exhibiting the decomposition of water by galvanism is to fill with water a glass tube, (see *fig*. 17.) to each end of which

Fig. 17.

a cork has been fitted so as to confine the water, and to introduce into the tube two metallic wires, by passing one at each end through the cork which closes it, allowing the extremities of the wires, that are in the water, to come so near each other as to be separated by an interval of only a quarter of an inch. The wires being then respectively made to communicate with each of the two poles of a voltaic battery, the following phenomena will ensue. If the wire connected with the positive pole of the battery consists of an oxidable metal, it is rapidly oxidated by the water surrounding it—while at the same time a stream of minute bubbles of hydrogen gas arises from the surface of the other wire, which is in connection with the negative pole. But if we employ wires made of a metal which is not susceptible of oxidation by water, such as gold or platina, gas will be extricated from both the wires, and by means of a proper apparatus may be collected separately. This may be accomplished by taking two glass tubes, or receivers, closed at one end, and filled with water; this fluid is retained by inverting them over a sufficient quantity of water contained in a glass vessel, as is shown in *fig*. 18. Each tube is to be

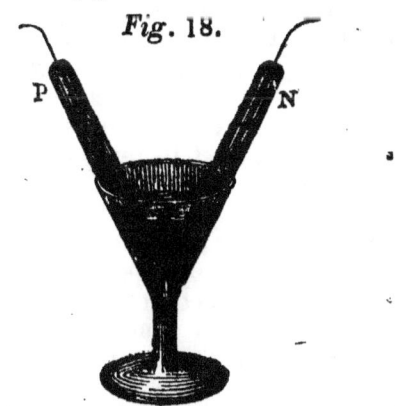

Fig. 18.

furnished with a platina wire, P and N, passed through the closed extremity, and descending within it through its whole length. The open ends are then to be placed as near to each other as their position in the water will allow; and the wires are to be connected respectively with the opposite poles of a voltaic battery. Gas will immediately be seen to rise from each of the wires, but in different quantities. The tube containing the negative wire, N, will be soon filled with hydrogen gas, while the other, which is traversed by the positive wire, P, will, in an equal time, be only half filled with oxygen gas. This arises from the circumstance that the volumes of the two gases, which form water when combined, or which are the products of the decomposition of water, are in the above proportion; that is, the volume of the hydrogen is to that of the oxygen gas as two to one. That the water is in this experiment perfectly resolved into its two elements is satisfactorily proved by mixing together the gases thus obtained, and firing the mixture by the electric spark; when the whole instantly loses its gaseous form, and is reconverted into water.

(46.) If the water employed in the preceding experiment be not perfectly pure, other substances besides oxygen and hydrogen will also make their appearance at the two wires, and the apparent formation of such substances from water was the occasion of great perplexity to the earlier experimentalists. But Sir H. Davy succeeded in proving, by a most masterly train of investigation, that when every precaution is taken to ensure the purity of the water subjected to the operation of galvanism, the only products obtained are the two gaseous elements of water, oxygen, and hydrogen.

(47.) In these experiments it became manifest, that under the influence of voltaic electricity neutral salts, existing in any solution, were decomposed, the acid portion being accumulated around the positive wire, on the same points where the extrication of oxygen took place; while the bases, whether earthy, alkaline, or metallic, were, at the same moment, transferred along with the hydrogen to the negative wire. The best mode of exhibiting these decompositions, is to employ two cups, made either of glass, or, where great precision is requisite, of agate, or of gold; the liquids contained in these cups being connected together by a few fibres of moistened asbestos, and subjected to the action of the voltaic battery. If the liquid contain any soluble saline compound, such as sulphate of soda, or common Glauber's salt, and the operation be continued a sufficient time, the whole of the acid contained in the salt will be found collected in the positive cup, and the whole of the alkali in the negative cup. Nor is any considerable solubility in the body placed in the circuit necessary for its decomposition by galvanism. Two cups made of compact sulphate of lime, containing pure water, were connected together by fibrous sulphate of lime, moistened by pure water, and the voltaic current transmitted through them. After an hour the fluids were accurately examined, when it was found that the negative cup contained a pure and saturated solution of lime, partially covered with a calcareous crust; while the positive cup was filled with a moderately strong solution of sulphuric acid. Sulphate of strontites, and fluate of lime, subjected to the same process, yielded similar results: sulphate of barytes, from its greater insolubility, proved more difficult of decomposition; but the difficulty was at length overcome. The analysis of many mineralogical specimens, of which the composition was much more complicated, was greatly elucidated by the application of voltaic electricity, which effected the extraction of all the acid and alkaline matters they contained.

(48.) For the production of these effects it is immaterial in what part of the fluid line of circuit the decomposable body happens to be situated. This will appear by placing three cups, side by side, in a line (*fig.* 19.), and connecting

Fig. 19.

them together by moistened asbestos. Let a solution of sulphate of potash, or any other neutral salt, be put into the middle cup, and blue infusion of cabbage into the other cups. When these fluids are placed in the circuit of the voltaic battery, by immersing the wires into the fluid in the outer cups, the sulphuric, or other acid, will collect in the positive cup, and render its blue infusion red, while the alkali will pass into the opposite cup, and tinge its blue contents green.

(49.) When metallic solutions are subjected to the decomposing action of galvanism, a deposition of the metal, generally in the form of minute crystals, takes place on the negative wire, and oxide is also deposited around it; while the acid passes over, as before, into the positive cup. This effect takes place with solutions of iron, zinc, and tin, as well as with the more oxidable metals.

(50.) When a solution of nitrate of silver has been placed on the positive side, and distilled water on the negative, the whole of the connecting asbestos becomes covered with a thin metallic film of silver. We have been the more particular in noticing these effects, because, as was before observed (§ 41.), they occur to a greater or less extent in the fluids which occupy the cells of the battery, and have a considerable influence in modifying, and ultimately destroying the power of the instrument.

(51.) Phenomena of a still more extraordinary nature, presented themselves to Sir H. Davy in the further prosecution of these inquiries. It was discovered that the elements of compound bodies were actually conveyed by the influence of the electric current through solutions of substances, on which, under other circumstances, they would have exerted an immediate and powerful chemical action, without any such effect being produced. Acids, for example, may be transmitted from one cup, connected with the negative pole, to another cup on the opposite or positive side, through a portion of fluid in an intermediate cup tinged with any of the vegetable coloured infusions, which are instantly reddened by the presence of an acid, without occasioning the slightest change of colour. The same happens also with alkalies. If three cups be arranged as before, (see *fig.* 19.) and connected with each other in a series by moistened cotton, the middle cup, and also the one next to the positive side of the battery, being filled with blue infusion of cabbage, or of litmus; and the cup next to the negative side containing a solution of sulphate of soda; on the series being placed in the voltaic circuit, a red tinge will soon be perceived in the water of the positive cup, which will become strongly acid. It is evident that the sulphuric acid so transferred must have passed through the fluid in the middle vessel, but without affecting the coloured solution in its passage. By reversing the connections with the poles of the battery, a similar transfer of the alkali will be made; it will be collected in the tinged water of the negative cup, which it will render green; but the intermediate portion of fluid will not, either in this or in the former case, exhibit any trace of the substance which is carried through it by the influence of electricity.

(52.) No union, under similar circumstances, is found to take place, between acids and alkalies, when either of these active chemical principles is transmitted by voltaic electricity through the other, provided the compound which they would form by their union remains soluble; for should the compound be insoluble, the union takes place, and the product, on falling to the bottom of the fluid by its superior gravity, is removed from the line of the electric action. When, for example, sulphuric acid is attempted to be passed through a solution of barytes, or *vice versâ*, barytes through a solution of sulphuric acid, sulphate of barytes is formed, which being insoluble in the fluid, falls down as a precipitate, and being removed from the action of the electric current, proceeds no further in its course. If some basis of mechanical support be provided, whereby this removal from the voltaic influence can be prevented, the transfer may sometimes be continued, notwithstanding the body has assumed a solid form; thus magnesia or lime will pass along moist asbestos, from the positive to the negative sides; but if a vessel of pure water be interposed, they do not reach the negative vessel, but sink to the bottom. In like manner when nitrate of silver was on the positive side, and distilled water on the negative, the silver, as we have already seen, passed along the transmitting fibres of the asbestos, so as to cover it with a thin metallic film.

(53.) When the fluids placed in the same voltaic circuit are connected, not by fluids, but by pieces of metal, such as wires, the changes above described take place in each separate portion of fluid, each alternate metallic surface performing the functions of a positive and negative polarity, according to its place in the circuit of the electric current. Those parts into which the electricity is entering possess properties corresponding to those of the negative wires or poles of the battery; and those which are giving exit to the electricity, act as positive wires. The former will collect around them the several bases of neutral and metallic salts, and the hydrogen of the decomposed water; the latter will collect oxygen, and the compounds in which oxygen predominates, such as the acids.

(54.) The decomposition of the alkalies and of the earths, which crowned this brilliant career of discovery, is, in point of theory, only a particular instance of the general fact above stated, namely, that combustible substances are carried to the negative wire, and oxygen evolved at the positive wire. Various other applications have been made of the voltaic battery to the purposes of chemical decomposition. Sulphuric acid is resolved by its means into oxygen gas and sulphur. Phosphoric acid, in like manner, yields oxygen gas and phosphorus. Ammonia separates into hydrogen and azote, with a small proportion of oxygen. Oils, alcohol, and ether, when acted on by a powerful battery, deposit charcoal, and give off hydrogen, or carburetted hydrogen. But it would be encroaching too far on the province of chemistry to extend our illustrations of this subject to any greater length.

§ 6. *Physiological effects of Galvanism.*

(55.) The action of voltaic, as well as of common electricity, on a living animal is chiefly exerted on the functions of the nervous system. It is shown in the production of sensation, in the excitation of muscular contraction, and in altering the products of secretion.

(56.) If any considerable part of the human body form part of the circuit of a voltaic pile or battery, a separate shock is experienced every time a connection is made with the poles of the apparatus; provided the skin through which the electric current is to pass be sufficiently moist to allow of its being transmitted: for in its usual dry state the cuticle, or outer skin, is scarcely pervious to electricity of such low intensity as that afforded by galvanism. The most effectual method of receiving the whole force of the battery is to wet both hands with water, or what answers still better, with a solution of common salt, and to grasp a silver spoon in each; the circuit is then to be completed by touching one pole of the battery with one spoon, and the opposite pole with the other spoon. Another mode is to plunge a finger of each hand into two separate vessels filled with water, into which the extremities of the two wires from the battery have been immersed. The shock received from the voltaic pile is similar to that resulting from a large electrical battery very weakly charged: and its intensity is greater in proportion to the number of series of elements composing the pile. Twenty pair of plates are generally sufficient to give a shock, which is sometimes felt in the arms: with a hundred pair it extends to the shoulders.

(57.) Independently of the shock felt on the first impression of voltaic electricity communicated from the battery, the continued flow of the current through the body, as long as it forms part of the circuit, is generally accompanied by a continued aching pain. If it pass through any external part deprived of cuticle, it produces a severe smarting or burning sensation, which, if the exposed surface be large, continues to increase till it is scarcely supportable. This painful feeling is experienced if the slightest cut, burn, or excoriation of any kind, happen to be in the path of the electrical current: and it will be excited in these parts, even by a single pair of plates, forming a galvanic combination. It has been remarked by Volta that the pain is of a sharper kind on those sensible parts of the body, included in the circuit, which are on the negative side of the pile; that is, where the electricity flows out from the body, than where it enters: a fact which has also been noticed with regard to the pungency of the common electrical spark.*

(58.) The impression made by voltaic electricity on some of the nerves of the face, when they form part of the circuit, is accompanied by the sensation of a vivid flash of light. The simple application of a piece of zinc and one of silver to the tongue or lips, frequently gives rise, at the moment of the contact of the metals, to this perception of a luminous flash: but the most certain way of obtaining this result is to press a piece of silver as high as possible between the upper lip and the gums, or to insert a silver probe into the nostrils; while, at the same time, a piece of zinc is laid upon the tongue; and then to bring the two metals into contact. Another mode is to introduce some tinfoil within the eyelid, so as to cover part of the globe of the eye, and place a silver spoon in the mouth, which must then be made to communicate with the tinfoil by a wire of sufficient length; or conversely, the tinfoil may be placed upon the tongue, and the rounded end of a silver probe applied to the inner corner of the eye; and the contact established as before. The flash which results from the action of a pile, applied in this way, is very powerful; and if the plates were numerous, the experiment might occasion permanent injury to the sight. This phenomenon is evidently produced by an impression communicated to the retina, or optic nerve, and is analogous to the effect of a blow on the eye, which is well known to occasion the sensation of a bright luminous coruscation, totally independent of the actual presence of light. In like manner the flash from galvanism is felt whether the eyes be open or closed, or whether the experiment be made in day-light or in the dark. If the pupil of the eye be watched by another person when this effect is produced, it will be seen to contract at the moment when the metals are brought into contact. A flash is also perceived at the moment the metals are separated from each other.

(59.) The peculiar taste which is perceived when different metals are applied to different parts of the tongue, and made to touch each other, has already been noticed. It is essential to the success of the experiment, that the surface of the tongue should be moist; for when the tongue is previously wiped very dry, the effect is considerably diminished, and it is not at all perceptible, if the surface is absolutely dry. The quality of the metal laid upon the tongue influences the kind of taste which is communicated; the more oxidable metal giving rise to an acid, and the less oxidable metal to an austere or alkaline taste. Similar differences have been observed by Berzelius, with regard to the sensations excited in the tongue by common electricity, directed in a stream upon that organ, from a pointed conductor; the taste of positive electricity being acid, and that of negative electricity caustic and alkaline. This circumstance would tend to prove that the taste perceived in the galvanic experiment is owing to the actual presence of acids and alkalies, derived from the chemical decomposition of the salts contained in the saliva, by the galvanic

---

* Nicholson's *Journal*, 4to. iv. 180.

action; and that it is not merely the effect of a direct impression of the electric current on the nerves of the tongue.

(60.) When the current of voltaic electricity is made to pass along a nerve distributed to any of the muscles of voluntary motion, these muscles are thrown into violent contractions of a convulsive kind. It was an observation of this kind that led the way, as we have already seen, to the discovery of the galvanic influence. The muscles of a frog are, indeed, peculiarly sensible to this influence, and are therefore the fittest for the exhibition of this phenomenon, with very weak galvanic powers. The susceptibility of some of the animals belonging to the class of *vermes*, is also very great. If a crown piece be laid upon a plate of zinc of larger size, and a living leech be placed upon the silver coin, it will suffer no inconvenience as long as it remains in contact with the silver only; but the moment it has stretched out its head so as to touch the zinc, it suddenly recoils, as if it had experienced a painful shock. An earthworm will also exhibit the same kind of sensitiveness; and the same effect is still more strikingly exhibited by the *nais*, which is an aquatic worm. Humboldt found that the *lernæa*, or water-serpent, and even the *tænia*, *ascaris*, and other species of intestinal worms, had their movements accelerated by the influence of galvanism, which also speedily destroyed their life. Powerful shocks from a voltaic battery are no less immediately fatal to animals, than discharges from an ordinary electric battery.* Small animals are easily killed by discharges which would only produce a temporary stunning effect on larger animals.

(61.) Convulsive movements may be excited by galvanism in the muscles of an animal, after its death, as long as they retain their contractility. These effects become exceedingly striking, when large animals are made the subjects of experiment, and when powerful batteries are employed. Thus if two wires, connected with the poles of a battery of a hundred plates, be inserted into the ears of an ox, or sheep, when the head is removed from the body of the animal recently killed, very strong actions will be excited in the muscles of the face every time the circuit is completed. The convulsions are so general, as often to impress the spectator with a belief that the animal has been restored to the power of sensation, and that he is enduring the most cruel sufferings. The eyes are seen to open and shut spontaneously, they roll in the sockets as if again endued with vision; the pupils are at the same time widely dilated. The nostrils vibrate as in the act of smelling; and the movements of mastication are imitated by the jaws. The struggles of the limbs of a horse galvanised, soon after it has been killed, are so powerful as to require the strength of several persons to restrain them.

(62.) It is needless to enter into the details of experiments of a similar kind performed in hospitals on limbs removed by amputation; or on the bodies of criminals soon after their execution. A great number of these are stated to have been made at Turin, on the victims of the guillotine; and in this country, Aldini, by operating with a considerable number of plates on the body of a criminal executed at Newgate, produced effects very similar to those already described in the sheep and ox; but which were necessarily of a more impressive character, from their conveying the more terrific expressions of human passion and of human agony.

(63.) Muscles whose actions, like those of the heart, are not under the guidance of the will, are less easily affected by galvanism than the muscles of voluntary motion. But Fowler, Vassali, Humboldt, Nysten, and others, have sufficiently proved that even these muscles may, by the proper application of this power, be made to contract.

(64.) The most curious and hitherto unexplained of the physiological effects of galvanism, are those on the functions of secretion, especially on that of the gastric juice, a fluid which is essentially subservient to the process of digestion. But these topics appertain more to physiology than to the subject of the present treatise.

Chapter V.

Theory of Galvanism.

(65.) The various attempts which have at different times been made to explain the phenomena of galvanism, by the application of the laws which are known to govern those of ordinary electricity, have on the whole been attended with very indifferent success; and the theory

---

* See Treatise on Electricity. § 182.

of this science remains, even at the present day, involved in considerable uncertainty and obscurity. No very distinct or satisfactory account has yet been given of the nature of that force, which originally disturbs the electrical condition of the different parts of the voltaic apparatus, and constitutes the primary source of galvanic power. It was long the prevailing hypothesis, that this force was the same with that which gives rise to the developement of electricity during the contact of dissimilar metals; a fact, the principal circumstances attending which have been stated in the treatise on Electricity. (§ 203.) But in proportion as a more extensive acquaintance with the phenomena afforded the means of a more accurate analysis, the insufficiency of this, which was termed the *Electrical Theory*, became more apparent; and it is now fully established, that the primary agent in the evolution of electricity, is the force of chemical attraction. This latter view of the subject, has led to what may be called the *Chemical Theory of Galvanism*.

(66.) Every scientific theory must have for its basis some general fact, comprehending a multitude of subordinate phenomena, which are its more or less direct consequences. The chemical theory of galvanism assumes the following as the most general fact in that science: namely, that chemical action, occurring between a fluid and a solid body, is always accompanied by the disturbance of electric equilibrium; in consequence of which a certain quantity of electricity is developed, or, in other words, converted from a latent into an active state. So intimate, indeed, is the connection between the electrical and the chemical changes, that the chemical action can proceed only to a certain extent, unless the electrical equilibrium which has been disturbed be again restored. The oxidation of metallic bodies (that is, their combination with oxygen) is more especially accompanied by the developement of large quantities of electricity. Thus it has been ascertained, that when a plate of zinc is chemically acted upon by dilute sulphuric acid, which produces first oxide, and then sulphate of zinc, the metal becomes negatively electrified, while the liquid is in the same degree positively electrified. This fact, when stated conformably to the hypothesis of Franklin, implies the abstraction of the electric fluid from the zinc, and its transference to the liquid product of the combination: but, when translated into the language of the hypothesis of a double fluid, must be understood as the separation of the two electricities by the chemical action, and the determination of the resinous or negative electricity in the direction of the zinc, and of the vitreous or positive electricity in the direction of the oxidating liquid. In order to avoid perplexity, however, we shall continue to adhere to the simpler of these hypotheses; and advert only to the conditions and movements of positive electricity. (§ 4.)

(67.) That two conducting bodies, such as zinc and acid, thus remain, the one in a negative, and the other in a positive electrical state, notwithstanding their being in contact, is known to us as a matter of fact; but it is a fact which is not explicable by any of the laws of ordinary electrical phenomena, or, in other words, it is not reducible to any other more general fact. We must for the present, therefore, be content to leave it as a subject of future inquiry, to determine to what peculiarity in the circumstances attending the changes of chemical composition it is owing, that the electric equilibrium is permanently disturbed, and what is the unknown obstacle that prevents its restoration. A similar difficulty occurring in the case of the electricity produced by contact, has been noticed in the treatise on Electricity. (§ 204.)

(68.) As long as the chemical action proceeds, the transfer of electricity from the metal to the fluid continues; but the rapidity of the process is checked by the circumstance, that as soon as the quantity transferred has accumulated so as to reach a certain degree of intensity, which is generally exceedingly low, all action ceases, the chemical affinities being balanced by an opposing electrical force. But in consequence of the gradual absorption of electricity by the metal from surrounding bodies, and the gradual dissipation of the superabundant electricity of the fluid, this state is never reached; or, if attained, does not long subsist: and the chemical affinities continue to produce their effects, though more slowly than if their operation were uncontrouled by the electrical force. But if, on the other hand, by the interposition of good conductors, a ready passage be afforded for the electricity from the fluid, where it is accumulated, to the metal where it is deficient, then the obstacle to the further exertion of the chemical affinities between these two bodies will be removed, and the action will now proceed with much greater energy. This is precisely what is accomplished by galvanic combinations. Some metal, such as copper, silver, gold, or platina, not susceptible of oxidation by the fluid employed, is applied to this fluid, collects from it the redundant electricity, and then being brought into contact with the zinc, or metal acted upon by the fluid, communicates to it this electricity, and thus continually restores the electric equilibrium, the very instant after it has been disturbed. We find, accordingly, that under these circumstances, that is, whenever the galvanic circuit is completed, the oxidation of the zinc proceeds with renewed activity; but ceases, or at least takes place more slowly, whenever this circuit is interrupted.

(69.) In order to take a more comprehensive view of the subject, we may state the following as the conditions that are essential to galvanic action. First, the presence of three elements is required, which we shall designate by the letters A, Z, and C. Between the two first of these, A and Z, some chemical affinity must exist, adequate to produce combination and developement of electricity; while the same action, or at least the same degree of that action, is not exerted between the third element C, and either of the former. Secondly, it is necessary that one of the two first bodies, which we shall suppose to be Z, be a solid,* and that it possess a high degree of conducting power with regard to electricity. As it is a general law in chemistry that no chemical action can take place between two bodies, unless one of these bodies be in a fluid state, it follows that as Z is a solid, so A must be a fluid body; on the other hand, the body C may be either solid or fluid. Thirdly, it is requisite that all the three bodies be in mutual contact, so as to compose a kind of circular arrangement, as is represented in *fig* 20. If all these conditions be fulfilled, it is found that a continued stream or current of electricity will circulate in a determinate direction through the bodies thus placed, as long as the chemical action continues. If the bodies Z, A, and C, be respec-

Fig. 20.

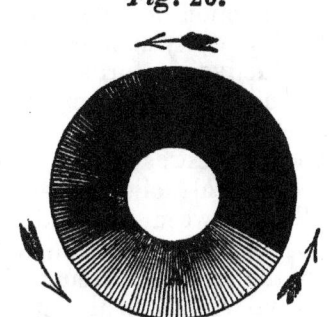

tively zinc, acid, and copper, the surface of contact between Z and A will be that at which the chemical action and consequent developement of electricity takes place; for C may be considered as acting merely the part of a conductor of that electricity between A and Z; and the current will circulate in the direction denoted in the figure by the arrows, that is, from A to C, and thence to Z.

(70.) The absolute quantity of electricity which is thus developed, and made to circulate, will depend upon a variety of circumstances, such as the extent of the surfaces in chemical action, the facilities afforded to its transmission, &c.,—causes the operation of which we shall afterwards have occasion to examine. But its degree of intensity, or *tension* as it is often termed, will be regulated by other causes, and more especially by the energy of the chemical action. In a single galvanic circle, however, it is necessarily very low, being limited by the nature of the process to which it owes its origin, and to which it is in some respects opposed. It may be much increased, however, by combining together the power of a number of circles, as is done in the pile and voltaic battery. Taking the common trough battery as an example, and tracing the several steps of the process, we shall find that the electricity which the liquid in the first cell has acquired from the first plate of zinc exposed to its action, is taken up by the copper plate belonging to the second pair, and transferred to the second zinc plate, with which it is connected. This second plate of zinc, having thus acquired a larger portion of electricity than its natural share, is capable of supporting a more intense chemical action than it would otherwise have done; and hence it communicates a larger quantity of electricity to the fluid in the second cell. This increased quantity is

---

* Sir H. Davy has shown that chemical action taking place between two fluids, although intense, is not attended with the disturbance of the electric equilibrium. *Philosophical Transactions* for 1826, p. 399, 400.

again transmitted to the next pair of plates, and renders the third zinc plate capable of maintaining a still more powerful chemical action than the preceding plate; and thus every succeeding alternation is productive of a further increase, both in the quantity and intensity of the electricity developed.

(71.) The simplest cases are those in which no chemical action whatever is exerted either between the fluid A and the body C, or between C and Z; and the force of the electric current will then be proportional simply to the energy of the chemical action taking place between A and Z. But either A and C, or C and Z, may also have some chemical action on one another; and it will depend on the nature of that action whether the electric force to which it gives rise opposes or concurs with the force resulting from the action between A and Z. If the two actions be of the same kind, as, for example, if they should both be oxidating actions, the electric forces resulting from them will be in opposition to each other; for while the one is impelling the current from Z to A, the others will tend to impel it from C to A, or from Z to C, that is, in a contrary direction. The effective electromotive force will, in all these cases, be equal to the difference between the two that are thus opposed to each other. On the other hand, if the chemical actions between A and C, or between Z and C, should happen to be of an opposite kind, with regard to their electrical tendencies, to that between Z and A, they will communicate to the developed electricity an impulse in the same direction, and the resulting electromotive force will be equal to the sum of the conspiring forces.

(72.) We have seen that the third element C may be either a solid or a fluid body, and we may therefore distinguish galvanic circles into two kinds, according as C has the one or the other of these two forms. In the first, the circle is composed of two solids and one fluid; in the second, of one solid and two fluids. Of the solid elements capable of forming galvanic combinations, the most efficacious are the metals, and charcoal. Of fluid elements, those which exert a powerful chemical action upon the former, such as the mineral acids, alkaline solutions, sulphurets, solutions of neutral salts, and water containing oxygen gas, or atmospheric air. The energy of the galvanic power will depend altogether upon that of the chemical action, and can never be excited when the latter condition is wanting. Thus silver and gold evolve no galvanic influence when in contact with pure water, which is incapable of acting chemically upon either of these metals; but the addition of nitric acid, or any other fluid decomposable by silver, to the water, immediately renders this combination of elements an active galvanic circle.

(73.) With regard to the direction given to the electrical current by the chemical action of two bodies, we may lay it down as a general rule, to which there are but few exceptions, that the electricity is determined from the solid to the fluid which acts upon it chemically. This we have already seen exemplified in the instance so frequently referred to of the ternary arrangement of zinc, acid, and copper. Another, and very common mode of expressing the same fact is, to say that the zinc is rendered positive with regard to the copper, and, *vice versâ*, the copper negative with reference to the zinc. In this sense, that is with relation to the action of acids and other oxidating fluids, every oxidable metal is positive with regard to a metal which is oxidable in a less degree.

In order to determine beforehand the effect of any combination of two metals in a galvanic circle with any of the acids, it will be convenient, therefore, to arrange the metals in the order of their oxidability. With this view the following catalogue has been given by Sir Humphry Davy:* viz.

Potassium and its amalgams.
Barium and its amalgams.
Amalgam of zinc.
Zinc.
Cadmium.
Tin.
Iron.
Bismuth.
Antimony (?).
Lead.
Copper.
Silver.
Palladium.
Tellurium.
Gold.
Charcoal.
Platina.
Iridium.
Rhodium.

(74.) In a ternary galvanic arrangement with acids, then, each metal in the above list is positive to all those which

* *Philosophical Transactions* for 1826, p. 408.

follow it; and the more so in proportion as the two metals are more distant from each other in the scale. Thus zinc and iron will compose a weaker circle than zinc and silver; and zinc and platina will form one of still greater power. It may be observed, however, that the precise order in which the metals stand in such a scale as the above, must be understood as only strictly true with relation to the particular acid employed, and even to the particular degree of dilution that has been given to the acid. For we find slight variations in the order of relation of the metals with different acids, or even with the same acid in different states of concentration.

(75.) When alkaline solutions are employed as the fluid agent, instead of acids, the same general order is observed in the metals, with regard to their mutual electrical relations. The principal exception is with regard to iron, which is here found to occupy a place intermediate between copper and silver. Thus a combination of iron and copper will, by immersion in an acid, form a circle in which the electricity will be determined from the iron to the acid, thence to the copper, and thence to the iron; that is to say, the iron will be positive with regard to the copper. But if the same combination of iron and copper be acted upon by an alkaline solution,* and more especially by ammonia, the iron is negative with regard to the copper; for here the chemical action of the fluid upon the copper is stronger than upon the iron, and the electricity is therefore determined to the fluid from the copper, and not from the iron as in the former case. The same results are obtained when tin is employed in conjunction with copper, and with ammonia.†

(76.) With solutions of hydro-sulphurets, the several metals stand also nearly in the same order, as to their electrical relations, as with acids—with a few exceptions, however, as will appear from the following catalogue, given by Sir H. Davy:—

    Zinc.
    Tin.
    Copper.
    Iron.
    Bismuth.
    Silver.
    Platina.
    Palladium.

---

* Davy, *Elements of Chemical Philosophy*, p. 148.
† De la Rive, *Annales de Chimie*, xxxvii, 232.

    Gold.
    Charcoal.

We may observe, that here also copper is positive with regard to iron; so that when these two metals form a circle with a solution of hydro-sulphuret, the electrical current is in an opposite direction to what it is when the same combination of metals is plunged in acids.

(77.) It need hardly be observed, that every thing that has been stated with regard to single galvanic circles applies also to compound circles, whether in the form of the pile, or the trough battery, composed of the same elementary parts.

(78.) We have next to consider the second class of galvanic circles; those, namely, which are composed of a single solid and two fluid elements.

The arrangement assumed in this case by the three elements of the circle, may be represented by the same diagram as before, *fig.* 20. Z will then denote the solid; A the acting fluid, and C the conducting fluid. As there is a necessity for separating the two fluids, they may be contained in separate vessels, and be made to communicate by means of a bent tube, inverted like a syphon, full of some conducting liquid, and passing over from the one to the other of the two fluids. Sir H. Davy uses, in many of his experiments, fibres of moistened asbestos in place of the tube, for establishing a communication between the fluids. Two plates of the same metal are then to be immersed in the fluids, and made to communicate by wires, or slips of the same metal.

(79.) Sir H. Davy has distinguished three different kinds of circles of the second class.*

The first and most feeble is composed of single metallic plates, arranged in such a manner, that two of their surfaces are in contact with different fluids, one capable, and the other incapable, of oxidating the metal. Zinc, acid, and water, occupying the situations of Z, A, and C, in the diagram, may be taken as an example; and it will be seen that the only difference between this arrangement and those of the former class, consists in the substitution in the circle of water for copper; but the function of each of these parts is essentially the same, namely, that of simply conducting electricity between the other

---

* *Philosophical Transactions* for 1801, p. 398.

two elements. As the conducting power of fluids, however, is much inferior to that of metals, the electrical indications will be more feeble than in circles of the first class; and, indeed, will scarcely be sensible unless we employ the more easily oxidable metals, such as tin and zinc. But powerful effects may be obtained by combining a number of such circles in a pile or battery. For constructing an instrument of the former kind, Sir H. Davy directs pieces of polished tin, about an inch square and one-twentieth of an inch thick, to be piled up with woollen cloths of the same size, moistened some in water, and some in dilute nitric acid, in the following order,—tin, acid, water, and so on. It is proper to observe the precaution of placing the cloth moistened with acid underneath the one which is moistened with water; for, as the acid is specifically heavier than the water, little or no mixture of fluid will then take place. Twenty such alternations will produce a battery capable of acting weakly on the organs of sense, and of slowly decomposing water. When zinc is the metal used, it is necessary, on account of its rapid oxidation in water containing atmospheric air, to use three cloths; the first moistened with a weak solution of hydro-sulphuret of potash, which has no power of acting upon zinc, and which prevents it from being acted upon by the water; the second moistened with a solution of sulphate of potash, of greater specific gravity than the solution of hydro-sulphuret; and the third wetted with an oxidating fluid, such as an acid, specifically heavier than either of the solutions. In this case, if, proceeding upwards, the order be as follows — zinc, — oxidating solution,—solution of sulphate of potash,—solution of hydro-sulphuret of potash, very little mixture of the fluids, or chemical action between them will take place; and an alternation of twelve series of this kind, forms a battery capable of producing sensible galvanic effects. The direction of the electrical current is, as usual, from the zinc to the oxidating fluid.

(80.) It has often been remarked that porter drank out of a pewter pot has a brisker taste than when taken out of a glass. Professor Robison ascribed this to the influence of galvanism, arising from the circle formed by the metal and two different fluids. He considered that, in the act of drinking, one side of the pewter pot is exposed to the action of the saliva which moistens the lip, while the other side of the metal is touched by the porter; the circle being completed when the latter fluid comes in contact with the tongue.

(81.) The second kind of galvanic combinations with a single metal, consists of a series of plates composed of a metal capable of being acted upon by sulphuretted hydrogen, in contact with solutions of hydrosulphurets on the one side, and water on the other, placed in a regular order of alternation. Under these circumstances, a current of electricity is produced, the direction of which is the reverse of what it is in the former case, the surface of the metallic plate in contact with the solution of sulphur being positive, while that in contact with acid is negative. Eight series will produce sensible effects. Copper, silver, and lead are each capable of forming this combination; their comparative activity being in the order in which they are here enumerated, that is, copper the most, and lead the least.*

(82.) A familiar instance of the operation of galvanism in promoting the combination of sulphur with silver, occurs in the employment of a silver spoon in eating the yolk of an egg; a galvanic circle of the second kind being formed by the yolk, which contains sulphur, the silver spoon, and the saliva of the tongue.

(83.) The third kind of combinations unite the power of the two former, and consist of a single metal, acted upon on one side by an acid, and on the other side by the hydro-sulphurets. Copper, silver, or lead may here be employed, and the order of their powers is the same as in the preceding instance. The pile may be constructed in the same manner as the pile with zinc in the first kind of combination; the cloths moistened with acid being separated from those moistened with solution of hydrosulphuret by an intermediate cloth soaked in solution of sulphate of potash. Three plates of copper, or silver, arranged in this manner, in proper order, produce sensible effects; and a pile composed of twelve or thirteen series is capable of giving weak shocks and of rapidly decomposing water. The current of electricity is determined as in the two former cases.

(84.) Greater permanency may be

---

* *Philosophical Transactions* for 1801, p. 400.

given to the effects of these combinations of a single metal with two fluids, by a disposition of the plates similar to the trough of Cruickshanks, with partitions alternately of metal and of horn or glass; and with the cells filled alternately with the different solutions, according to the kind of combination employed; these fluids being connected in pairs with each other, by slips of moistened cloth, carried over the nonconducting plates.

(85.) Efficient galvanic circles may also be formed with a single metal and with the same fluid solvent, (an acid, for example,) provided the action of the latter is different on the two sides of the metal, by being of different degrees of strength. Thus, if one of the branches of a tube, bent in the form of a V, contain concentrated sulphuric acid, while the same acid in a diluted state occupies the other branch, in which case the two fluids will, on account of the difference in their specific gravities, remain without mixing with each other; and two portions of the same metal, zinc for instance, be then immersed in these fluids, and made to communicate with each other, galvanic electricity will be evolved, and determined from the metal to the diluted acid, in consequence of the action of this portion of acid upon the zinc being greater than that of the concentrated acid. But with those metals, which are more acted upon by the latter than by the former, the influence of the concentrated acid will preponderate, and the current will be determined in an opposite direction. In like manner it has been observed, that two solutions of common salt, the one concentrated, the other diluted, form a galvanic circle with copper; that metal being more acted upon by the latter than by the former, became negative to the one and positive to the other.*

(86.) The application of these principles will explain a variety of apparently anomalous facts, which are continually presenting themselves in the course of experimental researches. Sir H. Davy observed, for instance, that when two pieces of the same polished copper were introduced at the same moment into the same solution of hydro-sulphuret of potash, there was, as might be expected, no action; but if they were introduced in succession, there was a distinct, and often, if the interval of time was considerable, a violent electrical effect; the piece of metal first plunged in being negative with relation to the other. This is owing to the rapid formation at the surface of contact of sulphuret of copper, which, by its presence, prevents, or at least diminishes, the further action of the fluid; the clean surface of the plate last introduced is therefore attacked comparatively with greater force, and determines a galvanic effect.* Many singular and apparently capricious changes of electric states occur in these and other experiments of the same kind, whenever new substances are produced by the chemical action, which at first adhere to the metal, but are liable to be detached in smaller or larger portions, and thus occasion sudden alterations in the conditions of the galvanic elements.

(87.) Having thus seen how, under certain circumstances, it is possible to form various galvanic combinations with a single metal and a single fluid, it remains for us to notice the attempts that have been made to produce the same effect without the aid of any metallic substance, or even of charcoal. Lagrave announced that by placing upon each other alternate layers of muscle and of brain, from a human body, with pieces of moistened cloth or leather interposed, he formed a pile which produced galvanic effects.† Dr. Baconio, of Milan, composed a galvanic pile entirely of vegetable substances: namely, discs of red beet-root, two inches in diameter; and discs of walnut-tree, of the same size, divested of their resin by digestion in a solution of cream of tartar in vinegar. With a pile so constructed, and with a leaf of scurvy-grass as a conductor, he is said to have excited galvanic convulsions in a frog.‡ Aldini also succeeded in producing the same effect without the intervention of any metallic substance; sometimes by bringing into contact the nerve of one animal with the muscle of another, and at other times by employing the nerves and muscles of the same animal. In some of his experiments the most powerful contractions were excited, by bringing the parts of a warm-blooded animal into contact with those of a cold-blooded animal. On introducing, for

---

* Becquerel, *Annales de Chimie et de Physique*, xxxv. 120.

* *Philosophical Transactions* for 1826, p. 393.
† *Journal de Physique*, lvi. 235; and Nicholson's *Journal*, v. 62.
‡ Nicholson's *Journal*, xviii. 159.

example, into one of the ears of an ox recently killed a finger of one hand, moistened with a solution of salt, and holding in the other hand a prepared frog, when the spine of the frog was made to touch the tongue of the ox, convulsions took place in the limb of the frog. In like manner, when he held a prepared frog by one hand, moistened with solution of salt, and applied the crural nerves of the animal to the tip of his own tongue, convulsions were produced.* Many of these experiments were made in presence of the members of a commission of inquiry appointed by the French Institute: and they have since been repeated with success in London, at the Anatomical Theatre in Great Windmill Street.

(88.) It is well known that several fishes, such as the *torpedo*, which is a species of ray; the *gymnotus electricus*, or the electric eel; the *silurus electricus*, a species peculiar to some of the rivers in Africa; and also the *trichiurus indicus*, and *tetraodon electricus*, which are fishes found in the Indian ocean, possess the power of giving electrical shocks to animals that touch them, or communicate with them by electrical conductors. Anatomical investigation has shown that this power resides in organs of a very peculiar construction. In the torpedo they are composed of a great multitude of vertical and parallel membranous plates, arranged in longitudinal columns of quadrangular, pentagonal, or hexagonal forms, with a loose net-work of tendinous fibres passing transversely and obliquely between the columns, and uniting them firmly together. Each column is, moreover, divided by a great number of thin horizontal partitions, placed over each other at very small distances, and forming numerous interstices, which appear to contain a fluid. All these parts are supplied by a great abundance of blood-vessels, and by a still more extraordinary proportion of nerves.

(89.) In the regular arrangement of their plates these organs have a marked resemblance to a voltaic battery; we know nothing, however, of the immediate source from which they derive electrical properties. Mr. Cavendish compared the action of the torpedo to that of a large electrical jar very weakly charged: and Volta considered it as still more analogous to that of the galvanic pile. Sir Humphry Davy, with a view to ascertain the justness of Volta's comparison, passed the shocks given by living torpedos through the interrupted circuit made by silver wire through water, but could not perceive that it produced the slightest decomposition of that fluid. The same shocks made to pass through a fine silver wire less than one thousandth of an inch in diameter did not produce ignition. Volta, to whom Sir H. Davy communicated the results of these experiments, considered the conditions of the organs of the torpedo to be best represented by a pile, of which the fluid substance is a very imperfect conductor, such as honey; and which, though it communicated weak shocks, yet did not decompose water. Sir H. Davy also ascertained that the electrical shocks given by the torpedo, even when powerful, produced no sensible effect on an extremely delicate magnetic electrometer. In a paper recently read at the Royal Society, he explains these negative results by supposing that the motion of the electricity in the organ of the torpedo is in no measurable time, and wants that continuity of current requisite for the production of magnetic effects.

(90.) Mr. Geoffroy St. Hilaire has found an organic structure very similar to that of the torpedo in other animals of the ray genus, which, nevertheless, do not possess any electrical powers.

(91.) Electrical effects are obtained from a pile composed of thin plates of different metals in the usual order, with discs of writing paper interposed between them. This species of pile was the invention of Mr. De Luc, who gave it the name of the *electrical column*. It may be constructed of pieces of paper, silvered on one side, by means of silver leaf, and alternated with thin leaves of zinc; taking care that the silvered surfaces of the paper discs are always in the same direction. A very large number of these may be contained in a glass tube of moderate length, previously well dried, having its ends covered with sealing-wax, and capped with brass. The most extensive instrument of this kind was made by Mr. Singer, and consisted of twenty thousand series. Each of the two ends or poles of the column affect the electrometer, and exhibit electrical attractions and repulsions; the apparatus will even give sparks, and communicate shocks of considerable force: but it possesses no sensible power of chemical decomposition when applied to fluids in the interrupted circuit. If two

* Nicholson's *Journal*, iii. 298.

upright electrical columns be placed side by side, with their poles in opposite directions, and connected at their upper ends, while a small bell is attached to the lower end of each; the whole will act as one column, and each bell will, in consequence of the electrical actions, be alternately struck by a brass ball suspended between them; and thus a continual ringing will be produced as long as the machine remains in action, which is generally for a considerable time. This action is, however, kept up solely by the presence of moisture in the paper, for it does not take place at all when the paper is perfectly dry; and although the process of oxidation is very slow, the more oxidable metal is in process of time found to be tarnished.

(92.) An apparatus somewhat analogous to that of De Luc was constructed by Hachette and Desormes with pairs of metallic plates, separated by layers of farinaceous paste, mixed with common salt. To this instrument, although it evidently owed its efficacy to the moisture of the paste, they gave the very inappropriate name of *dry pile*. It has the same properties as the electric column, except that it is unable to give a shock. A pile having nearly similar powers was also constructed by Professor Zamboni, of Verona, with discs of paper, gilt or silvered on one of their sides, while the other side was covered with a layer of pulverized black oxide of manganese, mixed with honey. Both this and the former instrument retained their power for a great length of time.

(93.) Piles formed simply of discs of copper and moistened card, placed alternately, were found by Ritter to have no power of developing electricity by their own action, but to be capable of receiving a charge by being placed in the circuit of a powerful voltaic battery, and of thus acquiring, though in an inferior degree, all the properties of the battery itself from which it derived its activity. The properties of these *secondary piles*, as they have been called, are obviously the effect of a series of electrical inductions, extending from end to end; and the apparatus is found to retain its charge for a very considerable time, provided it be kept insulated, and the communications between the two poles are not renewed too frequently.

(94.) Having thus traced the various ways in which galvanic power may be excited, we have next to examine the influence of different circumstances, by which its quantity, intensity, and mode of action are regulated. We have already seen that the intensity of the electricity developed by a single galvanic circle, bears no relation to the extent of surface of the elements which compose that circle. It follows, therefore, that however much we may increase the quantity of electricity by employing very large plates, as in the calorimotor, we cannot obtain from such an instrument any of those effects which require for their production a certain intensity, as well as quantity of electricity. In order to obtain these latter effects, we must employ the compound battery, consisting of a considerable number of alternations of the same elements. The former of these instruments, accordingly, will be capable of producing such effects as depend upon mere quantity, without regard to intensity; such as the evolution of heat, the ignition and deflagration of the metals, and electro-magnetic phenomena. The compound apparatus, on the other hand, will afford the more ordinary electric appearances, (such as the spark, and the phenomena of attraction and repulsion,) will affect the electrometer, or condenser, and will communicate a charge to a Leyden jar; for in all such operations, intensity of electricity is the most essential requisite, and the power of the battery to produce them is found to be augmented by every increase in the number of the alternations. But there is also a third class of effects, more peculiarly appertaining to galvanism, which take place by the transmission of the electric current through bodies of inferior conducting power; such as liquids of various kinds, and living organized structures, both animal and vegetable: producing in the former chemical decomposition, and in the latter various physiological effects, such as nervous excitation, muscular contraction, and affections of secretion. For the production of these effects it is necessary, not only that the electricity be sufficiently powerful, both in respect to intensity and to quantity, but also that it should flow in a continuous current. It is from the difficulty of supplying this latter requisite, that the electricity derived from the common electrical machine, is, under ordinary circumstances, incapable of decomposing water in the way that is so readily accomplished by voltaic electricity. It is from deficiency of intensity, on the other hand, that we are unable to obtain the same effects from the calorimotor, which amply fulfils the conditions of quantity and continuity. The electricity which it furnishes, however abundant in quantity, does not possess sufficient intensity to overcome the obstacle presented by the smallest thickness of water, or other liquid of low conducting power; and is, for the same reason, incapable of penetrating through the skin, or traversing through any other part of an animal body. Hence we can obtain from it neither chemical nor physiological effects. The electricity furnished by the electric column of De Luc, again, though of sufficient intensity to produce the shock and other effects of a sudden influx, is too deficient in quantity to produce chemical action; and the same general observations apply to the electricity of the torpedo.

(95.) Every circumstance that facilitates the passage of the electric current in all parts of the circuit, will tend to increase the quantity that circulates. The degree of conducting power possessed by the fluid parts of the circle, will, therefore, have an important influence on the power of the apparatus. Hence the addition of various saline bodies to the fluid is found to increase the efficacy of the voltaic battery, probably, in part at least, by increasing the conducting power of the fluid; but as such substances generally also promote chemical action, it is always in some degree doubtful what part of the effect is to be ascribed to the one or the other of these causes.

(96.) As the fluid element of the circle is the part having the smallest conducting power, the electric current will be retarded by having to pass through any considerable extent of fluid. With a view to augment the activity of the battery, it is an object to bring the two metallic surfaces of Z and C very near each other, so that the distance the electricity has to pass from the one to the other, through the fluid, shall be as small as possible; and for the same reason the surface of C, which collects the electricity from the fluid, should be sufficiently extensive to effect this purpose completely. We hence perceive the reason of the advantage derived from employing in the common trough battery, according to the suggestion of Dr. Wollaston, a double plate of copper to each plate of zinc, so that each surface of the latter metal acted upon by the fluid, may have a surface of copper opposite to it, (§ 18.); and also of enveloping each coil of zinc plate, in the calorimotor, by a coil of sheet copper, (§ 8.) Mr. Marianini has extended this principle still further, and has found that the maximum of effect takes place when the surface of the copper is no less than eight times greater than that of the zinc.

(97.) There is yet another cause of impediment to the motion of the electric current of a singular kind, and which produces very considerable effect. It appears from the experiments of Mr. Augustus De la Rive, that voltaic electricity, in passing out of one conducting body into another of a different kind, always sustains some loss of its intensity.* The amount of this loss varies much in different cases, according to the nature of the two conductors; and it is different with different degrees of intensity. In the case of the passage of the electricity from a fluid to a metal, or *vice versâ*, it is very great, and it is sensible even when it has to pass from one liquid to another, or along a mixed conductor composed of two different kinds of solids. The impediment arising from the mere change of conductor is quite independent of the peculiar conducting powers of the one or the other of the substances through which the electricity passes. Mr. De la Rive found, for example, that a much greater obstacle existed to the transmission of the electricity between sulphuric acid, especially when concentrated, and platina, than between nitric acid and the same metal; and accordingly, on sending the electric current from a voltaic battery through a number of portions of sulphuric acid, contained in separate glasses, and connected by arcs of platina wire, it proved to be a much worse conductor than when nitric acid was employed in a similar arrangement. But the conducting powers of each system of compound conductors were immediately rendered equal by dipping the ends of the platina wires in nitric acid, before immersing them in the sulphuric acid.†

(98.) In general the more readily a metal is acted upon by liquid conductors, the less is the diminution of intensity which is sustained by the passage of electric currents through them. Mr. De la Rive states it to be a general

---

* *Annales de Chimie et de Physique*, xxxvii. 267.
† Ibid. p. 273.

law, that, independently of the effects of chemical action, the influence of the obstacle opposed to the passage of electricity from a fluid to a solid conductor, is such, that when two metallic surfaces, either of the same or of different metals, are immersed in a fluid, so as to form a galvanic circle, that metal which transmits the electricity with the least loss of intensity is positive with respect to the other metal.*

(99.) The influence of this retarding cause varies also with the intensity of the current itself. The loss of electricity, from its passage through a number of metallic plates, is scarcely sensible when the current is very energetic, as, for instance, when it proceeds from a battery composed of a great number of plates; but it becomes more and more perceptible, according as the original intensity of the current is less considerable. It is also remarkable that the current is disposed to pass more readily through imperfect conductors, which present a great degree of resistance, when it has previously been made to traverse a great number of metallic plates. This was illustrated in two comparative experiments, in the first of which a current, originally of high intensity, was reduced, by passing through a considerable number of plates, till it was equal in intensity to one originally weaker, that had, in the second experiment, passed through a smaller number; of the two currents, thus apparently rendered equal in every respect, it was nevertheless found that the one which had previously passed through the greater number of plates, was thereby rendered capable of passing through any succeeding plate with less loss of intensity than the other current. The phenomena, he states, correspond to those which would take place, if we could imagine that there were two distinct kinds of electric current—the one capable of passing indiscriminately through all sorts of conductors, good or bad; the other capable of passing through good conductors alone. The passage of the currents through successive plates gradually effect the separation of these two portions, the plates arresting the one which cannot pass so readily through bad conductors, and giving free passage to the other portion.

(100.) M. De la Rive has applied this theory to the explanation of the different effects resulting from the increase of the number of the plates. If the pile, he says, consist only of a small number of plates, the electricity produced by it, not having undergone the above process of *filtration*, as it may be called, only one part of it will be capable of passing through an imperfect conductor, which is presented to it, and the other part will be arrested; but if a good conductor be presented, the whole of the electricity finds a ready passage, and will produce corresponding effects. Electricity of the former kind only will be capable of producing chemical decompositions, and of passing through organized bodies; but, in the latter case, it will be adequate to the production of all the calorific and magnetic effects. These modifications of electricity would, if this theory were established, have a remarkable analogy with those of light and of heat, under circumstances somewhat parallel.

(101.) It must be observed, however, that one source of the diminution of effect consequent on the multiplication of surfaces, exists in the transfer of elements which takes place in the fluid from galvanic action. This transfer, as is remarked by Sir H. Davy, in as far as it has actually occasioned the deposit of a positive element on the negative surface, and *vice versâ*, has an immediate influence in checking the further progress of the galvanic action; and arrests it completely when it has proceeded to a certain extent. Hence the powers of batteries are found to diminish by the continuance of their action, and ultimately to cease. This change we have already noticed in treating of the chemical actions of the simple galvanic circle. (§ 41.)

(102.) It is obvious that the several causes of retardation now stated render it exceedingly difficult to determine, previous to actual experiment, the relative powers of different batteries, composed of different materials, and consisting of different numbers of alternations of its parts.

(103.) It is not easy to understand the manner in which the chemical elements of a body decomposed by galvanism, are carried to their respective stations in the voltaic circuit. Thus if the influence of a powerful battery be transmitted through water, it will operate in decomposing that fluid, although the wires which form the communication with the poles be at a considerable distance from each other. They may even be placed in separate vessels, provided the portions of water in which

* *Annales de Chimie et de Physique*, xxxvii. 284.

they terminate are made to communicate with one another by means of a syphon full of water, or even by moistened threads. We find, under these circumstances, the whole of the oxygen of the decomposed water transferred to the positive, while the hydrogen is collected at the negative wire. Two questions may here be asked: first, in what part of the circuit does the decomposition take place? secondly, in what mode are the elements of the decomposed particles transferred to such distant points, without any indication being afforded of their movements, which must be exceedingly rapid, in order to traverse through so long a space? The velocity of this transfer would appear to be very considerable from the following experiment made by Dr. Roget, in the year 1807. The ends of two platina wires, communicating with the poles of a powerful battery, were introduced into two separate vessels of water, communicating by means of a long tube, bent into the form of a syphon, and filled with a solution of common salt. The whole length of the fluid part of the circuit between the two wires was 46 inches. Microscopes were applied to the ends of the wires, for the purpose of enabling the observer and an assistant, (who was the late Mr. Sylvester,) to ascertain the precise moment when the gases made their appearance at the respective wires. No sensible interval of time could be perceived between the appearance of the oxygen gas at the positive, and of the hydrogen gas at the negative wire, when the communications with the battery were made.

(104.) The transfer of material and ponderable substances, such as those which constitute the elements of water, might be expected, even with a moderate velocity, to occasion visible currents in the fluid through which they pass; for their motion, by whatever force produced, must be accompanied by a certain momentum, sufficient to displace the particles of the fluid through which they pass. Dr. Roget could, however, detect no appearance of current or displacement of fluid; such as would be indicated by movements among the minute globules of dust, or other extraneous matters suspended in the water, even with the assistance of the microscope. Mr. Wilkinson and Professor de la Rive, have also arrived at the same conclusion, by employing microscopes of high magnifying power.

(105.) These phenomena of transfer have appeared to some so inexplicable, upon the commonly received doctrine of the composition of water, that they have had recourse to a new hypothesis in order to solve the difficulty. Professor Ritter was led to consider water as a simple substance, forming oxygen by its combination with positive electricity, and hydrogen by its union with negative electricity; and this theory was adopted by several other philosophers. Monge endeavoured to account for the phenomena, by supposing that water formed compounds with excess of oxygen on the one hand, or excess of hydrogen on the other; which compounds passed in opposite directions between the two wires, each depositing on their arrival the superabundant ingredient. Dr. Bostock conceived that the water was decomposed at the positive wire only, where its oxygen was disengaged; and its hydrogen, uniting with electricity, was carried invisibly along with it to the negative wire, where this union being dissolved, the electricity passed on through the wire, and the hydrogen appeared in its gaseous form.

(106.) The following mode of explaining these phenomena was suggested by Dr. Roget, in a paper which was read to the Philosophical Society of Manchester, in 1807.

"We may conceive the agency of electricity to extend throughout the whole of the fluid line connecting the two wires. The hydrogen existing in every particle of water in this line, will, if it possess a positive electrical polarity, according to the hypothesis of Mr. Davy, be repelled by the positive, and attracted by the negative wire. We may consider the row of particles of hydrogen abstractedly from those of oxygen. While the former are moving together, by the agency of the electricity, in a direction towards the negative wire, all those particles which have not yet reached that wire, will merely have to pass over in succession from one particle of oxygen to the next, among those of the other row. They will not appear in the form of gas, because the instant each has quitted the particle of oxygen with which it was associated, it meets with another to combine with; and this process will be continually repeated, until it has arrived at the end of the line, when, finding no oxygen to unite itself with, it will make its appearance in the form of gas. In like manner, the first particle of hydrogen, in the series, by its abandoning the first particle of oxygen, which finds no other particle of hydrogen to replace it, causes the oxygen to appear at that point in the form of gas. We have thus the two gases formed at each end, not from the same individual particle of water, but from the two which happen at that moment to be in contact with the wires. The production of the two gases will take place at the same instant in both places, each particle having only to move one step, that is, from one particle to the adjoining one, instead of having to traverse the whole extent of the line, and no current will be perceptible in the fluid. If this theory be correct, the operation of gravity in favouring the descending current of the heavier element, namely oxygen, might be rendered sensible; and that this is actually the case appears by an observation of Mr. Sylvester, that when the wire giving out oxygen is placed at a much lower level than that which gives out hydrogen, the effect is sensibly greater than when the positions are reversed."

(107.) Similar explanations of the mode of transfer have been given by Dr. Henry, and by Grotthus; and from the following passage in Sir H. Davy's last paper on the subject,* it would seem that he entertained views somewhat similar. "If it be supposed that the fluid is divided into two zones, directly opposite in their powers to the poles of the battery, the virtual change may be regarded as taking place in the two extremities of these zones nearest the neutral point; so that by a series of decompositions and recompositions, the alkaline matters and hydrogen separate at one side, and oxygen, pure, or in union, at the other. In this way the electricity may be regarded as the transporter of the ponderable matters, which assume their own peculiar characters at the moment when they arrive at the point of rest." That visible motions are sometimes produced in fluid conductors when transmitting the electric current, has been shown by Sir H. Davy, who noticed the very singular convulsive agitations into which mercury is thrown, when placed within the circuit of a powerful voltaic battery discharged through water.† These motions, which are frequently of a violent and capricious kind, have also attracted the attention of Mr. Herschel, and he has made them the subject of an interesting research, of which an account is contained in the Philosophical Transactions.*

(108.) The following singular fact has been noticed by Mr. Porrett:—If a vessel be divided by a membranous partition into two compartments, of which the one is filled with water, and the other contains but a very small quantity, and if the positive wire from a voltaic battery be inserted into the former, and the negative wire into the latter, the water will be impelled from the first compartment into the second, through the partition, and will at length rise to a higher level in the latter than in the former.† Mr. A. De la Rive, upon repeating these experiments, arrived at the same result, when he employed distilled or river water, which has but a small conducting power; when, however, a saline solution of sufficient strength was used, no such effect of impulsion was perceptible. But the reality of such an effect under the above circumstances, is sufficient to establish the existence of a mechanical force derived from the current of voltaic electricity.

(109.) We have already had occasion to observe that a theory, founded upon totally different views of the sources of galvanic power from those which have now been stated, has been applied to the explanation of the phenomena. As this, which has been termed the *electric theory of galvanism*, has been adopted by several eminent philosophers, it ought not to be considered as undeserving of notice in this place.

(110.) It was conceived by Volta, the original author of this theory, that the primary source of the electricity liberated during the action of a galvanic apparatus, might be traced to the contact of the dissimilar metals. He assumed as a fundamental fact, that during the whole time that these metals are in contact, a certain force is in constant operation, tending to effect a transfer of electricity from the one metal to the other. To this force he gave the name of *electromotive force*. When, for example, zinc and copper are in contact, the alleged operation of this force is to impel the electricity from the copper to the zinc, so as to maintain in the latter a positive state, when compared with the former, which will, consequently,

---

* *Philosophical Transactions* for 1826, p. 416, 417.
† *Elements of Chemical Philosophy*, p. 172.

* For 1824, p. 163.
† Thomson's *Annals of Philosophy*, viii. 74.

itself be in a negative state with relation to the zinc. If either of these states be reduced to a more neutral condition by communication with other bodies; that is, if the redundant electricity of the zinc be carried off, and the deficiency of electricity in the copper be supplied from other sources, the electromotive force will, he conceived, immediately renew this difference of condition, and thus maintain a continual and rapid current of electric fluid, flowing always in the same direction.

(111.) It was further assumed in this theory that liquids have no electromotive power when in contact with metals: and that this negative property enabled them to transmit the electricity evolved by the contact of the zinc and copper, and which is accumulated in the zinc, back again to the copper; whence it is again transferred to the zinc; and so on in a perpetual circle. In compound galvanic circles, the electromotive force residing in the surfaces of contact between the two metals in each pair of plates, are all tending in the same direction; and the several impulses they give to the electricity conspire together to increase the effect, which will therefore be the sum of all the forces taken separately. Thus will a continued and powerful stream of electricity be determined from the negative to the positive pole of the battery, ready to circulate through any conducting line of communication extending between the two poles. The office of the fluid is considered, in this theory, as simply that of conducting the electricity from the one metal to the other: its chemical action on either of these being regarded as a mere accidental circumstance, not in any way concerned in the production of galvanic or electrical effects. The effective quantity of electricity which actually circulates in the voltaic battery is supposed to be determined altogether by the degree of conducting power possessed by the liquid: for it is assumed that the quantity which the electromotive force existing at even the smallest surface of contact between dissimilar metals could set in motion, if the movements of that electricity were not impeded by the difficulty of its transmission through fluids, would be incomparably greater than that which any conducting fluid can discharge.

(112.) Such is the general outline of the electric theory, which it is scarcely necessary to pursue in its various applications, because there are several facts which appear so totally at variance with the immediate consequences of its fundamental hypothesis, as to warrant us in rejecting it. Chemical action between some of the elements of a galvanic combination is so invariably connected with the production of electrical effects, that it would be a violation of all just rules of philosophy not to consider these two classes of phenomena as standing to each other in the relation of cause and effect. The quantity of galvanic effect is always in proportion to the energy of the chemical action. The extent of contact between the two metals, on the other hand, appears to have no relation to the quantity of electricity which is developed. Combinations producing galvanic effects may be formed, as we have seen, with a single metal only, when two fluids are present; and indeed, on other occasions, without the presence of any metallic substance whatever. We have also seen that the same metals do not in all cases stand in the same invariable electrical relation to each other; but that this relation is determined by the chemical properties of the fluid with which they are placed in contact. (§ 75.) All these facts are irreconcilable with the electric theory.

(113.) Were any further reasoning necessary to overthrow it, a forcible argument might be drawn from the following consideration. If there could exist a power having the property ascribed to it by the hypothesis, namely, that of giving continual impulse to a fluid in one constant direction, without being exhausted by its own action, it would differ essentially from all the other known powers in nature. All the powers and sources of motion, with the operation of which we are acquainted, when producing their peculiar effects, are expended in the same proportion as those effects are produced; and hence arises the impossibility of obtaining by their agency a perpetual effect; or, in other words, a perpetual motion. But the electro-motive force ascribed by Volta to the metals when in contact, is a force which as long as a free course is allowed to the electricity it sets in motion, is never expended, and continues to be exerted with undiminished power, in the production of a never-ceasing effect. Against the truth of such a supposition, the probabilities are all but infinite.

MAGNETISM.

CHAPTER I.

General Facts and Principles.

(1.) THE attractive power of the loadstone for iron was known in times of very remote antiquity, and has been, in all ages, a subject of curiosity and of wonder. It is a property which seems, at first sight, so unconnected with every other, as to form of itself a separate class among natural phenomena: and, although an immense mass of knowledge relating to Magnetism has been accumulated by the labours of successive generations, and embodied into a science of high rank and importance, yet the field it comprises is of comparatively limited extent. This arises from the great simplicity which characterises both the phenomena and the laws that govern them; a quality, however, which peculiarly invites a philosophic mind to undertake their investigation. A still more powerful motive to this inquiry will present itself when we reflect on the signal benefits mankind has derived from magnetism as applied to the purposes of navigation. The discovery of the compass, by the aid of which, the mariner, however distant from land, amidst cloudy skies, or in the darkest nights, is enabled, at all times, to steer his course with certainty, and traverse in all directions the wide expanses of ocean which separate the countries and continents of our globe, must unquestionably rank among the great discoveries that have essentially contributed to advance the civilization of the human race.

(2.) The term MAGNETISM expresses the peculiar property occasionally possessed by certain bodies, more especially by iron and some of its compounds, whereby, under certain circumstances, they mutually attract or repel one another, according to determinate laws.

(3.) This property was first noticed in a mineral substance called the *native magnet*, or the *loadstone*, which is an ore of iron, consisting chiefly of the two oxides of that metal, together with a small proportion of quartz and alumina. Its colour varies in different specimens, according to minute differences in the proportion of the oxides, and the nature of the other substances with which they may be found united: but it is usually of a dark grey hue, and has a dull metallic lustre. It is found in considerable masses in the iron mines of Sweden and Norway, and also in different parts of Arabia, China, Siam, and the Philippine Islands. Small loadstones have occasionally been met with among the iron ores of England.

(4.) There are several modes in which a piece of iron may be rendered magnetic, or converted into what is called *an artificial magnet*; and for all purposes of accurate experiment such a magnet is much to be preferred to a loadstone. The following is a simple and ready method of obtaining artificial magnets with a view to the investigation of the magnetic properties.

Let a straight bar of hard tempered steel, devoid of all perceptible magnetism, be held in a vertical position (or still better, in a position slightly inclined to the perpendicular, the lower end deviating to the north,) and struck several smart blows with a hammer; it will be found to have acquired, by this process, all the properties of a magnet.

(5.) These properties are the four following:—viz. 1. Polarity. 2. Attraction of unmagnetic iron. 3. Attraction and repulsion of magnetic iron. 4. The power of inducing magnetism in other iron. These we shall now explain and illustrate.

§ 1. *Polarity.*

(6.) If a bar, which has been rendered magnetic, be supported in such a manner as to have entire freedom of motion in a horizontal plane, and be removed from the neighbourhood of all ferruginous bodies which might influence it, it will spontaneously turn round, and, after a few oscillations, will finally

B

settle in a position directed nearly north and south. If it be disturbed from this situation and placed in any other direction, it will, as soon as it is again at liberty to move, resume its former position. The end of the bar which points to the north, is that which was lowermost at the time it acquired its magnetism by hammering: the end which, during that operation, had been the upper one, is consequently that which, when the magnet is free to move, directs itself to the south. The two ends of a magnet of this form are called its *poles:* the one which spontaneously turns to the north, being distinguished as the *north*, and the other as the *south pole:* and the tendency of the magnet to assume the above described position is called its *Polarity*. The straight line joining the two poles of a magnet is called its *axis*.

(7.) There are several ways of supporting a magnet so as to enable it to manifest its polarity. The readiest mode is to suspend it by a thread, fastened

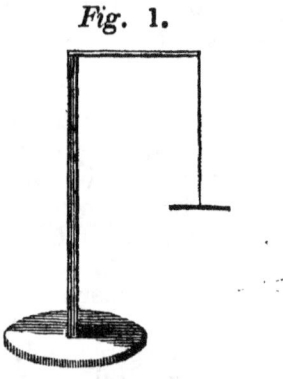

Fig. 1.

round it at the middle, so that it may be sufficiently balanced to preserve its horizontal position as it turns freely round its centre. It cannot, indeed, turn thus, without, at the same time, either twisting or untwisting the thread by which it hangs; and the reaction of the thread, the fibres of which tend to resume their original situation, or the force of torsion, as it is called, may prevent the magnet from assuming the precise position to which its polarity would have brought it. But by employing a very slender thread, and taking it of sufficient length, the force of torsion may be so much reduced as to be quite insensible in the experiments about to be described.

(8.) Another convenient mode of examining the horizontal movements of the magnetized bar is to poise it on its centre, hollowed into a cap, which is made to rest on a fine point fixed in a stand.

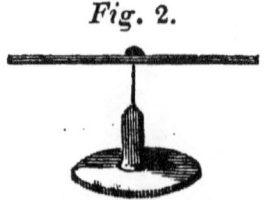

Fig. 2.

When thus fitted up, it acts like the needle of a mariner's compass; and in its principle is identical with that instrument.

(9.) We may sometimes find it more expedient to fix the magnet on a piece of cork, and thus make it float on water,

Fig. 3.

in a basin. In this case, we must take care, however, that it be kept at a sufficient distance from the sides of the vessel to prevent its being affected by the capillary attractions of the water.

The same precaution must be used if the magnet be made to float on the surface of mercury, which is an excellent mode of giving it complete liberty of motion. But the vessel containing the mercury should be at least six inches in diameter, in order to guard against the effects of the curvature of the surface of the mercury near the sides. When the surface of the mercury is very clean and bright, which happens only when the metal is very pure, it allows of the ready motion of pieces of iron floating upon it. But it soon tarnishes, and the film of oxide which forms on the surface, becomes a great impediment to the freedom of motion of the floating body. The best way of rendering it clean, is to strain it through a funnel of paper, rolled up into a cone, having a small aperture at the point, of about the fortieth of an inch in diameter.

§ 2. *Attraction of Iron.*

(10.) If either pole of a magnet be brought near any small piece of soft unmagnetic iron, it will be found to attract it. Iron filings, for instance, are immediately collected together when a magnet is placed among them; and they adhere more especially to the poles (as shewn in *fig.* 4, A), from which,

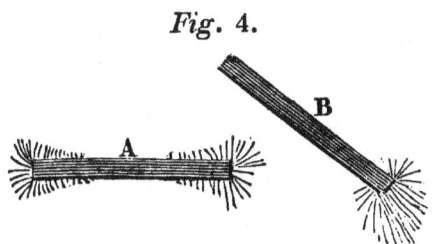

Fig. 4.

when the magnet is lifted up, they remain suspended in thick clusters. (*Fig. 4, B.*) A small number of filings are also found adherent to the intermediate parts of the bar, but they are evidently attracted much more feebly than those at the ends; it may also be remarked that there is a part of the magnet, generally mid-way between the two ends, to which the filings have no tendency to adhere at all, and which appears therefore to have no power of attraction. Thus it appears that the attractive forces, whatever be their nature, reside chiefly at the poles.

(11.) It is an established law of nature, the knowledge of which we have derived by induction from a vast variety of phenomena occurring in every part of the material universe, that all *action* is attended by a corresponding *reaction*, equal in degree, but opposite in its kind, to the action itself. Mechanical philosophy, in all its departments, abounds with exemplifications of this fundamental principle; many of these, indeed, are matters of familiar observation. The stretched rope pulls back with equal force at both its ends; the compressed spring resists equally in two opposite directions; the exploding powder, at the same moment that it propels the ball, gives to the gun its recoil. In all the effects resulting from cohesion, from elasticity, from caloric, from animal force, from gravitation, whether actuating the minutest particles of matter, or the largest masses; whether exerted on the rolling waters of the ocean, or displayed on the grander scale of the planetary movements, the same universal law is rigidly observed. To every physical force there is opposed another and a similar force. No material agent can produce an effect upon another, without being at the same time subjected to an equal reaction from that other agent. An attracting body must of necessity be itself attracted, and a repelling body repelled. This perfect reciprocity of action takes place in all the agencies of electricity;—it exists also in those of magnetism.

(12.) If the two bodies exerting a mutual action upon one another, be very different in their size, the smaller of the two will necessarily exhibit the effects of this action more strongly than the larger, because, its mass being less, the same force will communicate to it a greater velocity of motion. We find, accordingly, that the small fragments of iron in the experiment just described, appear to fly towards the magnet, while their reciprocal action on the magnet itself is imperceptible. But this latter action may be rendered sensible by trying its effect on a magnet poised or suspended in any of the ways above mentioned; and we shall find that on presenting a piece of soft iron to either of the poles of the magnet, the latter is slowly attracted by the iron. The attraction, therefore, between the magnet and the iron is reciprocal.

Let us next see what influence magnets have upon one another.

§ 3. *Attraction and Repulsion of Magnetic Iron.*

(13.) For the purpose of examining the mutual action of two magnets, we may either present to the poised magnet another magnet held in the hand, or we may place two poised magnets in different positions with respect to each other. We shall find by sufficiently varying these positions, that when the poles of different magnets are brought near one another, they in some cases appear to be attracted towards each other, while in others they manifest a mutual repulsion. This, however, does not happen capriciously; for if we mark the poles according to the distinction already pointed out, we shall find that two north poles always repel each other:—that two south poles also repel each other:—but that the north pole of one magnet invariably attracts, and is of course attracted by the south pole of another magnet.

(14.) It thus appears that there are two species of magnetic powers, the northern and the southern, which in their mode of action are perfectly similar, but in their effects are directly opposite.

(15.) Such of our readers as have studied our Treatise on Electricity must here be struck with the pointed analogy which subsists between the phenomena of magnetic attraction and repulsion, and those of electricity. In both there exists the same character of double agencies of opposite kinds, capable, when separate, of acting with great energy, but being, when combined together, perfectly neutralized and exhibiting no sign of activity. As there were two electrical powers, the positive and the negative, or, as some prefer denominating them, the vitreous and the resinous, so there are two magnetic powers, distinguished as the northern and the southern polarities; or, as some choose to designate them, the austral and the boreal. The parallel is most exact. Both sets of phenomena are governed by the same characteristic law, which may be expressed by the following concise and general formula, namely,—between like powers there is repulsion; between unlike, attraction.

§ 4. Induction.

(16.) The communication of magnetic properties to iron or steel by the mere approach of the poles of a magnet, is also analogous in its principal circumstances to electric induction.

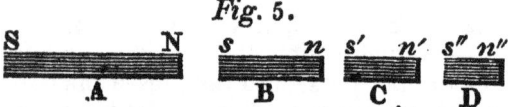

Fig. 5.

If the north pole, N, of a magnet A (*fig.* 5), be brought near to the end *s* of an unmagnetized bar of iron, B, that end will immediately acquire the properties of a south pole, while the opposite, or distant end, *n*, will at the same time be converted into a north pole. If, instead of the north pole, N, the south pole, S, had been presented to the bar, the changes effected in B would have been just the reverse; the adjacent end would have acquired the northern, and the distant end the southern polarity.

(17.) Thus we may observe that each pole of a magnet induces the opposite kind of polarity in that end of the iron which is nearest to it, and the same kind on the remotest end; just as happens in the induction of electricity, in which the positive state induces the negative, and the negative the positive state, in those parts of an insulated conductor which are nearest to the electrified body; and a similar state of electricity in the distant end.

(18.) That the iron, while it remains in the vicinity of the magnet, possesses the magnetic properties, may be shown by a variety of experiments.

First, it attracts other iron. If we take, for instance, a key (*fig.* 6), and

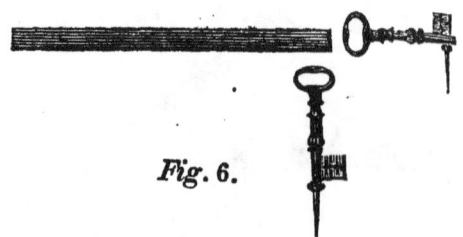

Fig. 6.

hold it horizontally near one of the poles of a strong magnet, also lying in a horizontal position, but not touching the key; and if we then apply another light piece of iron, such as a small nail, to the other end of the key, the nail will hang from the key, and will continue to do so while we slowly withdraw the magnet horizontally from the key. When the magnet has been moved beyond a certain distance, the nail will drop from the key, because the magnetism induced on the key becomes, at that distance, too weak to support the weight of the nail. That this is the real cause of its falling off may be proved by taking a still lighter fragment of iron, such as a piece of very slender wire, and applying it to the key. The magnetism of the key will still be sufficiently strong to support the wire, though it could not support the nail: and it will continue to support the wire, even when the magnet is yet further removed; at length, however, when the distance is still greater, the wire, in its turn, drops off.

The same effects may be observed if the nail be placed in contact with the near end of the key; but they are generally less distinct, on account of the direct influence which the magnet exerts on the nail, and which interferes in some degree with the action of the key, so that the results become complicated.

(19.) The same series of phenomena take place when the key is held above or below the pole of the magnet, or on either side of it. The key will hold the nail or wire suspended from either end, as long as the magnet is near enough to exert sufficient influence on the key.

(20.) If the key be laid upon a piece of paper on a table, and several small bits of wire, or iron filings, be strewed round one end of the key, which we suppose to be devoid of all magnetic properties, no adhesion will be perceptible between the fragments of iron and the key. Let us now approach the pole of a magnet to the other end of the key; we immediately observe the filings and lighter pieces of iron spontaneously, and of one accord, move towards the key, and adhere to it just as if the key had itself become a magnet. They also collect and cohere together, as if animated by a common sympathy. When this has taken place, let us suddenly remove the magnet: that moment all these effects cease at once, the key returns to its natural or unmagnetic state; the bits of iron which had attached themselves to it immediately fall off, and show no tendency either to cohere among themselves, or to adhere to the key.

(21.) Secondly, the vicinity of a magnet to a piece of iron gives it the property of attracting and repelling the respective poles of another magnet, in the same way as a magnet would have done. The truth of this proposition may easily be proved by placing a small compass needle poised as in *fig.* 2, in various situations relative to the ends of the key or any other piece of iron of a lengthened shape, while in the vicinity of the magnet. It will be seen by this examination that the piece of iron has acquired by induction two poles, the qualities of which will be discovered by their attractions or repulsions of the poles of the compass needle, as they are respectively presented to each; and it will be found that these two poles are disposed in the manner specified above.

(22.) Thirdly, the iron, which has become magnetic by induction, has at the same time acquired the power of inducing a similar state of magnetism on the iron in its neighbourhood. Thus, while the bar B, *fig.* 5, is rendered magnetic by the influence of the magnet A, it exerts itself a similar power on another bar C, rendering it also magnetic. The bar C, in its turn, will act in like manner upon another bar, D, and so on. In this way the influence of the magnet A may be made to extend along a series of iron bars or pieces of any other shape, each acquiring magnetism by the inductive power of the preceding piece; and in its turn inducing magnetism on the next.

(23.) But this is not all. The piece of iron which has been rendered magnetic by the vicinity of a magnet, not only acts upon the other iron that is near it, but also reacts upon the magnet from which its power is derived, and increases the intensity of its magnetism. The power of a magnet is, in fact, augmented by the exertion of its inductive influence on a piece of iron in its neighbourhood. A simple experiment is sufficient to prove this fact.

Let a piece of iron be suspended from one of the poles of a straight magnet; and let the weight which this magnet will carry be ascertained by attaching to the iron a scale, capable of holding the weights necessary for this trial, and which may be gradually increased till the piece of iron drops off from the magnet. Repeat this experiment, having previously placed a bar of iron in contact with the other pole of the magnet, and it will be found that the magnet will now support a much greater weight; showing the increase of power it has derived from the presence of the bar of iron which has been applied to the other pole, and the induced magnetism of which, although solely derived from the magnet, reacts, by a kind of secondary induction, upon that magnet. We have already had occasion, in the Treatise on Electricity, to notice the same kind of reaction in the case of electric induction. The increased intensity which a magnet acquires by induction often leads to the permanent acquisition of power by the magnet. Hence we may understand the reason why a magnet that is employed for magnetizing a neutral bar of steel, by means of its inductive power, becomes itself stronger by the operation.

(24.) It is a necessary consequence of the law of magnetic induction that it is accompanied by attraction: for the polarity of the adjacent end of the piece of iron on which the magnetism is induced, is always of the opposite kind to that of the pole of the piece which induces it: according to the fundamental law of magnetism, therefore, a mutual attraction must take place between them. The remote end of the piece on which the magnetism has been induced is indeed repelled, because its polarity is similar to that of the inducing pole: but it is evident that the attractive action of the adjacent and dissimilar poles will always be stronger than the repulsive action of the more distant poles; and will therefore always prevail.

(25.) This remark leads us to a very important step in the generalization of the magnetic phenomena. We have hitherto spoken of the attractive power of magnets for iron as one of the primary facts in the science: but we now see that it is merely a necessary result of a more general law, namely, that of induction, together with the law of action of the two polarities upon each other:— or, in other words, that it is itself comprehended in these more general facts. A magnet attracts a piece of unmagnetic iron, not from any inherent disposition to attract it in that state, but in consequence of its inductive influence, which converts it, for the time, into a second magnet, having its poles so disposed with relation to the first magnet, that the adjacent parts have always opposite polarities; and attraction, therefore, takes place between them. Thus the pieces A and B, *fig*. 5, attract each other, simply because the induced magnetism of the end *s* is of the opposite kind to that of the pole N. In like manner B and C attract each other, because the polarities of the adjacent poles *n* and *s'* being of a dissimilar kind, their mutual action is attraction. With respect to this ultimate effect, the inductive influence of either pole is exactly alike, and leads to the same result.

(26.) We may now understand the reason why, when a magnet is placed in a heap of iron filings, and then lifted up, the filings attach themselves in clusters to the poles, arranging themselves in lines, and adhering together by a force of attraction which extends from each individual particle to those which precede and follow it. They form, indeed, by their mere juxtaposition, under the influence of the large magnet, a series of minute magnets, of which the poles are similarly situated in each, and being alternately north and south, the adjacent ends attract one another.

(27.) This disposition of the poles may be verified by making an experiment of the same kind on a larger scale, suspending from the end of a strong magnet a piece of iron, such as a key (*fig.* 7), from the lower end of which a smaller key may be made to hang in consequence of its induced magnetism. To this may be appended a still smaller piece of iron, such as a nail; and we may thus proceed, adding piece after piece, till the lower one will exert only sufficient attraction to sustain a very small weight of iron, such as a small needle. The polarities of the lower ends of each piece, if examined previously to each additional piece being appended to it, will be found to be constantly of the same kind as that of the lower end of the magnet from which the whole is suspended. This may be ascertained by its attracting or repelling the poles of a small magnetic needle balanced on a point, and supported on a stand, as shown at M, *fig*. 7.

Fig. 7.

(28.) The knowledge of the general fact, that magnetic induction always tends to produce attraction between the adjacent parts of the bodies which act upon each other, enables us to explain many phenomena, which might otherwise appear to be at variance with the simple laws of attraction and repulsion already stated. Thus we find that the dissimilar poles of two magnets attract each other with a force which is greater than the repulsion exerted between the similar poles of the same magnets; and this happens because, in the former case, the tendency of induction is to strengthen the magnetic power of the adjacent dissimilar poles; but, in the latter case, where the poles are similar, each pole tends, by its inductive influence, to weaken the magnetism of the other. This is exemplified in a still more striking manner, when a weak magnet is brought near to a much more powerful one: in which case we find that, although when they are at a moderate distance from each other, either pole of the weaker magnet is repelled by the similar pole of the strong one; yet, if it be brought very near, and especially if it be made to touch the latter, it is attracted, and will even adhere with some force to the strong magnet. This effect evidently results from the powerful inductive influence of the strong magnet, which, for the time, destroys the feeble polarity of the weak magnet at the part immediately adjacent, and impresses upon it a polarity of an opposite kind: whence attraction follows as a necessary consequence of contrary polarities.

(29.) The intensity of magnetic power developed by induction in an iron bar, was found by Mr. W. S. Harris to be inversely as the distance of the inducing pole from the adjacent end of the bar on which it acts. It would also appear, from the experiments of the same gentleman[*], that the intensity of the magnetism induced on the remote end of the bar, is, with the same inductive power acting on the nearer end, inversely as the length of the bar.

Magnetic induction is not confined in its operation to any particular direction; thus a bar of iron will be rendered magnetic if placed at right angles, or at any other inclination to the axis of the mag-

---

[*] Transactions of the Royal Society of Edinburgh for 1829.

net, or line joining its two poles, as in the situations represented in *fig.* 8. The

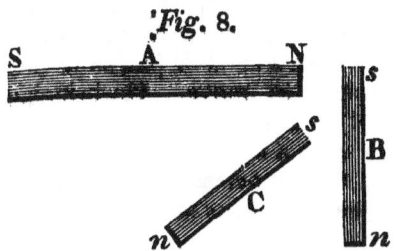

Fig. 8.

ends, *s*, *s*, of the bars B, C, adjoining the north pole N of the magnet A, will still become south poles by induction, and the ends *n*, *n*, north poles. Under these circumstances, if the inclination be less than a right angle, as in the case of C, the opposite pole of the magnet *s* begins to exert an inductive influence on the other end of the bar *n*, which concurs with that of the pole N in rendering *n* a north and *s* a south pole. The most favourable position for the bars receiving the full inductive influence of both poles is that of parallelism with the magnet A, as shown in *fig.* 9.

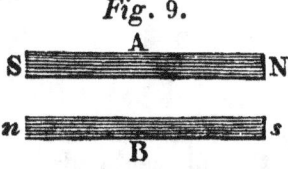

Fig. 9.

(30.) Complicated effects result from bringing the magnet in contact with other parts than the ends of a piece of iron. Thus, if the north pole of a magnet be placed in the middle of an iron bar, as in *fig.* 10, both extremities of the bar are rendered north poles, while the middle is a south pole.

(31.) If the north pole of a magnet be placed on the centre of a round iron plate (*fig.* 11), so that its axis may be

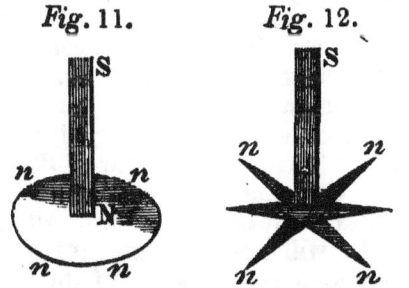

Fig. 11. Fig. 12.

perpendicular to it, the plate will have a south pole in its centre, and every part of its circumference will have the properties of a weak north pole. If the plate have the form of a star (*fig.* 12), each of the points will have a stronger northern polarity than in the last case. Analogous effects may be observed in pieces of iron of an irregular shape when acted upon by a magnet; the part immediately adjoining to the north pole of the magnet acquires the properties of a south pole, and all the remote protuberances have a feeble northern polarity.

§ 5. *Complex Induction.*

(32.) When two magnets are placed so as to exert an inductive influence on the same bar, it will depend on their relative position, whether they shall conspire to produce the same polarities in the ends of the bar, or whether they shall oppose each other, and produce contrary polarities. If the bar B, *fig.* 13, lie between the two magnets A and

Fig. 13.

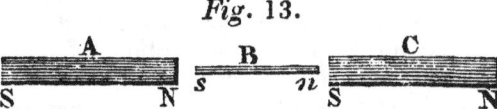

C, and be in the same line with them, and if N, the north pole of A, be adjacent to S, the south pole of C, the intermediate bar B will receive a magnetism of the same kind from the inductive power of both the magnets, its south pole *s* being adjacent to N, and its north pole *n* to S. Its magnetic power will, therefore, be considerably greater from the united influence of the two magnets, than it would have been from the influence of one only.

(33.) It may here be observed that the order in which the poles of these pieces A, B, and C, succeed one another, is exactly the same as that which obtains in the successive induction of magnetism along a series of iron bars, as in *fig.* 5. Now the same consequences follow from this arrangement in the one case as in the other. We have just seen that when C is a bar already rendered magnetic, the magnetism of the iron bar B, which the magnet A had induced upon it, is increased by the presence of C. In like manner, we find that the magnetism of the bar B, in the case above referred to, *fig.* 5, is increased by the presence of another piece of iron C, placed at its end, although that piece, previously to its being so placed, was entirely free from magnetism. This increase is owing to the piece C having become magnetic by its position with respect to B, which had itself been rendered magnetic by the vicinity of the magnet A. C having thus become a temporary magnet by the action of B, reacts upon B, and, exerting a new inductive influence, tends to increase its magnetism in the same manner as if it had been a permanent magnet. Thus it is that in a series of iron bars held together by induced magnetism, each piece tends to increase the strength of the preceding piece, and the whole coheres together with greater force than if no such reaction took place. This circumstance affords a further explanation of the strong cohesion we observe among the particles of iron filings, which hang in long threads from the poles of a magnet.

(34.) A closer attention to the consequences which flow from magnetic induction, will also enable us to explain another remarkable fact, which the adhesion of the strings of iron filings presents. It is that each separate filament, although composed of parts that attract each other in the direction of their length, yet shew a tendency to keep distinct from the neighbouring filaments, and even appear to repel one another. In order to understand this, let us consider the condition of several slender iron bars placed side by side, and adhering to the north pole of a magnet, as shewn in *fig.* 14. The inductive power of the magnet, as we have seen, will render each of the ends in contact with that pole, a south pole, while all the remote ends will be north poles. Hence, the bars will all have their similar poles near each other, and this will happen at both their extremities, and they will accordingly repel one another. As long as they adhere to the magnets by one end, this repulsion will be prevented by that adhesion from shewing itself; but at the other ends, which are at liberty to move, it will be strongly manifested, and the bars will be observed to separate or diverge from one another. Now this is very nearly the condition of the filaments composed of particles of iron. The polarities of those parts of each which are in contact, are neutralized and become scarcely sensible; but those of the extremities, being uncompensated, exert their full power, and produce the observed repulsion of the filaments.

(35.) This effect of induction is exceedingly well illustrated by the following experiment of Cavallo: let two short pieces of iron wire, *fig.* 15, be each fastened to a thread, the threads being joined at their other ends and formed into a loop, by which they are to be suspended from a hook or pin, so as to have full liberty to move. On bringing the pole of a magnet, the south pole for instance, at a certain distance below the wires, it will occasion them to recede from each other, as shewn in *fig.* 16, in-

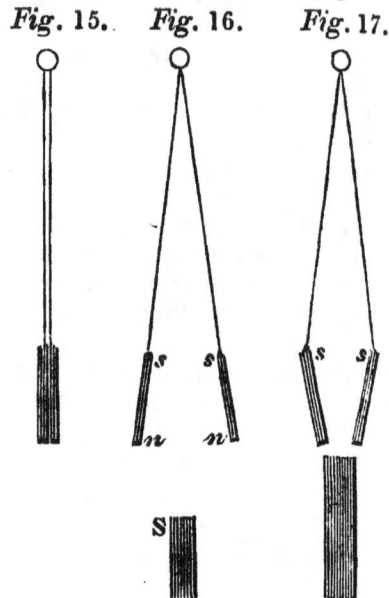

Fig. 15.   *Fig.* 16.   *Fig.* 17.

dicating the repulsion which takes place between the adjacent ends of the wires, in consequence of their being similarly affected by the inductive power of the magnet; the lower ends of both being rendered north poles, and the upper ends south poles. This divergency of the wires will continue to increase until the magnet has approached to a certain limit. But if the magnet is brought nearer than this limit, its own attractive force becomes so strong as to overpower the repulsion that exists between the lower ends of the wire; and therefore brings them nearer to each other, as shewn in *fig.* 17; while the repulsion of the upper ends s, s, still continues to manifest itself, by keeping them remote from one another. On removing the magnet entirely, the wires immediately collapse, their magnetism being only of a transitory nature. But if the same experiment be made with sewing needles, instead of soft iron wires, the needles will often continue to repel each other after the removal of the magnet, having acquired some degree of permanent magnetism by the circumstances in which they have been placed.

(36.) If four wires be suspended in a manner similar to those in the last experiment, each by its separate thread, the induction of a similar magnetism upon all of them will produce a mutual repulsion among them, and they will of course all diverge from one another. But if the wires be made of steel, so as to retain whatever magnetism may be communicated to them, and a northern polarity be given to the lower ends of two of the wires, but a southern polarity to the lower ends of the other two wires, when each of these pairs is kept apart, the wires will repel each other; but if both pairs are brought together, all the four wires will unite and adhere together. The reason is that those wires which have opposite polarities attracting each other, unite to form a pair in which the polarities are balanced, and the repulsion each had before exerted towards those which were similar in the other pair, is now entirely neutralized. The same thing will happen, however numerous are the pairs of wires that are dissimilarly magnetized.

(37.) In order that a bar of iron may receive the combined inductive influence of two magnets, it is not necessary that they should all be situated in the same line as in the example already given. The same effect will result if the bar be at right angles to the two magnets, as in the following figure (18), provided the

Fig. 18.

two ends be immediately acted upon respectively by the poles of opposite denominations of the magnets. The attraction of a bar in this situation is much increased by the conspiring inductive influence of the two magnets; and the force exerted is more than double of that by which it would have adhered to either of the magnets when singly employed. This may be verified by attaching the scale of a balance to the bar (*fig.* 19,) and adding weights till its adhesion to the magnets is overcome: these weights will be found to exceed the sum of the weights which the two magnets would have supported, by means of the adhesion of the same iron bar, if they had been applied separately.

(38.) While such is the effect of the application of the dissimilar poles of two magnets to the ends of a bar of iron, namely, that of conspiring to induce the same kind of magnetism, it is likewise evident that an effect of an opposite kind must result when the dissimilar poles of

Fig. 19.   *Fig.* 20.

the magnets are both applied to the same end of a bar. These poles, being of different kinds, will produce contrary effects; their inductive influence will oppose, instead of assisting, each other, and the magnetism induced on the bar will be only that resulting from the difference, instead of the sum of their intensities. If the bar be of some length, and if the magnets be of equal strength, and applied close to each other, their actions upon the remoter parts of the bar will be so nearly equal, that they will almost entirely neutralize each other, and no sensible degree of magnetism will be excited. Thus if while a key is supported by a magnet as in *fig.* 20, we gradually bring down upon it a second magnet, with its lower pole of the opposite kind to the lower pole of the first magnet, it will tend to induce in the key a polarity of an opposite kind to that which it has received from the first magnet. In as far as it exerts that influence it diminishes this magnetism, and consequently weakens the attraction. Another cause also operates in diminishing the attraction. The polarity induced upon the adhering end of the key is of the contrary kind to that of the pole of the first magnet; it is therefore of the same kind with that of the second magnet which is brought near it, and which, therefore, as far as the key retains its induced magnetism, must repel it. Accordingly, it happens that when the second magnet, if sufficiently powerful, is brought within a certain distance from the upper end of the key, it destroys its power of adhering to the magnet, and the key drops off.

A similar counteraction of magnetic induction will take place, when the other pole of the second magnet, that is the pole of the same denomination as that of the first magnet to which the key adheres, is applied to the lower end of the key. The first action of the lower magnet, as it approaches the key under these circumstances, is to repel it; but on being brought still nearer, its inductive influence becomes so great as to reverse the poles of the key, which is now attracted by the pole which before repelled it: it then generally drops off and adheres to the lower magnet.

(39.) The effect of applying similar poles to the two ends of a bar of iron is generally that of inducing the opposite polarity on both ends of the bar, and the same polarity at the middle. Thus, *fig.* 21, the north poles N, N, of the two mag-

Fig. 21.

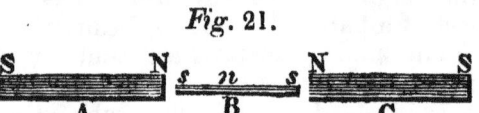

nets A and C being applied lengthwise to the ends of an intermediate bar B, will render it a magnet with three poles, those at the end being south poles, and the middle being a north pole. In this case the bar will be attracted by both the magnets, though less powerfully than when the acting poles of the latter are of opposite kinds, as in the situation shewn by *fig.* 13. In more complicated cases, and more especially when the form of the piece of iron is irregular, it is difficult to predict the exact mode in which the poles will arrange themselves when magnetism is induced upon it by a single magnet, and still more when the operation of two or more magnets, especially if they be of unequal strength, is to be estimated. The following, however, is one of those cases in which the process that takes place is more obvious, and which furnishes an amusing illustration of the general principle.

(40.) Take a piece of iron, C (*fig.* 22), formed into the shape of a fork, or of the letter Y, and suspend it by one of the branches of the fork to the north pole of a magnet A; its lower end will immediately acquire a northern polarity, and will attract another small piece of iron, such as a key, which may therefore easily be supported by it. While the key is thus hanging from its lower end, apply to the other branch of the fork the

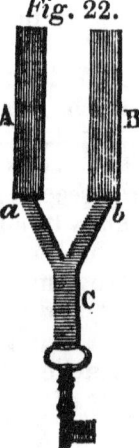

Fig. 22.

south pole of another magnet B, the key will instantly drop off. The reason is that the magnet B tends to induce upon the remote or lower end of the fork, a contrary polarity to that which is induced upon it by A, and thus destroys its power of attracting. The fork will have a south pole at *a*, a north pole at *b*, while its lower end will be neutral. If, on the contrary, the north pole of the magnet B had also been applied to the branch *b* of the fork, its influence would have conspired with that of A in inducing a northern polarity at C, and the key would have been more strongly attracted.

§ 6. *Different Qualities of Iron and Steel with regard to Magnetic Susceptibility and Retentiveness.*

(41.) All the effects we have hitherto described, as attendant on the induction of magnetism on iron, are of a temporary nature, depending altogether on the influence excited by the neighbouring poles of a magnet; for we find that, the moment the magnet is removed, all these effects cease, and the iron returns to its original state of neutrality, and loses all its magnetic properties. But the case is different when steel is made the subject of experiment. Magnetism, it is true, may be induced on steel; but the induction proceeds very slowly, and is, at first, much more feeble than it is with iron. On the other hand, steel does not, like iron, lose what it has acquired; for, on the removal of the magnet which gave it the magnetic properties, it retains these properties permanently: it has, in fact, become itself a real magnet.

(42.) This remarkable difference existing between iron and steel in their respective susceptibility to receive, and capacity to retain magnetism, must, no doubt, arise from some peculiar arrangement of their particles, the exact nature of which is at present entirely unknown.

It is, however, exceedingly analogous to the difference in the qualities of electrics and non-electrics with regard to the power of conducting electricity; and the magnetic phenomena depending upon it admit of being explained on an hypothesis very similar to that by which we are enabled to account for the electrical phenomena which correspond to them. The two magnetic polarities may be conceived to reside constantly in all iron or steel, and in the natural or neutral condition of these bodies, may be regarded as in a state of equilibrium, and as equally distributed throughout the whole mass. But this state of equilibrium in a bar is disturbed by the influence of a magnetic pole in the vicinity, which exerts an inductive influence. This new force which comes into play, tends to transfer one kind of polarity to one end of the bar, and the opposite polarity to the other end. In iron, these changes are readily effected, on account of the facility which its peculiar texture affords for the transmission of these agencies in both directions. No sooner is the cause which has produced these changes, and maintains the separation of the polarities, removed, than all the effects cease; for there exists no obstacle to the return of the two polarities to their original situations: they revert, therefore, to their former state of equal distribution, and the condition of neutrality is restored in every part. But it is not so with steel; the constitution of which is such as to interpose impediments to the transfer of the polarities from one part to another. It requires a certain time before the obstruction, whatever be its nature, can be overcome; and before the new state of distribution, which induction tends to establish, can be completed; nor can the changes themselves ever be accomplished to the same extent as they are in bodies which present no such obstacles. It is also a necessary consequence of the resistance which the texture of steel presents to any changes taking place in its magnetic condition, that these conditions, when once induced, tend to remain in a great degree fixed. Hence we see the reason why steel bars admit of being rendered permanently magnetic, while the magnetism induced upon iron is only temporary. A steel bar, which has as great a degree of magnetic power as it is capable of retaining, is said to be *saturated* with magnetism.

(43.) In order to obtain an exact knowledge of the progress of magnetic induction in steel, we should place a bar of this material very near to the pole of a strong magnet, and in the same line with

Fig. 23.

it, and provide ourselves with a very small and delicate compass needle, poised on its centre, as in *fig.* 2, by which the polarity of each part of the bar may be examined in succession. It will be evident that an inductive action commences immediately on the magnet's being presented to the bar; for the latter is attracted and adheres very strongly to the magnet from the very first.

The end next the magnet has, therefore, acquired a polarity of a contrary nature to that of the magnet. For the sake of greater clearness of illustration, we shall suppose the actual pole of the latter to be a north pole. The near end of the steel bar is at once converted into a south pole; but if we examine the remote end we do not find it so immediately converted into a north pole. A sensible time is required for effecting the change in the latter; and it will be found, upon a more careful investigation, that the different parts of the bar from south to north, acquire, in succession, this northern polarity, which at last settles in the extremity. If the bar be of considerable length, it

Fig. 24.

often happens that the northern polarity never reaches thus far, but stops at a nearer point; and in that case, we generally find a weaker south pole appearing at some greater distance; and this pole also travels slowly onwards till it attains its furthest limit. This is often succeeded by another north pole, and even a greater number of alternations will sometimes take place; each successive pole, however, becoming weaker and more diffused in proportion as they are more numerous and more distant. The points where the polarities thus change from the one kind to the other have been called *consecutive points*. It is evident that alternations of this kind must very much disturb the regularity of the magnetic actions of bars in which they exist, and complicate the resulting phenomena.

It would appear, from a variety of facts hereafter to be detailed, that a certain time is in all cases required for the complete operation of magnetic induction.

(44.) There are certain circumstances and modes of treatment which tend to quicken the progress of this induction. The first of these is concussion. Whatever excites a tremulous or vibratory motion among the particles of the steel, promotes the transmission of the magnetic polarities, and favours the induction of magnetism. Striking on the bar with a hammer is found to produce this effect in a remarkable degree; and the more so if it occasion a ringing sound in the steel, which is an indication that its particles are very generally thrown into vibratory motion. But any other cause producing agitation among the particles assists in the induction of magnetism.

(45.) The transmission of an electric discharge through a steel bar under the influence of a magnet, is sufficient to produce permanent magnetism. That the electricity acts here only by its mechanical operation, is proved by the effect being the same, whatever be the direction in which it is transmitted; that is, whether the positive stream of electricity be made to pass from right to left, or from left to right, along any part of the steel bar; or whether it be passed longitudinally or transversely through it. This mechanical operation of electricity is, however, to be carefully distinguished from an influence of a totally different description, which it is capable of exerting in producing magnetism, and the operation of which will be the subject of a distinct treatise hereafter to be published.

(46.) Heat also appears to act by removing the obstructions to the transmission of magnetism which exist in steel, in its ordinary state, and by thus reducing it nearly to the condition of soft iron. Accordingly, if a steel bar be heated, and placed in circumstances favourable to magnetic induction, if it be placed, for example, in the immediate vicinity of a magnet, and then suddenly cooled, it will be found, on its removal from the magnet, to have become strongly and permanently magnetic. The greatest degree of magnetism is produced by heating the steel to redness, and, while it is under the influence of a strong magnet, quenching it suddenly with cold water.

(47.) It will readily be understood that since the magnetism of a steel bar remains permanent, only because the peculiar texture of the steel presents an insuperable obstacle to its resuming its natural state of uniform distribution, all the causes which diminish this obstructing force, will give occasion to the escape of portions of this imprisoned magnetism, and will make the bar approach nearer to a neutral condition. In other words, its magnetism will be impaired and weakened, by the very same causes which favoured its acquisition when under the inductive process. It is accordingly found that any mechanical concussion, or any rough usage, has a tendency to destroy the power of a steel magnet. Dr. Gilbert, who was one of the earliest discoverers in this science, found that a magnet which he had impregnated very strongly was very much impaired by a single fall on the floor: and it has been observed since his time, that a magnet is more injured by falling on a stone pavement, or receiving blows which cause it to sound or ring, than by being struck with any soft or yielding substance.

(48.) In like manner the application of heat to a magnet is invariably attended by a dissipation of its magnetic power. It is even sensibly affected by the heat of boiling water; and a red heat totally destroys its magnetism. It has been observed by Mr. Canton, that if the temperature of the magnet has been raised only to that of boiling water, although it loses much of its power during the operation, yet that a great part of it is again recovered on its becoming cool. But after it has been heated to redness, no part of its magnetism is recovered on cooling.

(49.) The precise nature of the influence which heat has upon magnetism is far from being clearly understood; and there appears to be much discordance in the accounts given by different authors on this subject. This appears to have arisen in a great measure from a want of attention to the circumstance that the operation of heat is of two kinds: for while, on the one hand, it facilitates the induction of magnetism, on the other it weakens magnetic action. In those cases where the effects depend upon the readiness with which a piece of iron receives magnetism by induction, heat will favour this process; thus, soft iron is more disposed to be attracted by a magnet when hot than when cold, provided the heat be not excessive. But in as far as relates to permanent magnetism, the action of heat is to impair or destroy it; so that steel, when heated, is less capable of retaining its power than it is when cold. This happens in consequence of its being brought nearer to the condition of soft iron, by the separation of its particles. By raising the temperature sufficiently high, to a red heat for instance, the whole of its permanent magnetism is at once destroyed, though it will still be susceptible, while in that state, of receiving temporary magnetism by induction, and therefore of being attracted by another magnet.

(50.) The direct tendency of heat to diminish magnetic power must also be taken into account in our estimate of the preceding phenomena. It not only promotes the destruction of permanent magnetism, but diminishes likewise the effects of that which is of a temporary nature. The degree in which heat possesses this direct influence, can be estimated only under circumstances in which no permanent change has been produced in the magnetism of a bar subjected to the change of temperature; that is, provided we find on the return of the bar to its former temperature, that it has retained all the power it had before the experiment. The limit beyond which no proper distinction can be accurately drawn between the effects of this twofold operation of heat, appears, according to the experiments of Mr. Christie, to be below 100° of Fahrenheit. From this temperature downwards the power of a magnet increases as it becomes colder; and this augmentation proceeds as far as the lowest temperature that has been tried.

(51.) The following are the results of an extensive series of experiments upon this subject made by Mr. Christie*. Commencing with a temperature of −3° of Fahrenheit, up to one of 127°, the intensity of magnetic power decreased as the temperature of the magnets increased. From an experiment he made at the Royal Institution, in conjunction with Mr. Faraday, in which a small magnet, enveloped in lint, well moistened with sulphuret of carbon, was placed on the edges of a basin containing sulphuric acid, under the receiver of an air-pump, he found that the intensity of the magnet increased to the lowest point to which the temperature could be reduced, and that the intensity decreased on the admission of air into the receiver, and consequent increase of temperature. This, he observes, is in direct contradiction to the notion which has been entertained of intense cold destroying the magnetism of the needle. Captain Middleton had announced† his having frequently observed that a compass appeared to be deprived of all magnetic power from cold, while he was navigating among the ice in Hudson's Bay; but recovered its power when brought into the cabin and warmed by the fire: and that this repeatedly occurred. There can be no doubt that this must have been owing to some other cause than the one he assigned.

With a certain increment of temperature, the decrement of intensity is not constant at all temperatures, but increases as the temperature increases. From a temperature of about 80° the intensity decreases very rapidly as the temperature increases, and beyond the temperature of 100°, a portion of the power of the magnet is permanently destroyed.

(52.) The effects produced on unmagnetized iron, by changes of temperature, were observed by Mr. Christie to be directly the reverse of those produced on a magnet; an increase of temperature causing an increase in the magnetic power of the iron, the limits between which, he observed to be 50° and 100°. This is in perfect conformity with the views we have above explained, of the nature of the operation of heat with regard to magnetism.

(53.) Although the direct tendency of heat to diminish magnetic power may, in a red hot bar, be not sufficient to prevent its receiving induced magnetism, yet when the temperature is still further raised, even this capability is destroyed; and accordingly we find that, at a white heat, iron appears to be totally insusceptible of any magnetic action. There are still, however, some curious anomalies occurring in the magnetic action of iron at these very high temperatures, of which further investigation alone can furnish the explanation.

(54.) In the account we have now given of the properties of iron and of steel, with regard to their capabilities of acquiring and of retaining magnetism, we have all along referred to those of pure metallic iron in its softest and most ductile state, and to those of steel which has been brought to its greatest degree of hardness by immersion in cold water after being heated; for it is in these two states that they exhibit the strongest contrast in these respects. We often, however, meet with this metal in states possessing intermediate degrees of the above qualities; that is, acquiring magnetism with less facility than soft iron, and retaining less of it than hard steel. It may be laid down as a general propo-

---

* Philosophical Transactions for 1825, p. 62.
† Philosophical Trans. for 1738, vol. xl. p. 310.

sition, liable however to some exceptions, that the power of retaining magnetism in any specimens of iron or steel, is in proportion to its hardness.

(55.) But some of the combinations of iron with other substances affect its capacity for magnetism, independently of the hardness of the compound. A slight degree of oxidation pervading the mass of iron appears to increase its power of retaining magnetism; but a greater degree renders it totally insusceptible of being affected by the magnet, or of possessing any magnetic properties whatsoever. Combinations with phosphorus, with arsenic, or with tin, were found by Mr. Gay Lussac to produce compounds somewhat resembling those of carburet of iron or steel in their capability of retaining magnetism. Every thing depends, however, upon the proportions in which these several substances are united with the iron; for if they exceed a certain quantity, they totally incapacitate the compound from acquiring any magnetic properties.

(56.) It is only the finest and purest soft iron, free from all knots and veins, that returns to the state of perfect neutrality after it is removed from all extraneous magnetic influence. Iron is seldom found in this perfectly pure state; but even the purest iron may be rendered capable of permanently retaining magnetism, if it has been twisted or hammered violently. The slight superficial oxidation it undergoes by the action of the atmosphere, will also make it susceptible of some degree of fixed magnetism. But in its common state, iron may, on the whole, be regarded as incapable of any long retention of the magnetism which it may have received by induction.

(57.) It would appear from the experiments of Mr. Scoresby[*], that the texture of all iron, even the most malleable, presents a certain degree of resistance to the transmission of magnetic power; for if a bar of iron be placed in circumstances favourable to its acquiring magnetism by induction, it does not acquire it in the degree of intensity of which it would be capable, were there no such internal obstructions to the transmission. If, under these circumstances, it be subjected to percussion, which, as we have seen, favours the transfer of magnetism in obedience to the attractive and repulsive forces that act upon it, it is found to acquire a much higher intensity of magnetic power than it would have received without such percussion. Nor is the whole of this power lost on the removal of the inducting cause; a part is retained by the iron, the internal structure of which appears to have undergone some alteration by the percussion.

As connected with this subject, we may notice the following curious observation of the same experimentalist[*]. Bars which had been strongly magnetized, and had their magnetisms destroyed or neutralized, either by hammering, heating, or by the simultaneous contact of the two poles of another magnet placed transversely, were always found by him to have a much greater facility for receiving polarity in the same direction as before, than in the contrary direction. Hence, it generally happened in his experiments, that one blow with the original north end downward, produced as much effect as two or three blows did with the original south end downwards. He also observed, that the polarity of *pokers*, generally supposed to be permanent, and considerable in intensity, was rather transient and weak; for in no instance did he meet with a poker the magnetism of which he could not destroy by a blow or two with a hammer on the point; and in general, two blows, even when the poker was held in the hand, and not rested upon any thing, were sufficient to invert the poles.

(58.) Soft steel is not much more retentive of magnetism than iron in its ordinary state. It is only when hardened that its magnetic powers become in any degree sensible. Dr. Robison states, that when steel is tempered to that degree which fits it for watch springs, it may acquire a strong magnetism, which it exhibits immediately on the removal of the magnet. But it dissipates very rapidly; and in a very few minutes it is reduced to less than one half of the intensity it manifested while in contact with the magnet, and to less than two-thirds of what it was immediately on removal from it. It continues to dissipate for some days, though the bar be kept with care; but the dissipation diminishes fast, and it retains at least one-third of its greatest power for any length of time, unless carelessly kept or injudiciously treated.

(59.) Steel tempered for cutting-tools

---

[*] Transactions of the Royal Society of Edinburgh, vol. ix. p. 252.

[*] Philosophical Transactions for 1822, p. 251.

(the same author observes), such as chisels, punches, and drills for metal, acquires magnetism still more slowly by induction, and receives less of it while in contact with the magnet; but it is less disposed to lose it, and finally retains a larger portion of what it had acquired. Steel made as hard as possible is still longer in acquiring all the magnetism which simple juxtaposition can give to it. It acquires less than the former; but ultimately retains a much greater proportion. The loadstone, or native ore of iron, resembles very hard steel in these respects; that is, in the time necessary for its greatest impregnation, and in the durability of the acquired magnetism.

(60.) We have seen that iron, or any of its compounds, when free from magnetism, is attracted by a magnet only in consequence of the induction of magnetism upon it by the magnet which attracts it. It follows, therefore, that the degree of susceptibility to induction may be accurately measured by the attraction which results from this property. With this view Mr. Barlow made a series of experiments to ascertain the relative attraction which different species of iron and steel had for the magnet; and obtained the following specific results, the relative magnetic power of each substance being expressed by numbers*.

Malleable iron	100
Soft cast steel	74
Soft blistered steel	67
Soft shear steel	66
Hard blistered steel	53
Soft shear steel	53
Hard cast steel	49
Cast-iron	48

§ 7. Fracture.

(61.) We have hitherto been able to trace a very close analogy between the phenomena of magnetism and electricity, as far at least as relates to the law of action, and the influence of induction; but in pursuing it beyond this point it fails us entirely. Electricity, whether positive or negative, is not only capable of being excited by induction, but may be actually transferred from one body to another; but the transference of the magnetic polarities is a phenomenon which was never, in a single instance, known to take place. A body may, without difficulty, be rendered positively or negatively electrified; that is, it may be charged with a redundance of one or other of the two kinds of electricity; and the influence or agency, call it by what name we please, that has been gained by one body, is the same as that which has been lost by the other. It is not so with magnetism. There is never any transfer of properties, but only the excitation of those which were already inherent in the body operated upon. We always find in the same magnet, that the intensities of the two polarities, although each may occupy different portions of it, or be concentrated in some points, and diffused over others, yet still on the whole exactly compensate each other. We never can obtain a portion of iron or steel endowed wholly with either the northern or the southern polarity. Each appears to be strictly confined within the boundary of the surface of the body which contains it.

(62.) When a conductor of electricity, of an oblong shape, is placed near an electrified body, but not sufficiently near to receive any part of its electricity, it becomes electric by induction, the two ends of the body having opposite electricities. If, under these circumstances, the conductor be divided across the middle, and the two portions removed to a distance from one another, we obtain the two electricities separate; each portion retaining the electricity that had been induced upon it. The condition of a magnet appears to be exactly analogous to this in reference to the distribution of magnetic power; for the northern polarity appears to be collected in one half of its length, and the southern polarity in the other; and each of these agencies seems, indeed, to be almost entirely concentrated in the very extremities of the bar. What, then, ought to happen conformably with this analogy, were we to break a magnet (A, *fig.* 25,)

Fig. 25.

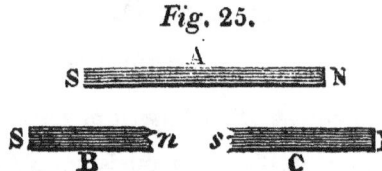

across its middle? Might we not expect by this means to obtain the two polarities separate, each still contained in the same portions where they had before resided?

(63.) The result of this experiment is exceedingly curious, and what certainly

---
* Philosophical Transactions for 1822, p. 117.

no previous reasoning could have led us to anticipate. Each portion, B C, of the fractured magnet is at once converted into a magnet, perfect in itself; that is, each respectively has a north pole at one end, and a south pole at the other. That end of the magnet which, previously to the fracture, was a north pole N, continues to be a north pole, while the other end of that fragment *s*, that is, the broken end, becomes a south pole. The converse is true of that fragment B which originally contained the south pole of the magnet. It thus appears that the two fractured surfaces *n* and *s*, are now converted, the one into a north, and the other into a south pole, although that part had, in the original magnet, been apparently in a neutral state.

(64.) Similar consequences ensue from the subdivision of one of these fragments into any number of portions, however great; each lesser fragment constituting in itself a complete magnet furnished with its two poles.

(65.) It is observed by Æpinus, who made many experiments on the effects of the fracture of magnets, and the observation has been confirmed by others, that the neutral point in each fragment of the broken magnet is at first much nearer to the place of their former union than to their other ends. He states that in the space of a quarter of an hour after the separation, the neutral points advance nearer to the middle of each, and continue to do so, by small steps, for some hours, and sometimes days, and finally become stationary at the centre.

When a magnet is split according to its length, the two portions will have sometimes contrary, and sometimes the same poles as they had when they formed one piece. When one portion is much thinner than the other, the slender fragment generally has its poles reversed*.

Chapter II.

Laws of Magnetic Forces.

§ 1. *Relation of Intensity to Distance.*

(66.) It would be inconsistent with the elementary views to which we are at present confining ourselves, to engage in the investigation of the mathematical law which regulates the variations of intensity of the magnetic forces, both attractive and repulsive, at different distances. We shall here only observe that this law has been made the subject of diligent and careful inquiry by some of the most eminent philosophers of modern times; and shall content ourselves with merely stating the final result of their labours. It has been ascertained most satisfactorily that the same law of variation obtains in magnetic attractions and repulsions with relation to proximity, as in the electrical: namely, that the intensity of the force by which magnetic polarities act upon each other is inversely as the square of their distance. In this respect, therefore, they agree, not only with the electrical forces, but also with that of gravitation; and it would appear, indeed, to be a property common to all forces which emanate in every direction from a central agent.

(67.) The variations of the intensities of magnetic attractions and repulsions exerted between any two poles depend solely upon the distances at which they are placed; and are in no degree affected or interfered with by the interposition of other bodies which are not themselves magnetic. Numerous experiments have been made with a view of discovering whether there exists any substance which can modify or intercept the action of magnets when placed between them and the body acted upon; but the result has been uniformly the same: namely, that the intervening bodies, of whatever kind they were, provided they were not susceptible of magnetism, occasioned no difference in the observed effects.

This subject, however, involves a question, hereafter to be discussed, as to the magnetic susceptibilities of substances which are not of a ferruginous nature.

§ 2. *Mutual Action of Two Magnets.*

(68.) The general law of magnetic force with relation to distance being once established, it becomes interesting to follow its consequences and applications under a variety of circumstances. These consequences are always, even in the simplest cases, more complicated than electrical arrangements; because in magnets the two polarities are always conjoined, and their influence is never perfectly isolated. In studying the mutual actions between two magnets, or even between one magnet and the smallest conceivable piece of iron, we have always four polarities in activity, the two residing in one body, and the two residing in the other; these polarities are

---

* Derham, Philosophical Transactions, vol. xxiv. p. 2138.

not strictly confined to particular points in the magnet: for although much concentrated at the two ends, they exist with less intensity in other parts of the magnet.

(69.) Let us, however, suppose, for the sake of simplification, that the magnetic forces emanate solely from the two poles at the extremities of the magnet M, *fig.* 26, with its axis placed hori-

Fig. 26.

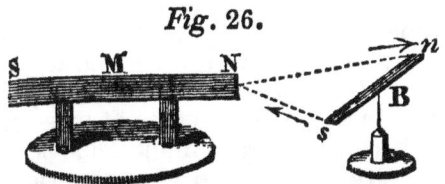

zontally, while a smaller magnet B suspended on a point, or in other words, the needle of a mariner's compass, and which we shall therefore designate as *the needle*, is presented to it in the vicinity of its north pole, N, and with its centre in a line with the axis of the magnet. The north pole of the magnet attracts the south pole of the needle, and tends to turn it in the direction indicated by the arrow at *s*. It also repels the north pole of the needle, turning it in the direction indicated by the arrow at *n*. These two actions, it will be seen, both conspire to give the needle a rotatory motion in the same direction with regard to its centre, and to bring it into the position represented in the next figure, (27,)

Fig. 27.

in which the south pole of the needle is turned directly towards the north pole of the magnet.

The influence of the south pole, S, of the magnet operates in a manner exactly contrary to that of its north pole; but being at a greater distance, its intensity is less; and all that it can effect is to subtract somewhat from the forces with which the needle would have been impelled, if the north pole of the magnet had acted alone. The general result as to the rotatory motion, is therefore determined by the predominance of the actions of the north pole of the magnet, and remains as before stated.

(70.) The tendency in one magnet to assume a particular position with relation to another magnet, is termed its *directive force**. It results, as we have seen, from the conjoined influence of two forces, the one acting on the north, and the other on the south pole, and is therefore equal to the sum of these forces.

(71.) If we now consider what tendency the needle has to approach to, or recede from the magnet, we shall find the same forces, which in the former instance conspired together, now opposing each other. It is, in the first place, evident that while the needle is in the position shewn in *fig.* 26, that is, at right angles to the magnet, the attraction of the adjoining north pole of the magnet for the south pole of the needle, is balanced by its repulsion for its north pole; and the needle, although strongly urged by these forces to turn round its centre, has no tendency, on the whole, to recede from, or approach the magnet. When, however, it arrives at the position shewn in *fig.* 27, its south pole *s* being nearer to N than its north pole *n*, the attractive action is more powerful than the repulsion, and the needle is, consequently, now impelled towards the magnet. But the force which thus impels it results from the difference only of two contrary forces, the one attractive, the other repulsive.

(72.) Hence we may conclude that the directive force, which consists of the sum of two forces, is in all cases considerably greater than the attractive force exerted upon the whole needle; this latter force being only equal to the difference between the same forces. The ratio between the directive and attractive forces will be increased, either by diminishing the length of the needle, or increasing that of the magnet. Hence the polarity of a small needle may be considerable, while its attraction is quite insensible.

(73.) Let us next transfer the needle to the situation shown in *figs.* 28 and 29, in which its centre is in a line drawn from the centre of the magnet, and at right angles to its axis; the needle being supposed, as in the former case, to be so balanced as to turn freely in a plane which passes through the centre of the needle, and both poles of the magnet. Let it be placed in the position indicated in *fig.* 28, with one of its poles directed towards the middle of the magnet. The directive force is here compounded of four forces: the attractions of N for *s* and of S for *n*; and

---

* Dr. Gilbert expressed it by the term *verticity*.

Fig. 28.

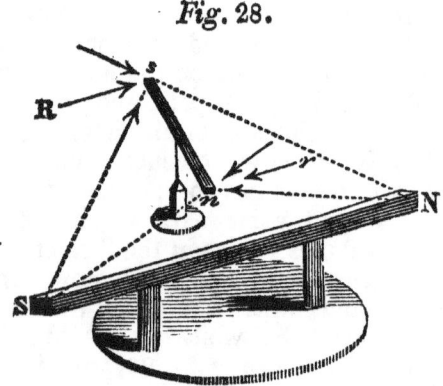

the repulsions of N for *n*, and of S for *s*. They respectively impel the poles *n s* of the needle in the directions denoted by the small arrows parallel to the lines in which these forces act. Those which act upon the remote pole of the needle *s*, compose a resultant having the direction of the upper horizontal arrow R, at right angles to the length of the needle, which is also the radius of its revolution. Those forces which act upon the opposite pole *n*, compose another resultant force in the opposite direction, expressed by the lower horizontal arrow *r*. Now these two resultant forces having opposite directions, and acting at the opposite ends of the needle which turns upon its centre, conspire in producing a rotation in the same direction with relation to that centre; and will tend to bring the needle into the position shown in *fig.* 29, in

Fig. 29.

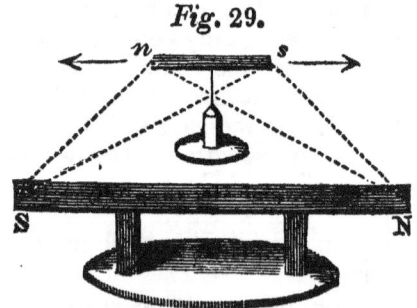

which its direction is parallel to that of the magnet, but in which its poles are reversed when compared with those of the magnet; that is, the north pole of the needle being on the side of the south pole of the magnet, and its south pole on the side of the north pole of the magnet. This relative situation has been called by some authors *the subcontrary position*.

(74.) Here also it may be remarked, that in consequence of the greater proximity of the poles of the different denominations, compared with that of the poles of the same name, the sum of the attractive forces exceeds that of the repulsive; the former will therefore prevail, and the needle will have a tendency to move towards the magnet in the direction of the line connecting their centres.

(75.) A similar process of reasoning, derived from the same principles, will enable us to determine the resultants of the forces which act upon the needle when its centre is situated in different directions relatively to the axis of the magnet: and consequently what will be its movements, and what its final position of equilibrium. In oblique positions, indeed, the process of investigation becomes more complicated, for it is necessary to take into consideration the different intensities of each of the four forces concerned, with reference not only to the respective distances of the poles of the needle from those of the magnet, but also to their respective directions in the plane of rotation.

(76.) If the plane of rotation, to which the movements of the needle is limited, be one which does not pass through the poles of the magnet, the complication of the problem becomes still greater. There are, however, three general results at which we may arrive, which tend very much to simplify the resolution of questions relating to this subject.

(77.) The first is, that if we suppose the needle to be at perfect liberty to move on its centre in all directions, the position of equilibrium at which it will arrive by the conjoint action of all the forces which impel it, will always be situated in the plane which includes the poles of the magnet and the centre of the needle. This plane may be called, for the sake of distinctness, *the magnetic plane*; and the position assumed by the needle in this plane may be called its *magnetic* position.

(78.) Secondly, when the movements of the needle are limited to any particular plane, its position of equilibrium is that which makes the nearest approach to the magnetic position that the case will admit of. It will therefore be situated in a plane passing through the magnetic position, and at right angles to the plane of revolution.

(79.) Thirdly, if the plane of revolution be perpendicular to the magnetic position, the needle will be in a state of equilibrium with regard to the forces exerted upon it by the magnet, in all positions. Such a plane may be called *the plane of neutrality*. An example of this is shown in *fig.* 30, where the needle,

MAGNETISM.

Fig. 30.

turning on a horizontal axis in a line with the magnet, is limited in its motion to a vertical plane perpendicular to its position of equilibrium. In this case it will have no tendency to assume any one position in preference to another, in this plane.

§ 3. *Magnetic Curves.*

(80.) In order still further to generalize our views, let us conceive the needle to be exceedingly short when compared with the length and distance of the magnet; and we shall then arrive at still more simple conclusions with regard to its positions of equilibrium in the magnetic plane. The two poles of the needle may, with regard to the action of the magnet, be considered as coincident; the intensities of the actions of any one of the poles of the magnet upon them are so nearly equal that their differences may be regarded as infinitely small. The attraction of the magnet for this minute needle, an attraction which, as we have seen, depends upon their difference, must accordingly be inappreciable. But the directive force, on the contrary, depending on the sum of these actions, must be very effective; and it is to the operations of the latter of these forces only that we need direct our inquiries.

(81.) The problem to be solved is this: given the position of the magnet M, (*fig.* 31,) and of its two poles N and S,

Fig. 31.

and also the place of the centre C of the needle, which is supposed to be at liberty to revolve only in the magnetic plane, to find the direction C T, at which the rotatory force resulting from the action of the north pole N of the magnet on the two poles of the needle in the direction C N, exactly balances that resulting from the action of the south pole S of the magnet on these poles, in the direction C S, each force having an intensity reciprocally proportional to the squares of these respective lines.

It may be mathematically demonstrated * that if such be the law of the magnetic forces, the direction of the needle is that of the tangent of a peculiar curve of an oval shape, which has been denominated the *magnetic curve*. Every magnet having two poles N and S (*fig.* 32) has a system of mag-

---

* Demonstrations of this and of the other fundamental properties of the magnetic curves are given in the Journal of the Royal Institution, for Feb. 1831, by the author of this Treatise.

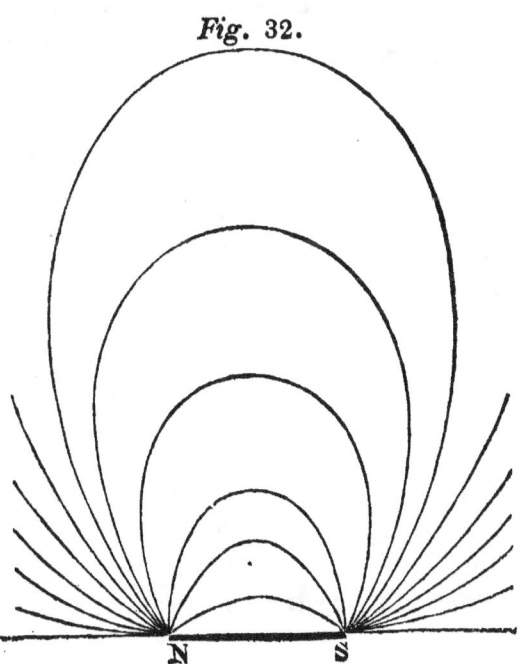

Fig. 32.

netic curves related to the line joining these poles, and which may be called its axis. The general form and disposition of these curves, according to their different distances from the magnet, is shown in the figure.

(82.) The magnetic curves have the following remarkable property; namely, that the difference of the cosines of the angles, which lines, drawn from any point in the curve to the two poles, make with the axis, taken on the same side, is constant. Thus, in the curve S C C' C'' N, *fig.* 33, the sum of the

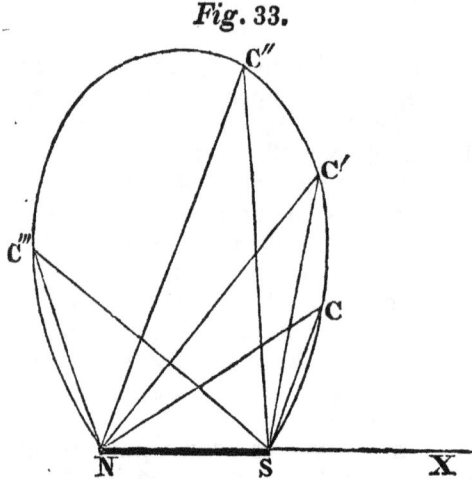

Fig. 33.

cosines of the angles C N X and C S X, is equal to the sum of the cosines of the angles C' N X and C' S X. When, however, the angle C'' S X exceeds a right angle, its cosine being negative, it will be the sum (instead of the difference) of the cosines of the polar angles C'' N S, C'' S N, that is constant. When the angle C''' N X is also obtuse, both the cosines being negative, it is again their difference that is constant.

(83.) If two radii of equal length, N *n*, S *s*, *fig.* 34, be made to revolve in the same

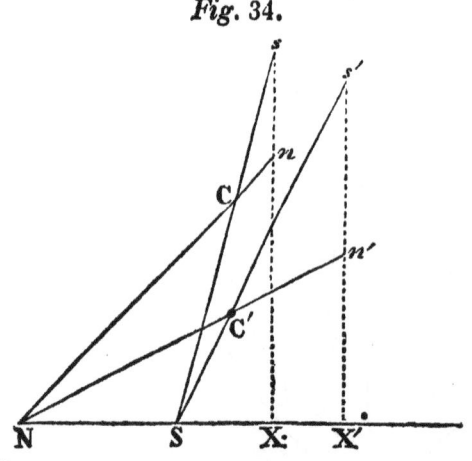

Fig. 34.

direction round their respective centres N and S, while their other extremities, *n* and *s*, are kept continually in such a relative position as that a line drawn through them shall always be perpendicular to the axis N X, then the line, constituted by the successive points of intersection C, C' of the radii, will be a magnetic curve*.

(84.) The most expeditious method of delineating a great number of magnetic curves related to the same base, in order to obtain a general view of the entire system of these curves, is to describe from each pole, N, S (*fig.* 35), as a centre, the equal circles or semi-circles, A A, B B, with as large a radius as the paper will conveniently admit of; and, dividing the axis, produced till it meets both circles, into any number of equal parts, to mark off, on the circumferences of both the circles, the points where they are cut by perpendiculars from these points of division; then, drawing radii from the centre of each circle to the divisions of its respective circumference, the mutual intersections of these radii will form different series of points indicating the course of the magnetic curves which pass through them. In the present case these curves are composed of a succession of diagonals of the lozenge-shaped interstices formed by the intersecting radii, as is shown in the upper half of *fig.* 35.

(85.) The forms and disposition of these curves are elegantly illustrated by the lines in which iron-filings arrange themselves when acted upon by a powerful magnet. In order to exhibit them, we need only place a sheet of paper or pasteboard immediately over a straight magnetic bar laid flat upon a table, and scatter lightly some very fine iron-filings over the pasteboard; which is best done by shaking them through a gauze bag. If we then tap gently upon the paper, so as to throw them into a slight agitation, they will arrange themselves with great regularity in lines, which exactly follow the course of the magnetic curves, extending from one pole of the magnet to the other. These minute fragments of iron, being rendered magnetic by induction, have their dissimilar poles fronting each other, and therefore attract one another, and adhere together

---

* The author of this Treatise has constructed a system of rulers by which magnetic curves may be mechanically delineated, founded on the principle stated in the text. The description of this instrument is contained in the paper above referred to in the Journal of the Royal Institution.

MAGNETISM.

Fig. 35.

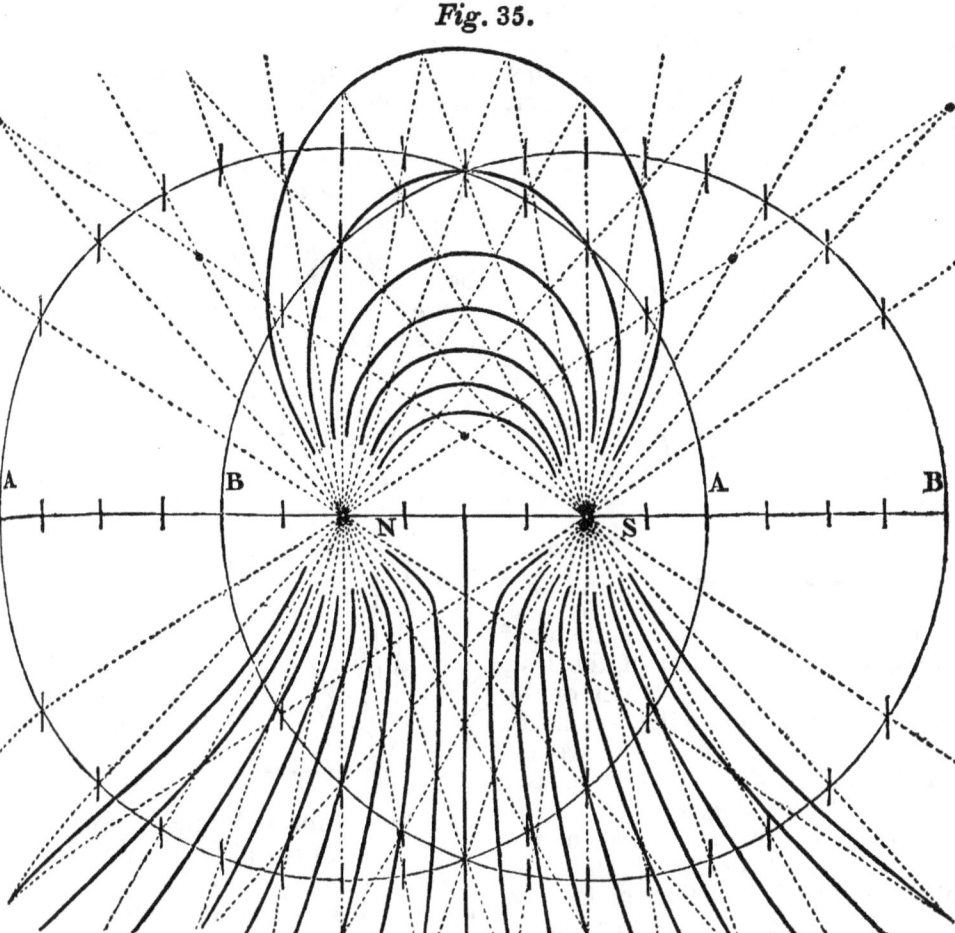

in the direction of their polarities, which is that of the tangent to the magnetic curve: thus affording a beautiful ocular exemplification of the mathematical properties of these curves.

(86.) By continuing to tap upon the paper, the filings arrange themselves still more visibly into separate lines; but here a curious, and perhaps unlooked for phenomenon presents itself. The lines gradually move and recede from the magnet, appearing as if they were repelled, instead of attracted, as theory would lead us to expect. This arises from the circumstance that each particle of iron, or cluster of particles, is thrown up into the air by the shaking of the paper, and, while unsupported, immediately turns on its centre, and acquires a position more or less oblique to the plane of the paper. This is shown in *fig.* 36, in which M represents a section of the magnet, P P a section of the paper, and *ff* the position of the filaments of iron thrown up into the air. The end of each filament nearest to the magnet is thus turned a little downwards, and the filament falls upon the paper at a point a little more distant than that which it before occupied; and thus, step by step, it moves further and further from the magnet, till it reaches the edge of the paper and falls off.

(87.) When the magnet, instead of being beneath the paper, is held above it, the effect is just the reverse. In this latter case, the lower ends of the filaments having a tendency to turn towards the magnet, the filings gradually collect under it, when made to dance by the vibrations of the paper, instead of falling outwards as they did before. This will be rendered apparent by *fig.* 37, where the letters indicate the same objects as in the preceding figure.

Fig. 36.

Fig. 37.

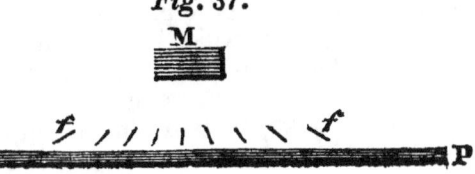

(88.) Magnetic curves of a different kind are constituted by the balanced actions of two poles of the same denomination placed near to each other. When, for instance, a second north pole N′ (*fig.* 38) is substituted, instead of the south pole S, both poles will act in a similar manner, and in directions not very different.

Fig. 38.

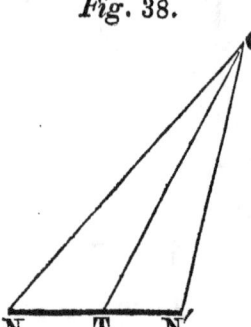

In order to render the conditions of this case as simple as those of the last, we must suppose that the action of the south poles belonging to the two north poles N, N′, whose action we are examining, is, from their remoteness, too feeble to influence the results. In the former case, where the actions of the two poles were of a contrary kind, the resultant of their joint action, or the line C T (*fig.* 31) passed in a direction intermediate between N C prolonged and C S, and therefore cut the axis N X at some point in the prolongation of N S. But in the present case, the two magnetic poles being of the same kind, their action is similar, and their resultant is a force of which the direction is intermediate to the lines C N and C S; and this line produced must cut the axis somewhere between N and N′. In consequence of this change of position, which produces a change in the sign of the cosine of the angle C S T, which is now C N′ T, the relation of the cosines of the polar angles is as follows; namely, that the sum (and not, as before, the difference) of the cosines of the angles which lines, drawn from any point in the curve to the two poles, make with the axis, taken on the same side, is constant. This applies to the case in which the angle formed by C N′ with the produced axis is acute, and its cosine positive. When it is obtuse (or C N′ N acute), the cosine becoming negative, it is their difference which is constant.

(89.) The intersections of the radii, drawn according to the method above described, § 82, will also point out the course of those curves which belong to the case where the acting poles are similar. For this purpose they must be taken in a different order of arrangement, and followed in the lines of the other diagonals of the lozenge-shaped intervals between the intersecting radii; that is, of the diagonals which cross those constituting the curves in the former case, as is shown in the lower half of *fig.* 34. These *divergent* curves, as they have been called in contradistinction to the former or *convergent* ones, are delineated in *fig.* 39; and may, in like man-

Fig. 39.

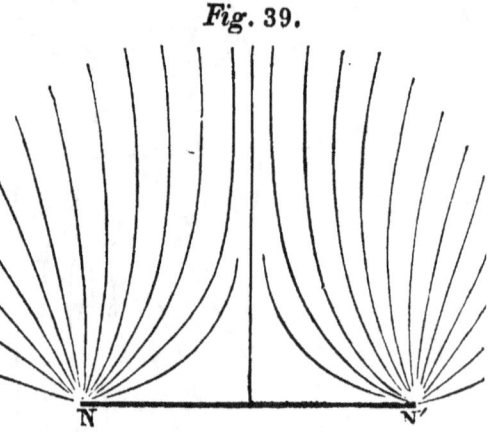

ner, be exhibited by the arrangements of iron-filings round two similar poles.

(90.) When the actions of the four poles of two magnets are taken into account, the magnetic curves expressive of the direction of a needle influenced by them, become, of course, much more complicated.

Chapter III.

Terrestrial Magnetism.

§ 1. *Variation of the Compass.*

(91.) It has been already stated (§ 6), that if a magnetic bar be poised on its centre so as to move freely in a horizontal plane, and if no ferruginous body be sufficiently near to affect it sensibly, it will assume, when left at liberty, a direction nearly north and south. When disturbed from this situation, it returns, after several oscillations, to the same position. On this property is founded the mariner's compass, which is of such essential use in navigation. In moving horizontally towards the position which it thus tends to assume, the needle of the compass is said to *traverse*.

(92.) It is found that in this country, as well as throughout Europe, the north pole of the compass deviates a certain number of degrees to the westward of the exact northern direction. This deviation from the true geographical meridian has been called the magnetic *declination;* but it is more usually known by the term *Variation of the Compass.* The vertical plane which passes through the direction of the horizontal needle at any particular place is termed the *magnetic meridian* of that place, in contradistinction to the *geographical* or *true meridian,* which is a vertical plane passing through the poles of the earth.

(93.) There are but few places on the earth where the compass points directly to the poles; that is, where it exhibits no variation. As far as observation has extended, these places are situated in a line which encompasses the globe, and is called *the line of no variation.* In many of its portions it appears to form part of a great circle of the sphere, but in others it deviates much from regularity, presenting many flexures in its course. It may be considered as commencing from a point which may be designated as the principal arctic magnetic pole of the earth, and the exact situation of which is not yet perfectly ascertained, although the late voyages of discovery in these regions have enabled us to form a tolerable approximation to the precise spot, which appears to be a point somewhere to the westward of Baffin's Bay. After crossing the United States of North America it passes along a tract of the Atlantic, a little to the eastward of the windward West India Islands, till it touches the north-eastern point of the South American continent. Thence it stretches across the Southern Atlantic towards the south pole, where navigators are unable to follow it. It re-appears in the eastern hemisphere to the south of Van Dieman's Land, and passing across the western part of the Australian continent, is again found in the Indian Archipelago. Here, according to Biot, it divides into two branches, one of which crosses the Indian Sea and enters Asia at Cape Comorin; it then traverses Hindostan and Persia, and passing through the western part of Siberia stretches over to Lapland and the Northern Sea. The second branch pursuing a more directly northern course, traverses China and Chinese Tartary, and makes its exit from Asia in the eastern division of Siberia, where we again lose it in the Arctic seas. Between these there must exist an intermediate line of no variation in some part of the continent of Asia; but the observations we possess regarding it are, as yet, too imperfect to admit of any attempt to trace it correctly.

(94.) If we consider these Asiatic lines of no variation as composing a single band, we may then consider the globe as divided by this and the corresponding American line into two hemispheres. In that hemisphere which comprehends Europe, Africa, and the western parts of Asia, together with the greater portion of the Atlantic, the variation is to the west. In the opposite hemisphere, which comprises nearly the whole of the American continents, both North and South, and the entire Pacific Ocean, together with a certain portion of Eastern Asia, the variation is to the east.

§ 2. *Dip of the Magnetic Needle.*

(95.) But in order to arrive at a knowledge of the real influence which the earth exerts on a magnetic needle, it is not sufficient to ascertain the position it assumes when its movements are confined to a horizontal plane, as it is in the mariner's compass of the ordinary construction: we must place it in such circumstances as will allow it to move freely in a vertical plane also. But to effect this in an unexceptionable manner is extremely difficult. The great obstacle with which we have to contend is the force of gravity, which by acting in one direction, interferes with the operation of the force of terrestrial magnetism, which acts in a different and in an oblique direction.

(96.) The readiest mode of removing the influence of gravity, is to affix a steel needle to a cork, or other buoyant substance, and to immerse it in water, adjusting the specific gravity of the two bodies, so that they may remain suspended in the middle of the fluid without any tendency either to float or to sink; taking care at the same time that the centre of gravity of the whole coincides with the centre of its figure, so that, when the needle is unmagnetic, and united to the cork, the two together, placed in any position in the fluid, shall have no tendency to take any other position. If the needle be now rendered magnetic, and replaced as before, it is found to assume a position nearly vertical, that is, making an angle with the plumb line of about 20 degrees, the north pole of the needle being turned about 25 degrees to the westward of the true north. Its deviation from the plane of the meridian is equal to the variation of the horizontal needle. Its inclination to the horizontal plane, or 70°, is called the dip. But this method, though well fitted for illustrating the general fact, and the principle on which it depends, is not adapted for accurate measurement. For this purpose we must have recourse to other contrivances.

(97.) The magnetic force may, by the ordinary dynamic method of the resolution of forces, be resolved into two forces, the one acting vertically, the other horizontally. The latter of these forces, namely, the horizontal force, is the only one with the action of which gravitation does not interfere; and accordingly, the mariner's compass indicates by its motions, the effects of this part of the terrestrial magnetic force, and this only. In order to ascertain the vertical force, we must proceed in a different manner. The needle must be furnished with an axis, at right angles to its length, and adjusted very carefully, so that it may pass as exactly as possible through its centre of gravity. This, of course, can only be done when the needle is wholly free from magnetism, and secured, in the manner hereafter to be pointed out, from all magnetic influence which the earth might exert upon it. The axes should be supported horizontally in such a manner as to allow the needle complete freedom of motion in a vertical plane. The needle being thus balanced, will have no tendency to incline to one side rather than to another, and will remain at rest in any position in which it may happen to be left, as long as no extraneous force is applied to it. When this has been accomplished, the needle is to be magnetized, by the methods hereafter to be described, as strongly as possible, and it is then to be replaced on its supports, which are to be turned so that the plane in which the needle is allowed to move, may coincide with that of the magnetic meridian. It will be found that, in this situation, the end of the needle to which a northern polarity has been imparted, will preponderate, or *dip*, as it is called, and after a certain number of oscillations, will settle at a determinate point. The line which its axis assumes under these circumstances, is termed the *magnetical direction*, or *position*. The dip of the needle was first observed by Norman.

(98.) The inclination of the needle, or *dip*, like the variation, differs in different parts of the globe. The latest accurate observation of the dip in London, of which we have any record, is that of Captain Sabine, who ascertained it, in August, 1828, to be 69° 47'.* As a general rule, to which, however, there are many exceptions, the dip diminishes as we approach the equator, and increases as we recede from it on either side. Towards the polar regions it is very great, and as we come near to the poles, it approaches to a right angle. At the magnetic poles themselves, the dipping needle would, of course, be exactly perpendicular to the horizon. Those places on the earth where the needle is perfectly horizontal, that is, where there is no dip, are in a line that encircles the globe, and is termed the *magnetic equator*.

(99.) As the magnetic poles are not situated exactly at the poles of the earth's rotation, but at some little distance from them; so, the magnetic equator does not coincide with that of the earth; though it does not in any part deviate widely from it. In a general way we may consider it as a great circle of the globe inclined to the terrestrial equator at an angle of about 12 degrees; its intersections with it being situated at the longitudes 113° 14' west, and 66° 46' east from the meridian of Greenwich. Such, at least, is the result given by all the observations made for an extent of more than one half of its circuit, in the Atlantic and Indian Oceans, and that part of the Pacific which is nearest to the South American continent, as appears from a table of these observations given by Biot*. But a remarkable anomaly is met with when we trace the course of the magnetic equator across the Pacific Ocean. This line is found in the southern hemisphere in the American continent, and joins the equator as before-mentioned, at a longitude of about 113°; but still further to the westward, at longitude 156° 30' it is again met with at a distance from the equator and to the south of it. In the Sea of China at 116° east longitude, it is found to the north of the equator, which it must therefore have crossed at some intermediate point; and it is again inflected towards the south, so as to traverse the equator at the eastern node already mentioned.

It appears, therefore, from these observations, that there are at least three points in the terrestrial equator where the magnetic equator coincides with it; and the probability is, that there are four: because, if the latter curve passes to the northern side of the equator at its western coincidence, it must again cross it before

---

* Philosophical Transactions for 1829. Since the above was written, we are informed that the dip has been ascertained by Capt. Segelcke to be 69° 38' at Woolwich, in Nov. 1830.

* Traité de Physique, tome III. p. 130.

it can arrive at the southern situation in which it has been met with in longitude 156½°. These inflexions will, therefore, assume a figure, with relation to the terrestrial equator, somewhat like that represented in *fig*. 40, where the dotted line *m m m*, is the magnetic, and the continuous line, *e e*, the terrestrial equator.

Fig. 40.

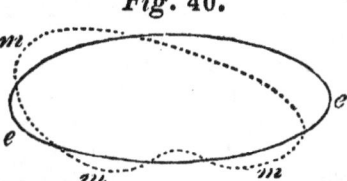

§ 3. *Variations in the Intensity of Terrestrial Magnetism.*

(100.) Besides the variation and the dip, which together constitute the magnetic position, and which differ much in different situations, there is also a third circumstance highly deserving our attention in connexion with this subject, namely, the intensity of the force which directs the needle towards this position. Extensive observations of the relative intensities of the magnetic force of the earth in different parts of its surface, are of greater value in enabling us to understand the 'general system of terrestrial magnetism than those in the dip or variation. We know that this force varies greatly in different latitudes; but our information with regard to the exact amount of this variation is exceedingly scanty, both from its importance not having been felt, and the consequent omission of the proper observations with regard to it, and also from the greater difficulty there is in conducting the experiments which are required to ascertain it.

(101.) The best mode of estimating the comparative intensities of the magnetic action in the same needle in two different places, is to count the number of oscillations which it makes in a given time, a minute for example, on its being disturbed from its position of equilibrium, while it is resuming that position. The movements of the needle being regulated by the same dynamical laws which govern the oscillations of the pendulum, it is a necessary consequence of those laws, that the intensity of the force producing the oscillations, is proportional to the square of the number of oscillations performed in a given time. Mr. Graham appears to have been the first who devised this method of measuring the magnetic intensities.

(102.) The first accurate observations of this kind were those made by Humboldt, and by De Rossel: who have completely established the general fact, that the intensity of the force of terrestrial magnetism increases as we recede from the equator, where it is weakest, till we approach the poles: at the magnetic poles themselves, it is probably greater than at any other spot. We have every reason to expect that great light will be thrown on this department of the science from the labours of Professor Hansteen of Christiana, who is now travelling at the expense of the King of Sweden, and with the permission of the Emperor of Russia, for the purpose of observing the magnetic dip, variation, and intensity, over the whole of the North of Europe and of Asia. He has especially directed his attention to trace the course of the lines of equal intensity, or *isodynamic lines* as they have been called: that is, the lines connecting those places where a needle freely suspended in the magnetic direction, and drawn a certain number of degrees from this position, makes the same number of vibrations round the point of rest in an equal time.

§ 4. *Hypothesis of the Magnetism of the Earth.*

(103.) From a consideration of the general facts that have now been stated with respect to the influence of terrestrial magnetism, it will be sufficiently evident that the earth acts upon magnetised bodies in the same way as if it were itself a magnet; or rather as if it contained within itself a powerful magnet lying in a position nearly coinciding with its axis of rotation. This hypothesis was originally proposed by Dr. Gilbert in his work entitled "Physiologia nova de Magnete, et de Tellure magno magnete," published in the year 1600; and Kepler ranks this hypothesis among the greatest discoveries in the annals of science.

(104.) In order to make this hypothesis agree with facts, we must assume that that pole of the terrestrial magnet which is situated in the northern regions of the earth, attracts the north pole of the compass needle, and consequently that it has the same properties as the south pole of an ordinary magnet. The opposite pole of the earth, or that situated in the antarctic regions, has the contrary properties, for it attracts the south pole of the compass; and therefore corresponds in its properties to the north pole of a common magnet.

(105.) It may be necessary to remark that this circumstance of the south pole of the terrestrial magnet being situated near the north pole of the earth, and *vice versa*, has occasionally created a confusion of terms. Some authors have taken a fancy to reverse the names we have hitherto given to the magnetic polarities: assuming that it is more correct to set out by calling that property which distinguishes the pole of the terrestrial magnet situated in the northern regions, the northern polarity: and consequently to give the name of the south pole to that pole of the compass, or ordinary magnet, which is attracted towards it, and which of course has the opposite polarity. For the same reason they would call the antarctic pole of the magnet of the earth, *the south pole*, and that end of the needle which is turned towards it, *the north pole*. Mr. Savery* endeavoured to avoid this confusion of terms by using the word *end*, in contradistinction to that of *pole*; and this phraseology is adopted by Mr. Christie in his papers in the Philosophical Transactions, as appears from the following passage: "To prevent any ambiguity, I must here state, that by the *south pole* of a magnet, I understand always the end which, when the magnet is freely suspended, points towards the north pole of the earth; so that the *north end* is the *south pole*, and the *south end* the *north pole* of a magnetic needle†." It matters little which set of terms are used, provided they are clearly defined, and all persons agree to abide by these definitions. But whereever a diversity of practice exists, it is then best to adhere to that which most generally prevails: in the present case the authorities in favour of the nomenclature we have adopted are much the most numerous.

(106.) Some have attempted to avoid the confusion which the changes just mentioned would lead to, by the introduction of the terms *Boreal* and *Austral* instead of *north* and *south:* the former set of terms having reference to the natural magnetism of the earth, the latter to that of the needle, or artificial magnet: that is, they would express what we have all along called the *northern polarity*, by the term *Austral polarity;* and the *southern polarity*, they would translate by the expression *Boreal polarity*. We should not have dwelt upon this comparatively unimportant topic, were it not that this change of language is sanctioned and adopted by Biot and most of the Continental writers on magnetism.

(107.) Assuming it, then, as an hypothesis, that the earth contains in its axis, or near it, a powerful magnet, let us note the consequences which follow from it, and compare them with the facts. We shall begin with those that relate to the inductive power of the earth's magnet: a power which will be exerted in the direction which a magnetised needle, at perfect liberty to move, would assume in consequence of the action of terrestrial magnetism; that is, in the direction of the magnetic position. In this part of the globe this position is, as we have seen, not very far from the perpendicular to the horizon. A bar of unmagnetised iron placed in the vertical position, or near it, ought therefore to become magnetic from the influence of the earth, and merely in consequence of its position. Its lower end should exhibit the properties of a north pole, and its upper end those of a south pole. All this agrees perfectly with experience. An iron bar held nearly upright will be found, at its upper end, to attract the north pole of a compass needle, and repel the south pole: it is, therefore, itself a south pole. Its lower end, on the contrary, will attract the south, and repel the north pole of the compass: and has therefore a northern polarity. That these properties of the ends of the bar depend altogether on the position of the bar itself, is proved by reversing its position; when the two ends will be found to have exchanged polarities merely by their change of situation: the upper end being always a south, and the lower end a north pole. On the other hand, if the bar be placed in a position at right angles to the magnetic position, (for example, horizontally, and with the ends directed to the east and west,) it will not exhibit any characteristic magnetism.

(108.) The magnetism which a soft bar of iron derives from its position with relation to the earth, is, as we have just seen, of a transitory kind; immediately lost on turning the bar so that it makes a right angle with the magnetic position; and again acquired, but with contrary poles, when its position is reversed. But this is not the case with harder bars, for, by remaining for a considerable time in a vertical position, they are found to ac-

---
* Phil. Trans. for 1730, p. 295.
† Ibid. for 1823, p. 344.

quire a sensible and permanent magnetism. This is generally the case with the stationary iron bars belonging to a building, and even with pokers and other fire-irons which have long been kept in an upright position. This circumstance will also readily account for the permanent magnetism of that class of iron ores to which the loadstone belongs. Indeed it is perhaps not going too far to assert with Professor Robison that all the magnetism which we observe, whether in nature or art, is either the immediate or the remote effect of the magnetism of the earth.

(109.) All the phenomena which we have already described as the consequences of induced magnetism proceeding from ordinary magnets, are exemplified also in the case of that derived from the magnetism of the earth. It is most readily induced, but soonest lost, in the softest kinds of iron and steel; it is slowly acquired, but more permanently retained in hard-tempered steel. Percussion promotes the change, of whatever kind it may be, which the position of the bar relatively to the earth has a tendency to produce. Hence we see the reason why the steel bar described in § 6 became permanently magnetical by being struck, while in a vertical position, with a hammer. Mr. Scoresby found that even a bar of soft iron, held in any position, except in the plane of the magnetic equator, may be rendered magnetical by a blow with a hammer or other hard substance; and both ends seem to acquire, by this treatment, an equal degree of magnetism.

On the other hand, an iron bar, possessing permanent polarity, when placed any where in a direction at right angles to the magnetic position, and struck several times, has its magnetism always much weakened, and may even be deprived of the whole of its magnetism by a single blow. This affords, indeed, an excellent method of depriving iron of its magnetism. Rough treatment of any kind, such as filing or scouring the surface of iron, and more especially bending or twisting it, when in the magnetical position, tends to impart to it the magnetism corresponding with that position; or to destroy its previous magnetism, if it be subjected to the same treatment in a position at right angles to this.

Iron heated to redness, and quenched in water, in a vertical position, was found by Mr. Scoresby to become magnetic; the upper end acquiring the southern, and the lower end the northern polarity. Hot iron, according to the same experimentalist, receives more magnetism of position than the same when cold. An iron bar is rendered magnetical by passing an electrical discharge through its axis, provided it be in a position favourable to induction by the earth: and the polarity it acquires corresponds with the effects of this induction. Electricity appears to act, in this instance, merely by its mechanical agency, and independently of a peculiar influence of another kind which it possesses, and which will be the subject of future inquiry.

(110.) Let us now examine how far Dr. Gilbert's hypothesis corresponds with the actual phenomena of the variations of magnetic position in different parts of the globe. For this purpose, it will be necessary to revert to what was explained in a former chapter regarding the positions which a small needle assumes when under the influence of a strong magnet in its vicinity, and variously situated with respect to it. These positions, we have seen, are tangents to a magnetic curve passing through the two poles of the great magnet, and through the centre of the needle. The direction of the tangent, which is the same as that of the dipping-needle, together with that of a vertical line, or one perpendicular to the horizon, will determine the plane of the magnetic meridian, for it is the plane which includes both these lines. The compass-needle, which turns in an horizontal plane only, will arrive at its position of equilibrium when it is situated in the plane of the magnetic meridian, because it then makes the nearest approach of which it is susceptible, to the position of the dipping-needle, which is that towards which the magnetic influence of the earth tends constantly to bring it.

(111.) In those parts of the globe where the dip is very small, the horizontal needle is capable of taking a position very nearly approaching to that of the dipping-needle: hence the terrestrial magnetism is exerted in bringing it to this position with very little loss of its force. This happens in the equatorial regions of the earth. In high latitudes, on the contrary, where the dip is great, the forces which actuate the horizontal needle, act more obliquely, and therefore to great disadvantage: hence the compass-needle is more feebly impelled; the point of rest is less decidedly marked, and the compass traverses slowly. The absolute intensity of the terrestrial force is, indeed, greater in the latter case than in the former; but the increase is not sufficient to compensate for the greater obliquity of its action. If we could place ourselves exactly over the north or south magnetic pole of the earth, the dipping-needle would take a vertical position, and the horizontal compass would no longer be sensible to the influence of terrestrial magnetism, but would remain at rest in any position in which it might happen to be placed.

(112.) All these consequences of the hypothesis which ascribes terrestrial magnetism to the influence of a magnetic power in the central regions of the earth, and of which the direction nearly coincides with its axis of rotation, may be experimentally illustrated by placing a strong magnet in the centre of an artificial globe. The points on the surface which are opposite to the poles of the magnet, are to be marked as the terrestrial magnetic poles. A great circle being traced equidistant from these poles, will be the magnetic equator, dividing the globe into the northern and southern magnetic hemispheres. Great circles passing through the poles, and crossing the equator at right angles, will be magnetic meridians; of which the one which also passes through the poles of the earth's rotation will be the lines of no variation. Smaller circles parallel to the magnetic equator, will indicate situations when the dip is the same in all. The lines of equal variation will be curves of particular forms less easily determinable. The accordance of fact with theory may now be verified by placing in different situations, on the surface of a globe so prepared, a small needle suspended as freely as possible by a fine thread, which holds it balanced as nearly as possible at its centre of gravity, and observing the positions it assumes in each situation.

(113.) But when we come to compare the regular lines thus traced from theory, on the supposition of a single central magnet, with the lines which observation points out as those indicating the actual variations of the magnetism of the earth, we meet with very remarkable discordances. Many have been the attempts made to explain the irregularities and anomalies in the course of the magnetic lines by suppositions of various kinds. There is reason for believing that the northern and the southern magnetic poles do not occupy points on the globe diametrically opposite to each other, which would be the case if the magnetic influence emanated from the centre of the earth. It has been supposed, in consequence, that the terrestrial magnet, or centre of magnetic force, was eccentric. But this supposition alone will not suffice; for there are various indications of the influence of more than one pole in each hemisphere of the earth; and the probability is that these poles are of very unequal intensities. Other irregularities exist which appear to owe their existence to the influence of causes entirely local and of limited extent, such as might be supposed to be derived from large masses of iron situated at different depths beneath the surface of the earth.

(114.) The observations best calculated to decide the important question of the existence of secondary magnetic poles, appear to be those of the variations of magnetic intensity, from which we derive the knowledge of the isodynamic lines already adverted to (§ 102); for these lines will necessarily arrange themselves in regular order around the point or points in each hemisphere when the intensity is greatest, that is around each respective pole. If these poles were single, and placed opposite to each other in the globe, one in the northern and the other in the southern hemisphere, the lines of equal intensity would form parallel circles, analogous to those of geographic latitude. Captain Sabine remarks* that the observations on this subject, made previously to those of Professor Hansteen, appeared to corroborate such an hypothesis; for, although they extended widely over the magnetic parallels in the northern hemisphere, namely, from the least almost to the greatest intensity, yet they were confined, in respect to longitude, to a space little more than a quarter of a hemisphere; and to that quarter which is immediately opposite to the countries visited by Professor Hansteen. Within the space that had been thus examined, the isodynamic curves appeared to arrange themselves with comparative insignificant deviations, in parallel circles around a point situated in the north-eastern part of Hudson's Bay, and, as nearly as could be judged, about the intersection of the sixtieth degree of geographical latitude

---

* Quarterly Journal of Science, Sept. 1829, p. 3.

with the meridian of 80° west of Greenwich.

But M. Hansteen was led by a more careful consideration of the slight apparent deviations which had been noticed, and of the general disposition on the globe of the lines of dip and variation, to infer the existence of a second point of principal magnetic action in the northern hemisphere. This fact may now, indeed, be regarded as fully established by his recent observations; the isodynamic curves being found to arrange themselves systematically round two poles, the one in Hudson's Bay and the other in Siberia; and to be governed in the courses which they follow, partly by their distances respectively from those points, and partly by a disparity in the absolute attractive force at the points themselves: the maximum intensity in Siberia appearing to be weaker than that in Hudson's Bay, and existing at a point situated in longitude 102° east of Greenwich, which is as nearly as can be judged, 180° from the present position of the corresponding point in Hudson's Bay, and in a latitude somewhat to the north of 60°, but which, it is to be hoped, will soon be more particularly determined.

§ 5. *Progressive Changes of Variation and of Dip.*

(115.) The most singular and unaccountable circumstance relative to terrestrial magnetism remains yet to be noticed; namely, that it does not remain constantly the same in the same place, but undergoes a slow and progressive change. The variation of the compass is itself variable, not merely in different regions of the globe, but at different periods of time. Thus, the needle in London, in the beginning of the seventeenth century, was inclined a few degrees to the eastward of the true north. In 1659 or 1660, it pointed exactly north; or in other words, the variation was reduced to zero; and, of course, London was at that time one of the points of the line of no variation. After this, the variation became westerly, and has continued so to the present time. The line of no variation, therefore, has been progressively, but slowly moving in a westerly direction, and has now passed over to North America.

Similar changes have taken place at Paris; but the line of no variation appears to have passed over that city rather later than it did over London: for it was not till the year 1664 that the magnetic coincided with the true meridian. In 1814, it was 22° 34′ west. In October, 1829, the variation at Paris was ascertained, by M. Arago, to be 22° 12′ 5″ west*.

At London, the westerly variation continued to increase till the year 1818, when it amounted to 24° 30.′ This appears to have been its maximum; for since that time it has somewhat diminished, and is at present about 24°.

It appears, from the table given by Mr. Gilpin†, that the annual change in the variation has diminished, in each successive period, since the beginning of the last century. In the preceding century, that is from 1622 to 1692, the annual change was about 10′; from 1723 to 1773, it was about 8′; from 1787 to 1795, about 5′; from that time to 1802, only 1′.2: in 1818 it was reduced to zero.

(116.) The dip has also undergone corresponding changes, though less considerable ones than the variation. In 1680, the dip in London was 73° 30′; in 1723 it was 74° 42′: since which time it has been observed to diminish progressively, though, as it would seem, not quite regularly.

Authorities and Localities.

Year		Dip	Authority
In 1773 it was	72°	19′	Dr. Heberden.
1786	„	72 8	Gilpin, Royal Society's Rooms Phil. Trans. for 1806, p. 419.
1805	„	70 21	
1818	„	70 34	Capt. Kater, Regent's Park.
1821	„	70 3	Captain Sabine, Chiswick.
1828	„	69 47	Ditto.
1830	„	69 38	Capt. Segelcke, Woolwich.‡

On the continent of Europe the dip has undergone a similar diminution of late years. The dip at the observatory at Paris, in the year 1814, was 68° 36′, according to the determination of M. Bouvard. In June, 1829, it was ascertained by M. Arago to be 67° 41′.3.

(117.) Captain Sabine, by comparing the present dip with that observed for the last fifty years, concludes that the

---

* Annuaire pour l'An 1830.
† Phil. Trans. for 1806, p. 395.
‡ For the information relative to the last of these determinations, we are indebted to the kindness of Professor Barlow, of Woolwich, who states that Captain Segelcke, of the Norwegian Navy, and a friend of Professor Hansteen, employed in this determination of the dip, the same needle which the latter had with him in his recent tour in Siberia.

mean annual diminution is about 3'. Mr. Barlow finds that these observations accord much more nearly with what would take place on the supposition of a uniform motion of revolution in the magnetic pole round the pole of the earth. From the most authentic observations on the dip and variation of the needle in London, he calculates that the longitude of the northern extremity of the magnetic polar axis which it obeys was, in 1818, 67° 41' west, and its latitude 75° 2' north. If we suppose that the motion of this pole has been uniform since the year 1660, when, from the disappearance of variation, its longitude must have been zero, and that it has preserved the same distance from the terrestrial pole, its annual motion of revolution must have been about 25'. 4. It would, therefore, require eight hundred and fifty years to make an entire revolution of 360°. Computing from these data, it would follow that the variation ought to reach its maximum when the longitude of the magnetic pole is 70° 23' west. It would have arrived at this situation about the year 1823; about which time, as it would appear, the variation was stationary, having attained its real maximum, and having, since that period, actually retroceded.

(118.) On calculating what the dip should be in 1823, according to Mr. Barlow's hypothesis, a very near agreement with actual observation is found to take place. It follows, however, from this hypothesis, that the dip has not an uniform decrease, but that it is changing much more rapidly at this present time than it has ever done since magnetical observations have been made. Its decrease, during the five years preceding 1824, has been nearly half a degree, and it ought to have diminished to an equal extent during the following five years. Mr. Barlow* has computed that in

	The Variation should be	and the Dip
1828	24° 29'	69° 43'
1833	24 26	69 21

The near accordance of these results with what has actually been observed, is considered by him as a strong confirmation of the truth of his hypothesis.

(119.) It would appear, then, both from observation and from theory, that the dip is at present changing more rapidly than the variation; and the theory leads to the expectation that it will continue to decrease together with the dip, for about two hundred and fifty-five years, at the end of which period, that is in 2085, the longitude of the magnetic pole will be 180°; the variation will then be nothing, and the dip only 56°, which will be its minimum; they will then both increase together for the next two hundred and sixty years, when the needle will have its greatest easterly variation, and will then again return towards the north, the variation decreasing, but the dip still increasing, for one hundred and sixty-five years longer, namely, till about the year 2510, when the magnetic pole will be again in the meridian of London; the variation will then be zero, and the dip will amount to 77° 43'. It is to be observed, however, that Mr. Barlow advances this merely as an hypothesis, the truth of which remains to be determined by future experience.

(120.) A curious hypothesis was advanced by Dr. Halley, and supported with some ingenuity, in order to explain the progressive changes that take place in the variation of the compass. He supposes the globe we inhabit to be a mere external shell, enclosing, towards its centre, a detached magnetic nucleus, of a spherical shape, which revolves with the external shell on a similar axis, with nearly the same velocity. He supposes both these spheres to be magnets, having each two poles; but the poles of the one not exactly corresponding in situation with the poles of the other. The difference of the periods of rotation of the two spheres, he conceives to be exceedingly small, yet sufficient to become sensible after the lapse of years, and to occasion a change in the relative situation of the two sets of magnetic poles; and hence would arise changes in the direction of their resulting actions, and corresponding changes in the variation of the magnetic needle. However ingeniously this hypothesis may have been framed, it was too bold and fanciful to have been ever generally adopted. Its author, indeed, has the candour to acknowledge that it is beset with numerous difficulties, which further experience, extended over a long period of time, can alone enable us to remove. He concludes his paper in the Philosophical Transactions in which he has developed his theory, with the following sentence: ' But whether these magnetical poles move altogether with one motion, or

---

* See his Essay on Magnetic Attractions, 2nd Edition, p. 218.

with several—whether equally or unequally—whether circular or libratory; if circular, about what centre; if libratory, after what manner; are secrets as yet utterly unknown to mankind, and are reserved for the industry of future ages*.'

§ 6. *Diurnal Changes of Variation and Intensity.*

(121.) Independently of the changes already noticed, the position of the magnetic needle is liable to certain slight variations, according to the time of the day, and also according to the season of the year. The daily change in the variation was discovered in 1724 by Mr. George Graham, and has been confirmed by many subsequent observers. This change, however, is exceedingly minute, and requires the most careful observation, and the most delicate instruments to render it sensible, even in the horizontal needle; and it is still more difficult of detection in the dipping needle, which does not admit of the same degree of delicacy of suspension.

(122.) Professor Barlow, to whom the science of magnetism is so much indebted for its more recent improvements, has devised a mode of rendering these diurnal oscillations much more perceptible, by diminishing the ordinary directive power of the needle, through the influence of one or two magnets, placed in such positions with respect to the needle as to counteract, and thereby neutralize, as it were, the terrestrial action. The effect of the ordinary action being thus removed, he was led to expect that the extraordinary cause, whatever it might be, which produced the daily variation, would exhibit its effects much more perceptibly; and thus not only the amount of the changes it produces, but also the period of their taking place, and of the maximum of their operation, might be ascertained with great precision. These expectations have been amply realized by the success of his own experimental researches, and also by those of Mr. Christie, which are detailed in several papers in the ' Philosophical Transactions †.'

(123.) The general result of the experiments of the latter of these observers was, that the deviation of the horizontal needle from the mean position was easterly during the forenoon, and was of greatest amount at about eight o'clock, thence returning quickly to its mean position, which it attained between nine and ten o'clock, after which it became westerly; at first increasing rapidly, so as to reach its maximum at about one o'clock in the afternoon, and then slowly receding during the rest of the day, and arriving at its mean position by about ten o'clock at night. The state of the weather, and more particularly that of the temperature, had considerable influence on the nature and extent of the changes.

(124.) Mr. Christie remarks that the changes which are observed to take place cannot be explained by a change in the directions alone of the terrestrial forces, but that their characters agree, as nearly as we can possibly expect, with the effects that would take place from an increase of intensity at the time that the direction deviates towards the west.

(125.) The occurrence of diurnal changes of intensity at Christiana in Norway have been ascertained by M. Hansteen; the same conclusion being deducible from his observations of the vibrations of a needle very delicately suspended; and also from those of Mr. Christie, made with a different apparatus, and by a totally different method.

(126.) M. Hansteen found that the minimum intensity occurs about half past ten o'clock in the morning, that is, about two hours after the westerly deviation has commenced, and the maximum intensity at half-past seven in the evening, that is, about the same time after the return towards the east. Mr. Christie * found that the terrestrial magnetic intensity is the least between ten and eleven o'clock in the morning; the time, nearly, he observes, when the sun is on the magnetic meridian; that it increases from this time until nine and ten o'clock in the evening; after which it decreases, and continues decreasing, during the morning, until it attains its minimum already stated.

(127.) The general dependence of these variations of magnetic position on diurnal changes of temperature is sufficiently apparent from the results hitherto obtained. But the prosecution of the inquiry involves considerations of another kind, connected with a subject we have not yet touched upon, namely, electro-magnetic and thermo-magnetic phenomena.

(128.) The mean diurnal changes of variation were found by Mr. Canton to

---

* Phil. Trans. for 1683, p. 220.
† For 1823, 1825, and 1827.

* Philosophical Transactions for 1825, p. 51.

differ at different seasons of the year, being greatest in June and least in December*, and he has given the results of his observations in a tabular form. Mr. Gilpin investigated this subject at a later period, and gives also tables of the diurnal changes of variations in each month, which he found to be very different in different years. The following table contains the results of these different observations*.

Mean Diurnal Changes of Variation.

Months.	Canton in 1759.		Gilpin in 1787.	Gilpin in 1793.
January	7′	8″	10′.2	4′.3
February	8	58	10.4	4.6
March	11	17	15.	8.5
April	12	26	17.4	11.7
May	13	0	18.9	10.4
June	13	21	19.6	12.6
July	13	14	19.6	12.5
August	12	19	19.4	12.1
September	11	43	15.5	9.8
October	10	36	14.3	7.0
November	8	9	11.1	3.8
December	6	58	8.3	3.8

Chapter IV.

Theories of Magnetism.

§ 1. *Mechanical Theories.*

(129.) In the general view we have now given of the present state of our knowledge with regard to magnetism, we have strictly confined ourselves to the statement of facts, unmixed with hypothetical speculations as to the nature of the powers from which they proceed. We have solely endeavoured to generalize the facts, as far as their nature and extent would warrant. The result has been their reduction to a small number, such as the mutual attractions and repulsions of magnetic iron according to certain laws,—the induction of these properties on other iron,—the differences in the capacities of receiving and of retaining these properties, existing in different kinds of ferruginous bodies,—and the magnetic influence of the globe of the earth.

(130.) But the human mind is so constituted as to refuse being restrained within the boundaries of a rigid inductive philosophy. Incited by an irresistible desire of exploring the secrets of Nature, it scruples not as to the means of forcing her to disclose them; and borne on the wings of imagination and conjecture, presses forwards with an eagerness which often betrays it into courses widely deviating from the truth. Yet good is often found to result from these erratic excursions of our faculties: they infuse fresh interest into the pursuit of knowledge; they inspire with the hope of success; they invigorate those powers which must be exerted to attain it. The spark which kindles a train of light is sometimes struck out in the conflict of discordant speculation; and amidst a multitude of attempts, some effort, more happy than the rest, elicits an important discovery. No great or comprehensive fact in science was ever established, without being preceded by a bold though sagacious conjecture. Hypothesis of some kind or other is invariably the precursor of truth.

(131.) Magnetism, ever since it occupied the attention of philosophers, has been a fertile soil for hypothesis. That a shapeless and unorganized lump of metal should have the power of drawing towards itself another equally rude and unfashioned piece lying at a distance, or of forcing it to move away, as if both were alive, and animated by some principle of active sympathy; and that all this should take place, whatever may be the number or kind of the intervening bodies, nay even in the apparent absence of any connecting medium, are phenomena of too remarkable a nature not to excite in us a lively curiosity to learn their cause. No wonder that the ancients, who had but imperfect notions of the real objects of philosophy, were impressed with a vague notion of their connexion with immaterial agency. Mag-

---

* Phil. Trans. for 1759, p. 398.

* Phil. Trans. for 1806, pp. 416, 417.

netic attraction was ascribed by Thales to the secret influence of a species of mind, or soul, residing in magnets. This was also the doctrine taught by Anaxagoras, who extended it to many other phenomena in nature. Others endeavoured to account for the attraction between the loadstone and iron by the vague notion of a kind of sympathy existing between these two bodies. In later times Cornelius Gemma imagined that the connexion between them was established by what he calls invisible rays. Cardan asserted that the iron was attracted because it was of a cold nature, and Costeo de Lodi, because iron was the natural food of the magnet.

(132.) But, consigning these wild vagaries to the oblivion they merit, let us consider whether the phenomena of magnetism are capable of being reduced to any class of physical actions with which we are more familiar. In accounting for a motion which we see take place, we have a natural repugnance to admit of the existence of a power of action at a distance; or, in other words, to conceive that a body can act where itself is not: and we always incline to that supposition which implies the motion to be the effect of impulse. We naturally ask, agreeably to this prepossession, whether the movements of magnetic bodies may not be occasioned by the impulse of some subtile ethereal fluid impinging on their surfaces; emanating, for instance, from one end, and passing into the other, or circulating in invisible currents around the magnets from pole to pole. This fluid might, for instance, be conceived to emanate from one pole, to enter at the other, and permeating the substance of the magnet, again to issue from its former outlet.

Such was the train of thought that obviously occurred to those who first witnessed the arrangement which iron filings, loosely scattered around a magnet, assume in consequence of its influence. The filings have the appearance which would be given by a stream of fluid brushing by them, and turning each individual filament in the direction of its course; which course might accordingly be easily traced in the regular and symmetric curves that are exhibited to the eye. In the infancy of the science, and in the absence of any other hypothesis, many were the speculations advanced as to the mode in which these supposed streams of magnetic fluid produced the observed effects. Descartes was the foremost among those philosophers who laboured to account for all the unexplained movements in nature by the impulsion of fluids circulating in vortices; and he naturally viewed the phenomena of magnetic action as strongly corroborating his system. Euler also, who sought to explain various natural appearances by the intervention of an ethereal fluid, did not fail to apply his favourite hypothesis to the elucidation of magnetism. He even went so far as to imagine the possibility of there existing in the substance of iron numerous canals, through which the ether circulated, furnished with valves which regulated the direction in which it moved. It was not until the phenomena had been examined with greater care, and were rigorously subjected to the inductive process, that juster notions of the nature of the magnetic forces came to be entertained. With the knowledge we now possess of the actual law of magnetic attraction and repulsion, it must be at once perceived that all hypotheses founded on the impulse of a fluid in motion, are irreconcileable with that law, and must therefore be totally discarded.

§ 2. *Theory of Æpinus.*

(133.) The obvious analogy which presents itself between the phenomena of magnetism and those of electricity, naturally suggested the probability that the same mode of explanation might apply to both, and laid the foundation of the first rational theory of magnetism. While Æpinus was intent upon improving the beautiful electrical theory of Franklin, he was struck with the remarkable similarity in the attractions and repulsions exhibited by the tourmaline, when it is heated, to those of magnetic bodies; and it occurred to him that the phenomena of magnetism might be derived from the agency of a peculiar fluid, having properties very similar to those of the electric fluid, but which acted exclusively upon iron. The principal difference between the two sets of phenomena was, that, in the case of electricity, the agent, whatever be its nature, is actually transferred from one body to another; but in magnetism there is merely induction, but never any transference. In as far, however, as respects mere attraction, repulsion, and induction, electricity and magnetism present phenomena that are perfectly pa-

D

rallel to one another. Franklin's ingenious theory of the two modes of electric agency, the one consisting in an excess, the other in a deficiency of fluid, and the happy explanation it afforded of the opposite electrical states resulting from induced electricity, and its accumulation in the Leyden phial, were applied with great ingenuity by Æpinus to the contrariety of magnetic polarities in the opposite ends of a magnet, and the induction of similar magnetic states in an unmagnetized bar of iron. His system of magnetism, when digested into a series of propositions, may be stated as follows:—

(134.) 1. There exists in all bodies capable of acquiring magnetic properties, a subtile fluid, which may be called the magnetic fluid.

2. The particles of this fluid repel one another with a force which decreases as the distance increases.

3. The particles of the magnetic fluid attract, and are attracted by the particles of iron, with a force varying according to the same law.

4. The particles of iron repel one another according to the same law.

5. The magnetic fluid is incapable of quitting the body in which it is contained, but it is capable of moving within the substance of pure iron and of soft steel without any considerable obstruction. It is more and more impeded in its motion as the steel is tempered harder; and in very hard tempered steel, and in some of the ores of iron, it moves with the greatest difficulty.

(135.) In order to judge of the degree in which the theory is qualified to represent the facts, we must study the several consequences which flow from the above suppositions, and then compare them with the actual phenomena which are presented to our observation.

(136.) Each particle of iron, by the hypothesis, attracts a particle of magnetic fluid, placed at any particular distance, with a certain force. We may conceive that magnetic fluid is gradually added to the particle, until the quantity thus added is such that the force of repulsion which the fluid exerts upon any distant particle of magnetic fluid, exactly balances the attractive force of the iron for that same particle. This quantity may be regarded as the natural quantity of fluid belonging to that particle of iron. According to this definition, therefore, a mass of iron, all the particles of which contain their natural quantity of fluid, must be neutral with regard to its action on any other particle of fluid, and also on any other particle of iron. Such is the condition of unmagnetical iron or steel. Its magnetism is neutral, or in a state of equilibrium.

(137.) But should, from any cause, this state of equilibrium be destroyed, and magnetic fluid be either accumulated beyond its natural quantity as relates to the iron, or reduced below that proportion, the part where this excess or this deficiency exists becomes active —that is, acquires the properties of either a north or a south pole. As the fluid can never pass beyond the surface of the mass of iron in which it is contained, the total quantity residing in that mass must remain precisely the same, whatever be its mode of distribution; and therefore the excess of fluid in those parts where it is accumulated or redundant, must be exactly compensated by the redundant iron, if we may so express it, in those parts where the fluid is deficient. In all cases it will be only the redundant fluid or the redundant iron that constitutes the active parts of the magnet.

(138.) It follows as a direct consequence of the second condition of the hypothesis, that the pole of one magnet in which the fluid is redundant will repel the pole of another magnet in which it is also redundant; because the fluid in each is mutually repulsive of the other.

(139.) From the third condition of the same hypothesis, it likewise follows that the pole having an excess of fluid, or the overcharged pole, as we may call it, of one magnet, will attract and be attracted by the pole in which the fluid is deficient, or the undercharged pole of the other; and this action must be reciprocal.

(140.) It is also a necessary consequence of the fourth condition that the redundant iron in the undercharged pole of one magnet repels every similarly constituted pole in other magnets; because, by the hypothesis, iron repels iron.

(141.) Hence we deduce the general law that similar poles repel, and dissimilar poles attract one another,—a law identical with that we have already deduced from experiment.

(142.) Let us next see what account the theory gives us of the induction of magnetism. If the overcharged pole of a magnet be brought near the end of a bar of iron in its natural or unmagnetical state, the redundant fluid in the former, exerting a repulsive influence on the fluid at the nearest end of the latter, will give it a tendency to move towards the remote end. It will obey this tendency, provided the texture of the iron offers no obstruction to its transmission; and a certain portion of the fluid will accordingly be transferred from the near to the remote end. The bar will now exhibit magnetic properties; its near end being undercharged, will possess a polarity of an opposite nature to that of the magnetic pole presented to it; the remote end, being overcharged, will have a polarity of the same kind as the pole of the magnet.

(143.) A series of changes exactly the converse of these will take place when, instead of the overcharged pole, we present the undercharged pole of the magnet to the bar. The redundant iron now attracts the magnetic fluid of the bar, and draws it towards the adjacent end, converting it into an overcharged pole, while the other end, from which the fluid has been drawn, becomes the undercharged pole.

(144.) The effects, however, do not end here. The bar, thus rendered magnetic, reacts upon the magnet from which it had derived its power, and tends to increase the magnetism it originally possessed. This increased magnetism, in its turn, tends to produce an augmentation of the induced magnetism of the bar; and these alternate actions and reactions proceed till all action is balanced and every thing remains quiescent. In soft iron this is accomplished almost in a moment: but in steel the process is somewhat different; for its texture presenting great impediment to the motion of the magnetic fluid, the changes of distribution take place much more slowly, and to a less extent than they do in iron. The adjacent end of a steel bar soon acquires a degree of polarity opposite to that of the end of the magnet presented to it; but the polarity of the same kind travels slowly onwards, and does not reach the other extremity of the bar till after a considerable time; and if the bar be very long, may possibly never reach it.

In this last case, we have a curious phenomenon produced from the influence of a secondary induction; namely, the appearance of a second set of poles, at a certain distance from the first. Thus, if a north pole has been presented, the adjacent end of the bar will be a south pole; at a little distance from this we shall have a north pole; beyond this again will appear another south pole, and perhaps at the furthest end a second north pole. Sometimes, indeed, there will be only three poles, the middle one being of an opposite character to those at the two ends, which are similar to one another.

(145.) Let us now remove the magnet; what will happen to the iron bar? The cause which maintained the magnetic fluid in the forced state of excess at one end, and of deficiency at the other, no longer operating, the fluid will now tend to resume its original state of uniform distribution over the whole mass of iron; and if no obstacle exist in the structure of the iron to impede its motion, it will immediately revert to that state. But if the bar be of steel, which presents obstacles to the passage of the fluid, which the force derived from its tendency to equable diffusion is insufficient to overcome, the fluid which had passed will remain stationary, and the induced magnetism will continue as at first—that is to say, the bar will have been converted into a permanent magnet.

(146.) On the same principle may be explained the effect of hammering, or any other kind of mechanical concussion, in impairing the magnetism of a steel bar; for the tremulous motions excited among the particles will open a passage for the fluid, which will thus escape from the situations where it is condensed, and return to those where it is rarefied.

(147.) Heat, as we have seen, weakens and finally destroys magnetic power; its operation may in like manner be understood, by its occasioning the separation of the particles of iron to a greater distance than before. Hence the interstices will be enlarged, and the obstacles to the motion of the fluid will be diminished, or even entirely removed. The magnetic fluid will thus be enabled to regain its natural state of uniform diffusion among the particles. But independently of its mechanical operation, there are yet many other ways in which heat may be conceived to contribute to the destruction of magnetism. It may change the action of the particles of iron on those of the fluid, or of the fluid on each other, and by altering the distribution of the fluid with respect to the particles of iron, may greatly affect the law of action between one magnet and another.

D 2

§ 3. *Correction of Æpinus's Theory.*

(148.) Thus far do the facts accord with the hypothesis of Æpinus, and thus far may we admit that hypothesis to be a satisfactory explanation of these facts. But in one important application it entirely fails; it does not explain the consequences that are observed to follow on the division of a magnet at the neutral point. Theory would lead us to expect that we should, in this case, obtain the different polarities separate, one in one piece, and the other in the other. The fact we know to be totally different: each part becomes a regular magnet with two poles, one of which retains the character it had before the separation.

Æpinus attempted to remove this difficulty by supposing that, in the act of fracture, a portion of the fluid actually escaped from the overcharged pole, while another portion entered into that which was undercharged,—effects which he conceived might result from the sudden change in the balance of magnetic forces consequent upon the fracture. But this explanation, as Professor Robison remarks, is far from satisfactory.

(149.) The only rational mode of reconciling this fact with the system of Æpinus, is to consider a magnet as an aggregate of small particles of iron, each of which individually has the properties of a separate magnet; that is, has two poles of its own: the arrangement of these particles being such that all the poles are disposed in a regular order of alternation; so that in every part of the mass of iron, each pole of one particle is in contact with the contrary pole of the next in the series. These adjacent poles of course neutralize one another, with regard to their magnetic action, and it is only those which are situated at the extremity of the line, and which are not associated with any other, that constitute the active poles of the entire magnet. Hence it is at the surface, and more particularly at the extremities, that polarity is manifested; and hence when a magnet is broken across, the fractured ends at once exhibit the opposite polarities they had before possessed, but which had been masked by their cohesion.

(150.) A practical illustration of this view of the subject may be afforded by placing a number of small magnets of equal strength in a line, with their opposite poles in contact, as exhibited in *fig.* 41. It will be found that almost the only polarity that is sensible, appears

Fig. 41.

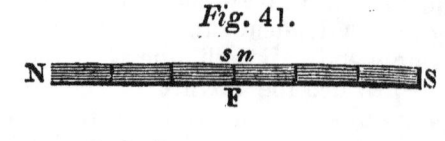

at the two extremities N and S; the intermediate portions formed by the junction of the opposite poles *n* and *s* being, to all appearance, neutral. If the series be broken at any one point as at F, the two portions G and H will immediately present the properties of separate magnets, and the new poles N^1 and S^1 being now separated, exhibit their natural activity.

(151.) According to this view of the subject, the induction of magnetism will consist, not in the actual transference of the magnetic fluid from one extremity to the other of the iron bar which has been rendered magnetic; but in a change of this nature taking place in every particle individually, and by which each particle is converted into a separate magnet.

§ 4. *Theory of two Magnetic Fluids.*

(152.) The theory with respect to magnetism which has of late more generally prevailed, is founded on the supposition, that its phenomena are occasioned by the agency of two magnetic fluids, residing in the particles of iron, and incapable of quitting them; one of which fluids imparts the northern and the other the southern polarity. They have been denominated respectively the *Austral* and *Boreal* fluids. The particles of each of these two kinds of fluids attract those of the other, but repel those of the same kind. When in combination with each other, these fluids are neutral and inert; each becoming active only when separate. The decomposition of the united fluids is effected by the inductive influence of either the one or the other when acting independently. It is obvious that, as far as regards the distribution and action of the two magnetic fluids in each individual particle, this theory is precisely similar to that of the two electric fluids, of which an account has been already given in our Treatise on Electricity; it is therefore unnecessary to pursue its development in those particulars, for the reader need only refer to that treatise, and substituting the terms austral and boreal fluids for those of vitreous and resinous electricities, will find that all the details of the electrical theory will apply to that of magnetism.

(153.) But however the laws of the theory of a double magnetic fluid may be analogous or identical with those of the theory of a double electrical fluid, their application is somewhat different in the two cases, in consequence of the difference of circumstances under which they act. The electrical fluids, when decomposed or separated from each other, are capable of being extensively transferred along the particles of bodies, and of being collected and accumulated at the surfaces, where they have a tendency to escape; and where, if that tendency exceed a certain limit, they actually do escape, either passing into the bodies in immediate contact, or flying off through the air to distant bodies. In this manner each kind of fluid may be separately, and in any quantity, transferred from one body to another. Nothing of this kind takes place with regard to magnetism; the magnetic fluids are never found to quit the bodies to which they are attached, however small those bodies, however intimate the contact with other iron, however long the contact may be continued, and however powerful the forces by which the fluids are impelled. The phenomena consequent on the division or fracture of a magnet lead us also to the conclusion that no sensible quantity of either austral or boreal fluid is ever transported from one part to another of the same piece of iron or steel. Hence, in order to accommodate the theory to these facts, we must introduce as a new condition of the hypothesis on which it is founded, that within the substance of a magnetized body, the two magnetic fluids, when they are decomposed by the influence of magnetizing forces, undergo displacements to an insensible distance only.

(154.) It is not necessary to determine whether the extremely small spaces, within which these displacements and motions of the magnetic fluids are restricted, be actually the same as the spaces occupied by the constituent molecules of the iron; it is sufficient for the purposes both of theory and of the calculations founded upon that theory, that they be extremely small in comparison with the whole volume of the body, or even with the smallest dimensions that ever come under the cognizance of our senses. Poisson, who has given us a beautiful developement of this theory*, designates these very minute spaces or portions of a magnetic body by the name of the *magnetic elements* of that body. There is also no necessity for making any particular supposition with regard to the form or respective disposition of these elements, provided we simply consider them as insulated from each other by intervals impermeable to either of the magnetic fluids.

(155.) The quantities of each kind of fluid contained in every magnetic element must be considered, with reference to all our experiments, and to all the powers we can apply, as without limit; that is to say, the forces we can command, in any magnetizing process, are never sufficient to exhaust or separate the whole of the fluids. For, when a body is magnetized by the inductive influence of a neighbouring magnet, the intensity of its magnetic state, as shown by its effects, increases without limit, in proportion as we employ a magnet of greater force; which, of course, implies that we have not yet effected the decomposition or separation of the whole quantity of the neutral or combined fluid which that body contains. In like manner, we find it impossible to separate completely the two electric fluids contained in any particular body.

(156.) Besides the obstacles, which appear to be insuperable, to the transmission of the magnetic fluids from one magnetic element to another, there must exist, in the substance of certain bodies, some impediment of another kind, which obstructs the motion of the fluids from one part to another of the same magnetic element. The effect of this power, which is somewhat analogous to the force of friction, is to arrest the particles of both fluids in the situations which they occupy; and thus to oppose, in the first place, the separation of these fluids, and, in the next, their return to the situations from which they had been displaced, and where they would unite to recompose a neutral fluid. This force is termed, by Poisson, the *coercive force*. In soft iron the coercive force is either wanting, or is extremely feeble; in steel and in the loadstone it is very energetic; and it exists in various degrees of intensity in

---

* Mémoires de l'Institut de France, tome v., p. 247. The introduction to this memoir is given in the Annales de Chimie, tome xxv., p. 113.

different kinds of steel. This coercive force, which exists in iron with regard to the magnetic fluids, is analogous in all respects to the resistance which glass, resin, and other non-conducting bodies, present to the passage of the electric fluids through their substance. Having thus established the foundations of the hypothesis of a double magnetic fluid adopted to the particular circumstances of the case, we must next endeavour to ascertain precisely the distribution of the austral and boreal fluids in magnetized bodies, conformably with these principles; and afterwards examine the nature of their combined actions upon bodies at a distance.

(157.) For this purpose, we may first take the simpler case of a cylindrical needle of soft iron, of very small diameter, and of any given length, as representing an elementary longitudinal filament of that metal. In the natural state of the needle, the two fluids it contains are united in equal proportions throughout its substance, so that their actions, being equal and opposite at all distances, totally destroy each other, and no sign of magnetism is exhibited. If we next suppose these fluids to be subjected to the action of magnetizing forces, proceeding from one or more centres, situated in the line of the axis of the needle produced, these forces will now cause the fluids to separate from each other; but each particle of austral or boreal fluid can, by the hypothesis, move only a very short distance from its primitive situation; and the two fluids, in their new arrangement, will succeed each other alternately, throughout the length of the needle, which will, accordingly, be divided into very small portions, composing a series, each part of which will contain, as it did in the neutral state, the two fluids in equal quantities. The united actions of every particle of decomposed fluid in this series upon a particle of magnetic fluid in any particular situation, compose a resultant force, the intensity and direction of which remain to be determined by the application of mathematical analysis.

(158.) We may now proceed to consider the more complicated case of a magnetized body of indeterminate form and dimensions. Attention must here be paid to the lines or directions in which the separation of the two fluids takes place throughout its substance, and in which they are arranged alternately, as we have just seen exemplified in the case of the simple filament. These lines or filaments will, in general, be curved; the nature of the curvatures depending on the form of the body, and on the external forces which act on the two fluids. They are termed by Poisson *lines of magnetization*, and may be considered as constituted by series of magnetic elements, following one another in the same regular consecutive order of polar arrangement. We have to determine, then, for each point of the body which is the subject of investigation, the direction of the line of magnetization, which is also the line of polarity; and the action of the magnetic element on any other point given in position, either within or without the body. This action is the difference of the forces exerted by the two fluids contained in the element, arising from the slight separation of the austral and boreal particles, which constitutes the state of polarity. It may excite surprise that forces depending on such small differential distances as those of the two centres of austral and boreal forces in each magnetical element, should, nevertheless, be capable of producing mechanical effects so considerable as those exhibited by the magnetic attractions and repulsions of bodies. By applying to the subject the methods of analytical investigation, Poisson arrived at the conclusion, that the result of the action of all the magnetical elements of a magnetized body is a force equivalent to the action of a very thin stratum, covering the whole surface of the body, and formed of the two fluids, the austral and the boreal, occupying different parts of it. We have a similar instance in the case of electrical attractions and repulsions of mechanical effects, sometimes very powerful, being produced by strata of fluids collected at the surfaces of conductors, and having a thickness so exceedingly minute as to be inappreciable by any of our senses. As these observed effects of the two magnetic agents result only from the differences of two contrary powers, we can form no estimate of the real magnitude of the forces belonging to each separate power, that is, to each of the two portions of austral or boreal fluid belonging to the same magnetic element; but can only infer that they are incomparably greater than the resulting forces which are actually in operation, and of which we witness the effects.

(159.) In the memoir on the Theory

of Magnetism, already referred to, M. Poisson deduces, from the theory above stated, the analytical equations which express, for all possible cases, the laws of the distribution of magnetism within bodies that are rendered magnetical by induction, and those of the actions, whether attractive or repulsive, which they exert on points given in position. The first problem to be resolved is to reduce the resultants of all the attractions and repulsions of the magnetic elements of a magnetized body, of any imaginable form, on such points, situated either within or without the surface, to three directions at right angles to one another. By adding to the resultants which relate to any interior point those of the external magnetic forces which act upon the body, he obtains the whole forces which tend to separate the two fluids that are united at that particular point. Were the matter of the body to oppose no sensible degree of resistance to the displacement of the fluids in each magnetic element, or, in other words, if there were no coercive force, it would be necessary, in order that there might be an equilibrium, that the attractions and repulsions should destroy one another; or, speaking algebraically, that their sum should be equal to zero; since, if any of them were uncompensated, they would effect a new decomposition of the neutral fluid, which may be regarded as inexhaustible, and the magnetic state of the body would be altered. The sum of the resultants must, therefore, be made equal to zero, with respect to each of the three rectangular directions to which they are referred. The equations of equilibrium, thus formed, will always be possible, and they will serve to determine, for each point of a magnetized body, the three unknown quantities which they comprehend; namely, the intensity of the action of a magnetic element on a given point, and the two angles which determine the corresponding direction of the line of polarity. At the extremities of each element, these joint resultants will not vanish; they will give rise to pressures from within each element, tending outwards, and counterbalanced by the obstacle, of which the nature is unknown, but which opposes the passage of the fluid from one element to another, and also its escape from the surface.

(160.) When the coercive force of the magnetized body is also taken into account, it will then be sufficient for the magnetic equilibrium that the resultant of all the exterior and interior forces, acting upon any point of the body, nowhere exceeds the given magnitude of the coercive force: so that, in this case, the equilibrium may take place in an infinitude of different ways, and the problem is, in this respect, wholly indeterminate. This indeterminateness is a source of considerable difficulty in the resolution of questions of this nature. The following general consequence, however, may be deduced from the equations of magnetic equilibrium formed in the manner above described; namely, that although in a solid body, magnetized by induction, the austral and boreal fluids are distributed in an active state throughout the whole mass of that body, yet the attractions and repulsions which it exerts externally are precisely the same as if they proceeded from a very thin stratum of each fluid, occupying the surface only, both fluids being in equal quantities, and distributed in such a manner as that their total action upon all the points in the interior of the body is equal to nothing. If the body be hollow, or contain an empty space within it, and if the centres from which magnetic forces proceed be situated within this space, the body must be considered as terminated by two thin strata of fluid, situated, the one on the external, and the other on the internal surface; and the action of these two strata on any point within the substance of the body, joined to that of all the given centres of magnetic action, must produce a perfect equilibrium; and, in this case, the two fluids may be in different quantities in each of the thin strata, provided that they be always in equal quantities in the two surfaces taken together.

(161.) Thus it appears, that the theory of magnetic attractions and repulsions is reduced to the same principles, and leads to the same formulæ, as the theory of electric forces in conducting bodies; and the perfect correspondence between the two may be illustrated in the following manner. We may suppose an aggregate mass composed of minute grains of metal, or other conductor of electricity, each grain being of so small a size that its dimensions may be neglected in comparison with the whole mass, and each being surrounded by a substance impermeable to electricity, but not sensibly adding to its bulk. On bringing a body thus constituted near an electrified body, every one of the grains would immediately become electrical by induction; and, in this condition of the body, it has been mathematically proved that the attractions and repulsions which the body would exert externally, would be the same with those of a homogeneous conducting body of the same form and size, subjected to the same external forces: although, in the latter case, the two electric fluids would be transferred to the opposite extremities of the body, while, in the former, they would be obliged to remain in the constituent masses to which they originally belonged. An electrical body, constituted in the manner here supposed, presents us with a disposition exactly analogous to that of a magnetical body; and is therefore calculated to give us a very distinct idea of the distribution of the magnetic fluids when that body is magnetized. The electricity inherent in the tourmaline appears to be disposed in the manner above described; and this stone accordingly affords an excellent illustration of the hypothesis under our consideration. See *Electricity*, § 197.

(162.) Another general consequence of the theory is, that a magnetic needle, placed in the interior of a hollow sphere of soft iron, and so small as not to exert any sensible influence on the sphere, will not be subject to any magnetic action from a magnetic force proceeding from a point external to the sphere; or, in other words, all magnetic action, whether of the earth or of any number of magnets placed without the hollow sphere, will be completely intercepted by the sphere with reference to all magnetic bodies contained in its interior. And conversely, such hollow sphere will totally prevent the action of a magnet placed within it from being exerted on any body placed without the sphere.

(163.) The formulæ derived from this theory have been applied by Poisson to another case, which, as we shall afterwards find, is one of considerable practical importance in navigation, namely, that of a hollow sphere of iron, magnetized by the influence of the earth, that is, by the action of a force of which the origin is very remote, and which may, therefore, be considered as uniform in magnitude, and acting in parallel directions on all the points of the body in question. From the resolution of the equations of magnetic equilibrium obtained in this case, it appears that although the magnetism is by no means confined to the superficial strata of the sphere, and although its intensity may be determined for any particular point of the solid mass of the shell, yet the magnitude of the three component forces produced by it is wholly independent of the thickness of the shell, and is determined only by the radius of the external surface, and by the co-ordinates belonging to the position of the point on which the forces act. When the distance of this point from the centre of the sphere is very great, compared with the radius, each of the three forces is very nearly as the cube of the radius directly, and as the cube of the distance inversely. We shall have occasion, in a future chapter, to notice the remarkable coincidence of the results of observation with the deductions from this theory, affording a very important confirmation of the accuracy both of the analysis itself, and of the theory from which it is derived.

(164.) In a subsequent memoir[*], M. Poisson extends his researches so as to obtain a more diversified comparison of the theory with the phenomena; and with this view resolves the general equations he had before established, in the case of bodies having forms less simple than that of the sphere. Such a resolution, however, is attainable only in a very limited number of cases, of which the elliptic spheroid is an example. After giving the formulæ relating to a spheroid of which the axes have any imaginable relations to each other, he particularly considers the two opposite cases of spheroids extremely flattened and extremely elongated. The former may represent a plate, of which the thickness varies very slowly near the centre, and decreases from the point to the circumference; for its action on points near its centre must be sensibly the same as that of any other plate of uniform thickness and of very great extent. The latter, or the extremely elongated spheroid, approaches very nearly to the form of a needle or bar, of which the diameter decreases from the middle to the extremities, varying at first very slowly; and its action on points near its middle can differ but little from that of a bar of which the diameter is constant, and very small in proportion to its length. The consideration of these three cases, which readily admit of the application of the analytical formulæ, is of considerable

---

[*] Mémoires de l'Institut, tome v., p. 481.

importance, as they allow of a strict comparison of the results of experiment with the deductions from theory; and the accurate accordance which has been obtained between them, in every instance in which such a comparison has been instituted, affords the strongest evidence of the correctness of the views on which that theory is founded.

(165.) It has already been observed that we have no data for determining the question as to the size of the magnetic elements, compared with that of the constituent molecules: we know not whether they are coincident with these molecules, or whether they occupy only the interstices between the molecules: neither can we determine whether they do not actually comprehend certain definite aggregates of molecules, or whether they are constituted in the intervals of these aggregates. All that we can be certain of is, that the sum of all the magnetic elements, added to the sum of all the unmagnetic elements (that is, the spaces, whether occupied by matter or not, which are devoid of magnetic fluid), must together make up the total apparent volume of the body under consideration. Now the ratio between these two sums may vary, not only in different kinds of bodies, but also in the same body, in different circumstances. It may, for instance, be very materially affected by changes of temperature; and this consideration will probably furnish a key to the explanation of many of the anomalous appearances we have already had occasion to notice in § 49.

(166.) The hypothesis of two magnetic fluids was first propounded by Wilke and Brugmann; but the first real foundations of the theory were laid by Coulomb, who, by the exercise of singular perseverance and sagacity, prepared and established all the physical principles upon which it rests. It has recently occupied the attention of Poisson, and appears to have received its last finish from his masterly hand; for by applying to it the refinements of modern analysis, this distinguished mathematician has succeeded in discovering formulæ which represent, numerically, all the principal phenomena of the science, even in their minutest details, and which furnish us with a ready and consistent explanation of the physical mode by which they are produced.*

* A popular view of this theory is given by Biot, in a note to his French translation of Fischer's Physique Méchanique, 4th edition, page 342.

(167.) Professor Prevost, of Geneva*, has laboured to frame a theory of magnetism which shall dispense with all attractive or repulsive agencies, and in which all the phenomena shall be resolvable into the effects of impulsion. For this purpose he admits two magnetic fluids, each giving its respective polarity to the two ends of a magnet, and neutralizing each other by combination; but adopting the hypothesis of Le Sage, as to the existence of another infinitely more subtile fluid, pervading all space, and giving rise by its inconceivably rapid movements to all the phenomena of gravitation, cohesion, and chemical attraction, he supposes the magnetic fluids themselves to be set in motion by this primary and universal agent. But it would be impossible in this place to engage in the development of so abstruse and complicated a system as this.

Chapter V.

Methods of making Artificial Magnets.

§ 1. General Principles.

(168.) The art of communicating magnetic power to bodies capable of retaining it, is founded on the proper application of the principles already explained; and the practical results of experience in this art have, as might be expected, furnished some of the most interesting illustrations of the theory of magnetism. We have seen that acquired magnetism of every kind, whether temporary or permanent, of which the origin can be traced, has been derived, by induction, from a similar power already existing in some other body. In this respect, then, it differs from electricity, which may be elicited from bodies all of which were previously in a neutral state, by a variety of processes either of a mechanical or chemical nature. But the body which is the cause of magnetism in another body must itself be in an active state of magnetism, and may be either a magnet, whether natural or artificial, or else it must be the globe of the earth itself: it is therefore highly probable, that the magnetism of the earth is the original source of all other magnetism. This view of the subject excludes, of course, all consideration of electro-magnetic influence, which belongs to another division of the science, hereafter to be treated of. It will then be shewn that electricity in

* Sur l'Origine des Forces Magnétiques. 8vo. Genève, 1788.

motion is a source of magnetism, and that strong grounds exist for the belief, that even the magnetism of the earth has its origin in electric currents circulating round the equatorial regions.

In giving an account of the methods of procuring artificial magnets, we shall begin with those which depend solely on this source of magnetic power, and which would enable us to obtain them if we were unprovided with any instrument previously magnetized.

(169.) The success of every plan that can be put in practice for obtaining magnets must depend on two circumstances: first, the efficacy of the induction; and, secondly, the fixation of the magnetism that has been induced. That quality and temperament of steel which is most favourable to the former, is least favourable to the latter of these objects; but various methods may be devised which shall answer both these intentions. The particular purposes intended to be answered by the magnetic instrument we are constructing, will frequently determine our preference of one or other of these methods, as well as guide us in the choice of the material to be used, and of the form and dimensions to be given to it.

(170.) Magnetism is most readily communicated to an unmagnetic bar of iron or steel by means of certain combinations of steel bars already magnetized to saturation, which combinations may be regarded as highly-charged magnetic batteries ready for action, and capable of exerting a powerful influence, in inducing magnetism, on all the iron in their vicinity. But an apparatus of this kind cannot at all times be commanded, nor can it at once be constructed: it must be the result of a long preliminary process, of which the object is to impart to each single bar additional quantities of magnetism, until it has acquired, by gradual steps, the full measure it is capable of retaining. We shall first, then, point out the methods of magnetizing those bars which are to compose the apparatus or battery just mentioned.

§ 2. *Method by Percussion.*

(171.) The most advantageous form for the steel bars that are to be employed for this purpose, is that of a rectangular prism, of which the length is about ten times the breadth, and about twenty times the thickness. Six or eight bars of this kind, and of equal size in every respect, should be provided. We have already seen that a certain degree of magnetism may be given to each of these bars by a few blows with a hammer, while they are held in a vertical position (§ 6). This effect results, as we have also seen (§ 107), from the direct inductive power of the earth. But the efficacy of this power will be very considerably increased, if it be combined with the inductive influence of other masses of iron placed near it, or in contact with it: notwithstanding the iron itself, which thus adds to the effect, derives its own power from the same source, namely, the magnetism of the earth. Thus, Mr. Scoresby found that a steel bar which acquired a feeble magnetism by being hammered vertically when resting upon stone or pewter, received a considerable accession of power when subjected to the same degree of hammering while it was placed upon a parlour poker, also kept in a vertical position. The poker, under these circumstances, became strongly magnetic, and in this state exerted upon the bar a much more powerful inductive influence than the earth alone could have done. Hence the magnetism of an iron bar, although temporary and dependent on position alone, may serve as a very important auxiliary in the development of the magnetism in steel bars, which is capable of being permanently retained. This is, in fact, the great principle on which the art of making artificial magnets of high power is founded.

(172.) The effect of the auxiliary iron bar, or of the poker used in the above experiment, is greater in proportion as it is longer; but as it would not be convenient to employ a bar of iron beyond a certain length, the magnetizing process may be continued by the aid of a still more powerful auxiliary, namely, very long bars of soft steel. Mr. Scoresby provided himself with two bars of this description, thirty inches long, and one inch broad; and also with a large bar of soft iron. This iron bar was first hammered in a vertical position. It was then laid on the ground, with its acquired south pole towards the south, and upon that end of it the large steel bars were made to rest while they were hammered; they were also hammered upon each other. On the summit of one of the large steel bars, each of the small bars (which were eight inches long, and half an inch broad), held also vertically, was hammered in succession. In a few minutes they had all received considerable magnetic power. He then had recourse to other methods, of which we are presently to speak, for still further increasing their power, till they were saturated with magnetism.

(173.) It may here be remarked, that in this, as well as in every other method for procuring artificial magnets, we advance only by successive steps, gaining a little additional power by each successful process, and employing that which has been acquired by one bar in contributing to the increase of the power of another; while this in its turn gives us the means of reacting upon the first. This we are enabled to do in consequence of the remarkable circumstance attending the induction of magnetism, and to which we have already adverted (§ 23), namely, that the power of the magnet which excites magnetism in another body, is itself increased, instead of being diminished, by such excitation. Hence, by proper management, the power of the several parts of the apparatus is capable of continual increase, limited only by their capacity for receiving and retaining magnetism.

(174.) After having in this way magnetized, by the help of terrestrial magnetism, a certain number of steel bars, we may proceed with them in imparting magnetism to others; and being thus provided with a stronger power, may, in our subsequent operations, dispense with that which we had at first employed.

§ 3. *Method by simple Juxtaposition.*

(175.) Simple induction by juxtaposition with one or more powerful magnets may suffice for the impregnation of very small magnets. But, for this purpose, it is not sufficient to place the latter in contact with one of the poles of a magnet, in the manner represented in the following figure (*fig.* 42); be-

Fig. 42.

cause, although the small bar or needle becomes magnetic by remaining a sufficient time subjected to the influence of the large magnet, yet we find that its two ends do not exhibit a magnetism of equal strength. That which has been in contact with the magnet appears to be the most powerful, in consequence of its magnetism being more concentrated at the very extremity; while in the remoter end it is more diffused and therefore less energetic. This inequality is in a great measure remedied by employing two magnets of as nearly equal power as possible, with their dissimilar poles fronting each other, and placing the needle to be magnetized in a line between them; as shown in *fig.* 43.

Fig. 43.

The effect of such a combination is always more than twice as great as that of each of the magnets when employed singly. It is difficult, however, even with every precaution, always to avoid the superinduction of consecutive poles in the intermediate parts of the needle.

(176.) The principle we have already referred to, of the increase of power which a magnet acquires by inducing magnetism on other bodies, may here again be applied in augmenting the influence of the magnets we employ in the preceding case. If a long bar of soft iron be applied to each of the poles of these magnets which are most distant from the needle to be subjected to their action, the power of the magnets will be greatly augmented. A more convenient, and perhaps equally efficacious method, is to place the magnets A and B, parallel to each other (*fig.* 44), while the small

Fig. 44.

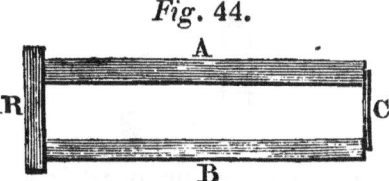

bar C, to be magnetized, is in contact with the two dissimilar poles at one end; and to unite those at the other end by a bar of soft iron, R. This bar becomes strongly magnetical by the joint induction of both the magnets, and the magnetism it thus acquires reacts powerfully in strengthening the magnets themselves; and the needle which connects their other poles participates in this augmentation of effect. These auxiliary pieces of soft iron, which serve to retain and concentrate the magnetism of steel bars, are called *armatures*.

(177.) Were the theory of Æpinus, in its original form, perfectly correct, nothing more would be required for impregnating steel bars with all the magnetism they are capable of receiving, than following the methods we have now pointed out. But we have seen reason to conclude that this theory can be applicable only to the minutest individual particles of which magnetic bodies are composed, and that a magnet should really be viewed as an aggregate of an indefinite number of minute magnets. This consideration cannot but have an important influence on the art of imparting magnetism to such an aggregate; as it will lead us to apply our means to effect, as far as it is in our power, a change in the magnetic state of each portion of the aggregate. The greater the proximity of the pole of the magnet which is to effect this change, to the part in which the change is to be produced, the greater will be the effect produced. Agreeably to this view of the subject, we shall succeed in converting a steel bar into a magnet of greatest power, by subjecting every part of the surface of the bar successively to the contact of the magnetizing pole. Let us trace the consequences of the practical application of this principle.

§ 4. *Method by the Single Touch.*

(178.) One of the earliest methods which was employed for giving magnetism to a bar C (*fig.* 45), was to lay it flat

Fig. 45.

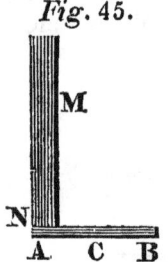

on a table, and placing an artificial magnet, M, on one of its ends, A, and at right angles to it, to slide it along the surface of the bar till it arrived at the other end B; and then, lifting it cautiously to a sufficient height to render its inductive influence insensible, to bring it down again to its former situation, and renew the operation. This was repeated several times on each of the surfaces of the bar, the pole of the magnet being always passed in the same direction, and the same pole employed.

It is evident that when the magnet is first applied to the end of the bar, it will induce in that end a polarity of the opposite kind to that of the pole N of the magnet which is in contact with it. Let us suppose, for the convenience of explanation, that this is a north pole; the end A of the bar to which it is first applied will first become a south pole, and the portions at a little distance from that end will acquire an equal degree of northern polarity. But as the magnet advances along the bar, a similar change will be induced in each successive particle of the surface which it approaches and touches; that is, each particle will now be converted into a south pole, although it had before been rendered a north pole. In as far as this takes place, therefore, the advance of the magnet reverses the effect it had at first produced. In like manner, the magnet has no sooner quitted the end to which it was first applied, than it tends to induce in it the northern polarity, at the same time that it renders the part which it then touches, a south pole. The same succession of changes, and reversal of the magnetism of each part, takes place during the whole of the progress of the magnet along the bar, with the exception of the end which it touches last. It leaves this end of the bar in the state of a south pole, while the other end remains a north pole. The intermediate parts may be considered as constituting a series of small magnets, with all their north poles turned towards A, and their south poles towards B.

(179.) However conformable to theory this method of magnetizing may appear to be, experience shows that it is very little superior to that by simple contact. It has also, like that method, the disadvantage of frequently producing consecutive poles; and these more especially occur when the bar to be magnetized is of some length, or consists of very hard steel. They are also very readily produced if care be not taken to prevent the magnet from resting for a longer time on some portions of the bar than on the rest; for in this case the poles are multiplied very much in the manner stated in a former chapter (§ 30, 31); a pole of one kind being formed at the point where the contact has been too long protracted, and two others of the contrary denomination in the immediate vicinity.

(180.) A singular circumstance characterizes this method of magnetizing by *touching*, as it is called. If, after a bar has been impregnated with as much magnetism as it is capable of receiving by this method from a strong magnet, an attempt be made to increase the effect by renewing the same operation upon the bar with a weaker magnet than the one that was first employed, the immediate result is a loss instead of an augmentation of power; and the bar remains only magnetized to a degree corresponding with the lesser power of the last magnet by which it has been touched. The reason of this will easily be understood, when we consider that the first effect produced by the second magnet is, to reverse the poles which already exist in the bar, and afterwards to induce the same kind of polarity; but this last effect it can produce only in a degree corresponding to its own strength. It therefore destroys, during the former part of the operation, more than it can supply in the latter.

The only exception which might be conceived to exist to this destructive action of a weaker magnet, would be in the case where the latter was composed of a very soft material, so that the magnetism of the bar was capable of affecting its polarity, so as to destroy it when of a similar kind to the part of the bar with which it came in contact, and convert it into an opposite polarity.

(181.) An attentive consideration of the stages of the process we have detailed, will show us that the destructive operation of the second magnet is produced chiefly in the first half of the bar; for if the weaker magnet were first applied to the middle of the bar, and then made to slide on to the end in the same direction as before, over the latter half, its effect on the first half would only tend to strengthen the polarity already impressed upon it. Nor would there, in that case, be any injurious effect produced if the second magnet were sufficiently soft in its texture to admit of having its polarity changed by the magnetism of the bar. This consideration leads us to another important stage in the progress of improvement in the art we are studying.

§ 5. *Dr. Knight's Method.*

(182.) This improvement consists in employing two magnets in the same operation, applying two dissimilar poles of these magnets each to a different half of the bar to be impregnated, and confining its action to that portion of the bar, which of course should be much smaller than the magnets. For this purpose the two magnets are to be joined lengthwise, with their dissimilar poles in contact, and laid on the bar to be magnetized, in the manner represented in *fig.* 46, where A and B are the magnets, and C the bar to be magnetized; so that the

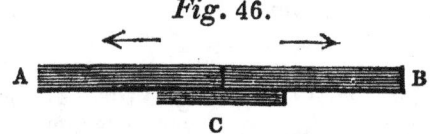

Fig. 46.

point of junction of the magnets shall be immediately over the middle of the bar. Then separating the magnets, by drawing them opposite ways in the direction of their length as far as the extremities of the small bar, they are next to be removed to a considerable distance, and again joined; and afterwards laid a second time on the middle of the bar, in the same manner as at first. This operation is to be repeated several times on each of the sides of the bar. By this method, which was first practised by Dr. Gowan Knight about the middle of the last century, steel bars could be rendered much more powerfully magnetic than by any of the means before in use.

(183.) The great superiority of Dr. Knight's method is owing, not merely to the circumstance before noticed—that each pole of the magnets acts only upon that half of the bar which is intended to receive a magnetism of an opposite kind, and that its inductive effect on the other half has never to be destroyed,—but also to the inductive influence of the two poles being combined together during the whole of the operation. In every portion of the bar which lies between the two poles of the magnets that are thus applied, their influence conspires to induce the kind of magnetism that it is desired to produce. In those portions of the bar, indeed, which lie on the other sides of the poles of the magnets, they oppose each other: but it will be perceived that their effect is here only that resulting from the difference of their respective influences; while, in the former case, when they act upon the intermediate portions, it is as the sum of that influence. The superiority of the combined influence is even greater than the united powers of the single magnets, as we have already had occasion to point out.

§ 6. *Duhamel's Method.*

(184.) If the magnets employed be large and powerful, and the bars very short and slender, it is easy, by the preceding method, to magnetize them to saturation. Soon after the publication of Dr. Knight's method, small bars thus magnetized were distributed over Europe, and were eagerly sought after by the cultivators of natural philosophy. It was soon found, however, that the attempt to magnetize bars of a greater length by this process was generally less successful, or at least failed in giving to them all the power of which they were susceptible. Philosophers therefore renewed their efforts to devise methods of greater and more universal efficiency. M. Duhamel, of the French Academy of Sciences, in conjunction with M. Authcaume, at length devised the following plan, which was found to succeed even with bars of considerable dimensions.

(185.) He first laid the two bars of steel intended to be magnetized, and which were made of equal length, parallel to each other, C D (see *fig.* 47), and

Fig. 47.

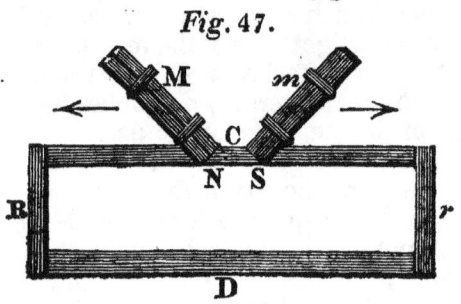

connected their extremities by two shorter bars of soft iron, R r, so as to form altogether a right-angled parallelogram. Then taking two parcels of bars already magnetized, M m, the separate bars of each parcel being placed with their respective poles in the same directions, and firmly tied together, he brought the poles of opposite kinds, N, S, into contact over the middle of one of the steel bars forming the parallelogram, giving them a certain inclination to the bars as seen in the figure. The angle they formed with each bar was generally about forty-five degrees, so that they formed with each other a right angle. Then separating them from each other, he made them slide gently, and with an equable motion, towards the extremities of the bar. This operation was repeated on the same bar as often as appeared requisite. The inclined parcels of magnets were then taken to the opposite bar of the parallelogram, and applied to them in the same manner; taking care, however, to reverse the disposition of the poles of the magnets, so that the side on which the north pole was placed in the one case, was occupied by the south pole in the other. After the bars had been rubbed sufficiently on the one side, they were turned on the other side, and the same operations repeated on them in that situation.

(186.) It is evident, that in as far as the magnets exert their conjoined influence on the portions of the bars that lie between them, and act only upon their respective halves of the bars, the method of Duhamel possesses all the advantages of that of Dr. Knight. The combination of many separate magnets in each bundle, however, gives them greater power in operating the requisite inductions—a power, indeed, which appears to be considerably greater than that which a single magnet of the same size as that of the combined magnets would possess. But the principal improvement in Duhamel's plan consists in the disposition of the bars in a parallelogram in conjunction with connecting pieces of soft iron, which, acting as armatures, afford an advantage of a similar kind to that already explained in § 176. In proportion as the steel bars acquire magnetism, these connecting pieces participate in the acquisition of a similar power, and serve to retain it in the bars themselves; just as the electricity which is imparted to the inner coating of a Leyden jar is retained by the reciprocal influence of the induced and contrary electricity of the outer coating. The magnetism of the bars is retained by a similar influence, and greater facility is thus afforded to increase its amount by the subsequent additions it is receiving from the action of the magnets as they pass along the surface.

§ 7. *Method by Double Touch: Process of Mitchell.*

(187.) While Duhamel was endeavouring to perfect his method in France, the same object was occupying the attention of experimental philosophers in England; and much about the same period new processes for magnetizing bars were invented by Mitchell and by Canton.

(188.) Mr. Mitchell, of Cambridge, published his improved method in 1750. He employed two parcels of strongly magnetized bars (M m, *fig.* 48), joined

Fig. 48.

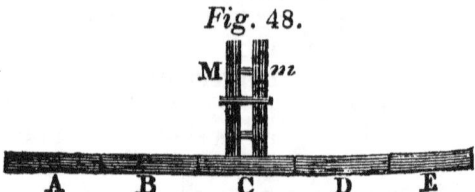

in a manner similar to those above described, and placed them parallel to each other, but with the poles of each parcel reversed, leaving between the two parcels an interval of about a quarter or a third of an inch. He then arranged a number of equal steel bars (A, B, C, D, E) in a straight line, and made one extremity of the conjoined magnets slide at right angles over the line of steel bars. He did not, however, limit himself to one direction, but moved them backwards and forwards the whole length of the united surfaces of the bars; repeating the operation on each side until he had obtained as great an effect as possible.

In order to equalize as much as possible the magnetic power of the two ends of each bar, it is expedient to commence each operation by laying the conjoined magnets on the middle of the line of bars, and to pass the magnets over each half of the line an equal number of times; at the conclusion of which, the magnets being brought again to the middle, they should be raised perpendicularly, so as not to disturb the lateral effects which had been produced. Mr. Mitchell found that the steel bars B, C, D, which were intermediate in the series, acquired by this process a very great degree of magnetic power. Those which formed the extreme bars of the series A, D, were much less impregnated; but by removing them from this situation, and transferring them to the middle of the series, and then repeating the same operations, they quickly acquired the same degree of magnetism as the rest.

(189.) The process above described, which soon acquired much celebrity, was called *the method by double touch;* and it is asserted by its inventor, that two magnets will impart more magnetic power to a bar of their own size, when employed in this peculiar mode, than a single magnet of five times the strength of the former, when applied after the manner of the single touch. The operation of the two poles of the conjoined parcels of magnets on those portions of the bars over which they pass will readily be understood from what has been said with respect to the methods of Knight and Duhamel. They act by the sum of their inductive powers on those parts of the bar that are situated between them, but with the difference of those powers on all those parts which lie beyond them; and the former is therefore always greatly more efficient than the latter. The superiority is the more considerable in the present case, inasmuch as the magnets are nearer to each other, and therefore act with much greater power when they co-operate, but are nearly inefficient when they oppose one another. The latter of these forces, therefore, will never have sufficient energy to destroy, or even much diminish, the effect which had been produced by the former; and thus the magnetism of each portion receives continual accessions of strength every time the magnets are made to pass over it. The long line of bars operates in a manner similar to the pieces of soft iron at the extremities of those in the parallelogram of Duhamel—that is, the external bars act as armatures to those which lie between them; and hence may be understood why these intermediate bars receive the strongest impregnation.

(190.) The different processes for communicating magnetism which we have now described, comprise all those methods that are essentially different in their principle; all others which have been proposed may be regarded as varieties merely in the combinations of which these principles are susceptible. We shall only, therefore, notice those which have been most in repute.

(191.) Mr. Canton published, in 1751, a method which he considered as superior to any of those previously employed. He placed the bars intended to be magnetized so as to form a parallelogram with connecting bars or armatures of soft iron, as in the method of Duhamel. He then had recourse to the method of double touch as prescribed by Mitchell; after which he separated the two bundles of magnets, and inclining them to the bars in contrary directions, as Duhamel had done, he completed the operation by making them slide from the middle towards the extremities. The combination of these two processes was considered by Canton as an improvement upon the method of Mitchell. There is, however, great reason to think, as Coulomb and Biot have remarked, that these successive operations are quite superfluous, and that the bars are left at the end of them precisely in the same state as if only the last had been employed.

§ 8. *Æpinus's Method.*

(192.) Æpinus introduced modifications into the process of the double touch, of greater importance and much more judiciously conceived. He first formed the parallelogram of steel bars in the manner of Duhamel; but in place of the auxiliary cross bars of soft iron, he connected the ends of the steel bars by means of other steel bars which had previously been rendered powerfully magnetic. He next placed the two compound magnets end to end, with their dissimilar poles adjoining each other, but separated by a small piece of wood (*fig.* 49),

Fig. 49.

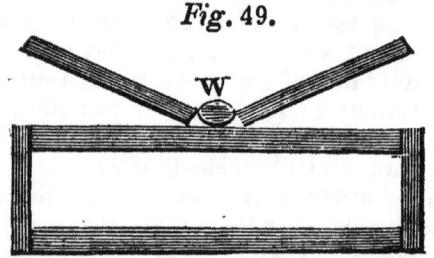

which kept them asunder for a short space; and then, inclining them so that they formed a very obtuse angle with each other, he placed them on the middle of one of the steel bars, and, without separating them, made them slide backwards and forwards along the surface of the bar; repeating the operation, with the usual precautions as to the direction of the poles, on the other bar, and on both sides of each.

With regard to the position of the magnets, it is evident that this process is analogous to that of Duhamel; but as the magnets, during the whole time they are rubbed upon the bars, are kept in the same relative situation with respect to each other, their operation depends upon the principle of the double touch peculiar to Mitchell's process. Æpinus tried different angles of inclination for the magnets, with a view to discover that which gave the greatest effect; and concluded that the maximum of effect was obtained when the magnets made angles of fifteen or twenty degrees on each side with the steel bar on which they were to act.

(193.) When an inquiry was instituted as to the comparative efficacy of the methods of Duhamel and of Æpinus, the latter was found to possess this advantage—that it enabled the experimenter to magnetize bars of considerable length and thickness by means of bars which themselves possess no great power, which was not the case with the process of Duhamel. At the same time the method of Æpinus is liable to many inconveniences; in the first place, we scarcely ever obtain, by its means, an equal degree of magnetic power in the two ends of the bars to which it is applied. This will appear by placing any one of these bars on a table, and laying on it a sheet of paper, on which are strewed some very fine iron filings;

when it will be seen, by the manner in which the filings arrange themselves, that the neutral point of the bar does not occupy the exact middle of the bar, but is sensibly nearer to that end to which the magnets used in the operation of touching it had been last applied.

In the second place, magnets formed by the process of Æpinus are much more liable to have consecutive poles than those obtained by Duhamel's process; and this is especially the case if the magnets are of some length. These consecutive poles, which are irregularly formed in various parts of the magnet, are, it is true, in general extremely feeble; but still they must always impair very considerably the directive force, which becomes a very serious objection when the magnets are intended for compass-needles. The inequality of strength or of diffusion of the two principal poles is also disadvantageous with a view to the same object. Hence the process of Duhamel will always be found preferable for the construction of compass-needles; while that of Æpinus is more serviceable when it is wished to obtain a very considerable magnetic power in large bars, for the purpose of batteries, or other magnetic combinations, where it imports little whether the neutral points be exactly coincident with the centres of each individual piece.

§ 9. *Coulomb's Process.*

(194.) The attention of M. Coulomb, already distinguished by his researches in electricity, was engaged for a considerable period in perfecting the art of making magnets; and his numerous communications to the French Academy and Institute contain a great mass of valuable observations on this subject. Some of the results of his experiments are given by Biot, in his "Traité de Physique."*

(195.) The magnetic apparatus for impregnating a steel bar consists, as we have seen, of two parts; the first is that which is fixed, and applied to the bars in such a manner as to act by its continued inductive operation; this includes the armatures of soft iron, as well as the fixed magnets that may be substituted for them: and the second is the moveable magnetic bars, or combinations of bars, which are made to slide and rub over the bar to be magnetized. For the construction of the fixed part of the apparatus, Coulomb employed bars of

---
* Tome iii. p. 57.

MAGNETISM.

steel tempered at a cherry-red heat, and from twenty to twenty-four inches in length, of rather more than half an inch in breadth, and one-fifth of an inch in thickness. These he first magnetized to saturation by means of other magnets procured by any of the methods already described; then, placing them parallel to each other, and uniting them by their poles of the same denomination, he arranged them into two assemblages, composed of five bars in each, separated by small parallelopipeds of soft iron, which projected a little beyond their extremities, and performed the office of an armature, common to the whole set (see *fig.* 50).

Fig. 50.

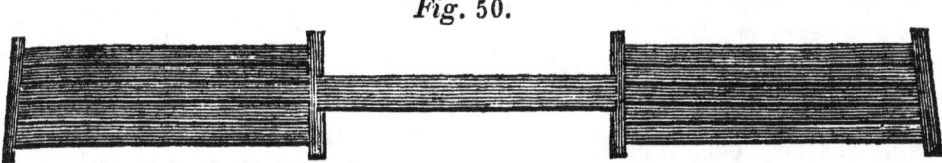

The moveable part of the apparatus he usually formed of four bars of steel, tempered at the same heat as the preceding, and of the same dimensions as to breadth and thickness, but only sixteen inches long. After magnetizing them as strongly as possible, he united two of them by their widths, and two others by their thicknesses, forming a packet consisting of four magnets placed as close as possible.

(196.) In proceeding to operate with this apparatus, the large assemblages of magnets, with their armatures, are placed opposite to each other; so that the magnets which compose them shall lie in the same line, with their north and south poles opposite to each other, but separated by a space nearly equal to the length of the bar to be magnetized, which latter bar is to be laid between the two sets of magnets, resting on the cross bars or armatures, for the space of about the fifth of an inch. Then the moveable magnets are laid upon the centre of the bar, and inclined on each side in opposite directions, so as to form with each half of the bar an angle of twenty or thirty degrees.

Every thing being thus prepared, it is at the option of the experimenter to proceed according to the manner of Duhamel, by drawing each packet of the moveable magnets away from the middle of the bar, along that half of it which lies on its own side, as far as the extremity; or, following the directions of Æpinus, to retain the magnets in their relative situation, by placing between them a piece of wood or of copper, so as to keep their poles at an invariable distance of one quarter or one fifth of an inch from each other, and preserving their inclinations, to slide them backwards and forwards from the centre to each extremity of the bar, until each half of it shall have been subjected to an equal number of frictions. After the last movement has been completed, when the magnets will have been brought back to the centre, where the movement had commenced, they are to be raised perpendicularly to a height sufficient to obviate all sensible disturbance of the magnetic state of the bar, and the operation repeated on its other side.

(197.) If the pieces which compose the moveable magnets have not previously received all the magnetic power of which they are susceptible, as will generally happen if we have not previously the command of a sufficient apparatus for that purpose, their united power, when assembled in the manner already described, will still produce in the bars subjected to their action in the above process, a degree of magnetism greater than that which they themselves possess. We may therefore avail ourselves of the latter of these bars for composing a new set of magnets, which will accordingly be more powerful than the former: and then, obtaining by their means still more highly impregnated magnets, we may again disunite them, and subject them to the action of still more energetic combinations, formed by the bars last impregnated. By the continued repetition of these processes, employing one set of magnetic bars alternately in raising the intensity of those of another set, it is evident that we shall finally succeed in effecting their complete saturation.

(198.) When it is required to magnetize bars of very considerable size, Coulomb recommends that the moveable apparatus of magnets should be composed of a much greater number of pieces than in the instance above given; and that these pieces should be disposed in rows, each successive row projecting beyond the last, as shown in *fig.* 51: thus the pole of each, which generally resides at the very extremity of the bar, will

E

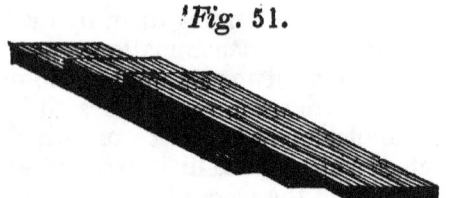

Fig. 51.

come immediately in contact with the bar to be magnetized, when the compound magnet is applied to it with the proper inclination, and the whole will powerfully conspire in producing the same effect.

(199.) The parallelograms of steel bars and soft iron should be kept firm by wedges, in the manner of printers' types, and the extremities of the magnetic bars should be perfectly cleaned. In rubbing the bars, it is recommended by some authors to apply considerable pressure; but Captain Kater found increased pressure rather injurious than beneficial. Dr. Robison conceived that by wetting their extremities he obtained a greater effect; but he found that the least drop of oil between the bars greatly obstructed the operation of the magnets, as was also the case when the smallest piece of the thinnest gold leaf intervened. He found that bars which were rough received a more powerful magnetism than those which were moderately polished; but that, if moderately rough, they acquired the first degrees of magnetism more expeditiously than smooth bars, but did not ultimately receive so strong an impregnation as the latter.

§ 10. *Comparative Advantages of the different Processes.*

(200.) An account of Coulomb's experiments on the comparative advantages of the different methods of magnetizing bars of different thicknesses, lengths, and forms, is given by Biot in his " Traité de Physique." The strength of each magnet was estimated by the number of oscillations which it performed in a given time on each side of the magnetic meridian by the influence of terrestrial magnetism. The following are some of the results of his inquiry.

He found that steel wires of small diameter may be rendered magnetic to an equal degree, whether touched by the method of Duhamel or of Æpinus, or even when simply rubbed with the single pole of a strong magnet, for in all these cases they became magnetized to saturation. When a plate of unannealed steel of greater width than the wires, but of equal length and thickness, was subjected to experiment, a slight difference was perceptible in the degree of magnetism resulting from the different methods, those of Duhamel and Æpinus being the most efficacious. The difference was more perceptible when the steel was made of a harder temper, and increased still more when thicker plates of steel were tried. The processes of Duhamel and of Æpinus, when applied to plates of which the thickness is less than one twelfth of an inch were nearly of equal power; but when they exceed this thickness, that of Æpinus was decidedly the most efficacious. In the case of bars sixteen inches long, one inch broad, and about one third of an inch thick, the comparative intensities of the magnetism produced by the methods of Æpinus and Duhamel were nearly in the proportion of nine to eight.

(201.) Captain Kater also made a series of valuable experiments on the effects of different methods of magnetizing, and on the influence of extent of surface, independently of the mass, on the directive force.[*] The directive force was estimated by means of the balance of torsion of Coulomb. This instrument consists of a fine wire terminated above by an index at right angles to it, which is moveable round a circle divided into degrees. To the lower end of the wire a cradle is attached for receiving the needle which is the subject of experiment. The instrument being adjusted so that the needle was in the magnetic meridian when the wire had no torsion, the index was turned, and the wire consequently twisted, until the needle was made to deviate 60° from its original position. The number of degrees passed over by the index would then be the measure of the directive force of the needle.

The needles to be magnetized were right-angled parallelograms, five inches long; the one seven-tenths of an inch broad, and the other of half this breadth. The broadest was reduced in thickness till it was of the same weight as the other, namely, one hundred and forty-two grains. The magnets employed were first placed perpendicularly on the centre of the needle, their opposite poles being joined; their lower extremities were then separated and kept asunder by placing between them a piece of wood a quarter of an inch thick, their upper extremities remaining in contact.

---

[*] Philosophical Transactions for 1821, p. 104.

The magnets were then slid along the needle backwards and forwards from end to end, and this was repeated on both sides, till it was conceived that the full effect had been produced; and the directive force of the magnet thus obtained was noted. The process was repeated with the same apparatus, excepting that the magnets were separated at the top by a piece of wood of the same thickness as that at the bottom. The effect was considerably diminished by this change. When the lower extremities of the needle were separated by a piece of wood to the distance of half the length of the needle, the upper extremities remaining in contact, the effect was greater than in the first experiment. A further augmentation of power was obtained when the magnets were joined and placed perpendicularly, as before, on the centre of the needle, and then moved in opposite directions from the centre to the extremities, keeping each magnet perpendicular to the needle; afterwards rejoining them at a distance from the needle, replacing them on its centre, and thus continuing the operation. The needles were then magnetized according to the method of Duhamel, the magnets being inclined at an angle of about forty-five degrees, and carried as before from the centre to the ends of the needle. This was attended with a still greater increase of effect; but it was increased still further when the magnets formed with the needle an angle of about twenty degrees. The maximum of effect took place when this angle was reduced to about two or three degrees; for when the magnets were laid flat on the surface of the needles, and drawn from the centre to the ends, the effect was not so great as in the last case.

(202.) On the whole, Captain Kater concludes that the best mode of communicating magnetism to a needle, is by placing it in the magnetic meridian, joining the opposite poles of a pair of bar magnets (the magnets being in the same line), and laying the magnets so joined, flat upon the needle with their poles upon its centre; then having elevated the distant extremities of the magnets, so that they may form an angle of about two or three degrees with the needle, they are to be drawn from the centre of the needle to the extremities, carefully preserving the same inclination; and having joined the poles of the magnets at a distance from the needle, the operation is to be repeated ten or twelve times on each surface.

(203.) We have seen (§ 171), that terrestrial magnetism may be made available for procuring artificial magnets by the help of percussion; and it now remains that we point out the methods of employing it, in the absence of all other magnetized bodies, in exciting magnetism by friction, either by the single touch or by a method analogous to that of Dr. Knight.

(204.) Let the needle to be magnetized be placed horizontally in the magnetic meridian and fixed in that situation, and apply to the middle of it the lower end of a long iron bar, a poker, for instance,

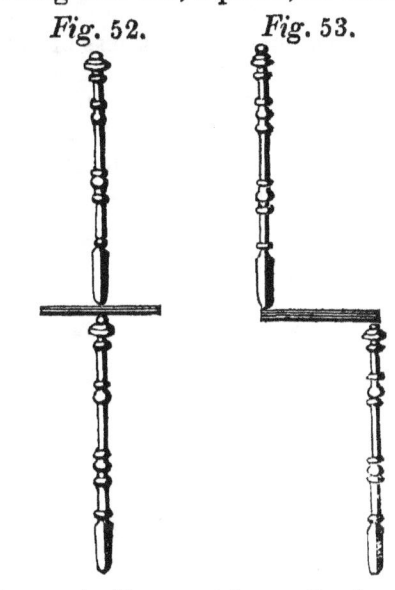

Fig. 52.   Fig. 53.

held vertically; and immediately opposite, at the lower side of the needle, apply the upper end of a second bar of a similar description to the first, as seen in fig. 52. Then draw each bar, still kept in a vertical position, towards the opposite ends of the needle (fig. 53), taking care that the upper bar be drawn towards the side of the needle intended to be its south pole, and the lower bar towards the intended north pole; then, separating the bars, remove them to a distance, and bring them again perpendicularly to the middle of the needle; and repeat this operation a sufficient number of times on each side. This simple process will often, if the needle be small, be sufficient to magnetize it to saturation. The principle on which it is founded is sufficiently obvious.

§ 11. *Canton's Process.*

(205.) The process of Canton, already alluded to, proceeds upon the same principle, and does not require the previous possession of any magnet. As the knowledge of it, therefore, may be of use to those who are not provided with any magnetic apparatus, we shall present the following outline of that part of it which appears to be the really efficient process.

(206.) Six bars of soft steel are to be provided, each three inches long, one quarter of an inch broad, and one twentieth of an inch thick, together with two pieces of iron, each half the length of one of the bars, but of the same breadth and thickness; and also six bars of hard steel, each five inches and a half long, half an inch broad, and three twentieths of an inch thick, together with two pieces of iron of half the length, but the whole breadth and thickness of one of the hard bars. All these bars are to be marked at one end by a line quite round them, in order to distinguish the poles.

(207.) Two bars of iron, or an iron poker and tongs (*fig*. 54), are to be taken:

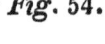

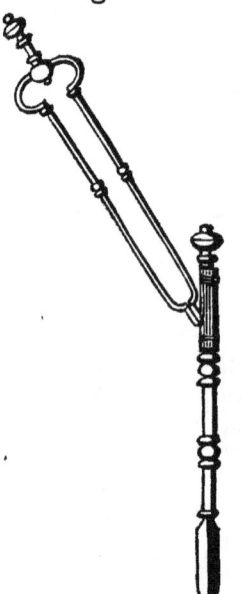

the larger they are, and the longer they have been used, so much the better. Let the poker be fixed upright, and held by the knees, and let one of the soft steel bars, having its marked end downwards, be tightly fastened to it by a piece of sewing silk, and held with the left hand; then grasping the tongs with the right hand a little below the middle, and holding them in a vertical position, let the bar be rubbed with the lower end, from the bottom to the top, about ten times on each side. This will give it sufficient magnetic power to lift a small key from the marked end, which will, of course, be a north pole.

(208.) Having magnetized four of the soft bars in this manner, the other two (*fig*. 55) are to be laid parallel to each other, at the distance of about one fourth of an inch between the two pieces of iron belonging to them, a north and a south pole against each piece of iron. Two of the four bars that have been already made magnetical are then to be united, so as to make a double bar in thickness, the north pole of one even with the south pole of the other; and the remaining two being placed next to these, one on each side, so as to have two north and two south poles together, the north and south poles are to be separated at one end by a large pin put between them; they are then to be

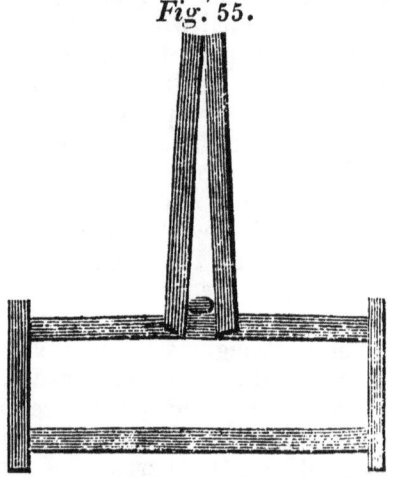

Fig. 55.

placed perpendicularly with that end downwards, on the middle of one of the parallel bars—the two north poles towards that end intended to be made the south pole, and the two south poles towards the intended north poles. Next slide them backwards and forwards three or four times the whole length of the bar, and removing them from the middle of this bar, place them on the middle of the other bar as before directed, and go over that in the same manner. Then turn both the bars the other side upwards, and repeat the operation.

Having done this, remove the two bars from between the pieces of iron, and placing the two outermost of the touching bars in their stead, let the other two be the outermost of the four to touch these with. This process being repeated till each pair of bars have been touched three or four times over, they will thus acquire a considerable magnetic power.

Next put together the six bars, as was done with the four, and touch with them two pair of the hard bars, placed between their iron armatures, at the distance of about half an inch from one another. The soft bars may now be laid aside, and two of the hard bars, placed between their iron armatures, may be magnetized by means of the other four, which should be held apart at the lower end, at an interval of about one fifth of an inch; to which distance they are to be separated after they are set on the parallel bar, and brought together again after they are taken off. The same process as that above described is now to be continued until each pair has been touched two or three times over.

The whole of this process may be gone through in less than half an hour; and each of the larger bars, if they had been previously well hardened, may be made to lift twenty-eight troy ounces, or even more. Bars thus impregnated will give to a hard bar of the same size its full virtue in less than two minutes; and may, therefore, answer almost every purpose in natural philosophy much better than the natural loadstone, which has seldom sufficient power to impregnate hard bars.

§ 12. *Horse-shoe Magnets.*

(209.) Magnets in the form of a straight bar are less convenient when the action of both the poles is wanted, as happens in various experiments, especially such as concern the raising of weights by the force of magnetic attraction. In order to bring the two poles near each other, artificial magnets are often made in the shape of a horse-shoe, (*fig.* 56,) or sometimes a more semicircular form is given to them (*fig.* 57). These horse-shoe magnets, as they are called, may be rendered magnetic by the same process as a straight bar; the magnets by which they are rubbed being, of course, made to follow the curvature of the bar. The method of Æpinus is best suited for the communication of magnetism to bars of this shape.

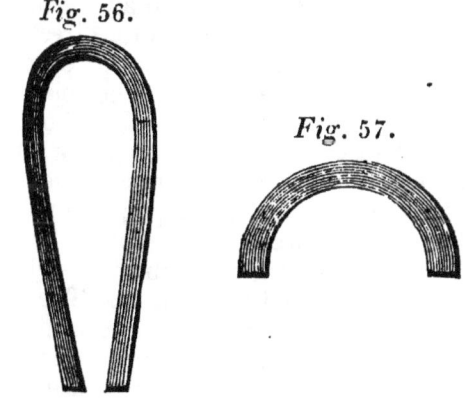

Fig. 56.

Fig. 57.

(210.) Horse-shoe magnets, that have their poles brought very near to each other, are exceedingly convenient as substitutes for the compound magnets employed in the process of magnetizing by the double touch. They fulfil, indeed, all the purposes of compound magnets in this operation; and if placed at once on the middle of the needle to be magnetized, with the poles turned in a direction the reverse of that of the poles intended to be given to the needle, and then moved backwards and forwards along the surface of the needle, taking care to pass over each half of it an equal number of times, and repeating the same operation on the other side, the needle is speedily and effectually rendered magnetic. The readiness with which this may be put in practice, and the absence of all previous preparation, are strong recommendations in favour of this form of magnet.

(211.) Powerful magnetic batteries are sometimes constructed by uniting a number of horse-shoe magnets, laying them one over the other with all their poles similarly disposed, and fastening them firmly together in a leathern or copper case.

§ 13. *Preservation of Magnets.*

(212.) From what has been already said respecting those circumstances which tend to produce or to destroy magnetism, we may easily devise rules for the preservation of magnets, for, unless kept with care, and with the observance of certain precautions, they soon lose their power.

(213.) If a single magnet be kept in an improper position, that is, one differing much from that which it would assume in consequence of the action of terrestrial magnetism, in process of time it becomes gradually weaker; and this deterioration is most accelerated when its poles have a position the reverse of the natural one. Under these circumstances, indeed, unless the magnet be made of the hardest steel, it will in no long time lose the whole of its magnetic power. Two magnets may also very much weaken each other if they be kept, even for a short time, with their similar poles fronting each other. The polarity of the weaker magnet, especially, is rapidly impaired, and sometimes is found to be actually reversed. More frequently, however, there arises, from this opposition of powers, considerable irregularity and confusion in the poles of both magnets. Heat, as we have seen, impairs magnetism: care should therefore be taken to avoid exposing magnets to a high temperature. We should likewise be very cautious to avoid all rough and violent treatment of a magnet; for we have seen how quickly its virtue is lost by any concussion or vibration among its particles. A fall on the floor, especially if it strike against any hard substance, will materially weaken it: rubbing with coarse powders, for the purpose of polishing it, and grinding, in order to bring it to any required form, are equally injurious. A natural loadstone will, in like manner, suffer by such an operation; hence we should attempt to alter its natural form as little as possible; and when it is necessary to do so, it should be effected very rapidly by cutting it briskly in the thin discs of a lapidary's wheel.

(214.) Although the loadstone retains its magnetic virtue more tenaciously than any artificial magnet that can be constructed, yet even this body requires a certain management for the permanent preservation of its power. For this purpose it should be *armed*, as it is called; that is, an armature of iron should be applied to both its poles. In order to do this most effectually, we must first ascertain the situation of the poles of the loadstone; and cutting off all the superfluous parts, give it the shape of a parallelopiped, having the poles in the middle of two opposite surfaces, and at the same time taking care to preserve the axis, which passes through the poles, of as great a length as can be obtained: for it has been observed, that any curtailment of the magnet in the direction of this line deprives it of force in a greater degree than when shortened in any other direction.

(215.) Two plates of very soft iron must next be provided, equal in breadth to the surfaces containing the poles, and a little longer than those surfaces; so that, when applied to them, a portion of each plate shall project beyond the loadstone to a small extent. In *fig*. 58, R *r* represents the sections of these iron plates affixed to the opposite sides of the loadstone L; and P *p* the projecting pieces. These projecting pieces should be much narrower than the other portion of the plates. For loadstones weighing less than an ounce, the lower surfaces

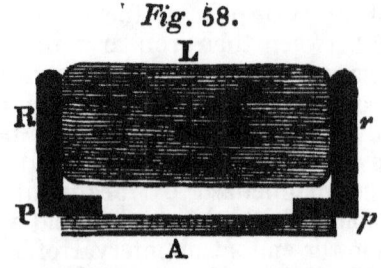

Fig. 58.

of the projections need not exceed the tenth of an inch; and so in proportion for larger loadstones. The thickness of the plates, also, must be regulated by the strength of the loadstone, and can scarcely be determined without previous trial in each particular case. The best way, therefore, is to make them tolerably thick at first; and then file off successive layers, until we find, by actual experiment on the power of the loadstone after each reduction, that we cease to obtain any advantage; for the power increases gradually to a certain limit, at which the filing ought to be discontinued. The armature of a loadstone should be fixed on it very firmly, by wires, or by an external case, which should be made of any metal which is not susceptible of magnetism. Loadstones are sometimes cut into a spherical shape, in imitation of the earth, and are then called *terrellæ*. Their armatures should, in that case, be adapted to the curvature of the surface, and should each cover about a quarter of that surface.

(216.) The addition of armatures to a loadstone is found to have a very favourable effect in augmenting its strength, and this increase of strength goes on for a considerable time after they have been applied. But there is another, and a still more important advantage resulting from them, in enabling us to direct the power of the loadstone, and to concentrate it into a small space. The polarities of loadstones are often diffused over a considerable part of their surface; and these scattered forces could never be made to bear upon any point on which they are required to act, unless by the intermedium of some substance which might collect and unite them. The iron armatures supply this intermedium. They receive at their expanded part the inductive influence of all the scattered poles residing in the surfaces to which they are applied; and this influence being transferred to the narrow extremity, is there concentrated, and acts with full effect. By this expedient also, the resultant forces, derived from each single pole, are brought near to each other, and their directions rendered parallel: they are, therefore, made to conspire in various actions which require the joint operation of both poles, such as that of eliciting magnetism by the double touch. The same advantages, indeed, are procured by this construction as we have already seen obtain in the case of horse-shoe magnets when compared with straight magnetic bars. Thus we find that a loadstone which, in the natural state, would appear to be exceedingly feeble, will possess, when properly armed, very considerable magnetic powers.

(217.) The armature of a loadstone not only contributes to exalt its magnetic virtue, but also furnishes us with the means of preserving it uninjured. Its two poles, being now transferred to the extremities of the armatures, or to each *foot* of the armature, as it has been called, on connecting these poles, by applying to them a bar of soft iron, A (*fig.* 58), we may effectually prevent the dissipation of their magnetism. This crossbar performs a similar function with relation to these poles that the iron plates do to the loadstone itself—it acts as a secondary armature; and we find, after applying this bar, that the apparatus gradually acquires greater power up to a certain limit. Such therefore is the mode in which loadstones, when not in use, should always be kept, with a view to the preservation of their powers.

(218.) Directions of a similar kind, and derived from the same principles, apply also to the preservation of artificial magnets. Horse-shoe magnets should have a short bar of soft iron (A, *fig.* 59)

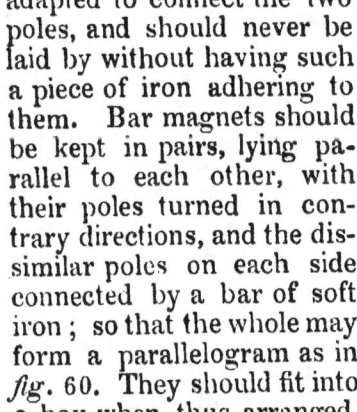

Fig. 59.

adapted to connect the two poles, and should never be laid by without having such a piece of iron adhering to them. Bar magnets should be kept in pairs, lying parallel to each other, with their poles turned in contrary directions, and the dissimilar poles on each side connected by a bar of soft iron; so that the whole may form a parallelogram as in *fig.* 60. They should fit into a box when thus arranged, so as to guard against accidental concussions, and to preserve them from the dampness of the atmosphere. Magnets should be polished, not indeed with a view to the increase of their magnetism,

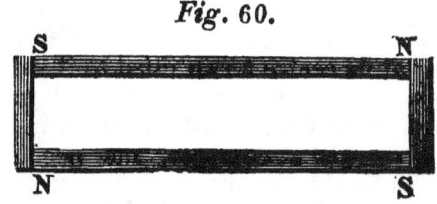

Fig. 60.

but because they are then less liable to contract rust. It is convenient that those ends which have the northern polarity should be marked with a line all round, in order to distinguish the respective poles in each magnet.

CHAPTER VI.
Magnetic Instruments.

(219.) In every branch of science, the value of a correct theory is best estimated by the extent and importance of its practical applications. The nearer its approach to perfection, the greater the assistance we derive from it in constructing instruments for the accurate measurement of spaces, of times, or of forces, and for the accomplishment of the objects which relate to that particular science. It is thus that in magnetism, if the theory, developed in the preceding part of this treatise, be correct, it ought to furnish principles for the construction and management of magnetic instruments, such as the compass, dipping-needle, &c. Our limits permit us only to point out the leading principles which particularly deserve attention in the case of each kind of instrument.

§ 1. *Of the Compass.*

(220.) The term *compass* is a general name for all instruments calculated to indicate the position of the magnetic meridian, or of objects with reference to that meridian, whether adapted for being used on land, and in the bottoms of mines, where we have a stable support at command, or for observation at sea, where the perpetual agitation of the surface deprives us of that advantage.

The first class, which merely show us the direction of the magnetic meridian, includes the *Land Compass*, the *Mariner's Compass*, and the *Variation Compass*; the second, or those which mark the angular distances of objects from this meridian, are called *Azimuth Compasses*.

(221.) Whatever modifications may be rendered necessary by the particular purpose of the compass, the essential parts of which it consists are the same in all—namely, a magnetised bar of steel, generally termed *the needle*, having at its centre a cap fitted to it, which is supported on a sharp-pointed pivot fixed in the base of the instrument. In the mariner's compass, the needle is also affixed to a circular plate, or *card*, the circumference of which is divided into degrees, while an inner circle described upon it is marked with the thirty-two points of the compass, or *rhumbs*, as they are called. The pivot of support rises from the bottom of a circular box, which contains the needle and its card, and is covered with a piece of glass,* in order to protect them from dust, and prevent their being disturbed by the agitations of the external air. The compass box is suspended within a larger box, by means of two concentric brass circles, or *gimbals*, as they are called; the outer one being fixed by horizontal pivots, both to the inner circle which carries the compass box, and also to the outer box; and the two sets of axes being in directions at right angles to one another. By the combinations of movements determined by these axes, the inner circle, with the compass box and its contents, always retains a horizontal position, during the rolling of the ship.

(222.) The qualities required in the needle of the compass, for the perfect performance of its office, are these:—first, its directive force compared with its weight, or with the mass which that power has to set in motion, should be as great as possible; while, secondly, the impediments to the exertion of that force, and which consist principally in the friction between the cap and pivot, should be as small as possible. Hence it becomes important to consider the relation subsisting between these opposing forces, and to ascertain those conditions which give the greatest preponderance to the directive force.

(223.) The friction that takes place between the pivot and the cap which rests on it, will, in different compasses, bear a certain proportion to the pressure on the points of support, provided these parts are constructed precisely in the same manner in each case. This pressure is proportional to the weight of the needle and the parts which turn with it. Coulomb concluded, from a set of experiments he made with a view to ascertain this particular point, that when the pivots terminate in a sharp point, and the caps are made of very hard materials, the friction is very nearly proportional to the square root of the cube of the weights. But after long use, the point of the pivot becomes blunted, and the surface of contact with the bottom of the cap is considerably enlarged. In this state the friction is found to be simply proportional to the pressure.

(224.) Assuming this, then, to be the law of relation between them, let us take a magnetized needle of any given size and shape, and support it upon a pivot in the usual manner. Let us next place upon it another needle, precisely similar in all its dimensions, and magnetized to the same degree. The pressure on the pivot will now be double what it was before; and therefore the friction, which is proportional to that pressure, will be double also. But the directive force, though increased, will not be twice as great as with the single needle; because, as was formerly shown, the reaction of the similar poles of the two magnets tends to diminish the power of each. Hence the ratio between the directive force and the resistance is diminished, and the compound needle is less sensible to the magnetic influence of the earth, and less fitted for indicating the magnetic points of the compass. The same mode of reasoning applies to any increase of thickness that may be given to the needle. Hence it appears, that when all other conditions are the same, needles of very small thickness possess the greatest sensibility to terrestrial magnetism. To this general proposition there is, however, a limit; inasmuch as excessive thinness in the needle would endanger its bending by its own weight, which would be attended with a considerable loss of power.

(225.) With regard to the most advantageous length for a compass needle, it appears that when we have passed a certain limit, which is about five inches, an increase of length is accompanied by an increase in the directive force in the same proportion; but when the thickness remains the same, the weight, and consequently the friction, increases in

---

* An electrical state of the glass cover, accidentally excited by friction, has been known to occasion a sensible disturbance of the needle, by attracting its ends. This attraction, when it exists, may be at once destroyed by moistening the surface of the glass. See Phil. Trans. for 1746, p. 242. See also the observations on the local and electrical influences on compasses by Lieutenant Johnson, in the 21st volume of the Quarterly Journal of Science, p. 274.

the very same ratio; no advantage, therefore, as to directive power can be obtained by any increase of length. Beyond the limit just mentioned, therefore, all needles having the same transverse dimensions should, according to theory, be equally sensible, whatever be their lengths. But it is found in practice, that needles which exceed a very moderate length are liable to have several consecutive poles, attended, as we have seen, with a great diminution of directive force. On this account, short needles, made exceedingly hard, are generally preferable.

(226.) The next object of attention in the construction of a compass needle is the shape which is most favourable to the acquisition of the greatest directive power. Various have been the forms given to compass needles; the choice having been regulated more by the whim and fancy of the maker, than by any reference to scientific principles. The forms most frequently met with are the cylindric, the prismatic, that of a rhombus or parallelogram, and that of the flat bar, tapering like an arrow at the extremities. Coulomb, who made many experiments on the subject, gave a decided preference to the last mentioned of these, as being that which, with a given weight of needle, retains the strongest directive force. On the other hand, he found, that any expansion of the needle at its extremities, a form which has sometimes been recommended, is attended with a sensible diminution of power. From the whole of his experiments, he was led to the general conclusion, that in needles of the same form, their directive forces are to each other as their masses.

(227.) This inquiry has been still further pursued by Captain Kater, whose paper in the Philosophical Transactions, already alluded to (§ 201), contains an account of a series of experiments for determining the best kind of steel for a compass needle, and the best form that can be given to it. He found, on comparative trial, that the directive force is little, if at all, influenced by extent of surface, but depends almost entirely on the mass of the needle, when magnetized to saturation. Two needles were prepared of that kind of steel which is called blistered steel, and two of spur steel, each weighing 66 grains. They were of the form of a long ellipse, five inches in length and half an inch in width. One of each kind was pierced, as shown in *fig.* 61; the weight so lost being made up by

Fig. 61.

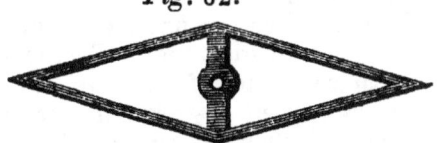

additional thickness. It is evident that these pierced needles had, though of equal mass, much less extent of surface than those which remained solid. Having formerly had in his possession a compass of extraordinary power, the needle of which was composed of pieces of steel wire put together in the shape of a rhombus, he procured two needles of this form (*fig.* 62), made from a

Fig. 62.

piece of clock spring, which is of that kind of steel called shear steel. In one, the cross piece was of brass; in the other, formed of part of a clock spring. They weighed only 45 grains.

(228.) The results of the inquiry were, that shear steel is capable of receiving the greater magnetic force; and that the pierced rhombus is the best form for a compass needle. Needles of cast steel were also tried, but were found so very inferior, as at once to be rejected. In the same plate of steel, of the size of a few square inches only, portions are found, varying considerably in their capability of receiving magnetism, though not apparently differing in any other respect.

(229.) Captain Kater next endeavoured to determine the effects of various modes of hardening and tempering the needles. He found that hardening a needle throughout considerably diminishes its capacity for magnetism. The greatest directive force was obtained by a needle which was soft in the middle, and its extremities hardened at a red heat. He at first thought that the most effectual means of increasing its retentive power, would be first to soften it throughout, and then harden it at the extremities, instead of first entirely hardening it, and afterwards softening it in the middle. But subsequent experience induced him to attribute the difference of effect to a difference in the degree of heat to which the needle is exposed in softening it in the middle. Repeated exposure to heat was found considerably to impair the susceptibility of the needle to retain the magnetic power communicated to it; an effect which does not appear to be owing to any decarbonization of the steel. Captain Kater suggests that this deterioration may arise from a permanent expansion produced in the texture of the steel by the repeated application of heat; for the springs of clocks, which was the material used in his experiments, being made by passing the steel through rollers, when it undergoes great compression, it is probable that the state of condensation thus induced is exceedingly favourable to the retention of magnetism.

(230.) The process which, on the whole, he recommends as the most effectual for giving to a needle the greatest susceptibility of directive power, is first to harden it throughout at a red heat, and then to soften it from the middle to within an inch of each extremity, by exposing it to a heat sufficient to cause the blue colour which arises again to disappear.

(231.) The effect of previously polishing the needle to be magnetized was not found by Captain Kater to have any sensible influence on its capacity for receiving directive power. Neither did any advantage result from the employment of increased pressure in applying the magnets over the surfaces of the needle during the process for magnetizing them; but, on the contrary, in one instance it seemed to be attended with a diminution of effect.

(232.) It is an important requisite in a compass needle that its polarities should be concentrated as much as possible in its two extremities, and undisturbed by the action of any consecutive poles existing at intermediate points. We have already had occasion to remark (§ 193) how much the directive force of a needle is impaired by irregularities in the distribution of its magnetism, attended either by a multiplicity of poles, or by an inequality in the strength of the two principal poles. It is on this account that Duhamel's process of magnetizing is so much preferable to that of Æpinus for imparting magnetism to compass needles; being more conducive to uniformity of effect in every portion of the needle. But even with all the care that can be bestowed, we cannot always be certain of obtaining perfect regularity in the disposition of the magnetic power of a steel bar, whatever shape we may give to it, or whatever process we may employ for its magnetization.

(233.) The consequence of the unequal distribution of magnetism on the two sides of the needle, is evidently to produce a deviation of its axis from the true magnetic meridian; and the instrument will therefore fail to point out the real direction of this meridian. There is only one way of discovering the existence and the amount of the deviation proceeding from this cause; it is to reverse the needle, that is, to turn upwards that surface which was before the under surface; and when thus reversed to balance it as nearly as possible in the same point in its axis as that on which it was before supported. If the needle, in this new state of suspension, finally settles in a position somewhat different from that it before assumed, we may conclude that the axis indicated by its figure is not its true magnetic axis; and that the latter, which alone tends to arrange itself in the magnetic meridian, lies in a situation exactly bisecting the two positions assumed by the needle in these two different modes of suspension.

(234.) When compasses are constructed of two separate pieces of steel bars, slightly bent at an obtuse angle in the middle, so as to allow a space for the placing of the brass cap on which it is to be suspended at the centre, and the two pieces joined by their extremities so as to compose a lozenge-shaped combination, they are exceedingly liable to the imperfection just noticed. For, unless the ends of the separate pieces which compose such a needle have been brought, by tempering, to an exactly equal degree of hardness, that side which is the hardest will retain more magnetic power than the other side; and will, consequently, have a stronger tendency to place itself in the magnetic meridian. The needle will, accordingly, incline on the side which favours this tendency, and the line joining its extremities, and which must be regarded as the axis of its figure, will deviate from the magnetic meridian. This evil will have a tendency to increase by time: for the stronger magnetism of one side, will tend first to impair, and at length destroy, or even finally to reverse, the polarities of the parts on the other side to which they are adjacent.

(235.) The mode in which compass

needles are to be suspended, is well deserving of attention. In order to provide a concave surface, by which the needle may rest on the pivot which is to support it, such, that the point of suspension may be just above the centre of gravity, it is generally necessary, in the straight needle, to make a perforation in its centre, and to rivet into the hole a piece of hammered brass, the lower side of which has been hollowed into a conical cavity, while its upper convex surface is allowed to project a little above the level of the upper surface of the needle. It is found, however, that brass is not capable of being rendered sufficiently hard to resist the continued action of the point against which it rubs in every motion of the compass. In process of time it is worn into an irregular hole, giving rise to great friction, and loss of mobility in the compass. This defect is usually remedied by inserting in the upper part of the brass, a piece of polished agate, ground concave, with a decided centre. The best compasses, made for nautical use, are thus furnished with agate caps.

(236.) Some have considered the perforation of the needle at the centre, for the purpose of suspension, as prejudicial to the regularity of the magnetic power, and as tending to the creation of an additional number of poles. But, in reality, the derangement occasioned by the perforation of a magnetic bar at the point of neutrality, is not found to be attended with any sensible inconveniences in practice*. If the shape given to the needle be that of the pierced rhombus, as recommended by Captain Kater, no such objection will arise, since the cross-bar which connected the obtuse angles of the rhombus has nothing to do with the magnetism of the steel bars forming the sides of the parallelogram. It would, no doubt, be easy to balance a straight bar, without removing any part of its substance, by the addition of a rim of copper, or other non-magnetic substance, to the circumference of the card, so that the centre of gravity of the moveable part of the instrument may be brought sufficiently low to be under the point of suspension. But a little reflection will show, that more would be lost than gained by this expedient; for every addition that is made to the weight of the parts which have to move along with the needle, lessens the efficacy of the magnetic force which gives them motion, and the friction also, being augmented in the same proportion, conspires to diminish the freedom of the motion of the needle, and to impair its sensibility.

(237.) The best precaution to be taken for ensuring the steadiness of the movements of the compass, under all circumstances, is to balance the needle accurately upon its centre, before the card is applied. Care should be taken that the card is uniform throughout in its thickness and texture, and be perforated with a circular hole in its centre, so that when united to the needle, the equilibrium of the whole may be perfectly preserved. In order to fix it to the needle, the latter is tapped with two small screw-holes, at the distance of about half an inch from each end; and the card being placed so that the meridian line marked on it is in the same vertical plane with the axis of the needle, and holes being made in it opposite to those in the needle, small screws are introduced, so as firmly to fasten them together. In order to secure the steadiness of the compass during the violent and irregular movements to which the ship is liable, the suspension of the box by the gimbals should be made with great care; the several axes of motion being so adjusted as that the point of suspension on which the needle, with its card, is supported, be exactly in the same line with both these axes.

(238.) Complaints are frequently made by seamen, that, in a rough sea, the ordinary compasses are so unsteady as to prevent their being easily observed; an inconvenience, which they are apt to ascribe to the needle's being too strongly magnetic, and therefore too easily disturbed by the irregularities in the motion of the vessel. This supposed defect they endeavour to remedy by adding a weight to the card: and this is often done, very injudiciously, by loading it with sealing-wax. Sometimes they stick a few pieces of paper on the under side of the card, to serve as vanes which, acting upon the air, may create a resistance to the oscillations of the needle. It has even been proposed, with a similar design, to make the needle move in oil, or other liquid, keeping it still suspended, as usual, on its pivot—the fluid serving to check the vibrations. But all these expedients, calculated to diminish the mobility of the needle, by counteracting the opera-

---

* Coulomb, Mémoires de Mathématique et de Physique présentés à l'Académie. Tom. ix., 1780.

tion of its directive force, are productive of an evil of a much more serious kind, than any that can arise from mere unsteadiness: for it is evident that the very same cause which makes the compass partake of the irregular motions of the ship, forces it, in the same degree, to deviate from its proper position in the magnetic meridian. While the card remains apparently steady, the steersman will pursue his course, unsuspicious of danger, until the first warning of his error may, perhaps, be the sudden appearance of a shore, from which he had imagined himself at a considerable distance. The real remedy for the inconvenient vacillations of the compass is that we have already pointed out, namely, the accurate adjustment of the point of suspension in the line of the axis of rotation of the gimbals, which, as we have before observed, ought to intersect one another at right angles, in that same point. In addition to this, it may be advantageous to increase the weight of the magnet, provided its directive force be at the same time augmented. This may be effected by employing, as the compass needle, a magnet of greater thickness, or by combining several needles together, laying them parallel to one another; for if both the magnetic power and the weight, (and consequently the friction,) increase in the same proportion, the directive power will remain the same as before; and the compass, thus constructed, being heavier, will be deranged to a less extent by the same disturbing force; and when deranged, will be brought back by the directive force to its proper bearing, with the same facility as in an instrument of the ordinary construction.

(239.) It is to be recollected that if a needle, in its unmagnetic state, be so constructed as that it shall be accurately balanced when resting on a point at its centre, and shall maintain itself in a horizontal position, and if it be afterwards magnetized, the influence of terrestial magnetism will cause it to assume an inclined position, one of its ends preponderating, as if it had acquired additional weight. In order, therefore, to restore the equilibrium, and bring it back to the horizontal plane, it will be necessary to add a corresponding weight to the other end of the needle.

The degree of inclination in the unbalanced needle, depends upon the amount of the dip, which, as we have seen, varies in different parts of the world, according to the situation of the place with regard to the magnetic poles of the earth. Hence, when the compass is transported to a distant part of the globe, a different adjustment must be made of the weight applied to correct the tendency to dip. These adjustments are best effected by means of a sliding piece of brass placed under the needle, and the position of which may change, according to circumstances, on the one side or the other, to any distance that may be necessary. In long voyages, during which the changes of latitude are considerable, the position of this regulating weight requires to be frequently shifted, in order to accommodate the needle to the varying changes of inclination incident to the variations of latitude.

(240.) The Azimuth Compass differs from the ordinary Mariner's Compass only in the circumference of its inner box being provided with sights, through which any object, either in the horizon, or above it, may be seen, and its bearings from the magnetic points of the compass determined, by reference to the position of the card, with respect to the sights. For this purpose the whole box is hung in detached gimbals, which turn on a strong vertical pin, fixed below the box, which is thus capable of being moved round horizontally, and of the sights being directed to whatever object is to be viewed through them. On one side of the box there is usually inserted a nut or stop; which, when pushed in, presses against the card and stops it; this is done to enable the observer to read off the number of degrees of the card, which correspond with an index, or perpendicular line, drawn in the inside of the box. They are also sometimes read off by means of a wire stretching from one sight to the other across the centre of the card.

(241.) Analogous to this instrument is the land or surveying-compass, which is also furnished with sights, and means for reading off the degrees on the card. This latter object is effected in a very ingenious manner, by a contrivance of Mr. Schmalcalder, for which he procured a patent. The card is balanced in the usual manner, and contained in a round brass box, with two sights, the one to which the eye is applied being furnished with a triangular prismatic lens, and the other being an open sight, with a vertical horse-hair line extending along its middle.

The pupil of the eye being bisected by the upper edge of the prism, as in the Camera Lucida, the object and that part of the circumference of the card on which the degrees are marked, are seen at the same time; the former by direct vision, the latter by reflexion from the internal surface of the inclined face of the prism: and thus the coincidence of the two may be accurately noted. A prism of the same kind is also applied in Gilbert's patent Azimuth Compass.

(242.) The Variation Compass, designed to exhibit the diurnal changes of variation in the horizontal magnetic needle, has generally a needle of much greater length, than those of other kinds of compasses; and as it is not required to move round the whole circumference, the box, instead of being circular, is oblong, so as to admit of a deviation of only 20 or 25 degrees from the middle line. A vernier scale, with a magnifier, is usually applied in order to estimate the changes of position of the needle with greater precision.

§ 2. *Of the Local Attraction of Vessels.*

(243.) The indications of the mariner's compass at sea are liable to error from a cause which, till lately, had never been supposed capable of affecting the needle. It consists in the attraction which the large quantity of iron, contained in various parts of the ship, exerts upon the magnetic needle: for although the action of each individual piece of iron may, at the distance at which it is placed, be quite insensible; yet the united action of the whole quantity dispersed in every part of the vessel, may amount to a considerable sum, and occasion a very perceptible deviation of the compass from its true position in the magnetic meridian. This will happen more especially in ships of war, which contain a large number of guns, of iron-shot, and of water-tanks, and various parts of the frame-work of the ship which are now made of iron.

(244.) If we suppose each particle of iron to exert a certain attractive force upon the magnetic poles of the compass needle, according to a certain law, hereafter to be determined, it is easy to understand how the combined effect of all these forces may be considered as equivalent to one simple resultant force acting in a certain direction. If the quantity of iron be considered as equally distributed on both sides of the ship, and the compass be placed, as is usual, in the binnacle, in the after part of the ship, this resultant force, which represents the combined action of the iron, will be situated in a vertical plane passing through the compass, and through the axis of the ship, and will, moreover, have a certain inclination to the horizon. In the northern regions of the globe, the inductive influence of the earth on unmagnetic iron consists in carrying the southern polarity upwards, and the northern polarity downwards, (§ 107,) in a direction parallel to that of the dipping needle. The action on the compass of a piece of iron thus brought into a state of induction will, therefore, be precisely similar to that of a magnet having the position of the dipping needle, and placed at a considerable distance from the compass. If it be placed, with relation to the compass, exactly in the magnetic meridian, (that is, to the magnetic north or south of the compass,) it can have no effect in disturbing its position. This will generally be the case when the course of the ship coincides with the magnetic meridian, and the needle of the compass is in the direction of the axis of the ship. But if the ship's head be turned to the eastward, and the resultant force of the iron in the ship be directed in a line downwards from the compass, that force will be represented by a magnet placed in the same oblique line; and the south pole of that magnet, being uppermost, will act with most power, and will attract the north pole of the compass needle, causing it to deviate towards the east. The same magnet, placed to the westward of the compass, which would correspond with the ship's head being turned to the west, would occasion a westerly deviation of the compass needle. In the southern hemisphere, when the inductive influence of the earth has a contrary direction, the opposite effects would result from the action of the iron in the ship; for the action would then be represented by a magnet, having a position with respect to its poles, the reverse of what it had in the former case.

(245.) The earliest record of any observation of the effect of this local attraction of vessels, occurs in the voyages of Captain Cook; but the reason of the deviation of the needle does not appear to have been suspected. The first distinct statement of the real cause of this anomaly is contained in a report from

Mr. Downie, Master of H.M.S. Glory, in which there is the following passage:—'I am convinced that the quantity and vicinity of iron in most ships have an effect in attracting the needle; for it is found by experience that the needle will not always point in the same direction when placed in different parts of the ship. Also, it is rarely found that two ships steering in the same course, by their respective compasses, will go exactly parallel to each other; yet these compasses, when compared on board the same ship, will agree exactly *.'

(246.) The next observations on this subject were those of Captain Flinders †, who, whilst surveying the south coast of New Holland, in H.M.S. Investigator, in 1801 and 1802, remarked considerable differences in the direction of the magnetic needle, when there was no other apparent cause for them, than the differences in the direction of the ship's head. This occasioned much perplexity in laying down the bearings, as it was very difficult to find the proper allowances to be made for this deviation of the compass in estimating them. With a view of trying how far an alteration in the disposition of the iron might tend to remedy this source of error, Captain Flinders first removed two guns, which had stood near the compass, into the hold, and afterwards fixed the surveying compass exactly a-midships upon the binnacle; for at first it was occasionally shifted to the weather-side as the ships went about; but neither of these two arrangements produced any material effect in preventing the deviations of the compass. When the ship's head was to the east, the deviation was westward; and the contrary, when the ship's head was to the west: when it was nearly north or south, no deviation was perceptible. These differences, arising from a change in the direction of the ship with regard to the points of the compass, were less considerable as he proceeded to lower latitudes; and on approaching the line of no variation, upon the south coast of New Holland, the deviations of the compass were smaller than either before or afterwards. In reasoning on the cause of these deviations, he supposes 'the attractive power of the different bodies in the ship, which are capable of effecting the compass, to be collected into something like a focal point, or centre of gravity; and that this point is nearly in the centre of the ship, where the shot are deposited, for here the greatest quantity of iron is collected together.' He further supposes that this point is endowed with the same kind of attraction as the pole of the hemisphere where the ship is; consequently, in New Holland, the south end of the needle would be attracted by it, and the north end repelled. On this hypothesis, which appears to be the true one, he explains the phenomena he had observed, and also deduces from it as a necessary consequence, that the deviations of the compass, arising from the attraction of the iron in the ship, must, when the ship is on the north side of the magnetic equator, be directly the reverse of those he had observed in the southern hemisphere; that is, the north end of the needle would be attracted, and the south end repelled. This theory was confirmed by other observations, made in the same ship, in the British Channel.

(247.) The observations of Captain Flinders excited considerable attention at the time they were published; and a course of experiments was, in consequence, made, by order of the Admiralty, in various ships in the Nore. It was found that, in every ship a compass would vary considerably in its position on being removed from one part of the ship to another. Although the general fact was completely established by these experiments, they did not then lead to any further investigation, until the subject was again brought into notice by Mr. Bain, who, in a useful treatise which he published on the Variation of the Compass, placed in a striking point of view the fatal consequences which might attend this source of error. The attention of the public was also particularly drawn to the subject at this time, in consequence of the proposed expeditions to the Arctic regions, from which it was expected that much important information would result with regard to terrestrial magnetism. The local attraction of the vessels sent out on these expeditions was made a particular object of inquiry; and the results of the numerous experiments made for that purpose, are detailed by Captains Ross and Parry in their accounts of their respective voyages; and also by Captain Sabine, in a paper in the Philosophical Transactions *. It is

---

* Walker's Treatise on Magnetism, published in 1794; quoted by Mr. Barlow in his Essay on Magnetic Attractions.
† Philosophical Transactions for 1805, p. 186.

* For 1819, p. 112.

stated by the last of these observers that, in the Isabella and Alexander, the binnacle compasses of the two ships were soon found to differ very materially from one another, in indicating the course steered. The difference was frequently one point, or eleven degrees and a quarter. No dependence whatever could be placed on the agreement of compasses in different parts of the ships, or, of the same compass with itself, if removed but a few inches. Even in the neighbourhood of the binnacles, the variation, as observed amidships, was from 8° to 10° greater than the result of azimuths taken by a compass placed between two and three feet on the larboard side, and an equal difference, in a contrary direction, took place, on removing the compass to the starboard side; all of which introduced great difficulties in the ship's reckoning.

(248.) An extensive investigation of the subject was now instituted by Mr. Barlow, with a view of discovering some principle of computation, or other method, for correcting this source of error, in all parts of the world. The results of the first experiments he made for this purpose, were published by him in 1820*; and, in 1824, there appeared a second and greatly extended edition of the same work, developing the mathematical principles which regulate the action of unmagnetic iron upon a magnetized needle. His situation, as Professor of the Royal Military Academy of Woolwich, gave him the means of pursuing his experiments upon a very extended scale; as he could procure, with facility, considerable masses of iron, such as balls and shells of every denomination, and having that regularity of figure which was most favourable to the application of mathematical formulæ. As the inquiry is important, not merely from its application to the subject of the local attraction of vessels, but also in its bearings on the whole theory of magnetism, we shall briefly state the principal results which he obtained.

(249.) Mr. Barlow ascertained, that a ball of iron produces no disturbance of the compass needle, when the latter is situated in any part of a plane passing through the centre of the ball, and at right angles to the direction of the dipping needle, in the place where the experiment is made. The angle of the inclination of this plane to the horizon is, therefore, the complement to the angle of the dip. In London, where the latter may be taken at 70°, this angle is consequently 20°. The section of this *plane of neutrality*, as it may be called, by a horizontal plane, passing through the centre of the ball, will be a line directed to the magnetic east and west. If a hollow sphere, of considerable diameter, be supposed to extend around the ball, and to be concentric with it, the plane above defined will, by its intersection with the sphere, form a great circle, which may be regarded as the *magnetic equator* of that sphere, with relation to the magnetic action of the ball.

(250.) Another plane of neutrality is constituted by a vertical plane, also passing through the common centre of the ball and sphere, and including the magnetic direction, that is, the line of the dip: this plane is evidently that of the magnetic meridian; and it also intersects a great circle on the imaginary sphere.

We have termed these two planes the planes of neutrality, in preference to adopting the name of *planes of no attraction*, by which Mr. Barlow has designated them, because, as Poisson has remarked, it is not the whole of the attractive force exerted by the iron ball that vanishes in these planes; but only that part of this force which occasions deviations in the natural position of the needle, which, indeed, is the only force of which we are now studying the effects. Strictly speaking, however, there remains another force, acting in a direction parallel to the dipping-needle, but of an opposite nature to the action of the earth, and tending, therefore, to retard the oscillations of the needle. There is, indeed, no plane in which the attraction of a sphere, or, in general, of any body magnetized by the earth's influence, becomes evanescent.

(251.) In like manner, other meridional great circles may be conceived on the sphere cutting the equator at right angles, and meeting at the two poles of that equator; and the situation of any point at the surface of the sphere, may be designated by its distance from the equator, measured on the meridional circle which passes through the point, and which may be defined its *magnetic latitude;* together with its distance from any one meridian, fixed upon as the first meridian, measured on a smaller circle

---

* Under the title of 'An Essay on Magnetic Attractions.'

parallel to the equator, and passing through the point in question, which distance might be termed its *magnetic longitude*. Mr. Barlow assumes as his first meridian, the circle which passes from the pole to the magnetic east and west points of the horizontal plane instead of the vertical meridional plane.—We cannot help thinking, however, that the multiplication of these planes would have been better avoided, by assuming the latter, necessarily referred to on so many occasions, as the first meridian.

(252.) Having settled these definitions, the law of action deducible from the experimental investigation of Mr. Barlow, may be very simply expressed. The amount of the angular deviation of a compass needle, the motion of which is limited to a horizontal plane, from the true magnetic meridian, at any point on the surface of the sphere, is such, that the tangent of the angle of deviation is directly proportional to the rectangle of the sine and cosine of the latitude of that point multiplied into the cosine of its longitude. As it is extremely convenient to express propositions of this kind in the concise and perspicuous language of algebra, we shall present the above proposition in that form; denoting the angle of deviation by the symbol Δ; the latitude by λ; the longitude by l. The formula will then be as follows,

$$\tan. \Delta = \sin. \lambda \cos. \lambda \sin. l.$$

But since the product of the sine and cosine of an angle is equivalent to the sine of twice that angle, the formula admits of this simplification, and it will then be,

$$\tan. \Delta = \sin. 2\lambda \cos. l.$$

(253.) The results of a numerous series of experiments made by Mr. Barlow, when the centre of the compass was placed in every variety of position, with respect to an iron ball, approximated so closely to those which were given by computation from the above formula, that no doubt can remain of the accuracy of the law from which it is deduced. They have been further verified by Mr. Christie, by a somewhat different method of procedure, of which he has given an account in the Transactions of the Cambridge Philosophical Society*.

(254.) The next object of inquiry was the law of attraction, with relation to distance; and the result at which Mr. Barlow arrived was, that, when the position, with regard to latitude and longitude, remains the same, the tangents of the angles of deviation are reciprocally proportional to the cubes of the distances. Now as it has been established, that the magnetic force varies inversely as the square of the distance, it will follow, that the square of the tangent of deviation is directly as the cube of the force; or, that the tangent of deviation is directly proportional to the $\frac{3}{2}$ power of the force. In order to convert this proportionality into an equation, it is necessary to introduce a certain constant co-efficient for the number expressing the distance. This co-efficient, when the distance is estimated in inches, Mr. Barlow finds to be .00080382. If this be called A, and the distance denoted by d, the formula, comprising all the variable quantities in one equation, becomes,

$$\tan. \Delta = \frac{\sin. 2\lambda \cos. l}{A\, d^3}$$

(255.) The influence of the mass, and also of the surface with relation to the mass, of the iron sphere in modifying its action, were next made the subjects of investigation. Having at first employed solid balls, weighing, respectively, 288 and 128 pounds, the results appeared to lead to the conclusion, that the tangents of the deviations were proportional to the cubes of the diameter, that is, directly as the masses. But when similar experiments were made with hollow shells, of the same diameter as the former balls, Mr. Barlow was not a little surprised to find that no difference was perceptible between the results of these and of the former trials. Hence he concluded, that the power of attraction was independent of the mass, and resided wholly in the surface of the metal; and all subsequent experiments confirmed the accuracy of this conclusion. The inference he drew was expressed in the following proposition, namely, that the tangents of the deviation are proportional to the cubes of the diameters, or to the square root of the cube of the surfaces, whatever may be the weight or thickness of the sphere. Subsequent experience, however, taught him that this law is subject to a limitation in respect to the thickness of the metal in which the magnetic power resides; for if that thickness, be less than the thirtieth of an inch, the power is not fully developed, and its action is diminished. This conclusion has been since verified by Captain Kater, who found, on

---

* Vol. i. p. 147.

employing three cylinders of iron, the one being solid, and the other two hollow, but all equal in surface, that the deviation of the compass needle, occasioned by the attraction of soft iron, depends on the extent of surface of the iron, and is wholly independent of the mass; excepting a certain thickness, amounting to about two-tenths of an inch, which is requisite for the full development of its attractive energy*. It may be remarked, by the way, that the circumstance of the effective power being limited to the surfaces of bodies, or nearly so, is another striking instance of the analogy which subsists between the magnetic and the electric agencies. These inductive results of observation are all in strict conformity with the theoretical deductions of Poisson already adverted to, § 163.

Introducing into the general formula this new variable quantity, namely, the diameter, or radius, of the sphere of iron, which we shall express by r: it becomes

$$\tan. \Delta = \frac{r^3 \sin. 2 \lambda \cos. l.}{A\, d^3}$$

(256.) These rules and formulæ are capable of being applied in another manner; for, instead of conceiving the imaginary sphere to surround the iron ball, we may imagine a similar sphere concentric with the point of suspension of the needle; and it will then be obvious that the centre of the ball will have the same relative position in the latter sphere, as the pivot of the compass has with respect to the former; so that the reference may be made indifferently to either: and when the mass of iron is irregular, which is the more usual case, it will be more convenient to refer the common centre of attraction of the iron to an imaginary sphere circumscribing the compass.

(257.) It must be observed, however, that in every instrument a limit exists within which the above law ceases to obtain. This limit arises from the influence which the inductive power of the needle may exert upon the iron presented to it; for we have already seen that the consequence of this induction is attraction of the adjacent pole of the magnet, whichever pole that may happen to be. Hence it follows that when the compass is brought so near to the iron, as to act upon it by induction, the laws above determined are superseded by those dependent on this latter cause, and are therefore no longer applicable. In all the experiments made by Mr. Barlow, care was taken that the distances should be such as to be entirely exempt from this disturbing cause.

(258.) Having established the law of action on the compass, as far as regards masses of iron of regular geometric forms, the next object was to determine whether the same law obtains with masses of irregular shapes. This would evidently not be the case, if the popular notion were true, that the poles of a piece of iron, under the influence of terrestrial induction, reside exclusively at the opposite extremities of the mass; whereas if the entire action admits of being referred to one common centre of attraction, in the same manner as the combined effect of the gravitation of all the particles of a body of irregular figure may be considered as directed on a single point, known by the name of the centre of gravity, it is reasonable to expect that the same laws are common to both. Experiments tried, with this view, upon a twenty-four pounder, showed the existence of a plane of neutrality in the most irregularly-shaped masses of iron, and completely established the identity of the operation of the attractive and repulsive forces in all cases, whether the iron was presented in isolated masses, or dispersed in every variety of situation throughout the ship.

(259.) The actual amount of deviation produced in the ship's compass by its local attraction, will, of course, be different in different vessels. With an easterly or westerly course, it has been observed in these latitudes to vary from five to twelve or fourteen degrees: it is of greater amount as the ship is in higher latitudes; and diminishes, without however vanishing, at the equator; and again increases as we approach the south pole. Mr. Barlow, in a paper lately published in the 'Philosophical Transactions*,' gives the following table of the deviation observed in different ships, on the best authorities, from which a general idea may be formed of the extent of error that may thus arise, and also of its average amount.

---

*Philosophical Transactions for 1819, p. 129.

* For 1831, p. 217.

Ship.	Commander.	Place.	Local Attraction.
Conway	Capt. Basil Hall	Portsmouth	4° 32'
Leven	Capt. Owen	Northfleet	6 7
Barracouta	Capt. Cutfield	Do.	14 30
Hecla	Capt. Sir E. Parry	Do.	7 27
Fury	Capt. Hopner	Do.	6 22
Griper	Capt. Clavering	Nore	13 36
Adventure	Capt. King	Plymouth	7 48
Gloucester	Capt. Stuart	Channel	9 30

giving a mean of 8° 44' at the east and west points in these latitudes.

(260.) The last of these ships, the Gloucester, was reported as being 'invariably drawn, in consequence of this deviation, to the southward of her intended place, notwithstanding the greatest care being taken in steering her.' Had it not been ascertained, by taking an observation, that this error was altogether the effect of local attraction, it would probably have been ascribed to the influence of an unknown current. The real deviation, estimated in distance, would occasion the vessel, after running ten miles, to be more than a mile and a half to the southward of her reckoning; and so on in proportion as the distance increased. An error of this magnitude, occurring in a narrow channel and in a dark night, were it unknown or disregarded, might lead to the most disastrous consequences. The wreck of his Majesty's ship Thetis, which lately happened on the coast of Brazil, has been ascribed, with some probability, to a mistake of this kind. The following is the account given of this accident in the ' United Service Journal:'—' The Thetis sailed from Rio Janeiro on the 4th of December, with a million of dollars on board, besides other treasure, and every prospect of a fine passage, stretching away to the south-east. The next day, the wind coming rather favourable, they tacked, thinking themselves clear of land; and so confident were they, that the topmast studding-sails were ordered to be set, the ship running at the rate of nine knots; and the first intimation they had of being near land, was the jib-boom striking against a high perpendicular cliff, when the bowsprit broke short off, the shock sending all three masts over the side; thus in a moment bringing utter destruction on this fine vessel and her valuable cargo.' Mr. Barlow shows, in the paper above referred to, that the deviation of the compass, arising from the attraction of the vessel, was exactly of the kind that was likely to occasion this great mistake in the ship's reckoning: for the distance run by the Thetis being about eighty miles, if the local attraction of the vessel had been equal to that of the Gloucester, she would have passed five miles nearer to Cape Frio than had been calculated upon; an error quite sufficient to account for the fatal catastrophe.

(261.) It is obvious that, when the cargo of the ship consists chiefly of iron, the error in the reckoning may be even more considerable than what has been now stated. The most fatal consequences might arise in a few hours to a vessel in the Channel, under these circumstances, in a dark and blowing night, having for its only guide a compass, subject to an error of fourteen degrees in opposite directions at east and west, the very courses on which she would be endeavouring to steer. How many of the mysterious wrecks that have taken place in the Channel might not be traced to this cause! The loss of the Thames Indiaman is given as an example by Mr. Barlow*. This vessel, besides the usual appointments of guns, &c., had a cargo of more than four hundred tons of iron and steel. The influence of such an enormous magnetic mass would alone be quite sufficient to explain the otherwise unaccountable circumstance, that after leaving Beacheyhead in sight at six o'clock in the evening, the ship was wrecked upon the same spot between one and two o'clock in the morning, without the least apprehension of being near the shore.

(262.) The practical application of the principles above established to the correction of the actual deviations of the compass in a ship, being, as we have seen, of such great importance in navigation, Mr. Barlow bent his mind to the discovery of a method of effecting so desirable an object. His first idea was, that since the guns and other iron of a vessel must produce exactly the same deviation of the needle as a smaller mass of iron placed in a similar situation, but as much nearer as its mass is smaller, it might be possible to place such a body of iron aft of the compass, as would exactly counterbalance the action of the guns, &c., forward, and consequently leave the needle as free to move, as if no such action existed: but he soon found that, for this purpose, the position of the compensating ball of iron would require to be

---

* Essay on Magnetic Attractions, p. 367.

shifted for every different position of the ship, which would, of course, be impracticable. He therefore had recourse to the following expedient, which was found to answer perfectly under all circumstances of situation. Since it is possible to place a ball of iron in the same line of direction, with regard to the compass, as that in which the combined action of the iron of the ship is exerted, and to bring it to the exact distance at which its action shall be equal to that of the ship's iron, it is obvious that a ball so placed will, instead of destroying the deviation of the compass, double its amount; and that this will be the case under all circumstances, and in every part of the world. Instead, therefore, of fixing the ball, let its proper place be first determined, and the ball itself laid aside; then, at any time when it is desirable to ascertain what effect is due to the magnetic attraction of the ship, let it be applied in the situation so determined, and observe how many degrees it draws the needle of the compass from the direction it had previously to the application of the ball. This will be the amount of the actual deviation produced by the iron of the ship; and the correction in the course of the vessel may be applied accordingly. Strictly speaking, it is not the angle of deviation which is doubled by the action of the ball, but the tangent of that angle; but as, in small angles, the tangents are very nearly in the ratio of their arcs, they may in most cases be taken, without sensible error, as the same.

(263.) As the effect to be obtained depends on the surface, and not on the mass of the iron which acts, Mr. Barlow has found it more expedient to employ plates of iron, instead of balls. The form he recommends is a double plate, composed of two thin plates of iron, screwed together in such a manner as to combine any strong irregular power of one plate, with a corresponding weak part of another; by which means a more uniform action is obtained. These plates are of a circular form, twelve or thirteen inches in diameter, with a hole in their centre, through which is passed a brass socket, with an exterior screw; a brass nut, about an inch and a half in diameter, screws on the exterior of each end of the socket, thereby pressing the plates together; with an interposed thin circular piece of board, which is intended to increase in some degree the thickness of the plate, without adding to its weight. It would appear also that the compound plate is more powerful when the two, of which it is formed, are thus separated from each other *. The proper position of the plate, with regard to the compass, must be ascertained by trials on shore; comparing its effects, in different relative situations, with the observed deviation of the compass on board the ship.

(264.) Although the method proposed by Mr. Barlow be exceedingly ingenious, and will, no doubt, to a certain extent, prove highly useful, several causes exist in practice which must interfere with the regularity of its operation. Changes of temperature will probably affect the compass-needle, the compensating plates, and the large masses of iron contained in the ship, in very different degrees; and many of the latter bodies will be more or less susceptible of acquiring permanent magnetism in the different circumstances in which they are placed. In the course of a long voyage, extending to very different latitudes, these causes are liable to considerable variation, and must introduce a degree of uncertainty in the amount of the changes induced. Still, however, the method of Mr. Barlow will furnish a most valuable approximation to the correct determination of the influence which the ship exerts on the needle of the compass. Certain it is that the proper estimate of the disturbing force arising from this cause has, of late years, acquired increased importance from the very large proportion of iron now employed in the construction of ships of war, and of the machinery for their guidance. Independently of the guns, shot, and iron water-tanks, the knees of the ship, the capstans, and cables are now made of iron, so that the whole forms a very large and powerful magnetic mass.

(265.) In all situations, but more especially in high magnetic latitudes, experience has shown the advantage of adopting an expedient originally suggested by Captain Flinders: namely, the selection of some particular spot in the ship as the permanent position of a standard compass, in which it should be invariably placed for use, whether in observing azimuths, or bearings of land, or in directing the ship's course: so that if, on any particular occasion, it

* Barlow's Essay on Magnetic Attractions. Second edition, p. 100.

should be necessary to use a compass in any other part of the ship, a reference should be made to the standard of comparison, and the difference, if any, in its pointing noted and allowed for; a certain degree of uniformity being found to obtain in the effects of the local attraction on a compass thus confined to one spot, enabling a navigator to form a sufficiently correct judgment of the different amounts of variation to be allowed with it on each change in the direction of the ship's head *.

(266.) Not only are the compasses on ship-board disturbed by the magnetic attraction excited by the iron existing in the vessel; the chronometers also are affected by the same influence. The sudden alteration in the rates of chronometers at sea had been frequently noticed by intelligent seamen, but had been generally ascribed to the motion of the vessels. The true cause was first pointed out by Mr. George Fisher, who accompanied Captain Buchan in his voyage to the Arctic Regions, in the year 1818, and who gave an account of his observations on this subject to the Royal Society †. He found that the chronometers on board the Dorothea and Trent had a different rate of going from what they had on shore, even when these vessels had been frozen in, and therefore when their motion could not have contributed to that variation. It appeared that this effect could be attributed only to the magnetic action exerted by the iron in the ships upon the inner rim of the balance of the chronometers, which is made of steel. A similar influence was perceptible on placing magnets in the neighbourhood of the chronometers. This conclusion was confirmed by the experiments made for this purpose by Mr. Barlow, who ascertained that masses of iron, devoid of all permanent magnetism, occasioned an alteration in the rates of chronometers, placed in different positions in their vicinity. The alterations varied according to the positions of each chronometer with relation to the magnetic equator of the masses of iron to whose influence it was subjected, and was always uniform in the same position. In the case of the chronometers on board the Dorothea and Trent, their rate was always accelerated. Mr. Barlow found, however, that this depends on the circumstances of the case, for in other instances they were retarded. He suggests that great care ought to be taken to keep the chronometers on board of any ship out of the immediate vicinity of any considerable mass or surface of iron. They ought not, for instance, to be kept in the cabins of the gun-room officers, which are on the sides of the vessel; as probably a strong iron knee, or even a gun, will be found at a very inconsiderable distance from the spot where the watch is deposited.

Mr. Barlow proposes to rectify this error by a method similar to that which he employs for the correction in the compass, namely, by previously ascertaining what the effect of the ship's iron is upon the rate of the chronometer. This may be done by means of a box or pedestal, on the top of which is a convenient receptacle for the chronometer, and in the side of which a brass pin is fixed, to carry the compensating double iron plate, employed to represent the action of the ship's iron on the compass. Then, having ascertained the rate of the chronometer in the usual manner, let the rate be again taken while it is placed on the pedestal. The plate should generally be kept at the distance of about a foot from the vertical line, through the centre of the dial; and its centre should be about the same depth below the plane of its balance. The rate thus obtained will be a very close approximation to the ship's rate of the instrument, provided care be taken to keep it out of the immediate action of any partial mass of iron, and to place it in the same direction with respect to the ship's head as it had with respect to the iron plate when its rate was determined *.

§ 3. *Of the Azimuth Compass.*

(267.) The purposes to which the azimuth compass is applied, and the general principles of its construction, have already been stated in § 240; but, for the sake of those who are desirous of making practical use of it, it will be necessary to enter into a fuller detail.

The ordinary azimuth compass is represented in *fig.* 63. The semicircle AB is fixed by a screw at its middle, or lowest point, to a stand at the bottom of the outer box, containing the whole apparatus, in such a manner as to ad-

---

* Parry's Journal of a Voyage for the Discovery of a North-West Passage, &c., Appendix, p. cxviii.
† Philosophical Transactions for 1820, p. 196.

* Barlow's Essay on Magnetic Attractions, p. 125.

MAGNETISM.

mit of its being turned round horizontally, and placed in all azimuths. To the upper extremities of this semicircle, a brass circle, CD, is fixed by two pivots GG, constituting a horizontal axis of motion; while the inner cylindrical brass box, PQ, containing the compass itself, is attached to the brass

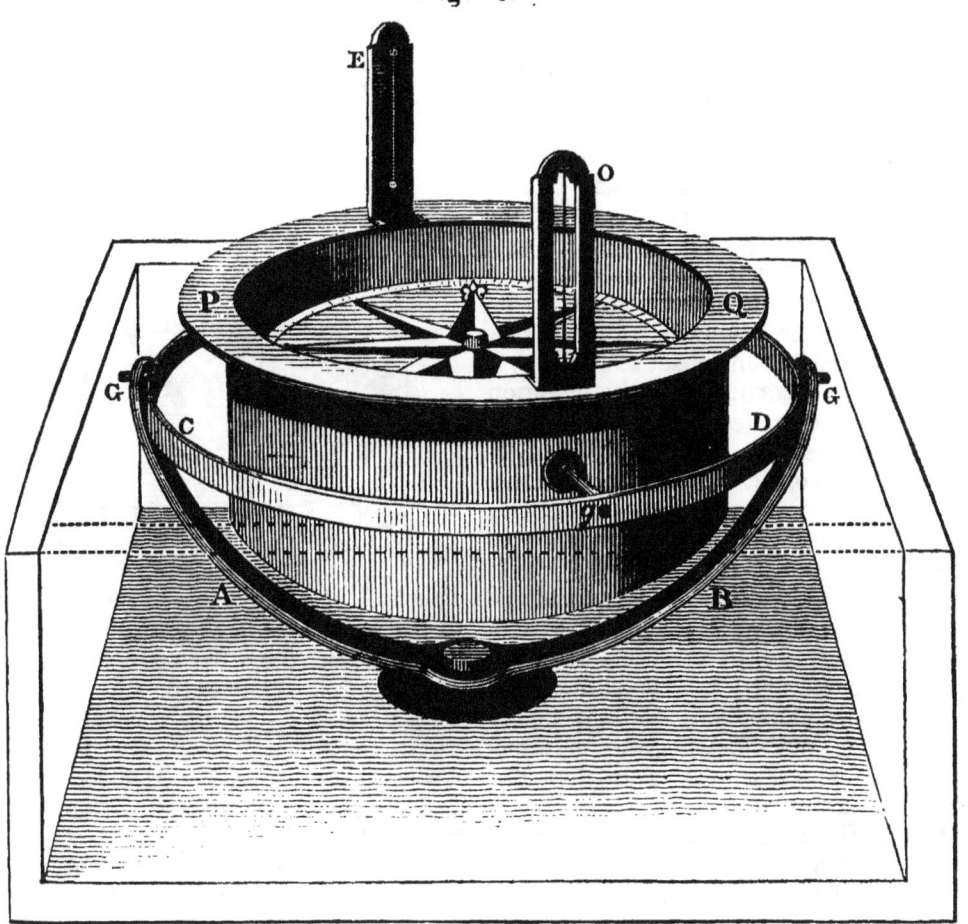

Fig. 63.

circle, CD, by similar pivots, of which one is seen at *g*, forming a horizontal axis at right angles to the former, and both together acting as gimbals. The compass, with its card, is balanced in the usual manner on a pointed pivot rising from the centre of the bottom of the inner box, the upper side of which is covered with a circular piece of glass. The two sights, E and O, are fixed vertically on the upper side of the cylinder of this box, diametrically opposite to each other; the one, E, to which the eye is intended to be applied, consists of a brass slip, having a narrow vertical slit; the other, O, which is turned to the object, is a similar slip, having an oblong aperture containing a fine thread, or horse hair, passing along the middle of the open space in a vertical direction. Two vertical lines are also marked on the inside of the box, which are prolongations of the slit in the sight for the eye, and of the thread in that for the object. These lines are intended as indexes for the measurement of the angular distance in azimuth of an object viewed through the two sights, from the place of the magnetic meridian, as shown by that portion of the graduated edge of the card, which coincides with the line with which it is compared. The degrees are reckoned from the north point of the compass, which is marked zero, all round the circle, in the direction from left to right, that is from north to east, and thence to south and west.

(268.) Sometimes a wire is placed between the two sights, stretching horizontally from the foot of the one to that of the other. This is intended as an index to ascertain coincidences with the degrees marked on the card, when they are viewed from above: but as this is a mode of using the instrument that is seldom practised, this wire is usually omitted, and observations made solely by means of the vertical lines.

(269.) On one side of the box containing the compass there is frequently inserted a nut or stop, which, when pressed, bears, by means of a lever within the box, against the card, and arrests its movement: thus giving the opportunity of reading off the number of degrees more at leisure, and therefore more correctly, than could be done at the moment of observation.

(270.) Sometimes the sights are, for the convenience of carriage, made, by means of joints at their feet, to fold down over the glass which covers the box, when the compass is not in use. In other cases, they are united by a transverse bar, and made so as to be capable of being removed from the box when the instrument is set aside.

(271.) The instrument, in its common form, as above described, is still exceedingly defective, and incapable of affording any very accurate observations. Sufficient evidence of its imperfections may be collected from the narrative of Captain Phipps's voyage; from which it appears that, although the observations were made with all possible care, yet differences in the variation were frequently occurring, in the same place and at the same time, amounting to two, three, and four degrees. In one instance, the error was even five degrees ten minutes.

(272.) The azimuth compass contrived by Captain Kater is a much more perfect instrument, combining all the advantages of the ordinary construction, together with those of being extremely portable, and of being adapted to every purpose of observation, whether at sea or on land. A short description of this compass, but without any figure, is given in the Instructions for the Adjustment and Use of the Instruments intended for the late Northern Expeditions, which were printed by order of the Royal Society in 1818. We have been enabled to illustrate the following account of this instrument by the annexed figures, exhibiting its construction; for the opportunity of drawing which we are indebted to the kindness of Captain Kater.

AB, *fig.* 64, is a brass cylindrical box, containing the compass, of which the card, CD, is five inches in diameter. The needle, which is perforated in its centre to admit of an agate cap, set in brass, for the purpose of suspension, is fixed to a circular piece of talc, over the circumference of which a narrow circular ring of card is laid; the outer margin of this card is accurately graduated into half degrees. The breadth of the cylindrical box is exactly one inch, and it is covered as usual by a piece of

Fig. 64.

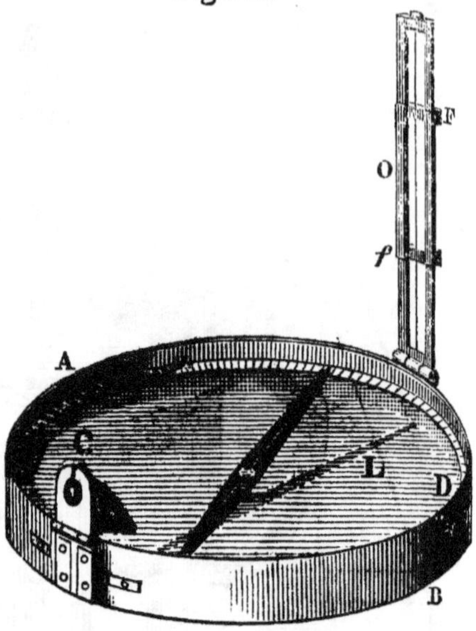

glass. A slanting piece of ivory is fixed to the inner side of the box, so as just to come over the outer edge of the graduated circle of the card: a line, at right angles to the circumference of this circle, is marked upon the ivory, to serve as an index for reading off the degrees in the manner to be presently mentioned.

To the opposite side of the box, at O, a sight is affixed, consisting of a brass frame, in the form of a parallelogram, five inches long. To this frame is adapted a shorter frame, F f, two inches in length, which slides upon it, and carries the segment of a glass cylinder, ground to a radius of five inches. By means of this piece of glass, when presented to the sun, the rays are collected into a linear focus; the line of light being thrown on the index on the piece of ivory, may be seen at the same time as the degrees on the card.

This sight has a hinge where it is connected with the box, by means of which it can be folded down upon the glass cover of the box, as seen in *fig.* 66: and when thus folded, it raises the needle of the compass by means of a lever under its centre, seen at L, so as to press it against the glass cover, and prevent its moving.

The sight, to which the eye is applied, and which is shown separately in *fig.* 65, is an inch in height from its hinge to its upper point; but it may be raised somewhat higher by means of an upright piece, which slides between two grooves in the side of the box; it consists of an upright plane, P, having a

Fig. 65.

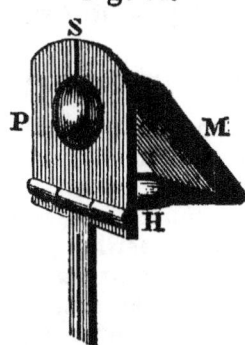

narrow vertical slit, S, in its upper part; below this is a circular aperture, in which a convex lens is placed: a horizontal plane, H, proceeding from the lower edge of the former, and also furnished with a convex lens, and a mirror, M, is placed behind P, and inclined at an angle of forty-five degrees. By means of this combination of lenses with the mirror, the degrees on the card are seen by reflexion, considerably magnified, and in a reversed position, together with the index on the ivory, which is contiguous to the part viewed. The image of the card, being produced by one reflexion, is reversed; on this account it is requisite that the figures expressing the number of degrees should themselves be reversed, so that they may read correctly when viewed through the lenses. This sight may be raised or lowered as much as is necessary to adjust its focus; and the whole is made to turn back, by means of a hinge, so as to lie in the same plane with the box when the instrument is placed in its case, as represented in *fig.* 66, which admits of its being carried in the pocket.

Fig. 66.

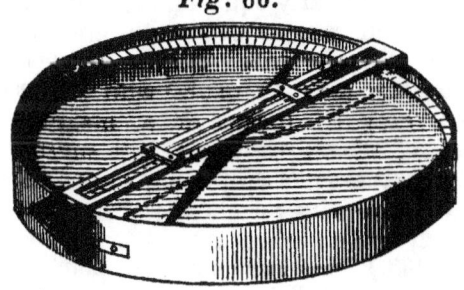

(273.) The following is the method of using this instrument, when the azimuth of the sun is to be taken. Elevate the object-sight, and turning it towards the sun, slide the glass along it till the line of light is thrown on the ivory index. The sight next the eye is then to be adjusted, by raising it from the position in which it lies when flat in the case, till its horizontal lens is over the edge of the card; and the proper focal distance obtained by sliding it in the dove-tailed groove till the index line is seen distinctly. Next observe whether the line of light from the sun seen on the piece of ivory through the lens appears narrow and well-defined; and if it does not, incline the sight furthest from the eye towards the compass, till the requisite distinctness is attained. Be careful that the sight leans neither to the right nor left, but is held perpendicular to the horizon, in the direction between the sun and the observer; for the neglect of this precaution is the principal source of error to be apprehended. Let the compass be now inclined towards the observer, so as to check the oscillations of the card, by bringing it in contact with the index and two pins fixed near it for the purpose. Do this repeatedly, till the card is steady, the compass being sufficiently inclined from the observer just to free the card from the index. The line of light being then accurately bisected by the index line, the degree and fractional parts also indicated by this line may be read off at the moment that an assistant takes the altitude of the sun. If the card should happen not to be perfectly steady, the mean of its vibrations may be readily estimated. The degrees on the card are read from the north towards the east, and are carried round to 360°, in order to obviate the possibility of error in this respect. To the degrees and minutes thus obtained, must be applied the correction written on the card, and the result will be the true magnetic position of the sun, from which, and the observed altitude, the variation of the needle may be obtained in the usual manner. When the variation is to be determined for the purpose of correcting the ship's course, it is sufficient, and indeed necessary, that the magnetic azimuths should be taken without any reference to the local attractions which may affect the needle; but for scientific deductions, after a certain number of observations have been obtained with the ship's head in one direction, she should be put on an opposite course, and another set of observations taken from the same spot: the mean of the two results will be the true variation of the needle.

(274.) Captain Kater's azimuth compass is also well adapted for surveying, for which object, indeed, it was originally invented. To apply it to this purpose, nothing more is necessary than to slide the frame containing the segment of the glass cylinder to the top of the sight, when the hair will be seen, which must be made to bisect the object viewed by direct vision at the moment that its bearing is also read off by reflexion.

(275.) There is also another mode of using this compass, which may, perhaps, be found more convenient and accurate than that already described. It is simply to turn back the reflecting sight, and to view the line of light, and read off the degrees by direct vision; and it has this decided advantage, that if the compass should not be in a horizontal position, the observer may readily perceive and correct the error. Some care, however, is necessary not to mistake in reading the figures indicating the degrees, they being inverted as marked upon the card: this may be prevented by viewing them also by reflexion.

(276.) On approaching the north pole of the earth, the north end of the needle will incline downwards; but the card may again be readily balanced by taking out the ring and glass, and attaching a small bit of wax to the south pole of the needle.

(277.) When it is considered how great is the diminution of the power with which the magnetism of the earth acts upon the horizontal compass needle in very high magnetic latitudes, the satisfactory results which have been obtained, even under such extreme circumstances as those of the late arctic voyages,—in Davis's Straits, for instance, and Baffin's Bay,—from the employment of Captain Kater's azimuth compass, which gave correct observations when other instruments became useless, afford the best testimony of its excellence, and of the precision which may be expected from its employment in the ordinary course of observation *.

(278.) In some azimuth compasses, for which patents have been taken, a triangular glass prism is substituted for the mirror in the above instrument, acting evidently on the same principle of reflexion, and evidently borrowed, with a trifling alteration of form, from the original invention of Captain Kater. Coloured glasses are sometimes provided for making observations on the sun; they are placed so as to be readily interposed between the eye and the nearest sight when wanted, and are removeable at pleasure when not required.

§ 4. *Of the Variation Compass.*

(279.) A magnetic needle intended to indicate the minute changes that take place in the direction of terrestrial magnetism, should, as already noticed (§ 242), be of somewhat greater length than an ordinary compass, in order that the extent of the variations of angular position may be more conspicuous.

(280.) For the same purpose, the following method was practised by Du Hamel:—At each extremity of a long needle, a slender, pointed piece of steel was erected perpendicularly, which served as sights for observing its position with reference to the divisions of a graduated limb, six feet in length, fixed to a pillar at the distance of nearly sixty feet from the needle, and in the direction of its axis *.

(281.) Analogous to this was the construction employed by Mr. Prony, consisting of a long magnetic bar, on which was fixed a telescope, moving along with it; its motion being observed by looking through it at a distant object, the image of which would have a corresponding motion in the field of the telescope. Humboldt, who made many observations with this instrument, considered it to be a very accurate method.

(282.) But a point of much greater importance is that the magnetism of the needle should be uniform, and that its magnetic axis should remain permanent. Hence its form should be of the simplest kind, such as that of a slender needle of nearly equal diameter throughout, and magnetised with great care. The observation of minute changes of position may be made with sufficient accuracy by means of a magnifying glass; which expedient will supersede the necessity of employing sights, or of giving to the needle any extraordinary length.

(283.) Another material point is to obtain great delicacy of suspension, so that the needle shall immediately obey the slightest change of direction in the force of terrestrial magnetism, or of

---

* See Captain Sabine's observations in the Philosophical Transactions for 1819, p. 141.

* Histoire de l'Académie Royale des Sciences de Paris, for 1772, part ii., p. 50.
† Biot, Traité de Physique, tom. iii., pp. 143, 144.

any other extraneous magnetic force. This object can hardly ever be sufficiently attained by balancing the needle upon a point, as in the common compass; because, however small the friction may be, it is still a force which is required to be overcome at the beginning of every new motion, and which must even prevent all motion until the moving power has increased to a certain amount. This objection does not apply in the same degree to the suspension of the needle by a fine thread, which is accordingly the best plan of construction for a variation compass. Care should, of course, be taken that the force of torsion be as small as possible. Mr. Bennet proposed a spider's thread as the best material for obtaining great delicacy of suspension, and procuring the greatest magnetic sensibility: for although twisted through many thousand turns, it occasioned no sensible deviation in a needle suspended by it; showing that its force of torsion is insensible *.

(284.) The thread should be contained in a vertical tube, fitted to the middle of the upper side of an oblong box, the remaining parts of which are to be completed by glass plates, for the purpose of protecting the needle from agitation by the air. With a graduated arc adapted to each end of the needle, and magnifiers to observe the exact position of the extremities when referred to these arcs, this simple form of the instrument, which is the one employed by Captain Kater, is calculated to answer every practical purpose that can be desired. Its superiority to the ordinary construction was shown on the occasion of the late Northern Expeditions, when it was found that the friction on the metal point in the variation needle belonging to Mr. Browne, made by Dollond, nearly a foot in length, and suspended in the usual manner by an agate cap on a metal point, was, in the high magnetic latitudes reached by Captain Parry, too considerable to be overcome by the directive power of the magnet; and accordingly it happened that at Winter Harbour the instrument was quite useless, while the one furnished by Captain Kater still traversed †.

(285.) Considerable light, however, may be thrown upon the causes that produce the minute diurnal or monthly changes in the variation, by adopting the expedient suggested by Mr. Barlow, and which we have already slightly alluded to, § 122. From a variety of considerations, we are warranted in concluding that the direction assumed by the magnetic needle is the result of a great number of magnetic forces acting upon it, some of which are of a nature more permanent than the rest. Thus, while the average direction is the resultant of some cause of very general operation, affecting extensive portions of the globe, many occasional changes are effected by causes of a more transient nature, some of which are periodical in their influence, but of which others are, as it were, accidental, or at least very irregular and fluctuating in their action. Innumerable observations have proved that the compass-needle is more or less agitated during the prevalence of the aurora borealis *. Its deviation from this cause has been known to amount to six or seven degrees. Volcanic eruptions have been at various times observed to occasion considerable disturbance in the position of the needle: this was particularly noted during the eruptions of Mount Hecla and of Vesuvius†. Atmospherical changes, such as violent winds, or a fall of snow, have, in like manner, been known to affect the needle. The electrical conditions of the atmosphere, and especially those connected with the approach or occurrence of thunder-storms, have a powerful influence on magnetic polarity.

(286.) It is evident that as the needle in its ordinary states is urged to move by a force resulting from the influence of these variable forces, combined with those that are of constant operation, the effect of the former would be much greater if the latter were withdrawn; and this can only be effected by neutralizing the operation of these constant forces. Mr. Barlow effected this by applying one or more magnets in the requisite positions, so as to counteract almost entirely the natural magnetic influence of the earth. In illustration of which he gives the following example ‡. Supposing that a finely suspended hori-

---

* Philosophical Transactions for 1792, p. 81.
† Parry's Journal of a Voyage for the Discovery of a North-West Passage, &c. See Appendix, p. cxvi.

* See Wargentin's Memoir in the Philosophical Transactions for 1751, p. 126.
† The Abbé de la Torre observed changes of several degrees in the declination of the needle, during an eruption of Vesuvius.
‡ Philosophical Transactions for 1823, p. 327.

zontal needle, under the natural influence of the earth, makes one vibration in two seconds; and that by masking the terrestrial influence by magnets properly adjusted, the time of vibration is increased to eight seconds; then it would follow that the directive power was reduced to one-sixteenth of the former; and, consequently, that any lateral magnetic force acting upon the needle would produce an effect sixteen times greater than before; so that if the former were twelve minutes, the new effect on deviation might be expected to amount to between three and four degrees, and therefore be such as to admit of distinct and satisfactory observation. Thus he found that when the needle was kept in its natural position, and then deprived of nearly the whole of its directive power by bringing a magnet near it, the daily variation might be magnified almost to any amount. The same result was obtained when the north pole of the needle was directed to the south, east, or west, or, indeed, any required position, at least within certain limits. With this view, Mr. Barlow first deflected the needle, by the repulsion of a magnet, into a certain position, and then, by means of another magnet, modified its directive power in the same way as when it was in its natural position in the magnetic meridian.

(287.) Thus, by combining different sets of observations, in different positions of the needle, information may be obtained as to the direction as well as intensity of the extraneous forces that interfere with the general directive influence of the earth. Mr. Christie, in prosecuting these investigations, preferred applying two magnets, placed one above and the other below, and on different sides of the needle, in the line of the dip, or that in which it would arrange itself if freely suspended by its centre of gravity, instead of retaining them in the same horizontal plane with the needle, conceiving that a more equable distribution of the forces acting on the needle would thus be obtained; for a portion of the forces acting upon the horizontal needle in the line of these magnets would be destroyed, and it would still be acted upon by forces in the same direction as before, but of less intensity; whereas by even applying the poles of two magnets to the corresponding poles of the needle, and in the same plane with them, the horizontal directive force of the needle would be diminished by increasing the angle which the resultant of the terrestrial forces and those of the magnet made with the horizon, and which would be nearly equivalent to increasing the angle of the dip. This arrangement also procured the further advantage of obtaining various modifications of effect, by altering the distances of the neutralizing magnets from the needle, whereby inferences might be deduced as to the variations in the intensities of the deflecting forces occasioning the deviations of the needle at different times. It would exceed the limits of this treatise to attempt even a short abstract of the mode of investigation pursued by Mr. Christie in this inquiry, and for the details of which we must refer our readers to his paper in the Philosophical Transactions*. The general results to which he arrived have already been given in §§ 123, 124.

(288.) In observations for determining the exact variation, great care should be taken that the compass employed be unaffected by any local causes of attraction from iron in the neighbourhood. In the account given of the meteorological instruments used at the Royal Society's house †, Mr. Cavendish points out the method he employed in order to ascertain whether this cause of error existed; and if so, to determine its amount. He removed the variation compass from the apartments of the Society, into a large garden belonging to a house in Marlborough-street, about a mile and a quarter to the west of Somerset House, where there seemed to be no danger of its being affected by any iron-work. Here it was placed exactly in the meridian, and compared for a few days with a very exact compass, placed in an adjoining room, and kept fixed constantly in the same situation. It was then removed back to the Society's house, and compared again with the same compass. By a mean of these observations, the difference between the position in the two stations was ascertained, indicating the amount of the local influence of the iron in the house and adjacent buildings, and consequently the error of the instrument.

§ 5. *Of the Dipping-Needle.*

(289.) The principle on which the dipping-needle acts has already been

---

* For 1823, p. 342.
† Philosophical Transactions for 1776, p. 391.

explained (§ 97), as also the general form of the instrument.

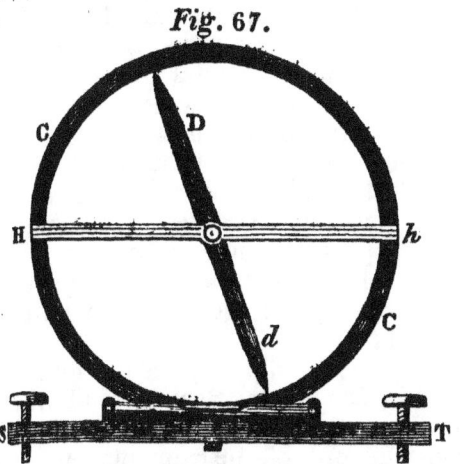

Fig. 67.

(290.) The simplest construction is that represented in *fig.* 67. The needle D *d* is a flat oblong piece of steel, broader at the middle, and tapering to a point at the extremities. A slender cylindrical axis is passed at right-angles through its centre, and moves freely in circular apertures made in the middle of the lateral horizontal bars, H *h*, fastened to a vertical graduated circle, CC, indicating the angle which the needle makes with the horizon. This circle is fixed to a flat stand, ST, provided with one or more levels; the horizontality of which is adjusted by means of screws placed at the corners of the stand. The usual mode of observing with such an instrument is first to ascertain the direction of the magnetic meridian by a common compass, and then, removing the compass to a sufficient distance, so that it may not affect the position of the dipping-needle, to fix the circle of the latter in the plane of this meridian, and then to render it perfectly level by means of the screws of the stand. For the adjustment of the instrument in the meridian, in any particular place where the bearing of a distant object is exactly known, the frame containing the needle is occasionally provided with two sight vanes, placed on an index moving horizontally on the top of the vane, and which may be directed to that object.

(291.) Great care should be taken that no iron or steel enters into the construction of any part of the frame-work of the apparatus, as such material might produce a sensible action upon the needle: great attention should even be paid to the purity of brass that may be employed in its construction, and to its exemption from all magnetic properties.

(292.) It was formerly deemed an advantage to make the needles of considerable dimensions, so as even to exceed a foot in length. But experience has shown that more is lost than gained in point of accuracy by giving to them a length greater than six or eight inches; and considerable convenience, of course, results from this reduction of size, as the instrument is thus rendered more portable, as well as less expensive.

(293.) With a view to diminish friction, Mr. Mitchell, in the year 1772, proposed that the two ends of the axis of the dipping-needle should be supported on friction-wheels; and two instruments with this improvement were executed for the Board of Longitude by Mr. Nairne. The needles were a foot in length, and the ends of the axes were made of gold alloyed with copper, and the friction-wheels on which they rested were four inches in diameter, these wheels being themselves balanced with great care. The ends of the axes of the friction-wheels were likewise made of an alloy of gold and copper, and moved in small holes made in bell metal; and opposite to the ends of the axes of the needles and of the friction wheels, were placed flat agates, finely polished. Each magnetic needle vibrated in a circle of bell-metal, divided into degrees and half degrees; and a line passing through the middle of the needle to the ends pointed to the divisions. The needles were nearly balanced before they were rendered magnetical; and by an ingenious contrivance of Mr. Mitchell, of a cross fixed on the axes of the needles, on the arms of which were cut very fine screws, to receive small buttons, admitting of being screwed nearer to or farther from the axis, the needles could be adjusted both ways, to a great nicety, after being magnetised, by reversing the poles, and changing the sides of the needle. The frame of the instruments were provided with levels for the horizontal adjustment, after they had been placed in the plane of the magnetic meridian [*].

(294.) In a subsequent volume of the Philosophical Transactions [†], a dipping-needle is described by Dr. Lorimer, calculated for making observations on the dip at sea, where, from the unsteadiness of the supports, the difficulty of attaining any degree of accuracy is very great. The needle was of the

---

[*] Philosophical Transactions for 1772, p. 476.
[†] For 1775, p. 79.

usual shape and size, and moved vertically on its axis, which had two conical points, slightly supported in two corresponding hemispherical sockets, inserted into the opposite sides of a small upright brass parallelogram, about an inch and a half broad, and six inches high. Into this parallelogram was fixed, at right angles, a slender brass circle, about six inches diameter, silvered and graduated to every half degree, on which the dip is indicated by the needle. This, for the sake of distinction, he called the *circle of magnetic inclination*. This brass parallelogram and, consequently, the circle of inclination, also turned horizontally on two other pivots, the one above and the other below, with corresponding sockets in the parallelogram. These pivots were fixed in a vertical brass circle, of the breadth and thickness of two-tenths of an inch, and of such a diameter as to allow the circle of inclination and the parallelogram to move freely round within it. This second circle he calls *the general meridian*. It was not graduated, but had a small brass weight fixed to the lower part of it, to keep it in a vertical position; and the circle itself was screwed, at right angles, into another circle, of equal internal diameter, of the same thickness, and twice the breadth, which was silvered and graduated on the upper side to every half degree. It represented the horizon: for it swung freely in gimbals, and was, consequently, always horizontal. The whole was contained in a mahogany box, of an octagon shape, with a glass plate at the top, and one on each side for some way down. That part of the frame which contained the glass could be lifted off when requisite. The whole box turned round upon a strong brass centre, fixed in a double plate of mahogany, glued together cross-wise, to prevent its warping or splitting; and this again was supported by three brass feet, frosted so as to prevent their slipping when the vessel rolled considerably. When not wanted for use, it was enclosed in an outer square box, in order to preserve it effectually.

The peculiar advantage of this instrument consists in the freedom which is allowed to the needle of obeying the tendency, impressed upon it by terrestrial magnetism, of placing itself in the line of the dip, in consequence of the power which it has of moving in different planes at right angles to one another. Its position with respect to the respective circles points out also, upon simple inspection, not only the inclination, or dip, but also the magnetic bearings in a horizontal plane. Hence by directing the vertical circle to the sun, or other object in the heavens, the magnetic amplitude of the object is also readily determined. Dr. Lorimer's compass, though exceedingly plausible in theory, presents such difficulties in its practical execution, as can scarcely be overcome by the most exquisite workmanship.

(295.) The dipping-needle formerly used by the Royal Society, and which has been regarded as the model for the construction of instruments of this kind, is described by Mr. Cavendish, in the 66th volume of the 'Philosophical Transactions*.' In this instrument, the ends of the axis roll on horizontal agate planes; and a contrivance is applied, by which the needle may, at pleasure, be lifted off from the planes, and laid down on them again in such a manner as to be supported always by the same points of the axis resting on the same parts of the agate planes, the motion by which it is let down being very gradual and without shake. The general form of the instrument, the size and shape of the needle, and the cross used for balancing it, were the same as in the dipping-needle constructed by Nairne on the plan of Mr. Mitchell, already described, § 293. The mode of using the instrument was as follows: the dip was observed first with its front to the west, and then with its front to the east; after which the poles of the needle were reversed, and the dip observed both ways as before. Care was taken that the needle was rendered equally magnetical after the poles were reversed, as it has been before; this equality being ascertained by counting the number of vibrations made by the needle in a given time in both cases. The mean of these four observations was the true dip.

(296.) In order to estimate the influence of the several causes of error which might singly vitiate the result, but which may be made to compensate one another by combining these different modes of observation; let us suppose *fig.* 68 to present us with a front view of the needle; and S N to be the direction of the magnetic axis, or line according to which its magnetism is exerted; and let

---

* For the year 1776, p. 375.

M *m* be drawn at right angles to S N, and passing through the centres of the cylindrical ends of the axis, and representing therefore the axis of motion. If the needle were truly balanced, its centre of gravity would coincide with

Fig. 68.

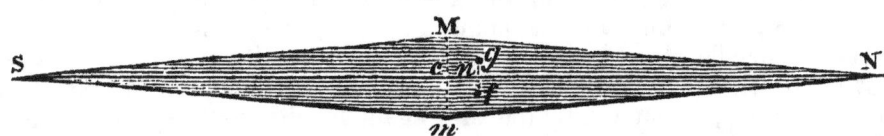

the intersection of these lines at *c*. But supposing this not to the be case, and that in consequence of an error in the suspension the centre of gravity is at *g*; draw *gf* perpendicular to S N, cutting it in *n*, and make *nf* equal to *g n*. When the instrument is turned half way round, so that the opposite face of the needle is presented to us, the edge S M N will now be in the place before occupied by S *m* N, and the centre of gravity will be situated at that part where point *f* was before; therefore the mean between the forces by which the needle is drawn out of its true position in these two situations, in consequence of its not being truly balanced, is accurately the same; and the mean between the two observed dips is very nearly the same as if the centre of gravity had been at *n*. But if the centre of gravity were at *n*, the dip would be very nearly as much too great in the one position of the needle, or it would be too little when the poles are reversed; or *vice versâ*. Therefore the mean of the observed dips in these four situations will be very nearly the same as if the needle were truly balanced.

(297.) In the second place, if the planes on which the axis rolls are not horizontal, the dip will be very nearly as much greater than it would otherwise be, when one face is turned to the west, as it is less when the other is; for if these planes dip towards the south in one case, they will dip as much towards the north in the other, supposing the levels by which the instrument is set to remain unaltered. Consequently, the mean of the two observations will be very nearly the same as if they had been placed in a truly horizontal plane.

(298.) The same method of reasoning will show, in the third place, that the mean of the two observations abovementioned will not be altered, although the index-line joining the mark by which we observe with the axis of motion be not parallel to the axis of the needle; that is, although the index line do not coincide with the continuation of the line SN; or although the line joining the two divisions of 90° be not perpendicular to the horizon; or although the axis of motion do not pass through the centre of the divided circle, provided it be in the same horizontal plane with it. Should it happen, indeed, that the axis of motion is not in the same horizontal plane with the centre of the divided circle, the error thence arising will not be compensated by this method of observing; unless the position of both ends of the needle be taken as checks upon one another. This, however, is of no consequence, since it is easy to examine whether or not they are in the same horizontal plane.

(299.) But the error that is most difficult to be avoided in the construction of the instrument, is that which arises from the ends of the axis not being truly cylindrical. It is, accordingly, essential that the parts of the axis which rest in the agate planes should be exactly the same. The instrument, however, is so contrived as to admit, on occasion, by giving the axis a little liberty in the notches by which it is lifted up and down, of our making these planes bear against a part of the axis distant about a hundredth or a fiftieth of an inch from their usual point of bearing. Mr. Cavendish found that, when the axis is confined, so as to have no such liberty, and when care is taken, by previously making the needle stand at nearly the right dip, that it shall vibrate in very small arcs when let down on the planes: that then, if the needle be lifted up and down any number of times, it will commonly settle exactly at the same point each time; at least the difference is so small as to be scarcely sensible. But if it be not so confined, there will often be a difference of twenty minutes in the dip, according as different parts of the axis rest on the planes; and that, although the greatest care be taken to free the axis and planes from dust; which can be owing only to some irregularity in the axis. If the needle vibrate in arcs of five degrees, or more, when let down on the planes, there will frequently be as great an error in the dip. It is true that the part of the agate planes on which the axis rests when the vibrations are stopped, will be a little different, according to the point at which the needle stood before it was let down; which will make a small difference in the dip, as shown by the divided circles, when only one end of the needle is observed, though the real dip, or inclination of the needle to the horizon is not altered; but this difference is far too small to be perceptible; so that the above-mentioned error cannot be owing to this cause. Neither does it seem to arise from any irregularity in the surface of the agate planes, for they were ground and polished with great accuracy; but it most likely proceeds from the axis slipping in the large vibrations, so as to make the agate planes bear against a different part of it from what they would otherwise do. Mr. Cavendish gives it as his opinion that this irregularity is not owing either to want of care or skill in the execution, but to the unavoidable imperfection of this kind of work. He imagines, therefore, that this instrument is at least as exact, if not more so, than any which has yet been made.

(300.) Thus it appears, that in general the indications afforded by the dipping-needle are liable to two principal sources of error: first, the axis of the magnet's length may not be the exact axis of its magnetic forces; and, secondly, its point of suspension may not, in every position, be exactly coincident with its centre of gravity. Different modes of observation must be resorted to, in order to ascertain the amount of the errors arising from these causes. We must first assure ourselves that the axis of rotation of the needle is perfectly level, so that the needle shall turn in a plane exactly vertical: we must next see that it is placed accurately in the plane of the magnetic meridian; and we have then to observe carefully the positions at which it settles, after being repeatedly disturbed, and allowed to oscillate freely. The mean of these positions may then be taken as the true position of the needle under these circumstances. We are next to turn the whole instrument horizontally till it has described a complete semicircle, or 180°; that face of it which was to the east being now to the west, and *vice versâ:* and then, taking similar observations on the dip, we get a mean of these, for this new position. Comparing these two means, we obtain a resulting mean, which is free from the first source of error. In order to exclude the operation of the second cause of error, we must now remove the needle from its supports, and after destroying its magnetism, magnetize it again in the contrary sense; namely, rendering that end a north pole, which before was south, and *vice versâ;* then, replacing it upon its supports, we must make with it similar sets of observations to those made before, turning it first on one side and then on the other. The mean thus obtained, combined with the former mean, will give the mean of the whole; which may be considered as the true dip, at the place and at the time of observation.

(301.) The error produced by the want of coincidence between the axis of motion and the centre of gravity of the needle may be removed by the following method, devised by Daniel Bernouilli, and which, being easily executed, deserves to be generally known. Let a dipping-needle be constructed with as much correctness as can be effected by the ordinary methods of workmanship, and balanced as exactly as possible before it is rendered magnetic: when impregnated, therefore, it will arrange itself tolerably nearly in the line of dip. Carefully note the position it takes under these circumstances, and then destroy its magnetism. When it has thus returned to its natural state, alter the point of suspension, or adjust the centre of gravity, in such a manner as that it shall arrange itself in the same position as that above noted by the sole influence of gravity. Now impregnate it again, imparting to it the same poles as before. It is evident that it will now approximate still more nearly to the true line of the dip, since nearly the whole of that portion of the force of gravity which before produced a deviation from the position no longer operates. If we find that this approximated position differs several degrees from the former one, the operation may be repeated, until we have arrived so near to the true position, that no further difference can be perceived. It will rarely happen that the third approximation will give an error of half a degree.

(302.) This simple instrument was adapted by its author to observation in all situations, in the following ingenious manner:—A very light brass graduated circle, ABC, *fig.* 69, is fixed to one side of the needle SN, concentric with its axis, and the whole is balanced as nicely as possible before impregnation. A very light index, R r, is then fitted on the axis so as to turn stiffly upon it. This will

Fig. 69.

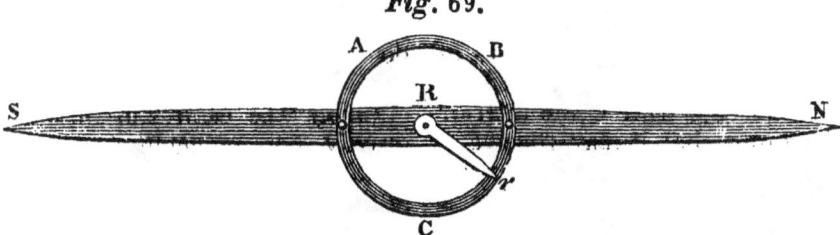

destroy the equilibrium of the needle. If the needle had been made with perfect accuracy, and perfectly balanced, the addition of this index would cause it always to settle with the index perpendicular to the horizon, whatever degree of the circle it might chance to point at. But as this is not to be expected, the index is to be set at various degrees of the circle, and the position which the unmagnetic needle takes, corresponding to each place of the index, must be observed, and the result of all these observations recorded in a table. Suppose, for example, that when the index is at 50°, the needle inclines 46° from the horizon: if in any place we observe that the needle, rendered magnetic by juxtaposition between two powerful magnets, having the index at 50°, has an inclination at 46°, we may be certain that this is the true dip at that place; for the needle is not deranged by magnetism from the position which gravity alone would give it. As we generally know something of the dip that is to be expected in any place, we must set the index accordingly. If the needle do not show the expected dip, the position of the index must be altered, and the inclination of the needle again observed. Examine whether this second position of the index, and this dip, form a pair which is in the table: if they do, then we have obtained the true dip; if not, we must try another position of the index. Noticing whether the agreement of this last be greater or less than those of the former pair, we learn whether to change the position of the index in the same direction as before, or in the opposite direction. Professor Robison had a dipping-needle of this kind, made by a person totally unacquainted with the making of philosophical instruments. He used it at Leith, at Cronstadt in Russia, at Scarborough, and at New York, and the dip indicated by it did not in any single trial differ a degree and a half from other trials, or from the dip observed by the finest instruments. He tried it in Leith Roads in a rough sea; and did not think it inferior, either in certainty or dispatch, to a needle of the most elaborate construction. Professor Robison deems it worthy of its ingenious author, and of the public notice, because it can be made for a moderate expense, and, therefore, may be the means of multiplying observations on the dip, which are of immense value towards perfecting the theory of terrestrial magnetism.

(303.) In a dipping-needle recently made by M. Gambey, at Paris, intended to be used at St. Petersburgh, the axis, instead of being a cylinder, is a knife-edge, as in a fine hydrostatic balance. This edge is placed exactly in the centre of gravity of the whole compound needle, and is so fixed that when the needle dips 71°, the edge rests perpendicularly on two agate plates. It is evident that such a needle, however sensible, is adapted for use only in those situations in which the dip is nearly 71°. It is, however, well calculated for ascertaining minute variations of inclination in the same place *.

(304.) Another mode of dispensing with the condition that the axis of motion should accurately pass through the centre of gravity, a condition which it is next to impossible ever strictly to fulfil, is that adopted in the dipping-needle invented by Professor I. Tobias Mayer, in his treatise, *De Usu accuratiori acus inclinatoriæ Magneticæ* †.

The centres of motion and of gravity are, in this needle, designedly separated, so that the inequalities of workmanship in the axis, or in the planes of suspension, are rendered of less effect, being opposed by the joint influence of gravity and magnetism; whilst, by a peculiar process of observation, and an appro-

---

* Annales de Chimie et de Physique.
† Published in the Transactions of the Royal Society of Sciences at Göttingen, for 1814.

NOTE

This volume has a very tight binding and while every effort has been made to reproduce the centres, force would result in damage

priate formula, the joint operation of the two forces is resolvable, and the position which the needle should assume from that of magnetism alone is deducible with great precision *. This intentional separation of the centres of gravity and suspension is effected by tapping the needle with a fine interior screw, in order that it may receive a fine steel screw, projecting at some distance from the needle, and on which a small brass ball traverses. By this contrivance, the needle may be deflected from the true dip, in any degree that may be desired, and the terrestrial action, which varies as the sine of the angle of deviation from the line of dip, may be increased in almost any proportion.

(305.) The following is the description of the needle constructed on this principle, which was employed by Captain Sabine in the determinations of the dip, as reported in the work already quoted. This needle was a parallelopipedon of eleven inches and a half in length, four-tenths in breadth, and one-twentieth in thickness; the ends were rounded; and a line marked on the face of the needle, passed through the centre to the extremities, answering the purpose of an index line. The cylindrical axis on which the needle revolved was of bell metal, terminated, when it rested on the agate planes, by cylinders of less diameter; the finer these terminations can be made, as long as they do not bend with the weight of the needle, the more accurate will be the oscillations. Small grooves in the thicker part of the axis received the Y's, which raised and lowered the needle on its supports, and insured that the same parts of the axis rested on the planes in each observation.

A small brass sphere traversed on a steel screw, was inserted in the lower edge of the needle, as nearly as possible in the perpendicular to the index line passing through the axis of motion; by this mechanism, the centre of gravity of the needle, screw, and sphere may be made to fall more or less below the axis of motion, according as the sphere is screwed at a smaller or greater distance from the needle, and according as spheres of greater or less diameter are employed. The object proposed in thus separating the centres of motion and of gravity, was to give to the needle a force, arising from its own weight, to assist that of magnetism in overcoming the inequalities of the axis; and thus to cause the needle to return, after oscillation, with more certainty to the same point of the divided limb than it would do were the centres strictly coincident.

(306.) The centres of motion and of gravity not coinciding, the position which the needle assumes, when placed in the magnetic meridian, is not that of the dip; but the dip is deducible by an easy calculation from observations made with such a needle, according to the following directions:—

(307.) If the needle has been carefully made, and the screw inserted truly as described, the centres of motion and of gravity will be disposed as in the lever of a balance, where a right line joining them will be a perpendicular to the horizontal passing through its extremities, that is, to the index line. This condition is not, indeed, a necessary one; but it is desirable to secure it, because it shortens the observations, as well as the calculation from whence the dip is deduced. Its fulfilment may be ascertained with great precision, by placing the needle on the agate planes before magnetism is imparted to it, and observing whether it returns to a horizontal direction after oscillation, in each position of the axis; if it do not, it may be made to do so at this time with no great trouble.

(308.) With a needle in which this adjustment can be relied on, two observations made in the magnetic meridian are sufficient for the determination of the dip. The two faces of the needle are in succession turned towards the observer, by reversing the position of the axis on its supports, in such a manner that the edge of the needle which is uppermost in the one observation, becomes lowermost in the other. The angles which the needle makes with the vertical in these two positions being read, the mean of the tangent of those angles is the co-tangent of the dip.

(309.) But when needles are used in which this previous adjustment has not been made, or when its accuracy cannot be relied on, four observations are required; two being those that have been already directed; and the other two being similar to them, but made with the poles of the needles reversed.

Calling, then, the first arcs F and f and those with the poles reversed G and g, calling the dip δ, and taking

---

* See Captain Sabine's Account of Experiments to determine the figure of the Earth, p. 467.

tang. F + tang. f = A
tang. F − tang. f = B
tang. G + tang. g = C
tang. G − tang. g = D

Then the dip may be calculated by the following formula:—

$$\frac{A \cdot D}{B+D} + \frac{B \cdot C}{B+D} = 2 \text{ cotang. } \delta.$$

(310.) In reversing the poles, it is not necessary that the magnetic force imparted to the needle should be the same in degree as it possessed previously to the operation. The coincidence of the poles with the extremities of the longitudinal axis may always be insured by adopting the precaution of placing the needle in a groove, to prevent its lateral motion, and by confining the sides of the magnet by parallel strips of wood, so that in moving along the needle they may preserve its direction.

(311.) If the distance between the centres of motion and of gravity be considerable, the arcs in the alternate observations will be on different sides of the vertical, especially when the dip is great; in such cases the arcs to the south of the vertical are read negatively. The arcs in each of the four positions, forming the data from which the dip is deduced, are the arithmetical means of several observations, usually six, half of which should be made with the face towards the east, and half with the face towards the west; the needle being lifted by the Y's and lowered gently on its supports between each observation. The arcs indicated by both ends of the needle should also be read, in order to correct the errors arising from inequality in the divisions, or from the axis of the needle not passing correctly through the centre of the circle.

(312.) In order to insure the perfect horizontality of the agate planes which supported the axis of the dipping-needle on Mayer's construction, employed by Captain Sabine, a spirit level was attached to a circular brass plate, of the proper diameter to be placed upon the planes themselves, with adjustments to bring it parallel to the plate. The errors of the level were shown by placing the plate in various positions horizontally; and the errors of the planes by turning the whole instrument upon its horizontal centre. When these errors were adjusted, and the planes and plate perfectly horizontal, the apices of two cones, which proceeded perfectly at right angles from the plate uniting them at their base, and were equal to the diameter of the divided circle of the instrument, ought to have coincided with the divisions 90° and 90° of the circle; when they did not, the cones afforded, in this case also, the means of correcting the adjustment.

(313.) The dipping-needle affords a method of determining the position of the magnetic meridian, independently of the horizontal needle; for if we turn round the whole instrument horizontally (so as to place it successively in different azimuths), till we find that in which the needle assumes an exactly vertical position, the plane of its motion is then exactly at right angles to the magnetic meridian; and the latter may therefore be determined from the former.

(314.) By comparing the inclination of the dipping-needle to the horizon, in two different positions, such that the planes of its rotation are perpendicular to each other, we may, by the following trigonometrical formula, deduce the dip. If the inclinations, observed in the two azimuths, be represented respectively by δ' and δ'', and the dip itself (or the inclination in the magnetic meridian) by δ, then,

Cot. $^2\delta$ = cot. $^2\delta'$ + cot. $^2\delta''$

By multiplying observations of this kind in different azimuths, and taking the mean of all, we may arrive at a very accurate determination of the dip.

(315.) Mr. Scoresby has proposed an ingenious method of finding the dip, by observing the situation in which bar-iron, void of permanent magnetism, loses all power of affecting the compass placed at a certain distance from it; for, as Mr. Barlow has ascertained, its position must then be in the plane of the magnetic equator. The inclination of the plane to the horizon is, of course, equal to the complement of the dip. Mr. Scoresby has described an instrument calculated for making this species of observation, in the Transactions of the Royal Society of Edinburgh*.

(316.) Other methods, of a nature somewhat more refined, exist for discovering the dip, which depend on the admeasurement of the intensities of the magnetic forces by which the needle is urged in different positions of the axis and plane of rotation. The magnetic force derived from the influence of the earth, and acting in the direction of the dip, may be resolved into other forces, which will bear to one another the same ratios as the sides of the triangles

* Vol. ix. p. 247.

which represent them. The angles of these triangles, the dip being one of these angles, may be determined by the trigonometrical relations of these lines when two of them are given. All that is required for this purpose is to ascertain the ratio of the forces which act in directions parallel to these lines, and are proportional to them. Of the methods by which the intensity of these forces is to be measured, we shall proceed to treat in the next section.

§ 6. *Methods of determining the intensities of the Magnetic Forces.*

(317.) When a magnetic needle is moveable in any plane on an axis that passes through its centre of gravity, so that its movements are simply the effects of the magnetic forces of the earth acting upon the two polarities of the needle (which may be considered as concentrated in its poles), it takes a certain position, which is that in which the forces are in equilibrium. Let needle SN, *fig.* 70, for example, be moveable on an axis at X, perpendicular to the plane of the figure; and let

Fig. 70.

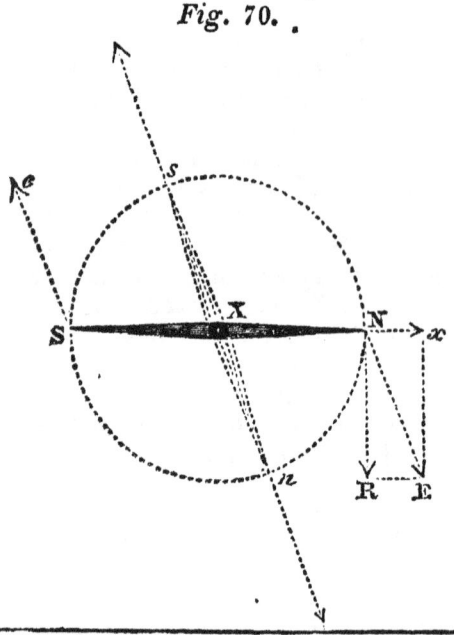

NE be the direction in that plane of the force of terrestrial magnetism acting upon the pole N; while S *e*, opposite and parallel to NE, is the direction of the force in the same plane, acting upon the pole S. The position to which the needle is brought by these forces is *s n*, parallel to the common direction of these forces, when they are in direct opposition to each other, and therefore in equilibrium. In order to estimate the rotatory efficiency of the forces in operation in any other position, as SN, we must resolve the force represented by the line NE into two others; the one, N *x*, in the direction of the radius of rotation XN, prolonged; and the other in the direction NR, perpendicular to it. The force N *x*, being opposed by the fixed axis at X, contributes in no respect to produce motion; NR is the only part of the terrestrial force that turns the needle upon its axis. Now it is evident that NR is to NE, as the sine of the angle NER, or its equal EN*x*, to the radius; but the force represented by the line NE being a constant force, the rotatory force NR will, in every position of the needle, be invariably as the sine of the angle EN*x*, made by the needle, on its prolonged direction, with the direction of the terrestrial force. The same reasoning, in all respects, applies to the force S *e* acting on the pole S; but since it acts on the other side of the axis in a contrary direction, it will concur with the force acting on the pole N, in giving the same rotatory motion to the needle. The effect will, therefore, be equal to the sum of these two rotatory forces, and will be twice as great as either of them taken separately; and the resultant will still be proportional to the sine of the angle of inclination.

(318.) A little consideration will enable us to perceive that the condition of the needle, with regard to the magnetic forces, is analogous to that of a lever moveable on a horizontal axis, and acted upon by the force of gravity. If we suppose a straight lever, AB, *fig* 71, moveable upon an axis X, at right angles to it, to be raised from the vertical position *a b*, which is that of equilibrium, inasmuch as gravitation acts in

Fig. 71.

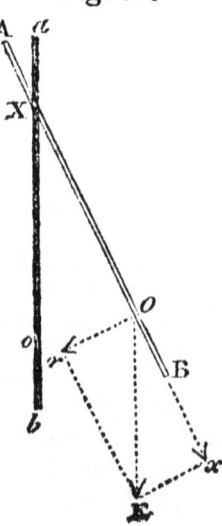

that direction, and placed in the inclined position AB, it is well known that the rotatory action of the force of gravity acting upon all its particles is equivalent to a single force acting upon a point, O, which is called the centre of oscillation; and also that, in order to estimate what portion of that force OE contributes to its rotation on its axis, we must resolve it into one in the direction O x, and another in the direction O r, at right angles to it; this latter force being in all cases proportional to the sine of the angle EOx, or its equal BXb. The only difference between this case and the one we have been considering, is that here the force is single, whereas there are two forces acting upon the magnetic poles.

(319.) These two forces being always precisely equal and in opposite directions, perfectly balance one another with reference to any motion of the *whole needle*, either towards or from the earth. This admits of experimental proof; for, in the first place, were there any balance remaining in favour either of the attractive or repulsive forces emanating from the earth, the effect would be shown by an apparent change in the weight of the needle; if, when magnetised, it were on the whole attracted to the earth, it would appear heavier than before; if repelled, lighter. But no such change is observed to take place. Neither is there any tendency manifested in a magnetised bar to a lateral or horizontal motion. This may be proved by placing it at the end of a light frame of wood, AB, *fig.* 72, which is suspended at its centre C by means of a fine silk thread, T; a weight, W,

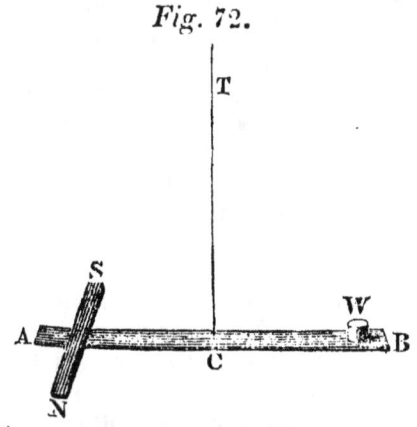

Fig. 72.

being placed at the other end to act as a counterpoise to the magnet NS. When left to itself, it will be found that the whole apparatus will turn round until the direction of the needle coincides exactly with the plane of the magnetic meridian, just as if it had been suspended by its own centre. Had there existed any force impelling it horizontally, it would have occasioned a deviation from this plane, acting as it must have done with the advantage of the lever AC. But the two equal forces acting differently upon the two magnetic poles, though opposed with respect to any motion of translation, yet concur in their rotatory action, and may, consequently, as far as relates to this action, be regarded as a single force of twice the intensity of either of them taken singly.

(320.) It is evident, then, that the same dynamical laws which regulate the motions of a compound pendulum, actuated by terrestrial gravity, will also regulate those of a magnetic needle, balanced on its centre of gravity, and actuated by terrestrial magnetism. The same pendulum, it is well known, performs all its vibrations in equal times, whatever be the length of the arc in which they are performed, provided that arc be not too great. If we estimate the length of a pendulum by the distance between its centre of motion and its centre of oscillation, then, in pendulums of different lengths, and in situations where the force of gravity is different, the squares of the times of performing a given number of vibrations are directly proportional to the lengths of the pendulums, and inversely proportional to the force of gravity. Now the number of vibrations performed in a given time is inversely as the time employed in each vibration; therefore, the square of the number of vibrations in a given time will be inversely proportional to the length, and directly proportional to the force of gravity.

(321.) The same formula being applicable to the vibrations of magnets, a very simple computation will enable us to arrive at an estimate of the comparative forces acting on the same magnet in different inclinations of the axis, and in different situations with respect to the position of equilibrium in the plane of motion. We have only to disturb it slightly from this position, and count the number of vibrations it makes in a given time, a minute for example, in different cases: then, taking the squares of these numbers, they will be proportional to the intensities of the terrestrial magnetic forces that are in operation in these several instances.

(322.) The preceding reasoning is founded upon the supposition that the axis of motion passed accurately through the centre of gravity of the magnet; so that the effect of gravity was removed, and could not in any way interfere with the rotatory force of magnetism. This, however, is a condition, which it is next to impossible practically to fulfil; and if it be not exactly fulfilled, then, whenever the centre of gravity is not in the precise line passing vertically through the centre of suspension, the effect of gravity is to impart to that side of the magnet, on which the centre is found, a tendency to preponderate; and its oscillations are no longer produced by the simple action of the magnetic forces, nor directed to the exact line of their action. The only method of correcting this source of error, when it is not very considerable, is to reverse the polarities of the magnet, and make a new set of observations on the inclination and intensity in this state of the magnet; and then to take the mean of the corresponding observations, which, in consequence of the compensation of the opposite errors existing in the two modes of estimation, will express the true value of the quantity sought.

(323.) In order to compare the results of two sets of observations on magnetic intensity in different parts of the world, it is necessary to employ the same needle in both cases; since the application of the various formulæ necessary to be employed for comparing the action of the same force on two different needles would be attended with great difficulty and uncertainty.

(324.) The oscillations of the compass-needle, which moves in a horizontal plane, furnish data for the calculation of the intensity of that part only of the terrestrial force which acts in that plane; whereas those of the dipping-needle, moving on a horizontal axis and consequently in a vertical plane, when that plane coincides with the magnetic meridian, indicate the full amount of the force of the terrestrial magnetism at the place of observation. The ratio between these two quantities is that of the base and hypothenuse of a right-angled triangle, inclined at an angle equal to the dip; that is to say, the intensity of the horizontal force is to the intensity of the whole force as the cosine of the angle of the dip is to the radius. Let SN, *fig.* 73, be the horizontal needle;

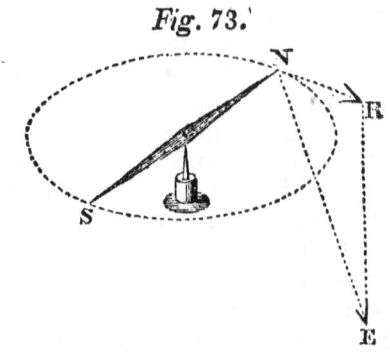

Fig. 73.

NE the line of dip; NR a horizontal line perpendicular to SN. The force NE is resolved into RE, perpendicular to RN, and which being out of the plane of motion, and perpendicular to it, does not contribute to the motion of the needle, and NR the horizontal force; which latter is to NE as the cosine of the angle ENR is to the radius. This force, NR, is constant in all positions of the needle in the horizontal plane; and acts always in parallel directions. Its rotatory action, however, will, of course, depend upon the deviation of the needle from the position of equilibrium, that is, upon the angle which it makes with the plane of the meridian; being proportional to the sine of that angle. The oscillations are therefore isochronous, that is, performed in equal times, whether the arc be large or small, like those of a pendulum; and are governed by the laws above stated as applying to those of pendulums; and the same remark applies equally to the oscillations of the dipping-needle performed in the plane of the magnetic meridian.

(325.) When the position of the axis of the dipping-needle is changed, so that the plane in which the needle moves is no longer that of the magnetic meridian, though still vertical, the force by which it is actuated is in like manner to be estimated by that portion of the terrestrial force which, on being resolved, has the direction of that plane: that portion which is perpendicular to the plane being of no effect.

Let the circle SANB, *fig.* 74, represent the plane of the motion of the needle SN; NE being the line of dip, or the direction of the terrestrial forces. The force represented by NE may be resolved into the two forces NV and NH, the one perpendicular to the horizon, and the other parallel to it. Let the former be denoted by the letter v, and the latter by h; and let us call the

Fig. 74.

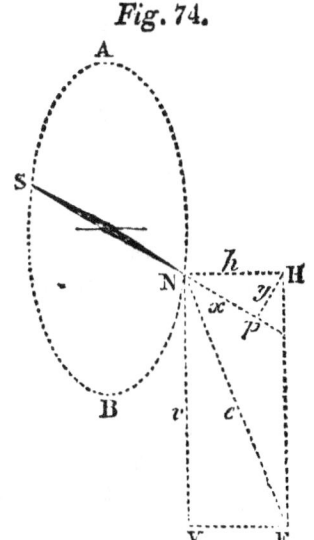

force of the earth e. Let δ be the angle of the dip ENH, and d the complement of that angle, or ENV.

Then by the properties of the triangles NVE, or NEH, we have

$v = e \cos. d$; and $h = e \sin. d$.

(326.) The force v, being vertical, acts wholly in the plane of the needle's motion, SANB: but the force h is out of that plane, and must be decomposed into two others; the one, HP, perpendicular to that vertical plane, and which we shall call y; the other NP, which we shall call x, directed horizontally in that plane. The angle HNP is equal to the deviation of the vertical plane SANB from the magnetic meridian; let us call this angle α.

We shall thus have

$y = h \sin. \alpha$; and $x = h \cos. \alpha$;

or, substituting for h its value as expressed in the former equation, and joining the value of v, we have,

$v = e, \cos. d.$
$y = e, \sin. d. \sin. \alpha.$
$x = e, \sin. d, \cos. \alpha.$

Of these, the force y is destroyed, being resisted by the axis of motion; and the forces v and x are those only which are effective in giving motion to the needle. Let R express the resultant of these forces, and φ the angle which it makes with a vertical line. We shall have

$R^2 = x^2 + v^2;$

and tang. $\varphi = \dfrac{x}{v}$,

or, substituting for x and v their respective values, as above found,

$R = e \cos. d \sqrt{1 + \text{tang.}^2 d, \cos.^2 \alpha};$
tang. $\varphi = $ tang. $d, \cos. \alpha.$

(327.) From these equations many important consequences may be derived.

In the first place we may deduce, that the intensity of the force R diminishes as the angle α increases; or in other words, as the plane of motion deviates more from that of the magnetic meridian. It is greatest when these planes coincide, being then equal to e; it is least when they are at right angles to one another, for then $\alpha = 90°$, and cos. $\alpha = 0$, whence

$R = e. \cos. d.$

(328.) The direction of the resultant, and consequently the position into which it brings the needle, also vary in the different azimuths in which it is placed. In proportion as the angle α increases, the cosine of that angle diminishes; and therefore the tangent of the angle φ, which expresses the angle the resultant makes with a vertical line, also diminishes. Hence, in proportion as the plane of motion comes nearer to a position perpendicular to the magnetic meridian, the position of the needle will approach more nearly to the vertical position; and it is exactly vertical when its plane of motion has arrived at that situation. This has been already noticed as affording a method of determining the position of the magnetic meridian, independently of the horizontal needle (§ 313).

(329.) We may deduce also the formula given in § 314, from the foregoing equations; for when the two azimuths in which the observations are made differ by 90 degrees, the tangents of φ in the two cases will be respectively

tang. $\varphi' = $ tang. $d \cos. \alpha$
tang. $\varphi'' = $ tang. $d \sin. \alpha$.

By taking the squares of each term of these equations, and adding them, we obtain

tang.$^2 d = $ tang.$^2 \varphi' + $ tang.$^2 \varphi''$;

which, when δ, δ' and δ'' express the angles of the dip, or the complements of d, φ, and φ'', respectively, become

cot.$^2 \delta = $ cot.$^2 \delta' + $ cot.$^2 \delta''$.

(330.) The same formula is derivable more simply from the following considerations:—

Let XD, *fig.* 75, be the line of dip in the magnetic meridian; and let XVFA, XVGB, be the two vertical planes at right angles to each other. From D, draw the lines DF and DG, perpendicular to these planes; and also FV and GV, perpendicular to XV. The lines XF and XG will be the positions of the needles in these planes, according to the law already stated, § 78. Taking XV as radius, the lines VF, VG, and

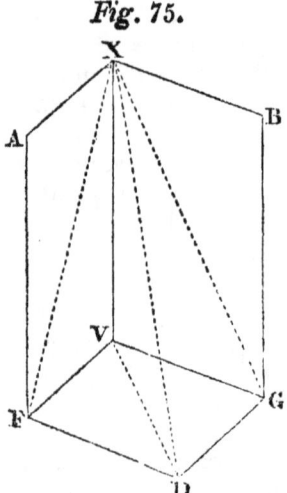

Fig. 75.

VD are the tangents of the angles VXF, VXG, and VXD, respectively; and in the right-angled triangle VDF,
$$VD^2 = VF^2 + FD^2;$$
that is (FD being = VG)
$$VD^2 = VF^2 + VG^2:$$
or tang.^{2} VXD = tang.^{2} VXF + tang.^{2} VXG; which is the formula above given.

(331.) On the other hand, the determinations of the relative intensities of the magnetic forces in different planes furnish data for the computation of the angles which those planes make with the line of the dip, or the direction of terrestrial magnetism. Thus the amount of the dip may be determined by comparing the number of oscillations in a given time made by the same needle, when vibrating in the plane of the magnetic meridian, and also in a vertical plane at right angles to it. For the squares of these numbers being as the intensities of the forces which respectively act in these planes, and the force in the former case being to that in the latter as the radius to the cosine of the angle d, which the line of dip makes with a vertical line, we obtain the latter by a simple proportion when the former are given. Resuming the notation before employed, let e be the total terrestrial force acting in the plane of the magnetic meridian, and v that part of it which acts in a vertical plane at right angles to the magnetic meridian; and let N and n express the number of oscillations, in a given time, which the dipping-needle performs in these two planes respectively: $v = e \cos. d$, or, d being the complement of δ;

$$v = e \sin. \delta;$$
$$\sin. \delta = \frac{v}{e}.$$
But $\quad v : e :: n^2 : N^2;$
therefore $\quad \dfrac{v}{e} = \dfrac{n^2}{N^2}$
and $\quad \sin. \delta = \dfrac{n^2}{N^2}.$

(332.) We shall give the following example of the application of these formulæ to the observations of magnetic intensity, made by Humboldt, near Quito, exactly at the terrestrial Equator, and at longitude 81° 2′ west from Paris. The number of oscillations made by the dipping-needle vibrating in the magnetic meridian, during ten minutes, was 220; the number of oscillations, made in the same time, when it vibrated in a plane perpendicular to it, was 109. Substituting these numbers in the formula for N and n respectively, we obtain

$$\sin. \delta = \frac{109^2}{220^2} = \frac{11881}{48400}$$

From log. 11881 = 4.0748530
Subtract log. 48400 = 4.6848454
there remains log. sin. δ = 9.3900076

whence we get $\delta = 14° \ 12′ \ 35″.$ The direct observation of the dip, by the dipping needle, was
$$\delta = 14° \ 25′ \ 5″,$$
the difference between the two methods being only 12′ 30″.

(333.) The angle of the dip with the horizon may, in like manner, be obtained by comparing the relative intensities of the forces, as determined by the squares of the number of oscillations in a given time, executed in the plane of the magnetic meridian, and also in a horizontal plane: for they are in the proportion of the radius to the cosine of the dip; or, if we call the number of oscillations made by the horizontal needle ν, while N is that made by the same needle, suspended as a dipping-needle, and placed in the plane of the magnetic meridian; then
$$\cos. \delta = \frac{\nu^2}{N^2}.$$

(334.) Methods have been devised for determining the dip, from the result of observations made with the horizontal needle alone, by comparing its number of oscillations with the weight of the counterpoise necessary for maintaining it in the horizontal position when magnetized. But the formula and mode of computation are much more complicated than those we have given; and we must therefore refer our readers for the details to Biot's Traité de Physique*.

(335.) The determination of the intensity of terrestrial magnetism may, in general, be made with much greater accuracy, by observing the oscillations of a needle moving horizontally, than in any other way: because the mode of suspension we can employ for obtaining a horizontal motion is much more delicate, and much less impeded by friction, than any other motion on a fixed axis can be. The greater duration also of the period through which the oscillations continue enables us to ascertain with greater exactness the average time of the vibration. Hence a silken suspension is much to be preferred for delicate experiments with horizontal needles, to that of balancing them on a point by an agate cup.

(336.) The following description of the apparatus used by Captain Sabine, in the voyages to the arctic regions in the year 1822 and 1823, may furnish valuable practical information to those who may hereafter conduct experiments of the same nature†. A mahogany box was provided, made, for convenience, of an octagonal shape, with a top of stout glass; its height was fifteen inches, and its diameter sufficient to allow a horizontal bar of seven inches in length to vibrate freely when suspended by a silk line passing through a brass button, inserted in a perforation in the middle of the glass top. A metal circle, fixed in the bottom of the box, of rather more than seven inches diameter, measured the arc of vibration. The bar was carried in a light stirrup, into which it was slid until correctly balanced. The silk thread, from which the stirrup was suspended, was fifteen inches long, and consisted of a sufficient number of silk fibres to sustain the weight. In order to remove all influence from the tendency in the silk to untwist, a brass bar, equal in weight to the magnetic bar, was first introduced into the stirrup in place of the latter, and the silk thread allowed to untwist itself, and then adjusted by turning the button in such a manner as that the brass substitute should settle, when at rest, in the magnetic direction. This being now removed, the magnetic bar was replaced in the stirrup, and its horizontality ascertained by its accordance with the circle, the degree to which it settled being registered as the zero. It was then drawn about forty degrees out of the meridian, and retained by a copper wire passing through the glass top, and capable of being moved in azimuth from its outside, and of being raised so as to release the needle at pleasure, in order to commence its oscillations. These were not noticed until the arc had diminished to thirty degrees, when the registry of them commenced, and was repeated at the close of every tenth vibration, until the arc had still further diminished to ten degrees, when the experiment was concluded. The box was usually placed on the ground, in a sheltered situation, far from buildings, or other sources of local interference; the only adjustment required, besides that of the silk thread, was to render the graduated circle horizontal, which was accomplished by a pocket spirit level, and wooden wedges placed beneath the box.

(377.) Six bars were used in this apparatus, differing from each other considerably, both in rapidity of vibration, and in the duration of the interval of oscillation between thirty and ten degrees. They were seven inches long, a quarter of an inch broad, 0.15 inches thick, and strongly magnetized. When not in use, they were kept in pairs, in the usual manner, as described in § 218, *fig.* 60, being combined, with their opposite poles united, in separate boxes; and each bar was placed by itself in the direction of the meridian for two or three hours before its time of vibration was ascertained. The times were registered to fractional parts of a second by the beats of a chronometer, having a rate inappreciable in the interval.

(338.) It should be observed, however, that comparative experiments on magnetic intensities, made by the oscillations of needles balanced horizontally, are liable to a source of error when they are made in places in which the dip is considerably different. For one of the poles having a tendency to incline below the horizon, the axis of suspension must, in order to compensate for this tendency, pass through a point on that side of the centre of gravity, so as to give an equal preponderance to the other side. Hence arises a difference between the two arms of the lever, and consequently a difference

---

* Tom. iii. p. 33.
† Account of experiments to determine the figure of the earth, p. 477.

in the effect of the force applied to them. This circumstance has escaped the attention of the most skilful observers, although it is of sufficient importance to destroy all confidence in the comparison of experiments made in places where the dip is very different*.

(339.) We have seen the method by which the amount of the dip may be determined from the comparative intensities of magnetic force in the plane of the magnetic meridian, and in the horizontal plane. It is easy to see how, by reversing the process, we may arrive at the knowledge of the force of terrestrial magnetism in the magnetic meridian, from observations of the intensity in the horizontal plane, when the dip is previously known; for we have only to augment the former in the proportion of the cosine of the dip to the radius: or, what comes to the same thing, to multiply it by the secant of the dip. For since

$$\cos. \delta = \frac{v^2}{N^2} = \frac{h}{e};$$

it follows that

$$e = \frac{h}{\cos. \delta} = h. \sec. \delta$$

(340.) The method of oscillations is not the only mode of determining the intensity of magnetic forces; for the same object may be attained by employing the balance of torsion: but in general the former method is, on many accounts, preferable.

(341.) It would conduce much to the future advancement of the science of Magnetism, if the absolute intensity of the terrestrial magnetic forces could be ascertained by a standard equally determinate as those by which we estimate the atmospheric pressure, or the temperature of different climates; for by repeating the same process of observation, in the course of successive centuries, we might learn whether the intensity of these forces experienced any variation similar to what we know takes place in their direction.

(342.) The method which first suggests itself, would be to observe the variation, the dip, and the intensity, by means of three needles, respectively appropriated to these objects, and carefully preserved, with a view to a repetition of the same experiments at distant periods of time. As it is possible that their magnetic power may become impaired by these long intervals of time, it would probably be necessary to magnetize them afresh, employing for that purpose the most efficacious methods, so as to induce a degree of magnetism which shall at first be considerably greater than what they are capable of retaining permanently. When left for a certain time to themselves, they will then return to their natural state of saturation, and in this state they may be subjected to the experiments in question. Our assurance of their attaining this determinate degree of magnetism may be increased by preserving a great number of needles, brought to this state, and noting their respective powers; which records may afterwards be compared with similar observations made at a future period; for if they should be found to have preserved among each other the same relative degree of strength, we may confidently conclude that no alteration has taken place in their magnetic constitution, and that they are well adapted to the determination of the absolute force of terrestrial magnetism.

(343.) If a method could be discovered of obtaining a material for the making of magnets of perfectly uniform composition and qualities, there would be no necessity to employ in this comparison the same identical magnets at the several times of observation. Steel would evidently be unfit for the purpose, its composition being necessarily variable. Nothing would answer so well as iron alone, which might be obtained in a state of perfect purity by proper chemical processes; for Coulomb found that pure iron, however soft, may be rendered nearly as retentive of magnetism as steel, by merely twisting it. All that would then be necessary, would be to regulate the degree of twist, so that it might be constantly the same for different pieces of iron: this might easily be accomplished, by taking them exactly of the same dimensions, and measuring the number of turns in the twist given to them. Each of the bars might then be magnetized to saturation, and employed either separately or in defined combinations, and their magnetic forces examined, both by the torsion balance, and by the method of oscillations*.

(344.) Poisson has also attempted to resolve this problem by considerations of a mathematical nature, for which we must refer to his memoir, read to the

---

* Pouillet, Elémens de Physique Expérimentale tom. i. p. 482.

* Biot, Traité de Physique, tom. iii. p. 144.

Academy of Sciences at Paris, in Nov. 1825, and of which an account is contained in Pouillet's Elémens de Physique*.

§ 7. *Experiments on the Magnetic Intensities at different Heights above the Surface of the Earth.*

(345.) In the year 1804, Messrs. Gay-Lussac and Biot undertook, at the desire of the French government, an aërostatic voyage, expressly for the purpose of ascertaining whether the magnetic force experiences any perceptible diminution at considerable elevations above the surface of the earth. De Saussure had inferred, from some experiments which he made on the Col du Géant, near Mont Blanc, the height of which is 3435 metres (about 11,270 feet), that the magnetic force of the earth was reduced to four-fifths of what it was in the plains below. The instrument with which he made these experiments was simply a magnetic needle, suspended by a very fine silk thread. Messrs. Gay-Lussac and Biot carried with them a needle, carefully constructed by Fortin, and magnetized by Coulomb, according to Æpinus's process. No iron was allowed to enter into the construction of the car of the balloon; the only articles of iron they carried with them, were a few knives and a pair of scissors, which were suspended in a basket below the car, at a distance of from twenty-five to thirty feet, so that they could have no sensible influence on the magnetic needle. The continual rotation of the balloon on its axis, during its ascent, seemed at first to present an insuperable obstacle to their observing the oscillations of the needle. But, by bringing themselves in a line with terrestrial objects and the sides of the clouds, they perceived that they did not always turn round in the same direction, the rotatory motion gradually decreasing, and then taking place in a contrary direction. By watching the short intervals during which they remained stationary between these opposite motions, they were enabled to observe five, or at most ten oscillations at a time; they were obliged, however, to be very careful not to agitate the car, for the slightest motion, such as that produced by letting the gas escape, or even that of the hand in writing, was sufficient to turn the balloon aside. With all these precautions, which required a great deal of time, they found means to make ten experiments in the course of the voyage, and at different altitudes. The conclusion they deduced from the average of all their observations is, that the magnetic force experiences no appreciable diminution at any distance from the surface of the earth, as far as 4000 metres, or 13,124 feet.

(346.) Many important facts relating to this question have lately been established by M. Kupffer, in the course of a journey to the neighbourhood of Mount Elbrouz, in the Caucasus, undertaken by order of the Emperor of Russia, in the year 1829, and of which an account has been given in a paper published in the Memoirs of the Imperial Academy of Sciences of St. Petersburgh*. M. Kupffer found that the intensity of terrestrial magnetism really decreased as he rose above the level of the sea; and that this decrease was much more considerable than is conformable with the commonly received hypothesis of a focus of magnetic forces situated at the centre of the globe. He even thinks that the experiments of Gay-Lussac and Biot, in the voyage just mentioned, should have led to the same conclusion, because, although they could not detect any difference in the apparent intensity, yet since the temperature of the elevated regions of the atmosphere in which they made their observations is exceedingly low, it is probable that the magnetic power of the needle itself was greater than in the warmer atmosphere at the surface of the earth; so that, unless the terrestrial force had really diminished, an increase of magnetic intensity would have been apparent, and would have been indicated by the increased frequency of the vibrations in a given time. As this increased frequency was not observed to take place, M. Kupffer concludes that the force of terrestrial magnetism is, in fact, less at the height to which they had reached, than it is at the surface of the earth. It is certain that, in all experiments of this kind, the temperature should be accurately noted, as constituting an essential element in the reasonings to be founded on them †.

CHAPTER VII.

Of the Magnetism of Bodies that are not ferruginous.

(347.) It has long been suspected that besides iron, other metallic substances

---

* Tom. i., p. 494.

* For 1830, p. 69.
† See Journal of the Royal Institution, vol. i. p. 610.

are capable of exhibiting magnetic phenomena. Nickel, and also cobalt, have occasionally been found obedient to the action of the magnet; and sometimes to possess considerable degrees of polarity. Brass, which is a compound of copper and zinc, has likewise been observed to be magnetic under certain circumstances, especially after it has been hammered. Cavallo states* that, when quite soft, brass has generally no perceptible degree of magnetism; and even those pieces which have acquired this property by hammering, again lose it by annealing or softening in the fire. He seems to have ascertained that the magnetism acquired in the former state, is not owing to any particles of iron or steel imparted to the brass by the tools employed in the hammering; and that those pieces of brass which have that property retain it without any diminution after having been hardened and softened several times in succession. If one end only of a large piece of brass be hammered, that end alone is rendered magnetic. He found, however, that the magnetic power which brass acquires by hammering has a certain limit, beyond which it cannot be increased by further hammering; and that this limit is different in pieces of brass of different quality or thickness.

(348.) Cavallo next examined various pieces of copper by means of a delicately suspended needle; but never found them magnetical, except occasionally in those parts where a file had been applied, and where, consequently, some particles of steel, detached from the file, may have adhered to the copper. On hammering other pieces, both in the usual way, and also between flints, he failed in obtaining any decisive result. Zinc, whether hammered or not, showed no sign of magnetism whatever. Platina was found to possess a degree of magnetic power nearly equal to that of brass.

(349.) The magnetic power of brass is sometimes so considerable as to interfere very sensibly with the movements of the needle in compasses, in the construction of which brass is employed. A remarkable instance of this is given by Mr. Barlow †. Seebeck has recommended an alloy of two parts copper with one of nickel, as admirably adapted for the manufacture of compasses, from its being entirely void of magnetism*. We have seen, in the case of brass, that two ingredients, which in themselves, when separate, are devoid of magnetic susceptibility, acquire that property by combination. Mr. Hatchet ascertained that a large proportion of either carbon, sulphur, or phosphorus, combined with iron, enables it fully to receive and to retain the magnetic properties: but that there is a limit beyond which an excess of either of these substances renders the compound totally insusceptible of magnetism †. On the other hand, instances occur where the admixture of the minutest quantity of another body will entirely destroy the magnetic power of a metal possessing that power when in a pure state. Mr. Chenevix found that the addition of arsenic, in very small proportion, deprived a mass of nickel, which had previously manifested strong magnetic power, of the whole of its magnetism ‡. Dr. Matthew Young states that the smallest admixture of antimony is sufficient to destroy the polarity of iron §.

(350.) In the mineral kingdom a great variety of substances, and even some of the precious stones, as the emerald, the ruby, and the garnet, exert a feeble yet sensible attraction on the magnetic needle; and sometimes even acquire a slight degree of polarity ‖.

(351.) Later inquiries appear to have established the fact that all bodies whatsoever are, in a greater or less degree, susceptible of magnetism. We owe this discovery to Coulomb, who exhibited his experiments in proof of it at a sitting of the French Institute, in 1802. The bodies examined were cut into small cylinders, or bars, about a third of an inch in length, and about the thirtieth of an inch in thickness: but those which were metallic were formed into needles of about the hundredth of an inch in diameter. Each of these cylinders was suspended by a thread of raw silk, which, being exceedingly fine, could scarcely support more than from 100 to 150 grains without breaking: on this account it was necessary to reduce the needles to very small dimensions. They were placed, when thus suspended, between the opposite poles of two steel

---

* Philosophical Transactions for 1786, p. 62; and also in his Treatise on Magnetism.
† Essay on Magnetic Attractions, second edition, p. 17.

* Annales de Physique, 1826.
† Philosophical Transactions for 1804, p. 315.
‡ Nicholson's Journal, 8vo. vol. iii. p. 287.
§ Seebeck discovered that an alloy of one part on with four parts of antimony exercised no power over the magnetic needle, even when in motion.
‖ Cavallo's Treatise on Magnetism, p. 73.

magnets, arranged in the same line, and separated about a quarter of an inch more than the length of the needle that was to oscillate between them. Whatsoever was the substance of which the needles were formed, they always ranged themselves accurately in the direction of the magnets; and if disturbed from this position, returned to it with oscillations, which were often as frequent as thirty or more in a minute, and considerably more frequent than when the magnets were removed: thus indicating a very decided force of attraction. Needles made of tin, lead, copper, silver, and gold, and cylinders of glass, chalk, bone, and different sorts of wood, together with a great variety of other organic substances, both animal and vegetable, were tried in succession, and with the same result.

These experiments were repeated in England, by Dr. Young, at the Royal Institution, but with less decided success: the force of attraction indicated was estimated at rather less than the two-thousandth part of the weight of the substance employed.

(352.) There are but two ways of explaining these phenomena: they are either owing to the presence of minute quantities of iron entering into the composition of all the bodies which manifest magnetic properties, or else they warrant the inference that all these bodies possess a certain degree of inherent magnetism. If the former mode of explanation be the true one, we shall be forced to admit that iron may exist in bodies, in quantities so minute as to elude detection by the severest chemical examination, and yet have sufficient power to be sensibly affected by a magnet. A set of very delicate experiments was undertaken by Coulomb with a view to determine this point: in the course of which he satisfied himself, that a smaller quantity of iron than can be discovered by any chemical test yet known, will, when added to a body, impart to it a very decided magnetic susceptibility. This is the case when a metal contains only the 130,000th part of its weight of iron. The magnetic powers of different specimens of metals were found to differ materially according to the methods employed for their purification. Hence he concluded that the greater part, if not the whole, of the effect observed, is to be ascribed to the presence of iron. So confident was he of the truth of this theory, that he imagined the magnetic action of all substances might safely be taken as a criterion of the proportion of iron they contain.

(353.) On the other hand, the indications of magnetic power given by nickel and by cobalt are far too considerable to be accounted for by the agency of any ferruginous admixture. Biot was in possession of a needle made of nickel, which Thenard had exerted all his chemical skill in rendering as pure as possible: the directive force of this needle, when magnetized, was not less than one-third of a similar needle made of steel[*]. Now the proportion of iron which, if added to the nickel, would be required to impart an equal degree of magnetic power, is far beyond what can ever reasonably be supposed to enter into the composition of nickel so purified. It is certainly just possible that nickel may be a compound metal, containing iron as one of its ingredients; but we are not justified in admitting an explanation so extremely hypothetical, especially as there are other facts besides those above mentioned, which tend strongly to corroborate the universality of magnetism. Of this nature are the evidences of an influence exerted by bodies not reputed magnetic, in controlling the oscillations of a magnetic needle placed in their immediate vicinity; and also the phenomena of the mutual influence exerted between these bodies and magnets, when the one is revolving rapidly, in exciting sympathetic rotation in the other. These very curious phenomena will be described in the ensuing chapter.

Chapter VIII.
On the Magnetism of Rotation.

(354.) Considerable light has lately been thrown upon the question of the universality of magnetism, by the discovery of the unexpected effects which result from the reciprocal action of magnets upon other bodies, when the one or the other is maintained in a state of rapid rotation. In the year 1824 M. Arago showed that if a plate of copper, or of any other substance, be placed immediately under a magnetic needle, it exerts sufficient influence upon its movements to diminish sensibly the extent of its oscillations, without, however, affecting their duration; and the needle is brought to rest in a shorter time than happened when no such substance is placed under it. The con-

---
[*] Traité de Physique, tom. iii., p. 126.

verse of this experiment was attended with still more striking effects. When a plate of copper, for example, is made to revolve with a certain velocity under a magnetic needle, supported on its centre, and contained in a vessel closed on all sides, the needle is found to deviate from its natural position in the magnetic meridian; and the deviation is greater in proportion as the rotation of the plate is more rapid. If the rapidity of revolution be sufficiently great, the needle will be brought to revolve also, and always in the same direction in which the plate is made to revolve *. The experiment was varied in the following manner:—A circular plate of copper, balanced on a point at its centre, was placed immediately under a strong magnet, to which a rapid rotatory motion was given; the copper-plate soon began to turn in the same direction, and acquired by degrees a very rapid velocity of revolution. It was found, also, that the oscillations of a copper-plate in a vertical plane, when suspended by an axis which passed at a small distance from its centre of gravity, were much impeded, and soon destroyed, when the plate was inserted between the two poles of a very powerful horse-shoe magnet. M. Arago was of opinion that these phenomena are inexplicable upon principles of ordinary magnetism, and considered them as the effects of some hitherto unknown power in nature. But subsequent inquiry seems to render it probable, that they are all reducible to the operation of known laws of magnetism.

(355.) Mr. Christie having observed a permanent change in the magnetism of an iron plate in consequence of a mere change of position on its axis, it occurred to Mr. Barlow that this change would be increased by rapid rotation. But on trial this was found not to be the case, the effect produced being merely temporary. The first experiments were made with a mortar-shell fixed to the mandril of a powerful turning lathe, worked by a steam-engine. When the ball was made to revolve at the rate of 640 times in a minute, the needle was deflected several degrees from its natural position, and there remained stationary during the motion of the ball; whenever the rotation ceased, the needle immediately returned to its original situation. On inverting the motion of the shell, an equal and contrary deflection took place. But although numerous trials were made under various circumstances, the law of the phenomena could not be deduced until the influence of the earth's action had been neutralized by means of other magnets perfectly adjusted. All the anomalies before met with now disappeared, and the following law was rendered manifest. When the needle and ball are both in the same horizontal plane, whatever may be the direction of the axis of rotation of the ball, if its motion at its upper part be made towards the needle, the north pole of the latter will be attracted; and if the contrary way, repelled. Hence he concluded, that when an iron body is put in rapid rotation on any line not coinciding with its magnetic axis, a temporary derangement takes place in its magnetic powers, equivalent in effect to the influence of a new axis of polarization, perpendicular to the planes passing through its axes of rotation and of ordinary polarization.

(356.) The next series of experiments on this subject are those of Mr. Christie*, who ascertained that a plate which, in a given position, produced a certain deviation of the compass, no longer produced the same deviation, after it had been carried round one entire revolution in its own plane, although brought to rest, and every part of the apparatus restored to its former place. This change in the directive power of the plate, produced by rotation, was greatest when its plane was parallel to the line of dip, and at the same time as little inclined to the horizon as this condition would allow; or, in other words, when the axis of rotation was in the plane of the magnetic equator, and also in a vertical plane, that is, in the magnetic meridian. Hence he deduced a law which may be thus expressed:— If we conceive a dipping-needle to lie in the centre of an imaginary sphere, having an equator situated in a plane intersecting perpendicularly the direction of the dipping-needle, and a circular plate of iron to be placed with its centre in the surface of that sphere, its plane being a tangent to that surface, when the plate revolves, the effect of its revolution upon the dipping-needle will be such that each side of the equator of the latter (that is, the portion of the equator which is situated in a line at right angles to the line joining the centres of the needle and plates)

---

* Bulletin Universel, vol. iii., p. 328; Annales de Chimie, xxviii., 325.

Philosophical Transactions for 1825, p. 347.

will be deflected in a direction contrary to the direction in which that edge of the plate which is nearest to it moves. The deviations of the horizontal needle may be easily deduced from this law, by reference to the motions of this imaginary dipping-needle, for they will be such as tend to bring them into the same vertical plane with the latter, which is the situation in which it makes the nearest approach to its line of direction.

(357.) The investigation of this curious subject was further prosecuted by Mr. Babbage and Mr. Herschel, who, in conjunction, undertook to verify M. Arago's experiments*. After a few trials they succeeded in causing a compass to deviate from the magnetic meridian, and finally to revolve, by placing under it plates of copper, zinc, or lead, which were put into very rapid rotation. In order to obtain more visible and regular effects, however, they found it necessary to reverse the experiment, by setting in rotation a powerful horse-shoe magnet with its poles uppermost, the line joining them being horizontal, and its axis of symmetry being placed vertically; while a circular disc of the substance to be examined was suspended over this magnet. The disc was found to follow the motion of the magnet with various degrees of readiness, according to the substance of which it was made. They obtained in this way signs of magnetic susceptibility from copper, zinc, silver, tin, lead, antimony, mercury, gold, bismuth, and carbon, in that peculiar metalloid state in which it is precipitated from carbonated hydrogen in gas-works. Great care was taken, in the case of mercury, to secure the exclusion of iron. In other bodies which were tried, such as sulphuric acid, rosin, glass, and other non-conductors, or imperfect conductors, of electricity, no positive evidence of magnetism was obtained.

(358.) They next endeavoured to determine the comparative intensities of action of these different bodies. Two methods were used for this purpose; first, by observing the deviation of the compass over revolving plates of great size, cast to one pattern; and, secondly, by the times of rotation of a neutralized system of magnets suspended over them; and it is remarkable, that the places of zinc and copper in the scale, according as the one or the other of these two methods was employed, were the reverse of each other; although the same order was assigned to all the other bodies by both methods.

(359.) On trying the effect of the interposition of different bodies as screens, in cutting off or modifying the influence of the rotating bodies, they could not detect any interceptive power, except, as might be expected, in the case of an iron plate, which, when of sufficient thickness, completely destroyed all perceptible effect from rotation.

(360.) The magnetic energy developed by rotation was found to be much diminished by any interruption of continuity in the plate which was acted upon. This fact had previously been noticed by Arago; but the experiments of Mr. Babbage and Mr. Herschel have verified it in more detail, and have added the curious circumstance, that re-establishing the metallic contact with other metals, restores, in a great measure, the force which had been lost by the division of the substances; and this happens even when the metal used for soldering has, of itself, but a very feeble magnetic power; thus affording a means of magnifying weak degrees of magnetism. The reduction of the metals to filings, or to powder, was found to produce a still more remarkable diminution of their magnetic energy. The law of diminution of force by increase of distance was next investigated; but it appeared to follow no constant progression according to any fixed power of the distance, but to vary between the square and the cube.

(361.) The explanation of these curious phenomena has been attempted on the following principle—namely, that in the induction of magnetism, time enters as a necessary element; or, in other words, that a certain appreciable time is required both for the acquisition of magnetic polarity, communicated by induction from a magnetized body, and for its loss, when the body in which it has been induced returns to the neutral state by the subtraction of all extraneous influence.

(362.) In order to trace the operation of this principle, let us conceive the north pole of a magnet to move horizontally, at a little distance above a plate of metal, or other substance, having a very low degree of magnetic susceptibility, and also a very low degree of retentive power. The points over which it passes in suc-

---
* Philosophical Transactions for 1825, p. 467.

cession will not instantly receive all the magnetism which the magnet is capable of exciting in them; their state of maximum polarity, therefore, will not be attained until the magnet has passed for some small distance beyond them. Neither will they lose their polarity at the same instant that the magnet is still further removed. Thus, from both causes, there will always be, in the rear of the magnet, a space both more extensive and more strongly impregnated with the opposite polarity than in advance of it. Hence, there will arise an oblique action between the pole of the magnet and the opposite pole of the plate, thus lagging behind it, which will urge it to move in the direction of the magnet's motion. The development of the more distant polarity, similar in kind to that of the magnet, being more diffused, that pole will be both weaker and less oblique in its action, and will be much inferior in power to that of the nearer attracting pole. It is evident that the converse will also be true when the magnet is at rest, but free to move horizontally; and when the different parts of the plate are passed in succession under it, the latter will tend to drag the former after it with a velocity continually accelerating, till they move on together with the same velocities. It is also manifest, that the greater the relative velocity, the more will the pole, developed in the plate, lag behind the magnet, or the magnet (in the reverse case) lag behind the pole; the more oblique, therefore, will be the action, and the greater the velocity produced. The application of these principles to circular motion, or to the rotation of plates, is sufficiently obvious; but in this case, if the velocity be excessive, compared with the retentive power of the revolving substance, the latter may have completed a revolution before there has been time for its being affected to a degree sufficient to occasion motion in the magnet; the induced polarity will then be weakened, and its effects rendered insensible. This diminution of the total effect by a more general diffusion of polarity was imitated by sticking a great number of magnetized needles, vertically, through a light cork circle, having their north poles downwards, so as to form a coronet of magnets. This apparatus, suspended centrally over a revolving copper disc, was not sensibly affected; for the poles of all the magnets, acting in rapid succession upon all the points below them, produced nearly a uniform circle of southern polarity, whose equal and contrary actions on the needles would destroy one another.

(363.) Plausible as this theory may appear, it is yet embarrassed with many serious difficulties. It does not give any satisfactory explanation of the mode in which an attractive force, resulting from induction, between one pole of a magnet and the consequent polarity of the adjacent parts of a piece of copper—a force which is so feeble as not to produce any sensible effects when both these bodies are at rest—is immediately so greatly increased on their separation and continued removal from one another, so as to occasion a very considerable motion. The force producing that motion is, according to the theory, an attractive force; but Arago has shown that the general resultant of all the forces, which operate between the pole of the magnet and the plate, is a repulsive force, with relation to the line perpendicular to the surface of the plate. The following experiment proves this:—Suspend a long magnet by a thread, in a vertical position, to the beam of a balance, and counterpoise it by weights on the opposite side; if the plate be then revolved under the magnet, the equilibrium will cease, and the magnet will rise, or appear to become lighter, indicating its repulsion from the plate*.

(364.) The latest experiments on this subject are those of Mr. W. S. Harris, of Plymouth, of which he communicated an account to the Royal Society, in June 1830†. Finding that the vibrations which attend bodies in rapid rotation are propagated to a remarkable extent along the solid parts of the apparatus by which a magnetic needle is suspended, and that they are also conveyed to great distances by the surrounding air, even when highly rarefied, he took great pains to obviate these two sources of fallacy. He accordingly conducted all his experiments in an exhausted receiver, the parts to be acted upon being effectually secured from the influence both of vibrations from solids and of aërial vortices. He conceives that, in general, sufficient care had not hitherto been taken to eliminate these several causes of error, and that we cannot repose that implicit confidence in the conclusions deduced from them which is required in

---

* Annales de Chimie, xxxii. 213.
† It has been since published in the Philosophical Transactions for 1831, p. 67.

a subject of so delicate a nature. He finds that the influence of a rotating body on the magnet is real, but more feeble than had previously been imagined; and that the law of intensity of action is directly as the rapidity of rotation, and inversely as the squares of the distances between the attracting bodies.

(365.) From some experiments which Mr. Harris lately exhibited at the Royal Institution of London, it appears, that a magnetic needle, partly neutralized with regard to the earth's action, and made to vibrate while surrounded by a massive ring of copper, or other substance of very weak magnetic energy, had its oscillations sensibly repressed by the presence of that substance, and that it arrived much sooner at a state of rest than when the ring was removed. The magnetic influence of rotating bodies was found to be intercepted by a variety of substances interposed between them.

(366.) His last communications to the Royal Society contain an account of experiments tending to show that every substance susceptible of magnetism by induction, when interposed as a screen, tends to arrest the action excited by a magnet on a third substance; and that this interceptive power is directly as the mass of the intervening substance, and inversely as its susceptibility to receive induced magnetism. A single plate of iron, for instance, about the sixteenth of an inch thick, is found effectually to intercept the action of a revolving magnet on a disc of copper; but the same result is not obtained when the disc acted upon, instead of being copper, is also of iron, unless the mass of interposed iron be very considerable. He afterwards determined that this interceptive influence depends, not merely upon the surface of the interposed iron, but is in proportion to its mass. Hence he was led to suspect that indications might be obtained of a similar influence, exerted by substances not of a ferruginous nature, if they were interposed in considerable masses; and this conjecture was verified on trying the experiment. He found that the action of a revolving magnet upon a disc of tinned iron was completely intercepted by masses of about four inches in thickness, of either copper, zinc, or silver, interposed between them.

(367.) It would appear, then, that this interceptive property is common to all matter, though possessed, in various degrees, by different kinds of substance; and that, in order to render it sensible, it is only requisite to employ them in masses proportionate to their respective magnetic susceptibilities. Lead, for example, which has a weaker magnetic susceptibility than copper, must be employed in a larger mass in order to produce an equal effect. By an extension of this principle, it would require a thickness of above thirty feet of ice, in order to render its interceptive power sensible.

(368.) It is not necessary, however, that the substance which exerts this controlling power over the action of a revolving magnet should be actually interposed between the magnet and the metallic disc. Mr. Harris found that, in the case of iron, a mass of that metal, when placed very near to that surface of the magnet most distant from the disc on which it was acting, had the effect of neutralizing its power. With regard to non-ferruginous bodies, it is very difficult to render this influence sensible, unless they are interposed in the direct line of action.

(369.) The temporary induction of magnetism may be conceived as taking place in two different ways: first, by the immediate action of the magnet upon each individual particle of the body on which magnetism is induced; or, secondly, by the action of each particle on the next adjoining to it in succession, constituting a continued and successive propagation of magnetism from the one to the other. Although both these kinds of induction may take place at the same time in the same substances, yet the degrees in which they are exerted seem to be in some inverse ratio the one to the other: for when the absorbing or retentive power of the substance is considerable, the power of the magnet is soon checked: because the particles of that substance first acted upon begin to operate as screens to the succeeding particles; and the induction, after a certain point, proceeds entirely by communication from particle to particle, until the whole has attained a state of permanence. When, on the contrary, the retentive power of the given substance is small, little or no interceptive influence can exist among its particles; and the induction will be produced solely by the direct action of the magnet on all the particles. Accordingly it is only by the succession or multiplication of effect, resulting from the action of a great number of particles, that the controlling power of such a substance becomes sensible. To this cause is apparently owing the diminution of the action of a revolving magnet on a disc of copper, when the latter is intersected by radiating grooves: since a portion of the substance, every part of which is concerned in the full development of induced magnetism, is thereby removed. In confirmation of this reasoning, Mr. Harris found that the number of oscillations made in vacuo in a given arc, by a delicately suspended bar, surrounded by several concentric copper rings, did not materially differ from the number performed, in similar circumstances, by the same bar, surrounded by a solid mass of copper.

(370.) The effects of various metals in diminishing the oscillations of a magnetic needle, have been determined with considerable accuracy by Professor Seebeck. An account of his experiments is given in the Annales de Physique for 1826*.

(371.) With regard to the theory of magnetism, Poisson has remarked that there is no necessity for supposing that the phenomena of magnetism are produced in all bodies by a fluid, or fluids, possessing everywhere the same intensity of attractive or repulsive action, and therefore requiring to be considered as the same fluid in different substances. No doubt can exist as to the identity of the electric fluid; because we see it passing from one conducting body into another, and at the same time preserving all its properties, and exercising, in like circumstances, the same attractions and repulsions. But we have no evidence of this kind in the case of the magnetic fluids, because they are always confined to the same particles; and we cannot, by mere reasoning, decide whether the magnetism of two different bodies, such as pure iron and pure nickel, should be considered as the same imponderable substance. It would assist us in the determination of this question, were it ascertained that similar and equal needles of iron and of nickel, when submitted to the magnetic influence of the earth, or of any other magnet, would make an equal number of oscillations. An experiment was made by M. Gay-Lussac with this view, from which it would appear that the mutual action of the magnetic fluids contained in steel and in soft iron is decidedly greater than the mutual action of the fluids belonging to steel and to nickel. This experiment, however, is not decisive of the question, because we may still consider the magnetic elements of a body as not actually in contact, but as constituting assemblages of particles, in which the two fluids reside, and are separated by intervals not greater than the dimensions of those elements; and, as we formerly observed (§ 165), the ratio between the sum of the volumes of all these elements, and the total volume of the body, may be different in different substances, and at different temperatures, in the same substance. This diversity may explain the result of Gay-Lussac's experiment, without the necessity of the supposition of a difference in the intensity of the magnetic power in substances differently susceptible of magnetism*. But the interest which attached to speculations of this kind, are now, in some measure, superseded by the new theory of magnetism, proposed by Ampère: for an account of which, we must refer to the forthcoming Treatise on Electro-Magnetism.

---

* See Quarterly Journal of Science for January, 1828, p. 456.

* Mémoires de l'Académie Royale des Sciences, tom. v. pp. 252, 254.

ERRATA.
Page 64, line 35, *for* sin, *read* cos.
    37, .. to the ..... to half the.
    41, .. sin. ..... ½ sin.

ELECTRO-MAGNETISM.

CHAPTER I.
History of the Science prior to Oersted's discovery.

(1.) THE analogies that exist between the phenomena of magnetism and those of electricity, in their general character, in the laws which govern them, and in the various combinations they present, are so extensive and so remarkable, as naturally to suggest the notion that the agencies themselves from which they proceed must be allied to one another by some close and intimate relation. Adventurous theorists have advanced the doctrine, that each of these principles is merely a modification of the other, and that both may be regarded as ultimately identical in their nature, constituting, instead of two separate and primary powers, a single power of a higher order of simplicity.

(2.) The connexion between magnetism and electricity was a favourite subject of speculation and inquiry among philosophers in the middle of the last century. Many were the efforts made to resolve this seductive problem, which continued, however, to baffle the labours of each succeeding experimentalist, who multiplied his attempts, and varied his processes, without approaching nearer to the point he aimed at; and also to elude the reasonings of those who theorized upon every new fact until they bewildered both themselves and their readers in the mazes of visionary and conflicting hypotheses.

(3.) In the year 1774, the following question was proposed by the Electoral Academy of Bavaria as the subject of a prize dissertation:—'Is there a real and physical analogy between electric and magnetic forces; and, if such analogy exist, in what manner do these forces act upon the animal body?' The essays received by the Academy on that occasion, were collected and published, ten years afterwards, by Professor Van Swinden, of Franeker, the author of one of the essays for which the prizes were awarded*. The conclusion to which he arrived, after a long and elaborate discussion of the subject, was, that the similarity between electricity and magnetism amounts merely to an apparent resemblance, and does not constitute a true physical analogy; whence he infers, that these two powers are essentially different and distinct from one another. The opposite opinion, on the other hand, was maintained by Professors Steiglehner and Hubner, who contended that so close an analogy as that exhibited by these two classes of phenomena, indicated the effects of a single agent, varied only in consequence of a diversity of circumstances. So many new facts have been brought to light since the time in which these authors wrote, that the reasonings adduced on either side in this controversy have now lost their interest, excepting that it is still curious to observe by what devious paths they were led away from the truth, at the moment when they had nearly reached it, and when a very slight variation in the form of their experiments would at once have disclosed it to their view.

(4.) Subsequent discoveries relating to the laws of electric and magnetic action, both as respects attraction and repulsion, and also induction, have tended to confirm the analogy between them, and to corroborate the opinion that they ultimately emanate from a common source. Electricity, it is true, affects every species of matter with which we are acquainted, in nearly an equal degree; while magnetism, although perhaps equally universal in its operation, yet acts very feebly, and probably unequally, upon most kinds of matter, and certainly exerts its principal energy upon iron, a circumstance which has, to

---

* His work is entitled 'Recueil de Mémoires sur l'Analogie de l'Electricité et du Magnétisme, couronnés et publiés, par l'Académie de Bavière, &c.' par J. H. Van Swinden. En trois tomes, 8vo. A la Haye, 1784.

B

this day, remained inexplicable, although we have acquired the knowledge that electricity, under certain modifications, will produce every effect of magnetism. Electricity, we know, may be transferred from one body to another, but magnetism can be excited by induction only, and is incapable of any similar kind of transference. Still, however, there existed many positive facts, which, independently of all analogy, demonstrated that the magnetic needle was occasionally influenced in its movements by the action of electricity; and that, in certain cases, the magnetic properties could be excited by electric explosions. The appearance of the aurora borealis, which has all the characters of an electric phenomenon, has been very frequently observed to be accompanied by a disturbance in the position of the compass; and a delicately suspended magnetic needle has generally exhibited, on these occasions, very frequent oscillations. Lightning, which is still more decidedly electric, has been known, in numberless instances, to destroy, and sometimes to reverse the polarity of the compass-needle; and many disastrous accidents happening to ships, in consequence of their mistaking their course, may very probably have been owing to this cause. In confirmation of this, we meet with a narrative recorded in one of the early volumes of the Philosophical Transactions[*], in which the ship Alexander, being one hundred leagues from Cape Cod, in latitude 48°, encountered a violent thunder-storm; the mast was struck by lightning, which also reversed the poles of all the compasses in the ship, a change which was not discovered till the ensuing night, when the stars appeared, and it was found that they had been steering in the opposite course to that which they intended. It is also stated, that in one of the compasses, the end which had before pointed to the north now pointed to the west. Another instance is recorded in the same work[†], where a stroke of lightning passed through a box containing a great number of knives and forks, melting some, and scattering the rest about the room. It was found that all those which were not melted had been rendered strongly magnetic, so as to take up large nails, and other pieces of iron, placed near them.

(5.) Experiments were tried with the electrical battery, in imitation of these effects, and in order to ascertain the circumstances on which they depended. But although steel bars were easily rendered magnetic by passing strong electric shocks through them, yet the results were by no means uniform, and no general law could be traced as governing the production and distribution of the polarity thus induced. A large proportion of the effects appeared to be referable to the concussion which the particles of the bar received in consequence of the violence with which the accumulated torrent of electricity rushed through them, thereby giving efficacy to the inductive influence of the earth. This influence, it is well known, depends altogether, as was explained in the Treatise on Magnetism (§ 109), on the position of the bar with relation to the direction of the dipping needle, which is the same as that of the action of terrestrial magnetism. The experiments of Mr. Scoresby[*], made with a view of determining the amount of this influence when aided by electric concussion, fully confirmed the principle upon which that mode of explaining the phenomenon rests, by showing that the action of a powerful electric shock is, in a great measure, similar to that of a blow from a hammer, or to the forcible twisting of the iron, or any other kind of mechanical violence.

(6.) There still, however, remained many anomalous appearances, to the explanation of which this principle did not furnish the most slender clue. These anomalies presented themselves more especially when the electric discharge was made to pass transversely, or in oblique directions, through the bar; for it was found, in those cases, impossible to predict what direction the induced poles would assume, or even whether any distinct polarity would be communicated to the bar when so treated.

Nothing illustrates more forcibly the proneness of the human mind to draw general conclusions from insufficient data, than the various opinions so confidently maintained by different experimentalists on this subject. D'Alibard thought he had demonstrated, by his experiments, that the electric discharge imparts a northern polarity to that point of a steel bar at which it enters, and a southern polarity to that at which it

---

[*] Vol. xiv. p. 520.   [†] Vol. xxxix. p. 74.

[*] Transactions of the Royal Society of Edinburgh, vol. ix.

makes its exit; and this quite independently of the position of the needle with respect to the magnetic poles of the earth. Wilke, on the contrary, imagined that he could establish the existence of an invariable connexion between the negative electricity and the northern polarity. The laborious series of experiments which were undertaken by Van Swinden, with the express view of reconciling these strange discrepancies, instead of settling the dispute, seemed only to leave it more than ever embarrassed with difficulties. About the year 1777, the celebrated Beccaria engaged in a similar investigation; and although he, like his predecessors, failed in discovering the true nature of the magnetic influence of electricity, yet he noticed a singular fact which occurred to him in the course of his experiments, but of which he does not appear to have appreciated the value. He found that a needle, through which he had sent an electric shock, had, in consequence, acquired a curious species of polarity; for, instead of turning as usual to the north and south, it assumed a position at right angles to this, its two ends pointing to the east and west. There is little doubt, that if he had followed up the inquiry which this important fact had opened to him, he would soon have arrived at the great discovery which was made about half a century afterwards by Oersted, and which has dispelled the whole mystery.

(7.) As nothing had been gained by following the more violent operations of highly condensed charges of electricity, other philosophers occupied themselves in the attentive study of the more tranquil influence of this agent, when merely accumulated in insulated conductors, and exerting simply its attractive and repulsive powers in conjunction with those of magnetism. But however these actions might be combined, nothing could be detected that indicated any interference of agency or modification of effect consequent on the combination. An electrified body is found to exert the same attractions and repulsions on a magnetized needle as it does on the same needle when devoid of magnetism; nor does it, like magnetism, exhibit any decided preference for iron, compared with its action on other metals. When the two agencies are united in the same body, as when bars of steel, already rendered magnetic, are also charged with electricity, and placed so as to act upon one another, their electrical and their magnetic actions appear to be perfectly distinct, and in no respect to influence or modify one another.

(8.) The discovery of galvanism, and the invention of the Voltaic apparatus, opened a new field of inquiry; for, by furnishing the experimentalist with the means of maintaining a continuous current of electricity in very large quantity, it enabled him to study the effects of this powerful agent under circumstances of a very different kind from those he had previously had under his command. The electro-chemical phenomena, brought to light by its application to another branch of physical science, for a long time occupied the talents and absorbed the attention of scientific men in every part of Europe; and many years elapsed before Voltaic electricity was applied with any success to determine the influence which it so directly exerts over magnetized bodies. The few inquirers who sought to establish a relation or identity between these two powers, excited but little attention, in consequence, either of the obscurity of their reasonings or the inaccuracy of their experiments. The various hints interspersed among the journals of this period, respecting movements having been observed in the magnetic needle by the action of the Voltaic pile, were too vague and uncertain to warrant any determinate conclusion. The most definite and authentic narrative relating to this subject was that of Ritter, who asserted that a needle, composed of silver and zinc, had arranged itself in the magnetic meridian, and had been slightly attracted and repelled by the poles of a magnet. He also stated, that by placing a gold coin in the Voltaic circuit, he had succeeded in giving to it positive and negative electric poles; and that the polarity so communicated was retained by the gold after it had been in contact with other metals, and appeared, therefore, to partake of the nature of magnetism. A gold needle, placed in similar circumstances, acquired still more decided magnetic properties. These experiments suggested to Ritter some vague idea that electrical combinations, when not exhibiting their electric tension, were in a magnetic state; and that there existed a kind of electro-magnetic meridian depending on the electricity of the earth, at right angles to the magnetic poles. But these speculations were of too crude a nature to throw any distinct light on the true connexion between magnetism and electricity.

Chapter II.
Account of Oersted's Experiments.

(9.) The real discoverer of the magnetic properties of electric currents was M. Oersted, Professor of Natural Philosophy, and Secretary to the Royal Society of Copenhagen. In a work which he published in German, about the year 1813, on the identity of chemical and electrical forces[*], he had thrown out conjectures concerning the relations subsisting between the electric, galvanic, and magnetic fluids, which he conceived might differ from one another only in their respective degrees of tension. If galvanism, he argued, be merely a more latent form of electricity, so magnetism may possibly be nothing more than electricity in a still more latent form; and he therefore proposed it as a subject worthy of inquiry whether electricity, employed in this, its most latent form, might not be found to have a sensible effect upon a magnet. It is difficult clearly to understand what he means by the expression of *latent states*, as applied to electricity, but it may be sufficient for us to know that in the various endeavours he subsequently made to verify his conjectures, he was led to such forms of experiment as afforded decisive indications of the influence of Voltaic currents on the magnetized needle. Yet, even after he had succeeded thus far, it was a matter of extreme difficulty to determine the real direction of this action, and it was not till the close of the year 1819 that his perseverance was at length rewarded by complete success.

(10.) The first account of his discovery that appeared in England is contained in a paper, which he himself communicated, in Thomson's Annals of Philosophy, for October, 1820[†]; and in which the following experiments are described:—The two poles of a powerful Voltaic battery were connected by a metallic wire, so as to complete the galvanic circuit. The wire which performs this office he called the *uniting wire;* and the effect, whatever it may be, which takes place in this conductor, and in the space surrounding it, during the passage of the electricity, he designates by the term *electric conflict*, from an idea that there takes place some continued collision and neutralization of the two species of electric fluids, while circulating in opposite currents in the apparatus. Then taking a magnetic needle, properly balanced on its pivot, as in the mariner's compass, and allowing it to assume its natural position in the magnetic meridian, he placed a straight portion of the uniting wire horizontally above the needle, and in a direction parallel to it; and then completed the circuit, so that the electric current passed through the wire. The moment this was done, the needle changed its position, its ends deviating from the north and south towards the east or west, according to the direction in which the electric current flowed, so that by reversing the direction of the current the motion of the needle was also reversed. The general law he expressed as follows:—'That end of the needle which is situated next to the negative side of the battery, or towards which the current of positive electricity is flowing, immediately moves to the westward.'

(11.) The deviation of the needle is the same, whether the uniting wire, instead of being immediately above the needle, be placed somewhat to the east or west of it, provided it continue parallel to and also above it. This shows that the effect is not the result of a simple attractive or repulsive influence, for the same pole of the magnetic needle which approaches the uniting wire when placed on its east side recedes from it when placed on its west side.

(12.) If the uniting wire be placed in a horizontal plane *under* the magnetic needle the latter is affected to an equal degree as in the former case, but the motions are made in the contrary direction; for the pole of the needle next to the negative end of the battery now deviates towards the east.

(13.) The effects above described will

Fig. 1.

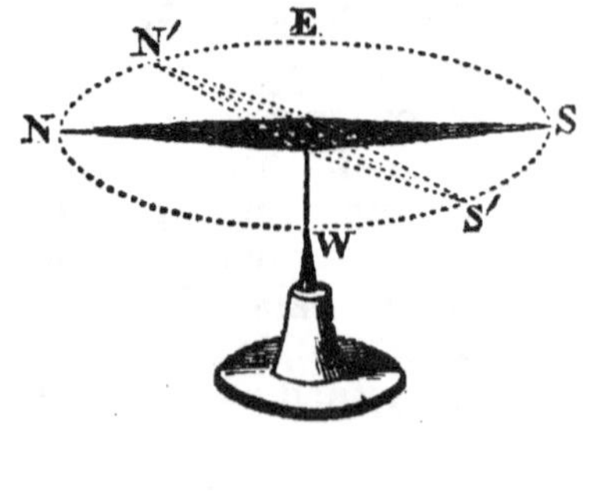

---

[*] This work was translated into French by Marcel des Serres, under the title of 'Recherches sur l'Identité des Forces Chimiques et Electriques. Paris, 1813.' See the 8th Chapter of that work.
[†] Vol. XVI. of the first series, p. 273.

be more clearly understood from an inspection of *Figs.* 1 and 2, where N, S present the two opposite poles of the magnetic needle, balanced upon its pivot; and *p n* the uniting wire; the end *p* being connected with the positive or copper end of the simple galvanic battery, and the other end, *n*, being connected with the negative or zinc end of the same battery. (See the Treatise on GALVANISM, § 15.) So that the direction of the positive electric current is from *p* to *n*, as described by the arrows in the figure.

Fig. 2.

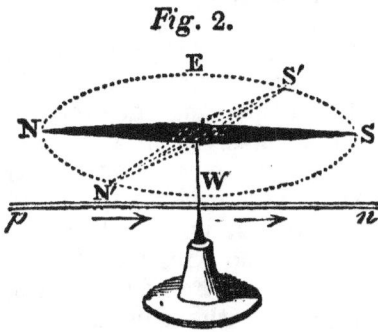

When the uniting wire is above the needle, as in *fig.* 1, the pole S, which is next to the negative side of the battery, or towards which the current of positive electricity is flowing, will move towards W, the western side of the horizontal dotted circle; and the needle will assume the position N′ S′. When the wire is below the needle, as in *fig.* 2, the same pole S will move towards E, the east point of the horizon; and its new position will be N′ S′, inclined in a direction the reverse of that which it assumed in the former case.

(14.) For the more easy retention of these facts in the memory Oersted used the following formula: namely, ' *the* pole *above* which the *negative* electricity enters, is turned to the *west;* under which, to the *east.*' Another, and more convenient formula, however, will presently be given, comprehending not only these but many other facts, which are derived from a more universal principle applicable to all of them.

(15.) When the uniting wire is situated in the same horizontal plane as that in which the needle moves, and is at the same time parallel to it, no declination takes place either to the east or west; but the needle is inclined, so that the pole next to the end of the wire at which the negative electricity enters is depressed, when the wire is situated on the west side, and elevated when situated on the east side.

Thus, if the uniting wire *p n, fig.* 3,

be placed on a level with the needle NS and parallel to it, on its eastern side, the pole S, next to the negative end of the wire *n*, will be elevated, and the pole

Fig. 3.

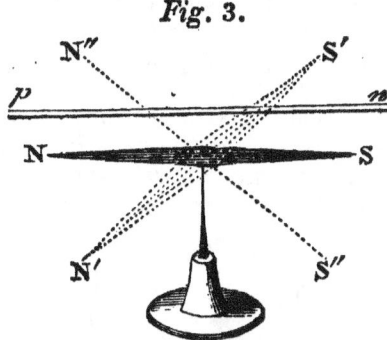

N depressed, so as to assume the position represented by the dotted needle N′S′. If the uniting wire had been placed on the western side of the needle the pole N would have been elevated, and S depressed; and the axis of the needle would have been in the position N″S″.

(16.) If the uniting wire, instead of being parallel to the needle, be placed at right angles to it, that is, extending from east to west, whether above or below it, the needle remains at rest, unless it be brought very near to one of the poles; in which case the pole is elevated when the entrance of the negative electricity

Fig. 4.

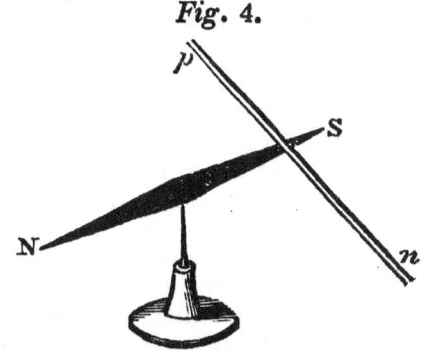

is from the west side of the wire, and depressed when from the east side. Thus the pole S, *fig.* 4, is elevated when the current of positive electricity proceeds from *p* to *n*; that is, when the entrance

Fig. 5.

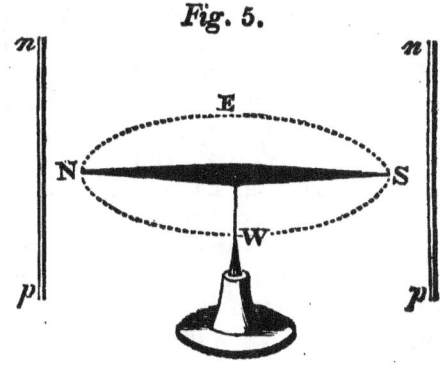

of the negative electricity is from the west side of the wire.

(17.) When the uniting wire, instead of being horizontal, is placed vertically, as shown in *fig.* 5, either to the north or south of the needle, and then brought near to the adjacent pole, if the upper extremity of the wire receives the negative electricity, that pole moves towards the east; but when the wire is brought opposite to a point between the pole and the middle of the needle, as in *fig.* 6, the

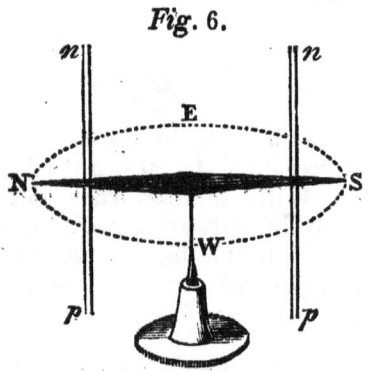

Fig. 6.

same pole deviates to the west. When the upper end of the wire receives positive electricity, the phenomena are reversed.

(18.) Oersted found that these experiments succeeded equally well if the uniting conductor consisted of one or of several wires, or metallic ribbons, connected together. Neither is the effect altered in its kind, though it may vary somewhat in degree, when different metals are used: thus, platinum, gold, silver, brass, iron, lead and tin, and even mercury contained in a tube, when employed as the conductors of the electricity, have a similar influence on the magnetic needle. The conductor still exerts this power, although it be interrupted by water, provided the interval between the metals does not extend to several inches in length. The magnetic influence of the wire on the needle is not prevented by the interposition of glass, metals, wood, water, resin, stones, or any other substance that was tried. The effect produced, nevertheless, is referable purely to magnetism, for it is exerted on magnetic bodies only, and has no influence on needles of brass, glass, or gum lac. It appears to depend, not upon the intensity of the circulating electricity, but solely on its quantity; and accordingly Oersted found that he could, with a single galvanic arc, repeat all the experiments which he had at first made with a compound Voltaic battery. In his way, also, he was enabled to detect the reciprocal action which the poles of a magnet exert on the conducting wire; for, by placing a plate of zinc, six inches square, between two plates of copper formed into a trough, in order to hold the acid which is to act upon the former, but kept from touching them by small pieces of cork interposed on each side, on forming a communication between the two plates by an extended wire, and then suspending the whole apparatus by a thread, the effect of a magnet in moving the wire could be readily ascertained.

(19.) The announcement of the important discovery of Oersted excited the greatest interest among all the philosophers of Europe, and they immediately occupied themselves in repeating and extending his experiments. Among those who were early distinguished by their zeal and activity in this research were Ampère and Arago, in France, and Sir H. Davy and Faraday, in England. So many were the cultivators in this new field of inquiry, and so eagerly did they pursue the path thus unexpectedly opened, that a great number of interesting facts were speedily brought to light; and where all were pressing forward in the same career, it is scarcely possible to adjust the claims to priority of discovery, with respect even to the most important facts. Instead, therefore, of attempting to give a chronological view of the progress of knowledge in this department of science, we shall adopt the following more didactic, and, we trust, more instructive plan. We shall first state those general principles to which philosophers have arrived by gradual and successive inductions; secondly, we shall trace the various combinations of those principles in different ways, and under different circumstances, and the effects resulting from them; and lastly, point out the explanations which they afford of particular phenomena, in the order which appears most conducive to clear and comprehensive views of the whole subject of electro-magnetism.

Chapter III.
Fundamental Law of Electro-Magnetic Action.

(20.) An attentive examination of the facts described in the preceding chapter will soon convince us that the magnetic force which emanates from the electrical conducting wire is entirely different in its mode of operation from all the other forces in nature with which we are acquainted. It does not act in a direction parallel to that of the current which is passing along the wire, nor in any plane passing through that direction. It is evidently exerted in a plane perpendicular to the wire, but still it has no tendency to move the poles of the magnet, in a right or radial line, either directly towards or directly from the wire, as in every other case of attractive or repulsive agency. The peculiarity of its action is that it produces motion in a circular direction all round the wire; that is, in a direction at right angles to the radius, or in the direction of the tangent to a circle described round the wire in a plane perpendicular to it. Hence, as Mr. Barlow has expressed it, the electro-magnetic force exerts a *tangential action*.

(21.) The direction, in the circumference of these circles, of the action exerted on any one pole of a magnet by the electrical current which is moving at right angles to the plane of the circles, is determined by the direction of the current. If we suppose the conducting wire to be placed in a vertical situation, as shown in *fig. 7, p n*, and the current of positive electricity to be descending through it, or moving from *p* to *n* (the negative electricity moving, of course, in the contrary direction, or ascending), and if through any point C in that wire, the plane NN be taken perpendicular to *p n*, that is, in the present case, a horizontal plane; and lastly, if any number of circles be described in that plane having C for their common centre, then the action of the current in the wire upon the north pole of a magnet, situated any where in that plane, will be to move it in the line of the tangent to the circle which passes through it, and in the direction denoted by the arrows in the figure; that is, from left to right in the remote part of the circle, and from right to left in the nearer part. In other words, the motions impressed will be in a direction corresponding to those of

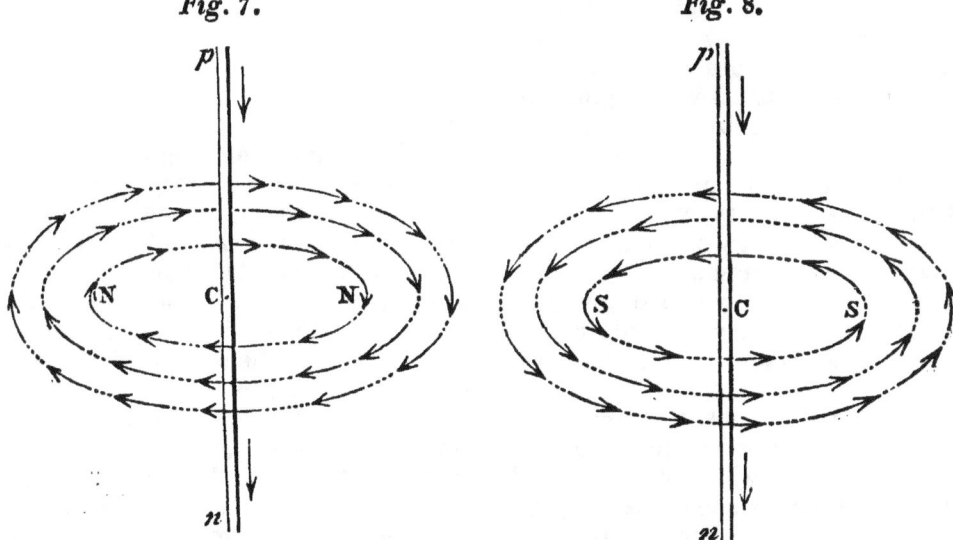

Fig. 7. *Fig. 8.*

the hands of a watch having the dial towards the positive pole of the Voltaic battery.

(22.) When the direction of the current is reversed, the wire still preserving its vertical position, the direction of the action is also reversed; and the circular motions produced correspond to the movements of the hands of a watch with its face downwards; that is, still looking towards the positive electrical pole.

(23.) The actions of either the descending or ascending electrical current upon the south pole of a magnet are exactly the reverse of those which are exerted on the north pole. *Fig.* 8 represents the action of the current moving from *p* to *n*, on the south pole; which is directed, as may be seen, from right to left in that part of the circle which is opposite to the wire, and which would, therefore, impel the south pole in a direction contrary to that of the hands of a watch. On reversing the direction of the current these effects will again be reversed.

(24.) It is evident that in the course of experiments on electro-magnetism, the current and magnetic poles may be presented to our observation in a great variety of relative positions; and it will be found not very easy to retain a perfect recollection of the way in which the force should act conformably to the rule above stated. Ampère has hit upon an ingenious device for imprinting this rule more firmly in the memory, and enabling us to apply it under a great diversity of circumstances. The electric currents are not only characterized as positive and negative, and as flowing in one or other of two directions along the wire that conducts them, but may be actually personified and conceived as endowed with a head and feet, with a face and back, and with a right and a left hand. In order to turn this idea to the best account, and being at liberty to choose, with respect to the various kinds of conditions belonging to the subject, one or other of two alternatives, we shall select in each case those which seem naturally entitled to the preference: and it fortunately happens that, on combining these conditions so selected, they accord exactly with nature, and are therefore well calculated to answer the purpose of a kind of artificial memory.

(25.) First, it is more natural to fix our attention on the current of *positive*, than of negative electricity. Secondly, in a vertical wire, a *descending* current will occur to us more readily than an ascending one: or, if we imagine ourselves borne along by the current, it would be more natural to conceive ourselves moving with our *feet* foremost; but if, on the contrary, we suppose ourselves to be at rest, we should conceive the current to be passing from our head to our feet. Our *face* would, of course, be turned *towards* the magnetic pole to which we are directing our attention; we should attend to the *north* pole in preference to the south; and the movement with which we are most familiar, is that which we perform with our *right* hand, as in writing for instance, that is, *from left to right*. Combining these conditions, then, we may always recollect, that *if we conceive ourselves lying in the direction of the current, the stream of positive electricity flowing through our head towards our feet, with the magnet before us, the north pole of that magnet will be directed towards our right hand.* If any one of these conditions be reversed, the result is reversed likewise.

(26.) The action of the conducting wire on the pole of a magnet is necessarily accompanied by a corresponding and opposite action of the magnet on the wire. When the wire impels the pole from left to right, the pole impels the wire from right to left, and *vice versâ*. Thus we have seen that a positive current, descending along a wire, of which W, *fig.* 9 A, represents the sec-

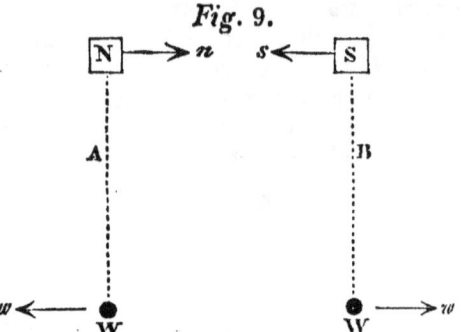

Fig. 9.

tion by a horizontal plane, urges the north pole N to the right, in the direction N *n*, but the wire itself is also urged in the direction W *w*, to the left. The contrary action takes place between the south pole S, *fig.* 9 B, so that if either pole of a magnet were fixed, and the wire moveable, the motion of the latter would, as in the case we have already considered, be circular, and the force which impels it tangential. This is shown in *figs.* 10 and 11, where *pn, pn,* &c. show the successive positions of the wire urged to move in the direction shown by the arrows, by the influence

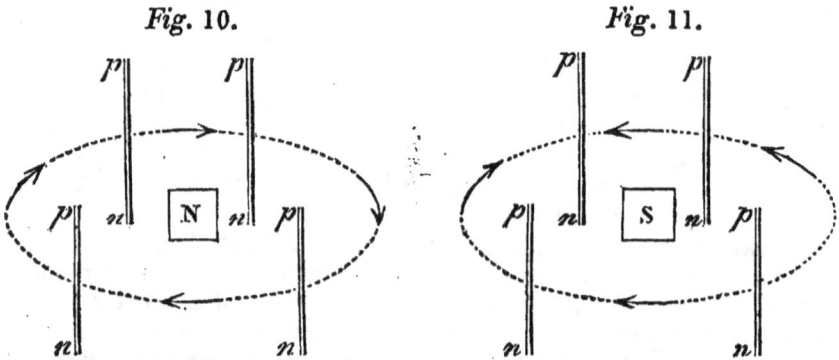

Fig. 10.   Fig. 11.

of the north or south poles N or S. The influence exerted on the same current by the one being in the opposite direction to that exerted by the other. When the currents are reversed, all the effects just described are again reversed.

It is also to be observed, that the motion of the wire, whatever be its relative position to the magnet, is always moved parallel to itself; that is, in the direction of a line at right angles to it.

(27.) The direction of the electro-magnetic force being thus determined, we have next to ascertain the exact law, according to which its intensity varies, with relation to the distance of the electric current from the point on which it acts. The most reasonable conjecture we can form on this subject, prior to experimental investigation, is, that this law is the same with that which is followed in the case of electric and magnetic actions, namely, that the intensity of the force is every where inversely as the square of the distance. But if this be the real law of action, it must apply to the elementary portions of the two agents which thus mutually act upon each other; or, to adopt the more convenient language of theory, it must obtain only among the elementary particles of the electric and magnetic fluids. In the magnet, the action of the latter may be regarded as concentrated in the points, which are the poles of the magnet; but in the conducting wire, the electric fluid which is passing through it, acts in an equal degree along the whole line of its motion; and admitting the hypothesis of the action being inversely proportional to the squares of the distances of each individual particle, we have to deduce the law which will result from the combined actions of all the points of a line directed upon a point out of that line. Now, it may be mathematically demonstrated, that if the line in question be perfectly straight, and its length be exceedingly great in proportion to the distance of the point on which it acts, then the intensity of action will be inversely proportional, not to the square, but to the simple distance of the point, so that at three times the distance, for example, the force shall be one-third, at four times the distance, one-fourth, and so on. That this law is conformable to observation, has been proved by the experiments conducted by Biot and Savart, in which the intensities of the force at different distances were accurately ascertained, by observing the number of oscillations performed by the needle in a given time, and taking the squares of those numbers.

Chapter IV.
Direct consequences of the Law of Electro-magnetic Action.

(28.) Let us now inquire into the consequences of this law. So different is the action of the electro-magnetic force from that of the other forces in nature, with the effects of which we are more familiar, that a particular train of investigation is required, in order to trace its exact operation under every combination of circumstances. It is not easy, even in the simpler cases, where a single magnetic pole is subjected to the action of a conducting wire, at once to pronounce upon the precise motion that will result, especially if the motion of the magnetized body is limited to a fixed plane, and restrained to mere rotation; but the difficulty is much increased, when, as most frequently happens in actual experiment, the investigation is complicated by the necessity of including the combined actions of several poles of different kinds. The only mode of obtaining clear views of the subject is to examine the several cases in their order of simplicity, commencing with each force taken singly, and afterwards studying their several combinations.

§ 1. *Effects on the Directive Property of a Magnetic Needle.*

(29.) Confining our attention, then, for the present, to a single magnetic pole, the north pole for instance, we have to examine the effects produced upon it by a conducting wire of indefinite length, acting upon it with a tangential force inversely proportional to its distance, when the movements of that wire are limited to the circumference of a circle, in a given plane, perpendicular to the wire. The case under consideration may, in a great measure, be exemplified, by placing a magnet, SN, *fig.* 12, on a flat support, AB, resting, at its centre, on the pivot P, and balanced by a counterpoise at the opposite end, so that the south pole, S,

Fig. 12.

of the magnet may be exactly above the centre of motion.

In this situation, the action of any electrical current upon the pole S, can have no influence in turning the bar, AB, in any particular direction; and the motion of the bar will be determined solely by the action of the current upon the north pole, N.

(30.) Let A B C D M N O, *fig.* 13,

Fig. 13.

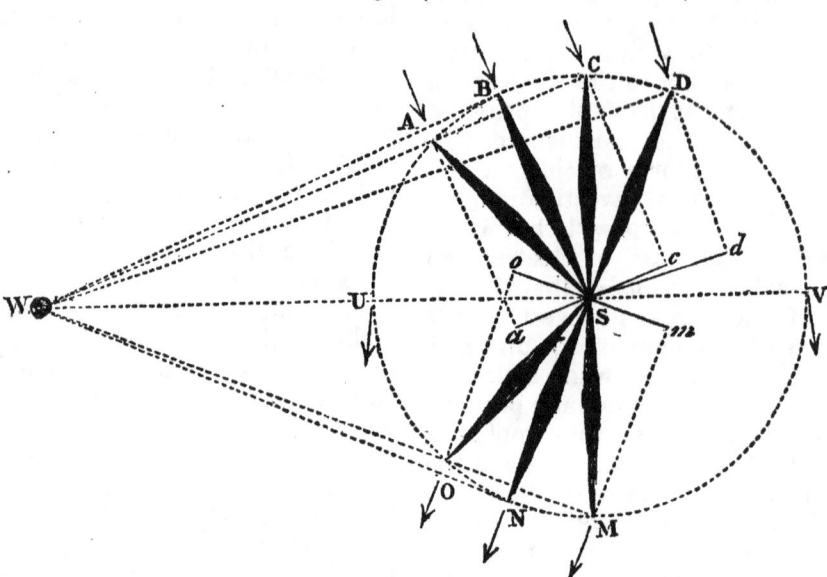

be the horizontal circle in which the needle NS revolves, S being the centre of its revolution; and let W be the horizontal section of the conducting wire, which acts upon the needle, and along which the positive electric current is descending. In every position of the needle, the tangential force, acting upon the pole in the circumference of the circle, takes the direction of a line to the right hand, perpendicular to that which connects the pole and the wire. At D, for instance, it has the direction of the line D *d*, perpendicular to DW. Its tendency to produce rotation in the needle, by turning it round S, will be proportional to the cosine of the angle formed between WD and the radius DS; or it may be represented by the line S *d*, drawn parallel to WD, and meeting the perpendicular D *d*, to which it is, of course, also perpendicular; for it will readily be seen, that the rotatory effect of the force we are considering is the same, whether applied on the needle at D, or at *d*, on the arm of a lever S *d*, rigidly connected with the needle. The needle, then, will be urged by this force to move towards V, and as the length of the lever by which it acts continually increases until it reaches this point, so also will the rotatory power increase. After the needle has passed V, it will again diminish; when it comes to M, its measure is S *m*, and on arriving at N, where the position of the needle NS is at right angles to NW, it is reduced to nothing. This, therefore, will be a position of equilibrium, and the equilibrium will be a stable one, for, on disturbing the position of the needle by pushing it onwards to O, for example, the rotatory force, in this new position, acts upon it by the lever S *o*, on the opposite side of S *m*, and, therefore, tends to give it rotation in the contrary direction; that is, to bring the pole of the needle back again to N. After performing a few oscillations, the needle will, therefore, finally settle in the position SN.

(31.) When the arcs of vibration are small, the forces which tend to bring the needle to its point of rest, are very nearly proportional to the arcs themselves; so that, in this respect, its movements are governed by the same law as those of a pendulum. They accordingly furnish very accurate means of determining the comparative intensities of the electro-magnetic forces which act upon the same needle under different circumstances of distance from the wire, or of intensity of the electric current, for the force will always be proportional to the square of the number of oscillations which the needle performs in a given time.—(See *Treatise on Magnetism*, § 320.)

(32.) When the needle is still further

deflected towards the wire, the force that tends to bring it back to the position of rest increases till it reaches its maximum at the position SU, where the needle points directly to the wire. Carrying it still further to the left, the rotatory force again diminishes, till it arrives at the position BS, perpendicular to BW, where, being directed to the exact centre of motion, it is reduced to nothing. This position of the needle, therefore, is also one of equilibrium; but it differs from the former in being an unstable equilibrium; for if the needle be disturbed ever so little from its position on either side, it will acquire a tendency to proceed onwards in that direction, and will move away from the point B. At A, for instance, the rotatory force acts upon it by the lever S a, urging it towards U, and causing it ultimately to settle at N. At C, again, it is urged towards D by a similar force, proportional to S c, and which, increasing as the needle advances, carries it to V, and finally brings it round to N.

(33.) It may here be remarked, that the rotations of the needle are in opposite directions in these two portions of the circumference; for, in the remote part, BVN, the motion is similar to that of the hands of a watch; in the nearer part, BUN, it is in the contrary direction. The lines WB and WN, drawn from W to the points where the needle is in equilibrium, being at right angles to the respective radii BS and NS, are tangents to the circle at B and N, and the circumference is divided by these points into two unequal portions, so that the needle, in passing from B to N, by the operation of the tangential force emanating from W, as indicated by the arrows in the figure, has to traverse a longer distance when moving in the remote than in the nearer part of the circle. The disproportion between these two arcs continually increases as the wire is brought nearer to the circle. When very near, as shown in *fig.* 14,

Fig. 14.

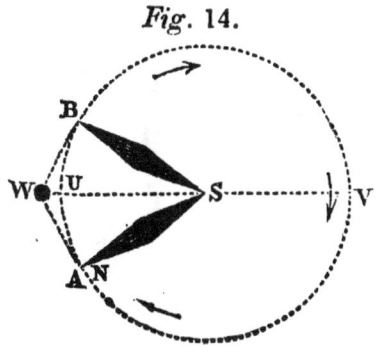

the arc BUN is very small, compared with BVN; yet, if the needle be placed ever so little on the other side of B, it will immediately recede from that point, as if repelled by the wire, and will proceed to describe the larger portion of the circle, in order to arrive at N, a position which it might have reached by a much more direct course had it described the arch BUN.

(34.) The singular preference thus shown by the needle for a very circuitous path, in reaching its destination, when it appeared free to take the shorter line that leads to it, appeared exceedingly paradoxical to those who first observed it, and excited much astonishment. But the explanation we have given shews clearly that it is nothing more than the direct result of the peculiar law of electro-magnetic force, which is characterized by the tangential direction of its agency.

(35.) If the wire be supposed to pass through the circumference itself, as in *fig.* 15, that portion of the circumfer-

Fig. 15.

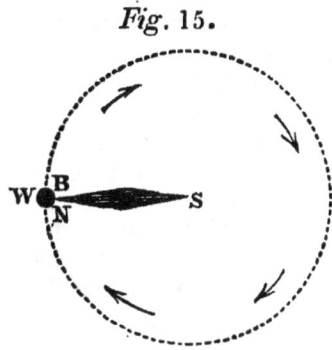

ence BN, which was comprehended between the two tangents, and in which the needle was urged to turn in a direction contrary to that of its revolution in the rest of the circle, is now reduced to a mere point; and the needle, when placed ever so little to the left of that point, will move round the entire circle, and even when it arrives at this point, can hardly be said to settle there, for the slightest movement in the same direction will again place it under the influence of the same impulse, which will, therefore, carry it round a second time. The very momentum it has acquired in this motion will be sufficient to transport it beyond this neutral point, and to maintain it in a state of perpetual revolution. Should the wire be actually within the circle, as in *fig.* 16, then the rotatory force will remain constantly in the same direction in every part of the circle, and, according to theory, the needle will revolve in perpetuity in the same constant direction. It is obvious, however, that in the circumstances under which an experiment of this kind can be made, this can never happen, because the wire being a solid substance, and passing perpendicularly through the plane of the circle in which the needle turns, its presence must arrest the motion of the needle as soon as it comes in contact with it. The only position which the needle can take, therefore, is that of resting against the wire in the manner represented in *fig.* 16. In any

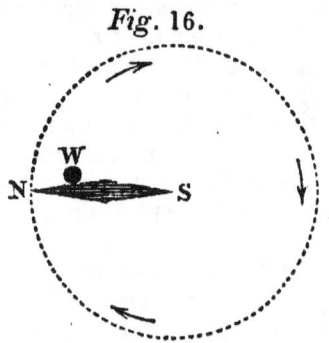

Fig. 16.

other part of the circle, it will move onwards in the direction indicated by the arrows.

(36.) Having thus investigated the action of an electric current on a single pole, we are now prepared for the consideration of its combined action upon the two opposite poles of a magnetized needle, balanced in the ordinary way on its centre. In this case, the current, descending through the wire W, *fig.* 17,

Fig. 17.

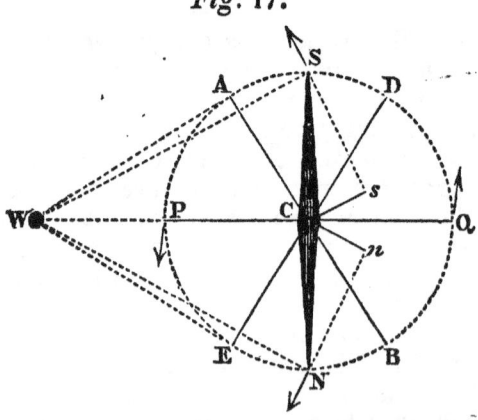

exerts a contrary action upon the two poles, N and S, of the needle. When the needle is in the position PQ, that is, in the same line with W, these two contrary forces, acting at right angles to the radius, and on opposite sides of the centre, concur in their rotatory effect, and the needle is urged by the sum of these forces to turn in the direction indicated by the arrows placed at these points. When the needle is in the position SN, at right angles to the line WC, the rotatory forces, being directed perpendicularly to WS and WN, as indicated by the arrows, oppose one another, and acting by the levers C*s* and C*n*, which are equal in length, are in exact equilibrium. The equilibrium is stable, as will be evident from considering that the displacement of S, in the direction of D, increases the length of the lever C*s*, while the accompanying motion of N towards E, diminishes the length of C*n*. The force represented by the former, will, therefore, preponderate over that represented by the latter, and will carry back the pole S to its former situation. The same would happen, were the displacement made on the other side of S, for in that case, the force which impels the pole N would have the advantage over that which acts on the pole S, and would restore the needle to its position of rest SN. This opposition of forces occurs when the needle is situated any where between the lines AB and DE, which are respectively perpendicular to the tangents to the circle, WA and WE; for, in either of these situations, AB or DE, the rotatory force exerted in one of the poles, is, as we have before seen, § 30, reduced to nothing. Beyond these positions, the rotatory force changes its direction, so that in any part of the arcs APE, and DQB, the forces acting upon the two poles conspire in producing a similar effect of rotation.

(37.) In proportion as the wire W, *fig.* 18, is brought nearer to the needle, the arcs ASD and ENB, in which the two forces oppose each other, form a larger portion of the circle, while those in which they concur, AE and DB, become smaller. Here it may also be

Fig. 18.

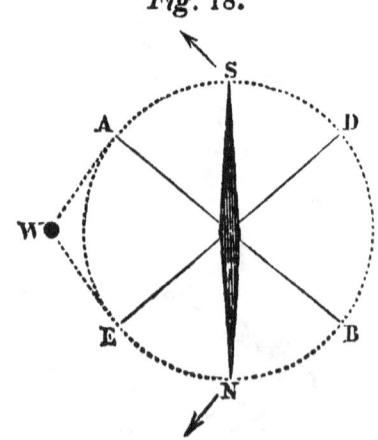

observed, that when the position of the needle differs much from that of SN, the two poles, N and S, will be at very different distances from the wire, and the intensity of the force being inversely as the distance, the forces acting upon the two poles will, in consequence, differ materially. When the forces concur in their rotatory effect, the result will not be affected by this difference; but when they oppose each other, the increase of force acting on the nearer pole, will go far towards compensating for the greater obliquity of its direction, and will bring it more nearly to an equality with the smaller force, which acts with greater mechanical advantage on the distant pole. This equality is actually attained when the wire passes through the circumference of the circle; for now the force acting upon S, *fig.* 19, in the direc-

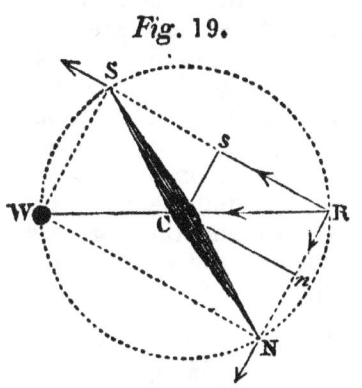

Fig. 19.

tion RS, is to the force acting upon N, in the direction RN, inversely as the distances WS and WN; that is, they are as WN to WS: but as the former acts by the lever C *s*, and the latter by the lever C *n*, which are themselves in the proportion of WS to WN, they must, by the laws of statics, be exactly in equilibrium.

To place the matter in another point of view, the forces RS and RN, when combined together, produce, as their resultant, the force RW, which, being directed to the centre of motion C, can have no tendency to produce rotation. Hence it follows, that the needle, whatever be its position in the circumference, will appear to be totally uninfluenced by the wire; the action of the latter, on both poles, exactly balancing each other.

(38.) This state of equilibrium no longer remains when the wire is within the circle, *fig.* 20. It will now be found, that in no position of the needle do the two forces conspire to produce the same rotatory motion, and that they oppose one another in every part of the circle. The only position in which the equilibrium is stable, is that of NS, the north pole being to the left, and the south pole to the right of the wire; a position which, it should be observed, is exactly the re-

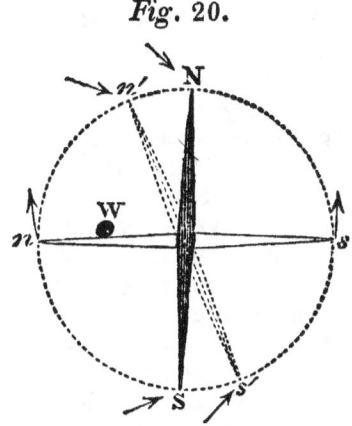

Fig. 20.

verse of that which the needle assumes when the wire is out of the circle, as in *figs.* 17 and 18. When disturbed from this position, and brought to $n'\, s'$, for example, the force urging the pole n', which is nearest to the wire, becomes more effective than that acting upon the more distant pole s', and, therefore, brings back the needle to its station. But if the pole N were placed on the opposite side of the wire, as at n', the tangential force which carries it towards the wire, is, here also, more effective than that which acts upon the distant pole s', and which tends to move it in the contrary direction; the needle, therefore, strikes against the wire, and being unable to pass it, remains in contact with it. If the needle be carried still further from the wire, however, the superiority of this force will continually diminish, and cease entirely when the needle is in the transverse position SN, shown in *fig.* 21, where the two poles, S and N, are equi-distant from W. Here there is again an equilibrium, but it is of

Fig. 21.

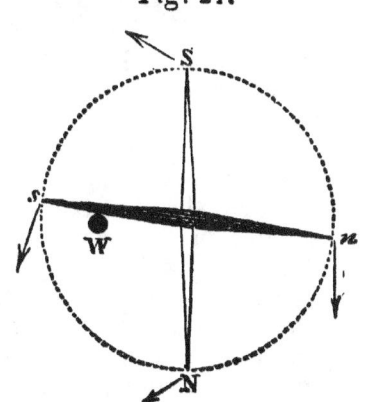

the unstable kind, for as soon as N is removed further from the wire, the force acting on S gains the advantage, and turns the needle round till its revolution is arrested by its coming against the wire, in the position *s n*.

(39.) Although, strictly speaking, the tangential force exerted by an electrical current upon either pole of a magnet, has no tendency to cause the pole to approach to, or recede from it, and, therefore, does not possess the character either of an attractive or of a repulsive force, yet the movements of a needle, in the circumstances we have just been considering, often resemble those of attraction and repulsion. But if viewed with reference to such a cause, they would appear exceedingly anomalous; and accordingly the sudden changes from attraction to repulsion, which take place from a slight alteration in the relative positions of the wire and needle, appeared to the earlier experimentalists to be very capricious and unaccountable.

(40.) In order fully to understand these transitions, we may arrange the results of the preceding investigation, as they refer to any one given position of the needle SN, *fig.* 22, varying the

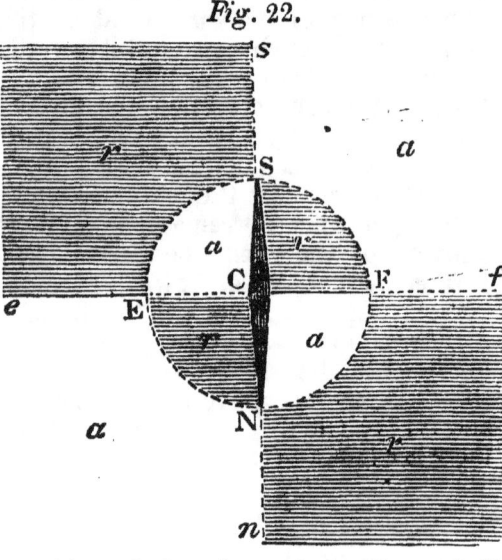

Fig. 22.

position of the wire only, and we shall then find that the lines which form the boundaries between the positions of apparent attraction and repulsion are the circumference of the circle of which the needle is a diameter, together with the prolonged axis of the needle *n s*, and another line crossing it, at the centre, at right angles, *e f*. The circumference indicates the positions of the wire when no apparent effect is produced on the needle, or the positions of neutrality.

The line *e f* is that in which an equilibrium obtains. When the wire is in any continuous part of the line *e f*, namely CF and E *e*, the equilibrium is stable; when in any of the dotted parts E C or F *f*, of the same line, unstable; on the line *s n*, the action is at the maximum. The letters *a, a, a, a*, show the spaces where an apparent attraction takes place between the wire and the nearest pole, when the former is situated in the respective spaces bounded by the above lines; and *r, r, r, r*, the spaces where there is apparent repulsion. These latter spaces are shaded for the sake of distinction. Thus within the quadrant SCE there is apparent attraction of the pole S; in the shaded quadrant SCF there is an apparent repulsion of that pole; in the shaded quadrant ECN, the pole N moves from the wire; in NCF, towards it. In the spaces exterior to the circle the actions are exactly the reverse of those in the interior; in the shaded space bounded by *s* S, *e* E, and the circumference, the action in S is apparently repulsive; in the white space on the other side of S, bounded by the lines S *s*, F *f*, and the circumference, it is attractive; and the contrary obtains with regard to the spaces on the other side of the line *e f*.

§ 2. *Movements of the Magnetic Needle in free space.*

(41.) In the preceding investigation our attention has been exclusively directed to the determination of the effects of the electro-magnetic forces on a magnetized needle, so restricted in its motion as to be capable of only turning on its centre; and we have had to consider only the forces which tended to produce the rotation of the needle. A part of the forces, however, which act on the poles is exerted in another direction, and would, were the needle at liberty to obey them, occasion the displacement of the whole needle, that is, would produce a motion of its centre. The needle being confined by its pivot, the only effect produced by these forces is pressure upon this pivot. But if this obstacle be removed, and the needle be allowed to move freely in any direction, the action of these remaining forces will become manifest; the motion of the centre of the needle being determined in its quantity and direction by the magnitude and direction of the resultant force estimated by referring the two component forces to that point.

(42.) When the conducting wire W, fig. 23, is situated in any part of the line WC, at right angles to the axis of the needle, the tangential force acting on the pole S, in the direction represented by the arrow, at right angles to WS, may be supposed to be transferred to the centre, C, of the needle, and to be represented by the line Cs. The force acting upon N being in like manner represented by Cn; the resultant of these two forces will be a force represented by the diagonal Ca of the parallelogram, having Cs and Cn for its two sides, and these sides being equal, and equally inclined to the line WC, this diagonal will coincide with that line: hence the force will be such as to move the centre of the needle directly towards W, that is, the needle will appear to be attracted by it. If either the current had followed an opposite course, or the poles of the needle had been reversed, the forces would have acted in the opposite direction, and would have been represented by the lines Cs', Cn', forming a parallelogram, of which the diagonal is Cr, indicating a motion of the centre of the needle from the wire, and resembling repulsion. This effect also takes place under the original circumstances of the experiment when the wire is on the other side of the needle, that is, in any part of the line CW; so that the needle will always appear to be attracted by the wire on one side and repelled on the other.

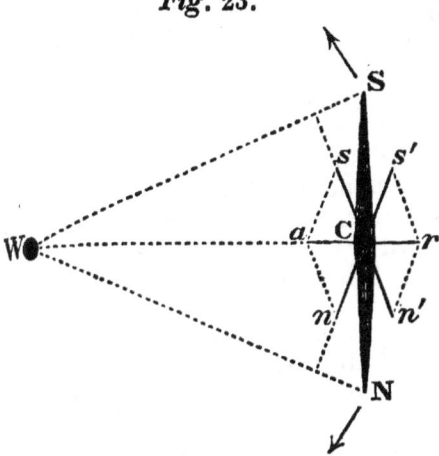

Fig. 23.

(43.) The intensity of the force which thus impels the needle, either towards or from the wire, diminishes as their distance is increased. Two causes conspire to produce this diminution; the one is that the component forces themselves are inversely proportional to the distances of the points on which they act from the wire; and the other is that the angles they form with one another become more obtuse as that distance increases. Mathematically speaking, the tangential force applied to each pole, when referred to the direction of the line joining the wire and the centre of the needle, is directly as the cosine of the angle formed between the axis of the needle and the line connecting the pole and the wire; and it is also inversely as this line; so that calling the force referred to that direction a, the distance from the wire to the centre of the needle d, the distances of the wire from the respective poles S and N, s and n, and the length of the needle m; and α and β being the angles between the axis of the needle and the lines connecting the respective poles with the wire, we have the following equation:

$$a = \frac{\cos.\alpha}{s} + \frac{\cos.\beta}{n}.$$

But as we have taken the case of W being placed on the line drawn from the centre of the needle at right angles to its axis, the two angles above mentioned are equal, and every part of the line is equidistant from S and N, that is,

$$\alpha = \beta, \text{ and } s = n;$$

hence the equation becomes $a = \dfrac{2 \cos.\alpha}{s}$. Now

$$\cos.\alpha = \frac{\text{CS}}{\text{WS}} = \frac{\frac{1}{2}m}{s};$$

which value of cos. α being substituted in the former equation, the formula becomes

$$a = \frac{m}{s^2},$$

that is, the force of apparent attraction is directly as the length of the needle, and inversely as the square of the distance of the wire from each pole.

(44.) In order to estimate the attraction with relation to the distance of the wire from the centre of the needle, or d, we must substitute for s^2 its equal $d^2 + \frac{1}{4}m^2$; so that the formula becomes

$$a = \frac{m}{d^2 + \frac{1}{4}m^2}.$$

But when the distance of the wire is very great compared with the length of the needle, the quantity $\frac{1}{4}m^2$ may safely be neglected; and $\dfrac{m}{d^2}$ may be taken without any sensible error as the expression of the attractive force.

(45.) This may be experimentally illustrated by suspending a magnetic needle, SN, fig. 24, from its centre by a thread, so that it may be balanced horizontally, and bringing it within a certain distance of a vertical conducting wire P n; if the electrical current be descending in that

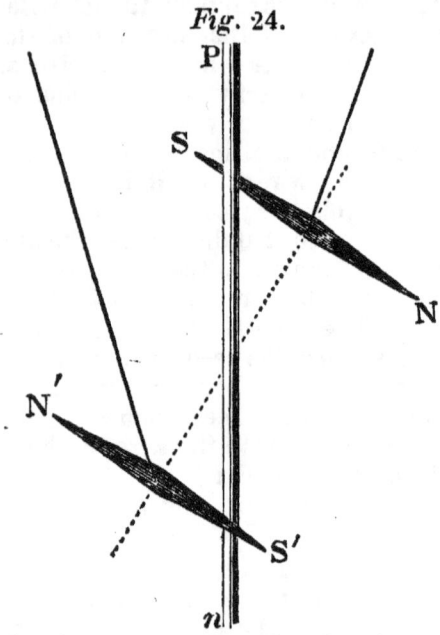

Fig. 24.

wire the needle will place itself so that the north pole N will be to the right, and the south pole to the left of a spectator conceived to be placed in the situation of the wire and looking towards the needle, as shown in the figure; whereas if the needle be before the wire as at N'S' the poles will have a reverse position. In both cases the needle will be impelled towards the wire, as shown by the inclination of the thread by which it is suspended.

(46.) When, on the other hand, the needle is removed to a considerable distance from the wire, or what comes to

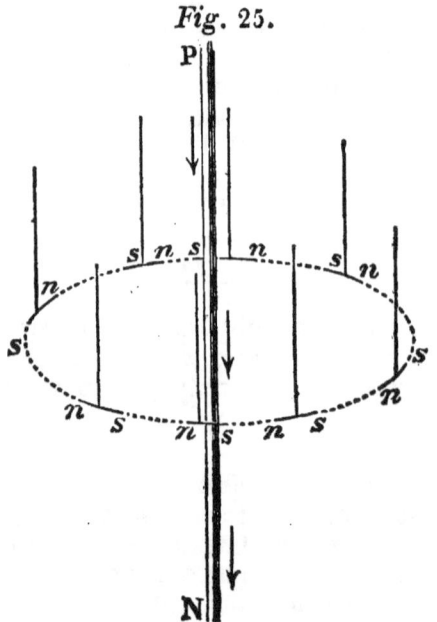

Fig. 25.

the same thing, when a very short needle, $s\,n$, is taken and carried round the wire P N, *fig*. 25, in a circle, its poles will always preserve the same relative situation, as indicated by the letters in the figure, each being turned in the direction in which they are respectively urged to move round the circumference by the tangential force. But the tendency to approach the wire will be quite insensible, in consequence of the angle formed by the directions of the two forces being so nearly equal to two right angles.

(47.) When the wire is placed in any part of the circumference of the circle, having for its centre the centre of the needle, and passing through the poles, the resultant of the two forces C s and C n (*fig*. 26), has the exact direction of the line CW; and therefore, neither

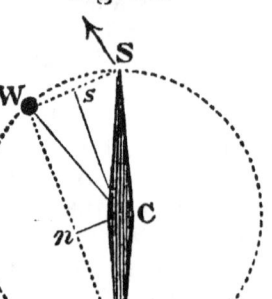

Fig. 26.

in this, nor in the preceding case, is there any rotatory force in operation. But, in the present case, the force CW being oblique to the axis of the needle SN, a part of that force is exerted in moving the needle in the direction of its length, from C towards S, and in bringing the centre C opposite to W; so that it will not rest until that centre comes in contact with the wire, as shown in *fig*. 27. A similar tendency in the centre of the needle to move towards the wire takes place in all other situations

Fig. 27.

of the wire on that side of the needle; but the direction of the motion produced is more or less oblique to the line connecting the centre of the needle with the wire. This direction may, in all cases, be easily found by drawing the lines C s and C n (*fig.* 28), respectively perpendicular to WS and WN, and com-

Fig. 28.

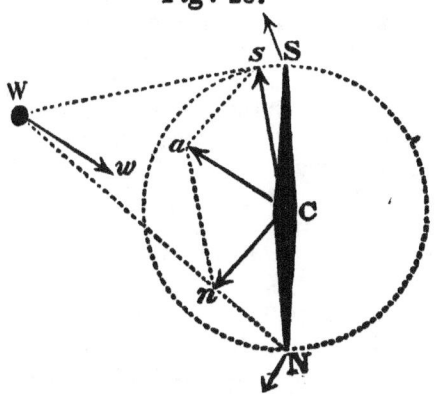

pleting the parallelogram C *s a n*; of which the diagonal, C *a*, will be the direction of the resultant force acting upon C. For the forces at S and N, being inversely as the distances WS and WN, are in the ratio of WN to WS, which is equal to the ratio of the sines of the opposite angles WSC to WNC of the triangle WSN; that is, in the ratio of C *s* to C *n*, which are the actual sines of those angles with the equal radii SC and NC. The lines C *s* and C *n* will, therefore, correctly represent, both in their directions and in their relative proportions, the tangential forces in question.

(48.) The actions exerted between the wire and the poles of the needle, are, as we have seen, reciprocal; the wire being urged by a force equal in intensity, and parallel in its direction, to that which acts upon the centre of the needle; hence the determination of this resultant force will also give us the measure and direction of the resultant of the two forces which act upon the wire. Thus the needle SN, *fig.* 28, being urged by a force represented by C *a*, the wire W will, in like manner, be impelled by a force represented by the line W *w*, equal and parallel to C *a*, but having an opposite direction.

(49.) The direction of the force impelling the wire by the joint action of the poles of the needle, may be found geometrically, by describing a circle W *b* S *r* N *a*, *fig.* 29, which shall pass through the position of the wire, and also through the two poles; for the diameter W *r* of that circle will be the direction required. This will appear from the following demonstration:—

Fig. 29.

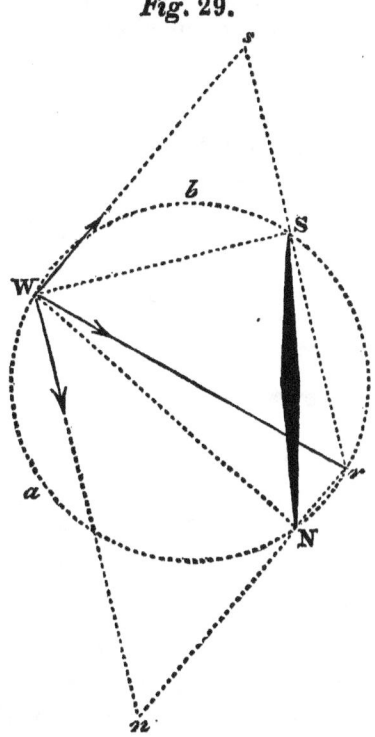

Through S and N draw S *r* and N *r*, respectively perpendicular to WS and WN, and which will, of course, meet at *r*, the extremity of the diameter W *r*; and through W, draw W *s* and W *n*, parallel respectively to *r* N and *r* S, meeting them, when produced, in *s* and *n*, and forming a parallelogram, of which W *r* is the diagonal. The triangle W *r s*, or its equal, W *r n*, is similar to the triangle WSN, because the angles WNS and W *r* S, which subtend the same arc W *b* S, are equal; as also the angles WSN and *s* W *r*, or its equal W *r* N, which subtends the same arc W *a* N. The sides of these triangles are, therefore, proportional; that is,

WN : WS : : *s r*, or its equal W *n* : W *s*.

But the tangential forces impelling W in the directions W *n* and W *s*, from the actions of the poles S and N, are inversely as the lines WS and WN; that is, directly as WN to WS, and therefore in the ratio of the line W *n* to the line W *s*. These lines will, therefore, represent, in their magnitudes as well as in their directions, the two tangential forces by which W is impelled; and consequently the diagonal W *r* of the parallelogram of which they are the sides, or the diameter of the circle, will represent the direction of the resultant force in question.

C

(50.) Hence it follows that the wire is, in all situations, impelled to move in the direction of the tangent of a circle having its centre in the prolongation of the axis of the magnet, and of which the radius is a mean proportional between the distances of its centre from the two poles. Thus the wire at W, *fig.* 30, is impelled by the

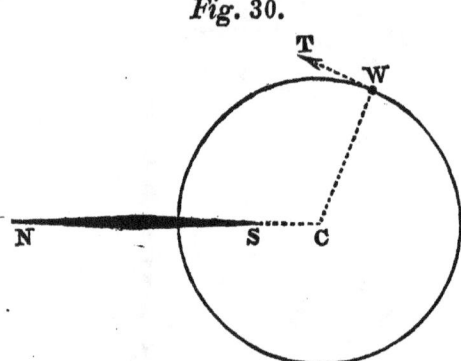

Fig. 30.

action of the two poles N and S, in the direction of the tangent of the circle of which the centre is at C, in the line NS prolonged, and of which the radius WC is a mean proportional between CS and CN. It will, therefore, revolve in that circle, which will stand in the same relation to the magnetic poles N and S, with regard to the law of electro-magnetic action, that the magnetic curves (See *Magnetism*, § 81) do with regard to the law of magnetic action.

CHAPTER V.

Application of the principles to the explanation of particular facts.

(51.) The principles we have derived from the preceding investigation are the foundations of the whole science of electro-magnetism, and furnish the key to the explanation of a vast variety of facts, some of which might appear, without an accurate attention to the circumstances of the case, exceedingly anomalous and perplexing. It is evident that they completely accord with the results obtained in the original experiments of Professor Oersted, which could not for some time be clearly understood.

(52.) In these experiments it will be recollected the wire was horizontal, and applied either above or below the needle, and in a direction parallel to it. In this case the action of the wire is exerted in the tangent to the circumference of a vertical circle, having the wire for its centre; and this action being in opposite directions upon the two poles, conspire to give the needle a motion round its axis. But the needle, having already a tendency to place itself in the plane of the magnetic meridian, in consequence of the influence of the earth, will arrange itself in a position intermediate between this plane and the position to which it tends by the action of the electric current. The greater the intensity of the latter force, the greater will be the deviation of the needle from the magnetic meridian; and both the amount and the direction of the deviation will be found on an attentive examination of the results of Oersted's experiments, as already detailed, to be exactly conformable to theory.

(53.) When the wire, still kept in a horizontal position, was placed by Oersted at right angles to the needle, and over its centre, no visible effect took place, because the actions of the wire upon the two poles were then exactly balanced. But whenever it was brought nearer to one of the poles than to the other, the vertical action being more strongly exerted upon that pole, occasioned its elevation or depression, according to the direction of that action, precisely in the manner which the theory would lead us to expect.

(54.) Mr. Barlow undertook a series of experiments to determine the deviations of a magnetic needle from its natural position, produced by a vertical conducting wire under different circumstances, and deduced from the theory various formulæ, by which its amount may be calculated. For the details of his researches, the reader is referred to Mr. Barlow's Essay on Magnetic Attractions*.

(55.) Of the speculations and hypotheses to which these extraordinary facts gave rise we shall defer the consideration to a future place, and, confining our attention to the facts themselves, we should here notice the observations of Mr. Faraday, which led to the more striking illustrations of the theory of tangential action we are about to describe. Mr. Faraday states† that on placing the wire perpendicularly, and bringing the needle towards it, in order to ascertain its positions of attraction and repulsion with regard to the wire instead of finding these to be four, one attractive and one repulsive for each pole, he found them to be eight; that two attractive and two repulsive for each pole. Thus, allowing the needle to tak

---

* Second edition, p. 240.
† Quarterly Journal of Science, vol. xii. p. 75.

its position of equilibrium across the wire, and then drawing away slowly the support of the needle from the wire, so as to bring the north pole, for instance, nearer to it, there was attraction; but on moving it a little farther, so that the end of the needle was the point nearest to the wire, repulsion took place, although the wire was still on the same side of the needle. When the wire was on the other side of the same pole of the needle, it repelled it when opposite to most parts between the centre and the end; but there was a small portion, at the very end, where attraction took place.

(56.) *Fig.* 31 exhibits a compendious view of the relative situations of the needle and wire in these experiments;

Fig. 31.

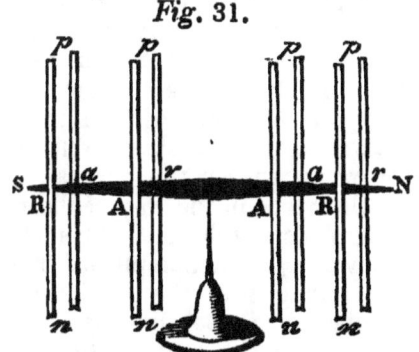

the electric current being supposed to descend along the vertical wire, *p n*, represented in eight different positions; the letters A, *a*, R, *r*, denoting respectively the apparent action (whether attractive or repulsive) exerted in each of these positions. A reference to *fig.* 22, and the general results stated in § 40, will sufficiently explain the facts mentioned by Mr. Faraday, if we take into account a circumstance which very generally obtains in needles of the pointed shape of those employed in the experiment; namely, that the centre of the active portion of each half of the needle, or its true pole, is not situated at the very extremity, but at some point near it, and towards the centre of the needle. Thus the wires in the extreme positions at the ends of the needle were in fact placed beyond the poles, and corresponded in their situation to points out of the circle passing through those poles, which is the circle given in *fig.* 22.

(57.) The reaction of the needle on the wire in these situations was also pointed out by Mr. Faraday, and illustrated by reference to the following figure (32), which represents horizontal sections of the wire in different positions with regard to the needle, balanced in its centre C. They are marked A or R,

Fig. 32.

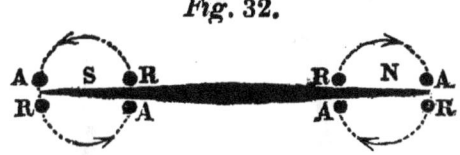

according as they appear to attract or repel the adjacent poles S and N; and the arrow-heads indicate the directions of the circular motion which resulted.

(58.) Mr. Faraday justly concluded from these facts, that there is no real attraction or repulsion between the wire and either pole of a magnet, the actions which imitate these effects being of a compound nature; and he also inferred that the wire ought to revolve round a magnetic pole, and a magnetic pole round a wire, if proper means could be devised for giving effect to these tendencies, and for isolating the operation of a single pole. For the first idea of the possibility of the rotations of an electromagnetic wire round its axis by the approach of a magnet, we are indebted to the sagacity of Dr. Wollaston[*], who did not, however, succeed in producing this effect in the experiments which he made for that purpose.

Chapter VI.
Electro-magnetic Rotations.

(59.) The continued revolution of one of the poles of a magnet round a vertical conducting wire was produced by Mr. Faraday in the following manner[†]:—That the action of the wire might be limited to the pole in question, the whole magnet, with the exception of that extremity in which the pole was situated, was immersed in mercury, its lower end being attached by a thread to the bottom of the vessel which contained the mercury, the conducting wire being made to pass down into the mercury, immediately above the place where the copper wire was fixed to the vessel. This apparatus is represented in *fig.* 33, and a section of it shown in *fig.* 34.

For the purpose of directing the electrical current through the mercury, a hole was drilled at the bottom of the cup, into which a copper pin was ground tight, projecting upwards a little way into the cup, and rivetted to a small

---
[*] Philosophical Transactions for 1823, p. 158.
[†] Quarterly Journal of Science, xii. p. 283.

round plate of copper, forming part of the foot of the vessel. A similar plate of copper was fixed to the turned wooden base on which the cup was placed, and

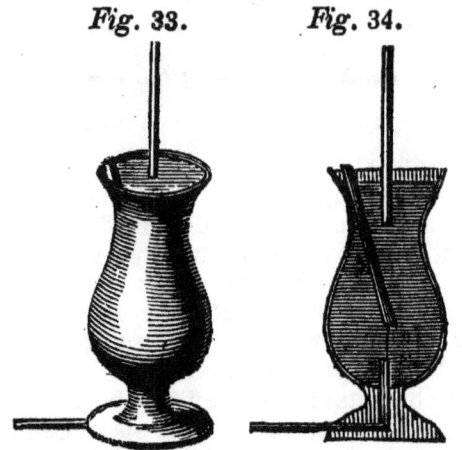

Fig. 33.   Fig. 34.

another piece of strong copper wire, attached to it beneath, after proceeding downwards a little way, was made to turn horizontally. The surfaces of these two plates, intended to come together, were tinned and amalgamated, that they might remain longer clean and bright, and afford better contact. The magnet used was of a cylindrical shape, and very powerful, and had its lower pole fastened by a piece of thread to the copper pin at the bottom of the cup. The height of the magnet and length of the thread were so adjusted, that when the cup was nearly filled with clean mercury, the free pole floated almost upright on its surface. The upright wire, communicating with one of the poles of the voltaic battery, and conducting the electrical current intended to act on the upper pole of the magnet, passed downwards from the upper branch of a stand, so as to descend to a small depth below the surface of the mercury. Its lower end was amalgamated, in order to ensure perfect contact; the circuit was completed by making a communication between the lower wire and the other pole of the battery. As soon as the current is thus established through the apparatus, the upper pole of the magnet immediately revolves round the wire which dips into the mercury. As the force which impels it continues to act without diminution, notwithstanding the motion of the magnet, it operates as an accelerating force; but the motion of the magnet in a circle giving rise to a centrifugal force, the magnet is carried to a greater distance from the wire, until its increased momentum is compensated by the increased resistance of the mercury, at which period the velocity becomes uniform.

(60.) The direction of the motion depends on the direction of the current, and on the denomination of the pole that is moved by it. If the current descends, the north pole of a magnet revolves from left to right; that is, in the direction of the hands of a watch. If the revolving pole be the south pole, it moves in the contrary direction. All this is in perfect conformity with what has already been explained in § 21, 22, and 23, and illustrated by figs. 7 and 8.

(61.) With a view of diminishing the resistance to the revolution of the magnet, which must necessarily take place when it has to revolve in mercury, attempts have been made to devise a method of suspending the magnet on a pivot; but the difficulty has always been to provide a proper channel for carrying off the current after it has acted upon one pole of the magnet. It became evident that no solid conductor would answer the purpose, as it would always be in the way of the magnet during its revolution. This object may, however, be accomplished by employing a magnet of the peculiar shape represented in fig. 35, having a double bend in the middle, so that this part is horizontal while the two extremities are kept in a vertical position. The magnet, so shaped, is furnished with an agate cap fixed to the lower side of the middle horizontal portion, resting on a fine point of an upright wire, which is fixed to the base of the apparatus, and upon which the magnet is balanced, so as to allow of its turning freely round. In order to steady its motion, however, a wire loop is attached to the magnet lower down, which embraces the upright wire, and retains that part of the magnet in a position nearly vertical. A small cistern, holding mercury, is also fixed upon the magnet at the middle of its upper side, just above the point of suspension. A bent wire, pointed and amalgamated at the end, passes out from this cistern, and dips into a circular trough of mercury, which is open in the centre, to allow the magnet to pass freely through the opening, and which is supported on a stage, sustained by means of legs connecting it with the base. A wire, proceeding from the interior of this circular cistern, passes out of it, and terminates in a cup with mercury. The electrical current, intended to act exclusively upon the upper half of the magnet, is to be conducted by a vertical wire of sufficient thickness, which is fixed so as just to dip into the small cistern attached to the magnet. Having reached this point, the current is then diverted from its course by the wire which dips into the large cistern, and is thence carried away by the wire which terminates in the cup last described, to such a distance, and in such a direction, as to prevent its acting on the lower pole of the magnet. The magnet will in this manner be made to revolve with great rapidity. It is scarcely necessary to remark, that the direction of the rotation will depend both on the direction of the current and on the nature of the pole which is acted upon; so that reversing either of these conditions will occasion a change in the direction of the rotation. Mr. Watkins describes an apparatus by which these opposite rotations may be exhibited in two magnets at the same time, and by the same current, by placing the poles of the one in a contrary position to those of the other*. But it is unnecessary to dwell upon these obvious combinations of the more simple forms of the experiment.

Mr. Faraday accomplished by employing the apparatus represented in *fig.* 36. The glass cup holding the mercury is shallow, and has a tubular stem; but instead of being filled with a plug, as was the aperture in the former vessel, a small copper socket is placed in it, and retained there by being fastened by a circular plate below, which is cemented to the glass foot, so that no mercury can pass out by it. This plate is tinned and amalgamated on its lower surface, and stands on another plate and wire, just as in the former apparatus. A small cylindrical magnet is placed in the socket, at any convenient height, and then mercury poured in until it rises so high that nothing but the projecting pole of the magnet is left above its surface at the centre. The forms and relative positions of these parts are seen in the section *fig.* 37. The wire which dips into the mercury, and has its lower end amalga-

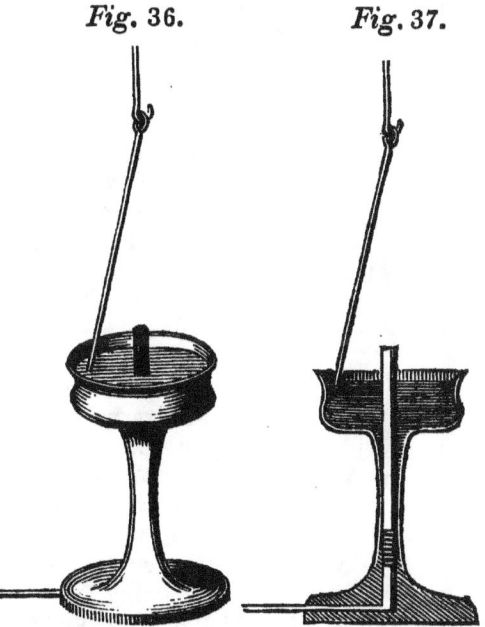

Fig. 36.   *Fig.* 37.

Fig. 35.

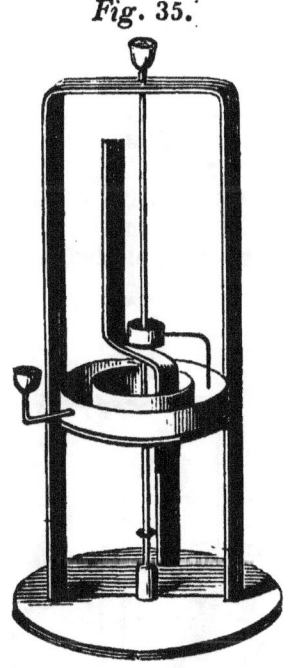

(62.) In the preceding examples, the wire was fixed, and the magnet at liberty to move. But in order to exhibit the revolution of the conducting wire round one of the poles of a magnet, this arrangement must be reversed, that is, the wire must have freedom of motion, and the magnet must be fixed. This

mated, may be suspended to a fixed wire, either by a ball and socket joint, constructed so as to ensure a continuity of metallic conductors, or more simply by means of loops. The best mode of obtaining a perfect contact, is to make the fixed wire terminate in a small cup containing mercury, with its mouth upwards, and to bend the moveable wire into the form of a hook, of which the extremity must be sharpened, and must rest in the mercury on the bottom of the cup, as shown in *fig.* 38. This latter wire, having full liberty to move, revolves round the pole of the magnet which is above the surface of the mercury, with an accelerated velocity, which afterwards

---

* A popular sketch of Electro-magnetism and Electro-dynamics. By Francis Watkins. 1828.

becomes uniform, from the increasing resistance of the fluid; the direction of the motion being determined by the principles already laid down in § 26, and exemplified by *figs*. 9, 10, and 11.

Fig. 38.

(63.) Mr. Faraday also contrived a small apparatus, answering a similar purpose with the last, and in which the wire revolves very rapidly, with a very small voltaic power. It consists of a piece of glass tube, GG, *fig*. 39, the lower end of which is closed by a cork,

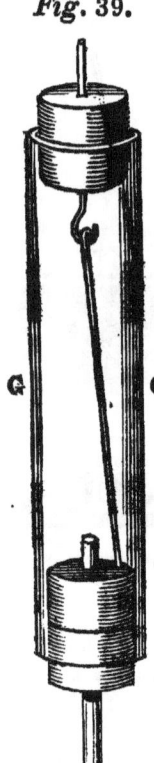

Fig. 39.

through which a small piece of soft iron wire is passed, so as to project above and below the cork. A little mercury is then poured in, to form a channel between the iron wire and the glass tube. The upper orifice is also closed by a cork, through which a piece of platinum wire passes, and terminates below by a loop; another piece of wire hangs from this by a loop, and its lower end, which dips a very little way into the mercury, being amalgamated, it is preserved from adhering either to the iron wire or to the glass. When even a feeble voltaic combination is connected with the upper and lower ends of this apparatus, and the pole of a magnet is placed in contact with the external end of the iron wire M, the moveable wire within rapidly rotates round the temporary magnet thus formed by induction at the moment, and by changing either the connexion or the pole of the magnet in contact with the iron, the direction of the motion itself is changed. This apparatus has been made so small as to produce rapid revolutions, by the action of two plates of copper and zinc, containing not more than a square inch of surface each.

(64.) A still more simple mode of exhibiting the rotation of the wire, is to employ, instead of a pierced cup, a wide and very shallow vessel, as a tea-saucer, for containing the mercury, and to bring a strong magnet underneath as near to it as possible. It may even be placed under the table on which the vessel is laid. Under these circumstances, the revolution of a wire, allowed to dip into the mercury as before, will take place as soon as it is placed in the voltaic circuit. The effect is the same, whether the magnet be held in a horizontal or vertical position, or inclined at any angle, provided the magnet be of sufficient length, so that the influence of the other pole may not act sensibly upon the wire.

(65.) An apparatus was constructed by Mr. Griffiths, for exhibiting, in like manner, the simultaneous revolution of two conducting wires round the opposite poles of magnets. Two copper wires, suspended so as to move freely, were made to dip into a shallow vessel containing mercury, in which were fixed two bar magnets, with their opposite poles raised above the surface. On making the connexion between the battery and the apparatus, the wires revolved round the magnets simultaneously, but in opposite directions[*].

(66.) The two forms of electro-magnetic rotation which have now been described, were exhibited at the same

Fig. 40.

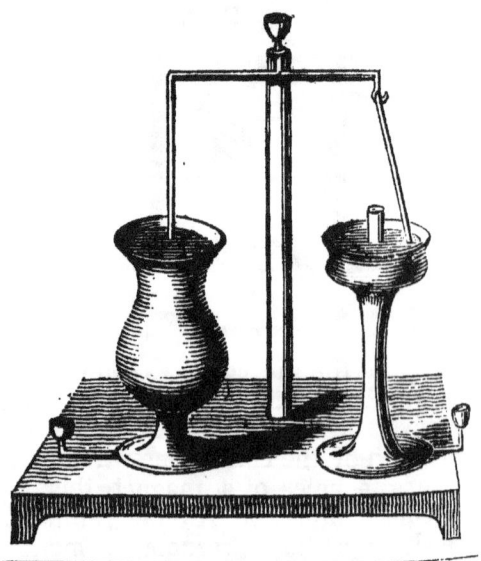

[*] An apparatus of this kind was exhibited by Mr. Barlow, at the London Institution, in 1823, in a course of lectures which he there gave on Electro-magnetism.

time, by an apparatus contrived by Mr. Faraday, in which the cups employed in the two first experiments are both acted upon by the same voltaic battery. This compound apparatus is shown in *fig.* 40. The cups in which the lower wires proceeding from the bottom of each cup respectively terminate, are made to communicate by means of wires with the opposite poles of a battery. The upper wires communicate by a cross wire, supported by an upright pillar fixed in the middle of the stand. The current of electricity, therefore, will ascend through the mercury and wire in one of the cups, and descend in the other, and produce at the same moment a revolving motion of the magnet in the one case, and in the other case, a revolution in the moveable wire. A cup is also placed over the middle of the cross wire for the convenience of sending the electric current in the same direction along both the wires, by making it communicate with one of the poles of the voltaic battery, while the lower cups both communicate with the other pole. The adoption of this arrangement will produce a corresponding change in the direction of one of the rotations.

Fig. 41.

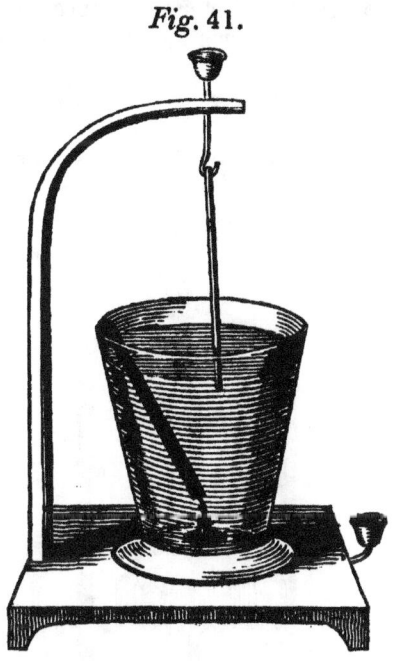

(67.) The two phenomena may even be shown in the same vessel, if, in that containing the moveable magnet, *fig.* 33, the wire which dips into the mercury be rendered moveable, as in *fig.* 38, by a mode of suspension adapted to that purpose. The wire and the magnet will then both revolve in the same direction round a common centre of motion, each appearing to pursue and be pursued by the other round the circumference of the circle described by their revolution. (See *fig.* 41.)

(68.) After the discovery of the revolution of a magnet round a conducting wire, and of the wire round a magnet, many attempts were made to obtain the rotation of a magnet, or of a conductor, round their own axes. Ampère was the first who accomplished the former of these objects, which may be effected by the following method:—The cylindrical magnet seen in the section, *fig.* 42, terminates at its lower extremity in a sharp

Fig. 42.

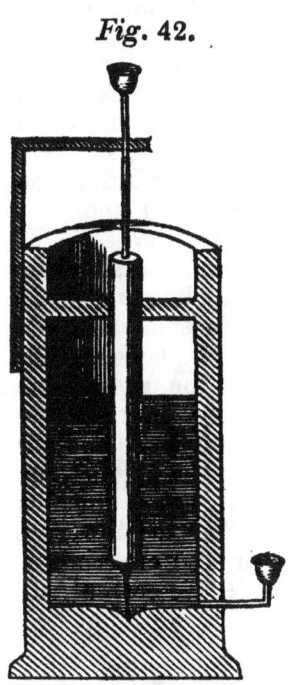

steel point, which rests in the centre of a conical cavity of agate, in the bottom of the vessel, which may be either of glass or wood. The upper end of the magnet is supported in a perpendicular position, by a thin slip of wood, passing across the upper part of the vessel and resting against its sides, having a hole through which the magnet passes freely. A piece of quill is fitted on the upper extremity of the magnet, so as to form a cup or reservoir above it for receiving a small quantity of mercury. Into this mercury is inserted the lower end of a wire which is amalgamated, in order to obtain a perfect metallic contact, while its upper end terminates in a cup holding a globule of mercury, for the purpose of forming a communication with one of the poles of the voltaic battery. The vessel being filled with mercury, so as to cover the lower half of the magnet, the galvanic circuit is completed by means of a thick copper wire proceeding from the bottom of the vessel, coming out through the side, and terminating in another cup holding a small quantity of mercury, by which a communication may be established with the other pole of the battery. As soon as this connexion is effected, the magnet begins to revolve round its axis with great rapidity, the rotation continuing as long as the connexions with the battery are preserved and the battery retains its power.

(69.) In the original experiment of Ampère, the magnet was allowed to float without support in the mercury, being kept in a vertical position by a weight of platina attached to its lower end. But this addition to the whole mass to be moved occasions a great diminution of effect, so that the apparatus above described gives a much greater velocity of motion with the same galvanic power.

(70.) The same phenomenon has been exhibited in various ways; the principle on which it depends is that the electric current should descend through the upper half of the magnet only, so as to act exclusively on the pole which is situated in that half, and afterwards be diverted from the magnet, and made to pass away in such a direction as that it shall not affect the lower pole of the magnet. In the experiment above related, the electric current, after traversing the upper half of the magnet, passes into the mercury, and being diffused through it, acts in no sensible degree on the lower pole of the magnet, and does not interfere with the rotation produced by its influence on the upper pole. There are several circumstances, however, to be taken into account, in explaining this experiment, which cannot now be easily rendered intelligible, and the notice of which must be reserved for a future part of the Treatise.

(71.) The same object is attained in the following manner, by an apparatus represented in *fig.* 43, and in section in *fig.* 44. A magnet, pointed at both ends, is supported below by an agate cup fixed on a stem rising from the bottom of the stand; while its upper point is lightly pressed upon by a screw, with a milled head, passing through a screwed hole at the top of an arched beam, which forms part of the sustaining frame-work of the apparatus. Near the middle of the magnet, this frame supports a stage in the form of a ring, through the centre of which the magnet passes freely, and carrying a circular cistern of mercury, which also surrounds the magnet, without touching it. A similar cistern of mercury surrounds the lower stem, which supports the agate cup. A copper wire, projecting into the interior of each of these cisterns, passes out through its sides, and, being bent upwards, terminates in a small cup, holding a little mercury, for

Fig. 43.

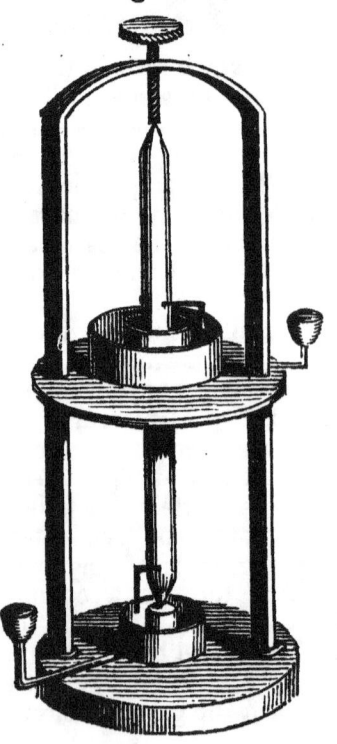

Fig. 44.

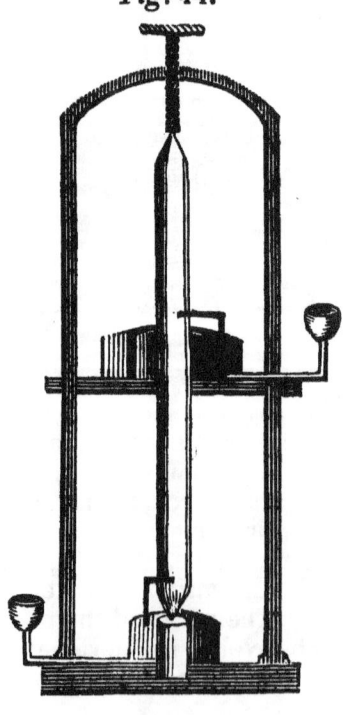

effecting the communication with the voltaic battery by wires, in the usual manner. A small wire, pointed and amalgamated at its end, is affixed to the middle of the magnet, immediately above the cistern, and is bent so as just to dip into the mercury contained in the cistern. A similar wire, proceeding from the lower end of the magnet, is made to dip into the mercury contained in the lower cistern. The lower half only of the magnet being thus made to form part of the galvanic circuit—which is continuous from one cup through the cistern of mercury, the wire belonging to the magnet, the magnet itself, the other wire, the other cistern of mercury, and the wire terminating in the other cup—receives the exclusive influence of the electric current which passes through it, and begins to rotate with considerable velocity round the axis, which is constituted by its upper and lower points of support. The degree of rotatory effect will depend very much on the delicacy of the suspension of the magnet, so that the friction at the points may be as small as possible.

(72.) When the magnet is large, it has been proposed to gain additional rotatory power by directing another electrical current to be supplied from a second battery along the upper half of the magnet, but in a direction contrary to that which passes through the lower pole. This might certainly be effected by removing the milled head of the vertical screw, and supplying its place by a small cup to hold mercury, and by carefully amalgamating the lower end of the screw where it touches the magnet. But since the rotatory force is proportional to the power of the voltaic battery used, it is very doubtful whether the second battery required in this latter method might not be equally efficacious if it were employed in increasing the strength of the first battery, by being joined to it, in the former mode of conducting the experiment.

(73.) Having thus succeeded in making the magnet revolve on its own axis, it next became an object to effect, in like manner, the rotation of a conducting body round its axis. As in the former case it was necessary to apply the electric agency in the interior of the magnet, so in the present instance some means were to be devised for procuring the action of the magnet from the interior of the conducting body: hence it was necessary to discard the wire, and employ in its place a hollow cylinder of metal, capable of receiving the pole of a magnet in its axis. Such an arrangement, which was devised by Mr. Barlow, is exhibited by *fig.* 45, which represents a section of the apparatus. A bar magnet is fixed upright in a solid stand, which has a cavity adapted to receive it, and which also supports a circular trough of mercury, surrounding

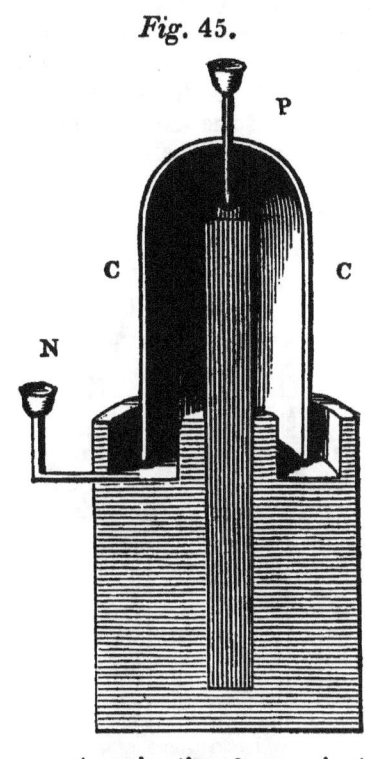

Fig. 45.

the magnet as in the former instances. C C is a light hollow copper cylinder, the lower edge of which dips into the mercury in the trough; and the upper part is supported by an arch of the same metal, from the middle of which there proceeds a steel-pointed wire, passing downwards so as to rest in an agate cup fixed to the top of the magnet, and also passing upwards and terminating in a small cup P, holding a little mercury, for the purpose of effecting a communication with the voltaic battery. A wire proceeds from the inside of the trough, and passing out, is bent upwards, so as to terminate in another cup with mercury N, for establishing the connexion with the other pole of the battery. It is evident that, in this arrangement, the electric current, which we may suppose to descend from the positive wire of the battery introduced into the cup P, being prevented from passing into the magnet by the interposition of the agate cup, can find no other channel than the copper cylinder, down the sides of which it will descend into the mercury in the trough, and thence, passing out by the wire below, will proceed through the cup N, and be received by the wire communicating with the negative end of the battery. The cylinder may therefore be regarded as consisting of a collection of parallel wires, each of which receives from the pole of the magnet placed in the interior an impulse to move in a direction parallel to itself.

Those on opposite sides of the magnet will be urged to move in opposite directions; but as their forces act on opposite sides of the axis of motion, they will all concur in their rotatory effect. The whole cylinder is accordingly found to commence revolving as soon as the

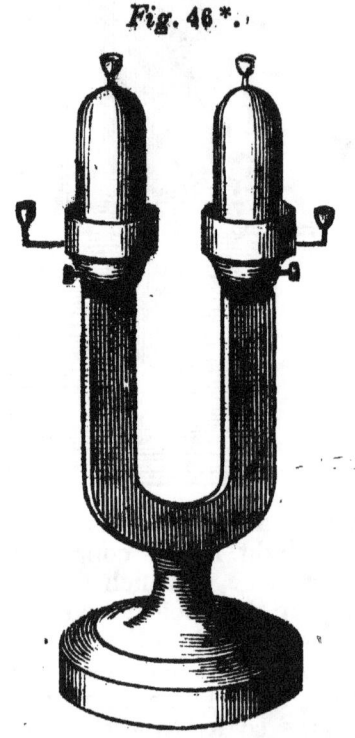

Fig. 46.*

electric current is sent through it; and the resistance it meets with being slight, its velocity soon becomes very considerable. After what has formerly been said, it is scarcely necessary to add, that the course of its motion is from left to right, or the same with that of the hands of a watch, when the electric current is descending along the cylinder, and when the enclosed part of the magnet is its north pole.

(74.) The motion is reversed when either of these conditions is reversed. This may be conveniently exemplified in the two poles of the same magnet by employing a horse-shoe magnet, supported vertically in a stand, as shown in fig. 46. Two wooden circular troughs are fixed upon the arms of the magnet, and secured by binding screws. These troughs contain the mercury into which the lower margins of the hollow cylinders dip. The upper part of each cylinder is formed into a hemispherical cup, which is traversed in the middle by a pointed wire, resting below in a small cavity in the centre of the extremity of the magnet contained within the cylinder, and having at its upper end a small cup to hold mercury. Two other cups, also containing a small quantity of mercury, are supported upon the external ends of bent wires, which pass through the sides of the circular troughs into the mercury contained in them. Thus a continuous metallic communication is established from one cup to the other, on each side, through each cylinder which surrounds the different poles of the magnet. If a stream of electricity from a voltaic battery be made to pass in the same direction in both the cylinders, they will revolve in contrary directions, being acted upon in an opposite manner by the two poles which they surround. But if the two upper cups be united by a short wire dipping its two ends in the mercury they contain, and the lower cups be connected, the one with the positive, and the other with the negative poles of the battery, the same stream will traverse both sides of the apparatus, passing upwards in one cylinder, and downwards in the other; and the rotations thence arising will now, from the contrary influences of the two poles, be in the same direction in both the cylinders.

(75.) The rotation of a conducting body round its own axis, as exhibited in the experiments just related (§ 73), throws considerable light upon the circumstances of the experiment before described, in which a magnet was made to rotate about its axis; for the explanation of that experiment will very much depend upon the course which we suppose taken by the electrical current during its passage through the magnet. If we supposed it to pass through the interior of the magnet, that is along the axis, and parts adjacent to it, it would occasion rotation by its influence on the parts of the magnet that are situated nearer to the surface, and further from the axis. On the other hand, if we suppose the course of the electric current to be nearly superficial, then it will

---

* See Mr. Watkins's Sketch, p. 74.

ELECTRO-MAGNETISM.

itself be influenced by the polarity of those portions of the magnet which lie near the axis, and the rotatory tendency impressed upon it will produce the rotation of the magnet, which will, of course, be carried along with it. On the latter supposition, it will correspond, in all its circumstances, with the experiment § 73, in which the conducting body is urged to rotate by the influence of a magnetic pole situated within it: excepting only, that in the former case the magnet and the conducting body were one and the same, while in the latter they were different and separate. Mr. Faraday has shown, however, that the circumstance of the magnet and conductor being immoveably joined together makes no difference in the results. Thus let the magnet M, represented in section, *fig.* 47, be loaded at its lower end with a platina weight, and fixed at its upper end on a piece of card or wood, having two branches of a strong wire, W W, descending from its upper edge

Fig. 47.

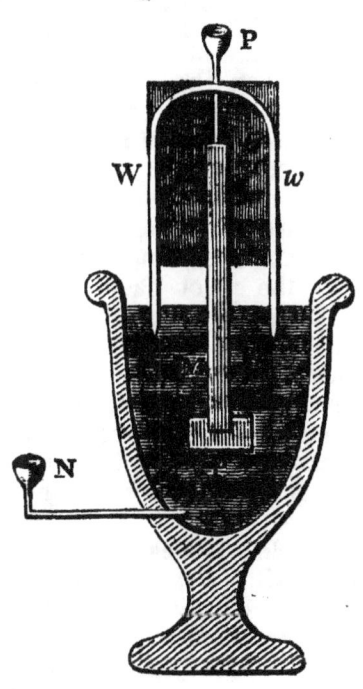

along its two vertical edges, and terminating below in points: so that the whole may float, in a vertical position, in a vessel full of mercury, from the bottom of which a wire proceeds, supporting the cup N; another cup, P, being placed upon the upper edge of the wires W W. The whole moveable part of this apparatus will rotate by the transmission of an electric current through the wires, on making the proper communications with a voltaic battery by means of the two cups containing mercury. This experiment is important, inasmuch as it appears to show that the action is the same, whether the magnet from which it proceeds be in motion or at rest. We shall have occasion, however, in a future part of this treatise, to point out another mode of explanation arising out of a different view of the subject.

(77.) On the other hand, when a hollow cylinder of metal, balanced on a point on the upper end of a vertical axis of wood, and its lower edge dipping into a trough of mercury, is acted upon by one of the poles of a magnet placed on the outside, and brought near it, as shown in the section *fig.* 48, where M is the magnet applied to the cylinder C, balanced in the wooden stand S, the rotatory force is very feeble, compared with that which takes place when the mag-

Fig. 48.

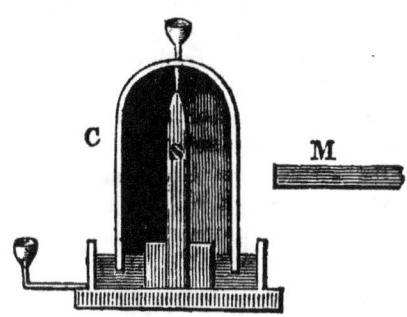

net acts from within the cylinder. The reason is, that the tendencies to motion of those portions of the moveable conductor which are most remote from the magnet, and of those which are nearest to it, are in opposite directions with respect to the centre of motion; and, if the conductor be cylindrical, and the current equally distributed on every side of it, must always exactly counterbalance one another. This will be evident when it is considered that, although these latter portions are, in consequence of their greater proximity to the magnet, acted upon more strongly, this advantage is compensated by the greater extent of the portion on the remote side, which is acted upon more feebly. But this equilibrium will not obtain if, as generally happens, the electric current be unequally distributed. If, for instance, it pass along one side only, the cylinder will revolve when the magnet is brought opposite to it on that side.

(78.) It appears, by the result of the experiment related in § 73, that the electro-magnetic influence of the conductor takes place equally when the current of electricity is diffused over a considerable surface, as when it is concentrated in a slender wire. The effects will, of course, be weaker in proportion as it is diffused; but when the whole of these scattered forces can be brought to bear in the production of any effect, the amount will be the same as when they are concentrated in a smaller space. Thus every filament of which the cylinders in these experiments may be supposed to be resolved, conducts its respective portion of the electric current, and contributes its share in the production of one common effect, namely, the revolution of the cylinder.

In like manner it has been found that the stream of electricity, which is passing through the voltaic battery itself from its negative to its positive pole, exhibits the same electro-magnetic properties that it does while passing along the wire which completes the circuit by connecting the two poles; for a magnetic needle placed in the vicinity of the battery, and in circumstances equally favourable to the action of the current, will be affected in the same way as it is by the wire itself. Now as all action implies a corresponding and equal reaction, it is reasonable to infer that, as the battery produces motion in the magnet, so the magnet might be made to move the battery, if a sufficiently delicate suspension could be contrived for the latter, so as to render its motion sensible. This could scarcely be effected with a compound battery of any size: but by reducing it to a single plate, making it as light as possible, and supporting it on a single point, in the way in which the cylinder was sustained in the last experiment, this object has been accomplished by Ampère.

(79.) The apparatus he employed for this purpose is represented in section, in *fig.* 49. It consists of a double cylinder of copper, C C, about two inches and a half in diameter, and the same in height, closed at the bottom, so as to form a vessel capable of holding diluted acid. The whole is supported by an arched plate of metal, which passes across the upper orifice of the inner cylinder on the upper end of a strong magnet, M, which is introduced through the middle of the cylinder. A cylinder of zinc, Z Z, made as light as possible, and supported by an arched wire, A, having a steel point proceeding downwards from the middle of its curvature, is introduced between the two plates of the double copper cylinder, so that the steel point

Fig. 49.

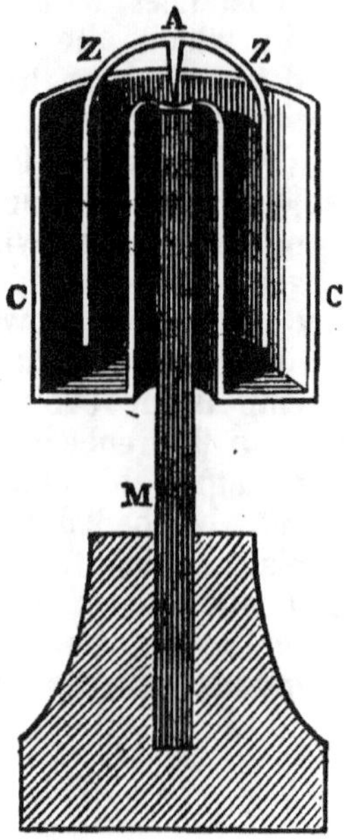

may rest upon the arched plate of the inner cylinder, and remain balanced in this position. On introducing diluted acid into the copper vessel, a galvanic action immediately commences; the electric current passing from the zinc to the acid, and ascending from the copper through the pivot back again to the zinc. Hence the zinc is in the situation of a conductor conveying a stream of electricity downwards, and under the influence of the magnetic pole which it surrounds. It will consequently revolve with an accelerated motion, which is at length rendered uniform by the friction of the fluid.

Mr. Barlow states that he has frequently, with this simple apparatus, produced a velocity of one hundred and twenty revolutions in a minute.

(80.) The theory just explained is prettily illustrated by an addition to the preceding apparatus which was made by Mr. J. Marsh; and which consists in having a second steel point fixed underneath the upper part of the arch which sustains the copper cylinder: the copper vessel may, by means of this point, be itself balanced on the top of the magnet, while the zinc cylindrical plate is balanced on the former; and each may thus turn round its own centre independently of the other. This arrangement

ELECTRO-MAGNETISM.

is represented in the section *fig.* 50. As the electric current ascends in the copper cylinder, while it descends along the zinc, the former will be urged by the magnet in its interior, to revolve in a direction contrary to the motion of the zinc cylinder. The velocity of the copper vessel is, however, much smaller than that of the zinc, not only from its greater weight, and from carrying besides the whole quantity of acid, but also from the friction of its pivot being increased by the weight of the zinc plate which that pivot has to support. In this double revolution, also, the velocity of the zinc plate is further retarded by the increased resistance it meets with from the fluid which is moving in a contrary direction.

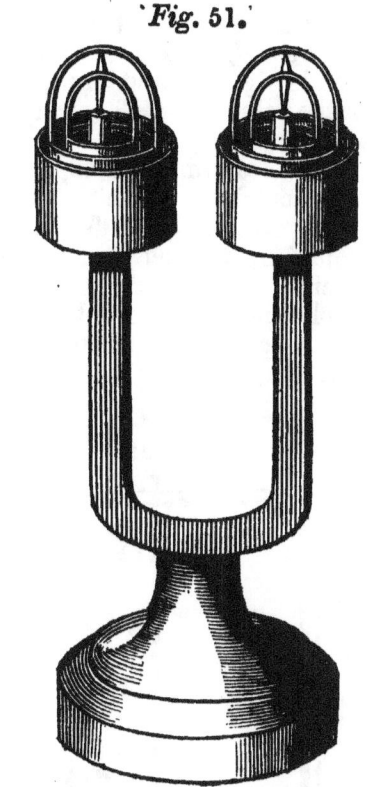

Fig. 50.

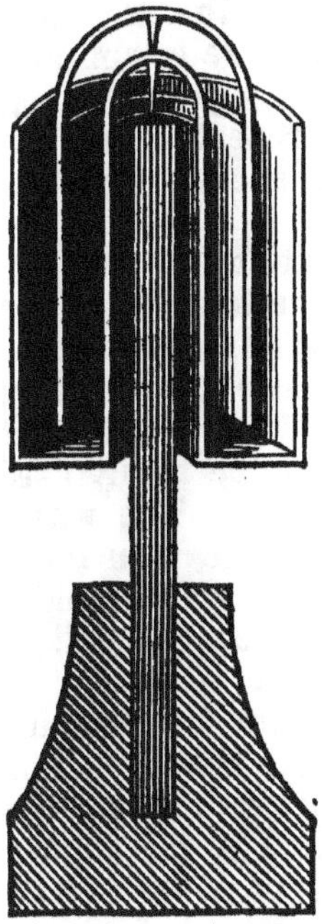

(81.) Mr. Watkins has applied an apparatus of this kind to each of the poles of a horse-shoe magnet, firmly fixed in a metal stand at its bent part, as shewn in *fig.* 51. The upper ends of the magnet are furnished with agate cups for receiving the steel points on which the apparatus is supported. The wire itself traverses the arch affixed to the copper vessel, and terminates in a point at its upper extremity also, so that the arch connected with the zinc plate rests upon it. When the apparatus is brought into action by charging the vessels with acid, the four cylinders are seen to revolve on their axes, the two copper vessels turning in opposite directions, and the two zinc cylinders turning in directions opposite to these, and of course also contrary to each other: the rapidity of their revolutions depending on the power of the magnet, on the strength of the diluted acid, and on the delicacy of their suspension.

(82.) Horse-shoe magnets may also be conveniently employed for combining the effects of both poles in giving motion to a conducting wire. The operation of the two poles being in contrary directions at their opposite sides, they will, on the other hand, conspire in producing the same effect upon a wire placed between them. Thus each of the conducting wires $p\,n$, $p'\,n'$, *figs.* 52, 53, in which the electric current is

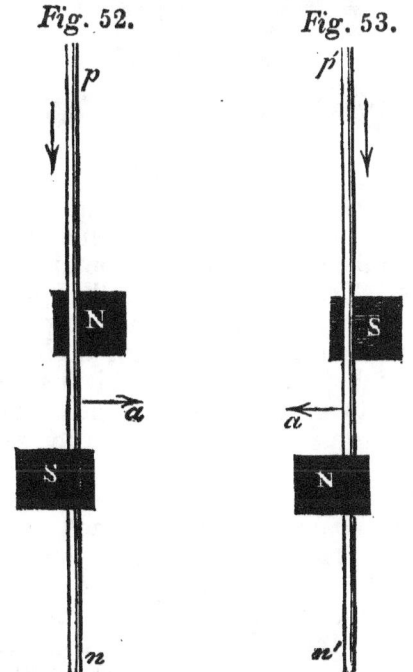

Fig. 51.

Fig. 52.   Fig. 53.

descending from p to s, when placed between the magnetic poles N and S, the former being north, and the latter south, and which, for the sake of illustration, we may conceive to be insulated, will be urged by their united influence to move parallel to itself, in the direction denoted by the arrows *a, a,* in the figures; that is, from right to left, if the north pole be behind, and the south pole before, as in *fig.* 52; and from left to right, if the poles are in a contrary position, as in *fig.* 53.

(83.) Several amusing experiments have been contrived, in which vibratory or rotatory motions of different kinds are obtained by various applications of this principle.

The following is the invention of Mr. Marsh. A conducting platina wire W, *fig.* 54, is suspended by a loop from a

Fig. 54.

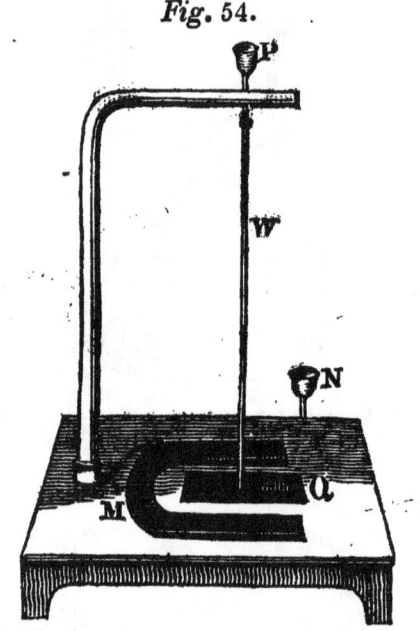

metallic hook at the lower end of another wire, which is fixed to the end of the arm of a stand; and which supports above the small cup P, to contain mercury. The lower end of the platina wire, which thus hangs freely, dips into a small cistern of mercury, Q, formed out of the wooden base, and is just midway between the two poles of a horseshoe magnet, M, laid flat upon the same base.

The mercury in the trough is placed in electrical continuity with another cup, N, by means of a wire passing out from the side, and supporting the cup. On making a communication with the two ends of the voltaic battery by means of these cups, the current passing along the loose platina wire, being influenced by the magnet, urges the wire either forwards towards Q, or backwards towards M, according to the position of the poles, and the direction of the current. In either case it is thrown out of the mercury; and the circuit being thus broken, the effect ceases, until the wire falls back again by its own weight into the mercury; when the current being re-established, the same influence is again exerted, the phenomenon is repeated, and the wire exhibits a quick succession of vibratory motions.

(84.) This reciprocating movement of the wire may be converted into one of rotation, by adapting, as proposed by Mr. Barlow, a spur-wheel, as shewn in *fig.* 55, to the lower part of the upright wire, which must then be firmly fixed to the arm of the pillar. The wheel, being constructed so as to turn round freely, will revolve with great rapidity as soon as the contacts are made with the battery: for this purpose, however, the wheel must dip so far into the mercury, as that each of the rays shall touch the surface before the preceding ray has quitted the mercury. The direction of the motion depends, of course, on the same circumstances as were before mentioned: Mr. Barlow observes, however, that in general the experiment succeeds best when the wheel revolves inwards.

Fig. 55.

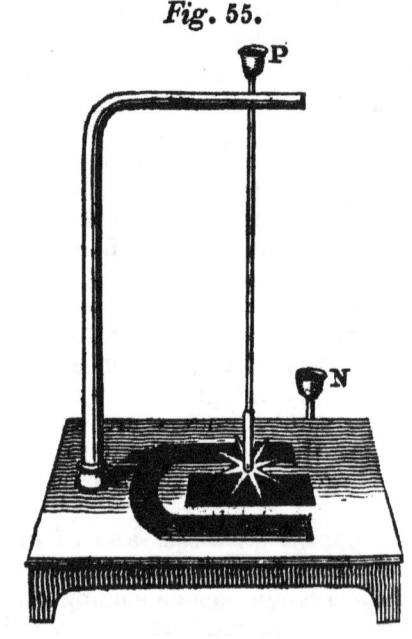

(85.) But it is not necessary to divide the wheel into rays in order to produce the effect above described; for a circular metallic disc substituted for the spur-wheel will revolve equally well, when it is traversed by an electrical current passing into mercury between the poles of a horse-shoe magnet. For this purpose the circumference of the disc should merely touch the mercury in the trough. It is necessary also that it be well amalgamated; this is best done by removing it from its centres, and cleansing the edge thoroughly by a file, and then dipping a piece of wire into nitrate of mercury, and taking up with it a portion of the mercury contained in the nitrate, transferring it to the edge of the disc, by rubbing the wire, coated with mercury, round it. This substitution of a continuous for a divided disc was suggested by Mr. Sturgeon.

(86.) The same current may be employed to turn two wheels with radii, by disposing them in the manner shewn in fig. 56, at the extremities of a horizontal wire which is supported on two pillars arising from the stand, and which serve as the common axis of the wheels.

Fig. 56*.

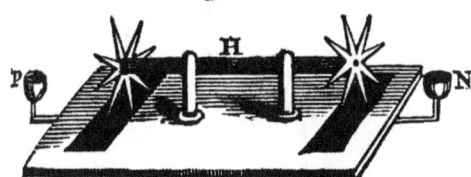

The lower ends of the rays dip into troughs of mercury, each lying between the poles of horse-shoe magnets. Each trough has its respective wire and cup P and N for making communications with the voltaic battery. The current passing from the one cup to the mercury in the trough on the same side, rises along the radius, which dips into it, and passing along the axis, arrives at the other wheel; then descending along its radius into the mercury, it makes its exit by the cup on that side. The electric currents, moving in opposite directions in the two wheels, require a contrary disposition of the poles of the two magnets by which they are to be acted upon: that is, the poles of the two magnets that are within the wheels must both be of the same kind; as must also be those that are exterior to them. The velocity of the wheels thus revolving by the united action of both magnets is very great.

(86.) The experiments on electro-magnetic rotation we have described, do not require for their successful performance a voltaic battery of any considerable size or power. If the magnets be sufficiently energetic, nothing more will be required than a single pair of plates. The most convenient form of a battery of this kind, is that described by Mr. Watkins, and which is represented in fig. 57.

It consists of a double cylindrical vessel made of thin copper, with a bottom of the same metal. A plate of zinc rolled into a cylinder, of a diameter intermediate between those of the copper cylinder, is introduced between them, but prevented from touching them in any part, by three wooden feet placed at the bottom of the vessel, and also by pieces of wood interposed as wedges between the sides.

A copper wire is soldered to the inside of the top of the outer copper cylinder, and

Fig. 57.

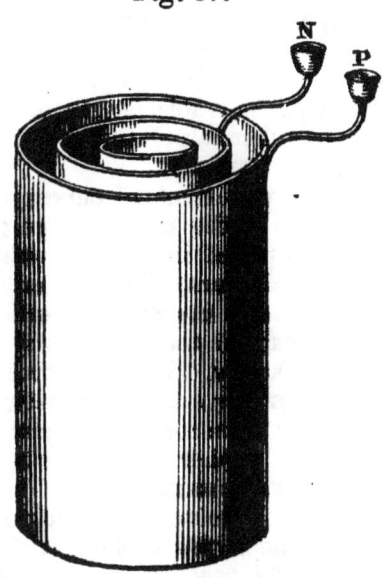

has a small cup P, fixed at its extremity; the wire passing through the bottom of the cup in order to come in contact with the mercury placed in it. Another and similar wire N, is also affixed to the upper edge of the zinc cylinder, likewise terminating in a cup which holds mercury. The battery is charged by filling the copper vessel with diluted acid; and the electric current, which is the effect of the voltaic action thence arising, may be easily transmitted to the apparatus where it is wanted, by means of two bent copper conducting wires, one end of the one being inserted into the mercury contained in the cup proceeding from the zinc cylinder, and the other in the cup fixed to the copper cylinder; while the other ends are immersed in the mercury placed in the cups attached to the apparatus. The current may be arrested or renewed at

---

* The engraver has forgotten to insert the horse-shoe magnets in this wood-cut. They should have been placed as the one in fig. 55.

any moment, by removing one end of either connecting wire from its cup, or by replacing it. The direction of the current may also be readily changed, by merely exchanging the situation of the wires in two of the cups. The extremities of the connecting wires should be made perfectly bright, and the ends of the wire arms which support the cups and enter the mercury in them, ought also to be in a similar state, so that a perfect metallic contact may be preserved.

(87.) In making electro-magnetic experiments, where numerous repetitions of contacts between wires are often required, it is extremely useful, if these wires are of copper, to rub the ends over with a little nitrate of mercury; an amalgam is thus formed on the surface of the copper, which does not oxidate or become dirty, as copper itself does, but remains bright, and fit for voltaic contact for a considerable length of time. For this useful manipulation we are indebted to Mr. Faraday.

(88.) The movement of currents by the influence of the pole of a magnet may be exemplified in fluid as well as in solid conductors. Thus mercury, while conducting a current of electricity, is made to exhibit these motions with the greatest facility. By immersing the points of the positive and negative wires into a shallow basin containing mercury, a magnet held either above or below the line of communication will cause the mercury to revolve round the points from which the currents diverge. This motion may be rendered more evident by covering the mercury with a very dilute acid solution, which occasions the disengagement of bubbles of air which are moved along with the mercury. The same phenomenon may also be exhibited in the following manner. If the positive wire terminate in a steel point which is dipped into mercury contained in a shallow basin, so as to convey into it an electric current, which, passing in radiating lines through the mercury, is received by a copper ring surrounding the steel point, and so transferred to the negative pole,—by placing the pole of a strong magnet underneath the basin immediately below the steel-pointed wire, the mercury will be seen to revolve rapidly in a vortex round the point from which the currents diverge. The revolution is in the contrary direction, if either the direction of the current be reversed, or the opposite pole of the magnet be applied.

(89.) Sir Humphry Davy found that the arched stream of electrical light which extends between two points of charcoal that are placed in the voltaic circuit, as described in the Treatise on GALVANISM, § 27, is thrown into a rapid rotatory motion by the action of the pole of a magnet placed near it *.

CHAPTER VII.
Concentration of Effects.

(90.) We have already seen, § 82, that when a conducting wire is placed between the contrary poles of a magnet, it receives a similar influence from these poles, and is urged to move in one particular direction by the united force of both. A similar combination of powers will occur when the pole of a magnet is placed between two parallel conducting wires, in which the electric currents are moving in opposite directions. Thus, if the needle N S, *fig*. 58, balanced as a

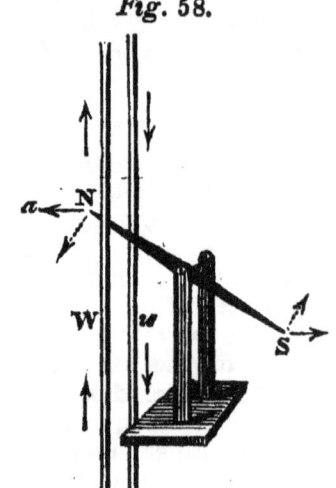

Fig. 58.

dipping needle, be placed between the two wires W, *w*, in the former of which the current is ascending, and in the latter descending, the north pole of the needle will be urged in the same direction, denoted by the arrow *a*, by both the wires, in a plane parallel to the wires, and at right angles to the plane in which they are both situated. The south pole will also be urged in the contrary direction by both wires; and the needle will, by the combination of these forces, have a strong tendency to turn upon its centre.

(91.) If the wires be joined together at either end, or, what comes to the same thing, if a continuous wire be bent back upon itself, an electric current

---
* Philosophical Transactions for 1821, p. 427.

sent through such a wire will affect a needle placed between its two branches with twice the force that a single wire would have exerted. This effect may be exhibited by the following simple apparatus, represented in *fig.* 59; where the two cups terminating the bent wire W A *w* B which passes above and be-

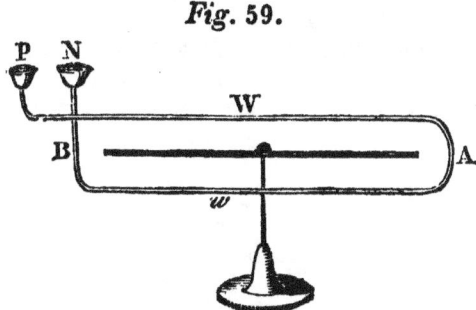

Fig. 59.

low a magnetic needle balanced on a point, enable us to transmit through it an electric current in any direction we please. This current, moving in opposite directions in the upper and lower horizontal portions of the wire, will conspire, in both cases, to deflect it from its natural position in the same direction, and to bring it into a position nearer to a right angle to the plane of the wires.

(92.) The force with which each pole is impelled in a line at right angles to the plane in which the wires are situated, is directly as the intensity of the current, (supposing it to be equal in both wires,) and directly as the length of the interval between the wires, and also inversely as the square of the distance of the pole from the wires. This will appear from the following considerations. Let A and B represent the sections of two wires passing perpendicularly through the plane of the figure, C being

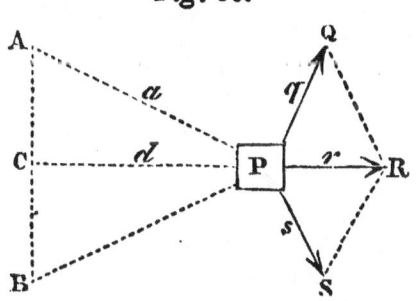

Fig. 60.

the middle point of the line A B, which constitutes the interval between them. Let the magnetic pole P be placed at various distances along the line C R, perpendicular to A B, and consequently perpendicular to the vertical plane which passes through A B, and comprehends the two wires. Supposing the wires to be of indefinite length; the law of action is such, that the intensity of the tangential force exerted on the pole P by the wire A, is inversely as the distance A P, which we shall call *a*, and is in the direction P Q, perpendicular to A P. In like manner, the wire B exerts upon the pole P, a force in the direction of P S, and which, on the supposition of an equal intensity in the two currents, is equal to the former force. If these two forces be represented by the lines P Q and P S, which we shall call *q* and *s*, the resultant force will be represented by the diagonal P R of the parallelogram, having P Q and P S for its sides. Calling PR, *r*, and AB, *i*, we have this proportion,

$$a : i :: q : r,$$

that is, $r = \dfrac{iq}{a};$

but, in different positions of P along the line C R, *q* will vary inversely as *a*; and therefore *r* will be as $\dfrac{i}{a^2}$; that is, the force by which the pole P is urged in the direction of the line C R, by the conjoined action of the two wires A and B, varies, in different situations in that line, inversely as the square of its distance from either of the wires, and directly as the length of the interval between the wires.

(93.) In order to estimate the rotatory force exerted on a needle constrained to move round a fixed axis in a plane perpendicular to that of the wires, as in the examples above given, §§ 90, 91; it will be necessary to resolve the force above found into one acting in the direction of the tangent to the circumference of rotation; that is, to reduce it in the proportion of radius to the cosine of the angle which the needle forms with the plane of the wires.

(94.) In the situation of the magnet represented in *fig.* 59, where the wires, instead of extending indefinitely in the horizontal direction, enclose the magnet also on the sides, the influence of the lateral portions A and B require to be taken into account in estimating the effect produced. A little consideration will satisfy us that the action of these parts concur with those of the horizontal portions in giving the same directive tendency to the needle; and that, in fact, if we suppose the wire to be bent

D

into a circular form, as shewn in *fig.* 61, the magnetic pole P, placed in the centre

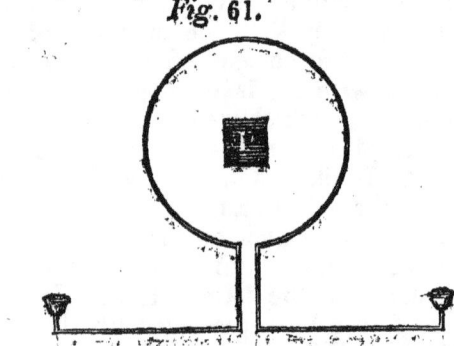

Fig. 61.

of the circle, or in a line passing through that centre, and at right angles to its plane, would be impelled in one uniform direction by an electric current transmitted through the wire, in every part of its course along that circular bend.

(95.) Supposing it were possible for the current to move in a perfect circle, its direction being that indicated by the arrows in figures 62 and 63, the north pole of a magnet placed in its centre would move to the right, and the south

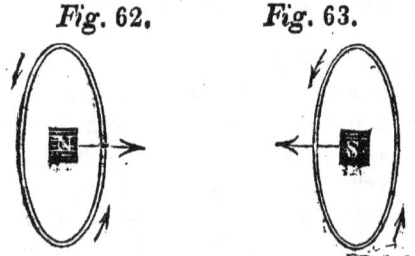

Fig. 62.   *Fig.* 63.

pole to the left; as shewn by the arrows at N and S. If the north pole of a magnet, therefore, were presented to the right hand side of this circular current, it would tend to move away from it, having the appearance of being repelled: and since a similar and reciprocal action takes place between the magnetic pole and the electric current, the latter, together with the wire which conveys it, will, if at liberty to move, recede from the magnet, or appear to be repelled by it. Just the contrary would happen if the south pole of a magnet were presented on the same side; that is, there would be the appearance of a mutual attraction between them. But when either of these poles is presented on the other side of the plane of the circular current, effects of an opposite kind are produced: the north pole appears to attract, and the south pole to repel. If the north pole, which thus appears to attract on one side, be brought nearer and nearer to the plane of the circle, the apparent attraction goes on increasing, till it reaches that plane; but the moment it passes through it and comes on the other side, a repulsion equally strong with the former attraction commences, gradually diminishing as the distance from the plane increases.

(96.) This hypothetical case may in some measure be realized in a very ingenious apparatus invented by M. De la Rive *, and which is shown in *fig.* 64. It consists of a small galvanic battery, formed by a pair of zinc and copper plates, Z and C, attached to a cork of

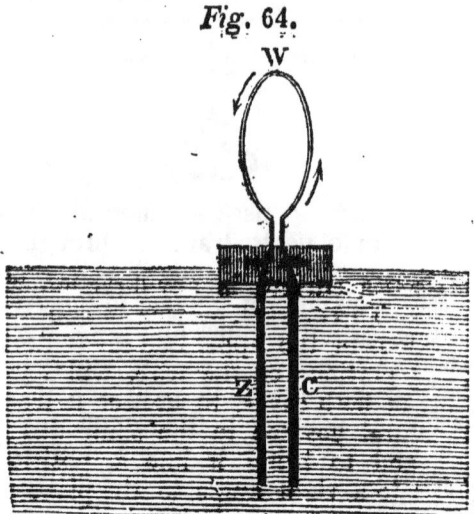

Fig. 64.

sufficient size to enable the whole apparatus to float on the acidulated water which is to act upon the zinc. Each of the metallic plates is about half an inch wide, and extends nearly two inches below the cork, through which its upper end is made to pass. A piece of copper wire, W, covered with silk thread, is affixed to the copper plate, and passing upwards through the cork, is bent into the form of a circle of about an inch in diameter, so that the other end returns into the cork and may be soldered to the plate of zinc. In the galvanic circuit which is thus formed by the acid and the plates of zinc and copper connected by the wire, an electric current is determined from the copper plate, along the circular wire, to the zinc plate, as shown by the arrows; and the mobility of the floating apparatus affords the best opportunity of exhibiting all the effects of the attractive and repulsive tendencies we have just been describing, when a magnet is brought near it on either side. It is proper to remark that the instrument is rendered more powerful by causing the wire to

* This apparatus is described in the Bibliothèque Universel, vol. xvi. p. 201; and in the Quarterly Journal of Science, vol. xii. p. 184.

make five or six turns in the circle, and then tying the coils together so as to form a ring, which being thus composed of a number of concentric circles, the action of each is combined, and the power as it were multiplied by the number of turns.

(97.) This difference in the effects which the two sides of the plane of the ring in this instrument have on the same pole of a magnet, presents a very striking phenomenon, and exhibits a strong analogy with the magnet itself. We may in fact consider it as a flat magnet, having its two poles in the centre of it, two surfaces, the one on one side, and the other on the other: so that if, on looking at one of these surfaces, the current is moving in the same direction as the hands of a watch move when we face the dial, then the side on which we are looking may be regarded as having the properties of the *south pole;* and the other side that of the *north pole.* The former attracts and is attracted by the north pole of a magnet; the latter attracts and is attracted by the south pole, and *vice versâ.*

(98.) A very curious phenomenon is seen when a magnet is presented horizontally to the vertical electro-magnetic ring of M. De la Rive; supposing the magnet to be sufficiently slender to pass easily through the ring. If the pole be presented to it on the side where attraction takes place, the ring will move towards it, till it arrives at the pole, and then proceeds onwards in the same course, the magnet being held in the axis of the ring, till it reaches the middle of the magnet; but there it seems inclined to stop; and then, after a few oscillations, it settles, as in a position of equilibrium: for if purposely displaced by bringing it forwards towards the other pole, it returns with a force which shows that it is repelled from that other pole. Let us now withdraw the magnet, and turning it half round, so that its poles are in directions the reverse of what they were at first, and holding the ring in one hand, let us again introduce the magnet into it with the other hand, until it is half-way through. Under these circumstances it is just possible that we may have brought it into such a situation as that the ring may again be in equilibrium, undetermined in what direction to move; but the slightest change in this position causes it to move with an accelerated velocity towards that pole which is nearest to it; and getting entirely clear of the magnet, it is projected to a considerable distance from it. At length, however, it stops, and, gradually turning round, presents the opposite face to the magnet; attraction now takes place, and the ring returns to the magnet with a force equal to that with which it had before fled from it; and passing again over its pole, finally rests in its position of equilibrium, encircling the middle, or what may be termed the equator of the magnet. In the former position it was equally attracted by the two poles of the magnet; in the latter it is equally repelled: and accordingly the first was an unstable, and the last a stable equilibrium. The ring is represented in this last situation in *fig.* 65, surrounding the middle of the magnet, S, N.

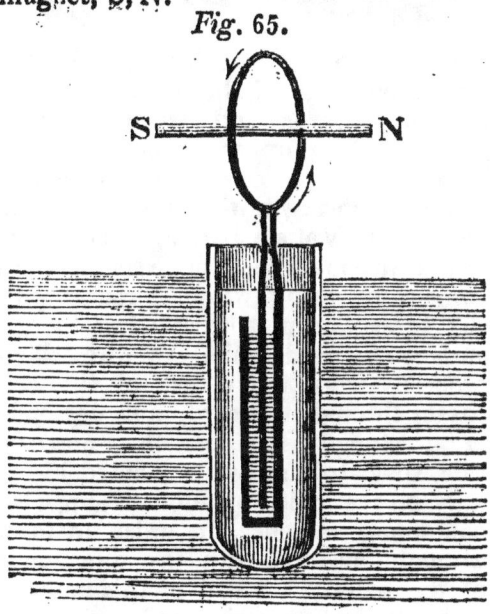

Fig. 65.

(99.) M. De la Rive's apparatus may be constructed so as not to require the liquid in which it floats to consist of the acid; for if the copper plates be double, and pass round the zinc plate, so as to form a cell capable of holding the acid and the zinc plate, the whole combination may be enclosed in a glass cylinder, which will enable it to float in water. Both the surfaces of the zinc are thus opposed to a surface of copper, as in the construction proposed by Dr. Wollaston. (See Galvanism, § 18.) This addition was first suggested by Mr. Marsh, and is represented in the preceding figure (65). The tube for this purpose may be made out of the neck of a Florence flask.

(100.) The magnetic properties of circular conductors may be exhibited in a striking manner by bending the wire

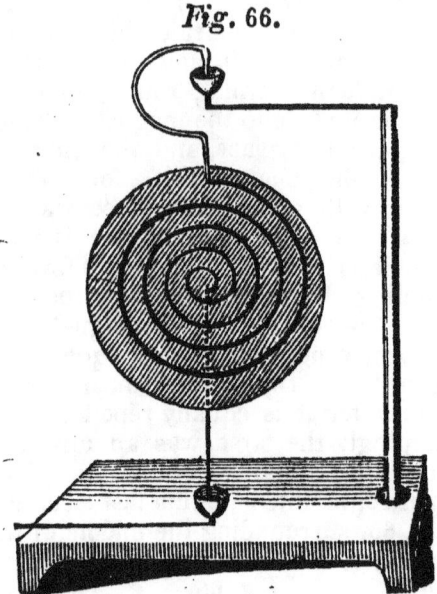

Fig. 66.

into the form of a spiral, see *fig*. 66. The upper end of the wire should be bent downwards and terminate in a point, for the purpose of being inserted in a cup containing mercury, which communicates by a wire with one of the poles of the Voltaic battery. The coils of the wire may be either secured from contact by being wrapped round with silk thread, or may be attached to one surface of a card, while the wire which proceeds from the centre of the coil passes through the card, and descends in a straight line on the opposite side, so as to rest by its pointed extremity on the inside of another cup, also containing mercury, in order to form a communication with the other pole of the battery. A coil of this description, all the successive coils of which conspire together in producing the opposite polarities on its two sides, imitates still more decidedly the effects of a magnet, whose poles might be supposed to be situated in the centre of each disc.

(101.) A still closer imitation of a magnet is obtained by making the turns of the wire not in the same plane, as in the spiral just described, but on a cylindrical surface, like the turns of a corkscrew; a figure which mathematicians have termed a *helix*: an arrangement which possesses many remarkable properties, both as regards its interior and its exterior action.

In *fig*. 67, the several turns of the helix are represented as separated to a distance from each other, in order that the direction of the turns, and the position of a magnet placed in the axis may be distinctly seen. The electro-magnetic influence exerted by each turn is, as we have seen, to urge the north

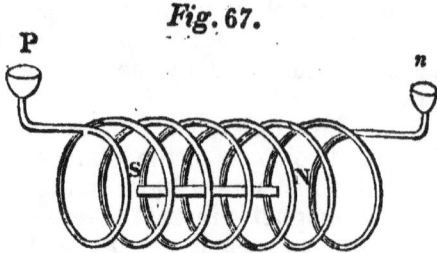

Fig. 67.

pole of a magnet placed in its axis, to move in one direction along that axis, and the south pole in the contrary direction. The force thus exerted is, of course, multiplied in degree and increased in extent, by each repetition of the turns of the wire; and a magnetic needle in every part of the interior of the helix will have a powerful tendency to place itself in the axis, and to turn its poles in a manner conformable to the nature of the force that is in operation.

(102.) Now this force depends on two circumstances: first, the direction of the current with reference to the axis of the helix; and, secondly, the direction of the circumvolutions which compose it. It is well known that screws are of two kinds, distinguished as right-handed or left-handed screws. In the former, as shown in *fig*. 68, the turns proceed

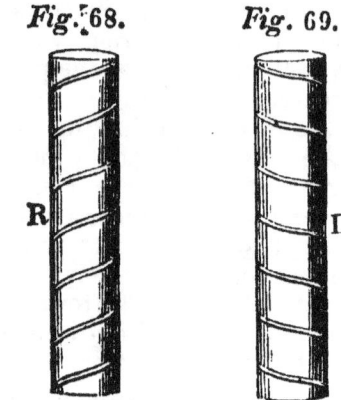

Fig. 68.   Fig. 69.

downwards, (if the screw be placed with its axis vertical) from right to left, on that side which is next to the spectator. In the left-handed screw (see *fig*. 69), the turns proceed in the contrary direction. Now the magnetic polarity of the electric helix, which is exerted in the space it encircles, depends on the direction in which the current is moving with reference to a plane at right angles to the axis; for if the current be descending on the side next to the spectator, (in the horizontal helix, *fig*. 67,) the north pole of a magnet in the axis will be determined to the right, and the south pole to the left; and this tendency will be given in the right-handed helix if the current be transmitted through it from left to right; but in the left-handed helix from right to left. It requires but a slight effort of attention to these particulars to perceive the influence they have on the phenomena; yet unless this effort be made mistakes may easily be committed.

(103.) When the needle lies exactly in the middle of the axis of the helix, the opposite forces which impel the two poles in contrary directions, derived from each coil of the wire, exactly balance one another, and the needle remains in equilibrium. When disturbed from this position, by being pushed nearer to one end, the forces derived from the turns of the wire collectively act with more power upon that pole which is nearest to the middle point of the axis, both because they are nearer, and because they act less obliquely. These forces will, therefore, prevail over those that urge the more distant pole in the contrary direction; and the magnet will be brought back to its former position in the middle of the axis. This is illustrated in *fig.* 70, which represents a section of the helix; S N being the

Fig. 70.

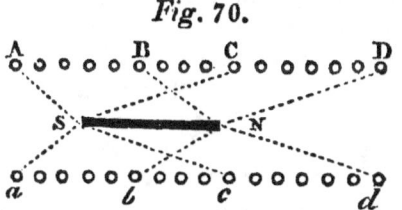

position of the magnet, a little to one side of the middle point of the axis. It will be evident that, in as far as the pole S is acted upon by forces derived from the turns of the wire situated between A *a* and C *c*, its tendency to move outwards is exactly balanced by the forces arising from the action of the wires between B *b* and D *d* upon the pole N, urging it in the contrary direction; because these wires have exactly the same relative situations to these respective poles. But the pole N is besides acted upon by all the wires that are situated between B *b*, and the end A *a*, and the pole S by all those situated between C *c* and D *d*. These two actions are in opposite directions; but the former is more powerful than the latter; first, because the wires between A *a* and B *b* are nearer to N, than those between C *c* and D *d* are to S; and secondly, because they act with less obliquity: they will therefore impel the whole magnet towards the middle of the axis.

(104.) So powerful is the action of a helix of this description, that if a small magnetized needle, or bar, be placed within it, so as to rest upon the lower portions of the wire, the moment the connexion is made with the Voltaic battery, so that the electric current circulates through the wires, the needle is seen to start up, and place itself in the axis, remaining suspended in the air in opposition to the force of gravity. This will even take place in a vertical position of the helix, presenting the singular spectacle of a heavy body raised by an invisible power, and maintained, like the fabled statue of Theamides, in a situation totally free from any material connexion and support.

(105.) The magnetic actions of a helix at its two extremities, and at some distance beyond them, agree with those of the sides of a single circle, or spiral coil already explained; one end having properties similar to the north, and the other to the south pole of a magnet. But the imitation may be rendered still more complete if the two portions of the wire which has formed the helix, and are situated at its two extremities, be bent back as shown in *fig.* 71, at N, S, so as to return in a straight course along the axis till they arrive at the middle point, where they are again bent at right angles, in order to pass out between the coils, rising parallel to one

Fig. 71.

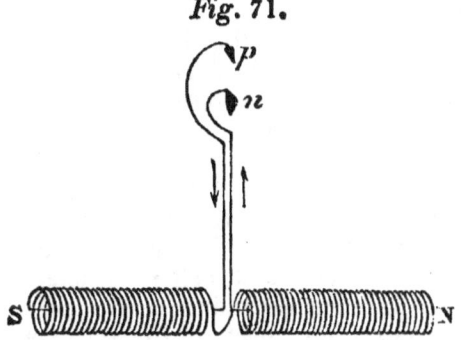

another, and terminating in points for the purpose of suspension in cups, as already described in the case of the spiral wire. Sometimes one of these wires, instead of being bent upwards, is made to descend vertically, and terminate in a sharp point below, where it is inserted into a cup.

(106.) What constitutes the peculiar excellence of this arrangement—which has been termed by Ampère an *electro-dynamic cylinder*, with a view to its assimilation with the condition of a magnetic cylinder—is this; that whatever magnetic action the turns of the heliacal part of the wire may have in a longitudinal direction, (that is parallel to the axis,) is counterbalanced by the contrary action of the returning wire. For the direction of each of the heliacal portions of the wire, that of W w, for instance, *fig.* 72, being necessarily somewhat oblique, and the magnetic force it exerts being along M m, at right angles

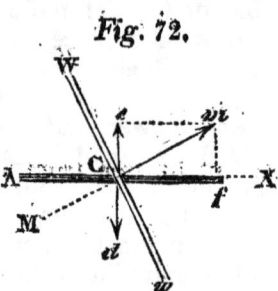

Fig. 72.

to that direction, the whole of the force is not exerted in the direction of the axis A X, but only that part of it represented by C f, while another part, C e, is directed at right angles to the axis. But that portion of the straight wire which passes along the axis, and corresponds in its length to the interval between the two adjoining spiral turns, exerts a force C d, precisely equal, and in an opposite direction to C e. These two forces, therefore, exactly destroy one another; and there remains only the force C f, in the direction of the axis.

(107.) Experiment has fully confirmed the accuracy of this theoretical deduction: and the heliacal arrangement just described is found to be a tolerably exact representation of what may be conceived to be a simple or elementary magnetical filament; for it has opposite poles at the two ends, the one being north, the other south. It obeys the action of magnets that may be presented to it, being attracted and repelled, and assuming determinate positions with respect to the poles of the magnet, just as if it were itself a magnet, of which, indeed, it appears to possess all the essential properties, and for which it may be substituted in almost every form of experiment. It is hardly necessary to observe that the polarity of these *Voltaic magnets*, as we may call them, is entirely of a conditional nature, dependant on the passage of the electric current through them, ceasing the instant that current is arrested, and capable of being suddenly reversed by changing the direction of that current.

(108.) In order to facilitate the comparison of the properties of Voltaic magnets with those of ordinary magnets, it will be found convenient to adapt them to the simple floating galvanic apparatus devised by M. de la Rive. Such is the one represented in *fig.* 73.

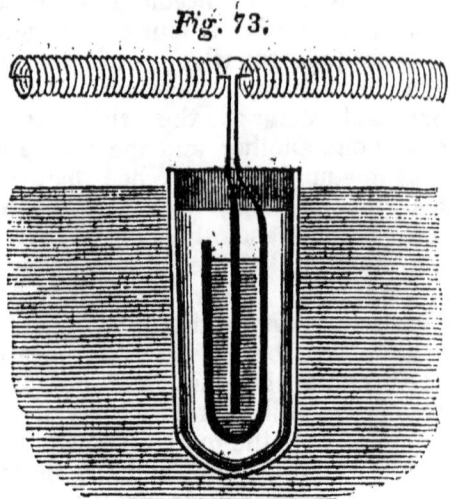

Fig. 73.

Both the ends of the wires are here made to descend through the cork, the one being soldered to the zinc, and the other to the copper plates; and the whole being enclosed in a glass cylinder adapted for floating it in water.

(109.) A very simple apparatus acting on the same principle, is that of Professor Vanden Boss, represented in *fig.* 74. It consists of a plate of copper about an inch square, and a similar plate of zinc, placed parallel to the former, their contact being prevented by a small piece of cork interposed between them. To the upper part of one of these plates a slender brass wire is at-

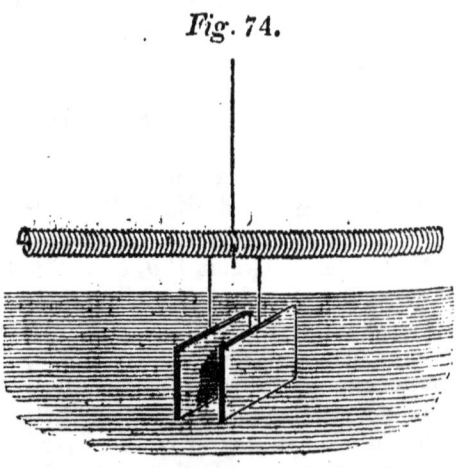

Fig. 74.

tached, which ascends, and is inserted into an opening made in the side of a long quill, or a tube formed of portions of quills inserted successively into each other, and about six or seven inches long. The wire, passing along the interior of the quills, comes out at the end, and being then wound round the outside of the tube in a helix, along its whole length, is made again to enter the quill at the other end; and proceeding back along the axis, is brought out near the middle, and made to descend till it meets the other plate, to which it is soldered. The whole apparatus is suspended at its centre of gravity by a piece of untwisted silk-thread. The plates being dipped into dilute acid, while thus supported, the galvanic action excited in them is sufficient to render the helix magnetical.

Heliacal Rotations.

(110.) An ingenious mode of exemplifying the rotatory action of a magnet on a conducting wire, when coiled into a helix, was contrived by Mr. Watkins, and described in his Popular Sketch of Electro-Magnetism*. The apparatus, represented in *fig.* 75, consists of a horse-shoe magnet, firmly secured to a wooden stand. Each of the poles of the magnet

Fig. 75.

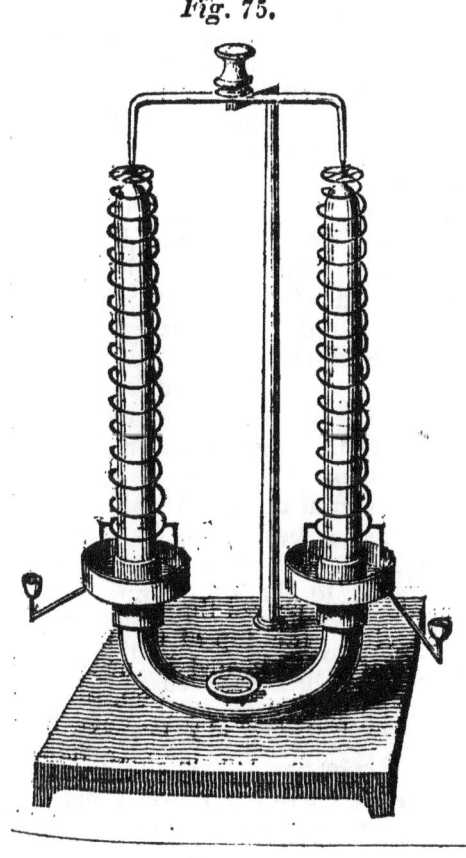

* P. 78.

is encircled by a heliacal coil of copper wire, having a slender bar across its top, with a needle point in its centre, turning in a conical hole drilled in the end of the magnet, with a small platina cup above it, in order to hold a globule of mercury. The lower end of each of these coils terminates in slender, pointed wires, which are soldered to them, and which are intended to dip into mercury contained in a wooden cistern below it, fixed by screws to the leg of the magnet. A wire also proceeds from the lower part of each cistern, and, being bent upwards, terminates in a small cup, also capable of holding mercury. A brass standard rises from the basis of the apparatus, having a forked piece attached to its upper end, with two points descending into the two platina cups upon the tops of the coils; and there is also another cup placed at the top of the forked piece, holding mercury. The voltaic circuit may thus be completed in various ways; either by placing wires in the mercury contained in the small side cups, and connected with one pole of the battery, while other wires, communicating with the other pole, are placed in the cup on the top of the apparatus; or else, directing one and the same stream of electricity through the whole of the apparatus, by joining one of the side cups with the positive, and the other with the negative side of the battery. In the former case, the current, passing in the same direction, whether upwards or downwards, in the two coils, and being acted upon by the different poles of the magnet, will be urged to revolve in opposite directions: in the latter case, the contrary directions of the currents in both wires, ascending in the one, and descending in the other, being respectively acted upon in opposite modes by the contrary poles of the magnet, the combination of these two contrarieties will produce rotations in the same direction in both the wires.

Chapter VIII.
Galvanometers.

(111.) The action of a circular or spiral coil has been applied to the construction of an instrument for detecting small quantities of galvanic electricity, or *Galvanoscope*; and also of a *Galvanometer*, or instrument for measuring the intensity of any galvanic current. For this purpose, the diameter of the circle must exceed the length of the needle which it surrounds, in order to allow the latter to place itself in the plane of the circle which is to act upon it. Thus, if the needle *n s*, *fig.* 76, be placed in the same plane with the wire W *w*, proceeding from the two cups, P, N, and bent in a circular

Fig. 76.

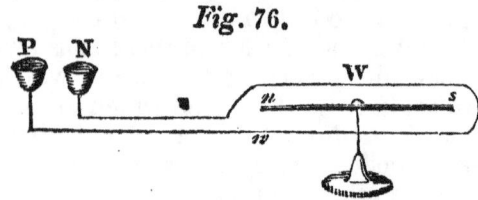

or oval form, so as to enclose it, the influence of every part of the wire when it so surrounds the needle, will be to turn both its poles in the same rotatory direction, until it takes a position at right angles to the plane of the figure. Let this plane be directed to the magnetic north and south—that is, coincide with the direction which the needle naturally assumes by the influence of the earth when left to itself, and undisturbed by the action of any electric influence; and let a feeble current of electricity be now sent through the wires: the effect of this current will be to occasion such a deviation of the needle from the plane of the magnetic meridian as will balance the force which the magnetism of the earth exerts in bringing it towards that plane. In proportion as the needle recedes from the meridian, the terrestrial force increases in intensity, while, at the same time, the electromagnetic force diminishes; the number of degrees at which it stops, and which mark where the equilibrium between these two forces takes place, will therefore indicate, with tolerable precision, the intensity of the galvanic current circulating through the wires.

(112.) The effect of a single turn, or coil of the wire may be increased by multiplying the coils; for in this way the same current is made to act repeatedly, in its course through the convolutions of the wire, upon the poles of the same needle. It is true that the electromagnetic force of the current is somewhat weakened by such an extension of the line of its course; but its diminution from this cause will scarcely be sensible, if the total length of the wire be not very considerable in comparison with the whole circuit of the current including the voltaic battery. In order to prevent the electric current from taking a shorter course than the one intended, it is necessary to secure the adjacent portions of the wires from coming in mutual contact; for such contact would allow of the direct passage of the current from the one to the other. For this purpose the wire must either be wrapped round with silk thread, or coated with sealing wax, throughout the whole length of the coil.

(113.) A galvanometer, constructed on this principle, was invented by Professor Schweigger, of Halle, very soon after the first discovery of Electro-Magnetism, and was called by him an *Electro-Magnetic Multiplier*. Various forms have been given to this instrument, either with a view to increase its sensibility, or to adapt it to different modes of application under particular circumstances.

(114.) One of the simplest forms of the instrument is that represented in *fig.* 77, in which a common compass-needle is suspended on a pivot proceeding from a wooden stand, and enclosed by a

Fig. 77.

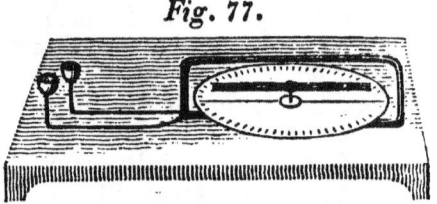

great number of turns of wire, bent into the shape of a vertical parallelogram, and the two ends of which terminate, as usual, in small metallic cups, containing mercury, for the purpose of establishing connexions with any galvanic combination of which we are desirous to ascertain and measure the electrical state. A graduated circle, having a dark line across it, coinciding with the plane of the wires, is to be fixed to the pivot, immediately under the needle, in order to estimate its deviations in either direction from that plane.

(115.) Greater mobility may be given to the needle by the more delicate mode of suspension employed in the balance of torsion. With this view, it may be suspended at its centre by a fine thread, or, what is best of all, by a single filament of silk, enclosed in a tube, and attached to the lower end of a short metallic wire, passed through the cover which closes the top of the tube, and capable of being turned in the aperture with some degree of friction, so as to bring the needle to any required horizontal position. The angular turning requisite for this purpose is marked by an index fixed upon the upper end of the wire, by reference to a small graduated circle immediately below it, in the upper side of the cover. All these parts are represented in the vertical section, *fig.* 78. The other parts of the apparatus, as far as relates to the coils of wire which

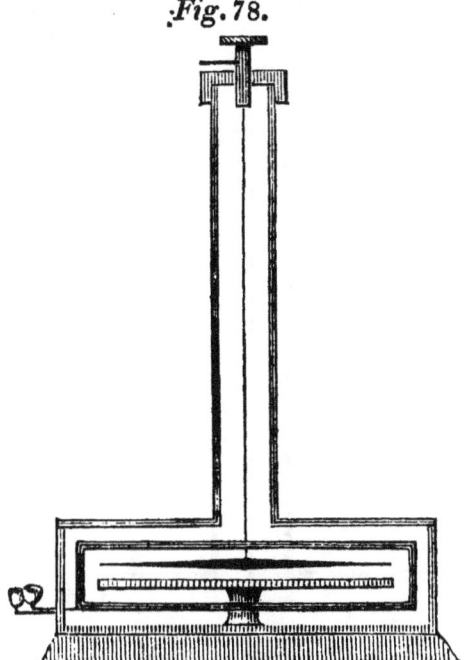

Fig. 78.

Fig. 79.

encircle the needle, are similar to those of the former instrument: excepting that the wires in the middle of the upper part of the coil must be separated a little, in order to leave an opening for the free passage of the thread that supports the needle. A graduated circle, equal in diameter to the length of the needle, is placed, as in the former case, immediately below the needle. The compass, wire, and card, are enclosed in a box, in order to secure them from the agitations of the air; and the cover, from the middle of which the upright tube rises, should be of glass, in order to allow of our seeing the position of the needle.

(116.) Mr. Ritchie has lately proposed a torsion galvanometer, in which he employs a thread of glass as the material for suspending the needle*. *Fig.* 79 is a vertical section of his instrument, of which he gives the following description:—Take a fine copper wire, and cover it with a thin coating of sealing-wax. Roll it about a heated cylinder, an inch or two in diameter, ten, twenty, or any number of times, according to the delicacy of the instrument required. Press together the opposite sides of the circular coil, till they become parallel,

* Philosophical Transactions for 1830, p. 218.

and about an inch, or an inch and a half long. Fix the coil in a proper sole, and connect the ends of the wires with two small metallic cups, for holding each a drop of mercury. Paste a circular slip of paper, divided into equal parts, horizontally on the upper half of the coil, and having a black line drawn through its centre, and in the same direction with the middle of the coil. Fix a small magnet, made of a common sewing-needle, or piece of steel wire, to the lower end of a fine glass thread, whilst the upper end is securely fixed with sealing-wax in the centre of a moveable index, as in the common torsion balance. The glass thread should be inclosed in a tube of glass, which fits into a disc of thick plate glass, covering the upper side of the wooden box, containing the coil and magnetic needle.

(117.) This instrument enables us to estimate the comparative intensities of currents of electricity circulating along the wires of the coil. For this purpose, the needle is to be placed directly above the meridian line drawn on the paper circle, and consequently directly above, and in the direction of the wires forming the upper side of the coil. As soon as a current of electricity is made to circulate along the wires, the needle will of course be deflected. The glass thread must then be twisted, by turning the index, until the needle is brought to its former position; and the number of degrees of torsion must be noted. A similar experiment may next be made with another current, the thread having previously been untwisted, so that the needle is again restored to its former position. The quantities of electricity circulating round the wires will be directly proportional to the number of degrees through which the thread has been twisted.

(118.) In the common galvanometers, in which the force of the current is estimated by the degrees of the deviation of the needle, this deflecting force acts with mechanical disadvantage as the needle deviates from the coil. When it has been deflected nearly ninety degrees from its original position, an addition to the power will produce scarcely any addition to the effect; and consequently the instrument ceases to give indication of a more energetic current. Hence Mr. Ritchie's instrument is better entitled to the appellation of a *galvanometer*, or measurer of galvanic electricity, than the former, which are mere *galvanoscopes*, or indicators of the presence of a galvanic current. It has, however, the disadvantage of not being so sensible to the influence of feeble voltaic electricity; since the needle, being on the outside of the coil, is acted upon only by the difference of the two contrary electro-magnetic forces, arising from the opposite currents in the upper and lower parts of the coil. In the former arrangement, the needle, being between these two parts of the coil, is deflected by the sum of these forces.

(119.) The sensibility of the galvanoscope may be very much increased by neutralizing the directive force of the needle arising from the magnetic influence of the earth. Professor Cumming employed for that purpose a magnetized needle placed immediately beneath the moveable needle *. Nobili improved upon this idea by attaching the neutralizing needle to the principal one, placing them one above the other, and parallel to each other, but with their poles in opposite directions. They are fixed by being passed through a straw, suspended from a thread, as in the apparatus formerly described. The distance between the needles is such as to allow of the upper coil of the wires to pass between them, an opening being purposely left, by the separation of the wires at the middle of that coil, for allowing the middle of the straw to pass freely through it. A graduated circle, on which the deviation of the needle is measured, is placed over the wire on the upper surface of the frame of the instrument, having an aperture in its centre for the free passage of the needle and straw. The whole of this arrangement may be understood by a reference to *fig.* 80, which represents a section of the apparatus: *s n* is the lower needle

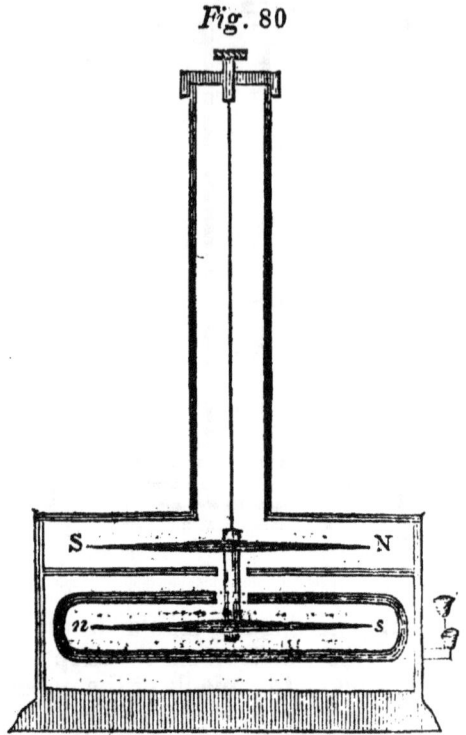

Fig. 80

surrounded by the coil of wire, and connected with the upper needle N S, by the intermediate straw shaft which is seen to pass through the upper horizontal coil of the wires, and also through the central aperture of the card immediately above it, on which the graduated circle is drawn. In Nobili's instrument, the frame was twenty-two lines long, twelve wide, and six high. The wire was of copper, covered with silk, one-fifth of a line in diameter, and from twenty-nine to thirty feet in length; making seventy-two revolutions round the frame. The needles were twenty-two lines long, three lines wide, a quarter of a line thick, and they were placed on the straw five lines apart from each other.

(120.) The adjustment of the opposing polarities of the two needles should be such, that the directive power of the combination resulting from the magnetism of the earth is very nearly balanced; the compound needle being allowed to retain only sufficient power to bring it to a constant position when uninfluenced by any electrical current. But the peculiar excellence of the contrivance

---

* Transactions of the Cambridge Philosophical Society, vol. i. p. 279.

is, that both needles are acted upon in the same manner, as far as the rotatory tendency is concerned, by the adjoining wires. The lower needle, being in the situation similar to that in the simple apparatus already described, § 91, is acted upon by the sum of the forces of the currents in every part of the coil. The upper needle, placed, with regard to the wires, in the same situation as in Mr. Ritchie's galvanometer, is acted upon by the excess of force in the upper current which is nearest to it. This force acts upon it in a direction the reverse of that in which it acts upon the lower needle, because it is situated on the opposite side; but since the poles are also in a reversed position, the rotatory action becomes the same in its direction on both needles. Hence, besides the increase of sensibility in consequence of the removal of the greater part of the opposing force derived from the magnetic influence of the earth, we have also an increase of power from the addition of the upper needle. There is also a convenience in employing the upper needle as an index; for by allowing of the graduated circle being placed above, instead of within the frame, the folds of the wire may be brought much nearer to each other than in the common instrument: this renders it more compact, and, from the greater approximation of the lower needles to the wires, also more powerful. The estimation of the deflection of the needle by reference to the graduated circle, can also be more conveniently made, from the view not being obstructed by the presence of the wires above the needle, as in the ordinary construction. It is hardly necessary to observe, that when fixing the graduation, the zero point should be placed so as to accord with the position of the upper needle, when left to the undisturbed action of the magnetism of the earth.

(121.) It is evident that if the magnetic powers of the two needles employed in Nobili's galvanometer were perfectly equal, they would exactly neutralize each other, as far as regards the directive influence of the earth; and the system of needles would be indifferent to any position. This would, however, defeat the purpose of the instrument, the object of which is to measure a feeble electro-magnetic force, by putting it in equilibrium with another force, likewise feeble, but still acting, and susceptible of measurement. If, therefore, a perfectly astatic needle, that is, one which retains no directive power whatever, be employed, it will be necessary to find some other weak, but variable and easily-measurable force to obtain this equilibrium. Such a force is that of torsion; and accordingly the greatest degree of perfection attainable in the measurement of minute electro-magnetic forces, would appear to be obtained by applying to the apparatus of Nobili, the needles being previously rendered perfectly astatic, the principle of the torsion suspension adopted by Mr. Ritchie.

(122.) An extension of the principle of Nobili's galvanometer has been proposed by M. Lebaillif; who employs a combination of four needles instead of two; one pair being applied to the upper part of the coil, and one pair to the lower, in the manner exhibited in the section, *fig.* 81, where N S, S N, represent the upper

Fig. 81.

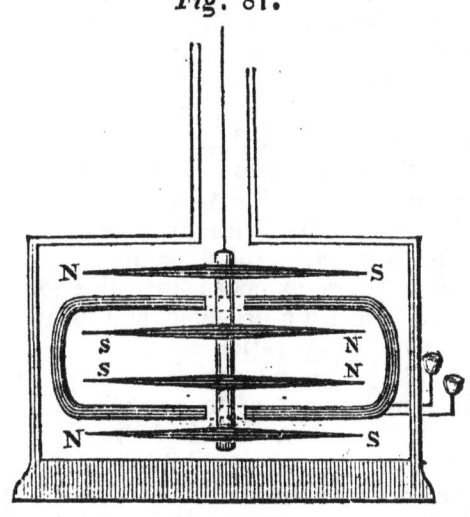

pair of the magnets, having their poles in opposite directions; and S N, N S, the lower pair, likewise reversed in their polarities; the two intermediate magnets, which are within the coils of the wire, having their poles similarly situated, as is likewise the case with the uppermost, and lowermost magnets; and the whole being affixed to the same vertical axis, which is a piece of straw, passing freely through the wires, and through the graduated circle, which forms the top of the frame enclosing both wires and needles. An index is fixed in the upper end of the axis to point out the positions of the needles. The axis itself is suspended from the end of a horizontal arm, proceeding from an upright pillar at the side of the apparatus. In order to form the coil, M.

Lebaillif employs, instead of a single wire, having, for instance, a length of 300 feet, five parallel wires, each sixty feet long, the ends of which are stripped of their silk coverings and united in a bundle by being pressed together with considerable force. In this way the electric current which enters at one extremity is divided into five parts, and made to flow, as it were, through five separate channels. It is alleged, in favour of this arrangement, that by thus multiplying the channels of transmission, a proportionally larger quantity of electricity is conveyed; while the diminution of intensity arising from the transmission of the same fractional part of that current which passes through one of the wires, along a great length of wire, is avoided*. But experiments of sufficient extent, and conducted with sufficient care, appear to be wanting to enable us to deduce any certain conclusions with regard to this subject. The only researches on this point, of which we have been able to find an account, are those of Dr. Kaerntz, who came to the conclusion that the power of the instrument to deflect the needle is exactly in proportion to the number of convolutions of the wire: six convolutions giving six times the power of one convolution†. But it would require a much more extended investigation to establish such a principle, and to fix the limits of its operation.

(123.) The advantage arising from the employment of four needles instead of two, in Mr. Lebaillif's instrument, appears extremely dubious; for it should be recollected that if, on the one hand, greater power is gained by the action of the wire on the additional needle, an equal addition is, on the other hand, made to the weight that is to be moved; so that probably nothing is thereby gained as to the motion indicating that power.

(124.) On account of the superior conducting power of silver, wires of that metal should be employed in preference to those of copper; and they may then be even as slender as the sixtieth of an inch in diameter, which will allow of a greater number of turns being included in the same space.

(125.) For the purpose of comparing the intensities of two electrical currents, an instrument has been contrived, which has been termed the *Differential Galvanometer*. Two wires of equal size are twisted together, so as to form a compound wire, which is coiled round the compass needle, as in the instruments already described; and the four extremities of the wires are immersed in four cups filled with mercury. By this means the two currents which are to be compared with one another, may be transmitted in opposite directions throughout the whole extent of the coil. These opposite currents, acting upon the needle under precisely similar circumstances, will, if they be equal, exactly counteract each other, and the needle will remain in equilibrio between the equal and contrary forces; but if the currents be unequal in intensity, the needle will be affected only by their difference, which it will therefore indicate by its movements.

(126.) When, on the contrary, we wish merely to ascertain the existence and direction of an electric current, it becomes an object to bring the current as near as possible to the needle, so that its action on the poles may be extremely powerful. The following form has, with this view, been given to the Galvanoscope. The needle is suspended from its centre by a fine thread, between four vertical spiral coils, the centres of which are brought very near to the poles of the

Fig. 82.

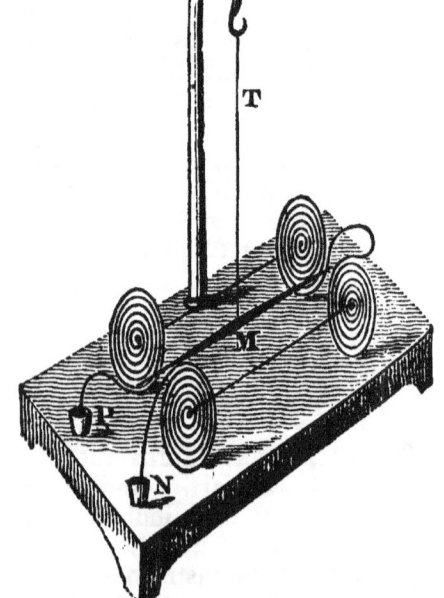

needle. The same current is made to circulate through all the four spirals, the turns of which are directed so as to produce repulsion of the contiguous pole

---

* See Pouillet's Elémens de Physique Expérimentale, tome i., p. 696.
† Philosophical Magazine, vol. lxii., p. 441.

ELECTRO-MAGNETISM.

on the one side, and attraction of the same pole on the other side. This arrangement is shewn in *fig.* 82, where M is the magnet suspended by the thread T, between the four spiral discs, composed of the convolutions of the wire proceeding from the cup P, and terminating in the cup N. In each disc, the force acting perpendicularly to the plane of the discs, is multiplied in proportion to the number of the circumvolutions of the wire; and the spiral turns being made in the same directions in all the discs, their actions will concur in producing in the needle a deviation in the same direction; and the total force will be four times that of a single disc. This arrangement allows also of a very close approximation of the needle to the discs.

(127.) The lightness and extreme flexibility of gold leaf have enabled electricians to employ this material for the construction of a very sensible electrometer. (See *Electricity*, § 73.) The same properties may be applied with great advantage to the purposes of a Galvanoscope, the electro-magnetic force of the current being estimated, not by the movements of a magnet on which it is made to act, but by those of a moveable conductor through which it is transmitted, under the influence of a powerful magnet. The construction of the *Gold-leaf Galvanoscope* is similar to that of Bennet's electrometer, excepting that the leaf is single, and there is added a forceps to retain the lower end of the gold-leaf, and complete the galvanic circuit. The slip of gold-leaf *g, fig.* 83, is suspended loosely from the forceps *f*,

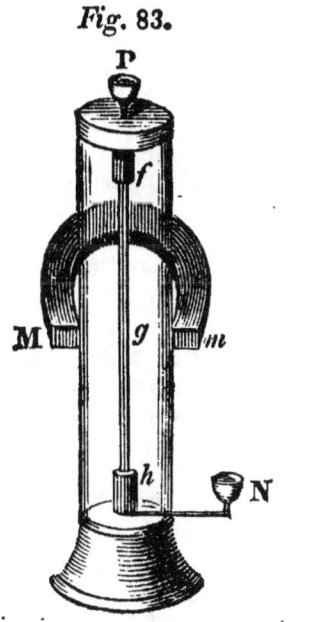

Fig. 83.

while the lower end is laid hold of by another forceps *h*; each forceps terminating in a cup, the one, P, being above, and the other, N, below, for establishing the communications by which the current is transmitted through the gold-leaf. The whole is enclosed in a cylindrical glass case, the middle of which is placed between the poles of a strong horse-shoe magnet M *m*, so that the gold-leaf may be nearly equidistant from them. When the circuit is completed through the gold-leaf, the latter will be attracted or repelled laterally by the poles of the magnet, according as the current is ascending or descending; the broad surface of the leaf becoming convex towards the magnet in the one case, and concave in the other. The curvature of the gold-leaf may be viewed through a lens in a direction at right angles to the line of its motion, and may be referred to a fine line drawn upon the tube in the direction of its axis. This instrument is, perhaps, the most delicate test possible of the existence and direction of a weak galvanic current [*].

Chapter IX.

Electro-magnetic Effects of Terrestrial Magnetism.

(128.) Since the earth acts as if it were endowed with a magnetic power, or rather as if it contained a powerful magnet in its centre, it naturally occurred to those who explored the new realms of science which the discovery of Oersted had laid open, that a current of voltaic electricity would itself be influenced by the magnetism of the earth. It was at first found extremely difficult, however, to devise means of rendering this action visible, in consequence of the great feebleness of the earth's action, compared with that of such artificial magnets as we are in the habit of employing. Ampère at length succeeded in obtaining decisive evidence that the conducting wire possessed a directive power by the following contrivance. Two wires A and B, *fig.* 84, bent at right-angles, are made to pass through a cylindrical piece of wood ᴜ, fixed at the end of an arm proceeding from the basis of the apparatus. They are made to terminate at both their extremities in small cups, designed to hold mercury, the cups P and N being intended to receive the wires communi-

---

[*] Cumming's Manual of Electro-Dynamics, p. 178.

cating with the poles of the voltaic battery; and the others, n and p, which are placed the one immediately above the

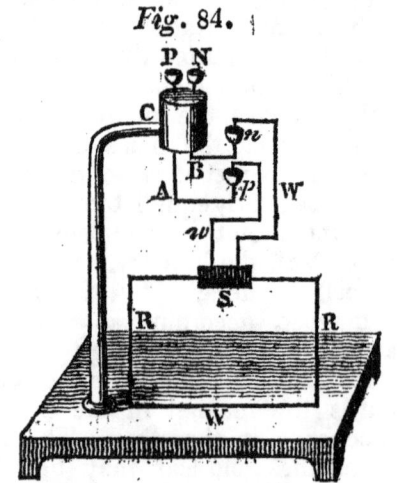

Fig. 84.

other, receiving the two ends of the wire W W w, which passes through a small piece of wood at S and is bent below into a square or rectangle R R. The upper point of the wire rests on the bottom of the cup n; the lower point being merely made to dip into the mercury in the cup p, without touching it, so that the whole of the wire, with its connecting piece S, has perfect freedom of motion round a vertical axis passing through the point of support in the uppermost of the two cups, n. When a connexion is made with the battery by means of the cups P and N, so as to direct an electric current through the wire W W w, it will, from the extreme delicacy of its mode of suspension, obey the magnetic influence of the earth, and arrange itself so that the plane of the rectangle R R shall be perpendicular to the plane of the magnetic meridian; and it will always return to this position when turned aside from it by the hand, or any other cause.

(129.) Another arrangement which exhibits the same effect is the one already described, § 100, and represented in *fig.* 66; where the electro-magnetic force is increased by the number of coils composing the spiral wire. This spiral, as in the last case, immediately assumes a position in a plane perpendicular to the magnetic meridian, as soon as it is made the channel for the transmission of a current of voltaic electricity. The mode of suspension here described is that of Professor Van den Boss*.

(130.) The apparatus invented by M. De la Rive, and described § 96, with the improvement described in § 99, is also exceedingly well adapted for the exhibition of the directive power of the galvanic current; for in consequence of the perfect freedom of motion allowed it, while floating in a fluid, it very readily assumes the position due to the magnetic influence of the earth. When the plates are immersed in acidulated water, as in M. De la Rive's original experiment, the gas liberated by the action of the acid on the plates, prevents them from taking a steady position; but when put into a little floating cell, the whole readily takes the position above mentioned, and even slowly vibrates about it. The same phenomenon is also obtained by the arrangements described in § 108 and § 109, which have also the advantage of exhibiting the strong resemblance which these instruments, actuated solely by electrical currents resulting from galvanic action, have to artificial magnets. For in consequence of their lengthened cylindrical form, the magnetic forces are directed along the axes, and the heliacal cylinder places itself, like a magnet, with its axis in the magnetic meridian; whereas, when a single circle, or combination of circles in a single plane is taken, that plane will arrange itself so as to be at right angles to the plane of the meridian, that is, will be in a plane passing east and west; the face of the plane only looking to the north and south.

(131.) In all the cases above described, the multiplication of the spiral or circular turns of wire is not productive of the advantage that might be expected, because, as already remarked with regard to the galvanometer of Lebaillif, § 123, although the power is increased, yet the weight to be moved by that power is increased nearly in the same proportion; and the resulting motion is therefore nearly the same.

(132.) The next point of comparison between the action of the earth on the conducting wire, and on the magnetized needle, relates to the dip. Since the direction of the force of terrestrial magnetism is in a line situated in the magnetic meridian, and inclined about seventy degrees to the horizon, the operation of this force on a Voltaic wire, bent in a plane so as to describe a circle, square, parallelogram, or any other figure which terminates where it commenced, forming what has been termed a *closed circuit*, is to bring it into a position where it is perpendicular

---

* Edinburgh Journal of Science, No. XII.

to this direction; that is, perpendicular to the position of the dipping needle.

(133.) The following was the apparatus, by which Ampère succeeded in exhibiting the effect now described. A

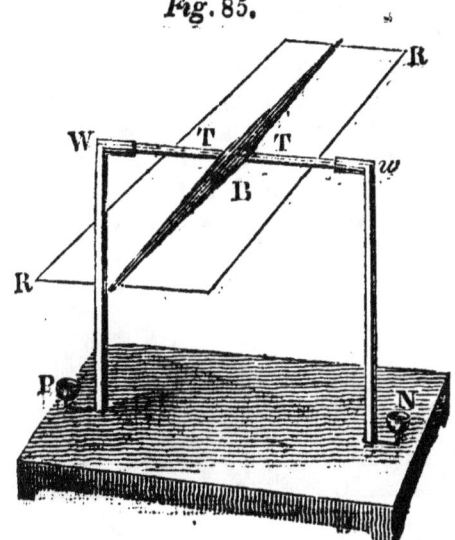

Fig. 85.

wire bent in the shape of a rectangle R R, *fig*. 85, is supported by a tube of wood, T T, passing directly across the middle of its longest sides, and serving as an axis. The two shorter sides or ends of the rectangle are supported by a light wooden beam, B, in the form of a lozenge, the middle of which is perforated by the tube just mentioned. One end of the wire, W, which forms the rectangle, is fixed to a steel pivot, which turns horizontally on a small metallic plate fixed upon the top of an upright metallic pillar, rising from the side of the basis of the apparatus. A little mercury is laid upon the plate in order to render the contact more perfect. The wire, after it has completed a circuit of the rectangle, and returned to the same point W, where it had commenced it, is bent so as to pass through the tube, and to come out at the other end, *w*, where it terminates in another steel point, turning in a like manner upon a metallic plate, fixed on the top of a pillar on the other side of the apparatus. The lower ends of both pillars, where they are fixed to the stand, are continuous with wires supporting cups with mercury, P and N, in the usual manner. On establishing a communication between the Voltaic battery and the cups, the electric current will ascend in the pillar which is next to the positive pole of the battery, and circulating along the rectangular wire, will pass out by its other extremity, descend by the other pillar, and make its exit through the cup on that side. As the rectangle is at perfect liberty to move around the axis formed by the two points by which it rests on the plates, and this axis being horizontal, it will be limited to a vertical motion. If the axis of motion be placed so as to be at right angles to the magnetic meridian, and the moveable part of the apparatus be exactly balanced, so as to retain any position in which it may be placed, then on directing the electric current through the wires, the rectangle will, after a few oscillations, place itself steadily in the plane of the magnetic equator; that is, in a plane perpendicular to the line of the dip; being the exact position which the theory would assign to it. On reversing the direction of the current, the magnetic polarity of the wire becomes immediately reversed, and turns completely round, so as still to place itself in the same plane as before, but with its faces turned in opposite directions to those they before assumed.

(134.) It is evident that, by adopting a similar mode of suspension, a voltaic magnet, formed by a helical coil of wire, as described in § 105, would exhibit the phenomena of the dipping needle, as completely as a magnetized needle.

(135.) Thus has the analogy between the action of terrestrial magnetism on wires conducting an electric current, and magnetized needles, been completely established. We have next to inquire whether a straight wire is affected by the earth in the same manner as it would be by the corresponding pole of a magnet placed near it. In order to make this comparison, we must first clearly deduce from the theory formerly laid down, what effects are to be expected on a straight conducting wire from the magnetism of the earth, or what is equivalent to it, from a south magnetic pole, acting at an indefinite distance, in the direction of the line of the dip. The electro-magnetic force being tangential, is exerted at right angles to this direction, which is that of the line connecting the wire with the magnetic pole, or origin of the force. Its action upon a current, whether ascending or descending, which moves in this exact line, or the line of the dip, is reduced to nothing: and it must act with greatest intensity upon a current which moves in a direction perpendicular to the line of the dip. Now, in order that a straight wire may be perpendicular to this line, it must be situated in the plane of the magnetic equator. Such, then, is the direction in which it receives the full influence of the earth's magnetism; and this influence is exerted in urging it to move in a direction parallel to itself, and at the same time perpendicular to the line of the dip; that is, it tends to continue in the plane of the magnetic equator. The direction of its motion to the one side or the other must depend altogether upon the course of the electric current which is passing through it. If the wire, for example, be placed horizontally, and have the direction of the magnetic east and west, and the current of positive electricity be flowing through it from west to east, the tendency to motion in the wire, in consequence of the influence of the earth, which acts like a south pole, is towards the *north*, that is *ascending* in the plane of the magnetic equator, which plane, it may be recollected, dips downwards towards the south, with an inclination to the horizon of about twenty degrees, equal to the complement of the dip.

This will be more clearly understood by reference to *fig.* 86, in which N, E, S, W represents a horizontal plane. D *d*, which has an inclination to this plane of 70°, is the line of dip, to which the plane M Æ, representing the plane of the magnetic equator, is perpendicular. W E is a straight portion of conducting wire, along which an

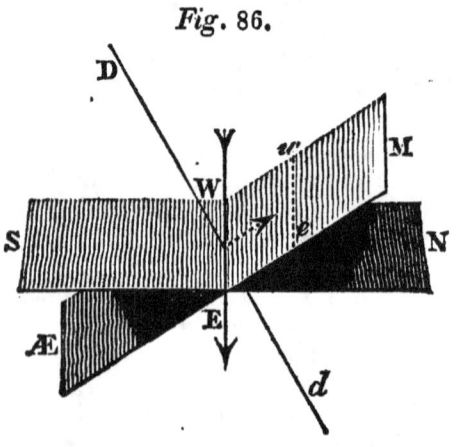

Fig. 86.

electric current is flowing in the direction from W to E. Under these circumstances, the effect of the electro-magnetic force exerted by the earth is to give the wire a tendency to move parallel to itself, in the plane M Æ, and towards M, as denoted by the arrow; so that were it at liberty to obey this impulse, it would next be found to occupy the position marked by the dotted line *w e*. If the electric current had been made to pass from E to W, the direction of the motion would have been altered, and the wire would have moved downwards in the same plane, still, however, preserving its parallelism.

(136.) If the wire extend in the magnetic plane from north to south, as, for instance, along the line M Æ in *fig.* 87, N S, as before, being the horizontal plane: and if the electric current move in the direction M Æ, that is,

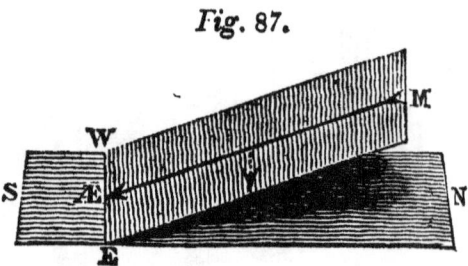

Fig. 87.

from north to south, the wire will tend to move towards the east, as shewn by the arrow, still keeping in the same plane, and remaining parallel to itself. If, on the contrary, the current move from south to north, the wire will be impelled to move from east to west.

It need hardly be observed that all these statements relate to what happens in the northern magnetic hemisphere of the earth, and when the dip is about 70 degrees, as is the case in England. In the southern hemisphere, where the northern polarity of the earth is in activity, the effects are of course reversed. At the magnetic equator, where the dip is nothing, the plane M Æ is perpendicular to the horizon, and the tendency to motion of a horizontal wire must be directly upwards, or directly downwards; and the effect of the terrestrial magnetism must be merely that of opposing or conspiring with gravitation, that is of producing either an increase or a diminution in the apparent weight of the wire. In these high latitudes the inclination of the magnetic equator to the horizon is too small to produce any very sensible effect of this kind. It has, however, been rendered perceptible in very nice experiments.

(137.) In consequence of the plane of the magnetic equator being not very far removed from a horizontal plane, wires placed horizontally, and being free to move in a horizontal plane, may be made to exhibit the actions of terrestrial magnetism without much difficulty. Mr.

ELECTRO-MAGNETISM.

Faraday succeeded in obtaining this effect in the following manner*. A piece of copper wire, about .045 of an inch thick, and fourteen inches long, has an inch at each extremity bent at right angles in the same direction, as shown at W *w*, in *fig*. 88, and the ends amalgamated; the wire is then to be suspended horizontally, by a long silk thread *s*, from the ceiling. Two grooves G *g* are cut in the sides of a rectangular piece of hard wood, parallel to the sides, and about half an inch in depth, and filled with mercury. P and N are wires fixed in the board, passing each into its respective groove, so as to come in contact with the mercury, and terminating at their other ends in cups for making the connexions with the voltaic battery. The points of the wires are now to be slightly immersed in the mercury contained in the respective grooves; and in order to obviate the inconvenience arising from the film of oxide which is apt to form upon the surface of the mercury, and impede the motion of the wires, it is advisable to cover the surface with a stratum of diluted nitric acid, which, by dissolving the oxide, removes this obstacle to free motion. As soon as the connexions are made with the battery, and the electric current passes along the wire, it will be seen to move laterally, being carried across the field until the points strike against the ends of the grooves. On breaking the connexion, the wire resumes its first position; on restoring it, motion is again produced. On changing the position of the apparatus with respect to the points of the compass, the same effect still takes place; and the direction of the motion is always the same relatively to the wire, or rather to the current passing through it, being at right angles to it. Thus, when the wire is east and west, and the electric current flowing from west to east, the motion is towards the north; when the current passes from east to west, the motion is towards the south. When the wire hangs north and south, and the current moves from north to south, the wire is directed towards the east, and when the current is reversed, towards the west. In intermediate positions the motions of the wire are in intermediate directions.

(138.) These different motions corresponding to the different positions of the wire, and directions of the current, are exhibited by the lines in *figs*. 89, in which N and S express the north and

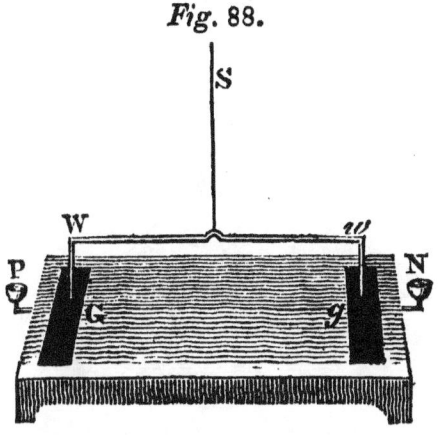

Fig. 88.

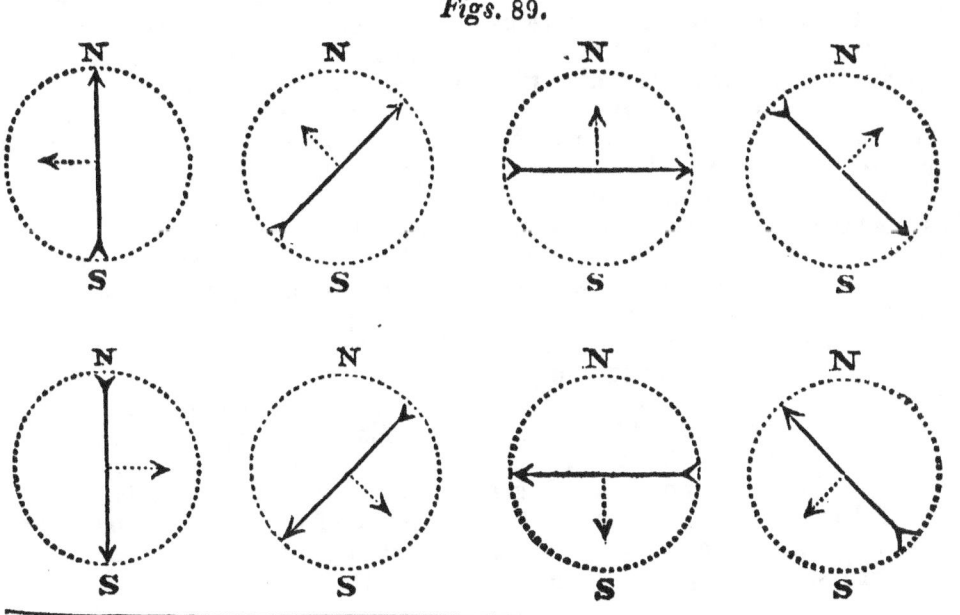

Figs. 89.

---

* Quarterly Journal of Science, &c., Vol. XII. p. 417.

south; the arrow-heads at the end of the lines shew the direction of the current in the wire; and the short arrows proceeding laterally from the middle, the direction of the motion induced in the wire.

(139.) It is evident that, in all these cases, the wire is moving in obedience to the same law, which produces the revolution of a wire round a magnetic pole in Mr. Faraday's first experiment on magnetic rotations, already described (§ 59). It is a direct and necessary inference from this law, that were the two troughs of mercury continued to ever so great a length, and even were they carried round the globe in a circle round the acting magnetic pole of the earth, the wire would continue to move along them, and after describing the whole circle, and returning from the point at which it had set out, would resume its course, and perform perpetual revolutions. In the very limited space compatible with actual experiment, the wire appears to move in a plane; but theory shews that it is in reality a small portion of a cylinder, of which the radius is the distance of the magnetic pole of the earth from the wire. It is amusing to compare this incipient revolution of the wire with the complete rotations effected in experiments with artificial magnets; and, considering it as part of a similar experiment upon a much vaster scale, to view the wire as setting out on its voyage of circumnavigation of the globe, although it is in the next moment arrested in its progress.

(140.) It is also a consequence deducible from the same law, that the force by which the horizontal conducting wire is urged is the same in all azimuths.

(141.) A real rotation, visible in all its course, may however be exhibited, as the effect of terrestrial magnetism. This has been accomplished also by Mr. Faraday, who, reflecting that in the experiment of rotation round the pole of a magnet, the pole is perpendicular to but a small portion of the wire, and more or less oblique to the rest, thought it probable that a wire, very delicately hung and connected, might be made to rotate round the line of dip by the earth's magnetism alone; the upper part being restrained to a point, in the line of the dip, and the lower being made to move in a circle surrounding it. With this view, a piece of copper wire, about 0.018 of an inch in diameter, and six inches long, well amalgamated all over, was hung by a loop to another piece of the same wire, at W, see *fig.* 90, so as to allow of very free motion; and its lower end w, was thrust through a small piece of

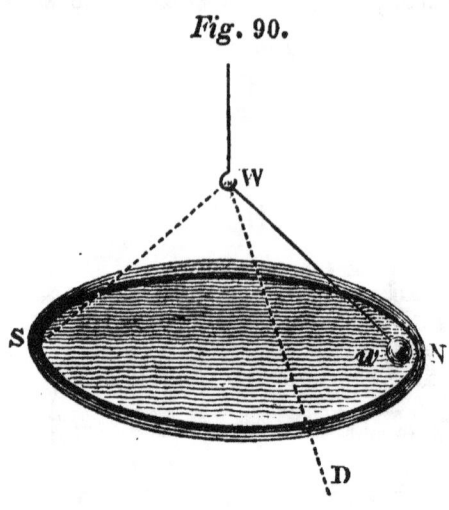

Fig. 90.

cork, in order to render it buoyant when placed on mercury. A glass basin, ten inches in diameter, was filled with pure clean mercury, and a little dilute acid poured on its surface. The thick wire which communicated with one of the poles of the voltaic battery was then hung over the centre of the glass basin, and depressed so low, that the thin moveable wire, having its lower end resting on the surface of the mercury, made an angle of about 40 degrees with the horizon. On the circuit through the mercury being completed, the wire immediately began to move and rotate, and continued, whilst the connexions were preserved, to describe a cone, which though its axis was perpendicular, had, evidently, from the varying rapidity of its motion, relation to a line W D, parallel to the dipping-needle, as being that of the force by which it was actuated. The direction of the motion was, of course, the same as that communicated in the experiment described § 64, when a south pole is placed beneath the apparatus. If the centre from which the wire hung was elevated, until the inclination of the wire was equal to that of the dip, no motion took place when the wire was parallel to the dip; and if the wire was less inclined than the dip, the motion in one part of the circle capable of being described by the lower end was reversed; results that necessarily follow from the relation between the dip and the moving wire*.

(142.) It is evident that by restraining the motion of one of the ends of the horizontal wire in the experiment described in § 137, and represented in *fig.* 88, so as to render that end a fixed axis, and providing a circular mercurial trough for the other end to move in, the same force which produced a parallel progressive motion in the former case, will now produce a rotatory motion; because the force producing a horizontal motion is the same in all positions of the wire. This equality is proved by making the experiment with two connected horizontal wires instead of one; placing them the one immediately above the other, each being furnished with its separate mercurial trough, into which the moveable end may dip. This arrangement is represented in *fig.* 91, where the current entering by the cup P, and traversing the mercury in the upper trough, ascends through the wire A, passes on through the upper horizontal wire to the central wire C, placed in the

Fig. 91.

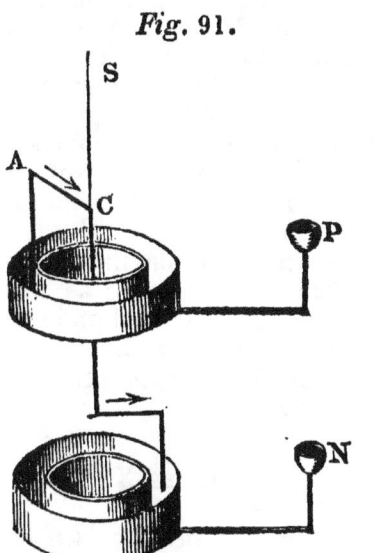

axis of suspension, (the wire being hung by the slender thread S,) along which it descends, and passes *outwardly* through the lower horizontal wire, and thence through the mercury in the lower trough, to the cup N, whence it escapes to the voltaic battery. When this has been effected, it is found that the suspended wires exhibit no tendency to rotate, in whatever azimuth they may be placed. Hence it may be inferred that the tendency to revolution which the earth communicates to the current

* Quarterly Journal of Science, XII. 418

moving from the circumference to the centre in the upper horizontal wire, is exactly counterbalanced by an opposite rotatory force in the lower wire, in which the current passes from the centre to the circumference; and as this equality is preserved in every azimuth, it follows that the rotatory force is constant in every position of the wire.

(143.) A vertical current in a conductor moveable round a vertical axis is also impressed by the influence of the earth with a horizontal force, which carries it towards the magnetic east, when the current is descending, and towards the west when it is ascending. This will be made apparent by suspending a wire bent as shown in *fig.* 92, A, and terminating above and below in the points P and N, for the purpose of being placed in their respective cups, and

Fig. 92, A.

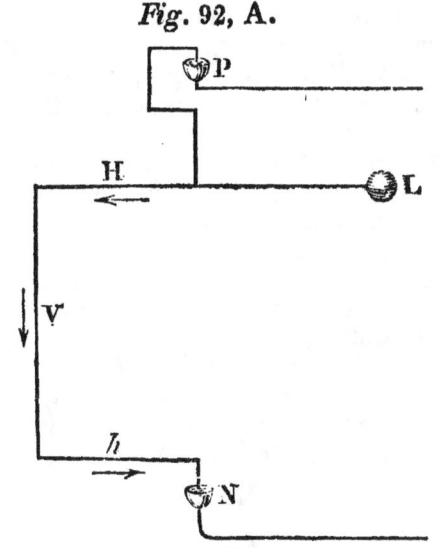

balanced by a counterpoise, L. When the current is passed through this wire, the direction of its course along the two horizontal branches, H and *h*, being opposite, will counterbalance each other; but that in the vertical portion, V, will take a position either to the east or west of the axis, according as the current descends or ascends through it.

(144.) If the wire, instead of having the shape just shown, has the figure of a complete square or parallelogram, as shown in *fig.* 92, B, the second vertical branch will conspire with the first in making the wire assume the same position, namely, that in which the current descends, (as V,) to the east, and that in which it ascends, (*v*,) to the west.

(145.) From an attentive consideration of the facts that have now been stated, we are enabled to understand why a vertical circular current, urged by the

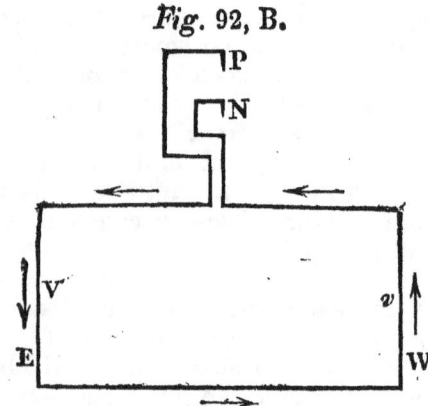

Fig. 92, B.

electro-magnetic force of the earth, tends to arrange itself in the plane of the magnetic equator. If at liberty to do so, it will assume this position; but if its motion be restricted to any other directions, it will place itself as nearly as possible in that plane. If, for instance, it be constrained by a vertical axis to turn horizontally only, it will place itself in a plane perpendicular to that of the magnetic meridian; that is, directed east and west, or fronting to the north and south. In its movements to attain this position, it is urged by the tendencies of the currents, in as far as their motion is vertical, whether ascending or descending; for the tendencies of the horizontal portions exactly balance one another, and produce no rotatory effect. Thus if in the circle A D, fig. 93, which turns on the vertical axis, X Y, the current descend in the branch D, and ascend in the branch A, the former

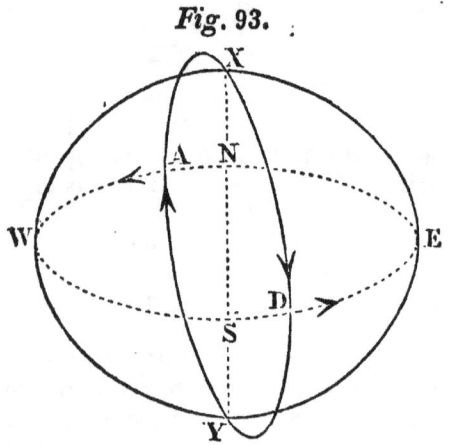

Fig. 93.

will be impelled in the direction D E, and the latter in the direction A W, by forces which cease only when they have attained the positions E and W. The horizontal portions at X and Y neutralize each other, with regard to their rotatory tendency. Hence the circle will revolve until it takes the position shown by the circle at E and W, where the forces are in equilibrium. The nature of this equilibrium will appear from fig. 94, in which the circle is represented as seen from above; and the arrows point out the horizontal direction of the forces, which when the circle is in the line W E pass through the vertical axis and are exactly balanced. The same letters denote the corresponding points in the two figures.

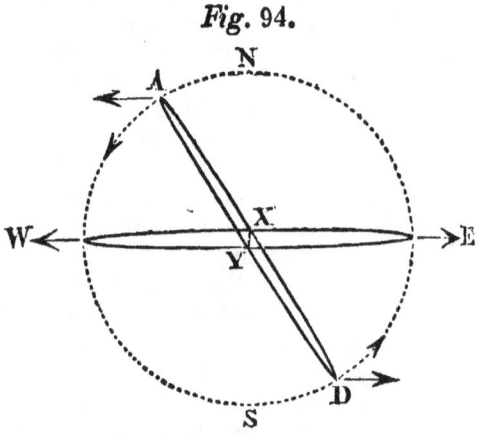

Fig. 94.

(146.) When, on the other hand, the axis of revolution is horizontal, and the motion vertical, the position is determined by the forces that act on the horizontal parts of the circle, which now conspire in determining a rotation towards the plane of the magnetic equator, if the plane of motion coincide with the magnetic meridian; or if not, as near to it as the restrictions to the motion will allow.

(147.) On the whole, then, it appears that a heliacal coil, such as that described in § 105, balanced on its centre, will assume all the positions, and exhibit all the directive properties of the magnetic needle.

Chapter X.

Electro-Magnetic Induction.

(148.) Thus far we have considered the electro-magnetic phenomena that result from the reciprocal action of galvanic currents on magnetized bodies. We have next to examine that class of effects which arise from the action of the former on iron, or other ferruginous bodies that have not previously been rendered magnetic. Experiment has proved that a conducting wire, during the passage of an electric current through it, tends to induce magnetism in such bodies as are in the vicinity, and in which that state is capable of being excited. *Induction*, therefore, is one of the phenomena of electro-magnetism, and must be enumerated among the properties of electricity in motion.

(149.) It was discovered both by Sir Humphry Davy and by Mr. Arago, nearly at the same time, that the connecting wire of a galvanic battery has a sensible attraction for iron filings, and that it will hold them suspended like an artificial magnet, as long as the electric current circulates through the wire; but the moment the galvanic circuit is interrupted, the action ceases, and the filings immediately fall off. In Sir H. Davy's experiments, the filings adhered to the wire connecting the poles of a voltaic apparatus, consisting of a hundred pairs of plates of four inches, in such considerable quantities as to form a mass round it ten or twelve times the thickness of the wire*.

The transverse magnetic action of the electric current upon iron in its vicinity is beautifully illustrated by the following experiments, which were devised by Mr. Watkins, and which he was so obliging as to show us. A copper wire of considerable thickness is extended between the poles of a voltaic battery; and upon sifting over it very gently some fine iron filings, they are observed to adhere to the wire all round its circumference, in the form of distinct transverse bands, the particles of which mutually cohere, as long as the current is maintained. When a broad and thin copper ribbon is substituted for the wire as the conductor of the voltaic electricity, and iron filings are carefully sifted upon it in small quantities, they are seen to arrange themselves in parallel lines at right angles to the length of the ribbon; and their magnetic properties are further evinced by the quick changes of position and general disturbance occasioned by the approach of a magnet brought underneath the conducting plate.

(150.) It might naturally be expected from these experiments with soft iron, that steel, under the same circumstances, would receive a permanent magnetism. Sir Humphry Davy, having fastened several steel needles, in different directions, by fine silver wire, to a wire of the same metal, of about the thirtieth of an inch in thickness, and eleven inches long, some parallel, others transverse, above and below, in different directions, placed them in the electrical circuit of a battery of thirty pairs of plates of nine inches by five, and tried their magnetism by means of iron filings. They were all magnetic; those that were parallel to the wire attracted filings in the same way as the wire itself; but those in transverse directions exhibited each two poles. All the needles that were placed under the wire when the positive end of the battery was east, had their north poles on the south side of the wire, and their south poles on the north side; while those that were over the wire had their south poles to the south, and their north poles to the north; and this was the case whatever was the inclination of the needles to the horizon. On breaking the connexion, all the steel needles that were on the wire in a transverse direction retained their magnetism, which was as powerful as ever, whilst those that were parallel to the silver wire appeared to lose it at the same time as the wire itself.

(151.) All the needles placed transversely *under* the communicating wire, the positive end being on the right hand, had their north poles turned towards the face of the operator; and those *above* the wire, their south poles. Contact with the wires was not at all necessary for the magnetization of the needles; for this effect is produced instantaneously, by the mere juxtaposition of the needle in a transverse direction, and that through very thick plates of glass. A needle that had been placed merely for an instant in this transverse direction with regard to the wire, was rendered as powerful a magnet as one that had long been in communication with it.

(152.) The intensity of the induced magnetism was found to be proportional to the quantity of electricity transmitted through the wire in a given time. Hence a wire electrified by a common machine, however powerful, produces no sensible effect; a feeble magnetism only is obtained by the reception of large sparks: but on passing the discharge from a Leyden battery through the wire, the needles placed transversely to the wire are rendered permanently magnetic. The discharge of an electrical battery of seventeen square feet, highly charged, through a silver wire of the twentieth of an inch in thickness, rendered bars of steel two inches long and from one-twentieth to one-tenth of an inch in thickness, so magnetic, as to enable them to attract small pieces of

---

* Philosophical Transactions for 1821, p. 9,

steel wire or needles; and the effect was communicated to a distance of five inches above or below laterally from the wire, through water, or thick plates of glass or metal electrically insulated.

(153.) The efficacy of electro-magnetic induction is, as might be expected, greatly increased by employing a helical coil of wire, and placing the needle or bar to be magnetized in the axis of the helix, in the situation represented in *fig.* 67. Mr. Arago first employed this method, and was enabled to produce the maximum effect on the needle almost instantaneously. It is not necessary, however, that the bar to be magnetized should be exactly in the axis of the helix, as it may lie in any situation within it, or be inclosed in a tube of glass, or of any other material which is not a good conductor of electricity. Such a tube will also be convenient as a support for the coils of the wire, as well as for admitting of the introduction of different needles in succession. The needle should not be allowed to remain beyond a moment in the tube, for the magnetizing effects of the helix are produced nearly instantaneously; and it sometimes happens that if the needle be left there a few minutes, the polarity it had at first acquired becomes impaired, or confused, and even occasionally destroyed.

(154.) If a long steel wire be placed in the axis of a helix, the direction of the turns of which change at different points, the wire will be found to have a number of consecutive points, corresponding to those at which these changes take place.

(155.) Mr. Watkins observes that the needle to be magnetized, if it be not very hard, need not have its whole length inserted into the glass tube; for if held in the hand so that only half of it is within the helix, it will become magnetic equally with one that has been wholly acted upon; because the portion of the needle that has received the magnetism communicates it to the other portion. When a small part of a needle, very highly tempered, is introduced into the glass tube, the induced magnetism will be found to extend to about twice the length of the part so introduced.

(156.) A very powerful temporary magnet may be obtained by bending a thick cylinder of soft iron into the form of a horse-shoe, and surrounding it with a coil of thick copper wire, secured from communication among its several parts by a covering of silk, or other non-conducting material. When the wire is made part of the galvanic circuit of a battery, even of moderate power, the iron is rendered powerfully magnetic, and will lift up a very heavy weight by means of a piece of iron applied to its poles, which act precisely like those of a horse-shoe magnet. *Fig.* 95 exhibits an arrangement of this kind; W *w* being the two ends of the wire, coiled round the iron to be magnetized, and bent so as to dip into the cups P and N, for forming connexions with a battery.

Fig. 95.

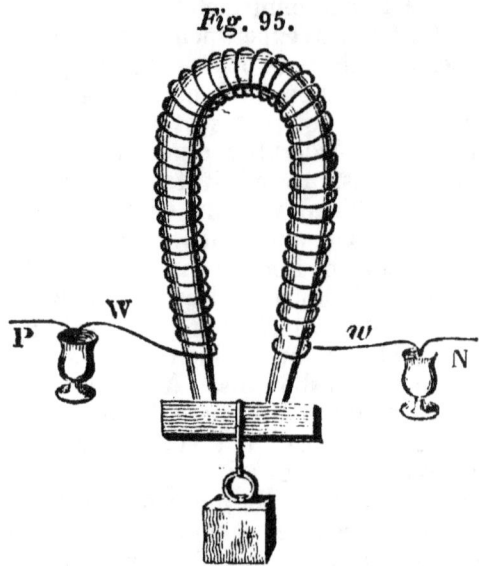

(157.) This experiment has been made upon a very large scale by Professor Moll with an apparatus constructed by Mr. Watkins*. It consisted of a cylinder of soft English iron, an inch in diameter, bent into the form of a horse-shoe, the interval between the ends being eight inches and a half. The copper wire forming the spiral was one-eighth of an inch in diameter, and made eighty-three convolutions; the weight of the whole was five pounds. A connecting piece of iron was placed in contact with the two extremities of the horse-shoe; and the ends of the spiral wire dipped in mercury, so as to form a voltaic circuit with a simple battery, consisting of a zinc plate, which exposed a surface of eleven square feet to a very diluted mixture of sulphuric and nitric acids, in a copper cell. In the first experiment the apparatus sustained, first, fifty pounds, and afterwards, with care, seventy-six pounds, by the magnetism induced upon it.

(158.) When the weight suspended to

---

* Bibliotheque Universelle, 1830, p. 19.

the transverse bar of iron is small, it is found that the iron retains its magnetism for some time after the voltaic communication is broken. If, instead of merely breaking the connexion, the electric poles are changed so as to reverse the direction of the current, then the reversion of the magnetism takes place with extraordinary rapidity. The weight, indeed, falls off, but is instantly again attracted and sustained with the same force as before. The rapidity of this change is the more extraordinary when it is compared with the slowness and difficulty of changing the poles of a magnet of equal force by the ordinary method. If, instead of a heavy weight, a light steel needle be in contact with the poles of the electro-magnet, the needle never falls off; the attractive force being destroyed and re-established before the weight of the needle has time to effect its removal.

(159.) An extraordinary sensation is experienced when the piece of soft iron connecting the poles is held in the hand during this change. At first a powerful attraction is felt; this on a sudden fails, and the iron gives way; but the force is so instantaneously renewed, that the hand is violently drawn up again by an attraction as strong as before. The moment the voltaic circuit is completed, the iron is magnetized to a maximum, and sustains its greatest weight. No increase of magnetic power is obained by augmenting the force of the voltaic battery.

(160.) With a larger horse-shoe magnet of soft iron, weighing twenty-six pounds, and of which the diameter was two inches and a half, the chord of the arc being twelve inches and a half, and the spiral wire being of brass, one-eighth of an inch in diameter, and making forty-four turns, and with the same voltaic battery as in the former experiment, the magnet supported 139 pounds. When an iron wire was used, instead of a brass one, this was increased to 154 pounds.

(161.) However great these effects may appear, they are much increased by augmenting the number of coils, without extending the length of the wire. Professor Henry, of the Albany Academy, in the United States, and Dr. Ten Eyck, employed for the construction of the magnet a soft iron bar, two inches square, and twenty inches long, having the edges rounded, bent into the form of a horse-shoe. Five hundred and forty feet of copper bell-wire was wound round it, in nine coils of sixty feet each. These coils were not continued from one end of the magnet to the other, but each of them was wound round a portion of the horse-shoe about an inch in length, leaving the ends of the wires projecting, and properly numbered. The alternate ends were soldered to a copper cylinder, and the others to a smaller cylinder of zinc, containing only two-fifths of a square foot, and forming a voltaic arrangement with dilute acid. When the armature of soft iron was placed across the ends of the horse-shoe, it was found capable of supporting 650 pounds; an astonishing effect for so small a battery, which required a charge of only half a pint of dilute acid. With a larger battery, the weight sustained was 750 pounds, which seemed to be the maximum of magnetic power that could be developed in that bar by voltaic electricity. It is remarkable that when the ends of the wires were united so as to form a continuous wire of 540 feet, the weight raised was only 145 pounds.

In a subsequent experiment, a magnet was wound with twenty-six strands of copper bell-wire, covered with cotton thread, thirty-one feet long; about eighteen inches of the ends were left projecting, so that only twenty-eight feet of each actually surrounded the iron. The aggregate length of the coil was, therefore, 728 feet. Each strand was wound on a little less than an inch; in the middle of the horse-shoe it formed three thicknesses of wire; and on the ends, or near the poles, it was wound so as to form six thicknesses. With a battery nearly five feet square, this electro-magnet suspended 2063 pounds, or nearly a ton weight. This appears to be the most powerful single magnet ever constructed, either by the ordinary modes of magnetizing steel bars, or by the voltaic current.

(162.) Trials were also made to procure a small temporary magnet, which should raise the greatest weight, compared with its own weight. A small horse-shoe of round iron, slightly flattened, one inch in length, and six tenths of an inch in diameter, wound round with three feet of brass wire, raised, by means of a cylindrical battery, 420 times its own weight. Sir Isaac Newton describes a magnet weighing three grains, which he wore in a ring, and which is said to have raised 746 grains, or 250 times its own weight, and this is the greatest relative strength of any magnet yet recorded. It is evident, therefore, that a much greater degree of magnetism can be developed in soft iron, by a galvanic current, than in steel of the same dimensions, by the ordinary processes of magnetizing *.

Mr. Watkins informs us that, in order to obtain magnets of any power by the above described method, great care must be taken to ensure the purity of the iron employed to form the horse-shoe-magnet; and after it has been welded and reduced to the proper shape, it is advisable, in order thoroughly to destroy any magnetism it may have accidentally acquired and retained during the process, to heat it in a furnace, and afterwards cool it very gradually, by allowing it to remain undisturbed till the furnace itself has grown cold. But, even after every precaution has been taken to ensure success, we are still liable to be baffled by causes which we cannot explain, and which, when all circumstances seem to be the same, produce great and unexpected variations in the results. It should be borne in mind, indeed, that similar embarrassments are often experienced in conducting almost every other experiment in electro-magnetism, their results appearing to be more or less capricious in proportion as the conditions necessary to be fulfilled, before uniformity can be obtained, are numerous and delicate.

(163.) The best form of a conducting-wire for exhibiting its attraction for iron filings is that of a flat spiral coil, similar to what is represented in *fig.* 66, which, however, for this purpose need not be rendered moveable. A wire of this form, through which an electric current is made to circulate, will collect a prodigious quantity of iron filings, and their relative positions and arrangement, while they remain attached, present many singular appearances. If the rings of wire are not continued quite to the centre, but leave an opening there, the particles of iron are observed to arrange themselves in lines, passing through the ring parallel to the axis, and then closing up as radii round the edge. The particles of iron in the centre erect themselves into a perpendicular filament, in the direction of the axis of the spiral, while the intervening particles form filaments inclining from the centre in proportion to their distance from it *. The reason of this will be evident from the principle explained in § 50.

(164.) There appears to be a very essential difference in the effects of the shock of an electrical battery discharged through a wire, and that of a voltaic battery, in communicating permanent magnetism to steel bars or needles. Mr. Savary has brought to light several very curious particulars relating to this subject, which have hitherto received no explanation †. When the discharge from a Leyden battery is made through a straight wire, different needles, though equal in size, and parallel to each other, and placed transversely on the same side of the wire, but at different distances, have their polarities not disposed in all of them in the same manner. In some the poles have the same relative situation as those of a needle previously magnetized, and free to move, which has taken the position it would have when under the influence of a continued voltaic current passing in the same direction along the wire.

But in others the position of the induced poles is the reverse of this. For the sake of conciseness of expression, we shall call the action which produces an arrangement of poles similar to that resulting from a voltaic current, *positive magnetization*; the contrary effect being that of *negative magnetization*. Thus, in a series of experiments in which the needles were placed at distances from the wire which increased by equal intervals, at the point of contact with the wire the needle was magnetized positively, at a small distance negatively; a little further off it had acquired no magnetism whatever; at a distance somewhat greater than this, it exhibited positive magnetism; and this effect continued for a certain interval, beyond which the magnetization was again negative. When still more remote, it was positive, and continued so to all greater distances that were tried. Hence the action appears to be periodical with relation to the distance at which it is exerted.

(165.) The number of periods in these alternations, as well as the distances at which they occur, appear to depend upon a variety of circumstances of which it

---

* Silliman's Journal, quoted in the Journal of the Royal Institution, I. 609; and II. 182.

* Watkins, Popular Sketch of Electro-Magnetism, p. 46.
† Annales de Chimie, tome. xxxiv.

is difficult to appreciate singly the effect: such as the intensity of the electric discharge, the length of the straight wire, its diameter, the thickness of the needles, and their degree of coercive force. In general, when the wires are very slender, and the coercive force of the needles feeble, the periodical alternations above noticed are less numerous; and it even frequently happens, with these conditions, that the magnetization is every where positive, and that the only differences observable at different stages of distance, are those of greater or less intensity.

(166.) When the discharge from the electric battery is transmitted through a wire coiled into the form of a helix around glass or wooden tubes, a similar diversity is met with in the effects produced on different needles successively placed in the interior of the tubes, and in different situations relative to the axis. By varying the intensity of the charge of the battery, or the length or thickness of the needles, the nature of the result is changed. The maximum of magnetic intensity which may be produced by a given wire, depends on the ratio between its thickness and its length; so that the degree of magnetization amounting to saturation, bears a relation to the value of this ratio. The degree of magnetic power that a needle receives from the influence of an electric discharge, and even the direction of its magnetization, depend also on the nature and the dimensions of the bodies that are in contact with it, or that surround it.

(167.) The magnetizing influence of a helix through which an electric discharge is passed, is completely intercepted by a cylinder of copper, of sufficient thickness, inclosing the needle, and introduced within the helix. When the interposed cylinder is of less thickness, some magnetic effect becomes perceptible; and when the thickness of the copper cylinder is still farther reduced, the needle is rendered even more strongly magnetic than when exposed to the action of the helix without any interposed substance. Tin, iron, and silver, placed round the needle, produce a similar modification of the electro-magnetic action of the helix; when interposed in very thin plates, they increase this action; when of a certain thickness, they entirely intercept it. Cylinders composed of metallic filings do not produce this effect; whereas we again meet with the intercepting property, if the interposed substance is composed of concentric layers consisting alternately of metallic and of non-metallic bodies. It would thence appear that solutions of continuity in a direction perpendicular to the axis of the needle, or to the axis of the helix, have a considerable influence on the magnetizing effects of the latter upon the former. An influence of a similar kind has been observed from metallic plates of different thickness, placed in contact with a needle properly disposed with regard to a straight conducting wire receiving the discharge of an electric battery; being found, according to their size or position, to modify the intensity and even the direction of the magnetism acquired by the needle.

(168.) All these phenomena appear to depend on the suddenness of the action exerted by the electric shock, either directly on the particles it meets with in its course, or on objects that are situated at a distance in the surrounding space. But the direction of the magnetization, as to its being of the positive or negative kind, depends essentially on the intensity of the discharge; so that discharges of different intensities develope in the metal a set of opposite states analogous to the polarities of contrary signs, acquired at different distances from a conducting wire, or by different intensities of electricity.

Chapter XI.

Mutual Actions of Electric Currents.

§ 1.—*Action of Parallel Rectilineal Currents.*

(169.) The discovery of Oersted, and all the consequences we have developed from the fundamental law that appears to regulate the reciprocal action between electric currents and magnetic bodies, belong to that division of the subject to which the term *Electro-Magnetism* is more properly applied: for they refer to the relation subsisting between the two agencies of electricity and of magnetism, which we have been accustomed to consider as distinct from one another. But electric currents are also found to have a mutual action on one another: and this general fact, which was ascertained by Ampère, soon after the discovery of Oersted, established another great division of the science; and the law on which it is founded is no less prolific in its consequences, and important in its applications, than that we have hitherto been occupied in investigating. To this branch of the subject Ampère has given the name of ELECTRO-DYNAMICS.

(170.) When two conducting wires are suspended or supported in such a manner as to be capable of moving, either towards or from one another, at the time that electric currents are passing through them, they manifest a mutual attraction or repulsion, according as the currents are moving in the same or in opposite directions in the two wires. This action is variously modified, when the relative inclinations and positions of the currents are varied.

(171.) We shall begin by considering the simplest case, which is that in which the two currents are running in parallel directions. The attraction or repulsion of currents, under these circumstances, admit of being exemplified in a great number of ways, according to different modes in which the conducting wires are suspended and rendered moveable. Thus the wires in the apparatus described § 143 and 144, *figures* 92 and 93, may be employed for that purpose, by bringing either the vertical or the horizontal branches sufficiently near a straight wire, through which an electric current is also passing.

The following is also an apparatus for the direct exhibition of this phenomenon. T, *fig.* 96, represents a rectangular table from which arise four upright pillars supporting two cross pieces of wood, having a row of holes for receiving four cups, two on each piece, the

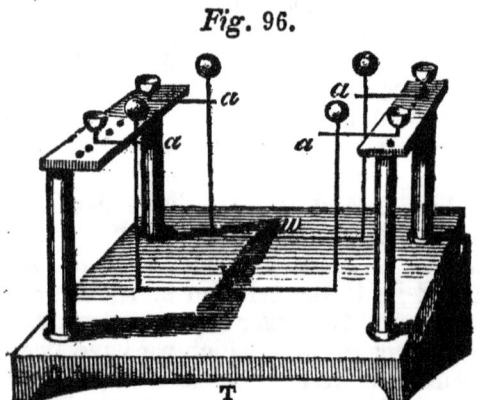

Fig. 96.

distances of which from each other may by means of these holes be varied at pleasure. Short wires, *a, a, a, a,* proceed horizontally from the bottoms of the cups, and serve as pivots round which the two wires, W, *w*, bent twice at right angles, are made to turn at the upper part of their vertical branches, having small holes drilled through them for that purpose. These wires, thus hung freely upon their pivots, carry on their upper ends small weights, which, bringing the centres of gravity as nearly as possible in coincidence with the points of suspension, enable them to be moved by a very slight force. Conducting wires, proceeding from a voltaic battery, are then inserted into the cups previously filled with mercury, in such a manner that the galvanic current shall pass in the same direction through both the parallel wires;—the moment this is done, the wires move towards each other, even from a distance of several inches, exhibiting a powerful mutual attraction. When the currents are transmitted in directions opposite to each other in the two wires, which they may be made to do by transposing the communicating wires inserted into the cups leading to one of the moveable wires, while the others are left as before, the moveable wires immediately recede from each other, manifesting a repulsion as powerful as the attraction was in the former case.

(172.) The electro-magnetic forces obtained from voltaic batteries of the ordinary strength are so feeble when compared with the force of gravity, that, in devising experiments for exhibiting their action, it becomes necessary, in order to succeed, so to contrive the apparatus as that the parts to be moved by these forces may be as light as possible, and be also suspended in such a way as to occasion the smallest amount of friction. Attention should be given not to encumber the conductors, or the magnetic bars which are to be set in motion, with any superfluous materials capable of adding to their weight; and we should avoid such dispositions as require them to move in opposition to their own gravity. The surfaces which are intended to move through mercury should be as much as possible reduced; not only on account of the friction which takes place between the solid and the fluid, but also because the surface of the mercury rapidly oxidates, and the film of oxide thus formed opposes considerable resistance to the motion of a solid body, and greatly impedes the mechanical action of the apparatus. In general, it will be found that a vertical suspension by a point is preferable to suspension by a horizontal axis, as the former occasions less friction. Thus Mr. Watkins finds, that the attractions and repulsions of wires transmitting voltaic currents are exhibited with more facility when they are suspended vertically, their two ends terminating respectively in upper and lower cisterns, than when turning horizontally, as in the apparatus exhibited in the preceding figure.

These attractions and repulsions may also be exhibited with a very feeble current of electricity, by means of the gold-leaf galvanoscope, already described, § 127. By removing the magnet, and inserting within the instrument a thick wire, inclosed within a glass tube, parallel and near to the gold leaf, a strong current may be passed through the wire, at the same time that a feeble current is transmitted through the gold leaf, which will then exhibit the attractions or repulsions of parallel currents, according as they are in the same or in opposite directions; for these actions take place equally whether the two currents are obtained from separate voltaic combinations, or whether they are merely two portions of the same current in different parts of its course.

(173.) This latter case occurs whenever a wire is coiled round in a spiral or heliacal form, so as to bring different portions of the same current, passing in the same direction, very near to one another. It occurred to the author of this treatise, soon after hearing of Ampère's discovery of the attraction of electrical currents, that it might be possible to render the attraction between the successive and parallel turns of a heliacal coil very sensible, if the wires were sufficiently flexible and elastic; and, with the assistance of Mr. Faraday, this conjecture was put to the test of experiment, in the laboratory of the Royal Institution. A slender harpsichord-wire bent into a helix, being placed in the voltaic circuit, instantly shortened itself whenever the electric stream was sent through it; but recovered its former dimensions the moment the current was intermitted. It was supposed that possibly some analogy may hereafter be found to exist between this phenomenon and the contraction of muscular fibres, which seems to be regulated by some properties of the nervous system, not unlike those of electric agency. Messrs. Prevost and Dumas have advanced a similar theory of muscular contraction, founded on a supposed distribution of nervous filaments, through which they imagine a current of electricity is sent, for the purpose of determining the action that precedes contraction. This theory, they conceive, is supported by microscopic observations; but it is far too hypothetical in its present form to deserve serious discussion.

(174.) The general fact of the mutual action of electric currents being established by these and similar experiments, we must proceed to consider the different modifications it receives by a variation of circumstances regarding the quality and direction of the currents.

(175.) We possess as yet but an imperfect knowledge of the peculiar affections which electricity experiences when in motion, and which enable it to exert the singular species of action we are here investigating, so different from its attractive and repulsive powers when at rest. These two classes of effects obey laws not only different, but in some respects of an entirely opposite nature. Accumulated electricity, when not in motion, acts in a degree proportioned to its tension; but the wires, which are silently conducting a current of electricity in motion, exhibit no sign whatever of electric tension; they produce no change in the electrometer, and neither attract nor repel light bodies in their vicinity. The law of action in the state of rest is, that dissimilar electricities attract, and similar electricities repel one another. When in motion, on the contrary, it is between similar currents, that is, currents moving in a similar manner, that attraction takes place; while a mutual repulsion is exerted between dissimilar currents. The electro-statical effects of electric tension cease when the atmospheric pressure is removed; but the electro-dynamical effects of currents take place equally whether the conductor be surrounded by the air or placed in *vacuo*.

(176.) Since the effects of electric currents are the consequences of the motion of the electricity, it is natural to suppose that they will be in proportion to the velocity with which it moves, as well as to the quantity that is set in motion. But we are in utter ignorance of the real velocity with which the electrical effects are propagated along a conducting body, during the completion of the voltaic circuit: nor do we even know whether this velocity varies in different cases, nor have we any distinct idea of the causes that are likely to produce such variation. We can perceive, however, that the mode of transmission has a considerable influence on the results. The currents transmitted by perfect conductors are *continuous*; that is, their intensity is either constant, or varies insensibly during two consecutive instants. When the conductors are imperfect, the currents are *discontinuous*; for the electricity is allowed to accumulate for a certain time, and until the insulating force is overcome, when it escapes, and passes on with a sudden impulse, analogous to an explosion. The electro-motive power continuing to act, gives rise to a second accumulation, and a fresh explosion, and so on successively. These alternations may become sufficiently rapid to escape our senses, and thus produce the appearance of an uninterrupted current, although it be really discontinuous. The distinctive character of such currents is, that they are incapable of producing a deviation in the magnetic needle. This is the case with the current produced by the common electrical machine, when a communication is established between its positive and negative conductors: and also with the currents established in what have been called the *secondary piles* of Ritter (see *Electricity*, § 93), or piles constructed with a series of metallic discs separated by humid conductors. Discharges from the Leyden vial, in like manner, although they induce a degree of permanent magnetism in steel bars near which they pass, yet scarcely leave any traces of their effects on the needle of the galvanometer, when transmitted through the wires of that instrument.

(177.) The continuity of the electric current being the quality most immediately concerned in the production of the effects that are the subject of our present consideration; and it being impossible for us to discriminate differences of velocity or of quantity, in any other manner than by the total effects that result from the passage of the current through a conducting body, we shall distinguish continuous currents only in respect to their *intensity*, and pretend to judge of the degrees of intensity solely by the amount of the effects produced on the galvanometer.

(178.) In order to arrive at the fundamental law of electro-dynamic action of currents upon one another, it is necessary to consider the total action of each as resulting from the combined actions of every one of its parts. As it is not possible to institute a direct measurement of those elementary forces exerted by each indefinitely small portion, the one upon the other, the inquiry can only be made by assuming some hypothesis relative to the law of diminution according to distance, and prosecuting the consequences of such an hypothesis, when applied to such finite portions of current as occur in our experiments, and to compare them with actual observation, their accordance with which will be a test of the admissibility of the hypothesis.

(179.) Guided by the analogy of all the other known forces in nature, we shall assume that the mutual actions of the elementary portions of electric currents are inversely as the squares of their relative distances; and this is, in fact, the supposition which agrees best with all the facts that have hitherto been ascertained. If we suppose A, for instance (*fig.* 97), to be an indefinitely small portion of the rectilineal current P N, moving from left to right, it will act upon another elementary portion, B,

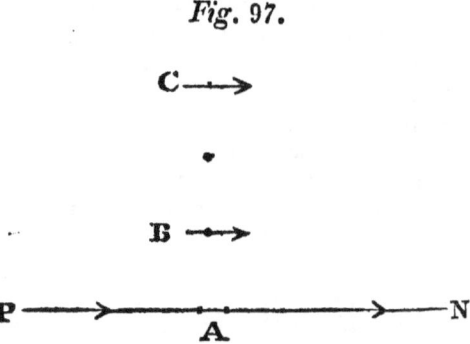

Fig. 97.

of a current placed at a given distance with nine times the energy that it exerts upon a similar portion of current placed at C three times further removed from it. If we call the force of attraction f, the intensity of the first current a, and of the second current b, and the distance between them, or the line B A, d, the following equation will express the law just enunciated:—

$$f = \frac{a\,b}{d^2}$$

(180.) It may be demonstrated mathematically, that such being the law of elementary action, it will follow as a necessary consequence that the total action of a current, P N, extended to an infinite length, upon an elementary portion of a parallel electric current placed at any given distance from it, is in the simple inverse ratio of the shortest distance between them—that is, of a line drawn from the one to the other, and perpendicular to both. Thus, in the example just given, where the distance C A is three times the distance B A, the action of the indefinite current P N is three times greater upon B than upon C. So that if this total action be expressed by F,

$$F = \frac{ab}{d}.$$

(181.) The action, whether attractive or repulsive, of two elementary portions of current, must be conceived as exerted in the direction of the line which joins them, and which, for the sake of distinctness, we shall call the *medial line*. So that in the case of the parallel currents A and B, *fig.* 98, moving in the same direction, an attraction denoted by the short arrows *a* and *a*, takes place in the

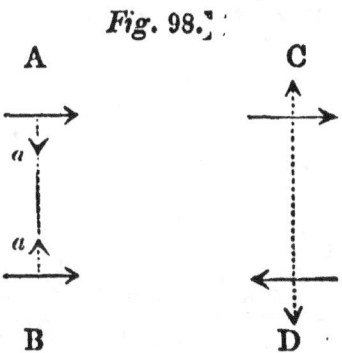

Fig. 98.

direction of the medial line A B; and in the case of the currents C and D, likewise parallel, but moving in opposite directions, a repulsion takes place, as shown by the short arrows, in the direction of the same line. It should be observed that, in both cases, the *action on each current is perpendicular to the direction of that current.*

§ 2. *Action of inclined Rectilineal Currents.*

(182.) Let us next suppose that the two currents, still remaining in the same plane, the direction of one of them, A, *fig.* 99, is changed from parallelism to the position C *c*, the action will still be perpendicular to that position—that is, the current A will be urged to move in the line A *a*, at right angles to C *c*; but the force which thus impels it will be diminished in the ratio of radius to the sine of the angle B A C, which the di-

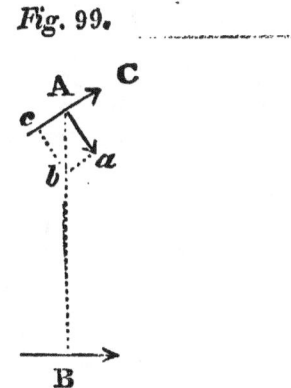

Fig. 99.

rection of the current makes with the medial line A B. This will readily appear by resolving the force A *b* into the two forces, A *a*, A C, of which the latter, acting counter to the direction of the current, is destroyed, while the only effective force is A *a*, which is to A *b* as the sine of B A C to radius.

(183.) A similar diminution of the force by which the current A reacts upon B, takes place in consequence of its obliquity; for the portion C *n*, *fig.* 100, which, when it was parallel to B, acted with its full power, has only the

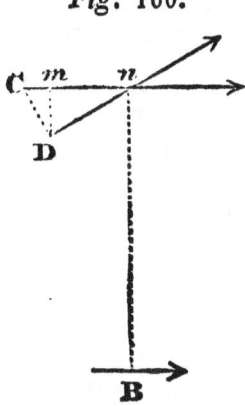

Fig. 100.

force of the portion *m n*, when acting in the oblique position D *n*, the diminution being proportional to the cosine of the angle C *n* D, or, what is the same, to the sine of the angle D *n* B. The mutual action of the current, therefore, situated in the same plane, but in oblique positions, may, in as far as this obliquity is concerned, be expressed by the following equation, in which α and β denote the angles made by the directions of the currents respectively with the medial line.

$$f = \sin. \alpha . \sin. \beta.$$

(184.) Let us now inquire into the modification the formula must receive when the two currents are in different planes. We have seen that in the last instance, the effective force of an oblique current, in its action on another current, is obtained by reducing that force to a direction at right angles to the medial line. Let us suppose this to be done with regard to both the currents A and B, *fig.* 101, the former being reduced to the line *a a*, and the latter to the line *b b*, situated respectively in planes perpendicular to the medial line A B. The force

Fig. 101.

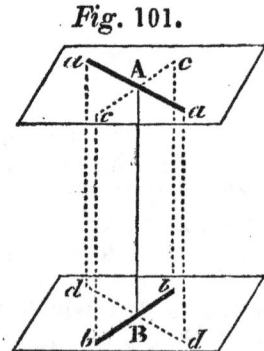

a A, estimated in the direction A *c*, drawn parallel to B *b*, or the force B *b* estimated in the direction of B *d*, drawn parallel to A *a*, will, in either case, be reduced in the proportion of radius to the cosine of the angle *a* A *c*, or *d* B *d*, which is equal to it, and which may be defined, the angle between two planes passing through the medial line and each of the currents respectively. Calling this angle μ, the formula, including all possible relative positions of the currents, either in the same or in different planes, becomes when the intensities and distance between the currents are also taken into account,

$$f = \frac{a\,b\,(\sin.\alpha.\sin.\beta.\cos.\mu)}{d^2}$$

which should express the action of the currents estimated in the direction of the medial line, provided the hypothesis with which we set out were correct.

(185.) But experiment, the only criterion of the soundness of physical theories, shows that an element is still wanting in this process for estimating the value of the forces. It would follow from the above formulæ that when an elementary portion of a current A, which has the precise direction of the medial line, that is, when it proceeds in a straight line, either towards or from another elementary portion of a current B, *fig.* 102, no action can take place between them; for the angle α being reduced to nothing, its sine likewise vanishes: and the same result should also obtain when the planes in which two currents are situated are at right angles to one another; for

Fig. 102.

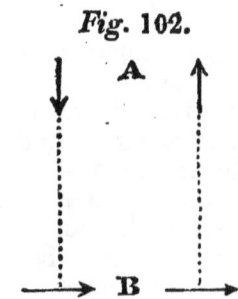

in that case the cosine of μ vanishes, and the whole function expressing the value of f is reduced to zero. This destruction of force ought to take place, whatever be the position of the force B.

(186.) This, however, is not found to be the case, excepting only when the current B is at right angles to the medial line. If it be in any other position, and more especially if it also coincide in direction with the medial line, a repulsion is manifested. This will appear from the result of the following experiment:—

(187.) Let a flat oval dish of glass, or porcelain, *fig.* 103, be separated into two divisions by a glass partition, fixed with cement, and the divisions filled with mercury. Insert into each of these troughs, the sides of a copper wire, bent in the manner shown in *fig.* 103, so that they may be parallel to the partition,

Fig. 103.

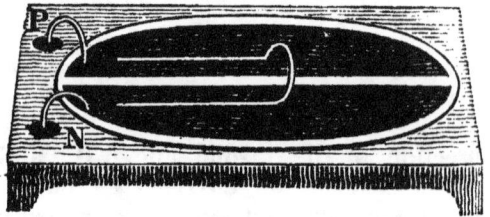

over which the arc passes, joining the two parts of the wire which float in the mercury. Every part of this wire, excepting the steel points soldered to its extremities, is to be covered with silk. Two wires, forming connexions with the two poles of a powerful voltaic battery, being inserted in the cups P and N, which communicate with the mercury in the basin, in the directions of the straight branches of the wire produced, the current from the one will pass through the mercury in the adjoining partition to the steel point belonging to one of the extremities of the wire, and then, circulating through the whole extent of the wire, will pass out into the mercury of the partition, and be carried off by a third wire. It is found that at the instant this current is established, the wire moves in the direction of the long branches until it is stopped by the end of the vessel *. This repulsion is exerted, not only at the indefinitely small distance that occurs between the parts immediately in succession, but also at finite distances between all the parts of the same current.

(188.) Since it appears, from this and other experiments, that portions of the same, or of different currents, moving in the same continuous line, or at oblique angles, repel one another, Ampère found it necessary to introduce another term in the formula. Since the action due to this cause is greatest when the two currents are in the same continuous line, as A B, *fig.* 104, and vanishes when the medial line is at right angles to both of them, as in the positions A and C, he inferred that in all intermediate positions, as at D, for instance, the action would be proportional to the cosine of the angle B A D, between the direction of the current A, and the medial line A D, which we have already expressed by the symbol α. The same reasoning applies to

Fig. 104.

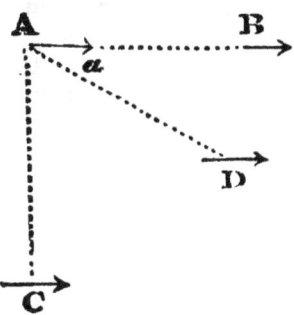

the current D, when the variations of its position are taken into account. The term to be added to the force, as formerly determined, must therefore be some function of the cosines of the angles α and β, and may be expressed by prefixing to them the indeterminate coefficient k. So that we now have

$$f = \frac{ab}{d^2}(\sin.\alpha.\sin.\beta.\cos.\mu + k\cos.\alpha.\cos.\beta).$$

(189.) In his earlier speculations, Ampère had regarded the value of k as so small that it might safely be neglected; but subsequent researches led him to the conclusion that it is in reality equal to $-\frac{1}{2}$, so that the whole of this second term of the formula is negative, when the cosines of the two angles are themselves positive.

---

* Ampère, Théorie des Phénomènes Electro-Dynamiques, p. 39.

(190.) The electro-dynamic forces which are thus called into action by voltaic currents, and of which the intensities and directions are determined according to the laws above defined, are subject to the same laws of composition and resolution as all other mechanical forces, and present the same facilities for the application of mathematical reasoning. It would of course be impossible to attempt giving, within the limits of this treatise, even an outline of the analytical investigations by which various important conclusions have been deduced. We must content ourselves with stating merely results, referring such of our readers as desire further information on the subject to the works of Ampère, Biot, and Savary.

(191.) It follows evidently from what has been said, that when two electric currents, situated in the same plane, are inclined to one another at any angle, they are always mutually repulsive when one of them approaches to, and the other recedes from, the summit of the angle; and, on the contrary, they attract one another when they both approach to, or both recede from, that angular point. When the intensities and positions of the currents are the same in the two cases, and the only difference is in the change of the direction of one of the currents, then the attractive force in the latter case will be found to be precisely equal to the repulsive force in the former case. And, universally, whatever be the action of a system of fixed conductors upon a moveable conductor, it is immediately changed into an equal and contrary action, by reversing the direction of the current, through either the moveable or the fixed part of the system. If the direction of the current through both the parts be reversed at the same time, the original action is reproduced. In this way we obtain a criterion by which the mutual actions of different parts of any electro-dynamical apparatus may be distinguished from those depending on the influence of the earth. The former effects are permanent, but the character of the latter is changed by reversing the direction of the current throughout the whole system.

(192.) It is hardly necessary to enter into any minute description of the apparatus by which these conclusions may be experimentally verified. The modes of suspension adapted to the particular object of the experiment will readily occur to any one who has made himself acquainted with the details we have already given of analogous experiments. It will be sufficient to observe that there are, in general, two kinds of rotation of which the moveable parts of the apparatus are susceptible, the one on a vertical axis, as in figures 66, 71, 84, 91, 92, 93, and the other on a horizontal axis, as in figures 85 and 96.

(193.) Care should always be taken, in nice experiments, to guard against the errors that might arise from allowing the influence of the earth to interfere with the actions we are examining. This disturbing force may, in general, be neutralized, and rendered ineffective by particular dispositions of the conducting wires. Thus the moveable conductor, *fig.* 92, may be rendered *astatic* or independent of terrestrial influence, by forming a second parallelogram below the first, composed of wires, so turned as to oblige the current to pass in opposite directions in corresponding parts of each. This is shown in *fig.* 105, in which P and N represent the steel points affixed to the extremities of the wires for the purpose of being placed in cups with mercury; and the directions of the currents in the several portions of the wire are indicated by arrows, whereby it appears that the action of the earth upon any one part is neutralized by its equal and opposite effect in another cor-

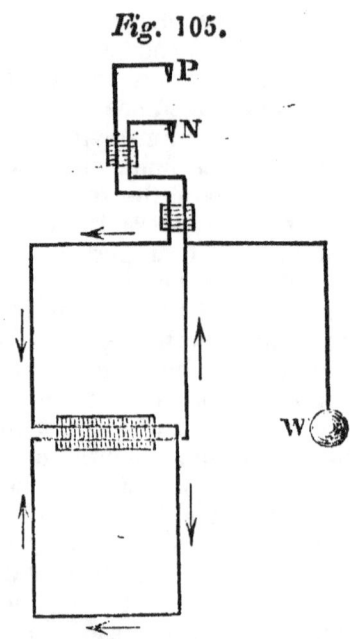

Fig. 105.

responding part, similarly situated with regard to the axis of rotation. The wires should be covered with silk thread, in order to prevent metallic contact in the parts where they are brought together. The shaded parts represent the branches that may be conveniently tied, or simply twisted together, after this precaution has been taken, for the sake of greater firmness. The weight W is applied as a counterpoise on the other side of the axis of rotation.

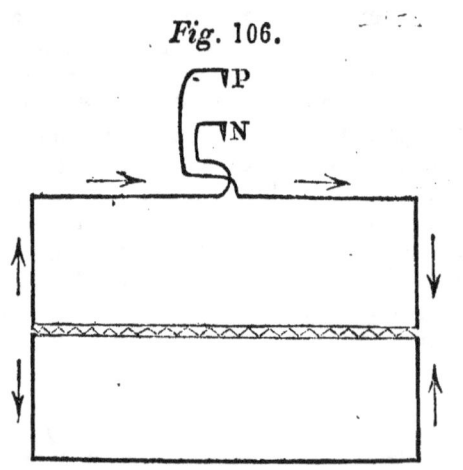

Fig. 106.

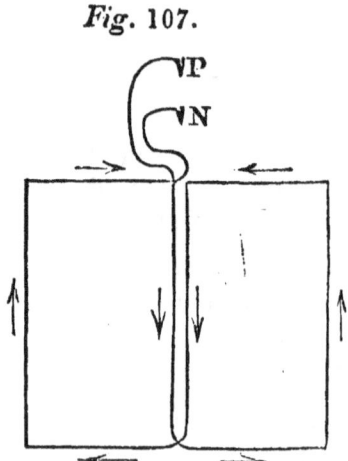

Fig. 107.

(194.) *Fig.* 106 represents another form of an astatic conductor, having the same properties as the preceding, but better adapted for the examination of the actions on the lower horizontal branch.

(195.) *Fig.* 107 shows an arrangement of a similar kind, in which the horizontal branches neutralize one another, but in which the interior vertical branches, being in the axis of motion, have no influence in producing rotation; and the exterior vertical branches are therefore uncompensated, as far as relates to the action of any current presented to them; although being in opposite sides of the axis, they neutralize one another as far as regards the influence of the earth.

ELECTRO-MAGNETISM.

(196.) It follows, as a consequence of the principles already laid down, that the action of a small portion of conducting wire, bent into any number of flexures, provided they extend to no considerable distance, upon another current, anywhere situated, is equivalent to the action of a similar wire proceeding in a straight course between the two extreme points of the contorted wire. The action, for example, between a conducting wire, A B, *fig.* 108, and an elementary portion, C D, the one pursuing a sinuous course, the other rectilineal, is precisely the same as if the former, instead of being contorted, had passed in a straight line from the point A to the point B; that is, along the dotted line A B.

Fig. 108.

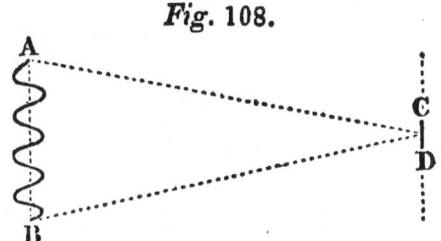

(197.) By an extension of the reasoning which led to the conclusion just stated, it may be proved that the action of a current traversing the contorted line A B, *fig.* 109, (and which we have seen is equivalent to that of a current

Fig. 109.

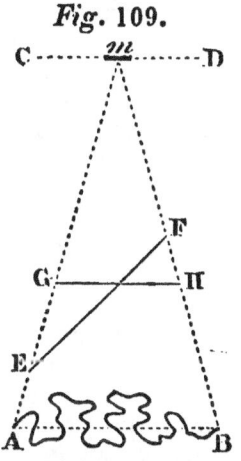

of equal intensity passing in a direct line from A to B,) on any elementary portion *m* of a distant current C D, will be to the action of a similar current E F, (comprehended within the angle A *m* B, which A B subtends at the point *m*, the middle of the elementary current,) in the inverse proportion of their mean distances from the point *m*; that is, drawing G H, making equal angles with A *m* and B *m*, through the middle of E F, the action of A B is to the action of E F, inversely as A *m* to G *m*.

(198.) If the electric currents be conceived as spread over a given surface, A, *fig.* 110, instead of being confined to a single line; then the action of this superficial stratum of currents on the elementary current *m*, which is a part of

Fig. 110.

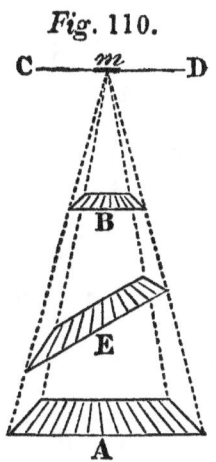

the current CD, will be precisely equal to that of B, or E ; or of any other superficial stratum composed of similar currents, situated at any distance from *m*, and inclined at any angle, provided it be comprehended by the sides of the same pyramidal or conical figure, having the surface A for its base, and *m* for its apex. This, indeed, follows as a necessary consequence of the preceding law: the diminished influence of the currents in A, resulting from their greater distance, being exactly compensated by their greater number. It may be derived still more directly, indeed, from the general law of the action of electric currents being inversely proportional to the squares of the distances. We shall have occasion hereafter to make important applications of this principle.

§ 3. *Action of Terminated Currents.*

(199.) We have seen that the action of a rectilineal current of infinite length on a short portion of current at a distance, situated in the same plane, and wholly on one side of the former, tends to give it motion in a line perpendicular to itself, and either in the same direction as the extended current, or in the opposite direction, according as it is receding from or approaching to it. The same applies to a current of any length, provided it be situated wholly on one side of the cur-

F

rent that acts upon it, and which it will be convenient to designate a *terminated current*. Thus, the current A B, *fig.* 111, lying wholly on one side of the extended current C D, and which is therefore a terminated current, will be urged

Fig. 111

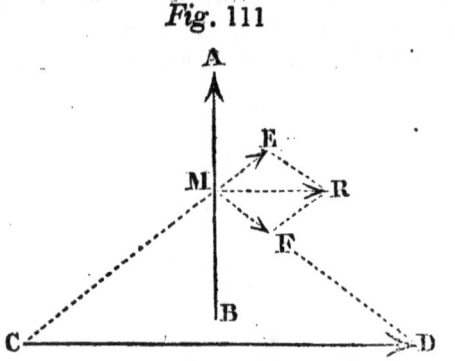

in the direction of the dotted line M R. For since the current A B is moving from the angular point B towards A, while the current C D is, in the part C B, moving towards B, the former will be repelled by the latter during the whole of that part of its course. The resultant of all the repulsive forces thus operating on A may be represented by the line M E. On the contrary, the currents passing along the lines A B and B D, are both moving in a direction from the angular point B; consequently they attract one another; and the resultant of these attracting forces may be expressed by the line M F, which, when combined with M E, gives the total resultant M R, perpendicular to A B.

(200.) Applying this principle to various positions of a terminated current with relation to the extended one, we obtain results which are expressed in the annexed diagram, *fig.* 112; where, as before, C D is the extended current passing from C to D, and the upper lines represent various positions of the terminated currents, of which the directions are marked by the terminal arrows; while the dotted arrows point out the directions of the resulting mo-

Fig. 112.

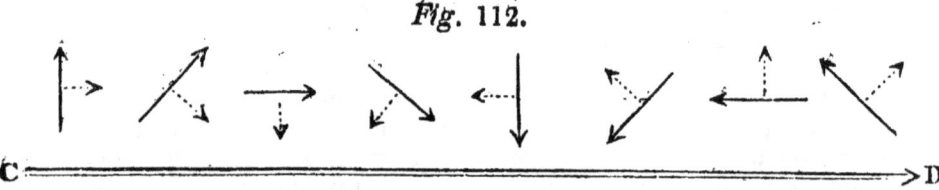

tions. As a general rule, whenever the direction of the terminated current is *from* the line of the extended current, it is urged to move in the same direction as the extended current moves; when its current is *towards* the extended current, it is urged to move in the contrary direction.

(201.) It is easy to perceive that if, instead of allowing the conducting wire transmitting the terminated current to obey its tendency to move parallel to itself, its motion were restricted to rotation round a fixed axis at one of its extremities, as shown in *fig.* 113, the force arising from the action of the in-

Fig. 113.

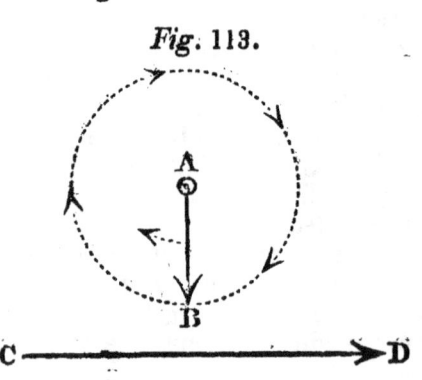

definite current C D, will carry the terminated current round the whole circumference of the circle. This rotatory force is independent of the angle of inclination of the currents, and is, consequently, uniform in every position of A B; and will accordingly act as an uniformly accelerating force, causing the wire to revolve with continually increasing velocity, until checked by friction and other mechanical obstacles.

(202.) The direction in which the wire revolves depends, of course, upon the relation between the directions of the two currents concerned. When the terminated current is passing from the centre to the circumference in the shorter wire, its revolution will be as represented in the figure; that is, in a direction contrary to that of the unlimited current, in that part of the circle which is nearest to it, but similar to it in the more distant part of the circle. The reverse takes place when the current in A B is passing from the circumference to the centre.

(203.) While such is the action of the

extended current upon the one that is terminated, an equal but contrary reaction is necessarily exerted by the terminated one upon the extended current. Thus, while the current A B, *fig.* 114,

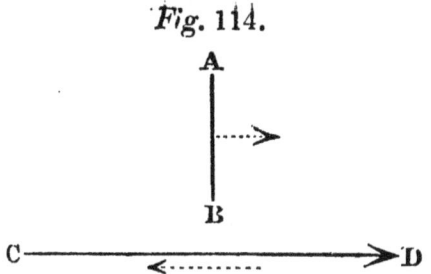

Fig. 114.

tends to move in the direction of the upper arrow, its reciprocal action on the current C D, urges the wire that conducts it in the contrary direction, from D to C, as denoted by the lower arrow; and the same principle applies to all the other cases.

§ 4. *Action of Diverging and Converging Currents.*

(204.) Since the rotatory force is the same in all positions of the wire, it is evident that if wires, or other conducting bodies, be so disposed as to cause the currents to radiate from a centre in all directions, they will tend to revolve in the same manner as any one of them singly would have done, by the influence of a rectilineal current in the vicinity, and in the same plane; provided this latter current be wholly without the circumference of the circle of revolution. The same thing will happen when the currents converge from the circumference to the centre, only the direction of the motion will be reversed. These two conditions of the experiment are represented in *figs.* 115 and 116, where the arrow-heads in the paths of the currents denote their direction; and the exterior dotted arrows the direction of the revolution of the conductors.

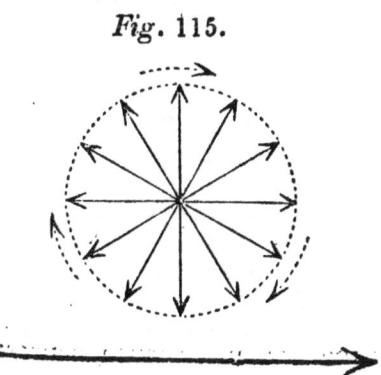

Fig. 115.

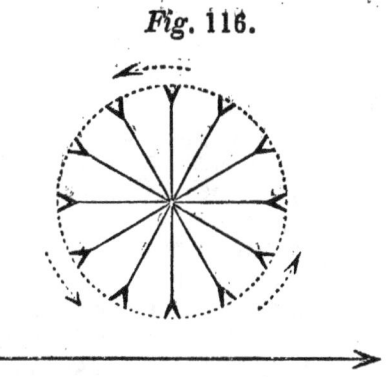

Fig. 116.

(205.) Examples of this kind of divergence or convergence of currents frequently occur in electro-dynamical experiments. They are met with whenever a fluid conductor, such as mercury, is the medium of communication between the point of a conducting wire dipped into the fluid and a circular rim of metal; in which case there is always more or less of diffusion of currents while they are passing through the fluid; and generally there is a tolerably regular radiation or concentration of the currents, of which some idea may be formed by *fig.* 117; where the current passing from P to N, through mercury contained in the cylindrical vessel V, will radiate from the point of the wire towards every part of the circumference of that vessel. If the current pass from N to P, it will converge towards the wire. In either case the action of a strong current, passing along the straight horizontal conductor C D, will give rise to a revolving motion in the mercury, the direction of which, corresponding with the directions of the two currents, is indicated by the arrows at w, D, and m.

(206.) It is not easy to exemplify by direct experiment the theoretical deductions applicable to the case of the action of a straight current of indefinite

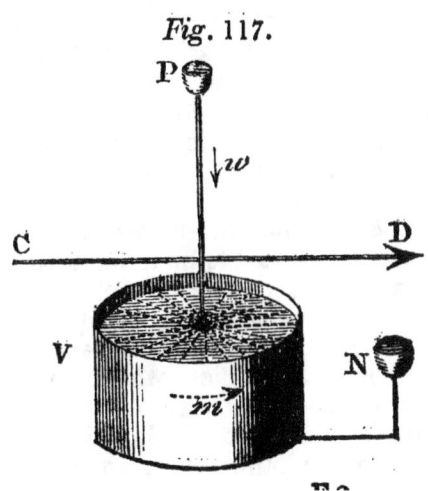

Fig. 117.

length on a terminated current; that is, on a portion of another current, situated on one side only. The difficulty arises from the impossibility of limiting the actions to those parts of the currents to which we wish to confine them, while studying their effects, and of excluding the action of the remaining portions of the currents necessary for completing the circuit. The only mode of preventing the interference of the latter, is to neutralize them by opposing one part to another; this may in a great measure be accomplished by providing for the subdivision and branching off of the currents in different directions, so that their actions may destroy one another. If, for instance, the ends of the smaller wire that is to be rendered moveable, be made to dip into a vessel of mercury, of sufficient width to allow of the electric currents to diverge and spread over a considerable surface, they will not materially interfere with the actions we are examining.

(207.) In the cases we have just considered, (§ 204,) the axis of rotation in the shorter wire was supposed to be at its extremity. If its situation were different — were it, for example, in the middle of its length, as at X, *fig.* 118, it is evident that when the current is passing from A to B, it moves in the first portion towards the

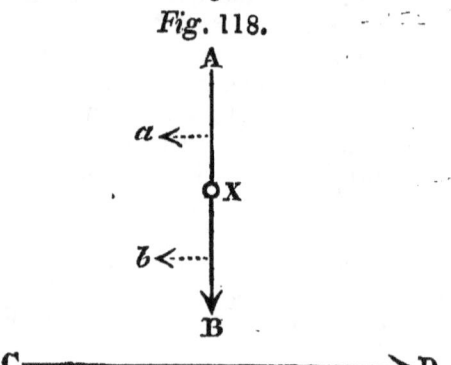

Fig. 118.

centre, and in the second portion from it; hence the rotatory forces, denoted by the arrows *a, b*, counteract one another, and the wire is urged to revolve only by the difference, if there be any, between them.

(208.) If the current, which we have hitherto supposed to be terminated, that is, altogether on one side of the rectilinear current, were prolonged so as to cross the latter (without, however, joining it), that portion which extended beyond it would have a tendency to move in an opposite direction to the part on the other side; so that these rotatory forces would oppose each other; and as the strongest would prevail, it would bring the conductor into a position where they are in equilibrium. See *fig.* 119, where the portion *f* B of the limited

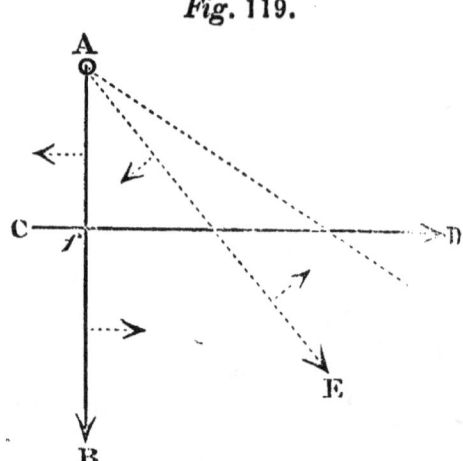

Fig. 119.

rectilineal current A B, turning on the axis A, and crossing the unlimited current C D, tends to move in a contrary direction to the portion A *f*, the position of equilibrium being that of A E.

(209.) If the current A B be traversed by the current C D passing through the axis itself, A, the position of equilibrium is that of parallelism between the two wires. In either case there can be no revolution round the axis.

§ 5. *Action between Currents situated in different Planes.*

(210.) Let us now consider what will happen when the two currents A B and C D, *fig.* 120, are in different planes, both being of an indefinite length, and extending on both sides of the perpendicular line P Q, which is common to the directions of both currents, and divides each into two portions. At-

Fig. 120.

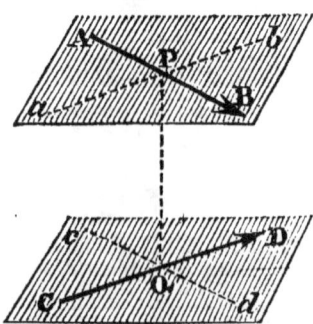

traction will take place between those portions in which the current is passing towards P or Q, the points at which the currents are nearest to each other; that is, in the present instance, between the portions A P and C Q. The portions P B and Q D will also attract one another, because the currents are proceeding from the points P and Q, in each respectively. But the portions A P and Q D will repel one another, as will also the portions P B and C Q; because the currents are moving in a different manner in the two that compose each of these pairs.

All these forces concur in producing a rotatory motion round the axis P Q. The wire A B will tend to assume the position ab, parallel to C D; and the wire C D will be urged to take the position cd parallel to A B. If only one of these be moveable, it will place itself in a line parallel to the other; if both be moveable, they both will take an intermediate position; so that, in either case, they will become parallel to one another. That part of the force which produces this rotatory effect, and acts in a plane perpendicular to the axis, may be termed the *directive force*. It varies as the sine of the angle A P a; but another part of the force still remains, namely, that which acts in a direction perpendicular to this plane—that is, parallel to the line P Q, the nearest distance of the wires. It is evident that this force varies as the cosine of the angle A P a. Whenever that angle is less than a right angle, this force is attractive; and as it tends to bring the currents nearer to each other, it may be distinguished from the former by the designation of the *approximative force*. Commencing when the positions of the wires, from being perpendicular, are slightly inclined to each other, this latter force attains its maximum when they have been brought by the directive force into a parallel position. When the corresponding portions of the wires, on the other hand, form an obtuse angle, the approximative force is negative, and is so in the greatest degree when the wires are parallel, so that their currents move in opposite directions. This is an obvious consequence of the change of sign which the cosine of the angle A P a experiences when the latter changes from an acute to an obtuse angle.

(211.) If the movements of either of the wires be restricted to rotation round an axis different from P Q, such as X, *fig.* 121, some part of the directive force will be destroyed by the opposing action of the current passing through the portion X P, which intervenes between the axis and the perpendicular. This opposition of forces will increase according as the axis is further removed from the perpendicular: so that all action may

Fig. 121.

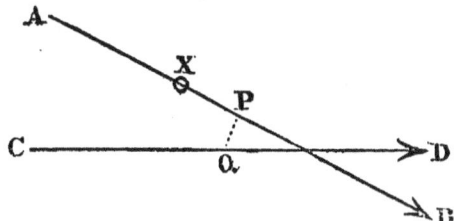

come to be entirely neutralized, if its distance is sufficiently great in proportion to the length of the other branch, P B, of the current situated on the other side of P Q. In estimating the resulting effect, however, it is necessary to take into account the mechanical advantage which the rotatory force, impelling the remote part P B, has over that which impels X P, in consequence of the greater length of lever by which it acts. When the contrary rotatory momenta thence arising are equal, the currents will be in a position of equilibrium, which position will tend the more nearly to coincide with that of parallelism, in proportion as the axis approaches to a coincidence with the perpendicular P Q. This result may be verified by employing the apparatus *fig.* 106, which, from its construction, is, as we have seen, astatic, and by which we may study the action of a transverse current upon either of the horizontal branches to which it is presented.

§ 6. *Mutual Action of Rectilineal and Curvilineal Currents.*

(212.) If a terminated current, which describes a curve line, be subjected to the action of an unlimited rectilinear current, its different portions will be urged in different directions, each being perpendicular to the respective portion of the curve. Thus the different parts of the circular conductors A B, *fig.* 122,

Fig. 122.

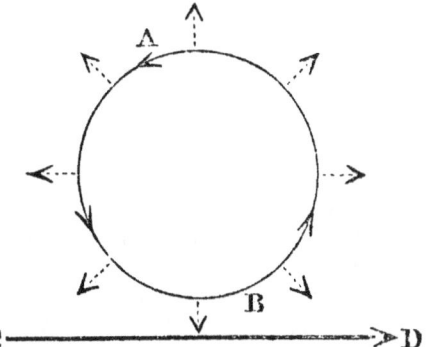

or E F, *fig*. 123, through which an electric current is passing, will be urged by the straight current C D, situated in the same plane with it, in the various directions indicated by the dotted arrows. If these forces were all equal, or nearly

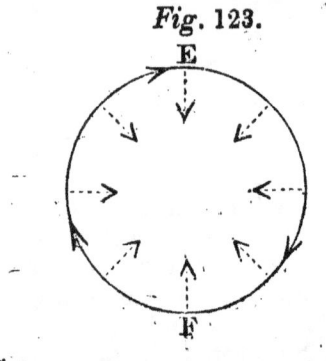

Fig. 123.

so, which could only happen when C D was at an infinite distance, or one incomparably greater than the diameter of the circle, they would all be in equilibrium. But, in all other cases, portions of the circles nearest to the current will be more powerfully acted upon than the remoter parts, and the forces by which they are impelled will therefore prevail, and the whole circle will tend to approach or recede from C D, according as the direction of the currents in that part is similar or contrary to that of the current C D. Thus it appears that the *approximative* force is equal to the difference between the resultants of the attractive and repulsive forces.

(213.) If the circular conductor be now made to revolve on an axis X Y, *fig*. 124, parallel to C D, and if it be

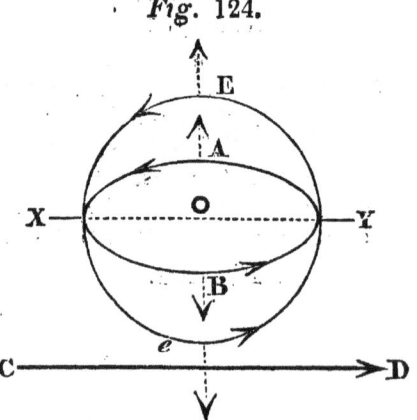

Fig. 124.

turned on this axis so that its plane is inclined to that which passes through its centre O, and the rectilinear current C D, the directions of the forces at A and B, being out of the plane of the circle, may be decomposed each into a force in that plane along the radius of rotation, and into one at right angles to it. The latter of these forces will tend to produce rotation, and to bring back the circle into its position of stable equilibrium E *e* in the plane common to it and to the current C D. Hence the *directive* force, or that which tends to bring the circle into this position, by turning it on its axis, is composed of the sum of the resultant forces acting upon the portions on each side of the axis. As the two sets of forces conspire to produce the same rotation, it matters not, as to the ultimate effect, whether or not the axis pass through the centre of the circle, provided it be parallel to C D, and either within the circle or beyond it; because, in the latter case, where there is an opposition of rotatory forces, the force acting on B being greater than that which acts on A, and also acting at a mechanical advantage, will always prevail.

(214.) Let us next suppose the axis X Y of the circular conductor to be at right angles to C D, as represented in *fig*. 125. The position of equilibrium will, under

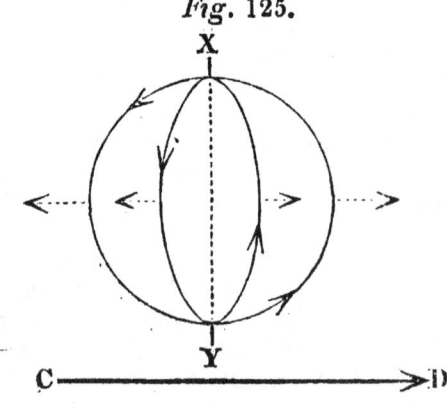

Fig. 125.

these circumstances, be precisely the same as the former: for any disturbance from the situation of the circle in which its plane includes the current C D, would give rise, in the portions of the circle nearest to it, to rotatory forces that tend to bring it back to that plane, as may be understood from what was explained in § 210. These forces will be aided by those that act on the lateral portions of the circle, in which an attraction exists towards those portions of the straight current where the directions correspond, as far as regards the approach to, or recession from the nearest points of the two conductors. The only forces opposing these are the forces acting upon the remoter parts of the circle, which are of course too weak to change the nature of the effect resulting from the former.

(215.) Whatever be the action which the circular current receives from the rectilineal one, a similar and opposite action is exerted by it on the latter, which is urged to assume a position in the plane of the circle, and such that the adjacent currents in each may be moving in similar directions.

(216.) The action of a circular current upon a rectilinear, but *terminated* current, situated wholly on one side of the plane of the circle, and inclined to it at a given angle, requires especial notice. If the direction of the straight current, when prolonged, pass near the centre of the circle, the forces that act upon it are nearly balanced, and neither action nor reaction is perceptible. If it be near the circumference, the action of the adjacent portion of that circumference will predominate, and effects, similar to those taking place between a terminated and an unlimited current, will be produced, with this modification, however, that the unlimited current being circular, the motion of translation in a straight conductor at right angles to the plane of the circle, following the course of the circumference, becomes itself circular; and if the conductor be attached to an axis perpendicular to the plane of the circle, and passing through its centre, that conductor will be made to revolve continually around that axis, as shown in *fig.*126, where C D is the circular current, and A B the straight moveable, but terminated current. This rotatory force

Fig. 126.

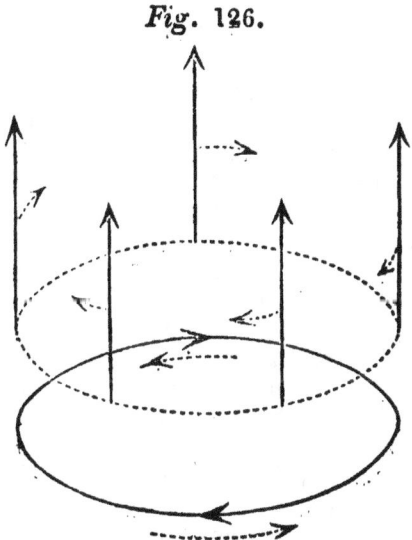

extends its influence beyond the interior of the circle to any distance, provided the straight current do not pass beyond the plane of the circle. The reaction of the straight current on the circular conductor impels the latter to revolve in the contrary direction, as marked by the dotted arrows parallel to it.

(217.) All these effects will be considerably increased if a great number of similar currents be moving in the same direction in the different parts of the circuit, described by the straight current in the last paragraph. This may be obtained by making currents traverse a number of wires placed in the surface of a cylinder, and parallel to its axis, which is also that of the rotation; or, what will be equivalent to this arrangement, by making a current pass along the surface of a hollow conducting cylinder, in the direction of its length; for in that case, the current may be considered as dividing itself into an infinite number of parallel filaments.

(218.) A similar augmentation of power may be obtained by multiplying the circular currents, either by employing a wire coiled into the form of a ring, or into that of a flat spiral. When these rings or spirals are combined with the cylinders above mentioned, the effects are again proportionably increased.

(219.) The modes of exemplifying these conclusions experimentally are various. Thus, a wire, as shown in *fig.* 127, consisting of two vertical branches, united above by a transverse arch, to

Fig. 127.

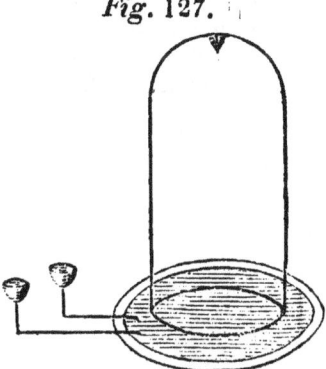

the centre of which is affixed a steel point turning downwards, for the purpose of suspension, may be united below to a circular rim, which dips into a shallow trough of mercury, so as to enable us to transmit currents through the wire, that will move in both the vertical wires in the same direction; that is, either upwards or downwards in both. If, while so suspended and connected, a circular current be made to act upon it from below, whether by means of a single circle, as shown in the same figure, or by a spiral coil, as that of *fig.* 128, the wire will revolve round its axis of suspension, in a direction determined by the relative direction of the current.

Fig. 128.

(220.) A hollow cylinder, *fig.* 129, balanced in a similar manner as that of *fig.* 123, may be substituted for the wire; but its revolution will in general

Fig. 129.

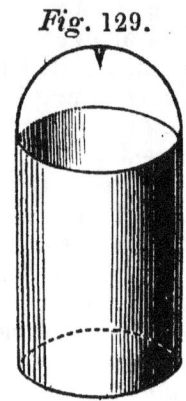

not be so rapid as the wire, because, although it may convey a more powerful current, the weight to be moved is also proportionably increased.

(221.) The rotation of the circular or spiral conductor may in like manner be exhibited by suspending either of them from a point in the axis of the circle, as in *fig.* 130, and subjecting it to the action of

Fig. 130.

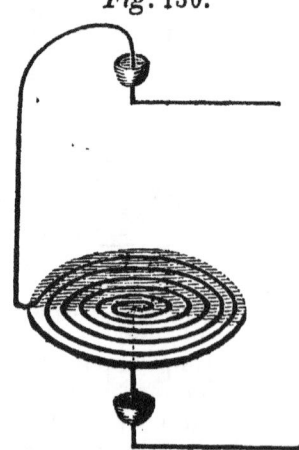

a terminated vertical current, that does not extend to both sides of its plane.

(222.) The effect is the same at whatever angle the direction of the straight current is inclined to the plane of the circular current, provided the axis on which it revolves be perpendicular to that plane and pass through its centre. Thus, if the wire A B, *fig.* 131, moveable round on an axis, A X, be subjected to the action of a circular current C D, the plane of which is wholly below it, it will revolve, describing a conical surface.

Fig. 131.

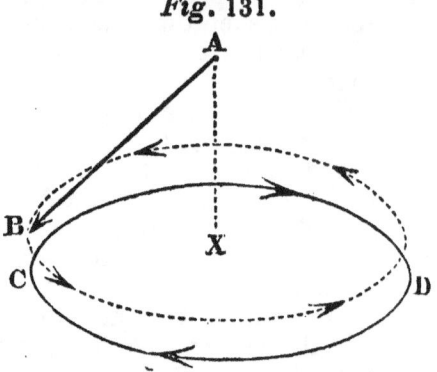

(223.) Pursuing this investigation, it becomes evident that a revolving motion will equally take place, if the straight conductor be parallel to the plane of the circle, provided it does not exceed in length the radius of the circle. Thus, the straight conductor A B, *fig.* 132, which is wholly within the circle C D, revolves round the axis A, in the

Fig. 132.

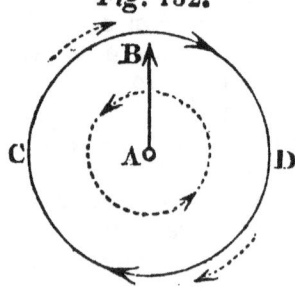

same direction as the current in that circle, when its own current is passing from the circumference to the centre. When its current passes from the centre to the circumference, it will revolve in a direction contrary to the motion of the current in the circle. On the other hand, if the straight current be fixed, and the circle moveable round its centre, the action of the former will cause the latter to revolve in directions opposite to those which have been just stated.

(224.) It may be observed that we have limited this proposition to the cases in which the current A B does not extend beyond the circumference of the circle; for if it did, as seen in *fig.* 133, the exterior portion A B, being affected in an opposite manner from the interior portion B C, there would arise an opposition among the rotatory forces; and the amount as well as direction of the resulting motion would be regulated by the difference between them. This contrariety of effect will, on the other hand, be removed, if the straight current be wholly exterior to the circle, as A B, *fig.* 134, though still moveable round the same axis as before. The revolution will now be performed in a

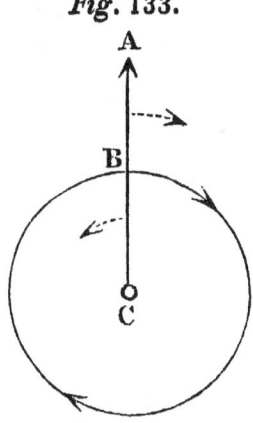

Fig. 133.

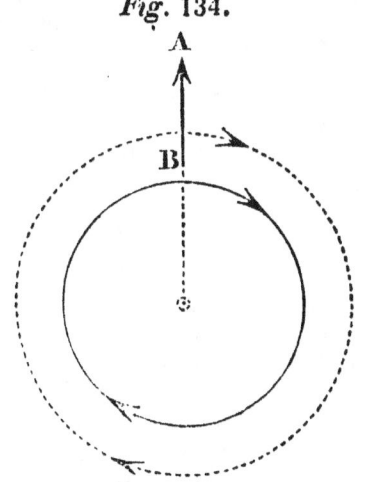

Fig. 134.

direction contrary to that of the interior current in the former case. The reaction of an exterior current on the circular conductor will likewise be in the opposite direction to what it was before.

(225.) It is obvious that every thing that has been stated with regard to straight currents, the direction of which is towards or from the centre of the circular current, applies also to a number of radiating or converging currents.

Hence if the cylinder, *fig.* 129, communicating by its point with one of the poles of a voltaic battery, have its lower rim immersed in a flat dish containing mercury, communicating by a wire from its centre with the opposite pole of the battery, radiating or converging currents will be established in the mercury, which, acting on the vertical currents existing in the sides of the cylinder, will cause it to revolve. If the currents tending to or from the cylinder be exterior to it, which may be obtained by surrounding the cylinder with a metallic ring of larger diameter, and making this ring the medium of communication with the battery, the revolution of the cylinder will be made in the opposite direction to what it was before.

§ 7. *Reciprocal Action of Circular Currents.*

(226.) The mutual actions exerted between two circular currents, may readily be collected from the application of the general law of attraction among those parts in which the directions of the currents are similar, and of repulsion where they are dissimilar. If one of the circles be fixed and the motion of the other be limited to revolution round an axis, the effects of their mutual action will depend on the position of the centre of the moveable circle with regard to the plane of the fixed circle, and also upon the position and inclination of the axis with relation to the line joining both centres.

(227.) If the centre of the moveable circle be in the same plane with the fixed circle, or not far removed from it, whatever be the inclination of the axis, a directive force will arise, tending to bring the whole of the circumference into that plane, and to make it assume such a position as that the currents in the adjacent portions of the circle shall be in the same directions. Thus C D, (*figs.* 135 and 136,) being the fixed,

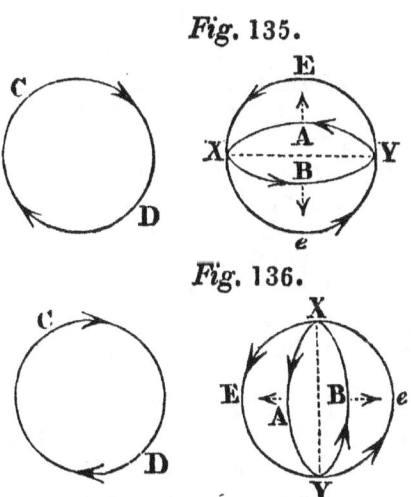

Fig. 135.

Fig. 136.

and A B the moveable circle, on the axis X Y, the directive force will bring the latter into the position E *e*, that is, in the same plane with C D; and this will happen equally, whether the axis be at right angles to the line joining their centres, as in *fig.* 135, or coincide with it as in *fig.* 136, or have any other inclination to it.

228. If the centre of the moveable circle be any where in a line drawn through the centre of the former, and perpendicular to its plane, the moveable circle will tend to arrange itself in a plane parallel to the fixed circle, and having its currents moving in a similar direction. This is evident from *fig.* 137, in which the same letters as before are used to denote the corresponding points.

Fig. 137.

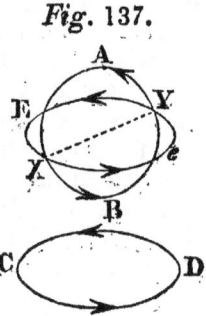

(229.) In both cases an approximative force takes place, whenever the moveable circle has arrived at its position of equilibrium; which force, in the latter case, is particularly strong, inasmuch as the attraction of the corresponding parts of the circles is uniform throughout the whole circumference.

(230.) For each position of the centre of the moveable circle, intermediate to those above described, there exists a particular position of equilibrium, the line of which, if prolonged, would intersect the plane of the fixed circle at a certain distance beyond it.

(231.) All these positions of equilibrium are determinate, and exclude the possibility of any continued rotatory or revolving motions.

(232.) When an electric current, after traversing a certain line of conducting bodies, returns upon itself, so as to arrive at the point from which it had set out, or very near it, it has been denominated a *closed circuit*. Such is the case with the circles we have been considering. One of the most important facts on which the theory of electro-dynamics rests, is that the mutual action of two closed circuits cannot produce, in either of these circuits, a continued rotatory motion in an invariable direction; and, consequently, no assemblage of closed circuits can ever be made to produce such rotatory motion, in whatever manner they may be disposed.

(233.) Experiments on the mutual actions of circular currents, either on each other or on straight conductors, are most advantageously made by means of a flat spiral rendered *astatic*, by opposing to it a similar coil on the opposite arm of the lever, from the middle of which they are both suspended, as shown in *fig.* 138, the spiral turns being in

Fig. 138.

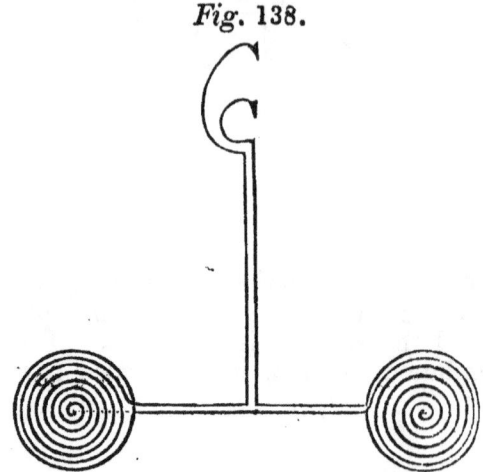

different directions in each, so that the rotatory influence of the earth on the one shall be exactly balanced by its influence on the other.

§ 8. *Mutual Action of Heliacal and Rectilinear Conductors.*

(234.) We have seen that the action of conducting wires rolled into the form of a flat spiral is similar almost in every respect to that of a simple circular wire; but when coiled round the surface of a cylinder, so as to constitute a helix, its action becomes much more complicated. When the extremities of the wire, after completing the helix, are made to return along the axis, as described in § 105, and shown in *fig.* 71, constituting what has been termed by Ampère an electro-dynamic cylinder, the whole may be considered as equivalent in effect to a succession of circles, whose planes are perpendicular to the axis, and occupy the whole length of the cylinder. In determining the forces that are called into operation by such an apparatus, we may, therefore, put out of consideration the slight obliquity which the turns of the spires have to the axis, and the effect of which is completely neutralized by the corresponding portion of the wire that passes along the axis; and we may regard the whole as composed of currents circulating at right angles to the length of the cylinder.

(235.) Since we have seen that the

influence of a single circular current C D, *fig.* 126, on a straight terminated current A B, perpendicular to the plane of the circle, is to induce in it a tendency to revolve with a motion parallel to itself, round the line drawn from the centre of the circle perpendicularly to its plane, it is evident that the addition of similar circles, placed in succession exactly below the first, (supposing the axis vertical, as in the figure,) will tend to increase this force of revolution. The effect of each additional circle, it is true, is less than the preceding, not only because its distance is greater, but also because its action is more oblique, and because the difference between the actions of the nearer and more remote portions of the circle continually diminishes as the angle between the lines drawn from the several points in the straight conductor, and the centres of the respective circles, increases, which is the case as they are further removed from the extremity of the straight conductor. From all these considerations, the force by which the current A B, *fig.* 139, is urged to revolve round the axis,

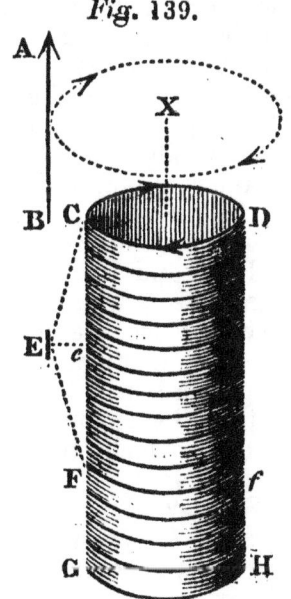

Fig. 139.

X, in consequence of the action of the lowermost circle G H, is plainly less than that exerted by the circle F *f*, and still less than that exerted by C D.

(236.) On the other hand, if we add in succession a number of circular currents *above* C D, they will conspire with the lower circles in their effect of producing a tendency to revolution in the straight conductor; but each will do this only by its action on that part of the conductor that is above its own plane; for its operation in any portion situated below that plane is to produce a revolution in the contrary direction. So that the action exerted upon any elementary portion of a vertical current, at E, for example, is, as far as it depends upon the circles above that which is nearest to it, exactly balanced by an equal number of circles below it; that is, the circles lying between C and *e* are counterbalanced by those lying between *e* and F, the whole of that portion of the cylinder between C and F being neutralized; and the only portion that is active being that which lies beyond F, that is, between F and G. This active part of the cylinder becomes smaller in proportion as the element is situated nearer to the plane which divides the cylinder into two equal parts; and at this point the action is reduced to nothing: on the contrary, it increases as the element comes nearer to either extremity of the cylinder, where it is the greatest of all. These extremities may accordingly be considered as the *active poles* of the cylinder, round which the revolution of the conductor is made: the resultant of all the forces called into action by every part of the cylinder has the direction of the tangent of the circle of revolution; that is to say, is at right angles to the line joining the straight conductor and the pole.

(237.) It is hardly necessary to remark that the action in this, as in every other instance, is reciprocal between the straight conductor and electro-dynamic cylinder; so that if the conductor be fixed and the cylinder moveable, the latter will revolve round the former; or, if restricted to a motion round its own axis, it will perform a rotatory movement round that axis.

(238.) The same tendency to revolution about the poles of an electro-dynamic cylinder, arising from a force of a tangential kind, apparently emanating from these poles, is observed to take place, whatever be the angle of inclination between the straight conductor and the axis of the cylinder. In order to explain this curious fact, the application of which is of considerable importance in a theoretical point of view, we must avail ourselves of the principle enunciated above (§ 198), namely, that the electro-dynamic action of currents that occupy in a similar manner two different surfaces, subtending the same angular extent, and lying in the same direction with reference to any point, on an elementary portion of current situated at that point, are equal. It will also be convenient to analyze the actions of each circular current into those exerted in planes at right angles to each other, a mode of viewing them which, being analogous to the artifice of the resolution of forces constantly resorted to in dynamics, will make no difference in the results. Conceive, then, that the currents, instead of moving in the circumference of a circle, traverse the four sides of a square, and that the cylinder is represented by a square prism. S N, *fig.* 140, is intended to convey the idea of a prism, so constituted, the surface of which is

Fig. 140.

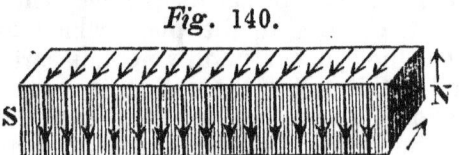

occupied by electric currents circulating round each of the laminæ, into which it may be divided by planes perpendicular to its axis, the direction of the currents being marked in the two sides which come into view, by the arrows. On the sides opposite to them, and which are not seen, the currents are, of course, moving in the contrary directions.

(239.) Let us now examine the effects of currents in each side upon a straight conductor, whose direction is at right angles to the axis, and which is placed in various positions with regard to the prism.

Let P Q R S, *fig.* 141, be the upper surface of this prism, its axis being horizontal; let W be the section of a vertical conducting wire, of indefinite

Fig. 141.

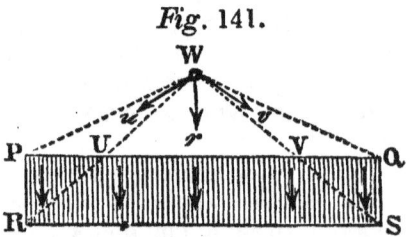

length, perpendicular to the plane of the figure; and let the current be moving in this wire in the same direction as those currents which traverse the adjacent vertical side of the prism, of which the upper edge is P Q. We shall suppose, for example, that the currents are ascending in the wire, and also in the side adjacent to it, whence they traverse the upper side from P Q towards R S (as denoted by the arrows), descending again on the side opposite to W, and of which the edge is R S, and returning on the lower side in a direction from R S towards P Q.

Since the currents are passing in opposite directions in the upper and lower surfaces of the prism, their effects on W (as far as any horizontal motion is concerned) are completely neutralized; and we need, therefore, only examine the actions of the vertical surfaces P Q and R S. Let R W and S W be the sections of two vertical planes, drawn from W to R and to S, cutting P Q in U and V respectively. It follows from the proposition above referred to that the actions of the currents in that portion of the surface P Q, adjacent to W, which is included between U and V, are exactly balanced by the currents in the whole of the surface R S, opposite to it, and which run in contrary directions. The resulting action, therefore, will be determined only by the currents in the remaining portions of the surface P Q, situated between P and U on the one side, and between V and Q on the other, both of which attract the current in W: the former in the direction of W *u*, the latter in the direction W *v*. These two forces combine in giving a resultant in the direction W *r*, indicating an attraction towards the centre of the prism.

(240.) In proportion as the situation of the vertical conductor is taken nearer to either of the extremities of the prism, such as Q S, for instance, the portion P U of the side P Q, intercepted between the plane R W and the extremity P, increases in extent, while the portion V Q diminishes. Consequently the forces arising from the attractions of the former portion are proportionally increased, and those from the latter diminished, and the resulting force gradually becomes more inclined towards P.

(241.) When W is situated in the plane of the side Q S, as in *fig.* 142, the force arising from the currents adjoining

Fig. 142.

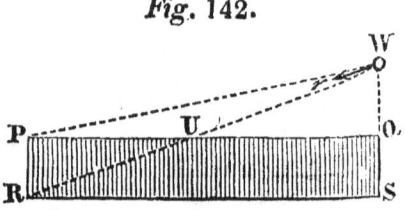

to Q vanishes entirely, and the action upon the wire depends solely upon the currents in the remoter division of the side P Q, namely, that comprehended between P and U. The resultant force will therefore be directed towards these

ELECTRO-MAGNETISM.

currents, being nearly at right angles to the line W Q.

(242.) When W is situated on the other side of this line, as shown in *fig.* 143, the extent of the active portion of the surface P Q has increased considerably, for it now occupies the large space P U; but its power has not increased in the same proportion, because

Fig. 143.

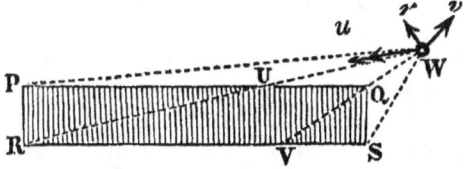

its action is more oblique, as well as more distant than it was before. The resultant of this action is in the direction W *u*. It is combined, however, with another set of forces, those arising from the uncompensated portion V S, of the surface R S, situated between S and the vertical plane W Q V. The currents in this portion are moving in a direction contrary to that in W: their action upon it is therefore repulsive, and the force thence arising may be represented by W *v*, which, combined with W *u*, gives, as a final resultant, the force W *r*.

(243.) When W is placed in the prolongation of the axis of the prism, as in *fig.* 144, it is attracted by the whole of the currents in the side P Q, and repelled by the whole of those in R S,

Fig. 144.

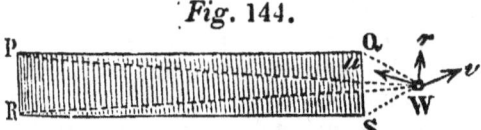

the former giving rise to the force W *u*, the latter to the force W *v*, their resultant being W *r*.

(244.) When W is in the situation represented in *fig.* 145, the currents situated between V and S are neutralized by those between P and U. Those

Fig. 145.

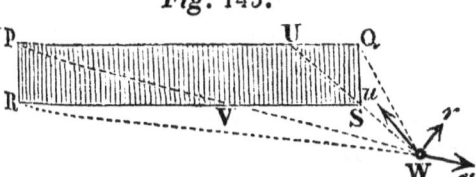

between R and V repel W in the direction of W *v*, while those between U and Q attract it in the direction W *u*, forces which produce the resultant W *r*.

(245.) When W is in the prolongation of the line Q S, *fig.* 146, the currents between P and Q being neutralized by

Fig. 146.

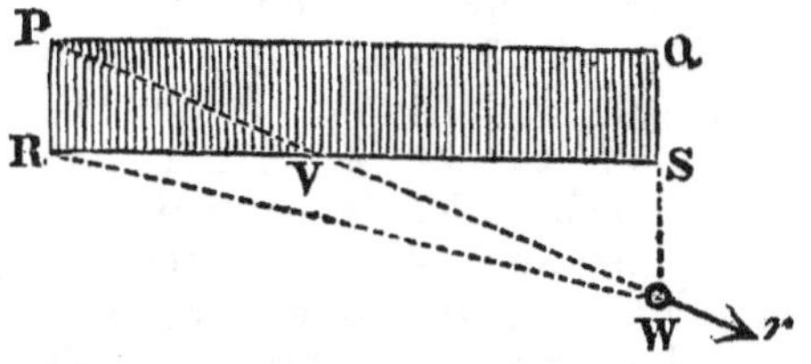

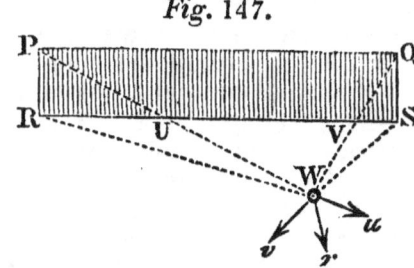

those between V and S, the only active currents are those between R and V, which being repulsive, the resultant is in the direction W *r*.

(246.) When the situation of W is as shown in *fig.* 147, the active portions of the currents are those occupying the spaces R U and V S, which being both repulsive, and acting according to the directions W *u* and W *v* respectively, join in producing the resultant W *r*.

Fig. 147.

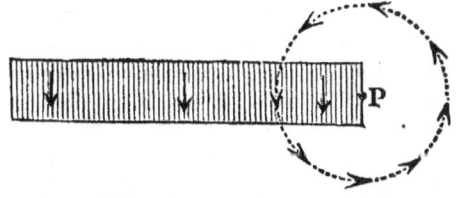

(247.) Thus it appears that, combining all the results of this induction, the conducting wire is, in every situation, urged by a force impelling it in the direction of a tangent to the circumference of a circle, C, *fig.* 148, round the extremity of the prism, P, which may therefore be considered as having the functions of

Fig. 148.

a pole. The force thus arising possesses the same character of being rotatory and tangential as that which was exerted on the same wire when its direction was parallel to the axis: and if it possess this character in two directions that are at right angles to each other, it may fairly be inferred that the law is general, and that it applies to all the intermediate inclinations.

(248.) The explanation above given will be sufficient to convey a general idea of the application of the theory to the phenomenon in question. But the subject has been investigated with all the rigour of mathematical analysis, and the results determined with all the precision that can be required for comparison with actual experiment. We have purposely omitted several of the minuter details which were even compatible with the popular view we have presented, but which would have required more complicated diagrams for their exposition, and considerably lengthened the inquiry, but which have no material influence on the ultimate conclusions. Thus, if the straight conductor, instead of being indefinite in length, were terminated, and wholly above the horizontal prism, it would be found that there is no longer that exact compensation between the currents in the upper and lower surfaces; for when the conductor is immediately above the prism, the upper currents have a much more considerable influence on it than the lower currents, and urge it on its revolution in the same direction as that in which it was moving from the effect of the other forces in operation. At the remotest part of the circle, the lower currents come more into operation from their acting with less obliquity than the upper currents, and concur, in their turn, in augmenting the tendency to revolution in the same direction.

(249.) The following laws are obtained as the results of the mathematical investigation of the subject:—

i. The action of a very slender electro-dynamic cylinder upon an elementary portion of a current may be resolved into two forces, acting in directions perpendicular to the direction of the current, and also respectively perpendicular to the lines drawn from it to each of the extremities of the axis of the cylinder; each of these forces being inversely as the squares of these distances.

ii. The action of an electro-dynamic cylinder upon an indefinite conductor, perpendicular to its axis, may, in like manner, be reduced to two tangential forces, as in the former case; but these forces are in the simple inverse ratio of the distances from the extremities of the cylinder.

iii. If the length of the electro-dynamic cylinder be supposed to be indefinite, its action upon an elementary portion of a current will depend entirely upon the relative positions of the element, and that extremity of the cylinder to which it is referred, and is influenced in no respect by the relative position of the axis of the cylinder.

iv. The action of this cylinder upon conductors, of whatever form or magnitude, is subject to the same conditions, being dependent solely upon the position of that extremity, which is referred to the conductor, and remains the same whatever be the direction of the axis of the cylinder *.

(250.) The conclusions thus deduced from the evidence of observation, combined with the deductions from theory, indicate the strongest analogy, and almost perfect identity, between the agency of electro-dynamic cylinders and that of magnets. The law of their action upon an electric current, and of the reaction of the latter upon both, is precisely the same; so much so, that if we had the command of sufficiently powerful currents, the electro-dynamic cylinder might be substituted for the magnet in all the experiments we have described in the last Chapter, and the same results, whether of attraction, repulsion, or revolution, would be obtained from them. The two extremities of an electro-dynamic cylinder exhibit all the properties possessed by the poles of a magnet: that end in which the current of positive electricity is moving in a direction similar to the movements of the hands of a watch, acting as the *south* pole of a common magnet; and the other end, in which the current is moving in a contrary manner, manifesting a *northern* polarity.

(251.) It will be readily anticipated, from the known resemblance between the action of electro-dynamical cylinders and of magnets on electric currents, that two such cylinders will act upon each other precisely in the same way as magnets do. Theory confirms the exactness of this general conclusion; for the following is the law to which mathematical examination conducts us, namely, that the mutual action of two electro-dynamic cylinders may always be represented by four forces, having the directions of lines drawn from each extremity of the one to both extremities of the other, and being to one another in the reciprocal ratio of the squares of these lines, provided these distances be not exceedingly small †.

---

* Ampère, Recueil d'Observations Electro-dynamiques, p. 343. See also Demonferrand's Manuel d'Electricité Dynamique; or Cumming's Translation, pp. 66, 67, 138, and 140.

† Ampère, Recueil d'Observations Electro-dynamiques, &c. p. 343.

(252.) The mutual action of electro-dynamic cylinders on magnets is the same as that of two magnets on each other, so that in any experiment the one may be substituted for the other without affecting the nature of the result.

Chapter XII.

Theories of Electro-Magnetism.

§ 1. *Electro-Magnetic Theory of Oersted.*

(253.) The discovery of the remarkable phenomena of electro-magnetism naturally gave rise to the invention of a variety of hypotheses for their explanation. Adopting the theory which ascribes the electric phenomena to the agency of two fluids, composing by their union a neutral fluid, and exhibiting their peculiar powers when that union is decomposed, and when they are obtained separately, Professor Oersted conceived that a distinct class of effects resulted during the act of their reunion; which was marked, not only by mechanical agitations among the particles of bodies, by the production of sound, by the evolution of light, and by the disengagement of heat, but also by the disturbance of the magnetic equilibrium. These phenomena seemed to indicate the occurrence of great and sudden changes taking place in the conditions of two powerful agents at the moment of their coalescence, and suggested to Oersted the idea that something analogous to a shock takes place when the fluids rush together from a distance. During galvanic action, the separation of the two electric fluids, proceeding without intermission in one part of the apparatus, and their reunion being in like manner effected in perpetual sequence along the conducting bodies which complete the circuit, he conceived that a continued series of electric shocks took place throughout the whole line of conductors; a condition which he expressed by the term *Electric Conflict*.

(254.) If these views be correct, it must follow that the electric fluids, which, whether at rest or in motion, have, when isolated, no apparent influence on magnetic bodies, acquire, during their conflict, the power of affecting these bodies. This hypothesis was expressed by Oersted in the following words: "The electric conflict acts only on the magnetic particles of matter. All non-magnetic bodies appear penetrable by the electric conflict, while magnetic bodies, or rather their magnetic particles, resist the passage of this conflict. Hence they can be moved by the impetus of the contending powers. It is sufficiently evident that the electric conflict is not confined to the conductor, but dispersed pretty widely in the circumjacent space.

"We may likewise collect that this conflict performs circles; for without this condition, it seems impossible that one part of the uniting wire, when placed below the magnetic pole, should drive it towards the east, and when placed above it, towards the west—(see § 13, *figs.* 1 and 2): for it is the nature of a circle that the motions in opposite parts should have an opposite direction. Besides, a motion in circles, joined with a progressive motion, according to the length of the conductor, ought to form a conchoidal or spiral line; but this, unless I am mistaken, contributes nothing to explain the phenomena hitherto observed.

"All the effects of the north pole are easily understood by supposing that magnetic electricity moves in a spiral line bent towards the right, and propels the north pole, but does not act on the south pole. The effects on the south pole are explained in a similar manner, if we ascribe to positive electricity a contrary motion and power of acting on the south pole, but not upon the north *."

(255.) The views entertained by Oersted were very generally adopted by philosophers who prosecuted the path of discovery he had laid open. It was the prevailing belief that electricity in motion had magnetic properties, or rather that it imparted to the body that conducted it a species of transverse magnetism. Some conceived that the action resembled that of a series of magnets placed around the axis of the conductor, at right angles to each other, their poles being situated in four lines parallel to the axis, and forming a square, as represented in *fig.* 149, which

Fig. 149.

exhibits a section of the conducting wire, and four magnets with their poles

* Annals of Philosophy, vol. xvi. p. 276.

marked *n*, *s*, respectively, succeeding each other in a regular order of alternation round the wire. But this hypothesis cannot be a faithful representation of the phenomena; for it is found on experiment that the action of the conducting wire upon a magnetized needle is exactly the same in every part of its circumference. If the wire be vertical, for instance, its effect is the same in all azimuths, and has no relation to any rectangular planes passing through the axis of the wire.

(256.) With this correction, the hypothesis that a conducting wire acts as if a series of minute magnets were placed in succession round its circumference, with their opposite poles facing each other, will account for a large class of phenomena. It explains why a compass needle assumes its peculiar position at right angles to the axis of the wire, in obedience to the directive influence of that particular portion of the imaginary series of magnets which is the nearest to the needle, see *fig.* 150; and also the mutual attraction between the needle

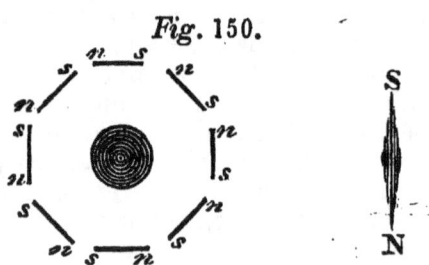

Fig. 150.

and the wire under these circumstances. It also explains the other fundamental fact in the science; namely, the mutual actions exerted between two conducting wires: for when the currents are passing in the same direction in both the wires as in A and B, *fig.* 151, the polarities

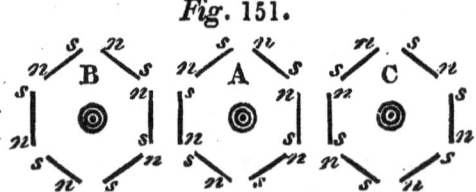

Fig. 151.

of the minute magnets on the sides adjacent to one another will be reversed, and they will consequently attract one another. The contrary will happen when the currents are passing in opposite directions in the two wires, as in A and C; for then the polarities of the magnets belonging to each, which are adjoining to each other, are the same in kind, and, therefore, repulsive of each other.

(257.) But there is still one class of phenomena which the hypothesis we are considering is totally inadequate to explain; that comprising the rotatory movements either of magnets or of conductors, and which movements may be maintained with uniform velocity notwithstanding the retardation from friction, or the impediments of a resisting medium; exhibiting, in fact, the extraordinary spectacle of a really perpetual motion. The supposition of a series of magnets encircling the conducting wire will not account for this continued motion; for it is certain that no actual combination of magnets, nor even any conceivable arrangement of magnetic particles, could ever, consistently with the known laws of magnetic action, produce any approach to perpetual rotation. In order to obtain such movements, the agent from which the force emanates must itself be in motion, and must revolve round the axis of the wire, while traversing it from end to end, with the utmost rapidity. Such was the peculiar kind of movement, partly longitudinal, and partly circular, which Dr. Wollaston attributed to the electro-magnetic agent, and which he termed its *vertiginous motion*.

(258.) A further emendation must, therefore, be made in the hypothesis in order to adapt it to the phenomena, by supposing that the two magnetic fluids, which accompany the electric fluids, when the latter are set in motion, and in a state of conflict, (if we choose to adopt the phraseology of Oersted,) acquire a *vertiginous motion* in opposite directions transversely to the axis of the conductor; that is, the boreal fluid revolving in one direction, and the austral fluid in the other; these determinations being given to them by the direction in which the electric fluids are moving in the conductor, dependent, of course, upon the relative positions of the poles of the voltaic apparatus from which they proceed. There will result from this peculiar kind of movement, not only all the effects that we have just seen to be the consequence of quiescent circles of magnets, but also those of a rotatory nature, which nothing but an agent in motion could produce. The tangential action of a conductor upon a magnet is a necessary consequence of the transverse motions of the magnetic fluids in the conductor; and the rotation of a magnetic pole round that conductor, or conversely, the revolutions of the conductor round a magnet, are phenomena also naturally resulting from the vertiginous circulation of the two fluids.

(259.) The mutual attractions and repulsions of parallel conductors, are at once referred, as in the former case, to the action of parallel magnets having their poles in the same or in opposite directions. If, for example, the electro-magnetic current be moving in the same direction in two parallel conducting wires, the stream of austral magnetic fluid belonging to one wire will be flowing in the same direction as the boreal magnetic fluid belonging to the other wire, in that part which is adjacent to it; and, on the other hand, the direction of the boreal fluid of the former will coincide with that of the austral fluid of the latter wire, in the adjacent part. According to the known laws of magnetic action, attraction must be the result of such a state of things; for the boreal and austral fluids attract one another. If W and *w*, *fig*. 152, represent sections of the conducting wires in both of which the current of positive electricity is descending, the arrows in the circumference of the outer dotted circles

Fig. 152.

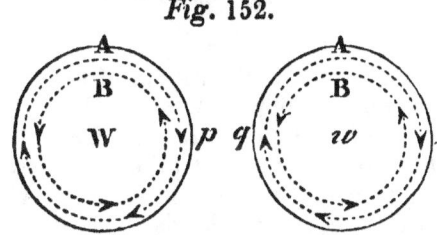

A A, will point out the directions in which the austral magnetic fluids circulate on the surface of the wires; and those on the inner circles B B, the directions in which the boreal fluids circulate, and it will be seen that in the parts *p* and *q*, when they are nearest to each other, the austral fluid in the one is moving in the same direction as the boreal fluid in the other, and we may, therefore, expect that they will attract each other.

(260.) If the electric currents be moving in contrary directions in the two wires, as represented in a similar manner in *fig*. 153, opposite effects will

Fig. 153.

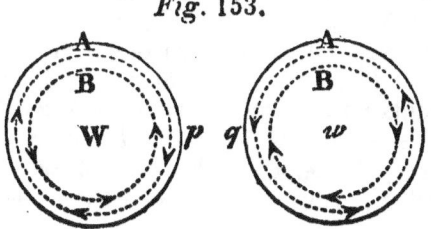

result; for in that case both the streams of austral fluid are moving in the same direction in the adjacent parts of the wires, and must consequently repel one another; and the same thing happens with regard to the streams of boreal fluid, which flow in the contrary direction to those of the austral fluid.

(261.) Such, then, is the hypothesis that has been, after proper emendations, made to correspond with the phenomena, and which may be assumed as a correct representation of them. It must, at the same time, be admitted to be an exceedingly strained and artificial hypothesis, at variance with the analogy of all other physical forces, and repugnant to our ideas of that simplicity which seems to pervade all the operations of the material world. All other known accelerating forces, emanating from a certain point, and exerted upon another point, act in the direction of the line joining these two points. Such is the case with the electric and with the magnetic actions, in all the cases that belong exclusively to the one or the other of these two classes of phenomena. When two conducting wires, bent into helices, act upon one another, which they do in a manner that imitates very exactly the mutual action of two magnets, the action is purely electrical, and is exerted in the lines of direction that join the acting points. The same is the case with two magnets, when magnetism alone is concerned. But when a helix and a magnet act upon one another, and present the very same phenomena as in either of the preceding cases, the theory assigns a tangential direction to the forces then called into operation. That a mode of action which is simple and intelligible in the case of actions either purely electric or purely magnetic, should be so suddenly and so completely changed when the electric and magnetic fluids act mutually upon one another, would be a strange and scarcely conceivable anomaly in physical science.

(262.) We may avoid all these difficulties by adopting the theory of electro-magnetism devised by the genius of Ampère, and ably supported by his mathematical, in conjunction with his experimental researches. Of this theory we shall proceed to give an account.

§ 2. *Electro-Dynamic Theory of Ampère.*

(263.) The phenomena relating to the

science of electro-magnetism may, as we have seen, be reduced to three classes, or general facts: the first being the evolution of a tangential and rotatory force usually exerted between a conducting body and a magnet; the second, the transverse induction of magnetism by the former in such bodies as are susceptible of receiving it; and the third, the attractive or repulsive force exerted between two electric currents traversing different conductors. In the magnetic theory already discussed, the first of these is considered as being the most general fact, and the other two as being merely its consequences. Ampère, on the contrary, assumes the last of these facts—that is, the mutual attractions and repulsions of electric currents, as the primary or fundamental fact, to which, by the help of a particular hypothesis as to the constitution of magnets, all the other facts, not only of electro-magnetism, but of magnetism also, are reducible.

(264.) His supposition is, that all bodies that possess magnetic properties, the globe of the earth being included among the number, derive those properties from currents of electricity continually circulating among the parts of which they are composed, and having, with relation to the axes of these bodies, one uniform direction of revolution, in planes perpendicular to those axes.

(265.) The striking resemblance which exists between the action of magnets, and that of electro-dynamic cylinders already described, and which extends through a wide range of phenomena, very naturally suggested the hypothesis on which this theory is founded; for since the circular currents in the latter are observed to produce effects similar to magnetic polarity, it is but an extension of the analogy to consider a magnet as deriving its properties from similar currents continually circulating in its substance.

(266.) In the account we have given of magnetism it will be seen that the phenomena attending the fracture of a magnet oblige us to consider magnetized iron as an aggregate of small particles of iron, each of which has the properties of a separate magnet (see MAGNETISM, § 141). In like manner, the hypothesis just stated, relative to the circulation of electric currents in the substance of a magnet, must receive a similar modification to that given to the theory of magnetism. Since the fragments detached from a magnetic bar are themselves complete magnets, the electric currents, from which it derives its properties, must be conceived as circulating round each of these fragments separately, or rather round particles smaller than any that can be obtained by mechanical division. Each particle, or magnetic element, may be regarded as constituting a voltaic circuit, analogous to a voltaic pile of which the two ends are united by conductors; the vitreous and the resinous electric fluids being separated at one point of the circuit, circulating in contrary directions round the particle, until they meet together, and by their reunion again forming the neutral fluid. The course of the fluids during this circulation is represented in *fig.* 154; V and R denoting respectively the paths of the vitreous and resinous electricities emanating from the point E in the particle of iron P, and flowing in the directions indicated

Fig. 154.

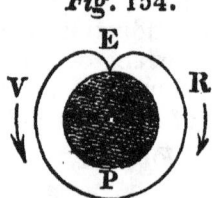

by the arrows, till they meet and coalesce on the opposite side. But as the effects of the one fluid are exactly the reverse of those of the other, the result is equivalent to the continued circulation of one of the fluids, the vitreous, for example, in one constant direction, E V P R.

(267.) A magnet, then, is to be considered as composed of an assemblage of parallel filaments, each of which is constituted by a series of particles, round which electric currents are circulating in the manner just described, all of them flowing in the same direction with reference to the axis of the filament, and moving in planes perpendicular to that axis. That extremity of the filament in which, when uppermost, the current of positive electricity is moving in a direction similar to that of the hands of a watch (the dial of which is also uppermost), has the properties of a south magnetic pole, and *vice versâ*. If the filament be placed horizontally, its north pole pointing to the north, then the currents on the western side are ascending, pass from west to east in the upper surface, descend on the eastern side, and return from east to west in the lower part. This is shown in *fig.* 155, which represents one of these elementary magnetic filaments, the eastern side being presented to the spectator.

Fig. 155.

(268.) These currents which exist in each particle of a magnet, may therefore be considered as constituting closed circuits (see § 232), the effects of which on all bodies exterior to the circuit will depend on the difference between the actions of the nearest and the most remote parts of the circle described by the current. The united effects of a great number of these circular currents will almost entirely depend on those parts of the current which occupy the exterior surface of the mass.

(269.) Thus, supposing the magnet to be cylindrical in its shape, and its section shown in *fig.* 156, to consist of the sections of each of its component filaments a, b, c, d, &c., and round each of

Fig. 156.

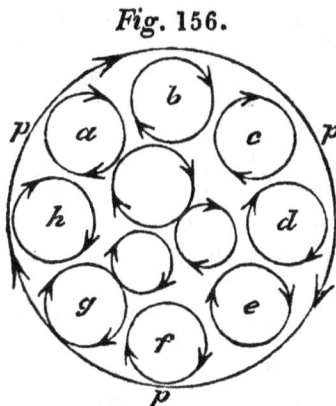

which electric currents are circulating in the directions indicated by the arrows, it is evident that the currents of all the interior parts will nearly, if not exactly, compensate one another, and that their action will be neutralized. But the currents that pass near the circumference are differently circumstanced, inasmuch as they are not compensated by any others; and their action is, therefore, fully exerted on the bodies that are near them, and is equivalent to that of a single circular current flowing uniformly round the circumference, p, p, p, of a circumscribing circle, in the same direction. Hence, in estimating the effects of the whole assemblage, we may confine our attention to that of a superficial current.

(270.) It is obvious that in order to institute an exact comparison between the action of a magnet, and that of an artificial assemblage of electric currents similar to that which is supposed by the theory to exist in the magnet, our imitation must be made by collecting together a great number of similar helices, in parallel directions, and uniting them in one mass. Such an arrangement is called by Ampère *an Electro-dynamic Solenoid**.

(271.) The tendencies which a magnet and conducting wire have to place themselves in positions at right angles to one another, was deduced from the electro-magnetic theory as a consequence of the supposed transverse situation of magnetic fluids resulting from the electric conflict—that is, accompanying the movements of the electric fluids. In Ampère's theory the transverse direction of the action is ascribed to the transverse movements of the electric currents in the magnet itself, which act upon the current in the conductor, and are also acted upon by that current, and tend constantly to establish a parallelism between them. Thus, since the currents in the magnet N S, *fig.* 157, move in planes perpendicular to the axis of the magnet, their action, being in those planes, is transverse to the axis, and tends to bring a straight conducting-

Fig. 157.

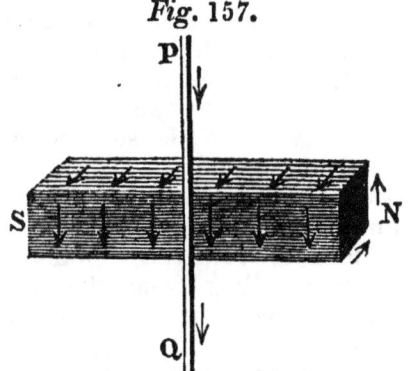

wire, P Q, into the transverse position represented in the figure, in which the direction of the current of the conductor is parallel to that of the current in the nearest part of the magnet. On the other hand, if the wire be fixed, and the magnet moveable, the forces will tend to bring the plane of that current, which occupies the middle of the magnet, into such a position as may include the straight conductor; and as the axis of the magnet is perpendicular to that plane, so also must it be at right angles

---

* Théorie des Phénomènes Electro-dynamiques, p. 95.

to the wire which acts upon it. When the magnet and wire have attained this relative position, it is evident that, since the adjacent currents move in the same direction in both, an attraction will take place between them. All this, as we have seen, is in perfect accordance with the observed phenomena.

(272.) It is unnecessary to pursue the application of this theory to the endless variety of cases of the mutual actions of magnets and conducting bodies, because, having already fully gone into the details of the explanation which is afforded of these facts by the principle of a tangential force emanating from both these agents, it will necessarily follow that they are all equally explicable on the electro-dynamic theory, if it be once proved that the basis of the former theory, namely the tangential force, is itself a direct consequence of the latter. Now this has already been established experimentally by the phenomena exhibited by the helices and electro-dynamic cylinders described in a former Chapter, § 107, and the same has also been deduced from theory, according to what was stated in § 249. It has been shown that the same tangential force results from the heliacal disposition of the current, whatever be the position of the axis of the helix relatively to the conductor on which it acts. We are warranted, therefore, in transferring this conclusion to the action of the circular currents assumed as existing in magnets, and as being the sole source of their activity.

(273.) Guided by these principles, we find no difficulty in explaining the phenomena of revolving motions so frequently resulting from the mutual actions of magnets and conducting wires; and which take place in exactly the same manner when helices or electro-dynamic cylinders are substituted for the magnets. It is instructive, however, to examine the particular cases we have already given in exemplification of the rotatory tendency arising from a tangential force, by applying to them the more general principles of electro-dynamic action. In many instances it will be found that the rotatory motions, although in part produced by the action of the currents in the magnet upon the current in the straight wire, are also in a still greater extent dependant on the influence of those portions of the current that traverse the mercury into which the conducting wires or the magnets are immersed.

(274.) This is exemplified in the following arrangement represented in fig. 158, where the bent wire, proceeding

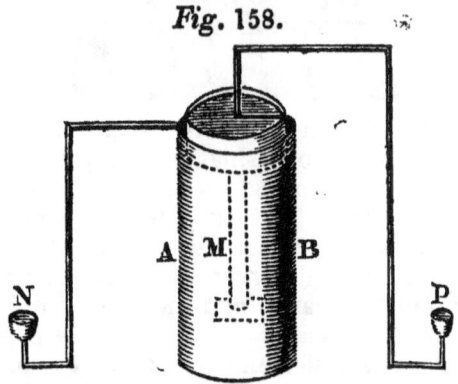

Fig. 158.

from the positive cup P, terminates in a steel point that is made to dip into the surface of a quantity of mercury contained in the vessel A B, in the centre of which a magnet, M, is kept floating in a perpendicular position by being loaded with a weight of platina at the lower end. A ring of copper is placed on the surface of the mercury, from the side of which proceeds a wire, which terminates in the cup N. The electric current, in passing from the steel point to the ring of copper, traverses the mercury, radiating from that point as from a centre, and consequently giving a revolving tendency to the currents in the magnet below them. The magnet, under these circumstances, revolves on its axis. A similar effect, but in a contrary direction, takes place when the course of the electric stream is reversed, and is made to traverse the mercury from the copper ring towards the steel point, producing converging instead of diverging currents. The explanation of these phenomena is obvious, from what has been said in § 203, 204. For let M in fig. 159, be one of the currents at the

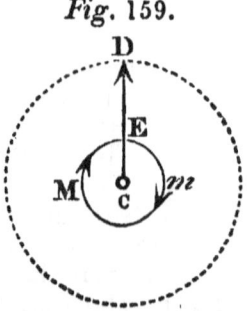

Fig. 159.

upper end of the magnet, and C D one of the diverging currents; the action of the portion E D will be to produce a revolving motion of the magnet in the direction m E M, because the current in m is attracted, and that in M repelled by the current in E D.

(275.) If the point P were inserted, not, as before, in the centre of the fluid above the magnet, but to one side of it, the action of the currents would be more complicated, some being attractive and others repulsive, according to their situations relative to the magnet. The resultant force will be one at right angles to the line joining the centre of radiation with the axis of the magnet, and the effect of this force will be a motion of translation of the whole magnet; that is, of revolution round a line parallel to its axis, and exterior to its surface.

(276.) The presence of transverse currents in every part of the surfaces of magnets is well illustrated by their conjoined influence, when a number of magnets are placed horizontally, as in *fig.* 160, like the spokes of a wheel, with their similar poles turned towards the

Fig. 160.

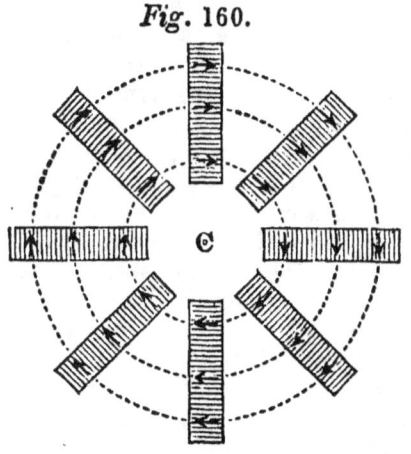

centre C. In this situation all the currents on the upper sides of the magnets are passing in the same direction with reference to the circumference of circles described from the centre C. They will therefore produce continued rotation in a vertical conductor, whose axis passes through that centre, but is terminated—that is, does not extend beyond that side of the plane in which the magnets are situated.

(277.) The theory of Ampère would lead to the conclusion that no mechanical arrangement of the parts of an electro-magnetic apparatus can give rise to rotatory movements, unless fluid conductors form some part of the voltaic circuit; and accordingly no attempt to obtain practically such movements has ever been successful.

(278.) It is, accordingly, impossible to obtain the revolution of a magnet round its own axis, either by the action of other magnets, or by that of an electric current, which traverses neither the magnet, nor a body that is so fixed to it as to move along with it. This is a direct consequence of the law derived from the electro-dynamic theory, that the mutual action of two closed circuits cannot produce in one of these circuits a continued rotatory motion in one constant direction; for it is evident that if this be true with regard to two single currents, it must also be true with regard to any assemblages of such closed currents, in whatever way they may be arranged. The utmost that can result is a tendency in one of them, if moveable, to assume a fixed position of equilibrium; if, therefore, the system be so constituted that it can only revolve round an axis, about which the circuits composing it are symmetrically arranged, it will acquire no motion whatever by the action either of a single closed circuit, or of an assemblage of such circuits. A magnet susceptible of no other motion than rotation round its axis is in this condition; and hence, if it derive its magnetic properties from electrical currents, it must be impossible to produce in it such a rotation by the action of other magnets.

(279.) On the other hand, a detached portion of a voltaic circuit moveable on an axis that coincides with that of a magnet may be set in motion, and made to revolve by the action of the closed currents, in the magnet itself. Thus let V v, *fig.* 161, represent a section of a voltaic pile, with its positive and nega-

Fig. 161.

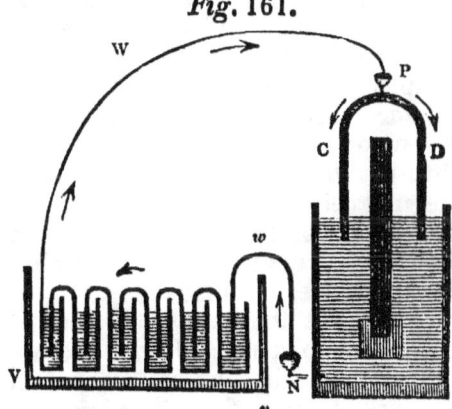

tive wires, W, w, proceeding from its two poles, and inserted into the cups P and N respectively; the former being placed at the top of an arch of wire, of which the two branches descend on each side, and terminate under the surface of a quantity of mercury, contained in the vessel, also seen in section; and the latter being at the end of a wire proceeding from the lower part of the vessel, and in contact with the mercury; while a magnet is made to float in an upright position in the axis of the vessel, by a weight of platina fixed to its lower end. The magnet, it will be seen, being unconnected with the wires, forms no part of the voltaic circuit, and remains unmoved by it; yet it excites movements in the conductors which surround its upper portion. For since, in the parts C and D, the currents of the wires are approaching those of the magnet, they will be impelled (see § 200) to turn round it in a direction opposite to that of the currents in the magnet: a reaction is at the same time exerted by the currents of the wires upon those of the magnets, which therefore tend to move the magnet *progressively*, or in the same direction as its own currents. (§ 203.) But the currents which pass from the lower ends of the wires through the mercury to the exterior of the vessel, recede from the magnet, and tend to impress on the mercury a motion of revolution in the direction of the magnetic currents; and, consequently, by the reaction of this force the magnet receives a tendency to revolve in the opposite direction. The two forces resulting from these contrary tendencies of the descending and the receding currents, oppose and partly destroy each other, as far as regards their effect on the magnet; and when the rotatory effects of the whole of the remaining part of the current composing the whole circuit, and including that of the pile itself, and its two wires, W and w, are taken into account, the compensation becomes complete, and the total effect reduced to nothing. Hence we see that, although the wires are made to revolve in one direction and the mercury in another, the magnet itself, being acted upon by equal and contrary rotatory forces, and unattached to any part of the circuit, remains perfectly unmoved.

(280.) But the case is altered if the magnet be so connected with the apparatus of the wires as to form a part of the circuit, even for a portion only of the current; for that portion of the current which thus passes through the magnet no longer exerts upon it any rotatory tendency, and may, therefore, be considered as suppressed: and since the action of this portion exactly counterbalanced the equal and opposite action of the remainder of the circuit, that equilibrium can no longer subsist, when this portion is removed, and the remainder of the current becoming effective, will produce a rotation of the magnet on its own axis. The direction of this rotation will be the same as that of the descending wires; hence the magnet may be connected with these wires, without altering the nature of the action, as in the experiment of Mr. Faraday, described in § 76.

(281.) It follows, also, from the principles of Ampère's theory, that when the moveable portion of the circuit which is attached to the magnet has both its extremities in the axis, no motion of this kind will take place; because no action can result between a system of closed currents and another current terminating at both extremities in the axis of the system.

(282.) The theory of Ampère implies a perfect identity in the mode of action of a magnet and of an electro-dynamic cylinder. A remarkable difference, however, has been observed between them. In the electro-dynamic cylinder, the poles are situated at the very extremities of the cylinder; whereas, in ordinary magnets, they are always found to be nearer to the centre than the ends; the distance varying in different magnets. This circumstance was long considered as invalidating the truth of the theory[*]. It may, however, be explained consistently with the hypothesis, in two ways; either by supposing that the intensities of the currents gradually diminish from the middle to the extremities; or else by assuming that they acquire a degree of obliquity when at a distance from the centre of the magnet; that is, that they move in planes which are not exactly perpendicular to the axis of the magnet, but differently inclined in different parts. These effects are, indeed, not only quite consistent with Ampère's hypothesis, but follow as the natural consequences of the established laws of electro-dynamic action[†].

These positions of the different currents, according to their positions relative to the axis, will be best understood from *fig.* 162, which represents a longitudinal section of a magnet by a plane passing through the axis; the directions of the currents being marked by short

---

[*] This was urged as an objection by Mr. Faraday, in the Quarterly Journal of Science, vol. xii. p. 76.
[†] Ampère, Recueil, &c. pp. 257 and 340.

arrows. The elementary currents of those particles of the magnet which are situated in the axis, that is, along the line X Y, will, of course, on account of the symmetry of the figure, move in planes perpendicular to the axis; as also those in the medial plane M m,

Fig. 162.

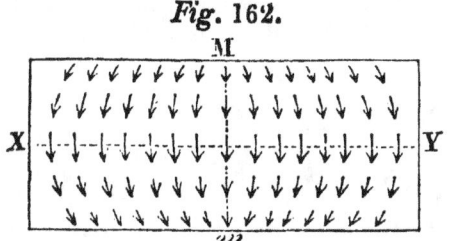

passing through the centre of the magnet. But with regard to the currents nearer to the surface, they will, by the action of the interior currents, be turned towards the middle of the magnet, while those parts of the same currents that are nearest to the axis will be repelled from the middle towards the adjacent extremity; and the planes of their inclination will therefore be more or less inclined to the axis, as they are more or less remote either from the axis, and from the middle of the magnet, in the manner represented by the arrows in the figure. The total amount of inclination in the lateral currents will be greater in proportion to the intensity of the action of the interior currents, and also in proportion to their number; it will, therefore, be greater in proportion as the thickness of the magnet is greater compared with its length. We may conceive this relative thickness to be so excessive as that the forces tending to produce this inclination of the currents will at length overcome the coercive force, and prevent the development of magnetism. This consideration will easily explain the difficulty that is experienced in magnetizing a bar in such a manner as that the poles may be in the direction of the shorter diameter*; a remark which leads us to the subject of the induction of magnetism. Let us examine with what success the hypothesis of Ampère may be applied to this class of phenomena.

(283.) We have already seen that an electric current communicates magnetic properties by induction to such bodies in the vicinity as are susceptible of acquiring them. If these properties are owing to electric currents circulating in the particles of the magnetized body, or in the magnetic elements, as they have been called, (see Magnetism, § 154,) there are two suppositions, either of which will account for this phenomenon. The first is, that electric currents, which did not before exist, are produced, or called into action, by the influence of another current in the vicinity. The second hypothesis is, that the electric currents pre-exist in all the particles of iron, or other bodies susceptible of magnetism previous to their acquiring this property, but without having any uniform direction; under these circumstances, their actions upon any external body counteract and balance one another, so as to constitute the neutral state. When, on the other hand, they are under the influence of an external electric current of sufficient power, they are all turned by it towards the same quarter, and assume a common direction; they will now co-operate in their action upon external bodies, and exhibit magnetic properties. This change is analogous to what takes place in the rays of ordinary light when, from being polarized in all possible directions, they become suddenly polarized in one particular direction.

(284.) It is implied in the first of these hypotheses, that every electric current tends to produce currents in a similar direction in other bodies. Ampère has proved, by the following curious experiment, that a powerful voltaic current possesses this power of exciting currents in neighbouring bodies that are not generally considered as susceptible of magnetism. A copper wire of considerable length, covered with silk thread, was rolled round a cylinder, so as to form a coil of some thickness. Within this coil, placed in a vertical position, a copper ring of smaller diameter was suspended by a fine silk thread, passing through a small glass tube, which was thrust between the threads of the copper coil. The circumference of the ring was thus brought, in every part, very near to the conducting coil, through which a very powerful voltaic current was sent. When a magnet was presented to the ring, under these circumstances, the latter was attracted or repelled in the same manner as if it had formed part of the same circuit as the coil. Hence it was inferred, that an electric current tends to induce in conductors, placed in its immediate vicinity, currents that move in similar directions,

---

* See Cumming's Translation of Demonferraud, Manual of Electro-Dynamics, p. 167 to 170, and also p. 250.

This tendency, indeed, is but feeble; and the first endeavours of Ampère to discover it failed, in consequence of his employing inadequate means; but, on repeating the experiment with more powerful batteries and magnets, he perfectly succeeded in rendering the action sensible.

It were much to be desired that this important experiment, upon the accuracy of which so much is made to depend in accounting for magnetic induction in Ampère's theory, were carefully repeated, and with every possible variation in its circumstances, so as to determine whether the effect which he observed is uniformly sustained, is invariably connected with its supposed cause, and is always proportioned to it; or whether it be not dependent upon some particular conditions in the current with relation to its tension, velocity, or intensity, or upon some temporary variation taking place in these conditions. In the particular form in which the experiment has been tried, it seems scarcely to warrant the very general conclusion which Ampère has deduced from it.

(285.) Even if we admit it to be established as a general fact, that electric currents, circulating in one body, are attended by similarly directed currents in neighbouring conductors, we are still not in a condition to decide the question, whether, in imparting magnetism to metals, there is an actual production of electric currents, or simply a change effected in the directions of currents previously existing in their particles. There is, however, no inconsistency in the supposition that the effect may be due to both these causes; for the action of an electric current may consist in giving a common direction to pre-existing currents, while it, at the same time, augments their intensity.

(286.) It is unnecessary to enter into long details as to the modes in which, according to the theory we are considering, an electric current, passing through conductors of different forms, whether straight, or bent into spirals, or helices, or a magnet, in which currents are supposed to circulate, induce magnetic polarity in the adjacent parts of pieces of iron or steel brought within the sphere of their influence, when we regard that polarity as consisting in the establishment of circular currents of the same description as those of the inducing magnet. It will be sufficient to show that the fundamental fact, namely, that either pole of a magnet tends to induce the opposite polarity in the adjacent end of a magnetizable body in its vicinity, is the direct and necessary consequence of the hypothesis. That this is the case will readily appear from considering that when the elementary magnetic filament A B, *fig.* 163, is brought near to a similar elementary filament, C D, in a neutral

Fig. 163.

state, the currents which circulate in the former will excite in the latter a circulation of currents in the same direction, thereby rendering it magnetic. But since, according to the theory (§ 267), the kind of polarity manifested at either end of a magnet depends altogether upon the direction of the currents with respect to the axis at the extremity, it is evident that if the current at the end B revolves, as seen by a spectator looking at that end, in the direction of the hands of a watch on the dial, constituting the southern polarity, the current induced at the end of the other piece, C, revolving in the same direction in space, will appear to a spectator looking at that end to move in the contrary direction; it will therefore have a northern polarity, that is, one contrary to that of the adjacent end B, but similar to that of the remote end A. In like manner the polarity of D, if the inductive influence extend to that distance, will be the same as that of B; for the circumstances attending the revolution of its current are precisely the same in both.

(287.) When, on the other hand, the neutral bar is placed near and parallel to the inducing magnet, the action of the currents on the adjacent side of the latter will prevail over that of the currents on the remote side, on account of their greater proximity to the bar, and induce in its adjacent side currents running in the same direction; but these two sets of currents, being situated in different sides of their respective axes, will constitute magnetic currents in contrary directions, and, therefore, of opposite properties. Hence the poles of the induced magnet are reversed with relation to those of the inducing magnet. This will readily appear from an inspection of *fig.* 164. The same opposition of direction takes place when two parallel rollers turn upon one another, in consequence of the parts in contact moving in the same direction.

Fig. 164.

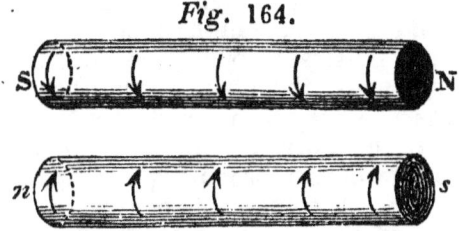

(288.) After the removal of the current which originally determined them, these induced currents continue to circulate with more or less permanence, according to the degree of coercive force inherent in the body. In soft iron they disappear almost immediately: in steel they continue to maintain themselves, and constitute permanent magnets. The action of heat is either to weaken or destroy the currents altogether, or else to derange the uniformity of their direction, so that they cease to act in concert, and the steel reverts to its neutral state. It is found, in conformity with the theory of Ampère, that all the effects of magnetic induction are produced equally well by electric currents circulating through spiral or heliacal conductors, as by artificial magnets.

(289.) The theory of Ampère furnishes a key to the explanation of a variety of facts attending the conversion of steel bars into magnets by the ordinary processes of magnetization, which are not intelligible on any other hypothesis. It accounts for the peculiar circumstances already noticed in the Treatise on Magnetism, regarding the relative advantages of the single or double touch, according to the inclinations given to the magnet when applied to the bar to be magnetized; and it more especially explains the frequent occurrence of consecutive points when certain methods are employed. Thus, let one of the poles of a magnet, the north, for instance, be placed on the middle of a steel bar, at right angles to it: see *fig.* 165. The form of the steel bar will, as

Fig. 165.

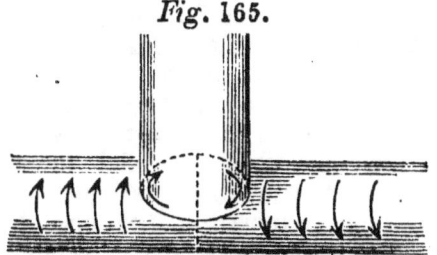

already remarked, give greater facility to the induction of currents in a direction transverse to its length; and the currents in the magnet running in this direction are those situated on the opposite sides of the magnet, supposed to be divided by the dotted line perpendicular to the length of the steel bar. But these portions of currents are themselves moving in contrary directions; the currents they respectively induce in the parts of the bar which they touch, and in the neighbouring parts, must therefore, in like manner, have opposite directions, giving rise to opposite polarities. Thus the two ends of the bar will be converted into north poles, while the point immediately under the centre of the magnet will be a consecutive point, or south pole.

(290.) The phenomena attending the division or fracture of a magnet follow very naturally from the constitution assigned to it by Ampère's hypothesis; for, as the currents circulate in the same direction in the divided ends while they were united, they will appear to circulate in opposite directions with reference to the two sides of the plane which divides them, and which become the terminal planes of each fragment when separate. The polarities of the two ends must, therefore, be of opposite kinds; for the same reason that the adjoining ends, B and C, *fig.* 163, of two magnets placed in the same line, with their currents having similar directions, have opposite polarities. At the poles of a horseshoe magnet, the currents revolve in opposite directions with respect to the two ends of the bent axis; but the directions of the adjacent part of each current, as well as of the remote parts, are similar. See *fig.* 166.

Fig. 166.

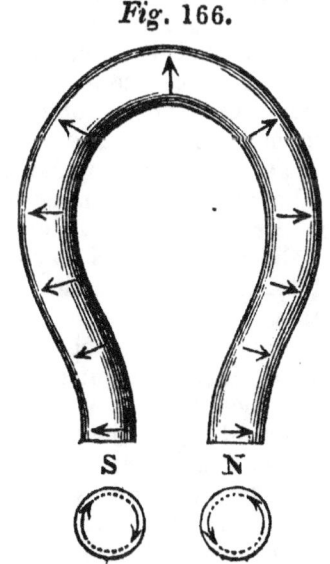

(291.) If a steel bar, instead of being bent into the form of a horseshoe, be formed into a complete ring, *fig.* 167,

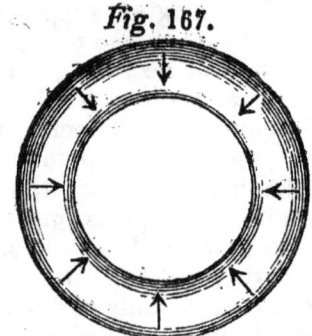

Fig. 167.

and then magnetized, it exhibits no magnetic properties as long as the ring is entire; but when broken into any number of portions, each part has two poles, and possesses all the properties of an ordinary magnet. This experiment suggested the theoretical investigation of the properties of a system of small circular currents situated in planes perpendicular to another circle, passing through all their centres. The result of the investigation of this problem led to a mathematical theorem exactly conformable to observation; a ring so constituted, or an *electro-dynamic ring*, as it has been called, being found, both from theory and experiment, to exert no action upon a voltaic conductor or magnet, at whatever distance from it, or in whatever situation it may be placed.

(292.) In viewing the application of Ampère's theory to the mutual action of two magnets, we might content ourselves with the observations already made as to the mutual action of two electro-dynamic cylinders, which may be taken as their representatives; and simply refer to the general principle deduced from theoretical considerations, § 251, namely, that the resultants of all the actions may be reduced to forces emanating from the poles, and inversely proportional to the squares of the distances. Yet as a more popular view of the actual operation of the forces derived from the attraction or repulsion of currents in the simpler cases may be more satisfactory, we shall examine a few of these cases.

(293.) It will be evident that when two magnets are presented to each other, with their axes in the same line, it must depend upon the similarity or contrariety of the directions of the currents at the adjacent ends, whether these ends will attract or repel each other. The former, it is well known, happens when poles of opposite denomination front each other; the latter when similar poles are brought together. The motion of the currents in the first case may be aptly illustrated by two watches laid the one above the other, so that the dial of the one may be in contact with the back of the other, for the hands in both watches will then be moving in the same direction. We may obtain a representation of the second case, by placing the watches either face to face, or back to back; for in either of these situations, the motion of the hands in the two watches are in opposite directions. The electric currents in the former case will exert a mutual attraction; and in the last, a mutual repulsion.

(294.) In estimating the attractive or repulsive forces which arise in other relative positions of the magnets, we must take into account, not merely the terminal currents, but those which exist along the whole length of both magnets. The general resultants of all the forces thus arising may be reduced to attractive or repulsive forces between the whole of each of the sides of one magnet, and the whole of each of the sides of the other magnet. Thus, supposing two magnets to be situated horizontally nearly in the position to which they would be brought by the influence of terrestrial magnetism, the east side of the one will attract the east side of the other, and repel the west side; the west side will, in like manner, attract the west and repel the east. Hence the general tendency of all these actions is to turn the magnets so as to bring the two eastern sides, for example, as near together as possible, and parallel to each other; that is, into a relative position, such that the north pole of each magnet shall be adjoining to the south pole of the other; and in this situation the greatest amount of attractive force will be exerted.

(295.) In positions intermediate to these, and especially when much inclined to each other, the estimation of the resultant force in each individual case is often difficult, from the complex operation of the numerous forces that are in action in a variety of directions. Thus, if one of the magnets, situated as just described, parallel to each other, and with their dissimilar poles adjacent, be moved in the line of its axis till the two ends, having similar poles, are brought into the same plane, as shown in *fig.* 168, a strong repulsion takes the place of the attraction before observed, notwithstanding the similarity of the currents in the two edges at S and s that are nearest each other. The reason is, that the attraction of the ad-

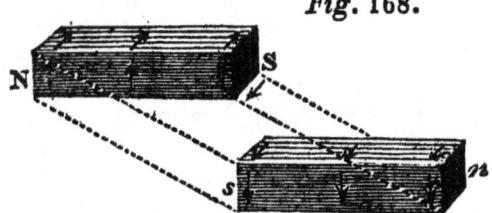

Fig. 168.

jacent sides is now much weakened both by the greater distances of their remoter portions at N and n, and also on account of the great obliquity of that action. The repulsions, on the contrary, exerted between the adjacent side of the one and the remote side of the other magnet, become very powerful, both from their increased proximity and more direct action; and they predominate accordingly. A similar account may be given of the attraction which takes place between dissimilar poles placed in a similar situation. The reasoning in both instances being analogous to what was stated (§ 236) with respect to the action of a helix upon an elementary portion of current placed in different situations with respect to the helix.

(296.) In the case of magnets that are not of a prismatic or cylindric shape, nor terminated by plane surfaces perpendicular to their axes, the estimation of the resultant force becomes much more complicated. All that we have now said on this subject, indeed, can only afford approximations to the solution of the problem of finding this resultant. The rigorous investigation of this problem would involve mathematical considerations of too great an extent for a treatise of this kind. The reader who may wish to prosecute the inquiry is referred more especially to the works of Ampère, in which the subject is treated with a masterly hand.

(297.) The magnetic influence of the earth being so perfectly analogous to that of other magnetic bodies, the theory of Ampère with respect to the constitution of such bodies must, if founded in truth, apply also to terrestrial magnetism, which must, according to that theory, be derived from electric currents circulating in the globe from east to west in planes parallel to the magnetic equator. The united effect of such currents would be to produce a southern polarity on the northern side of these planes, and a northern polarity on the southern side. It is scarcely necessary to point out how exactly the phenomena described in Chapter IX. (§ 128 to 147,) accord with the consequences of such an hypothesis. The magnetic axis of the earth, according to this view of the subject, is merely an imaginary line, perpendicular to the planes of the electric currents circulating in the earth, and passing through the centres of the circles described by those currents; and the directive power of the globe which acts on iron and on magnets on its surface, is the result, not of any real influence proceeding from those portions of the earth to which their poles point, but of the electro-dynamic action of currents circulating in the plane of the magnetic equator, in obedience to which the corresponding currents which circulate in the magnet place themselves, so as to approach to parallelism with the former; that is, to attain the position of equilibrium between the forces in operation. This position is that of a plane perpendicular to the line of magnetic direction, or the line of dip: and accordingly, since the currents in the magnet are themselves perpendicular to its axis, they will tend to bring that axis in that very line. Hence the phenomena of the dipping-needle, and hence the position assumed by the compass-needle, in the plane of the magnetic meridian, as being the nearest approach which its mode of suspension will allow it to make to the line of dip.

(298.) All the effects of terrestrial magnetism may be imitated by distributing wires round the surface of an artificial globe, so as to direct a galvanic current through them. Mr. Barlow, in a paper lately read at the Royal Society, describes the following experiment which he made with this view. A hollow wooden globe, sixteen inches in diameter, was furnished with copper wires passing in grooves along each parallel of latitude for every tenth degree. When an electric current was made to pass through these wires, in the same direction in each, it was found that a magnetic needle, properly neutralized with regard to the earth's action, and suspended in different situations near the surface of the artificial globe, arranged itself in positions perfectly analogous to those actually assumed by the dipping-needle in corresponding regions of the earth. It is probable that if we could indefinitely multiply these electric currents on a globe so prepared, the apparatus might be made to represent with great accuracy every circumstance of magnetic dip and direction; and by employing, instead of a magnetic needle, an electro-dynamic cylinder, all the phenomena of terrestrial magnetism might be exhibited, without the intervention of magnetism, by means of electricity alone.

(299.) The origin of these electrical currents permeating the interior of the earth, and more especially its external layer, may possibly be traced to the action of the solar rays on successive parts of the torrid zone, which taking place from east to west, may excite currents of positive electricity in that direction, and in planes corresponding with the magnetic equator. The probability of such an effect being produced, and the inference from analogy that similar currents may be excited, and even exist permanently in iron and steel, is greatly increased by the recent discoveries of Professor Seebeck, that electric currents may be produced and maintained in circuits formed exclusively of solid conductors, by the partial application of heat. This discovery, which leads to a separate department of this science, to which the name of *Thermo-Electricity* has been given, will be treated of in the next Chapter.

(300.) A further confirmation of the electro-dynamic theory of magnetism is derived from its applicability to the curious phenomena of magnetic rotations, which have been described in the eighth chapter of the Treatise on Magnetism (§ 354 to 360). Soon after the discovery of this new class of facts, M. Arago suggested to M. Ampère the substitution of electro-dynamic cylinders for the magnetic bars in these experiments on the effects of rotation. The first trials made by these two philosophers in conjunction did not lead to any decisive result, in consequence of some defects in the apparatus they employed; but when these defects were obviated in the subsequent experiments which they made with M. Colladon, in which a very short double helix, forming a coil of about two inches in diameter, was used, they succeeded perfectly in obtaining the same results as if magnets had been employed*. Hence we may infer the complete identity between all the effects of a common magnet and an electro-dynamic cylinder.

(301.) We thus find that the theory of Ampère satisfies every condition that is required of a true theory, inasmuch as it affords a complete explanation of all the phenomena, even in their minutest details. It unites the character of simplicity in principle, and comprehensiveness in its applications; and by suggesting new combinations, it has led to the discovery of new facts. It also has an important advantage over the theory of tangential forces in presenting greater facility of mathematical investigation, and for the comparison of the analytical formulæ thence obtained, with the results of experiment; and thereby affording the most severe test of its accuracy. If the truth of the theory be established, it will effect an important step in the generalization of physical phenomena, by showing that all those formerly referred to the operation of an unknown principle, considered as distinct from electricity and denominated magnetism, are, in fact, essentially electric, and that the two principles are identical, and instead of being the bases of two separate departments of knowledge, are merely branches of a single and more extended and comprehensive science.

(302.) It must at the same time be acknowledged that much still remains to be done towards removing the difficulties opposed to this as well as other electro-magnetic theories, which are presented by the singular and apparently capricious phenomena of the induction of magnetism by electrical currents transmitted along conductors, and derived either from the voltaic or the common electrical batteries. We allude particularly to the results of the experiments of Savary, already noticed in § 164 to 168, and which have not yet been sufficiently generalized to admit of being explained on any hypothesis.

Chapter XIII.

Thermo-Electricity.

(303.) Professor Seebeck, of Berlin, discovered, in the year 1822, that currents of electricity might be produced by the partial application of heat to a circuit composed exclusively of solid conductors. The original experiment which established this fact was first announced in this country, in the Annals

---

* Ampère, Théorie des Phénomènes Electro-dynamiques, p. 196.

of Philosophy*. A bar of antimony, about eight inches long and half an inch square, was taken, and its extremities connected by twisting a piece of brass wire round them so as to form a loop, each end of the bar having several coils of the wire. On heating one of the extremities, for a short time, with a spirit-lamp, electro-magnetic effects were produced in every part of a circuit so formed.

(304.) Thus it appears that for constituting a circuit of this kind, two elements only are requisite; which may be represented in the diagram, *fig.* 169, by the conductors A and B, consisting

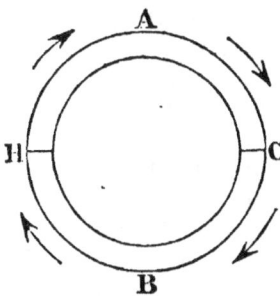

of two different metals, in contact in two points H and C, so that a circuit is formed in H A C B.

(305.) The electrical current thus excited has been termed *Thermo-electric*, in order to distinguish it from the common *galvanic current*, which, as it requires the intervention of a fluid element as one of its essential components, was denominated a *Hydro-electric current*. The term *Stereo-electric current* has also been applied to the former, in order to mark its being produced in systems formed of solid bodies alone. It is evident that if, as is supposed in the theory of Ampère, magnets owe their peculiar properties to the continual circulation of electric currents in their minute parts, these currents will come under the description of stereo-electric currents.

(306.) The chief evidence we possess of the existence of thermo-electric currents consists in the production of electro-magnetic effects. A compass-needle placed either within or without the circuit, and at a small distance from it, is deflected from its natural position in a direction conformable to its situation with regard to the circuit. Still stronger indications of electro-magnetic action are obtained by placing two ends of one of the metallic arcs in contact with the wires of a galvanometer. The thermo-electric current has also been found to excite contractions in the muscles of a frog: but as far as experiments have yet been tried, it is inadequate to effect chemical decompositions, the ignition of metals, or to exhibit sparks, or any other of the phenomena of ordinary electricity.

(307.) If the metallic arcs, through which a thermo-electric current is made to pass by the application of heat to one of the points of contact of the different metals, be delicately suspended, they will obey the action of a magnet brought near it. If the opposite poles of two magnets be placed on the outside of a circuit moving in a vertical plane, and turning on a vertical axis, the conductors may be made to revolve by continuing to apply the heat on the same side. Thus if the circular arrangement of bars represented in *fig.* 169 be suspended by a thread at A, and opposite magnetic poles be applied at H and C, out of the circle, while the flame of a spirit-lamp is held steadily at H, the combined actions of the two magnetic poles upon the adjoining ascending current at H, and descending current at C, will be to move the circle till its plane is at right angles to its former position. But the impulse it has acquired by the joint action of the magnets is sufficient to continue the motion until the side C arrives at the flame. This part of the circle being thus heated, while the part H is at the same time becoming cool, an electric current is now determined from C through A to H, and back again through B to C, which direction, with reference to the magnets, is the same as before, and the circle is urged onwards in its revolution. When it has completed an entire revolution, all the circumstances being the same as at first, another impulse will be given, and the circle will continue incessantly to revolve; the current moving alternately in opposite directions at every semi-revolution of the circle.

(308.) On the other hand, the pole of a magnet placed within the circuit will have no tendency to produce rotation; because the current in the opposite branches of the circle moves in contrary directions; and being, therefore, urged by the magnet to revolve in opposite directions, the circle will remain in equilibrium. But two systems of circles supported each by a point on the ends

---
* New Series, vol. iv., p. 318.

of a horseshoe magnet, placed vertically, with the poles uppermost (that is, fixed as in *fig.* 50), and a lamp being placed half way between the poles, each of the circles will revolve by the action of that pole which is exterior to it.

(309.) It appears from these and other experiments of a similar kind*, that the mutual action of a magnet and a thermo-electric current is subject to the same laws as those of magnets and galvanic currents; and hence all the phenomena of the attraction, repulsion, or rotation of conductors conveying galvanic currents, may be exhibited by a thermo-electric current transmitted through the same conductors.

(310.) The two metals of which the combination and contact produce the most powerful thermo-electric currents, are antimony and bismuth, which we shall accordingly take as the representatives of their respective classes. As in the galvanic circuits, where the current of positive electricity is flowing directly from the copper to the zinc (see *Galvanism*, § 4), the latter is generally said to be positive with respect to the former (see *Galvanism,* § 73); so, in the thermo-electric circuit, the bismuth is generally said to be positive with regard to the antimony, because, in the colder portion of the circuit, the electric current is passing from the antimony to the bismuth†.

(311.) In the Treatise on Galvanism, we have given (§ 73) a list of metallic substances in the order of their oxidabilities, or rather in the order of their electrical relations, when united in galvanic circuits, with interposed acids. A number of experiments have been made by Professor Cumming, for the purpose of determining the comparative thermo-electric relations of the different metals by forming circuits of them taken in pairs. From these the following series has been deduced, descending from the extreme positive, as we have already defined it, which is bismuth, to the extreme negative, which is antimony.

Bismuth,	Cobalt, }
Mercury, }	Manganese, }
Nickel, }	Tin,
Platina,	Lead,
Palladium,	Brass,
Rhodium,	Charcoal, }
Gold,	Plumbago, }
Copper,	Iron,
Silver,	Arsenic,
Zinc,	Antimony.
Cadmium,	

(312.) In this series every metal is positive with respect to all those below it, and negative to those above. Hence any two metals occupying situations intermediate between the two extremes will together compose a thermo-electric circuit similar to, though of less power than that formed by bismuth and antimony.

(313.) The order in which the metals stand in the above series does not continue the same at all temperatures: thus gold, silver, copper, brass, and zinc, should be placed below iron in high temperatures, though they rank above it in a low heat.

(314.) On comparing the series above given, which represents the thermo-electric relations of the metals, with that given in the Treatise on *Galvanism*, § 73, which represents their galvanic relations, it will be evident that there is no correspondence between them.

(315.) The contact of the metals in these experiments is most completely secured by soldering them together; but in most cases it will be sufficient, if they are in the form of wires, to twist them closely together. Mercury may be conveniently employed as the intermedium between other metals: the mercury being previously heated, the extremities of each piece composing the pair being dipped into it at the same moment, and the other extremities being applied to a galvanometer. Even a small fragment of any metallic substance is sufficient to afford indications of its thermo-electric relations, if placed upon a disc of the metal with which it is to be compared, and touched with a hot wire; the circuit being completed through the wire and the disc. But it is found that the results of experiments so made do not always accord with those obtained by employing larger pieces, for it appears that the effect is much influenced by the relative dimensions of the heated surfaces. Even when the experiment is made by plunging the metals to be examined in heated mercury, the direction of the current will be determined, in many cases, by the order in which they have been immersed.

(316.) Considerable diversities take

---

* For a more detailed account of these, see Cumming's Manual, already quoted.

† There is still some confusion in the application of the terms positive and negative to the different parts of the circuit, by different authors, and sometimes even by the same author in different places.

place in the directions of the current when the metals contain any alloy, or are not in a state of perfect purity. Thus, although bismuth and tin are each positive with regard to copper, yet an alloy of the two former is found to be negative with regard to the latter metal.

(317.) We are yet far from possessing any theory by which the whole of the facts belonging to *thermo-electricity* can be satisfactorily explained. The most intelligible account of them appears to be that given by Becquerel*, which proceeds upon the hypothesis, that whenever a particle of a metal receives heat from a body of a higher temperature than itself, part of the neutral electric fluid which is attached to it is decomposed, the vitreous fluid being retained, and the resinous fluid driven off, and passing into the adjoining particles of metal. In proportion as the heat extends, by communication from particle to particle, similar effects take place in each of those that are acquiring heat, while contrary effects are taking place in all those that are losing heat. Thus, the simple diffusion of that portion of heat which was originally received by the first particle, produces only an oscillatory movement of the electrical fluids between adjacent particles, attended by a series of decompositions and combinations of the two electric fluids. But if the source of heat be permanent, so that the temperature of the first particles which receive it be uniformly maintained, the retrograde movements of the decomposed electric fluids are prevented, and a continued current of each takes place in opposite directions; the negative electricity being impelled forwards from the parts where the temperature continues high to those which continue to be colder, and a positive current moving in the contrary direction. It follows, from this hypothesis, that when two different metals are placed in contact, so as to constitute a circuit, the currents from the heated parts that are conjoined will be urged in opposite directions; but the strongest will prevail, and the thermo-electric current actually observed is that which results, and of which the intensity is equal to the difference between the two that are simultaneously developed.

(318.) Thermo-electricity does not appear to have its source in any chemical changes taking place in the materials composing the circuit. Oxidation, at least, has no share in the effect; for Becquerel has repeated the experiments of Seebeck and others, relating to this mode of action, when the apparatus was surrounded by hydrogen gas, without any sensible difference in the results.*

(319.) The great peculiarity which distinguishes thermo-electric currents from those produced by galvanic action, is that the *quantity* of circulating electricity is much greater compared with its *intensity*. They are, in this respect, still further removed from the condition of streams of electricity produced in the common electrical machine, which possess a much greater intensity, though they are much less considerable in quantity than galvanic currents. Hence it is chiefly by their effects in producing deviations in the magnetic needle that the existence of thermo-electric currents is recognised. The low state of intensity of these latter currents occasions great loss of power whenever they have to traverse any considerable line of conductors,—even of metals, which are the most perfect conductors. On this account it is that very little advantage is gained by forming compound circuits; that is, arranging their elements in a series of alternations analogous to those of the voltaic pile. Messrs. Fourier and Oersted made trials of this kind; first combining three bars of bismuth with three bars of antimony, placed alternately, so as to form the sides of a hexagon, and with their contiguous ends soldered together, thus composing a thermo-electric circuit, which included three pair of elements. The length of the bars was about four inches and a half, their breadth about half an inch, and their thickness one-sixth of an inch. This circuit was placed upon two supports, and in a horizontal position, one of the sides of the hexagon being in the magnetic meridian. A compass-needle was placed below this side, and as near to it as possible, and was very sensibly affected when one of the solderings at the junctions of the bars was heated with the flame of a lamp. The deviation was considerably increased on heating two of the alternate angles of the hexagon; and a still greater deviation was produced when the heat was applied to the three alternate angles. Similar effects were produced when, instead of

---

* See Annales de Chimie, tome xli. p. 353.

† Annales de Chimie, tome xli. p. 359.

applying heat, the temperature of one or more of the other angles of the hexagon was reduced by means of ice. When the action of the ice was combined with that of the flame, applied at the same time to the alternate angles all round the hexagon, the effect was still more considerable, the deviation of the needle amounting to sixty degrees.

(320.) By continuing these experiments with more numerous alternations, it was found that the total effect of a compound thermo-electric circuit is very inferior to the sum of the effects which the same elements could produce when employed in the formation of simple circuits, so that the electro-magnetic forces called into action increase in a much less ratio than the number of alternations constituting the series *.

(321.) The latest thermo-electric experiments are those of Messrs. Nobili and Melloni, of which an account was read to the French Academy of Sciences in September last (1831.)† A thermo-electric pile, consisting of thirty-six pairs of plates of bismuth and antimony, having a galvanometer with two needles attached to it, was found to be so sensible as to be affected by the warmth of a person at the distance of thirty feet. A number of delicate experiments were made with this apparatus on the permeability of bodies to radiant heat, on the temperature of insects, and on the powers of different bodies of emitting, reflecting, and absorbing heat. Considerable doubt is also thrown by these inquirers on the conclusions of Fourier and Oersted with respect to the limited effect of increasing the number of alternations in augmenting the intensity of the current.

(322.) It would appear also, from the observations of Professor Cumming, that although the hydro-electric and thermo-electric currents may both be regarded as continuous, when compared with those of common electricity, excited by the electrical machine, which are manifestly discontinuous (see *Galvanism*, § 21 and 94), yet when the hydro-electric and thermo-electric currents are compared with one another, the continuity of the latter is by far the most complete. This will appear evident from the consideration that, as it is necessary that one of the three elements of a galvanic circuit must be a fluid (see *Galvanism*, § 69), it will, therefore, be a more imperfect conductor than the metals, and will oppose some degree of resistance to the passage of the electric currents circulating through the whole assemblage.

(323.) There are, therefore, strictly speaking, three states of electricity. That derived from the common electrical machine is in the highest state of tension, and accumulates till it is able to force a passage through the air, which is a perfect non-conductor. In the galvanic apparatus the currents have a smaller degree of tension; because, although they pass freely through the metallic elements, they meet with some impediment in traversing the fluid conductor. But in the thermo-electric currents the tension is reduced to nothing, because throughout the whole course of the circuit no impediment exists to its free and uniform circulation.

(324.) These considerations serve also to explain why the latter species of current is inadequate to effect any kind of chemical decomposition, or even to produce any degree of permanent magnetism. It has hitherto been found impossible to magnetize steel bars by means of thermo-electricity, although the apparatus employed for that purpose was capable of producing a strong effect on the magnetic needle.

(325.) It is probably owing to some quality of this kind in the currents, which theory assigns as the source of magnetism (namely, from deficiency in tension), that all the endeavours which have so many different times been made by various experimentalists to obtain from magnetism any effects that may be considered as exclusively electrical, have uniformly failed. Although a magnet is powerfully affected by a current of electricity proceeding from a voltaic battery, it does not appear that the magnet is capable of augmenting or diminishing either the intensity or velocity, or any other of the qualities of the electric current. The only way in which the reaction of the magnet is shown, is by giving the electric current a tendency to lateral deflexion, as if urged by tangential forces proceeding from the poles of the magnet. If the wire of a galvanometer form part of the voltaic circuit, and a powerful magnet be applied to other parts of the circuit, whether bent into a helix or not, no indication of any action from the magnet is afforded by the needle of the galvano-

---

* Quarterly Journal of Science, xvi. 126.
† Bulletin des Sciences, No. II. for 1831.

meter*. We understand, however, that Mr. Faraday is at present engaged in an experimental inquiry upon this subject, which cannot fail, in such able hands, to lead to important results.

Chapter XIV.

Influence of Light on Magnetism.

(326.) Professor Morichini of Rome announced, in the year 1813, his having discovered that steel, exposed in a particular manner to the concentrated violet rays of the solar spectrum, became magnetic; but the uniform failure of the experiment, when tried by every other person, had created great doubt of the accuracy of the result as reported by Morichini. In the course of some experiments made by Mr. Christie, in the year 1824, he was led to the conclusion that the solar rays actually do exert a sensible influence on magnetism, which is shown by their affecting the vibrations of a magnetized needle exposed to them, quite independently of the effects produced by the heat which they impart. A needle, six inches long, contained in a brass compass box with a glass cover, was suspended by a fine hair, and made to vibrate, alternately shaded and exposed to the sun. He found, from a number of trials, that the vibrations of the needle, when exposed to the sun, ceased in a much shorter time than when they took place in the shade. That this greater slowness of the vibrations was not attributable to an increase of temperature, was proved by the needle's being observed to vibrate more rapidly when its temperature was raised by other means†.

(327.) In the summer of 1825, Mrs. Somerville was induced, by the unusual clearness of the weather, to investigate this subject‡. Having at that time no information of the manner in which Morichini's experiments had been conducted, it occurred to her that if the whole needle were equally exposed to the violet rays, it was not probable that the same influence which produced a south pole at one end, would, at the same time, produce a north pole at the other. She therefore covered half of a slender sewing-needle, an inch long, with paper, and fixed it in such a manner as to expose the uncovered part to the violet rays of a spectrum thrown, by an equiangular prism of flint glass, on a pannel at five feet distance. As the place of the spectrum shifted by the motion of the sun, the needle was moved so as to keep the exposed part constantly in the violet ray. The sun being bright, in less than two hours the needle, which before the experiment showed no signs of polarity, had become magnetic, the exposed end having the properties of a north pole.

The season continuing favourable, afforded daily opportunities of repeating and varying the experiments with needles of different sizes, and placed in different positions with respect to the meridian, and at different distances from the prism. The results were nearly uniform, and similar to that above stated. It was not found necessary to darken the room, provided the spectrum was thrown out of the direct solar rays.

(328.) Mrs. Somerville next endeavoured to ascertain whether the other prismatic rays had the same property as the violet. Needles, previously ascertained to be unmagnetic, exposed to the blue and green rays, sometimes acquired magnetism, though less uniformly and less quickly than in the violet ray: when magnetism was thus communicated, it seemed to be equally strong as in the former case. The indigo ray succeeded nearly as well as the violet. The exposed end, in almost every case, became a north pole. In no one instance was magnetism produced by the yellow, orange, or red rays, though in some instances the same needles were exposed to their influence for three successive days; neither did the calorific rays of the spectrum produce any sensible effect.

(329.) Pieces of clock and watch spring were next tried with similar success, and were found to be even more susceptible of this peculiar magnetic influence than needles, possibly on account of their blue colour, or greater proportional surfaces. The violet rays concentrated by a lens produced magnetism in a shorter time than the prism alone.

(330.) Experiments were next instituted by transmitting the solar rays through coloured media. Needles, half covered with paper, were exposed on a stone outside a window, under a blue glass coloured by cobalt, to a hot sun for three or four hours. They were found to be feebly magnetic; but their

---

* See Quarterly Journal of Science, xix. 338.
† Philosophical Transactions for 1826, p. 219.
‡ Ibid. p. 132.

magnetism was not permanently retained. In subsequent experiments, by an exposure of needles under the same circumstances, for six hours, a very sensible degree of magnetism was acquired, and remained permanent. The rays transmitted through the blue glass employed in this experiment blackened muriate of silver as powerfully as those transmitted through uncoloured glass; thus proving that it was freely permeable to the chemical rays of the solar spectrum. Green glass was also tried; and the rays which had penetrated it were likewise found to communicate magnetism. The white light of the sun produced no magnetic effect whatever on needles exposed to its influence.

(331.) Although the experiments, of which we have just stated the results, are minutely detailed in the paper above referred to in the Philosophical Transactions, yet, in many trials made by other experimentalists, no success has been obtained. The experiments on the oscillations of the needle were repeated by Messrs. P. Riess and L. Moser without any satisfactory result*. We may, therefore, consider the subject as still open to inquiry, and as requiring a more minute and scrupulous investigation.

Chapter XV.

Origin of Terrestrial Magnetism.

(332.) SEVERAL causes have been assigned for the magnetic influence which the globe of the earth is found to exercise, not only over the magnetic needle, but also, as we have seen, over currents of voltaic electricity transmitted through conductors. (*See* Chapter IX. § 128, *et seq*.) Among the various substances which occupy the interior of the globe it is extremely probable that chemical actions of different kinds are incessantly occurring. These actions will, for the most part, however, be very slow, and will continue with a certain degree of uniformity for very extended periods of time. They will occur more especially in the superficial strata of the earth, where the combined agencies of water, of atmospheric air, and of heat are in constant operation. The influence of the solar rays on a surface of such vast extent must be very considerable: and excepting in the vicinity of the poles, every portion of that surface is exposed in succession to their action, and acquires during that exposure a certain degree of heat; which heat is again lost by nocturnal radiation. Although the effect of these alternate changes of temperature may extend only to a small depth below the surface, yet considering their immense superficial extent, they may be sufficient to give rise to thermo-electric currents of considerable power. It has been conjectured, also, that these effects may be combined with an influence of another kind, more directly derived from the rotation of the earth on its axis, on the principle that all bodies have been found to exhibit magnetic polarity by rotation.†

(333.) That electric currents do really circulate in different parts of the solid strata of the earth, is not merely matter of conjecture: the existence of such currents has been lately proved, in the most satisfactory manner, by Mr. Robert Fox, in a paper "On the Electro-magnetic properties of metalliferous veins," which has been recently published in the Philosophical Transactions*. Having been led from theory to entertain the belief that a connexion exists between electric action in the interior of the earth, and the arrangement of metalliferous veins, he was anxious to verify this opinion by experiment. The first trials he made with this view were unsuccessful: but by persevering in his attempts, he soon obtained decisive evidence of considerable electrical action in the mine of Huel Jewel, in Cornwall. His apparatus consisted of small plates of sheet copper, which were fixed in contact with ore in the viens by copper nails, or else wedged closely against them by wooden props stretched across the galleries of the mine. Between two of these plates, at different stations, a communication was made by means of copper wire, one twentieth of an inch in diameter, which included a galvanometer in its circuit. In some instances three hundred fathoms of copper wire were employed.

(334.) The intensity of the electric currents was found to differ considerably in different places. It was generally greater in proportion to the greater abundance of copper ore in the veins, and in some degree also to the depth of the station. This curious fact may possibly afford the miner some useful indications as to the relative quantities of ore which the vein contains, and also as

---

* Annales de Chimie, xlii. 304.

* Cumming's Manual, &c. p. 231.
† For 1830, page 399.

to the directions in which it is most productive. The electricity thus perpetually in action does not appear to be in any respect influenced by the presence of the workmen and their candles; nor even by the explosions of gunpowder in blasting.

(335.) Mr. Fox observes that ores which transmit electricity have generally some conducting material interposed in the veins between them and the surface: a structure which appears to bear some analogy to the ordinary galvanic combinations. These electrical currents which pervade mines were found to have various and frequently opposite directions in different parts of the same mine.

(336.) The metals are probably not the only substances capable of giving rise to electrical currents in the earth; for it is well known that galvanic combinations may be formed by arrangements of elements that are not metallic. (*See* Galvanism, § 87.) The direction of each current will of course be determined by the relative positions of the elements from which it is derived; but even if we suppose the arrangement of these elements to be fortuitous, a prevailing current will still result, arising from the difference of their actions; for it is infinitely improbable that, without a designed arrangement, the currents in opposite directions should be exactly equal, so as to destroy one another. Irregularities of distribution probably exist with regard to the materials composing the interior of the globe; the resultant electro-magnetic action of the whole combination being that of which we witness the effects, and which may be considered as due to electrical currents circulating in directions parallel to the magnetic equator round the surface of the earth.

(337.) Even in the irregularities incident to the magnetic forces derived from the earth we may discern the operation of causes which are periodical in their operation. Thus the diurnal and annual changes of the variation of the needle may be traced to corresponding changes in the position of the different parts of the earth with regard to the sun, in as far as these electric currents are dependent upon solar influence. The progressive changes in the variation, which embrace longer periods of time, are less easily accounted for, and appear referable to causes which act at greater depths below the surface of the earth; and are probably connected with chemical changes taking place in the interior of the globe, of which we can possess no certain knowledge.

(338.) On the whole, then, it must be allowed, that there are strong grounds for the belief that there subsists some mutual connexion, or rather an intimate relation and affinity, between the several imponderable agents, namely, *Heat*, *Light*, *Electricity*, and *Magnetism*, which pervade in so mysterious a manner all the realms of space, and which exert so powerful an influence over all the phenomena of the universe.

NOTE. Since the above was sent to the press, a paper, by Mr. Faraday, has been communicated to the Royal Society, disclosing a most important principle in electro-magnetism, of which, I regret, I can only give the following brief statement.

By a numerous series of experiments, Mr. Faraday has established the general fact, that when a piece of metal is moved in any given direction, either in front of a single magnetic pole, or between the opposite poles of a horse-shoe magnet, electrical currents are developed in the metal, which pass in a direction at right angles to that of its own motion. The application of this principle affords a complete and satisfactory explanation of the phenomena observed by Arago, Herschel, Babbage, and others, where magnetic action appears to be developed by mere rotatory motion, and which have been erroneously ascribed to simple magnetic induction, and to the time supposed to be required for the progress of that induction. The electro-magnetic effect of the elective current induced in a conductor by a magnetic pole, in consequence of their relative motion, is such as tends continually to diminish that relative motion; that is, to bring the moving bodies into a state of relative rest: so that, if the one be made to revolve by an extraneous force, the other will tend to revolve with it, in the same direction, and with the same velocity.

POSTSCRIPT.

The design of the last four Treatises has been to offer a condensed and methodical work on that important department of Natural Philosophy which comprises the diversified phenomena of Electricity and Magnetism. These phenomena, which were formerly regarded as the effects of two perfectly distinct agents, are now discovered to have an intimate relation to one another, and, in all probability, to be dependent on one and the same principle: in like manner, as it was found by Newton that the simpler mechanical phenomena of the universe are the results of the single principle of gravitation. A succinct and connected account of the numerous discoveries which the exertions of philosophers have recently brought to light on this highly interesting branch of physical science, collected from the various scientific journals and transactions through which they are dispersed, and digested in a didactic order, seemed to be particularly wanting, and to be especially calculated to further the objects of the *Society for the Diffusion of Useful Knowledge*. In pursuance of this design, I have aimed at giving to the subjects treated as much condensation as was compatible with perspicuity. I have endeavoured to conduct the student, by a regular progression, from the simpler to the more complex topics of research; and I have also been anxious, by placing constantly before his view the distinction which exists between ascertained facts, and the hypotheses and theories devised for their explanation, to illustrate the precepts of Bacon by examples, and to foster that genuine spirit of philosophical inquiry by which alone error can be avoided, and truth attained.

For the many deficiencies which I fear the reader will discover in the completion of this design, I have to plead, in extenuation, the very scanty portion of leisure, which the continual pressure of my professional duties leaves at my disposal. When I undertook this task, at the request of the Society, above four years ago, I was far from anticipating the extent of the labour it has imposed upon me; and from the multiplied interruptions to which I have been subject, I have been compelled to prosecute the work in a desultory manner, and at irregular and uncertain intervals.

Since the publication of the earlier Treatises, many valuable researches have been made, both in Electricity and in Galvanism, which deserve to be recorded in their proper places. This, however, is an inconvenience which, in the present age of improvement, must be incident to every scientific Treatise; for while so many accessions are daily accruing to the stock of information, it is hardly possible to keep pace with the rapid growth of knowledge; nor can we ever hope to incorporate the whole of the discoveries, which have been made up to the last moment of publication, in a systematic work on any science. To wait till perfection is attained would be vain and fruitless presumption; for the architecture of science has this peculiarity, that the foundations must be prepared, and the superstructure begun, long before the plans and elevations are completed. To posterity will be left the task of adding the key-stone, and of removing the scaffolding which interrupts the symmetry of the perfect edifice.

P. M. Roget.

39, *Bernard-Street, Russell-Square,*
December 12*th,* 1831.

EXPLANATION OF SCIENTIFIC TERMS

MADE USE OF IN THIS VOLUME.

N.B. Many of the terms are common to both Volumes; but those explanations that were given in the former Glossary will be merely referred to in the present; except, in a few cases, where the definitions were not supposed to be sufficiently explicit. Several omissions may be supplied by consulting the Indexes.

ABERRATION.—See GLOSSARY I.

—————, SPHERICAL. — See Gloss. I.

ABSCISSA.—See *Conic Sections*. Gloss. I.

ACCELERATION.—See Gloss. I.

ACCELERATED FORCE is the increased force, or impetus, which a body exerts when stopped, in consequence of the acceleration of its motion. Some object to the expression, and propose to substitute the term *Accumulated Force*.

ACCELERATED MOTION.—See *Acceleration*.

ACCIDENTAL COLOURS.—See Gloss. I.

ACHROMATIC.—See Gloss. I.

ACIDS. The term acid was originally confined to denominate those bodies only which have a sour taste; but recently the name is given to other substances. The present characteristic of an acid is, that it changes the blue, green, and purple juices of vegetables to a red colour, and that it unites with alkalis and metallic oxides to form salts.

ACID, CARBONIC.—See *Carbon*.

———, NITRIC.—See *Azote*.

ADAMANTINE SPAR.—See *Corundum*, Gloss. I.

AFFINITY.—See *Chemical Affinity*.

ACTING POINT.—See *Machine*.

ACTION.—See Gloss. I.

ACTIVE FORCE.—See Gloss. I.

ACUTE ANGLE.—See *Angle*.

ADULARIA.—See *Feldspar*, Gloss. I.

AERIFORM FLUIDS.—See *Gas*, Gloss. I.

AGATES.—See Gloss. I.

AIR, GENERAL, CONDENSED, ETHERIAL, &c. See Gloss. I.

AIR, PRESSURE OF, a term sometimes used in place of the weight or the pressure of the atmosphere.—See *Atmosphere*.

AIR, INFLAMMABLE.—See *Oxygen*.

AIR-TIGHT, that degree of closeness in any vessel or tube, which prevents the passage of air, under the circumstances in which it is placed.

AIR-VESSEL, a vessel in which air is condensed by pressure, for the purpose of employing the re-action of its elasticity as a moving, or as a regulating power.

ALCHEMY, the name of that fanciful department of chemical science which, for many centuries, was occupied in the search for the philosopher's stone, and the *Elixir Vitæ*; by the former of which the baser were to be transmuted into the precious metals, and by the latter, human life was to be indefinitely prolonged. Sir Richard Steele was one of the latest of the followers of that phantom.

ALCOHOL. That portion of a vegetable substance which is sweet to the taste, or which is capable of becoming sweet under certain circumstances, or by certain manipulations, is termed *Saccharum* or *Saccharine matter*. This, when sufficiently fluid, readily enters into an intestine motion called the *Vinous fermentation*, emits *Carbonic Acid Gas*, and becomes of less and less specific gravity during the action. This lessening of weight is called *Attenuation*, and the product is a *Vinous liquor*. From this vinous liquor another liquid is procured by distillation. It is lighter than water, and called *spirituous*; and this, by re-distillation, (termed *Rectification*,) is brought to the state of pure spirit, rectified spirit of wine, or *Alcohol*, which are different names for the same thing. *Alcohol* always retains a portion of water, and its purity is calculated by its freedom from flavour and its lightness. The strongest alcohol yet procured has the specific gravity of 792, taking water at 1000.

ALKALIES are substances that have an acrid taste, change blue vegetable colours to green, and form salts by their union with acids. There are three alkalies: *Potash*, called the *Vegetable Alkali*, and *Soda* the *Mineral Alkali* are said to be *Fixed Alkalies*; and *Ammonia*, which is termed the *Volatile Alkali*, because it exists in the form of a gas. Potash and Soda are understood to be the oxides of two substances, called *Potassium* and *Sodium*, which are classed among the metals. Lime and certain other minerals, having some of the properties of an alkali, are called *Alkaline Substances*.

ALTITUDE of the sun or a star.—See *Horizon*.

AMALGAM (from the Greek *ama*, together, and *gameo*, I marry) is a chemical term signifying the union of any metal with mercury, which is a solvent to various metals.

AMETHYST.—See *Corundum*.

AMMONIA.—See *Alkalies*.

AMPLITUDE.—See *Horizon*.

ANALCIME is a stone which is found in grouped crystals, deposited by water, in the fissures of hard lavas. It melts under the blowpipe into a semi-transparent glass. It is also called *Cubizite*.—See Vol. I., *Polarization of Light*, p. 39.

ANALYSIS is the separation of the parts of a compound, so as to be able to examine them apart. SYNTHESIS is the opposite, signifying the composition of parts into one whole.

ANAMORPHOSIS (Greek *ana*, again, and *morphosis*, a form) is a distorted representation of an object; but which is so made as to appear in its proper shape by viewing it in a particular direction, or through a particular medium. The figure is also restored, in some cases, by causing the anamorphosis to be reflected from specula with certain surfaces, such as those of cones and cylinders.

ANGLE.—See *Gloss*. I.

ANGLES of *Incidence*, of *Reflexion*, and of *Draught*.—See *Gloss*. I. for these terms respectively.

ANHYDROUS.—See *Hydrate*, Gloss. I.

ANIMAL ELECTRICITY.—See *Galvanism*.

ANNEALING OF METALS consists in making them red hot, and then letting them cool gradually, in order to restore their malleability, which they are apt to lose under the operation of hammering. The *Annealing of glass* is conducted in the same manner, and is necessary to its perfection; for, otherwise, it would be apt to fly into pieces by the slightest scratch.—See *Rupert's drops*.

ANTECEDENTS.—See *Ratio*.

APHELION is that point of the orbit of a planet in which it is farthest from the sun (Greek *helios*, the sun); and the *Perihelion* is the point of the planet's nearest approach.

APLANATIC (Greek *a* privative, and *plane*, error) signifies free from error. The term is applied to those optical instruments in which the spherical aberration is completely corrected.—See *Aberration, Spherical*, in Gloss. I.

APOGEE (Greek *apo*, from, and *ge*, the earth) is that point of the moon's orbit in which she is at the greatest distance; and the *Perigee* is that point in which she is nearest to the earth. At the time when the earth was regarded as the centre of the system, the terms apogee and perigee were applicable to the places of all the planets, and also to the sun, with respect to their variable distances from the earth; but now they refer only to the moon. What was then called the sun's *Apogee* is now the earth's *Aphelion*, and the *Perigee* of the former has become the *Perihelion* of the latter.—See *Aphelion*.

APOPHYLLITE, or FISH-EYE-STONE is a scarce mineral, having a pearly lustre like to the species of feldspar called moon-stone. Its crystals are various and often tessellated with thick tables irregularly piled and grown together. It has a white milky colour, but in its divided portions it is usually transparent. This mineral is found in the iron mines of Uto, in Sudermania, a province of Sweden.

APPARENT TIME.—See *Time*.

AQUA FORTIS.—See *Azote*.

AQUEOUS VAPOUR, the vapour of water.—See *Vapour*.

ARC OF A CIRCLE.—See *Angle*.

AREA. The Roman *area* was a threshing floor, but the word is used by geometricians to denote any surface of a determinate extent. This extent is ascertained by calculating how many times larger the surface is than that of another smaller surface of the size of which we have an idea, such as a square inch, a square foot, &c., which we use as *superficial measures*.

ARITHMETICAL PROGRESSION.—See *Progression Arithmetical*.

ARRAGONITE, an impure species of carbonate of lime, brought from Arragon in Spain.

ARTIFICIAL MAGNETS.—See *Magnet*.

ASTRONOMICAL HORIZON.—See *Horizon*.

ASYMPTOTES OF AN HYPERBOLA.—See *Conic Sections* in Gloss. I.

ATMOSPHERE.—See Gloss. I.

ATMOSPHERES. One, two, three, &c.—See Gloss. I.

——————— REFRACTION OF. The atmosphere, which thus surrounds the earth like a shell, is more dense than the medium (whether ethereal or a vacuum) that intervenes between it and the celestial bodies; and, consequently, the rays of light are refracted when entering this shell. This refraction varies with the density of the atmosphere, and also with the direction in which the rays enter. The atmosphere gradually increases in density from the higher to the lower strata; and, therefore, a ray of light will be more and more refracted in its passage to the earth's surface, so as to descend in a curve line. The curve, too, varies with the direction of the ray; that coming from the zenith alone being a straight line.

ATOM.—See *Molecule*.

ATTENUATION.—See *Alcohol*.

ATTRACTION IN GENERAL, CAPILLARY, and of Cohesion.—See Gloss. I.

——————— ELECTIVE.—See *Chemical Attraction*.

——————— MAGNETIC.—See *Magnetism*.

AXINITE, a mineral commonly found in crystals of four-sided prisms, so flattened that some of its edges become thin and sharp; and hence its name from the Greek *axine*, an axe.

AXIS OF AN ELLIPSIS, PARABOLA, or CONE, &c.—See Gloss. I.

AXIS OF REFRACTION.—See *Refractive Power.*

——— OF A MAGNET.—See *Magnetism.*

AZIMUTH.—See *Horizon.*

——— COMPASS.—See *Horizon.*

AZOTE, or AZOTIC GAS, (Greek *a* privative, and *zoe* life,) so called because if inhaled alone it would be instantly destructive of life, is combined with oxygen in the atmosphere, of which it constitutes seventy-three parts in the hundred. This gas is also called *Nitrogen*, because it is believed to be the basis of *Nitric acid* or *Aqua Fortis.*

BALANCE.—See Gloss. I.

BAROMETER.—See Gloss. I.

BASIL LEATHER, tanned sheep skin.

BATTERY, ELECTRICAL.—See *Leyden Phial.*

———, VOLTAIC.—See *Galvanic Circle.*

BERYL.—See *Emerald.*

BLACK-LEAD.—See *Carbon.*

BODY is any determinate portion of matter which may act, or be acted upon, by other bodies.

BOILING.—See Gloss. I.

BOILING-POINT.—See Gloss. I.

BURNING-GLASS.—See Gloss. I.

CAIRNGORM.—See *Quartz.*

CALAMINE, an ore of zinc.

CALCAREOUS SPAR.—See Gloss. I.

CALORIC, latent, specific, &c.—See Gloss. I.

CALORIFIC RAYS.—See Gloss. I.

CALX.—See *Oxygen.*

CAOUTCHOUC, or INDIAN RUBBER, is an elastic resin or dried juice of certain trees and plants, growing in South America and the East Indies: the *Hevæa caoutchouc* and *Iatropha elastica* of the former; and the *Urceola elastica* of the latter. In some parts of those countries boots and shoes are made of that material.

CAPACITY FOR HEAT.—See Gloss. I.

CAPILLARY TUBE.—See Gloss. I.

——————ATTRACTION.—See Gloss. I.

CARBON is the chemical name for *charcoal*, supposing it to be pure; but pure carbon is understood to exist only in the diamond. *Charcoal* (the carbon of the arts) is the coaly residuum of vegetable substances which have been burnt in close vessels, and is an *oxide of carbon*. Carbon unites readily with oxygen, forming a gas called *Carbonic Acid*. It is this which is produced by the *vinous fermentation*. The union of this acid with alkalies, and alkaline substances, or with metals, forms what are called *Carbonates:* thus we have *Carbonate of Potash, Carbonate of Lime, Carbonate of Iron*, &c. Carbon enters into direct combination with iron. Nine parts carbon to one of iron is *Carburet of Iron;* what has erroneously been called *Plumbago* or *Black-lead*. In the proportion of about a forty fifth of the weight of the iron it forms *Cast-iron. Steel* is a combination of about one part of carbon to two hundred of iron. This union of carbon and iron is called *Carbonization*, and to *decarbonize* the cast-iron, or steel, is to drive off its carbon, in the form of *Carbonic Acid Gas.* Iron is said to be *Case-hardened* when its outer surface is converted into steel.—See *Steel.*

CASE-HARDENING.—See *Carbon.*

CAST-IRON.—See *Carbon.*

CATOPTRICS, that part of the science of optics which treats of the reflexion of light.

CENTIMETRE.—See *Metre.*

CENTRE OF GRAVITY.—See *Gravity.*

——— OF GYRATION.—See *Gyration.*

——— OF PERCUSSION.—See *Percussion.*

——— OF PRESSURE.—See *Pressure.*

CENTRIFUGAL FORCE.—See Gloss. I.

CENTRIPETAL FORCE is that force which draws a body towards a centre, and thereby acts as a counterpoise to the centrifugal force in circular motion. Gravity is a centripetal force, preventing the planets from flying off in a tangent, as the stone does from the sling.

CHARCOAL.—See *Carbon.*

CHEMICAL ATTRACTION, CHEMICAL AFFINITY, AND ELECTIVE ATTRACTION are different names for that unaccounted-for action by which the particles of one class of bodies, when presented to those of certain other classes, conjoin to form new compounds, making, apparently, a choice or election, of those with which they unite.

CHEMICAL COMBINATION is that intimate union of two substances, whether fluid or solid, which forms a compound, differing in one or more of its essential qualities from either of the constituent bodies.

CHORD OF AN ARC.—See *Angle.*

CHROMATICS (from the Greek *chroma*, colour) is that division of the science of optics which treats of the colours of light, their several properties, and the laws by which they are separated.

CHROMATIC VERNIER.—See *Vernier.*

CIRCLE OF GYRATION.—See *Gyration.*

CIRCUMFERENCE.—See *Perimeter.*

COHESION.—See Gloss. I.

———, ATTRACTION OF.—See Gloss. I.

COLOUR.—See Gloss. I.

COLOURS, PRIMARY.—See Gloss. I.

COMBINATION OF BODIES.—See *Chemical Combination.*

COMMENSURABILITY.—See *Ratio.*

COMPASS, AZIMUTH.—See *Horizon.*

———, MARINER'S.—See *Mariner's Compass.*

COMPASS, VARIATION OF.—See *Mariner's Compass.*
COMPOSITION OF FORCES. — See *Forces.*
COMPRESSIBILITY.—See Gloss. I.
CONCAVE MIRRORS.—See *Mirrors.*
——— LENSES.—See *Lenses.*
CONDENSATION.—See Gloss. I.
CONDUCTORS OF CALORIC. — See Gloss. I.
——— IN ELECTRICITY. If a body be *over-saturated* with the electric fluid, that fluid will endeavour to escape into other bodies; or, if *under-saturated*, the body will attract the fluid from other bodies. If the positively, or negatively, electrified body be surrounded by other bodies through which the fluid cannot pass, it is said to be *insulated*,—to be in a state of *insulation;* and substances which thus oppose the egress or ingress of the fluid are said to be *Non-conductors.* Those through which the passage is unobstructed are *Conductors.*
CONE.—See Gloss. I.
CONJUGATE DIAMETERS.—See Gloss. I. in *Conic Sections.*
——— HYPERBOLAS. — See Gloss. I. in *Conic Sections.*
CONOID.—See Gloss. I.
CONSECUTIVE POLES.—See *Magnet.*
CONSEQUENTS.—See *Ratio.*
CONVERGING RAYS.—See *Aberration.*
CONVEX LENSES AND MIRRORS.—See *Lenses* and *Mirrors.*
CORUNDUM.—See Gloss. I.
CRYSTALLIZATION.—See Gloss. I.
CUBIZITE.—See *Analcime.*
CURVE AND CURVATURE. — See Gloss. I.
CURVES, EVOLUTES, AND INVOLUTES.—See Gloss. I.
———, EQUATION OF.—See Gloss. I.
———, MAGNETIC.—See *Magnetism.*
CURVILINEAL.—See Gloss. I.
CYANOMETER, an instrument invented by Saussure, for comparing the different shades of blue, of which a good description is given in *Optics*, pp. 65, 66.
CYCLOID.—See Gloss. I.
CYLINDER.—See Gloss. I.
D'ALEMBERT'S PRINCIPLE. — See *Principle*, &c.
DEAD LEVEL.—See *Level.*
DECAMETRE.—See *Metre.*
DECARBONIZATION.—See *Carbon.*
DECIMETRE.—See *Metre.*
DEGREES AND MINUTES.—See *Angle.*
DENSITY (Latin *densitos*, closeness) is a relative term, and denotes the comparative quantity of matter in different bodies, which is contained in the same space (see *Volume*). Gravity is understood to act in proportion to the relative quantity of the matter of bodies; and, hence, the specific gravities of bodies are presumed to be the measure of their densities.—See *Gravity.*

DE-OXIDATION is the depriving a substance of the oxygen, or vital air, which it contains. Concerning the *de-oxidizing* power of the solar rays, see *Optics*, p. 29.
DESCARTES'S OVALS.—See *Ovals of Descartes.*
DIAGONAL, in geometry, is a straight line, drawn through a figure from one corner to another. A four-sided figure has two diameters, which, when the angles are right angles, are equal.
DIAMETER OF A CIRCLE, a right line passing through the centre, and terminating at both ends by the circumference.
DIAMETERS, TRANSVERSE AND CONJUGATE. See *Conic Sections.*
DIAPHANOUS (from the Greek *dia*, through, and *phäino*, to shine) is that quality of a substance which allows a passage to the rays of light. *Translucent* is a more ordinary term, of the same import. *Transparent* rises above *translucent*, by admitting not only the passage of light, but the vision of outward objects. *Semi-translucent* and *semitransparent* are occasionally written to express weaker degrees of those qualities.
DIFFRACTION, or INFLEXION OF LIGHT. Light, when it meets with no obstacle, proceeds in straight lines; but, if it be made to pass by the boundaries of an opaque body, it is turned from its rectilineal course, which deviation is termed *diffraction*, or *inflexion*. See *Newton's Optics*, p. 10.
DIGESTER, a strong vessel of iron or other metal, having a screwed-down and air-tight lid, into which animal or other substances are inclosed immersed in water, and submitted to a higher degree of heat than could be had in open vessels, whereby the solvent power of the water is so increased that bones (for which it was originally invented) are converted into a jelly.
DIOPTRICS is that division of the science of optics which treats of the refraction of light.
DIPPING NEEDLE, a magnetic needle poised so as to move freely in a vertical direction, points downward, or dips, less or more, towards the earth; except it be situated on some part of a line which surrounds the globe, and is called the *magnetic equator*. On this line the needle remains horizontal. This equator, which intersects the geographical equator at an angle of about twelve degrees, has its *magnetic poles* at a short distance from the true poles of the earth.
DIRECT PROPORTION, or DIRECT RATIO.—See *Ratio.*
DIRECTION, LINE OF.—See *Force, Direction of.*
DIRECTIVE FORCE, in magnetism, is the tendency in one magnet to assume a

particular position with relation to another magnet.

DIRECTRIX OF A PARABOLA.—See *Conic Sections.*

DISTILLATION is a process by which a fluid, or portion of a liquid, is converted into vapour by means of heat; and that vapour returned into a liquid state by cold, or, as some say, by the abstraction of caloric. Distillation is *evaporation*, that is, raising a liquid to the state of vapour; but the latter term does not include the idea of preserving that vapour and condensing it again into a liquid. The chief object of distillation is either to separate mixed liquids, where the steam of one rises at a lower heat than the other; or to free a simple liquid from dregs or impurities. In the distillation of vinous liquors, alcohol is produced, which boils at a much lower heat than water; but it is not yet perfectly ascertained whether this alcohol existed ready formed in the liquor, or owes its formation to a chemical action during the process. The grosser liquor remaining in the still, after the *spirit* is all exhausted, is called *spent wash*, and is food for hogs.

DIVERGING RAYS (of light) are the opposite of *converging* (which see). They separate in their progress further and further asunder, as the radii of a circle do from its centre.

DODECAHEDRON.—See *Rhombus.*

DOGMATISM—See *Empirical.*

DOUBLE REFRACTION.—See *Refraction.*

DUPLICATE RATIO.—See *Ratio, Compound.*

DYNAMICS (Greek, *dynamis*, force) is that division of the science of mechanics which considers bodies as acted upon by forces that are not *in equilibrio*. It, therefore, treats of bodies in motion.—See *Equilibrium.*

DYNAMETER (a Greek compound signifying a measurer of power) is an instrument so contrived as to measure, with accuracy, the magnifying powers of microscopes and telescopes. It is described at page 11 of the treatise on *Optical Instruments.*

EBULLITION.—See *Boiling.*

ELASTICITY (from a Greek word signifying *to push*, or drive back) is that quality of a substance, whether solid or fluid, by which, when compressed, or when forcibly expanded, it endeavours, in either case, to reassume its former bulk.

ELASTIC FLUIDS.—See *Fluids* and *Gas.*

ELECTIVE ATTRACTION.—See *Chemical Attraction.*

ELECTRICITY. If a dry piece of amber be rubbed by the hand, it will acquire the property of alternately attracting and repelling light bodies, such as bits of straw, paper, or feathers. This power continues only for a short time, when it becomes exhausted and ceases to act. If the experiment be made in the dark, sparks of light will be observed, passing between the light bodies and the amber. Glass and several other substances have similar properties; and the collection of phenomena which have been observed concerning them is called *electricity*, from the Greek *electron*, amber. Bodies that are capable of being endowed with this power of attraction and repulsion and the emission of light are termed *electrics*. They are said to be *excited* by the friction; and a machine contrived to produce this *excitation* in an easy and rapid manner, by means of a peculiarly-constructed *cushion*, called a *rubber*, is an *electrical machine*. Bodies that are not excitable by such means are *non-electrics*.

ELECTRIC FLUID. In order to account for the various phenomena of electricity, it has been supposed that there is a subtile fluid, identical with lightning, which pervades the pores of all bodies, and is capable of motion from one body to another. When the natural quantity belonging to a particular body (then said to be *saturated*) is increased, that body is said to be *positively electrified*; and, when that quantity is diminished, it is *negatively electrified*. These two states have also been called *plus* and *minus electricity*; and the former being obtained from *glass* and the latter from *sealing-wax*, the two are sometimes distinguished by the terms *vitreous* and *resinous electricity*.

ELECTRICITY, ANIMAL.—See *Galvanism.*

————— —————, VOLTAIC.—See *Galvanism.*

————— —————, POSITIVE AND NEGATIVE.—See *Electric Fluid.*

————— —————, RESINOUS AND VITREOUS.—See *Electric Fluid.*

ELECTRICS AND NON-ELECTRICS.—See *Electricity.*

ELECTRICAL BATTERY.—See *Leyden Phial.*

ELECTRO-MAGNETISM is a science which comprehends the phenomena shewing the connexion between Electricity and Magnetism.

ELECTROMETER, an instrument used for ascertaining the quantity and quality of the electricity in an electrified body.—See *Index.*

ELECTROSCOPE, an instrument for exhibiting the attractive and repulsive agencies of electricity.—See *Index.*

ELIXIR VITÆ.—See *Alchemy.*

ELLIPSIS.—See *Cone and Conic Sections.*

ELLIPSOID.—See *Conoid* and *Spheroid.*

EMERALD. The emerald is ranked among the gems, and is now found only in Peru. It is of a green colour, rather harder than quartz, and always in crystals, which are translucent and generally transparent. What is called *oriental emerald* is a *green* sapphire. The *beryl* is a variety of the emerald, of a paler green, frequently passing into blue, and is much less prized. It is found in various countries, sometimes in Scotland. The *emerald* of *Brazil* is a *tourmaline*, which see.

EMPIRICAL (Greek *en*, and *peirao*, I try) designates any assertion or act which is made or done as an experiment, independently of hypothesis or theory. The term is generally used in a bad sense; especially in the science of medicine, in which an *empiric* is synonymous with a *quack*. The empiric is supposed to set up his own short-lived experience to the collected knowledge of ages, which is understood to guide the regular practitioner; and which the empiric, in his turn, vilifies by the name of *dogmatism*, a Greek derivative, denoting a fixed and positive opinion.

EQUATION OF A CURVE.—See *Conic Sections*.

EQUATOR, MAGNETIC.—See *Dipping Needle*.

EQUILIBRIUM. When two or more forces, acting upon a body, are so opposed to each other that the body remains at rest, although either would move it if acting alone, those forces are said to be *in equilibrio*, which is a Latin term signifying *equally balanced*.

ERIOMETER, an instrument, invented by Dr. Young, for the purpose of measuring the diameters of minute fibres. It is described in the treatise on *Optics*, pp. 37, 38.

ETHER.—See *Air, Ethereal*.

———— (in chemistry) is the name of an extremely volatile liquid, formed by the distillation of some one of the acids with alcohol. There are, of course, several modes of production, according to the acid employed; as *nitric ether, sulphuric ether*, &c.; but, when well rectified, the ether is the same whatever acid has been employed.

EUCLASE, a scarce species of emerald, remarkably brittle; and hence its Greek name.

EVAPORATION is the conversion of water or other liquids into vapour or steam, which becomes dissipated in the atmosphere in the manner of an elastic fluid. When the evaporation is spontaneous, that is, at an ordinary temperature of the atmosphere, and without artificial heat, it is commonly called *exhalation*, whereas evaporation is often understood to be produced artificially, and preceded by *boiling*.—See *Boiling, Steam,* and *Vapour*.

EVOLUTE OF A CURVE.—See *Curves*.

EXCENTRICITY. The distance between the *foci* of an ellipsis is called its excentricity, and sometimes its *ellipticity*. It is in this way that we speak of the *excentricity* of the orbits of the planets which are supposed to move in ellipses.

EXCITATION.—See *Electricity*.

EXHAUSTED RECEIVER.—See *Vacuum*.

EXPANSIBILITY.—See Gloss. I.

FAHRENHEIT'S THERMOMETER.—See Gloss I.

FELDSPAR.—See Gloss. I.

FIRST, or PRIME MOVER, in mechanics.—See *Machine*.

FIXED ALKALIES.—See *Alkali*.

FLUID, ELECTRIC.—See *Electric Fluid*.

————, MAGNETIC.—See *Magnetic Fluid*.

FLUIDITY.—See Gloss. I.

FLUIDS, ELASTIC, NON-ELASTIC, &c.—See Gloss. I.

FLY-WHEEL.—See Gloss. I.

FOCUS.—See Gloss. I.

———— REFRACTED AND GEOMETRICAL. The point in which the rays of light (according to their known laws) ought to be concentrated, when reflected from a concave mirror, or refracted through a lens, is termed the *Geometrical Focus*; that in which they are actually found is the *Refracted Focus*. These foci are separated from one another in proportion to the degree of spherical aberration.

FORCE.—See Gloss. I.

———— CENTRIFUGAL.—See *Centrifugal*.

———— CENTRIPETAL.—See *Centripetal*.

———— DIRECTION OF.—See Gloss. I.

———— COMPOSITION.—See Gloss. I.

———— ACCELERATION OF.—See *Acceleration*.

———— DIRECTIVE.—See *Magnets, Artificial*.

FORMULA, a short general form, or rule, easily to be remembered, directing how certain things may be done. The word is a Latin diminutive, and has often the plural *formulæ* in place of *formulas*.

FREEZING-POINT.—See Gloss. I.

FRICTION.—See Gloss. I.

FRIGORIFIC.—See Gloss. I.

FULCRUM.—See *Lever* and *Balance*.

FUSION.—See Gloss. I.

GALVANISM, so named after its discoverer, Professor Galvani of Bologna, "includes all those electrical phenomena, arising from the chemical agency of certain metals with different fluids[*]." Volta discovered the means of multiplying those effects: hence the science has also been called *Voltaism*; and (from its action on the muscles of animals newly killed) *Animal Electricity*.

GALVANIC CIRCLE. If, between two plates of different metals, a fluid be interposed which has a chemical effect on one of the metals, and little or none on the other; and if a communication be made between other parts of the plates, by means of a conducting substance (as a

---

[*] For a definition which involves no hypothesis, see *Galvanism,* § 1.

wire), a continued current of Electricity will be produced, through the conductor, from one plate to the other, as long as the chemical action is exerted. This is the simple *Galvanic Circle.* A number of similar pairs of plates, placed alternately with an acting fluid intervening between each, and the two ends of the series connected by a wire, multiplies the effect, and is called a *Galvanic,* or *Voltaic, pile.* For the construction of such *piles,* and of *batteries* of various forms, see *Galvanism,* Chapters II. and III. The end of the galvanic pile which gives out the electric fluid is called the *positive pole,* and the other end, in which the wire terminates, and which receives the electric matter, is called the *negative pole* of the pile.

GALVANIC PILE.—See *Galvanic Circle.*

GAS.—See Gloss. I.

GASEOUS signifies that the substance spoken of has the nature of gas; and thus *gaseous fluids* are distinguished from other fluids.

GAS, AZOTIC.—See *Azote.*

—— CARBONIC ACID.—See *Carbon.*

—— HYDROGEN.—See *Oxygen.*

—— NITROGEN.—See *Azote.*

GEOMETRICAL PROGRESSION.—See *Progression.*

GLASS DROPS.—See *Rupert's Drops.*

——ANNEALING OF.—See *Annealing.*

GLAUBERITE.—See Gloss. I.

GONIOMETER.—See Gloss. I.

GOVERNOR.—See Gloss. I.

GRAVITY.—See Gloss. I.

—————— CENTRE OF. The centre of gravity of a solid body is a point so situated with respect to it, that if the body could be suspended from the point in question, the whole body would remain at rest (with respect to its tendency to the earth) in whatever situation the surrounding parts may be turned. Thus, the centre of gravity of a globe, if of uniform density, is its common centre; and that of a balanced beam is the pivot on which it turns. See this further illustrated in the *Popular Introductions,* pages xviii. xix. and xx.

—————— RELATIVE AND SPECIFIC. The comparative or relative gravities of different bodies towards the earth are measured by a general standard called *weight,* and one substance is said to have a greater *specific gravity* than another, when a less portion of its bulk is of equal weight to that other. Thus, a cubic inch of platina is nearly twice the weight of a cubic inch of silver; and, therefore, is said to have double its *specific* gravity,—the *specific* gravity of platina, *relative* to that of silver, is as two to one. In this mode of comparison, the gravities are relative; but a standard is assumed with which both may be compared. That standard, for solids and liquids, is water, which is reckoned unity, and compared with that fluid, silver is 10.5 and platina 21.4: that is, equal bulks of water, silver and platina, would have weights in these proportions. In designating the specific gravities of gases, the standard, or unity, is atmospheric air.

GRAVITY, LINE OF DIRECTION OF, is that right line which passes through the centre of gravity of a body in a direction towards the centre of the earth.

GYRATION (Latin *gyrus,* a circle) is the action of turning round a centre, in the manner of a wheel.

——————, CENTRE OF, is a point in a revolving body, into which, if all its matter could be collected, it would continue to revolve with the same energy as when its parts were in their original places.

HALO, "a luminous and sometimes coloured circle, appearing occasionally around the heavenly bodies, but more especially about the sun and moon."—See *Parhelia.*

HARDNESS is the resistance to impression. It is *incompressible,* but limited to solids.—See *Compressibility.*

HEAT.—See *Caloric.*

——, CAPACITY FOR.—See *Caloric, Capacity for.*

—— CONDUCTORS OF.—See *Conductors.*

—— LATENT.—See *Caloric, Latent.*

—— RADIATION OF.—See *Radiation.*

—— SPECIFIC.—See *Caloric, Specific.*

HECATOMETRE.—See *Metre.*

HELIX, the scientific name for a spiral.

HERMETIC SEAL.—See Gloss. I.

HEXAHEDRON.—See *Rhombus.*

HETEROGENEOUS.—See Gloss. I.

HOMOGENEOUS.—See Gloss. I.

HORIZON is a Greek word signifying a boundary, and was employed to denote the circle in which the apparent plane of the earth terminated in the concave of the sky. This is now called the *sensible horizon,* to distinguish it from the *true* or *astronomical horizon,* which is parallel to the *sensible,* but is conceived to be a plane passing through the centre of the earth and dividing the whole celestial sphere into the upper and lower hemispheres. That the ancients believed the earth to be an extended plain is obvious from the words which they employed in its description. They believed, too, that it was longer from east to west than from north to south: calling the former its *length* and the latter its *breadth,* and hence we have our terms *longitude* and *latitude.* A line or plane in, or parallel to, the horizon, is *horizontal.* Planes passing through the *zenith* (or point which is directly over our head) and the centre of the earth are called *vertical planes;* and the circles in the heavens marked by such planes are *vertical circles,* or *azimuths.* All these circles cut the horizon at right angles; and it is in an arc of one which passes through a star that the *altitude* of the star above the horizon is measured. The vertical circle which passes through the place of the sun at noon, cuts the horizon at the north and south points, and is called the *meridian* of the place where it is supposed to be drawn. Any other vertical plane which may be imagined to pass through the sun, or a star, when not in the meridian, will make an angle with the plane of the meridian, which will be measured by the portion of the circle of the horizon which it cuts off to the east or west of that meridian. This angle, or portion of the circle of the horizon is called the *Azimuth* of the sun, or star, at that time and place. The *Magnetic Meridian*, as pointed out by the *Mariner's Compass*, differs from the true (or real north and south) by the amount of the *Variation of the Compass*, and so does the apparent or *Magnetical Azimuth*. The *Azimuth Compass* is constructed so as to find easily the magnetical azimuth.—See *Magnetism*, pages 60, 68—72. An arch, intercepted between the east or west point of the horizon, and the point (of the same circle) of the rising or setting of the sun or of a star, on any particular day, is called the *Amplitude* of the sun, or star, for that day. The distances of the points of rising or setting from the east and west, as shown by the compass, is the *Magnetical Amplitude*.

HYACINTH.—See *Zircon*.
HYDRATES. Chemical compounds, particularly salts, which contain water as one of their ingredients, have been termed *Hydrates*. If water is not a constituent, they are said to be *Anhydrous:* a Greek compound which signifies *without water*.
HYDROUS, watery, or containing water in its composition.
HYDROGEN.—See *Oxygen*.
HYGROMETER, an instrument, of which there are various forms of construction, for measuring the relative degree of moisture which exists, at any particular time and place, in the atmosphere.
HYPERBOLA.—See *Cone*, and *Conic Sections*.
HYPERBOLOID.—See *Conoid*.
HYPOTHESIS.—See *Induction*.
ICELAND SPAR.—See *Calcareous Spar*, and *Spar*.
ICOSAHEDRON.—See *Rhombus*.
IDOCRASE, a name sometimes given to *Vesuvian*, which see.
IMPENETRABILITY.—See Gloss. I.
IMPULSE.—See Gloss. I.
INCIDENCE, POINT OF.—See Gloss. I.
INCOMMENSURABLE.—See *Ratio*.
INSTRUMENT.—See *Machine*.
INDEX OF REFRACTION.—See *Refractive power*.

INDIAN RUBBER.—See *Caoutchouc*.
INDUCTION, in philosophy, is the collecting, or bringing into one focus, a multitude of observations on any particular subject, and drawing conclusions from an examination and general survey of the whole. It is the opposite of *Hypothesis*, which is to lay down a theory in the outset, and trusting to future experiments, or example, for its proof.
——— IN ELECTRICITY is that effect of an *insulated* electrified body which tends to produce an opposite electric state in neighbouring bodies.
——— IN MAGNETISM is analogous to electric induction; for illustrations of which see *Magnetism*, page 4.
INERTIA.—See *Vis Inertiæ*.
INFLAMMABLE AIR.—See *Oxygen*.
INFLEXION OF LIGHT.—See *Diffraction*.
INSULATION.—See Gloss. I.
INVERSE PROPORTION, or RATIO.—See *Ratio*.
INVOLUTE OF A CURVE.—See *Curves*.
IRON, CARBURET OF.—See *Carbon*.
ISOCHROMATIC, &c.—See Gloss. I.
ISODYNAMIC, having equal power.
JARGON.—See *Zircon*.
LATENT HEAT.—See *Caloric*.
LAW OF THE SINES.—See *Refractive Power*.
LENS POLYZONAL.—See *Polyzonal*.
LEVEL.—See Gloss. I.
LEUCOCYOLITE, a name given to a variety of *Apophyllite*, which see.
LEVER (Latin *levare*, and French *lever*, to lift, or raise) is one of the mechanical powers. It is an inflexible bar, supported and moveable in one point of its length on a pivot, or prop, called the *fulcrum*. One end of the lever is applied to the weight to be raised, while a force is applied to the other end. The power of this instrument depends on the proportion between the lengths of the parts of the lever on each side of the *fulcrum*.—See *Balance*.
For a plain account of the different kinds and applications of levers, see *Popular Introductions*, pages xx.—xxiv.
LEYDEN PHIAL. The *Leyden Phial*, or *Leyden Jar*, (so called because it was first constructed in that city,) is a cylindrical glass vessel, coated to a certain height, inside and outside, with some conducting substance, which is capable of being charged with electrical fluid, accumulated for various experiments. A combination of such phials is an *electrical battery*. See those words in the Index for more complete explanation.
LIGHT, RAYS OF REFLEXION OF, &c.—See Gloss. I.
LIGNUM NEPHRITICUM (Latin *lignum*, wood, and Greek *nephros*, a kidney) is a bitter tasted wood, so called because it was once believed to be a sove-

reign remedy in *nephritis*, or inflammation of the kidneys. It is chiefly imported from Mexico. The wood, when cleared of its bark, is of a dirty yellow colour; but its infusion in cold water has a sky-blue tinge, when viewed by a false light, and a gold colour by a true one. A small portion of any acid being mixed with the tincture, both these colours disappear; but the sky-blue may be restored by means of potash.

LIMIT.—See Gloss. I.

LIQUIDS, and LIQUIDITY.—See Gloss. I.

LOADSTONE.—See *Magnet, Native*.

MACHINE (Latin *machina*, a frame or contrivance). Any complication of artificial bodies acting upon one another by contact, through the medium and motion of which any effect is produced, is a machine. The initial force which puts the machine in motion is called the *First* or *Prime mover*. The *point* at which that force is applied is the *Acting point*; and that in which the effect is produced is the *Working point*: the machine being the medium through which the power is transferred, and by which it is modified so as to answer the intended purpose. When a simple body is the medium between the *acting* and the *working points*, it is an *Instrument*.

MAGNETISM " is that peculiar property occasionally possessed by certain bodies (more especially by iron and some of its compounds), whereby, under certain circumstances, they mutually attract or repel one another, according to determinate laws."

MAGNET, NATIVE, or LOADSTONE, is an ore of iron, found in the iron mines of Sweden and other places.

MAGNETS, ARTIFICIAL, are made of small bars of iron or steel, which, when placed at perfect liberty, turn one end towards the north, and the other, consequently, in a southerly direction. These two points are termed the *North* and the *South Poles* of the magnet; and a line, supposed to connect these points, is its *Axis*. The tendency to acquire a direction nearly north and south is its *Polarity*. Either pole of the magnet attracts iron. Slight poles formed at irregular points of the bar, and which tend to disturb the attraction of the real ones, are termed *Consecutive poles*.

MAGNETIC CURVES. For the forms of these curves, and diagrams illustrative of their properties, see *Magnetism*, pages 19—22.

MARINER'S COMPASS, a well-known instrument, consisting of a small magnetic bar, called a needle, poised on its centre of gravity, so as to be enabled, with the greatest ease, to turn every way in an horizontal direction. After a few vibrating motions, during which it is said to *traverse*, the needle takes its direction nearly north and south, which direction is said to be in the plane of the *Magnetic Meridian* of the place where the compass happens to be. The true *Geographical Meridian* is a plane passing through the zenith and the poles of the earth. The angle, which the magnetic meridian is east or west from the geographical, or true north and south, is different in different places and at different times; and this is called the *Variation of the Compass*.—See *Dipping Needle*.

MAGNETIC FLUID is a hypothetical fluid, by which the phenomena of magnetism have been accounted for. Some have supposed two such fluids, a *Boreal* or northern, and an *Austral* or southern.

MASS (of matter).—See *Volume*.

MAXIMUM. In a variable *quantity* or *effect*, that quantity or effect which is *the greatest possible*, under the circumstances in which it is placed, is termed a *maximum*. Thus, in respect to the sails of a windmill, they may be placed at any angle, but there is one angular direction on which the wind will have more power than on any other, and this is, therefore, termed a *maximum*. There are other cases, in which we seek for a *minimum*, that is, *the least possible*.

MECHANICS is that science which investigates the nature, laws, and effects of motion and moving powers.

MECHANICAL POWERS are the simple instruments or elements of which every machine, however complicated, must be constructed: they are the *Lever*, the *Wheel* and *Axle*, the *Pulley*, the *Inclined Plane*, the *Wedge*, and the *Screw*.

MELTING POINT. That point of the thermometer which indicates the heat at which any particular solid becomes fluid, is termed the *melting point* of that solid.

MENISCUS (Greek *mene*, the moon) a lens which is concave on one side, and convex on the other; and so called because it resembles the appearance of the new moon.

MERIDIAN, MAGNETIC.—See *Mariner's Compass*.

METALS, annealing of.—See *Annealing*.

METAPHYSICS.—See *Physics*.

METRE. A *metre* is the French standard measure of length, equivalent to 39.371, or very nearly $39\frac{3}{8}$, English inches. The French measures ascend and descend in a decimal progression. Thus,

	English Inches.
A Millimetre is	.03937
Centimetre	.39371
Decimetre	3.93710
Metre	39.371
Decametre	393.71
Hecatometre	3937.1
Chiliometre	39371
&c.	

MICA is a mineral of various colours, but usually gray. It is chiefly distributed, in very thin plates, through quartz, feldspar, and other fossils; but it is also found in the form of prismatic crystals. It constitutes a principal ingredient in many of what are termed primitive rocks. The plates are sometimes large (as much as eighteen inches diameter), and extremely thin. They are employed in Russia for window-panes; and, in that state, are called *Muscovy Glass*.

MILLIMETRE.—See *Metre*.

MINERAL ALKALI.—See *Alkali*.

MINIMUM.—See *Maximum*.

MIRRORS, PLANE, CONCAVE, and CONVEX.—See Gloss. I.

MOCHO STONE.—See *Agate*.

MOLECULE is a diminutive, formed from the Latin *moles*, a mass, and denotes one of the minute particles of which the mass or body is composed. *Molecules* differ from *Atoms* in this, that they are never considered but as portions of some aggregate. An *Atom* (from the Greek *a* privative, and *tamno*, I cut) is accounted as one of the simplest particles in nature,—what is incapable of further division.

MOMENTUM, or MOMENT, is the impetus, or force of a moving body. The comparative *momenta* of bodies are in a compound ratio of their quantity of matter and their velocity: that is, they are in proportion to the products of the matter and velocity, *when expressed in numbers*. Thus a ball of four pounds weight, moving *uniformly* at the rate of eighteen feet in a second, would have double the momentum,—that is, it would strike against an object with twice the force that a ball of three pounds weight, moving at the rate of twelve feet per second, would do; because the first product (4 multiplied by 18) is double that of 3 multiplied by 12. *Momentum* is the *force of percussion*.—See *Percussion*.

MOONSTONE.—See *Feldspar*.

MOTION is the passing of a body, or any parts of a body, from one place to another: we say *parts* of a body, because in the cases of a globe turning on its axis, or a wheel revolving on a pivot, the parts of the body change their situation, while the bodies themselves are stationary.

MOVING POWER.—See *Power*.

MUSCOVY GLASS.—See *Mica*.

NATIVE MAGNET.—See *Magnet*.

NEGATIVE ELECTRICITY.—See *Electric Fluid*.

NITRIC ACID.—See *Azote*.

NITROGEN.—See *Azote*.

NON-CONDUCTORS.—See *Electric Fluid*.

NON-ELECTRICS.—See *Electricity*.

NON-ELASTIC FLUIDS.—See *Gas* and *Liquids*.

NONIUS.—See *Vernier's Scale*.

OBLATE and OBLONG SPHEROIDS.—See *Spheroid*.

OBTUSE ANGLE.—See *Angle*.

OCTAHEDRON.—See *Rhombus*.

OCULAR SPECTRA.—See *Accidental Colours*.

OPACITY (Latin *opacus*, dark), a state impervious to light.

ORDINATE, of an *Ellipse, Parabola,* and *Hyperbola*.—See *Conic Sections*.

OSCILLATION (Latin, *oscillatio*, swinging) is particularly applied to designate the motion of a pendulum.

——————, CENTRE OF. "The centre of oscillation in a pendulous body is a point in the line passing through the centre of suspension, and the centre of gravity. If all the matter of the body could be collected in that point, any force applied there would generate the same angular velocity, in a given time, as the same force would generate in the same time, by acting similarly at the centre of gravity of the pendulum, when all the parts thereof are situated in their respective places." This point differs from the *Centre of Gyration*, because the motion of the body is produced by the gravity of its own particles, whereas in *Gyration*, the body is put in motion by some other force, acting at one place only.—See *Centre of Percussion*.

OVALS. These figures have their name from their resemblance to the transverse section of an egg, Latin *ovum*. Ellipses are ovals which are formed by a fixed law, but the latter is a popular term for any curved figure, approaching to that shape. The carpenter's oval, for example, is made up of circular arcs, that unite without leaving any angular appearances at their junctures.

OVALS OF DESCARTES. These, though not Ellipses, are governed by a determinate law, which constitutes them as varieties of that curve. As in the Ellipse the two lines drawn from the foci to any point of the circumference vary, so that the increment of one shall always be equal to the simultaneous decrement of the other; so, in the *Cartesian Ovals*, these increments are in an invariable ratio. "These curves may therefore be defined the *locus* (place) of the vertex of a triangle, on a given base, one of whose sides bears a given ratio to the sum or difference of a given line and the other side."

OVERSHOT WHEEL.—See *Water-Wheel*.

OXYGEN, or OXYGEN GAS, is that portion (something more than a fourth) of the atmospheric air, which is capable of supporting flame, and is essential to the respiration of animals. Oxygen is generally diffused throughout nature, but always in combination with other substances. United with *Hydrogen Gas* (*Inflammable Air*) it forms water. It was at one time supposed to be a necessary ingredient in the composition of all acids; and hence its name, which is derived from the Greek, and signifies *a generator of sours*; but acids have been since discovered, which contain no oxygen. It unites with metals and other substances during their combustion, and forms *Oxides*, what were formerly called *Calces*. Hence we say that those substances are *Oxydable*, and speak of the *Oxides* of iron, of lead, &c.—See *De-oxydation*.

PARABOLA.—See *Cone* and *Conic Sections*.

PARABOLOID.—See *Conoid*.

PARALLEL LINES.—When two straight lines, in the same plane, are so directed that, however much they might be lengthened, they would never approach nearer to, nor recede from one another, they are said to be parallel.

PARALLELOGRAM is a right-lined and four-sided figure, whose opposite sides are parallel, and consequently equal. When its angles are right-angles, the figure is usually called a *Rectangle* or *Oblong*. If all its sides, as well as angles, are equal, it is a *Square*.—See *Rhombus*.

PARALLELOPIPED.—A parallelopiped is a solid having six sides, each of which is a parallelogram, and consequently always equal to and parallel to its opposite. It is a prism whose base is a parallelogram.—See *Prism*.

PARHELIA, PARHELIUM, or PARHELION (Greek *para*, near, and *helios*, the sun), is a *mock sun*; an appearance similar to the sun, which occasionally accompanies *halos* (See *Halo*.) There have been sometimes seen six or seven of these *mock suns* at the same time, which, in that case, are denominated by the plural, *Parhelia*.

PENCIL OF LIGHT.—See *Light, Ray of*.

PENUMBRA (Latin *penè*, almost, and *umbra*, a shadow) is a partial shadow; that is, a shadow which only receives a portion of the rays of a luminous body, when that body has a measurable diameter. This is well explained in *Newton's Optics*, at page 23.

PERCUSSION, CENTRE OF. Percussion is a forcible stroke given by a moving body. In taking any particular body, such as a rod of equal thickness, held at one end, and swung forcibly by the hand, so as to strike upon a resisting object, the force of the stroke will be greater or less, according to the part of the rod that shall hit the object. There is one point of the rod in which the whole force of the stroke is concentrated, and the resistance to which would neutralize the blow. That point is termed the *Centre of percussion*. When the percutient body revolves round a fixed, the centre of percussion is the same with the *Centre of oscillation*, and if all the parts of the percutient body be carried forward with the same celerity (which is not the case of the pendulum), the centre of percussion is the same with the *centre of gravity*.

PERCUSSION, FORCE OF.—See *Momentum*.

PERIGEE.—See *Apogee*.

PERIHELION.—See *Aphelion*.

PERIMETER. The length of the whole bounding line of any plane figure, of whatever parts or shapes that line may consist, is termed the *perimeter* of the figure. The length of the bounding line of a circle (and, perhaps, of any curve which returns upon itself) is its *circumference*.

PERPENDICULAR.—See *Angle*.

PETUNTSE.—See *Feldspar*.

PHENOMENON (plural *Phenomena*) is a Greek word, signifying an *Appearance*, and is limited, in our language, to denote those appearances in nature, whether discovered by direct observation or experiment, for which there is no obvious cause. An *Hypothesis* is an assumed cause, by which we endeavour to account for a particular class of phenomena; and that hypothesis is best which solves the greatest number.

PHLOGISTON (from the Greek *phlego*, to burn) is a name given by the older chemists to an imaginary substance, which was the principle of inflammability. According to them, every combustible body was formed of an incombustible base, united to this phlogiston, which escaped into the atmosphere during the *combustion*. This process is now attributed to the union of certain known substances (chiefly oxygen), which are therefore called *Supporters of Combustion*.

PHOTOMETER (Greek *phos*, light, and *metron*, a measure) is an instrument for measuring the different intensities of light. These instruments are variously constructed; but those of Rumford and Leslie are the most generally known.

PHYSICS (Greek *physis*, nature) is that science which is employed in observing the phenomena, and investigating the constitution, powers, and effects of the several bodies in nature. Aristotle, that celebrated Greek, whose writings formed the text-books of the schools for so many centuries, after having treated of Physics, or Nature, added certain disquisitions, concerning Being in general, the Soul of Man, and the Deity. These were termed his *Metaphysics* (*meta*, beyond), because they were distinct, or *beyond* what he understood by *Physics*, or Nature.

PILE, GALVANIC, or VOLTAIC.—See *Galvanic Circle*.

PISTON.—See Gloss. I.

PLANE, TANGENTIAL—See *Tangent*.

————, HORIZONTAL.—See *Horizon*.

————, VERTICAL.—See *Horizon*.

PLUMBAGO.—See *Carbon*.

PLUNGER.—See *Piston*.

POINT, ACTING.—See *Machine*.
———— BOILING.—See *Boiling point*.
———— FREEZING. — See *Freezing point*.
———— OF INCIDENCE.—See *Refractive Power*.
———— WORKING.—See *Working point*.
POLARITY (of a magnet).—See *Magnet, Artificial*.
POLES, of a magnet.—See *Magnet, Artificial*.
———— OF A GALVANIC PILE.—See *Galvanic Circle*.
POLYHEDRON.—See *Rhombus*.
POLYZONAL designates, literally, what is composed of many *zones*, or belts. The term is applied in this volume to certain lenses, composed of pieces united in rings which are therefore called *Polyzonal lenses*.
PORES (of matter.)—See *Volume*.
POWER is that principle which is capable of effecting a change in the state or condition of a body. When power is exerted, as in mechanics, it is force, applied for the purpose of producing or preventing motion. In the former case it is termed a *moving power*, or *force*, and in the latter a *sustaining power*, or *force*. *Power is latent force*.
———— ANIMAL, or ANIMATE, is the power of a man, or other animal.
———— INANIMATE, is that of *air, fire, water*, or other inanimate bodies.
———— MECHANICAL.—See *Mechanical Power*.
———— IN OPTICS expresses the effect producible by lenses, or other instruments, as *magnifying power, heating power, &c.*
PRESSURE is the application of force to a resisting body, when that force is in continued contact with the body upon which it is exerted.—See *Impulse* and *Percussion*.
———— ATMOSPHERIC.—See *Atmospheric Pressure*.
———— CENTRE OF. When a fluid presses upon a surface, there is a *point* in that surface, at which, if a force be applied in the same line with the pressure of the fluid, and equal to the whole of that pressure, but in a contrary direction,—this counter-force will exactly balance the whole pressure of the fluid, —and that *point* is called the *centre of pressure*.
PRIME MOVER.—See *Machine*.
PRIMARY COLOURS.—See *Colours, primary*.
PRINCIPLE, D'ALEMBERT'S, in *Mechanics*, is this:—If several *non-elastic* bodies have a tendency to motion, with velocities, and in directions which they are constrained to change, in consequence of their reciprocal action on each other, then these motions may be considered as composed of two others;—one which the bodies actually take; and the other such, that, had the bodies been acted on by such alone, they would have remained in equilibrium.—See *Equilibrium* and *Forces, composition of*.
PRINCIPLE OF VIRTUAL VELOCITIES. "When a system of material points, solicited by any force, is in equilibrium, if the system receive a small alteration in its position, by virtue of which every point describes an infinitely small space, the sum of each force multiplied by the space described by the point to which it is applied, according to the direction of the force, is always equal to *zero*." This is the *general principle of virtual velocities*, referred to at page 2 of MECHANICS, Treatise II.
PRISM. A prism is a solid contained by plane figures, of which two are parallel, and the rest are parallelograms.
PRISMATIC SPECTRUM is the various-coloured *appearance* (Latin *spectrum*) which a ray of white light exhibits when separated by refraction through a glass prism. The prism of the opticians is triangular; that is, its two ends are parallel, equal and similar triangles, and consequently its other faces are three parallelograms.
PROGRESSION, in a general sense, is merely *going forward*, but as the word is understood, it is presumed that the progress is in a determinate order. It is motion measured by some scale whatever that scale may be.
———— ARITHMETICAL, is a series of numbers, or quantities, in which each term differs from that which precedes it by a fixed number, or quantity, called the *ratio*. Thus 3, 5, 7, 9, 11, &c. is an arithmetical progression having the ratio, two; that being the number by which each term differs from the adjoining one.
———— GEOMETRICAL, is a series of numbers, or quantities, in which every two consecutive terms differ by a multiplier which is common to the whole series: this multiplier is the ratio. Thus 2, 4, 8, 16, 32, &c. is a geometrical progression, of which every term is double an adjoining one, and whose *ratio* (or rate of increase) is 2. Whether arithmetical, or geometrical, progressions increase or decrease, that is, *ascend* or *descend*, the principle, or order of progression, is the same.
PROPORTION, direct and inverse.—See *Ratio*.
PROPORTIONALS.—See *Ratio*.
PYRAMID.—See *Cone*.
PYROMETER.—See *Thermometer*.
PYROSCOPE.—See *Thermometer*.
QUADRANT.—See *Angle*.
QUARTZ.—See Gloss. I.
RADIATION.—See Gloss. I.
RARITY, in bodies, is the opposite of *Density*, which see.

RATIO. In comparing two subjects, with regard to some quality which they have in common, and which admits of being measured, that measure is their *ratio*. It is the *rate* in which one exceeds the other. *Proportion* is the *portions*, or parts of one magnitude that are contained in another. When the ratio is *commensurable*, (that is, when it is reducible to numbers,) it is equivalent to *proportion;* but the latter term is usually employed in the comparison of *ratios*, in which case, two equal ratios are said to be *proportionals*. Thus 3 has to 4 (written 3 : 4) a certain *ratio*, or *proportion;* but the expression 3 is to 4 in the same proportion as 6 to 8, denotes that the ratios of 3 to 4 and 6 to 8 are equal; 3 being the same proportion of 4 as 6 is of 8, that is, three-fourths. Ratios, however, may be unequal. Thus it is said that the ration of 9 to 4 is greater than that of 7 to 6, because $\frac{9}{4}$ is greater than $\frac{7}{6}$: it being thus that ratios are measured.

————— DIRECT AND INVERSE. When two quantities, or magnitudes, have a certain ratio to each other, and are, at the same time, subject to increase or diminution; if, while one increases, the other increases in the same ratio, or, if while the one diminishes, the other diminishes in the same ratio, the *proportions*, or comparisons of ratios, remain unaltered, and those quantities, or magnitudes, are said to be in a *direct* ratio or proportion to each other. Thus, if a yard of cloth be worth a pound, ten or any number of yards will be worth so many pounds, and the proportion of value continues unaltered.

But, if the magnitudes are such, that, when one increases, the other necessarily diminishes; and *vice versâ*, when the one diminishes the other increases, the *ratio*, or proportion, is said to be *inverse*. Thus, there is, at any moment, a certain ratio of the length of the day to that of the night; but this is an *inverse ratio;* for, in proportion as the length of either *increases*, that of the other must *diminish*.

RATIO, *Compound*. A compound ratio is made up of the product of two, or more, simple ratios; that is, of the product of their first terms, which are called *Antecedents*, compared with the product of their second terms, called *Consequents*. Thus 24 : 3 is a compound ratio of 4 : 1 and 6 : 3; this being made up of two simple ones is called a *Duplicate Ratio*. When three simple ratios are compounded, they form a *Triplicate Ratio;* if four, a *Quadruplicate Ratio*, and so of other compounds.

RAY is a single radiation from a body which sends out emissions in all directions.— See *Radiation* and *Light*.

RAYS, ABERRATION OF.—See *Aberration*.

RAYS, CALORIFIC.—See *Calorific Rays*.
————— COLOURED.—See *Colours* and *Prismatic Spectrum*.
————— CONVERGENT.—See *Reflexion, Laws of*.
————— DIVERGENT. — See *Reflexion, Laws of*.
————— PARALLEL. — See *Reflexion, Laws of*.
————— REFLEXION OF.—See *Reflexion*.
————— REFRACTION OF.—See *Refraction*.
————— ORDINARY AND EXTRAORDINARY.—See *Refraction, Double*.
RE-ACTION.—See *Action*.
REFLEXION.—See Gloss. I.
REFLECTING *Microscopes*, &c. — See Gloss. I.
REFRACTION.—See Gloss. I.
————— DOUBLE.—See Gloss. I.
REFRACTING *Microscopes*, &c. — See Gloss. I.
REFRANGIBILITY.—See Gloss. I.
RELATIVE GRAVITY.—See *Gravity*.
REPULSION.—See Gloss. I.
RESINOUS ELECTRICITY.—See *Electric Fluid*.
RESISTING FORCE.—See *Force*.
RESOLUTION OF FORCES. — See *Forces*.
RESULTANT.—See *Forces, Composition of*.
RHOMBUS.—See Gloss. I.
RIGIDITY.—See Gloss. I.
ROCHELLE SALT.—See Gloss. I.
RUBBER.—See *Electricity*.
RUBY.—See *Corundum*.
RUPERT'S DROPS (so called because they were first brought to England by Prince Rupert, a German prince, and grandson of James I.) are a sort of glass drops with long and slender tails. They will bear a smart stroke of a hammer, but burst into atoms with a loud report if the surface be scratched, or the tip of the tail broken off. They are made by dropping melted glass into cold water, which condenses the outer surface, and imprisons the heated particles while in a state of repulsion.—See *Annealing of Glass*.
SAFETY-VALVE (a necessary appendage to a steam-engine) is a valve opening outwards from a boiler, and loaded with a weight sufficient to withstand the pressure of the steam until it rise to a certain required height; but which would be forced open before the steam could burst the boiler.
SAPPHIRE.—See *Corundum*.
SATURATED SOLUTION.—See *Solution*.
SATURATION.—See *Electricity*.
SCALE.—See Gloss I.
SCREW.—See Gloss. I.
SECTOR. A sector is any portion of a circle (less than a semicircle) contained between two radii and a part of the circumference: such as the triangular spaces A C B and A C D, the former of which is an *acute-angled*, and the latter an obtuse-

EXPLANATION OF SCIENTIFIC TERMS.

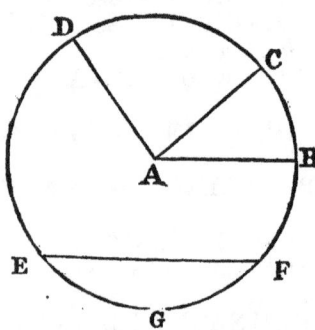

angled sector. When the angle contained between the radii is a right angle, the sector is a *quadrant*, and is so called. A *sector* is also the name given to a mathematical instrument, composed of two flat rulers connected with a joint, which allows them to open in the form of radial lines, so as to include a sector.

SEGMENT OF A CIRCLE is any portion cut off by a straight line. Thus, in the preceding figure, E F G is a segment cut off by the line E F. When this line passes through the centre it divides the circle into two equal segments, or *semicircles*.

SEMI-TRANSLUCENT.—See *Diaphanous*.

SEMI-TRANSPARENT.—See *Diaphanous*.

SHEAR-STEEL (so called because fitted for making *clothiers' shears*, scythes, &c.) is prepared by laying several bars of common steel together, and heating them in a furnace until they acquire the welding temperature. The bars are then beaten together with forge hammers, after which they are drawn anew into bars for sale.

SILEX.—See Gloss. I.

SINE.—See *Angle*.

SINES, LAW OF THE.—See *Reflective Power*.

SODA.—See *Alkali*.

SOLIDS.—See Gloss. I.

SOLID OF LEAST RESISTANCE.—See *Conoid*.

SOLUTION.—See Gloss. I.

SOUND.—See Gloss. I.

——— RAYS OF.—See *Reflexion*.

SPAR.—See Gloss I.

SPAR, ADAMANTINE.—See *Corundum*.

——— ICELAND.—See *Calcareous Spar*.

SPECIFIC denominates any property that is not general, but is confined to an *individual* or *species*.

——— GRAVITY.—See *Gravity, Specific*.

——— HEAT.—See *Caloric, Specific*.

SPECTRA, OCULAR.—See *Ocular Spectra*.

SPECTRUM, PRISMATIC.—See *Prismatic Spectrum*.

SPECULUM.—See *Mirror*.

SPHERE.—See Gloss. I.

SPHERICAL ABERRATION.—See Gloss. I.

SPHEROID.—See Gloss. I.

SPIRAL.—See Gloss. I.

SPIRIT OF WINE.—See *Alcohol*.

STATICS is that division of the science of mechanics which considers bodies as influenced by forces that are in equilibrium. It therefore treats of bodies at rest. The word is formed from the Greek *statos*, standing still. What belongs to statics is *statical*.

STEAM is generally used to signify the visible cloudy vapour arising from water, and which at low temperatures is supposed to be the consequence of a chemical solution of water in air; but steam, as it is used in the arts, denotes water, in an elastic form, at or above the temperature of the boiling point, when it is invisible.

STEAM-TIGHT is that degree of closeness which, in any particular case, prevents the escape of steam.

STEEL.—See *Carbon*.

——— TEMPER OF.—The different *tempers*, or degrees of hardness, of rigidity, or of elasticity, are given by means of the different degrees of heat to which the metal is exposed in the operation.

STEELYARD.—See *Balance*.

STRAIGHT LINE, the same as a right line.—See *Curve*.

SUCTION. The action of sucking is performed by the child's making a vacuum in its mouth, which exhausts the air from the pores of the nipple; and the milk is consequently ejected from the breast by the unresisting elasticity of the air within. The raising of liquids through a tube, by means of a piston which lifts and sustains the weight of the atmosphere from that part of the well which is covered with the tube, leaving it to press on the other parts of the surface, is also, metaphorically, termed *suction*.

SYNTHESIS.—See *Analysis*.

TABASHEER.—See Gloss. I.

TANGENT.—See Gloss. I.

TELESCOPE, ACHROMATIC.—See Gloss. I.

TEMPERATURE.—See Gloss. I.

THERMOMETER.—See Gloss. I.

THERMOSCOPE, a name given by some inventors to their particular kinds of thermometers; as *pyroscopes* are names of some sorts of pyrometers.

TOPAZ.—See *Corundum*.

TORSION-BALANCE, a delicate electrometer, so called because its principle consists in the *torsion* or *twisting* of a silk fibre.

TORRICELLIAN VACUUM.—See Gloss. I.

TOURMALINE.—See Gloss. I.

TRANSLUCENT.—See *Diaphanous*.

TRANSPARENT.—See *Diaphanous*.

TRANSVERSE DIAMETER.—See Gloss. I.

VALVE.—See Gloss. I.

VAPOUR.—See Gloss I.

VARIATION OF THE COMPASS.—See *Mariner's Compass.*
VEGETABLE ALKALI.—See *Alkali.*
VELOCITY.—See Gloss. I.
VERNIER.—See Gloss. I.
———— CHROMATIC.—See Gloss. I.
VERTEX.—See *Cone and Conic Sections.*
VERTICAL CIRCLE.—See *Horizon.*
———————— PLANE.—See *Horizon.*
VESUVIAN, or IDOCRASE, is a stone, generally of a reddish-brown colour, similar in appearance to common *garnet*. It is found, crystallized, among substances thrown out of volcanoes; and, as its name indicates, particularly by Mount Vesuvius.
VOLTAISM.—See *Galvanism.*
VOLTAIC BATTERY, &c.—See *Galvanic.*
VORTICES, the plural of the Latin *vortex*, a whirlpool. The primary hypothesis of the natural philosophy of Descartes was that the universe is a *plenum* (Latin *plenus*, full); that is, without any vacuum, or unoccupied space; and that the *atoms* of matter moved in numerous *vortices* which carried the heavenly bodies around their several centres of motion; such as the planets about the sun, and, perhaps, similar planets around the fixed stars.
WEATHER-GLASS. The barometer is popularly termed a weather-glass, because its variations are commonly believed to prognosticate the approaching state of the weather. In former times, the same appellation was given to the thermometer.
ZENITH.—See *Horizon.*
ZIRCON is a heavy, hard, sparkling, and transparent stone, susceptible of a fine polish, and having a strong double refraction. It is usually divided into the two varieties of *hyacinth* and *jargon;* the former having a yellowish-red colour, and the latter being most esteemed when colourless.

GENERAL INDEX.

The references are given to the treatise, or treatises, in which the article is to be found. Of the contractions, POP. INT. stands for *Popular Introductions*; NEW. OPT. for *Newton's Optics*; OPT. INST. for *Optical Instruments*; THERM. for *Thermometer and Pyrometer*; ELECT. for *Electricity*; GALV. for *Galvanism*; MAGN. for *Magnetism*; and ELECT.-MAGN. for *Electro-Magnetism*.

			Page
ABERRATION, spherical account and cause of	NEW. OPT.		7, 8
,, ,, effects of in lenses	———		28
,, ,, effects of in mirrors	OPT. INT.		11
,, ,, minimum of, in lenses	———		14
,, ,, in inverse ratio of the magnifying power	———		12
,, ,, comparative in glass, sapphire, and diamond	———		13
Academy del Cimento, their improvements on the thermometer	THERM.		3
,, French, their attempted improvements on	———		6
Account, Oersted's, experiments on electro-magnetism	ELECT. MAG.		4—6
Accumulated electricity, experiments on the motion of	ELECT.		39—41
,, ,, by induction	———		31—36
Accumulation of water in hills, cause and consequence of	POP. INT.		62
Achard's pyrometer, description of	THERM.		9, 10
Achromatic telescopes, principles and description of	OPT. INST.		27
,, ,, the largest ever known, described	———		23
,, eye-pieces for astronomical telescopes	———		27
,, opera glasses, construction of	———		27, 28
Acids decomposed by the voltaic pile	GALV.		17
Action, chemical, connection between, and electricity	ELECT.		57, 58
,, mutual, of two magnets, experiments on	MAGN.		16—19
,, and reaction, their equality an established law of nature	———		3
,, electro-magnetic, fundamental law of	ELECT. MAGN.		6—9
Action and Reaction, that their equality is one of the laws of motion, illustrated	POP. INT.		11—20
,, of a bird in flying described	———		13
,, of the oar in raising a boat described	———		13
,, of the fly-wheel explained	———		29
,, of gravity, and the pressure of fluids, explained	———		57, 58
,, of sonorous bodies illustrated	———		71, 72
Actions, electric and magnetic, emanate from a common source	ELECT. MAGN.		1
,, mutual, of electric current, concerning generally	———		57—76
,, ,, ,, ,, particularly, described. (See *Electric Currents*.)			
ÆPINUS, his amendments of Franklin's theory of electricity	ELECT.		12
,, his theory of magnetism	MAGN.		33—35
,, corrections of his theory of magnetism	———		36
,, his method of making artificial magnets	———		47, 48
Aerial vibrations, their reflexions the cause of echoes	POP. INT.		72
Age, the decay of sight consequent upon, how remedied	———		97
,, its effect upon thermometers	THERM.		12
Air, in what it differs from liquids	POP. INT.		1
,, atmospheric, its mechanical properties	———		7
,, elasticity of, experiments to prove	———		65
,, its enormous pressure on the human body	———		65
,, its resistance to falling bodies	———		7

GENERAL INDEX.

		Page
Air, its resistance to moving bodies proportionate to the squares of their velocities	Pop. Int.	17—18
.. its tremulous motion the cause of sound		71
.. means of weighing a small quantity of		66
Air-pump, experiments with, described		65, 66
Air-pyrometer, of Schmitz, construction of	Therm.	31
Air-thermometer, Kinnersley's Electrical, described	Elect.	43
Air, currents of, alway accompany the discharge of electricity		26
Alcoholic and mercurial thermometers, comparative table of at different temperatures	Therm.	54, 55
Alkalis, decomposed by the voltaic pile	Galv.	17
Amalgams for the rubbers of electrical machines	Elect.	16
Amician reflecting telescopes described	Opt. Inst.	48
Amanton's thermometer, description of	Therm.	6
.. .. objections to		8
Ampere's electro-dynamic theory	Elect. Magn.	81—92
Analogy between the electric spark and lightning	Elect.	59
Anamorphoses restored by reflection from cylindrical surfaces	Opt. Inst.	3
Anatomical description of the torpedo	Galv.	26
Anatomy of the eye explained	Pop. Int.	94
Ancients had no instruments for measuring heat	Therm.	1
.. their opinions respecting the cause of magnetic attraction	Magn.	33
Angle, the smallest under which an object is visible	Pop. Int.	80
Angles of incidence and reflexion, equality of, known to Plato	New. Opt.	1
.. .. known with precision by Ptolemy		2
.. .. particular explanation of	Opt. Inst.	2
.. .. defined	Pop. Int.	14, 15
.. account of telescopes for measuring	Opt. Inst.	25
Animal life equally destroyed by shocks from the electric or the voltaic battery	Galv.	19
Animals, dead, excited into convulsive muscular action by galvanism		19
.. warm-blooded and cold-blooded, galvanic effects of the contact of parts of one class with those of the other		25
.. experiments of the effects of electricity upon	Elect.	49, 50
Annual motion of the earth explained	Pop. Int.	30—33
Antimony and bismuth, the metals best fitted for producing thermo-electric currents	Elect. Mag.	94
Aplanatic diamond lenses, Pritchard's	Opt. Inst.	13
.. telescopes, Clairault's and Herschel's, described		20
.. .. table for object-glasses of		21
Apparatus for producing electro-magnetic rotations	Elect. Magn.	22
Apparent place and size of the image in plain mirrors	Opt. Inst.	2
.. dimensions of objects of sight	Pop. Int.	79
.. velocity of bodies, limit of		80
.. situation of the heavenly bodies		87
Arago's experiments on the magnetism of rotation	Magn.	91, 92
Archimedes' burning mirrors, account of	New. Opt.	1
Aristophanes, his description of burning glasses		2
Aristotle attempted to investigate the phenomena of the rainbow		2
Armatures for retaining and concentrating magnetism	Magn.	43, 54, 55
Arrangement of iron filings under magnetic influence		21
.. mechanical, of microscopes	Opt. Inst.	44
.. of the prismatic colours exhibited	Pop. Int.	91
Artificial cobwebs for micrometers	Opt. Inst.	57
.. magnets, various methods of making	Magn.	41—45
.. .. general principles of		41
.. .. method of making by percussion		42
.. .. .. juxtaposition		43
.. .. .. single touch		44
.. .. less retentive of their virtues than loadstones		54
.. .. ready method of forming		1
Ascent of fluids in capillary tubes, cause of, explained	Pop. Int.	5
.. of smoke, steam, &c., cause of		8
.. of balloons		8

		Page
Astronomical telescopes, achromatic, described . . .	New. Opt. 6. Opt. Inst.	10
.. .. eye-pieces for . . .	———	27, 28
Astronomy, popular introduction to . . .	Pop. Int.	30—55
.. objections to the presently-received system answered . . .	———	37, 39
Atmosphere, experiments on the electricity of . . .	Elect.	59, 60
.. its pressure on the human body, how counteracted	Pop. Int.	65
.. tides in, as well as in the ocean . . .	———	71
Atmospheric air, its mechanical properties . . .	———	7
.. refraction observed by Ptolemy . . .	New. Opt.	3
.. pressure, variation of, its effects on the boiling point of water . . .	Therm.	8
.. .. its effects on the bulbs of thermometers	———	13
Attraction in bodies defined and illustrated . . .	Pop. Int.	3
.. of cohesion . . .	———	3, 4
.. of gravitation . . .	———	5
.. of mountains upon a plummet . . .	———	6
.. of houses and churches by neighbouring hills	———	6
.. and repulsion, electrical, explained . . .	Elect.	2, 3
.. .. experiments on .	———	4, 17—20
.. .. of magnetic iron .	Magn.	3
.. .. of magnetism analogous to that of electricity . . .	———	3, 39
.. of iron by the magnet, illustrations of .	———	2, 3
.. .. opinions of the ancients respecting its cause . . .	———	33
.. local, of vessels, general account of .	———	61—68
.. .. .. Barlow's experiments on that subject . . .	———	63—65
.. .. .. cause of the loss of certain ships	———	66
.. .. .. Barlow's proposed remedy for the evil . . .	———	67
.. .. .. chronometer disturbed by .	———	68
Aurora Borealis affects the magnetic needle . . .	Elect. Magn.	2
Axioms, Newton's, respecting light . . .	New. Opt.	11
Azimuth compass, construction of . . .	Magn.	60, 68, 70
.. .. Kater's, described . . .	———	70—72
Babbage and Herschel's experiments on the magnetism of rotation . . .	Magn.	93, 94
Bacon, Friar, his description of magnifiers and combined lenses . . .	New. Opt.	3
.. .. the inventor of the camera obscura . .	Opt. Inst.	52
Balance, thermometer, description of . . .	Therm.	47, 48
.. electrometer . . .	Elect.	38, 39
.. (torsion) . . .	———	19, 21
Balloons, cause of their ascent . . .	Pop. Int.	8
.. the earth appears to sink from under them	———	38
Barlow's hypothesis concerning the variation of the needle	Magn.	30
.. experiments on the local attraction of vessels .	———	63—65
.. proposed remedy for ..	———	67
Barometer, table of the effects of its different states on the boiling point of water . . .	Therm.	15
.. its principle and construction . . .	Pop. Int.	66—67
Barometrical thermometer described . . .	Therm.	48, 49
Bartolinus's experiments on Iceland spar . . .	New. Opt.	9
Battery electrical, description and construction of .	Elect.	36—39
.. .. and galvanic, different effects of .	Galv.	9
.. voltaic or galvanic. See *Galvanic*.		
Beautiful experiment of the combustion of Mercury .	———	13
Bennet's gold-leaf electrometer described . .	Elect.	19
Bernouilli's method of obviating an error in the dipping-needle . . .	Magn.	78, 79
Biot's experiments on electricity . . .	Elect.	22
Bird, action of in flying . . .	Pop. Int.	13
Bismuth and antimony best fitted for producing thermo-electric currents . . .	Elect. Magn.	94
Blackander's Register thermometer described . .	Therm.	38, 39
Blind man, his feelings when first endowed with sight .	Pop. Int.	80, 81

GENERAL INDEX.

		Page
Boat, action of the oar in rowing	Pop. Int.	13
Bodies, their general properties explained	———	1—8
.. their impenetrability illustrated	———	1
.. .. extension and figure, or shape	———	2
.. .. divisibility, examples of	———	2
.. .. inertia defined and illustrated	———	3
.. attraction of	———	3, 4
.. density and rarity of explained	———	4
.. falling, resistance of the air to	———	7
.. experiments on	———	8, 10
.. moving, general effect on the resistance of the air to	———	17, 18
.. their elasticity illustrated	———	11—13
.. centre of gravity of, defined and illustrated	———	9, 18—20
.. their weight different at different parts of the earth's surface	———	43
.. momentum of, defined and illustrated	———	11
.. in motion, measure of the resistance of the air to	———	17, 18
.. specific gravity of explained	———	59, 60
.. their sonorousness owing to their elasticity	———	71
.. at what degree of velocity their motion ceases to be apparent	———	80
.. heavenly, why their apparent situation differs from the real	———	87
.. various, tables of their expansion, by heat	Therm.	61, 62
.. what shape of, is most favourable for retaining electricity	Elect.	7
.. effects of electricity upon different	———	41—51
.. pointed, phenomena of entrance or issue of electricity in	———	27
.. mechanical effects of electricity upon	———	42—45
.. not ferruginous, on the magnetism of	Magn.	89—91
.. of all kinds are, more or less, susceptible of magnetism	———	90
.. become more obscure by excess of light	New. Opt.	10
.. reflect, more copiously, rays of their own colour	———	37
.. magnitude of their corpuscles investigated	———	55
.. colour or opacity of depends on their pores	———	53
.. light not reflected from their solid surfaces	———	55
Boiling point of water affected by atmospheric pressure	Therm.	8
.. .. table of its height in different states of the barometer	———	15
Books upon optics and optical instruments, list of	Opt. Inst.	60
Bores, elliptical, of thermometer tubes, their use	Therm.	11
Boyle's thermometer described	———	3, 4
.. proposed scales for thermometers	———	4
Brass has sometimes a considerable magnetic power	Magn.	90
Breezes, sea and land, accounted for	Pop. Int.	70, 71
Breguet's pyrometer described	Therm.	32, 33
Brewster's improvements of lenses	Opt. Inst.	40
.. lenses built of circular rings	———	78
.. kaleidoscope, construction of	———	55
.. compound microscope for objects of Natural History	———	47
.. reflecting telescope described	———	16
.. telescope for measuring distances described	———	25
Buffon, his burning mirrors described	———	3
Bulk, apparent, of images accounted for	———	2
Burning-glasses described by Aristophanes	New. Opt.	2
.. lens, Parker's large one described	Opt. Inst.	7
.. mirror of Archimedes	———	1
.. .. of Buffon and Villette with their experiments	———	3
Calcareous spar, experiments on	New. Opt.	9
Calorimeter, description and use of	Therm.	52, 53
.. Hare's described	Galv.	4
Camera lucida, description of	Opt. Inst.	53, 54
Camera obscura, accounts of the invention of	New. Opt. 3. Opt. Inst.	52
Canton's method of making artificial magnets	Magn.	47, 51—53
Caoutchouc, (India rubber) its use in making thread for microscopes	Opt. Inst.	57

		Page
Capillary tubes, cause of the ascent of fluids in	Pop. Int.	5
Cartesian ovals, account of	New. Opt.	8
Cassegrainean telescope, description of	Opt. Inst.	17
Cause of opacity in bodies, investigated	New. Opt.	53, 54
.. of magnetic attraction, opinions on	Magn.	33
.. meaning of the word in Natural Philosophy	New. Opt.	44
Cavallo's electroscope described	Elect.	3
Cavendish, his improvements on Franklin's theory of electricity		12
.. his register thermometer described	Therm.	34, 35
Celsius's thermometer described		8
.. Reaumur's and Fahrenheit's scales respectively converted into one another		10
Centering of lenses, directions for	Opt. Inst.	31
Centigrade (Celsius's) thermometer	Therm.	9
Centre of gravity of bodies explained and illustrated	Pop. Int.	9, 18—20
Centrifugal force, explanation of		16, 31
Centripetal force, explanation of		16, 31
Charcoal, splendid exhibition of electric light from	Galv.	10
.. galvanic ignition of, at the Royal Institution, described		10, 11
Chemical effects of electricity, experiments on	Elect.	47, 48
.. and electrical action, connexion between		57, 58
.. changes effected by galvanism	Galv.	13
.. effects of galvanism exemplified in the case of copper and zinc		14
.. theory of galvanism		20
.. properties of elastic fluids differ with their species	Pop. Int.	65
.. changes in the materials not the cause of thermo-electricity	Elect. Magn.	95
Children's galvanic battery, construction of	Galv.	8
Christie's experiments on the magnetism of rotation	Magn.	92
Chromatic dispersion illustrated	Opt. Inst.	14
Chronometers disturbed by the local attraction of vessels	Magn.	68
Circles, galvanic, simple, formation of	Galv.	2—4
.. .. compound		4—9
Circuit of electricity, meaning of the term	Elect.	37
Circular conductors, exhibition of their magnetic properties	Elect. Magn.	34
.. rings formed into lenses	Opt. Inst.	7, 8
Clairault's aplanatic telescope described		20
Cobwebs, artificial, their use in microscopes	New. Opt.	41
Cohesion, attraction of, defined and illustrated	Pop. Int.	3, 4
Cold, however intense, does not impair magnetism	Magn.	13
Coloured rings, phenomena of	New. Opt.	41
.. .., reflected from coloured plates, table of		52
.. shadows, account and explanation of		61
.. .. hyperbolic curves		62
Colourless topaz of New Zealand used for prisms	Opt. Inst.	25
Colours, Newton's theory of	New. Opt.	33
.. mixture of		33
.. spectral, re-composition of		35
.. of transparent liquors vary with their thickness		37
.. reflected, Newton's scale for determining		46
.. reflected and transmitted by thick transparent plates		56
.. of natural bodies, cause of investigated		54
.. of thin plates of air, water, and glass, tables of		52
.. prismatic, obtained from voltaic light	Galv.	11
.. .. their arrangement	Pop. Int.	91
.. .. exist originally in the light		90
.. reflected, theory of		92
.. produced by the combustion of different metals	Galv.	13
.. of electrical light, various exhibitions of	Elect.	24
Combination of lenses, and their magnifying power, known to Friar Bacon	New. Opt.	3
Combination of sulphur and silver promoted by galvanism	Galv.	24
Combustion of mercury, beautiful phenomena of		13
Comets, observations on	Pop. Int.	36, 37
Communication of the electric shock, extraordinary examples of	Elect.	39, 40

GENERAL INDEX.

		Page
Comparative table of alcoholic and mercurial thermometers at different temperatures	Therm.	54
Comparison of the processes of making artificial magnets	Magn.	50
Compass, mariner's, construction of	—	55—60
.. azimuth ..	—	68—72
.. variation ..	—	72—74
.. land ..	—	60, 61
.. on the variation of	Magn.	22, 23
.. progressive changes of its dip and variation	—	29—31
Complex magnetic induction, experiments on	—	7—10
Component parts of bodies, investigation concerning	New. Opt.	53
Composition of Forces, explanation of its effects	Pop. Int.	16—18
.. .. which produce the earth's motion round the sun	—	30
Compound microscopes, principles and theories of	Opt. Inst.	43
.. .. proper size of	—	48
.. .. for the purposes of natural history	—	47
.. galvanic circles, formation of	Galv.	4—9
.. .. battery	—	5
Concave and convex mirrors, concerning	Opt. Inst.	2
.. .. popular explanation of their effects on the rays of light	Pop. Int.	83, 84
.. mirrors for burning glasses	Opt. Inst.	3
.. .. images formed by, and curious experiments on	—	3
Concentration of the effects of electro-magnetism	Elect. Magn.	32—38
Concord of sounds, how produced	Pop. Int.	73
Condenser, Volta's, described	Elect.	52
Conductors and non-conductors of electricity distinguished	—	5, 6
.. metallic, for the safeguard of ships and buildings	—	59, 60
Cones of electric fluid passing from a positive to a negative point, representation of	—	27
Connecting wire of a galvanic battery attracts iron filings	Elect. Magn.	52
Consequences of the law of electro-magnetic action	—	9—18
Construction of the Leyden jar	Elect.	34, 35
.. of an electrical battery	—	36—39
.. of the common thermometer, and history of the improvements in	Therm.	1—10
.. of register thermometers, and history of	—	33—39
.. of thermometers, precautions to be observed in	—	10—15
.. of pyrometers, and history of their improvements	—	15—32
Convex lenses, radii of the surfaces of	Opt. Inst.	6
.. mirrors, images formed by	—	3
Convulsive agitations of mercury under galvanic influence	Galv.	31
.. muscular motions in dead animals excited by galvanism	—	24
Copper, effects of dilute sulphuric acid on	—	14
.. .. nitric acid on	—	14
.. *sheathing* of ships prevented from being corroded by sea water	—	14
Correspondence of different thermometric scales, tables of	Therm.	57—60
Coulomb's Electrometer, or torsion-balance, described	Elect.	19, 20
.. .. its extreme sensibility	—	20, 21
.. experiments on the magnetism of different bodies	Magn.	90, 91
.. method of making artificial magnets	—	48—50
Crichton's metallic thermometer described	Therm.	30, 31
Cruickshank's trough battery, construction of	Galv.	7
Cruquius's thermometer described	Therm.	8
Cumming's statical thermometer described	—	45—47
.. hygrometer described	—	50, 51
Current of voltaic electricity passing through the human body, sensation produced by	Galv.	18
Currents of air always accompany the discharge of electricity	Elect.	26
Current electrical, their mutual action. [See *Electrical Currents*.]	Elect. Magn.	57—76
.. .. transmitted by perfect conductors, are continuous	—	57
.. thermo-electric, distinguished from galvanic	—	93
.. .. chiefly recognised by their effects on the magnetic needle	—	95

K

		Page
Curvature of lenses, method of calculating their force	Opt. Inst.	6
Curves, magnetic, properties of, and means of delineating	Magn.	19—22
Cushions for electrical machines, first used by Winkler	Elec.	15
.. amalgams, recommended for	———	16
Cuthbertson's balance electrometer described	———	38, 39
Cylinder, reflecting surface of, used in restoring anamorphoses	Opt. Inst.	3
Daniell's pyrometer, description of	Therm.	16
.. hygrometer	———	49, 50
.. table of temperatures	———	32
Dark chamber, (*camera obscura*), invented by Friar Bacon	Opt. Inst.	52
Day telescopes, account of their construction	———	10
Day and *night* thermometer of Rutherford	Therm.	36, 37
Days and Nights, why they vary in their lengths	Pop. Int.	44—48
Dead animals, muscular motions excited in by galvanism	Galv.	19
Decay of sight in age, how remedied	Pop. Int.	97
De Butt's differential thermometers described	Therm.	41
Decomposition of solar light, experiments on	New. Opt.	11, 12
.. and re-composition of water by the voltaic pile	Galv.	15
.. of water, why not effected by the common electric machine	———	27
.. of neutral salts by the voltaic pile	———	15
.. of metallic solutions by	———	16
.. of acids, alkalis, and earths, by	———	17
De Dominis, his theory of the rainbow	New. Opt.	4
Definition of magnetism	Magn.	1
De la Land's proposed thermometer	Therm.	9
De Lisle's thermometer as used in Russia	———	9
De Luc's microscopic pyrometer	———	23, 24
.. metallic thermometers	———	24
.. electrical column described	Galv.	26
Density and rarity of bodies defined	Pop. Int.	4
Desaguliers' pyrometer, description of	Therm.	16
.. his theory of the rainbow	New. Opt.	9
.. his unfair plagiarisms from Snellius	———	7
Development of Electricity by changes of temperature and form	Elect.	53—55
.. by contact, compression, and other mechanical means	———	55—57
Deviation of the Compass on account of local attraction, experiments and observations on	Magn.	61—65
.. Table of, observed in different ships	———	66
Dew, vapours, and rain, their distinction and causes	Pop. Int.	5
.. temperature at which it falls	Therm.	49
De Wildt's table of expansions of spirit and of mercurial thermometers	———	55
Diameters of the planets proportionally represented	Pop. Int.	35
Diamond aplanatic lenses	Opt. Inst.	13
.. microscopes, Pritchard's	———	39
Different effects of the electric and the galvanic batteries	Galv.	9
Differential thermometers and their modifications	Therm.	39—45
.. of Leslie	———	40
.. of De Butt	———	41
.. hygrometer and photometer, improvements suggested on	———	45
.. galvanometer, description of	Elect. Magn.	44
Diffraction of light, account of	New. Opt.	60, 63
.. Grimaldi's discovery of	———	10
Dip of the magnetic needle, observations on	Magn.	23—25
.. its progressive changes	———	29—31
Dipping-needle, description and construction of, &c.	Magn.	74—82
.. remarks on that formerly used by the Royal Society	———	76—78
.. sources of errors to which it is liable	———	78
.. method of obviating those errors	———	78—79
.. Gambey's, described	———	79
.. Mayer's	———	79, 80
.. Sabine's	———	80, 81

GENERAL INDEX.

		Page
Dipping-needle, Scoresby's instrument for finding the dip	Magn.	81
.. phenomena of, exhibited by voltaic magnets	Elect. Magn.	47
Directive properties of the magnetic needle exhibited by helical coil	—	52
Discharge of Electricity always accompanied with currents of air	Elect.	26
Discharger (universal) of Henley described	—	37
Discharging electrometer, Lane's, described	—	38
Discovery of the laws of refraction	New. Opt.	7
.. of the diffraction of light	—	10
.. of the polarity of light	—	64
.. of Saturn's sixth satellite, time of	Opt. Inst.	17
Disguised electricity, described	Elect.	30, 31
Dispersive powers of different substances with respect to light, tables of	Opt. Inst.	25
Distances, telescope for measuring	—	25
Distinction between the geometrical and the refracted focus	—	7
Distribution of electricity, concerning	Elect.	4, 11, 20—23
Diverging and *converging* electric currents, action of	Elect. Magn.	64, 65
Divided object-glass of micrometers	Opt. Inst.	57
Diving-bell, Halley's, observations on light in	New. Opt.	38
Divisibility of bodies, illustrations of	Pop. Int.	2
Diurnal changes of variation and intensity of the magnetic needle	Magn.	31
Double image telescope, description and use of	Opt. Inst.	25
.. *refraction*, particularly of Iceland spar	New. Opt.	9
.. .. Huygen's theory of	—	—
Doublers, or multipliers of electricity	Elect.	53
Drebbel's improvement on the thermometer described	Therm.	2
Drops, Prince Rupert's, their fracture attended with electrical light	Elect.	58
Dry Pile of Hatchetts and Desormes, described	Galv.	27
.. of Zamboni	—	27
Du Fay's theory of galvanism	—	3
Duhamel's method of making artificial magnets	Magn.	45, 46
Duration of the impression of light on the eye ascertained	New. Opt.	35
Dynameter, that instrument described	Opt. Inst.	11
Ear-trumpet, principle and construction of	Pop. Int.	73
Earth, hypothesis of its magnetism	Magn.	25
.. magnetic intensities at different heights above its surface	—	87
.. rises to meet a falling stone	Pop. Int.	6
.. account and cause of its annual motion	—	30—33
.. why it moves in an ellipsis	—	31
.. describes equal areas of its orbit in equal times	—	32
.. is nearer to the sun in winter than in summer	—	32
.. its threefold motion described	—	34
.. appears to sink under an ascending balloon	—	38
.. general account of its motions and their effects	—	40—49
Earths, decomposition of by the voltaic pile	Galv.	17
Echoes produced by the reflection of aërial vibrations	Pop. Int.	72
Eclipses of the sun and moon, their causes explained	—	51, 52
.. of Jupiter's satellites described	—	52
.. .. method of finding the longitude by	—	52, 53
Ecliptic tropics and zodiac described	—	40, 41
Effect of atmospheric pressure on the bulbs of thermometers	Therm.	13
.. of age on thermometers	—	12
Effects of galvanism, general	Galv.	9—19
.. of the galvanic and electric batteries, different	—	9
.. of dilute sulphuric acid on copper and on zinc	—	14
.. of nitric acid on ditto ditto	—	14
Egg, its sulphur unites with a silver spoon by means of galvanism	—	24
Elastic fluids differ in their chemical but not in their mechanical properties	—	65
Elasticity of air, experiments to prove	—	65
.. of bodies the cause of sound	—	71
.. .. examples of	—	11—13

GENERAL INDEX.

		Page
Electric excitation, phenomena of	Elect.	2
.. attraction and repulsion, phenomena of	———	2, 3
.. .. experiments on	———	4, 17—20
.. .. similar to magnetic	Magn.	3, 39
.. *fluid*, hypotheses concerning	Elect.	10
.. .. whether there be one or two fluids	———	12—14
.. .. phenomena observed on its passage or transference	———	23—28
.. .. velocity of the transmission of	———	23
.. .. the sound which accompanies its transference variously modified	———	25
.. .. representation of the pencils and stars of light, visible on its escape or entrance from or to a pointed body	———	27
.. .. representation of the cones passing from a positive to a negative point	———	27
.. .. objections to the theory of a single fluid	———	63, 64
.. *light* has the same properties as common light	———	24
.. .. its brilliancy proportioned to the conducting power of the body through which it passes	———	24
.. .. its colours vary with circumstances	———	24
.. .. whether it actually proceeds from the fluid itself	———	25
.. .. elicited by the fracture of Prince Rupert's drops	———	58
.. .. exhibited in the combustion of charcoal	Galv.	10
Electric spark, its zig-zag progress in a long passage	Elect.	23
.. .. and lightning, analogy between	———	59
.. *shock*, extraordinary examples of its communication	———	39, 40
.. .. received from different species of fishes	Galv.	26
.. *battery*, construction of	Elect.	36—39
.. .. and galvanic battery, different effects of	Galv.	9
.. *machines*, various kinds of described	Elect.	14—17
.. .. Winkler, the first who used cushions for	———	15
.. .. Nairn's described	———	15
.. .. Ingenhouz's described	———	16
.. .. peculiar odour proceeding from when wrought	———	25
.. *discharge* through a steel bar renders induced magnetism permanent	Magn.	12
.. induction analogous to magnetic induction	———	4—7
.. effects of galvanism	Galv.	9
.. theory of galvanism	———	20, 31, 32
.. columns of De Luc and Singer	———	26
.. air-thermometer described	Elect.	43
.. stone, or *Lapus electricus*, described	———	53
.. qualities of various stones	———	54
.. *currents*, mutual actions of	Elect. Magn.	57—76
.. .. parallel rectilineal	———	57—61
.. .. inclined rectilineal	———	61—65
.. .. terminate	———	65—67
.. .. diverging and converging	———	67, 68
.. .. situated in different planes	———	68, 69
.. .. rectilineal and curvilineal	———	69—73
.. .. circular	———	73
.. .. transmitted by perfect conductors are continuous	———	60
.. .. tend to produce currents in a similar direction in other bodies	———	88
Electricity, the phenomena first generalized by Gilbert	Elect.	1
.. early cultivation of by the Royal Society	———	—
.. distribution and transference of	———	4, 11, 20—23
.. conductors and non-conductors of	———	5, 6
.. insulation of	———	5—7
.. shape of bodies most favourable for retaining	———	7
.. vitreous and resinous distinguished	———	8, 9
.. induction of explained	———	9, 10, 12
.. theories of	———	10, 60
.. Franklin's theory, amended by Æpinus and Cavendish	———	12
.. positive and negative distinguished	———	13
.. resides wholly on the surface of bodies	———	20, 21

GENERAL INDEX.

			Page
Electricity, transference of	Elect.		4, 11, 23—28
.. phenomena of, in its passage through a vacuum	———		25
.. currents of air always accompany its discharge	———		26
.. Nicholson's instrument for distinguishing positive from negative	———		27, 28
.. disguised, description of	———		30, 31
.. accumulated, experiments on the motion of	———		39—41
.. accumulation of by induction	———		31—36
.. circuit of, meaning of the term	———		37
.. on the lateral explosion of	———		41
.. its effects upon bodies generally	———		41—51
.. its mechanical effects on bodies	———		42—45
.. its chemical effects	———		47, 48
.. its effects upon animals	———		49, 50
.. its effects upon vegetables	———		50, 51
.. evolution of heat by	———		45—47
.. instrument for collecting weak	———		51—53
.. doublers or multipliers of	———		53
.. development of, by changes of temperature and form	———		53—55
.. by contact, compression, and other mechanical means	———		55—57
.. three states of distinguished	Elect. Magn.		96
.. and magnetism identical	———		92
.. of the atmosphere, experiments on	Elect.		59, 60
.. metallic conductors of, for the safeguard of ships and buildings from lightning	———		59, 60
.. materiality of, experiments to prove	———		60—62
.. and magnetism found to be identical	Magn.		1, 88
Electrometers, principles of those instruments	Elect.		19
.. Henley's described	———		19—37
.. Bennet's gold-leaf	———		19
.. Coulomb's, or torsion-balance	———		19, 20
.. Cuthbertson's balance	———		38, 39
.. Lane's discharging	———		—
Electroscope, different kinds of	———		—
.. Henry's described	———		—
.. Cavallo's	———		—
Electrophorus, Volta's, described	———		51, 52
Electro-magnetism, history of prior to Oersted's discoveries	Elect. Magn.		1—4
.. experiment of Ritter, account of	———		3
.. .. Oersted	———		4—6
.. fundamental law of explained	———		6—9
.. direct consequence of the law of	———		9—18
.. its effects on the directive property of the magnetic needle	———		9—14
.. concentration of its effects	———		32—38
.. theories of	———		75—88
.. theory of Oersted	———		75—78
Electro-magnetic rotations	———		19—32
.. multiplier	———		40
.. effects of terrestrial magnetism	———		45—52
.. induction, concerning	———		52—57
.. effects of galvanism	Galv.		13
Electro-dynamic theory of Ampère	Elect. Magn.		81—92
.. sclenoid described	———		83
.. ring, effect of	———		90
Electro-motive force, meaning of the term	Galv.		31
Elementary galvanic battery of Wollaston	———		3
Ellicot's pyrometer described	Therm.		16, 17
Elliptical bores of thermometer tubes, their use	———		11
Ellipsis, why the earth revolves round the sun in that curve	Pop. Int.		31
Equality of the angles of incidence and reflection known to Plato	New. Opt.		1
.. of action and re-action, a law of nature	Pop. Int. 11—20. Magn.		3
Equator, magnetic, explanation of the term	———		24
Euclid, his explanation of the phenomena of the rainbow	New. Opt.		2
Evolution of heat by electricity, experiments on	Elect.		45—47
.. .. by the voltaic battery	Galv.		12
Excitation, electrical, phenomena of	Elect.		

		Page
Exhibition of electric light from charcoal	GALV.	10
Expansibility of glass rods and tubes, table of	THERM.	53
Expansion, relative, of different metals, from the freezing to the boiling point of water, table of	————	20
,, ,, of seven different metals, table of	————	17
,, ,, of seven different solids, table of	————	27
,, of spirit and mercurial thermometers, tables of	————	53
,, of various bodies by heat, tables of	————	61, 62
Experiments on Iceland spar by Bartolinus	NEW. OPT.	9
,, on the decomposition of light	————	11, 12
,, on the reflexibility of light	————	20, 22
,, on the inflexion of light	————	60
,, on the images of concave mirrors	OPT. INST.	3
,, on burning mirrors	————	3
,, on the phenomena exhibited by thin transparent plates	NEW. OPT.	40, 41
,, on galvanism by Roget	GALV.	30, 31
,, on the mutual attraction of electric currents by Roget	ELEC. MAG.	59
Explosion, lateral, of electricity	ELECT.	41
Eye, anatomical description of . . POP. INT. 94.	NEW. OPT.	3
,, preserves the impression of light for a time	————	35
,, how objects are rendered visible to the, illustrated	POP. INT.	77, 78
Eye-piece, Ramsden's micrometical	OPT. INST.	14
FACTS and general principles of magnetism	MAGN.	1—16
FAHRENHEIT'S mercurial thermometer described	THERM.	7
,, scale, principle of its division	————	—
,, Reaumur's and Celsius's scales, formulæ for converting into degrees of each other	————	10
Falling of a magnet on a stone pavement impairs its power	MAGN.	12
,, bodies, resistance of the air on	POP. INT.	7
,, ,, experiments on	————	8, 10
,, ,, the earth rises to meet	————	6
FARADAY'S electro-magnetic experiments	ELECT. MAG.	19—23, 97, 99
Fatal experiment of Professor Richman	ELECT.	33, 59
,, consequences of the local attraction of vessels	MAGN.	68
FERGUSON'S pyrometers described	THERM.	21—23
Ferruginous bodies, not the only ones susceptible of magnetism	MAGN.	87—91
Fibres for micrometers, various kinds of	OPT. INST.	57
Figures of bodies, illustrations of	POP. INT.	2
Fishes, electric shocks received from several kinds of	GALV.	26
Fits of easy reflection and transmission of light	NEW. OPT.	44
FITZGERALD'S metalline thermometer	THERM.	20, 21
Fixed stars, their distance and bulk unknown	POP. INT.	37
Florentine Academy, their improvement of the thermometer	THERM.	3
Fluid, electric. [See *Electric Fluid*.]		
,, microscope described	OPT. INT.	42
Fluids, methods for inclosing objects in for observation	————	52
,, magnetic, theory of two	MAGN.	36, 41
,, heat considered as one of them	POP. INT.	4
,, cause of their rise in capillary tubes	————	5
,, mechanical properties of	————	56—60
,, effects of gravity more observable in than in solid bodies	————	56
,, gravitation and pressure of, explained	————	57—58
,, elastic, mechanical properties of	————	65—69
,, ,, differ in their chemical properties	————	65
Fly-wheel, its mode of action explained	POP. INT.	29
Foci of lenses, calculation of	OPT. INST.	6
,, geometrical and refracted, distinction between	————	7
Fog, why the sun appears red through one	POP. INT.	93
Force, definition of	————	9
,, centrifugal, centripetal, and tangential, distinguished	————	16, 17, 31
Forces, composition of, laws of	————	15, 18
,, ,, how they produce the earth's annual motion	————	30—33
,, magnetic, laws of	MAGN.	16—22
,, ,, intensity of, in relation to distance	————	16
,, ,, method of determining their intensities	————	82, 87

GENERAL INDEX.

		Page
Forcing-pump, principle and construction of	Pop. Int.	69
Form of the specula of reflecting telescopes	Opt. Inst.	10
Formulæ for converting the scales of Reaumur's, Fahrenheit's, and the centigrade thermometers into degrees of each other	Therm.	10
Fountains and springs, origin and effect of	Pop. Int.	61—64
.. .. phenomena of intermitting, accounted for	——	64
Fracture of magnets, experiments on the effects of	Magn.	15, 16
Franklin's theory of electricity, as amended by Æpinus and others	Elect.	12
.. discovery of the identity of lightning with electricity	——	59
French Academy, their attempted improvements of the thermometer	Therm.	6
Friction described and illustrated	Pop. Int.	28, 29
Fringes (coloured) of shadows, concerning	New. Opt.	61
.. .. hyperbolical curves of	——	62
Frogs, experiments upon by Galvani	Galv.	1
Froteringham's pyrometer described	Therm.	18
Fulcrum, explanation and application of	Pop. Int.	20—24
Functions and structure of the eye	New. Opt.	3
Fundamental law of electro-magnetism	Elect. Mag.	6—9
Galilean telescope described	New. Opt. 6. Opt. Inst.	24
Galvani's experiments upon frogs	Galv.	1
Galvanism first noticed by Sulzer		1
.. experiments on the various effects of	——	9—19
.. electric effects of	——	9
.. luminous effects of	——	10
.. ignition of metals by	——	12
.. .. heat more intense than by any other means	——	12
.. electro-magnetic effects of	——	13
.. chemical changes effected by	——	14—17
.. physiological effects of	——	17—19
.. theories of	——	3, 19, 20, 31
.. combination of sulphur with silver by	——	24
.. Volta's theory of	——	31, 32
Galvanic battery, elementary, by Wollaston	——	3
.. of the London Institution described	——	4
.. of piles, construction of	——	5
.. children's, described	——	8
.. Hart's	——	8
.. difference between, and electric battery	——	9
.. its power best determined by experiment	——	29
.. the connecting wire of, attracts iron filings	Elect. Magn.	52
Galvanic circles, simple ones described	Galv.	2—4
.. compound ones, construction of	——	4—9
.. pile Volta's, described	——	4
.. formed of animal substances	——	25
.. formed of vegetable substances	——	25
.. trough battery of Cruickshank, &c.	——	7
.. theory of Du Fay	——	3
.. electricity not dependent on the magnitude of the surfaces of the plates	——	10
.. experiments by Roget	——	30, 31
.. influence upon mercury	——	31
.. current distinguished from the thermo-electric	Elect. Magn.	96
Galvanometers, various kinds of, described	——	39—45
.. differential	——	44
.. Ritchie's, torsion one	——	41
Galvanoscope, description of	——	42
.. gold-leaf, described	——	45
Gamby's dipping-needle described	Magn.	79
General facts and principles of magnetism	——	1—16
.. principles of artificial magnets	——	41
Generalization of electrical phenomena, when first attempted	Elect.	1
Geometrical and refracted focus distinguished	Opt. Inst.	7

		Page
Georgium Sidus and his six moons, account of	Pop. Int.	36, 37
GILBERT, the earliest scientific electrician	Elect.	1
GILPIN and Canton, their table of the variations of the compass	Magn.	32
Glass, comparison of the aberration of light by, with that of sapphire and diamond	New. Opt.	13
.. globules substituted for small lenses, or microscopes	Opt. Inst.	38
.. description of a thermometer with	Therm.	3
.. rods and tubes, table of expansibilities of	———	63
.. *prism*, on the transmission of light through	Pop. Int.	90
Globe, terrestrial, representation and description of	———	40
Gold-leaf electrometer, description of	Elect.	19
.. galvanoscope, description of	Elect. Magn.	45
Graduation of the scales of thermometers, directions for	Therm.	13—15, 56
Graphic telescope, description of	Opt. Inst.	26
Gravitation defined and illustrated	Pop. Int.	5
.. Newton's, discovery of its universality	———	39
.. and pressure of fluids, explanation of their action	———	57, 58
Gravity, centre of, explained and illustrated	———	9, 18—20
.. specific, of bodies, explained	———	59, 60
.. its effects more obvious in fluids than in solid bodies	———	56
Gregorian telescope, description of	New. Opt.	10, 16
GRIMALDI's discovery of the inflexion, or diffraction, of light	———	10
Grinding of specula and lenses	Opt. Inst.	30
.. of microscopic lenses	———	35
HATCHETT's dry galvanic pile, account of	Galv.	27
HALE's thermometer described	Therm.	9
HALLEY, Hooke, and Boyle, their proposed scale for thermometers	———	4, 5
.. observations on the light in a diving-bell	New. Opt.	38
Hardness of iron and steel favourable to their magnetic power	Magn.	14
HARE's calorimeter, description of	Galv.	4
Harmony of sounds, how produced	Pop. Int.	73
.. distinguished from melody	———	73
HARRIS's experiments on the magnetism of rotation	Magn.	94, 95
HART's galvanic battery described	Galv.	8
HAUY's electroscope described	Elect.	3
Heat, effects of, described	Pop. Int.	4
.. of the seasons, its diminution caused by the obliquity of the sun's rays	———	46, 47
.. the ancients had no means of measuring	Therm.	1
.. imperfections common to all instruments for measuring	———	51—56
.. table of the expansion of bodies by	———	61, 62
.. table of various points of, according to Wedgwood	———	29
.. its effects upon the powers of a magnet	Magn.	12, 13
.. favours the progress of magnetic induction, but impairs its permanency	———	12
.. produced by the voltaic battery to a great intensity	Galv.	10
.. experiments on its evolution by the voltaic battery	———	12
Heavenly bodies, on the apparent situation of	Pop. Int.	87
Height of the boiling point of water in different states of the barometer	Therm.	15
Helical rotations, exhibition of	Elect. Magn.	39
.. coil (balanced) assumes the positions and directive properties of the magnetic needle	———	52
.. and rectilineal conductors, mutual action of	Elect. Magn.	74—79
HENLEY's universal discharger described	Elect.	37
.. electrometer described	———	19, 37
HERSCHEL's periscopic combination of lenses	Opt. Inst.	41
.. front-view reflecting telescope	———	17
.. aplanatic telescope	———	20
.. table of dimensions of a double aplanatic object glass	———	21
.. experiments on the magnetism of rotation	Magn.	93, 94
Hills, why their attraction does not draw houses towards them	Pop. Int.	6
.. accumulation of water in	———	62
History of the discovery of the local attraction of vessels	Magn.	61—63

		Page
History of electro-magnetism	Elect. Magn.	1—4
.. and construction of the common thermometer	Therm.	1—10
.. .. register thermometers	——	33—39
Homogeneous light, method of obtaining	New. Opt.	23
.. law of refraction of	——	26
Horse-shoe magnets and batteries described	Magn.	53
Houriet's pyrometer, or metalline thermometer, described	Therm.	32, 33
Huggins's theory of the double refraction of light	New. Opt.	9
Hydro-electric current defined	Elect. Magn.	93
Hydrometer, description of that instrument	Pop. Int.	60
Hydrostatics, popular introduction to	——	56—64
Hygrometer, thermometric, described	Therm.	41, 42
.. and photometer, Leslie's, described	——	39, 40
.. .. suggested improvements in	——	45
.. Daniell's description of	——	49, 50
.. Jones's ..	——	50
.. Cumming's ..	——	50, 51
Hyperbolic curves formed by coloured shadows	New. Opt.	62
Hypotheses, different, on the nature of light	Pop. Int.	74, 75
Hypothesis of the earth's magnetism	Magn.	25
.. .. illustrated by means of an artificial globe	——	28
.. Barlow's, concerning the variation of the magnetic needle	——	30
.. Halley's curious one on the same subject	——	30
.. invariably the precursor of truth	——	33
Iceland *spar*, observations on	New. Opt.	9
Identity of magnetism and electricity	Elect. Magn.	88
Ignition of charcoal, by galvanism, splendid exhibition of	Galv.	10
.. of metals, .. phenomena of	——	12
Images formed by plane mirrors, their place and bulk	Opt. Inst.	2
.. .. by concave and convex mirrors, with curious experiments	——	3
Imitation of terrestrial magnetism by means of wires round an artificial globe	Elect. Magn.	91
Impenetrability of bodies, illustrations of	Pop. Int.	1
Imperfections common to all instruments for measuring heat	Therm.	51—56
.. of refracting telescopes	New. Opt.	26—30
Impression of light, duration of, on the eye	——	35
Incidence and *reflection*, equality of the angles known to the ancients	——	1
.. .. on the angles of Pop. Int. 14, 15.	Opt. Inst.	2
Inclined plane, account of it as a mechanical power	Pop. Int.	28
Inconvenience of the *plus* and *minus* degrees of the thermometer	Therm.	9
India-rubber, its use for microscopes	Opt. Inst.	57
Induction in *electricity*, described	Elect.	9, 10, 12
.. development of the law of	——	28—31
.. accumulation of electricity by	——	31—36
.. magnetic, analogous to electric induction	Magn.	4—7
.. .. complex experiments on	——	7—10
.. .. means of quickening its progress	——	11
.. .. its progress favoured, but its permanency impaired, by heat	——	12
.. explained on the theory of Ampère	Elect. Magn.	87
.. the only means of exciting magnetism	——	2
.. electro-magnetic, account of	——	52—57
Inertia of bodies defined and illustrated	Pop. Int.	3
Inflection, or diffraction of light, observations and experiments on	New. Opt.	60, 63
Influence of light on magnetism	Elect. Magn.	97, 98
Ingenhouz's electrical machine described	Elect.	16
Instrument, Nicholson's for distinguishing negative from positive electricity	Elect.	27, 28
.. invented by Ptolemy to measure the degree of refraction	New. Opt.	2
Instruments for collecting weak electricity	Elect.	51—53
.. magnetic, various ones described	Magn.	55—87
.. for measuring heat, imperfections common to all	Therm.	51—56

			Page
Insulation in electricity described	. . . .	ELECT. .	57
INTENSITY of terrestrial magnetism, variations of	.	MAGN. .	25
.. of heat producible by the voltaic battery	.	GALV. .	10
.. of *magnetic forces* in relation to distance	.	MAGN. .	16
.. .. method of measuring	. .	———	25
.. .. methods of determining	.	———	82—87
.. .. at different heights above the earth's surface	. . . .	———	87
Intermitting springs, phenomena of, accounted for	. .	POP. INT.	63
Introduction to mechanics	. . . . .	———	1—29
.. to astronomy	. . . . .	———	30—55
.. to hydrostatics	. . . .	———	56—64
.. to pneumatics	. . . . .	———	65—73
.. to optics	. . . . .	———	74—100
Inversion of the images of objects on the retina, why not observed	———	78, 79
Iron, illustrations of its being attracted by the magnet	.	MAGN. .	2, 3
.. magnetic, attraction and repulsion of	. .	———	3
.. and *steel*, different qualities of, how they affect the magnetic power	. . . .	———	10
.. .. retain magnetic power in proportion to their hardness	. . . .	———	14
.. .. table of the relative magnetic power of different species of	. . . .	———	15
.. why it is less retentive of magnetic power than steel	———	11
.. Scoresby's experiments on its magnetism	.	———	14
.. *filings*, curious arrangement of, when under magnetic influence	. . . .	———	21
.. .. attracted by the connecting wire of a galvanic battery	. . . .	ELECT. MAGN.	52
JONES's hygrometer described	. . . .	THERM.	50
Jupiter and his four moons described	. . .	POP. INT.	36
.. eclipses of his satellites, and method of finding the longitude by	. . . .	———	52, 53
Juxtaposition, a method of making artificial magnets	.	MAGN. .	43
KALEIDOSCOPE, principle of its construction	. .	OPT. INST.	55
KATER's remarks on the processes for making artificial magnets	MAGN.	51
.. azimuth compass described	. . .	———	70—72
KEITH's register-thermometer described	. .	THERM.	37, 38
KENNERSLEY's electrical air-thermometer described	.	ELECT.	43
... theory of the phenomena of the rainbow	NEW. OPT.	5
.. astronomical telescope	. .	———	6
KEWLEY's balance thermometer described	. .	THERM.	47, 48
KNIGHT's method of making artificial magnets	.	MAGN. .	45
LAND COMPASS, construction of	. . .	MAGN. .	55, 60, 61
LANE's discharging electrometer	. . . .	———	38
Lapis electricus, description of that stone	. .	ELECT. .	53
Lateral explosion of electricity	. . . .	———	41
Law of induction, experiments for the development of	.	———	28—31
.. of electro-magnetic action	. . . .	ELECT. MAGN.	6—9
.. .. direct consequences of	.	———	9—18
.. .. its effects on the magnet needle	———	9—14
.. of inductions, its application to the explanation of particular facts	. . . .	———	18—19
.. of refraction of light discovered by Snellius	.	NEW. OPT.	7
.. of refraction of homogeneous light	. .	———	26
.. of magnetic forces	. . . . .	MAGN. .	16—22
Layers, alternate, of muscle and brain from a galvanic pile	GALV. .	25
LEBAILIF's improved galvanometer described	. .	ELECT. MAGN.	43
Lenses defined and severally described	POP. INT. 89.	OPT. INST.	4
.. effects of their combination	. . .	———	3
.. tables of the magnifying powers	. . .	———	35
.. spherical aberrations of light in, and in mirrors	———	11, 12
.. minimum of spherical aberration in	.	———	24
.. method of calculating the foci of	. .	———	6
.. .. of grinding	. . . . .	———	30
.. .. of polishing and centering	. . .	———	31

GENERAL INDEX.

		Page
Lenses, method of grinding for microscopes	Opt. Inst.	35
.. Brewster's improvements in		41
.. polyzonal, or built of zones		7, 8
.. parabolic of Newton		14
.. periscopic, combination of		41
.. Parker's large one described		7
.. sapphire and diamond of Pritchard		13, 39
.. .. table of their magnifying power		40
Leslie's hygrometer and photometer described	Therm.	39, 40
.. differential thermometer		40
.. thermometrical hygrometer		41, 42
.. photometers		42—44
.. pyroscope		44, 45
Lever, principle of, and description of the several sorts of	Pop. Int.	20—24
.. species of, distinguished according to the place of the fulcrum		22—24
Leyden jar, construction of	Elect.	34, 35
Light, different hypotheses concerning its nature	Pop. Int.	74, 75
.. why its rays are visible in their passage		77
.. refraction of, theory concerning		85, 86
.. .. its effects on the apparent places of the stars		87
.. .. through lenses of various forms		89
.. transmission of through a glass prism		90
.. prismatic colours exist in, and not formed in the medium through which it passes		90
.. how its rays are refracted to the retina		95
.. nature and principles of, and axioms concerning	New. Opt.	9, 11
.. rays of, always proceed in straight lines		1
.. experiments on its composition and decomposition		11, 12
.. homogeneous, method of obtaining		2, 3
.. .. law of its refraction		26
.. reflexibility of, general laws concerning		20—22
.. not reflected by infringing upon the solid parts of bodies		55
.. reflected by bodies chiefly of their own colour		37
.. duration of its impression on the eye		35
.. Halley's experiments upon in a diving-bell		38
.. its fits of easy reflection and transmission		44
.. diffraction of, explained, with experiments		60
.. dispersive powers of by different bodies, table of	Opt. Inst.	25
.. refraction of through different lenses		13, 35, 40
.. rays of, their primary colours	New. Opt.	11, 12, &c.
.. their different refrangibilities		32
.. their interference		10
.. undulations of, account of that theory		44
.. its polarity suspected by Newton		64
.. electric. [See *Electric Light*.]		
.. its influence on magnetism	Elect. Magn.	97, 98
.. stars and pencils of, exhibited on the passage of the electric fluid from or to a pointed body	Elect.	27
.. electric, exhibited in the ignition of charcoal, &c., by galvanism	Galv.	10, 11
Lightning, analogy between it and the electric spark	Elect.	59
.. safeguard for ships and buildings from		59, 60
.. affects the magnetic needle, and sometimes reverses its polarity	Elect. Magn.	2
Line of no variation of the compass, traced	Magn.	23
Liquids, in what they differ from air	Pop. Int.	1
.. sound conveyed by their undulation		71
Liquors, transparent, their colours vary with their thickness	New. Opt.	37, 38
Loadstones, or native magnets, where found	Magn.	1
.. retain their virtue more tenaciously than artificial magnets		54
.. how they should be armed		54, 55
Local attraction of ships, remarks concerning		61—68
.. history of its discovery		61—63
.. Barlow's experiments concerning		63—68
.. table of deviation on account of, observed in different ships		66

			Page
Local attraction, consequence of, in the wreck of vessels	MAGN.		66
.. Barlow's proposed remedy for			67
.. chronometers disturbed by			68
London, Institution, galvanic battery belonging to	GALV.		4
Longitude, method of finding from the eclipses of Jupiter's satellites	POP. INT.		52, 53
Lucernal microscope, account of	OPT. INST.		52
Luminous effects of galvanism described	GALV.		10
MACHINES, considerations with regard to	POP. INT.		20
.. effect upon, of the medium in which they are worked			29
.. electric. [See *Electric Machines*.]			
Magic-Lantern, principles and construction of	OPT. INST.		52
Magnet, revolution of one of its poles round a vertical wire	ELECT. MAGN.		19—23
.. made to revolve round its axis			23, 24
.. voltaic, description of			38
.. .. made to show the phenomena of the dipping-needle			47
.. method of making a very powerful temporary one			54
.. one which sustained 750 pounds			55
.. Newton's small one, which raised 250 times its own weight			51
.. either pole of, tends to produce opposite polarity in the adjacent end of a neighbouring magnetizable body			88
Magnets, native, or loadstones, where found	MAGN.		1
.. artificial, ready method of forming			1
.. .. various methods of forming			10—15
.. .. method of forming by percussion			42
.. .. .. by juxtaposition			43
.. .. less tenacious of their virtue than loadstones			54
.. .. general principles of			4!
.. impaired or destroyed by heat			12
.. impaired by falling on a stone pavement			13
.. experiments on their fracture			15, 16
.. lose their power by rubbing			54
.. on the preservation of			53
.. polarity of, and other properties described and illustrated			1—3
.. horse-shoe, formation of			53
Magnetism, definition of	MAGN.		1
.. general facts and principles of			1—16
.. (induced) rendered permanent by the electric discharge			12
.. not impaired by cold, however intense			13
.. of iron, experiments on			14
.. terrestrial, concerning			22—32
.. .. variations in its intensity			25
.. .. hypothesis concerning			25
.. different theories of			32—41
.. mechanical theory of			32, 33
.. of steel bars retained and concentrated by armatures			43
.. of bodies which are not ferruginous			87—91
.. all bodies in some degree susceptible of			90
.. of rotation, various experiments on			91—96
.. excitable only by induction	ELECT. MAGN.		2
.. induction of, explained in Ampère's theory			87
.. and electricity identical			92
.. terrestrial, exhibited by means of an artificial globe			87
.. influence of light upon			97, 98
Magnetic theories, observations on	MAGN.		96
.. attraction and repulsion, similar to electric			3, 39
.. attraction, opinions of the ancients concerning			33
.. fluids, theory of two			36—41
.. .. Brewster's theory respecting			41
.. forces, laws of			16—22

		Page
Magnetic forces, relations of their intensities to distance	MAGN.	16
.. methods of determining their intensities	—	82—87
.. method of measuring	—	25
.. at different heights above the earth's surface	—	87
.. induction analogous to electric induction	—	4—7
.. .. complex, experiments on	—	7—10
.. .. means of quickening the progress of	—	11
.. iron, attraction and repulsion of	—	3
.. susceptibility and retentiveness, less in iron than in steel	—	10, 11
.. power of steel, below a certain heat, increases as it cools	—	13
.. of iron, or steel, retained in proportion to the hardness	—	14
.. .. .. table of different species	—	15
.. curves, their remarkable properties and method of delineating	—	19—22
.. batteries, concerning	—	53
.. instruments, description of various	—	55—87
.. equator, explanation of the term	—	24
.. needle, its proper proportion, weight, &c.	—	53—58
.. on the dip of	—	23—25
.. affected by the Aurora Borealis	ELECT. MAGN.	2
.. affected by lightning, so as to reverse its polarity	—	2
.. how affected by electro-magnetism	—	9—14
.. its movements in free space	—	14—18
.. its properties exhibited by a helical coil	—	52
.. suspended in the air without a visible agent	—	37
.. effects of thermo-electric currents upon	—	95
.. properties of circular conductors exhibited	—	34
Magnifiers, Friar Bacon's description of	NEW. OPT.	3
Magnifying power of lenses, table of	OPT. INST.	35
.. of sapphire lenses, table of	—	40
.. of telescopes and microscopes, method of determining	—	11, 45
Magnitude of the corpuscles of bodies investigated	NEW. OPT.	55
Man, why he can see himself at full-length in a plane mirror, which is only half his height	POP. INT.	81
Mariners' compass, construction of	MAGN.	55—60
Mars, account of that planet	POP. INT.	36
Materiality of electricity, experiments in proof of	ELECT.	60—62
Materials, size and form proper for magnetic needles	MAGN.	56—58
Matter is never annihilated	POP. INT.	2, 3
MAUROLYCUS, his description of the structure and functions of the eye	NEW OPT.	3
MAYER's dipping-needle, described	MAGN.	79, 80
Measures of heat, unknown to the ancients	THERM.	1
.. imperfections common to all instruments constructed for that purpose	—	51—56
Measuring of distances, telescope for	OPT. INST.	25
Mechanical properties of atmospheric air	POP. INT.	7
.. powers, description of	—	20—29
.. properties of fluids, described	—	56—60
.. .. of elastic fluids	—	65—69
.. theories of magnetism	MAGN.	32, 33
.. effects of electricity on bodies	ELECT.	42—45
.. development of electricity	—	55—57
.. effects, different in Voltaic from those of common electricity	GALV.	13
Mechanics, popular introduction to	POP. INT.	1—29
Melody, cause of given, and the effect distinguished from harmony	—	73
Melting of platina and other metals by galvanism	GALV.	11—14
Meniscus a species of lens, described	OPT. INST.	4
Mercury, beautiful experiments of its combustion	GALV.	13
.. its convulsive agitations under galvanic influence	—	31
Mercurial thermometer of Roemur	THERM.	7
.. and *alcoholic* thermometers compared at different temperatures	—	54

GENERAL INDEX.

		Page
Mercurial and *alcoholic* thermometers, by De Witt	Therm.	55
Mercury, account of that planet	Pop. Int.	35
Meridians, defined and described	—	41
Metals, table of the relative expansion of different	Therm.	17
.. tables of their different degrees of oxidability	Galv.	22, 23
.. ignited and melted by the galvanic battery	—	11, 14
.. colours produced by their combustion	—	13
.. tables of their comparative thermo-electric relations	Elect. Magn.	94
Metallic solutions decomposed by galvanism	Galv.	16
.. thermometers of De Luc	Therm.	24
.. .. Regnier	—	29
.. .. Crichton	—	30, 31
.. conductors for the safeguard of ships and buildings	Elect.	59, 60
.. .. of Fitzgerald	—	20, 21
Metalline thermometer, or pyrometer, of Breguet	Therm.	32, 33
.. .. of Houriet	—	33
Microscopes, their principles and construction	Pop. Int.	98
Micrometer-pyrometer of Smeaton, described	Therm.	18—20
Micrometers of various kinds, construction of	Opt. Inst.	56, 57
.. circular construction of	—	59, 60
Micrometrical eye-piece, by Ramsden, described	—	14
Microscopes, on their invention and antiquity	—	33
.. theory of single	—	33
.. .. of compound	—	43
.. singly-reflecting	—	43
.. reflecting, proper form of their mirrors	—	48
.. Amician reflecting	—	48
.. compound, proper size of	—	48
.. mechanical arrangement of	—	44
.. method of determining their magnifying power	—	45
.. object-glasses for	—	46, 47
.. test-objects for	—	49
.. fluid	—	42
.. small, made of glass globules	—	38
.. diamond and sapphire	—	39
.. table	—	36
.. for objects of natural history	—	47
.. periscopic, of Dr. Wollaston	—	40
.. opaque	—	50
.. solar	Pop. Int. 99. Opt. Inst.	50, 51
.. lucernal	Opt. Inst.	52
.. smallest magnitude visible by	—	32
Microscopic lenses, method of grinding	—	35
.. pyrometer of De Luc	Therm.	23, 24
.. .. of Ramsden	—	24, 27
Middleton's experience of the effects of cold on magnetism	Opt. Inst.	14
Minimum of spherical aberration in lenses	Magn.	13
Mirrors, description of the different kinds and their effects	Pop. Int.	80, 85
Mirrors, plane, their images and reflections, concerning	Opt. Inst.	2
.. concave	—	2
.. .. curious experiments with their images	—	3
.. .. used as burning-glasses, Archimedes's, &c.	—	1, 3, 7
.. convex, images of	—	3
.. of reflecting microscopes, proper form of	—	48
.. .. telescopes	—	15
.. spherical aberrations in	—	11
Mitchell's method of making artificial magnets by double touch	—	46, 47
Modifications of differential thermometers	Therm.	39—45
Momentum of bodies defined and illustrated	Pop. Int.	11
.. .. measurement of	—	11
Monsoons, description and cause of	—	70
Moon, general account of	—	49—55
.. her motion and phases explained	—	50, 51
.. concerning the eclipses of	—	51, 52
Moons of Jupiter, Saturn, and the Georgium Sidus	—	36
Mortimer's pyrometer, described	Therm.	17
Morveau's platina pyrometer, description of	—	29, 30
.. table of temperatures	—	30

		Page
Mother-of-Pearl micrometers, described	Opt. Inst.	57
Motion of bodies, absolute, relative, uniform, retarded and accelerated, defined	Pop. Int.	9, 10
.. perpetual, exists only in the heavens	—	10
.. reflected, explanation, and illustrations of	—	13—15
.. compound, explained	—	15—18
.. the earth's annual, produced by the composition of forces	—	33
.. threefold, of the earth described	—	34
.. of the moon explained	—	50, 51
.. of a body may be insensible on account of its great velocity	—	80
Mountains, their attraction of a plummet	—	6
.. accumulation of water in	—	62
Moving bodies, resistance of the air to, how measured	—	17, 18
Multipliers and doublers of electricity	Elect.	53
Murray's proposed scale for a thermometer	Therm.	9
Muschenbrock's pyrometer described	—	15
Muscle and brain, galvanic pile formed by alternate layers of	Galv.	25
Muscular motions in dead animals produced by galvanism	—	19
Nairn's electrical machine described	Elect.	15
Nature of light, theories of	New. Opt.	9
Natural bodies, cause of the colours of	—	54
.. history, microscopes adapted to objects	Opt. Inst.	47
.. magnets or loadstones, where found	Magn.	1
Needle, magnetic, see *Magnetic Needle*, compass, and variation		
Needle, Dipping, see *Dipping-Needle*.		
Negative and *positive* electricity described	Elect.	13
.. .. instrument for distinguishing	—	27, 28
Near-sightedness, cause and remedy of pointed out	Pop. Int.	96
Neutral salts decomposed by the galvanic pile	Galv.	15
New Holland, colourless topaz of, its use	Opt. Inst.	25
Newton's experiments on the oil thermometer	Therm.	5
.. axioms concerning light	New Opt.	11
.. reflecting telescope described	Opt. Inst. 15. New. Opt.	10—30
.. queries concerning the inflection of light	New. Opt.	63
.. scale for determining reflected colours, &c.	—	46
.. suggestions of the polarization of light	—	64
.. table of the colours of thin plates and films	—	52
.. theory of colours	—	31
.. theorems concerning refraction	—	33
.. small, but powerful, magnet, account of	Elect. Magn.	55
.. discovery of the universality of the principle of gravitation	Pop. Int.	39
Nicholson's instrument for distinguishing negative electricity	Elect.	27, 28
Night telescopes, account of	Opt. Inst.	10
Nitric Acid, its effects on copper and on zinc	Galv.	14
Nobili's galvanometer described	Elect. Magn.	42, 43
Non-conductors of electricity described	Elect.	5, 6
Oar, its action in rowing a boat described	Pop. Int.	13
Objects of natural history, microscopes for	Opt. Inst.	47
.. (test) for microscopes	—	49
.. the shadowed side of, by what means visible	Pop. Int.	77
.. manner in which they become visible to the eye	—	77, 78
.. their images inverted on the retina	—	78, 79
.. on the apparent dimensions of	—	79
.. smallest angle under which they can be seen	—	80
Object-glasses for microscopes, formation of	Opt. Inst.	46, 47
Objections to the present system of astronomy answered	Pop. Int.	37—39
.. to Amonton's thermometer	Therm.	8
.. to Volta's theory of galvanism	Galv.	32
.. to the theory of a single electric fluid	Elect.	63, 64
Obliquity of the sun's rays a cause of the diminution of their heat	Pop. Int.	46, 47
Observations on magnetic theories	Magn.	96
.. by Halley on light in a diving-bell	New. Opt.	38

GENERAL INDEX.

		Page
Odour, peculiar, proceeding from a worked electrical machine	Elect.	25
Oersted, history of electro-magnetism prior to his discoveries	Elect. Magn.	1—4
.. account of his discoveries	———	4—6
.. his electro-magnetic theory	———	79—81
Oil-*thermometer*, Newton's improvements on	Therm.	5
Opacity of bodies, probable cause of	New. Opt.	53
Opaque microscopes, description of	Opt. Inst.	50
Opera-glasses, achromatic description of	———	24
Opinions of the ancients respecting the cause of magnetic attraction	Magn.	33
Optics and optical instruments, books upon	Opt. Inst.	60
.. popular introduction to	Pop. Int.	74—100
Orbits of the planets proportionally represented	———	35
Oxidability of different metals, tables of	Galv.	22, 23
Paraboloidal surface proper for the mirrors of reflecting microscopes	Opt. Inst.	15
Parker's large burning-mirror described	———	17
Particles, minute, of bodies, separated by pores	New. Opt.	53
Pearl (mother of) micrometer	———	57
Percussion, artificial magnets made by	Magn.	42
Periscopic combination of lenses	Opt. Inst.	41
.. microscope described	———	42
.. spectacles	———	9
Perpetual motion exists only in the heavens	Pop. Int.	10
Phantasmagoria, that exhibition explained	Opt. Inst.	52
Phenomena of the rainbow, different theories of	New. Opt.	4
.. .. examined and investigated by Aristotle and Euclid	———	2
.. of refraction accurately investigated by Ptolemy	———	2
.. of coloured rays, description and laws of	———	41
.. prismatic, singular account of	———	38
.. exhibited by thin transparent plates	———	39—41
.. observable in the passage of the electric fluid	Elect.	23—28
.. .. on the passage of the electric fluid through a vacuum	———	25
.. of intermitting springs accounted for	Pop. Int.	63
Photometer and hygrometer, description of	Therm.	39, 40
.. improvements in, suggested	———	45
Photometers, different, by Leslie, described	———	42—44
Physiological effects of galvanism	Galv.	17
Pile, galvanic, discovery of	———	4
.. .. formed by layers of muscle and brain	———	25
.. .. formed of vegetable substances	———	25
Piles, galvanic, secondary formation of	Galv.	27
.. .. battery formed by a combination of	———	5
Pith-balls, experiments with, on electrical attraction and repulsion	———	17—20
Planets, probability of their being inhabited by rational beings	Pop. Int.	33, 36
.. general account of	———	33—40
.. their orbits and diameters proportionally represented	———	35
.. primary, why the satellites revolve round them	———	34, 35
.. vicissitudes of seasons in	———	48
Plates, galvanic electricity not dependent on the magnitude of their surfaces	Galv.	10
.. thin, thick, &c. colours of	New. Opt.	39—41, 52—54
.. .. tables of	———	52
Platina pyrometer described	Therm.	29, 30
.. phenomena exhibited on its combustion	Galv.	11
Plato, his knowledge of the equality of the angles of incidence and reflexion	New. Opt.	1
Plummet attracted by mountains	Pop. Int.	6
Plus and *minus* degrees of the thermometer, inconvenience of	Therm.	9
Pneumatics, popular introduction to	Pop. Int.	65—73
Polarisation of light first suggested by Newton	New. Opt.	64
Polarity of a magnity described and illustrated	Magn.	1, 2
Pole of a magnet made to revolve round a vertical wire	Elect. Magn.	1S—2

		Page
Pole of a magnet tends to induce opposite polarity in adjacent bodies	Elect. Magn.	88
.. sometimes reversed by lightning	———	2
Polishing of lenses and specula, method of	Opt. Inst.	30, 31
Polyzonal lenses described	———	7, 8
Porta said to have invented the *camera obscura*	New. Opt.	3
Porter, its taste when drunk out of a pewter pot	Galv.	24
Positive and negative electricity, concerning	Elect.	13
Power of a magnet at 100° Fahrenheit increases as it cools	Magn.	13
.. lost by rubbing	———	54
.. of a galvanic battery best determined by experiment	Galv.	29
Powers, mechanical, individually described	Pop. Int.	20—29
Precautions in constructing thermometers	Therm.	10—15
Preservation of magnetic power, means for	Magn.	53
Pressure of fluids, action of explained	Pop. Int.	57, 58
.. of the atmosphere on a man's body, amount of	———	65
Prevost's theory of magnetic fluids	Magn.	41
Primary colours of the rays of light	New. Opt.	15, 33
Prisms, refraction of the rays of light through	Pop. Int. 90, New. Opt.	12—31
Prismatic spectrum, arrangement of	——— 91, ———	15
.. observed by Seneca	New. Opt.	1
.. phenomenon, singular account of	———	38
.. colours, exhibited in the combustion of metals	Galv.	11—13
.. exist in the light, and are not produced by the prism	Pop. Int.	90
Pritchard's diamond and sapphire lenses, account of	Opt. Inst.	13
Progress of magnetic induction, method of quickening	Magn.	11
.. .. by heat, remarks on	———	12
Progressive changes of dip and variation of the magnetic needle	———	29—31
Properties of bodies in general	Pop. Int.	1—8
.. mechanical, of atmospheric air	———	7
.. .. of fluid	———	56—60
Ptolemy, his knowledge of the laws of refraction	New. Opt.	2, 3
Pulley, the principle of, illustrated	Pop. Int.	24, 26
Pump, common, principle and construction of	———	67, 68
.. forcing	———	69
.. air, description of, and experiments with	———	65, 66
Pyrometer, history and construction of various kinds	Therm.	15—32
.. by Achard described	———	9, 10
.. by Muschenbrock	———	15
.. by Desagulier	———	16
.. by Ellicot	———	16, 17
.. Mortimer's	———	17
.. Froteringham's	———	81
.. Smeaton's	———	18—20
.. Ferguson's	———	21—23
.. Microscopic, of De Luc	———	23, 24
.. Ramsden's	———	24—27
.. Wedgewood's	———	27—29
.. Platina one, of Morveau	———	29—30
.. Schmidt's air-pyrometer	———	31
.. Daniell's	———	31, 32
.. Breguet's, or metalline thermometer	———	32, 33
.. Houriet's, or metalline thermometer	———	33
Pyroscope, by Leslie, described	———	44, 45
Queries, Newton's, concerning the inflexion of light	New. Opt.	63
Rain, dew, and vapours, distinguished, and their causes pointed out	Pop. Int.	5
.. snow, and hail	———	61
Rainbow, the phenomena of investigated by Aristotle and Euclid	New. Opt.	2
.. .. different theories of	———	4, 5, 9
Ramage's reflecting telescope, description of	Opt. Inst.	18
Ramsden's micrometrical eye-pieces described	———	14
.. microscopic pyrometer	Therm.	24—27
Rays of light proceed in straight lines	New. Opt.	1
.. primary colours of	———	11, 12, &c.

			Page
Rays of light, reflected from bodies of their own colour	New. Opt.		37
.. general laws of their reflexion	———		11
.. interference of	———		10
.. refraction of and its laws	———		7, 33
.. how they become visible in their passage	Pop. Int.		77
.. effects of their transmission through glass prisms	———		90
.. in what manner they are refracted to the retina	———		95
Re-action and action, their equality a law of nature	Pop. Int. 11—20. Magn.		3
Reaumur's thermometer, account of	Therm.		8
.. Fahrenheit's and the Centigrade scales of thermometers, formulæ for converting into each other	———		10
Recomposition of the spectral colours produce white light	New. Opt.		35
Reflected colours, cause of investigated	Pop. Int.		92
.. motion explained and illustrated	———		13—15
.. colours, Newton's scale for determining	New. Opt.		46
Reflecting microscopes	Opt. Inst.		43, 48
.. telescopes New. Opt. 10, 30.	———		11, 15—18
.. .. their peculiar advantages	Pop. Int.		100
.. surfaces of cylinders, their application	Opt. Inst.		3
Reflexibility of light, Newton's experiments on	New. Opt.		20—22
Reflexion of the rays of light, general laws of	———		11
.. and transmission of light, fits of easy	———		44
.. of aërial vibrations the cause of echoes	Pop. Int.		72
Refracted and geometrical focus, distinction between	Opt. Inst.		7
Refraction of light, Snellius's discovery of its laws	New. Opt.		7
.. .. Newton's theorems respecting	———		33
.. .. theory of	Pop. Int.		85, 86
.. .. its effects on the apparent situation of distant bodies	———		87
.. .. through lenses of different forms described	———		89
.. of homogeneous light, law of	New. Opt.		26
.. double, explained	———		9
Refractive power of diamond and sapphire lenses	Opt. Inst.		39, 40
.. and dispersive powers of different transparent substances	———		25
.. power and spherical aberration, in the inverse ratio to each other	———		12
Refrangibility of the rays of light	New. Opt.		32, 33
Register thermometers, history and construction of	Therm.		33—39
.. .. of Cavendish	———		34, 35
.. .. Six's	———		35, 36
.. .. Blackadder's	———		38, 39
.. .. Trail's	———		39
.. .. Keith's	———		37, 38
Regnier's metallic thermometer	Therm.		29
Relative magnetic power of iron and steel, table of	Magn.		15
.. .. with respect to distance	———		16
Representation of the proportion of the orbits of the planets	Pop. Int.		35
.. of .. of the diameters	———		35
.. and description of the terrestrial globe	———		40
.. of different appearances on the passage of the electric fluid	Elect.		27
Repulsion and attraction, electrical, concerning	———		2, 3
.. .. .. experiments on	———		4, 17—20
.. .. of magnetic iron	Magn.		3
.. .. .. similar to electric	———		3, 39
Resinous and *vitreous* electricity distinguished	Elect.		8, 9
Resistance of the air, its effects on falling bodies generally	Pop. Int.		7
.. .. on moving bodies	———		17, 18
Retina, the images of objects inverted upon	———		78, 79
.. in what manner the rays of light are refracted to	———		95
Revolving camera obscura, description of	Opt. Inst.		53
Richman, fatal consequences of his electrical experiments	Elect.		33, 59
Ring, electro-dynamic, effects of	Elect. Magn.		90
.. Saturn's, described	Pop. Int.		36
Rings, coloured, phenomena of	New. Opt.		41—43
Ritchie's torsion-galvanometer	Elect. Magn.		41
Ritter's experiments on electro-magnetism	———		3
Robinson's method of finding the radii of the surfaces of convex lenses	Opt. Inst.		6

GENERAL INDEX.

		Page
Rochon's telescope for measuring angles and distances	Opt. Inst.	25
Roemur's mercurial thermometer described	Therm.	7
Roget's galvanic experiments, account of	Galv.	30, 31
.. demonstrations of the properties of the magnetic curves	Magn.	19
.. invention of a machine for the mechanical delineation of the magnetic curves	———	20
.. experiments on the mutual attraction of the coils of a helical conducting wire	Elect. Magn.	59
Rotations caused by electro-magnetism	———	19—32
.. of a magnet round its axis	———	23, 24
.. helical, by electro-magnetism	———	39
.. rendered visible in terrestrial magnetism	———	50
.. on the magnetism of	Magn.	91—96
Rotatory and vibratory motions, experiments on	Elect. Magn.	30—32
Royal Institution, voltaic battery	Galv.	7
.. experiments made at	———	10—13
Royal Society, their early attention to electricity	Elect.	1
.. description of a dipping-needle belonging to them	Magn.	75—78
Rumford's thermoscope described	Therm.	40, 41
Russia, thermometer used in	———	9
Rutherford's day and night thermometer	———	36, 37
Sabine's dipping-needle described	Magn.	80, 81
Sapphire and diamond lenses, their aberration compared with those of glass	Opt. Inst.	13
.. lenses and microscopes	———	39, 40
Santorio, the maker of the first thermometer, described	Therm.	2
Satellites, why they revolve round their primary planets	Pop. Int.	34, 35
.. of Jupiter, their eclipses, and advantages of	———	52
Saturn, with his seven moons and ring, described	———	36
Saturn's sixth satellite, when discovered	Opt. Inst.	17
Scale, Fahrenheit's, principle of its division	Therm.	7
.. Newton's for determining reflected colours	New. Opt.	46
Scales of thermometers, directions for graduating	Therm.	13—15, 56
.. for .. proposed by Boyle, Halley, and Hooke	———	4, 5
.. .. .. by Murray	———	9
.. of Reaumur's, Fahrenheit's, and Celsius's thermometers converted into each other	———	10
.. tables of the correspondences of different thermometrical	———	63
Schmidt's air-pyrometer described	———	31
Schweigger's electro-magnetic multiplier	Elect. Magn.	40
Scoresby's experiments upon the magnetism of iron	Magn.	14
.. instrument for finding the dip of the needle	———	81
Screw, its effect as a mechanical power explained	Pop. Int.	28
Sea and land breezes, their causes described	———	70, 71
Seasons, causes of their variation explained	———	44—48
.. their vicissitudes in the planets	———	48
Secondary galvanic piles described	Galv.	27
Seneca, his knowledge of optics . . New. Opt. 2.	Opt. Inst.	33
Sensation produced by a current of voltaic electricity	Galv.	18
.. of taste occasioned by the galvanic and electric fluid	———	18
Shadowed side of an object, by what means visible	Pop. Int.	27
Shadows, their nature defined and illustrated	———	75, 76
.. coloured, phenomena of	New. Opt.	61
Shape and figure of bodies, illustrations of	Pop. Int.	2
Ship's copper, its corrosion prevented	Galv.	14
Shock, electric. See Electric shock.		
.. .. communicable to vast numbers of persons at a time and through great distances	Elect.	39, 40
Shocks, powerful, from voltaic and electric batteries, equally destructive of animal life	Galv.	19
.. electric, received from different species of fishes	———	26
Sidereal and solar time, distinction between	Pop. Int.	48, 49
Sight acquired by a man who had been blind from infancy, its effects upon him described	———	80, 81
.. cause and remedy of its decay in old age	———	97
Signs of the zodiac described	———	37, 42
Silver and sulphur, their combination assisted by galvanism	Galv.	24

		Page
Simple microscope, theory of	Opt. Inst.	33, 43
.. galvanic circles described	Galv.	2—4
Sines, the law of, explained	New. Opt.	7
Singer's electrical column	Galv.	26
Singular prismatic phenomenon, account of	New. Opt.	38
Six's register thermometer	Therm.	35, 36
Smeaton's micrometer-thermometer described	Therm.	18—20
Smoke and steam, cause of their ascent	Pop. Int.	8
Snellius's discovery of the laws of refraction	New. Opt.	7
Snow, hail, and vapour, cause of	Pop. Int.	61
Solar microscope, description of .. Pop. Int. 99.	Opt. Inst.	50, 51
.. rays, their influence on magnetism	Elect. Magn.	97
.. and sidereal time distinguished	Pop. Int.	48, 49
Solenoid, electro-dynamic, description of	Elect. Magn.	79
Solid parts of bodies not touched by the rays of light	New. Opt.	55
.. bodies less affected by gravity than fluids	Pop. Int.	56
Solids, tables of the comparative expansions of seven, by heat	Therm.	27
.. capable of conveying sounds by the vibration of their particles	Pop. Int.	71
Sonorousness of *bodies* owing to their elasticity	——	71
.. .. effects of, illustrated	——	71, 72
Sound which accompanies the transference of the electric fluid, variously measured	Elect.	25
.. various remarks on	Pop. Int.	69—73
.. caused by the tremulous motion of the air	——	71
.. conveyed by the undulation of liquids	——	71
.. .. the vibration of the particles of solid bodies	——	71
.. its velocity about 1142 feet in a second	——	72
.. .. not materially different, whatever is the direction of the wind	——	72
.. harmony, or concord of, how produced	——	73
Spar, Iceland, its double refraction discovered by Bartolinus	New. Opt.	9
Spark, electric. See *Electric spark*.		
Speaking trumpet, principle of its construction	Pop. Int.	72, 73
Specific gravities of bodies explained	——	59, 60
Spectacles, when invented	Opt. Inst.	8
.. periscopic, described	——	9
Spectral colours, when re-united, produce white	New. Opt.	35
Spectrum, prismatic, described	——	15
Specula, qualities and proportions of, metals for	Opt. Inst.	29
.. method of grinding and polishing	——	30
Spherical aberration in lenses, cause of .. New. Opt. 7, 8, 27.	——	11
.. in mirrors	——	11
.. is in the inverse ratio of the magnifying power	——	12
.. in lenses, minimum of	——	14
.. comparison of, in glass, sapphire, and diamond	——	13
Springs and fountains, their origin, &c.	Pop. Int.	61—64
.. intermitting, accounted for	——	63
Stands, or supports, for telescopes, construction of	Opt. Inst.	29
Stars, fixed, their size and distances unknown	Pop. Int.	37
Statical thermometer, description of	Therm.	45—47
Steel. See *Iron*.		
Steel-bar, effects of a transmission of electric fluid through	Magn.	12
Steelyard, its principle and application	Pop. Int.	21
Stereo-electric currents, definition of	Elect. Magn.	93
Stone, falling, is met on its way by the earth	Pop. Int.	6
Stones, electrical quality of some species described	Elect.	54
Structure and functions of the eye .. Pop. Int. 94.	New. Opt.	3
Substances, transparent, table of the refractive and dispersive powers of	Opt. Inst.	25
Sulphuric acid, dilute, its action upon copper and on zinc	Galv.	14
Sulzer, the first author who noticed any of the effects of galvanism	——	1
Sun, the earth nearer to in winter than in summer	Pop. Int.	32
.. eclipses of, explained	——	51, 52
.. why he appears red through a fog	——	93
Sun's rays, their obliquity the cause of the diminution of their heat	——	46, 47

GENERAL INDEX.

		Page
Surfaces of bodies, light reflected from without touching them	New. Opt.	55
.. of cylinders, their use in optical experiments	Opt. Inst.	3
Syphon, description and principle of	Pop. Int.	62, 63
System of astronomy, Copernican, objections to, answered	———	37, 39
Table of the height of the boiling-point of water in different states of the barometer	Therm.	15
.. of the relative expansions of different metals at different heats	———	15
.. of the expansion of rods of different substances between the freezing and the boiling point of water	———	20
.. of the expansion of seven different solids by heat	———	27
.. of various points of heat according to Wedgewood	———	29
.. of temperatures according to Daniel	———	32
.. .. .. to Morveau	———	30
.. of expansibilities of glass rods and tubes	———	53
.. comparative, of alcoholic and mercurial thermometers	———	54, 55
.. of correspondence of different thermometrical scales	———	57—60
.. of expansions of bodies by heat	———	61, 62
.. of remarkable temperatures, according to Fahrenheit's scale	———	63
.. of the refractive and dispersive powers of various substances	Opt. Inst.	25
.. of the colours of thin plates of air, water, and glass	New. Opt.	52
.. of dimensions of an aplanatic double object-glass	Opt. Inst.	21
.. of the magnifying powers of lenses	———	35
.. of the comparative thermo-electric relations of different metals	Elect. Magn.	94
.. of the relative magnetic powers of different species of iron and steel	Magn.	15
.. of changes of variation and intensity of terrestrial magnetism	———	32
.. of the local attractions observed in different ships	———	66
Table-microscope, description of	Opt. Inst.	36
Tangential force described	Pop. Int.	17, 31
Taste of porter affected by galvanism	Galv.	24
Teinoscope, description of	Opt. Inst.	54, 55
Telescope, different accounts of the invention of	New. Opt.	5, 4
.. astronomical, described	New. Opt. 6. Opt. Inst.	10
.. night and day	———	10
.. Newton's reflecting	New. Opt. 30. ———	15
.. achromatic, by Dollond, Blair, &c.	———	23
.. .. theory of	———	19
.. Cassograinean and Gregorian	———	16, 17
.. front-view reflecting	———	17, 30
.. reflecting, by Ramage	———	18
.. .. proper form of the specula of	———	11
Telescopes, method of ascertaining their power	———	11
.. for measuring angles and distances	———	25
.. Varley's graphic	———	26
.. double-image	———	25, 26
.. imperfections of refracting	New. Opt.	26—30
.. achromatic, eye-pieces for	Opt. Inst.	27, 28
.. stands or supports for	———	29
.. general observations respecting	———	31
Telescopes, principle and construction of	Pop. Int.	100
.. reflecting, advantages of	———	100
Temperature, Morveau's table of	Therm.	30
.. Wedgewood's	———	29
.. Daniell's	———	32
.. table of, according to Fahrenheit's	———	63
.. at which dew falls	———	49
Terrestrial globe, representation and description of	Pop. Int.	40
.. magnetism, observations on	Magn.	22—32
.. .. variations in its intensities	———	25
.. .. electro-magnetic effects of	Elect. Magn.	45—52
.. .. exhibits a visible rotation	———	50
.. .. imitated by means of wires on an artificial globe	———	91

GENERAL INDEX.

		Page
Test-objects for microscopes	Opt. Inst.	49
Theorems, Newton's, concerning refraction	New. Opt.	33
Theories of the nature of light	———	9
.. of the rainbow	———	4, 5
.. of electricity	Elect.	10—14, 60—62
.. of magnetism	Magn.	32—41
.. .. general observations on	———	96
.. of electro-magnetism	Elect. Magn.	79—92
Theory, magnetic	———	79—81
.. of the winds explained	Pop. Int.	69
.. of the trade-wind	———	70
.. of the Monsoons	———	70
.. of the sea and land breezes	———	70—71
.. of the sonorousness of bodies	———	71
.. of the nature of light	———	74—75
.. of reflected colours	———	92
.. electro-dynamic of Ampère	Elect. Magn.	81—92
.. .. induction of magnetism, explained by	———	87
.. of colours, Newton's	New. Opt.	31
.. of the undulations of light, Newton's	———	63
.. of achromatic telescopes	Opt. Inst.	19
.. of the single microscope	———	33
.. of the compound microscope	———	43
.. of galvanism, by Du Fay	Galv.	3
.. .. by Volta	———	31, 32
Theories of Galvanism, electrical and chemical	———	19—20
Thermometer, history and construction of	Therm.	1—10
.. the first made by Santorio, described	———	2
.. improvement of, by the Florentine academy	———	3
.. .. by Drebbel	———	2
.. with glass globules, described	———	3
.. Boyle's, described	———	3, 4
.. (oil) of Newton, described	———	5
.. Roemur's mercurial, described	———	7
.. Amonton's	———	6
.. .. objections to	———	8
.. Craquius's	———	8
.. centigrade, or Celsius's	———	9
.. Reaumur's	———	8
.. Hales's	———	9
.. De Lisle's, used in Russia	———	9
.. De Laland's proposed	———	9
Thermometers, precautions requisite in the construction	———	10—15
.. effects of age on	———	12
.. of atmospheric pressure on	———	13
.. directions for filling	———	11, 12
.. .. graduating the scales	———	13—56
.. perfect vacuum in, not essential	———	12
.. tables of correspondences of various scales	———	57—60
Thermometer, Register, history and construction of	———	33—39
.. .. Cavendish's described	———	34, 35
.. .. Six's	———	35, 36
.. .. Keith's	———	37, 38
.. .. Blackadder's	———	38, 39
.. .. Trail's	———	39
.. *Differential*, history and modifications of	———	39—45
.. .. Leslie's described	———	40
.. .. De Butt's	———	41
.. Metalline, by Fitzgerald described	———	20, 21
.. .. by De Luc	———	24
.. .. by Regnier	———	29
.. .. by Crichton	———	30, 31
.. .. by Breguet	———	32, 33
.. .. by Houriet	———	33
.. peculiar applications of	———	45—51
.. air of Kinnersley	Elect.	43
.. statical by Cumming	Therm.	45—47
.. balance, by Kewley	———	47, 48
.. barometrical by Wollaston	———	48, 49

GENERAL INDEX.

		Page
Thermometer, alcoholic and mercurial, table of comparison at different temperatures	THERM.	54, 55
.. day and night, of Rutherford	———	36, 37
Thermometric Hygrometer, Leslie's, described	———	41, 42
Thermoscope, Rumford's described	THERM.	40, 41
Thermo-electricity, definition of, and experiments on	ELECT. MAGN.	92—96
.. the phenomena of not, hitherto reduced to a theory	———	95
.. does not appear to arise from any chemical change in the materials	———	95
Thermo-electric currents distinguished from galvanic	———	93
.. .. metals best fitted for producing	———	94
.. .. chiefly recognized by their effects on the magnetic needle	———	95
Threefold motion of the earth described	POP. INT.	34
Tides, cause of, explained	———	54, 55
.. exist in the atmosphere as well as in the ocean	———	71
Time, solar and sidereal, distinguished	———	48, 49
Topaz, colourless, of New Holland, use of double refracting prisms	OPT. INST.	25
Torpedo, anatomical description of	GALV.	26
Torsion-balance, description of	ELECT.	19—21
.. its extreme sensibility	———	20, 21
Torsion-galvanometer, described	ELECT. MAG.	41
Tourmaline, its electrical properties	ELECT.	54
Trade-winds, description and cause of	POP. INT.	70
Transference of electricity	ELECT.	4, 11, 23—28
Transmission and reflection of light—easy fits of	NEW. OPT.	44
.. .. colours from transparent plates	———	56
Transparent liquors, their colours vary with their thickness	———	37
.. plates, their phenomena	———	39—41
.. substances, tables of refractive and dispersive powers	OPT. INST.	4—6—25
Tropics, described	POP. INT.	40, 41
Trough battery, galvanic, described	GALV.	7
.. .. Cruikshank's	———	7
Trumpet, the speaking-trumpet and ear-trumpet constructed on the same principle	POP. INT.	72, 73
Truth, invariably preceded by hypothesis	MAGN.	33
Tubes, capillary, cause of the ascent of fluids in	POP. INT.	6
UNDULATIONS of liquids convey sounds	———	71
.. of *light*, account of the theory of	NEW. OPT.	63
Universal discharger, description of	ELECT.	37
VACUUM, phenomena on the passage of electricity through	ELECT.	25
Vapour, dew and rain, cause and distinction of	POP. INT.	5—61
Variation of the seasons accounted for	———	44—46
.. of atmospheric pressure, effects of on boiling water	THERM.	8
.. *of the compass*, concerning	MAGN.	22, 23
.. .. line of, traced upon the earth's surface	———	23
.. in the intensity of terrestrial magnetism	———	25
.. .. and dip, progressive changes in	———	29—31
.. .. diurnal changes in	———	31
Variation-Compass, construction of	———	61—72—74
VARLEY's graphic telescope, account of	OPT. INST.	26
Vegetable substances, galvanic piles formed entirely of	GALV.	25
Vegetables, effects of electricity upon	ELECT.	50, 51
Velocity, absolute, relative, &c., defined	POP. INT.	9, 10
.. multiplied by weight—the measure of momentum	———	11
.. of sound, its medium amount	———	72
.. of a moving body, if to a certain extent, becomes imperceptible	———	80
.. of the transmission of the electric fluid	ELECT.	23
Venus, account of that planet	POP. INT.	36
Vibrations of the particles of solid bodies convey sounds	———	71
Vicissitudes of the season in the different planets	———	48
VILLETTE, experiments with his burning mirror	OPT. INST.	3
Visible objects, duration of, on the eye	NEW. OPT.	35

GENERAL INDEX.

		Page
Vitreous electricity distinguished from resinous	Elect.	8, 9
Volta's galvanic pile, construction of	Galv.	4
.. theory of galvanism, arguments for and against	——	31, 32
Voltaic battery of the Royal Institution	——	7
Voltaic battery, intense heat produced from	Galv.	10
.. .. experiments with	——	10—13
.. pile, decomposition and recomposition of water by	——	15
.. .. different decompositions by	——	15—17
.. and common electricity, different mechanical effects of	——	13
.. electricity, sensation of in passing through the human body	——	18
.. .. transferable to the common electrical battery	——	10
Voltaic magnets, description of	Elect. Magn.	38
.. made to exhibit the phenomena of the dipping needle	——	47
Water, accumulation of in hills and mountains	Pop. Int.	62
.. its boiling point affected by atmospheric pressure	Therm.	8
.. height of its boiling point in different states of the barometer	——	15
.. decomposed and recomposed by the voltaic pile	Galv.	15
.. why not decomposable by the common electrical machine	——	27
Water-level, description of that instrument	Pop. Int.	57
Wedge, a mechanical power	——	27
Wedgewood's *pyrometer*, description of	Therm.	27—29
.. .. table of temperatures according to	——	29
Weighing-beam, principle and construction of	Pop. Int.	20, 21
Weight multiplied by the velocity, the measure of momentum	——	11
.. of bodies different at different parts of the earth's surface	——	43
Wheel and axle, account of that mechanical power	——	26, 27
White produced by the reunion of all the spectral colours	New. Opt.	33, 35
.. light, decomposition of	——	—
Winds, general and particular remarks on	Pop. Int.	69—73
.. causes of, investigated	——	69
Winkler first used cushions in electrical machines	Elect.	15
Winter, the sun nearer the earth in than in summer	Pop. Int.	32
Wollaston's barometrical thermometer described	Therm.	48, 49
.. elementary galvanic battery	Galv.	3
.. periscopic spectacles described	Opt. Inst.	9
.. camera lucida, construction of	——	53, 54
Zamboni, description of his dry galvanic pile	Galv.	27
Zig-zag progress of the electric spark when passing to a long distance	Elect.	24
Zinc and copper, different effects of certain acids upon	Galv.	14
Zodiac, signs of described	Pop. Int.	37, 41, 40

www.ingramcontent.com/pod-product-compliance
Lightning Source LLC
Chambersburg PA
CBHW080555240426
43664CB00051B/2772